P9-DGL-423

THE ROUGH GUIDE TO

Germany

This third edition updated by

Jeroen van Marle, James Stewart, Neville Walker and
Christian Williams

ROUGH
GUIDES

roughguides.com

Contents

Introduction to
Germany

The paradox of Germany is that it is simultaneously one of the most rewarding and most overlooked travel destinations in Europe. You'd think the continent's third largest country – a nation at the geographical, cultural and political heart of Europe long before it was defined as a single entity, which has fathered some of the world's greatest thinkers, artists and scientists, and pioneered an A to Z of inventions, from automobiles to Zeppelins – would be better known. Instead, a travel press that prides itself on winkling out secrets in countries like France or Italy resorts to cliché for Germany. It is the country of Berlin and the Black Forest; the land of river cruises down the Rhine Valley, of traditional festivals like Munich's Oktoberfest knees-up or the Christmas markets. It is, in short, the place of beer and sausages and oompah. That Germany exists, of course (yes, even the Lederhosen). Yet that it does so within one of the most dynamic, progressive, cultural nations in Europe – and more importantly a nation that is at ease with itself for the first time in decades (see box, p.11) – is just one more reason why contemporary Germany may be more rewarding today than it has been for decades.

If it is misunderstood by outsiders, recent history is to blame. It is not even three decades since the Berlin Wall was chipped away to end a turbulent and agonizing century for Germany, ill-served at crucial points in its brief history as a united nation-state by rulers who twice led it into disaster: in 1918, as Kaiser Wilhelm II's vainglorious dream of empire ended in defeat, starvation and revolution; and at the end of **World War II**, as Hitler's vile race-war rebounded in terrible fashion on the German people who had chosen him as their leader. There followed a period of 45 years in which not one Germany but two faced each other across a tense international divide – the so-called Iron Curtain – throughout the years of the **Cold War**.

ABOVE CHINESISCHEN TURM BIERGARTEN, ENGLISCHER GARTEN, MUNICH **RIGHT** CYCLISTS IN MEADOW, UPPER BAVARIA

Political fragmentation is nothing new in Germany. From the tenth century until the early nineteenth, the Holy Roman Empire provided only a loose semblance of sovereignty over a vast **collection of states**, and it's this jumbled history, as much as the country's varied geography, that explains Germany's sheer diversity. For centuries many of Germany's cities governed themselves without feudal overlords, while elsewhere the feudal states ranged from substantial kingdoms like Prussia, Saxony or Bavaria to tiny landgraviates and prince-bishoprics. Yet each made its contribution to Germany's heritage, in the architectural and cultural splendour of many a former Residenzstadt. The **Lutheran Reformation** and its aftermath left their mark too: northern Germany is predominantly Protestant, the south more Catholic.

Germany's contribution to the world of **classical music** is undeniable, and provides a powerful pretext for a visit for many, whether to experience the glories of the Berlin Philharmonic or of Wagner's *Ring* at Bayreuth, or to follow in the footsteps of great composers: Bach in Leipzig, Beethoven in Bonn. Germany's reputation as the cradle of **modernism** is also well deserved, and a pilgrimage to the Bauhaus in Dessau or the Weissenhofsiedlung in Stuttgart is sure to please design fans. German modernism was preceded by the older traditions of the Romanesque, Gothic, Renaissance, Baroque and Rococo, each of which left a rich legacy of artistic and architectural treasures. Germany's **fine art** is less well known, yet from the pioneering realism of Albrecht Dürer to the ethereal Romanticism of Caspar David Friedrich, it's well worth discovering. Most German cities of any size have excellent galleries, with Berlin and Cologne hubs of the European contemporary art scene.

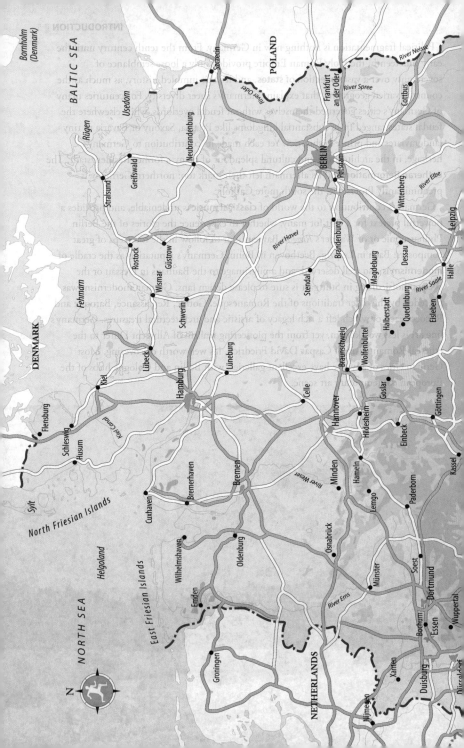

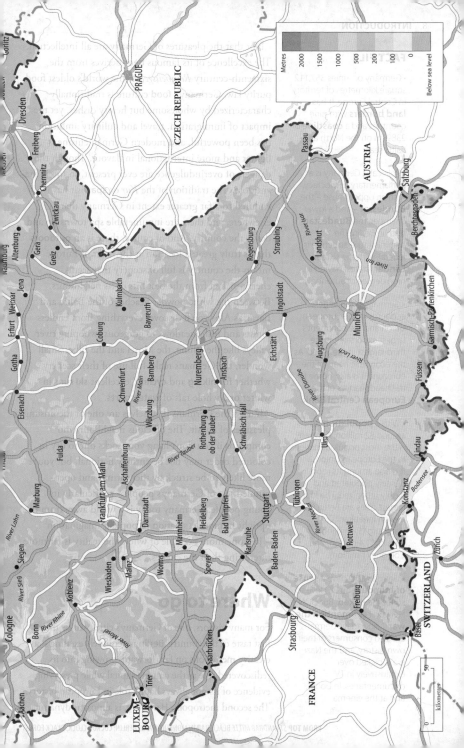

FACT FILE

• Germany occupies 357,112 square kilometres of territory in Central Europe. It has **land borders** with nine countries and a **coastline** of 2389km on the North and Baltic seas.

• Politically, Germany is a parliamentary democracy, with an upper house – the **Bundesrat** – and a lower chamber, the **Bundestag**, both in Berlin. The administrative structure is federal, with the sixteen **Länder** (states) having a high degree of autonomy.

• Germany is the largest economy in the European Union and the continent's largest exporter; it is the third-largest in the world. As the economic heart of the eurozone it is also home to the headquarters of the **European Central Bank**.

• With a **population** of around 82 million, Germany is the most populous nation in the European Union, and it is also among its most densely populated and highly urbanized. The four largest cities are Berlin (3.5 million inhabitants), Hamburg (1.8 million), Munich (1.4 million) and Cologne (1 million).

• Germans DO have a **sense of humour** and DO love to sunbathe **naked**. But DON'T feel you can't **mention the war** – nowadays Germans are avid consumers of their own history, and the Nazi era is picked over exhaustively in TV documentaries, in books, and at the cinema.

Not that the pleasures of Germany are all intellectual. The excellence of its famous **beer** derives from the sixteenth-century *Reinheitsgebot*, the world's oldest food purity law. Germany's **food** culture is traditionally characterized by wholesome but hearty dishes, yet the impact of immigration, travel and culinary ambition has been powerful, and modern German cuisine is lighter and more international in flavour. Though the dangers of overindulgence are ever present, so too is the antidote. The tradition of the *Kur* or **spa** visit has endured to a far greater extent in Germany than elsewhere, and there are innumerable spa towns up and down the country. And of course, there is an **outdoors** that is truly great: a location at the heart of Europe means the country is full of scenery that seems cherry-picked from the best bits of its neighbours. Between the white powder beaches of the Baltic and Bavaria's Alps you'll discover everything from endless forests and lush meadows to gorgeous swooping river valleys like the Rhine, the Mosel and the Elbe. Small wonder, the Germans make full use of their scenery, whether for **hiking** and **cycling**, excellent **ski runs** in winter or a whole raft of **watersports**.

Indeed the Germans themselves are one of the unsung pleasures of a visit. The officious neighbour who complains if you don't hang your socks out to dry in coloured order may not be entirely fictional, but you're more likely to be struck by the warmth and open-mindedness of Germany's people – particularly its young people. Germany today is a world away from the uptight humourless nation of popular imagination – just one more example of where the reality is far more interesting than the clichés.

Where to go

For many visitors, one of Germany's cities will be their first taste of the country. **Berlin** is genuinely exciting – a creative metropolis on fast-forward, growing into its rediscovered role as the nation's capital while preserving evidence of its not always happy role in European history. The second metropolis, **Hamburg**, is almost as dynamic

THE GREAT OUTDOORS

Goethe eulogized it. Caspar David Friedrich painted it. Even politicians saluted it when they established the world's first Green Party in 1979. A love of the great outdoors is hardwired into the national psyche, and with more than ninety nature reserves, fifteen national parks and sixteen biosphere reserves to choose from, there's no shortage of unspoilt landscapes in which to hike, cycle, ski, climb, canoe, swim or simply stroll.

TOP 5 NATIONAL PARKS

Jasmund Ⓦ nationalpark-jasmund .de. Situated on the Baltic Sea island of Rügen, Jasmund is blessed with the country's sunniest climate and celebrated for the white chalk cliffs of the Königstein. p.836

Berchtesgaden Ⓦ national park-berchtesgaden.de. Legend claims the mountains of the Berchtesgadener Land – the nation's only Alpine park – appeared when angels dropped the best bits of the world. It's certainly heavenly, an area offering stupendous hiking among soaring peaks, impossibly emerald lakes and pristine forests. p.402

Saxon Switzerland Ⓦ nationalpark-saechsische-schweiz.de. The distinctive sandstone plateaux of the Elbsandsteingebirge (Elbe Sandstone Mountains), near Dresden, are beloved of rock-climbers as well as hikers. p.153

Bavarian Forest Ⓦ national park-bayerischer-wald.de. A low range of mountains and pine forests that extends over the Czech border and harbours deer, otters and pygmy owls – as well as many good mountain-bike and hiking trails. p.408

Harz Ⓦ nationalpark-harz.de. Sleepy and brooding, with steam trains and half-timbered villages huddling amid spectres and witchcraft, this is Germany's most fabled national park. p.217

and arguably more prosperous, shaped by its twin roles as Germany's great port and its rich media city. Many other cities have proud histories as independent city-states or as capitals in their own right. There's nothing remotely "provincial" about ancient, liberal **Cologne**, **Dresden**'s restored Baroque splendour or the proud Bavarian metropolis of **Munich**. The financial capital, **Frankfurt**, impresses with its dynamism and international spirit, while **Bonn**, the former West German capital, charms with its scenic setting and excellent museums. Elsewhere, chic **Düsseldorf** and laidback **Stuttgart** embody aspects of the German economic miracle, while the eastern city of **Leipzig** fizzes with fresh energy. **Nuremberg** evokes the triumphs and tragedies of Germany's past.

Cultural attractions of capital-city quality are not limited to the bigger cities, and many of the most rewarding places are quite small: the cathedral cities of **Bamberg** and **Regensburg**; the Hanseatic ports of **Lübeck**, **Stralsund** and **Wismar**; the "Prussian Versailles" of **Potsdam**; and micro-capitals like **Weimar**, **Schwerin** and **Eichstätt**. Germany has university towns as evocative as any: **Heidelberg** is the most famous, but **Freiburg**, **Marburg** and **Tübingen** are just as charming. As for the spa towns, at their best – in **Baden-Baden**, **Bad Homburg** or **Wiesbaden** – they combine health benefits with turn-of-the-century elegance and lovely natural settings. For a potted digest of Germany's cultural riches the **Romantic Road** is deservedly popular, a road journey linking Rococo churches with medieval cities and eccentric royal castles. Other themed "roads" are devoted to fairy tales, half-timbering or wine. Often, the most magical places – a fortress on a crag, a placid village rising above vineyards, an ancient market square of improbable quaintness – await discovery on such routes. And surrounding all is Germany's undeniable natural beauty – as good a reason to visit as any city. The **Bavarian Alps**, the **Black Forest** and the valleys of the **Rhine** and **Mosel** have long

REINVENTING GERMANY

If it is possible to specify when modern Germany emerged, June 2006 is as good a date as any. The **football World Cup** held in Germany was something of a turning point. When football fans descended from around the world, they discovered a friendly, multiethnic and multicultural nation that was, for the most part, at ease with itself and happy to fly its flag for the first time since the war. Germans were almost as surprised as the visitors.

The decade since has only generated more plaudits. "Why can't we be more like Germany?" asked the cover of Britain's *New Statesman* magazine in 2013, and who can blame it. At a time when many first-world countries have abandoned their industrial base, Germany – Europe's richest country – is the world's third largest **exporter** after China and the US, and has the most highly waged, highly skilled workers in Europe. Even its **federal system** that devolves power to regions is championed by more centralized economies.

But back to the football. In the 2006 and 2010 world cups a young German team came a solid third. Then in 2014, Germany ripped through the groups, trounced home-nation Brazil 7–1 and won its final with a display that blended power, teamwork, flair and, yes, the famed German efficiency. Modern Germany in a nutshell.

been celebrated, but the talcum-powder softness of **Rügen**'s beaches, the chic village resorts of **Sylt** and the bucolic backwater of **Mecklenburg**'s lakes have yet to make it onto the international agenda. The world's loss is, for the time being, the independent traveller's gain.

When to go

Much of the country receives its maximum rainfall in **midsummer**, so although the weather in June, July and August can be very warm, it can also be unpredictable. For more settled weather with sunshine and comfortable temperatures, **late spring** and **early**

autumn – May, September and early October – are well worth considering: the Germans don't call the harvest season "goldener Oktober" for nothing. The **ski season** in the Alps runs between Christmas and the end of March. Germany's climate straddles the maritime climates of the western European seaboard and the more extreme conditions found further east. The prevailing wind is from the west, so that the mild climate of the Rhineland and North Sea coast quite closely resembles that of the UK or Ireland. Winters are more severe further east, while heading south the effects of steadily increasing altitude ensure Munich's summers are no warmer than those of Berlin. The balmiest climate in Germany is found in the wine-growing southwest, where it's not unusual to see lavender, Mediterranean pine, almond and even lemon trees.

A WINE-MAKING RENAISSANCE

Germany's **wine growers** did themselves no favours when, in the 1970s, they responded to growing demand from abroad by exporting the cheapest and worst of what they produced. German wine was saddled for decades with a reputation for poor quality.

All that is now changing. A new generation of wine makers is eschewing high technology, chemicals and the mass market in favour of organic production that reflects the *terroir*, or soil and climate conditions of the region. It helps that **Riesling** – Germany's most popular grape – strongly reflects the conditions in which it has been grown. The result is a resurgence of light, drinkable, dry white wines that range from elegant crispness to the subtly mineral. German wines are increasingly common on wine lists in North America and in parts of Asia, where they match the cuisines well.

Germany's major **wine regions** are mostly in an arc that follows the course of the Rhine from the Mosel in the west to Baden in the south. To the east, wine is grown in more challenging climatic conditions in Franconia, Saale-Unstrut and along the Elbe near Dresden.

ABOVE VINEYARDS ABOVE BACHARACH, ROMANTIC RHINE

Author picks

Germany has its poster places: the Brandenburg Gate in Berlin or Bavaria's gloriously over the top Schloss Neuschwanstein. But the cherished memories of a country are usually more personal discoveries. Rough Guides' authors made many of their own as they sallied down every backroad to research this book. Here are their favourites:

Bathtime With wonderful nooks, fin-de-siècle tiles and cutting-edge sauna facilities, the baths at Bad Wilbad really are something special. p.494

Military marvels The subject could be deathly (no pun intended), yet Dresden's new Militarisches Museum is superb, its thematic exhibitions as unexpected as its striking modern building. p.142

Backroads by the beach Wild powder-sand beaches, birdlife, and art in modern galleries and old barns – what's not to like about the Darss-Zingst peninsula? p.830

Ulm's Münster You don't normally associate churches with exercise and adrenaline, but you'll get both climbing the world's tallest spire, with its views to the Alps. p.449

Biking the Rosskopf Mountain-bike trails for every level of ability fan out from Freiburg, but the climb up the Rosskopf is the most satisfying. p.504

The Venus Grotte, Linderhof "Mad" King Ludwig's Wagnerian underground lake, complete with gilded barge and waterfall. Every home should have one. p.391

Wines in Würzburg Franconian wine, with its traditional rounded glass bottle and distinctive grape varieties, is a great delicacy unknown outside Germany. p.317

The great escape Unleash your inner Huckleberry Finn on canoe-and-camp trips through the maze-like Mecklenburg lakes. Expect birds and butterflies, woods and meadows, a campsite every few kilometres and a fire at night. Magic. p.853

> Our author recommendations don't end here. We've flagged up our favourite places – a perfectly sited hotel, an atmospheric café, a special restaurant – throughout the Guide, highlighted with the ★ symbol.

FROM TOP SWIMMERS NEAR WAREN, MECKLENBURG LAKE DISTRICT; MILITARISCHES MUSEUM, DRESDEN

31

things not to miss

It's not possible to see everything that Germany has to offer in one trip – and we don't suggest you try. What follows, in no particular order, is a selective taste of the country's highlights: iconic landscapes, captivating architecture, and legendary drinking and dancing. All entries have a page reference to take you straight into the Guide, where you can find out more. Coloured numbers refer to chapters in the Guide section.

2

1 CARNIVAL IN COLOGNE

Page 630

Banish the winter blues, Rhineland style, with costumes and ritual silliness – but be sure not to wear a tie.

2 SCHLOSS NEUSCHWANSTEIN

Page 386

"Mad" King Ludwig's maddest creation combines Wagnerian inspiration with a superbly dramatic Alpine site to create a romantic fantasy from the age of chivalry.

3 LENBACHHAUS, MUNICH

Page 347

The masterpieces of Munich's Blaue Reiter embody all the colour-saturated excitement of the time when European art turned towards abstraction.

3

29

30

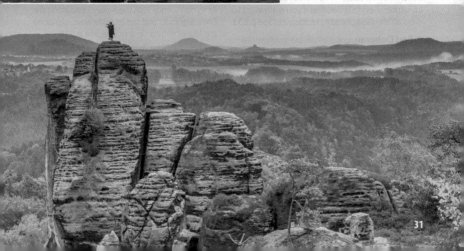

31

Itineraries

With its highlights dotted rather than clustered, Germany rewards touring, be it a classic vineyard-and-castle-studded route down the country's western flank; a picture-postcard circuit of Bavaria's cathedral towns; or even a northern coastal tour.

COAST AND CULTURE

Berlin and Hamburg bookend a circuit that includes beach resorts and pretty medieval ports. Set aside ten days to do it justice.

❶ **Berlin** No longer "poor" as claimed by its mayor in 2003, the capital remains "sexy" nevertheless, with superlative culture and clubbing. **See p.58**

❷ **Stralsund** Overlooked by most holidaymakers, Stalsund's Altstadt is stuffed with architecture from its peak as a medieval trading port. **See p.830**

❸ **Rügen** Travel on the Rasender Roland steam train or just laze on some of the finest white beaches in the Baltic – this holiday island was irresistible even to Hitler. And if you really want to drop off the radar, head to Hiddensee. **See p.833**

❹ **Bad Doberan** Just a small spa town, yet its twelfth-century minster is a pinnacle of brick Gothic in the Baltic. **See p.824**

❺ **Schwerin** A fairy-tale castle straight from *Cinderella* is the highlight of the state capital, along with the gentle art of walks around its lake. **See p.846**

❻ **Lübeck** The queen of the medieval Hanseatic League is a Venice of the Baltic, with architecture that speaks of former greatness. **See p.783**

❼ **Hamburg** Great galleries, gourmet eating and glitzy-to-grungy nightlife – what else to expect of a city that is simultaneously a hip media metropolis and Germany's largest port? **See p.757**

THE MOSEL, RHINE AND BLACK FOREST

This classic itinerary wheels around western Germany to include some of its most famous rivers, castles and wine-growing regions as well as the relatively wild swathe of hills known as the Black Forest. Allow ten days.

❶ **Trier, Rhineland-Palatinate** Tour well-preserved Roman remains in one of Germany's oldest cities. **See p.548**

❷ **The Mosel, Rhineland-Palatinate** Follow the Mosel River, with stops at the idyllic wine towns of Bernkastel-Kues and the hidden Burg Eltz. **See p.543**

❸ **The Romantic Rhine, Rhineland-Palatinate** At its confluence with the Mosel, head along the Rhine's grander and busier waterways, exploring the Marksburg castle en route. **See p.534**

❹ **Mainz and Worms, Rhineland-Palatinate** Discover two venerable imperial Rhine cities with their impressive churches and worthwhile museums. **See p.528 & p.524**

❺ **Heidelberg, Baden-Württemberg** Nip over the state line to an attractive old town that wowed Mark Twain. **See p.471**

❻ **Baden-Baden, Baden-Württemberg** Spend time perambulating dignified streets and de-stressing in the venerable baths. **See p.484**

❼ **Schwarzwaldhochstrasse, Baden-Württemberg** Drive from Baden-Baden through mountains via Freudenstadt and the

Kinzig Valley to cuckoo-clock country around Triberg. **See p.496**

❽ Freiburg, Baden-Württemberg Return to the Rhine Valley to visit this attractive medieval city with its wanderable old town. **See p.501**

BAVARIA

Bavaria has it all, from high culture to viticulture and beer to breathtaking scenery. This circular tour takes in the highlights. Allow two weeks at a leisured pace.

❶ Munich A rich and vibrant metropolis with a seductive lifestyle. No wonder Germans would rather live here than anywhere else. **See p.332**

❷ Berchtesgadener Land A country within a country, dazzling in its scenery and chilling in its reminders of a one-time holiday home for the Third Reich's elite. **See p.402**

❸ The Bavarian Alps Head west from Berchtesgaden along the northern flank of the Alps through idyllic mountain resorts like Reit im Winkl, Bayrischzell and Walchensee. **See p.380**

❹ The Romantic Road Dawdle along Germany's most famous tourist road, past Baroque churches, pastoral landscapes and lost-in-time walled towns. **See p.310**

❺ Bamberg A charming historic core and distinctive smoked beer make this compact but beautiful city a tempting spot to linger. See **p.302**

❻ Bayreuth This pint-sized cultural hotspot is the product of two strong-willed individuals – Frederick the Great's sister Wilhelmine and the composer Richard Wagner. **See p.292**

❼ Nuremberg The triumphs and tragedies of German history, from the monuments of the city's imperial zenith to the still-recognizable reminders of the Nazi era. **See p.280**

❽ Altmühltal Hike, cycle or paddle through the Jurassic landscapes of one of Germany's biggest nature reserves. **See p.367**

❾ Regensburg Journey's end is one of the best-preserved medieval cities in Central Europe. **See p.414**

SAUSAGE SHOP, HAMBURG

Basics

Getting there

The quickest and easiest way to reach Germany from outside continental Europe is by air. The national carrier is Lufthansa, but dozens of other major airlines fly to Germany too. The wide spread of airports throughout the country – many served by budget airlines – means air is also the cheapest method of arrival. However, a location at the heart of continental Europe opens up the possibility of road and rail travel, both more eco-friendly and, at least in the case of road travel, an option that may be cheaper than flying and then renting a car.

The principal hub for international long-haul flights is Frankfurt – whose airport has its own major train station for onward connections – followed by Munich and Düsseldorf. Prices vary considerably by **season**, with the highest being around June to August. Fares drop during "shoulder" seasons – September, October, April and May – and you'll get the best prices during the low season: November to March, excluding Christmas and New Year when prices are hiked up. As ever, early bookers snatch the best deals. Note too, that midweek prices are the cheapest.

Most points of arrival are well linked to city centres via cheap and efficient public transport. If you plan to use public transport throughout a city stay, then multi-day tickets that include your journey from the airport are available, the only exceptions being the remote airports used by budget airlines, although even these are always linked to a major destination by bus services.

Flights from the UK and Ireland

Numerous airlines fly daily to destinations throughout Germany from UK and Irish airports. The two major players are British Airways and Lufthansa, though budget flights by the likes of Ryanair, easyJet, Air Berlin and Germanwings have significantly expanded the route network. Low-cost operators have also slashed the price of getting to the country. While a published single from the UK with the major carriers can be around £300, you can usually pick up similar flights with the budget carriers for around £50, or from as little as £20 if you book a couple of months in advance. Competition and tight margins mean that flight routes are particularly vulnerable to change, which makes search engines such as Ⓦ kayak.co.uk, Ⓦ momondo.com or Ⓦ skyscanner .net invaluable.

Flights from the US and Canada

Thanks to competition between carriers, prices have reduced from the US and Canada in recent years. Most major North American gateways have direct flights and many others offer convenient connecting flights. Lufthansa has the most extensive network, but other major carriers include Continental, Delta, Singapore Airways and United. Meanwhile budget carriers such as Air India, Air Berlin and Condor tend to concentrate on direct services to smaller regional airports; the latter two only operate in summer.

Most transatlantic flights are bound for **Frankfurt**, with a handful to **Munich** and **Düsseldorf**. However, domestic connections are cheap and plentiful, by air or train.

East-coast flights are marginally cheaper than those from the west coast. The lowest discounted scheduled return flight to Frankfurt you're likely to find in low/high season, flying midweek, is US\$475/650 from New York, US\$600/900 from Chicago and US\$700/1100 from Los Angeles.

There are fewer direct-flight options from Canada. The widest selection of flights, operated by Air Canada, Condor, Air Transat, LTU and Lufthansa, are out of Toronto, followed by Vancouver with a handful of flights from Ottawa, Calgary and Montreal. Again, Frankfurt is the premier destination, then Munich. You are unlikely

---

A BETTER KIND OF TRAVEL

At Rough Guides we are passionately committed to travel. We feel that travelling is the best way to understand the world we live in and the people we share it with – plus tourism has brought a great deal of benefit to developing economies around the world over the last few decades. But the growth in tourism has also damaged some places irreparably, and climate change is exacerbated by most forms of transport, especially flying. All Rough Guides' trips are carbon-offset, and every year we donate money to a variety of charities devoted to combating the effects of climate change.

to make major savings by flying to the US first: low-/high- season fares to Frankfurt from Toronto are Can$750/1100; from Vancouver expect to pay from Can$950/1600.

Flights from Australia and New Zealand

Nearly all "direct" flights from Australia take around 22 hours to travel from Sydney, Melbourne or Perth to Frankfurt, via Singapore. Qantas, British Airways and Singapore Airlines command the bulk of flights, with other carriers providing routes that require a transit and change of planes in the operators' hub city – usually in Asia or the Middle East – before continuing to Germany, though these cheaper fares can bump up journey times by a good ten hours – reputable agents such as STA come into their own here. Other stopover possibilities include the US and Canada, though North American routes tend to be more expensive.

The lowest **prices** from Sydney or Melbourne to Frankfurt in (European) high/low season are A$2200/1400, with those from Perth generally around A$200 cheaper, and those from Adelaide more expensive by the same margin. From New Zealand, low-season scheduled fares from Auckland start at around NZ$2400 and rise to NZ$2600 and up in high season. Again Qantas, British Airways and Singapore Airlines are the big three carriers, with most flights stopping at Singapore. Consequently **round-the-world tickets** often offer good-value fares compared with a standard return, not to mention a chance to break up the journey for some travel en route. For roughly the price of a long-haul return, you can buy multi-stopover or round-the-world tickets. A good agent such as STA is able to devise a travel plan pieced together from various airlines, with Germany just one destination on a ticket that is generally valid for a year. Prices for the basic Australia–Asia–Europe–US–Australia itinerary start from as little as A$1400. It's also possible to route overland segments into the journey.

Trains

The high-speed rail links of Eurostar (Ⓦeurostar.com) run from St Pancras International, London, to Brussels (1hr 55min) in Belgium where you'll need to switch to a French-run Thalys or InterCity Express (ICE) express train to Germany. Like air travel, prices vary according to the season, day and time, class of travel and also how far in advance tickets are booked. For example, a last-minute standard-class return for London–Cologne can easily rise above £300, but advance fares start at around £120. This means train travel has begun to compete with the price of flying if you take into account baggage fees and the cost of travel into cities to and from airports, not to mention the annoyance and time spent in airport security. The environmental benefits of train travel are also huge.

Sleeper carriages (*Schlafwagen*) appeal for overnight journeys, permitting the romance of waking up at your destination and saving on a hotel overnight. When arriving by train, you'll find that the **Hauptbahnhof** (main train station) of almost every city is an easy walk from the centre, and generally preceded by a string of outlying stations which might be more convenient for your accommodation.

Long-distance train advice website Ⓦseat61.com is invaluable for planning.

Rail passes

If you plan to use the train extensively, look into rail passes. Since, with some planning, travel by train within Germany can be very good value, it's worth doing the sums via the website of national operator **Deutsche Bahn** (Ⓦbahn.com) to ensure that a pass that gets you to Germany from abroad and provides travel within the country, is cheaper than an international flight to Germany plus a national rail pass (see p.32).

There are two types of railway pass depending on if you have been resident in Europe for the last six months or not. The **Eurail Pass** is for those from outside Europe, and it comes in a variety of forms: the Global Pass permits unlimited travel within 24 countries from ten days (US$955) to three months (US$2240); the Select Pass allows five (US$573) to ten days' travel (US$834) in 27 countries within a two-month period; and the Benelux-Germany Pass provides five (US$368) to ten days' (US$557) travel within a two-month period. Under-26s are eligible for "Youth" passes, which are cheaper by about a third and only valid for second-class seats. Group passes are also available.

European residents can purchase a time-honoured **InterRail** pass, which comes in formats that are either valid continuously or only for specified days within a set period. Prices start at £233 for five days' second-class travel within a ten-day period and rise to £553 for a month's continuous travel. First-class passes cost around half as much again, while under-26s pay a third less. All passes require supplement payments for high-speed trains and couchettes.

Buses

Compared with low-cost airlines, travelling to Germany by bus is not particularly cheap and will involve a long and uncomfortable journey. The only real advantages are the smaller carbon footprint; the chance to buy an open return at no extra cost; and the fact that passes around Germany are a good bit cheaper than the rail equivalents. Services to all major cities in Germany are run by **Eurolines** from Victoria Coach Station in London, and are bookable through most travel agents and any National Express agent. As an idea of times and advance prices, London–Cologne takes thirteen hours and costs around £70 one-way, London–Berlin twenty hours and £100.

Eurolines Passes, priced by season, cost €215–355 for fifteen days' travel or €320–465 for thirty days. Under-26 passes are €30–75 cheaper. Another alternative is the Eurolines bus pass which provides a 25 percent discount on tickets for fifteen or thirty days, and is priced at £23/43 in the UK.

Another option for a European tour is backpacker-friendly bus service **Busabout**, which operates a hop-on, hop-off network of routes throughout the continent. Berlin, Dresden, Munich and Stuttgart are on the "North Loop" tour (as are Bruges and Amsterdam which are close to the arrival of UK ferry services – see below). A one-loop pass costs €559. The pass is valid for an entire season that lasts from May to October.

Ferries and the Channel Tunnel

There are no longer any direct **ferry services** from the UK to Germany, so you'll have to pass through France, Belgium or the Netherlands, depending on your start point and destination. The most useful routes from **southern England** run to France: the Newhaven–Dieppe ferry (DFDS; 2 daily); the Dover–Calais/Dunkirk ferry (DFDS & P&O; hourly); and the Folkstone–Calais car-carrying Eurotunnel train (4 per hour). From **eastern England** the best option is the Harwich–Hoek van Holland ferry (DFDS & Stena Line; 2 daily). From **northern England** there's the choice of two ferries: Hull–Rotterdam/Zeebrugge (P&O; daily) and Newcastle–Amsterdam (DFDS; daily). Year-round sea links to the German Baltic

coast also exist from **Scandinavia**, notably Sweden and Denmark (Stena Line; daily), and **Baltic nations** such as Lithuania. From **Ireland**, Cherbourg and Roscoff, in northwest France, are as close as services get to Germany, both accessed from Dublin and Rosslare respectively and served by P&O Ferries. Fast it is not. The website ⊛ directferries.co.uk presents a useful overview of all routes, ports and operators.

As a general guide of **driving times** from Calais, allow eight hours to Hamburg (6hr from Hoek van Holland), six hours to Frankfurt, ten hours to Berlin and ten hours to Munich.

Finally, you may be able to pick up a faster ride – and often a cheaper one – via the German **Mitfahrzentralen** car-share system (see p.34).

AGENTS AND OPERATORS

Harvey World Travel New Zealand ☎ 0800 758 787,
⊛ harveyworld.co.nz. Great deals on flights, hotels and holidays.
Martin Randall Travel UK ☎ 0208 742 3355, ⊛ martinrandall
.com. Small-group cultural tours, usually accompanied by lecturers; an
eight-day Berlin, Potsdam and Dresden package costs around £2500.
North South Travel UK ☎ 01245/608 291, ⊛ northsouthtravel
.co.uk. Friendly, competitive travel agency, offering discounted fares
worldwide. Profits are used to support projects in the developing world,
especially the promotion of sustainable tourism.
STA Travel UK ☎ 0333 321 0099, US ☎ 1800 781 4040, Australia
☎ 134 782, New Zealand ☎ 0800 474 400, South Africa ☎ 0861
781 781, ⊛ statravel.co.uk. Worldwide specialists in independent
travel; also student IDs, travel insurance, car rental, rail passes, and more.
Good discounts for students and under-26s.
Trailfinders UK ☎ 0207 368 1200, Ireland ☎ 021 464 8800
⊛ trailfinders.com. One of the best-informed and most efficient agents
for independent travellers.
Travel CUTS Canada ☎ 1800 667 2887, US ☎ 1800 592 2887,
⊛ travelcuts.com. Canadian youth and student travel firm.
USIT Ireland ☎ 01 602 1906, Northern Ireland ☎ 028 9032 4073,
Australia ☎ 1800 092 499 ⊛ usit.ie. Ireland's main student and youth
travel specialists.

RAIL CONTACTS

Deutsche Bahn UK ☎ 0871 880 8066, ⊛ bahn.com.
Eurail ⊛ eurail.com.
Eurostar UK ☎ 08432 186 186, International ☎ +44 (0)1233 617
575, ⊛ eurostar.com.
Rail Europe UK ☎ 0844 848 4064, US ☎ 1800 622 8600, Canada
☎ 1800 361 7245, ⊛ raileurope.co.uk.

THE TUNNEL ON TWO WHEELS

Though all ferry operators will take **bicycles** to the continent, hands-down the cheapest and quickest service is Eurotunnel. They only charge £16 per person one-way, all-in. Curiously motorbikes tend to be even cheaper, with rates starting at £12.

BUS CONTACTS

Busabout UK ☎ 0845 026 7514, ⊛ busabout.com.
Eurolines UK ☎ 0871 781 8178, Textphone for deaf UK customers
☎ 0121 455 0086, ⊛ eurolines.com.

FERRY CONTACTS

DFDS Seaways UK ☎ 0871 522 9955, ⊛ dfdsseaways.co.uk.
Irish Ferries Ireland ☎ 0818 300 400, UK ☎ 0871 730 0400,
⊛ irishferries.com.
P&O Ferries UK ☎ 08716 642 121, International ☎ 01304 863
000, ⊛ poferries.com.
Stena Line UK ☎ 0844 770 7070, ⊛ stenaline.co.uk.

CHANNEL TUNNEL

Eurotunnel UK ☎ 0844 335 3535, International ☎ 03 2100 2061,
⊛ eurotunnel.com.

Getting around

Planes, trains and automobiles, not to mention buses, boats and bikes: Germany deals in the full deck of options for travel within the country, with one of the finest public transport systems in Europe. Unusually for a largely landlocked nation, it also affords considerable opportunities for travel on its arterial rivers – slow travel at its best, in which the getting there is as much a reason to travel as the destination. Services operate on arterial rivers such as the Rhine, Mosel and Elbe, generally from April to October; details are provided in relevant destinations. Prices are more expensive than those for rail, but that's not really the point.

By air

Alongside national carrier Lufthansa (⊛ lufthansa .com), budget airlines such as Air Berlin (⊛ airberlin.com) and Germany Wings (⊛ germanwings.com) offer daily routes throughout the country, with single fares for as little as €30 including taxes. Lufthansa flights are more expensive but still good value, with the greatest number of routes and the most frequent departures. These can be hourly on popular routes such as Hamburg–Munich, a flight that saves five hours compared to the same journey by train. Advance bookings – at least two weeks prior – provide substantial discounts.

By train

The much-lauded national rail system operated by **Deutsche Bahn** is superb, but not quite faultless. Trains can be a few minutes late and strikes are not unknown. Nevertheless, trains remain the workhorse of public transport and the nation has good reason to be proud of its efficient privatized system. Its 43,900km of track is the most extensive in Europe; trains are frequent – generally hourly, with extra services at rush hours; invariably clean; and prices are fair, with weekend, regional and other discounts often helping to sweeten the deal.

Kings of the rails are the flagship **Intercity-Express** (ICE) trains, which travel at speeds up to 300km/hr and offer the most comfort, including a bistro. When making a reservation you can also request a seat in areas with boosted mobile-phone reception or none at all. Not as fast or flash are **Intercity** (IC) and international **Eurocity** (EC) trains, though these hurtle along at 200km/hr, and still have electricity terminals throughout and a buffet carriage. Local trains come as swift **InterRegio-Express** (IRE), the steady **Regional-Express** (RE) trains and the slowish local **Regionalbahn** (RB), which tend to stop at every station en route. In cities, **Stadt-Express** (SE) trains or the commuter S-Bahn trains also operate.

In addition to Deutsche Bahn, a handful of other companies also operate train services. These include various Netinera (⊛ netinera.de) and Veolia Verkehr (⊛ veolia-verkehr.de) brands. Most are not of interest to the visitor, with the exception of the Interconnex (⊛ interconnex.com) service from Berlin to Leipzig to the Ostsee, since its prices are always very low.

Standard and discounted tickets

Standard **tickets** (*Fahrkarten*) – not restricted to any particular train and refundable for a small charge – are priced according to the distance travelled, so returns cost twice as much as singles. Reservations (€4 per journey) are worthwhile for peak long-distance trains, especially the popular Friday late-afternoon getaway.

You can **buy tickets** over the counter at the *Reisezentrum* (travel centre) of larger stations or, at

> ### TRIP PLANNING IN GERMANY
> The Deutsche Bahn website (⊛ bahn.com) is superb for planning, with its online timetable even covering local bus connections.

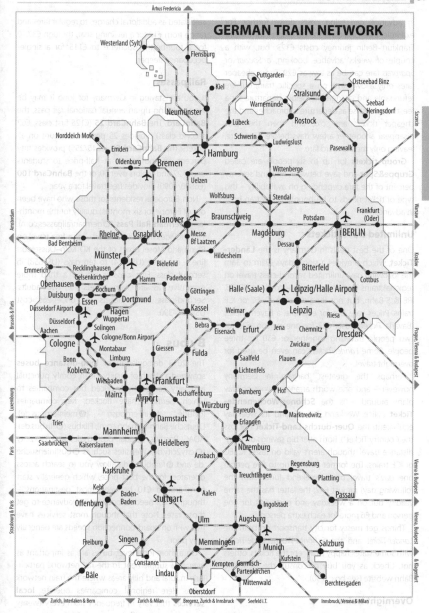

GERMAN TRAIN NETWORK

all but the rural stations, from touchscreen vending machines with English instructions. You can also buy tickets on board for a nominal service charge – all trains now accept major credit cards. Telephone reservations are on ☎01805 99 66 33; registered users can buy tickets online at 🌐bahn.com at no

surcharge up to ten minutes before departure – you'll require a print-out of the ticket and your credit card as proof of purchase.

Flexible standard tickets are reasonably priced (though the use of ICE trains can be a little expensive), but **Spezial** or **Sparpreis** fares, booked in advance, can bring costs down further. For example, a second-class standard ticket for the 5hr Frankfurt–Berlin journey costs €123, but, with a couple of weeks' advance booking, a *Spezial* or *Sparpreis* fare can be as low as €29. These cheaper fares only allow travel on a specific train, but are refundable and changeable before departure for a fee; the prices rise as departure approaches and the cheaper tickets are sold, and then the fares disappear altogether a few days before departure, leaving only the Standard fare.

Group tickets for up to six people are called **Gruppe&Spar** and save between fifty and seventy percent of the fare depending on availability – this type of ticket needs to be bought at least an hour in advance.

Unlimited travel tickets

One of the best deals in Germany is the **Länder-Ticket**, which provides a single day's (9am to 3am the following day) unlimited second-class travel on regional trains in a single region – covering RE, RB, IRE & S-Bahn, but not long-distance IC, EC or ICE trains. Prices vary, but for example, a Bayern Ticket (Bavaria Ticket) costs €22 for one person, €26 for two people travelling together or €30 for three people. Some *Länder-Tickets* can even be used for overnight travel.

Perhaps the greatest bargain in Germany however – and one worth arranging your holiday plans around – is the **Schönes-Wochenende-Ticket** ("Nice Weekend Ticket") and its weekday equivalent, the **Quer-durchs-Land-Ticket** ("Across the Country Ticket"). Both offer big savings on long-distance travel, though aren't valid on faster IC, EC or ICE trains. The former permits up to five people one day's travel on a weekend (until 3am the following day) for just €42; the latter has the same validity but on a weekday and costs €44 for one person and €6 more for each extra person.

Things get messy for city transport on both the *Länder-Ticket* and the *Schönes-Wochenende-Ticket*, with some states happy to accept the tickets, others not. Check as you buy or consult the Deutsche Bahn website (see box, p.30).

Overnight trains

Deutsche Bahn's **City Night Line** (CNL Ⓦcitynightline.de) trains to the Netherlands, Austria and Switzerland and destinations throughout Germany offer travel in reclining seats, couchette or comfortable sleeper carriages, with soothing curved corridors, soft lighting, shower and toilet or a wash-basin inside compartments. Ticket prices are calculated as additional charges to regular fares and range from €12 for a reclining seat, through €37.50 for a four-berth couchette to €115 for a single-occupancy sleeper.

Rail passes

If you are staying in Germany for long it may be worth picking up an annual national rail pass, the **BahnCard**. The **BahnCard 25** (€125 first class, €62 second class) provides 25 percent discount on all tickets; the **BahnCard 50** (€515/255) provides fifty percent off and comes at half-price to students under 27 and seniors over 60; or the **BahnCard 100** (€6890/4090) provides free travel for a year.

Non-European residents (or those who have been out of Europe for six months) qualify for the month-long **German Rail Pass** (Ⓦgermanrailpasses.com). This provides free rail transport – plus free travel on Rhine and Mosel boats of the KD Köln–Düsseldorf line – for three (US$374) to ten days (US$658) in second class. First class is around a third more expensive, as are twin tickets for two adults. Second-class Youth tickets for under-26s cost US$221–390.

By bus

The 2013 deregulation of **long-distance buses** spawned a clutch of quality, clean, comfy, punctual and very competitively-priced bus companies to which Germans have flocked. Key companies include MeinFernbusn (Ⓦmeinfernbus.de), Deutsche Bahn (Ⓦbahn.com), Flixbus (Ⓦflixbus.de), ADAC Postbus (Ⓦadac-postbus.de) and city2city (Ⓦcity2city.de). Websites such as Ⓦbusliniensuche.de and Ⓦfernbusse.de allow you to search across operators for the best price, which generally start from around €10 between most destinations – though you'll need to book well in advance to get those rates. Note that though most services have free wi-fi on board, connection speeds are generally very poor.

On a more local level, buses are as important as ever as a supplement to the rail network, particularly in rural and hilly areas where the train network thins. Here regional companies operate **local services** that vary in frequency from every twenty minutes or so to daily or even fewer, with most routes scheduled to serve commuters from early morning to early evening; services can dry up entirely at weekends. In addition, buses need not adhere to strict schedules, so may leave earlier than times published – use the printed timetables as a guide only and arrive early. The exception to this is departures from the terminus, known in cities as a **Busbahnhof** or **Zentral Omnibus Bahnhof** (ZOB) and ubiquitously located near the train station. **Tickets** are bought either from kiosks or from the driver. If you intend to travel widely in a region ask about a day-card (*Tageskarte*) or week-card (*Wochenkarte*).

By car

Holders of any home national – or international – driving licence are permitted to drive in Germany provided they have this to hand. If driving your own car you will also require vehicle registration documents and a valid third-party insurance certificate. If bringing your own car, be aware, too, that a growing number of cities – 48 as of 2014 – have implemented **Low Emission Zones** to reduce exhaust fumes. Vehicles in a central "Green Zone" must display an "Emission Badge" (*Umwelt Plakette*), which is bought for around €5–10 from repair centres, dealers and MOT (*Tüv*) stations, or via websites Ⓦtuev-nord.de (northern Germany) and Ⓦtuev-sued.de (southern Germany) for an additional €15. In practice this means pre-'93 petrol models and pre-'97 diesels will not pass unless retro-fitted with a catalytic converter. Vehicles caught entering a Green Zone without a badge will be fined.

Germany's most celebrated principal roads are its **Autobahnen** (motorways), indicated with blue signs and an A prefix. These roads have two or three lanes in each direction and, famously, have no overall speed limit, although many stretches, particularly near towns and cities, do have speed limits imposed (white sign with red edge), and the use of electronic signboards on many stretches mean that limits can quickly be imposed when authorities feel weather or traffic conditions warrant it. A round white sign with three diagonal stripes indicates that you're entering a section with no speed limit, though 130km/hr is the recommended limit. But even here you can generally forget fantasies of barrelling along at 200km/hr in your BMW, since traffic can be heavy and east–west routes packed with pan-European truckers. Major roadworks and accidents also frequently seem to be problems, helping to explain the national obsession with traffic jams (*Staus*). Perhaps all this is just as well, since if you have an accident at what your insurer regards as an excessive speed they may not pay out; and the police will take speed into account when apportioning blame.

Secondary **B routes** (*Bundesstrassen*) are often dual carriageway, with three lanes on heavy sections, and have a speed limit of 100km/hr. Speed limits in **urban areas** are 50km/hr. All routes are toll free.

On-the-spot **speeding fines** are issued on a sliding scale depending on the speeds involved. Traffic police are fair but determined – don't expect to weasel out of a fine with pleas of innocence. The maximum blood **alcohol** limit is 0.5mg/l. Penalties for those over the limit are severe – fines are steep, licences can be revoked – and even those involved in an accident but under the limit can have licences and vehicles confiscated temporarily. The use of mobile phones while driving is forbidden except with a hands-free set.

On Autobahnen, emergency telephones are located every 1.5km for **breakdown services**; ask for *Strassenwachthilfe*. Phones connect to Germany's principal automobile organization, Allgemeiner Deutscher Automobil Club (ADAC; breakdown line ☏01802 22 22 22, Ⓦadac.de), affiliated to the British AA, American AAA and Canadian CA, though check the extent of cover with your own breakdown service.

On the road

Driving is on the right, overtaking on the left, and **seatbelts** compulsory for all, including those on back seats – whoever isn't wearing one will be fined, a law which extends to taxis though isn't rigorously enforced. Some states request (but not demand) that headlights are always on when driving. Carrying a reflective **hazard-warning triangle** is mandatory and should be set up 100m behind the vehicle on the hard shoulder if required. In southern Germany snow chains are a good idea if you intend to venture onto Alpine backroads in winter, but most routes are kept snow-free with grit, salt and snowploughs.

For first-time foreign drivers, remember that anything approaching from the right has **right of way**, unless posted otherwise. This is generally only an issue in cities, where trams make things a little more difficult by having right of way regardless of their direction. Since tram stops are at the roadside, overtaking stationary trams is forbidden. Pay special attention to pedestrians and cyclists in cities – you might receive a green light to pull away from a junction, but the road you turn into is often green for a cycle and pedestrian crossing. Treat every junction with caution and double-check before you turn. Signs for Stadt Mitte (city centre) or Altstadt (old town) lead you to a town's heart; orange signs announce an *Umleitung* (diversion), which can lead you a merry dance but will get you there in the end.

Car parks (*Parkhaus*) are generally on the edge of pedestrianized centres, and marked by a blue "P". While most car parks offer flat-rate overnight parking, some spring surprises – check to avoid a shock in the morning. **Street parking** is either pay-and-display or free for a specified time beneath a blue P, in which case cardboard "clocks" bought from petrol stations are left on the dashboard to indicate the time of arrival.

Petrol – all *Bleifrei* (unleaded) and either Super Plus (98 octane) or Super (95 octane) – is available every 50km or so on Autobahnen, where major players are open 24 hours a day. All petrol stations are self-service.

Car rental

Car rental (*Autovermeitung*) is widely available, with multinational chains operating desks at all airports and either in or around the Hauptbahnhof of most cities. Rack rates are steep – around €80 a day without a promotional deal or a fly-drive deal – and, if you don't care too much about the car's looks, smaller local outfits can be better value. The best rates are generally found on aggregator sites like ⓦ rentalcars.com and ⓦ novacarhire.com.

CAR RENTAL AGENCIES

Alamo ⓦ alamo.com.
Apex ⓦ apexrentals.co.nz.
Auto Europe ⓦ autoeurope.com.
Avis ⓦ avis.com.
Budget ⓦ budget.com.
Dollar ⓦ dollar.com.
Enterprise ⓦ enterprise.com.
Europcar ⓦ europcar.com.
Hertz ⓦ hertz.com.
Irish Car Rentals ⓦ irishcarrentals.com.
National ⓦ nationalcar.com.
Nova Car Hire ⓦ novacarhire.com.
Rental Car Group ⓦ rentalcargroup.com.
Rentalcars.com ⓦ rentalcars.com.
SIXT ⓦ sixt.com.
Skycars ⓦ skycars.com.
Thrifty ⓦ thrifty.com.

By taxi

Taxis – nearly always cream-coloured – will only save money over well-priced public transport if you are in a group; even then savings will be minimal. Available cabs have rooftop lights lit, though it's rare to hail one on the street. Most gather at city centre ranks, at the edge of the pedestrian centres and at train stations. Fares are metered, priced per kilometre and rise slightly between 11pm and 6am and on Sunday. Large items of luggage may attract a small extra charge.

Car shares

Eco-aware Germany has a shared-car system called **Mitfahrzentralen** that operates as a form of organized hitchhiking (which we cannot recommend for obvious safety reasons, though most hitchhikers rate Germany highly for the speed of pickups and friendliness of drivers). Agencies in cities connect drivers with passengers, who usually split fuel costs. Most agencies publish searchable online journeys lists, many of them international – and since all drivers are required to provide details of addresses and registration numbers, the ride should be safe. Prices vary according to passenger numbers, but you can expect to pay around €35 from Hamburg to Berlin. Check websites ⓦ mitfahrzentrale.de, ⓦ mitfahrgelegenheit.de, ⓦ mfz.de, ⓦ drive2day.de, ⓦ blablacar.de and ⓦ bessermitfahren.de.

By bike

Cyclists have an easy ride in Germany: many small roads have dedicated cycle-paths, as do cities where cycle lanes are often built into the pavement. When you are forced onto the road in towns, you will be treated with respect by drivers rather than rammed into the curb. A network of **long-distance cycle-paths**, often following major rivers, such as the Elbe, Danube or Rhine, make cycling between destinations an appealing prospect, though distances can be large. All trains bar ICE services accommodate bikes so long as you have purchased an additional **Fahrrad-Karte** (bicycle ticket), which costs €9 (or €6.50 with a rail card) on IC and EC services (which generally have a dedicated carriage), and €5 or free on local services and the S-Bahn, depending on the state. You'll also find bike racks on the buses in popular touring areas such as Rügen or Sylt, and bikes are permitted on just about all ferry services. Many of Germany's long-distance buses will also carry bikes, though a small fee is usually involved.

Bike rental is widely available in cities, usually from the Hauptbahnhof (main train station) and any train station served by ICE trains. A convenient innovation introduced and run by DB is **Call-a-bikes**. These silver-and-red, full-suspension bicycles can be rented at any time of day for €0.08 per minute (up to €15 for 24hr and €48 for a week), with no deposit or minimum charge. To use one you first need to register a credit card (**☎**0700 05 22 55 22, **ⓦ**callabike-interaktiv.de). Registering your mobile will mean your account will be debited automatically when you call. Once you've registered, it's just a matter of calling the individual number on the side of a bike and receiving an electronic code to open the lock. To drop it off, leave it on any street corner then ring up for a code to lock the bike and leave its location as a recorded message. This can all also be done using the Call-a-bike smartphone app. Participating cities are Berlin, Frankfurt, Cologne, Munich, Stuttgart and Karlsruhe. Otherwise, hostels are an excellent source of bike rental, or many cycle shops offer rental for around €10–15 a day; enquire at local tourist offices.

City transport

Municipal transport in Germany is almost always efficient and fairly priced. The cornerstones of most systems in major cities are two rail systems, supplemented on the streets by buses and trams. Once on board any of them, illuminated signs and announcements ensure it's easy to find the right stop. Tickets are available from machines at stations, on trams or from bus drivers – but be sure to validate them by punching the ticket when you travel. An unvalidated ticket is as good as no ticket at all and will result in a fine at spot checks.

The mainstay of most city-centre systems is the **U-Bahn**, which is clean, punctual and rarely crowded. Running both under- and overground, these cover much of the centre: trains tend to run from 4am to around 12.30am, and all night on Friday and Saturday in the metropolises. Out of these hours, their routes are usually covered by night buses – denoted by a number with the prefix "N". The **S-Bahn** systems are a separate network of suburban trains that run largely overground, and are better for covering long distances fast, with generally larger distances between each stop. Within small and medium-sized towns, the **tram** or **bus** replaces the U-Bahn as the heart of city transport, operating a network of circuits. Otherwise, the modus operandi remains the same, the only exception being that you may have to buy tickets direct from the driver rather than from a vending machine at your stop.

Transport networks are usually divided into zones – A, B, C or 1, 2, 3, etc – and **ticket prices** vary according to their reach. Basic singles are called *Einzeltickets*, or you can usually buy a cheaper *Kurzstrecke*, a short-trip ticket that permits travel for a limited number of stops (no return journeys or transfers). Buying a day-ticket (*Tageskarte*) will generally work out cheaper still – look out for group tickets (*Gruppenkarten*). Another possibility for short-term city visitors are the cards promoted by city tourist offices that provide 48 or 72 hours' unlimited travel alongside discounted entry to city sights. If not named after its city, it is often called a Welcome Card.

Accommodation

Finding a bed is rarely a problem in Germany and the range of accommodation – from half-timbered hostel to high-rise designer hotel, pension to palace – means there's something to suit all budgets and tastes. There are two caveats: during major festivals and high season in premier resorts you may struggle to find a room; and when expense accounts roll into town during Messen (trade fairs), prices skyrocket.

In the past decade or so the country's fairly frumpy stock of small hotels has largely been updated and supplemented by some fairly modern, bland and cheap hotels of a similar quality to American motel chains. Another trend is the emergence of an **independent hostel** sector. Though targeted at the backpacker market, these convivial hostels are open to all comers and often offer cheerful modern doubles for around €30.

While the strength of the euro means hotel accommodation is not quite the bargain of a decade or so ago, Germany remains reasonable value. **Prices** vary hugely, but you can expect to pay around €80–120 for a double in an average mid-range hotel. Many city hotels, especially those that target the executive market, offer cheaper weekend rates. Hostels charge about half that price for a double room, and under €30 for a dormitory. The other source of a cheap bed is **private houses** or **farms offering rooms** – those in more remote regions such as the Black Forest and Bavarian Alps abound in country character and provide bargains to boot.

A peculiarly German quirk is the enduring love affair with the **sauna and spa** or "wellness" centre, which you'll find even in dated hotels – worth remembering before you thrill to the notion of a "spa hotel". Another national tradition is the

ACCOMMODATION PRICES

All the accommodation listed in this guide is followed by a price which represents the cost of the cheapest double room in high season, quoted at the official rack rate, although prices outside high season will fall dramatically. Single rooms are sometimes half-price but more usually around two-thirds the price of a double.

Kurtaxe, which is charged in spa towns and "health" resorts, a definition extended to encompass most coastal resorts. This adds €2–4 to your hotel bill on the grounds that facilities are laid on for the resort's tourists.

For **reservations** most tourist offices will book all forms of accommodation either for free or for around €2–4 per person. Those in resorts are a good first port-of-call if you arrive without a reservation in peak season. Many tourist offices in destinations with a high visitor rate have touchscreen info-points outside, sometimes with a free telephone. And if you make a reservation be sure to notify staff about an expected arrival time after 6pm – or else your room may be given away.

Hotels

Many hotels in Germany have aligned themselves with a voluntary five-star **Deutschen Hotelklassifizierung rating system** based on the assessment of 280 criteria by an independent body. This ensures that participating one-star establishments have rooms of up to 12m squared, with en-suite toilet and shower; that 3-star hotels offer larger rooms, a minibar and 24-hour call on reception even if they are not manned; and that in five-star places, you will enjoy rooms of at least 18m squared and luxuries such as 24-hour room service and reception, and laundry services. Most hotels have a restaurant – those named a *"Hotel garni"* serve breakfast only.

Whether aligned to the *Deutschen Hotelklassifizierung* system or not, German hotels are generally comfortable enough for you to have few complaints; they are clean, generally en suite except in the cheapest establishments, and rooms nearly always come with a TV. In the lower and mid-range, you can expect either a fairly anonymous business style or a dated 1980s throwback. Budget hotel chains Etap and Ibis provide functional modern rooms at rates comparable to a room in an independent hostel (see opposite). That said, a growing number of style hotels in the cities also offer interior style at affordable prices, and at the upper end you can have a pick of hotels with wow factor, with many luxury outfits installed in historic palaces or castles. All hotels provide **breakfast**, generally buffet-style and included in the price of your room, but do double-check.

Pensions, inns, private rooms and farmstays

A real step away from the formality and anonymity of blander hotel chains is the **pension**: by and large smaller, cheaper establishments, often in large houses or in city apartment blocks. What they lack in mod-cons – you'll usually have to share bathroom amenities, for example – they make up in character in the form of personal service and homely decor. In Bavaria they are often called a **Gästehaus**. A similar style can be found in a **Gasthof** or a **Gaststätte**, which roughly translates into English as an inn. Accommodation is generally above a traditional restaurant – and the fact that it is often in a historic building is all part of the charm

---

ACCOMMODATION ALTERNATIVES

To find private rooms and apartments on the web try the tourist information websites for the town or region you are interested in; or try one of these commercial sites:

9flats Ⓦ 9flats.com. Berlin internet startup that aims to help you find "affordable private accommodations, rented out by friendly locals all over the world".

Airbnb Ⓦ airbnb.de. A full variety of properties and timescales are offered via this international agency.

Be My Guest Ⓦ be-my-guest.com. Short-stay apartments, bed & breakfasts and guest rooms for all budgets.

Citybed ☎ 030 23 62 36 10, Ⓦ citybed.de. Online accommodation booking, with prices starting at around €20 per person.

Couchsurfing Ⓦ couchsurfing.org. Relies on the goodwill and trust of members to provide free accommodation to each other.

Vacation Rentals by Owner Ⓦ vrbo.com. World leader in vacation rentals.

Wimdu Ⓦ wimdu.com. Another big international database for apartments, holiday homes and bed & breakfast deals.

of a stay, although bear in mind that this means room dimensions are historic, too. For obvious reasons these are especially prevalent in small towns and in the countryside. Both pensions and inns will provide breakfast.

A step down from the pension or inn is a **private room** in a local house. Normally priced €15–30, they are a viable alternative to hostels for budget travellers. At their best, private rooms offer a chance to dip a toe into everyday life and to glean the insider information from a local host. Such intimacy may not be to all tastes, however. Tourist information offices can book rooms, or look for signs advertising *Zimmer frei* or *Fremdenzimmer*; alternatively, you can source rooms (and apartments) online at Ⓦ bed-and-breakfast.de, Ⓦ bedandbreakfast.de and the websites in the box opposite.

One of the most notable developments in German accommodation in the past decade is the rise of **farmstays**. Beloved by city families as a rural escape, and often good bases for country pursuits such as walking or riding, these are classified either as *Landurlaub* (country holiday) – former farms or country houses with typical regional charm – or as *Urlaub auf dem Bauernhof* (farm holiday) which provide rooms on working farms and vintners. Many of the latter feature home-made produce for breakfast and, on occasion, evening meals – but you'll obviously need your own transport. Again, local tourist offices can recommend farmstays, or try farmstay organizations, all of which sell brochures or guidebooks.

FARMSTAY ASSOCIATIONS

Bauernhof and Urlaub Ⓦ bauernhofurlaub-deutschland.de.
Landtourismus Ⓦ landtourismus.de.
Zentrale für den Landurlaub Ⓦ bauernhofurlaub.com.

Youth hostels

Since 1912, the pioneering German Youth Hostelling Association (Deutscher Jugendherbergswerk, or **DJH**) has been providing clean and basic accommodation and now has over six hundred hostels throughout Germany. This means you'll find a DJH hostel in most towns. The majority have been refurbished to provide modern accommodation with facilities such as internet access. Most have also relaxed their institutional feel a little, making them more welcoming for families – with en-suite rooms available and the lunchtime lock-out and 11pm curfew eliminated in city hostels. The bad news is that they are immensely popular with school groups and often a bus ride from a town centre.

To stay at a hostel you must be a member of the Hostelling International association (see above). Nonmembers can join for €21 (€7 for under-27s) or buy a night's membership known as a Welcome Stamp for €3.50 – collect six stamps to become a member. The price of a dorm bed in Germany hovers around the €21 mark, with over-26s charged €3 extra; throughout the Guide we quote the price for members under 26. The DJH website (Ⓦ jugendherberge.de) acts as a portal for all hostels as well as regional websites. Many DJH hostels permit online booking.

Linen and breakfast are included in the price, and cheap half- or full-board is almost universally available; many hostels also provide packed lunches and a bistro. Opening hours vary: while those in large cities are generally open 24/7, many outside cities close at 11pm. Reception times are generally morning and late afternoon only. Note, too, that unless otherwise confirmed reservations are held until 6pm; after that, a reserved room may be given to another guest. Many hostels close between Christmas and New Year, sometimes even in January or February, and a few remote hostels only open in summer.

INTERNATIONAL YOUTH HOSTEL ASSOCIATIONS

Australian Youth Hostels Association Australia
☎ 02 9565 1699, Ⓦ yha.com.au.
Hostelling International–American Youth Hostels US
☎ 1301 495 1240, Ⓦ hiusa.org.
Hostelling International Canada Canada ☎ 1800 663 5777,
Ⓦ hihostels.ca.
Hostelling International Northern Ireland Northern Ireland
☎ 028 9032 4733, Ⓦ hini.org.uk.
Hostelling International South Africa South Africa
☎ 021 424 2511, Ⓦ hisouthafrica.com.
Irish Youth Hostel Association Ireland ☎ 01 830 4555,
Ⓦ anoige.ie.
Scottish Youth Hostel Association UK ☎ 0845 293 7373,
Ⓦ syha.org.uk.
Youth Hostel Association (YHA) UK ☎ 0800 019 1700,
Ⓦ yha.org.uk.
Youth Hostelling Association New Zealand New Zealand
☎ 0800 278 299 or 03 379 9970, Ⓦ yha.co.nz.

Independent hostels

No change in Germany has benefitted budget travellers as much as the rise of the independent hostel in the past decade or so. Unlike DJH hostels, these hostels target independent travellers rather than groups.

Independence makes generalizations tricky, but these hostels tend to be relaxed and friendly, with a young international clientele. Most are small, often in converted houses or apartments in a city's nightlife district, and will typically provide laundry facilities, a communal TV lounge, internet access (or wi-fi) and perhaps a games room. Accommodation is in mixed dormitories, typically from four- to (cheaper) ten-bed, as well as in double or twin rooms, and a handful of singles. Some hostels operate single-sex dorms – washrooms are nearly always segregated. Bed linen is generally included in the price and a simple buffet breakfast is available for around €3–5.

Many hostels have noticeboards advertising work and cheap activities and many also rent bikes. Staff are generally young, well-travelled and knowledgeable about the local area. The one negative to consider is that city dorm rooms are not conducive to early nights, especially those in bar districts.

Many independent hostels are listed at ⓦgerman-hostels.de and at ⓦhostelz.com.

Camping

As a nation besotted with the outdoors, Germany has over 2500 campgrounds, generally sited beside lakes or in the bosom of some inspiring landscape. Most are above average by European standards: even the most basic will have a dedicated reception, often with a mini-shop, and offer full washing facilities, while high-end sites will often have an outdoor pool, restaurants, a bar and a supermarket, and organized activities for kids. However, German campsites can be seriously uptight, often sterile places with row after tidy row of caravans and motorhomes sprouting satellite TV antennas.

Most campgrounds open between April and October, although some operate year-round. **Prices**, which vary according to the facilities, are by pitch and the number of people plus a car if you have one. Some charge a euro or two for showers – you may have to buy tokens from reception – and electricity, if required. The annual Camping Card (€10) of the European Federation of Campingsite Organizations (EFCO, ⓦcampingeurope.com) provides 25 percent discounts.

The website of the Federal Association of German Campsites (BVCD; ⓦbvcd.de) has a searchable database of 1300 sites organized by region, and publishes a highly condensed guidebook of sites (€7) that can be ordered through its website. Online database Cris 24 (ⓦcris24.com), with a similar number of campgrounds, permits reservations. You'll also find guidebooks in bookshops; that of national auto association the ADAC, *ADAC Camping-Caravaning-Führer*, is reliable. Wild camping is illegal on environmental grounds.

Finally a note about **campervanning**, a mode of holiday-making dear to German hearts. As well as

---

BIN THERE, DONE WITH THAT: RECYCLING IN GERMANY

Travel anywhere in Germany by train and you'll see an array of coloured bins on the platform, evidence that Germany takes recycling seriously. The recycling industry turns over around €50 million annually and Germans, who have a long tradition of social consciousness, recycle more of their rubbish than most other European nations. Using the **Grüne Punkt** (Green Dot) icon that indicates material can be recycled, they now recycle up to 70 percent of some materials, including 41 percent of plastics. In Bavaria, only 1 percent of rubbish goes to landfill. Visitors are expected to do their bit – novices placing items in the wrong container may be quietly reprimanded.

Bins – of which there are up to five – are colour-coded. One, usually green or blue, is for **paper** (*Papier*) and cardboard, including waxed cartons; boxes should be flattened and emptied of any plastic wrappers. **Plastic** goes into the yellow bin, along with milk cartons, cans, polystyrene and **aluminium** (marked with the Green Dot icon of two interlocking arrows). Straightforward enough, so long as you don't stuff different materials inside each other; this stuff gets sorted by hand, so a plastic cup hidden inside a tin is strictly *verboten*. There's no need to rinse items but most Germans empty cans and plastics. **Glass** is usually collected in hostels to be taken to bottle banks, commonly in supermarket car parks. However, most bottles – glass and plastic – usually have a deposit (*Pfand*) on them of around €0.30–0.50 per item to be cashed at specified re-collection centres, most conveniently supermarkets. It's standard practice to return items in bulk rather than singly. **Biodegradables** – including coffee grounds and teabags – go in another bin, usually brown, after which there's hardly anything left over. What is goes in the one bin that takes genuine *Müll* (rubbish) – grey or black and usually empty.

campsites, many towns and cities will provide a *Wohnmobil Parkplatz* (motorhome car park) for overnight stays; look for signs of a motorhome as you enter a town. These vary from free waste-ground car parks at the town outskirts to reserved areas with drinking water and waste disposal. The latter charge around €10 a night – still cheaper than a hostel for a night and often in the centre of a city.

Food and drink

Though neither as obsessive as the Italians nor as fussy as the French, Germans are serious about their food. Consequently standards are high. You'll rarely find cause to criticize the quality in Germany even if you don't share a taste for its national cuisine. For most outsiders that means a taste of tradition – *Bratwurst* (grilled sausage), assorted cuts of pork and, of course, *Sauerkraut*. All present and munched daily, but to brand German cooking as its time-honoured dishes only, is to overlook a foodie revolution that has rippled across the country over the last decade or so.

To complement the impressive range of regional cuisines from granny's cookbook, the nation's chefs have created a brand of light, modern cooking infused with international flavours. The *Michelin Guide* reviewers now rave about the contemporary **Neue Deutsche Küche** (New German Cuisine) of the nation's superstar chefs as much as they do the gourmet *Bratwurst* produced in Bavaria's *Wurst-küchen* (sausage kitchens). And menus throughout the country now show a taste for modern Mediterranean cooking as Germans look to reduce the calorie and cholesterol counts. Even the old oompah-and-*Schnitzel* joints have healthy salads these days. Indeed, even if not quite a gourmand's paradise, modern German cuisine is one of the great surprises of culinary Europe. Perhaps as importantly, the modern urban brasserie in Germany arguably represents better value than its French equivalent. On top of this, Germany keeps an excellent cellar of wine and spirits. And its beer should need no introduction.

Germany's share of **ethnic restaurants** tends to be those of its large immigrant groups – Italian, Greek and Turkish, with the ubiquitous Chinese thrown in and, in cities, the occasional Thai and sushi joint. Indian cuisine is less well represented, and often fairly mild.

Breakfast

It's rare for a hotel – or even a hostel come to that – not to include **breakfast** (*Frühstuck*) in the price of your accommodation or serve it separately for around €8–15 (around €5 in hostels). This usually proves excellent value for money, especially at the mid- and upper ends of the market. Most places allow you to browse at leisure from a Scandinavian-style *smorgasbørd* of mueslis and cereals, yoghurt, hard-boiled eggs, jams, marmalade and honey, as well as cheese and cold meats, usually ham and salami. Alongside this will be a regional assortment of the nation's three hundred varieties of bread – from simple crusty white rolls or brown rolls encrusted with sunflower or poppy seeds to damp, heavy *Schwarzbrot* (black bread), the gourmet's choice – the most famous is rye *Pumpernickel*. Watery orange juice aside, breakfast is usually washed down with coffee – always fresh and usually weaker than that of France and Italy – although you will also be offered tea, usually *Schwarz Tee* (black), or fruit teas.

Cafés also provide excellent breakfasts – for many younger Germans a café brunch is a weekend institution – though it's easy to spend €12–15 by the time you add in juice and coffee. A better budget option is to grab a coffee and sandwich at a bakery such as ubiquitous chain *Kamps* and use the stand-up counter (known as the *Stehcafé*) to eat it in the shop. These open from around 7am and you'll breakfast well for around €6.

Snacks and street food

Germany pretty much invented fast food: Hamburg's meat rissoles became the hamburger, its sausages in bread were exported as the hot dog. The difference with German snacks is their high quality, which makes bites on the go a mini-meal rather than a guilty filler. Most quick snacks are served at **Imbiss** stands, invariably located at transport hubs and market squares, where you eat standing. The standard fare is a range of sausages plus hamburgers and occasionally meatballs or perhaps a greasy *Schnitzel*. Some *Imbiss* stalls specialize in spit-roast chicken, which typically comes as a half-bird (*Halbes Hähnchen*) at low prices. Mustard (*Senf*) comes free, ketchup and mayonnaise may cost a few euros extra. Larger towns and cities often have market stalls in a dedicated **Markthalle**, with a wide range of delica-tessens under one roof, some rather upmarket and often with a few international cuisines. On the coast, fish replaces the traditional meat-fare in *Imbiss* stalls; often smoked and almost always served by the harbour, fresh fish comes in sandwiches (*Fischbrötchen*). Nationwide fish chain *Nordsee* prepares fast food alongside cheap meals.

In **bakeries**, there'll often be a corner to sit or else stand, known as a *Stehcafé*. Incidentally, German pretzels, known as *Brezeln* and covered in salt crystals, are a far superior snack to their American counterparts.

You'll find standard Italian and Asian **takeaways** everywhere, and also Turkish. It's no surprise that a country fond of fast food has embraced the kebabs of a large Turkish community; indeed, the idea of a kebab with salad in pitta bread is a German invention. Known as *Gyros* or *Döner*, these are generally of grilled lamb, sometimes chicken. British visitors will be pleasantly surprised.

Finally, a special word about **Kaffee und Kuchen** (coffee and cakes), a traditional Germanic treat equivalent to English tea. It is observed religiously by an older generation at late afternoon, and is best taken in an old-fashioned café. Most prepare fresh home-made gateaux piled with quantities of cream and chocolate to make dieters weep.

Traditional restaurants and meals

The tradition of lunch (*Mittagessen*) as the main meal of the day has been quashed by the pressure of modern work practices. Like most North Europeans, Germans are now as likely to grab a sandwich or snack and save the main meal until dinner (*Abendessen*). Nevertheless, cooked food (*warme Küche*) is served throughout the day except in more upmarket restaurants, which pause between meals, and on *Ruhetag* (day off), when the establishment is closed; Sunday or Monday is a favourite.

The first choice for honest traditional food should be a **Gaststätte** or **Brauhaus**. Traditional and convivial, these are roughly equivalent to the British pub, so are relaxed venues in which to drink as well as eat, many providing a **Biergarten**, or beer garden in summer. Others have a cellar in which to imbibe: a **Bierkeller**. The *Brauhaus* (literally, "brew house") also means fresh beers brewed in-house. The cuisine is almost always **gutbürgerlich Küche** – unpretentious home-cooking that's filling, tasty and generally good value. Similar but slightly more upmarket is the **Ratskeller**, a German institution in the often-historic cellars of the town hall. These are reliable and strong on regional specialities, if a little stuffy at times. Don't be surprised if you are asked to share a table in either, nor if your credit card is met with a dismissive shrug – most small *Gaststätten* only accept cash.

German **restaurants** serve anything from posh traditional food, to a lighter take on German cuisine, often with a polyglot of Mediterranean accents, to exquisite *Neue Deutsche Küche*, a sort of German *nouvelle cuisine*. Wherever you go, the **menu** (*Speisekarte*) will be displayed outside.

Notwithstanding regional variations (see opposite), traditional starters (*Vorspeise*) are soups of the thin variety, or pâté. Things get more interesting for the main course (*Hauptgericht*), usually meat (*Fleisch* – no flinch from the truth in Germany) with one or two vegetable dishes and sometimes a side salad. As a rule of thumb, the meat in question will be some part of a pig. Every possible cut, plus knuckles and offal is served in a baffling variety of ways; ubiquitous German pork dishes are breaded fillet **Schnitzel**, **Schweinbraten** (roast pork), **Schweinhaxe**, a huge crispy knuckle which could have graced a medieval banqueting table, and **Eisbein**, salted knuckle or shin. And, of course, pork comes as sausages (**Würste**) – grilled, fried, boiled and baked; all are excellent (see box opposite). The standard beef dish tweaked with regional variations is **Sauerbraten** (roast and marinated in vinegar). **Game** (*Wild*) – typically venison (*Hirsch*) or wild boar (*Wildschwein*), occasionally hare (*Hase*), and veal (*Kalb*) – also provides respite from the pork-fest. Lamb (*Lamm*) sometimes gets a look in, and chicken (*Hähnchen*) rarely. Except on the coast, **fish** is almost exclusively freshwater, typically salmon (*Lachs*), trout (*Forelle*) and *Zander* (a meaty pike-perch).

Vegetable side-dishes will nearly always feature some form of potato (*Kartoffel*), often the pub-favourite fry-up *Bratkartoffeln*, sometimes jacket potatoes (*Ofenkartoffeln*) or in traditional places stodgy potato dumplings (*Klösse* or *Knödel*). And, of course, there's **Sauerkraut**. The classic side-dish of green cabbage pickled in white-wine vinegar is an acquired taste – many outsiders find red-cabbage variety *Rotkohl* more palatable, especially as apple-spiced *Apfelrotkohl*. Worth a special mention is **asparagus** (*Spargel*), which is of the white variety and comes into season from April to late June to feature on dedicated menus throughout the land.

Desserts (*Nachspeise*) are usually light, often ice cream or fruit salad. The nation that brought the world Black Forest Gateau (*Schwarzwälder Kirschtorte*) tends to reserve cakes for late-afternoon *Kaffee und Kuchen* (see above).

FOR BETTER OR WURST: A GERMAN SAUSAGE PRIMER

Few foods are as iconic of their home country as the German sausage (**Wurst**). Part of the national cuisine since the Middle Ages, sausages are taken seriously in their home nation. Yes, you'll find Germans guzzling them down with a dollop of mustard as fast food – a tradition exported by nineteenth-century émigrés to give the world the hot dog – but Michelin critics also list *Wurst* kitchens in Bavaria. All *Würste* feature pork (and sometimes beef or veal), spices and peppercorns. What makes each distinctive are the herbs and spices. Aficionados say there are around a thousand regional varieties to sample. Good luck.

Blutwurst "Blood sausage" – black pudding. Eaten sliced and cold or fried.

Bockwurst A popular variety that is more fine veal than fine pork. Resembles a chubby frankfurter and is heated in liquid. Traditionally served with *Bock* beer in spring.

Bratwurst The common or garden sausage served countrywide. Varies by region – Bavaria's are finger-sized, Thuringia's are long and thin, for example – but usually made of finely minced pork and marjoram.

Braunschweiger Smoked liver sausage (*Leberwurst*) enriched with eggs and milk, so it is spreadable.

Currywurst A Berlin icon invented, they say, in 1949 by a bored *Imbiss* stall-holder. Basically a *Wiener* sliced, smothered in ketchup, then dusted with curry powder.

Frankfurter Not the same as the American variety, this contains fine, lean pork with a little salted bacon. Smoked then reheated in liquid.

Knockwurst (or Knackwurst). Short, plump, smoked sausage of finely minced lean pork, beef, spices and garlic. Typically poached or grilled then served with *Sauerkraut*.

Thüringer Rotwurst Speciality low-fat black sausage from Thuringia afforded protected geographical status under EU law.

Weisswurst Munich's "White sausage", so called for its being made of veal and fresh bacon. Flavoured with parsley, mace and cardamom, it is traditionally prepared before breakfast and eaten before lunch.

Wienerwurst Thought to be the source of the American frankfurter. Pork and beef flavoured with coriander and garlic, grilled or fried.

Regional dishes

What comes as a surprise for most visitors resigned to a pork-and-spuds diet is the tremendous variety of regional cuisines.

Fresh seafood is always worth investigating in the **north coastal regions**: *Matjes* (herring) and white *Rotbarsch* (like whiting) are common. Hamburg vies with Berlin for the title of gourmet capital of Germany, and is arguably more cosmopolitan in its range of restaurants. Nevertheless, you'll still find traditional sailor's dish *Labskaus*, a filling mash of beef, pork, salted herring, potato, beetroot and gherkin, topped with a fried egg. *Aalsuppe*, a piquant eel and vegetable soup with fruits such as pear and prunes, is another one for adventurous diners. More conservative tastes will prefer *Rotes Gruz*, a dessert of red berries, and keep an eye open for *Pharisäer*, coffee with a swig of rum and topped with cream. You'll also find widespread use of *Nordseekrabben*, tiny North Sea shrimps.

Further south, lamb from the heather-clad plains of the **Lüneburg Heath** is excellent, while a traditional dish in **Lower Saxony** and **Bremen** is *Grünkohl mit Pinkel*, curly kale with spicy sausage.

North Rhine-Westphalia is known for smoked hams and dishes such as *Himmel und Erde* (literally "heaven and earth"), a gutsy casserole of puréed apple, onion and potato with black sausage, or

winter-warmer *Dicke Bohnen*, a fava-bean stew cooked with a splash of vinegar.

South of here, in the **Rhineland-Palatinate**, look for *Saumagen*, pig's stomach stuffed with cabbage, like a German haggis. And around **Frankfurt** there's the marvellously named *Handkäse mit Musik*, cheese with onions in a spicy vinaigrette – the "music" in question refers to its effects on digestive systems.

Baden-Württemberg, also known as **Swabia**, in southwest Germany boasts a unique pasta-style cuisine – typically doughy *Spätzle* noodles coated in cheese or eaten pure as a side dish, and *Maultaschen*, like over-sized ravioli stuffed with meat, spinach, eggs or herbs. Beef, potato and *Spätzle* stew, *Gaisburger Marsch*, is another favourite. A regional form of pizza, *Flammkuchen*, is here too: generally topped with crème fraîche, onions and bacon bits, it's served in many hip pubs. In the **Black Forest**, smoked hams are always worth tasting, trout is excellent and there is, of course, *Schwarzwälder Kirschtorte*, which bears no relation to the stodgy Black Forest Gateaux dolloped onto foreign plates in the 1970s.

Bavaria, the Land of beer-hall-and-Lederhosen cliché, comes good with a no-nonsense pig-fest, typically great hunks of *Schweinehaxe* (roast knuckle) and *Rippchen* (roast ribs). This is also the sausage capital of Germany: short and thin, those of Nürnberg and Regensburg are acclaimed by gourmets, though Munich acclaims its veal *Weiss-wurst* as far finer. Franconia in north Bavaria is renowned for carp. **Thruringians** will tell you the state's charcoal-grilled *Rostbratwurst* (grilled sausage) is better than anything produced in Bavaria, made to a recipe that dates from 1404.

Classics from **Saxony** include marinated braised beef (*Sauerbraten*), *Quarkkeulchen* (sweetened potato pancakes) and *Eierschecke* – similar to cheesecake. Dresden is renowned for *Christstollen*, a local Christmas cake.

And finally to **Berlin**, which has the full glut of modern restaurants of a capital city. By common consent, traditional Prussian cuisine is solid rather than exciting – perhaps the most iconic taste of Berlin is the *Currywurst* (see box, p.41).

Vegetarians

While still a nation fond of its meat, Germany has modern European attitudes to vegetarianism – indeed, many large towns will have a vegetarian restaurant. Even if they don't, salads are always meat-free unless stated, the ubiquity of Italian cuisine means vegetarian pasta dishes abound, and even traditional *Schnitzel* joints will list at least one vegetarian dish even if they don't have a dedicated menu – short, admittedly, but there. Bear in mind, too, that even meat-obsessed Bavaria includes traditional German vegetarian options such as filling soups and potato dumplings as well as dedicated asparagus menus for much of the summer. Otherwise, modern bistros and cafés will always provide something tasty and wholesome, and more upmarket Turkish takeaways often provide cheap veggie dishes alongside the ubiquitous kebabs.

Drink

The standard beverage is **coffee**, always fresh and generally weaker than its counterparts from France or Italy unless you ask for an espresso. All the usual lattes and cappuccinos are on offer. **Tea** is most popular in the northern *Länder* of Lower Saxony, Bremen and Schleswig-Holstein where the Dutch influence is most pronounced.

Mineral water (*Mineralwasser*) usually comes sparkling (*mit Gas*), although the muscle of corporates such as Evian and Volvic has pushed still water (*stilles*) onto the shelves. Even so, fizzy mineral water still rules, and many drinks mix this with fruit juice and call themselves a **Schorle**. Most common is probably the apple juice variant: *Apfelschorle*. One

very successful and trendy brand basically bottling the *Schorle* – though with fancy varieties like *Holunder* (elderberry) and *Ingwer* (ginger) – is Bionade.

Beer will also merrily get mixed with various other drinks, the most popular and successful being *Radler*, a lemonade–beer shandy. Meanwhile, mixing orange soda (such as Fanta) with cola is also popular as a *Spezi*. American brands of **cola** are enduringly popular in Germany, but there is stiff competition from various home-grown forms: Club Cola is the East German variety, still going strong since 1967. Fritz-Kola, a brand announced by a black-and-white logo depicting the faces of the Hamburg duo behind the company, is particularly popular. The signs themselves are worn like badges by cafés and restaurants wishing to announce how with-it they are. Every bit as trendy is the Club Mate brand, a high-caffeine drink with mate tea extract.

Beer

And so to **beer**. Supped by all, *Bier* is not just the national drink but an integral part of German life, with distinct regional accents and seasonal quirks. Whether conglomerate or small **Hausbrauerei** (a brewery-cum-*Gaststätte*), 1200-plus brewers producing over 5000 brews adhere voluntarily to the 1516 **Reinheitsgebot**, a purity law that specifies that only barley, hops, water and yeast can be used for fermentation – perhaps the reason why delicious chemical-free brews slip down dangerously easily, and (so locals say) won't give you a hangover. (Not true, incidentally, but the morning after is noticeably less brutal.) Beer comes in volumes of between 0.2 litres and 0.5 litres, either as draught (*vom Fass*) or in the bottle (*Flasche*).

Pils is the most familiar beer for visitors, golden in colour and with a hoppy, refreshing flavour. Many will also know **Export**, stronger than *Pils* and named because its high alcohol content kept the beer fresh during travel. It is dry with a hint of sweetness, although not as sweet as **Helles**, a generic term for light brews. **Dunkel** is the generic name for dark beers, which are rich in malt and full-bodied, though not as heavy as catch-all name **Schwarzbier** (black beer). Its opposite is **Weissbier** (white beer, also *Weisse* or *Weissen*), a southern favourite now available countrywide. Brewed from wheat, it is pale, cloudy and tastes like fresh hay; *Hefeweissen* has a stronger kick of yeast and *Kristal-Weissen* is clearer with more fizz. In Berlin it comes with lactic acid as low-alcohol **Berliner Weisse**, often drunk *mit Grün* (with green woodruff syrup) and *mit Schuss* (raspberry syrup). Light or dark, **Bock**

beers should be treated with respect because of a 6.5–7 percent alcohol content, which makes super-strength festival brew **Doppelbock** positively dangerous. Lemonade shandy is known as **Radler**, or **Alsterwasser** in Hamburg.

Local specialities abound. Dortmund, Germany's beer capital in terms of volume, is renowned for its Export; Düsseldorf brews a malty **Alt** beer, served with fruit in summer as *Altbierbowle*; and Cologne is proud of its light, refreshing **Kölsch** beer, routinely dismissed elsewhere as a glorified shandy, not helped by the small measures served in narrow *Stangen* glasses. Bavaria, the spiritual home of German beer and the beer garden, produces all the usuals plus sweet **Malzbier** (malt beer), like stout; Munich specials are *Märzenbier*, a powerful brew fermented in March for September knees-up, the Oktoberfest, and **Hofbräu**, formerly supped only by the royal court. Bamberg's smoky *Rauchbier* is another state special.

Wine

Such is the German love of beer it would be easy to overlook its wines. The memory of sickly *Liebfraumilch* once exported to Britain may play its part. But in recent years Germany's better wines are being exported, prompting foreign wine-buffs to wax about a Renaissance in German wine-making. Quite simply, German wines of the past decade have been superlatively good, aided by global warming and a return to Riesling rather than exotic crossbreeds. Of the thirteen areas in which wine is produced, most in the southwest, the most

celebrated are those of the Rhine and Mosel valleys (see box below). Most areas produce wines that are *trocken* (dry) or *halbtrocken* (medium), though there are some *lieblich* (sweet) wines.

Another reason non-Germans may have steered away from German wine is that the classification system seems absurdly over-complicated alongside the classic French AOC standard. Basic plonk is sweetish **Tafelwein**; a better choice is **Landwein**, a dry, German *vin de pays*. By the **Qualitätswein** level you're in the good stuff, either *Qualitätswein bestimmter Anbaugebiete* (Qba) from defined regions, or *Qualitätswein mit Prädikat* from specific vineyards. Of the latter, **Kabinett** wines are reserve wines – unsugared dry wines of natural personality and occasionally sublime – while **Spätlese** are produced from late-harvested grapes to produce fuller, usually dry flavours. **Auslese** wines are a step up in strength and sweetness, their intensity often prompting comparisons with honey. **Eiswein**, sharp with a concentrated, often sweet flavour, is made from grapes harvested after being frozen. Sweeter still are rare **Beerenauslese**, produced from exceptionally ripe grapes.

Three-quarters of German wines are white (*Weisswein*), typically Rieslings, which comprise over a fifth of total wine output and at their best are sensational – light and elegant, often almost floral. *Silvaner* wines have more body, while *Gewürztraminers* are intense and highly aromatic in flavour. The German *Grauburgunder* is better known in English as Pinot Gris. Notable **reds** (*Rotwein*) are *Spätburgunder*, a German Pinot Noir, rich in colour,

GERMAN WINE REGIONS

Ahr Small wine-valley south of Bonn that specializes in reds – has a reputation for a light, sometimes elegant, *Spätburgunder*.

Baden Spread over a huge area from Heidelberg to the border and across to the Bodensee. Specializes in dry wines: *Spätburgunder*, Riesling and *Gewürztraminer*.

Franconia (Franken). Main valley and around. Grows dry wines as distinctive as the area's round-bellied *Bocksbeutel* bottles. Good *Silvaner*.

Hessiche Bergstrasse North of Heidelberg and west Germany's smallest area. Small producers, and reliable Riesling.

Mittelrhein More famous for scenery, the Middle Rhine grows a flinty, underrated Riesling around the villages of Boppard and Bacharach.

Mosel–Saar–Ruwer Germany's most acclaimed – and exported – region, with a subtly elegant Riesling grown on the Mosel's sun-soaked slopes and a brilliant one in the Saar tributary. Also known for exciting new producers who keep the old hands sharp.

Nahe Rhine tributary whose fresh, well-balanced Riesling doesn't get the attention it deserves.

Palatinate (Pfalz). The growing region formerly known as Rheinpfalz south of Rheinhessen. A warm climate and fully ripe grapes produce classic, rich wines – the dry Riesling is increasingly well made.

Rheingau West of Wiesbaden, this is the best area of the Rhine valley, with a classic if rather old-fashioned Riesling and good reds.

Rheinhessen Riesling is the pick of this huge region between Mainz and Worms, its reputation on the up nationally.

Saale-Unstrut Riesling and *Gewürztraminer* whites, *Silvaner* and a Cistercian-rooted *Portugieser* red, plus sparkling *Sekt* wines at the river confluence by Naumberg, west of Leipzig.

Saxony (Sachsen). Small region centred on Meissen west of Dresden. Best known for a distinctive Muscat-style *Müller-Thurgau*.

Württemberg Large and underrated area of small producers around Stuttgart. Go for reds – *Trollinger* and *Lemberger* – especially in the Neckar valley.

velvety in taste, and *Trollinger*, a light, fresh wine that's delicious in summer. **Rosé** (*Roséwein*) is less common. A notable addition to the cellar is Frankfurt's **Apfelwein** – cider – and at Christmas everywhere *Glühwein* (hot mulled wine, literally "glow wine"). More detail on German wines is published online at 🔵 germanwine.de.

Spirits

High-proof **Schnapps** spirits come in a range of regional flavours which rival that of beer: common varieties include *Kirschwasser* (cherry Schnapps), served with ham in the Black Forest, and in Berlin a *Doppelkorn* (corn Schnapps), traditionally tossed off with a knuckle of pork. Whether digestif, aperitif or simply a short, Schnapps is served in 2cl measures and locals delight in claiming it is medicinal, an idea handed down over a millennium since monks began distillation of fruits and herbs.

The media

The foreigner's image of Germany is of a land of books, a serious country of deep thought and highbrow ideas. Certainly 95,000 new books are published in Germany each year and nothing else in the world comes close to the immense annual Frankfurt Book Fair. Yet Germany also has dynamic printed, television and radio sectors. The best place to look for foreign media is at newsagents in the main train station – those in cities also carry a small stock of international magazines.

Newspapers and magazines

The German press is characterized by the number of titles. At the national level, the daily **newspaper** market is dominated by a small number of publishers. Largest, with 24 percent of the market, is Axel Springer group, which prints both heavyweight newspapers and the "**boulevard press**" as Germany calls its tabloids. The press is strongest at regional level, although many of the city-produced dailies are distributed nationwide. Germany's bestseller on the streets is sensationalist tabloid *BILD* (🔵 bild.de), which shifts four million units daily. Of the dailies, conservative *Frankfurter Allgemeine Zeitung* (🔵 faz.net) enjoys considerable prestige, presumably thanks to its weighty opinions and business focus rather than dry content – an English-

language version is included as a supplement in every issue of the *International Herald Tribune* – and Berlin-produced *Die Welt* (🔵 welt.de) has a great influence on public opinion.

At the other end of the political spectrum is the left-of-centre *Tageszeitung*, known as "*Taz*" (🔵 taz.de) – not so hot on solid news, but good in-depth articles on politics and ecology. It has the added advantage of being an easier read for non-native German speakers, since the German used is a little simpler. Other nationwide papers include Munich's *Süddeutsche Zeitung* (🔵 sueddeutsche.de) and *Frankfurter Rundschau* (🔵 fr-online.de). Incidentally, Berlin-produced *The Local* (🔵 thelocal.de) provides German news in English but is tricky to find even in its home town Berlin – there's a good online edition, though, with regional sections.

The German **magazine** sector is extremely buoyant, with around 2000 magazines and specialized periodicals on the market. Weekly news magazines with a model similar to American *Time* magazine are very popular. This sector is monopolized by the politically influential *Der Spiegel* (🔵 spiegel.de), which is known for its investigative journalism. It also has an excellent English-language website. In a similar vein is Hamburg-based left-wing weekly *Die Zeit* (🔵 zeit.de). Best seen as a weekly newspaper that focuses on analysis and background information, it appears every Thursday and, while left-wing in stance, includes a number of independently written reports on a variety of subjects.

Television and radio

While Länder are responsible for public broadcasting within each state, all contribute programmes for the nationwide principal **TV channels** (nicknamed "Das Erste", or "the first") – run by ARD (Arbeitsgemeinschaft der Rundfunkanstalten Deutschlands; 🔵 ard.de) and ZDF (Zweites Deutsches Fernsehen; 🔵 zdf.de); both approximate BBC or PBS channels. Both ARD and ZDF offer a range of free digital channels.

Otherwise major commercial channels dominate, foremost among them Sat, RTL and VOX. All channels seem to exist on a diet of US reruns dubbed into German. Germany has an above-average percentage of cable households – 53 percent. With cable TV, available in larger hotels, you'll be able to pick up the locally available cable channels, with over twenty to choose from, including MTV, BBC World, and the ubiquitous CNN.

Radio in Germany is very much a regional affair. According to the various broadcasting laws of the various states, some Länder prefer a variety of commercial radio stations, others opt for diverse programming within a limited number of stations. Spin a dial and you'll find some decent dance music, American rock and the occasional hip-hop show (mainly late at night) alongside classical, cheese and soft rock. The only nationwide English-speaking radio station is the BBC World Service (90.2FM). British Forces station **BFBS** (W ssvc.com/bfbs) pumps out programming modelled on BBC radio in localized areas – principally western Lower Saxony and Westphalia. BFBS has chart hits and classics plus hourly news, BFBS 2 has more chat plus BBC news programmes from Radio 4 and sport from BBC Radio Five Live. Frequencies vary by area – check the website or scan from (roughly) 95FM to 106FM.

Festivals

Germans like festivals. From city to village, wherever there are people there'll usually be a festival of some kind, whether a major event for thousands that programmes international artists or just a summer fair. The diversity is astounding – high-quality classical music and theatre events, wine festivals, unbridled parties and atmospheric Christmas markets. Notwithstanding the latter, most are staged from May to August, when you're almost sure to roll into a good-humoured town centre crammed with stalls and stages, with much food and beer being consumed by all. On top of local secular events, Germany observes a large number of pagan and religious festivals in its calendar. See individual town accounts in the Guide for more information of local events.

JANUARY AND FEBRUARY

Karneval (also known as Fasching or Fastnet). Seven weeks before Easter. Pagan-rooted pre-Lent speciality of the Rhineland and Bavaria, where it's known as Fasching. Warm-up events throughout late January climax in late February (or early March) with costumed parades and considerable revelry. Cologne (see p.616) has the most celebrated Karneval, followed by Düsseldorf and Mainz, or Munich's more jolly Fasching. Black Forest events are more traditional, the unique event in Rottweil, Baden-Württemberg, almost pagan.

Berlinale Early Feb, Berlin. The third largest film festival in the world, with around twelve days of new movies, art-house cinema and more mainstream entertainment. W berlinale.de.

MARCH AND APRIL

Leipziger Honky Tonk Saturday, usually mid-March, Leipzig. In theory a music festival in a hundred boozers, actually Europe's largest pub crawl. W honky-tonk.de/leipzig.

Easter Late March or early April. Sacred pomp throughout Catholic Germany – especially impressive in Bavaria.

Walpurgisnacht April 30, Harz. Celebration of the witches' sabbath with costumed parades and music throughout the Harz (see p.217) area.

MAY

Erste Mai May 1, Hamburg and Berlin. A combination of joyous and riotous behaviour takes over several city streets in the name of International Workers' Day.

Hafengeburtstag Weekend closest to May 7, Hamburg. Tall ships and flotilla parades in the world's largest harbour festival. W hafengeburtstag.de.

Africa Festival End of May, Würzburg. Europe's largest celebration of African culture: dance, music and parades. W africafestival.org.

Passionsspiele May–Sept, Oberammergau. Once-a-decade passion play by locals of a Bavarian village (see p.388), celebrated nationwide. Next is 2020.

Rhein im Flammen ("Rhine in Flames"). May–Sept, Rhineland. Start of the firework spectaculars along the Rhine from Bonn to Bingen; culminates in August in Koblenz (see p.541). W rhein-in-flammen.de.

JUNE

Wave-Gotik-Treffen Whitsun (first weekend in June or last in May), Leipzig. Around 25,000 Goths muster for the world's largest doom-fest (see p.176). W wave-gotik-treffen.de.

Karneval der Kulturen Early June, Berlin. Berlin celebrates its ethnic diversity in a "Carnival of Cultures" – expect around 1.5 million people. W karneval-berlin.de.

Bachfest Mid-June, Leipzig. Week-long celebration of the great composer in the city where he produced his finest works (see p.169). W bach-leipzig.de.

Kieler Woche Last week in June, Kiel . Long-standing fixture on the international sailing circuit: races, parades and parties (see p.797). W kieler-woche.de.

Christopher Street Day June–July, nationwide. Parades and parties for gay pride events, over thirty years young – the largest events are in Berlin, Munich and Cologne.

JULY

Schützenfeste Early July, Hannover. Biggest and best of the Marksmen festivals in Lower Saxony and the Rhineland area (see p.705). W hannover.de/schuetzenfest.

Kinderzeche Mid-July, Dinkelsbühl. Celebrated children's folklore pageant that re-enacts the town's capitulation to a Swedish siege in the Thirty Years' War (see p.323). W kinderzeche.de.

Mercedes Benz Fashion Week Mid-July, Berlin. Big fashion show which coincides with the more-offbeat Bread & Butter (W breadandbutter.com) fashion trade show, which takes place twice a year in July and January. W berlin.mbfashionweek.com.

CHRISTMAS MARKETS

Each December lights twinkle in the small wooden huts which gather across the country to celebrate local seasonal handicrafts and delicacies. But it's not just shopping: a **Christmas market** is as much about the pleasure of splitting a bag of roasted chestnuts with friends and soaking up Christmas spirit – including in the form of a mug or two of steaming *Glühwein*.

A BRIEF HISTORY

The first Christmas market seems to have gone unrecorded, but the **1294 Vienna market** was certainly among the earliest. Around this time the idea caught on among Czechs, and it was just over the Czech border, in Bautzen in 1384 that the first German Christmas market was recorded.

The earliest markets mainly sold meat, but over time they grew to include local handicrafts. This trade got a terrific boost from the sixteenth-century teachings of **Martin Luther**, who suggested the birth of Christ would be a better time to exchange gifts than the traditional saints' days of St Nicholas (December 6), or St Martin (November 11). But despite having roots in religious veneration, Christmas markets – usually held by the city's main church to attract church-goers – soon competed with the churches themselves. As early as 1616 a Nuremberg priest complained he'd had to abandon a Christmas Eve service because all of his congregation were at the market. This was also the time when **Christmas gift-buying** took off – and up until the nineteenth century the markets remained the main place to buy seasonal toys and treats. Today, Germany's markets attract a staggering 160 million visitors a year and market-related revenues are around €5 billion.

FOOD AND DRINK

Many towns keep their warming Christmas recipes a closely guarded secret, even trademarked, with Nuremberg's **Lebkuchen**, a soft spiced gingerbread that's been produced since the fourteenth century, probably the most famous. In the Rhineland and Westphalia, **Spekulatius** – cardamom and cinnamon biscuits – are common, while the heavy **Stollen** fruitcake is particularly associated with Saxony.

The seasonal drink of choice is **Glühwein** (mulled wine) and its nonalcoholic cousin **Kinderpunsch**. **Feuerzangenbowle** – red wine, flavored by a flaming rum-dipped block of sugar – and **Eierpunsch** (a sort of eggnog) are also popular.

CRAFTS

Traditional handmade **wooden crafts** are the most popular and include crib figurines, toys,

AUGUST

Bayreuth Festspiele Late July–Aug, Bayreuth. Prestigious Wagnerian opera spectacular in the composer's Festspielhaus. Buy tickets as far in advance as possible. Ⓦ bayreuther-festspiele.de.

Gäubodenfest Mid-Aug, Straubing. Hugely popular Bavarian folk jamboree – folk displays, beer, music, funfairs and more beer (see p.412). Ⓦ volksfest-straubing.de.

Weinfeste Late Aug to Sept, Rhine–Mosel area. Traditionally a celebration of the annual grape harvest, in fact an excuse for a knees-up. Three of the best are in Rudesheim, Mainz and Dürkheimer, which cites its mid-Sept Wurstmarkt as the biggest wine bash in the world.

SEPTEMBER AND OCTOBER

Oktoberfest Mid-Sept to Oct, Munich . Beer swilling takes on epic proportions at one of Germany's most famous annual events (see box, p.357) – which ensures legions of foreigners are among the six million drinkers. Ⓦ oktoberfest.de.

Berlin Marathon Late Sept, Berlin. With around 40,000 participants from over a hundred countries, and with the most marathon world records (for men and women) set here, this is one of the largest and most popular road races in the world. Ⓦ bmw-berlin-marathon.com.

Canstatter Volksfest Late Sept to Oct, Stuttgart. Two weeks of oompah bands in traditional costume and fairground attractions in the world's second-largest beer festival; a less touristy alternative to the Oktoberfest. Ⓦ cannstatter-volksfest.de.

Tag der Deutschen Einheit Oct 3. Day of German unity is celebrated with gusto, beer, sausages and music in many German cities.

NOVEMBER

Martinsfest Nov 10–11, north Baden and Rhineland. Festival to honour jovial fourth-century St Martin; marked by a goose lunch on the day and, in the Upper Rhine, preceded by evening children's lantern processions.

DECEMBER

Christmas markets (Weihnachtsmarkt or Christkindelsmarkt), nationwide. Traditional homespun Germany at its most charming (see box above).

marionettes and nutcrackers. Look out for the wooden *Weihnachtspyramide* – in which the heat from candles rotates a nativity scene – and the jovial little *Räuchermänchen* – figures that serve as incense holders and puff smoke from their mouths. Much of this woodwork comes from the Erzgebirge (see p.180) on the Czech border, where the Christmas market in Schneeberg is particularly good for such things.

CHRISTMAS FOR KIDS

Kids visiting Christmas markets will usually find a carousel, a few games or rides and sometimes an ice rink. Other draws often include street performers, nativity plays, puppet theatres and concerts; and there's always a **nativity scene** – sometimes populated by a petting zoo of real animals, such as sheep, donkeys and goats. But Germany's best kids' Christmas market is doubtless that of the Europa-Park (see p.496).

CHRISTMAS IN THE CITY

Though smaller towns often have particularly atmospheric markets (see the German tourist-board's ⓦ germany-christmas-market.org.uk), many of Germany's larger cities have great Christmas festivities. Among them are:

Bremen The attractive market on the main square aside, Bremen also has a medieval maritime market, where you can fire crossbows, have your fortune told and watch magic. Look out too for free outdoor performances of the *Stadtmusikanten* fairy tale (see p.741).

Cologne The main market is by the cathedral, which also forms the motif for much of its famed *Spekulatius*. Other novelties include the medieval Chocolate Museum market, which has acrobats, entertainers and stallholders in period costume. Look out for local speciality *Meth*, a honey wine.

Dresden Dresden's invention of the *Stollen* is celebrated in the jovial *Stollenfest*, in which a four-tonne example journeys through the city before being carved into more bite-sized portions.

Frankfurt Despite skyscrapers and banking, Frankfurt's Römerberg market, with its giant Christmas tree, vintage carousel and

half-timbered facades, is atmospheric and fun.

Hamburg Highlights include a cheerful circus-designed market, with wandering performers; the stylish Winterzauber market with ice bar, skating rink and puppet theatre; the Finnish-themed Fleetinsel market; and the irreverent Santa Pauli market in the red-light district, where Santas in lewd poses sit atop stalls selling kinky knickers and sex toys.

Munich The Marienplatz market is wonderfully atmospheric and great for handicrafts, but Münchener Freiheit is more relaxed and has better food.

Nuremberg Nuremberg's delightful huddle of red-and-white-striped canvas on an old square below the castle is deservedly popular, with two million annual visitors. The *Lebkuchen* is its hallmark, but look out for *Nürnberger Zwetschgamännla*: little figures made from prunes.

Sports and outdoor activities

From the soupy mudflats of the North Sea to the southern Bavarian Alps, there's a lot to enjoy in Germany's great outdoors, and the array of activities is just as varied – there's even a German surf scene. However, the most popular activity of all – even if only followed from a bar stool – is football. Tickets to Bundesliga matches are cheaper than for the UK's Premier League and the following just as passionate.

Hiking and walking

Germany has an abundance of scenic walks and long-distance hiking routes, so no matter where

you go there'll be a well-marked trail or short stroll. In recent decades the country has also developed a taste for so-called **Nordic walking**: purposeful walking using ski poles.

Popular areas include the Harz, Black Forest, Bavarian Alps, Saxon Switzerland and the Thuringian Forest, though many trails in any of these areas travel through thick forest, so views can be limited. The latter two are home, respectively, to arguably Germany's most scenic long-distance walk, the 112km **Malerweg**, and its most popular, the **Rennsteig** (168km). Details are in relevant chapters. A useful source of walking information is **Wanderbares Deutschland** (ⓦ wanderbares-deutschland .de), a marketing body whose German-language website provides details of walks nationwide, including trail information, plus links to other websites where relevant. Along many trails you'll find hotels and inns that provide specialized accommodation for hikers. Kompass publishes hiking

---

DON'T GET TICKED OFF

A serious and growing problem, **ticks** are fairly rampant in many German forests and are often the transmitters of a range of nasty and often incurable diseases, including tick-borne encephalitis and Lyme disease. As ever, prevention is better than cure and measures include wearing a hat when out in the woods and checking your body while showering for possible new friends; crotches, armpits and scalps are favourite locations. If one has embedded itself in your skin you're best to visit a hospital or see a doctor for its removal. If you can't, the right technique is to gently twist the creature off your skin, while trying to squeeze the body as little as possible. Whether or not any part is left inside, you should also take a course of antibiotics as soon as possible.

---

maps of popular walking areas (see p.55), and bookshops stock any number of walking guides (*Wanderführer*).

Cycling

Simply a joy. Over two hundred long-distance cycle routes across the country provide 42,000km of excellent touring. Dedicated cycle-paths off the main road typically follow river valleys – the classic is the **Elberadweg** (Elbe Cycle Route; Ⓦ elberadweg.de), which follows the river for 860km as it slices northwest from Schöna in Saxon Switzerland to Cuxhaven on the North Sea. However, there is an abundance of marked cross-country routes to choose from – pootling through the little-known water-world of the Mecklenburg Lakes Cycle Route, for example, or bowling along the Baltic coast, even exploring the Ruhrgebiet's industrial heart. Mountain biking is also good thanks to legions of dedicated forest trails, such as the **Mountain Bike Rennsteig**, which tracks through the Thuringian Forest parallel to Germany's most popular footpath.

The national tourist board has a good section on its website that provides a heads-up on many of the most popular touring routes, while the key contact is the **Allgemeiner Deutscher Fahrrad-Club** (ADFC; Ⓦ adfc.de), a national cycling federation that grades long-distance trails with one to five stars. It also publishes a handy brochure of five thousand cyclist-friendly accommodation options, *Bett & Bike* (Ⓦ bettundbike.de), available at bookshops. Cycle maps are widely available through local tourist offices. For details of taking a bike on the train, see p.34.

Winter sports

The German ski holiday is characterized by first-class facilities, low prices and a charmingly low-key après-ski with hearty German food in a country

Gaststätte. The premier resorts lie in the **Bavarian Alps** south of Munich, centred on Garmisch-Partenkirchen, a former Olympic town with a lively après-ski whose facilities were upgraded for the 2011 Alpine World Ski Championship. The pistes lie above on Germany's highest mountain, Zugspitze (2964m), on the Austrian border – with some 20km of pistes ranging from 700m to 3km and a snowboard park, as well as 40km of cross-country trails. The nearby ski village Oberammergau has the finest cross-country skiing in Germany – all 90km of it – as well as steep pistes on the Laber hills (1683m). Steeper still is the Dammkar-tunnel near Mittenwald on the other side of Garmisch-Partenkirchen, its forty-percent-incline hill one of the most challenging in Germany. The **Allgäu** area in southwest Bavaria offers the largest continuous ski area in Germany, with 500km of downhill slopes, including some deep-snow off-piste skiing, and two hundred ski lifts. Outside of Bavaria, the **Black Forest** offers good downhill skiing; the low-lying **Harz** and the **Sauerland** regions focus more on cross-country skiing, weather permitting; and there are lesser scenes in the **Thuringian Forest** highlands around Oberhof and on the Czech border in south **Saxony**. The season begins in mid-November in Bavaria (usually Dec elsewhere) and runs to around February – sometimes March in a good year.

Ski rental and lessons are widely available at the resorts, either at ski shops or at ski schools, often located on the pistes themselves. Costs are around €25 per day for a set of boots, poles and skis or snowboard, plus €30 for a day's lift-pass.

Watersports

Riddled by waterways, dotted with lakes and lapped by seas, Germany is generally a good watersports destination. Even in major cities, boat rental is available by the hour on most lakes and waterways, generally from April to September, sometimes to October.

Canoeing and river **kayaking** are also popular on most major rivers. The overlooked River Oder on the border of Poland appeals for its lack of development. Arguably the most appealing multi-day canoeing in Germany is in the **Müritz National Park** in Mecklenburg-Western Pomerania, where you can **canoe-and-camp** through a mosaic of lakes. Similar experiences are available in the Spreewald south of Berlin, and in the Schleswig-Holstein lakes from Eutin to Kiel. Rental is best sourced through local tourist-information centres – if you are renting equipment for river trips, try to find one that offers transport, thereby allowing a one-way trip. If your German is up to it, browse the websites of the Federal Association of Canoeing Tourism (Bundesvereinigung Kanutouristik; Ⓦ kanu-touristik.de) or whitewater-orientated Kajak Channel (Ⓦ kajak-channel.de).

Motor- or **houseboat** holidays are popular on Lake Müritz, Germany's second-largest lake, and in the waterways of Brandenburg, north of Berlin. Rental of leisure craft, which typically sleep up to eight people, is usually by the week; no licences are required for most waterways for craft under 13m. The regional tourist office website (Ⓦ vorpommern.de/house-boat-holidays.html) is useful, as is motor organization ADAC, which has a German-only section on watersports at Ⓦ adac.de/reise_freizeit/wassersport.

The coasts are playgrounds for **sailing**, **windsurfing** and **kitesurfing** – holiday resorts on Rügen and Sylt offer rental outfits, the latter a stop on the Windsurf World Cup tour. As a rule of thumb, you'll find flat water in the Baltic off Rügen and waves in the more challenging conditions of the North Sea off Sylt. Consequently, the latter is also home to Germany's **surfing** scene – generally wind-slop but which has its days when the weather allows. Again, rental is available locally.

Football

Without question football is Germany's number-one spectator sport, ever since *Fussball* was imported by an English expat to Dresden in 1874. The national team lifted the 1954 World Cup even before Germany had a professional national league. Fast-forward a few decades and the team cemented its reputation for invincibility with a style that emphasized teamwork over individual flair. Not only did Germany win the most recent World Cup finals in 2014, they have three others to their name, as well as three European championships. They have also not lost a penalty shoot-out since 1976, as millions of England fans rue.

All the same, club matches of the **Bundesliga** (Ⓦ bundesliga.de), the German premier league since 1963, can be a little disappointing – many of the most talented homegrown players are lured abroad to leagues in England and Italy. Nevertheless, a Bundesliga match is a must for any true football fan, not least because facilities in club stadiums are superb. The most successful club is Bayern Munich, regulars in the European Champions League with a record 24 league cups in its trophy cabinet. Other big names include Borussia Mönchengladbach, with five titles; Borussia Dortmund, whose 79,000 average attendance rivals that of FC Barcelona – the largest in Europe; Werder Bremen; and Hamburger SV, the only team never to have been relegated.

The league runs from mid-August to the end of May, and **tickets** for games, generally played on Saturday, can be bought at stadium gates on matchday or at ticket shops – often a dedicated fan shop – in the preceding week for all but the biggest games. The league website lists fixtures, grounds and links to online ticket sales. Expect to pay from €10–15 for the cheapest seats and around €50 for the best. Some fans may be fairly lumpen – with much boozed-up bellowing of club anthems – but generally nonviolent.

Culture and etiquette

Germany is a modern, cosmopolitan country, its society shaped by a plurality of lifestyles and ethnic and cultural diversity. If you had images of a conservative, homespun people in Lederhosen and feathered hats, dispense with them now. In cities Germans are traditionally quite reserved, in the countryside rather more open and welcoming. However, attitudes vary across the country too – southerners tend to be more gregarious and conservative, while the liberals of the north can be more introverted.

The country's metropolises, particularly Berlin and Hamburg, are famous for their live-and-let-live attitude. This tolerance comes in part from the cities' appeal for unconventional Germans who relocate from elsewhere in the country, and partly from their large immigrant populations with more laissez-faire attitudes.

This open-mindedness also extends to tolerating **smoking** far more widely than elsewhere in

Western Europe – with many bars frequently ignoring bans. That said, smoking is banned in many public places in Germany. Various states rule differently, but in general smoking is forbidden in most indoor public spaces, including hospitals, airports and train stations, restaurants, bars, cinemas and theatres. Bavaria has the toughest laws, with smoking banned practically everywhere (except at the Oktoberfest), but even here some bars have become designated "smoking clubs". Other states are laxer in both regulations and enforcement – particularly Berlin – but in general most bars are smoke-free or have a separate smoking room. This fluid situation makes it important to always ask before you light up, unless plenty of people around you are smoking.

Even here, however, foreigners should be aware of a few points of protocol. First is the use of **du** and **Sie** (you) to strangers, which, though not the cultural minefield of French, still requires careful negotiation. *Du* is used for friends – or between young people – only, and the formal *Sie* is expected from everyone else you speak to, whether waiters or shop assistants and especially the police and officialdom.

Whatever stereotypes may have you believe, Germans don't take themselves all that seriously –

and, yes, they enjoy a joke – nor are they prudish: indeed, the popularity of *Frei Korper Kultur* (FKK; nudism) is more likely to shock visitors. The country that introduced naturist flights to the world – from Erfurt to Usedom in January 2008 – also has dedicated nude areas on most beaches, and even in some public parks. Be aware, too, that mixed-sex nudity in spas is the norm.

Shopping

Quality and precision – the watchwords of German products – mean most visitors to the country will already be familiar with many of the smaller items it exports besides beer. Familiar names may include Adidas, Birkenstock, Boss, Nivea, Mont Blanc, Villeroy & Boch and Meissen. Prices for these brands are not significantly cheaper than elsewhere in Europe, although the choice is wider.

Most cities have a local **alternative quarter** with a quota of independent boutiques and vintage outlets for local hipsters. Those same quarters in Berlin and to a lesser extent Hamburg also support superb record shops – a good place to browse for cutting-edge electronica.

CLOTHING AND SHOE SIZES

WOMEN'S CLOTHING

American	4	6	8	10	12	14	16	18	
British	6	8	10	12	14	16	18	20	
Continental	34	36	38	40	42	44	46	48	

WOMEN'S SHOES

American	5	6	7	8	9	10	11		
British	3	4	5	6	7	8	9		
Continental	36	37	38	39	40	41	42		

MEN'S SHIRTS

American	14	15	15.5	16	16.5	17	17.5	18	
British	14	15	15.5	16	16.5	17	17.5	18	
Continental	36	38	39	41	42	43	44	45	

MEN'S SHOES

American	7	7.5	8	8.5	9.5	10	10.5	11	11.5
British	6	7	7.5	8	9	9.5	10	11	12
Continental	39	40	41	42	43	44	44	45	46

MEN'S SUITS

American	34	36	38	40	42	44	46	48	
British	34	36	38	40	42	44	46	48	
Continental	44	46	48	50	52	54	56	58	

And then, of course, there is the wonderland of German **crafts**. Wooden toys are excellent – ubiquitously beautifully crafted with superb attention to detail, and often a regional flavour. **Christmas markets** (see p.46) are excellent opportunities to pick these up. If you must buy one, **cuckoo clocks**, made in southern Germany since the eighteenth century, can be bought in shops throughout the Black Forest.

Travelling with children

Children and Germany are a good match. This is an orderly, safe country with an indulgent attitude towards youngsters. It's the land of familiar fairy tales, such as the Pied Piper of Hamlyn (Hameln); traditional folk festivals; hills dotted with castles steeped in gory legends; and commercial attractions and theme parks aplenty. Free entry or concession rates are standard practice (expect around thirty to fifty percent discount on sights and tours), the main problem being that the definition of child for discounts varies enormously – you're safe to assume under-12s count; under-16s often do; under-18s sometimes do.

Public transport provides discounts for children under 16, while under-4s travel free of charge. Group rail tickets also provide good value (see p.32). All major car-rental companies can provide child seats on request for around €5 a day. Motorway service centres have baby-changing facilities.

All but luxury **hotels** are child-friendly. Most can rustle up a cot and many have family rooms with a double bed and two singles, or can provide an extra bed for a small charge. Larger hotels may allow children to go free, otherwise the standard discount is thirty percent. **Farmstays** (see p.37) are an option worth considering – endless space to romp around and often with activities such as cycling and riding included.

Cafés and standard **restaurants** are relaxed about kids and menus offer few challenges. High-end restaurants are a different matter, particularly in cities, and especially at dinner. High-end places in the country tend to be more relaxed but double-check. **Baby-changing facilities** are common in public toilets; discreet breast-feeding is acceptable in public.

The best science **museums** offer interactive exhibits and most large cities have a **zoo**; see Ⓦ zoo-infos.de for a full list.

Travel essentials

Climate

German weather can be a real mixed bag at any time of year, thanks to the way in which continental and maritime air masses collide in this part of Europe. That said, those used to British variability and poor weather are likely to find German weather much better; while those used to the searing summer heat of much of North America will also be pleased. **Summer** temperatures rarely hit 30ºC and temperatures tend to stay comfortable well into the evening, allowing beer gardens and outdoor cafés to bustle as darkness falls as late as October. **Winter** tends to be cold enough to be a very different season, unlike the UK, but not so savage that many activities have to halt entirely, as in much of the US or Canada.

Costs

By European standards, prices in Germany are reasonable; Berlin, for example, is well short of the excesses of Paris and London and with quality to match. Nevertheless, the country has the potential to become expensive, especially if you're set on flashy nightspots, swanky restaurants and smart hotels. There can also be large differences in prices between regions and cities – Cologne is noticeably cheaper than near-neighbour Düsseldorf, for example.

Assuming you intend to eat and drink in moderately priced places, use public transport and stay at hostels, the bare minimum living-cost you could get by on is around €40 (£32/US$54) a day, including a hostel bed (around €20), snacks and an evening meal (€10), and a little for museums and entertainment. Make lunch the main meal of the day and you may save maybe €5 per day; but overall a more realistic **typical holiday budget** is about twice that of shoestringers: €80 per day.

Student discounts

Full-time students can expect **discounts** at almost all sights and attractions – often around thirty

AVERAGE DAILY TEMPERATURES

	Jan	Feb	Mar	Apr	May	Jun	Jul	Aug	Sep	Oct	Nov	Dec
BERLIN												
Max °C	2	3	8	13	19	22	24	23	20	13	7	3
Min °C	-3	-3	0	4	8	12	14	13	10	6	2	-1
Max °F	36	37	46	55	66	72	75	73	68	55	45	37
Min °F	27	27	32	39	46	54	57	55	50	43	36	30
Rainfall (mm)	42	33	41	37	54	69	56	58	45	37	44	55
FRANKFURT												
Max °C	3	5	11	16	20	23	25	24	21	14	8	4
Min °C	-2	-1	2	6	9	13	15	14	11	7	3	0
Max °F	37	41	52	61	68	73	77	75	70	57	46	39
Min °F	28	30	36	43	48	55	59	57	52	44	37	32
Rainfall (mm)	42	37	48	43	60	61	65	53	50	55	52	55
MUNICH												
Max °C	1	3	9	14	18	21	23	23	20	13	7	2
Min °C	-5	-5	-1	3	7	11	13	12	9	4	0	-4
Max °F	34	37	48	57	64	70	73	73	68	55	45	36
Min °F	23	23	30	37	45	52	55	54	48	39	32	25
Rainfall (mm)	48	45	58	70	93	128	132	111	86	65	71	61

percent – as well as being able to save money on transport such as rail travel (see p.28 & p.32). In general you'll need to be under 27 to qualify for many of the discounts, and in possession of some kind of proof of your status. The International Student Identity Card (ISIC; ⓦisic.org), available from student travel agents, is the most widely recognized way to prove your status.

Crime and safety

Crime is low by Western standards, but not nonexistent, and standard modern tensions exist. Statistically, crime is more prevalent in eastern states of the former GDR, fuelled by depressed economies. Small-minded attitudes also often exist here, and xenophobic neo-Nazi thugs can target those who look "foreign" – non-white. Paradoxically, eastern German city centres, and German cities in general, are safer in comparison with other European cities. **Petty crimes** such as pickpocketing or bag-snatching in shopping precincts or busy U-Bahns are the most likely crimes you'll encounter.

As far as **personal safety** is concerned, even the rougher city neighbourhoods feel more dangerous than they actually are. Those run-down U-Bahn stations or train stations with a crowd of drunks look alarming when compared to the rest of the country, but wouldn't stand out in most other European cities. The situation in city suburbs is a little trickier, in Berlin, for example. With caution it's fine, but muggings and casual violence do occur, particularly to those who stand out.

If you do have something stolen (or simply lost), or suffer an attack, you'll need to register the details at the local police station: a straightforward, but inevitably bureaucratic and time-consuming process. Note the crime report number – or, better still, get a copy of the statement itself – for your insurance company.

The two offences you might unwittingly commit concern identity papers and jaywalking. By law you need to carry proof of your identity at all times. A driver's licence or ID card is fine, but a passport is best. It's essential that you carry all your documentation when driving – failure to do so may result in an on-the-spot fine. Jaywalking is also illegal and you can be fined if caught.

Electricity

Supply runs at 220–240V, 50Hz AC; sockets generally require a two-pin plug with rounded prongs. Visitors from the UK will need an adaptor, and visitors from North America may need a transformer, though most portable electrical equipment – such as cameras, laptops and mobile phones – is designed to accommodate a range of voltages.

Emergencies

Police: ☎ 110
Fire and ambulance: ☎ 112

Entry requirements

British and other EU nationals can enter Germany on a valid passport or national identity card for an indefinite period. US, Canadian, Australian and New Zealand citizens do not need a visa to enter Germany, and are allowed a stay of ninety days within any six-month period. South Africans need to apply for a visa, from the German Embassy in Pretoria (see below), which will cost around ZAR260 depending on the exchange rate. Visa requirements vary for nationals of other countries; contact your local German embassy or consulate for information.

In order to **extend a stay** once in the country all visitors should contact the nearest Ausländeramt (Alien Authority): addresses are in the phone books. For more information on this process and finding a job, see p.54.

GERMAN EMBASSIES ABROAD

UK 23 Belgrave Square, London SW1X 8PZ ☎ 020 7824 1300, ⓦ london.diplo.de.

Ireland 31 Trimelston Ave, Booterstown, Blackrock, Co Dublin ☎ 01 269 3011, ⓦ dublin.diplo.de.

US 2300 M Street NW, Washington, DC 20037 ☎ 202 298 4000, ⓦ germany.info.

Canada 1 Waverley St, Ottawa, ON K2P 0T8 ☎ 613 232 1101, ⓦ ottawa.diplo.de.

Australia 119 Empire Circuit, Yarralumla, Canberra 2600 ☎ 02 6270 1911, ⓦ canberra.diplo.de.

New Zealand 90–92 Hobson St, 6011 Wellington ☎ 04 473 6063, ⓦ wellington.diplo.de.

South Africa 180 Blackwood St, Arcadia, Pretoria 0083 ☎ 012 427 8900, ⓦ pretoria.diplo.de.

Gay and lesbian travellers

Germany has a legendary gay and lesbian scene in its major cities and gay pride event **Christopher Street Day** is celebrated throughout the country. Along with the two metropolises of Berlin and Hamburg, Cologne is one of the world's great gay cities, with one in ten of the population either gay or lesbian. The scene in **Berlin** – home to the world's first gay organization in 1897 and ruled by openly gay mayor, Klaus Wowereit – centres around the districts of Schöneberg, Kreuzberg and Prenzlauer Berg. That of **Hamburg** is in St Georg, and in **Cologne** there are two main gay districts –

around Rudolfplatz and close to the river around Alter Markt and Heumarkt. Other thriving gay centres are in **Munich** and **Frankfurt**. Details of local scenes are provided in the sections on relevant destinations. Otherwise newsstand listings magazines have information on gay and lesbian clubnights and events.

Small-town Germany is inevitably more socially conservative. Staunch Catholic towns of Bavaria can be hostile, and physical assaults are not unknown in depressed towns of eastern Germany.

Health

German healthcare is world-class. For immediate medical attention, head for the 24-hour emergency room of a major **hospital**; details are provided in the "Directory" sections of major destinations. In the event of an **emergency**, phone ☎ 112 for an ambulance (*Krankenwagen*). For non-urgent issues, go to the nearest **doctor** who calls himself a *Hausarzt* (general practitioner); surgeries usually operate 9am to noon and 3 to 6pm weekdays except on Wednesday afternoon.

As a European Union member, Germany has free reciprocal health agreements with other member states, whose citizens can apply for a free **European Health Insurance Card** (EHIC; ⓦ ehic.org.uk), which provides free, or cut-rate treatment, but will not pay for repatriation. If you qualify, you will need to get the card in advance of your trip; without it, you'll have to pay in full (or claim from your travel insurance) for all medical treatment, which starts at about €35 for a visit to the doctor. Non-EU residents will need to insure themselves against all eventualities, including medical costs, and are strongly advised to take out travel insurance (see p.54).

Staff at **Apotheken** (pharmacies) provide over-the-counter advice, often in English, and basic medicines for minor health upsets. Marked by a green cross, pharmacies are generally open weekdays 8.30am to 6.30pm and on Saturday mornings. They also operate late opening hours (24hr in cities) by rota – a list of the current incumbent and its address is displayed in windows. For prescription medicines you must provide a *Rezept* (prescription) from either your home doctor or a local one.

Since pre-Roman days, Germany has sworn by the curative powers of **spa waters**, a fixation which peaked in the mid-1800s. Towns with a "Bad" prefix to their names, or which include Baden (baths) in their titles (spa doyenne Baden-Baden or Wiesbaden) still offer extensive spa facilities.

ROUGH GUIDES TRAVEL INSURANCE

Rough Guides has teamed up with WorldNomads.com to offer great travel insurance deals. Policies are available to residents of over 150 countries, with cover for a wide range of adventure sports, 24hr emergency assistance, high levels of medical and evacuation cover and a stream of travel safety information. Roughguides.com users can take advantage of their policies online 24/7, from anywhere in the world – even if you're already travelling. And since plans often change when you're on the road, you can extend your policy and even claim online. Roughguides.com users who buy travel insurance with WorldNomads.com can also leave a positive footprint and donate to a community development project. For more information go to ⓦ roughguides.com/travel-insurance.

Insurance

Even though EU healthcare privileges apply in Germany (see p.53), an insurance policy is a wise precaution to cover against theft, loss and illness or injury.

If buying a policy check small print for waivers on "danger sports" – common activities such as mountain biking can be classed among the likes of skiing and rock climbing. A supplemental payment provides cover. If you need to make a claim, keep receipts for medicines and medical treatment, and in the event you have something stolen, obtain an official statement (*Anzeige*) from the police.

Internet

Most German towns operate a municipal website with good visitor information and helpful event databases as well as accommodation booking engines. Larger cities provide an English-language version. Most museums, hotels and restaurants also have a website. Be aware when hunting addresses that letters with an umlaut are rendered with an e – ä becomes ae, ü becomes ue and ö becomes oe.

Online access is good in mid-sized towns and in cities, where **internet cafés** cost about €1–4 per half-hour. "Callshops" – discount international call centres – often in the streets around the main train station, usually have computers. Most hotels and hostels also provide a connection, often free, and a fair number of pensions, guesthouses, cafés, train and motorway-service stations also have **wi-fi hotspots** (referred to as W-LAN), though you may have to pay to access many of these.

One thing to be aware of when surfing are Germany's strict intellectual-property laws – downloading illegal torrents and the like could attract €1000 fines if, say, your hotel can pin the activity on you and is contacted by one of the specialist lawyers who take it upon themselves to police the system. This is one reason why many hotels and hostels protect themselves with access systems which require your registration with their provider first.

Laundry

Larger hotels generally provide a laundry service – but at a cost. Most hostels offer a cheaper wash-and-dry service for around €5 a load. **Launderettes** are a little cheaper still, with an average load costing around €4 to wash and dry. Hours tend to be daily 7am to 10pm; addresses can be found listed under "Waschsalon" in the *Yellow Pages* (*GelbeSeiten*). One popular nationwide chain is Schnell und Sauber, which sometimes have bars and free wi-fi.

Left luggage

Left-luggage lockers at the large main train stations allow storage for time periods of 24 to 72 hours. Charges for lockers are around €2 for 24 hours. Many hostels provide free storage for a few days if you have stayed or intend to.

Living in Germany

Of all Germany's towns and cities, Berlin is easily the most attractive to foreigners looking to live and work in Germany. The capital's reputation as a happening and tolerant city ensure there's a large English-speaking community – something that will work to your advantage when it comes to jobs and housing, and to your disadvantage in terms of competition.

But wherever you try to live you'll be at the mercy of the same regulations. **Work permits** (*Arbeitser-laubnis*) aren't required for EU nationals, but everyone else needs one and shouldn't, in theory, even look for a job without one. Long-term permits involve complicated and tedious bureaucracy, making advice from an experienced friend invaluable, especially when completing official forms. The best official place for advice is the **Auswärtiges Amt** (German Federal Foreign Office; Ⓦauswaertiges-amt.de), whose website has the latest information – in English – on entry into Germany and local contact details.

All who want to stay in Germany for longer than three months – including EU citizens – must technically first **register** their residence (*Anmeldung*) at an **Einwohnermeldeamt**. For non-EU nationals, finding legal work is extremely difficult, unless you've secured the job before arriving in Germany. The best advice is to approach the German embassy or consulate in your home country. Citizens of Australia, New Zealand and Canada between 18 and 30 can apply for a working holiday visa, enabling legal work in Germany for ninety days in a twelve-month period: contact German embassies for details.

The local press is the obvious place to find long-term **accommodation,** as is the dedicated website Ⓦwggesucht.de, but it can be useful to register with a **Mitwohnzentrale**, an accommodation agency specializing in long-term apartment sublets. Be warned, scams are increasingly common targeting foreigners looking for flats from abroad, so be sure not to part with any money until you have personally visited the apartment. When you find a place to live, you need to **register** your residence as above. The form for this requires a signature from your landlord.

Numerous **job agencies** offer both temporary and permanent work – usually secretarial – but you'll obviously be expected to have a good command of German. Useful internet sources are Ⓦstepstone.de, Ⓦmamas.de, Ⓦjobs.de, Ⓦjobnet .de and Ⓦmonster.de.

Mail

The bright yellow postboxes and post offices of **Deutsche Post** (Ⓦdeutschepost.de) pep up many German streetscapes. Many offices are near (or within) the main train station. Standard opening hours are Monday to Friday 9am to 6pm and Saturday 9am to 1pm, although the main office often has longer hours. Many post offices have separate parcel offices (marked *Pakete*) a block or so away. As well as at post offices, stamps can be bought from the small yellow machines beside some postboxes and at selected newsagents.

Mail to the UK usually takes three days; to North America one week; and to Australasia two weeks. A postcard or letter under 50g costs €0.75 to send worldwide. When posting a letter, you may have to pick between the slots marked for various postal codes. Boxes marked with a red circle indicate collections late in the day and on Sunday.

Maps

In addition to the maps in this guide a large foldable motoring map of the country can be useful. Michelin and the AA both make good, well-priced versions. In Germany most German tourist information offices offer free **town maps**; larger offices should have free **regional maps**. Both are generally fine for orientation, though don't rely on the latter for touring. Commercially produced maps available at larger bookshops are a joy. Falkplan and motor organization Allgemeiner Deutscher Automobil Club (ADAC; Ⓦadac.de) are consistently excellent. If you are a member of a foreign motoring organization, you will likely qualify for free maps from ADAC offices around Germany, though all their materials are in German. Kompass (Ⓦkompass .at) publish a full range of **walking and cycling maps**.

Money and banks

Germany uses the **euro** as its currency, which divides into 100 cents. There are seven euro **notes** – in denominations of 500, 200, 100, 50, 20, 10 and 5 euros, each a different colour and size – and eight different **coin** denominations, including 2 and 1 euros, then 50, 20, 10, 5, 2 and 1 cents. Euro coins feature a common EU design on one face, but different country-specific designs on the other. All euros can be used in the eighteen countries that share the currency (Austria, Belgium, Cyprus, Estonia, Finland, France, Germany, Greece, Ireland, Italy, Latvia, Luxembourg, Malta, the Netherlands, Portugal, Slovakia, Slovenia and Spain). At the time of writing, €1 was worth £0.81/$US1.36/AUS$1.48/ZAR14.15; for current rates go to Ⓦxe.com.

Debit and **credit cards** are widely used in Germany, though not as widespread as in the UK or North America. International services such as Visa or MasterCard are less common than the local Girocard system and should never be completely relied upon. Cash is still the currency of choice, particularly in bars and restaurants, and you should never assume that you can pay using a card.

The best way to get hold of cash is from one of the many **ATMs** and you should have no problem using either your credit or debit card, though sometimes a fee is levied by the local bank (a printed sticker on the machine or a screen warning should alert you to this). Your home bank will also likely charge you fees of at least two percent if your account is not in Euros. It's worth finding out about this, and checking your personal identification number (PIN) will work overseas, before you leave home.

Banks are plentiful and their hours usually weekdays 8.30am to 5pm. If you want to change cash, it may be worth shopping around several banks, as the exchange and commission rates vary. The latter tends to be a flat rate, meaning that small-scale transactions should be avoided. In any case, the **Wechselstuben** (bureaux de change) at the main train stations in cities, offer better rates, as well as being open outside normal banking hours and weekends, usually daily 8am to 8pm, a couple of hours longer on either side in the nation's principal travel hubs.

Opening hours and public holidays

Shops and markets: Business hours are generally Monday to Friday 9am to 6pm and Saturday 9am to 2pm, although some bakeries open on Sunday mornings, and department and chain stores will stay open till 8pm on weekdays and till 4pm on Saturday, both legal closing times. Conversely, many shops in smaller towns still close for lunch, generally from midday to 2pm. Outside of trading hours, small supermarkets in train and petrol stations supply the basics. Produce markets (usually weekdays in towns) operate between 9am and 1pm.

Tourist information: Typically Monday to Friday 9am to 6pm, Saturday 9am to 2pm, closed Sunday; but consult relevant chapters.

Museums and tourist attractions: Tend to open Tuesday to Sunday 9am to 6pm, though occasionally some open on Mondays too. Many museums close from November to March, particularly in very tourist-orientated regions like the Rhine and Mosel.

Restaurants: Generally open 10am to midnight, although smarter restaurants tend to take Sunday or Monday as *Ruhetag* (closing day).

Churches: Access is generally excellent, usually open all day and all week, though respect services.

Opening hours on **public holidays** generally follow Sunday hours: most shops will be closed and museums and other attractions will follow their Sunday schedules. **Public holidays** fall on January 1, Good Friday, Easter Monday, May 1, Ascension Day (40 days after Easter), Whitsun, October 3, November 3, and December 25 and 26.

CALLING HOME FROM ABROAD

Note that the initial zero is omitted from the area code when dialling the UK, Ireland, Australia and New Zealand from abroad.

Australia international access code + 61
New Zealand international access code + 64
UK international access code + 44
US and Canada international access code + 1
Ireland international access code + 353
South Africa international access code + 27

Phones

You can make local and **international calls** from most phone boxes – marked international – which are generally equipped with basic English instructions and which often require phonecards available from newsagents. Another option is to use one of the many **phone shops** offering cheap international calls and calling cards, usually alongside internet services, which can be found in cities. The cheapest time to call abroad is between 9pm and 8am.

Most British **mobile phones** should work in Germany, but if you haven't used your phone abroad before, check first with your phone provider. US and Canada tri-band phones will work outside North America.

If you are in Germany for a while, consider buying a local SIM card for your mobile phone. These are available through the phone shops and even corner stores and tend to cost around €15, often including some credit. Technically German SIM cards are only available to German residents and you will be required to register it at an address in Germany. In practice you can supply the address of your accommodation for this.

To use a different SIM card in your phone, it will need to be unlocked, if it isn't already, to accept the cards of different providers. The phone shops will be able to advise where this is possible locally. Expect to pay around €10 for this instant service. Top-up cards can be bought in supermarkets, kiosks and phone shops.

Calling Germany from abroad the **international code** is 🛈49. For **directory enquiries** in English call 🛈118 37; the service costs €1.99 per minute.

Time

Germany is in the Central European Time Zone, one hour ahead of British Greenwich Mean Time, six hours ahead of Eastern Standard Time and nine hours ahead of US Pacific Standard Time. Daylight savings time (summer time) applies from the end of March to the end of October, when clocks are put forward one hour. Use of the 24-hour clock is very common: for example, 1.30pm is 13.30.

Tipping

Service is, as a rule, included in the bill. Rounding up a café, restaurant or taxi bill to the next euro or so is acceptable in most cases, though when you run up a particularly large tab you will probably want to add some more.

Tourist information

The **national tourist board** (Ⓦgermany.travel) produces stacks of slick brochures on regions and holiday themes, which can be ordered for free from its website, which is also first-class. Most regional tourist boards, cities and small towns also maintain an online presence, most with pages in English. On the ground, you'll find a walk-in **tourist office** almost wherever you go, even in many villages. These typically stock a good spread of pamphlets and brochures – usually in English in larger towns and cities, where one member of staff will be near-fluent. Tourist information offices will reserve accommodation, either for free or for a nominal charge.

Travellers with disabilities

Access and facilities for the disabled (**Behinderte**) are fair to good in large towns and cities: most major museums, public buildings and much of the public-transport system are wheelchair-friendly, though the cobbled streets in older cities can be miserable. Nearly four hundred **Deutsche Bahn** train stations have lifting aides or ramps. The company also runs a 24hr helpline at ☏01805 99 66 33. Under certain conditions, the disabled and their escorts travel by train free or at reduced rates. For full information check on their English-language website, Ⓦbahn .co.uk, under "Services" and "Barrier-Free Travel".

The German Tourist Board website (Ⓦgermany .travel) has links to dedicated state providers. **NatKo** (Nationale Koordiationsstelle Tourismus für Alle; Ⓦnatko.de) handles accessibility enquiries, supported by the main German disabled associations. Its German-language website publishes information for state travel-advice centres for disabled tourists as well as a list of dedicated tour operators. For formal, in-depth information in Berlin, try disability activist group **Mobidat** (Ⓦmobidat.net). They provide information on wheelchair-accessible hotels, restaurants, city tours and local transport services. Finally if you speak German, you might like to browse the online version of quarterly magazine *Handicap* (Ⓦi-motio.de), for its hundreds of articles and active forums.

Berlin and Brandenburg

SONY CENTER, POTSDAMER PLATZ, BERLIN

1

Berlin and Brandenburg

As Germany's largest, most happening city, Berlin's lure is obvious. The pace here is brisk: new buildings sprout up; nightlife is frenetic, trends whimsical; graffiti is everywhere and the air crackles with creativity; even brilliant exhibitions and installations are quickly replaced. The results are mesmerizing and couldn't contrast more with the sleepy, marshy lowlands of the surrounding state of Brandenburg, whose small regional towns, empty rambling churches, crumbling Gothic monasteries and faded palaces hint at a mighty Prussian past.

Today, as the frantic forces of renewal and regeneration calm and Berlin enters the final phase of patching itself up after its tempestuous twentieth century, an exciting mix of modern buildings, thoughtful monuments and world-class museums has emerged from the jungle of cranes. Thankfully many fascinating reminders of the city's past have been left intact too. Yet it's not all heavyweight history and high culture; Berlin is also endlessly vibrant: there's always something new, challenging and quirky going on and every year it seems to be a little more cosmopolitan, international and mesmerizing.

Though rubbing shoulders with Berlin, Brandenburg's capital, **Potsdam**, is a staid and provincial world apart, if nevertheless attractive and rewarding thanks to generations of Hohenzollerns who favoured the city and effectively doubled its size with fabulous palaces and gardens, royal piles and follies. This provides a lovely breather from Berlin's unrelenting pace, as does the rest of its sleepy **Brandenburg hinterland**. Here the main workaday cities – including Brandenburg an der Havel, Frankfurt an der Oder and Cottbus – are best avoided in favour of cruising Brandenburg's flat, tree-lined minor roads through a gentle patchwork of beech forests, fields of dazzling rapeseed and sunflowers and heathland, all sewn together by a maze of rivers, lakes and waterways.

This landscape forms the backdrop for a disparate collection of attractions which include the former concentration camp **Sachsenhausen**; the bucolic town of **Rheinsberg**, with its palace, lakes, forests and earthy pottery; a dignified ruined monastery at **Chorin**; an impressive ship hoist at **Niederfinow**; and the **Unteres Odertal Nationalpark**, an ecologically important wetland environment on the Polish border. It's the countryside that's likewise the main attraction east of Berlin, where a series of low hills interrupt Brandenburg's plains, ambitiously known as the **Märkische Schweiz**, or the Switzerland of Brandenburg. Finally, Brandenburg's most

Highlights

❶ The Reichstag and the Brandenburg Gate Germany's two most famous landmarks are practically neighbours, and the view from the Reichstag's glass cupola provides a great handle on the city. **See p.68 & P.65**

❷ Museum Island The Greek Pergamon Altar and Babylon's Ishtar Gate are among the spectacular antiquities in Berlin's premier museum complex. **See p.74**

❸ Berlin Wall Memorial See the Wall as it once was, in the only remaining, completely preserved section. **See p.82**

❹ Bars and clubs You can party all night every night in Berlin's bewildering array of bars and clubs. **See p.102**

❺ Potsdam An easy day out from Berlin, Potsdam harbours several fine palaces, including the fabled park Sanssouci. **See p.110**

❻ Sachsenhausen The former concentration camp for both the Nazis and Soviets makes for a grim but rewarding day-trip from Berlin. **See p.119**

❼ Spreewald Mess around in a boat along lush and sleepy waterways, or cycle along their quiet banks. **See p.125**

❽ Tropical Islands For a quick and easy getaway from a cheerless Brandenburg winter try overnighting on the beach in this vast tropical dome; unmissable for kids. **See p.126**

HIGHLIGHTS ARE MARKED ON THE MAP ON P.62

1

heavily touristed area is the **Spreewald**, centred on **Lübbenau**. Its web of gentle waterways is particularly popular for punting and canoeing, and the region is made all the more interesting by the presence of Sorbs, Germany's largest indigenous non-German community, while the astonishing array of local gherkins, sold as snacks on the streets, adds an off-beat attraction.

Berlin

"Poor but sexy" is how hip Berlin mayor, Klaus Wowereit, proudly describes his city. Its poverty stems back to World War II devastation when bombs razed 92 percent of buildings and provoked serious debate about leaving the city in ruins and starting afresh nearby. Decades of rebuilding since have almost totally rejuvenated Berlin, but have also left it broke. Its sexiness dates back even further, to the debauched 1920s, but began to take on its present-day form during the Cold War when a military service loophole and

HIGHLIGHTS

1. The Reichstag and the Brandenburg Gate
2. Museum Island
3. Berlin Wall Memorial
4. Bars and clubs
5. Potsdam
6. Sachsenhausen
7. Spreewald
8. Tropical Islands

BERLIN & BRANDENBURG

the huge West German **arts** scene subsidies attracted hippies, punks, gays and lesbians, artists and musicians. Subsequent waves of economic immigrants from Greece, Italy and Turkey, together with those linked to the occupying American, British and French forces, plus a current crop of adventurous urbanites from all over the developed world, have together made Berlin Germany's most cosmopolitan city by far.

This multiculturalism is readily reflected in the excellent variety of **cuisines** in the city's restaurants, cafés and bars, but the "poor and sexy" combination has also created breathing room for cutting-edge designs and offbeat concepts to flourish, with both elements especially evident in Berlin's legendary, nonstop **nightlife**, and energetic **contemporary arts** scene. By day, however, it's the city's remarkable museums, memorials, historic sights and modern buildings that tend to capture the imagination of even those with little interest in history or architecture. The city's medley of architectural styles range from its reconstructed sixteenth-century core, the **Nikolaiviertel**, and a grand nineteenth-century Neoclassical imperial showpiece quarter, all the way through to neighbourhoods that were mainly crafted during, and by, the conflicting ambitions and philosophies of the Cold War. Then, when the German government decided to move back to Berlin, it both brought with it, and stimulated, a whole host of contemporary building projects.

Brief history

As heart of the Prussian kingdom, cultural centre of the Weimar Republic, headquarters of Hitler's Third Reich and a key frontline flashpoint in the Cold War, Berlin has long been a weather vane of European and even world history. Its story began in the twelfth century when violent settlement of Slavic regions by Germanic tribes in the Dark Ages led to the creation of the **margravate of Brandenburg** in 1157. Berlin slowly rose to become the capital of this marshy frontier territory and from 1415 Brandenburg became the possession of the Hohenzollern dynasty, who embraced Protestantism in 1538. Brandenburg merged with Prussia in 1618, then became entangled in the **Thirty Years' War**, which left the whole region devastated and depopulated. Rebirth was slow, but gathered momentum on the back of Prussia's social tolerance – towards Huguenots and Jews in particular – which helped produce rapid **industrialization** throughout the eighteenth and nineteenth centuries. With increasing economic power came military might and ambitions, which sparked two centuries of martial adventures and horse-trading diplomacy, bringing about German unity and the creation of a **second German Reich** in 1871.

The twentieth century

Within two centuries Berlin had gone from also-ran provincial town to Germany's capital, but these drastic changes would be matched the following century by its demolition in **World War II** and subsequent division in the **Cold War**. Brandenburg was radically transformed too, losing all its territory east of the Oder and falling under the sway of communism. Then, in November 1989, the world's media converged on the Brandenburg Gate to watch Berliners chipping away at the Berlin Wall and witness the extraordinary scenes of the border opening for good. This triggered a series of events which saw Germany's federal government re-established in the city, sparking a pace of urban change unrivalled in the developed world.

EXPLORING BRANDENBURG

Before you travel to Brandenburg it's worth taking a look at the website of **Tourismus Marketing Brandenburg** (☎ 0331 200 47 47, ⓦ brandenburg-tourism.com), which has a useful accommodation booking facility. Also worth investigating is the **Brandenburg-Berlin Ticket**, which allows up to five people to travel anywhere within Brandenburg for one day (9am to 3am the following day) on all regional trains (RE, IRE, RB) as well as the entire Berlin public transport network. The ticket costs €29 online at ⓦ bahn.de, or €31 from train stations.

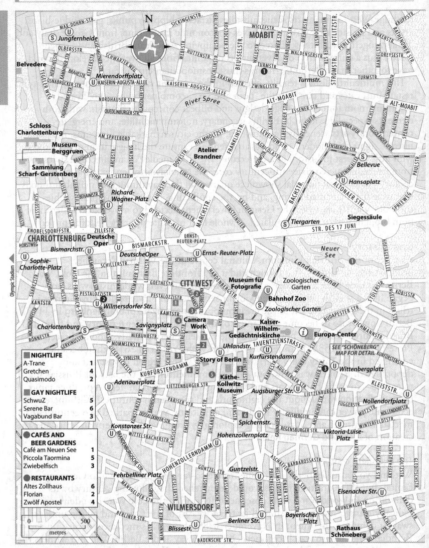

NIGHTLIFE
A-Trane	1
Gretchen	4
Quasimodo	2

GAY NIGHTLIFE
SchwuZ	5
Serene Bar	6
Vagabund Bar	3

CAFÉS AND BEER GARDENS
Café am Neuen See	1
Piccola Taormina	5
Zwiebelfisch	3

RESTAURANTS
Altes Zollhaus	6
Florian	2
Zwölf Apostel	4

Mitte

Berlin's Mitte district – literally "centre" – is huge, cosmopolitan, varied and packed with enough attractions and parks to keep you busy for days. The city's most famous landmark, the **Brandenburg Gate**, is here, as is its parliament and main train station, but what really sticks out on any Berlin map is the Tiergarten, a giant central park. At its southeastern corner lie the world-class art museums of the **Kulturforum** and the thrusting modern skyscrapers of Potsdamer Platz – Berlin's Piccadilly Circus or Times Square. Northwest of here along the city's premier boulevard Unter den Linden, Neoclassical Berlin asserts itself in districts built during the city's time as Prussian capital. Here Museum Island incorporates Berlin's most magnificent museums, while further

SEE "MITTE"
MAP FOR DETAIL

SEE "PRENZLAUER
BERG" MAP
FOR DETAIL

CENTRAL BERLIN

● SHOPS
| KaDeWe | 3 |
| ReSales | 1/2 |

■ ACCOMMODATION
Funk	5
Hollywood Media Hotel	4
Hotel Q!	2
Jetpak City Hostel	6
Kettler	3
Scandic	1

east again lies the GDR's 1960s socialist showpiece quarter, centred around the broad concrete plaza of **Alexanderplatz** and the distinctive **Fernsehturm** TV tower. The only real break from the area's modernity is the **Nikolaiviertel**, a tiny rebuilt version of old Berlin, and the **Spandauer Vorstadt**, an old Jewish quarter, with fascinating reminders of those days, though today better known for its fairly touristy restaurants, bars and nightlife, and a loosely-defined fashion district full of stylish urbanwear boutiques.

The Brandenburg Gate

Heavily laden with historical association, the **Brandenburg Gate** (Brandenburger Tor), modelled on the entrance of Athens' Acropolis, was built as a city-gate-cum-triumphal-arch

1

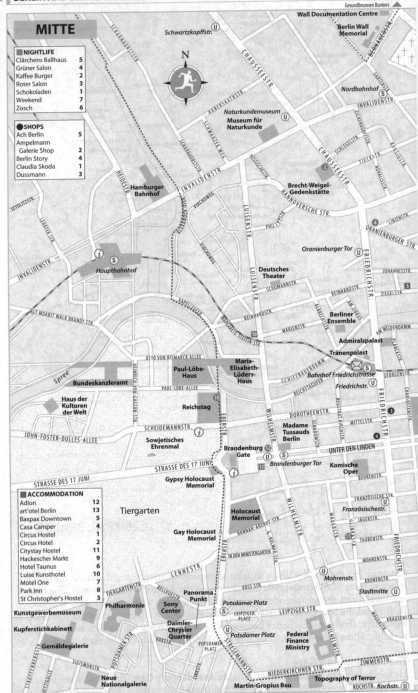

MITTE

NIGHTLIFE
Clärchens Ballhaus	5
Grüner Salon	4
Kaffee Burger	2
Roter Salon	3
Schokoladen	1
Weekend	7
Zosch	6

SHOPS
Ach Berlin	5
Ampelmann Galerie Shop	2
Berlin Story	4
Claudia Skoda	1
Dussmann	3

ACCOMMODATION
Adlon	12
art'otel Berlin	13
Baxpax Downtown	5
Casa Camper	4
Circus Hostel	1
Circus Hotel	2
Citystay Hostel	11
Hackescher Markt	9
Hotel Taunus	6
Luise Kunsthotel	10
Motel One	7
Park Inn	8
St Christopher's Hostel	3

1

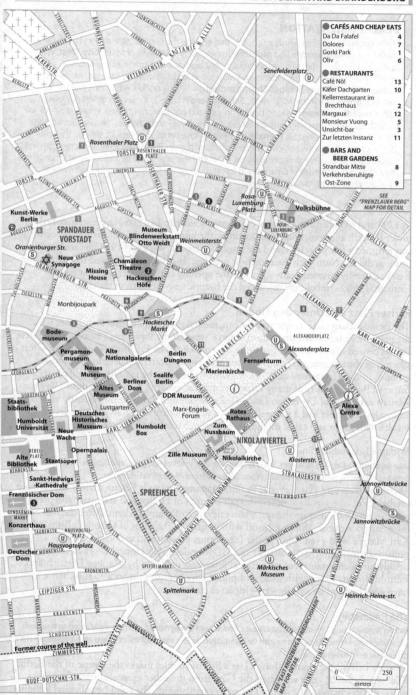

● CAFÉS AND CHEAP EATS
Da Da Falafel	4
Dolores	7
Gorki Park	1
Oliv	6

● RESTAURANTS
Café Nö!	13
Käfer Dachgarten	10
Kellerrestaurant im Brechthaus	2
Margaux	12
Monsieur Vuong	5
Unsicht-bar	3
Zur letzten Instanz	11

● BARS AND BEER GARDENS
Strandbar Mitte	8
Verkehrsberuhigte	
Ost-Zone	9

SEE
"PRENZLAUER BERG"
MAP FOR DETAIL

0   250
metres

SEE "EAST KREUZBERG & FRIEDRICHSHAIN" MAP FOR DETAIL

1

BERLIN ORIENTATION

The residential inner-city neighbourhoods that encircle the central Mitte district particularly shine for their **restaurants** and **nightlife**. Immediately southwest of Mitte, **City West**, West Berlin's old centre, is the most commercial neighbourhood and straddles the sedate, middle-class districts of Charlottenburg-Wilmersdorf and Schöneberg. Charlottenburg is the location of the Baroque **Schloss Charlottenburg** – Berlin's pocket Versailles – and the iconic 1930s **Olympic Stadium**. Meanwhile, **Schöneberg** is famous for Berlin's oldest gay village. East of here, **Kreuzberg** has long been a grungy and nonconformist district that's great for nightlife, as is its happening former East Berlin neighbour Friedrichshain. Also eastern and hip, but a little more grown-up is **Prenzlauer Berg**, whose cobbled streets are among the few places where the nineteenth-century tenements of prewar Berlin have been preserved. Berlin's suburbs also offer a few interesting sights, notably the former **Stasi** headquarters and prison in Lichtenberg, and the dense **Grunewald** forest on the city's southwestern fringe, which offers a perfect respite from the urban bustle.

in 1791 and soon became a symbol of German solidarity. In 1806 Napoleon marched under the arch and took home the **Quadriga**, the horse-drawn chariot that tops the gate. It was returned a few years later, and the revolutionaries of 1848 and 1918 met under its form, as did the Nazis with their torch-lit marches. The Berlin Wall placed the Gate in the East in a heavily guarded death-strip, and the opening of the border here just before Christmas 1989 symbolically re-created the historic east–west axis of the city.

Pariser Platz and Unter den Linden

The Brandenburg Gate looms over the ornamental gardens of **Pariser Platz**, from which the grand leafy boulevard **Unter den Linden** ("beneath the lime trees") runs east. The trees line its central island and the first saplings were planted by Friedrich Wilhelm, the Great Elector, in the seventeenth century, to mark the route from his palace to the hunting grounds in the Tiergarten (see p.70). It gradually became the main thoroughfare of Imperial Berlin and site of many foreign embassies, yet after the war and until 1989 the western extremity of Unter den Linden led nowhere and, lined by infrequently visited embassies, the street had a strangely empty and decorative feel. Today the boulevard bustles with shops and cafés, though their presence is relatively muted.

Madame Tussauds Berlin

Unter den Linden 74 · Daily: Aug 10am–9pm; Sept–July 10am–7pm · €21, combined tickets with Berlin Dungeon (see p.78), Sea Life Berlin (see p.78) and Legoland (see p.72) available · ⓦ madametussauds.com · U-Bahn Brandenburger Tor

The shiny faces and glassy eyes at Berlin's **Madame Tussauds** belong mainly to German celebrities of one sort or another, though a clutch of Hollywood stars past and present also get a look in, despite the uncertain relevance of many of them. After the inevitably long entrance queue, things kick-off with politics in the form of Otto von Bismarck; Karl Marx; a wild-eyed Adolf Hitler (no photos please); and various Cold War politicians including Willy Brandt and GDR leader Erich Honecker. Then things move briskly on to entertainment where local interest is provided by Marlene Dietrich and Bertold Brecht. Along with dozens of photo opportunities there's also the chance to have your hand preserved in wax – for an extra fee.

The Reichstag

Platz der Republik 1 · Daily 8am–midnight, last admission 10pm; advance booking required, either online or at a booth on the opposite side of Scheidemannstrasse (the road that separates the Reichstag from the Tiergarten); book at least a day in advance in summer · Free · ⓦ bundestag.de · U-Bahn Bundestag

Directly behind the Brandenburg Gate a line of cobbles marks the course of the Berlin Wall which for 28 years separated the Gate from the other great emblem of national unity, the **Reichstag** – the seat of Germany's parliament. The solid Neoclassical building was built for a sham parliament answerable only to the Kaiser, in 1918, but is more famous for being set alight in 1933, allowing the Nazis to impose martial law, suspend democracy and establish a totalitarian regime. In a show trial, an itinerant ex-communist Dutch bricklayer, Marius van der Lubbe, was successfully charged with arson and executed, but it's more likely that the Nazis started the fire themselves. Equally famously, the Reichstag became a symbol of the Allied victory at the end of World War II, when soldiers raised the Soviet flag on its roof – even though heavy fighting still raged below. Evidence of this fighting is still visible as scores of patched bullet holes around some windows. In 1999, the reunified German parliament moved back in after extensive renovations and the addition of a flashy cupola by British architect Sir Norman Foster.

A circular ramp spirals up the inside to a **viewing deck** with stunning 360-degree views of the city. Entry is by timed slot (advance booking required), but for more immediate entry, make a reservation at the *Käfer Dachgarten* restaurant (see p.100).

Regierungsviertel

Foreground views from the Reichstag are filled with the cutting-edge designs of Berlin's **Regierungsviertel**, or Government Quarter, which straddles a bend of the River Spree. The elegant offices and conference rooms of the **Paul-Löbe-Haus** and **Maria-Elisabeth-Lüders-Haus**, just north of the Reichstag and west and east of the Spree respectively, are joined via a footbridge over the former East–West border with deliberate symbolism, while an underground tunnel linking them to the Reichstag is meant to tangibly represent the interconnectedness of government.

Another tunnel was to connect them to the imposing **Bundeskanzleramt** (Federal Chancellery), opposite, but the money ran out. Cleverly designed by Axel Schultes and Charlotte Frank, the Bundeskanzleramt has as its centrepiece a nine-storey white cube that houses the chancellor's accommodation, and earns the building the nickname, "the washing machine".

The Holocaust memorials

Jewish Holocaust Memorial • Cora-Berliner-Str. 1 • Info centre Tues–Sun 10am–8pm, last admission 7.15pm • Free, audio tour €4 • ⓦ holocaustmahnmal.de • U-Bahn Brandenburger Tor

Lying beside the Brandenburg Gate, the dignified and surreal Jewish **Holocaust Memorial** was unveiled in May 2006 after 23 years of planning, debate and building work. It's the work of New York architect Peter Eisenman, who was inspired by the densely clustered gravestones in Prague's Jewish graveyard. The entire site – about the size of three football pitches – is covered with 2711 tightly spaced, oblong, dark grey pillars of varying heights. With no single entrance, visitors have to pick their own way through the maze to the centre where the blocks are well above head height and intended to convey a sense of gloom, isolation and solitude. The underground **information centre** in the southeast corner of the monument carefully relates the harrowing life stories of selected Jewish victims of the Holocaust; its **audio tour** is largely unnecessary.

Over the road from the Holocaust Memorial, the fringes of the Tiergarten park hold another concrete oblong, a **Gay Holocaust Memorial**, which remembers the eight thousand people convicted of homosexual acts and murdered in concentration camps by the Nazis. The 4m-high monument echos the Jewish memorial, but leans differently and contains a window behind which a looped film of two men kissing plays.

A third Holocaust memorial, the **Gypsy Holocaust Memorial**, lies a short walk away, by the Reichstag. Commemorating the half-million Roma and Sinti killed in the Third Reich, this memorial focuses on a circular pond surrounded by rough stone flags, with haunting violin music playing. A fresh flower is placed on the single rock at the centre of the pond every day.

1

The prewar Regierungsviertel

The Holocaust Memorial lies at the northern end of Berlin's **prewar Regierungsviertel**, or Government Quarter. From 1871 onwards government buildings stood shoulder to shoulder here, including the Chancellery and, after the Republic was established in 1918, the Presidential Palace. Today little remains, but information boards with photographs and descriptions of former buildings make figuring out what was where, compelling. One such board lies a couple of minutes' walk south of the Holocaust Memorial along Gertrude-Kolmar-Strasse at the site of Hitler's bunker, where the Führer spent his last days, issuing meaningless orders as the Battle of Berlin raged above. Here Hitler married Eva Braun and wrote his final testament. On April 30, 1945, he shot himself, and his body was hurriedly burned by loyal officers.

The Tiergarten

A huge swathe of peaceful green parkland smack in the middle of Berlin, the **Tiergarten** was originally designed by Peter Lenné as a hunting ground for Elector Friedrich III, but now provides a great antidote to city noise and bustle. Bus #100 between Bahnhof Zoo and Alexanderplatz crosses the park, but it's best appreciated on foot or by bike. At least wander along the Landwehrkanal, and the pretty little group of ponds of the grand-sounding **Neuer See**. In summer the popular beer garden here, *Café am Neuen See* (see p.102), rents out **boats** by the hour.

Siegessäule

Grosser Stern 1 • April–Oct Mon–Fri 9.30am–6.30pm, Sat & Sun 9.30am–7pm; Nov–March daily 10am–5.30pm • €2.20 • Bus #100

Approached by great boulevards at the centre of the Tiergarten, is the eye-catching **Siegessäule** (Victory Column). Topped with a gilded Winged Victory, the column celebrates Prussia's military victories. The mosaics at the column's base show the unification of the German peoples and incidents from the Franco-Prussian War. The four bronze reliefs beside depict the main wars and the victorious marching of the troops into Berlin. The Siegessäule's summit offers a good view of the surroundings, but is 285 stairs distant.

The Kulturforum

Matthäikirchplatz • *Bereichskarte* combined ticket to all museums €12 • ⓦ smb.museum • S- & U-Bahn Potsdamer Platz

The Kulturforum, literally "culture forum", is an umbrella term that covers several art museums and cultural venues in the southeast corner of the Tiergarten park, which could easily fill a day of your time. The big highlight is the Gemäldegalerie with its impressive collection of Old Masters, but the forum's modernist buildings are themselves worth a closer look.

The Philharmonie

Herbert-von-Karajan-Str. 1 • Tours in German daily 1.30pm • €5 • ⓦ smb.museum • S- & U-Bahn Potsdamer Platz

Many of the Kulturforum buildings were designed in the 1960s by Hans Scharoun, including the honey-coloured **Philharmonie**, home of the Berlin Philharmonic, with its complicated floor-plan and top-notch acoustics and views, regardless of your seat. Daily tours explore the interior of the building.

The Kunstgewerbemuseum

Matthäikirchplatz 1 • Tues–Fri 10am–6pm, Sat & Sun 11am–6pm • €10 • ⓦ smb.museum • S- & U-Bahn Potsdamer Platz

Over the road from the Philharmonie, the **Kunstgewerbemuseum** (Museum of Applied Arts) holds an encyclopedic but seldom dull collection of European arts and crafts from the Middle Ages on. Renaissance, Baroque and Rococo pieces (wonderful silver and ceramics), along with Jugendstil, Art Deco and Bauhaus objects are all present, as are sumptuous pieces from the Middle Ages and Early Renaissance collections. Highlights are Lüneburg's municipal silver and an eighth-century purse-shaped **reliquary** that belonged to Duke Widikund, leader of the Saxon resistance to Charlemagne.

1

The Gemäldegalerie

Matthäikirchplatz 4 • Tues–Fri 10am–6pm, Sat & Sun 11am–6pm • €10 • ⓦ smb.museum • S- & U-Bahn Potsdamer Platz

With its stupendous collection of early European paintings, the **Gemäldegalerie** (Picture Gallery) is the real jewel of the Kulturforum. Highlights include **German work** from the Middle Ages and Renaissance such as the large *Wurzach Altar* of 1437, from the workshop of the great Ulm sculptor Hans Multscher; landscapes by Albrecht Altdorfer; and several superbly observed portraits by Albrecht Dürer and Hans Holbein the Younger. The gallery's **Netherlandish section** includes fifteenth- and sixteenth-century works by Jan van Eyck, Jan Gossaert, Quentin Massys and Pieter Bruegel the Elder, whose *Netherlandish Proverbs* is an amusing, if opaque, illustration of over a hundred sixteenth-century proverbs.

The later **Dutch and Flemish collections**, with their large portraits of Van Dyck and fleshy canvases of Rubens, are another strong point. But the major highlights are several paintings by **Rembrandt**: though *The Man in the Golden Helmet* has been proved to be the work of his studio rather than the artist himself, this does little to detract from the portrait's elegance and power. Finally, the **Italian section** spanning the Renaissance to the eighteenth century has impressive paintings by Botticelli, Caravaggio, Poussin, Claude and Canaletto.

The Kupferstichkabinett

Matthäikirchplatz 4 • Tues–Fri 10am–6pm, Sat & Sun 11am–6pm • €6 • ⓦ smb.museum • S- & U-Bahn Potsdamer Platz

Sharing its main entrance with the Gemäldegalerie, the **Kupferstichkabinett** (Engraving Cabinet) holds an extensive collection of European medieval and Renaissance prints, drawings and engravings. The collection includes Botticelli's exquisite drawings for Dante's *Divine Comedy*.

The Neue Nationalgalerie

Potsdamer Str. 50 • Tues, Wed & Fri 10am–6pm, Thurs 10am–10pm, Sat & Sun 11am–6pm • €10 • ⓦ smb.museum • S- & U-Bahn Potsdamer Platz

At the southeast corner of the Kulturforum, and by far its finest building, is the **Neue Nationalgalerie**. Designed by Mies van der Rohe in 1965, the building comprises a severe glass box, its ceiling seemingly almost suspended above the ground. The gallery divides between the permanent collection, featuring works from the beginning of the twentieth century onwards, including pieces by **Braque**, **Gris** and **Picasso**, and temporary exhibits, often of contemporary art.

Potsdamer Platz

The skyscrapers of **Potsdamer Platz**, which soar beside the Kulturforum, represent Berlin at its most thrustingly commercial and cosmopolitan. Said to have been the busiest square in prewar Europe, **Potsdamer Platz** was once surrounded by stores, bars and clubs, and pulsed with life day and night. The war left it severely battered, though immediately afterwards it regained some vitality as a black market centre at the junction of the Soviet, American and British sectors. This ended with the coming of the Wall: all the buildings on the eastern side were razed to give the GDR's border guards a clear field of fire, while the West put no real money into restoring its battered survivors. For years western tourists could gaze at the East from a viewing platform here, and ponder the sight of prewar tramlines disappearing under the Wall. The Wall's dismantling then produced a premier lot, which was quickly carved up by multinationals who frantically built bold architectural forms for obligatory shopping malls with restaurants, cafés, a theatre, and a film multiplex with 3D cinema. Its tallest building – the red-brick skyscraper that's a nod to the Chicago school of architecture – has on its top floor **Panorama Punkt** (Tues–Sun 11am–8pm; €5.50; ⓦpanoramapunkt.de), an outdoor viewing deck with views to rival the Fernsehturm.

1

The Sony Center

Filmmuseum Berlin Potsdamer Str. 2 • Tues, Wed & Fri–Sun 10am–6pm, Thurs 10am–8pm • €7 • ⓦ filmmuseum-berlin.de **Legoland Discovery Centre** Potsdamer Str. 4 • Mon–Sat 10am–7pm • €16, discounts available online, combined tickets with Madame Tussauds (see p.68), Berlin Dungeon (see p.78) and Sea Life Berlin (see p.78) available • ⓦ legolanddiscoverycentre.de • S- & U-Bahn Potsdamer Platz

The bravely twenty-first-century glass cylinder of the Helmut Jahn-designed **Sony Center** is the most eye-catching building on Potsdamer Platz. Several glass-sheathed buildings surround an airy, circular courtyard, sheltered by a conical glass rotunda, creating a huge atrium. In one building the **Filmmuseum Berlin** provides a superb introduction to the history of German cinema and television using a bevy of clips, reconstructions and artefacts, many relating to Marlene Dietrich. In another corner of the complex, the **Legoland Discovery Centre** not only promotes a product, but also aims to entertain kids aged 3–10 with a cinema, castle, dragon rides and a workshop. A couple of things entertain adults too – particularly the Lego reproduction of Berlin's main landmark buildings.

The Topography of Terror

Niederkirchnerstr. 7 • Daily 10am–8pm (outside areas until dusk) • Free • ⓦ topographie.de • S- & U-Bahn Potsdamer Platz

Lurking behind central Berlin's most substantial but dilapidated stretch of Wall is the city block which from 1933 to 1945 headquartered the Reich security services, including the Gestapo and SS. Some ruined foundations remain, but the flawlessly sleek and silvery piece of memorial-chic architecture in the middle houses the **Topography of Terror**, Germany's most significant museum on the perpetrators of Nazi terror.

Inside, information panels retell the dreadful history (in both English and German) alongside many black-and-white photos of Nazis and their forlorn victims at miserable events: book burnings; public humiliations; Jewish property and synagogue destruction; and the rounding up of those to be murdered in concentration camps. It's all sadly familiar, but what many don't realize, and the exhibition goes out of its way to show, is that many of the perpetrators were never brought to justice. One exception was senior SS-man Adolf Eichmann, whose life story is extensively retold here, from his role in the Holocaust to his subsequent capture in Argentina in 1960 to his trial and hanging in Israel. Outside, in the Reich Security ruins, more info panels catalogue the history of the Third Reich in Berlin and reveal gruesome insights: the ground beneath the exhibition held the cellars where prisoners were interrogated and tortured. All this is overlooked by Berlin's best-preserved Third Reich government building: Hermann Göring's fortress-like **Luftfahrtministerium** (Air Ministry). It now houses the Federal Finance Ministry.

Friedrichstrasse

A block east of the Topography of Terror lies **Friedrichstrasse**, Unter den Linden's major cross-street, where bland modern offices, malls and high-end boutiques rub shoulders with more everyday shops, including good bookshops and antique shops near **Bahnhof Friedrichstrasse**.

The Tränenpalast

Auguststr. 68 • Tues–Fri 9am–7pm, Sat & Sun 10am–6pm • Free • ⓦ hdg.de/berlin • S-Bahn Oranienburger Strasse

In the days of the Wall, Bahnhof Friedrichstrasse was Berlin's key crossing point for all foot traffic passing in and out of East Berlin. The border complex's glass and concrete entrance hall, grimly nicknamed the **Tränenpalast** (Palace of Tears) by Berliners, was the scene of many a poignant farewell – an estimated eight million west-bound travellers passed through – as people took leave of relatives, friends and lovers. All this is remembered within the superb museum that occupies the building today, which explores the consequences and daily restrictions of the German division using many original artefacts, documents, photographs and old newsreels and exhibits devoted to personal stories. Taking all this in, it's easy to forget to have a good look at the bleak building itself.

Checkpoint Charlie

Friedrichstrasse's southern end is interesting as the former site of **Checkpoint Charlie**, an Allied military post and gateway between the two Berlins. It became the best-known Iron Curtain crossing and scene of repeated border incidents, including a standoff between American and Soviet forces in October 1961, when tanks from both sides growled at each other for days. A **replica** border post opposite Friedrichstr. 43 marks the original site.

The Gendarmenmarkt

The immaculately restored **Gendarmenmarkt** lies just off Friedrichstrasse. It's now hard to imagine that all its buildings were almost obliterated during the war and that rebuilding lasted well into the 1980s. The square was originally home to Berlin's main market until the Gendarme regiment set up their stables here in 1736. With the departure of the military, Frederick the Great ordered an architectural revamp to mimic the Piazza del Popolo in Rome.

Französischer Dom

Gendarmenmarkt 5 • **Tower** Daily 10am–7pm • €3 • **Hugenottenmuseum** Tues–Sun noon–5pm • €2 • ⓦ franzoesischer-dom.de • U-Bahn Französische Strasse

Frederick the Great's Gendarmenmarkt revamp resulted in Schinkel's 1817 Neoclassical Konzerthaus at the centre being flanked by two twin early-eighteenth-century churches: the Deutscher Dom built for the city's Lutherans; and the **Französischer Dom** designed for Berlin's influential Huguenots. Though built as a simple place of worship, the latter had an appealing Baroque **tower** added some eighty years later, which overwhelmed the church itself. A spiral staircase up the tower balcony provides good views of the square, though avoid it at noon, 3pm and 7pm when its bells chime. The **Hugenottenmuseum** at the base of the tower details the history of the Huguenots in France and their arrival in numbers in Prussia thanks to guarantees of rights and religious freedom.

Bebelplatz

At its eastern end, Unter den Linden's lime trees peter out at the imposing Neoclassical **Bebelplatz**, which was designed as eighteenth-century Berlin's showpiece quarter when, as capital of Brandenburg-Prussia, it competed with Paris, Vienna and Prague. Its buildings were intended to project an image of solidity, permanence and power, and after the heavy bombing and shelling of World War II they were extensively restored. Most were the work of architect **Georg Wenzeslaus von Knobelsdorff** under close supervision from **Frederick the Great**, who still overlooks proceedings as Christian Rauch's nineteenth-century equestrian monument at the centre of Unter den Linden.

Several noble eighteenth-century buildings overlook the plaza, among them the **Alte Bibliothek**, a former royal library with its curved Baroque facade; the **Sankt-Hedwigs-Kathedrale** (Mon–Sat 10am–5pm, Sun 1–5pm; free), a still-functioning Catholic church inspired by the Pantheon in Rome, whose 1963 reconstruction gave it an oddly modern interior; and Knobelsdorff's Neoclassical **Staatsoper**, one of Berlin's leading opera houses (see p.106). Meanwhile, behind the Staatsoper, a lawn dotted with dignified **statues of Prussian generals** leads to the Baroque **Opernpalais**, built as a palace for Friedrich Wilhelm III's three daughters.

The Empty Library

The most interesting feature of the rather bleak and unimpressive Bebelplatz is the **Empty Library**, a monument at its centre. It was here, on May 10, 1933, that twenty thousand books that conflicted with Nazi ideology went up in smoke, demonstratively in front of the university. The ingenious monument is simply a room of empty shelves set underground beneath a pane of glass; it's spectacular at night when a beam of light streams out.

Humboldt Universität

Across the Unter den Linden from the main part of Bebelplatz, the building that houses **Humboldt Universität** was built in 1748 as a palace for Frederick's brother, but in 1809 the philologist, writer and diplomat Wilhelm Humboldt founded a university here whose alumni include Karl Marx and Friedrich Engels. The philologists Jacob and Wilhelm Grimm, and Albert Einstein, are some of the best-known former members of staff.

Neue Wache

Adjacent to Humboldt Universität, **Neue Wache**, designed by Karl Friedrich Schinkel (see box below), resembles a Roman temple and was completed in 1818 as a guardhouse for the royal watch. In 1930 it became a memorial to World War I and now serves as a more general war memorial. Inside, a granite slab covers the tombs of an unknown soldier and an unknown concentration camp victim. At the head of this memorial stone is a statue, depicting a mother clutching her dying son, an enlargement of a small sculpture by Käthe Kollwitz (see p.85).

The Deutsches Historisches Museum

Unter den Linden 2 • Daily 10am–6pm • €8 • ⓦ dhm.de • S-Bahn Hackescher Markt

The old Prussian Arsenal or **Zeughaus**, one of Berlin's finest Baroque buildings and just east of Bebelplatz, became a Prussian army museum in the late nineteenth century and has been a museum ever since, though often at the mercy of extreme political ideologies. Today, as the **Deutsches Historisches Museum**, it uses an immense collection to present a balanced German history from the Dark Ages on. The **collection** of art and artefacts, and accompanying narrative, is arranged so that it's easy to skip epochs or immerse yourself; pick up the audio-guide if your German is minimal. Inevitably the museum focuses overwhelmingly on military escapades and though it does show how eras affected the masses, its Prussian-centric narrative fails to break much new ground or provide any real social history. So it's just as well that the eye-catching, swirling, glass building behind the Zeughaus (and also part of the museum), the **I.M. Pei Bau**, provides space for temporary exhibitions on German social history, using first-class exhibition techniques to explore frequently difficult subjects. The building is the work of American-Chinese architect I.M. Pei – famous for his glass pyramid at Paris's Louvre.

Museumsinsel and around

At its eastern end, Unter den Linden leads to the **Spreeinsel**, the island in the middle of the River Spree, which is famed for the gathering of museums in the **Museumsinsel** (Museum Island) at its northern tip. The museums were built during the nineteenth century by the Hohenzollerns, and really took off when German explorers and archeologists returned with bounty from the Middle East. Despite war losses and Soviet

---

KARL FRIEDRICH SCHINKEL

The incredibly prolific architect **Karl Friedrich Schinkel** (1781–1841) was one of the most influential German architects of the nineteenth century. Nearly every town in Brandenburg has a building that Schinkel had, at the very least, some involvement in, and a lasting testimony to his importance is the fact that even today the distinctively Neoclassical heart of Berlin is defined by his work. His first ever design, the **Pomonatempel** in Potsdam, was completed while he was still a 19-year-old student in Berlin, but his architectural career did not take off immediately, as he first worked as a landscape artist and theatre-set designer. Towards the end of the first decade of the nineteenth century he began submitting architectural designs for great public works and, in 1810, he secured a job with the administration of Prussian buildings. Between 1815 and 1830 he designed some of his most renowned buildings, including the Grecian-style **Neue Wache** (see p.74), the elegant **Schauspielhaus**, and the **Altes Museum** (see opposite).

MUSEUMSINSEL AND STATE MUSEUM TICKETS

1

Given how impressive the six Museumsinsel museums are (see below), it's remarkable to find out that the city-state of Berlin has another twelve **state museums** (ⓦ smb.museum). These include the Kulturforum museums (see p.70) as well as the Hamburger Bahnhof (see p.84), the Museum für Fotografie (see p.85), the Sammlung Scharf-Gerstenberg (see p.86) and the Museum Berggruen (see p.87). Any one of these can easily take half a day to explore, so choose carefully before you set out; note too that you have to book a time to visit the Museumsinsel's Pergamon and Neues Museum at their ticket desks, so arrive early to ensure you can go at the time you want.

If you plan to visit several state museums, you have the option of two different **combined tickets**. A **three-day pass** to all state museums costs €24 and can be bought at any of the museums. For several nearby museums on the same day buy a **Bereichskarte** ("area card"), which in the case of the Museumsinsel museums costs €18.

looting, some of the world's finest museums reside here and are becoming ever greater, thanks to a large-scale reorganization and remodelling that's due for completion in 2017. Some sections will be temporarily closed as part of this process in the meantime.

The Altes Museum

Am Lustgarten • Mon–Wed & Fri–Sun 10am–6pm, Thurs 10am–8pm • €10 • ⓦ smb.museum • U- & S-Bahn Friedrichstrasse

Overlooking the lawns of the Lustgarten, a former parade ground, lies one of Berlin's most striking Neoclassical buildings: Schinkel's impressive **Altes Museum** with its 87m-high facade and Ionic colonnade. As host to the city's **classical antiquities collection**, this is the place for fans of ancient Greek and Roman pottery and sculpture. Many are small works but nonetheless captivating, such as *The Praying Boy*, a lithe and delicate bronze sculpture from Rhodes dating back to 300 BC. The *Vase of Euphronios*, decorated with athletes in preparation, is among one of the finest surviving Greek vases in the world.

The Neues Museum

Bodestr. 1• Mon–Wed & Fri–Sun 10am–6pm, Thurs 10am–8pm • €14 • ⓦ smb.museum • U- & S-Bahn Friedrichstrasse

After decades on the move around Berlin, the city's impressive **Egyptian Collection** moved back into its original home in the **Neues Museum** in 2009. Built in 1855, the museum was badly damaged in the war then extensively rebuilt and remodelled under British architect David Chipperfield. He took pains to preserve as many original features as possible, including fluted stone columns and battered faux-Egyptian ceiling frescoes, as well as adding a few tasteful features – like the huge central staircase – to replace irreparably damaged parts of the building.

The museum's greatest prize is the 3300-year-old **Bust of Queen Nefertiti**, a treasure that's become a city symbol. There's no questioning its beauty – the queen has a perfect bone structure and gracefully sculpted lips – and the history of the piece is equally interesting. Created around 1350 BC, the bust probably never left the studio in Akhenaten in which it was created, acting as a mere model for other portraits of the queen (explaining why the left eye was never drawn in). When the studio was deserted, the bust was left, to be discovered some three thousand years later in 1912.

A bit of a comedown after all the Egyptian excitement below is the underwhelming **Early and Prehistory Collection** in the museum attic that mainly shows off archeological discoveries from around Berlin.

The Alte Nationalgalerie

Bodestr. 1–3 • Tues, Wed & Fri–Sun 10am–6pm, Thurs 10am–8pm • €10 • ⓦ smb.museum • U- & S-Bahn Friedrichstrasse

Tucked just behind the Neues Museum, the Neoclassical **Alte Nationalgalerie** is a grandiose interpretation of a Corinthian temple that houses a museum of European art that's particularly strong on nineteenth-century German Romantics, such as Liebermann, though it also has great works by Cézanne, Rodin, Monet and Degas.

1

The Pergamonmuseum

Am Kupfergraben 5 • Tues, Wed & Fri–Sun 10am–6pm, Thurs 10am–8pm • €14 • ⓦ smb.museum • U- & S-Bahn Friedrichstrasse

The largest of the Museum Island museums, the massive **Pergamonmuseum** was built in the early twentieth century in the style of a Babylonian temple, primarily to house the city's vast Middle-Eastern treasures. Highlights include the **Pergamon Altar** – a huge structure dedicated to Zeus and Athena, dating from 180 to 160 BC, and depicting a furious battle between the gods and the giants – as well as the enormous, deep-blue-tiled Ishtar Gate, a sixth-century-BC processional way from Babylon. The collection also numbers hundreds of other fascinating smaller items from as far back as 2000 BC.

The Bode-Museum

Am Kupfergraben 1 • Tues, Wed & Fri–Sun 10am–6pm, Thurs 10am–8pm • €10 • ⓦ smb.museum • U- & S-Bahn Friedrichstrasse

The stocky, neo-Baroque **Bode-Museum** at the northern tip of Museum Island suffered such heavy World War II damage that it was scheduled for demolition, until Berliners protested in the streets. Subseqent waves of renovation have resulted in opulent interiors that form a seamless backdrop for one of Europe's most impressive **sculpture collections**, which spans the third to the nineteenth centuries. A particular strength is the early **Italian Renaissance**, though the **German collection** is equally authoritative. Also in the building is a solid collection of **Byzantine art**, notably early Christian religious items; ornamental Roman sarcophagi and several intricate mosaics and ivory carvings; and around half a million coins of the city's **Numismatic Collection**.

The Schloss and the Humboldt Box

Humboldt Box Daily: April–Oct 10am–8pm; Nov–March 10am–6pm • €4 • ⓦ www.humboldt-box.com • S-Bahn Hackescher Markt

The Spreeinsel formed the core of the medieval twin towns of Berlin-Cölln, which from the fifteenth century onwards, by virtue of its defensive position, became the site of the **Hohenzollern Residenz** – the fortress-cum-palace of the family who controlled Berlin and Brandenburg. Originally this was a martial, fortified affair, but later it received a Baroque restyling, with virtually every local architect of note, including Schlüter, Schinkel and Schadow, contributing. On November 9, 1918, the abdication of the Kaiser brought the Hohenzollern era to an end, and after World War II the Schloss, a symbol of the imperial past, became an embarrassment to the GDR. They dynamited it in 1950, even though it was no more badly damaged than other structures that were subsequently rebuilt. In its place came the **Palast der Republik**, a piece of brutal 1970s modernism with bronzed, reflective windows that housed the GDR's parliament. Following the *Wende* – and a decade and a half of debate – this was dismantled to make way for transitional projects and ultimately a re-creation of the **Schloss**, due for completion in 2019; an exhibition centre on the site, the **Humboldt Box**, provides details.

The Berliner Dom

Lustgarten 1 • Daily: April–Sept Mon–Sat 9am–8pm, Sun noon–8pm; Oct–March Mon–Sat 9am–7pm, Sun noon–7pm • €7, audio-guide €3 • ⓦ berlinerdom.de • S-Bahn Hackescher Markt

The Spreeinsel's most striking building, the **Berliner Dom**, is a hulking symbol of Imperial Germany that managed to survive the GDR. Built at the turn of the twentieth century as a grand royal church, it was a fussily ornate affair. The huge dome, flanked by four smaller ones, was designed to resemble that of St Peter's in Rome, but heavy war damage resulted in a much simplified reconstruction. Its vault houses ninety sarcophagi containing the remains of various Hohenzollern royalty, including the particularly opulent ones of the Great Elector Wilhelm I, and his second wife, Dorothea. For an overhead view, head for the **Kaiserliches Treppenhaus** (Imperial Staircase), a grandiose marble staircase at the southwest corner of the building which leads past pleasantly washed-out paintings of biblical scenes, to a balcony.

The Nikolaiviertel

Just east of the Spreeinsel lies the site of the city's **medieval** core, the **Nikolaiviertel**, a district razed overnight on June 16, 1944, but which the GDR sought to re-create in the 1980s. Almost all the pastel four- or five-storey townhouses in the compact network of streets are replicas. Sadly, the district has barely taken seed, having the sterile feel of a living history museum that attracts only tourists and locals who work in the restaurants and *Gaststätten* serving reasonable, traditional German food.

Nikolaikirche

Nikolaikirchplatz • Tues & Thurs–Sun 10am–6pm, Wed noon–8pm • €5 • ⓦ stadtmuseum.de • U-Bahn Klosterstrasse

At the centre of the Nikolaiviertel lies the Gothic **Nikolaikirche**, a thirteenth-century church, restored to its twin-towered prewar glory. The Nikolaikirche is one of the city's oldest churches and it was here on November 2, 1539, that news of the Reformation was proclaimed to the citizens of Berlin. The distinctive needle-like spires are copies of those added in the nineteenth century, which were thoroughly wrecked during the war. The church **museum** tells this history and is also used for temporary exhibitions. Note the bright colouring of the vault ribbings above: they may look like a Sixties Pop Art addition, but actually follow a medieval pattern discovered by restorers.

The Zille Museum

Propststr. 11 • April–Oct daily 11am–7pm; Nov–March Tues–Sun 11am–6pm • €6 • ⓦ heinrich-zille-museum.de • U-Bahn Klosterstrasse

Running past Nikolaikirche to the River Spree is Propststrasse, where there are a couple of places associated with **Heinrich Zille** – the Berlin artist who produced earthy satirical drawings of local life around the turn of the twentieth century. At no. 11, the little **Zille Museum** provides a good insight into his life and work, but makes no allowances for non-German-speakers. A favourite watering hole of Zille's – and of another Berlin artist Otto Nagel – was the sixteenth-century *Gaststätte* **Zum Nussbaum**, in the days when it stood on Fischerinsel before it was destroyed by wartime bombing. The replica is a faithful copy, right down to the walnut tree in the tiny garden.

Alexanderplatz and around

During East Berlin's forty-year existence, while Unter den Linden was allowed to represent Berlin's glorious past, the area northeast of the Spreeinsel as far as major transport hub **Alexanderplatz**, was meant to represent the glories of a modern socialist capital. It's easily located thanks to its gigantic **Fernsehturm**, or TV Tower, and there's almost no trace of an earlier history. Postwar rebuilding projects saw whole streets and neighbourhoods vanish under vast and dreary concrete plazas and buildings housing missable shops and cafés. Exceptions include two large prewar buildings: the solid, nineteenth-century red-brick Rotes Rathaus, seat of Berlin's administration; and the **Marienkirche**, Berlin's oldest church.

The Marienkirche

Karl-Liebknecht-Str. 8 • Daily: April–Oct 10am–8pm; Nov–March 10am–6pm • Free • U- & S-Bahn Alexanderplatz

Over the large, open plaza from the Rotes Rathaus lies the appealing medieval **Marienkirche**. Its Gothic stone-and-brick nave dates to about 1270, but the tower was

---

THE U-5 EXTENSION AND THE MARX-ENGELS-FORUM

The huge building works in front of the Rotes Rathaus are impossible to miss and a part of a mighty project to extend the **U-5 underground line** between Alexanderplatz and the Hauptbahnhof across the heart of Berlin. Completion is planned for 2019, but in the meantime viewing platforms allow passers-by to inspect progress. Much of the work is taking place on the **Marx-Engels-Forum**, a severe plaza just west of the Rathaus. It's dedicated to the two revolutionary thinkers Karl Marx and Friedrich Engels, and their landmark commemorative bronze – about five times their former real sizes – will eventually reappear here.

added in 1466, with the verdigris-coated upper section tacked on towards the end of the eighteenth century by Carl Gotthard Langhans. A small cross near the main entrance of the church was erected by local citizens as penance, after a mob immolated a papal representative on a nearby marketplace. Just inside the entrance, look out for the fifteenth-century *Totentanz*, a 22m frieze showing the Dance of Death. It's very faded, but a reconstruction shows Death as a shroud-clad mummy popping up between all levels of society. The vaulted nave is plain and white but enlivened by opulent decorative touches, including Andreas Schlüter's magnificent **pulpit**, its canopy dripping with cherubs and backed by a cloud from which gilded sunrays radiate.

The Fernsehturm

Panoramastr. 1a • Daily: March–Oct 9am–midnight; Nov–Feb 10am–midnight • €12.50 • ⓦ tv-turm.de • U- & S-Bahn Alexanderplatz

Looming over the Berlin skyline like a giant olive on a cocktail stick, the **Fernsehturm** (Television Tower) is Western Europe's highest structure. This 365m-high transmitter was built during the isolationist 1960s, when East Berlin was largely inaccessible to West Germans, and was intended as a highly visible symbol of the GDR's permanence. Having outlasted the regime that conceived it, the Fernsehturm has become iconic, and though few would champion its architecture, it does have a certain retro appeal. The tower provides tremendous **views** (40km on clear days) from the observation platform and the café. There are usually long queues to go up – early evening is your best bet.

Sea Life Berlin

Spandauer Str. 3 • Daily 10am–7pm, last admission 6pm • €17.50, discounts available online, combined tickets with Madame Tussauds (see p.68), the Berlin Dungeon (see below) and Legoland (see p.72) available • ⓦ sealifeeurope.com • S-Bahn Hackescher Markt

The large modern touristy mall that overlooks the Marx-Engels-Forum from the north and incorporates the *Radisson Hotel*, contains **Sea Life Berlin**, an overtly commercial aquarium which showcases the relatively dreary regional aquatic life. At least the species, which include seahorses, jellyfish, small sharks and manta rays, are elegantly displayed, particularly in the **AquaDom**. This gigantic tubular tank, in the lobby of the *Radisson* next door, has an elevator through which Sea Life visitors slowly rise. Others might sneak a peek at it from the hotel lobby, with its swish bar and comfy chairs.

The DDR Museum

Karl-Liebknecht-Str. 1 • Mon–Fri & Sun 10am–8pm, Sat 10am–10pm • €6 • ⓦ ddr-museum.de • S-Bahn Hackescher Markt

At the hands-on **DDR Museum**, there are reminders of the old school system, of pioneer camps and of the razzmatazz that celebrated the feats of model workers. Less impressive are East Germany's awkward polyester rivals to western fashions. A section devoted to travel includes the chance to sit behind the wheel of a Trabi, where you'll quickly appreciate the "fewer parts mean less trouble" principle which guided the fibreglass car's design. But the museum's highlight is the chance to mooch around a tiny reconstructed GDR apartment, ablaze with retro browns and oranges, where you're invited to nose through cupboards and cosy up on a sofa to speeches by Honecker: *Vorwärts immer, rückwärts nimmer* ("Always forwards, never backwards"). Many of the remaining areas of the museum are gloomy but important, since they tackle the dark sides of GDR life – such as censorship and repression – and so help properly round off this snapshot of East German life.

Berlin Dungeon

Spandauer Str. 2 • 1hr tours daily 10am–7pm • €19, discounts available online, combined tickets with Madame Tussauds (see p.68), Sea Life Berlin (see above) and Legoland (see p.72) available • ⓦ thedungeons.com/berlin • S-Bahn Hackescher Markt

For a populist history of Berlin's gorier moments, visit the **Berlin Dungeon**. Here hour-long tours visit theatre sets of scenes from the last seven hundred years in the company of actors who try to scare and amuse with tales of torture, serial killings,

1

plagues and the like. Most tours are in German but regular English-language tours take place. Children under 10 are not allowed.

The Spandauer Vorstadt

The crescent-shaped area north of the River Spree between Friedrichstrasse and Alexanderplatz, known as the **Spandauer Vorstadt**, emerged after the *Wende* as one of the most intriguing parts of unified Berlin. A wave of artists' squats, workshops and galleries sprang up here in the early 1990s, and some still survive. But today the district's appeal is based on its history as Berlin's affluent prewar **Jewish quarter** and as a booming, if fairly touristy, **shopping**, **restaurant** and **nightlife** quarter, with fashionable boutiques, ethnic restaurants and stylish bars. The S-Bahn station and convivial square, **Hackescher Markt**, provides the main focus, along with the main drag **Oranienburger Strasse**. At its western end lies Berlin's nebulous theatre district, where **Bertolt Brecht** lived and worked.

Hackescher Markt and the Hackeschen Höfe

The small, jumbled and slightly chaotic crossroads at **Hackescher Markt** has become a major Berlin tourist hub, with restaurants and cafés crowding its pedestrian plaza. On the opposite side of the intersection, the **Hackeschen Höfe** are a series of beautifully restored, early twentieth-century Art Deco courtyards housing cafés, stores, galleries, theatres and cinemas. Though thoroughly gentrified today, these courtyards preserve a typical prewar-Berlin layout, where daily life was played out in a labyrinth of *Hinterhöfe*, or backyards, out of view of the main road. Within this warren, small-scale workshops lay cheek-by-jowl with rich and poor housing and commerce crammed together, creating a squalid turn-of-the-twentieth-century urban culture satirized by Heinrich Zille (see p.77).

Museum Blindenwerkstatt Otto Weidt

Rosenthaler Str. 39 • Daily 10am–8pm • Free • ⦿ museum-blindenwerkstatt.de • S-Bahn Hackescher Markt

A good place to picture Old Berlin is in a decrepit little alley between the network of Hackeschen Höfe, where the small but excellent **Museum Blindenwerkstatt Otto Weidt** occupies the former broom and brush workshop of one Otto Weidt, who did what he could to protect his mostly deaf and blind, Jewish employees from Nazi persecution. Luckily his workshop was considered important to the war effort, enabling Weidt to prevent the deportation of his workers to concentration camps. But in the 1940s, as pressure grew, he resorted to producing false papers, bribing the Gestapo, and providing food and even hiding places to keep them alive, all at considerable personal risk. One small room, whose doorway was hidden by a cupboard, was the refuge for a family of four until their secret was discovered and they were deported and murdered in Auschwitz. The exhibition has relics of the wartime factory: brushes, photos and letters from the workers. It's all in German but an English translation is available.

Oranienburger Strasse

Now principally known for its touristy restaurants and watering holes, before the war **Oranienburger Strasse** was the heart of Berlin's main **Jewish quarter**. During the initial waves of Jewish immigration, from the seventeenth century on, the area was densely populated and desperately poor, but by the nineteenth century many of Berlin's Jews were wealthy, which enabled the building of a grand Neue Synagoge (see opposite),

---

> ### STOLPERSTEINE
>
> Look at the ground around the entrances to some of the Hackeschen Höfe and you'll see brass-plated cobblestones known as **Stolpersteine**, or "stumbling blocks" (⦿ stolpersteine .com). These are some of the nine thousand laid into footpaths around Germany as a memorial to Nazi victims: each carries a name, birth date and fate.

halfway down Oranienburger Strasse. The stretch further west is the street's busiest, with cafés, bars and restaurants crammed together, which after dark are joined by prostitutes openly soliciting; their presence alongside gawping visitors is faintly reminiscent of Amsterdam's red-light district.

The Neue Synagoge: the Centrum Judaicum

Oranienburger Str. 28/30 • March & Oct Mon & Sun 10am–8pm, Tues–Thurs 10am–6pm, Fri 10am–2pm; April–Sept Mon & Sun 10am–8pm, Tues–Thurs 10am–6pm, Fri 10am–5pm; Nov–Feb Mon & Sun 10am–6pm, Tues–Thurs 10am–6pm, Fri 10am–2pm • €4.60 • ⓦ cjudaicum.de • S-Bahn Oranienburger Strasse

The **Neue Synagoge** was inaugurated in the presence of Bismarck in 1866, a gesture of official recognition that – in a time when Jews in Russia were still enduring official pogroms – must have made many feel that their position in Germany was finally secure. The Neue Synagoge was built in mock-Moorish style, particularly apparent in its bulbous gilt-and-turquoise dome, and was Berlin's central synagogue for over sixty years, serving also as a venue for concerts, including one in 1930 by Albert Einstein in his lesser-known role as a violinist. Though badly damaged on Kristallnacht, the synagogue escaped destruction and remained a place of worship until 1940 when it was handed to the Wehrmacht for use as a warehouse until it was gutted by bombs in 1943. The building's facade remained intact until 1988, when it was restored as **Centrum Judaicum**, a Jewish museum and cultural centre, its reconstructed gilded dome once again a Berlin landmark. Inside are two permanent exhibitions, one on the synagogue itself and another on local Jewish life and culture.

Grosse Hamburger Strasse

The most intriguing side-street off Oranienburger Strasse is undoubtedly **Grosse Hamburger Strasse**, close to its eastern end. Here you can see what's left of Berlin's oldest **Jewish cemetery**, established in 1672, and the site of its first **Jewish old people's home**, which the Nazis used as a detention centre for people awaiting deportation to concentration camps. A memorial tablet and a sculpted group of haggard figures, representing deportees, mark the spot where the home stood. The grassed-over open space behind is the site of the cemetery itself. In 1943 the Gestapo dug up the remains of those buried here and used gravestones to shore up a trench they had excavated through the site. A few cracked headstones with Hebrew inscriptions remain. The only freestanding monument, erected after the war, commemorates **Moses Mendelssohn** on the spot where he is thought to have been buried; the philosopher and German Enlightenment figure founded one of Berlin's first Jewish schools on this street in 1778.

The Missing House

Further north along Grosse Hamburger Strasse is the **Missing House**, a unique and effective monument to Berlin's wartime destruction. A gap in the tenements marks the spot where house no. 15–16 stood until destroyed by a direct hit during an air raid. In 1990 the French artist Christian Boltanski put plaques on the walls of the surviving buildings on either side, recalling the names, dates and professions of the building's former inhabitants.

The Brecht-Weigel-Gedenkstätte and Dorotheenstädtische Friedhof

Brecht-Weigel-Gedenkstätte Chausseestr. 125 • Tues 10am–3.30pm, Wed & Fri 10–11.30am, Thurs 10–11.30am & 5–6.30pm, Sat 10am–3.30pm, Sun 11am–6pm; guided tours (German only) at least every hour • €3 • **Dorotheenstädtische Friedhof** Chausseestr. 126 • Daily: May–Aug 8am–8pm; Sept–April 8am–4pm • Free • U-Bahn Oranienburger Tor

The **Brecht-Weigel-Gedenkstätte** preserves the final home and workplace of Bertholt Brecht (see box, p.82) and his wife and collaborator Helene Weigel. The guided tours take in the seven simply furnished rooms – an absolute must for Brecht fans, but not so fascinating if you're only casually acquainted with his work. The basement is home

1

BERTOLT BRECHT

Bertolt Brecht (1898–1956) is widely regarded as one of the leading twentieth-century German dramatists. Born in Augsburg, he studied medicine, mainly to avoid full military service in World War I. Working as an army medical orderly in 1918, his experiences helped shape his passionate anti-militarism. Soon he drifted from medicine into the fringes of the theatrical world, eventually winding up as playwright in residence at the Munich Kammerspiele in 1921, and moving to Berlin a few years later. It wasn't until the 1928 premiere of *Die Dreigroschenoper* ("The Threepenny Opera"), co-written with composer Kurt Weill, that Brecht's real breakthrough came. This marked the beginning of a new phase. A couple of years earlier he had embraced Marxism, an ideological step that led him to espouse a didactic "epic" form of theatre. The aim was to provoke the audience, perhaps even move them to revolutionary activity. To this end he developed the technique of **Verfremdung** ("alienation") to create a sense of distance between spectators and the action unfolding before them. By using effects such as obviously fake scenery, monotone lighting and jarring music to expose the sham sentimentality of love songs, he hoped to constantly remind the audience that they were watching a play – and so make them judge, rather than be drawn into, the action. The result was a series of pretty heavy-going plays.

In 1933, unsurprisingly, Brecht went into self-imposed exile, eventually ending up in America. His years away from Germany were among his most productive. The political message was still very much present, but somehow the dynamic and lyrical force of his writing meant that it was often largely lost on his audience – at the Zürich premiere of *Mutter Courage* in 1941, Brecht was dismayed to learn that the audience in fact identified with his heroine, whom he had intended to serve as an unsympathetic symbol of the senselessness of wartime sacrifice. Returning to Europe, he finally settled in East Berlin in 1949. His decision to try his luck in the Soviet-dominated East Germany was influenced by the offer to take over at the **Theater am Schiffbauerdamm**, the theatre where *Die Dreigroschenoper* had been premiered over twenty years earlier. However, before heading east, Brecht first took the precaution of gaining Austrian citizenship and lodging the copyright of his works with a West German publisher. The remainder of Brecht's life was largely devoted to running what is now known as the Berliner Ensemble and facing his own tensions with the fledgling GDR.

to the *Kellerrestaurant im Brechthaus* (see p.100), which dishes up Viennese specialities, supposedly according to Weigel's recipes. Both Brecht and Weigel are buried beside the Brecht-Weigel-Gedenkstätte in the **Dorotheenstädtische Friedhof**, eastern Berlin's VIP cemetery.

The Berlin Wall Memorial

Bernauer Str. 119 & 111 • Tues–Sun: April–Oct 9.30am–7pm; Nov–March 9.30am–6pm • Free • ⓦ berliner-mauer-gedenkstaette.de • S-Bahn Nordbahnhof

Opposite S-Bahn Nordbahnhof, on Bernauer Strasse, is the first of two buildings dedicated to the **Berlin Wall Memorial** (Gedenkstätte Berliner Mauer). The memorial contains a **visitor centre**, which screens an introductory film and has a good bookshop. Bernauer Strasse was literally bisected by the Wall; before the Wall was built you could enter or exit the Soviet Zone just by going through the door of one of the buildings, which is why, on August 13, 1961, some citizens, who woke up to find themselves on the wrong side of the newly established "national border", leapt out of windows to get to the West. Over the years, the facades of these buildings were cemented up and incorporated into the partition itself, until they were knocked down and replaced by the Wall proper in 1979. A short section of Wall as it once was – both walls and a death-strip between – remains preserved opposite Bernauer Str. 111, where the associated **Wall Documentation Centre** keeps the story of the Wall alive using photos, sound recordings and information terminals, and has a useful viewing tower that you can climb to contemplate the barrier and the way in which it once divided the city.

The Hauptbahnhof

Just west of the Spandauer Vorstadt and north of the Reichstag and Regierungsviertel, lies a sizeable area recently colonized by Berlin's **Hauptbahnhof**, Europe's largest train station. The ultramodern, sparkling and sterile, five-level glass-and-steel station was completed in 2006 at the crossing point of an old **east–west** track along an 1882 viaduct between Bahnhof Zoo to Alexanderplatz – which provides a superb vantage point for many Mitte sights – and a new underground **north–south** line. The building's shape symbolically mirrors the crossing point: the glass hall follows the east–west line, while the gap between the two huge administrative blocks indicates the direction of the underground north–south track.

The station has many shops and services with conveniently long hours, while nearby hangouts are slowly emerging along the Spree, where in summer sightseeing boats cruise past the bars, cafés and deckchairs on its banks.

THE BERLIN WALL

After the war, Berlin's administration was split between Britain, France, the US and the USSR. Each sector was to exist peacefully with its neighbours under a unified city council. But antagonism between the Soviet and other sectors was high. Only three years after the war, Soviet forces closed the land-access corridors to the city from West Germany in what became known as the **Berlin Blockade**: it was successfully overcome by a massive **airlift** of food and supplies that lasted nearly a year. This, followed by the 1953 uprising, large-scale cross-border emigration (between 1949 and 1961, the year the Wall was built, over three million East Germans – almost a fifth of the population – fled to West Germany) and innumerable "incidents", led to the building of what the GDR called "an antifascist protection barrier".

BACKS TO THE WALL

The Wall was erected overnight on **August 13, 1961**, when, at 2am, forty thousand East German soldiers, policemen and workers' militia went into action closing U- and S-Bahn lines and stringing barbed wire across streets leading into West Berlin to cordon off the Soviet sector. The Wall followed its boundaries implacably, cutting through houses, across squares and rivers, with its own cool illogicality. Many Berliners were rudely evicted from their homes, while others had their doors and windows blocked by bales of barbed wire. Suddenly the British, American and French sectors of the city were corralled some 200km inside the GDR.

Most people in West and East Berlin were taken by surprise. Crowds gathered and extra border guards were sent to prevent trouble. A tiny number – including a few border guards – managed to find holes in the new barrier and flee west. But within a few days the barbed wire and makeshift barricades were reinforced with bricks and mortar. Additionally, West Berliners were no longer allowed into East Berlin. From 1961 onwards the GDR strengthened the Wall, making it almost impenetrable – in effect two walls separated by a *Sperrgebiet* (forbidden zone), dotted with watchtowers and patrolled by soldiers and dogs. It was also known as the *Todesstreifen* (death strip), as border troops were under instructions to shoot anyone attempting to scale the Wall: any guard suspected of deliberately missing was court-martialled, and his family could expect severe harassment from the authorities. Over the years, over two hundred people were **killed** trying to cross the Wall.

THE WALL CRUMBLES

An oddity of the Wall was that it was built a few metres inside GDR territory; so the West Berlin authorities had little control over the **graffiti** that covered it. The Wall was an ever-changing mixture of colours and slogans. Late in 1989 the East German government, spurred by Gorbachev's glasnost and a tense domestic climate, realized it could stay stable no longer. To an initially disbelieving and then jubilant Europe, travel restrictions for GDR citizens were lifted on November 9, 1989 – effectively, the Wall ceased to matter, and pictures of Berliners, East and West, hacking away at the detested symbol filled newspapers and TV bulletins around the world.

Today, it's only possible to tell exactly where the Wall ran by the simple row of cobbles placed along much of its former course. Few significant stretches remain, the sections devoted to the East Side Gallery (see p.90) and the Berlin Wall Memorial (see p.82) being the most notable.

THE GESUNDBRUNNEN BUNKERS TOURS

Just north of Berlin's Mitte district – two stops north on the S-Bahn from the Nordbahnhof and the Berlin Wall Memorial – lies U- and S-Bahn **Gesundbrunnen**, around which several underground passages and **bunkers** are open for fascinating and unusual tours. The nonprofit organization **Berliner Unterwelten** (☎030 49 91 05 17, ⊕berlinerunterwelten.de) offers eight tours around Berlin, though all their core tours are in the vicinity of the Gesundbrunnen. Their ticket office lies in the southern entrance hall of the station, and tickets are available from 10am on the day; the tours start within easy walking distance of the office. **English-language tours** are listed below, but further tours take place in German, Spanish, French, Italian, Dutch and Danish and are listed on the website.

Breaching the Berlin Wall Investigates some of the tunnels used by some three hundred people to escape to the West (April–Oct Mon–Wed 3pm; 2hr; €12).

Dark Worlds Berliner Unterwelten's key tour explores a large, well-preserved World War II bunker (daily Mon 11am & 1pm, Thurs–Sun 11am; March–Nov also Wed 11am; 90min; €10).

Flak Towers A tour around an anti-aircraft gun tower that proved too beefy for the Soviets to destroy (April–Oct Thurs–Sun 3pm; 90min; €10).

Subways and Bunkers in the Cold War A tour of tunnels and bunkers designed to protect West Berliners from nuclear strikes (Thurs–Sun 1pm; March–Nov also Tues 11am & 1pm & Wed 1pm; 90min; €10).

The Hamburger Bahnhof: Museum für Gegenwart

Invalidenstr. 50–51 • Tues, Wed & Fri–Sun 10am–6pm, Thurs 10am–8pm • €14 • ⊕ www.hamburgerbahnhof.de • U- & S-Bahn Hauptbahnhof

On the northern side of the Hauptbahnhof, the **Hamburger Bahnhof** is home to Berlin's premier contemporary art museum: the **Museum für Gegenwart** (Museum for Contemporary Art). Housed in former railway station buildings, it is a spacious, effective setting for an impressive survey of postwar art from Rauschenberg, Twombly, Warhol, Beuys and Lichtenstein right up to Keith Haring and Donald Judd. The Warhol collection is excellent.

City West

Immediately southwest of Mitte, **City West** is West Berlin's old centre and still a neighbourhood where shopping streets showcase Cold War building projects between rows of **department stores**. Berlin's **zoo** populates the western fringes of the Tiergarten park and lends its name to Bahnhof Zoo opposite, the main transport hub of the neighbourhood which technically straddles the districts of Charlottenburg-Wilmersdorf and Schöneberg (see p.87).

The district's two main shopping streets are **Kurfürstendamm** (universally called **Ku'damm**), its litany of shops and cafés dazzling with the neon of big labels; and **Tauentzienstrasse**, a rather bland chain-store drag, with Europe's largest department store, the venerable **KaDeWe**, at its eastern end. KaDeWe's excellent top-storey food court is an ideal stop after a hard shop.

The Zoologischer Garten

Zoo Hardenbergplatz 8 • Daily: late March to mid-Sept 9am–7pm; mid-Sept to late Oct 9am–6pm; late Oct to late March 9am–5pm • **Aquarium** Budapester Str. 32 • Daily 9am–6pm • Zoo €13, aquarium €13, combined ticket €20 • ⊕ zoo-berlin.de • S- & U-Bahn Zoologischer Garten

Berlin's zoo, or **Zoologischer Garten**, harks back to 1844, surviving World War II to become one of Europe's most important zoos. It's a pleasantly landscaped place with reasonably large animal compounds, some peaceful nooks for quietly observing animal behaviour, and lots of benches that are ideal for picnicking. Unusual highlights are the nocturnal **Nachttierhaus**, whose principle attraction is the bat cave, and a large glass-sided hippo-pool.

The zoo's **aquarium** is fantastic and an excellent rainy-day option. The large, humid crocodile hall is the most memorable part, though most tanks are attractive. Despite the attractive price of the combined day-ticket, getting around both zoo and aquarium in a day is a rush.

Museum für Fotografie

Jebenesstr. 2 • Tues–Sun 10am–6pm • €10 • ⓦ smb.museum • S- & U-Bahn Zoologischer Garten

Opposite the back door of Bahnhof Zoo, the excellent **Museum für Fotografie** is the home of the **Helmut Newton Foundation** which focuses almost entirely on the work of this world-famous and locally born fashion and nude photographer. Artefacts include Newton's camera collection, a reconstruction of his quirky Monaco office, and his oversized made-to-measure beach-buggy – complete with monogrammed steering wheel. But the mainstay of the museum is Newton's extraordinary work: his heavily stylized portrait, glamour and nude photography, his celebrity portraiture and penchant for Amazonian women.

Kaiser-Wilhelm-Gedächtniskirche

Breitscheidplatz • Daily 9am–7pm • Free • U-Bahn Kurfürstendamm

A short two-block walk east of Bahnhof Zoo, the angular concrete **Breitscheidplatz** – a magnet for vendors, caricaturists and street musicians – encircles the **Kaiser-Wilhelm-Gedächtniskirche** (Kaiser Wilhelm Memorial Church), a grand church built at the end of the nineteenth century and destroyed by British bombing in November 1943. Left as a reminder, it's an effective memorial, the crumbling tower providing a hint of the old city. It's possible to go inside the remains of the nave where a small exhibit shows wartime destruction and a "before and after" model of the city centre. Adjacent, a modern **chapel** contains a tender, sad charcoal sketch by Kurt Reubers, *Stalingrad Madonna*, dedicated to all those who died during the Battle of Stalingrad.

Käthe-Kollwitz-Museum

Fasanenstr. 24 • Daily 11am–6pm • €6 • ⓦ kaethe-kollwitz.de • U-Bahn Uhlandstrasse

Just off the Ku'damm's consumer jungle, the **Käthe-Kollwitz-Museum** displays the moving, early twentieth-century antiwar art of Käthe Kollwitz. Born in 1867, she lived almost all her life in Prenzlauer Berg and following the death of her son in World War I, her woodcuts, lithographs, prints and sculptures became explicitly pacifist, often dwelling on the theme of mother and child. With the death of her grandson in World War II her work became sadder yet and more poignant. She died in 1945, shortly before the end of the war.

The Story of Berlin

Ku'damm 207–208 • Daily 10am–8pm • €12 • ⓦ story-of-berlin.de • U-Bahn Uhlandstrasse

Just west of the Uhlandstrasse U-Bahn, **The Story of Berlin** contains an excellent and inventive multimedia exhibition – extensively labelled in English – that's an ideal first step in unravelling Berlin's history. On the way around you'll be confronted with life-size dioramas, film clips, noises, flashing lights, smoke and smells, which illustrate the trawl through the city's turbulent past. It's great for kids, though it takes at least two hours to do it justice, not including a bonus tour of a 1970s Allied-built Cold War nuclear bunker below – which can be done another day on the same ticket if you've run out of time or energy in the museum.

Charlottenburg-Wilmersdorf

The rather sedate, predominantly white and middle-class district of **Charlottenburg-Wilmersdorf** is inner-city Berlin at its most affluent and restrained. However, Charlottenburg has its own gathering of fairly high-profile attractions, particularly the Baroque **Schloss Charlottenburg** – Berlin's pocket Versailles with its opulent chambers, wanderable gardens, and several excellent nearby **museums** – along with the iconic 1930s **Olympic Stadium**.

1

Schloss Charlottenburg

Spandauer Damm 10–22 • **Altes Schloss** Tues–Sun: April–Oct 10am–6pm; Nov–March 10am–5pm • €12 • **Neuer Flügel and the Concert Room** Mon & Wed–Sun April–Oct 10am–6pm; Nov–March 10am–5pm • €6 • **Schloss Gardens** April–Oct Tues–Sun 10am–6pm; Nov–March Sat & Sun 10am–5pm • Gardens free, Neuer Pavillon €4, Belvedere €3, Mausoleum €2 • ⓦ spsg.de • Bus #M45 from Bahnhof Zoo

Schloss Charlottenburg comes as a surprise after the unrelieved modernity of the city streets. Commissioned as a country house by the future Queen Sophie Charlotte in 1695 (she also gave her name to the district), the Schloss was subsequently much expanded and modified to provide a summer residence for the Prussian kings.

The Altes Schloss

Immediately behind the statue of Friedrich Wilhelm is the entrance to the **Altes Schloss**, which includes the apartment of Friedrich Wilhelm IV and the Baroque rooms of Friedrich I and Sophie Charlotte. To see these you're obliged to go on the conducted **tour** in German – though free English audio-guides are available. The tour traipses through increasingly sumptuous chambers and bedrooms, filled with gilt and carvings. Look out for the **porcelain room**, packed to the ceiling with china, and the **chapel**, which includes a portrait of Sophie Charlotte as the Virgin ascending to heaven.

Neuer Flügel and the Concert Room

The Knobelsdorff-designed **Neuer Flügel** (New Wing) includes an elegant Golden Gallery and adjacent White Hall, whose eighteenth-century ceiling was replaced at the end of the nineteenth century by a marble-and-gold confection with full electric illumination. Next door, the **Concert Room** contains a superb collection of works by **Watteau**, including the outstanding *The Embarcation for Cythera*, a delicate Rococo frippery tinged with sympathy and sadness.

The Schloss Gardens

Laid out in the French style in 1697, the bucolic **Schloss Gardens** were transformed into an English-style landscaped park in the early nineteenth century, then restored to their Baroque form after severe war damage. Buildings here include the **Neuer Pavillon**, designed by Schinkel for Friedrich Wilhelm III, and where the king preferred to live, away from the excesses of the main building. Square and simple, it houses some of Schinkel's drawings and plans. Deeper into the Schloss Gardens, on the north side of the lake, is the **Belvedere**, built as a teahouse in 1788 and today housing a missable Berlin-porcelain collection. On the western side of the gardens a long, tree-lined avenue leads to the hushed and shadowy **Mausoleum**, where Friedrich Wilhelm III lies, the carved image on his sarcophagus making him seem a good deal younger than 70. He commissioned the mausoleum to be built thirty years earlier for his wife, Queen Luise. Later burials here include Kaiser Wilhelm I, looking every inch a Prussian king.

Sammlung Scharf-Gerstenberg

Schlossstr. 70 • Tues–Sun 10am–6pm • €10 combined ticket with Museum Berggruen (see p.87), audio-guide included • ⓦ smb.museum • Bus #M45 from Bahnhof Zoo

The old nineteenth-century stables of the palace's Garde du Corps-Regiments opposite the Schloss has been revamped at great expense to house the **Sammlung Scharf-Gerstenberg**, the personal collection of early twentieth-century insurance-magnate Otto Gerstenberg. He simply "liked looking at pictures", in the words of his grandson Dieter Scharf, who put the collection at Berlin's disposal. The collection suggests Gerstenberg had a penchant for the graphic arts and sculpture, particularly from the French Romantic and Surrealist schools, but there's no doubt Gerstenberg enjoyed the weird.

On show are massive structures by Giovanni Battista Piranesi, some odd island-like forms by Victor Hugo and a woman copulating with a beast in Henri Rousseau's *Beauty and Beast* – who apparently uses the depiction to play with notions of the active and the passive. Other oddities include Max Klinger's local dream-based roller-skating works, and experimental use of materials by Wolfgang Paalen, who painted with candle soot, and Jean Dubuffet, who used coal, cement and butterfly wings. Other works in the collection are perhaps more mainstream by Surrealist standards, but include impressive pieces by some of the greats, including Max Ernst, René Magritte, Salvador Dalí and Paul Klee.

Museum Berggruen

Schlossstr. 1 • Tues–Sun 10am–6pm • €10 combined ticket with Sammlung Scharf-Gerstenberg (see opposite) • ⓦ smb.museum • Bus #M45 from Bahnhof Zoo

Opposite Schloss Charlottenburg, the wonderful **Museum Berggruen** is unmissable for fans of twentieth-century art and specifically Picasso. Heinz Berggruen, a young Jew forced to flee Berlin in 1936, ended up as an art dealer in Paris, where he got to know Picasso and his circle and assembled a collection of personal favourites. In 1996 the city gave him this comfortable and uncrowded building to show off his revered collection. Most of the Picassos here have rarely been seen and steal the show – highlights include the richly textured Cubist *The Yellow Sweater* and large-scale *Reclining Nude* – but there's also a handful of Cézannes and Giacomettis and a pair of Van Goghs. The top floor is very strong on Paul Klee, with works spanning the entire interwar period and so offering a meaningful insight into the artist's development.

The Olympic Stadium

Olympischer Platz 1 • Daily: late March–May & mid-Sept to Oct 9am–7pm; June to mid-Sept 9am–8pm; Nov to late March 10am–4pm • €7 • ☏ 030 25 00 23 22, ⓦ olympiastadion-berlin.de • U- & S-Bahn Olympiastadion

Western Charlottenburg is best known for its **Olympic Stadium**, where the world watched the 1936 Games and then, after a big revamp, the 2006 football World Cup. It's one of Berlin's few remaining fascist-era buildings, and hugely impressive, despite being tainted by its past. This huge Neoclassical construction was a deliberate rejection of the modernist architecture fashionable in the 1930s. Inside, the stadium's sheer size comes as a surprise, since the seating falls away below ground level. As the home ground of Hertha BSC, Berlin's best football team, the stadium is sometimes closed for sporting events or team practice, so check before trudging out.

Schöneberg

Once a separate entity, **Schöneberg** (see map, p.88) was swallowed up by Greater Berlin in the late eighteenth and early nineteenth centuries. By the 1920s and early 1930s it had become the centre for Berlin's sizeable gay community: there were around forty gay bars on and near to the road and rail intersection **Nollendorfplatz** alone, and gay life in the city was open, fashionable and well organized, with its own newspapers and community associations. Local theatres were filled with plays exploring gay themes; homosexuality in the Prussian army was little short of institutionalized; and gay bars, nightclubs and brothels proudly advertised themselves – there were even gay working men's clubs. A block away from Nollendorfplatz, at Nollendorfstr. 17, stands the building in which **Christopher Isherwood** lived during his years in prewar Berlin. Under the Third Reich, however, homosexuality was brutally outlawed: gays and lesbians were rounded up and taken to concentration camps and often murdered. A red-granite triangle at Nollendrfplatz U-Bahn station commemorates this. Though the neighbourhood was blown to pieces during the war, Schöneberg's gay village has proved more robust, and its attendant nightlife (see p.107) is still first class.

Kreuzberg-Friedrichshain and around

Directly south of Mitte, the district of **Kreuzberg-Friedrichshain** loosely divides into the more middle-class and white **West Kreuzberg**, mostly of interest for its museums,

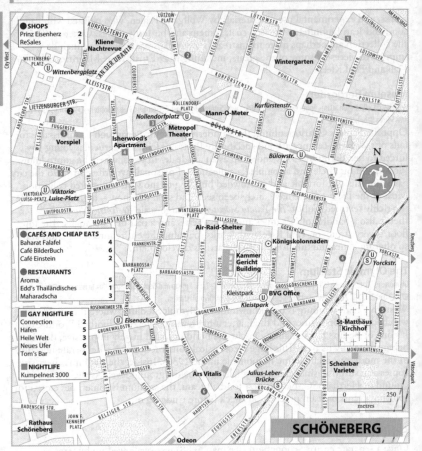

◄ City West

●SHOPS
| Prinz Eisenherz | 2 |
| ReSales | 1 |

●CAFÉS AND CHEAP EATS
Baharat Falafel	4
Café BilderBuch	6
Café Einstein	2

●RESTAURANTS
Aroma	5
Edd's Thailändisches	1
Maharadscha	3

■GAY NIGHTLIFE
Connection	2
Hafen	5
Heile Welt	3
Neues Ufer	6
Tom's Bar	4

■NIGHTLIFE
| Kumpelnest 3000 | 1 |

N

SCHÖNEBERG

0 — 250 metres

including the impressive **Jewish Museum**; unkempt, bohemian and heavily Turkish **East Kreuzberg**, great for wandering between café-bars, art galleries and clothes shops along its main drag **Oranienstrasse**; and **Friedrichshain**, a modern and fairly bland part of former East Berlin, whose low rents and central location have attracted Berlin's most happening bar and nightlife scene.

The Jüdisches Museum Berlin

Lindenstr. 9–14 • Mon 10am–10pm, Tues–Sun 10am–8pm • €5 • ⓦ jmberlin.de • U-Bahn Hallesches Tor or bus #248 from Alexanderplatz

An architectural burst of light in a bland residential part of Kreuzberg, the **Jüdisches Museum Berlin** (Jewish Museum Berlin) tackles the difficult topic of the history and culture of German Jewry. Designed by Daniel Libeskind, the museum's footprint resembles a compressed lightning bolt (intended as a deconstructed Star of David), while the structure itself is sheathed in polished metal, with windows – or, rather, thin angular slits – that trace geometric patterns on the exterior. All these uncomfortable angles and severe lines are intended to create a disturbed and uneasy space to mirror the painful history covered inside. Though expertly crafted, the exhibition is a bit convoluted – an irony of the deliberately disorientating building – and a bit too long.

The Berlinische Galerie

Alte Jakobstr. 124–128 • Mon & Wed–Sun 10am–6pm • €8 • Ⓦ berlinischegalerie.de • U-Bahn Hallesches Tor

Just northeast of the Jewish Museum, a vast former warehouse supplies the clinical home of the **Berlinische Galerie**, which gathers together some of Berlin's darkest and most tortured artwork. These include pieces by Lesser Ury, George Grosz and Otto Dix, with almost all from the twentieth century when movements such as Secessionism, Dadaism and the New Objectivity called Berlin home. But the gallery really thrives on its expertly presented temporary exhibitions (extra charge).

The Deutsches Technikmuseum Berlin

Trebbiner Str. 9 • Tues–Fri 9am–5.30pm, Sat & Sun 10am–6pm • €6 • Ⓦ sdtb.de • U-Bahn Möckernbrücke

Housed in a former railway station goods depot, the **Deutsches Technikmuseum Berlin** presents a comprehensive – possibly overwhelming – overview of German technology. The vast collection – which even includes trains and planes – is particularly strong on computers, radios and cameras. As well as presenting artefacts the museum also sheds interesting light on more disperate topics such as the development of the chemical and

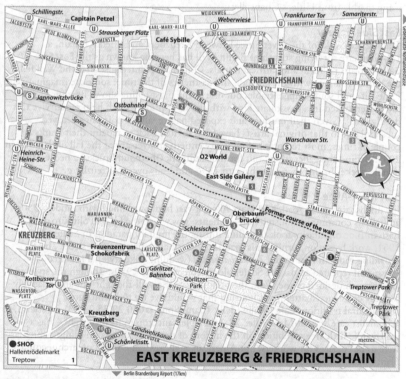

EAST KREUZBERG & FRIEDRICHSHAIN

▶ Berlin Brandenburg Airport (17km)

■ ACCOMMODATION		● CAFÉS AND CHEAP EATS		● BARS AND BEER GARDENS		Monarch	9
East Side Hotel	5	Burgermeister	3	Ankerklause	10	Rosi's	3
Eastern Comfort	6	Café V	5	Dachkammer	1	SO36	8
IntercityHotel Berlin	3	Kvartira Nr. 62	6	Kantine am Berghain	2	Tresor	4
Jetpak Alternative Hostel	8	Morgenland	9	White Trash Fast Food	7	Watergate	5
Michelberger Hotel	4					Wild at Heart	10
nhow	7	● RESTAURANTS		■ NIGHTLIFE			
Odyssee Globetrotter		Baraka	8	Berghain	2	■ GAY NIGHTLIFE	
Hostel	1	Café Jacques	11	Cassiopeia	1	Barbie Deinhoff	6
Ostel	2	Weltrestaurant Markthalle	4	Club der Visionaere	7		

● SHOP	
Hallentrödelmarkt Treptow	1

1

pharmaceutical industries and their impact on everyday life. Much of the museum is based on viewing life-sized reproductions and actual machines; an annexe around the corner at Möckernstr. 26, the **Science Center Spectrum**, is dedicated to interactive exhibits.

Treptower Park and the Sowjetisches Ehrenmal

Just south of East Kreuzberg, **Treptower Park** was designed as a place in which nineteenth-century tenement-dwellers could let off steam; by 1908 there were thirty-odd dance halls and restaurants here. A few beer gardens still exist, and boat rental is possible around the Insel der Jugend, the main hub of activity, but the park's main sight is the large and sobering **Sowjetisches Ehrenmal** (Soviet Memorial), which commemorates the Soviet Union's 305,000 troops killed in the Battle of Berlin in April and May 1945, and is the burial place of five thousand of them. It's best approached from the arched entrance on the south side of Puschkinallee which leads to a sculpture of a grieving woman representing the Motherland. A long sunken park of mass graves stretches out towards a vast statue of an idealized Russian soldier clutching a saved child and resting his sword on a shattered swastika – typical Soviet gigantism, and built using marble from Hitler's Chancellery.

East Side Gallery

Trailing the banks of the River Spree between Kreuzberg and Friedrichshain, a 1.3-kilometre surviving stretch of Berlin Wall has become known as the **East Side Gallery** for its political and satirical murals. Originally painted just after the Wall fell, the murals resonate with the attitude and aesthetics of the time: some are imaginative, some trite and some impenetrable, but one of the most telling shows Brezhnev and Honecker locked in a passionate kiss, with the inscription, "God, help me survive this deadly love". Given their outdoor and exposed nature, all the paintings decayed substantially, so that original artists have been invited back to repaint their works a couple of times, most recently before the twentieth anniversary of the fall of the Wall in 2009. Behind the gallery, look out for the landmark **Oberbaumbrücke**, a neo-Gothic double-decker bridge that dates back to 1896 and leads over to Kreuzberg.

Karl-Marx-Allee

Friedrichshain's main road, **Karl-Marx-Allee**, a vast boulevard lined with model 1950s and 1960s communist housing developments, was where the GDR Politbüro and Eastern Bloc dignitaries took the salute during the military parades. In September 1951, work began on turning this road into "Germany's first socialist street", by providing modern flats in the *Zuckerbäckerstil* (wedding-cake style), a mutated Classicism repeated across the Soviet bloc throughout the 1950s. Though the style was and is much derided in the West, the buildings were a well-thought-out and relatively soundly constructed attempt at housing that would live up to Berlin's great architectural tradition. **Café Sybille** (daily 10am–8pm; ☎030 29 35 22 03) – a stylish, minimalist café at Karl-Marx-Allee 72, and a pleasant stop in its own right – has a worthwhile little free **exhibition** on the history of the street and its buildings, which were to be "palaces for workers, not American eggboxes", and based on architectural plans direct from the USSR.

Prenzlauer Berg

Fanning out immediately east of Mitte, the residential working-class district of **Prenzlauer Berg** fared relatively well in the war, being fought over street by street, leaving many of its turn-of-the-twentieth-century tenement blocks battle-scarred but intact, and preserving the leafy cobbled streets and intersections that typified prewar Berlin. This sense of history helped make Prenzlauer Berg a bohemian centre even during the GDR days, when large numbers of artists and young people chose to live here. After the *Wende* these pleasant corners with low rents were quickly seized on as ripe for gentrification and settled by some of the best restaurants, cafés, bars and clubs in the city. These days the district is known for its young alternative population and their broods, giving it one of the highest densities of small children in Germany.

Schönhauser Allee and the Kulturbrauerei

Schönhauser Allee, Prenzlauer Berg's main drag, is traced by the route of the U-Bahn from Alexanderplatz en route to **U-Bahn Eberswalder Strasse**, the district's hub. Here, underneath the elevated railway tracks lies *Konnopke's*, Berlin's oldest and most famous sausage kiosk and as good a place as any for a quick *Currywurst*. North of the station, Schönhauser Allee becomes an old-fashioned shopping street, whose cobbles and narrow shop facades give it a vaguely prewar feel.

Wandering Prenzlauer Berg's maze of old streets, absorbing the atmosphere and looking out for Battle of Berlin bullet and shell marks on unrestored facades is an end unto itself, but for more structured sightseeing, start just southwest of U-Bahn Eberswalder Strasse at the **Kulturbrauerei** (see p.105), an agglomeration of cafés, bars, clubs, cinemas and venues in a former brewery built in the 1890s in the pseudo-Byzantine style then favoured by Berlin's architects.

Kollwitzplatz and around

A block southeast of the Kulturbrauerei lies the leafy green

● SHOP	
Flagship Store	1

■ ACCOMMODATION	
Acksel Haus	1

■ NIGHTLIFE	
Dunckerclub	1
Kulturbrauerei	3
nbi	2

● CAFÉS AND CHEAP EATS		● BARS AND BEER GARDENS	
Al Hamra	7	Prater	8
Intersoup	3	Zu mir oder zu dir?	5
Kietzkantine	9		
Morgenrot	10	● RESTAURANTS	
November	11	Gugelhof	12
Pasternak	13	The Bird	1
Wohnzimmer	4	Zum Schusterjungen	6
Zuckerfee	2		

PRENZLAUER BERG

triangle of **Kollwitzplatz**. The nineteenth-century tenement street running north from the platz, **Husemannstrasse**, was restored to its original glory in the late GDR days: raddled facades were covered with fresh stucco and new wrought-iron balconies installed, as has happened in neighbouring streets since. Meanwhile, a left turn from the southern corner of Kollwitzplatz leads to **Knaackstrasse**, where the huge red-brick **Wasserturm** (Water Tower) looms. Built in 1875 on the site of a preindustrial windmill,

1

its basement was briefly used by the Nazis as a torture chamber – the bodies of 28 victims were found in the underground pipe network – but today the tower houses quirky circular apartments.

The synagogue and Jüdischer Freidhof

From Knaackstrasse, a left turn into **Rykestrasse** brings you to an ornate, functioning **synagogue** in the courtyard of no. 53. Built in 1904–05, it survived both Kristallnacht and use as stables by the SA. Another main remnant of Jewish Berlin, on the opposite side of Kollwitzplatz, and entered from Schönhauser Allee 23–25, is the **Jüdischer Freidhof** (Jewish Cemetery: Mon–Thurs 8am–4pm, Fri 8am–1pm; free), opened when space ran out at the one on Grosse Hamburger Strasse (see p.81). Though there are over twenty thousand people buried here, for most their last resting place is anonymous: in 1943 most of the gravestones were smashed.

The suburbs

Exploring Berlin's **suburbs** completes a picture of the city, but is not always attractive, since many bland Cold War building projects have survived here. Old socialist silo-like apartment blocks and soulless shopping precincts look pretty desperate, particularly in the east. However, the sprawling working-class district of **Lichtenberg**, a mid-1970s model neighbourhood just southeast of Friedrichshain, is home to two sights of vital importance to anyone with an interest in the Stasi, the GDR's secret police: their remand prison at **Hohenschönhausen**, and their headquarters at **Normannenstrasse**.

All the other particularly worthwhile suburban destinations are on Berlin's rural fringes, particularly Grunewald forest and adjacent **Wannsee lake** in the southwestern corner of the city, which is famed for its summertime bathing beaches but sadly also as the location of the **Wannsee Villa**, where a Nazi conference initiated the Holocaust.

Gedenkstätte Hohenschönhausen

Genslerstr. 66 • Daily 9am–4pm; English-language tour 2.30pm, hourly tours in German • €5 • ⓦ stiftung-hsh.de • Tram #M5 from Hackescher Markt or bus #256 from U-Bahn Lichtenberg; get off at Freienwalder Strasse

A potent antidote to *Ostalgie* – nostalgia for the GDR – is a visit to the grim, former Stasi prison at **Gedenkstätte Hohenschönhausen** (Memorial Hohenschönhausen), which offers an insight into the fear and oppression upon which the regime was

---

THE STASI

East Germany's infamous Staatssicherheitsdienst (State Security Service), or **Stasi**, monitored everything in the GDR. It ensured the security of the country's borders, carried out surveillance on foreign diplomats, business people and journalists, and monitored domestic and foreign media. It was, however, in the surveillance of East Germany's own population that the organization truly excelled. Very little happened in the GDR without the Stasi knowing about it: files were kept on millions of innocent citizens and insidious operations were orchestrated against dissidents, real and imagined. By the *Wende* the Stasi had a budget of £1 billion and 91,000 full-time employees and 180,000 informers within the East German population, figures brought into context by the punier, albeit more ruthless, 7000-strong Nazi Gestapo.

At the beginning of 1991 former citizens of the GDR were given the right to see their Stasi files. Tens of thousands took the opportunity to find out what the organization had recorded about them, and, more importantly, who had provided the information; many a friendship and not a few marriages came to an end as a result. The process of unravelling truths from the archives also provided material for **books and films**, including Timothy Garton Ash's book, *The File: A Personal History* and the film, *Das Leben der Anderen* (*The Lives of Others*). Not all documents survived: many were briskly shredded as the GDR regime collapsed, resulting in an unenviable task for one government organization which spent literally years piecing them together to bring people to justice, thankfully with some success.

founded. Hohenschönhausen began life in 1945 as a **Soviet Special Camp**, with 4200 inmates penned in together in horrendous living conditions. By 1946 around 3000 had died. Officially most had been interned because of suspected Nazi links, but in most cases there was no evidence. This made torture chambers vital for acquiring "confessions" that would usually lead to decades of forced labour – though ultimately almost all prisoners were declared innocent by the Russian authorities in the 1990s.

In 1951 the Stasi (see box opposite) inherited the facility and turned it into a **remand prison** which was quickly blotted from city maps. The smallest sign of resistance or opposition to the state, including comments written in personal letters – which were all routinely steamed open – would earn you a spell inside. Typically, you'd be caught unawares on your way to work, bundled into a van and brought here. The former prisoners who lead tours deliver an absorbing insight into the psychological rather than physical abuse that followed in the solitary world of padded cells, tiny exercise yards, endless corridors and interrogation rooms.

Stasi Museum Berlin

Ruschestr. 103, Haus 22 • Mon–Fri 10am–6pm, Sat & Sun noon–6pm • €5, English booklet €3 • ⓦ stasimuseum.de • U-Bahn Magdalenenstrasse

Occupying a building in the huge, former Stasi headquarters complex, the **Stasi Museum Berlin** methodically unravels the massive surveillance apparatus of the GDR's secret police. Walking along the bare, red-carpeted corridors and looking at the busts of Lenin and Felix Dzerzhinsky – founder of the Soviet Cheka, models for both the KGB and the Stasi – it all seems part of a distant past, not an era which ended only in 1990. But then the obsessively neat office and apartment of **Erich Mielke**, the Stasi head from 1957 to October 1989, makes it all the more immediate. Everything is just as he left it: white and black telephones stand on the varnished wooden desk as though awaiting calls, and Mielke's white dress uniform hangs in a wardrobe. Other rooms have displays of Stasi surveillance apparatus described in German, but which mostly speak for themselves. The many bugging devices and cameras – some concealed in watering cans and plant pots – reveal the absurd lengths the GDR went to in order to keep tabs on its citizens.

Grunewald and the Wannsee

Few people associate Berlin with hikes through dense woodland or swimming from crowded beaches, but that's just what the **Grunewald** forests and the adjacent Wannsee lake offer. The main attraction here is Europe's largest inland beach, **Strandbad Wannsee**, a kilometre-long strip of pale sand that's packed as soon as the sun comes out. From here it's easy to wander into the forests and to smaller, less-populated beaches along the lakeside road, **Havelchaussee**. Usefully, bus #218 from S-Bahn Wannsee and Nikolassee goes this way and runs along 6km of sandy coves where there are few facilities.

The Wannsee Villa

Am Grossen Wannsee 56–58 • Daily 10am–6pm • Free • ⓦ ghwk.de • S-Bahn Wannsee, then #114 bus to "Haus der Wannsee-Konferenz"

The **Wannsee Villa** is infamous as the location of the Wannsee Conference in which the Nazis elected to gas millions of Jews as a "final solution". The villa is now a memorial to the conference and subsequent atrocities. Documents from the meeting are displayed and photographs of participants ranged around the walls, their biographies showing that many lived to a comfortable old age.

| ARRIVAL AND DEPARTURE | BERLIN |

BY PLANE

Berlin's two international airports (ⓦ berlin-airport.de) both lie within easy reach of the city centre via public transport. The closer of the two is Tegel airport (TXL); this is due to shut in 2016, when all traffic will land at the new Berlin Brandenburg International (BBI) – which will incorporate Berlin's other airport, Schönefeld (SXF).

Tegel airport From Tegel airport, the frequent #TXL express bus runs to the Hauptbahnhof and Alexanderplatz, while the #X9 express bus or local bus #109 run to Bahnhof

1

Zoo. A public transport zone AB ticket (€2.60) covers this. Given the frequency and efficiency of public transport, taxis are hardly worthwhile, but typical rates are around €20.

Berlin Brandenburg airport From Berlin Brandenburg/Schönefeld, S-Bahn line #S9 runs to Alexanderplatz, the Hauptbahnhof and Bahnhof Zoo (every 30min; 30min); bus #X7 runs to nearby U-Bahn Rudow. A public transport zone ABC ticket (€3.20) covers journeys from Schönefeld into the centre. Taxis cost around €35.

BY TRAIN

Long-distance trains arrive at the swanky Hauptbahnhof, which has late-opening shops and all the standard facilities. Many services also stop at other major stations such as Bahnhof Zoo, Alexanderplatz and the Ostbahnhof. A train ticket to Berlin may well include use of zones A and B of the city's public transport system (see below); check with the conductor or ticket office.

Destinations (Berlin Hauptbahnhof) Dessau (frequent; 1hr 30min); Dresden (12 daily; 2–3hr); Hamburg (frequent; 1hr 40min); Hannover (every 30min; 2hr 50min); Leipzig (frequent; 2hr 20min); Munich (15 daily; 6hr 30min); Potsdam (frequent – including S-Bahn; 30min).

BY BUS

Most international buses stop at the bus station (ZOB), which is linked to the Ku'damm area by many buses, including the #M49 service, and U-Bahn line #2 from Kaiserdamm station.

BY CAR

If arriving by car, you'll meet the Berliner Ring (A10), a circular motorway around the city which is worth following round to the side of town you need rather than deal with inner-city traffic.

GETTING AROUND

PUBLIC TRANSPORT

Berlin's efficient and inexpensive public transport network is run by the BVG (⑩bvg.de) and looks complicated at first glance but quickly becomes easy to navigate. Fast suburban (S-Bahn) and underground trains (U-Bahn) form the backbone of the system and are supplemented on the streets by buses and trams. Trains run all night on Fri and Sat but otherwise from 4am to around 1am when their routes are generally covered by night buses – whose numbers are prefixed by "N". Buses and trams called MetroBus or MetroTram run particularly frequently, often all night, and have numbers preceded by "M". On all services, onboard illuminated signs and announcements make finding the right stop easy.

BVG TICKETS

All BVG services share the same tickets, valid for transfers between different modes of transport as well as all other services within the regional system, including buses and trams in Potsdam, Oranienburg and even Regional Express trains (marked RE) within the city limits.

Types of ticket The network is divided into ticket zones A, B and C; a basic single ticket (*Einzelticket*) for zones A and B costs €2.60, a ticket for all three zones costs €3. Tickets are valid for two hours and allow unlimited transfers, but not return journeys. A *Kurzstrecke*, or short-trip ticket, costs €1.50 and allows you to travel up to three train or six bus stops (no transfers). A day-ticket (*Tageskarte*; €7.20 for zones A, B and C) is valid until 3am

BERLIN TOURS

In recent years English-language **walking tours** of Berlin have become a popular way to get a handle on the city. A four-hour city tour should cost around €12. Companies include Original Berlin Walks (☎030 301 91 94, ⑩berlinwalks.com), Insider Tours (☎030 692 31 49, ⑩insiderberlintours.com) and New Berlin Tours (☎030 510 50 03 01, ⑩newberlintours.com), who offer a free city-centre tour, though generous tips are expected. All companies also offer **special interest tours** such as the Third Reich, Jewish life, Potsdam and Sachsenhausen. Two companies offering something a bit different are Alternative Berlin (☎0162 819 82 64, ⑩alternativeberlin.com), which tours the graffiti art and squats of Berlin's underbelly, and Berliner Unterwelten, which offers tours (see box, p.84) around various underground installations such as a World War II bunker.

Insider and New Berlin also run **cycling tours**, as do specialist, Fat Tire Bike Tours (☎030 24 04 79 91, ⑩fattirebiketoursberlin.com), who charge €24 for a guided four-hour pedal around central Berlin astride a beach-cruiser bike.

Boats cruise Berlin's numerous city-centre canals and suburban lakes regularly in summer. Usually you can just turn up at quayside stops around the Spreeinsel and buy a ticket on the spot. One of several similar outfits picking up passengers around the Spreeinsel, Reederei Riedel (March to mid-Dec; ☎030 67 96 14 70, ⑩reederei-riedel.de) offers an hour-long *Stadtkernfahrt* (€11.50) and a three-hour *Brückenfahrt* (€20), which runs a loop around central Berlin.

the next morning. A seven-day ticket (*Sieben-Tage-Karte*) is €35.60 for all zones. Other money-saving possibilities include a small-group ticket (*Kleingruppenkarten*), valid for a whole day's travel for up to five people (€16.70 for zones A, B & C).

Buying tickets All public transport tickets are available from machines – which have an English-language option – on station platforms and on trams, but be sure to validate them by punching the ticket at the red or yellow machines before you travel; failing to do so results in €40 fines at spot checks. Bus drivers can also sell tickets, though only single and day-tickets.

CONCESSIONARY CARDS

A couple of travel cards include concessionary rates at a host of attractions and discounts at participating tour companies, restaurants and theatres: the Welcome Card, and the slightly cheaper City Tour Card (ⓦcitytourcard.com). Both are available in 48-hour, 72-hour and five-day versions, and range from €16.90 for 48 hours in zones A and B, to €36.50 for five days in zones A, B and C. The main difference between the two cards is their partners, so check to see which are more appealing. A Museum Island version of the Welcome Card also covers all of the Museum Island museums (see p.74): 72 hours in zones A and B costs €34.

TAXIS

Berlin's cream-coloured taxis are plentiful, cruising the city day and night and congregating at useful locations.

Fares Taxis are always metered: for the first 7km it's €3.20 plus €1.65 per kilometre, after which it's €1.28 per kilometre. Fares rise slightly between 11pm and 6am and all day Sun. Short trips, known as *Kurzstrecke*, can be paid on a flat rate of €4 for up to 2km or five minutes, though this only works when you hail a moving cab, and you must request it on getting into the taxi.

Taxi firms City Funk ⓣ030 21 02 02; Funk Taxi Berlin ⓣ030 26 10 26.

CYCLING

An extensive bike-path network makes cycling quick and convenient, and you can also take your bike on the U- and S-Bahn, with a *Fahrrad* ticket.

Bike rental One good bike-rental company is Fahrradstation (ⓦfahrradstation.com), with branches at Auguststr. 29a (Mon–Fri 10am–7pm, Sat 10am–3pm; ⓣ030 22 50 80 70; U-Bahn Weinmeisterstrasse), and at Bergmannstr. 9, Kreuzberg (Mon–Fri 10am–7pm, Sat 10am–4pm; ⓣ030 215 15 66; U-Bahn Gneisenaustrasse). Call-a-bikes – bikes from the public bicycle sharing initiative operated by Deutsche Bahn (see p.35) – are also scattered around the city and easy to find.

BY CAR

Car rental All major car-rental agencies are represented, along with better-value local operator Robben & Wientjes (ⓦrobben-wientjes.de), with branches at Prinzenstr. 90–91, Kreuzberg (ⓣ030 61 67 70; U-Bahn Moritzplatz), and at Prenzlauer Allee 96 (ⓣ030 42 10 36; U-Bahn Prenzlauer Allee).

INFORMATION

Visit Berlin (ⓦvisitberlin.de) provides the city with five **tourist information offices**, which all have a wide selection of material – including a useful what's-on magazine. They sell tickets to many upcoming events and offer free accommodation booking.

Brandenburg Gate South Wing, Pariser Platz (daily: April–Oct 9.30am–7pm; Nov–March 9.30am–6pm; U- & S-Bahn Brandenburger Tor).

Fernsehturm (TV Tower) Panoramastr. 1a (late May to Oct daily 10am–6pm; U- & S-Bahn Alexanderplatz).

Hauptbahnhof Europaplatz (daily 8am–10pm; U- & S-Bahn Hauptbahnhof).

Neuen Kranzler Eck Kurfürstendamm 22 (Mon–Sat 9.30am–8pm, Sun 10am–6pm; U-Bahn Kurfürstendamm).

Tegel airport Terminal A /Gate 2 (daily 8am–9pm).

ACCOMMODATION

Berlin has plenty of **hotels**, **pensions**, **hostels**, **private rooms** and **apartments** for short-term rent, and even **campsites**, but it's best to book at least a couple of weeks in advance. For quick results, try Visit Berlin (ⓣ030 25 00 25, ⓦvisitberlin.de), who specialize in hotels and pensions. They do have private rooms on their books, but there's a better selection via local accommodation agencies, where **private rooms** start at €20 per night: try Bed & Breakfast in Berlin (ⓣ030 44 05 05 82, ⓦbed-and-breakfast-berlin.de), Citybed (ⓣ030 23 62 36 10, ⓦcitybed.de); 9flats (ⓦ9flats.com); or Brilliant Apartments (ⓦbrilliant-apartments.de), who specialize in apartments in Prenzlauer Berg.

HOTELS AND PENSIONS

There's considerable overlap between what pensions and hotels – and even hostels (see p.97) – in Berlin offer, yet almost all accommodation is of a good standard, so deciding on which part of town to stay in is often the most important choice, despite the great public transport. Mitte is best for sightseeing, but its main restaurant and nightlife district, around Oranienburger Strasse, is a little touristy. To

1

get under the skin of the city one of the surrounding boroughs can be a good choice: genteel Prenzlauer Berg and Schöneberg are both happening neighbourhoods, but gritty Friedrichshain and Kreuzberg are home to the most cutting-edge nightlife. City West, the staid old centre of West Berlin, has plenty of accommodation, but may be a bit too far from Berlin's brightest lights for some.

MITTE

Adlon Unter den Linden 77 ☎030 226 10, ⓦhotel -adlon.de; U- & S-Bahn Brandenburger Tor; map pp.66–67. The jewel of Berlin's prewar luxury hotels has been re-created in all its excessive splendour. Prices are fit for a Kaiser – you'll part with at least €15,000 per night for the royal suite. **€221**

★**art'otel Berlin Mitte** Wallstr. 70–73 ☎030 24 06 20, ⓦartotel.de; S-Bahn Hackescher Markt; map pp.66–67. Smart, lively hotel with quirky decor – lots of contemporary and modern art, including an impressive range of Georg Baselitz paintings – in a quiet corner of Berlin, close to the U-Bahn. When reserving, you can pick the colour of your room: green, blue, red or aubergine. Breakfast not included. **€66**

Casa Camper Weinmeisterstr. 1 ☎030 20 00 34 10, ⓦcasacamper.com; U-Bahn Weinmeisterstrasse; map pp.66–67. Smart boutique hotel whose solid-wood interiors try to mirror a bit of Berlin's quirkiness. Wi-fi and breakfast are included in the rates, as are around-the-clock snacks and drinks at the hotel restaurant with its impressive rooftop views. With sauna and bike rental. **€191**

★**Circus Hotel** Rosenthalerstr. 1 ☎030 20 00 39 39, ⓦcircus-berlin.de; U-Bahn Rosenthaler Platz; map pp.66–67. The sister establishment of the *Circus Hostel* (just over the road – see opposite) is a more upmarket and more eco-friendly place. Sixty rooms include junior suites and apartments, decorated in striking colours with wooden floors and antique furniture. Restaurant *Fabisch* serves organic and locally sourced German cuisine. Buffet breakfast €4–8. With beer garden and free wi-fi. **€107**

Hackescher Markt Grosse Präsidentenstr. 8 ☎030 28 00 30, ⓦhotel-hackescher-markt.com; S-Bahn Hackescher Markt; map pp.66–67. Quirky little hotel on a quiet side street, in the midst of the Hackescher Markt bar scene. It has an eclectic mix of furnishings and some pleasant touches, including under-floor heating in the en-suite bathrooms. The rooms overlooking the courtyard are quieter. **€99**

Hotel Taunus Monbijouplatz 1 ☎030 283 52 54, ⓦhoteltaunus.com; S-Bahn Hackescher Markt; map pp.66–67. No-frills budget hotel with clean and simple if cramped rooms but at extraordinarily low prices for the location – arguably as good as it gets in central Berlin. There are some en-suite rooms for an extra €10. **€59**

Luise Kunsthotel Luisenstr. 19 ☎030 28 44 80,

ⓦluise-berlin.com; U- & S-Bahn Friedrichstrasse; map pp.66–67. Each room here is an eccentric, and impressive, work of art: one comes with bananas all over the walls and hot-pink velvet bedding, while another is an Alice in Wonderland-themed room with oversized furniture. The elegant rooms at the front tend to suffer from train noise (earplugs provided), while the quieter rooms at the back are a bit blander. Not all are en suite and breakfast costs extra. **€55**

★**Motel One** Dircksenstr. 36 ☎030 20 05 40 80, ⓦmotel-one.com; U- & S-Bahn Alexanderplatz; map pp.66–67. Countrywide hotel group whose stylish lobbies – flat-screen TVs and wacky modular '70s furniture – suggest far higher prices than its cheerfully straightforward en-suite rooms command. The location, a couple of minutes' walk from Alexanderplatz, helps make it a downtown bargain; the chain has seven other locations in Berlin. Free wi-fi. **€87**

Park Inn Alexanderplatz ☎030 238 90, ⓦparkinn.de; U- & S-Bahn Alexanderplatz; map pp.66–67. Big, ugly block bang in the middle of things, hard to beat for convenience, and with unbeatable views over the city. Of the nine hundred en-suite rooms, the newly renovated business-class ones are a clear notch above the rest. There's a gym, sauna and top-floor casino too. Breakfast not included. **€85**

Scandic Potsdamer Platz, Gabriele-Tergit-Promenade 19 ☎030 700 77 90, ⓦscandichotels.com; U-Bahn Mendelssohn-Bartholdy-Park; map pp.64–65. Smart yet informal homage to Scandinavian design in the no-man's-land south of Potsdamer Platz – very handy for the U-Bahn. Rooms and each floor are successfully themed by season, and this international hotel chain's eco-friendly policies are equally well thought out: the restaurant uses local ingredients; disposable sachets are absent; and the breakfast honey even comes from rooftop hives. There's a gym and bar, and bikes are available to rent. Breakfast costs extra. **€82**

CITY WEST

★**Funk** Fasanenstr. 69 ☎030 882 71 93, ⓦhotel -pensionfunk.de; U-Bahn Uhlandstrasse; map pp.64–65. Interesting re-creation of a prewar flat, with furniture and objects from the 1920s and 1930s, when this was the home of Danish silent-movie star Asta Nielsen. Given this, its location, and the included breakfast buffet, it's a bargain. The cheapest rooms share bathrooms. Breakfast and wi-fi included. **€89**

Hollywood Media Hotel Kurfürstendamm 202 ☎030 88 91 00, ⓦfilmhotel.de; U-Bahn Uhlandstrasse; map pp.64–65. Owned by German film producer Artur Brauner (*Bridge Over the River Kwai*), this hotel is a shrine to films of all sorts. But it's all classily understated: rooms, themed by movie star, are tastefully decorated with just one headshot and bio in each. The modern hotel boasts predictably sound

4-star standards, has a sauna and steam room and a huge buffet breakfast included in the rates. Wi-fi costs extra. **€99**

Hotel Q! Knesebeckstr. 67 ☎030 810 06 60, ⓦloock -hotels.com; S-Savignyplatz; map pp.64–65. A leader in the swankiness stakes, even in über-cool Berlin, this hotel is full of minimalist Bauhaus-inspired elegance and quirks like bathtubs built into bedframes and chocolate massages on offer. Great buffet breakfasts and extremely affable staff. **€185**

★**Kettler** Bleibtreustr. 19 ☎030 883 49 49; S-Savignyplatz; map pp.64–65. Tiny, charming 1920s-style pension on a lively, café-lined street. A multitude of knick-knacks, Berlinana and patterned wallpaper give the place character. Rooms are themed by artist or performer (choose between the likes of Callas or Toulouse-Lautrec) and have showers but share toilets. **€65**

EAST KREUZBERG–FRIEDRICHSHAIN

★**East Side Hotel** Mühlenstr. 6 ☎030 29 38 33, ⓦeastsidehotel.de; U- & S-Bahn Warschauer Strasse; map p.89. Small, laidback modern hotel just over the Spree from Kreuzberg in southern Friedrichshain, overlooking the East Side Gallery. The service is exceptional and the absence of rules refreshing: you can check in or out, order room service, or have breakfast in the café 24 hours a day. Original artwork in the hotel includes quirky murals by Birgit Kinder, who famously painted the Trabant on the East Side Gallery. **€85**

IntercityHotel Berlin Am Ostbahnhof 5 ☎030 29 36 80, ⓦberlin.intercityhotel.de; S-Bahn Ostbahnhof; map p.89. Sleek but budget-conscious business hotel at the Ostbahnhof, so very convenient for the S-Bahn and the Friedrichshain scene. Rooms are of the usual international business standard, and rates include buffet breakfast and a ticket for Berlin's public transport network (zones A, B & C) for the duration of your stay. Rates vary wildly depending on events and demand. **€65**

★**Michelberger Hotel** Warschauer Str. 39 ☎030 29 77 85 90, ⓦmichelbergerhotel.com; U- & S-Bahn Warschauer Strasse; map p.89. Modern, trendy and urbane, this relaxed haunt with its cool warehouse-style interior provides anything but workaday hotel accommodation. Apart from enjoying its improvised feel – cuckoo clocks on raw concrete walls, exposed wiring – you'll also likely find the all-night bar and lobby friendly, relaxing and unpretentious hangouts. The buffet breakfast (€9) is excellent. **€80**

nhow Stralauer Allee 3 ☎030 29 02 990, ⓦnhow -hotels.com; U-Bahn Warschauer Strasse; map p.89. This 4-star concept hotel merges a music theme with designer hotel rooms. Amenities include a health club, sauna and fitness facility, and some rooms have great views over the river. **€86**

Ostel Wriezener Karree 5 ☎030 25 76 86 60, ⓦostel .eu; S-Bahn Ostbahnhof; map p.89. Step back into the GDR of the 1970s amid a haze of browns and oranges at this themed budget hotel a short walk from the Ostbahnhof. The rendition is creepily accurate, but thankfully the whole thing's done with a sense of humour and just the thing for those needing a fix of *Ostalgie* (see box, p.878). Some rooms share bathrooms; also available is a six-person apartment (€120 per night). **€57**

PRENZLAUER BERG

★**Acksel Haus** Belforter Str. 21 ☎030 44 33 76 33, ⓦackselhaus.de; U-Bahn Senefelderplatz; map p.91. Small offbeat hotel on an attractive residential street in the midst of the lively Prenzlauer Berg scene. Besides rooms, it offers fully equipped and individually themed apartments with broadband access and spacious kitchens. **€130**

HOSTELS

Amazingly, there are well over one hundred hostels in Berlin; nearly all are independent and often smart, clean and quite sophisticated, with their own bar, social areas, internet terminals and buffet breakfasts. Many also have private rooms.

MITTE

Baxpax Downtown Ziegelstr. 28 ☎30 27 87 48 80, ⓦbaxpax.de; S-Bahn Oranienburger Strasse; map pp.66–67. Great hostel with busy communal areas in a handy, yet relatively quiet location, with all the usual facilities – internet, bar, breakfast buffet, games room, bike rental – and a relaxed vibe. Avoid the 24-bed dorm if you are a light sleeper in favour of an eight-bed or smaller dorm. Dorms **€17**, doubles **€98**

★**Circus Hostel** Weinbergsweg 1a ☎030 20 00 39 39, ⓦcircus-berlin.de; U-Bahn Rosenthaler Platz; map pp.66–67. Top-notch hostel in a fantastic location, with particularly helpful staff and good facilities. Rooms are plain though bright, with large windows and high ceilings, and with the advantage of not having bunk beds. The hostel has its own, decent bar, *Goldmans*, downstairs. Bicycles for rent and free walking tours too. Dorms **€23**, doubles **€100**

★**Citystay Hostel** Rosenstr. 16 ☎030 23 62 40 31, ⓦcitystay.de; S-Bahn Hackescher Markt; map pp.66–67. Berlin's best-located hostel for the sights – in easy walking distance of the S-Bahn, Hackescher Markt and Museum Island – is a large well-run place spreading over several immaculate floors. It also has a good stock of private rooms, some en suite, and pleasant communal areas, including a leafy courtyard. Facilities include an all-night bar, summer-only restaurant (serving great *Flammkuchen*) and free wi-fi. The hostel's also a hub for various walking and cycling tours and bar crawls. The breakfast buffet costs extra. Dorms **€19**, twins **€55**

St Christopher's Hostel Rosa-Luxemburg-Str. 39–41 ☎030 81 45 39 60, ⓦst-christophers.co.uk; U-Bahn

1

Rosa-Luxemburg-Platz; map pp.66–67. Well-run branch of a British hostel chain, with the perfect layout and opening times (24hr) for partying all night in its big bar, complete with chill-out areas and billiards. There's also pub grub, free wi-fi and occasional live events, but the staff and guests are a motley international crew, so there's little to remind that you're in Germany. Rates include a basic breakfast and linen. Some dorms are single-sex. Dorms €240, doubles & twins €78

CITY WEST
★**Jetpak City Hostel** Pariserstr. 58 ☎030 784 43 60, ⓦjetpak.de; U-Bahn Spichernstrasse; map pp.64–65. Western Berlin's best hostel is scrupulously clean and in a quiet residential neighbourhood a short walk from the Ku'damm shops area and close to the U-Bahn. Amenities include free internet and wi-fi; access to printers, iPod chargers and speakers; and a sociable café-bar with rock-bottom prices, plus a common room with all sorts of film and gaming entertainment. Breakfast included. Dorms €20, doubles €80

EAST KREUZBERG–FRIEDRICHSHAIN
Eastern Comfort Mühlenstr. 73–77, Friedrichshain ☎030 66 76 38 06, ⓦeastern-comfort.com; U- & S-Bahn Warschauer Strasse; map p.89. Sleep swaying on the River Spree in a range of accommodation – from spacious doubles, through cabin bunks all the way to bedding down on the deck in a tent. All cabins except dorms are en suite and the boat has internet and wi-fi. Highly unconventional and lots of fun, and there's a social area and bar that's lively until the small hours. Tents €12, dorms €16, doubles €78
★**Jetpak Alternative Hostel** Görlitzerstr. 38 ☎030

62 90 86 41, ⓦjetpak.de; U-Bahn Schlesisches Tor; map p.89. Slick branch of Berlin's best hostel chain that offers a pretty stark contrast to Kreuzberg's gritty but happening Wrangelkiez neighbourhood. All rooms have high-end fittings such as under-floor heating in en-suite bathrooms. Other perks include a cheap bar, free on-street parking, free wi-fi, and a buffet breakfast (included in price). Dorms €22
Odyssee Globetrotter Hostel Grünberger Str. 23, Friedrichshain ☎030 29 00 00 81, ⓦglobetrotterhostel .de; U-Bahn Frankfurter Tor; map p.89. Imaginatively decorated and sociable hostel hard by the Friedrichshain scene and with a happening bar of its own. Facilities include kitchen and free wi-fi. Dorms €16, doubles €78

CAMPSITES
None of Berlin's campsites are close to the centre and if you're looking to cut costs, bear in mind that hostels will probably work out cheaper once you've added the cost of travel to a campsite.
Campingplatz Am Krossinsee Wernsdorfer Str. 38, Schmöckwitz ☎030 675 86 87, ⓦcampingplatz-berlin .de; S-Bahn Grünar, then tram #68 to Schmöckwitz, then bus #733. Pleasantly located in the woods just outside the southeastern suburb of Schmöckwitz, Am Krossinsee offers easy access to local lakes. It's also possible to rent a bungalow here. Bungalows €75; pitch €5, plus €7.50 per person
Campingplatz Kladow Krampnitzer Weg 111–117, Gatow ☎030 365 27 97; U-Bahn Rathaus Spandau, then bus #134 or #X34 to stop "Alt-Kladow". Friendly campsite on the western side of the Havel lake, with good facilities including a crèche, bar, restaurant, shop and showers. Pitch €5.50, plus €7 per person

EATING AND DRINKING

Berlin has all the **restaurants**, **cafés** and **bars** you'd expect from a major European capital, with virtually every imaginable type of food represented; indeed, national food generally takes a back seat to Greek, Turkish, Balkan, Indian and Italian specialities. In line with Berlin's rolling nightlife timetable, you can pretty much eat and drink around the clock. The majority of restaurants will happily serve until at least 11pm, and it's not hard to find somewhere in most neighbourhoods. Eating at Berlin's restaurants is by international standards inexpensive: main courses start at around €7, and drinks aren't hiked up much in bars. For most of the restaurants you can just walk in, though on weekend nights or at expensive places, **booking** is recommended.

CAFÉS AND CHEAP EATS
MITTE
Da Da Falafel Linienstr. 132 ☎030 27 59 69 27, ⓦdadafalafel.de; U-Bahn Oranienburger Tor; map

pp.66–67. Tiny Middle Eastern *Imbiss* with sleek decor, some seating and excellent falafel and shawarma sandwiches – the best of a clutch of cheap and cheerful options at this end of Oranienburger Strasse. Mon–Thurs & Sun 10am–2am, Sat 10am–3pm.
Dolores Rosa-Luxemburg-Str. 7 ☎030 28 09 95 97, ⓦdolores-online.de; U-Bahn Rosa-Luxemburg-Platz; map pp.66–67. As good a burrito as you'll find in Berlin, dished up in a small, funky and generally overcrowded cafeteria at staggeringly low prices. You'll leave very full, €4–6 poorer and maybe a bit bewildered by the à la carte menu system. Mon–Sat 11.30am–10pm, Sun 1–10pm.

TOP 5 CAFÉS
Café BilderBuch see opposite
Café Einstein see opposite
Café V see opposite
Kvartira Nr. 62 see opposite
Wohnzimmer p.100

Gorki Park Weinbergsweg 25 ☎030 448 72 86, ⓦgorki-park.de; U-Bahn Rosenthaler Platz; map pp.66–67. Tongue-in-cheek Soviet-themed café with 1970s Eastern Bloc-style furnishings and tasty and affordable Russian dishes like blini and *pelmeni* (dumplings); mains average €9. A large *Milchcafé* comes with a delicious molasses cookie, and the weekend brunch buffet (€10) is a treat. Free wi-fi. Mon–Sat 9.30am–2am, Sun 10am–2pm.

Oliv Münzstr. 8 ☎030 89 20 65 40, ⓦoliv-cafe.de; U-Bahn Weinmeisterstr.; map pp.66–67. Pleasant spot with modern interior, great coffee and decent, unpretentious food (sandwiches, quiches, soups and cakes), very handy for a respite from boutique bashing. Cash only. Mon–Fri 8.30am–7pm, Sat 9.30am–7pm, Sun 10am–6pm.

CITY WEST

Piccola Taormina Uhlandstr. 29 ☎030 881 47 10, ⓦpiccola-taormina.net; U-Bahn Uhlandstrasse; map pp.64–65. Enduringly popular wafer-thin pizza specialist with a strange setup: order and pay at the bar, find a seat in the back room, listen up for a tannoy announcement, then head back to the bar to collect. It's all a bit chaotic and very Italian, but well worth it for the food – slices from €1.50. Daily 11am–2am.

Zwiebelfisch Savignyplatz 7 ☎030 312 73 63; S-Bahn Savignyplatz; map pp.64–65. Corner bar and 1970s throwback for would-be arty and intellectual types. Jazz, earnest debate and good cheap grub (€5–11) such as goulash and Swabian *Maultaschen* (ravioli), served until 1am. Daily noon–6am.

SCHÖNEBERG

★**Baharat Falafel** Winterfeldtstr. 37 ☎030 216 83 01; U-Bahn Nollendorfplatz; map p.88. The best falafel in Berlin is served in this bare-bones vegetarian *Imbiss*, with some seating. Dishes are freshly made and falafels fried to order so there can be a little wait, but it's well worth it. Daily noon–2am.

Café BilderBuch Akazienstr. 28 ☎030 78 70 60 57, ⓦcafe-bilderbuch.de; S-Bahn Julius-Leber-Brücke; map p.88. Lovely rambling café in the Viennese tradition. It doesn't look particularly special from the front, but the comfortable parlour in the back will likely hold you captive for hours. Great breakfasts, lovely cakes and elegant coffees, plus seating in a courtyard too. Mon–Sat 9am–midnight, Sun 10am–midnight.

Café Einstein Kurfürstenstr. 58 ☎030 261 50 96; U-Bahn Nollendorfplatz; map p.88. Housed in a seemingly ancient German villa, this is about as close as you'll get to the ambience of the prewar Berlin *Kaffeehaus*, with international newspapers and breakfast served until 2pm. Occasional live music, and a good garden. Expensive, though, and a little snooty. Daily 8am–1am.

EAST KREUZBERG–FRIEDRICHSHAIN

★**Burgermeister** Oberbaumstr. 8 ⓦburger-meister .de; U-Bahn Schlesisches Tor; map p.89. Cult burger joint in a converted old Prussian public toilets, by the elevated underground station at Schlesisches Tor, serving fresh and delicious burgers (€2–3.50) that could hold their own in far classier surroundings. Has a couple of places to sit, but mostly it's standing room only and often packed. Mon–Thurs & Sun 11am–3am, Fri & Sat 11am–4am.

Café V Lausitzer Platz 12 ☎030 612 45 05; U-Bahn Görlitzer Bahnhof; map p.89. Cosy, dimly lit, bohemian place beside a leafy Kreuzberg park – as good a hangout as restaurant. Though it serves fish, everything else is vegetarian, with plenty of tofu and seitan (wheat gluten) on offer, on pizzas and salads; the fennel nut salad is particularly good (mains €8–12). Menus change weekly. Daily 10am–2am.

Kvartira Nr. 62 Lübbener Str. 18 ☎0179 134 33 43; U-Bahn Schlesisches Tor; map p.89. Atmospheric Russian café with 1920s-era dark red and gold decor serving Russian classics such as *borscht* (stew; €3), delicious *pelmeni* (dumplings; €4.50) and tea flavoured with jam – as well as some great chocolate cake. Daily 4pm–late; food served 5–11pm.

Morgenland Skalitzer Str. 35 ☎030 611 32 91, ⓦmorgenland-berlin.de; U-Bahn Görlitzer Bahnhof; map p.89. Relaxed café with a welcoming vibe, serving a mix of European snacks. The amazing brunch buffet (Sat & Sun 10am–4pm; €11.50) seems to attract most of the neighbourhood. Mon–Fri 9am–late, Sat & Sun 10am–late.

PRENZLAUER BERG

Al Hamra Raumerstr. 16 ☎030 42 85 00 95; U-Bahn Eberswalder Strasse; map p.91. Comfortable Arab café with shabby decor but decent Mediterranean food, beer, water pipes, backgammon and chess, plus internet terminals and wi-fi. Daily 10am–3am.

Intersoup Schliemannstr. 31 ☎030 23 27 30 45, ⓦintersoup.de; S-Bahn Prenzlauer Allee; map p.91. Mellow den with an encyclopedic collection of excellent soups (€3.50–5) and a relaxing vibe. The place's trademark soup – Thai lemon grass, bean sprouts, noodle, coconut milk with chicken, tofu, fish or shrimp – is well worth a try. It's also one of the few bars in the area regularly promoting local and international DJs (upstairs) and bands (downstairs). Mon–Fri 6pm–3am, Sat & Sun 6pm–5am.

★**Kietzkantine** Oderberger Str. 50 ☎030 448 44 84; U-Bahn Eberswalder Strasse; map p.91. Choose from just two or three excellent daily specials at rock-bottom prices in this hugely popular bistro. There's always something vegetarian, and students get a discount. Order and pay at the till – the food will then be brought to your seat. Mon–Fri 9am–4pm.

1

★**Morgenrot** Kastanienallee 85 ☎030 44 31 78 44, ⓦcafe-morgenrot.de; U-Bahn Eberswalder Strasse; map p.91. Bohemian Berlin hits its stride in this collective café where G8 riots are planned and vegan breakfasts consumed. Everything is organic and the vegetarian buffet breakfast is excellent (until 3pm; €4–8): pay according to how wealthy you consider yourself. Tues–Thurs noon–1am, Fri & Sat 11am–3am, Sun 11am–midnight.

November Husemannstr. 15 ☎030 442 84 25, ⓦcafe-november.de; U-Bahn Senefelderplatz; map p.91. Uncluttered, exposed-wood place, just north of Kollwitzplatz, with imaginative German daily specials (€8–14), a reasonable Sun brunch (9am–4pm; €11) and outdoor seating in a pleasantly quiet residential street. Free wi-fi. Mon–Fri 10am–2am, Sat & Sun 9am–2am.

Pasternak Knaackstr. 24 ☎030 441 33 99, ⓦrestaurant-pasternak.de; U-Bahn Senefelderplatz; map p.91. Authentic upmarket Russian place that recalls the cafés and restaurants founded by Berlin's large Russian émigré community during the 1920s. A nice spot for caviar and champagne, a *Milchcafé* or a more substantial meal from the good selection of Russian dishes, including *borscht*, *pelmeni* (dumplings) and blini. The range of vodkas is suitably extensive. Daily 9am–late; food served until midnight.

Wohnzimmer Lettestr. 6 ☎030 445 54 58, ⓦwohnzimmer-bar.de; U-Bahn Eberswalder Strasse; map p.91. The rumpled and ramshackle living-room atmosphere helps make this café a relaxed and sociable hangout at any time of day – and the comfy sofas make leaving hard. At weekends a cocktail bar pops up between its two rooms. Breakfast served until 4pm, and you can get a filled roll and a coffee for €3 at anytime. Daily 9am–4am.

★**Zuckerfee** Greifenhagener Str. 15 ☎030 52 68 61 44, ⓦzuckerfee-berlin.de; U-Bahn Schönhauser Allee; map p.91. Gastronomic concept based on Tchaikovsky's *The Nutcracker* and named after the Sugar Plum Fairy. The immaculate interior – all Victorian dolls and tasteful ornamentation – reflects the menu, which features delicious waffles, cakes and uniquely presented breakfasts and lunches (book ahead at weekends). Tues–Sun 10am–6pm.

RESTAURANTS
MITTE

★**Café Nö!** Glinkastr. 23 ☎030 201 08 71, ⓦcafe-noe.de; U-Bahn Französische Strasse; map pp.66–67. This restaurant-wine bar serves very decent food for very reasonable prices. The menu includes *Flammkuchen* and the like, a huge mixed plate for two featuring almost everything on the menu is €23, and the wine list is vast enough for most tastes. Service is pleasant and not too formal. Mon–Fri noon–1am, Sat 7pm–1am (last orders midnight).

Käfer Dachgarten Platz der Republik 1 ☎030 22 62 99 33; U- & S-Bahn Brandenburger Tor; map pp.66–67.

Famous for its location on the roof of the Reichstag and its 180-degree view of eastern Berlin, this restaurant specializes in gourmet renditions of regional German dishes (mains €8–30). A reservation here also means you get to nip in a side entrance and avoid the consistently long line at the front entrance. Daily 9am–midnight (last orders 10pm).

Kellerrestaurant im Brechthaus Chausseestr. 125 ☎030 282 38 43, ⓦbrechtkeller.de; U-Bahn Oranienburger Tor; map pp.66–67. Atmospheric restaurant in the basement of Brecht's old house, decorated with Brecht memorabilia, including models of his stage sets. The Viennese specialities (mains €9–15) are from recipes dreamt up by Brecht's wife Helene Weigel, a busy actress with only East German ingredients at her disposal, so don't expect anything too elaborate or expensive. Reservations recommended. Daily 6pm–late.

Margaux Unter den Linden 78, entrance on Wilhelmstr. ☎030 22 65 26 11, ⓦmargaux-berlin.de; U- & S-Bahn Brandenburger Tor; map pp.66–67. Onyx walls, marble floors and burgundy upholstery set the stage for this upscale restaurant, whose daily menu is dictated by the quality of available supplies. The gracious maître d' will happily recommend wines from their selection of seven hundred); prices are harder to swallow, with mains from €26–45, but a good-value alternative is offered in the form of set meals, with three-course lunches (€35) and dinners (€95). Mon–Sat 7pm–late (last orders 10.30pm).

Monsieur Vuong Alte Schönhauser Str. 46 ☎030 30 87 26 43, ⓦmonsieurvuong.de; U-Bahn Weinmeisterstrasse; map pp.66–67. Snazzy Vietnamese place with delicious soups and noodle dishes (€8–11) from a tiny menu – look out also for the daily specials on the blackboard, which are available without meat. Bench dining means you'll sometimes have to squeeze together with other diners – expect queues at peak times. Don't miss the delicious jasmine and artichoke teas, or the zesty fruit smoothies. Daily noon–midnight.

Unsicht-bar Gormannstr. 14 ☎030 24 34 25 00, ⓦunsicht-bar-berlin.de; U-Bahn Weinmeisterstrasse; map pp.66–67. Hugely successful novelty restaurant run by an organization of the blind and visually impaired, where you eat in total darkness. First, pick from one of several three- or four-course fixed menus (€40–57), including a vegetarian option, then follow your blind or partially sighted waiter into the pitch black for your meal. The idea is that without your eyesight, your other senses will be heightened, but you're likely to make other discoveries, too, including how hard it is to judge the amount of food that's on your plate or fork, or even down your front. Mon–Thurs & Sun 5pm–1am, Fri & Sat 6pm–1am.

★**Zur letzten Instanz** Waisenstr. 14–16 ☎030 242 55 28; U-Bahn Klosterstrasse; map pp.66–67. Berlin's oldest *Kneipe*, considered so authentically German that foreign heads of state are often brought here: Mikhail Gorbachev dined at *Zur letzten* in 1989, as has, more recently, Jacques Chirac. There's a wonderfully old-fashioned interior, including a classic tiled oven, and a great beer garden. Reasonably priced traditional dishes, all with legal-themed names like *Zeugen-Aussage* ("Eyewitness account"), a reminder of the days when people used to drop in on the way to the nearby courthouse. If all the meaty dishes (€9–14) look too heavy, try the simple *Boulette*, Berlin's home-made mince and herb burger, done here to perfection. Mon–Sat noon–11pm, Sun noon–9pm.

CITY WEST

Florian Grolmanstr. 52 ☎ 030 313 91 84, ⍟ restaurant-florian.de; S-Bahn Savignyplatz; map pp.64–65. Leading light of the *Neue Deutsche Küche* movement in Berlin and as much a place for Berlin's beautiful people to be seen as it is a place to eat. The hearty and innovative South German food is only moderately expensive (mains €14.50–24.50), the interior coolly bland and the service excellent. Daily 6pm–3am (last orders 2am).

Zwölf Apostel Bleibtreustr. 49 ☎ 030 312 14 33, ⍟ 12-apostel.de; S-Bahn Savignyplatz; map pp.64–65. Deluxe and very popular pizzeria with a smart, Baroque-style interior and huge thin pizzas with unusual toppings like smoked salmon and cream cheese, plus five types of calzone (mains €7–20). The €6.50 weekday lunch (11.30am–4pm) is great value, while the brunch buffet on Sun is €18 but comes with a glass of sparkling wine and a hot drink. Booking recommended. Daily 8am–1am.

SCHÖNEBERG

Aroma Hochkirchstr. 8 ☎ 030 782 58 21, ⍟ cafe-aroma.de; U- & S-Bahn Yorckstrasse; map p.88. This rustic Italian gem, tucked away on a sleepy residential street, is the unofficial headquarters for Berlin's slow food movement. The antipasti spread at Sun brunch (until 4pm; €12) is legendary, while the likes of dried cod with polenta (€7.50) and squid with baby chard (€15.50) satisfy the dinner crowd. The terrace is a peaceful haven in summer. Mon–Fri 6pm–late, Sat 3pm–late, Sun 11am–late.

Edd's Thailändisches Lutzowstr. 81 ☎ 030 215 52 94, ⍟ edds-thairestaurant.de; U-Bahn Kurfürstenstrasse; map p.88. Huge portions of superbly cooked fresh Thai food make this sumptuous place popular all week. Bearing in mind the quality and authenticity – many family recipes stem from Edd's gran (including the signature banana blossom salad), who cooked in Bangkok's Royal Palace – the prices are reasonable, with mains around €16–25. Booking essential and credit cards not accepted. Tues–Fri 11.30am–3pm & 6pm–midnight, Sat 5pm–midnight, Sun 2pm–midnight.

Maharadscha Fuggerstr. 21 ☎ 030 213 88 26; U-Bahn Nollendorfplatz; map p.88. Though the ambience is that of a German farmhouse, the food here is pure Indian, with dishes (€7–11) from every part of the subcontinent. It gets packed out for the Sun buffet (noon–5pm; €9.90). Daily noon–midnight.

EAST KREUZBERG–FREIDRICHSHAIN

Altes Zollhaus Carl-Herz-Ufer 30 ☎ 030 692 33 00, ⍟ altes-zollhaus-berlin.de; U-Bahn Prinzenstrasse; map pp.64–65. Very classy place located in an old half-timbered building overlooking a canal, serving modern German food such as duck from Brandenburg with *Kartoffelpuffer*, and zander, a pike-like fish, from the Havel. The three-course set menus cost €38. Tues–Sat 6pm–1am.

Baraka Lausitzer Platz 6 ☎ 030 612 63 30, ⍟ baraka-berlin.de; U-Bahn Görlitzer Bahnhof; map p.89. One for North African food fans, with tasteful authentic decor and food – tagines, chicken skewers, *shawarma* – that's some of the best in town, and at decent prices (mains €5–12). The mixed plate for two is immense. Mon–Thurs 11am–midnight, Fri & Sat 11am–1am.

Café Jacques Maybachufer 8 ☎ 030 694 10 48; U-Bahn Schönleinstrasse; map p.89. Traditional French cuisine is the mainstay at this restaurant on the leafy banks of the Landwehr canal, but other foods like pasta and couscous also make an appearance; most mains around €10. Daily 6pm–midnight.

Weltrestaurant Markthalle Pücklerstr. 34 ☎ 030 617 55 02, ⍟ weltrestaurant-markthalle.de; U-Bahn Görlitzer Bahnhof; map p.89. Spacious restaurant that attracts a young crowd with its long communal tables and German food in hearty portions. Look out for the €8.50 daily special and leave space for the phenomenal cakes. Daily 10am–midnight.

PRENZLAUER BERG

Gugelhof Knaackstr. 37 ☎ 030 442 92 29, ⍟ gugelhof.de; U-Bahn Senefelderplatz; map p.91. Lively Alsatian restaurant put on the map by Bill Clinton's surprise visit in 2000. It serves inventive and beautifully presented German, French and Alsatian food (mains €8–18) – worth trying is the unusual *Flammkuchen*, a thin-crust Alsatian pizza. Mon–Fri 4pm–1am, Sat & Sun 10am–1am.

The Bird Am Falkplatz 5 ☎ 030 51 05 32 83, ⍟ thebirdinberlin.com; U-Bahn Schönhauser Allee; map p.91. Hugely popular New York-style steakhouse with punk-rock attitude, an international staff and gigantic tasty burgers, spicy chicken wings, steaks, hand-cut fries and so on. Mains are around the €10–20 mark, other dishes around half that. Cash only. Mon–Sat 6pm–late, Sun noon–late.

Zum Schusterjungen Danziger Str. 9 ☎ 030 442 76 54, ⍟ zumschusterjungen.com; U-Bahn Eberswalder Strasse; map p.91. Large portions of no-nonsense German

1

food served in the back room of a locals' *Kneipe*. The plastic and formica decor has echoes of the GDR and, at around €8 per dish, the prices are almost as cheap as back then, too. Daily noon–midnight.

BARS, BEER HALLS AND BEER GARDENS

The distinction between cafés, bars and clubs is notoriously fluid in Berlin, and many places morph from one type of venue into another throughout the day. A good place to slurp a morning coffee may well turn into a restaurant later on before rolling out the decks for a DJ until the small hours, when it closes to repeat the process all over again two or three hours later – so check places listed under "Cafés" on pp.98–100 and "Nightlife" on pp.103–105 too. Opening times are just as relaxed and bars typically close between 1am and 5am.

MITTE

The easiest place to bar-hop is Oranienburger Strasse, though you won't meet many Berliners here.

★**Café am Neuen See** Lichtensteinallee 2 ☎ 030 254 49 30, ⓦ cafeamneuensee.de; S- & U-Bahn Zoologischer Garten; map pp.64–65. A little piece of Bavaria smack in the middle of the Tiergarten; this beer garden is next to a picturesque lake where you can rent a rowing boat. The usual snacks – and superb pizzas – are served alongside frothing jugs. Daily 9am–late.

Strandbar Mitte Monbijoupark ⓦ strandbar-mitte .de; S-Bahn Oranienburger Strasse; map pp.66–67. Possibly Berlin's best beach bar, set in the Monbijoupark overlooking the Spree and the Bode-Museum. Grab a deckchair and a drink while watching the tourist boats float by, or join the fun on the dancefloor, with tango, swing, salsa and classic ballroom on alternating days. Summer daily 10am–late; closed in bad weather.

Verkehrsberuhigte Ost-Zone Monbijouplatz, Bahnbogen 153 ☎ 030 24 62 87 81, ⓦ veboz.de; S-Bahn Hackescher Markt; map pp.66–67. Great little bar if you are looking for a dose of *Ostalgie* with your beer, given the abudance of GDR memorabilia. It's hidden away in the arches of the S-Bahn overlooking the Spree, which might be what keeps it from being touristy. Daily 8pm–3am.

EAST KREUZBERG–FRIEDRICHSHAIN

Ankerklause Kottbusser Damm 104, Neukölln ☎ 030 41 71 75 12, ⓦ ankerklause.de; U-Bahn Kottbusser Tor; map p.89. This little café, perched by the Landwehr canal, turns into a hip and crowded funk and soul club by night. Thurs is Sixties night. Mon 4pm–4am, Tues–Sun 10am–4am.

Dachkammer Simon-Dach-Str. 39 ☎ 030 296 16 73; U- & S-Bahn Warschauer Strasse; map p.89. The largest and possibly most sociable place on the strip – the combination of a rustic bar downstairs and retro bar upstairs has made this a local classic. Free wi-fi. Mon–Fri noon–1am, Sat & Sun 10pm–1am.

Kantine am Berghain Rüdersdorfer Str. 70 ☎ 030 29 36 02 10; S-Bahn Ostbahnhof; map p.89. This venue's friendly atmosphere and tiny but jolly summer beer garden, mean it's started to go well beyond just offering a haven to those rejected by the neighbouring *Berghain* club (see p.104) – to which its music compares. Entry €5–10. Sat noon–late, Sun 9am–late.

White Trash Fast Food Am Flutgraben 2 ☎ 030 50 34 86 68, ⓦ whitetrashfastfood.com; U-Bahn Schlesisches Tor; map p.89. This perennially popular den of kitsch acts as restaurant, bar and club/live venue. In Wild-West-saloon-meets-Chinese-restaurant theme, the food here – mostly burgers and nachos – is decent enough and matches the informal crowd, who come to check out the regular DJs and bands who play mostly country, punk and Fifties- and Sixties-era tunes. Entry €1–8. Mon–Fri noon–late, Sat & Sun 6pm–late.

PRENZLAUER BERG

Prater Kastanienallee 7–9 ☎ 030 44 48 56 88, ⓦ pratergarten.de; U-Bahn Eberswalder Strasse; map p.91. In summer you can swig beer, feast on *Bratwurst* and other native food, and listen to 1970s German rock in the traditional beer garden (dates back to 1837); in winter the beer hall offers a similarly authentic experience. Mon–Sat 6–11pm, Sun noon–11pm.

Zu mir oder zu dir? Lychener Str. 15 ☎ 0176 24 42 29 40; U-Bahn Eberswalder Strasse; map p.91. Groovy, very Seventies-style lounge-bar with a sociable vibe and lots of

---

PUB CRAWLS

If the idea of venturing into Berlin's legendary nightlife seems overwhelming, or you fancy the company of young travellers, consider a **pub crawl tour**. For around €12 (cover charges included) you'll be taken to around half-a-dozen watering holes and a club at the end of it all. You'll be watered with free shots on the street along the way, so it's not the most dignified way to spend an evening, but it can be good fun if the crowd's right. Pub crawls trawl Berlin every night of the week and companies include: New Berlin Tours (ⓦ newberlintours.com); Insider Tours (ⓦ insiderberlintours.com); and Alternative Berlin (ⓦ alternativeberlin.com). The last of these offers something a bit different, hitting more unusual nightspots than the competition and trying to keep group sizes smaller.

sofas to crash out on. A good place to start an evening even if the cheeky name – translating as "your place or mine?"

NIGHTLIFE

Since the days of the Weimar Republic, and even through the lean postwar years, Berlin has had some of the best – and steamiest – nightlife in Europe, an image fuelled by the drawings of George Grosz and films like *Cabaret*. Today's big draws are world-class **techno clubs** in once-abandoned buildings around the former East–West border. Berlin also has a wide range of other clubs: from slick hangouts for the trendy to raucous dives, with **live music** of just about every sort. To find out **what's on** check the listings magazines *Tip* (ⓦ tip-berlin.de) and *Zitty* (ⓦ zitty.de), available at any newsstand. Club **opening hours** are very open-ended – they rarely get going before midnight and some stay open beyond 6am. With the **U- & S-Bahn** running nonstop on Fri and Sat nights – and restarting from about 4am on other nights – getting home or jumping between areas of town could hardly be easier. And don't worry too much about dress code as the prevalence of a shabby-chic aesthetic means you can get into most places with little effort.

MITTE

Clärchens Ballhaus Auguststr. 24 ⓣ 030 282 92 95, ⓦ ballhaus.de; S-Bahn Hackescher Markt; map pp.66–67. First opening in 1913 and providing a hedonistic venue throughout the 1920s before just about surviving fascism and communism, this dancehall is back in style. It now hosts a range of dance nights, with instruction provided (Mon salsa, Tues tango, Wed swing, Thurs waltz, disco or rumba; times on website), while weekends it's a bit of everything. Sun afternoons see the upstairs mirror room – unused during GDR days for being too glitzy – acting as the venue for concerts. Also dishes up great pizzas. Daily 10am–late.

Grüner Salon Rosa-Luxemburg-Platz 2 ⓣ 030 24 59 89 36, ⓦ gruener-salon.de; U-Bahn Rosa-Luxemburg-Platz; map pp.66–67. Club beside the *Roter Salon* (see below) that preserves something of the 1920s in its chandeliers and velvet. Renowned for salsa courses and Fri tango evenings, but with a varied programme of live music, comedy and cabaret besides. Entry €4–15. Thurs 9pm–4am, Fri & Sat 11pm–4am.

Kaffee Burger Torstr. 60 ⓣ 030 28 04 64 95, ⓦ kaffeeburger.de; U-Bahn Rosa-Luxemburg-Platz; map pp.66–67. Russian-owned smoky 1970s retro-bar legendary for its Russian-themed disco nights, but good any time, not least for the mad mix of genres – Balkan, surf rock, samba, rockabilly – that fills the small dancefloor. Readings and poetry often start evenings off, but it really fills up later on. Entry €1–5. Mon–Thurs 8pm–late, Fri & Sat from 9 or 10pm–late, Sun 7pm–late.

Roter Salon Rosa-Luxemburg-Platz 2 ⓣ 030 24 06 58 06, ⓦ volksbuehne-berlin.de; U-Bahn Rosa-Luxemburg-Platz; map pp.66–67. Tatty club within the Volksbühne theatre, with lurid red decor and chintzy furniture giving it the feel of a 1950s brothel. Readings, concerts and clubnights are held here. Wed is soul and funk night, other nights a mix of electronica, ska and Brit-pop. Entry €6–7. Mon & Wed–Sat 11pm–4am.

Schokoladen Ackerstr. 169–170 ⓣ 030 282 65 27, ⓦ schokoladen-mitte.de; U-Bahn Rosenthaler Platz;

– suggests you might end it here. Daily 8pm–late.

map pp.66–67. The spartan, bare-brick interior of this former chocolate factory is a hangover from its time as a squatted building in the early post-*Wende* days. Now it's a venue for theatrical and art events, live indie-pop and upcoming singer/songwriters. Mon–Thurs 8pm–4am, Fri & Sat 9pm–4am, Sun 7pm–4am.

★**Weekend** Alexanderplatz 5 ⓣ 030 246 25 93 20, ⓦ week-end-berlin.de; U- & S-Bahn Alexanderplatz; map pp.66–67. In the former GDR state travel agency, this is another of Berlin's creative transformations: the twelfth-floor views over central Berlin are spectacular, and the roof terrace is wonderful. All this makes up for the coolly offhand manner of many of its patrons as they groove to house and techno. Very popular Sun gay night. Entry €10–12. Thurs–Sat 11pm–late.

Zosch Tucholskystr. 30 ⓣ 030 280 76 64, ⓦ zosch -berlin.de; U-Bahn Oranienburger Tor; map pp.66–67. Alternative place that started as a squat when the Wall came down, and has retained much of the feel. A good place for gigs and clubnights in the cellar, where a fun-loving local Creole jazz band often plays amid the smoky ambience and constant chatter. Daily 4pm–5am.

CHARLOTTENBURG-WILMERSDORF

A-Trane Pestalozzistr. 105 ⓣ 030 313 25 50, ⓦ a-trane.de; U-Bahn Savignyplatz; map pp.64–65. Small and smoky jazz den and a good place for both up-and-coming and well-known jazz artists. Best during Sat-night jams, when musicians arrive from other venues and join in throughout the evening. Entry €6–21. Daily 9pm–late.

Quasimodo Kantstr. 12a, Charlottenburg ⓣ 030 312 80 86, ⓦ quasimodo.de; U- & S-Bahn Zoologischer Garten; see map pp.64–65. Casual cellar bar that's one of Berlin's best jazz spots, with black-and-white photos, low ceilings, intimate tables and nightly programmes. A high-quality mix of international (usually American) stars and up-and-coming names. Aside from jazz there's funk, blues and Latin. Often free on weekdays, otherwise €7–28. Daily 9pm–2am.

1

SCHÖNEBERG

Kumpelnest 3000 Lützowstr. 23, Schöneberg ☎030 261 69 18, ⓦkumpelnest3000.com; U-Bahn Kurfürstenstrasse; map p.88. Carpeted walls and a mock-Baroque effect attract a rough-and-ready crew of thirty- and forty-somethings to this erstwhile brothel, which gets going around 2am, when there's standing room only. The best place in the area, it's good fun and infamous as a hook-up bar for people of all sexual orientations. Daily 7pm–5am.

KREUZBERG–FRIEDRICHSHAIN

A short hop from Berlin's current clubland frontier, Friedrichshain's Simon-Dach-Strasse is a good place to start a bar hop. Kreuzberg is the best place for live rock.

Berghain Am Wriezener Bahnhof, Friedrichshain ⓦberghain.de; S-Bahn Ostbahnhof; map p.89. Housed in a vast, artfully scuzzy old power plant with a fantastic sound system, this club is considered the best in the world by many. Minimal techno and house cannonball around the gigantic dancefloors that are packed largely with shirtless guys, while more laidback bars and murky backrooms cater to other desires of an evenly mixed gay and straight crowd. The club ensures and abuses its legendary status with a picky, indefinable door policy: avoid looking like a tourist or arriving in any kind of group. And remember headline acts often start at noon, so there's no rush to get here early – about 5am is ideal, when the wait to get in generally drops below an hour. Entry €14. Fri & Sat midnight to usually late-afternoon the next day.

Cassiopeia Reveler Str. 99, Friedrichshain ⓦcassiopeia-berlin.de; U- & S-Bahn Warschauer Str; map p.89. A former squat, where the shambolic vibe has been preserved to produce a venue that's as odd, grungy, hip and nebulous as any: on-site there's a skate-park, climbing wall, outdoor cinema, beer garden and four dancefloors. Always worth a look. Entry €3–7, extra when bands play. Mon, Sat & Sun 3pm–late, Tues–Fri 6pm–late.

Club der Visionaere Am Flutgraben 1, Kreuzberg ☎030 69 51 89 42, ⓦclubdervisionaere.com; U-Bahn Schlesisches Tor; map p.89. Legendary summer-only techno bar that enjoys a unique setting at the intersection of the Spree and Flutgraben canals. The bar and DJ booth is in an old ceramic-tiled boathouse, and punters stand (and

dance) on the floating docks outside. It's minimal techno all the way and a fantastically upbeat place. Entry €1–5. Food served daily 6pm–1am. May–Sept Mon–Fri 2pm–late, Sat & Sun noon–late.

Gretchen Obentrautstr. 19–21, Kreuzberg ☎030 25 92 27 02, ⓦgretchen-club.de; U-Bahn Mehringdamm; map pp.64–65. A bit off the beaten track, but few clubs can boast that they occupy the 1854 stables of Queen Victoria's Prussian 1st Guards. This mid-sized club has a pedigree too, as it rose from the ashes of Prenzlauer Berg's famed *Icon* club. Here, too, drum'n'bass is big, but all species of innovative electronic music thrive. Entry €5–12. Hours vary, but usually Thurs–Sat 11.30pm–late.

Monarch Skalizerstr. 134, Kreuzberg ⓦkottimonarch .de; U-Bahn Kotbusser Tor; map p.89. Unpretentious and inevitably slightly ragged place that attracts a hip crowd who groove to a wide range of tunes – swing, rockabilly, folk, punk and indie (but no techno) – and enjoy views over Kotbusser Tor from the huge windows. Entrance is via an unmarked door and stairwell opposite the kebab shop *Misir Casisi*. Entry €3. Tues–Sat 9pm–late.

★**Rosi's** Revalerstr. 29 ⓦrosis-berlin.de; S-Bahn Warschauer Strasse; map p.89. Oddball, upbeat club that sports Berlin's classic unfinished and improvised feel in a mix of semi-derelict buildings. There's a definite sense of crashing a house-party here, with even a small kitchen and living room to hang out in between bouts on the dancefloors, where indie or techno pounds. Outside table tennis is also a big attraction. Thurs–Sat 11pm–late.

SO36 Oranienstr. 190, Kreuzberg ☎030 61 40 13 06, ⓦso36.de; U-Bahn Görlitzer Bahnhof; map p.89. This legendary club, named after the district's old postcode, has its roots in punk, post-punk and alternative music. A string of musical heroes have played here, including Iggy Pop, David Bowie and Einstürzende Neubauten. Nowadays it hosts alternative and electronic shows, including monthly parties like *Gayhane*, a Turkish "homoriental" party, and "Ich bin ein Berliner", where you can catch an exquisite array of Berlin-based artists playing everything from garage to synth-pop. Entry €3–10. Usually daily from 11pm.

Tresor Köpenicker St. Kreuzberg ☎030 229 06 11, ⓦtresorberlin.de; U-Bahn Heinrich-Heine-Strasse; map p.89. A key player in Berlin's electronic music scene, with trouser-shaking techno booming in every nook of the convoluted bunker-style club. The volume, intensity and light-show all have to be experienced to be believed. Attracts clubbers from all over Europe. Entry Wed €5–8, Fri & Sat €10–15. Wed–Sat midnight–late.

★**Watergate** Falckensteinstr. 49, Kreuzberg ☎030 61 28 03 96, ⓦwater-gate.de; U-Bahn Schlesisches Tor; map p.89. A top Berlin club, with a glorious riverside location by the Oberbaumbrücke and impressive light installations. It sprawls over two levels, with a large main floor and a floor

---

BERLIN'S TOP 5 OFFBEAT ODDITIES

Clärchens Ballhaus p.103
Morgenrot p.100
Ostel p.97
Graffiti art tour p.94
Unsicht-bar p.100

with a lounge, and the music is varied but mostly electronic. Attracts big-name DJs. Entry €8–15. Wed, Fri & Sat 11pm–late, occasional Tues & Thurs events.

★ **Wild at Heart** Wiener Str. 20, Kreuzberg ☎030 611 70 10, ⓦ wildatheartberlin.de; U-Bahn Görlitzer Bahnhof; map p.89. Cornerstone live music venue for rock'n'roll, indie and punk, with something always going on well into the small hours. Daily 8pm until late.

PRENZLAUER BERG

Though not cutting-edge by Berlin standards, many Prenzlauer Berg clubs are dependable choices, with at least a decade of success behind them.

★ **Dunckerclub** Dunckerstr. 64 ☎030 445 95 09, ⓦ dunckerclub.de; S-Bahn Prenzlauer Allee; map p.91. Indie, industrial and unashamedly Goth refuge from the mainstream and techno. Aptly enough it's located in a striking neo-Gothic church. Entry €3–5. Mon 9pm–late,

Tues, Thurs & Sun 10pm–late, Fri & Sat 11pm–late.

Kulturbrauerei Schönhauser Allee 36 ☎030 48 49 44, ⓦ kulturbrauerei-berlin.de; U-Bahn Eberswalder Strasse; map p.91. Nineteenth-century brewery that's been turned into a multi-venue arts and cultural centre, attracting a thirty-plus crowd and local and mid-level bands to its two clubs, *Alte Kantine* and *Soda* – the former specializes in mainstream pop and rock, the latter is best known for salsa nights, but also has regular house and R&B nights. Entry €3–8. Daily 10pm–late.

nbi Schönhauser Allee 36 ☎030 67 30 44 57, ⓦ neueberlinerinitiative.de; U-Bahn Eberswalder Strasse; map p.91. The residential neighbourhood keeps the volume of the music here down, which the lounge-cum-club has used to its advantage, creating a comfortable environment for the appreciation of cutting-edge electronic music. DJs come here to hear each other experiment. Entry €3. Daily 8pm–late.

THE ARTS

Though 1920s and 1930s Berlin was famed for its rich and intense satirical and political cabaret scene, the Nazis quickly suppressed it and the scene has barely recovered. Most of today's shows are either semi-clad titillation or drag shows, though a few places are increasingly worth trying despite their high bar prices. Berlin's greatest strength today is probably its vibrant **fringe arts** scene, which brims with experimental work.

ESSENTIALS

Listings magazines To find out what's on check the listings magazines *Tip* (ⓦ tip-berlin.de) and *Zitty* (ⓦ zitty .de), available at any newsstand, and the free magazine 030 (ⓦ berlin030.de), distributed in bars and cafés.

Tickets The first place to try for last-minute deals, especially for fringe-type theatre, less popular classical concerts and dance, is Hekticket (☎030 230 99 30, ⓦ hekticket.de), which sells half-price tickets from 2pm, with offices at Hardenberg Str. 29a (U- and S-Bahn Zoologischer Garten), and Karl-Liebknecht-Str. 12, Mitte (U- & S-Bahn Alexanderplatz). The city's tourist information offices (ⓦ visitberlin.de) also sell tickets online.

CLASSICAL MUSIC AND OPERA

The main venues can be expensive but the level of the performances is incredibly high. Several high-quality orchestras and troupes call them home, including the Berlin Philharmonic, one of the world's finest symphony orchestras, as well as many smaller orchestras who often perform chamber concerts. A major annual music festival is the Festtage in the first half of April, organized by the Staatsoper, but staged at the Berlin Philharmonic. Also significant is the Musikfest Berlin (ⓦ berlinerfestspiele .de), an acclaimed international music festival in the first half of September, when guest orchestras from around the world play innovative modern works.

Deutsche Oper Bismarckstr. 35, Charlottenburg ☎030 34 38 43 43, ⓦ deutscheoperberlin.de; U-Bahn

Deutsche Oper; map pp.64–65. Formerly West Berlin's premier opera house, built in 1961 after the Wall cut access to the Staatsoper. Once the city's most prestigious venue in terms of visiting performers, it now shares that honour with its eastern cousin. Tickets €17–167.

Deutsches Symphonie Orchester ⓦ dso-berlin.de. Under conductor Tugan Sokhiev since 2012, and with no permanent base, though often plays at the Philharmonie. Tickets €20–59.

Komische Oper Behrenstr. 55–57, Mitte ☎030 47 99 74 00, ⓦ komische-oper-berlin.de; U- & S-Bahn Brandenburger Tor; map pp.66–67. Less traditional than the Staatsoper (see p.106), but a reliable venue for well-staged operatic productions. The building doesn't look like much from the outside, but the interior is a wonderful 1890s frenzy of red plush, gilt and statuary and a great place to enjoy cutting-edge interpretations of modern works alongside the usual fare. Tickets €10–149.

Konzerthaus Berlin Gendarmenmarkt, Mitte ☎030 20 30 90, ⓦ konzerthaus.de; U-Bahn Stadtmitte; map pp.66–67. A super venue mainly for visiting musicians, orchestras and ensembles. Two concert spaces occupy the Schinkel-designed building: the Grosser Konzertsaal for orchestras, and the Kammermusiksaal for smaller groups and chamber orchestras. Look out for performances on the Konzerthaus's famed organ. Tickets €10–99.

Philharmonie Herbert-von-Karajan-Str. 1, Mitte ☎030 25 48 80, ⓦ berlin-philharmonic.de; U- & S-Bahn Potsdamer Platz; map pp.66–67. Home to the

1

world-famous Berlin Philharmonic, Hans Scharoun's indescribably ugly building is acoustically near-perfect, and while you'll have to pay fairly handsomely to enjoy it, it's definitely worth it. Conductor Simon Rattle has created his own distinctive sound with the orchestra, moving them away from their traditional Germanic comfort zone of Brahms and Beethoven and into more contemporary music like that of the Finnish composer Magnus Lindberg. The Philharmonie also contains the smaller Kammermusiksaal for more intimate performances. Your best chance of getting a ticket is when guest orchestras are playing. Tickets €34–138.

Staatsoper Unter den Linden 5–7, Mitte; box office ☎030 20 35 45 55, ⊕staatsoper-berlin.de; U-Bahn Friedrichstrasse; map pp.66–67. The city's oldest and grandest music venue, built for Frederick the Great in 1742 to a design by Knobelsdorff. During the GDR years, political isolation meant that performers didn't match the glamour of the venue, but the appointment of Daniel Barenboim in 1992 as musical director gradually helped bring the Staatsoper to the forefront of the international opera scene. Tickets €14–160.

THEATRE, CABARET AND DANCE

Admiralspalast Friedrichstr. 101, Mitte ☎030 31 98 90 00, ⊕admiralspalast.de; U- & S-Bahn Friedrichstrasse; map pp.66–67. The Admiralspalast provides much the same round-the-clock entertainment as it did in its 1920s heyday – though without the brothel it incorporated then. These days it draws in the punters with an eclectic events programme, including comedy, live music, burlesque and operas, plus a casino. Tickets €22–63.

Berliner Ensemble Bertolt-Brecht-Platz 1, Mitte ☎030 28 40 81 55, ⊕berliner-ensemble.de; U- & S-Bahn Friedrichstrasse; map pp.66–67. Brecht's old theatre still features a lot of his work, though thankfully the productions are a little livelier than in GDR days and much of the rest of the programme is given over to a range of reliable pieces by Henrik Ibsen, Friedrich Schiller and the like. There are also occasional experimental productions on the *Probebühne* (rehearsal stage). Tickets €5–30.

Chamäleon Rosenthaler Str. 40–41 (in the Hackeschen Höfe), Mitte ☎030 400 05 90, ⊕chamaeleonberlin.de; S-Bahn Hackescher Markt; map pp.66–67. Lively, innovative cabaret and vaudeville shows with jugglers, acrobats and the like. Seating is around tables and there's a bar, so there's no harm in turning up early. Tickets €36–49.

Deutsches Theater Schumannstr. 13a, Mitte ☎030 28 44 12 21, ⊕deutsches-theater.de; U-Bahn Oranienburger Tor; map pp.66–67. Good, solid productions taking in everything from Schiller to Mamet make this one of Berlin's best theatres, and productions are frequently sold out. The venue also includes a second theatre, the Kammerspiele. Tickets €4–48.

Tanzfabrik Berlin Möckernstr. 68, Kreuzberg ☎030 786 58 61, ⊕tanzfabrik-berlin.de; U- & S-Bahn Yorckstrasse; map pp.64–65. Experimental and contemporary works, usually fresh and exciting. This is also Berlin's biggest contemporary dance school. Tickets free–€13.

Volksbühne Rosa-Luxemburg-Platz, Mitte ☎030 247 67 72, ⊕volksbuehne-berlin.de; U-Bahn Rosa-Luxemburg-Platz; map pp.66–67. One of Berlin's most adventurous and interesting theatres, often with highly provocative performances: nudity and throwing things at audiences crop up fairly regularly. A second stage also shows modern adaptations of classics. Tickets €10–27.

Wintergarten Potsdamer Str. 96, Tiergarten ☎030 25 00 88 88, ⊕wintergarten-variete.de; U-Bahn Kurfürstenstrasse; map p.88. Glitzy attempt to re-create the Berlin of the 1920s, with live acts from all over the world – cabaret, musicians, dance, mime and magicians – with meals served while you watch. Tickets €26–60.

CONTEMPORARY ART

The Hamburger Bahnhof (see p.84) may be Berlin's flagship contemporary art venue, but investigating the local scene can be more rewarding. Many of Berlin's estimated five thousand artists-in-residence regularly open their studios or exhibit at the hundreds of galleries around town. A useful and comprehensive source of information about what's on in city galleries, and what's available in most of them, is the English and German monthly magazine, *artery berlin* (⊕artery-berlin.de).

Atelier Brandner Helmholtzstr. 2–9, Entrance E, Charlottenburg ☎030 30 10 05 75, ⊕atelier-brandner .de; U-Bahn Turmstrasse; map pp.64–65. Southern German Matthias Brandner is among the most successful of the many painters who have flocked to Berlin's energetic, liberal atmosphere and cheap studio space. Though famed for his murals on buildings, it's his powerful abstract watercolours and oils that are on show at his studio. Daily noon–8pm.

Camera Work Kantstr.149, Charlottenburg ☎030 310 07 73, ⊕camerawork.de; U-Bahn Uhlandstrasse; map pp.64–65. Hidden in a courtyard and blessed with huge north-facing windows and wonderfully even light, this relaxed photography gallery spreads over two floors. Exhibitions often focus on big names such as Man Ray, Irving Penn, Horst P. Horst, Peter Lindbergh and Helmut Newton, but the occasional up-and-coming name gets a look-in too. Visitors are welcome, even if you can't afford the work. Tues–Sat 11am–6pm.

Capitain Petzel Karl-Marx-Allee 45, Friedrichshain ☎030 24 08 81 30, ⊕capitainpetzel.de; U-Bahn Strausberger Platz; map p.89. Joint venture between two art dealers from Cologne and New York that's most eye-catching for its location in a Soviet modernist glass cube – in GDR days an Eastern Bloc showcase. It's now far more international and the cornerstone of a new area in the Berlin art scene. Tues–Sat 11am–6pm.

Carlier Gebauer Markgrafenstr. 67, Mitte ☎ 030 280 81 10, ⓦ carliergebauer.com; U-Bahn Kochstrasse; map pp.64–65. Superb art gallery where you never quite know if you'll find home-grown or international art, but it's sure to be cutting-edge. Tues–Sat 11am–6pm.

Kunst-Werke Berlin Auguststr. 69, Mitte ☎ 030 243 45 90, ⓦ kw-berlin.de; U-Bahn Oranienburger Tor; map pp.66–67. Large gallery in a former factory building, where exhibits vary from has-been American artists carpetbagging their way into the city arts scene, to astute reflections on contemporary Berlin. The gallery is the principal organizer of the Berlin Biennale (ⓦ berlinbiennale.de). Entry €6. Mon & Wed–Sun noon–7pm, Thurs noon–9pm.

GAY AND LESBIAN BERLIN

Berlin's gay and lesbian scene is world class, making it a magnet for gay men and women from all over Germany and Europe. This has been the case since the 1920s, when Christopher Isherwood and W.H. Auden were both drawn here to escape the fear of harassment and legal persecution in the rest of Europe. Weimar Berlin's gay scene in the 1920s and early 1930s was prodigious before it was outlawed and persecuted in the Third Reich. This is a distant memory today: the charismatic city mayor, Klaus Wowereit, nicknamed "Wowi", is openly gay and it's not uncommon to see glitzy transvestites dancing on tables at even conservative bashes. The monthly gay magazine **Siegessäule** (ⓦ siegessaeule.de) has listings of events and is free from most gay bars and venues. The best time to explore the hurly-burly is during the annual month-long **Pride Festival**, centred on the **Christopher Street Day parade** (ⓦ csd-berlin.de) at the end of June.

BOOKSHOPS, MUSEUMS AND VENUES

Frauenzentrum Schokofabrik Mariannenstr. 6, Kreuzberg ☎ 030 615 29 99, ⓦ schokofabrik.de; U-Bahn Kottbusser Tor; map p.89. One of Europe's largest women's centres, with its own café, a gallery, day care and sports facilities that include a women-only Turkish bath or hamam (ⓦ hamamberlin.de) and a diverse programme of events that includes readings and workshops. Mon–Thurs 10am–2pm, Fri noon–4pm.

Prinz Eisenherz Buchladen Lietzenburger Str. 9a, Charlottenburg ☎ 030 313 99 36, ⓦ prinz-eisenherz .com; U-Bahn Wittenbergplatz; map p.88. Friendly and informative gay bookstore with helpful assistants. Excellent for relaxed browsing, free magazines and what's-on posters and leaflets about current gay happenings in the city. Mon–Sat 10am–8pm.

Schwules Museum Lützowstr. 73, Schöneberg ☎ 030 69 59 90 50, ⓦ schwulesmuseum.de; U-Bahn Kurfürstenstrasse; map pp.64–65. Interesting gay museum with changing exhibitions (entrance €6) on local and international gay history, and library material to browse through. Mon, Wed–Fri & Sun 2–6pm, Sat 2–7pm.

BARS AND CLUBS

In addition to the places listed below, many largely straight clubs have gay nights – particularly *Berghain* and *Kumpelnest 3000* (see p.104). Nights not to miss are the stalwart GMF events (ⓦ gmf-berlin.de), which pop up at different venues around town – think stripped-to-the-waist revellers dancing to pounding house music.

BARS

Barbie Deinhoff Schlesische Str. 16, Kreuzberg ⓦ barbiedeinhoff.de; U-Bahn Schlesisches Tor; map

p.89. Colourful and funloving dive bar that attracts a heady mix of transvestites, gay men and curious onlookers. The decor runs from deliberately kitsch to colourfully futuristic and there are regular DJs and events. Popular two-for-one happy hour Mon–Fri 6–9pm, Sat & Sun from 4pm. Mon–Fri 6pm–6am, Sat & Sun 4pm–6am.

Hafen Motzstr. 19, Schöneberg ☎ 030 211 41 18; U-Bahn Nollendorfplatz; map p.88. Mixed place that's a long-established, cruisey bar for thirty- and forty-somethings, and always packed. It's known for its Mon quiz nights, drag shows and generally flamboyant events – a great place to start a night out. Daily 8pm–late.

★ **Heile Welt** Motzstr. 5, Schöneberg ☎ 030 21 91 75 07; U-Bahn Nollendorfplatz; map p.88. The youngest and trendiest bar in Schöneberg provides a second living room for many locals, with great cocktails and a convivial atmosphere. The front bar is packed shoulder-to-shoulder most nights, but there's also a sophisticated lounge that extends far into the rear, as well as outdoor seating. Daily 6pm–late.

Neues Ufer Hauptstr. 157, Schöneberg ☎ 030 78 95 97 00; U-Bahn Kleistpark; map p.88. Lovely neighbourhood gay bar, where Bowie used to drink in the 1970s when it was *Anderes Ufer*. Boasts very friendly service and superb coffee, which is best enjoyed on outdoor seating watching the world go by. Daily 11am–2am.

★ **Tom's Bar** Motzstr. 19, Schöneberg ☎ 030 213 45 70, ⓦ tomsbar.de; U-Bahn Nollendorfplatz; map p.88. Dark, sweaty and debauched cruising establishment with a large darkroom. Possibly Berlin's most popular gay bar, and a great place to finish off an evening. Drinks are two for the price of one on Mon night. Men only. Daily 10pm–late.

★ **Vagabund Bar** Knesebeckstr. 77, City West ☎ 030 881 15 06, ⓦ vagabund-berlin.com; U-Bahn Uhlandstrasse; map pp.64–65. This popular gay bar opened in 1968 but has recently had a facelift. It gets

1

crowded after 3am and has an anything-goes, trashy aesthetic – very flirty, very fun, and not only for men. Mon–Thurs 6pm–8am, Fri & Sat midnight–late, Sun midnight–8am.

CLUBS

Connection Fuggerstr. 33, Schöneberg ☎ 030 23 62 74 44; U-Bahn Wittenbergplatz; map p.88. Gay entertainment complex including refined American sports bar – *Prinzknecht* – that's all bare brick and gleaming chrome, attracting a broad range of middle-aged gay men and some women. Very popular house and techno club at weekends for late-night dancing and cruising in an extensive labyrinth of darkroom play-spaces. Daily 3pm–late.

SchwuZ Mehringdamm 61, Kreuzberg ☎ 030 69 50 78 89, ⊛ schwuz.de; U-Bahn Mehringdamm; map pp.64–65. Dance club well loved by all stripes of the gay community, and always crowded and convivial. One floor has the usual 1980s and disco mixes, the other more experimental tunes. Fri & Sat 11pm–late.

Serene Bar Schwiebusser Str. 2, Kreuzberg ☎ 030 69 04 15 80, ⊛ serenebar.de; U-Bahn Platz-der-Luftbrücke; map pp.64–65. Great lesbian hangout, particularly on Sat when the big dancefloor packs out. The bar is also used by many special-interest groups as a meeting point: table tennis, amateur photography and so on. The entrance is tucked away down an alley. Tues 6pm–late, Wed & Thurs 8pm–late, Sat 10pm–late.

SHOPPING

Multistorey **department stores** rule Berlin, but many small and quirky specialist shops have survived or emerged in neighbourhoods like **Prenzlauer Berg**, while ethnic foods and "alternative" businesses thrive in **Kreuzberg**, along Oranienstrasse and Bergmannstrasse. If you like browsing and foraging you'll find a second home in the city's many **flea markets**.

DEPARTMENT STORES

KaDeWe Tauentzienstr. 21, Schöneberg ☎ 030 212 10, ⊛ kadewe-berlin.de; U-Bahn Wittenbergplatz; map pp.64–65. Content rather than flashy interior decor rules the day here. From surprisingly well-priced designer labels to the extraordinary displays at the international delicatessen, there's everything the consumer's heart desires at this, the largest department store on the continent. Mon–Thurs 10am–8pm, Fri 10am–9pm, Sat 9.30am–8pm.

BOOKS AND MUSIC

Berlin Story Unter den Linden 26, Mitte ☎ 030 20 45 38 42, ⊛ berlinstory.de; U- & S-Bahn Friedrichstrasse; map pp.66–67. The city's most extensive Berlin-focused bookshop, with everything from travel guides to specialist histories, offered in a range of languages. There are various historical exhibits to look at too, including a 25min film on Berlin, a 1930 city model and an old Trabant car. Daily 10am–8pm.

Dussmann Friedrichstr. 90, Mitte ☎ 030 20 25 24 00, ⊛ kulturkaufhaus.de; U- & S-Bahn Friedrichstrasse; map pp.66–67. A huge emporium of books, music, films and software, including a large selection of new English-language titles. The music selection is also extremely strong for most genres, though the basement's entirely devoted to classical. Mon–Sat 10am–midnight.

CLOTHES

Claudia Skoda Mulackstr. 8, Mitte ☎ 030 40 04 18 84, ⊛ claudiaskoda.com; U-Bahn Weinmeisterstrasse; map pp.66–67. Berlin's knit-master and most famous designer, whose shop is filled with her renowned and instantly recognizable knitwear. Chic and expensive and geared mostly towards women. Mon–Sat 11.30am–7.30pm.

Flagship Store Oderberger Str. 53, Prenzlauer Berg ☎ 030 43 73 53 27, ⊛ flagshipstore-berlin.de; U-Bahn Eberswalderstrasse; map p.91. Great one-stop shop to peruse the urbane collections of some thirty local designers, with a vast range of clothing and accessories (for women and men), plus shoes, magazines and more. Mon–Sat noon–8pm.

ReSales Turmstr. 72, Mitte ☎ 030 39 87 52 98; U-Bahn Turmstrasse; map pp.64–65; Pestalozzistr. 82, Charlottenburg; U-Bahn Wilmersdorfer Strasse; map pp.64–65; Potsdamer Strasse 105, Schöneberg; U-Bahn Kurfürstenstrasse; map p.88; ⊛ second handandmore.com. Nationwide chain of secondhand stores with four branches in central Berlin and a vast array of garments at each that ranges from hip streetwear to silky evening wear. All tend to be at fair prices too. Opening times vary, but generally Mon–Sat 10am–7pm.

SOUVENIRS

Ach Berlin Markengrafenstr. 39, Mitte ☎ 030 92 12 68 80, ⊛ achberlin.de; U-Bahn Stadtmitte; map pp.66–67. Good source of offbeat Berlin memorabilia where classy designs celebrate local landmarks and life – among them cookie-cutters of the TV tower, brooms that look like the Brandenburg Gate and many stylish souvenir T-shirts. Mon–Sat 11am–7pm.

Ampelmann Galerie Shop Hackeschen Höfe 5, Mitte ☎ 030 44 72 64 38, ⊛ ampelmann.de; S-Bahn Hackescher Markt; map pp.66–67. Celebration of the traffic-light man (*Ampelmann*) that reigns supreme on

1

CYCLE, OR GET YOUR FLÄMING SKATES ON

What Brandenburg lacks in challenging cycling terrain it more than makes up for with its excellent **cycle-path network**. Long-distance routes include the **Berlin–Usedom** cycle path, a 337km route to the Baltic Sea island; the **Spreeradweg**, which follows Berlin's Spree River to its source, 407km away; and a 228km **Berlin–Leipzig** route that passes through Wittenberg (see p.201).

But nowhere in Brandenburg is better equipped for cyclists than the **Teltow-Fläming** district just south of Berlin. Here several communities have clubbed together to build a 220km network of cycle paths (⒲ flaeming-skate.de) that are smooth and flat enough to become a European-wide draw for **inline skaters**. An ideal gateway is the small regional town of **Jüterbog** (connected to Berlin by hourly trains; 50min), which has its own dedicated skate centre and race track. One of the best selections of skates for hire is at Sport 2000 Kuhlmey, Grosse Str. 56 (☎ 03372 40 52 52, ⒲ sport-kuhlmey.de), a 25-minute walk from the train station (or 17min on hourly bus #758).

The official website lists many more options in the region (under "Services") and has full accommodation listings. Jüterbog's tourist office, at Mönchenkirchplatz 4 (☎ 03372 463 113, ⒲ jueterbog.de), lies in the town centre, a five-minute walk from the skate shop.

the eastern side of the city. After being threatened with replacement by the svelte West Berlin counterpart he became the object of protests and a cult object. Pick up T-shirts, mugs, lights and so on at the original shop here; there are five other branches elsewhere in central Berlin. Mon–Sat 9.30am–10pm, Sun 10am–7pm.

FLEA MARKETS AND JUNK SHOPS

Flohmarkt am Arkonaplatz Arkonaplatz, Prenzlauer Berg; U-Bahn Bernauer Strasse. Small flea market that helps supply Berlin's constant craving for retro-gear, with all sorts of furniture and old-school clutter to be had for reasonable prices. Not bad for old

Eastern Bloc memorabilia either. Sun 10am–4pm.
Flohmarkt Str. des 17 Juni, near Ernst-Reuter-Platz, Charlottenburg; S-Bahn Tiergarten. Great for a Sunday-morning browse, though not a place for a bargain, rather somewhere you can paw over antiques and quality bric-a-brac from a couple of generations ago. Strong on jewellery, furs, embroidery and lace. Sat & Sun 10am–5pm.
Hallentrödelmarkt Treptow Eichenstr. 4, Treptow; S-Bahn Treptower Park; map p.89. Ideal rainy-day option: there's something of everything in this huge indoor flea market. The stalls are all permanent fixtures and thoroughly chaotic. From the S-Bahn head north along Hoffmannstrasse, walking parallel to the Spree River. Sat & Sun 10am–5pm.

DIRECTORY

Embassies Australia, Wallstr. 76–79 ☎ 030 880 08 80, ⒲ germany.embassy.gov.au; Canada, Leipziger Platz 17 ☎ 030 20 31 20, ⒲ canadainternational.gc.ca; Ireland, Jägerstr. 51 ☎ 030 22 07 20, ⒲ embassyofireland.de; New Zealand, Friedrichstr. 60 ☎ 030 20 62 10, ⒲ nzembassy .com; UK, Wilhelmstr. 70–71 ☎ 030 20 45 70, ⒲ britischebotschaft.de; US, Pariser Platz 2 & Clayallee 170 ☎ 030 830 50, ⒲ germany.usembassy.gov.
Health There's a 24hr pharmacy in the Hauptbahnhof. If you need a doctor, call English-language service ☎ 01805 32 13 03, ⒲ calladoc.com; calls cost €0.14 per min. There's an emergency room at Charité Universitätsklinikum, Charitéplatz 1, Mitte (☎ 030 450 531 000; S-Bahn Hauptbahnhof).

Internet Most hostels and hotels, as well as many cafés and main train stations, have wi-fi – and an internet café in the vicinity (which charge about €2/30min); there's a free hotspot in the Sony Center (see p.72).
Laundry Laundries ("Waschsalon" in the Yellow Pages) are dotted throughout the city, including Schell und Sauber, Oderberger Str. 1 (daily 6am–11pm; U-Bahn Rosenthaler Platz).
Police For emergencies call ☎ 110; otherwise call the 24-hour hotline ☎ 030 46 64 46 64.
Post office The post office (Postamt) with the longest hours is at Bahnhof Friedrichstrasse, under the arches at Georgenstr. 12 (Mon–Fri 6am–10pm, Sat & Sun 8am–10pm; ⒲ deutschepost.de).

Potsdam

For most visitors **POTSDAM** means **Sanssouci**, Frederick the Great's splendid landscaped park of architectural treasures, which once completed Berlin as the grand Prussian capital. However, Potsdam dates back to the tenth-century Slavonic settlement

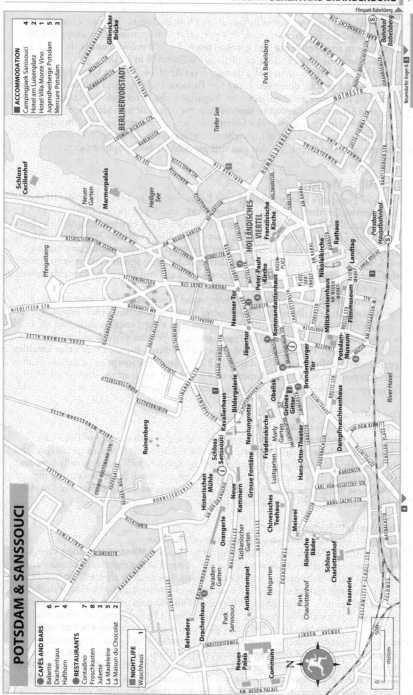

POTSDAM & SANSSOUCI

ACCOMMODATION

Campingpark Sanssouci	4
Hotel am Luisenplatz	2
Hotel Villa Monte Vino	1
Jugendherberge Potsdam	5
Mercure Potsdam	3

CAFÉS AND BARS

Babette	6
Drachenhaus	1
Haffhorn	4

RESTAURANTS

Contadino	7
Froschkasten	8
Juliette	3
La Madeleine	5
La Maison du Chocolat	2

NIGHTLIFE

Waschhaus	1

1

Poztupimi, and predates Berlin by a couple of hundred years. The castle built here in 1160 marked the first step in the town's gradual transformation from sleepy fishing backwater to **royal residence** and **garrison town**, a role it enjoyed under the Hohenzollerns until the abdication of Kaiser Wilhelm II in 1918.

World War II left Potsdam badly damaged: on April 14, 1945, a bombing raid killed four thousand people, destroyed many fine Baroque buildings and reduced its centre to ruins. Less than four months later – on August 2 – the victorious Allies converged on Potsdam's **Schloss Cecilienhof** to hammer out the details of a divided Germany and Europe. Potsdam ended up in the Soviet zone, where modern "socialist" building programmes steadily erased many architectural memories of the town's uncomfortably prosperous imperial past. Yet this past still provides its most popular sights.

The Alter Markt

North of Potsdam's Hauptbahnhof over Lange Brücke and on the fringes of the town centre, lies the large plaza of **Alter Markt**, which lies framed by the unmistakeably GDR-era *Mercure Potsdam* hotel and the elegant, Schinkel-designed, Neoclassical **Nikolaikirche** (Mon–Sat 9am–7pm, Sun 11.30am–7pm; free). Surging traffic and building work make the Alter Markt an unprepossessing city gateway, but it was once the focal point for a district of bustling squares and streets: it was here that the town's earliest fortifications were built and where the medieval town flourished.

The Alter Markt is best known, however, as the former site of the **Stadtschloss**, a Baroque residence built by the Great Elector between 1662 and 1669. World War II – specifically April 14 and 15, 1945 – reduced it to a bare, roofless shell, and the GDR demolished what remained in 1960 (around eighty percent of the building) to remove the last vestiges of Potsdam's grandest imperial buildings. Brandenburg's new **Landtag** (parliament building), completed here in 2014, copies the footprint of the old Schloss and incorporates many of its elements into its design, not least the domed Fortunaportal – the reconstructed gate to the palace forecourt.

The Rathaus

Am Alten Markt 9 • Daily Tues–Sun 10am–6pm • Free

Potsdam's former **Rathaus**, built during the mid-eighteenth century in Palladian Classical style, became an arts centre under the GDR, a role it retains to this day. The **obelisk** in front of the Rathaus was designed by Knobelsdorff and originally bore four reliefs depicting the Great Elector and his successors. When re-erected during the 1970s these were replaced with reliefs of the architects who shaped much of Potsdam: Schinkel, Knobelsdorff, Gontard and Persius.

The Marstall: Filmmuseum

Breite Str. 1a • Tues–Sun 10am–6pm • €5 • ☎ 0331 271 81 12, ⓦ filmmuseum-potsdam.de

Across from the Nikolaikirche lies the squat but elegant **Marstall**, the oldest town-centre survivor. Built as an orangerie towards the end of the eighteenth century and converted into stables by that scourge of frivolity, Friedrich Wilhelm I, the building owes its current appearance to Knobelsdorff, who extended and prettified it during the eighteenth century. Today it houses Potsdam's **Filmmuseum**, which draws on material from Babelsberg's UFA studios (see p.117) to present both a technical and artistic history of German film from 1895 to 1980, with some particularly fascinating immediate postwar material. There's a vaguely hands-on feel, with a few visitor-operated bioscopes and numerous screens playing clips. The museum **cinema** is Potsdam's best and there's also a good **café**. Just behind the Marstall, **Am Neuen Markt** leads to a few more handsome vestiges of old Potsdam, including some improbably grand eighteenth-century coaching stables entered through a triumphal arch.

The Altstadt

North beyond Alter Markt, **Friedrich-Ebert-Strasse** passes into an area once occupied by Potsdam's **Altstadt** before it was fairly comprehensively destroyed in the war. Luckily, a couple of residential districts survived substantially intact and slowly emerge along the north end of Friedrich-Ebert-Strasse. Brandenburger Strasse, today's main shopping street, is the key cross-street here.

Bassinplatz

Follow Brandenburger Strasse east of Friedrich-Ebert-Strasse to arrive at **Bassinplatz**, a grand plaza and park that's disfigured by a huge modern bus station, but dominated by the impressive nineteenth-century **Peter-Pauls-Kirche**, a replica of the campanile of San Zeno Maggiore in Verona. At the southeastern corner of the square lies the **Französische Kirche**, completed according to plans by Knobelsdorff in 1753, in imitation of the Pantheon in Rome, a recurring theme in German architecture of the period.

Holländisches Viertel

Just north of Bassinplatz lies the appealing **Holländisches Viertel** (Dutch quarter), where 134 gabled, red-brick houses were put up by Dutch builders for immigrants from Holland who were invited to work in Potsdam by Friedrich Wilhelm I. The quarter has seen periods of dereliction since, but recent restoration and gentrification has produced a small colony of trendy shops and cafés.

Brandenburger Strasse and Lindenstrasse

West of Friedrich-Ebert-Strasse, Brandenburger Strasse leads to Park Sanssouci and forms the backbone of a **Baroque quarter** – built between 1732 and 1742 on the orders of Friedrich Wilhelm I for tradespeople as Potsdam rapidly expanded. One major cross-street is **Lindenstrasse**, where the Dutch-style **Kommandantenhaus** at nos. 54–55 has uncomfortable associations: until the *Wende* it served as a Stasi detention centre known as the "Lindenhotel", and before that it had a spell as a Nazi prison and "hereditary-health court", where decisions about compulsory sterilization were made. It now houses **Gedenkstätte Lindenstrasse** (Tues–Sun 10am–6pm; €3 with tour, €1.50 without; ⓦgedenkstaette-lindenstrasse.de), where you can view the chilling cells and see an exhibition about the building's former uses.

Further north up Lindenstrasse is the **Jägertor** (Hunter's Gate), one of Potsdam's three surviving town gates, surmounted by a sculpture of a stag succumbing to a pack of baying hounds. Meanwhile, the triumphal **Brandenburger Tor** marks the western end of Brandenburger Strasse – built by Gontard in 1733 with a playfulness lacking in its Berlin namesake. The **Grünes Gitter** park entrance (see p.114) lies just beyond the northwestern corner of the adjacent **Luisenplatz**.

Park Sanssouci

Park daily 6am–dusk; main visitor centre daily: March–Oct 8.30am–6pm; Nov–March 8.30am–5pm • Park free, €2 donation suggested; *Tageskarte* €15 (access to all buildings except Schloss Sanssouci; sold at all palaces & the visitor centre), *Premium-Tageskarte* €19 (access to all buildings; sold only at Schloss Sanssouci) • ⓦ spsg.de • From the Hauptbahnhof, bus #X15 runs straight to Schloss Sanssouci; take #X5 or bus #605 to "Neues Palais" to walk from the furthest reaches of the park via its attractions back to the Altstadt

Stretching west from Potsdam's town centre, **Park Sanssouci** was built for Frederick the Great as a retreat after he decided in 1744 that he needed a residence where he could live "without cares" – "sans souci" in the French spoken in court. The task was entrusted to architect Georg von Knobelsdorff, who had already proved himself on other projects in Potsdam and Berlin. **Schloss Sanssouci**, on a hill overlooking the town, took three years to complete, while the extensive parklands were laid out over the following five years. As a finishing touch Frederick ordered the construction of the

1

Neues Palais at the western end of the park, to mark the end of the Seven Years' War, and there were numerous other additions over the following hundred and fifty years or so. The park is most beautiful in spring, when the trees are in leaf and the flowers in bloom, and least crowded on weekdays. The **Grünes Gitter** provides a southeastern entrance to Park Sanssouci and has an information kiosk; the main **visitor centre** is by the historic windmill (see opposite).

The Friedenskirche

Late April & early Oct Mon–Sat 11am–5pm, Sun noon–5pm; May–Sept Mon–Sat 10am–6pm, Sun noon–6pm; mid-Oct to late April Sat 11am–4pm & Sun 11.30am–4pm • Free

Immediately to the north of the Grünes Gitter is the 1850 Italianate **Friedenskirche**, designed by Persius for Friedrich Wilhelm IV. With its 39-metre-high campanile and lakeside setting, it conjures up the southern European atmosphere that Friedrich Wilhelm strove for by using the St Clemente Basilica in Rome as a model, and with the design centred on the magnificent Byzantine apse mosaic from Murano. Adjoining the church, the domed Hohenzollern **mausoleum** contains the tombs of Friedrich Wilhelm IV and his wife Elizabeth, and Friedrich III and his wife Victoria. The garden to the west is the **Marly-Garten**, once the kitchen garden of Friedrich I, who named it, with intentional irony, after Louis XIV's luxurious Marly park.

Schloss Sanssouci

Schloss Sanssouci Tues–Sun: April–Oct 9am–6pm; Nov–March 10am–5pm • €12 April–Oct, €8 Nov–March • **The Damenflügel** May–Oct Sat & Sun 10am–6pm • €2

To approach **Schloss Sanssouci** as Frederick the Great might have done, make for the eighteenth-century **obelisk** on Schopenhauerstrasse. Beyond, Hauptallee runs through the ornate Knobelsdorff-designed **Obelisk-Portal** – two clusters of pillars flanked by the goddesses Flora and Pomona – to the **Grosse Fontäne**, the biggest of the park's many fountains, around which a host of Classical statues stand, notably Venus and Mercury. The approach to the Schloss itself leads up through terraced ranks of vines that are among Germany's most northern.

Frederick had definite ideas about what he wanted and worked closely with Knobelsdorff on the palace, which was to be a place where the king, who had no great love for his capital, Berlin, or his wife, Elizabeth Christine, could escape both. It's a surprisingly modest one-storey Baroque affair, topped by an oxidized green dome and ornamental statues, looking out towards the high-rises of central Potsdam.

The interior

Inside the Schloss you'll find a frenzy of Rococo in the twelve rooms where Frederick lived and entertained his guests – a process that usually entailed quarrelling with them. The most eye-catching rooms are the opulent **Marmorsaal** (Marble Hall) and the **Konzertzimmer** (Concert Room), where the flute-playing king forced eminent musicians to play his own works on concert evenings. Frederick's favourite haunt was his library where, surrounded by two thousand volumes – mainly French translations of classics and a sprinkling of contemporary French writings – he could oversee work on his tomb. The **Damenflügel**, the west wing of the Schloss, was added in 1840, and its thirteen rooms housed ladies and gentlemen of the court. Nearby on the terrace is a wrought-iron summerhouse protecting a weather-beaten copy of a Classical statue, while just to the south an eighteenth-century sculpture of Cleopatra looks over the graves of Frederick's horses.

The Bildergalerie

May–Oct Tues–Sun 10am–6pm • €6

Overlooking the ornamental **Holländischer Garten**, or Dutch Garden, east of Schloss Sanssouci, is the restrained Baroque **Bildergalerie**, which, it's claimed, was the first

VOLTAIRE AT SANSSOUCI

One of Frederick's most celebrated house guests was **Voltaire**, who lived here from 1750 to 1753, acting as a kind of private tutor to the king. He finally left when he'd had enough of Frederick's moody and dictatorial behaviour, damning the king's intellect with faint praise and accusing him of treating "the whole world as slaves". In revenge Frederick had Voltaire's former room decorated with carvings of apes and parrots.

building in Europe built specifically as a museum. Unfortunately, wartime destruction and looting scattered the contents, but the new collection includes Caravaggio's wonderful *Incredulity of St Thomas* and several works by Rubens and Van Dyck.

The Neue Kammern and around

March Sat & Sun 10am–5pm; April–Oct Tues–Sun 10am–5pm • €4 with tour, €3 without

On the west side of the Schloss, from a point near the Cleopatra statue, steps lead down to the **Neue Kammern**, the architectural twin of the Bildergalerie, originally an orangerie and later a guesthouse. Inside lie a succession of opulently decorated ceremonial halls and private suites, the highlight of which is probably the fancy Ovidsaal: a grand marble-floored ballroom surrounded by gilded reliefs from Roman poet Ovid's *Metamorphosis*.

Frederick was prepared to go to some lengths to achieve the desired carefree rural ambience for Sanssouci and retained an old wooden windmill as an ornament just north of the Neue Kammern. Four years after his death, this was replaced by a rustic-looking stone construction, the **Historische Mühle**, now a restaurant.

The Sizilianischer Garten and Nordischer Garten

Immediately west of the Neue Kammern is the prim **Sizilianischer Garten** (Sicilian Garden), crammed with coniferous trees and subtropical plants, complementing the **Nordischer Garten**, another ornamental garden just to the north, whose most interesting feature is the strange-looking **Felsentor** or Rock Gate, a gateway fashioned from uncut stones and topped by an eagle with outstretched wings.

The Orangerie

April Sat & Sun 10am–6pm; May–Oct Tues–Sun 10am–6pm • €4

West of the Sizilianischer Garten, **Maulbeerallee**, a road open to traffic, cuts through the park past the **Orangerie**. This Italianate Renaissance-style structure with its belvedere towers is one of the most visually impressive buildings in the park. A series of terraces with curved retaining walls sporting waterspouts in the shape of lions' heads leads up to the sandy-coloured building, whose slightly down-at-heel appearance adds character.

It was built at the behest of Friedrich IV and, like the Friedenskirche (see opposite), was inspired by architecture seen on his Italian travels. The facade is lined with allegorical statues set in niches, such as "Industry", who holds a cog wheel. The western wing of the building is still used as a refuge for tropical plants in winter, and during the summer it's possible to ascend the western tower for views of the Neues Palais and vistas of Potsdam's high-rises. The Orangerie also houses a gallery, the **Raphaelsaal**, with copies of paintings looted by Napoleon.

The Belvedere, Drachenhaus and Antikentempel

From the western wing of the Orangerie, the arrow-straight Krimlindenallee, lined with lime trees, leads towards a Rococo **Belvedere**, the last building built under Frederick the Great. It was the only park building to suffer serious war damage, but has since been restored to its former glory. A couple of hundred metres short of the Belvedere, a path off to the left leads to the **Drachenhaus**, a one-time vintner's house

1

built in the style of a Chinese pagoda for the small vineyard nearby. Today the café inside (see p.118) is an ideal place to interrupt wanderings. Southwest of the Drachenhaus, a pathway leads to the **Antikentempel**, built in 1768 to house part of Frederick the Great's art collection. This domed rotunda is now the last resting place of a number of Hohenzollerns, including the Empress Auguste Victoria, and Hermine, the woman Wilhelm II married in exile, and who became known as the "last Empress".

The Neues Palais

Mon & Wed–Sun: April–Oct 10am–6pm; Nov–March 10am–5pm • €8

Rising through the trees at the western end of Park Sanssouci, the **Neues Palais** is another massive Rococo extravaganza from Frederick the Great's time, built between 1763 and 1769 to reaffirm Prussian might after the Seven Years' War. At the centre of the palace is a huge green-weathered dome, topped by a crown, while the edges of the roof around the entire building are adorned by mass-produced sculptures of Classical figures. The main entrance is in the western facade, and once inside, you'll find the interior predictably opulent, particularly the vast and startling **Grottensaal** on the ground floor, which is decorated entirely with shells and semi-precious stones to form images of lizards and dragons. The equally huge **Marmorsaal** is the other highlight, with its beautiful patterned marble floor. The southern wing contains Frederick's apartments and theatre where he enjoyed Italian opera and French plays. The last imperial resident of the Neues Palais was Kaiser Wilhelm II, who packed sixty train carriages with the palace contents before fleeing with his family in November 1918, following the revolution and abdication.

Facing the Neues Palais entrance are the **Communs**, a couple of Rococo fantasies joined by a curved colonnade. They look grandiose, but their purpose was mundane: they housed the palace serving and maintenance staff.

The Rehgarten, Park Charlottenhof and the Römische Bäder

From the Neues Palais, Ökonomieweg leads east between the **Rehgarten** or Deer Garden, the former court hunting ground (and still home to a few deer) and **Park Charlottenhof**, created by Friedrich Wilhelm III as a Christmas present for his son, and today one of Sanssouci's quieter corners. A path leads over a bridge past a small farm building to the **Römische Bäder** (May–Oct Tues–Sun 10am–6pm; €4), built by Schinkel and Persius in convincing imitation of a Roman villa.

Schloss Charlottenhof and around

May–Oct Tues–Sun 10am–6pm • €4

South across the lawns from the Römische Bäder, **Schloss Charlottenhof** is another Roman-style building, again designed by Schinkel and Persius for Friedrich IV. Though called a Schloss, it's little more than a glorified villa, but its interior, unlike most Sanssouci buildings, is original. The effect is impressive: the hallway is bathed in blue light filtered through coloured glass decorated with stars, a prelude to the **Kupferstichzimmer**, or Print Room, whose walls are covered in copies of Italian Renaissance paintings. Immediately east of Schloss Charlottenhof is the **Dichterhain** (Poets' Grove), an open space dotted with busts of Goethe, Schiller and Herder, among others. West of here through the woods and across a racetrack-shaped clearing called the **Hippodrom** is the **Fasanerie**, another Italian-style edifice built between 1842 and 1844.

The Chinesisches Teehaus

May–Oct Tues–Sun 10am–6pm • €2

On the Ökonomieweg – en route back to the Grünes Gitter entrance – you'll pass the slightly kitsch **Chinesisches Teehaus**, a kind of Rococo pagoda housing a small museum of Chinese and Meissen porcelain and surrounded by eerily lifelike Oriental statues.

Neuer Garten

Immediately northeast of Potsdam's centre lies another large park complex, the **Neuer Garten**. This lakeside park on the banks of the **Heiliger See** is a little less formal, more relaxed and less busy than Park Sanssouci, though its two sights are still worthwhile.

The Marmorpalais

Neuer Garten • April Sat & Sun 10am–6pm; May–Oct Tues–Sun 10am–6pm; Nov–March Sat & Sun 10am–4pm • €5

The stout Neoclassical **Marmorpalais** (Marble Palace) was built on the lakefront for Friedrich Wilhelm II, who died a premature death here in 1797, allegedly a consequence of his dissolute lifestyle. It has now been restored to an approximation of its original royal condition and the sumptuous rooms can be seen once again.

The Schloss Cecilienhof

Neuer Garten • Tues–Sun: April–Oct 10am–6pm; Nov–March 10am–5pm • €6 • ⓦ spsg.de • Tram #92 or #96 to stop "Reiterweg Alleestrasse" then change to bus #603 to Schloss Cecilienhof

In the grounds of the Neuer Garten, looking like a mock Elizabethan mansion, is **Schloss Cecilienhof**, the last palace commissioned by the Hohenzollerns. It was begun in 1913 and completed in 1917, the war evidently doing nothing to change the architectural style. Cecilienhof would only rate a passing mention, were it not for the fact that the **Potsdam conference** – confirming earlier decisions made at Yalta about the postwar European order – was held here from July 17 to August 2, 1945. The conference was heavily symbolic, providing a chance for Truman, Stalin and Churchill (replaced mid-conference by Clement Attlee) to show the world that they had truly won the war by meeting in the heart of the ruined Reich. As a result, the main attraction inside is the **Konferenzsaal**, or conference chamber, which resembles an assembly hall of a minor British public school, and is where the Allies worked out details of the division of Europe. Everything has been left pretty much as it was in 1945, with the huge round table specially made in Moscow for the conference still in place. It's also possible to visit the delegates' workrooms, furnished in varying degrees of chintziness.

Filmpark Babelsberg

Grossbeerenstrasse, Potsdam-Babelsberg • Late March to Oct daily 10am–6pm • €21 • ⓦ filmpark.de • Bus #690 or #601 from S-Bahn Babelsberg

On the eastern bank of the Havel lies **Babelsberg**, a former town that's now part of Potsdam and whose real claim to fame is as the one-time heart of the German film industry. Founded in 1917, it was here that the UFA film studios rivalled Hollywood during the 1920s. Today, the huge old complex is given over to **Filmpark Babelsberg**. It's mainly of interest to those with a good knowledge of the German film industry, with films produced here during its heyday including *Das Kabinett des Dr Caligari*, *Metropolis* and *Der Blaue Engel*. It has now reinvented itself as a theme park and visitors can wander through costume and props departments and watch technicians going through the motions of shooting film scenes. It's also possible to visit the hangar-like studio where Fritz Lang may have filmed *Metropolis* (no one is quite sure) and admire a reproduction of his futuristic set. Fairground rides and animal shows operate alongside the film-related attractions.

ARRIVAL AND GETTING AROUND   POTSDAM

By train All trains, including the S-Bahn from Berlin (around 30min) arrive in Potsdam's Hauptbahnhof. Destinations Lutherstadt Wittenberg (hourly; 1hr 33min); Magdeburg (hourly; 1hr 22min).

By bus and tram The city's main bus station lies beside the Hauptbahnhof, from where Verkehrsbetrieb Potsdam (ViP;

ⓦ vip-potsdam.de) buses and trams depart, including tram #92 to the Altstadt, though it's more interesting to simply walk 10min via Lange Brücke and Alter Markt. Potsdam's local bus and tram services are included in the BVG ticket (see p.94) that includes zone C, making an ABC day-ticket the most economical option for day-trips from Berlin.

1

Bike rental Potsdam per Pedales at the Hauptbahnhof (May–Sept daily 9.30am–7pm; ☏0331 748 00 57, ⓦpotsdam-per-pedales.de) rents bikes (€10.50/day), as well as Potsdam audio-guides (€6/day). However, you can only cycle on a single loop within the Park Sanssouci and are not allowed to park your bike within it.

INFORMATION

Tourist office In the Hauptbahnhof (April–Oct Mon–Sat 9.30am–8pm, Sun 10am–4pm; Nov–March Mon–Fri 9.30am–6pm, Sun 10am–4pm) and at Brandenburger Str. 3, by the Brandenburg Gate (April–Oct Mon–Fri 9.30am–6pm, Sat & Sun 9.30am–4pm; Nov–March Mon–Fri 10am–6pm, Sat & Sun 9.30am–2pm; ☏0331 27 55 88 99, ⓦpotsdam-tourism.com).

ACCOMMODATION

Summer accommodation in Potsdam can be scarce, so take advantage of the tourist office **booking hotline** (☏0331 27 55 88 99 or ⓦpotsdam-tourism.com – under heading "Hosts"). Private rooms start at €38.

HOTELS AND PENSIONS

Froschkasten Kiezstr. 4 ☏0331 29 13 15, ⓦfroschkasten .de. No-nonsense pine-furnished en-suite doubles above one of the oldest and most authentic inns in Potsdam, on the edge of the town centre. Breakfast included. **€75**

Hotel am Luisenplatz Luisenplatz 5 ☏0331 97 19 00, ⓦhotel-luisenplatz.de. Pleasant well-run hotel in an early eighteenth-century townhouse overlooking the quiet Luisenplatz, yet in the thick of things at the end of Brandenburger Strasse and just a couple of minutes' stroll from Park Sanssouci. Furnishings are vaguely in keeping with the building, giving the compact guest-rooms a historic feel; the suites are much roomier, but twice the price. Prices include a superb breakfast and wi-fi. **€134**

Hotel Villa Monte Vino Gregor-Mendel-Str. 27 ☏0331 201 33 39, ⓦhotelvillamontevino.de. Delightful family-run hotel in a sprawling villa located an easy walk from the Sanssouci gardens. Has its own tranquil gardens too, and the smart modern rooms are furnished with the occasional antique. A superb breakfast and wi-fi are included; bikes are available for rent. **€149**

Mercure Potsdam Lange Brücke ☏0331 27 22, ⓦmercure.com. Typical GDR-era high-rise with over two hundred rooms and a pool in a central location with superb views over town and surrounding parks and lakes. Rooms are standard modern and often available online at half the rack rate. Bike rental available. **€81**

CAMPSITES AND HOSTELS

Campingpark Sanssouci Gaisberg, An der Pirschheide 1 ☏0331 9 51 09 88, ⓦcampingpark -sanssouci-potsdam.com; tram #94. The closest campsite is just south of Potsdam, making it a good camping base for Berlin too. Also has wi-fi, bike and canoe rental and a reasonable regional restaurant. Open April–Oct. Pitch **€12.80**, plus **€13.50** per person

Jugendherberge Potsdam Schulstr. 9 ☏0331 581 31 00, ⓦjh-potsdam.de. Slick modern hostel around the corner from S-Bahn Babelsberg with bright but spartan twelve-bed dorm rooms, and a games room with billiards and table football. Linen and breakfast are included in the rates. Dorms **€23.50**

EATING AND DRINKING

CAFÉS AND BARS

Babette Brandenburger Str. 71 ☏0331 29 16 48. Pleasant café with outdoor seating, in the shadow of the Brandenburger Tor, that's a good place to rest weary feet and have an indulgent *Torte* after trekking around Park Sanssouci. The large menu is also available in English and features both simple snacks (€7) and main meals (€10), though the quality of both is fairly ordinary. Mon–Sat 9am–late, Sun 10am–late.

Drachenhaus Maulbeerallee 4a ☏0331 505 38 08. Genteel little café in the grounds of Schloss Sanssouci itself, housed in a pagoda-style building once used by royal vintners. You can also eat well here, with a choice of sturdy Brandenburg specialities or just a piece of florid *Torte*. March–Oct daily 11am–7pm; Nov–Feb Tues–Sun 11am–6pm.

★**Hafthorn** Friedrich-Ebert-Str. 90 ☏0331 280 08 20. Hip and happening pub with snacks in the €2–7 range, including superb burgers as well as *Rösti* and potato pancakes. A fashionable but very mixed crowd packs the place out until late, even when there's no live music, and there's also a busy beer garden. Daily 6pm–midnight.

RESTAURANTS

Contadino Luisenplatz 8 ☏0331 951 09 23. The casual surroundings overlooking a plaza and the Brandenburger Tor make this mid-priced Italian restaurant a perfect place to eat before or after tackling Sanssouci. Along with pasta and pizza there's a wealth of perfectly good alternatives: chops, steaks and some pan-fried Iberian and South American food. Some items and daily specials cost as little as €3.50. Daily noon–late.

Froschkasten Kiezstr. 4 ☎0331 29 13 15, Ⓦ froschkasten.de. One of the oldest and most authentic inns in Potsdam serves good, traditional German food, with several great fish dishes including a delicious grilled salmon fillet (€19). Mon–Sat noon–midnight, Sun noon–10pm.

★ **Juliette** Jägerstr. 39 ☎0331 270 17 91. Cosy gourmet place that's probably Potsdam's best restaurant thanks to its French flair (and wines) and its unpredictable range of dishes that might include the exotic likes of loach with couscous and avocado purée, or steak with truffles and foie gras. Expect to drop around €70 per person including drinks. Mon–Sun noon– 3.30pm & 6–10pm.

La Madeleine Lindenstr. 9 ☎0331 270 54 00. Smart *crêperie* with a good selection of delicous French crêpes: the buckwheat versions are particularly good – try the Nordic with salmon and radish, or the ratatouille version. Prices start at €8. Daily noon–10pm.

La Maison du Chocolat Benkertstr. 20 ☎0331 237 07 30. Café-restaurant with outdoor seating on the pavements of the pretty Dutch quarter. It's a good spot for breakfast, or regional and seasonal specialities (from around €9), but it's the rich, indulgent, and frankly unmissable hot chocolates that really put the place on the map. Great cakes too. Cash only. Daily 10am–10pm.

NIGHTLIFE AND ENTERTAINMENT

Waschhaus Schiffbauergasse 1 ☎0331 271 56 26, Ⓦ waschhaus.de. Large cultural venue where there's always something going on. It lies just off Berliner Strasse on the way into town from the Glienicker Brücke, and incorporates galleries, an open-air cinema, beer garden, live music stages and Fabrik (☎0331 280 03 14, Ⓦ fabrikpotsdam.de), a theatre for contemporary dance and music.

Gedenkstätte Sachsenhausen

Strasse der Nationen 22 • Daily: mid-March to mid-Oct 8.30am–6pm; mid-Oct to mid-March 8.30am–4.30pm • Free, audio tour €3, leaflet €0.50 • Ⓦ stiftung-bg.de • Train from Berlin-Hauptbahnhof (hourly; 25min) or S-Bahn from Friedrichstrasse (frequent; 45min) to Oranienburg train station, then signposted 20min walk or bus #M804 or #M821, stop "Gedenkstätte" (BVG zone ABC tickets valid for whole journey)

The former concentration camp of Sachsenhausen on the fringes of the small town of Oranienburg, 35km north of Berlin, has been preserved as the unremittingly miserable **Gedenkstätte Sachsenhausen** (Sachsenhausen Memorial), as a reminder of the crimes of two of the last century's most powerful and terrible regimes. This early Nazi camp was a prototype upon which others were based. It was never designed for large-scale mass extermination, but all the same around half of the 220,000 prisoners who passed through its gates never left, and at the end of the war the camp was used to systematically kill thousands of Soviet POWs and Jewish prisoners on death marches. After the war the Soviets used the infrastructure for similar purposes.

At the entrance to the camp, its largest structure, the impossibly detailed **New Museum**, charts the camp's origins from defunct brewery to a Nazi political prison; the local Nazis filled it with many of their former classmates, colleagues and neighbours.

The camp

The camp proper begins under the main watchtower and beyond a gate adorned with the ominous sign *Arbeit macht frei* ("Work frees"). Within the perimeter walls and former high-voltage fence – site of frequent inmate suicides – many parts of the camp have been chillingly well preserved or reconstructed: a number of **prison blocks** which now house a museum telling the stories of selected inmates; the **camp prison**, from which internees seldom returned; and the former **kitchen and laundry** where harrowing films show the camp on liberation. Just outside the perimeter lie pits where summary executions took place and bodies were incinerated.

Finally, at the northern tip of the camp, an exhibition in a **guard tower** investigates what the local populace thought and knew of the place, via video interviews, while the

1

jumbled hall next door examines the postwar Soviet Special Camp (1945–50), when the Russians imprisoned 60,000 people with suspected Nazi links – though most were innocent – of whom at least 12,000 died.

Rheinsberg

Some 50km northwest of Berlin, venerable tree-lined avenues home in on the rolling forests that cradle lakes on Brandenburg's border with Mecklenburg-Western Pomerania – where this landscape is protected as Müritz National Park (see p.852). But just south, on the languid shores of Grienericksee, lies the pretty little town of **RHEINSBERG**, where Frederick the Great claimed to have spent his happiest years as a young crown prince living in a modest Schloss, studying for the throne and giving occasional concerts.

Rheinsberg's tiny centre is worth a quick exploration, and though there are few real landmarks, it features genteel, leafy, cobbled streets and several **pottery** workshops on the south side of town, which carry on centuries-old local traditions. Digs south of the Schloss have traced the origins of the local industry to the early thirteenth century, and Rheinsberg continues to be known for ceramics and faïence (tin-glazed pottery), though today's most popular pieces are sturdy rustic ones with cream and dark blue glazes.

Schloss Rheinsberg

Schloss Rheinsberg Tues–Sun: April–Oct 10am–6pm; Nov–March 10am–5pm • €8 including English audio-guide, combined ticket with Tucholsky Literaturmuseum €10, gardens free • ☏ 033 931 72 60 • **Tucholsky Literaturmuseum** Tues–Sun 10am–5.30pm • €4, combined ticket with Schloss Rheinsberg €10 • ⓦ spsg.de

Even outside concert times (see box opposite) **Schloss Rheinsberg** remains a popular attraction, its gardens free to wander around. The Schloss was a sanatorium in GDR days, when much of its frivolity disappeared, but elegant surviving highlights include the Spiegelsaal (Mirror Hall), with its ceiling fresco by Antoine Pesne, and the Muschelsaal (Shell Hall) with its intricate Baroque detailing.

In the Schloss's north wing, the **Tucholsky Literaturmuseum** commemorates the life of pacifist and left-wing journalist Kurt Tucholsky (1890–1935), who also wrote as Kaspar Hauser and was a great champion of the Weimar Republic. He left Germany in the early 1930s, preferring self-imposed exile in Sweden – and died there before the World War he predicted broke out. Rheinsberg provided Tucholsky with inspiration for his novel *Rheinsberg: Ein Bilderbuch für Verliebte* – a cheerful love story laced with criticism of the bourgeoisie and nationalism.

ARRIVAL AND INFORMATION   **RHEINSBERG**

By train and bus Getting to Rheinsberg (Mark) by public transport can be a headache and requires a train and bus combination that can take almost three hours, but the quickest route from Berlin is by train via Neuruppin (7 daily; 2hr 15min); Rheinsberg's station is just southeast of town, 1.2km from the Schloss.

GRIENERICKSEE CRUISES AND TOURS

Rheinsberg's adjacent tranquil lake, **the Grienericksee**, can be explored with Reederei Halbeck (☏ 033 93 13 86 19, ⓦ schiffahrt-rheinsberg.de), at the lakeshore, whose two-hour cruises of three local lakes cost €12.50; they also rent out rowing boats and kayaks (from €5/hour or €20/day). Rheinsberger Adventure Tours (☏ 033 93 13 92 47, ⓦ rhintour.de), at the corner of Rhinstrasse and Mühlenstrasse, also hire out canoes and kayaks, and offer escorted tours too.

CLASSICAL RHEINSBERG

Though royal musicians have long gone, **concerts** continue to be one of the town's big draws, with the Musikakademie Rheinsberg (☎033 931 72 10, ⓦmusikakademie-rheinsberg.de) putting on concerts, ballet and musicals in the Schloss year-round, but particularly during the **Rheinsberger Musiktage** (May or June), which encompasses quite a range of genres, particularly jazz and chamber music, and the **Kammeroper Schloss Rheinsberg** (ⓦkammeroper-rheinsberg.de), an opera festival of international standing that promotes young talent, in late June or mid-August.

Tourist office Mühlenstr. 15a (Mon–Thurs 10am–5pm, Fri & Sat 10am–6pm, Sun 10am–4pm; ☎033 931 349 40, ⓦrheinsberg.de). The office has a list of private rooms (from €40), for which vacancy signs hang throughout town.

ACCOMMODATION AND EATING

EIS-Zauberei Kurt-Tucholsky-Str. 36. The unmissable local gastronomic quirk is *this* great local ice cream maker, renowned for unusual flavours – including garlic, parsley and radish – that taste far better than they sound. Daily 11am–11pm.

Pension Holländermühle Holländer Mühle 01 ☎033 931 23 32, ⓦhollaender-muehle.de. A 10min walk due south of the Schloss along Schanower Strasse, this pension has the novelty of being in an old windmill. Rooms are generally bright and simple, but each is individually decorated, some with coronet bed drapes. The restaurant serves good *Schnitzel*, pasta and trout mains for around €12. Restaurant Tues–Sun 11.30am–8pm. **€65**

Der Seehof Seestr. 18 ☎033 931 40 30, ⓦseehof-rheinsberg.de. This central mid-eighteenth-century former farmhouse just north of the Schloss has bright and cheerful upscale rooms, many of which have balconies with lake views. Rates include a free pass to a local gym and wi-fi. Mains at the lovely restaurant average €15 and include the delicious, perch-like local fish, zander, served here with local gherkins, salami and rosemary potatoes. Restaurant daily 6pm–late. **€110**

The Schorfheide

Large tracts of heathland increasingly assert themselves as you travel northeast from Berlin and into a region known as the **Schorfheide**. Its gentle charms may fail to draw the crowds, but as a UNESCO Biosphere Reserve it's certainly ecologically important, and within it a couple of sights are worth a detour, particularly the romantic Gothic ruins of the **Kloster Chorin** monastery, and an impressive industrial monument in the form of a giant 1930s barge hoist at **Niederfinow**.

Kloster Chorin

Kloster Chorin Amt Chorin 11a • Daily: April–Oct 9am–6pm; Nov–March 10am–4pm • €4 • ⓦkloster-chorin.org • **Choriner Musiksommer** €7–27 • ☎033 34 81 84 72, ⓦmusiksommer-chorin.de • Train from Berlin to the village of Chorin (hourly; 40min), then connecting bus to Kloster Chorin, or follow the signposted paths 3km south through the woods

The product of sixty years' hard graft by a group of thirteenth-century Cistercian monks, **Kloster Chorin** is one of Germany's grandest red-brick structures. Bristling with patterned brickwork, its impact in an age where such enormous buildings were rare must have been staggering, but after the monastery's dissolution in 1542, it gradually crumbled until its early nineteenth-century renovation in which Schinkel (see box, p.74) had a hand. A wander around it reveals sleek portals, gracefully elongated windows and a beautiful step gable on its western side, but its parkland setting – beside a pretty lake – is equally enchanting, particularly during the **Choriner Musiksommer**, a series of classical concerts held on summer weekends that showcase the building's fine acoustics.

1

Schiffshebewerk Niederfinow

Visitor centre Late Feb to Dec daily 10am–3pm • €1, parking €3 • ☎ 033 36 22 15, ⓦ schiffshebewerk-niederfinow.info •
Platform Daily 9am–6pm • €2 • **Fahrgastschiffahrt Neumann boat trips** March–Oct daily 11am, 1pm & 3pm • €7 • ☎ 033 342
44 05 • Train from U- & S-Bahn Lichtenberg station in Berlin (hourly; 1hr) to Niederfinow, then follow a signed 2km walk through
the countryside to the hoist

For a rare remnant of Prussia's mighty industrial legacy, travel 20km southeast of
Chorin to the small community of **Niederfinow**, whose **Schiffshebewerk** (ship hoist)
is visible for miles around. This gigantic steel trough within a lattice of enormous
girders raises and lowers boats the 36m between the Oder River and the Oder-Havel
Canal, providing a vital link for the regional shipping network. On completion in
1934 this engineering feat was the largest of its kind – the trough is almost 100m
long and can handle thousand-tonne barges – and cut a process that took several
painstaking hours to twenty minutes. You can watch the procedure from the
street-level base of the structure for free, but the view is better from the upper canal
platform. Better still is to join a **boat trip** and be lifted by the hoist; boat trips are
run by Fahrgastschiffahrt Neumann, whose ticket office is in a kiosk among the
small group of buildings by the adjacent car park. Also here are several *Imbiss*
stands and a **visitor centre**, which details the intricacies of the hoist's construction
and operation, and gives details on a new structure, half the size again, that's
planned for 2016.

ACCOMMODATION AND EATING
THE SCHORFHEIDE

Am Schiffshebewerk Hebewerkstr. 43, Niederfinow ☎ 033 36 27 00 99, ⓦ hotel-schiffshebewerk.de. To stay the night or eat a sit-down meal by the Niederfinow hoist, try this hotel with its clean and spacious en-suite rooms, and solid traditional meals (mains average €11) – as well as nice cakes – in its restaurant. Restaurant Mon–Sat noon–8pm, Sun 10–8pm. **€75**

Hotel Haus Chorin Neue Klosterallee 10, Chorin ☎ 033 36 65 00, ⓦ chorin.de. Lakeside hotel midway between the monastery and the village of Chorin, with bright modern rooms and a very good, mainly organic, restaurant which uses honey in every dish; try the delicious honey-marinated roast pork (mains €10–18). Restaurant daily noon–8pm. **€99**

The Unteres Odertal Nationalpark

Don't expect expansive untrammelled wilds in the **Unteres Odertal Nationalpark**
(Lower Oder Valley National Park), which lies on the Polish border in
Brandenburg's northeastern corner. The long, thin park – 60km long and as little
as 2km wide in places – centres on a huge island in the centre of the Oder whose
meadows, marsh and clusters of mixed woodland provide a peaceful habitat and
breeding ground for 100,000 geese and ducks as well as rare birds like sea eagles
and black storks. October is the most spectacular time to visit, when 13,000
migratory cranes pass through on their way south. Binoculars are extremely useful,
as is a bike since the park is crisscrossed by some 100km of flat and generally
smooth cycle paths.

The largest town in the area, and best public transport hub, is lacklustre **SCHWEDT**,
100km northeast of Berlin, while the main park focus is the **Nationalparkhaus**
information centre (April–Oct daily 9am–6pm; Nov–March Fri & Sat 10am–5pm;
€3; ☎ 033 322 67 72 44, ⓦ nationalpark-unteres-odertal.eu), in the hamlet of
Criewen, 8km southwest along the riverbank path and connected by bus #468 (10
daily; 14min). The centre has plenty of lively displays on local wildlife, including a
large aquarium.

ARRIVAL AND INFORMATION
SCHWEDT

By train Trains run from Berlin to Schwedt (hourly; 1hr 15min).

Tourist office Berliner Str. 47 (May–Sept Mon–Fri 9am–6pm, Sat 10am–2pm; Oct–April Mon–Fri

9am–5pm; ☎033 322 55 90, ⓦunteres-odertal.de). The office can help with accommodation.

Bike and canoe rental Fahrrad- und Touristikcenter

Butzke, Kietz 11 (☎033 32 83 95 00, ⓦkanubutzke.de), rents bikes from €7.50 per day.

ACCOMMODATION

Oder-Hotel Apfelallee 2, Schwedt ☎033 32 26 60, ⓦoder-hotel.de. Situated in a peaceful spot in the National Park, 4km from Schwedt, this hotel has 33 smart, modern rooms, all with pretty garden views, and a good onsite restaurant that specializes in fish and game. Wi-fi and breakfast included. **€80**

The Märkische Schweiz

Rolling hills, crisp, clean air, trickling streams and languid lakes: the **Märkische Schweiz** has long been a popular middle-class getaway from Berlin's hubbub. Predictably, nineteenth-century poet and writer Theodor Fontane (see box below) heaped praise on the region – though he conceded that the Switzerland epithet was a hyperbole too far. Bertolt Brecht and Helena Weigel also voted with their feet, spending several of their last summers together in a pleasant lakeside cottage in the delightful little spa town of **Buckow**.

Buckow

BUCKOW's disjointed geography comes from being wedged between three sizeable lakes. Its tiny **centre**, with its smattering of shops, huddles on the shores of one of them, the **Buckowsee**, though much of the action, at least in summer, happens 1km north on the shores of the **Schermützelsee**, by far the largest lake. This is where you'll find Strandbad Buckow, an organized bathing beach where you can rent rowing boats or **cruise the lake** with Seetours (April–Oct daily 10am–5pm; hourly; 1hr tour €7; ☎033 43 32 32).

THEODOR FONTANE AND HIS BRANDENBURG WANDERINGS

Widely regarded as Germany's most important nineteenth-century Realist writer, Huguenot novelist and poet **Theodor Fontane** (1819–98) pioneered the German social novel, most famously writing *Effi Briest* (1894), which became a film by Rainer Werner Fassbinder in 1974. Fontane's work offered insights into the lives of people across different social classes in an original style later dubbed Poetic Realism and often compared to Thomas Hardy. But he's far less well known for his contribution to travel writing, which was well ahead of its time for its fusion of literary style, historical insight and narrative adventure. It also challenged the notion that exploring the exotic reaps the greatest rewards, suggesting instead that with the right approach your immediate surroundings can prove as bountiful. This notion came to him during a stint in Britain, which, as an Anglophile in the service of the Prussian intelligence agency, he knew well. While rowing on a Scottish loch it occurred to him that corners of his native Prussia were every bit as beautiful – he came from near Rheinsberg – yet uncelebrated and generally considered among Germany's least appealing regions.

So between 1862 and 1889 he set out to champion his homeland, compiling the five-tome *Wanderungen durch die Mark Brandenburg* ("Wanderings through the Mark of Brandenburg"), based on his whimsical walks around the state: "I travelled through the Mark and found it richer than I dared to hope. The earth beneath every footfall was alive and produced ghosts … wherever the eye rested, everything bore a broad historic stamp." His project would marry Prussian national identity with Romanticism in ways that often mirrored the writings of Sir Walter Scott, whose style was in vogue at the time.

Fontane's wanderings are certainly worth dipping into, despite their off-putting length – at least they didn't end up as the twenty tomes he once planned – and as you travel around the region you'll certainly find enough quotes from his work on tourist office literature. Last respects can be paid at Fontane's grave in Berlin's Französischer Friedhof.

1

GET TANKED

The Märkische Schweiz may be best known as a place of tranquility, but just beyond its southern edge – 18km southeast of Bukow near the village of Schönfelde – the big attraction is quite the opposite. Here €145 buys you half an hour at the helm of a 40-tonne **T55 tank** – the cornerstone of the Warsaw Pact fleet during the Cold War. It'll set you back another €260 for the pleasure of crushing a car with it. For reservations contact Panzer Kutscher (☎033 637 38 32 89, ⓦ panzerkutscher.de).

Overlooking the beach from the south, a steep but narrow strip of land with grand lake views boasts Buckow's ritziest homes – mostly proud, prewar villas.

Many **hiking and cycling paths** fan out around the town, with lakeside paths easy to find, even without the free tourist office map. For more adventurous sorties through thick woodland and up steep hills, either on foot or by mountain bike, head to the northeastern part of town, where routes from the Schweizer Haus visitor centre (see below) fan out into the **Naturpark Märkische Schweiz**, a nature reserve.

The Brecht-Weigel-Haus

Bertolt-Brecht-Str. 30 • April–Oct Wed–Fri 1–5pm, Sat & Sun 1–6pm; Nov–March Wed–Fri 10am–noon & 1–4pm, Sat & Sun 11am–4pm • €3 • ☎033 43 34 67

Sandwiched between the Buckowsee and the Schermützelsee on the west side of town lies the **Brecht-Weigel-Haus**, where Brecht and his actress wife, Helene Weigel, summered in the mid-1950s. The home is a memorial to their time here, complete with simple rustic furnishings and pretty gardens all preserved much as they were then. Exhibits also chart their lives in photos and various documents, and include the covered wagon that was famously used in the 1949 premier of Brecht's play *Mother Courage and Her Children*.

ARRIVAL AND INFORMATION
BUCKOW

By train and bus Trains from Berlin-Lichtenberg station (hourly; 35min) pull in to the town of Müncheberg, from where bus #928 (hourly; 16min) runs 10km southeast to Buckow. On summer weekends (May–Oct), Müncheberg and Buckow are connected by the Buckower Kleinbahn (ⓦ buckower-kleinbahn.de), a small tourist train.

Tourist office Sebastian-Kneipp-Weg 1 (April–Oct Mon–Fri 9am–12.30pm & 1–5pm, Sat & Sun 10am–12.30pm & 1–5pm; Nov–March Mon–Fri 10am–12.30pm & 1–4pm, Sat & Sun 10am–2pm; ☎033 43 36 59 82, ⓦ maerkischeschweiz.eu). The office is at the centre of things by Buckow's tiny main square, and can arrange private rooms (from €43).

Park information Schweizer Haus, Lindenstr. 33 (Mon–Fri 10am–4pm, Sat & Sun 10am–6pm; ☎033 43 31 5841), has info on the adjacent Naturpark Märkische Schweiz.

ACCOMMODATION AND EATING

Bergschlösschen Königstr. 38 ☎033 43 35 73 12, ⓦ bergschloesschen.com. Late nineteenth-century villa with a terrace, restaurant and sauna, and classic if slightly stuffy and dated rooms, but rates that are keen considering the overall style. The restaurant serves excellent seasonal local food with gourmet twists; the menu often features fine cuts of wild boar, served with pumpkin, blood sausage and fried potatoes; mains average €14. Restaurant daily 5pm–late. €85

Castello Angelo Wriezener Str. 59 ☎033 43 35 75 13. The good and well-priced Italian dishes at *Castello Angelo* make its disturbing faux castle theme forgivable. Pizzas and pasta dishes are around €8 and there's fresh local fish on the menu too. Cash only. Mon & Wed–Sun noon–10pm.

DJH Buckow Berliner Str. 36 ☎033 43 32 86, ⓦ jh-buckow.de. Spick-and-span DJH hostel on the southern outskirts of town, 1km from the centre, with en-suite twins and eight-bed dorms. Rates include breakfast and sheets; lunches and dinners are available. Dorms €18

Fischerkehle Fischerberg 7 ☎033 43 33 74, ⓦ fischerkehle.de. If you're after fish, make a beeline for *Fischerkehle*, just south of the Schermützelsee and signposted off Berliner Strasse near the youth hostel, where you'll find fish and game dishes par excellence (mains €9–18). The rosefish with boiled, parsley-seasoned potatoes is excellent, as is the game ragout, served with *Spätzle* (Swabian noodles) and cranberries. The big terrace overlooking the Schermützelsee is also a big plus. Daily 11am–5pm.

The Spreewald

The **Spreewald** is Brandenburg at its most attractive and touristy. Designated a UNESCO Biosphere Reserve, this gentle landscape of meadows and meandering waters 80km southeast of Berlin is home to Germany's Sorbic community (see box below), but is every bit as well known for its market gardening: famously it produces 40,000 tonnes of pickled gherkins every year, in a staggering number of varieties. Gateway towns in the region include Lübben and Cottbus, but easily the most attractive hub is **Lübbenau**, where punting and canoeing are popular. But though canals, lakes and rivers may be what the region's known for, its single most popular attraction is **Tropical Islands**, an indoor water park and resort – housed in an old airship hangar – where tropical temperatures rule year-round.

Lübbenau

LÜBBENAU's unassuming Altstadt is crowded with hotels, restaurants and services, and with a million visitors a year strolling through its centre, it's a fairly touristy place worth avoiding on weekends and in the peak summer season. **Cycling**, **punting** and **canoeing** (see box, p.126) are the main draws, though two small musuems in town warrant a look if the weather is poor: the **Spreewald-Museum**, Am Topfmarkt 12 (Tues–Sun: April–Oct 10am–6pm; Nov–March 10am–5pm; €4; ☏035 42 24 72), in the brick former courthouse, jail and town hall, offers local cultural history; the **Haus für Mensch und Natur**, behind the tourist office at Schulstr. 9 (April–Oct Tues–Sun 10am–5pm; free; ☏035 428 92 10), explains, in German, why the area is a Biosphere Reserve.

THE SORBS

Numbering just 60,000 people, **Sorbs** are Germany's only indigenous ethnic minority and can trace themselves back to the Slavic Wends who settled the swampy lands between the Oder and Elbe rivers in the fifth century. Conquered by Germanic tribes in the tenth century they found themselves forcibly, often brutally, Germanized throughout the Middle Ages, until their homeland – known as Lusatia (Łužica or Łužyca in Sorbian) – became divided between Prussia and Saxony in 1815. Their language takes two distinct dialects: **lower Sorbian**, with similarities to Polish, was spoken in Prussian areas and generally suppressed; while **upper Sorbian**, a little like Czech, was mostly spoken in Saxony and enjoyed a certain prestige. But emigration from both areas was widespread throughout the nineteenth century, with many ending up in Australia and the USA, specifically a Texas town called Serbin.

THE TWENTIETH CENTURY AND BEYOND

Persecution heightened under the Nazis – who butchered around 20,000 Sorbs – then rapidly lessened in the GDR, even though Lusatia was overrun by resettling Germans expelled from Poland at the end of the war. The area subsequently became heavily industrialized, which hastened the erosion of old ways. But at least the Sorbs were allowed some **cultural autonomy**, with their language granted equal status with German and their folk traditions encouraged, albeit for tourist purposes. Since the *Wende* cultural interest has been stepped up and colourful Sorbian **festivals** like the Vogelhochzeit on January 25, the Karnival, and their variant of Walpurgisnacht on April 30, have become popular. Yet despite all this, and bilingual street signs throughout the region, Sorbian is rarely heard and the minority still feels underrepresented and underfinanced by the German state. They are petitioning the EU for greater recognition and are helped by the fact that Sorbian Stanislaw Tillich has been Minister President of Saxony since 2008.

1

PUNTING, CANOEING AND CYCLING IN THE SPREEWALD

Trips on a *Kahn* (**punt**) along the Spreewald's network of mellow waterways are offered by a clutch of similar operators (2hr trips €10), from either the Kleiner Hafen (small harbour), 100m northeast of the tourist office, or the Grosser Hafen (large harbour), 300m southeast. If punts seem overcrowded, consider renting a **canoe or kayak** from the same operators (around €6/hr).

If you'd rather stay on land and explore on two wheels then you'll find a good range of flat, quiet roads and **cycle paths** in the area. One marked route runs 250km to Berlin, and the tourist office has information on shorter marked local routes and tours. Bikes can be hired at Spreewelten, Bahnhofstr. 3d (☎035 42 88 99 77, ⓦspreewelten-bahnhof.de), at the train station.

Lehde and the Freilandmuseum

The most popular trip by punt, canoe or bike is to **LEHDE**, a protected village oft touted as the Venice of the Spreewald for its many waterways, and which lies 3km east via signposted paths from Lübbenau's Grosser Hafen (large harbour). Lehde's prime attraction is the excellent **Freilandmuseum** (daily: April to mid-Sept 10am–6pm; mid-Sept to Oct 10am–5pm; €4; ☎035 42 24 72), an intriguing open-air museum with a Sorbian village, whose houses and farmhouses have been brought here from other parts of the region and furnished with traditional Sorbic household objects. Unusual are the buildings' large foundation stones that rest on top of timber poles driven deep into the marshy ground, and inside, beds designed for a whole family.

ARRIVAL AND INFORMATION   LÜBBENAU

By train and bus Lübbenau's train and bus station lies on Poststrasse, about 500m south of the Altstadt.

Tourist office Ehm-Welk-Str. 15 (April & Oct Mon–Fri 10am–6pm, Sat 10am–4pm; May–Sept Mon–Fri 10am–6pm, Sat 9am–4pm, Sun 10am–4pm; Nov–March Mon–Fri 10am–4pm; ☎035 42 36 68, ⓦluebbenau-spreewald.com). The office is well signposted. It can arrange **private rooms** (from €30), which advertise with *Gästezimmer* signs around town.

ACCOMMODATION AND EATING

Am Alten Bauernhafen Stottoff 5 ☎035 42 29 30, ⓦam-alten-bauernhafen.de. Large family-run pension a short walk from the centre of Lübbenau, whose bright, modern riverside rooms include singles (€39) and triples (€69). The extensive breakfast buffet features many home-grown and organic items, including, of course, gherkins. **€49**

Hotel Schloss Lübbenau Schlossbezirk 6 ☎035 42 87 30, ⓦschloss-luebbenau.de. Classy hotel with elegant fin-de-siècle rooms in Lübbenau's palace. The spa, with vaulted ceilings and intricate mosaics, is as beautiful as it is relaxing. In the face of weak competition, the town's best restaurant is also here, serving regional foods (mains €17–28); the three-course set meal (€27) is good value. Restaurant daily 11.30am–10.30pm. **€140**

Naturcamping Am Schlosspark, Schlossbezirk 20 ☎035 42 35 33, ⓦspreewaldcamping.de. The best budget alternative to private rooms is this shaded campground, a 10min walk from town, which also has some cabins sleeping two people. Facilities include bike and canoe rental. Cabins **€50**; pitch **€5**, plus **€6.50** per person

Saloon Santa Fe Robert-Koch-Str. ☎035 42 36 00, ⓦsaloon-santafe.de. Not exactly what you'd expect to find in provincial Lübbenau – a Southwestern steakhouse – but justifiably popular. Choose from steaks, burgers and TexMex skillets and enjoy them in mock-Western surroundings – there's even a table in a covered wagon. Mains average €11. Mon–Thurs 5pm–late, Fri–Sun noon–late.

Tropical Islands

60km south of Berlin, off the A13 motorway from Berlin (exit Staakow) • Daily 24hr • €36, nudist sauna area additional €12; overnight tents €114 for two, including breakfast buffet; overnight at beach €20 per person, not including breakfast; outdoor campground tents €6, plus €8 per adult • ☎035 477 60 50 50, ⓦtropical-islands.de • Brand (Niederlausitz) train station, where free shuttle buses to the complex meet every train

Since 2004 an old hangar for zeppelins 60km south of Berlin has housed **Tropical Islands**, an indoor landscaped **water park** the size of four football fields containing pools, lagoons, water slides, waterfalls, whirlpools and saunas as well as a clutch of bars, restaurants and shops. The quality of the landscaping is first class, and the tropical shrubbery and birds that flit around its undergrowth get to luxuriate in the constant 27ºC temperature. A Disney-esque quality is added by interior buildings and monuments – like the Bali, Borneo, Thai and Samoan pavilions – and regular evening dance shows, but what really sets the place apart is its laidback air and convenience. A wristband received on entry handles all purchases electronically – to be paid on exit – but best of all, the place is open all day, every day, allowing you to **stay overnight**. Tents can be rented, but most people just crash on the beach with a mat and blanket, for an additional fee on top of the admission price. There's another one-off extra charge for use of the immense, nudist sauna area, and for the large adjacent outdoor campground for tents and caravans.

Saxony

THE ELBE RIVERFRONT, DRESDEN

2

Saxony

After several decades in a rut, Saxony (Sachsen), the one-time state of the Saxons, is back in the groove. Under the GDR, the three largest cities of the regime outside the capital – Dresden, Leipzig and Chemnitz – found their ambitions stifled, or, worse, were simply allowed to moulder. Government masterminds even attempted to re-create Mother Russia in Chemnitz. Nowadays, as its Baroque city reappears, Dresden is restored as a cultural marvel, while Leipzig is once again vibrant, in trade as much as in one of the most dynamic modern arts scenes in Europe. Of all the East German states outside Berlin, Saxony has benefited most from reunification.

With its economy secure, Saxony likes to promote itself as the **"state of the arts"**: the Land where Johann Sebastian Bach spent nearly half his life; which nurtured Robert Schumann; and whose distinctive landscapes in Saxon Switzerland inspired some of the finest work from Romantic painter Caspar David Friedrich. It is also the state that pioneered porcelain outside Asia and created some of the most ebullient Baroque architecture in Europe – both achievements down to eighteenth-century strongman Augustus the Strong, a Saxon Sun King under whose rule the state blossomed into an artistic powerhouse. His legacy is evident wherever you go.

However, the state capital **Dresden** is evidence that Saxony doesn't only live in its past. Since reunification it has set about re-creating the Baroque city that was shattered by the bombing raids of World War II, but it also fizzes with life in a bar and club scene that's as good a reason to visit as some of the biggest art blockbusters in Germany. **Leipzig** is similarly sized but entirely different in character: a dynamic mercantile city that has rediscovered its rhythm after off-beat decades. The Land's communist legacy is most evident in erstwhile "Karl-Marx-Stadt" **Chemnitz**, worth visiting for its art and a nearby castle. Of the small towns, the most appealing is cobbled charmer **Meissen**, closely followed by **Görlitz**, hard against the Polish border, and **Bautzen**, capital of the indigenous Slavic-speaking Sorbs. Yet Saxony also provides more visceral pleasures: pottering for crafts in small towns of the **Erzgebirge** and the fantastic cliffs of **Saxon Switzerland**, by far the most scenic corner of the state and a paradise for walkers and rock-huggers alike.

Dresden

For most visitors **DRESDEN** is synonymous with devastation; in fact, it's all about regeneration. Of the major cities, only Berlin and Hamburg suffered such total obliteration in the war, and Dresden had far more to lose. For two centuries before its Altstadt was reduced to a smouldering heap in February 1945, it was acclaimed the most beautiful city in Germany. Italian master Canaletto immortalized it as a "Florence on the Elbe". Visitors on the Grand Tour marvelled at a Baroque streetscape

THE ZWINGER COURTYARD, DRESDEN

Highlights

❶ Dresden Baroque 'n' roll in the former Florence on the Elbe – after the glorious architecture and dazzling artistry, go bar-hopping in one of the most enjoyable *Szene* neighbourhoods in Germany. **See p.130**

❷ Palaces around Dresden With Augustus the Strong's Baroque palaces accessible from Dresden by vintage train and steamship, getting there is half the fun. **See p.147**

❸ Meissen Never mind Europe's first and finest porcelain factory, Meissen's picture-book-pretty Altstadt is idyllic. **See p.150**

❹ Saxon Switzerland Spectacular views and sandstone massifs in the most scenic corner of Saxony, best savoured on a week-long walk that has been voted the most beautiful in Germany, but which can be sampled on a day-trip from Dresden. **See p.153**

❺ Leipzig The dynamic trade-fair city that led the peaceful overthrow of the GDR regime has channelled its energy into a vigorous contemporary art scene and boisterous nightlife. **See p.165**

HIGHLIGHTS ARE MARKED ON THE MAP ON P.132

THE BOMBING OF DRESDEN

Historians continue to debate the **bombing of Dresden**. Some describe it as immoral or a war crime, and no other Allied raid has attracted more condemnation than that launched on the night of February 13, 1945. Records show that RAF and USAF Command carried out an incendiary raid on a city that had hitherto escaped destruction. Thereafter the issue is contentious. Without doubt it was an annihilation: if the obliteration of the architectural gem of Germany does not put the raid in a different class, the **casualty figures** do. Around 25,000–35,000 people were killed in a city swollen by refugees; always sketchy at the time, the number of dead was exaggerated first by Nazi propagandists, who stated that 200,000 had died, then by the communists, who put the figure at 135,000.

The tragedy of Dresden is that the raid seems pointless. The stated **military aim** was to restrict movement of troops and armaments in order to aid the Russian advance west. As leaflets dropped on the city explained: "To the people of Dresden: we were forced to bomb your city because of the heavy military traffic your railroad facilities have been carrying. Destruction of anything other than military objectives was unintentional." (As it turned out, those key railroads were knocked out for barely two days.) Allied bombing of civilian targets was nothing new. Yet Dresden, a city whose tradition of arts and humanism was so anathema to the Third Reich that Hitler had only visited twice, was no military lynchpin, and passing comments by High Command about shattering German morale at the end game of the war did not help the military's case. Contemporary Allied journalists and intelligentsia sniffed something rotten, something punitive, and the raid provoked the first **public dissent** over High Command bombing policy. Churchill, who must have approved the plan, distanced himself from it, leaving Air Chief Marshall Arthur **"Bomber" Harris** to carry the can. Few historians now concur that the attack shortened the war. Just as depressing is the fact that "Dresden's Holocaust" is a cause célèbre of neo-Nazi parties; every year on February 13, thousands of disgusted citizens, rallied by the unions, churches, and even Dresden's mayor, protest against the annual neo-Nazi march.

unparalleled in Central Europe. Dresden's coming of age was thanks to Elector Augustus the Strong (August der Starke; 1696–1763). No matter that the regent had an ugly absolutist streak, nor that the city's rejuvenation was all about personal vanity – a transformation to reflect the glory of a self-styled Saxony Sun King. Augustus gathered to his court a brilliant group of architects and artists, and between them they created a city of extraordinary grace in which nobles rode through perfect squares, were serenaded by church bells in elegant spires, or drifted up the Grand Canal of the Elbe to alfresco balls in the Zwinger.

Then came the bombs (see box opposite). Several iconic buildings were rebuilt under the communists, but others were left as ruins or replaced by boxy prefab *Plattenbauten* blocks. From 1990, the city's reconstruction became a metaphor for reconciliation, not just for East and West Germany but among wartime enemies too. When the wraps came off the Frauenkirche in 2005, the last icon of Europe's most striking Baroque city was resurrected.

Part of the attraction of the Altstadt is that it remains in the act of creation as the GDR past is airbrushed and the Baroque streetscape of its glory days reappears – regime apparatchiks would be disgusted. Consequently the city fabric is patchy in places, except around the showpieces that extend behind the Elbe between the two axes of the Altstadt: civic space **Neumarkt**, home to the **Frauenkirche**; and the **Residenzschloss** and splendid **Zwinger** pleasure palace – the former with some of its finest museums, the latter not just the great glory of Baroque Dresden but a prize of Germany. The **Neustadt** on the north bank emerged from the war with much less damage. Originally the Baroque "new town" of its name, it splits between the Innere Neustadt south of Albertplatz and Äussere Neustadt, where most culture is of the bar variety.

Dresden today is as rooted in its past as ever, yet its two districts are effectively strangers. In one, the south-bank Altstadt, you have historic buildings and museums,

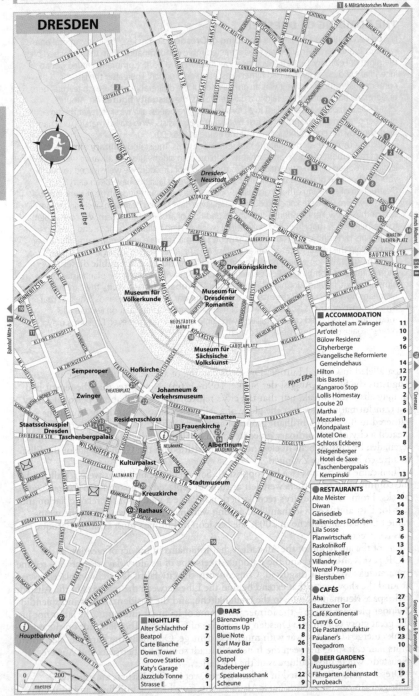

DRESDEN

1 & Militärhistorisches Museum

■ **ACCOMMODATION**
Aparthotel am Zwinger	11
Art'otel	10
Bülow Residenz	9
Cityherberge	16
Evangelische Reformierte Gemeindehaus	14
Hilton	12
Ibis Bastei	17
Kangaroo Stop	5
Lollis Homestay	2
Louise 20	3
Martha	6
Mezcalero	1
Mondpalast	7
Motel One	4
Schloss Eckberg	8
Steigenberger Hotel de Saxe	15
Taschenbergpalais Kempinski	13

● **RESTAURANTS**
Alte Meister	20
Diwan	14
Gänsedieb	28
Italienisches Dörfchen	21
Lila Sosse	3
Planwirtschaft	13
Raskolnikoff	13
Sophienkeller	24
Villandry	4
Wenzel Prager Bierstuben	17

● **CAFÉS**
Aha	27
Bautzener Tor	15
Café Kontinental	7
Curry & Co	11
Die Pastamanufaktur	16
Paulaner's	23
Teegadrom	10

● **BEER GARDENS**
Augustusgarten	18
Fährgarten Johannstadt	19
Purobeach	5

■ **NIGHTLIFE**
Alter Schlachthof	2
Beatpol	7
Carte Blanche	5
Down Town/ Groove Station	3
Katy's Garage	4
Jazzclub Tonne	6
Strasse E	1

● **BARS**
Bärenzwinger	25
Bottoms Up	12
Blue Note	8
Karl May Bar	26
Leonardo	1
Ostpol	2
Radeberger Spezialausschank	22
Scheune	9

tour groups and cafés. In the other, the north-bank Neustadt, is the best bar district south of Berlin and a young multicultural population for whom the historical city is just that – history. That they coexist happily accounts for much of Dresden's appeal as two cities in one.

The Frauenkirche

Neumarkt • **Church** Mon–Fri 10am–noon & 1–6pm, Sat & Sun times vary • Free • **Tower** Mon–Sat 10am–6pm, Sun 12.30–6pm; Nov–Feb closes 4pm • €8 • ⓦ frauenkirche-dresden.de

No monument is so potent a metaphor of reborn Dresden as the **Frauenkirche**. The church on Neumarkt was designed both as Germany's largest Protestant church and a piece of one-upmanship over the nearby Catholic Hofkirche by a town architect, Georg Bähr, and paid for almost entirely by public donation. Canaletto set up his easel wherever he could conspire to feature its landmark cupola, and the church was considered the pinnacle achievement of Protestant Baroque. Shattered by the 1945 raid, it lay in a heap of rubble as a communist memorial – a salute to the city's dead and an accusatory statement of the destruction wrought by the perfidious West. Plans to resurrect the church were discussed in the mid-1980s, and the council finally voted on a rebuild after the *Wende* in 1991; a year ahead of schedule, at 10am on October 30, 2005, with some of the €180 million cost funded by British and American associations, the bells rang over a crowd of thousands to celebrate the re-consecration.

As locals are keen to point out, this is less a new church than a return of the old – its beautifully balanced structure is faithful to the original plans and its café-au-lait sandstone is freckled with original fire-blackened blocks. Within what is probably the busiest church in Saxony, delicately marbled galleries crammed Escher-esque into the lantern cupola fight a losing battle for attention with the explosion of gilt that is the **high altar** depicting Jesus in the olive grove, jigsawed together from two thousand original pieces. The original twisted crucifix dug out from the rubble is displayed by the exit door. Poignantly, the cross of the new church was produced by a silversmith from Coventry whose father was a bomber pilot in the 1945 raid. A separate entrance at the rear provides access to the **tower** whose windy balcony provides unrivalled views over the city and river. The church has a busy schedule of **concerts** and events; check online for times.

With the church rebuilt, work on the revival of **Neumarkt** itself continues. Pictured by Canaletto as the handsome heart of the Altstadt, the square is returning to its role as a civic centre-stage, with townhouses serving as cafés, hotels and luxury stores.

Along Brühlsche Terrasse

When Augustus the Strong created a Baroque city to mirror his power and glory, he permitted a cabinet minister, the Earl of Brühl, a private garden on top of the city's ramparts. **Brühlsche Terrasse** was acclaimed the "balcony of Europe", a riverside belvedere that elbows behind the Frauenkirche as a grand terrace of steps, past showpiece buildings such as the Hochschule für Bildende Künste (Academy of Fine Art), balustrades and busts of German cultural heroes, providing views from 15m above river level – all in all the best promenade in town. Access is via steps at various points.

Museum Festung Dresden

Georg-Treu-Platz 2 • Daily 10am–6pm • €5 • ⓦ festung-dresden.de

Northeast of the Frauenkirche, by a sweeping staircase up to the Brühlsche Terrasse, you'll find the entrance to the **Museum Festung Dresden**, an atmospheric rummage through floodlit cannon rooms of what were highly advanced Renaissance fortifications. Audio-guides accompany you around the museum, except on Saturdays when there are guided tours only.

Albertinum

Brühlsche Terrasse • Tues–Sun 10am–6pm • Albertinum €10, Lipsiusbau temporary exhibitions, combined ticket €12.50 • Ⓦ skd.museum

The palatial **Albertinum** houses the excellent Galerie Neue Meister and Skulpturensammlung – and the main hall with the ticket office is worth a look in its own right. Creatively hung to forge links across artistic periods, the **Galerie Neue Meister** provides a superb haul of art that spans from Romantics like Caspar David Friedrich to recent works by living artists such as Georg Baselitz and Gerhard Richter: en route are excellent French and German Impressionists and Fauvist works by the Die Brücke movement plus classic Modernists such as Otto Dix, whose searing triptych, *War*, pulls no punches in its depiction of his experiences in the trenches. An exception to the museum's crisp white walls is the historical Klingersaal, a *fin-de-siècle* hall of sculpture by Max Klinger as well as contemporary painting and antiquities.

As thoughtfully curated is the **Skulpturensammlung**, beautifully spotlit in darkened rooms like a treasure hunt through artistic styles; keep an eye open for a bust of August the Strong by Balthasar Permoser, the sculptor behind the ornamentation of the Zwinger. A ground-floor space holds modern exhibitions.

The colonnaded palace next door to the Albertinum is the **Lipsiusbau**, with a distinctive glass cupola dubbed the "Lemon Squeezer". It's used for temporary exhibitions of contemporary art, which are changed every two or three months.

Johanneum: the Fürstenzug frieze and Verkehrsmuseum

Augustusstr. 1, entrance on Neumarkt • Tues–Sun 10am–6pm • €7 • Ⓦ verkehrsmuseum-dresden.de

Along Augustusstrasse, which leads northwest from Neumarkt, runs the 102m-long **Fürstenzug frieze**, mounted on the walls of the **Johanneum**, the former Schloss stables. The 24,000 Meissen-china tiles depict a procession of Saxony's rulers from 1123 to 1904; at the centre is the state's very own Sun King, Augustus the Strong – one of the few who gazes directly out from the medieval-styled pageant. The stables are worth a look for a colonnaded Italianate Renaissance courtyard – access is via an arch at the alley's east end. The front half of the ritziest stables ever built contains the **Verkehrsmuseum** (Transport Museum), with a wide range of land-, sea- and aircraft.

Schlossplatz

Schlossplatz, where Augustusstrasse terminates, has been a seat of power throughout Dresden's history: in the past, it was the swaggering Renaissance gateway to the

---

AUGUSTUS THE STRONG, SUN KING OF SAXONY

Dresden's Baroque brilliance is thanks to Augustus II (1670–1733). The Saxony Elector was nicknamed **"Augustus the Strong"** either because of his physical strength – they say he showed off in court by snapping horseshoes – or his potency. Even if contemporary rumours that he fathered around 370 illegitimate children are hyperbolic, his twelve or so mistresses – from aristocratic ladies to French dancers via an Ottoman noblewoman – suggest a man of considerable appetites. The sobriquet also suits a ruler with an absolutist streak. Impressed by Versailles and Italian courts as an 18-year-old, Augustus styled himself as a **Saxon Sun King** and began to transform his capital into a mirror of his own magnificence. The upshot was such fantastic fripperies as the Zwinger and outrageous collections of **porcelain** and jewels that were hoarded with an almost obsessive-compulsive need. Indeed, his passion for porcelain, a "white gold" that had to be imported until his alchemist, Johann Friedrich Böttger, cracked the secret while incarcerated in the Königstein fortress (see p.156), was directly inspired by the god-like rule of Oriental emperors. Yet Augustus was as ruthless as he was extravagant. Despite Saxony's role as a wellspring of the Reformation, he converted to Catholicism to claim the Crown of Poland in 1697 and spent huge sums on bribes for its nobility and clergy.

Residenzschloss; today it is the site of Saxony's parliament building, the Landtag, which boxes in the east side.

The Hofkirche

Schlossstr. 24 • Mon & Tues 9am–6pm, Wed & Thurs 9am–5pm, Fri 1–5pm, Sat 10am–5pm, Sun noon–4pm • Concerts Wed & Sat 11.30am–noon • Free • Ⓦ bistum-dresden-meissen.de

The **Hofkirche** (also known as the Kathedrale) graces Schlossplatz with a handsome dollop of Baroque. After Augustus the Strong had converted to Catholicism as a ruse to claim the Polish Crown, his son, Augustus III, commissioned a church to keep up appearances before the pope as the Protestant Frauenkirche inched into the sky. He also kept the plans for the Hofkirche secret – a wise move as it turned out, because the Protestant council refused to acknowledge the church after it was completed in 1755 nor allow its bells to peal.

A collaboration of an Italian and a German architect – the *Italienisches Dörfchen* restaurant across Theaterplatz recalls the "Italian village" of masons – results in a quirky hybrid of Italianate exterior (the decidedly un-Germanic two balconies crowded with posturing saints and a lantern-like spire) and a solid Germanic interior which is a bit of a letdown: impressive in scale but plainly whitewashed. Furniture includes a Rococo pulpit held aloft on boiling clouds of putti thanks to Zwinger sculptor Balthasar Permoser, and a prize organ by Gottfried Silbermann. In the crypt lie assorted members of the House of Wettin along with Augustus the Strong's heart in a casket.

The Residenzschloss

Schlossstrasse • Daily except Tues 10am–6pm; Hausmannsturm closed Nov–March • €12, or €21 including Historisches Grünes Gewölbe • Ⓦ skd.museum

Beyond a Renaissance gateway off Schlossplatz, flanked by muscled warriors to reflect the might of the incumbent House of Wettin, lies the **Residenzschloss**. The neo-Renaissance residence of electors and kings of Saxony until 1918, the palace has a Renaissance core at its colossal bulk, though most of what you see is a post-reunification rebuild. For forty years the GDR regime paid lip service to the idea of restoration of the bomb-damaged derelict site but twiddled its thumbs. Work finally began in 1985 and was completed to coincide with the 800th anniversary of the city's founding in 1206; the inner courtyard was canopied with a glass roof similar to that of London's British Museum. Restoration is still ongoing: the latest project, due for completion in 2015, is to display the Münzkabinett ducal coin collection in the restored Georgenbau.

Restoration returned the **Grünes Gewölbe** (Green Vault) collections to the palace for which they were intended. One of the most sumptuous treasuries on the planet, these fancies are a legacy of Augustus the Strong – a real-life Ali Baba's cave of gold, silver, diamonds, ivory and mother-of-pearl craftsmanship designed to express the Elector's wealth and authority and fed by his obsessive-compulsive appetite for luxury. The most fantastical objects are the work of Johann Melchior Dinglinger, Augustus's chief court jeweller who turned to Asian art in his later years to concoct ever more decadent fripperies to please his employer's jaded eye. Such is the scale of the collection – there are four thousand or so objects – they are split into two sections, the Historisches Grünes Gewölbe and the Neues Grünes Gewölbe.

The Historisches Grünes Gewölbe

The **Historisches Grünes Gewölbe** is displayed as Augustus the Strong knew it, in ever glitzier palace rooms of the west wing. Note that there's a cap on the number of tickets sold on any given day, with admission restricted to timed slots – buy in advance or come early. While the objects displayed on shelves and free-standing tables are less head-spinning than those in the Neues Grünes Gewölbe, seen in their mirrored, gilt-trimmed rooms they are intended as a *Gesamtkunstwerk* (total work of art).

2

Highlights are the intimate Eck-Kabinet crammed with the tiny curios that so tickled Augustus, and the Juwelenzimmer, intended to suggest the inside of a treasure chest, whose statuette of an African king bearing a tray of uncut crystal has become an icon of the collection's decadence.

Neues Grünes Gewölbe

The stand-alone dazzlers of the Grünes Gewölbe collection are in the **Neues Grünes Gewölbe**, a glut of objects that express better than words the grandiose and, ultimately, grotesque posturing of Augustus's Baroque. A cherry stone carved with 185 human faces or a jewelled miner's axe are typical. There's no faulting the workmanship, however. Highlights by Dinglinger include a chinoiserie coffee set that was four years in the making; and in the same room a representation of the Court of Delhi on the birthday of the Grand Mogul Aureng-Zab, consisting of 137 gold and enamel figurines encrusted with over five thousand jewels. This thinly disguised homage to absolutism cost Augustus more than the Moritzburg hunting lodge north of Dresden. More expensive still was a 400,000-thaler green diamond hat-clasp commissioned by Augustus III, who inherited his father's extravagant tastes. Dinglinger's personal favourite was the *Bath of Diana*, crafted with Balthasar Permoser.

Türckische Cammer

Geopolitics help explain the rooms that contain Augustus's **Türckische Cammer**, or Turkish collection. The late seventeenth century saw the Ottoman Empire push deep into Habsburg territory, its high-water mark the Siege of Vienna in 1683 – a large room contains weaponry and battledress collected from the conflict. Yet by the late 1720s, as Augustus wooed the empire to shore up his position as the King of Poland, he was seduced by the sultan's power and sheer decadence. On display are some of the objects that so bedazzled him: ornate ceremonial weaponry encrusted in jewels and gilded saddles. By 1731, Augustus commanded a three-month military parade be realized as a Turkish encampment. Dressed in silk kaftan and embroidered gold slippers, he sipped coffee beneath fabulous tents designed by his court architect Matthäus Daniel Pöppelmann – 20m long and unique to Dresden, one richly embroidered tent is the highlight of a collection later bolstered by future Saxony Electors.

Rüstkammer

The **Rüstkammer**, in the newly restored, 60m-long Riesensaal, is a hall of armour, its highlights the ceremonial swords of Saxony Electors and a suit of ornamental gold armour for Swedish king Erik XIV and his horse, embossed with the labours of Hercules.

Hausmannsturm

Originally from the fifteenth century but later enlarged and capped by a Baroque spire, the 100m-high **Hausmannsturm** palace tower is the oldest surviving part of the Schloss, and offers excellent views over the Zwinger and central Dresden.

The Semperoper

Theaterplatz 2 • Tours 4–5 daily; times vary by rehearsals, but there is usually one in English at 3pm • €10 • ⓦ semperoper-erleben.de

Boxed in by Baroque, **Theaterplatz** is, perhaps, the most handsome square in Dresden. Its name derives from the **Semperoper** opera house at its back. The original building in which Wagner premiered *Tannhäuser*, *Rienzi* and *The Flying Dutchman* also did wonders for the career of its creator, Gottfried Semper, who went on to become a superstar architect of Europe and also a close friend of Wagner. The busts of playwrights and sculpture of Dionysus in a chariot pulled by panthers were rescued from an earlier venue destroyed by fire. Tickets for performances and tours are sold at a desk in the Schinkelwache, a Neoclassical Schloss guardhouse.

The Zwinger

Theaterplatz 1 • Tues–Sun 10am–6pm • Courtyard and gardens free, combined ticket for all museums €10, Mathematisch-Physikalischer Salon only €6, Porzellansammlung only €6 • ✪ skd.museum

The **Zwinger** complex of buildings owes its name to an early "outer bailey" that guarded the Residenzschloss; thereafter the similarity ends. The great glory of Baroque Dresden, it was conceived as an alfresco ballroom for court high-jinks by Augustus the Strong, who entrusted the commission to architect Matthäus Daniel Pöppelmann and sculptor Balthasar Permoser. The duo came up with one of the prize buildings of Germany. While the symmetrical layout of lawns and fountains is a paean to the order of the Age of Reason, the Zwinger courtyard is Baroque at its most playful. A balustraded one-storey wing broken by a gateway capped by the Polish Crown runs to dumpy corner pavilions, while at either end are lozenge-shaped ceremonial gateways – the eastern **Glockenspielpavillon** with a peal of forty Meissen-china bells, and the **Wallpavillon** opposite, exuberant with heraldic froth and topped by a statue of Augustus as Hercules carrying the world on his shoulders. To the structure Permoser adds a sculptural carnival: festive putti, bare-breasted nymphs and satyrs who leer as caryatids. The only grouch in the party is a workmanlike north wing added in the mid-1800s to finally close the courtyard after work had stalled through lack of funds. It's worth circling the complex on the terrace to see it at its best; it's accessed via a stairway that zigzags within the Wallpavillon, behind which is the Nymphenbad fountain, an enchanting sunken nook whose nymphs are modelled on Tuscan Roman originals.

Gemäldegalerie Alte Meister

The big draw of the Zwinger's three collections is the Saxon Electors' exquisite collection of old masters in the **Gemäldegalerie Alte Meister** in the north wing. Rather shunted into a corridor as you enter are seven Dresden scenes by Canaletto that helped spread Dresden's fame as a Florence of the North. The most celebrated work is Raphael's touching *Sistine Madonna*; its radiant Virgin and Child, already haunted by the knowledge of the child's fate, are probably less well known than the two bored cherubs who lounge at its base, stars of numerous postcards. All the other big guns of Italian art are here – Titian, Tintoretto, Correggio, Botticelli and Veronese to name a few – plus an outstanding Flemish and Dutch collection that includes muscular works by Rubens, a room of Jan Bruegel the Elder, Van Dyke, and an intriguing Rembrandt self-portrait that depicts him carousing as the Prodigal Son with his surly new wife on his knee. Cranach and Dürer star for the Germans, but keep an eye out for a room of works by Dresden court painter Anton Raffael Mengs, which includes a fleshy image of Augustus III.

Mathematisch-Physikalischer Salon

The Zwinger's oldest museum, the **Mathematisch-Physikalischer Salon**, was opened in 1728, and presents Augustus the Strong's collection of over 1000 scientific instruments and technical oddities in the grand Festsaal hall. Highlights are a thirteenth-century Islamic celestial globe, a sixteenth-century astronomical clock, Blaise Pascal's 1650 mechanical calculator, and a unique fourteen-dial "La Grandiose" Swiss pocket watch.

Porzellansammlung

The Glockenspielpavillon serves as a historic backdrop for the **Porzellansammlung**, the world's largest collection of porcelain. Thanks to Augustus the Strong, Dresden produced the first porcelain in Europe in 1707 before manufacture shifted to the town of Meissen a year later (see p.150). Early works show how Meissen artists stuck faithfully to the Ming-Dynasty Chinese and Japanese role models. Things get far more interesting when Baroque forms develop, with menageries of fantastical animals and an extravagant centrepiece of Augustus on horseback atop a plinth. As appealing is the exhibition's interior design, its flamboyant styling by New York designer Peter Marino an attempt to evoke the shameless decadence of the original of 1730.

The Altmarkt

While Baroque rules in the central Altstadt, communism characterizes the area south. If you arrive at the Hauptbahnhof, your first impression of Dresden is Prager Strasse, a broad boulevard whose high-street shopping cannot quite cover the GDR style, complete with atom fountains. The **Kulturpalast**, a late 1960s cultural centre, skulks on the north side of Altmarkt – fans of communist kitsch will enjoy the propaganda mosaic at its west end which traces the doctrine from Marx to proletariat brothers-in-arms. The regime bulldozed away rubble from the oldest city square to extend Altmarkt into a grand civic space of megalomaniac dimensions. A block to the east at Wilsdruffer Str. 2 is a mildly diverting tale of town history in the **Stadtmuseum** (Tues–Sun 10am–6pm, Fri till 7pm; €5; ⓦstadtmuseum-dresden.de).

Kreuzkirche

An der Kreuzkirche 6 • Mon–Fri 10am–6pm, Sat 10am–3pm, Sun noon–6pm • €3 • ⓦ kreuzkirche-dresden.de

The one concession the GDR regime made to history in the Altmarkt was the blackened Protestant **Kreuzkirche**, whose architecture dithers between late Baroque and early Neoclassicism. A postwar rebuild, depicted in photos at the rear, re-thought the vaulted interior in rough concrete, an exercise in austerity that feels more cutting-edge gallery than church. It's especially dramatic during concerts of its acclaimed boys' choir, the **Kreuzchoir**; the choir gathers for vespers on Saturday at 6.30pm and Sunday service at 9am plus concerts advertised in the foyer. A hike up the **tower** offers views across the plaza towards the domes of the Schloss and Frauenkirche.

The Rathaus

Dr.-Külz-Ring 19 • Tower March–Oct daily 10am–6pm • €3 • ⓦ dresden.de

Behind the Kreuzkirche, past a modern restaurant strip, lies a **Rathaus** that's overweight even by German standards, worth a visit for the views 100m up from its **tower** and a foyer exhibition of ongoing beautification projects. The tower was closed for renovation as this book went to press, and is due to reopen in early 2015.

The Grosser Garten

Dresden's largest park, the **Grosser Garten**, rolls out a carpet of greenery southeast from the Altstadt. Its origins are as a pleasure garden of the ruling House of Wettin – a place for such idle pursuits as games, theatre or hunting – and it was laid out accordingly in formal Baroque style until the switch to the current naturalistic parkland in vogue in the late eighteenth century.

A student-run miniature steam train, the **Dresdener Parkeisenbahn**, runs a circuit of the park (every 20min: mid-April to Oct Tues–Sun 10am–6pm; July & Aug also Mon same times; €5; ⓦparkeisenbahn-dresden.de), stopping at five stations, including the Volkswagon factory, the palace and lake (for all, see below) and an above-average **zoo** (daily: summer 8.30am–6.30pm; winter 8.30am–4.30pm; €12; ⓦzoo-dresden.de) in the south of the park.

The Gläserne Manufaktur

Lennéstr. 1 • Daily 8.30am–7pm, Sat & Sun 9am–6pm; assembly-line tours in English Mon–Fri noon, 3pm & 5pm, Sat noon & 3pm, Sun 3pm • Tours (reservation required) €7 • ☏ 0351 420 44 11, ⓦ glaesernemanufaktur.de

The 40m glass-skinned tower on Lennéstrasse on the park's northwestern fringes is Volkswagen's **Gläserne Manufaktur**, a "transparent factory" unveiled by the motor giant in 2001 as a miniature of its celebrated centre in Wolfsburg, Lower Saxony (see p.725). At full tilt, 150 luxury-class motors roll out daily from a factory that is visible through the glass facade. Multimedia information terminals in the foyer – no small piece of architecture itself – guide you through the production process, or you can tour the assembly line.

The Palais

Grosser Garten • April–Oct Wed–Sat 10am–6pm, Sun 11am–6pm; Nov–March Sat & Sun 11am–6pm • ⓦ grosser-garten-dresden.de

Ruler-straight avenues of trees channel you directly east to the **Palais** at the park's centre, a residence that pioneered Baroque in Dresden and led to an entire cityscape. Though acclaimed in its day throughout Europe as a venue for extravagant festivities, the palace is currently in poor shape and serves as a shabby exhibition space. South of here lies a **boating lake** – rental is available at its west end.

The Panometer

Gasanstaltstr. 3b • Tues–Fri 10am–5pm, Sat & Sun 10am–8pm • €10 • ⓦ asisi.de • Tram #1 or #2 to Liebstädter Strasse

A good fifteen-minute walk behind the Grosser Garten via Winterbergstrasse leads to the **Panometer** on Gasanstaltstrasse. Inspired by the large panoramas of Dresden by Canaletto, artist and architect Yadegar Asisi created one of Dresden's most intriguing sights – a 105m-by-12m painting of Dresden that wraps 360 degrees around the inside of a former gasworks. The panoramic paintings on show alternate between Dresden circa 1756 and the city in ruins at the end of World War II.

The Neustadt

The north-bank Neustadt is only on nodding terms with the historic Altstadt even though its origins were as Augustus the Strong's Baroque "new town", planned after a fire obliterated an earlier settlement in 1685. Incidentally, the mosque-like building that brings an unexpected exoticism to the vista west as you cross the river is the Yenidze, a cigarette factory built in 1909 which today contains offices and a restaurant – it's most impressive when the coloured glass dome is illuminated at night.

Augustus was a vain ruler. With great ceremony, three years after his death in 1733, his new district – first christened "New King's Town" – was inaugurated with a larger-than-life statue of the ruler as a Roman emperor – the **Goldener Reiter statue** on the north end of Augustusbrücke. A few of his former palaces house museums, while ruler-straight Königstrasse has a hint of the Baroque glory of its heyday. Beyond it is the boisterous bar district, Äussere Neustadt.

The Jägerhof: Museum für Sächsische Volkskunst

Köpckestr. 1 • Tues–Sun 10am–6pm • €3 • ⓦ skd.museum

A short way east of the *Goldener Reiter* statue, the city's oldest Renaissance building, the **Jägerhof**, houses the **Museum für Sächsische Volkskunst**, which displays regional folkcraft and costume as well as toys, including collections from the Erzgebirge villages (see p.180), enjoyable working models and a valuable puppet collection.

The Japanisches Palais: the Museum für Völkerkunde

Palaisplatz 11 • Tues–Sun 10am–6pm • €4 • ⓦ voelkerkunde-dresden.de

Go west from the *Goldener Reiter* statue – take the riverside Elbe Meadows for views of the glorious Baroque city opposite – and you reach the **Japanisches Palais** on Palaisplatz. Augustus commissioned the palace as a venue for his prize Meissen and Chinese porcelain, which explains the chinoiserie flair to the roofline and courtyard. Appropriately, then, it is given over to an entertaining ethnology collection, the **Museum für Völkerkunde**. Among its colourful global displays are carved and painted house beams from the Micronesia region, acquired by court naturalist Carl Gottfried Semper in 1881 after he was shipwrecked on the Palau Islands. Their coloured mythical and erotic themes so impressed the Expressionist Die Brücke group that artist Max Pechstein set off to Palau for himself.

2

Königstrasse and Hauptstrasse

Broad boulevard **Königstrasse** spears northeast from Palaisplatz as an unbroken row of Baroque townhouses, many with the original courtyards – perhaps the finest picture of handsome old Dresden in the city. It's more successful than **Hauptstrasse** north of the *Goldener Reiter* statue, after GDR urban planners tinkered with it to create a pedestrianized precinct. Midway along at no. 13, Kügelenhaus offers a snapshot of the original residences in the second-floor quarters of Dresden Romantic painter Gerhard von Kügelgen, preserved as the **Museum für Dresdener Romantik** (Wed–Sun 10am–6pm; €4). A little further up at no. 23 is the **Dreikönigskirche** (tower March–Oct Tues 11.30am–4pm, Wed–Sat 11am–5pm, Sun 11:30am–5pm; Nov–Feb Wed–Sun noon–4pm; €3), a rebuild of a church by Zwinger mastermind Pöppelmann. The high altar, shattered in the war, catches the eye, as does a walloping Renaissance *Danse Macabre* frieze.

The Äussere Neustadt

The mood changes in the **Äussere Neustadt** north of Albertplatz. After reunification, artists and radicals moved into its then-tatty nineteenth-century quarter and so began this urban village's transition into the home of the city's alternative arts and nightlife scenes. The cappuccino classes have certainly arrived, but the area remains multicultural and nicely scruffy – a place of funky galleries and independent boutiques, and the best **bar scene** south of Berlin. The unofficial icon at the heart of the area is the **Kunsthofpassage** (enter at Alaunstr. 70 or Görlitzer Str. 21), a web of interconnecting themed courtyards designed by local artists.

Pfunds Molkerei

Bautzer Str. 79 • Daily 10am–6pm • Free • ⦿ pfunds.de • Tram #11

The coach tours are lured east to **Pfunds Molkerei**, acclaimed by the *Guinness Book of Records* as "the most beautiful dairy in the world", apparently. Crowds in the late nineteenth-century cheesery are especially heavy at lunchtimes, though there's no faulting the charm factor, with its walls and ceiling a blur of hand-painted tiles.

Militärhistorisches Museum

Olbrichtplatz 2 • Mon 10am–9pm, Tues & Thurs–Sun 10am–6pm, • €5, free Mon after 6pm • ⦿ mhmbw.de • Tram #7 or 8 to Stauffenbergallee

Ten minutes' walk north of Äussere Neustadt, the excellent **Militärhistorisches Museum** (Military Museum) – a grand old arsenal building dramatically cut in two by American architect Daniel Libeskind's strikingly modern giant wedge – has a permanent exhibition that ranges from the Middle Ages via the two world wars to modern-day peacekeeping missions. The wedge-shaped extension has twelve fascinating exhibitions on themes such as animals in the military, the language of war and "War and Memory", and is topped by a viewing platform overlooking the city.

ARRIVAL AND DEPARTURE	DRESDEN
By train Dresden has two main train stations: Hauptbahnhof south of the Altstadt and Dresden-Neustadt in the north. Dresden-Mitte station lies en route to Dresden-Neustadt at the far west edge of the Altstadt but is not especially convenient. Destinations Bad Schandau (every 30min; 25–45min); Bautzen (hourly; 40min–1hr); Chemnitz (hourly; 1hr–1hr	20min); Görlitz (hourly; 1hr 10min–1hr 40min); Leipzig (every 30min; 1hr 15min–1hr 40min); Meissen (every 30min; 35min); Zwickau (hourly; 1hr 35min–2hr 20min). **By plane** The airport (⦿ dresden-airport.de) is 9km northwest of Dresden, linked to the Hauptbahnhof by S-Bahn line S2; trains run every 30min and go via Dresden-Neustadt. Expect to pay €18 for a taxi.

GETTING AROUND

By tram and bus Municipal provider BVG (⦿ dvbag.de) operates a good public-transport system to get between the north and south banks of the city and outlying sights; a single costs €2 or a four-card strip (*Kurzstrecke*) for single journeys of up to 2km is €5. Single day-tickets (*Tageskarte*) cost €5; those for a family of four are €7 and for a group of

DRESDEN TOURS AND CRUISES

The tourist offices are your best source of information on myriad **bus** and **walking tours** of the city; among the latter are night-walk tours and Baroque strolls in the company of costumed actors. Ask at hostels about Neustadt **pub-crawls** should you need an incentive to explore the area's bar scene (unlikely). Self-drive tours in a convoy of dinky GDR Trabants are available through **Trabi Safari** (w trabi-safari.de); prices for a 90min tour vary from €60 per person for a couple to €34 per person for a group of four. Sächsische Dampfschiffahrt (w saechsische-dampfschiffahrt.de) runs Elbe **river cruises** on what it claims is the world's oldest and largest fleet of paddle-steamers – trips depart from Dresdener Terrassenufer beside the Augustusbrücke and ply to up- and downriver destinations such as Meissen (one-way/return €11/17.50) and Bad Schandau in Saxon Switzerland (one-way/return €22.50/25) respectively.

2

up to five people €23. Useful transport hubs are: the Hauptbahnhof; Postplatz, just south of the Zwinger; and Albertplatz in the Neustadt. Trams #3 and #7 go from the Hauptbahnhof to the Neustadt. Maps are available at DVB info points in the Hauptbahnhof, at the top of Prager Strasse on Waisenhausstrasse, and on Scheffelgasse west of Altmarkt.

By cycle rickshaw Rickshaws tout for custom at tourist hotspots; try the Hauptbahnhof and beside the Frauenkirche (w rikschataxi-dresden.de).

By bike Bicycles are a fast way to zip around town and along the Elbe: rental (from €6/day) is available at

MietStation, with branches near the Hauptbahnhof at St Petersburger Str. 33, and near Neustadt at Conradstr. 34 (daily 9.30am–1pm; June–Sept also 5–7pm; ☎ 0351 484 343 56, w mietstation-dresden.de).

By taxi Ranks in central Dresden are outside the Hauptbahnhof. To pre-book cabs call Taxi-Dresden (☎ 0351 211 211).

By car Avis, Friedrichstr. 24 ☎ 01806 21 77 02, w avis.de; Europcar, Strehlener Str. 5 (behind Hauptbahnhof) ☎ 040 520 18 76 54, w europcar.de; Hertz, Hauptbahnhof ☎ 01806 33 35 35, w hertz.de. All rental operators also maintain a desk at the airport.

INFORMATION

Tourist offices The helpful tourist office is at Neumarkt 2, inside the QF Passage next to the Frauenkirche (Mon–Fri 10am–7pm, Sat 10am–6pm, Sun 10am–3pm; ☎ 0351 50 15 01, w dresden.de/tourism); it has a cinema with free screenings of Dresden documentaries. It also has a booth in the Hauptbahnhof (daily 8am–8pm).

Discount cards The tourist offices and many hotels sell the Dresden-City-Card (1 day €9.90, 2 day €29.90; family €13.90/54.90) which is valid for most public transport; the two-day version also offers discounted or free entry to many museums. A four-day Dresden-Regio-Card (€79.90, family €119) extends coverage to the region and provides free transport on all Elbe River ferries.

ACCOMMODATION

With Dresden's revival, the international **hotel** names have moved in, allowing Dresden to stand toe to toe with anything in other major cities; some swish options aspire to Baroque splendour if your budget extends to it. A few excellent independent **hostels** take care of the budget scene, most in the thick of the Neustadt's nightlife. Note that Dresden's **visitor's tax** (€1.30/person/day) sometimes needs to be settled separately at reception.

HOTELS AND PENSIONS
ALTSTADT
Aparthotel am Zwinger Maxstr. 3 ☎ 0351 89 90 01 00, w aparthotel-zwinger.de. Located a 10min walk behind the Zwinger and good value for its larger-than-average rooms, all furnished in IKEA-esque style – think pale wood-laminate floors and crisp white and grey fabrics. It also has several apartments for two to four people. **€98**

Art'otel Ostra-Allee 33 ☎ 0351 492 20, w artotels.de. Located about 300m behind the Zwinger and showcasing art by Dresden's A.R. Penck, this design hotel is far more neutral than the giant golden egg in its atrium suggests.

Part business hotel, it has classic-modern decor in rooms, plus efficient staff. **€84**

Cityherberge Lingnerallee 3 ☎ 0351 485 99 00, w city-herberge.de. Simple funky decor, low prices and a 5min walk from the central Altstadt – small wonder this large budget hotel in an apartment block is hugely popular. You can choose between "hostel" rooms with shared bathrooms or "hotel" en suites. **€66**

Evangelische Reformierte Gemeindehaus Brühlscher Garten 4 ☎ 0351 43 82 30, w kanonenhofkirche-dresden.de. An ecclesiastical residence that's open to all and provides perhaps the best deal in the Altstadt: hotel-standard en suites with parquet

2

flooring, modern bathrooms and a location in the heart of the Altstadt at a bargain price. Reservations on weekdays during office hours only. **€75**

Hilton An der Frauenkirche 5 ☏ 0351 864 20, ⊚ hilton .de/dresden. A five-star *Hilton*, with all the requisite international-quality service plus a dozen bars and restaurants to choose from, as well as a spa and pool, all in an excellent location just behind the Frauenkirche. Standard prices do not include breakfast. **€161**

Ibis Bastei Prager Str. 5 ☏ 0351 48 56 20 00, ⊚ ibis -dresden.de. This is one of three hotels of the modern chain housed in adjacent GDR-era towerblocks. While accommodation is functional and far from spacious, all are affordable, reasonably placed for the sights and train station, and are hardly ever full. **€85**

Steigenberger Hotel de Saxe Neumarkt 9 ☏ 0351 48 60, ⊚ steigenberger.com/dresden. No hotel in Dresden has a finer view of the Frauenkirche than this Baroque-styled place on Neumarkt. Brisk, efficient and comfortable, it has all you expect of this upmarket German chain – modern decor in inoffensive neutrals and a spa. **€206**

Taschenbergpalais Kempinski Taschenberg 3 ☏ 0351 491 20, ⊚ kempinski-dresden.de. Five-star luxury in the Baroque manor where Augustus the Strong installed his mistress, restored into an effortlessly classy number whose public areas showcase features by Zwinger architect Pöppelmann. "Kurfürsten" rooms have the best views, and prices to match. **€247**

NEUSTADT

Bülow Residenz Rähnitzgasse 19 ☏ 0351 800 32 91, ⊚ buelow-residenz.de. Still the "fine corner house with a huge entrance portal" described in 1731 when it was the residence of Augustus the Strong's master builder. Now, however, also a classy hotel with immaculate service, classic elegant style and an excellent restaurant. **€135**

Martha Nieritzstr. 11 ☏ 0351 817 60, ⊚ hotel-martha-dresden.de. Tucked away in a smart quarter of the Neustadt, equidistant between the Altstadt and nightlife, this option provides one of the most comfortable mid-range stays in Dresden – friendly and with splashes of contemporary decor to pep up its Biedermeier style. **€133**

Mezcalero Königsbrücker Str. 64 ☏ 0351 81 07 70, ⊚ mezcalero.de. Quirky Mexican-styled guesthouse with bags of character for the post-backpacker market: expect bright colour-washes, wood floors and oddities in rooms such as a basin in a plastic tree-stump. Multi-bed rooms, plus one dorm; cheaper rooms share facilities. Dorms **€17**, doubles **€52**

Motel One Palaisplatz 1 ☏ 0351 655 73 80, ⊚ motel-one.com. The Dresden outpost of the popular German chain hotel is in a modern block, and ticks all the usual boxes – relaxed designer cool in public areas and modestly hip rooms, without ever breaking the bank. It lies a 20min walk from the Altstadt. **€69**

Schloss Eckberg Bautzner Str. 134, Dresden-Loschwitz ☏ 0351 809 90, ⊚ schloss-eckberg.de; tram #11. The romance of staying in this neo-Gothic castle in its own landscaped estate above the Elbe compensates for a location 3km east of Albertplatz. Pick of the rooms are the seventeen in the castle itself – antique-furnished and with marble bathrooms. Cheaper, blander accommodation is in the modernized Kavalierhaus in the grounds. Kavalierhaus **€122**, castle **€181**

HOSTELS AND CAMPSITES

Campingplatz Mockritz Boderitzer Str. 30 ☏ 0351 471 52 50, ⊚ camping-dresden.de; bus #76 from the Hauptbahnhof. In suburbs 4km south, a 15min walk from Mockritz. Facilities include a laundry, a small shop with a bakery and a pool in summer. Also offers bike hire. Pitch **€3.50**, plus **€6** per person

Kangaroo Stop Erna-Berger-Str. 8–10 ☏ 0351 314 34 55, ⊚ kangaroo-stop.de. A functional building near the Neustadt station, with large dorms and rooms, plus apartments for up to four in an adjacent villa. A quiet side-street location and garden for barbecues and bonfires add appeal. Dorms **€12.50**, doubles **€44**, apartments **€72**

★ **Lollis Homestay** Görlitzer Str. 34 ☏ 0351 810 84 58, ⊚ lollishome.de. Welcoming, small but quirky place operated by Neustadt locals, and with a communal vibe – there's a free dinner get-together weekly – and idiosyncratic themed decor: many rooms have platform beds or giant furnishings; one has a bed in a Trabant estate. *Lollis* also produces an excellent free activities map for Dresden with tips for young travellers. Dorms **€13**, doubles **€48**

Louise 20 Louisenstr. 20 ☏ 0351 889 48 94, ⊚ louise20 .de. Sited in a courtyard just off one of the main arteries of the Neustadt bar scene, this is more budget hotel in style than other hostel options in the area. Also offers an apartment that sleeps up to eight people. Dorms **€14**, doubles **€38**

Mondpalast Louisenstr. 77 ☏ 0351 563 40 50, ⊚ mondpalast.de. Space-themed hostel in a townhouse that's in the thick of the action in the Neustadt. Modestly cool if rather cosy en-suite doubles and clean dorms with shared facilities. Check-in is at the café beneath. Dorms **€13**, doubles **€37**

EATING AND DRINKING

Dresden's post-*Wende* revival has seen the resurgence of its **restaurant** scene. In broad terms, the Altstadt is traditional, while restaurants in the Neustadt are more contemporary and international in flavour. However, Weisse Gasse in the Altstadt is a globe-trotting precinct of modern (and fairly anonymous) restaurants and cafés. **Café-culture** is particularly atmospheric on summer evenings around the floodlit Frauenkirche. No city south of Berlin compares to Dresden for **bar-hopping**, if only because Neustadt packs such variety into so small an area: from cocktail bars to *Ostalgie* dives, jazz bars to grungy rock dens all within a 20min radius. Most places close around 4am at weekends, but some operate until the last man standing. On warm summer evenings join the crowds outside at the crossing of Görlitzer and Louisenstrasse, the so-called **Assi-Eck**, to drink cheap beer purchased from the late-night shops. Alongside the riverside **beer gardens** listed (all summer only; generally May–Sept) are two in the Grosser Garten – one at the west entrance, another on the north bank of the Carolasee lake.

CAFÉS AND CHEAP EATS

ALTSTADT

Aha Kreuzstr. 7 ☎0351 496 06 71, ⊛ladencafe.de. A mellow little café above a crafts shop at the side of the Kreuzkirche with an emphasis on organic ingredients. It rustles up light dishes, many vegetarian such as the goats' cheese with figs (€12.20) – a pleasant spot for breakfast. Daily 10am–midnight.

Paulaner's Taschenberg 3 ☎0351 496 01 74, ⊛paulaners-dresden.de. Traditional dishes such as *Schweinshaxe* (€14.90) or Munich *Weisswürste* (€7) are served in this reassuringly old-fashioned outpost of the Bavarian brewery chain; dining is either in the main bar, a side-cellar area or a large terrace. Daily 11am–1am.

NEUSTADT

Bautzener Tor Hoyerswerdaer Str. 37 ☎0351 803 82 02, ⊛bautznertor.de. This microbrewery pub is the last GDR throwback in the area, both in enjoyably tatty, traditional decor and the prices of its pub grub. Though embraced by a scruffy hipster crowd, it is still far from posy. Offers brunch on Sun. Mon–Sat 5–11pm, Sun 10am–2am.

Café Kontinental Görlitzer Str. 1 ☎0351 272 17 22, ⊛cafe-europa-dresden.de. Good breakfasts, baked potatoes, ciabatta sandwiches and a short daily Mediterranean menu in a quietly cool café at the heart of the Neustadt. It morphs into a laidback bar in the evenings. Daily 9am–2am.

Curry & Co Louisenstr. 62 ☎0173 966 54 97, ⊛curryundco.com. The *Currywurst* here is served with hip style, and covered with delicious home-made sauces such as satay or honey and mustard. There are Belgian-style fries too. Mon–Wed & Sun 11am–10pm, Thurs 11am–midnight, Fri & Sat 11am–2am.

Die Pastamanufaktur An der Dreikönigskirche 9 ☎0351 323 77 99, ⊛diepastamanufaktur.de. Minimalist bistro and takeaway beloved by Dresden's style-conscious yuppies, well-priced for home-made pasta with contemporary flavours that change by the season, such as spaghetti with shrimps and ginger for €14, or rigatoni with red pesto and Parmesan for €6. Daily 10am–10pm.

Teegadrom Louisenstr. 44 ☎0351 799 27 41, ⊛teegadrom.de. For a cup of tea and a change of pace in the Neustadt wind down in this sweet little café, whose potter-owner created many of the cups and pots. It has

everything from Jenga to Monopoly Star Wars among a good selection of games. Daily 4pm–2am.

BEER GARDENS

Augustusgarten Wiesentorstr. 12, Neustadt ☎0351 802 07 74, ⊛augustusgarten.de. There's always space at this vast beer garden above the Elbe meadows, whose expanses of tables enjoy a superb view of the Altstadt opposite – a magic spot for drinking at dusk. Good prices and grilled sausages too. Mon–Fri 11am–late, Sat & Sun 10am–late.

Fährgarten Johannstadt Käthe-Kollwitz-Ufer 23b ☎0351 459 62 62, ⊛faehrgarten.de. A 30min walk east of the Altstadt along the river, this lazy-paced traditional beer garden has been a local favourite since 1925. Canopied by birch trees, it spreads alongside the Elbe and has a mellow family atmosphere – there's a playground adjacent. Daily 1pm–1am.

Purobeach Leipziger Str. 15b ☎0351 795 29 02, ⊛purobeach.de. Ibiza comes to Dresden in the form of a hip chill-out-bar-cum-club on the north bank – ideal for loafing on canopied beds by a small pool before going to attached club and lounge bar, *Pier 15*. Daily from 11am; closed in rain.

RESTAURANTS

ALTSTADT

Alte Meister Theaterplatz 1a ☎0351 481 04 26, ⊛altemeister.net. Grilled pike-perch with organic black pudding (€18) and tagliatelle with duck breast and apricots (€14) are typical of international dishes served in this classy café-restaurant behind the Zwinger. Good lunch deals and a large terrace make it especially appealing on sunny days and warm evenings. Daily 10am–1am.

Gänsedieb Weisse Gasse 1 ☎0351 485 09 05, ⊛gaensedieb.de. The sole outpost of Saxon food in the Altstadt's restaurant strip, named after the "Goose Thief" fountain opposite – fried turkey liver (€11) and goose with market vegetables (€19) are available on a long modern-German menu. Daily 11am–1am.

Italienisches Dörfchen Theaterplatz 2–3 ☎0351 49 81 60, ⊛italienisches-doerfchen.de. Three historic rooms make this place worth braving the tour groups for: there's German cuisine priced €12–23 in the *Biersaal*; a handsome café in the *Kurfürstenzimmer*; and, upstairs, Italian in *Bellotto*. All have a terrace overlooking the Elbe. Daily 10am–midnight.

2

Sophienkeller Taschenberg 3 ☎0351 49 72 60, ⊛sophienkeller-dresden.de. A touristy but fun (if you're in the mood) medieval-themed restaurant, with waitresses in period costume and suits of armour in low-lit stone cellars. The menu of dishes like roast suckling pig changes every century or so. Daily 11am–1am.

NEUSTADT

Diwan Pulsnitzer Str. 18, corner Louisenstrasse ☎0351 320 54 05, ⊛diwan-dresden.de. A friendly "restobar" serving delicious Syrian and Middle Eastern meals in various Oriental-looking rooms. There's *fattah* (chickpeas with sesame sauce and fried bread), *mutabbal* (aubergines in sesame-yoghurt sauce) and home-made *labna* (Syrian curd); it's best to ask the owner to come up with a mixed dish. Tues–Sat 6pm–midnight.

★**Lila Sosse** Alaunstr. 70 ☎0351 803 67 23, ⊛lilasosse.de. Innovative takes on classic German cooking such as sweet potatoes in green sauce (€5.50) or oxtail stew with home-made *Spätzle* (€9.50), with specials served in sweet glass jars of various sizes, all in the arty courtyard of the Kunsthofpassage – a lovely spot when candlelit in summer. Daily noon–11pm.

Planwirtschaft Louisenstr. 20 ☎0351 801 31 87, ⊛planwirtschaft.de. A cosy café, bar and restaurant with a leafy garden, where organic and mainly regionally-sourced ingredients contribute to dishes such as *Schnitzel* in bread (€6.80) or *coq au vin* (€11.80). Drop by on Sun for the excellent buffet breakfast. Mon–Thurs 5pm–1am, Fri & Sat 5pm–2am, Sun 9am–6pm.

★**Raskolnikoff** Böhmische Str. 34 ☎0351 804 57 06, ⊛raskolnikoff.de. Beloved by a thirty-something clientele, this restaurant and bar is one of the originals of the Neustadt scene, as good for cheap dishes such as lemon chicken, chalked up on a daily menu, as for its boho vibe and its garden – one of the prettiest in the area. Also good for Sun brunch. Mon–Fri 10am–2am, Sat & Sun 9am–2am.

Villandry Jordanstr. 8 ☎0351 899 67 24, ⊛villandry .de. The finest dining in Äussere Neustadt is in this laidback gastropub, with a modern Mediterranean-style menu that includes dishes such as Baltic salmon with lemongrass and pak choi, or pork steak with chorizo and polenta (both €18.50). The vibe is cool without being forced, and the courtyard is idyllic in summer. Mon–Sat 6pm–midnight.

Wenzel Prager Bierstuben Königstr. 1 ☎0351 804 20 10. Waitresses in traditional dress and sturdy dishes such as beer goulash (€10.40) and Bohemian dumplings, all washed down with foaming glasses of *Krusovice* beer – all noisy good fun in a Czech-styled traditional beer hall. Mon–Thurs & Sun 11am–10pm, Fri & Sat 11am–11pm.

BARS

ALTSTADT

Bärenzwinger Brühlscher Garten ☎0351 495 14 09, ⊛baerenzwinger.de. One of the few options for a grungy night out in the centre is this student bar and club buried into the old town walls – think table football, squishy sofas, occasional gigs and cheap beer. It is accessed from "outside" the walls. Daily 7pm–midnight.

Karl May Bar Taschenberg 3 ☎0351 491 20, ⊛kempinski.com/en/dresden/hotel-taschenbergpalais. The bar of the *Taschenberg Palais* hotel is unrivalled for sophisticated drinking, all oak panelling, red-leather banquette seats and Native American paintings after its eponymous novelist. Cocktails are acclaimed some of the best in Germany, and live jazz tinkles Fri & Sat from 9pm. Daily 6pm–2am.

Radeberger Spezialausschank Terrassenufer 1 ☎0351 484 86 60, ⊛radeberger-spezialausschank.de. Cosy panelled bar with a handsome beer garden in an unrivalled position above the river on the Brühlsche Terrasse: the *Radeberger* refers to the beer, the *Spezial* to the fact some brews are produced under licence on-site. Daily 11am–1am.

NEUSTADT

Blue Note Görlitzer Str. 2b ☎0351 801 42 75, ⊛jazzdepartment.com. Sultry jazz club in the centre of the bar district that hosts live jazz plus occasional folk and roots gigs several times a week then segues into a (very) late-night bar. Fun even for non-jazzers. Daily 8pm–5am (later at weekends).

Bottoms Up Martin-Luther-Str. 31 ☎0351 802 01 58. One of the best bars in Neustadt, with friendly service, a quaint interior with wooden furniture, decent food, a good selection of beers and a lovely summer garden. Arrive early on weekends to grab a table. Mon–Fri 5pm–5am, Sat & Sun 10am–5am.

Leonardo Rudolf-Leonard-Str. 24 ☎0351 804 22 47, ⊛leonardo-im-hecht.de. In the upcoming Hecht neighbourhood, *Leonardo* is a lively pub with a quirky collection of locals that's worth looking up for its friendly service, reasonably priced meals and weekend brunch spreads. Mon–Fri 6pm–2am, Sat & Sun 10am–2.30pm & 6pm–2am.

Ostpol Königsbrücker Str. 47 ⊛ost-pol.de. If only the prices were as retro as the decor of this hip GDR-era bar that has been funked up with period furnishings – love the vintage arcade game. *Ostalgie* hipster heaven and occasional gigs too. Daily 8pm–late.

Scheune Alaunstr. 36–40 ☎0351 802 66 19, ⊛scheune.org, ⊛scheunecafe.de. A bastion of the alternative scene that has been going strong since it appeared as a GDR youth club. Ticks all boxes: an eclectic, studenty bar and beer garden in summer, tasty Indian food in huge portions, a cinema and occasional gigs. Mon–Thurs 4pm–midnight, Fri 4pm–1am, Sat 10am–1am, Sun 10am–midnight.

NIGHTLIFE AND ENTERTAINMENT

For the latest on Dresden's **club scene**, check the free *Dresdener* magazine or get the Cybersax app for your smartphone. The nightclubs listed here are all regulars, but clubnights at *Scheune* bar (see opposite) are also worth a look. Classical music buffs are well served thanks to two world-class **symphony orchestras**, the Dresdener Philharmonie and Staatskapelle – city churches also host concerts alongside the concert halls. The tourist office ticket desk covers most events.

CLUBS

Down Town/Groove Station Katharinenstr. 11–13, Neustadt ☎ 0351 802 95 94 ☯ downtown-dresden.de, ☯ groovestation.de. Attitude-free clubbing in two studenty venues in one courtyard in the central Neustadt: in *Down Town* there's party hits, while *Groove Station* bar-club hosts studenty indie, electro, world and gigs. Down Town Fri & Sat 11pm–late; Groove Station daily 7pm–late.

Katy's Garage Alaunstr. 48, Neustadt ☎ 0351 656 77 01, ☯ katysgarage.de. A good, gritty bar-club with eclectic nights every night at low prices (or free): rock, drum'n'bass, reggae and dub, electro disco. It also hosts occasional live bands. Look for the car on the roof. Daily 8pm–late.

Strasse E Werner-Hartmann-Str. 2 ☯ strasse-e.de; tram #7 or the S-Bahn to "Industriegelände". A cultural centre in an industrial area 1km north of the Neustadt, whose eight or so clubnights cover all bases: from disco and house to the dark side of Goth. *Strassencafe* bar is a good option to start the night. Strasse E Fri & Sat 10pm–late; Strassencafe Thurs–Sun 6pm–late.

LIVE MUSIC

Alter Schlachthof Gothaer Str. 11 ☯ alter-schlachthof .de; tram #4 or #9 to "Hafenstrasse". A renovated industrial slaughterhouse west of Neustadt schedules a broad programme of jazz and rock acts.

Beatpol Altbriesnitz 2a ☎ 0351 421 03 97, ☯ beatpol .de; tram #12 from Postplatz or bus #94 and alight on Alte Meissner Landstr. just past the Aral garage, or catch a train to Dresden-Cotta. Small venue 1km southeast of the Altstadt, always worth checking out for indie-rock and alt-folk acts, and regularly featuring major-name touring international acts.

Jazzclub Tonne Königstr. 15, Neustadt ☎ 0351 802 60 17, ☯ jazzclubtonne.de. The city's tiny leading jazz venue hosts gigs several times per week and features many international acts. Look to *Blue Note* at other times (see opposite).

THEATRE, CABERET AND CLASSICAL MUSIC

Carte Blanche Priessnitzstr. 10 ☎ 0351 20 47 20, ☯ carte-blanche-dresden.de. Sequins and ostrich feathers in shamelessly glitzy *Travestie* shows. Not cheap at over €25 a ticket but all good fun. The venue has cocktail bar *Zora* to make a night of it.

Kulturpalast Altmarkt ☯ kulturpalast-dresden.de. Under renovation as this book went to press, the hulking GDR concert hall at the heart of the Altstadt will reopen in 2017 as the home of the renowned Dresdener Philharmonie.

Sächsische Staatsoper Theaterplatz 2, Altstadt ☎ 0351 491 17 05, ☯ semperoper.de. Dresden maintains its international reputation for opera in the spectacular Semperoper building. It's a world-class act, with music from the city's finest orchestras and brilliant staging in a sumptuous concert hall. Also stages some ballet.

Staatsschauspiel Dresden Ostra-Allee 3, Altstadt ☎ 0351 491 35 55, ☯ staatsschauspiel-dresden.de. The city's premier stage divides between the main venue and intimate Kleines Haus. While including works by the likes of Goethe, Schiller or Shakespeare, the repertoire is strong on modern drama.

DIRECTORY

Books and media Thalia, Altmarkt 24, stocks international press and a good choice of foreign-language titles.

Hospital Krankenhaus Dresden-Friedrichstadt, Friedrichstr. 41 ☎ 0351 48 00, ☯ khdf.de.

Laundry Waschsalon Crazy, Louisenstr. 6 (Mon–Sat 6.30am–11pm; ☯ waschladen.de); Eco-Express Sb-Waschsalon, Königbrücker Str. 2 (Mon–Sat 6am–11pm).

Post office Annenstr. 10 and Altmarktgalerie (enter from Wallstrasse).

Swimming Georg-Arnhold-Bad, Helmut-Schön-Allee 2, at the western edge of the Grosser Garten (May to mid-Sept daily 9am–10pm) has indoor and outdoor pools. Locals swim in the Elbe in summer, though avoid when polluted after heavy rain.

Around Dresden

Three destinations within 15km of Dresden have made day-trips at least since Augustus the Strong's day: two summer palaces of the absolutist Saxon Elector, **Schloss Pillnitz** and **Schloss Moritzburg**, and small town **Pirna**. Although all are accessible by public transport, other options make the getting there as enjoyable as the destination: to Schloss Pillnitz and Pirna a river cruise along the UNESCO-listed Elbe Valley; to Moritzburg a vintage steam train. The **Elberadweg cycle trail** (ⓦelberadweg.de) is another option for Schloss Pillnitz and Pirna; S-Bahn trains and ferries will transport bikes off-peak to save a return cycle-ride.

Schloss Pillnitz

Augustus the Strong conceived **Schloss Pillnitz** as a love nest in which to dally with his mistress, the Countess of Cosel, an easy 10km southeast of court. But when their affair soured, Anna Constantia got the boot and in the early 1720s Augustus turned to his favourite architect, the Zwinger's Pöppelmann, to create a Versailles-inspired retreat spiced with a pinch of Oriental mystery; this was, remember, a ruler who admired the autocratic rule (and porcelain) of Chinese emperors. The complex's first two palaces – the Wasserburg, erected on the river bank in an allusion to Venice, and the Bergpalais – appear unexpectedly exotic in such a Middle European landscape. Baroque rooflines swoop to pagoda points and beneath the lintels are fanciful (and none too accurate) Oriental scenes.

The Wasserburg and Bergpalais: the Kunstgewerbemuseum

May–Oct Tues–Sun 10am–6pm • €8 combined ticket with Schlossmuseum • ⓦ skd.museum

Lying either side of a courtyard garden, the Wasserburg and the Bergpalais now serve as a fast-forward through the decorative arts as the **Kunstgewerbemuseum**. The **Wasserburg**, open as one wing of a museum of decorative arts, struggles to conjure much majesty in fairly spartan rooms that are bare except for the odd piece of Augustus's china and furnishings such as his gilded thrones. More successful are the restored rooms of the **Bergpalais** opposite, not least the opening main hall with its whimsical Oriental imagery or the Watteau-Saal; its table set for dinner and painted with scenes of courtly love, it is the pleasure-palace explicit. Other rooms are in Classical and Biedermeier style, one commemorating the Pillnitz Fürstentreffen of 1791, a meeting of European and Russian nobility fearful the recent French Revolution might prove contagious.

The Neues Schloss: the Schlossmuseum

May–Oct Tues–Sun 10am–5pm; Nov–March Sat & Sun by tour only 11am, noon, 1pm & 2pm • €8 combined ticket with Kunstgewerbemuseum • ⓦ schlosspillnitz.de

Following a fire in 1818, the closing wing of the U-shaped palace was rebuilt to create the Neoclassical **Neues Schloss**, today open as the **Schlossmuseum**. Displays on palace history act as a prelude to a court kitchen, the domed Neoclassical Festsaal and the palace chapel, whose rich decoration by a Nazarene court painter alludes to Italian old masters but without any of their insight.

The park

Park Daily 6am–dusk • April–Oct €2 including Palmenhaus, Nov–March free **Palmenhaus** Daily: April–Oct 9am–6pm; Nov–March 10am–4pm • April–Oct included in park entry, Nov–March €2

As much of an attraction as the palace is the **park**, mostly landscaped in naturalistic style except for a labyrinth of trimmed hornbeams opposite the Neues Schloss, designed by the ill-fated countess herself. Within you'll find the Venetian-style "Triton gondola" in which Augustus's son, Augustus III, processed upriver on Dresden's Grand Canal, the Elbe. Elsewhere, there are exotics in the restored **Palmenhaus** greenhouse.

ARRIVAL AND DEPARTURE

By bus and tram Bus #83 goes close to the palace from Comeniusplatz, north of the Grosser Garten. More conveniently, tram #2 goes from the city centre to its terminus, Kleinzschachwitz, from where it's a short walk to a river ferry (one-way €1.50, return €2) across to the Schloss.

By boat Sächsische Dampfschiffahrt ferries stop at Schloss Pillnitz on their route east along the Elbe (April–Oct 4–5 daily; one-way €11, return €17.50; ⓦ saechsische-dampfschiffahrt.de). Ferries depart from Dresdener Terrassenufer beside the Augustusbrücke.

Schloss Moritzburg

Daily 10am–5.30pm • €7, combined ticket with Fasanenschlössen €9.50 • ⓦ schloss-moritzburg.de

The village of Moritzburg 15km north of Dresden is another pleasure-park of Augustus the Strong, who was never going to be content with the hunting lodge he inherited from the House of Wettin. He ordered his beleaguered architect Pöppelmann to model it into a luxury Baroque palace along the lines of a French chateau. The product is pure theatre. **Schloss Moritzburg** rises like a wedding-cake decoration above an artificial lake spanned by a grand walkway on which stone trumpeters announce visitors. While the interior, on the whole, fails to live up to the outside promise, it is hugely impressive in places like the Speisesaal (dining hall), bristling with plaster hunting trophies or the Federzimmer, where the regent slept in a bed canopied by a tapestry of over a million multicoloured feathers like a fairy-tale prince. The surrounding naturalistic **Schlosspark** is tailor-made for lazy summer days.

The Fasanenschlösschen and around

Tours (max 10 people): May–Oct Mon–Fri hourly 11am–4pm, Sat & Sun every 30min 11am–4pm • €5.50 • ⓦ schloss-moritzburg.de

Drift to the east end of the Schlosspark and you stumble upon the pink **Fasanenschlösschen**, a charmingly dumpy Rococo lodge whose roofline nods to the fashion for Chinoiserie. The "Little Pheasant Castle" offers a glimpse of a royal household in miniature with such fancies as feather wall decorations in the bedroom. Just as decadent are the lighthouse and breakwater follies in the **lake** behind, where the landlocked Saxon princes commanded cannon volleys of fireworks as miniature frigates sailed in mock sea-battles.

Käthe-Kollwitz-Haus

Meissner Str. 7 • April–Oct Mon–Fri 11am–5pm, Sat & Sun 10am–5pm; Nov–March Tues–Fri noon–4pm, Sat & Sun 11am–4pm • €4 • ⓦ kollwitz-moritzburg.de

Although stripped of royal status in constitutional reforms in 1918, the House of Wettin continued to own Schloss Moritzburg. Prince Ernst Heinrich von Sachsen sheltered graphic artist and sculptor Käthe Kollwitz in 1944 after her house in Berlin was destroyed, and the great Expressionist remained for what transpired to be her final year in lakeside **Käthe-Kollwitz-Haus**, just south of the Schloss. Its displays of her works, haunted by the death of her son in Flanders in 1914, are typically compelling.

ARRIVAL AND DEPARTURE   SCHLOSS MORITZBURG

By train More enjoyable than the bus is a journey by the Lössnitzgrundbahn vintage steam train (one-way €6.70, return €12.70; ⓦ loessnitzgrundbahn.de). At least six departures a day leave from S-Bahn station Radebeul-Ost, east of Dresden.

By bus Bus #326 (towards Radeburg) to Moritzburg departs from Dresden-Neustadt bus station.

Pirna

After the high culture of Dresden, the pretty town of **PIRNA** is small and uncomplicated, with no pretentions to greatness. Yet the two are linked: just as Canaletto captured Dresden in its glory, so did he set up his easel to capture the splendour that was eighteenth-century Pirna. The difference is that the latter retains its original core. A chequerboard of Baroque streets shaded in dusty pastels, it is at its most picturesque on the cobbled **Markt**, painted from its west end by Canaletto to best frame a stocky Renaissance Rathaus and a sharp-peaked merchant house; today named

"**Canaletto-Haus**", the latter houses the tourist office and a copy of the Italian's work. The **Stadtkirche St Marien** that rises behind the square is worth visiting for its fabulously vaulted roof and a Renaissance pulpit adorned with coquettish cherubs.

DDR Museum Pirna

Rottwerndorfer Str. 45 • April–Oct Tues–Sun 10am–6pm; Nov–March Tues–Thurs, Sat & Sun 10am–5pm • €6 • ⦿ ddr-museum-pirna.de

A former barracks on the main road 1km south of central Pirna houses the **DDR Museum Pirna**, a well-ordered museum of the GDR. The regime's fraught politics practised by Erich Honecker, familiar even to foreigners due to the iconic Berlin Wall mural of the bespectacled regime leader locked in a passionate kiss with Brezhnev, are covered. Yet it's the everyday *Ostalgie* that appeals most: a dinky Trabant car, a fully furnished mid-1970s apartment and shop shelves packed with contemporary goods.

Gross Sedlitz

Heidenau • Daily: April–Aug 8am–8pm; Sept–March 8am–dusk • €4 • ⦿ barockgarten-grosssedlitz.de

Inevitably, Augustus the Strong reaches even to sleepy Pirna. Accessed by car or a 3.5km country walk southwest of Pirna (maps from the tourist office), **Gross Sedlitz** is his most grandiose pleasure garden. In 1719, the Saxony ruler forced a count to sell his retirement home in Heidenau village in order that he might create a Saxon Versailles. A lack of funds during construction put paid to that plan, but you can glimpse what Augustus had in mind in the garden's synthesis of late-Baroque Italian and French styles whose symmetry reflects the Age of Reason. The garden opens onto an immaculate green ringed by sculpture where our hero played bowls, then sweeps down to a festive lower garden divided by channels and backed by a handsome orangerie full of Tuscan orange trees in summer months.

ARRIVAL AND INFORMATION PIRNA

By train S-Bahn lines S1 and S2 run to Pirna; the station is a 5min walk west of the Altstadt.

By boat Sächsische Dampfschiffahrt ferries stop at Pirna en route east to Bad Schandau (April–Oct 4–5 daily; one-way €12, return €18.50; ⦿ saechsische-dampfschiffahrt.de). Ferries depart from Dresdener Terrassenufer beside the Augustusbrücke.

Tourist office Am Markt 7 (Easter–Oct Mon–Fri 10am–6pm, Sat & Sun 10am–2pm; Nov–Easter Mon–Fri 10am–4pm, Sat & Sun 10am–1pm; ☏ 0351 55 64 46, ⦿ tourismus.pirna.de).

Meissen

MEISSEN's fate is to be synonymous with porcelain. All its coach-tour day-trippers make a beeline for the prestigious china factory founded by Augustus the Strong in 1710. Even if you don't visit that outlet, it's hard to escape porcelain in the town that pioneered its large-scale production outside of East Asia. Yet Meissen, 25km northwest of Dresden, is better visited for its picture-postcard medieval **Altstadt**, complete with charming cobbled streets and the **Albrechtsburg** castle and a cathedral standing proud above the River Elbe on a rocky outcrop. Though hailed as the birthplace of Saxony because it has the earliest castle in the state, Meissen never developed into a major city. Adding to its appeal as a day-trip from Dresden is that you can reach the town by steam river-cruiser as well as S-Bahn.

The lower Altstadt

After over eight centuries of pulling at the threads, Meissen has knotted its **Altstadt** into a tight bundle of cobbled lanes. With no true sights, this is a place to explore by instinct, though your starting point is likely to be the Markt at its centre. North of the Markt stretches cobbled **Bergstrasse**, the former prestige street between the Markt's civic power-base and episcopal powers above.

Markt

The pretty **Markt** is boxed in on one side by a Late-Gothic **Rathaus** with a three-piece suite of step-gabled facades. Massive carved portals on surrounding houses that jostle for space are worth a look: the Markt Apotheke at no. 9 has a Renaissance tympanum of Icarus above a walled medieval Meissen on the Elbe.

The back of the square is framed by the **Frauenkirche** with the world's earliest carillon of what else but Meissen-china bells (played at 6.30am, 8.30am, 11.30am, 2.30pm, 5.30pm & 8.30pm). Within, beneath Gothic vaults is a gilded medieval altar, and you can ascend the tower (Easter–Oct daily 10am–4pm; €2).

Heinrichsplatz

East of the Markt is **Heinrichsplatz** with a statue of Heinrich I who founded the first castle on the Albrechtsburg in 929 AD; they say he earned his nickname "der Vogler" ("the fowler") because he was bird-catching when confirmed as Germany's first king. Also on the square is an erstwhile Gothic Franciscan monastery housing the **Stadtmuseum** (Tues–Sun 10am–6pm; €3), which provides a quick resumé of what makes Meissen tick; a colossal red wine press (1788), said to be the largest of its type in Germany, catches the eye.

The Albrechtsburg

Domplatz 1 · Daily: March–Oct 10am–6pm; Nov–Feb 10am–5pm · €8 · Ⓦ albrechtsburg-meissen.de

Climb several steep staircases from the end of Burgstrasse to enter the courtyard where Meissen made its debut a thousand years ago as Heinrich I's "Misni" castle, located on a defensive bluff above the Elbe. The current castle, the **Albrechtsburg**, Germany's first residential palace, is a late fifteenth-century replacement that dithers between stronghold and palace – slab sides that rise sheer from the rock outcrop seem at odds with prestige windows like drawn theatrical curtains. As good a reason to ascend is for the **views** across the river from a terrace beside the Dom, or over the Altstadt from several cafés.

The palace was commissioned as a symbol of Saxon power by two prince electors of the House of Wettin, Ernst and Albrecht. Unfortunately, the duo squabbled, work halted and by the time the palace was finished in 1520, the court had decamped to Dresden. It was then largely abandoned for two centuries until the ubiquitous Augustus the Strong installed within it Europe's first **porcelain manufacturer** in 1710. And what a factory: at the front is a French-styled octagonal Renaissance tower embedded with Old Testament imagery. A museum within tells a tale of the castle's past, though most impressive is the building itself. The staircase of the Renaissance tower is one highlight of an interior notable for eccentric stellar vaulting like a Cubist's take on Gothic. As impressive are halls revamped after the china factory moved to its current premises (see p.152) in 1864. It's a typically overenthusiastic interpretation of medieval roots, with murals of the Wettin rulers seemingly lifted from a *Boy's Own* adventure – all good fun.

The Dom

Domplatz · **Dom** Daily: April–Oct 9am–6pm; Nov–March 10am–4pm · €4 · **Tower** Tours hourly April–Oct daily 1–4pm · €6 · Ⓦ dom-zu-meissen.de

Arnold von Westfalen, the sixteenth-century architect who completed the Albrechtsburg, also tinkered with the **Dom**, which merges into the Albrechtsburg to update an early medieval structure into High Gothic – the landmark lattice spires were added in the early 1900s. The finest artwork is in the Fürstenkapelle, tacked onto the end of the nave as a mausoleum for the Wettin household, so protecting the original carved portal. German Renaissance heroes Cranach and especially Dürer are the

2

influences for the ducal bronzes set into the floor, the latter especially evident in that of Duke George the Bearded in a side chapel. Italian artists added the enchanting Renaissance stucco in the 1670s. Other artwork of note is the rood screen and astonishingly advanced statues of Emperor Otto I and his wife Adelheid in the nave, both sculpted by Naumberg masters (c.1260). Inevitably, the Baroque crucifix is of local porcelain, created by court master-artist Johann Joachim Kaendler.

The Porzellan-Manufaktur
Talstr. 1, 1.5km southwest of the centre • Tours (30min) daily: May–Oct 9am–6pm; Nov–April till 5pm; English audio-guides available • €9 • ⓦmeissen.de

The number-one destination of every tour group to Meissen is the **Porzellan-Manufaktur museum**, a twenty-minute walk southwest of the Altstadt; arrive early or at lunchtime to escape the worst of the crush. Augustus the Strong's china obsession is a tale of its own, the result of incarcerating alchemist Johann Friedrich Böttger in his mightiest stronghold, the Königstein (see p.156). While Dresden china – the first manufactured west of Asia – reflected the regent's aspirations to the omnipotence of Oriental emperors, it was also intended to fill coffers: "my golden pheasant", as Augustus put it. The formula of Meissen china, branded by blue crossed swords, remains secret.

Tours take in a demonstration workshop of the four stages of hand-produced manufacture and the Schauhalle, whose three thousand items span three centuries of manufacture in Meissen. Court artist Johann Joachim Kaendler stars, not least for the display's highlight, a 3.5m-high table decoration that graced the dining table of Augustus III. An on-site **factory outlet** (free) stocks more china than a bull could smash – from the usual coquettish dolls and tea sets, to contemporary streamlined pieces influenced by Japan.

The Nikolaikirche
Neumarkt 29 • May–Sept daily 10am–5pm • Free • ⓦsankt-afra-meissen.de

From the Porzellan-Manufaktur, a short walk back up Talstrasse then right on Kerstingstrasse brings you to the **Nikolaikirche**, an intimate church that takes Meissen's porcelain obsession to new heights. The largest Meissen-china figures ever cast, 2.5m-high, flank the altar of a church completely clad in china as a memorial to the dead of World War I.

ARRIVAL AND INFORMATION   MEISSEN

By train The Bahnhof, served by regional trains and frequent S-Bahn S1 from Dresden, is on the east bank of the Elbe; a second Bahnhof, Meissen-Triebischtal, is on the west bank near the porcelain factory. A footbridge from the main Bahnhof and road bridge Altstadtbrücke link the modern east-bank city to the Altstadt opposite. The Altstadtbrücke funnels you directly towards the Markt.

By boat Steamers of the Dresden ferry line Sächsische Dampfschiffahrt make two trips a day in summer (April–Oct 2 daily; one-way €13.50, return €17.50;

ⓦsaechsische-dampfschiffahrt.de). Ferries depart from Dresdener Terrassenufer beside the Augustusbrücke.
Tourist office Markt 3 (April–Oct Mon–Fri 10am–6pm, Sat & Sun 10am–4pm; Nov–March Mon–Fri 10am–5pm, Sat 10am–3pm; closed Sat in Jan; ☏03521 419 40, ⓦtouristinfo-meissen.de).

ACCOMMODATION

Meissen is an easy day-trip from Dresden – it looks its best on summer evenings and the S-Bahn permits late-night returns until long after the town has gone to bed. However, there's some appealing **accommodation** to choose from should you want to stay.

Burgkeller Domplatz 11 ☏03521 414 00, ⓦhotel-burgkeller-meissen.de. The smartest address in the old town is all about old-world elegance and a location overlooking the Altstadt from above; balcony rooms are worth the extra €10. The café/beer garden and restaurant boast the same views of the Altstadt's roofscape. **€160**

★**Fuchshöhl** Hohlweg 7 ☏03521 833 99 77, ⓦfuchshoehl.de. A 500-year-old townhouse at the top of Burgstrasse renovated into a small fairy-tale-themed pension and furnished with bags of personality by its artist owner. Tasteful rooms – four with kitchenettes – are individually styled, with a dash of artistic flair and the occasional antique. A bargain. **€56**

Goldener Löwe Heinrichsplatz 6 ☏03521 11 10, ⓦgoldener-loewe-meissen.com. Though it lacks the prestige and views, this is nonetheless a good option if the *Burgkeller* is full. A small pleasant hotel, it is sited just off the Markt and has a calm bygone ambience and antiques in some rooms. **€50**

Herberge Orange Siebeneichener Str. 34 ☏03521 45 43 34, ⓦherberge-orange.de. Small, private hostel with ten rooms that overlooks the river – and rents sit-on kayaks to guests. It's located at the town boundaries a 20min walk south of the Altstadt; call to confirm the owners are around first. Dorms **€15**, doubles **€44**

Welcome Parkhotel Meissen Hafenstr. 27–31 ☏03521 722 50, ⓦwelcome-hotels.com. A 4-star chain hotel split between a villa and two annexe blocks, among gardens on the Elbe's north bank. The Jugendstil villa at its core seems to have rubbed off on the decor, which has more character than the usual business chain. **€130**

EATING AND DRINKING

There are two must-dos when it comes to eating and drinking in Meissen. First is sampling **Meissner Fummel**, a slightly sweet inflated pastry that looks like a puff-pastry egg. It is notoriously fragile: local legend says Augustus the Strong invented it for his court messengers to carry to Dresden – only if it was intact could he be sure they had not been at the **local wines** (see box opposite), the second must-do of Meissen.

Am Hundewinkel Görnische Gasse 40 ☏03521 71 78 64. Tasty modern German cooking at good prices – expect the likes of pork medallions with asparagus risotto – plus friendly service and a sun-trap terrace make this place off the Markt a fine option. Wed–Sun 11.30am–2pm & 5.30–10pm.

Café Zieger Rote Stufen 2 ☏03521 45 31 47. Defiantly traditional *Konditorei* on a quiet square at the top of Burgstrasse that has been a fixture for over 150 years – the best place to sample *Meissner Fummel* assuming you don't succumb first to a menu of gateaux and fruit tarts. Mon–Sat 11am–6pm.

Domkeller Domplatz 9 ☏0352145 76 76, ⓦdomkeller-meissen.com. The oldest restaurant in Meissen prepares a good-value traditional menu – there are favourites such as home-made beef roulade with potato dumplings or goulash in beer – and has views over the Altstadt from two terraces. Daily 11am–midnight.

Vincenz Richter An den Frauenkirche 12 ☏03521 45 32 85, ⓦvincenz-richter.de. Beside the Frauenkirche and a mite touristy, this *Weinhaus* from 1523 is a charming option nevertheless, with a choice between snug rooms and a lovely terrace. Local produce features on the traditional menu, with mains priced €15–24. Tues–Sat noon–midnight, Sun noon–6pm.

Saxon Switzerland

The area from Pirna, 18km east of Dresden, to the Czech border is commonly known as **Saxon Switzerland** (Sächsische Schweiz), but that was always a conceit of the Romantics. This is classic Middle Europe – 275 square kilometres of rolling fields through which the Elbe River carves a broad steep valley, much of it protected as a national park. What comes closer to the nub of some of the most distinctive scenery in Germany is the area's second title, **Elbsandsteingebirge** (Elbe Sandstone Mountains):

2

HIKING AND OTHER ACTIVITIES IN SAXON SWITZERLAND

Day-hikes are numerous throughout the area: routes with sketch maps are printed in the free promotional booklet *Erlebnis-Kompass*, a useful area overview of basic walks around villages, available from tourist offices. From Königstein you can ascend to two plateaus or embark on a four- to five-hour hike up to the Bastei. The best base for day-walks, however, is Bad Schandau, with the Schrammsteine's fissured labyrinth in its backyard.

Long-distance route the **Malerweg** (Ⓦmalerweg.de) is one of Germany's most beautiful walks. Regardless of whether the 112km trail, marked with a brush-stroke "M", truly tracks the route taken by Romantic painters, the circuit from Pirna offers a loop around major sights and remote landscapes on both sides of the Elbe – all in all highly recommended. Most walkers average 15km a day (approx 5hr) on an eight-day circuit, but you could cut out two by starting at Stadt Wehlen, the start of the best scenery. Area tourist offices stock a booklet of the trail with lists of accommodation en route.

ROCK CLIMBING

Sandstone pinnacles make Saxon Switzerland hallowed ground among German **rock-climbers**. There are 1100 official climbing rocks, and over 11,000 routes, most in the Schrammsteine. Bergsport Arnold at Marktstr. 4 in Bad Schandau (Ⓦbergsport-arnold.de) has a respectable stock of climbing gear and guidebooks – staff are a good source of advice, too.

CYCLING

The long-distance **cycle** route Elberadweg (Ⓦelberadweg.de), mainly along the south bank, but crisscrossing the river to avoid busy roads, is a superb option for touring. The tourist office in Bad Schandau rents bikes.

ACTIVITY TOURS

Among the many operators offering activity tours or rental in the area are:

Elbsandstein Reisen Through Bad Schandau tourist office ☎ 035022 900 31, Ⓦbad-schandau.de. Climbing and walking tours in the superb Schrammsteine area above Bad Schandau; from one-day excursions (from €50 per person) to five-day walking and multi-activity weeks (from €220, includes accommodation).
Hobbit Hikes Fichtenstr. 1, Dresden ☎ 0173 380 06 75, Ⓦhobbit-hikes.de. Backpacker-friendly Dresden

outfit that provides bespoke tours priced by group size, including short 4hr fixed-rope trips on exposed ridges and sections of the Malerweg.
Kanu Aktiv Tours Schandauerstr. 17–19, Königstein ☎ 035021 59 99 60, Ⓦkanu-aktiv-tours .de. One of the area's leading rental outfits for canoes, kayaks and rubber dinghies. Transfers are possible for a modest fee should you only want to paddle one-way.

table-topped outcrops rise suddenly above the fields like miniature mesas, their summits sculpted over the aeons into fantastical pinnacles.

With a maze of gorges to explore and iron ladders that ascend sheer faces, this is superb **hiking** country, notably on the long-distance **Malerweg** (Painters' Way) track, if you have a week to spare. Indeed, the story goes that the area's name stuck after eighteenth-century Swiss artists Adrian Zingg and Anton Graff wrote postcards home from a walking holiday saying, "Greetings from Saxon Switzerland". Later hikers included Caspar David Friedrich, who added the picture to the postcard with works such as *Rambler Above a Sea of Fog*. **Rock climbing** is also excellent. At a push you could tick off the main sights on a long, rushed day-trip from Dresden – the **Bastei** area, then a brisk walk that skirts around the Lilienstein outcrop to **Königstein**, for example. However, these are landscapes to savour and are at their best away from the premier sights; set aside a couple of days at least.

ARRIVAL AND GETTING AROUND   SAXON SWITZERLAND

By train The S1 train from Dresden (and Meissen) tracks along the south bank of the river to Rathen, Königstein, Bad Schandau and Schmilka approximately every 30min; frequent passenger (and bike) ferries from each village ply

to north-bank destinations.
By boat An appealing way to access the area is on steam-cruisers of Dresden ferry line Sächsische Dampfschiffahrt, which run from Dresden to Bad Schandau via all

destinations en route (3 daily; 5hr 30min; one-way €22.50, return €25; @ saechsische-dampfschiffahrt.de).

By bus From late April to Oct, a bus service, Sächsisch-Böhmischen-Nationalpark-Express, shuttles from the Bastei to Königstein via Hohnstein and Bad Schandau, easing the logistics of a whistle-stop day-trip (late April–Oct 4–5 daily 9.40am–4.35pm; ☎ 035021 990 80, @ frank-nuhn-freizeit-und-tourismus.de).

By car Be aware if driving that the only traffic bridges are at Pirna and 2km west of Bad Schandau.

INFORMATION

Tourist offices Tourist offices at Rathen (see below), Königstein (see p.157) and Bad Schandau (see p.158) stock brochures and maps for walking. The NationalparkZentrum – the official national park centre – is at Bad Schandau.

Website There's information on the national park website @ nationalpark-saechsische-schweiz.de.

Maps There's a general 1:25,000 *Topographische Wanderkarte der Nationalparkregionen in der Sächsische-Böhmische Schweiz* or smaller area maps. In the region, they are best sourced in Bad Schandau at either the tourist office, the NationalparkZentrum or Bergsport Arnold, at Marktstr. 4 (@ bergsport-arnold.de).

The Bastei and around

Without question, the premier tourist destination in Saxon Switzerland is the **BASTEI**. Out of a pleasant pastoral landscape of rape fields springs a fortress of fantastical sandstone pillars that tower over 300m-high above the pine forests. Almost as impressive as this natural double-take – one of Germany's most distinctive landscapes – is a panorama that sweeps over a meander in the mighty Elbe and south to the table-top slabs of Lilienstein and Pfaffenstein, and the walls of the mighty Königstein (see p.156).

The Felsenburg and Basteibrücke

Felsenburg daily 9am–6pm • €1.50

The name Bastei refers to the thirteenth-century **Felsenburg** fortress, whose remnants are wedged among outcrops linked by wooden gangways. Signs point out carved stairways or the massive cistern at the core, but you'll need imagination or a peruse of a model of the castle as it looked around 1400 displayed at the centre – where a massive cistern is hewed out of the rock – to make sense of what was a medieval city in the sky. The staggering views make the spot insanely popular – visit early to appreciate the grandeur of a site that can be obscured by mass-tourism hell. As much of an attraction is the **Basteibrücke** that leapfrogs to the fortress on sheer outcrops – the picture-postcard view is from a lookout point reached via a path left before the bridge. Graffiti midway across reveals that tourists have visited since at least 1706.

Hohnstein

To make a day of it, you could walk to **HOHNSTEIN** 5km north of the Bastei, a photogenic village whose layers of half-timbering and crumbling houses fold down a hillside. It has its own castle, **Burg Hohnstein** (May–Oct daily 10am–5pm; €1.60; @ hohnstein.de), albeit fairly tatty after heavy-handed restoration following its use as a POW camp, but with good views. The village is accessed on the Knotenweg path (marked by a green stripe) from the Bastei.

ARRIVAL AND INFORMATION   THE BASTEI AND AROUND

By car In peak season, the inner car park is often full by mid-morning, so you have to park by the turn-off 2.5km from the site, then walk or catch the Bastei-Panorama-Express bus (€1.50 return).

By public transport Notwithstanding the tourist buses (see above) or bus #247 from Pirna (p.149), access by public transport is by S-Bahn to sleepy riverside resort Rathen; a rope-ferry links the Bahnhof to the north bank, from where it's a 30min ascent to the Bastei. Alternatively, get off the S-Bahn a stop earlier at Stadt Wehlen, cross the river on a foot-passenger ferry and follow the Malerweg footpath to the Bastei (2hr).

Tourist office In Rathen, in the Haus des Gastes at Füllhölzelweg 1 (Easter–Oct Mon–Fri 9am–noon & 1–6pm, Sat & Sun 9am–2pm; Nov–Easter Mon, Wed & Thurs 10am–noon & 1–3pm, Tues 10am–noon & 1–6pm, Fri 10am–2pm; ☎ 035024 704 22, @ kurort-rathen.de).

2

2

ACCOMMODATION AND EATING

THE BASTEI AND RATHEN

Berghotel At Bastei Bastei ☎ 035024 77 90, ⓦ basteiberghotel.de. The natural glory of the Bastei is marred somewhat by the clunking late-1970s architecture of this hotel at the site, although refurbishment has modernized its interior and added a sauna. Its affiliated restaurant, *Panorama*, makes up for so-so food and mass tourism with superb views. **€116**

Burg Altrathen Am Grünbach 10–11, Rathen ☎ 035024 76 00, ⓦ rathen-urlaub.de. A good choice below the Bastei is hillside *Burg Altrathen*, a hotel and pension romantically sited among the ruins of a medieval castle, with simple rooms of pine furnishings. **€80**

Elbschlösschen Kottesteig 5, Rathen ☎ 035024 750, ⓦ hotelelbschloesschen.de. The premier hotel in Rathen, this is a medium-sized resort number, with all the usual mod cons in its 4-star rooms, the best of which have balconies above the river. Facilities include a pool, spa and beauty salon. **€79**

HOHNSTEIN AND AROUND

Burg Hohnstein Markt 1 ☎ 035975 812 02, ⓦ burg-hohnstein.info. The castle has above-average hostel accommodation divided into en-suite rooms in the lower castle and a youth hostel with shared bathrooms. It promotes itself as a motorbikers' hostel, so expect male groups. Dorms **€28**, doubles **€76**

Luk Basteiweg 12, Rathewalde, 2km west of Hohnstein ☎ 035975 800 13, ⓦ luk-landhotel.de. Utter escapism in the most relaxing address in the area, less a hotel than a homestay in a pretty village, where the owners live in an adjacent house. All the pastel rooms have a balcony overlooking the garden. **€79**

★Zum Schwarzbachtal Niederdorfstr. 3, Lohsdorf, 7km east of Hohnstein ☎ 035975 803 45, ⓦ schwarzbachtal.de. En route to Sebnitz, this restaurant is a gem whose rustic charm belies the seasonal slow food of chef Barbara Siebert. Expect the likes of rump steak with a blue cheese sauce or lasagne with chanterelles and tomato, prepared from whatever ingredients are freshest, with mains between €13 and €19. Also rents four lovely cottagey rooms. Restaurant Mon–Wed & Fri 5–11pm, Sat & Sun noon–11pm. **€75**

Königstein and around

Around an S-bend meander of the Elbe, **KÖNIGSTEIN** is the next stop east from Rathen. An anonymous oversized village, it vies with the Bastei in popularity because of Festung Königstein, one of the largest hilltop fortifications in Europe, perched 240m above the Elbe on a sandstone plateau.

Festung Königstein

Daily: April–Oct 9am–6pm; Nov–March 9am–5pm • €8, Nov–March €7, includes lift • ⓦ festung-koenigstein.de

Began as a thirteenth-century fortress, **Festung Königstein** was beefed up by successive rulers into a mighty citadel. Potential enemies took one look at its eyrie – its massive walls that grew from the rock up to 42m high – and dismissed it as impregnable. No raid was even attempted. The result is an architectural encyclopedia of military thinking up to the Napoleonic era scattered across the plateau. A highlight of the thirty buildings, many with displays of weaponry, is a 152m-deep well ordered by Augustus the Strong. Without an offensive role, the citadel served as a refuge for Saxony rulers and, from 1591 as the most secure prison in the state, the **Georgenburg**. An ambitious 19-year-old apothecary apprentice, **Johann Friedrich Böttger**, found himself inside after he promised Augustus he could alchemize gold. He failed, of course, but, nudged towards achievable goals by court scholar Ehrenfried Walter von Tschirnhaus, magicked instead "white gold" – the first porcelain in Europe. Other names behind the Georgenburg's bars include nineteenth-century social democrat August Bebel. In World War II it served as a POW camp and storehouse for Dresden's art. More than exhibits, however, it's the views that impress.

The Lilienstein and Pfaffenstein

Both the **Lilienstein** (415m) and **Pfaffenstein** (434m) plateaus, north and south of the Festung Königstein respectively, are accessible on marked **trails** from Königstein village: they say Augustus the Strong hacked out the path to the Lilienstein (5km; 2hr) in 1708, while the fissured plateau of the Pfaffenstein (8km; 3hr), the highest in the region, is beloved by rock-climbers for the landmark 43m Barbarine column on its south side. Pick up sketch maps from the tourist office.

By train S-Bahn trains leave you a 10min walk east of the centre of Königstein village. To the fortress, it's a tough 30min walk west or a short trip on the free Festung-Express bus from the centre (April–Oct daily; 4–5 per day).

By car The fortress is signposted off the main road west of the village. Tourist trains (€2.50 one-way/€4 return) depart from the site car park if you can't face the 20min ascent on foot.

Municipal tourist office By the church at Schreiberberg 2 (May–Oct Mon–Fri 9am–6pm, Sat 9am–noon, Sun 10am–1pm; Nov–April Mon–Fri 9am–5.30pm, Sat 9–10.30am; ☎ 03521 682 61, ⓦ koenigstein-sachsen.de).

Private tourist office Zentrale Tourist-Info is in the village centre at Bahnhofstr. 1 (Mon, Tues & Fri–Sun 9am–4pm; ☎ 035021 59 96 99, ⓦ tourismusverein-elbsandsteingebirge .de).

ACCOMMODATION

Camping Königstein ☎ 035021 882 24, ⓦ camping-koenigstein.de. The campsite occupies a pleasant spot directly beside the river 500m beyond the centre; turn left if coming from the Bahnhof. Negatives are its popularity and the train line which runs behind the site until evening. Closed Nov–March. Pitch €4, plus €5.50 per person

Ferdinands Homestay ☎ 035022 547 75, ⓦ ferdinandshomestay.de. On the north bank of the Elbe, this hostel is ideal as a walkers' base or simply as a place to kick back – the ideal Dresden retreat. It also has the most tranquil campsite in the area. It's tricky to find, so check the website first if driving; the owners operate a shuttle from a wooden pavilion 100m from the jetty (free

noon & 6pm, otherwise €3; free calls from *Gästhof Müller*). Closed Nov–March. Dorms €15, doubles €41.50

Lindenhof Gohrischer Str. 10 ☎ 035021 682 43, ⓦ lindenhof-koenigstein.de. Something of a mid-80s timewarp with a decor scheme of pink and grey, and dark wood flashed with gilt, yet a passable option with river views from its hillside location 400m beyond the village centre. €76

Rock Hostel Schandauer Str. 36 ☎ 035021 596 16, ⓦ rock-hostel.de. A small family- and group-friendly hostel, created in the former national park headquarters. Five modern rooms and a nice communal area, plus table tennis. It's around 1km east of the centre. Dorms €19, doubles €38

Bad Schandau and around

A comprehensive tourism infrastructure makes pocket-sized **BAD SCHANDAU**, 5km east of Königstein, the best base in Saxon Switzerland. An injection of capital after GDR doldrums has helped revive this late nineteenth-century spa resort, and there's good walking in its backyard. A **museum** (May–Oct Tues–Fri 2–5pm, Sat & Sun 10am–5pm; Nov–April Tues–Sun 2pm–5pm; €3) on the east side of the central **Kurpark** documents the resort's history and Elbe shipping.

The Personenaufzug

Daily: April & Oct 9am–6pm; May–Sept 9am–8pm; Nov–March 9am–5pm • €1.80 one-way, €2.80 return

The main attraction of Bad Schandau was traditionally the **Personenaufzug** lift, a 1904-vintage tower which whisked spa-goers up to a viewing platform atop the rocks at 50m. The lift still operates today, and even without the appeal of river views, it remains a good starting point for forest walks; at the top there's also an enclosure for lynx.

The Schrammsteine

The obvious goal for a walk hereabouts (an hour east from Personenaufzug viewpoint) is the **Schrammsteinaussicht** viewpoint that looks across to the **Schrammsteine** area, the region's largest stretch of fissured upland, incorporating the bulk of the national park area – its labyrinth of columns attracts rock-climbers (see box, p.154). From the viewpoint it's worth picking up the spectacular **Gratweg trail**, which clings to a ridge in a route that offers scenery similar to the Bastei but without any of its crowds; pick up maps from the tourist office to make a day-hike circuit.

For shorter hikes take the historic tram, the **1898 Kirnitzschtalbahn** (April–Oct every 30min until 8.15pm; Nov–March hourly; one-way €5, day-ticket €8), which departs from the west side of the Kurpark and rumbles up through a wooded canyon to upper terminus, **Lichtenhainer Wasserfall**, 7km northeast, from where it's an easy walk to the eponymous waterfall and the Kuhstall (Cow Stall) rock arch. For tougher hikes, you could alight one stop before at **Beuthenfall** to access the Schrammsteine: up to viewpoints at Carolafelsen (459m) or Frienstein (455m), both around two and a half hours each way; or for a serious day-hike over the Alfensteine plateau, then down the thrilling Heilige Stiege (Holy Steps) – rungs hammered into the rock – to riverside village Schmilka on the Czech border, from where you can either catch the S-Bahn or a ferry back to Bad Schandau.

By car, **Ostrau village** offers the most direct access to the Schrammsteine trails. Maps are essential and it's worth seeking up-to-date advice from the NationalparkZentrum (see below).

Hinterhermsdorf

The end of the road 10km beyond Lichtenhainer Wasserfall is **HINTERHERMSDORF**, a farming village and base for walking trails among rolling hills. Nearby in the Kirnitzsch Valley (Kirnitzschtal) you can take an enchanting twenty-minute **river trip** (Easter–Oct daily 9.30am–4.30pm; €4 one-way, €6 return; ⊕hinterhermsdorf.de/obere-schleuse. html), in which you are paddled in a shallow-draft canoe through a wild river gorge clad in pines once harvested by loggers – an idyllic excursion that feels another world to the tourist mills elsewhere. The embarkation point is at Obere Schleuse, a thirty-minute signposted walk from a car park.

ARRIVAL AND INFORMATION

By train Bad Schandau's Bahnhof is on the opposite side of the Elbe; frequent ferries and buses cross to the town centre.

By bus Bus #241 links Bad Schandau and Hinterhermsdorf (6 daily; 50min).

Tourist office Markt 12 (April & Oct daily 9am–6pm; May–Sept daily 9am–9pm; Nov–March Mon–Fri 9am–6pm, Sat & Sun 9am–1pm, Jan & Feb closed Wed; ☏035022 900 30, ⊛bad-schandau.de). Also in the Bahnhof (April & Oct Mon–Fri 8am–5pm, Sat & Sun 9am–noon; May–Sept Mon–Sat

BAD SCHANDAU AND AROUND

8am–5pm, Sat & Sun 9am–4pm; Nov–March Mon–Fri 8am–5pm, Sat 9am–noon, Jan & Feb closed Wed; ☏035022 412 47). Also offers bike rental.

NationalparkZentrum Sächsische Schweiz Dresdner Str. 2b (April–Oct daily 9am–6pm; Nov, Dec, Feb & March Tues–Sun 9am–5pm; closed Jan; €4; ⊛lanu.de). A useful first stop in the area is the national park information centre west of the Markt, with enlightening displays on the area's distinctive geology and fauna. It's just as useful for the enthusiastic staff and a good stock of maps in its shop.

ACCOMMODATION AND EATING

Campingplatz Ostrauer Mühle 3km northwest of Bad Schandau on Hinterhermsdorf road ☏035022 727 42, ⊛ostrauer-muehle.de. Camping on a bend in the pine-wooded valley at Ostrauer Mühle, a stop on the Kirnitzschtalbahn. A popular walkers' base, it also has hikers bunks and budget rooms in a guesthouse. Dorms €10, doubles €65, pitch €4, plus €5.25 per person

Elbresidenz Markt 1–11 ☏0350 91 90, ⊛elbresidenz-bad-schandau.de. The premier hotel in the area is this luxurious pile, which provides stylish contemporary rooms that overlook the Markt or the river, plus a beauty spa. Its two restaurants offer hugely contrasting experiences: *Sendig* is a sophisticated address serving Michelin-starred international cuisine;

Elbeterrasse rustles up modern takes on Saxony classics like *Sauerbraten*, and is a great option on sunny days due to its raised terrace beside the river. Sendig Tues–Sat from 6pm; Elbeterrasse 11am–midnight. **€150**

Lindenhof Rudolf-Sendig-Str. 11 ☏035022 48 90, ⊛lindenhof-bad-schandau.de. This nineteenth-century spa hotel offers standard doubles – rather snug under the mansard roof – and superior rooms, which for an extra €10 provide more height and a balcony over the Kurpark. **€92**

Zum Rotes Haus Marktstr. 10 ☏035022 423 43, ⊛hotel-zum-roten-haus.de. Fairly frumpy but a passable budget option in a central half-timbered *Gaststätte* that offers good-value half-pension deals. Bland classic-modern decor in rooms, all of which are en suite. **€70**

Bautzen

BAUTZEN, 60km east of Dresden, is the capital of the **Sorbs**, Germany's only indigenous minority (see box, p.125); they're derived from the Slavic Wends who migrated west

RIGHT BASTEIBRÜCKE, SAXON SWITZERLAND (P.155) >

around fifteen hundred years ago. Apart from the thrill of exotic street-names and the occasional museum, however, you'd be hard pushed to know, unless your visit coincides with a Sorb weekend market five weeks before Easter or an Easter Sunday festival. Only five percent of the local population are native Sorb – the Czech-influenced dialect is heard more commonly in villages north, linked by a cycle route.

Instead, what defines Bautzen, a settlement that is a thousand years old, is its historic Altstadt – a maze-like kernel guarded by seventeen medieval bastions that march above a river valley. The Spree River flows north to second Sorb stronghold, Spreewald (see p.125).

Kornmarkt and around

As good a place to start as any is the viewing platform of the cylindrical **Reichenturm** (April–Oct 10am–5pm; €2), which watches over the eastern Altstadt like a Baroque lighthouse. Built for town defence in 1492, it assumed its 1.44m lean from the vertical within four decades – operations to shore up the tower in 1948 revealed that the foundations were only 80cm deep. The **Stadtmuseum** in an adjacent grand building at Kornmarkt 1 (Tues–Sun: April–Sept 10am–5pm; Oct–March 10am–6pm; €3.50; ⓦmuseum-bautzen.de) provides a Bautzen primer on three floors, organized into region, town and art.

The Hauptmarkt and around

Pedestrian high-street Reichenstrasse leads from the Reichenturm to **Hauptmarkt**, enclosed by colourful Baroque townhouses and a two-tiered **Rathaus** crowned by a tower. Its most handsome facade is that on Fleischmarkt behind, where you'll also find the Dom. A couple of **Sorb gift shops** are located near the Dom: Lausitzer Töpferwaren, behind the Dom at An der Fleischbänken 4, sells Sorb folk crafts, including traditional blue-and-white pottery and charming painted Easter eggs; Bautz'ner Senfladen at Fleischmarkt 5 specializes in mustard – a staple of Sorb cuisine.

Dom St Petri

Fleischmarkt • **Dom St Petri tower** Easter–Christmas Sat & Sun 1–6pm • €2 • **Domschatzkammer** Mon–Fri 10am–noon & 1–4pm • Free

The **Dom St Petri**, an otherwise plain cathedral, is notable for several quirks. The nave of the hall bends away to the right, presumably a ruse to squeeze extra length onto the plot. The Dom is also East Germany's only dual-denomination church. Because Catholics and Protestants agreed to share the cathedral when the Reformation rolled east from Thuringia, the nave divides halfway: at the back is the restrained church of Protestantism; in front Catholics celebrate the divine through decorative excess. **Tower** tours are conducted by the couple who live halfway up it; visitors pass through their apartment en route.

A Baroque gateway on which God and Jesus pose casually on a globe fronts the **Domstift**, a U-shaped residence of the cathedral dean. The building houses cathedral treasures in the **Domschatzkammer**.

The Nikolaiturm and Nikolaikirche

West of the Domstift (left from the gate) are cobbled lanes that are Bautzen at its most charming. The area's thoroughfare is Schlossstrasse, main street of the medieval Altstadt. At its top is the **Nikolaiturm** defence tower – they say the bust depicts a town clerk who attempted to betray the city to Hussites – and the entrance to the shell of the **Nikolaikirche**. A romantic ruin since it was shattered by cannonballs in the Thirty Years' War, it has a cemetery and an idyllic setting above the river; for the photo-album shot ascend to a viewpoint opposite via a path beyond the Nikolaiturm.

The Schloss Ortenburg and Sorbisches Museum

Ortenburg 3 • Museum April–Oct Mon–Fri 10am–5pm, Sat & Sun 10am–6pm; Nov–March closes 1hr earlier • €5 • ⓦ museum.sorben.com

Schlossstrasse ends at **Schloss Ortenburg**, sited at the northeast tip of the Altstadt where Bautzen made its debut as a border-fortress c.600 AD. While the current Renaissance-styled model dates from the 1640s, it retains the gateway of a fifteenth-century predecessor ordered by Matthias Corvinus, King of Hungary and Bohemia – that's him on the tower's sandstone plaque. A former Baroque warehouse within the courtyard houses the **Sorbisches Museum**, with a homespun world of Sorb folk costume and crafts, including the traditional painted Easter eggs rolled downhill on Easter Sunday.

The Alte Wasserkunst

Wendischer Kirchhof 3 • April–Oct daily 10am–5pm; Nov, Dec, Feb & March daily 10am–4pm; Jan Sat & Sun 10am–4pm • €2.50 •
ⓦ altewasserkunstbautzen.de

A few minutes' walk west of Hauptmarkt along Heringstrasse is the **Alte Wasserkunst**, a fortified tower with a dainty white cap that was built to pump river water 30m up and into pipes to over eighty troughs in the town. This was the main source of water in the Altstadt for almost five hundred years until 1965; nowadays the machinery generates electricity. You can climb five floors up to the summit for an idyllic view of fortifications which march along the riverbank, or three floors down to the waterworks.

Michaelskirche and around

Wendischer Kirchhof • May–Sept Mon–Fri 10am–5pm • Free

Adjacent to the Alte Wasserkunst tower is **Michaelskirche**; the story goes the Sorb church was erected because Archangel Michael came to Bautzen's aid against the Hussites in 1450. The picture-postcard view of the church and water tower above the Spree is from the Friedensbrücke to the south. It's well worth wandering Mühlstrasse along the Spree River towards Schloss Ortenburg; en route you'll pass a high-peaked cottage like something out of Hansel and Gretel, the oldest in Bautzen, which is said to have survived fire and wars due to the spell of a Gypsy, hence its nickname, the **Hexenhäuschen** (Witch's House).

The Gedenkstätte Bautzen

Weigangstr. 8a • Mon–Thurs 10am–4pm, Fri 10am–8pm, Sat & Sun 10am–6pm • Free • ⓦ stsg.de

The antithesis to the Altstadt's charm is the chilling **Gedenkstätte Bautzen**, fifteen minutes' walk east of the Hauptmarkt. Hard to believe, but Bautzen is synonymous in the former East Germany with GDR paranoia. Critics of the party, renegade agents, border escapees and even aspirant defectors, were incarcerated in Bautzen II, a prison under unofficial control of the Stasi secret police (and before that under the Nazis and the especially brutal Soviet NKVD). Of the 2700 people imprisoned during its operation from 1956 to 1989, many in solitary confinement, eighty percent were jailed as political "enemies of the state". Officially, however, it never existed and East German citizens remained ignorant of the oppression until prisoners were released in late 1989. In the former garages are the fake delivery vans used to transport terrified prisoners; in the prison itself are cells from various periods, exhibitions about the Nazi, Soviet and Stasi periods, and chilling prisoners' stories (in German).

ARRIVAL AND INFORMATION

BAUTZEN

By train Bautzen's Bahnhof is a 15–20min walk south of the Altstadt: go straight up Bahnhofstrasse, then right at the junction with Lauengraben to reach the Reichenturm. There's no convenient bus to the centre.
Destinations Dresden (every 2hr; 50min–1hr); Görlitz (hourly; 30–40min).

Tourist office Hauptmarkt 1 (April–Oct Mon–Fri 9am–6pm, Sat & Sun 9am–3pm; Nov–March Mon–Fri 9am–5pm, Sat & Sun 9am–2pm; ☏03591 420 16, ⓦ bautzen.de). The office rents out English audio-guides for city walks and also has an internet terminal available free for short intervals.

ACCOMMODATION

Alte Gerberi Uferweg 1 ☎ 03591 27 23 90, ⓦ hotel-alte-gerberei.de. There's charm by the pail-load in this pretty pension on the Spree – pleasing cottagey rooms, the best with a view across to the Alte Wasserkunst, and a verdant courtyard for its rear restaurant. Restaurant Mon–Sat from 6pm. **€70**

Camping Stausee Bautzen 2km north of Bautzen, beyond Burk village ☎ 03591 27 12 67, ⓦ camping-bautzen.de; bus #3 (Sat & Sun only). The nearest campsite is well-maintained, with pitches spread beside a lake. It also has tipis and a yurt for hire. **€7** per person, plus: pitch **€4**; tipis **€10–20**; yurt **€30**

DJH Bautzen Am Zwinger 1 ☎ 03591 403 47, ⓦ jugendherberge-sachsen.de. The town youth hostel is in the former armoury tower of the medieval fortifications, 100m from the Nikolaiturm and near the restaurants of Schlossstrasse. Dorms **€19.50**, doubles **€46**

Dom Eck Breitengasse 2 ☎ 03591 50 13 30, ⓦ wjelbik.de. A Sorb-owned hotel from the family behind the *Wjelbik* restaurant (see below). It is disappointingly bland in decor but comfortable and a great price for the location just behind the Dom. **€76**

Goldener Adler Hauptmarkt 4 ☎ 03591 486 60, ⓦ goldeneradler.de. Traditional four-star in a handsome Baroque townhouse on Hauptmarkt – fairly dated but comfortable enough and spacious. Facilities in the cellars include a restaurant, bar, and the most romantic wine-bar in Bautzen. **€110**

Schloss-Schänke Burgplatz 5 ☎ 03591 30 49 90, ⓦ schloss-schaenke.net. A fine friendly choice in the Altstadt's cobbled lanes, formerly a Franciscan medieval residence; it also has rooms in a medieval stone tower nearby. Furnishings are either simple modern or traditional charming. **€88**

EATING AND DRINKING

Bautzener Senfstube Schlossstr. 3 ☎ 03591 59 80 15, ⓦ senf-stube.de. Speciality Bautzen mustard comes with almost everything – turkey in mushroom-mustard sauce (€8.40) for example – in this spacious brasserie with a large terrace. It's located at the start of the Altstadt's restaurant strip. Daily 11am–midnight.

Monchshof Burglehn 1 ☎ 03591 49 01 41, ⓦ moenchshof.de. "A table in the Middle Ages" is the catchphrase of this jolly themed restaurant: think recipes that date to 1560, home-made unfiltered beer in

earthenware jugs, waiters in sackcloth and a menu of barely legible Gothic script. Good fun. Mon–Sat 11.30am–1am, Sun 11.30am–11pm.

Wjelbik Kornstr. 7 ☎ 03591 420 60, ⓦ wjelbik.de. Sorbish speciality restaurant behind the Dom that is, inevitably, a little touristy, but the quality is consistently high and prices are reasonable. A "Sorbish Wedding" feast of beef with horseradish (€11.80) from the Spreewald is typical. Tues–Sun 11am–3pm & 5.30–11pm.

Görlitz

"Simply the most beautiful city in Germany" say the tourism office brochures of **GÖRLITZ** – hyperbole, certainly, although the accolade was bestowed by the chairman of the German Foundation for the Protection of Historic Monuments. Geographically speaking, Görlitz is only *just* in Germany. The postwar redraw of the map shifted the German–Polish border onto the Neisse River, thereby cutting Görlitz off from its eastern suburbs. Perhaps that's apt for an **Altstadt** that is pure Central Europe: the town flourished on the east–west Via Regia route that linked Kiev to Santiago de Compostela, and in 1815 was amalgamated into Silesia, a definitively Central European province along the Oder River that took in slices of modern Poland and the Czech Republic. The GDR regime surveyed the town and slapped a preservation order on the entire Altstadt. **Untermarkt** is arguably the most romantic town square in eastern Germany – less a collection of buildings than a living Old Master, gorgeous at dusk. "At nightfall I long to be in Görlitz," Goethe once sighed. In recent years, **Hollywood** has taken notice: Görlitz featured in George Clooney's film *Monuments Men* (2014), in Quentin Tarantino's *Inglourious Basterds* (2009) and, most beautifully, in Wes Anderson's *Grand Budapest Hotel* (2014), featuring the gorgeous 1912 Karstadt department store as the hotel lobby. More than most towns in eastern Germany, the Altstadt rewards those who stray down whichever lane looks interesting.

Obermarkt

The appetizer to the Altstadt's main course is elongated **Obermarkt** square, whose Baroque looks are only marginally spoiled by its role as a car park. The square's west end is guarded by the **Reichenbacher Turm** (April–Oct Tues–Sun 10am–5pm; €3; ⓦ museum-goerlitz.de), former gateway to the Altstadt and a crammer in architectural style: a squat fourteenth-century square tower sprouts into a round tower from a century later, onto which is added a Baroque cap. The highest defence in the medieval city, it has history displays that are the epitome of tedium and, from within the former garret of a watchkeeper at its summit, views over Obermarkt. The squat circular **Kaisertrutz** (Tues–Sun 10am–5pm; €5) opposite is a one-time cannon bastion that now holds exhibitions of the Kulturhistorisches Museum Görlitz. The defining monument at the opposite end of the square is the **Dreifaltigkeitskirche** (Mon–Sat 10am–6pm, Sun 11.30am–6pm), expanded erratically over seven centuries to create an enjoyably idiosyncratic interior; the prize at the end of its elongated nave is a Gothic altar in the St Barbara chapel.

Untermarkt

All of Görlitz is, in essence, a prelude to **Untermarkt**. There can be few more handsome squares in Germany than that off the east end of Obermarkt, ringed by the residences of patrician merchants. At the corner of link-street Brüderstrasse – no mean patricians' parade itself – is the **Rathaus**, expanded through the centuries so it boxes in the west side. The best block is the original, with a carved, early Renaissance staircase and balcony from which the mayor addressed the populace. They say the knight that opens his mouth to mark the minutes on a Baroque clock was a marvel of its day. Untermarkt 22 around the corner is celebrated for its Flüsterbogen ("whisper arch") that transmits sounds around its Gothic span, and the Renaissance **Ratsapotheke** at no. 24 is unmissable for its spidery astrological charts. These face the building filling the centre of the square, the former Baroque merchants' hall **Alte Börse**, now a hotel (see p.164), and the sixteenth-century corner **Waage** (weigh house), its corbels carved into portraits of town dignitaries. The south flank beside the Rathaus, fronted by a Gothic colonnade, was the prestigious address of cloth merchants – so-called **Görlitzer Hallhausen** because of their bright hall-like atriums in which to inspect cloth.

Schlesische Museum zu Görlitz

Untermarkt 1 · Tues–Sun 10am–5pm · €5 · ⓦ schlesisches-museum.de

The Schönhof, Görlitz's oldest private Renaissance house (1526), has been restored to house the **Schlesische Museum zu Görlitz**, a brisk spin through the Central European region of Silesia. Displays track its turbulent history and showcase craftsmanship over several floors and two buildings – start at the top to follow displays chronologically and pick up an English-language audio-guide from the reception.

The Barockhaus and around

Neissstr. 30 · May–Oct daily 10am–6pm; Nov–April Tues–Sun 10am–5pm · €5 · ⓦ museum-goerlitz.de

Just off the Untermarkt, the **Barockhaus** re-creates a Baroque courtyard mansion, and holds a passable collection of furnishings and old masters by the likes of Dürer, Hans Holbein the Younger and Martin Schöngauer. Rear rooms pay homage to Jakob Böhme, a local-born sixteenth-century polymath and alchemist who straddled medieval mysticism and philosophy.

Adjacent **Biblisches Haus** impresses for Bible scenes on its facade. Downhill down Neissstrasse is the river and Poland – simply cross the footbridge and the language and food (and the price of cigarettes and booze) changes in former Görlitz suburb Zgorzelec.

The Peterskirche

Bei der Peterskirche 9 • **Church** Mon–Sat 10am–6pm, Sun 11.45am–6pm • Free, tower €2 • **Organ concerts** Year-round Sun noon, plus Tues & Thurs April–Oct • Free

Peterstrasse, punctuated intermittently by swaggering carved portals, tracks north off Untermarkt from the Ratsapotheke. Townhouses hem in the **Peterskirche** at the street's end – it is only inside the five-nave church that you appreciate a scale that testifies to the town's wealth in the early Middle Ages. Its pride and joy is the newly reconstructed **Sun Organ** that fills most of a rear wall with rosettes of pipes like sun beams. The 88 registers and 6095 pipes trump in weekly free **concerts**. Below it, parts of the original early eighteenth-century instrument are on display. Incidentally, only one stained glass window survived when the Nazis blew up the nearby Neisse bridge in May 1945.

Nikolaikirche and around

Grosse Wallstrasse • March Thurs–Sun noon–4pm; April–Oct daily 11am–5pm • €2, combined ticket with Heiliges Grab €3

West of the Peterskirche via Nikolaistrasse, the Late Gothic **Nikolaikirche**, refurbished in 1925 as an Expressionist war memorial, lies at the heart of the **Nikolaivorstadt**, an atmospheric former craftsmen's quarter outside the Altstadt's boundary. The hillside cemetery above is a Gothic horror fantasy – full of crumbling mausoleums – while Steinweg, which continues west from Nikolaistrasse, preserves a medieval streetscape.

Heiliges Grab

Heilige-Grab-Str. 79 • March & Oct Mon–Sat 10am–5pm, Sun 11am–5pm; April–Sept Mon–Sat 10am–6pm, Sun 11am–6pm; Nov–Feb Mon–Sat 10am–4pm, Sun 11–4pm; English notes available • €2, combined ticket with Nikolaikirche €3 • ⓦ heiligesgrab-goerlitz.de

A ten-minute walk west from the Nikolaikirche via Steinweg takes you to the **Heiliges Grab**. This intriguing site, commissioned by a fifteenth-century citizen, Georg Emmerich, is the only complete medieval reproduction of Jerusalem's **Holy Sepulchre**. The future mayor returned home from a pilgrimage to the Holy Land to build a replica from measurements he had taken on site; the original was destroyed in the sixteenth century, making this a particularly important copy. Hearsay has it that the pilgrimage was either in thanks for Emmerich's marriage to his sweetheart, the mayor's daughter, or in penance at having made her pregnant out of wedlock while a student in Leipzig. At the front is a simple two-storey chapel whose "crack" represents a legend that the Crucifixion took place on the grave of Adam – as graffiti from 1543 shows, it was a tourist attraction almost as soon as it opened. The Romanesque box topped with a Moorish pavilion behind is the tomb itself.

ARRIVAL AND INFORMATION

GÖRLITZ

By train The Hauptbahnhof is a 20min walk southwest of the centre: to reach the Altstadt go ahead on Berliner Strasse, cross An der Frauenkirche and Marienplatz, to reach Steinstrasse then Obermarkt.

Destinations Bautzen (every 30min; 30–40min); Dresden (hourly; 1hr 10–40min).

Tourist office Obermarkt 32 (April–Oct Mon–Fri 9am–7pm, Sat & Sun 9am–6pm; Nov–March Mon–Fri 9am–6pm, Sat 9am–4pm; ☎ 03581 475 70, ⓦ goerlitz .de).

ACCOMMODATION

Börse Untermarkt 16 ☎ 03581 764 20, ⓦ boerse-goerlitz .de. Antiques, modern art on the walls and restored parquet floors in an elegant but unstuffy hotel created from a Baroque merchant's hall with an unbeatable location on Untermarkt. "Luxury" class is worth the extra €20 for a splurge. Almost as glam is the hotel's *Gästehaus im Flüsterbogen* opposite (€85); check-in is at *Börse*. **€113**

Jugendherberge Görlitz Altstadt Peterstr. 15

☎ 03581 649 07 00, ⓦ goerlitz-city.jugendherberge .de. Budget beds don't come any more central than at this newly built hostel in a quiet courtyard just off the Untermarkt. All rooms have private facilities. Dorms **€28.50**, doubles **€61**

Picobello Pension Uferstr. 32 ☎ 03581 42 00 10, ⓦ picobello-pension.de. Large hostel-style pension in a former factory on the riverbank below Untermarkt; turn right on reaching the river. Plain rooms of the pine furnishings variety, but clean and with facilities such as bike rental and a sauna. €44

Tuchmacher Peterstr. 8 ☎03581 473 10, ⓦ tuchmacher.de. Kate Winslet is in the guestbook of this prestigious address in a patrician's Renaissance townhouse; some rooms feature restored painted ceilings. Tasteful decor is classic-modern, with warm tones of saffron and ruby to complement old wood. €132

Zum Hothertor Grosse Wallstr. 1 ☎03581 66 11 00, ⓦ zum-hothertor.de. Spotless en-suite rooms of rattan and pine furnishings and crisp white walls in an excellent-value small hotel in a renovated Baroque house. Located by the river between the Altstadt and atmospheric Nikolaivorstadt area. €54

EATING AND DRINKING

Dining in Görlitz divides neatly between **Untermarkt** – where upmarket restaurants on it and offshoot **Peterstrasse** lean towards international cuisine – and **Neissstrasse**, where pubs prepare cheaper traditional dishes. Keep an eye open for Silesian dishes such as *Schlesisches Himmelreich*, a "Silesian heaven" of pork loin with dried plums and apricots, usually with potato dumplings and a butter sauce. For Polish food, simply stroll across the bridge to one of the riverfront restaurants in Zgorzelec, where euros are gladly accepted.

Bürgerstübl Neissstr. 27 ☎03581 87 95 79, ⓦ buergerstuebl-goerlitz.de. Silesian specials such as *Schlesisches Himmelreich* (€9.90) and goulash (€7.90) in one of Görlitz's oldest inns, with a wood-panelled dining room. There's also a small garden behind. Mon–Fri 6pm–midnight, Sat & Sun noon–4pm & 6pm–midnight.

Destille Nikolaistr. 6 ☎03581 40 53 02, ⓦ destille-goerlitz.de. Excellent Mediterranean and regional Silesian cuisine such as venison goulash with red cabbage and potatoes (€12.90), served in a quaint inn beside an old defence tower. Daily 11.30am–2.30pm & 5.30&5.30-11pm–11pm.

Filetto Peterstr. 1 ☎03581 42 11 31, ⓦ filetto-goerlitz .de. A quietly stylish, modern Italian restaurant with an intimate candlelit dining room, and a small garden in summer. Steaks (€16.50) are precisely cooked, and pasta dishes are fresh, modern and good-value at around €8. Mon–Fri 5pm–midnight, Sat noon–3pm & 5–midnight, Sun noon–3pm & 5–10pm.

St Jonathan Peterstr. 16 ☎03581 42 10 82, ⓦ goerlitz-restaurant.de. An above-average menu of modern German cooking plus the historic ambience of dining under the vaults of a Gothic merchants' hall equals a hugely popular choice – buzzy at weekends, but expect to wait. Daily noon–11pm, till midnight Fri & Sat.

Vierradenmühle Hotherstr. 20 ☎03581 40 66 61, ⓦ vierradenmuehle.de. "The easternmost restaurant in Germany" is one of the selling points of this old watermill. Another is its veranda – complete with border post – that juts into the river, making this a popular choice for summertime drinking and eating (local trout €10.50). Service can be a misnomer when busy, however. Daily noon–11pm.

Leipzig

"Leipzig is the place for me! Tis quite a little Paris; people there acquire a certain easy finish'd air." So mused Goethe in his epic *Faust*, though in truth the second city of Saxony is no French *grande dame* – indeed, it's not much of a looker despite efforts to patch up the damage of war. But nor is it as languid. After decades in a socialist rut, **LEIPZIG** is back in the groove. Those architectural prizes that remain have been scrubbed up, and glass-and-steel edifices are appearing at lightning pace. No city in the former East Germany exudes such unbridled ambition, but then none has so firm a bedrock for its self-confidence. In autumn 1989, tens of thousands of Leipzigers took to the streets in the first peaceful protest against the communist regime. Their candles ignited the **peaceful revolution** that drew back the Iron Curtain and achieved what two decades of *Ostpolitik* wrangling had failed to deliver. Not bad for a city of just half a million people.

It's seductive to believe that Leipzig's achievement was inspired by the humanist call-to-arms *Ode To Joy* that Schiller had penned here two centuries earlier. In fact, the demonstrations were simply another expression of Leipzig's get-up-and-go. Granted market privileges in 1165, it emerged as a rampantly commercial city, a dynamic free-thinking place that blossomed as a **cultural centre** to attract names such as Bach, Mendelssohn, Schumann, Wagner and, of course, Goethe as a law student. Even the

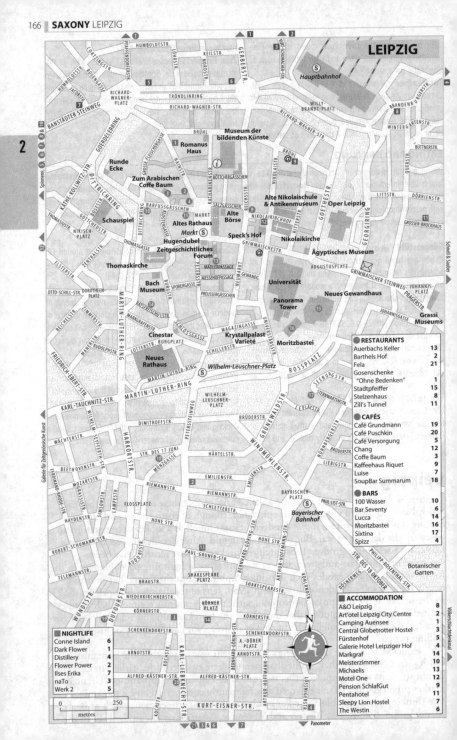

LEIPZIG

Hauptbahnhof

Museum der bildenden Künste

Romanus Haus

Runde Ecke

Zum Arabischen Coffe Baum

Alte Nikolaischule & Antikenmuseum

Oper Leipzig

Schauspiel

Altes Rathaus

Alte Börse

Markt

Hugendubel

Speck's Hof

Nikolaikirche

Zeitgeschichtliches Forum

Ägyptisches Museum

Thomaskirche

Bach Museum

Universität

Neues Gewandhaus

Panorama Tower

Grassi Museums

Cinestar

Krystallpalast Varieté

Moritzbastei

Neues Rathaus

Wilhelm-Leuschner-Platz

Bayerischer Bahnhof

Botanischer Garten

Panometer

RESTAURANTS	
Auerbachs Keller	13
Barthels Hof	2
Fela	21
Gosenschenke "Ohne Bedenken"	1
Stadtpfeiffer	15
Stelzenhaus	8
Zill's Tunnel	11

CAFÉS	
Café Grundmann	19
Café Puschkin	20
Café Versorgung	5
Chang	12
Coffe Baum	3
Kaffeehaus Riquet	9
Luise	7
SoupBar Summarum	18

BARS	
100 Wasser	10
Bar Seventy	6
Lucca	14
Moritzbastei	16
Sixtina	17
Spizz	4

NIGHTLIFE	
Conne Island	6
Dark Flower	1
Distillery	4
Flower Power	2
Ilses Erika	7
naTo	3
Werk 2	5

ACCOMMODATION	
A&O Leipzig	8
Art'otel Leipzig City Centre	2
Camping Auensee	1
Central Globetrotter Hostel	5
Fürstenhof	3
Galerie Hotel Leipziger Hof	15
Markgraf	14
Meisterzimmer	10
Michaelis	13
Motel One	12
Pension SchlafGut	9
Pentahotel	11
Sleepy Lion Hostel	6
The Westin	7

0   250
metres

GDR rulers cultivated trade fairs, allowing the city to maintain its dialogue with the West when others were isolated. In recent decades the same energy has found an outlet through one of the most exciting **contemporary arts** scenes in Europe and a **nightlife** that is refined and riotous by turns.

The Nikolaikirche

Nikolaikirchhof 3 · **Church** Mon–Sat 10am–6pm, Sun 9am–6pm · Free · **Tower tour** Sat 2pm · €2.50 · Ⓦ nikolaikirche-leipzig.de

The touchstone of modern history in Leipzig is the **Nikolaikirche** on Nikolaistrasse, whose sober, early Gothic looks belie a theatrical interior, its candy-coloured Rococo barely tempered by emergent Neoclassicism, and with shaggy palm leaves in place of Corinthian capitals. Its place in national history is as the wellspring of the *Wende*, when it became the site of the first peaceful protest against the GDR (see box below).

The Antikenmuseum

Nikolaikirchhof 2 · Tues–Thurs, Sat & Sun noon–5pm · €3 · Ⓦ uni-leipzig.de/antik

On the church's north side, within the Alte Nikolaischule, a former church school whose alumni include eighteenth-century philosopher Gottfried Leibniz and Wagner, the university-run **Antikenmuseum** holds a passable collection of antiquities. Highlights are a sculpted bronze mirror circa 450 BC and its collection of Attic vases.

Zeitgeschichtliches Forum Leipzig

Grimmaische Str. 6 · Tues–Fri 9am–6pm, Sat & Sun 10am–6pm · Free · Ⓦ hdg.de/leipzig

The **Zeitgeschichtliches Forum Leipzig** is a well-presented display that chronicles the rise and fall of the GDR from its response to the horror of the Nazi regime via communist propaganda, kitsch and into contemporary politics. There are only basic English-language notes available at the entrance desk, but archive footage of the GDR suppression of protest and the construction and destruction of the Berlin Wall packs a punch.

Speck's Hof and Mädler-Passage

Speck's Hof Reichsstr. 4 · Mon–Sat 10am–8pm · Ⓦ speckshof.de · **Mädler-Passage** Grimmaische Str. 2 · Mon–Sat 9.30am–8pm · Ⓦ maedlerpassage.de

On either side of the Zeitgeschichtliches Forum Leipzig museum are the most celebrated of around fifty covered **arcades** that burrow through blocks in the central Altstadt, a legacy of the city's mercantile past before trade fairs moved out of the centre.

Diagonally opposite the museum, **Speck's Hof** is a series of interconnecting courtyards which leads to a central atrium with colourful tiles and an embossed Art Nouveau bronze roof. At the entrance is a bowl "fountain": rub the brass handles to set up

---

LEIPZIG'S PEACEFUL REVOLUTION

In autumn 1989, the **Nikolaikirche**'s Monday services for peace – held since 1982 – assumed new significance as refugees fled the GDR states. Party stooges ordered to disrupt services paused instead to listen to sermons, then joined the protests. Things came to a head after a brutal **suppression of demonstrations** on October 7. A two-thousand-strong congregation filed out into the arms of ten thousand sympathizers holding candles – the police were powerless, the momentum unstoppable. A month later, the Berlin Wall fell. As one Stasi official recalled later, "We had been prepared for anything, but not prayers and candles." Twenty information panels across the Altstadt show where the **peaceful revolution** happened; the tourism office has a dedicated brochure.

resonance patterns in the water. Adjacent to the museum, **Mädler-Passage** is the doyenne of Leipzig's shopping arcades, an old-world Jugendstil mall whose expensive boutiques would have been unthinkable in GDR days. It also boasts literary connections – Goethe had Mephistopheles and Faust bamboozle a trio of ruffians with magic in its *Auerbachs Keller* restaurant (see p.174) before they rode away on a barrel, a scene commemorated in bronzes outside.

2 The Markt and around

The heart of the historic city is the **Markt**, the venue of the trade fairs that shored up Leipzig's prosperity as early as 1190; the stylish entrance to a 1924 underground trade fair hall was recently given new life as the entrance to the new S-Bahn station. Goethe, who knew Leipzig as a law student in the 1760s, strides from a plinth on Naschmarkt in front of the **Altes Börse**, a pleasingly tubby Baroque stock-exchange that doubles as a cultural centre.

Altes Rathaus: the Stadtgeschichtliches Museum Leipzig

Böttchergässchen 3 • Tues–Sun 10am–6pm • €6, free first Wed of month; temporary exhibitions €3 • ⓦ stadtgeschichtliches-museum-leipzig.de

The size of the Markt's **Altes Rathaus**, an impressive Renaissance structure, is a testimony to Leipzig's commercial clout – the inscription that wraps around its elongated length is said to be the longest of any building in the world. Long passed over as the town hall, it now contains the **Stadtgeschichtliches Museum Leipzig**, a sprint through early city history, and owns the only portrait of Johann Sebastian Bach painted in his lifetime. It's worth a visit for a magnificent 50m Festsaal lined with oils of assorted mayors. Temporary exhibitions are displayed in the Neubau cube on its north side.

Zum Arabischen Coffe Baum

Kleine Fleischergasse 4 • Museum daily 11am–7pm • Free

Off the west side of the Markt, via bar-and-restaurant strip Barfussgässchen, a Baroque portal of a cherub who proffers a cup to an Ottoman Turk under a coffee tree announces Europe's oldest coffee shop, **Zum Arabischen Coffe Baum** (1711). The carving is said to have been donated by Augustus the Strong in thanks for the hospitality he had received from the landlady. The fact that the Saxony Elector himself visited testifies to the coffee craze that swept Saxony from the late seventeenth century, even knocking beer off its pedestal as the favourite beverage. A top-floor **museum** spins through European coffee culture, and you can sup in historic rooms – see p.174 for the café review – just as former visitors Bach, Goethe, Wagner and Schumann did. The two leaders of a divided Germany, Helmut Kohl and Lothar de Maizière, also met here to discuss reunification.

Museum der bildenden Künste

Katharinenstr. 10 • Tues & Thurs–Sun 10am–6pm, Wed noon–8pm • €5, free second Wed in month • ⓦ mdbk.de

The Sachsenplatz area north of the Markt epitomizes modern Leipzig's go-ahead ambitions: communist eyesores have been replaced by a plastic-sheathed cube to house the excellent **Museum der bildenden Künste** (Museum of Fine Arts). Pure minimalism within – all white walls, pale oak and concrete – it is curated with a light touch, so that works are juxtaposed with a wit and flair that rewards slow exploration. If you're pressed for time seek out the big guns from the German late Middle Ages – Hamburg's Meister Francke, Cranach, whose *Adam and Eve* titillates under the pretence of Renaissance style, and Hans Baldung – and enjoyable works by Rubens and Hals, notably the latter's louche *Mulatto*, as well as a luminous seascape by Romantic Caspar David Friedrich. You're unlikely to miss Max Klinger's colossal marble sculpture of *Beethoven*, who is enthoned brooding and nude like a Greek god. Another Leipzig son, Max Beckmann, introduces a room of the Leipzig School, though don't miss large-format works on the top floor by Neo Rauch, a figurehead of the city's modern art movement.

The tangerine-and-cream **Romanus Haus** opposite the museum is the finest of the city's Baroque mansions. It was named after its mayor owner, Franz Conrad Romanus, a favourite of Elector Augustus the Strong, who modernized the city and dug its western canals. Unfortunately he also had light fingers – arrested for embezzlement, he ended his days incarcerated in the Königstein (p.156).

The Hauptbahnhof

Leipzig's massive **Hauptbahnhof** just north of the Altstadt is a sight in its own right: the grand 1915 building from the golden age of rail is one of the largest rail termini in Europe, with 21 tracks and a 300m-wide facade. More recently, a two-level underground mall and a handy S-Bahn tunnel running underneath the city centre were added. Several historical trains are parked at platform 24; on the first Saturday of the month, the same platform disappears beneath the stalls of an antique and flea **market**.

The Runde Ecke

Dittrichring 24 • Daily 10am–6pm • Free, English audio-guide €3 • ⓦ runde-ecke-leipzig.de

Ten minutes' walk from the Markt, at the western fringe of the Altstadt, the **Runde Ecke** is the former Leipzig headquarters of GDR secret police, the Stasi. Captured by citizens on December 4, 1989, the building was made famous by news footage of peaceful protesters placing candles on its steps. It is preserved as a museum, where surveillance equipment remains in drab offices and exhibits document the regime's oppression and paranoia – citizens rescued over six miles of documents from the shredder despite the pulping of files throughout November.

The Thomaskirche

Thomaskirchhof 18 • **Church** Daily 9am–6pm • Free • **Tower** Tours April–Nov Sat 1pm, 2pm & 4.30pm, Sun 2pm & 3pm • €2 • **Concerts** Motet services Fri 6pm, Sat 3pm • €2 • ⓦ thomaskirche.org

Off the southwest corner of the Markt rises the Gothic **Thomaskirche**, where **Johann Sebastian Bach** served as cantor for his last 27 years – nearly half the life of a composer who had previously flitted around princely courts in what is now north and east Germany. He was interred in the graveyard in 1750. Major renovation of the church in the 1880s provided an excuse to exhume what were thought to be his remains and bring scientific rigour to a long-standing debate about Bach's appearance. Measurements of the skeleton were used to create the bronze (1894) outside the church – the out-turned pocket is said to be a reference to his poor finances. The sculpture was paid for by Mendelssohn, then director of Leipzig's acclaimed Gewandhaus Orchester, who did much to rehabilitate a then underrated composer. Bach now lies interred beneath a plaque in the chancel, and the celebrated **boys' choir**, the Thomanererchor, sings works from his vast canon in motet services and in weekend concerts, often with the Gewandhaus Orchester.

The Bachmuseum

Thomaskirchhof 15 • Tues–Sun 10am–6pm • €8, free first Tues of the month • ⓦ bachmuseumleipzig.de

Opposite the Thomaskirche, the modern **Bachmuseum** strives to reveal the great composer's *Zeitgeist* and methods, alongside exhibits such as his household iron chest. There are displays on his often querulous relationship with ducal employers, iPods playing his work and an entertaining interactive exhibit that highlights his orchestral innovation. For Bach devotees all pales beside a darkened room of treasures such as the great man's handwritten manuscripts or items from what was thought to be his tomb displayed like holy relics.

The Neues Rathaus

Martin-Luther-Ring 4–6 • Foyer Mon–Fri 8am–4.30pm • Free

In the southwest corner of the Altstadt the behemoth that is the **Neues Rathaus** – a replacement for the town hall on the Markt – is an enjoyably overblown piece of Second Reich architecture from the late 1800s. Subtle it is not – monstrous in scale and so pompous its revivalist architecture even alludes to Venice's Bridge of Sighs. The foyer's staircase is just as preposterous.

Galerie für Zeitgenössische Kunst and GfZK-2

Karl-Tauchnitz-Str.11 • Tues–Fri 2pm–7pm, Sat & Sun noon–6pm • Galerie für Zeitgenössische Kunst €5, GfZK-2 €5, combined ticket €8 • ⊛ gfzk.de

Ten minutes' walk southwest from the Neues Rathaus (across the ring road), near the university arts departments, a gutted villa serves as the **Galerie für Zeitgenössische Kunst** (Gallery of Contemporary Art), with temporary exhibitions of avant-garde abstract art by contemporary artists of the **New Leipzig School** as well as work by post-1945 artists who didn't square with the GDR social-realist aesthetic. A striking glass-walled adjacent exhibition space, **GfZK-2**, also hosts a hip café that is redesigned (and renamed) by an artist every two years.

Augustusplatz

Nowhere in central Leipzig is so redolent of the GDR aesthetic as Augustusplatz at the eastern edge of the Altstadt. On either side is the regime's **Oper Leipzig** opera house to the north and the glass-walled **Neues Gewandhaus** concert hall, inaugurated in 1981, to the south. The enormous socialist-realist painting in the latter's foyer was by a regime-approved Leipzig university artist, Sighard Gille. The square was a venue for peaceful protest in 1989.

Panorama Tower

Augustusplatz 9 • Viewing platform Mon–Thurs 9am–midnight, Fri & Sat 9am–1am, Sun 9am–11pm • €3 • ⊛ panorama-leipzig.de

After reunification there was considerable debate about whether to keep GDR skyscraper the **Panorama Tower** beside the Gewandhaus. When it was built in 1970 the silver-grey book-shaped tower eradicated historic university edifices, doing little to endear it to locals. Today you can zip up to the 120m-high **viewing platform**, bar and restaurant. The university got payback when it rehoused a 33-tonne bust of Marx to its building on Jahnallee, west of the Altstadt; the demolished Paulinerkirche attached to the university has made a comeback too, as a striking building of glass shards.

Ägyptisches Museum

Goethestr. 2 • Tues–Fri 1–5pm, Sat & Sun 10am–5pm • €5 • ⊛ uni-leipzig.de/~egypt

Just north of the square on Goethestrasse is the university-owned **Ägyptisches Museum**. The highlight of its good collection of antiquities gathered by scholars since the mid-1800s is a cedar coffin of Hedbastiru (c.500–300 BC), richly carved with hieroglyphics.

The Grassi museums

Johannisplatz 5–11 • Tues–Sun 10am–6pm • Museum für Angewandte Kunst €5, Museum für Völkerkunde €6, Museum für Musikinstrumente €5, combined ticket for all three €12 • ⊛ grassimuseum.de

The doyennes of city museums are the three collections of **Museen im Grassi**, presented in an Art Deco complex 400m east of Augustusplatz.

Museum für Angewandte Kunst

By far the finest museum is the two millennia's worth display of decorative arts in the **Museum für Angewandte Kunst** (Museum of Applied Arts). Innovative presentation brings life to one of the richest collections of its type in Europe, ordered within permanent exhibitions themed as "Antiques to Historicism", "Asian Art" and "Art Nouveau to the present". You could lose several hours among over two thousand objects on display: starting at early Roman items, browsing through the treasures of the Leipzig council chamber, and lingering in highlights such as a cabinet room of Italian Renaissance majolica ceramics or the so-called Roman Hall, whose panels of painted ruins – the Romantic concept of beauty through decay – were rescued from a now-demolished palace near Leipzig, Schloss Eythla. Modern objects include works by the big guns of twentieth-century design such as Mies van der Rohe.

Museum für Völkerkunde

The opposite wing of the complex houses the **Museum für Völkerkunde** (Museum of Ethnology), whose displays roam across Asia, Africa, America, Australia and Oceania – if you're pushed for time, make a beeline for Northeast Asia with one of only nine Kurile-Ainu feather dresses in the world, an eye-catching village complex built by craftsmen from the Gujarat region of India, or a North African Bedouin tent.

Museum für Musikinstrumente

The five thousand instruments on show in the **Museum für Musikinstrumente**, among them what is said to be the world's oldest piano (1726), is small beer by comparison with the other two Grassi museums, though a "sound laboratory" entertains.

Plagwitz

If you want to tap into the energy of Leipzig's contemporary arts dynamo, **Plagwitz**, a former industrial area 3km west of the Altstadt, is the place to come. The Spinnerei arts centre (see below) is the main draw, but while you're in the area you could also head three streets north to the **Tapetenwerk**, Lützner Str. 91 (Wed–Fri 2–6pm, Sat 1–5pm; free; ⊛tapetenwerk.de; S-Bahn Leipzig-Lindenau or tram #15 to Henriettenstrasse), a five-gallery space created in a former wallpaper factory. Full listings of the exhibitions in over forty modern art galleries throughout the city can be found in the quarterly booklet *Kunstindex.Leipzig,* available at the tourist office and galleries, and online at ⊛rundgang-kunst.de.

Contemporary art aside, the Plagwitz district itself is well worth visiting. The **Weisse Elster** River is flanked by converted industrial-era buildings, best seen from the Industriestrasse bridge or on a boat tour (see box, p.172). The pretty, sunken **Karl-Heine-Kanal** branches off here, flanked by an attractive bike path which passes close by the Spinnerei. Nearby Karl-Heine-Strasse is an upcoming street with a dozen ethnic eateries and bars.

The Spinnerei

Spinnereistr. 7, Plagwitz · **Galleries** Tues–Sat 11am–6pm · Free · **Tours** Every hour on Sat · €10 · Book via ✉ archivmassiv@spinnerei.de · ⊛spinnerei.de, ⊛spinnereigalerien.de for gallery programme · S-Bahn or tram #14 to Leipzig-Plagwitz

The excellent **Spinnerei** arts centre is an impressive former cotton-yarn factory that was once the largest in Europe, with its own plantations in present-day Tanzania. It now provides workshop space for over a hundred artists (including Neo Rauch), whose work is displayed in its fourteen **galleries: Eigen + Art** (⊛eigen-art.com) in the former steam hall, and the nonprofit **Halle 14** (⊛halle14.org) remain two of the best.

2

WATERSPORTS AROUND LEIPZIG

The **Weisse Elster** River and **Karl-Heine-Kanal** among parkland and renovated old industry west of the city are a pleasant spot to lose a sunny afternoon. Bootshaus Klingerweg at Klingerweg 2 (April–Oct; ☎0341 480 65 45, ⓦbootstour-leipzig.de; tram #1 or #2 to "Klingerweg") has boat and **canoe rental and tours**. Alternatively, **gondola excursions** are available through *Da Vito* restaurant at Nonnenstr. 1b (☎0341 480 26 26, ⓦda-vito-leipzig.de; €70/hr for up to 5 people).

For more high-octane stuff there's **Kanupark Markkleeberg** (May–Sept Wed 4–8pm, Fri 3–8pm, Sat 10am–7pm, Sun 10am–6pm; ☎034297 14 12 91, ⓦkanupark-markkleeberg.com), Germany's premier **whitewater canoeing and rafting** facility. An hour on a 270m section of artificial rapids by kayak costs €15, or a dozen rafting rides are €38; reservations are required. To get there, take bus #141 (Mon–Fri) to "Auenhain Kanupark", or exit Leipzig-Südost off the A38; a taxi will cost around €25.

The Panometer

Richard-Lehmann-Str. 114 • Tues–Fri 10am–5pm, Sat & Sun 10am–6pm • €11.50 • ⓦasisi.de • Tram #9 or #16 to "Richard-Lehmann-Strasse"

Around 4km due south of Augustusplatz is the **Panometer**. It seems apt that artist and architect Yadegar Asisi has brought a city with a modern artistic bent what is claimed to be the world's largest panoramic painting, which wraps around the inside of a former gas storage-tower. The 360-degree panorama – over 100m long and 30m high – changes every fifteen months: the destination at the time of writing was Leipzig during the Battle of Nations in 1813; from autumn 2015 it's the Great Barrier Reef.

The Völkerschlachtdenkmal

Strasse des 18 Oktober 100 (parallel to Prager Strasse) • Daily: April–Oct 10am–6pm; Nov–March 10am–4pm • €6 • ⓦstadtgeschichtliches-museum-leipzig.de • Tram #15 to "Völkerschlachtdenkmal"

It's hard to believe from the surrounding suburbs, but in 1813 southeast Leipzig was the venue for the **Battle of Nations**, the defining clash of European superpowers that pitted the combined might of the Prussian, Austrian and Russian forces against the all-conquering army of Napoleon. The centenary of victory over the French army, which had hitherto romped unopposed all the way to Croatia, was commemorated by the **Völkerschlachtdenkmal**, a monument sited not far from where the diminutive French emperor issued the orders that lost the battle and, ultimately, saw him exiled on Elba. It's a colossus of a war memorial to the 54,000 allied dead, a concrete-and-granite construction 91m high, unyielding in style and with muscular 10m-high knights as guards of honour in the crypt. A lookout platform offers views, and at its base the **Forum 1813** museum provides context to the battle.

Belantis

Daily mid-April to Oct 10am–6pm • €27.90 • ⓦbelantis.de • Tram #3 to "Belantis"; by car take exit 30 on the A38

Welcome to the most popular family attraction in Leipzig – a large theme park at the city's southern limits, fifteen minutes from the centre by tram. Divided into themed adventure zones around a lake, **Belantis** has all the requisite thrills – a log flume down Europe's largest pyramid, roller coasters and a swinging pirate-ship – plus gentler pleasures like a Segway course, a kids' zoo, and canoes to paddle on the "Belantis Pacific".

ARRIVAL AND DEPARTURE   LEIPZIG

By train The Hauptbahnhof is north of the Altstadt, across the ring road.

Destinations Chemnitz (hourly; 55min); Dresden (hourly; 1hr 10min–1hr 40min); Grossbothen (hourly; 40min); Zwickau (hourly; 1hr 20min–1hr 40min).

By plane The airport, Leipzig-Halle (ⓦleipzig-halle-airport .de), 18km north, is linked by the Flughafen Express and slower Regional Express trains (€4.30). A taxi will cost around €30.

By car The cheapest central parking is on Querstrasse, one block east of Georgiring.

GETTING AROUND

By public transport The S-Bahn from Hauptbahnhof stops beneath the central Altstadt. Most tram routes pass outside the Hauptbahnhof; other transport hubs are Augustusplatz east of the Altstadt and Wilhelm-Leuschner-Platz south. A single ticket costs €2.40, a day-card €6.50. For schedules see ⓦ lvb.de.

By bike Bike rental is available from Zweirad Eckhardt (☎0341 961 72 74, ⓦ bikeandsport.de) at Kurt-Schumacher-Str. 4 on the west side of the Hauptbahnhof;

they even provide complete picnic sets.

By taxi The most reliable taxi rank is outside the Hauptbahnhof; to pre-book a cab try Funktaxi (☎0341 48 84) or Löwentaxi (☎0341 98 22 22).

By car All the major car rental companies maintain bureaux in or near the Hauptbahnhof and at the airport: Hertz ☎01806 33 35 35; Europcar (Wintergartenstr. 2) ☎040 520 18 76 54; Sixt ☎1805 25 25 25; Avis ☎01806 21 77 02.

INFORMATION

Tourist information Beside the Museum der bildenden Künste at Katharinenstr. 9 (Mon–Fri 9.30am–6pm, Sat 9.30am–4pm, Sun 9.30am–3pm; ☎0341 710 42 60, ⓦ leipzig.travel). The office has a brochure, a free app and audio-guides (€7.50) for the 5km Music Trail city walk, which links Leipzig's main music-related sites; the route is

marked by metal notes in the pavement.

Discount cards The tourist office sells the Leipzig Card (1 day €9.90, 3 days €19.90), providing free travel on all city public transport and discounts on museum entry, and the Leipzig Regio Card (1 day €16.90, 3 days €35.50), valid for the surrounding region, including Colditz and its castle.

ACCOMMODATION

Prices in hotels can rise sharply when major trade fairs roll into town. Where you stay may depend on your plans as much as your budget. Notwithstanding a couple of central options, most cheap accommodation is at the north edge of the Altstadt, while nightlife districts are to the south and west.

HOTELS

Art'otel Leipzig City Centre Eutritzscher Str. 15 ☎0341 30 38 40, ⓦ artotel-leipzig.com. Located in a block 500m from the train station, this design hotel is a quietly sophisticated number that features a warmed-up take on minimalism and artwork by local artists. **€85**

Fürstenhof Tröndlinring 8 ☎0341 14 00, ⓦ hotelfuerstenhofleipzig.com. Luxury hotel in an elegant mansion with a 200-year history of seamless service. Decor is an impeccable blend of traditional elegance and modern comfort and there's a stylish pool-spa area and a fine-dining restaurant. **€145**

Galerie Hotel Leipziger Hof Hedwigstr. 1–3 ☎0341 697 40, ⓦ leipziger-hof.de. One of the city's more individual addresses due to its original artwork in all rooms, much of it by major names of the New Leipzig School. Decor is not as sharp as the painting, however, and the location near Leipzig-Ost station is a mite isolated. **€76**

Markgraf Körnerstr. 36 ☎0341 30 30 30, ⓦ markgraf-hotel-leipzig.com. Pleasant enough and friendly if also fairly bland in style, this mid-range hotel appeals nevertheless for a quiet location in the midst of the Südvorstadt nightlife – a good option to party in comfort. **€69**

★ **Meisterzimmer** Spinnereistr. 7, Leipzig-Plagwitz ☎0341 30 67 70 99, ⓦ meisterzimmer.de. Four über-cool apartments for up to eight people in former factory buildings of the Spinnerei arts complex: think creative open-plan interior design and retro furnishings. Far from the action, 3km west of the centre, but fabulously original – and what a price. **€65**

Michaelis Paul-Gruner-Str. 44 ☎0341 267 80, ⓦ hotel-michaelis.de. This friendly small hotel near the nightlife of Südvorstadt brings an interior designer's eye to its modern en-suite rooms. There's a good restaurant, too. **€99**

Motel One Nikolaistr. 23 ☎0341 337 43 70, ⓦ motel-one.com. The German budget design chain comes up trumps again, both for its modest hipster style at an impressive price, and – most of all – for an unrivalled location in the heart of the Altstadt. **€79**

Pension SchlafGut Brühl 64–66 (Dussman-Passage) ☎0341 211 09 02, ⓦ schlafgut-leipzig.de. Simple one-to three-bed rooms in a central location, with standards somewhere between hostel and budget hotel. The cheapest accommodation shares amenities; you can save more by forsaking extras such as cleaning, a TV or breakfast. Also offers a budget apartment-hotel nearby. **€45**

Pentahotel Grosser Brockhaus 3 ☎0341 129 20, ⓦ pentahotels.com. A funky style number whose quirky touches include outsize furniture in public areas and a mirror-mosaic lift; the decor is restrained cool in the rooms. A good location on a quiet square, too, and facilities include a pool. **€117**

The Westin Gerberstr. 15 ☎0341 98 80, ⓦ westin-leipzig.com. What looks like a dreary GDR apartment block is actually a slick design-hotel. Some rooms boast astounding city views, and there is a selection of hip bars and restaurants that optimize the building's space. **€119**

HOSTELS & CAMPSITES

A&O Leipzig Brandenburger Str. 2 ☎0341 250 79 49 00,

2

ⓦaohostels.com. The usual IKEA-esque rooms are on offer from the German budget behemoth, which lacks the community vibe of a hostel but is popular with more mainstream visitors and rarely full. This outpost enjoys the spacious dimensions of its historic building. Dorms €12, doubles €43

Camping Auensee Gustav-Esche-Str. 51 ⓣ0341 465 16 00, ⓦcamping-auensee.de; tram #10 or #11 towards Wahren/Schkeuditz and alight at "Annaberger Strasse". The nearest campsite is this well-maintained place in woods 5km northwest of the centre that also offers budget rooms in cabins. Pitch €3.50, plus €6 per person; double cabin €22

Central Globetrotter Hostel Kurt-Schumacher-Str. 41 ⓣ0341 149 89 60, ⓦglobetrotter-leipzig.de. A communal vibe and good kitchen/lounge areas are the winners in this friendly, spotless hotel with a useful location behind the train station. Dorms have up to eight beds, all with shared bathrooms; the hostel also has some en-suite rooms. Dorms €12.50, doubles €42

★**Sleepy Lion Hostel** Jacobstr. 1 ⓣ0341 993 94 80, ⓦhostel-leipzig.de. Leipzig's oldest hostel has great modern dorms, all en suite and subdivided into smaller areas, in four- to ten-bed varieties (women-only dorms available). Seven spacious apartments sleep up to four. Dorms €12.50, doubles €42

EATING AND DRINKING

Leipzig's restaurant and bar scene splits into three districts. Smartest and most central is **Drallewatsch**, centred on Barfüssgässchen and Kleine Fleischergasse west of the Markt, which is chock-a-block with restaurants and bars and enjoyably buzzy in summer. Less touristy is the **Schauspielviertel** area along Gottschedstrasse west of the Thomaskirche, a laidback strip popular with a crowd of late-twenty- and thirty-somethings. More local still is the **Südvorstadt** 2km south of the centre around Karl-Liebknecht-Strasse (tram #10 or #11): the "Karli" is your spot for alternative bars and multi-ethnic restaurants.

CAFÉS AND CHEAP EATS

★**Café Grundmann** August-Bebel-Str. 2 ⓣ0341 222 89 62, ⓦcafe-grundmann.de. For a touch of class in the Südvorstadt visit this relaxed Art Deco café with superb coffee and a modern menu – the cakes and breakfasts are legendary. It swings to live jazz and chanson when the *Hot Club* band takes over on the first Tues of the month. Mon–Fri 8am–midnight, Sat 9am–midnight, Sun 9am–8pm.

Café Puschkin Karl-Liebknecht-Str. 74 ⓣ0341 391 01 05, ⓦcafepuschkin.de. Popular laidback café-bar at the heart of the Südvorstadt scene with a Russian theme and shisha smoking. It serves breakfasts till 4pm Mon–Sat, plus filling dishes like spuds and pasta in large portions. Student heaven. Daily 9am–2am.

Café Versorgung Spinnereistr. 7, Leipzig-Plagwitz ⓣ0341 351 37 75. The cosy café inside the Spinnerei complex has cheap pub food (*Schnitzel* with fries €6.50, lentil soup €3.30), occasional concerts and a lovely summer garden with scattered seating and table tennis. Mon–Fri 8.30am–7pm, Sat 10am–7pm, Sun 11am–7pm.

Chang Gottschedstr. 8 ⓣ0341 253 51 47, ⓦchang-leipzig.de. In a country which too often shies away from punchy exotic flavours, this simple restaurant and takeaway is the real deal, with delicious Thai curries and noodle dishes. Good-value lunch deals plus takeaway available. Mon–Fri noon–3pm & 5.30–11pm, Sat & Sun 5pm–midnight.

Coffe Baum Kleine Fleischergasse 4 ⓣ0341 961 00 60, ⓦcoffe-baum.de. Germany's oldest coffee house is a Leipzig institution (see p.168) frequented by Bach, Goethe, Liszt and now almost every tourist in Leipzig. The various floors cover most bases, with three cafés in French, Austrian and Arabic styles. It also has three expensive restaurants. Daily 11am–1am.

Kaffeehaus Riquet Schuhmachergässchen 1 ⓣ0341 961 00 00, ⓦriquethaus.de. Tucked away on a quiet street and usually quieter than other cafés, this is a smart little Vienna-style coffee house that's worth a visit for its Art Nouveau exterior – the building's first owner was an Orient importer, hence the elephant heads outside. Daily 9am–8pm.

Luise Bosestr. 4, corner Gottschedstrasse ⓣ0341 961 14 88, ⓦluise-leipzig.de. Always-busy café-bar that serves as the fulcrum of the Gottschedstrasse bar strip, which is perhaps why its laidback cool is beloved by a thirty-something crowd, especially in summer. Great to people-watch, though the food from a cheap bistro-style menu is only passable. Daily 9am–1am, Fri & Sat till late.

SoupBar Summarum Münzgasse 5 ⓣ0341 149 49 74, ⓦsoup-bar-summarum.de. Delicious home-made soups – from the usuals like carrot or mushroom with white wine to exotic flavours such as vanilla with forest berries – prepared fresh each day at low prices. Mon–Fri 11am–midnight, Sat 5pm–midnight.

RESTAURANTS

Auerbachs Keller Grimmaische Str. 2–4 (Mädler-Passage) ⓣ0341 21 61 00, ⓦauerbachs-keller-leipzig.de. A sixteenth-century tavern immortalized in Goethe's *Faust* – turn-of-the-twentieth-century murals celebrate its claim to fame – and already an institution in his time. Hugely touristy of course, but its many historic rooms can usually cope. The menu of traditional and regional food is upmarket; *Schnitzel* goes for €18.90. Daily 11.30am–1am.

Barthels Hof Hainstr. 1 ☎0341 14 13 10, ⓦbarthels-hof.de. Traditional Saxony dishes in a perennially popular restaurant in one of the prettiest courtyards off the Markt. There are three traditional dining rooms to choose from in the sixteenth-century building. Mon–Sat 11am–midnight, Sun 10am–midnight.

Fela Karl-Liebknecht-Str. 92 ☎0341 225 35 09, ⓦfela-in-leipzig.de. Head here for some style and creative cuisine along the "Karli"; expect the likes of char fillet fried with lime leaves, or a vegan parsley-root dish with cranberries and grilled cauliflower. Sun brunch is extensive and well worth the trip. Mon–Sat 5pm–1am, Sun 9.30am–3pm.

Gosenschenke "Ohne Bedenken" Menckestr. 5, Leipzig-Gohlis ☎0341 566 23 60, ⓦgosenschenke.de; tram #12 to Gohliser Str. An inn 1km north of the centre that's worth the effort for its rich *Gose* beer – brewed to a 1750s recipe – and beer garden as much as its charming historic rooms. Good food too: a weekly menu of seasonal home-cooking based on an early 1900s menu, plus a few more modern options. Easter–Sept daily noon–midnight; Oct–Easter Mon–Fri 4pm–midnight, Sat & Sun noon–midnight.

Stadtpfeiffer Augustusplatz 8 (in Gewandhaus) ☎0341 217 89 20, ⓦstadtpfeiffer.de. A Michelin-starred address with faultless service and superb modern cuisine that changes with the seasons; à la carte mains average €35–45, pre-concert menus are from €98. Shame about the soulless dining room, though. Tues–Sat 6pm–late; closed July & Aug.

Stelzenhaus Weissenfelser Str. 65, Leipzig-Plagwitz ☎0341 492 44 45, ⓦstelzenhaus-restaurant.de. The Plagwitz destination for a stylish older crowd is this hip minimalist box in a 1930s corrugated iron factory above the canal, 15min walk from the Spinnerei complex. It provides bistro and restaurant menus with mains around €15 – the weekday lunch buffet is good value – plus a bar. Mon–Sat 10am–1am, Sun 9am–1am.

Zill's Tunnel Barfussgässchen 9 ☎0341 960 20 78, ⓦzillstunnel.de. Today's restaurant, the current incarnation of a popular restaurant from 1841, spreads over several levels between a tunnel-like cellar and a formal top-floor wine restaurant. The traditional regional cuisine is the same on each. Daily 11am–midnight.

BARS

100 Wasser Barfussgässchen 15 ☎0341 215 79 27, ⓦ100-wasser.de. A bright explosion of colour, the playful design of this bar was inspired by the Austrian artist Friedensreich Hundertwasser, and in places it's like being trapped in a Kandinsky painting. It's popular with older, rather dressed-up drinkers: think Armani and sunglasses. Light meals and breakfasts are available. Mon–Fri 11am–late, Sat & Sun 9am–late.

Bar Seventy Karl-Heine-Str. 70, Leipzig-Plagwitz ☎0341 60 44 24 64, ⓦbarseventy.de. This Seventies-style joint is one of a number of studenty options en route to the Spinnerei. The soul food served up includes tasty burgers (around €7), chilli con carne and "groove salad". Mon–Fri 11.30am–1am, Sat & Sun noon–3am.

Lucca Ratsfreischulstr. 10 ☎0341 225 56 77, ⓦlucca-bar.de. A small, stylish Italian restaurant and café, with good food (ravioli €10.80), *tramezzini* sandwiches (€3.80), newspapers, coffee and cocktails. Mon–Sat 10am–1am.

Moritzbastei Universitätsstr. 9 ☎0341 702 590, ⓦmoritzbastei.de. This warren of cellars containing bars and gig and club venues has been a multipurpose bastion of student life ever since students dug out the former defence bastion in the 1970s. *Café Barbakane* in a well-like cocoon is a good central spot for Sun brunch. Keep an eye open for outdoor cinema and arts in summer. Mon–Fri 10am–late, Sat noon–late, Sun 9am–late.

Sixtina Sternwartenstr. 4 ☎0177 476 48 55, ⓦsixtina .net. Absinthe and Goths in a dark bolthole with antiques, cobwebs and an organ for playing the Dracula theme, all just across the ring road from the Moritzbastei; a focus of doom-laden fun for the Wave-Gotik-Treffen Goth-fest (see box, p.176). Mon–Thurs & Sun 6pm–2am, Fri & Sat 4pm–late.

Spizz Markt 9 ☎0341 960 80 43, ⓦspizz.org. Central café-bar popular with all ages; its terraces straddling the Markt and Barfüssgässchen are in a prime people-watching spot. The weekend club beneath, with jazz-funk, disco plus occasional house and soul nights, is a popular mainstream option in the centre. Bar daily 9am–late; club Fri & Sat 10pm–6am.

NIGHTLIFE AND ENTERTAINMENT

Central student bar *Moritzbastei* (see above) is always worth checking out for gigs and weekend clubs, otherwise the alternative club scene is in the **Südvorstadt** along arterial Karl-Liebknecht-Strasse (aka "Karli"), 2km south of the centre (tram #10 or #11). Keep an eye open too for **Bimbotown** (ⓦbimbotown.de), an occasional lunatic rock-club-cabaret extravaganza curated by artist Jim Whiting in the Spinnerei complex. Local publication *Kreuzer* (€2.50; ⓦkreuzer-leipzig .de) is the pick of the newsstand **listings magazines**; freesheet *Blitz* in bars and the tourist office provides a brief rundown of what's on. The tourist office operates a **ticket** desk, and a commercial outlet is in bookshop Hugendubel at Peterstr. 12–14 (Mon–Sat 9.30am–8pm; ☎0341 980 00 98). The city's **classical music** tradition is second to none thanks to Bach's Thomanerchor boys' choir (see p.169) and the world-class Gewandhaus Orchester. Other venues for classical music include the Bach-Museum and the Völkerschlachtdenkmal, whose crypt is renowned for superb acoustics.

2

ALL ABOUT THE MUSIC

In the city of Bach what else should you expect but music festivals? Europe's largest pub crawl, music festival **Leipziger Honky Tonk** (ⓦhonky-tonk.de), does the rounds of 100 boozers one Saturday in April or May; 25,000 Goths gather for the **Wave-Gotik-Treffen** (ⓦwave-gotik-treffen .de), the world's largest Goth doom-fest, over Whitsun (first weekend in June or last in May); and the week-long **Bachfest** (ⓦbach-leipzig.de) runs in the middle of June.

CLUBS

Conne Island Koburger Str. 3, Leipzig-Connewitz ☏0341 301 30 28, ⓦconne-island.de. Hardcore, drum'n'bass, techno and hip-hop in a (sub)cultural centre at the far end of alternative strip Karl-Liebknecht-Strasse. Also hosts regular gigs, usually of the indie, ska-punk and thrash variety – watch out for kamikaze stage-divers. *El Dry* opposite is a lovely pub to prepare for the grunge-fest. Café Tues–Sat 4pm–late, Sun 2pm–late; event times vary.

Dark Flower Hainstr. 12–14 ⓦdarkflower.de. The goth and darkcore sister of retro club *Flower Power* (see below), which occasionally strays into doom-pop and alt-rock. It's near the Museum für bildenden Künste. Thurs–Sat 9pm–6am.

Distillery Kurt-Eisner-Str. 91, corner Lössniger Strasse ☏0341 355 974 00, ⓦdistillery.de. Though house and techno are the mainstays, the oldest dance-music club in the GDR provides a mash-up of electro, dubstep, reggae, dancehall and old-skool funk and whatever else its DJs fancy. Always worth a look. Usually Fri & Sat 11.30pm–late, but dates vary.

Flower Power Riemannstr. 9 ☏0341 961 34 41, ⓦflowerpower.eu. Psychedelic little bar-club in the "Karli" with booze-fuelled parties of super-solid sounds from the Sixties to the Eighties, plus the occasional rock night or karaoke. Either way, it's at its best at weekends in the wee hours. If you just can't leave, the bar has two basic rooms upstairs with beds for €10. Daily 7pm–late.

Ilses Erika Bernhard-Göring-Str. 152 (Haus der Demokratie), ⓦilseserika.de. A block east of the "Karli", this attitude-free mainstay of student life hosts a regular programme of alternative clubs in its cellar venue, including midweekers, plus sweaty gigs. Wed–Sun, times vary.

LIVE MUSIC

naTo Karl-Liebknecht-Str. 46 ☏0341 301 43 97, ⓦnato-leipzig.de. A focus of the city's alternative scene whose manifesto of "Art + communication" translates into gigs of indie, alt-folk and jazz, including international touring acts. It also hosts theatre, cabaret and an art-house cinema.

Werk 2 Kochstr. 132 ☏0341 308 01 40, ⓦwerk-2.de. This alternative cultural centre at the bottom of Karl-Liebknecht-Strasse in a renovated factory hosts major German indie and alternative acts, plus occasional touring international names several times a week.

THEATRE AND CLASSICAL MUSIC

Krystallpalast Varieté Magazingasse 4 ☏0341 14 06 60, ⓦkrystallpalast.de. "New vaudeville" in Leipzig's premier variety venue whose tradition of acrobats and jugglers, *chanson* and comedy dates back to the 1880s.

Neues Gewandhaus Augustusplatz 8 ☏0341 127 02 80, ⓦgewandhaus.de. Never mind the ugly GDR building, this is the home of the acclaimed Gewandhaus Orchester, whose programmes in a 1900-seat hall have won critics' awards, plus a more intimate chamber-music venue, the Mendelssohn-Saal.

Oper Leipzig Augustusplatz 12 ☏0341 126 12 61, ⓦoper-leipzig.de. A celebrated venue formerly under the baton of Gustav Mahler now performs classic opera, for which the Gewandhaus Orchester are involved, as well as contemporary works. It also maintains a highly regarded ballet company, and stages a showbiz musical every few months.

Schauspiel Bosestr. 1 ☏0341 126 81 68, ⓦschauspiel-leipzig.de. The city's leading dramatic stage, a venue for classic works by major names, also serves as a front-of-house for associated contemporary venue Skala around the corner at Gottschedstr. 16.

Colditz

No matter that the Schloss was a Renaissance palace of the state's ruling House of Wettin. Never mind that the pretty provincial town provided prized white kaolinite clay for the Baroque china of Saxony Elector Augustus the Strong. **COLDITZ**, 50km southeast of Leipzig, is inextricably linked in British minds with one thing only: the high-security World War II POW camp Oflag IV-C. Mention Colditz to most Germans, however, and you'll be met with a blank look.

Schloss Colditz

Daily: April–Oct 10am–5pm, tours 10.30am, 1pm & 3pm, extended tours Mon–Sat 10.30am & 2pm; Nov–March 10am–4pm, tours 11am & 2.30pm, extended tours on demand • Museum only €4, tours €8.50, extended tours €15 • ⓦ schloss-colditz.com

The most famous of German POW camps among Britons, **Schloss Colditz** was popularized first in a book by former inmate Major Pat Reid, *The Colditz Story*, and later by a TV series and two films. It certainly looks the part, standing on a high bluff above the town, and probably would have been as secure as the Nazis believed were it not for the ingenuity of its 600–800 Allied officer inmates, most of them incarcerated here following their recapture after escapes from other camps. Wooden sewing machines manufactured fake German uniforms, forgers produced identification papers and banknotes. More astonishing were those plans that were never used: a 44m tunnel dug over eight months by French prisoners (they were just 14m short when it was discovered); or a glider plane built in the church attic, constructed with wood, bed sheets and porridge – in 2012, a replica built for a film crew was successfully catapulted from the roof without incident. Of the 300 **escape attempts**, only 31 succeeded. Over a third were made by the British, who scored 11 home-runs. French escapees boasted an impressive hundred-percent record for their 12 attempts.

Castle tours last an hour and focus on the war history and also permit a look at the French tunnel alongside documents and photographs in a **Fluchtmuseum** (Escape Museum); the extended tours are two hours and have even more on the POW history.

ARRIVAL AND INFORMATION

COLDITZ

By train and bus From Leipzig, take a train to Grimma and change on to bus #619 for Colditz (hourly connections daily; 1hr 30min); get off at "Colditz Sportplatz". The last bus back to Grimma departs around 8pm. The Schloss is unmissable above the town.

Tourist office Markt 11 (April–Oct Mon–Fri 10am–5pm, Sat & Sun 1pm–5pm; Nov–March Mon–Fri 10am–4pm; ☎ 034381 435 19, ⓦ zweimuldenland.de). The office has internet and wi-fi access for €2.50, and can give tips for pleasant forest walks and canoe rental to make a day of it.

ACCOMMODATION

Jugendherberge Schloss Colditz Schlossgasse 1 ☎ 034381 450 10, ⓦ djh-sachsen.de. One wing of the infamous POW camp has been renovated to serve as a modern youth hostel – as managers joke, "We let you out in the morning." Dorms **€23.50**, doubles **€47**

Chemnitz and around

CHEMNITZ (pronounced "kemnitz") is a curio after Leipzig. When the GDR regime wanted to create its own outpost of Stalinist Russia to celebrate Karl Marx's seventieth birthday in 1953, it turned to Saxony's third-largest city, probably inspired by an industrial heritage that had earned it the nickname of a "Saxon Manchester". In places, a city known for four decades as **Karl-Marx-Stadt** is a Soviet-style throwback that's as bizarre as it is controversial. Even reunification brought its own problems in the form of depopulation, although award-winning investment has reversed the trend and revived the city centre. Nowadays Chemnitz declares itself a "Stadt der Moderne". From a tourist's point of view it is a curio worth a detour partly because of its glimpse at a Soviet past that's all but absent from Leipzig, but also because of a brace of modern art **galleries and museums** and a good day-trip to nearby **Schloss Augustusburg**.

Kunstsammlungen Chemnitz

Theaterplatz 1 • Tues–Fri 11am–5pm, Sat & Sun 11am–6pm • €5, combined ticket with Museum Gunzenhauser €14 • ⓦ kunstsammlungen-chemnitz.de

The main arterial road into the centre is Soviet-style Strasse der Nationen. Off one side is Theaterplatz where the palatial **Kunstsammlungen Chemnitz** displays art that spans

2

from German Romantics such as Caspar David Friedrich to Expressionists of the Die Brücke group, notably a large collection of local son and group figurehead Karl Schmidt-Rottluff that tracks his shift from Impressionism into Expressionism. The gallery also hosts a fine sculpture collection from the late Baroque, and includes international names.

Karl-Marx-Monument

The town's iconic relic of communism is the **Karl-Marx-Monument** on Brückenstrasse, a 7m-high statue cast by a Russian sculptor, Lew Kerbel. The god-sized bust fixes an unswerving glare at the city centre above the *Communist Manifesto* exhortation "Working men of all countries, unite!" After reunification the town council mooted removing it, after over three-quarters of the population voted to revert from the city's communist moniker, Karl-Marx-Stadt, to the original Chemnitz. Instead, it was retained as a testament to the past, to the chagrin of some locals. Actually, it fits more easily into the streetscape than a medieval defence tower opposite.

The Markt

South of the Karl-Marx-Monument lies the Markt, pedestrianized heart of the Altstadt whose restoration won Chemnitz a European award for urban renewal – the glass-skinned Galerie Kaufhof department store is a cathedral to capitalism unthinkable in the 1970s. The Galerie Kaufhof faces the Gothic **Altes Rathaus**, fronted by a carved Renaissance portal and conjoined on its right-hand side to the Art Nouveau **Neues Rathaus**. The Gothic **Jakobikirche** behind received a makeover at the same time.

DAStietz

Moritzstr. 20 • Ⓦ dastietz.de • **Neue Sächsische Galerie** Mon & Thurs–Sun 11am–6pm, Tues 11am–7pm • €3 • Ⓦ neue-saechsische-galerie.de • **Museum für Naturkunde** Mon, Tues, Thurs & Fri 9am–5pm, Sat & Sun 10am–6pm • €4 • Ⓦ naturkunde-chemnitz.de

Across Bahnhofstrasse, behind the Galerie Kaufhof, a courtyard department store has received a new lease of life as a cultural centre with two museums: the **Neue Sächsische Galerie**, with rotating displays of 12,000 postwar artworks from Saxony; and child-friendly natural history centre the **Museum für Naturkunde**. Arguably the most intriguing exhibit, Europe's largest plant fossil, can be seen for free in the foyer – the copse of tree trunks is estimated to have been fossilized around 290 million years ago.

Museum Gunzenhauser

Zwickauer Strasse • Tues–Fri 11am–5pm, Sat & Sun 11am–6pm • €7, combined ticket with Kunstsammlungen Chemnitz €14 • Ⓦ kunstsammlungen-chemnitz.de

Finest of Chemnitz's galleries is **Museum Gunzenhauser**, set in a striking 1929 building south of the centre. Its classic Modernist collection picks up the baton from its sister museum, the Kunstsammlungen Chemnitz (see p.177), with more Expressionism – neo-primitive works of Die Brücke and the Blaue Reiter artists such as Kirchner and Russian-born Alexej von Jawlensky, who edges from the colour blocks of Gaugin towards the boundary of abstraction – and a floor of abstract works. All is a prelude to the world's largest collection of **Otto Dix**, leading light of the anti-Expressionist New Objectivity movement. Seared by his experiences in the trenches of World War I, his cynical and often comically grotesque images of 1920s Germany fell foul of the Nazis. He never lost that bite – outwardly tamer, later works are bitter allegories of suffering.

Staatliche Museum für Archäologie Chemnitz

Stefan-Heym-Platz 1, at the eastern end of Brückenstrasse • Tues, Wed & Fri–Sun 10am–6pm, Thurs 10am–8pm • €7 • ⓦ smac.sachsen.de

The new **Staatliche Museum für Archäologie Chemnitz**, or **SMAC**, has beautifully presented exhibits covering everything from the arrival of the Neanderthals 280,000 years ago to the early industrial age. Don't miss the 14,000-year-old depiction of horse heads on a slate, Saxony's oldest artwork, or the model of the Göltzschtalbrücke, built in 1851 with 26 million bricks – the largest of its kind. SMAC is housed in the curved 1930 Schocken department store, which was designed by architect Erich Mendelssohn and owned by Zionist and publisher Salman Schocken; an excellent exhibition about Schocken and Mendelssohn includes seventeen models of the architect's most famous designs.

ARRIVAL AND INFORMATION

CHEMNITZ

By train Chemnitz's Hauptbahnhof, on the Dresden and Leipzig lines, is a few hundred metres northeast of the centre. Destinations Dresden (every 30min; 1hr–1hr 20min); Erdmannsdorf-Augustusburg (hourly; 15min); Leipzig (hourly; 1hr).

Tourist office Markt 1 (Mon–Fri 9am–6pm, Sat 9am–4pm; ☏ 0371 69 06 80, ⓦ chemnitz-tourismus.de). The office stocks free listings magazines and sells Karl Marx T-shirts.

ACCOMMODATION

An der Oper Strasse der Nationen 56 ☏ 0371 68 10, ⓦ hoteloper-chemnitz.de. The most appealing address in the centre is this four-star opposite the Kunstsammlungen Chemnitz, not the GDR-era towerblock it appears but a smart business four-star with design leanings. **€99**

Biendo Strasse der Nationen 12 ☏ 0371 27 23 73 02, ⓦ biendo-hotel.de. A comfortable new business hotel on the top floor of an office block opposite the Karl-Marx-Monument; central and good value for money. **€70**

City Hostel Chemnitz Eins Getreidemarkt 1 ☏ 0351 27 80 98 97, ⓦ jugendherberge-sachsen.de. A new youth hostel, superbly located in a lane behind the Rathaus. If it's full, there's a second hostel 5km east of the city (☏ 0371 713 31; same website). Dorms **€23.50**, doubles **€47**

EATING AND DRINKING

Café Ankh Schönherrstr. 8 ☏ 0371 458 69 49, ⓦ cafeankh.de. A bustling, studenty restaurant in an old industrial complex 2km north of the centre. There's a wall of books, and Asian-inspired cuisine such as turkey stuffed with mango papaya chutney (€9.60) or falafel burger with yoghurt (€7.20). Mon–Fri 5pm–11pm, Sat 4pm–midnight, Sun 10am–midnight.

Kellerhaus Schlossberg 2 ☏ 0371 335 16 77, ⓦ kellerhaus-chemnitz.de. Not just the city's oldest restaurant, but its most charming, where affordable traditional meals are served in a rustic seventeenth-century dining room – nice beer garden in summer, too. It's in the Schlossviertel north of the centre. Daily 11am–midnight.

Turm-Brauhaus Neumarkt 2 ☏ 0371 909 50 95. Popular microbrewery with chunky pub-grub favourites such as *Schweinehaxe* (roast pork knuckle), *Schnitzel* and spare ribs. Fresh beers produced on-site slip down dangerously easily. Mon–Thurs 10am–midnight, Fri & Sat 10am–1am, Sun 9am–11pm.

Villa Esche Parkstr. 58 ☏ 0371 236 13 63, ⓦ restaurant-villaesche.de. Refined restaurant in the former coach-house of a villa by Art Nouveau pioneer Henry van de Velde. There's a seasonal menu of gourmet Italian and modern German cuisine – the finest dining in the city by far, with mains priced at €13–25. Tues–Sat noon–10pm, Sun noon–6pm.

NIGHTLIFE

Atomino Hartmannstr. 9 ⓦ atomino-club.de. One of the more alternative options in the centre, this student favourite hosts gigs plus weekend clubnights of indie, house and dubstep and the occasional ironic midweek bingo session. Wed & Thurs 9pm–late, Fri & Sat 10/11pm–late.

Brauclub Neumarkt 2 ⓦ brauclub.de. A basement venue opposite the Rathaus with mainstream clubnights – nothing cutting-edge but popular with a mainstream young crowd and a passable option for a drink and a bop. Thurs–Sat 7pm–late.

Schloss Augustusburg

Hasenhaus, museums, dungeon and tower Daily: April–Oct 9.30am–6pm; Nov–March 10am–5pm • Castle including Kutschenmuseum and Jagdtier- und Vogelkundmuseum €6, Motorradmuseum €6, dungeon €2, tower €1, combined ticket for all museums €12 • **Lindenhaus tours** Daily: April–Oct 10.30am, noon, 1.30pm, 3pm & 4.30pm; Nov–March 11am, 12.30pm, 2pm & 3.30pm • 50min • €3 • **Falconry displays** Mid-March to Oct Tues–Sun 11am & 3pm • €7 • ⓦ die-sehenswerten-drei.de

2

Just under 15km east of Chemnitz, the tiny town of Augustusburg drapes itself picturesquely over a rocky knuckle above lush rolling hills. The colossal white-and-pink wedding-cake decoration at its summit is **Schloss Augustusburg**, created as a hunting lodge by Saxony Elector Augustus in 1572. Guided tours explore historic apartments of the **Lindenhaus**; a sweet **Schlosskirche**, the high-water mark of Renaissance ecclesiastical architecture in Saxony, with an altarpiece by Cranach the Younger, of the Elector and family beneath a Crucifixion set before his castle; and the **Brunnenhaus** wellhouse, whose wooden machinery is still able to draw water from a 130m shaft, albeit without the two oxen originally required.

Other areas can be visited individually. For historical character there's former banqueting quarter **Hasenhaus**, which gets its name from the murals of anthropomorphized hares which gambol over the doorways, more appealing than the so-so hunting and regional nature displays of its **Jagdtier- und Vogelkundmuseum**. The former kitchen opposite houses the **Motorradmuseum**, a rev-head's paradise of shiny motorbikes – from Gottfried Daimler's 1885 boneshaker, capable of a giddy 12km per hour with stabilizers, to sports and classic roadsters of international marques, including a section on Saxony brand DKW, the world's largest bike producer in the 1920s and 1930s. The former stables behind contain a gilded Cinderella carriage (1790), which was pulled by six white chargers for the imperial coronation, among displays of coaches in the **Kutschenmuseum**; while the **Schlosskerker** dungeon is an orgy of torture instruments and grisly illustrations. There's also a **tower** for an elevated view over the quilt of fields and forest that roll back to the Erzgebirge south. By the castle gateway the **Sächsischer Adler- und Jagdfalkenhof** stages free-flight falconry displays in homage to the castle's hunting roots.

ARRIVAL AND INFORMATION
SCHLOSS AUGUSTUSBURG

By bus Bus #704 runs from Chemnitz Hauptbahnhof (5 daily; 40min).

By train Trains from Chemnitz run to Bahnhof Erdmannsdorf-Augustusburg, from where you can catch the vintage Drahtseilbahn funicular (€4 one-way, €5 return).

Tourist office Marienberger Str. 24, in the Rathaus on the main road beneath the Schloss (Mon–Fri 9am–noon & 1–5pm, foyer open Sat & Sun 9am–5pm; ☎ 037291 395 50, ⓦ augustusburg.de).

ACCOMMODATION

Jugendherberge Schloss Augustusburg ☎ 037291 202 56, ⓦ jh-augustusburg.de. A historic rear building of the castle near the old stables contains a popular youth hostel, with singles, doubles and family rooms plus up to eight-bed dorms. It's a hugely atmospheric stay once the tourists leave and the castle courtyard is yours alone. Check-in from 3pm. Dorms **€21.80**, doubles **€43.60**

The Erzgebirge

The Czech borderlands south of Augustusburg are pillowed in soft woodland and rolling fields. These are the **Erzgebirge**, literally the "Ore Mountains", whose rich deposits of silver, tin, copper and cobalt earned the fortunes of their handsome small towns. None are worth a trip in their own right, but with a car the region offers lovely backroads touring between Chemnitz and Zwickau. An added incentive is a strong **crafts heritage**: when reserves were depleted, miners turned to folk crafts, which is why the so-called **Sächsische Silberstrasse** (Saxon Silverstreet) offers both historical romance and an opportunity to buy beautiful Christmas and Easter wooden toys and lace. In December the region feels like a German Christmas card made real.

Annaberg-Buchholz

The first destination of note south of Augustusburg, Annaberg-Buchholz enjoyed the richest silver seams in the area and grand townhouses on the Markt suggest the hilltop

Altstadt is a place of some importance. Silver also funded the sixteenth-century **St Annenkirche**, uphill at Grosse Kirchgasse 21 (Jan–March Mon–Sat 11am–5pm, Sun noon–4pm; April–Dec Mon–Sat 10am–5pm, Sun noon–5pm; free, tower €2), whose rough exterior belies a beautiful interior fretted with stellar loop rib vaulting. The sculpture is as rich on the High Gothic miners' altar left of the main altar – notoriously superstitious, miners hoped their outlay would curry favour with St Anne, miners' patron saint. **Craft shops** line Grosse Kirchgasse, which links the Markt and church. South, below the Altstadt at Sehmatalstr. 3, the **Frohnauer Hammer** (daily 9am–noon & 1–4pm; €3) is a massive mid-seventeenth-century forge with steam-driven ore-hammers – the last of its type in Europe.

Schneeberg

Around 10km southeast of Zwickau, **SCHNEEBERG** is another former mining town – there are miners on the crest of the Baroque Rathaus and signs of "Glück auf", the traditional "good luck" salutation of miners. A more eloquent testament to Schneeberg's former status, however, is **St Wolfgangkirche** at the top of the Markt, a spacious, Late Gothic hall church whose vivacious large altar is by Lucas Cranach. Between the Markt and church, the **Museum für bergmännische Volkskunst** at Obere Zobelgasse 1 (Tues–Sun 10am–5pm; €3; ⓦmuseum-schneeberg.de) displays historic miners' folkcrafts.

INFORMATION

THE ERZGEBIRGE

Tourist offices In Annaberg-Buchholz just south of the Markt at Buchholzer Str. 2 (Mon–Sat 10am–6pm; ☎03733 194 33, ⓦannaberg-buchholz.de). In Schneeberg in the Rathaus on the Markt (Mon, Wed, Fri 9am–12.15pm & 12.45–4pm, Tues & Thurs until 6pm, Sat 10am–2pm, Sun 11am–2pm; ☎03772 203 14, ⓦschneeberg.de).

ACCOMMODATION & EATING

Büttner Markt 3, Schneeberg ☎03772 35 30, ⓦhotel-buettner.de. A pocket of relaxed country charm on the main square. Some of the twelve rooms feature old beams of the Baroque house; all are enjoyably snug. Its charming restaurant serves fine modern German cuisine. Restaurant closed Mon & Tues. **€70**

Jagdhaus Waldidyll Talstr. 1, Hartenstein, 30km southwest of Chemnitz ☎037605 840, ⓦromantikhotel-waldidyll.de. An elegant country retreat among woods south of Hartenstein. Created from a nineteenth-century hunting lodge, it is grown-up modern-country in decor, and four-star in facilities that include a spa centre and restaurant. **€128**

Wilder Mann Markt 13, Annaberg-Buchholz ☎03733 114 40, ⓦhotel-wildermann.de. This substantial sixteenth-century house on the main square has been transformed into a traditional four-star: old-fashioned yet comfortable, and decent value. It also has a good restaurant. **€82**

Zwickau

It seems rather unfair that a medium-sized city which gave to the world Romantic composer Robert Schumann and the prestigious Audi brand is known instead for the Trabant. Yet such is the ironic nostalgia for GDR kitsch – *Ostalgie* as it is known (see box, p.878) – that the plastic "people's car" used throughout the communist bloc is the most famous export of **ZWICKAU**, which lies in the foothills of the eastern Erzgebirge range. Such is the price of being the regime's **Motor City** for four decades. The tradition of motor manufacturing in Zwickau – ongoing in major Volkswagen plants in surrounding suburbs – was initiated in 1909 by August Horch, an entrepreneurial engineer who caught the wave of industrial success in the late 1800s. His legacy is an excellent **motor museum** north of the centre, the premier reason to visit; the centre of Zwickau is a pleasant enough but unremarkable assortment of historic islands, nineteenth-century grandeur and modern commercial shopping arranged around two squares, Marienplatz and Hauptmarkt.

The Altstadt

The core of the Altstadt is **Hauptmarkt**, an elongated "L"-shaped square lorded over by a huge castellated **Rathaus** and, adjacent, the **Gewandhaus**, a cloth-merchants' hall whose half-timbered upper level experiments with Renaissance style.

Robert-Schumann-Haus

Hauptmarkt • Tues–Fri 10am–5pm, Sat & Sun 1–5pm • Free • ⓦ schumannzwickau.de

At the southwest corner of Hauptmarkt, **Robert-Schumann-Haus** documents the career of the Romantic composer who was born in this house on June 8, 1810. Schumann was always a passionate figure, as tumultuous in his words to concert pianist and later wife Clara Wieck as he was in the wild hallucinations during an 1854 concert tour that induced his mental breakdown and subsequent death. No surprise, then, that Clara, a premier-division pianist of her day, is a recurring theme, nor that her Bösendorfer grand is on display.

Dom St Marien

Marienplatz • Daily noon–6pm • €2

A block across from Hauptmarkt, Marienplatz is named for the **Dom St Marien**, whose two-tiered Baroque tower serves as a homing beacon for the Altstadt if you arrive by train. Within the Gothic church is a blockbuster display of art. The focus is the largest altar in the area, a riot of female martyrs in fiddly gilt from the workshop of Nürnberg master Michael Wolgemut, Dürer's tutor. Other eye-catchers are rare Protestant confessionals that place the priest and sinner face-to-face at eye level – their carved panels are to prevent lip-reading by the congregation – and, at the side of the chancel a Renaissance tower up which twists a staircase double-helix. Look, too, for a fine Pietà (1502) by Zwickau son Peter Breuer, a grief-stricken work infused with the emergent spirit of Renaissance humanism. Interestingly, coal mining in the area has caused the whole church to sink 3.6m and shift 1.3m to the southeast over the past 75 years.

Priesterhäuser

Domhof 5–8 • Tues–Sun 1–6pm • Free • ⓦ priesterhaeuser.de

The stack of fourteenth- and fifteenth-century houses occupied by medieval artisans opposite the Dom's portal is the oldest terrace in the state. Church employees were housed in the three restored **Priesterhäuser** (Priest Houses) at the end. Some roughly plastered rooms furnished in medieval style, none more atmospheric than the soot-stained "black kitchens", have themed displays on contemporary crafts. A modern wing holds exhibitions.

Johannisbad

Johannisstr. 16 • Mon, Wed & Fri 10am–10pm, Tues 7am–10pm, Thurs 8am–10pm, Sat & Sun 9am–10pm • €4.50 • ⓦ johannisbad.de

Outside of the Altstadt, the mood changes in streets laid out during the town's rapid nineteenth-century expansion. Ten minutes' walk north of the Altstadt – across Dr-Friedrichs-Ring, then up Max-Pechsteinstrasse – the **Johannisbad** is a gorgeous Art Nouveau swimming pool, its galleries picked out in bottle-green tiles. No excuses: it rents towels and sells swimming costumes. There's nude swimming Thursday after 8pm.

Kunstsammlungen Zwickau

Lessingstr. 1 • Tues–Sun 1–6pm • Free • ⓦ kunstsammlungen-zwickau.de

About ten minutes' walk northeast from the Altstadt is a broad park that flanks main road Crimmitschauer Strasse. The Art Nouveau pavilion at its back houses the **Kunstsammlungen Zwickau** which displays the city's decent art collection and religious sculpture, including a Late Gothic altar of morose saints by Breuer.

August Horch Museum

Audistr. 7, 2.5km from the Hauptbahnhof • Tues–Sun 9.30am–5pm • €5.50 • ⓦ horch-museum.de • Tram #4 or #7 or bus #17 or #22 from the Hauptbahnhof, or train to Zwickau Pölbitz and then walk 700m

Signs on arterial routes into the city direct you to the northern suburb where August Horch opened the first Audi factory in 1909; the Audi name was a latinization of *horch* (literally, "hear" in imperative form). Now home to the **August Horch Museum**, it houses eighty or so landmark motors from the Horch stable whose marques Audi, Horch, Wanderer and DKW merged as Auto-Union in the 1930s to give modern Audi its interlocking four-rings logo. The result is a petrolhead's paradise, where the presentational flair of setting cars in period streetscapes makes this an enjoyable collection for all. Rather tatty after the vintage glories are assorted **Trabants** – a "*Horch*" marque that originated as the 1950s Zwickau P70 before it became the rattling 500cc workhorse of communism. Three million were exported in the 34 years until production ceased in 1991. The GDR army even commissioned an all-terrain Trabi – small wonder Zwickau has a concrete miniature Trabant memorial on Georgeplatz northwest of the Altstadt. All but forgotten is Horch's handsome restored Art Nouveau villa beside the museum (open by request at the ticket office).

ARRIVAL AND INFORMATION   ZWICKAU

By train The Hauptbahnhof lies due west of the Altstadt and southwest of the August Horch Museum.
Destinations Chemnitz (every 30min; 30–50min); Dresden (hourly; 1hr 30min); Leipzig (hourly; 1hr 20min).

Tourist office Hauptstr. 6, just off Hauptmarkt (Mon–Fri 9am–6pm, Sat 9am–4pm; ☎0375 271 32 40, ⓦzwickautourist.de).

ACCOMMODATION AND EATING

Brauhaus Zwickau Peter-Breuer-Str. 12–20 ☎0375 303 20 32, ⓦbrauhaus-zwickau.de. All the usual pub-grub in a brewery inn in the central Altstadt, with an adjacent beer garden overlooking Marienplatz – a fine spot for a summertime knees-up. The rooms above the restaurant are an appealing option, with many featuring the exposed bricks or beams of the half-timbered inn. It also puts you on the doorstep of Zwickau's bar strip. Restaurant daily 10am–midnight. €65

Holiday Inn Kornmarkt 9 ☎0374 279 20, ⓦholiday-inn .com. Zwickau's finest address is one block southwest of Hauptmarkt. It provides all you'd expect from the international chain; there's also free bike rental, and kids eat for free in its restaurant. €69

Mr. Meyers Diner Humboldtstr. 12 ☎0375 28 34 96 65, ⓦmeyers-diner.com. Just west of the Altstadt, this small American diner has seating in booths or on stools, and serves up tasty ribs and burgers (around €9), steak and pancakes. Wash it all down with lemonade or Californian wine. Mon–Thurs 10am–10pm, Fri 10am–midnight, Sat 9am–midnight, Sun 9am–10pm.

Wenzel Prager Bierstuben Domhof 12 ☎0375 273 75 42, ⓦwenzel-bierstuben.de. A rustic tourist favourite, with solid German and Czech food including excellent dumplings, pork goulash, hare and trout (€8–15), and four types of Czech beer. The weekday lunch menu is good value at €6.90. Mon–Thurs & Sun 11am–10pm, Fri & Sat 11am–11pm.

Saxony-Anhalt and the Harz

MARKT, QUEDLINBURG

Saxony-Anhalt and the Harz

Saxony-Anhalt (Sachsen-Anhalt) divides into two distinct landscapes: to the east sandy plains are scattered with farms, pastures, pine forests and bogs, and a series of gritty, postindustrial cities; while to the west the land suddenly rises into the gentle Harz mountains where sleepy villages nestle in dark forests. Though the range straddles the old border between East and West Germany and is today divided between Saxony-Anhalt and Lower Saxony (see p.690), for convenience the entire range is covered in this chapter.

State capital **Magdeburg** is relatively small and parochial, but does have a few interesting sights, particularly its cathedral, as well as some urban distractions and reasonable nightlife. North along the Elbe, the **Altmark** region is a real backwater, a thinly populated heathland, where a clutch of low-key towns – particularly half-timbered Tangermünde – preserve a very traditional feel.

East of Magdeburg along the Elbe is almost as rural, apart from two towns with heavyweight contributions to world history: Dessau, whose **Bauhaus** school invented Modernist architecture and design; and **Lutherstadt Wittenberg**, birthplace of the sixteenth-century Protestant Reformation which divided the Christian Church. In between the two, the English country gardens of Wörlitz provide an attractive respite.

Southern Saxony-Anhalt is focused on the postindustrial but upbeat university town of **Halle**, with its own small crop of attractions, and great dining and nightlife. It sits on the Saale River, upstream from which lies **Naumburg**, famous for its grand cathedral and Germany's most northerly wine region in nearby Freyburg. Meanwhile, just west of Halle, in the foothills of the Harz mountains, lies **Lutherstadt Eisleben**, the town where Martin Luther was born, died, and is now relentlessly celebrated.

The key eastern gateway to the **Harz mountains** is the half-timbered town of **Quedlinburg**, which is pretty enough to deserve a place on anyone's Germany itinerary. From here it's a short hop to northern Germany's premier mountain playground, whose main attractions are outdoorsy: **hiking** and **cycling** in summer and **tobogganing** and **skiing** – particularly cross-country – in winter. The Harz villages and towns are well equipped for all this, and noteworthy for some excellent **spas** to help you unwind at the end of the day. Some of the best of these lie on the northern fringes of the Harz in **Bad Harzburg**, while the nearby town of **Goslar** is another quintessential half-timbered gem, almost rivalling Quedlinburg in attractiveness.

Road and **rail** links are good throughout Saxony-Anhalt, with the entire eastern half a reasonable day-trip from Berlin. The Harz needs and rewards more relaxed exploration, ideally on foot, by bike, or on its network of charming old **narrow-gauge railways**.

Brief history
Extractive industries and large navigable **rivers** – particularly the Elbe and Saale – were of foremost importance in settling this region. Forestry, salt, copper, coal and lignite all

BAUHAUS FOUNDATION AND DESIGN SCHOOL, DESSAU

Highlights

❶ **Bauhaus** Heighten your aesthetic appreciation of clean lines and creative thinking at this seminal design school. **See p.197**

❷ **Lutherhaus Wittenberg** Discover the origins of the Protestant Reformation and the people who triggered it. **See p.201**

❸ **Händel Festival** Spoil your ears with the melodious work of George Frideric Handel in his home town, Halle. **See p.207**

❹ **Quedlinburg** Germany at its half-timbered best. **See p.215**

❺ **Sauna in Altenau** With facilities to rival any of the spas and saunas that dot the Harz, Altenau's saunas and outdoor pools also boast

splendid views. **See p.219**

❻ **Bode Valley** Hike a deep and verdant valley to see the Harz mountains at their most picturesque. **See p.220**

❼ **Rübeland** Atmospheric limestone caverns that can be explored without the need for risky speleology. **See p.221**

❽ **Walpurgisnacht** Let your imagination run riot during ancient celebrations of witches and the supernatural. **See p.221**

❾ **Skiing** The varied terrain of Braunlage is the Harz's largest resort, with its most dependable conditions. **See p.222**

HIGHLIGHTS ARE MARKED ON THE MAP ON P.188

played their part in shaping it over the centuries. As a rich industrious area, it has regularly been a battleground, with the **Thirty Years' War** badly battering the region and **World War II** levelling its largest cities. The state of **Saxony-Anhalt** was first formed after World War II when the occupying Russians cobbled together the former Duchy of Anhalt with the old Prussian province of Saxony. The union only lasted a few years before re-division, but was resurrected in the wake of German reunification in 1990, with **Magdeburg** the state capital. In the decade that followed, heavy industrial production – which the GDR had feverishly built – dropped by more than

SAXONY-ANHALT AND THE HARZ

HIGHLIGHTS

1. Bauhaus
2. Lutherhaus Wittenberg
3. Händel Festival
4. Quedlinburg
5. Sauna in Altenau
6. Bode Valley
7. Rübeland
8. Walpurgisnacht
9. Skiing

BIKE SAXONY-ANHALT

The easy gradients of the fine riverside cycle paths that join all its most rewarding towns have made Saxony-Anhalt popular for exploration by bike. The 980km **Elberadweg** (Elbe cycle path; Ⓦ elberadweg.de) is excellent for a long-distance tour of the state, as is the 410km **Saaleradweg** that runs along the Saale River from close to the Czech border to its confluence with the Elbe near Magdeburg. Meanwhile the 65km **Gartenreichtour Fürst-Franz** near Wörlitz and the **Unstrut Radweg** between Freyburg and Naumburg are both ideal for a leisurely, long weekend. The government-run website, Ⓦ radtouren-sachsen-anhalt.de, is the best place for information and tips – though all in German.

---

three-quarters and employment by more than nine-tenths, with high levels of unemployment particularly blighting the south of the state, where mining and chemical works had prevailed. The situation has since stabilized, but the state remains one of Germany's poorest.

Magdeburg

MAGDEBURG is sometimes described as Berlin in miniature and there's some truth to this, even if it's not much larger than one of the national capital's neighbourhoods. Certainly Magdeburg was destroyed to a similar extent, with World War II bombs levelling four-fifths of the city. Then, postwar rebuilding projects blighted it with large socialist buildings, soulless boulevards, loveless plazas and windswept parks. Yet tiny pockets of cobbled streets with nineteenth-century tenements did survive, notably at the southern end of the city around **Hasselbachplatz**, where a buoyant **bar and club scene** has taken hold. Magdeburg has also struggled economically and is propped up by generous federal funding – in this case thanks to the town's role as capital of Saxony-Anhalt. With this economic boost has come a major makeover of many parts of town: bold new architecture has been welcomed and Friedensreich Hundertwasser's Grüne Zitadelle has become a major landmark, offsetting the angular bleakness elsewhere.

Brief history

Its modernity aside, Magdeburg is not without reminders of its lengthy history. Established as a trading post by Charlemagne in the tenth century, it became great under Emperor Otto I who chose it as his main residence, making it a significant political and cultural centre in medieval times and giving it Germany's oldest cathedral. It was badly hammered by siege and fires in the Thirty Years' War when two-thirds of the population – around 20,000 people – lost their lives; some heavyweight city defences still stem from this time. In the seventeenth century Magdeburg slowly resurfaced thanks in part to the work of **Otto von Guericke**, who was famous for his physics experiments, and though it lost most of its political importance with the abolition of the city's bishopric in 1680, it continued to be a major port on the Elbe.

MAGDEBURG ORIENTATION

Ernst-Reuter-Allee, the town's major east–west thoroughfare, runs from the Hauptbahnhof to the Elbe. Partway along it – and beside the tourist office and giant Allee Center shopping mall – it intersects with **Breiter Weg**, the main north–south artery. Just northeast of the intersection lies the **Alter Markt**, the city's old marketplace, but most sights – including the **Dom** and Hasselbachplatz – are on or around Breiter Weg to the south.

The Alter Markt and around

Magdeburg's traditional centre, the **Alter Markt**, is the location of the **Magdeburger Reiter**, Magdeburg's most famous artwork, which has the distinction of being the earliest (1240) equestrian statue north of the Alps. The gilded statue is a copy of the sandstone original, now in the **Kulturhistorisches Museum** (see p.192). The rider is generally thought to be Otto I, with two wives alongside; he looks on at a *Roland* statue and the late seventeenth-century Baroque **Rathaus** behind. The lady on the facade of the Rathaus is the Magdeburger Jungfrau, symbol of the city; one of the Rathaus's main doors depicts scenes from Magdeburg's history carved by local artist Heinrich Apel. One scene is devoted to the experiments of **Otto von Guericke**, whose statue also commands attention on the square.

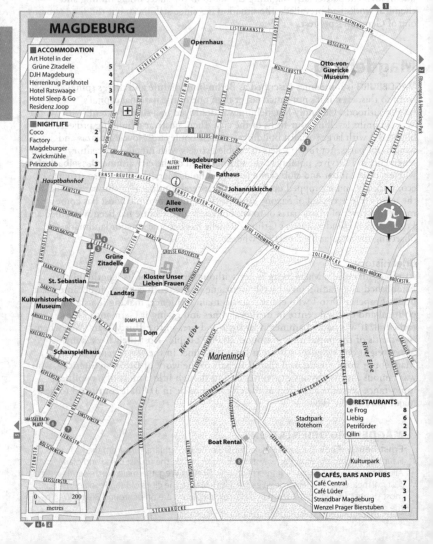

OTTO VON GUERICKE (1602–86)

So extraordinary was the life's work of Magdeburg-born Otto Guericke that he almost single-handedly wrote Magdeburg not only into the history books but also physics textbooks – accomplishments that earned him a knighthood and the surname von Guericke. His most important discovery came as the result of his **Magdeburg Hemispheres** experiments, which demonstrated the principle of a vacuum. Using a home-made pump, he sucked the air from two copper hemispheres which had been joined together, creating a vacuum so powerful that even two teams of sixteen horses couldn't pull them apart – to the amazement of the 1654 Reichstag of Regensburg. Guericke also pioneered the use of a barometer to predict weather and conducted early electrical experiments. All this activity was vital in promoting Magdeburg as the city rebuilt itself after its destruction in the Thirty Years' War. As if that wasn't enough, Guericke juggled his scientific investigations with his other job, as a diplomatic representative and later city mayor – though he was better known locally as a vet and a brewer.

Otto-von-Guericke Museum

Schleinufer 1 · Tues–Sun 10am–5pm · Free · ☏ 0391 541 06 16

The life and work of seventeenth-century scientist Otto von Guericke (see box opposite), and a reconstruction of his study, are the subject of the interesting little **Otto-von-Guericke Museum**, which lies five minutes' walk north from the Alter Markt along the Elbe in the **Lukasklause**, a fifteenth-century brick tower that was once part of the town's defences.

Grüne Zitadelle

Information office daily 10am–6pm; 1hr tours in German Nov–March Mon–Fri 11am, 3pm & 5pm, Sat & Sun hourly 10am–5pm · €6, English-language booklet €3.90 · ☏ 0391 620 86 55, ⊛ gruene-zitadelle.de

Walking south beside trams that rattle along the arterial Breiter Weg, the most eye-catching building is the **Grüne Zitadelle**, whose curvy, zany form is the unmistakeable work of Viennese architect Friedensreich Hundertwasser. The building – a mix of apartments, shops, offices and a hotel (see p.192) – was his last, completed five years after his death in 2005.

Kloster Unser Lieben Frauen

Regierungsstr. 4–6 · Tues–Sun 10am–5pm · €4 · ⊛ kunstmuseum-magdeburg.de

Behind the Hundertwasser building, along Erhard-Hübener-Platz, lies **Kloster Unser Lieben Frauen**, an austere, late eleventh-century Romanesque church and Magdeburg's oldest building. Inside it has been stripped of all ornamentation to serve as a concert hall, but the door is worth a look for Heinrich Apel's unusual bronze door-handles: knock with the woman's necklace, then push down the man's cap to enter. Inside a modest **sculpture museum** features works by Barlach and Rodin.

Dom St Mauritius und St Katharina

Am Dom 1 · Daily: Jan–March 10am–4pm; May–Oct 10am–6pm; April, Nov & Dec 10am–5pm; tours in German Mon–Sat 2pm & Sun 11.30am · €3 · ⊛ magdeburgerdom.de

A large square surrounded by Baroque mansions lead up to Magdeburg's impressive cathedral **Dom St Mauritius und St Katharina**, with its distinctive octagonal turrets and spires. One of Germany's most important Gothic structures, it was begun in 1209 on the site of an earlier monastery church that was founded by Emperor Otto the Great in 926 – there's some lopsided evidence of the original building on the south side – but it was largely built in the fourteenth century and completed in 1520. Inside, the vastness of the structure and its lofty ceilings immediately impress and serve to exaggerate its bleak emptiness. An English-language booklet sold at the entrance desk explains all the main features and artworks which span eight centuries. Don't miss the tomb of Otto I and his English wife Editha, Ernst Barlach's contemplative memorial to the dead of World War I and the sculpture of the Magdeburger Virgins.

The Kulturhistorisches Museum

Otto-von-Guericke-Str. 68 • Tues–Sun 10am–5pm • €5 • ⓦ khm-magdeburg.de

A five-minute walk west of the Dom, across Breiter Weg, lies the **Kulturhistorisches Museum**, Magdeburg's modest town history museum, whose most valuable treasure is the thirteenth-century **Magdeburger Reiter** equestrian statue, a copy of which stands on Alter Markt (see p.190).

The Marieninsel and Rotehornpark

What looks to be the eastern bank of the Elbe from Magdeburg's city centre is actually the Marieninsel, a large river island that's almost entirely filled by the **Rotehornpark**, a large public park with playgrounds, picnic areas, beer gardens and rowing boat rental, and the sort of place where there's often a fair or weekend flea market.

Elbauenpark

Elbauenpark Tessenowstr. 5a • May–Sept 9am–8pm; Oct–April hours vary • €3 • **Jahrtausendturm** April–Oct Tues–Sun 10am–6pm • Schmetterlingshaus April–Oct Tues–Sun 10am–6pm • ⓦ mvgm-online.de • Tram #6 to stop "Messegelände Elbauenpark"

On the eastern bank of the Elbe, some 2.5km from Magdeburg's Altstadt, lies the **Elbauenpark**, an extensive enclosed park with a couple of resident commercial attractions. The key one is the **Jahrtausendturm**, a funky piece of architecture in the form of a conical tower with an external walkway that spirals around it. Inside a hands-on museum celebrates scientific achievement, including of course that of local hero Otto von Guericke. It's great for kids, but a bit of a struggle if you can't read German. Otherwise the **Schmetterlingshaus** (Butterfly House) is the most interesting feature of the strollable gardens. For a larger and wilder park landscape, take tram #6 to its terminus at **Herrenkrugpark**.

ARRIVAL AND GETTING AROUND   MAGDEBURG

By train From the Hauptbahnhof it's a short walk east along Ernst-Reuter-Allee, to the tourist office.

Destinations Dessau (hourly; 1hr); Goslar (hourly; 2hr); Halle (hourly; 50min); Quedlinburg (hourly; 1hr 20min); Tangermünde (hourly; 1hr 10min).

By bus and tram The city is easily walkable, but a good bus and tram network can speed things up (singles €1.80, day-tickets €4).

Bike rental Little John Bikes, Alter Markt 13–14 (ⓣ 0391 555 62 03, ⓦ littlejohnbikes.de), has a large fleet of rental bikes from €10 per day.

INFORMATION AND TOURS

Tourist office Ernst-Reuter-Allee 12 (April–Oct Mon–Fri 10am–6.30pm, Sat 10am–4pm; Nov–March Mon–Fri 10am–6pm, Sat 10am–3pm; ⓣ 0391 194 33, ⓦ magdeburg-tourist.de). The tourist office has many private rooms on its books, useful given that accommodation in Magdeburg tends to be business-orientated.

Boat trips Boat company Weisse Flotte (ⓣ 0391 532 88 91, ⓦ weisseflotte-magdeburg.de) offers short cruises on the Elbe, with those that explore the Wasserstrassenkreuz – an unusual 918m aqueduct across the Elbe – the most interesting (2.5hr; €17). For longer jaunts on the river, including trips to the Altmark (see p.194), try Reederei Kaiser (ⓦ reederei-kaiser.de), whose day-trips (8hr; €25) stop at Tangermünde and Havelberg.

ACCOMMODATION

HOTELS AND PENSIONS

★ **Art Hotel in der Grüne Zitadelle** Breiter Weg 9 ⓣ 0391 62 07 80, ⓦ arthotel-magdeburg.com. Stay in the wobbly world of Hundertwasser (see p.191), where the decor in most rooms is curvaceous if restrained, though the bathroom mosaics are pure mayhem. Wi-fi is available and there's a sauna too. **€109**

Herrenkrug Parkhotel Herrenkrug 3 ☎0391 850 80, ⓦherrenkrug.de. Four-star pile set in a quiet bucolic park around 5km northeast of town, with a good spa and a well-respected and funky Art Deco restaurant, and extensive pool and sauna facilities. Wi-fi extra. **€124**

Hotel Ratswaage Ratswaageplatz 1 ☎0391 592 60, ⓦratswaage.de. Dependable and central 4-star hotel a short walk north of the centre, with pool, sauna and fabulous breakfast buffet. Weekday and online rates can be a third lower. **€80**

Hotel Sleep & Go Rogätzer Str. 5a ☎0391 53 77 91, ⓦhotel-sleep-and-go.de. Budget multistorey hotel with clean but fairly spartan rooms a 20min walk north of the Altstadt. Many rooms have balconies and there's free parking and wi-fi too. **€50**

Residenz Joop Jean-Burger-Str. 16 ☎0391 626 60, ⓦresidenzjoop.de. Elegant B&B in a small villa an easy walk from Hasselbachplatz, the nightlife district. The decor's a bit too floral and chintzy, but the breakfast buffet is excellent. Free wi-fi. **€114**

HOSTELS

DJH Magdeburg Leiterstr. 10 ☎0391 532 10 10, ⓦjugendherberge.de. Large, modern, central and well-equipped youth hostel offering bike rental, wi-fi and spacious en-suite dorm rooms with no more than four bunk beds. A good buffet breakfast is included. Dorms **€21.50**, doubles **€52**

EATING AND DRINKING

CAFÉS, BARS AND PUBS

★**Café Central** Leibnizstr. 34 ☎0163 237 39 86, ⓦcafecentral.cc. Opulent but relaxed *fin de siècle*-style hangout and a great place to play the board games that are supplied, or appreciate the varied programme of cabaret, readings, films and lectures. Daily 8pm–2am.

Café Lüder Allee Center ☎0391 562 07 52. Located on the top level of Magdeburg's biggest mall, it may lack ambience, but the quality of the cakes at this *Konditorei* is hard to argue with and the open-plan seating offers good people-watching at all hours. Daily 10am–6pm.

★**Strandbar Magdeburg** Petriförder 1 ☎0175 594 00 59, ⓦstrandbar-magdeburg.de. Get bright white sands between your toes while you lounge on a deckchair and sip a cocktail. This small, urban beach beside the Elbe has a number of food stalls, and various sociable and well-attended events – including films, DJs and beach-volleyball contests. April–Oct daily 11am–1am.

Wenzel Prager Bierstuben Leiterstr. 3 ☎0391 544 66 16. Branch of a dependable, regional chain of rustic Czech places that specialize in good beers and various, moderately priced, heavy meat meals (€7–14) – all of which should apparently be chased by a *Becherovka*, an aniseed and cinnamon herbal liqeur. Daily 11am–11pm.

RESTAURANTS

Le Frog Heinrich-Heine-Platz 1 ☎0391 531 35 56, ⓦlefrog-md.de. Brasserie in the Rotehornpark, whose large beer garden regularly hosts live music. Good for breakfast and even better for Sat and Sun brunch (€19), which tends to draw crowds. Otherwise the broad menu includes some local game and wild mushrooms along with a few good salads and veggie options. Mains average €12. Daily 10am–midnight.

Liebig Liebigstr. 3 ☎0391 555 67 54, ⓦliebig-lounge .de. Trendy spot that's as much a bar and café as restaurant, though the international food – from curries to steaks to Mediterranean dishes (all around €11) – is worth trying. Daily 10am–late (food until midnight).

Petriförder Petriförder 1 ☎0391 597 96 00, ⓦrestaurant-petrifoerder-magdeburg.eu. Large restaurant with a rather pleasant riverside location and a rambling menu that includes numerous Italian options (pizzas average a very reasonable €7) but also a good line in *Schnitzel* (€13) and Argentinian steaks (€17). Mon–Fri 11.30am–late, Sat & Sun 10am–late.

Qilin Leiterstr. 1 ☎0391 243 99 44, ⓦqilin-md.de. Stylish, modern pan-Asian restaurant with a wide spectrum of dishes from sushi to tempeh to stir-fries. All are reasonably priced (mains €10–15, half that at lunch) and MSG-free. Mon–Sat 11.30am–11pm, Sun noon–11pm.

NIGHTLIFE AND ENTERTAINMENT

In contrast to the town's eating scene, the busy and fairly studenty nightlife couldn't be more central, with most spots within a couple of blocks of Hasselbachplatz at the southern end of the town centre. For event listings check the magazine *DATEs* (ⓦdates-md.de), available at the tourist office.

BARS AND CLUBS

★**Coco** Otto-von-Guericke-Str. 56 ☎0391 636 08 88, ⓦcoco-md.de. Serving hands-down Magdeburg's best cocktails, and with a peerless selection (most around €5 mark). Consequently it's very busy and sociable, particularly on Wed when there's live music. Similar places dot adjacent city blocks. Daily 6pm–5am.

Factory Karl-Schmidt-Str. 26–29 ☎0391 59 07 95 30, ⓦfactory-magdeburg.de. Leading larger venue for all sorts of clubnights, live music and artsy events; always

3

worth a look. Hours vary, but most weekend nights 7pm–late.

Prinzzclub Halberstädter Str. 113 ⓦprinzzclub.de. Magdeburg's leading club, where most visiting celebrities and bands end up partying. It has two bars and a lounge and often as not hip-hop thundering across its dancefloor. Located 1km southwest of town along Halberstädter Strasse. Wed, Fri & Sat 11pm–late.

CABARET, THEATRE AND OPERA

Magdeburger Zwickmühle Leiterstr. 2a ⓣ0391 541 44 26, ⓦmagdeburger-zwickmuehle.de. Popular satirical cabaret bar, great if your German's up to it; tickets cost around €20. Also serves good pub-food from 6.30pm onwards: mains €9–15. Performances daily 8pm–late.

Opernhaus Universitätsplatz 9 ⓣ0391 540 65 00, tickets ⓣ0391 540 65 55, ⓦtheater-magdeburg.de. The town's main forum for high culture and home to opera and ballet companies and the Magdeburg Philharmonic. The strong point tends to be well-known works like Verdi's *La Traviata* or Mozart's *Don Giovanni* as well as Andrew Lloyd Webber musicals. Hours vary, most nights from around 6pm.

Schauspielhaus Otto-von-Guericke-Str. 64 ⓣ0391 540 63 00, tickets ⓣ0391 540 65 55, ⓦtheater -magdeburg.de. Run alongside the Opernhaus, this is the other main stage in Magdeburg. It focuses on theatre and well-known pieces like Goethe's *Faust* or Shakespeare's *Hamlet*, but also has regular jazz nights. Hours vary, mostly Fri & Sat from around 6pm.

The Altmark

North of Magdeburg, the Elbe flows into the secluded and gently rolling **Altmark** region where little disturbs the peace – and seemingly hasn't for centuries, with all its most significant towns being beautifully preserved medieval gems. The most atmospheric and interesting are the small fortified towns of **Tangermünde** on the banks of the Elbe and, 40km downstream at its confluence with the Havel, **Havelberg**. The region is only lightly visited, with few services and little going on, Havelberg's **Pferdemarkt** festival (see opposite) being the exception.

Tangermünde and around

The faded charm of **TANGERMÜNDE**, 65km northeast of Magdeburg, makes it the most delightful Altmark town. Its cobblestone central streets are lined almost exclusively by half-timbered houses, most hailing from the seventeenth century and built after the town was destroyed by a 1617 fire. This was blamed on one Grete Minde, who was subsequently burned as a witch, and celebrated for her suffering two centuries later in the eponymous Theodor Fontane novel. But the town's roots go back much further: it grew rapidly in medieval times when trade boomed with its membership of the Hanseatic League. For centuries it was also the seat of the Brandenburg margraves and then in the late fourteenth century, second royal residence to Charles IV, king of Bohemia, after Prague.

The Burg

Some of Charles IV's **Burg** remains as part of the town's foreboding riverside defences. The bulk of these defences are far younger though, being rebuilt versions of the originals which were destroyed by Swedes during the Thirty Years' War in 1640. Today the Burg is given over to a small public park and the town's finest hotel (see opposite).

St Stephanskirche

Almost beside the Burg lies the town's other grand building, the **St Stephanskirche**, a church built for the Augustinian monks brought into town by Charles IV in 1377. The magnificent Late Gothic structure was finally completed at the end of the fifteenth century, though many of its most interesting features came later, including a 1624 organ from the Hamburg workshop of Hans Scherer the Younger, a 1619 pulpit by Christopher Dehne and a font from 1508 by Heinrich Mente.

The Markt and around

Southeast of the Stephanskirche, reached via **Kirchstrasse** – one of the two main streets that run parallel through town, and featuring many of the finest half-timbered houses with richly painted doorways – lies the **Markt**. Its timber-framed **Rathaus** is one of Tangermünde's oldest buildings, built during its commercial zenith of the 1430s, and studded with a forest of gables and pinnacles. Further along, Kirchstrasse terminates beside the magnificent **Neustädter Tor**, another impressive remnant of the city walls from around 1300.

Jerichow Abbey

Jerichow • Tues–Sun: April–Oct 10am–5pm; Nov–March 10am–4pm • €3 • Bus #742 from Bahnhof Tangermünde (6 daily; 22min)

Lying 13km southeast of Tangermünde, **Jerichow Abbey** was founded by Premonstratensians in 1144 and – like Havelberg's Dom (see p.195) – was part of a spate of ecclesiastical and German expansion onto the right bank of the Elbe around this time. Built in a late-Romanesque style using local brick methods, it's one of northern Germany's oldest such buildings. It's also graceful enough to well justify a look as you pass through the eponymous village on your way to or from Tangermünde.

3

ARRIVAL AND INFORMATION

TANGERMÜNDE

By train Tangermünde's Bahnhof lies a short walk north of the Altstadt.
Destinations Hannover (hourly; 2hr); Magdeburg (hourly; 1hr 15min).
By boat Pleasure boats sail up the Elbe to Tangermünde

from Magdeburg (see p.192).
Tourist office Markt 2 (April–Oct Mon–Fri 9am–6pm, Sat & Sun 10am–6pm; Nov–March Mon–Fri 10am–5pm, Sat 10am–4pm, Sun 1–4pm; ☎039322 223 93, ⓦ tourismus-tangermuende.de).

ACCOMMODATION AND EATING

Alte Brauerei Lange Str. 34 ☎039322 441 45, ⓦ hotel -alte-brauerei.de. A solid mid-range accommodation choice and one of several German food options clustered around the church: its range of salads, steaks and fish dishes cost around €8, the excellent Sun brunch €15. Restaurant mid-April to mid-Oct daily 11.45am–late; mid-Oct to mid-April Mon–Fri 5.30pm–late, Sat & Sun 11.45pm–late. **€79**
★ **Exempel** Kirchstr. 40. ☎039322 448 99, ⓦ exempel .de/exempel. The intriguing *Exempel*, set in a former schoolhouse with original furnishings and various cheerful bits of clutter, serves old-fashioned dishes such as pea soup as well as the local *Kuhschwanz* beer. Most mains around

€10. Daily 11am–11pm.
Schloss Tangermünde Amt 1 ☎039322 73 73, ⓦ schloss-tangermuende.de. The town's most prestigious hotel, with attentive service, dark-beamed rooms and a sauna. It also has the town's most upmarket restaurant, which nonetheless tends to focus on traditional regional dishes like wild boar, *Eisbein* (pork knuckle) and zander. Mains are around the €14 mark, but the more gourmet four-course set meal is good value at €29. It also has wonderful terrace seating with river views, when the weather's good. Restaurant Mon–Fri 5.30pm–10pm, Sat & Sun 11.30am–1pm. **€137**

Havelberg

Founded by Otto I in 948 as a Christian missionary outpost, **HAVELBERG** centres on a dense cluster of crooked houses that cheerfully squeeze together on a small island in the Havel River. The time to be in Havelberg is during its **Pferdemarkt** – a huge fair on the first weekend in September. This one-time horse market now combines a flea market with beer tents, fairground rides and handicraft stalls to be one of eastern Germany's largest festivals, involving thousands of visitors.

Dom St Marien

Domstr. 3 • Mon–Fri 10am–5pm, Sat 10am–6pm, Sun noon–6pm; May–Sept closes 7pm daily • Free • ⓦ havelberg-dom.de

Dom St Marien, built between 1150 and 1170, dominates the town's skyline. A cheerless and forbidding structure, its many Romanesque and Gothic features are the result of several rebuilds following a huge thirteenth-century fire and several later redesigns. The chief treasure in its impressive interior is a fourteenth-century stone choir-screen carved with the Passion of Christ. An excellent English-language guide can be borrowed from the front desk to explain this and many other church features.

ARRIVAL AND INFORMATION HAVELBERG

By bus Buses from Tangermünde (6 daily; 1hr) stop on Uferstrasse, by the river close to the town centre.
By boat Pleasure boats sail up the Elbe to Havelberg via Tangermünde from Magdeburg (see p.192).

Tourist office By the river (April–Sept Mon–Fri 9am–6pm, Sat & Sun 1–5pm; Oct–March Mon–Fri 9am–5pm, Sat 1–5pm; ☎039387 790 91, ⓦhavelberg .de).

EATING

Das Bilderbuchcafé Am Markt 7 ☎039387 59 25 55. Lovely little café overlooking the town's marketplace serving superb coffees, breakfasts, various light meals

(soups, salads, *Schnitzel* €5–12) as well as superlative cakes. Also features changing exhibitions of local art. Daily 9.30am–9pm.

Dessau and around

DESSAU, 60km southwest of Magdeburg, was once an attractive town at the centre of a patchwork of palaces, parks and gardens. The latter have survived, but war damage, Stalinist rebuilding programmes and years of GDR neglect have made the actual town pretty bland. But what does justify the journey here are the town's remnants of the Bauhaus movement (see box opposite). Built here in 1925, the **Bauhaus design school** once made Dessau the hub of Modernism and the first place where many modern designs were implemented; these include the **Meisterhäuser**, the villas of the most influential thinkers, and the **Törten**, the first modern housing estate. All this makes it a place of pilgrimage for architecture students, but it is interesting enough to appeal to anyone inquisitive about the roots of modern design.

The belt of landscaped parks in and around Dessau have been collectively dubbed the **Gartenreich** (Garden Realm; ⓦgartenreich.com) and offer days of unhurried exploration and picnicking, with their attendant Baroque and Neoclassical mansions an additional draw. The most extensive and impressive of all the complexes is **Wörlitz** (see p.200), but the most convenient is **Park Georgium**, a short walk from the Meisterhäuser in central Dessau.

Stiftung Bauhaus Dessau

Gropiusallee 38 **Bauhaus Foundation** Mon–Fri 9am–6pm, tours in German Mon–Fri 11am & 2pm, mid-Feb to Oct also Sat & Sun noon & 4pm • Audio-guide in English €5, tour in German €5 • ⓦ bauhaus-dessau.de • **Ausstellung im Bauhaus** Mon–Fri 10am–5pm • €7.50, combined ticket with Meisterhäuser €16

The one-time hub of the worldwide Bauhaus movement was Dessau's **Bauhausgebäude**, which now houses the **Stiftung Bauhaus Dessau** (Bauhaus Foundation). The work of Walter Gropius, this white concrete building with its huge plate-glass windows was refurbished on its eightieth anniversary in 2006, making it look tremendously new. The famous Bauhaus logo graces the southern side; the photogenic "swimming pool" balconies its eastern wall.

---

24 HOURS OF BAUHAUS

If you're in Dessau on a Bauhaus pilgrimage, be sure to pick up a **24-hour ticket** (€22) at the Bauhausgebäude. It gets you into all publicly-accessible Bauhaus buildings and on all tours of them within a 24-hour period. Complete the experience by dining at the *Mensa* (see p.200) or the *Kornhaus* (see p.199) and sleep in the *Prellerhaus*, the school's former student accommodation (see p.199).

BAUHAUS

Bauhaus, whose literal meaning in German is "building-house", has become a generic term for the aesthetically functional designs that emerged from the art and design school at Dessau. The **Bauhaus movement** began with the **Novembergruppe**, founded in 1918 by Expressionist painter Max Pechstein to utilize art for revolutionary purposes. Members included Bertolt Brecht, Kurt Weill, Emil Nolde, Eric Mendelssohn and architect Walter Gropius. In 1919 Gropius was invited by Germany's new republican government to oversee the amalgamation of the School of Arts and Crafts and the Academy of Fine Arts in Weimar into the **Staatliche Bauhaus Weimar**. The new institution was to break down barriers between art and craft, creating a new form of applied art. It attracted over two hundred students who studied typography, furniture design, ceramics, wood-, glass- and metalworking under exponents like Paul Klee, Wassily Kandinsky and László Moholy-Nagy.

Financial problems and opposition from the conservative administration in Weimar eventually forced a relocation to Dessau, chosen because, as home to a number of modern industrial concerns, notably an aeroplane factory and a chemical works, it could provide financial and material support. Dessau's **Bauhausgebäude**, designed by Gropius and inaugurated on December 4, 1926, is one of the movement's classic buildings. Towards the end of the 1920s, the staff and students of the Bauhaus school became increasingly embroiled in the political battles of the time. As a result, Gropius was pressurized into resigning by the authorities and replaced by Swiss architect Hannes Meyer. He, in turn, was dismissed in 1930 because of the increasingly left-wing orientation of the school. His successor Ludwig Mies van der Rohe tried to establish an apolitical atmosphere, but throughout the early 1930s Dessau's **Nazi** town councillors called for an end to Bauhaus subsidies. Their efforts finally succeeded in 1932, forcing the school to close and relocate to a disused telephone factory in more liberal **Berlin**. However, after the Nazis came to power, police harassment reached such a pitch that in 1933, Mies van der Rohe decided to shut up shop for good. He and many of the staff and students subsequently went into exile in the USA, where they helped found a successor movement known as the **International Style**.

At the time of its construction the building was an architectural sensation and prototype for several construction techniques. A reinforced concrete skeleton allowed for curtain walling – outer walls designed to carry nothing but their own weight – and introduced wide-span building techniques that opened up more useable floor space by removing the need for supporting columns. These principles really flourished from the 1950s and 1960s and have dominated ever since – making them less of a spectacle for today's viewer.

Though still in use as a design school, the public can wander round much of the building, with the audio tour a useful accompaniment, particularly if you can't make the hour-long tours in German which access otherwise locked areas. Both can be organized at the first-floor front desk, which sells tickets to Dessau's other Bauhaus attractions and is the entrance to the **Ausstellung im Bauhaus** (Exhibition in the Bauhaus), which explores the experimental application of Bauhaus theory in just about every sphere of art and design, including ceramics, furniture, theatre and visual art. Finally, the well-stocked basement **book and gift shop** is also worth a look.

The Meisterhäuser

Ebertallee 69 • Daily: April–Sept 10am–5pm; Oct–March 10am–5pm; Tours Tues–Sun 12.30pm & 3.30pm, Sat & Sun also 1.30pm • €7.50, combined ticket with Ausstellung im Bauhaus €16, tours €5 • ⓦ meisterhaeuser.de

Several distinguished Bauhaus professors once lived in the **Meisterhäuser**, a series of Cubist villas a five-minute walk from the Bauhausgebäude: turn right up Gropiusallee then left onto Ebertallee. These quarters were supposed to espouse a philosophy of new industrial living, yet contained features and designs – such as large windows and complicated lighting systems – that put them well outside the pockets of the masses, so arguably contravened Bauhaus ideals. Sadly too, original Bauhaus furnishings are lacking, since they're now simply too expensive to buy, as the prices in the antique shop along Gropiusallee en route from the Bauhausgebäude confirm. However, in their absence, photos of original setups help give an impression, as do the informative German-language **tours**.

The Gropius Haus

The most important of the Meisterhäuser, the **Gropius Haus**, lies at the start of the street. As the director's house it was something of a model for the others, and indeed the whole Bauhaus movement. The design itself was inspired by children's building blocks and was initially filled by Gropius with all sorts of modern functional gadgetry: electric cookers and complete sanitation systems made it an advert for modern living, and Walter and Ilse Gropius operated something of an open-house policy to advertise it. Much of Gropius's work was chucked out by the next director, **Hannes Meyer**, who hated the house's complexity, and more changes were made by his successor, **Ludwig Mies van der Rohe**, who found the property's compartmentalization of life anathema in his quest to design free-flowing spaces.

An air raid in World War II destroyed the input of all three directors, but in 2014 the house was finally **reconstructed**, using structural elements of the original design but without faithfully reproducing every detail, which for the visitor craving an insight from original floor plans ends up being a bit unsatisfactory.

The Moholy-Nagy/Feininger Haus

The **Moholy-Nagy/Feininger Haus**, beside the Gropius House, is the first of three semidetached properties along the street that all champion homogeneity and design purity. Like the Gropius Haus, it was badly damaged in an air raid, but has been fairly faithfully rebuilt since. A scatter of photos of original studio and living room helps bring some impressive spaces to life.

The Feininger half of the property – belonging to German-American artist Lyonel Feininger – is now home to the **Kurt-Weill-Zentrum**, which celebrates the work of the versatile Dessau musician who's famed for cabaret pieces such as *Mack the Knife* in *The Threepenny Opera*, a collaboration between Weill and Brecht.

The Muche/Schlemmer Haus and Kandinsky/Klee Haus

The other two semidetached properties in the Meisterhäuser are known as the **Muche/Schlemmer Haus** and the **Kandinsky/Klee Haus**. The former, with its many intriguing prototype design features, is only open to the public on tours, while the latter – home to the artists Wassily Kandinsky and Paul Klee, and containing reproductions of the pastel walls chosen by them – can be visited independently. The Kandinsky/Klee Haus also contains some **background exhibitions** on the houses, which include various newspaper cuttings from the era that convey something of the excitement and realization, even then, of the importance of the design movement. Photos of a Bauhaus carnival – a woman dressed as a wing-nut and a man as a spoon soldier – show a little of the offbeat attitude and humour of the movement too.

Park Georgium

The large road junction just east of the Meisterhäuser – where Ebertallee, Gropiusallee and Kornhausstrasse meet – is presided over by some Neoclassical columns that announce the gateway to the **Park Georgium**, one of the Gartenreich parks in and around Dessau. The columns and other buildings in the park – which include a number of faux ruins – come across as strange frippery after the austere Bauhaus designs, particularly the ornate **Schloss Georgium** from 1780. It now houses the **Anhalt Art Gallery** (Tues–Sun 10am–5pm; €3; ☏0340 61 38 74), a collection of old masters that includes Rubens, Hals and Cranach. The rest of the park extends north to the banks of the Elbe, a little over 1km away, and includes over a hundred different kinds of tree.

From the northern edge of the Park Georgium, it's a five-minute walk west along the Elbe to the **Kornhaus**, Bauhaus architect Carl Fieger's wonderfully curved 1930 restaurant (see p.199), beer and dance hall overlooking the Elbe.

The Törten

Moses-Mendelssohn-Zentrum Mittelring 38 • Daily 10am–5pm • €2 • ☎ 0340 850 11 99 • **Information centre** Südstr. 5 • Tues–Sun: March–Oct 10am–6pm; Nov–Feb 10am–5pm; tours in German Tues–Sun 3.30pm • Free, German tours €5 • ☎ 0340 858 14 20 • **Konsumgebäude** Am Dreieck 33 • Tues–Sun 11am–3.30pm • €3 • Tram #1 from the Hauptbahnhof, direction Dessau Süd to "Damaschkestrasse", then follow signs

The **Törten**, a leafy 1920s prototype low-rise housing estate, lies 7km southeast of central Dessau. This estate was created as a model housing development that tried to combine the economy of prefabrication with airy designs, sizeable gardens and ultimately decent living conditions for the working classes. Sadly building standards were nowhere near as good as Gropius's designs, and many houses have since been altered – often in twee non-Bauhaus ways – by the owners. The only dwelling to have been restored to its original design – and the only one open to the public – is the **Moses-Mendelssohn-Zentrum**, where the life of this Dessau humanist and philosopher is explored. An English-language guide to the architecture is available at the front desk.

The **information** centre for the Törten is in the cheerless **Stahlhaus**, also the starting point for German tours of the estate. These tours also explore the outside of the **Laubenganghäuser**, a red-brick apartment block by Hannes Meyer, the second Bauhaus director; **Haus Fieger**, Carl Fieger's futuristic home; and the **Konsumgebäude**, Gropius's corner shop design. The latter can also be visited independently.

ARRIVAL AND GETTING AROUND
DESSAU

By train Arriving at the Hauptbahnhof, the Stiftung Bauhaus Dessau lies a 5min walk west via Schwabestrasse and Bauhausstrasse; the town centre is a similar distance east.
Destinations Berlin (frequent; 1hr 30min); Halle (frequent; 50min); Leipzig (frequent; 50min); Lutherstadt Wittenberg (hourly; 36min); Magdeburg (hourly; 1hr).

By bus and tram Buses and trams leave from the Hauptbahnhof for Dessau's outermost sights and Wörlitz (6 per day; 37min).

INFORMATION

Tourist office Zerbster Str. 2c, a signposted 10min walk southeast of the Hauptbahnhof (April–Oct Mon–Fri 10am–6pm, Sat 9.30am–1pm; Nov–March Mon–Fri 10am–5pm, Sat 10am–1pm; ☎ 0340 204 14 42, ⓦ dessau-tourismus.de). The office's accommodation hotline is ☎ 0340 220 30 03.

ACCOMMODATION

Fürst Leopold Friedensplatz ☎ 0340 251 50, ⓦ hotel-dessau-city.de. Glitzy modern hotel that's part of the Radisson chain, with central location, smart standard rooms and a good spa with sauna, steam room and whirlpool. Wi-fi and breakfast cost extra. **€60**
Hotel 7 Säulen Ebertallee 66 ☎ 0340 61 96 20, ⓦ hotel-7-saeulen.de. Friendly, family-run hotel in a quiet spot opposite the Meisterhäuser. The spotless en-suite rooms are smart, bright and modern and there's also free parking and a good breakfast buffet. **€65**
★**Prellerhaus** Gropiusallee 38 ☎ 0340 650 83 18, ⓦ bauhaus-dessau.de. Simple rooms in the former Bauhaus student accommodation in the iconic Bauhaus school building itself. Rooms have oodles of less-is-more minimalist style. **€60**

EATING AND DRINKING

Bauhaus Klub Gropiusallee 38 ☎ 0340 650 84 44, ⓦ klubimbauhaus.de. In the basement of the same building as the *Mensa*, the *Bauhaus Klub* offers daily salads and light fare (around €8) and drinks, and has occasional goings-on like tango evenings. Mon–Sat 8am–midnight, Sun 8am–6pm.
★**Kornhaus** Kornhausstr. 146 ☎ 0340 640 41 41, ⓦ kornhaus-dessau.de; bus #10 or #11 from the

Hauptbahnhof. For a full meal in Bauhaus surroundings try the *Kornhaus*, which has a balcony overlooking the Elbe and serves contemporary cuisine, with fish dishes such as marinated Alaskan shellfish and organic vegetables often part of its selection of well-priced three-course menus (around €18). If you're not taking the bus, it's a 1.5km walk along Kornhausstrasse. Mon–Sat 11am–11pm, Sun 10am–11pm.

L'Appart Zerbster Str. 8 ☎ 0340 661 59 75. Smart French brasserie with seating on the square that's as great for a quick crêpe or €5 lunch special as it is for lingering over a four-course set meal (€22–34). Other options, including traditional German restaurants and pizzerias, can be found elsewhere along main drag Zerbster Strasse. Daily 11.30am–9pm.

Mensa Gropiusallee 38 ☎ 0340 650 84 21, ⓦ bauhaus -dessau.de. To fully immerse yourself in Bauhaus eat in the school's *Mensa*, a canteen in the same wing of the school as the exhibitions and shop. Mains cost around €7, and are enjoyed on unforgiving benches in austere Bauhaus surroundings; there's always a veggie option. Mon–Sat 10am–4pm.

Wörlitzer Park

Wörlitz • **Park and buildings** Tues–Sun: April & Oct 11am–5pm; May–Sept Tues–Sun 10am–6pm • Schloss 1hr tours €6, Gotisches Haus €6, Insel Stein €5, synagogue €2, combined day-ticket €14 • **Gondola tours** Daily: April & Oct 11am–4pm; May–Sept 10am–6pm • 45min • €7 • ⓦ gartenreich.com

Wörlitzer Park, an attractive stately home and country garden midway between Dessau and Lutherstadt Wittenberg, is a place where Gothic follies and mock Classical statues dot manicured lawns, and swans and rowing boats bob on tranquil lakes. All this mentally transports you to the sort of English country parks that inspired Prince Leopold III and his favourite court architect, Friedrich Wilhelm von Erdmannsdorff, to create the place at the end of the eighteenth century.

The landscaped park grows fairly seamlessly out of the village of Wörlitz and all its main buildings cluster at the boundary of the two. These include the engaging Neoclassical **Schloss Wörlitz**, whose Baroque decoration is rather muted and which can only be visited on an hour-long tour, and the **Gotisches Haus**, the Prince's neo-Gothic residence. You can also visit the **Insel Stein**, a mock Italian landscape, and a **synagogue**, built for the local population at the Prince's expense.

Popular **gondola tours** of the park's central lake depart according to demand from behind the Schloss. Note the interesting array of bridges over the park waterways, each built in a different style and including a midget **Iron Bridge** – a quarter-size of the original over the Severn in Britain. Wörlitz gets rather too busy on summer weekends, though this is also when classical concerts are held.

ARRIVAL AND INFORMATION   WÖRLITZ

By bus Bus #334 connects the village of Wörlitz, adjacent to the park, to Dessau (6 per day; 37min), 17km away.

Tourist office Förstergasse 26 (daily: April–Oct 10am–6pm; Nov–Feb 9am–4pm; ☎ 034905 310 09, ⓦ woerlitz.de). Buses and trains stop a short walk from the office, which has useful maps of the park.

ACCOMMODATION AND EATING

Gastwirtschaft im Küchengebäude Wörlitzer Schloss ☎ 03495 02 23 38. Beer garden and restaurant in the old Schloss kitchens that's the only real option inside the park grounds. Serves interesting dishes such as goose and deer, gnocchi and steaks (mains €13–20). April–Oct daily 11am–8pm.

Zum Hauenden Schwein Erdmannsdorffstr. 69 ☎ 034905 301 90, ⓦ zumhauendenschwein.de. Traditional place with bright country-style rooms complete with floral duvet covers and exposed beams – as well as a wine bar, standard German restaurant (mains around €12) and beer garden. Restaurant daily 8am–10pm. **€75**

Ferropolis

Museum April–Oct Mon–Fri 10am–6pm, Sat & Sun 10am–7pm; Nov–March daily 10am–5pm • €4 • ⓦ ferropolis.com • From Dessau Hauptbahnhof take bus #331 (6 daily; 38min) to "Jüdenberg B107 Ferropolis"; by car follow signs from Dessau Ost motorway exit on A9

Only 15km to the north of Wörlitz, yet the complete antithesis to its preened bucolic parks and gardens, is **Ferropolis**, a landscape and venue ingeniously crafted from old GDR coal mines. Here gargantuan old coal-processing machines – the size of whole city blocks – have been artistically arranged around a 25,000-seat concert venue, with a sense of post-apocalyptic irony. Surrounding it, the old open-pit has been turned into a lake, all creating a postindustrial playground which draws crowds for **festivals** like Splash (mid-June; ⓦsplash-festival.de), one of Europe's biggest hip-hop and reggae festivals; and Melt (mid-July; ⓦmeltfestival.de), a huge electronica and alt-rock gig. At other times a museum in the former control centre of the site – where there are hundreds of lights and buttons and the faint smell of GDR-era linoleum – has exhibits that tell the site's story, but it's walking among the vast otherworldly machines that's the main attraction.

Lutherstadt Wittenberg

Gracing a scenic stretch of the Elbe, 84km southeast of Magdeburg, the neat little town of Wittenberg is so inextricably associated with Martin Luther that it renamed itself **LUTHERSTADT WITTENBERG**. It was here that in 1508 the Augustinian monk arrived to study at the university of a relatively obscure 3000-strong town and ended up sparking off one of the most important philosophical debates in world history, catapulting the town to prominence and triggering the Protestant Reformation. Now Wittenberg basks in the glory of its golden era by celebrating the homes, workplaces and graves of the cast of characters who together created the Protestant Rome. Among them were professor and theologian **Philipp Melanchthon**, who added intellectual clout, and painter and printmaker **Lucas Cranach the Elder**, who, with his son, created a tangible image for the whole movement, which could be widely disseminated thanks to the recently invented printing press. Elector of Saxony **Frederick the Wise**, who shielded them all from the Papacy, lies buried in the town's Schlosskirche.

Fittingly all the main **festivals** in Wittenberg revolve around Luther: the big events are the celebration of Luther's marriage in early June, and **Reformation Tag** on October 31, which celebrates the publication of his 95 theses. **Collegienstrasse**, Wittenberg's high street, becomes **Schlossstrasse** at its western end; together they join virtually every sight in town.

The Lutherhaus

Collegienstr. 54 • April–Oct daily 9am–6pm; Nov–March Tues–Sun 10am–5pm • €6, combined ticket with Melanchthonhaus €8 • ⓦ martinluther.de

At the eastern end of Collegienstrasse, beside a small park, lies the **Lutherhaus**, set within the Augustinian monastery that Luther entered before he brought about its dissolution during the Reformation and took one wing as his family residence. Today the reformer's quarters contain an extraordinary collection of items relating to him in a well-executed multimedia museum that's easily the best in town, particularly thanks to excellent signage in both German and English.

The museum is entered via the **Katharinenportal**, a gift to Luther from his wife in 1540. Among the collection's treasures are Luther's desk, pulpit and first editions of many of his books, along with some priceless oils by Cranach the Elder, particularly his much-celebrated painting of the Commandments. Other rooms include one apparently left bare as Luther had it in 1535, and one visited by Tsar Peter the Great in 1702, as his graffiti on the doorframe attests. One quirky section of the museum looks at the various biopic films of Luther's life and how they dramatized key events through the looking glass of their own times.

MARTIN LUTHER

As the founder of Protestantism and modern written German – a side effect of translating the Bible into German – Martin Luther's (1483–1546) impact on German society has equalled anyone's. Yet Luther's personality remains one of history's more elusive, in part because both he and generations of historians ever since have sought to manipulate his image.

THE ROAD TO WITTENBERG

Though born Martin Luder into the well-to-do family of Magarete and Hans Luder in Eisleben in 1483, Luther liked to talk of humble origins. He would talk of his father's hard mining life and how his mother carried wood home on her back. In fact his father owned a mine and smelting business and so his mother would rarely have needed to collect wood herself. Certainly, though, his upbringing was hard: "My parents always punished me severely and in a frightening way. My mother beat me for the sake of a single nut until blood flowed." His early life was governed by his father's ambition that he should become a lawyer. Luther began to study at the University of Erfurt until 1505, when, after a near miss from a lightning bolt, he swore he would become a monk if he survived the thunderstorm. He followed this up and became a model **Augustinian monk** in Erfurt, following the order's rules so strictly that he became a priest in just over eighteen months. He left to study in Wittenberg in 1508 and by 1512 had become a **Doctor of Theology**; by all accounts he was an excellent teacher and charismatic preacher.

LUTHER ATTACKS THE CHURCH

In 1517 he wrote his famous **95 theses**, a document in which he attacked the issue of **indulgences** by the Church. These certificates could be bought from the papacy to give the purchaser less time in Purgatory, while the funds were used to raise revenues, to fund Vatican building projects, great cathedrals and, ironically, Wittenberg's university. Martin Luther blew the whistle on all this and found widespread support, in part because the latest round of indulgence selling was part of a high-profile campaign to raise funds for rebuilding St Peter's in Rome, which struck a nationalist chord against foreigners bleeding Germanic states of their wealth. This principled stand against authority and injustice has later been celebrated with vigorous **embellishments**: Luther probably didn't nail his 95 theses on the door of the Schlosskirche but rather circulated them like a memorandum. Nor is there historical evidence that he boldly stated at the Diet of Worms *Hier stehe ich. Ich kann nicht anders.* ("Here I stand. I can't do anything else."), a slogan now on souvenir socks and T-shirts. He did, however, change his name to Luther, inspired by a Greek word for liberated.

UNDERSTANDING LUTHER

Luther was clearly pious and principled and courageously ventured into territory that had cost other would-be reformers, notably Jan Huss a century earlier, their lives. Yet his defiant and stubborn actions – such as openly burning the papal bull that called for his excommunication – were born out of a sort of academic pedantry, that the Bible and not the papacy was the only source of truth, rather than a desire for rebellion, as shown in his opposition to the Peasants' War (1524–25), which made him a hard figure for the GDR to swallow. Certainly Luther should be seen more as a conservative whose aim was to return to the original Church values, rather than someone who wanted to create a revolutionary new order. However the same cannot always be said of those who adopted the Reformation, who often had self-interest in change: his protector Frederick the Wise, Elector of Saxony, for one, must have been tired of emptying his coffers to the Catholic Church – he'd personally hoarded around five thousand indulgences to shorten his time in Purgatory by a reputed 1443 years.

The Luthereiche

Outside the Lutherhaus, and diagonally opposite the adjacent park, on the corner of Lutherstrasse and Am Hauptbahnhof, grows an old oak – the **Luthereiche**. It was planted in 1830 on the spot where in 1520 Luther publicly burned the papal bull threatening his excommunication. This was perhaps his best-documented display of courage and conviction – qualities that were probably his most important contribution to the Reformation.

The Melanchthonhaus

Collegienstr. 60 • April–Oct Tues–Sun 10am–6pm; Nov–March Tues–Sun 10am–5pm • €4, combined ticket with Lutherhaus €8 • ⓦ martinluther.de

Luther's closest Reformation associate was his friend Philipp Schwarzerd, a lecturer and humanist expert in Greek and Hebrew, known as Philipp Melanchthon. Many have argued that he was more the brains of the movement than Luther and that his assistance in translating original texts can't be overestimated. His house, the **Melanchthonhaus**, one of Wittenberg's finest surviving Renaissance houses, lies a short walk from Luther's. The museum – in which his quarters have been extensively re-created – gives an impression of this calmer and less-outspoken man whose greatest contribution was to draft the Augsburg Confession, which later served as the constitution for the Lutheran faith.

The Marktplatz and around

West of the Melanchthonhaus, Collegienstrasse broadens, bustles with shops and then empties into Wittenberg's large **Marktplatz** where two powerful nineteenth-century statues of Luther and Melanchthon stand: Luther's is the work of Berlin's Neoclassical designers Schadow and Schinkel. The Rathaus lies behind the statues.

Stadtkirche St Marien

Kirchplatz • April–Oct Mon–Sat 10am–6pm, Sun 11.30am–6pm; Nov–March Mon–Sat 10am–4pm, Sun 11.30am–4pm • Free • ☎ 03491 40 44 15

On the eastern side of the Marktplatz an alley cuts through a row of townhouses to the **Stadtkirche St Marien**, in which many landmark Protestant events took place. It was here that the first Protestant services took place in 1521, where Luther preached his Lectern Sermons in 1522. It was also here that he married Katharina von Bora and had all six of their children baptized in the imposing and well-preserved Gothic font. Architecturally, the church isn't particularly distinctive. It dates back to 1300, though wasn't completed until 1470, and its striking octagonal turrets weren't added until after the Reformation.

The interior

Inside, the main attraction is the fabulous **altar** (1547) by Lucas Cranach the Elder and his son, which depicts several Reformation figures, including Philipp Melanchthon and the artist, Frederick the Wise, in biblical contexts. In the central *Last Supper*, Luther is the disciple receiving the cup. At the back of the altar the painting of *Heaven and Hell* was subject to an irreverent local medieval tradition in which students etched their initials in one or other part of the painting depending on their exam results. Also worth seeking out is the fine epitaph to Lucas Cranach the Younger, whose work was as accomplished as his father's.

Cranachhöfe

Schlossstr. 1 • Mon–Sat 10am–5pm, Sun 1–5pm; Nov–March closed Mon • €4 • ☎ 03491 420 19 11

Cranach the Elder's studio now houses the **Cranachhöfe**, a cultural venue for musical performances and readings. This includes a good museum on the work Cranach produced to publicize and popularize the Reformation, along with exhibits on his life

3

WITTENBERG ENGLISH MINISTRY

Between May and October the **Wittenberg English Ministry** (☎ 03491 49 86 10, ⓦ wittenberg-english-ministry.com) offers the chance to worship in some of the same spaces as the first Protestants, but with services in English. Times vary so check the website or with the tourist office in advance.

as an artist, local businessman and politician: he was Wittenberg's mayor for several years. Cranach's residence – and birthplace of his son – the **Cranachhaus**, lies on the southern side of the Markt at no. 4.

Historische Druckerstube

Cranach-Hof • Mon–Fri 9am–5pm, Sun 10am–1.30pm • Free • ☎ 03491 43 28 17

The importance of the printing press in disseminating the Reformation can't be overstated, so it's fitting that the yard behind the Cranachhaus is home to the **Historische Druckerstube**, where you can see printing presses rattle out various lithographs and leaflets, and have staff explain the processes and sell you the results.

The Haus der Geschichte

Schlossstr. 6 • Daily 10am–6pm • €6 • ⓦ pflug-ev.de

An intriguing museum of life in the GDR, the **Haus der Geschichte** is almost the only sight in town not concerned with the Reformation. The GDR's commercial evolution is documented here by museum displays of various consumer durables from the time. One room shows basic refugee quarters (there was a huge influx of refugees from Poland at the end of the war); another the living room of a party bigwig; another a kitchen from the 1950s; and another a kindergarten from the 1980s. The throwback to the late twentieth-century decor is enlivened by humorous and insightful tour guides – the museum can only be visited on tours in German, although English speakers are given printed descriptions.

Schlosskirche

Schlossplatz • April–Oct Mon–Fri 10am–4pm, Sat 10am–5pm, Sun noon–5pm; music May–Oct Tues 3pm • Free • ⓦ schlosskirche-wittenberg.de

Schlossstrasse terminates in front of the old Schloss and the tourist office, where the most imposing building is the Gothic **Schlosskirche**. Repeatedly ravaged by fires and wars over the years, it's now largely the product of the nineteenth century. Even the door on which church notices were pinned – where Luther allegedly nailed his 95 theses on October 31, 1517 – has long since gone, although a bronze door has since been added with Luther's theses inscribed in Latin. Inside the church and beneath the pulpit lies Luther's tombstone, opposite that of Philipp Melanchthon. Most other tombs are devoted to powerful locals and include the bronze epitaph and statue of Frederick the Wise. All this is graced by free weekly choir and organ music.

ARRIVAL AND DEPARTURE

LUTHERSTADT WITTENBERG

By train The Hauptbahnhof, with connections to Berlin (hourly; 45min), is an easy 10min walk northeast of Collegienstrasse where most points of interest lie.

By bus The Hauptbahnhof is the hub for local and regional buses. Regular buses run to Wörlitz (6 daily; 45min).

INFORMATION AND TOURS

Tourist office Schlossstr. 16, just beyond the western end of Collegienstrasse (Jan Mon–Fri 10am–4pm; Feb Mon–Fri 10am–4pm, Sat 10am–2pm; March, Nov & Dec Mon–Fri 10am–4pm, Sat & Sun 10am–2pm; April–Oct Mon–Fri 9am–6pm, Sat & Sun 10am–4pm; ☎ 03491 49 86 10, ⓦ lutherstadt-wittenberg.de). The office can book one of the town's considerable stock of private rooms (from €38)

for you free of charge.
Boat trips There are various boat trips on the Elbe aboard the MS *Lutherstadt Wittenberg* (€10/90min; ☎ 03491 769 04 33, ⓦ ms-wittenberg.de); trips are bookable at the tourist office, which also has information on the ample canoeing in the region.

FROM TOP GRÜNE ZITADELLE, MAGDEBURG (P.191); BROCKENBAHN, THE HARZ MOUNTAINS (P.220) >

ACCOMMODATION

HOTELS AND PENSIONS

★**Alte Canzley** Schlossstr. 3 ☎03491 42 91 90, ⓦalte-canzley.de. The noble old Chancellery building overlooking Schlosskirche, where kings and emperors have stayed, has now been revamped with spotless upmarket dark-wood furniture and beige decor. There's also a sauna and superb organic restaurant (see below). **€89**

Best Western Stadtpalais Wittenberg Collegienstr. 56–57 ☎03491 42 50, ⓦstadtpalais .bestwestern.de. Large hotel with some sixteenth-century touches – headboards and lithographs on walls – but mostly devoted to providing modern luxury. Look out for well-priced "Luther" packages (from €149) which include a sixteenth-century-style meal in its restaurant, a ticket to the Lutherhaus next door and entry to the hotel sauna to bring you back to modern times. Stays of more than one night attract big discounts. Breakfast not included. **€92**

Pension am Schwanenteich Töpferstr. 1 ☎03491 40 28 07, ⓦwittenberg-schwanenteich.de. Small pension, 1min walk from the Marktplatz, with bright, airy and fairly minimalist en-suite rooms and wi-fi. Also has a good traditional restaurant and some great half-board packages for an extra €14.50. **€80**

Stadthotel Wittenberg Schwarzer Baer Schlossstr. 2 ☎03491 420 43 44, ⓦstadthotel-wittenberg.de. Modern central hotel in a venerable five-hundred-year-old building, with boutique-style modern hotel rooms, free parking and wi-fi. Also has a great pub – see below. **€75**

CAMPSITES AND HOSTELS

Brückenkopf Marina-Camp Elbe Brückenkopf 1 ☎03491 45 40, ⓦmarina-camp-elbe.de; Wittenberg-Elbtor station. Well-run holiday village with hotel, cabins and campsites, 1.5km from the city centre on a scenic spot on the banks of the Elbe. Facilities include a sauna. Doubles **€70**; pitch **€7**, plus **€7** per person

DJH Wittenberg Schloss Schlossstr. 14–15 ☎03491 40 32 55, ⓦwittenberg.djh-sachsen-anhalt.de. Good, clean and central lodgings, with the added attraction of occupying a castle, though interiors are institutional and 1970s. All rooms en suite. Dorms **€21**, doubles **€62**

EATING AND DRINKING

Wittenberg has a small range of restaurants; worth investigating is the local so-called *Lutherbrot*, a gingerbread with chocolate and sugar icing which has no real links to the reformer but is tasty all the same. There's little nightlife, though you may find something in local listings magazine *Ingo*.

CAFÉS, BARS AND PUBS

Brauhaus Wittenberg Markt 6 ☎03491 43 31 30, ⓦbrauhaus-wittenberg.de. Bustling brewpub, with an atmospheric courtyard just off the marketplace where dark, light, wheat and seasonal beers wash down basic hearty dishes like huge *Bratwurst* (€8) or spare ribs (€12). Daily 11am–11pm.

Marc de Café Pfaffengasse 5 ☎03491 45 91 14. Excellent café tucked in a quiet courtyard in the lane behind the tourist office. The fabulous cakes, great coffee and relaxed vibe encourage lingering far longer than you ever intended. Tues–Sun 10am–6pm.

★**Zum Schwarzen Baer Wittenberger Kartoffelhaus** Schlossstr. 2 ☎03491 41 12 00, ⓦstadthotel-wittenberg.de. Old-fashioned, dark-wood pub serving potatoes just about any way you could want them: fried, grilled, as salad, gratin and even potato cakes for dessert. Naturally there are various meat and fish accompaniments, and they're good too; mains average €9. Daily 11am–10pm.

RESTAURANTS

★**Alte Canzley** Schlossstr. 3 ☎03491 42 91 90, ⓦalte-canzley.de. First-rate organic restaurant under fourteenth-century arches with an experimental and oft-changing menu that includes the likes of orange-ginger soup, beef in a black-beer crust (€11) and the thoroughly refreshing but seriously oddball asparagus ice cream. April–Oct daily 10am–10pm; Nov–March Tues–Sun 10am–10pm.

Tante Emmas Markt 9 ☎03491 41 97 57, ⓦtante -emma-wittenberg.de. Traditional German food such as *Schnitzels* (mains €13) are served in this ramshackle place just off the Markt, that bursts with curios. In summer the outdoor seating overlooking the square is a huge bonus. Tues–Sun 9am–9pm.

Halle

Sprawling across a sandy plain on the right bank of the Saale River, 37km northwest of Leipzig, **HALLE** got its name from the pre-Germanic word for salt, the presence of which encouraged settlement and extraction during the Bronze Age. The city continues

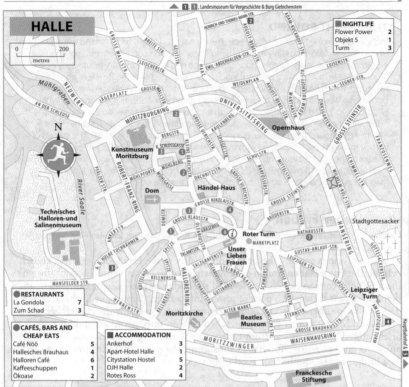

HALLE

0 — 200
metres

N

Mühlgraben

NEUWERK

AN DER SCHLEUSE

River Saale

Technisches
Halloren-und
Salinenmuseum

Kunstmuseum
Moritzburg

Dom

Händel-Haus

MANSFELDER STR.

Roter Turm

Unser
Lieben
Frauen

Opernhaus

Stadtgottesacker

Leipziger
Turm

Moritzkirche

Beatles
Museum

Franckesche
Stiftung

NIGHTLIFE
Flower Power | 2
Objekt 5 | 1
Turm | 3

RESTAURANTS
La Gondola | 7
Zum Schad | 3

CAFÉS, BARS AND CHEAP EATS
Café Nöö | 5
Hallesches Brauhaus | 4
Halloren Café | 6
Kaffeeschuppen | 1
Ökoase | 2

ACCOMMODATION
Ankerhof | 3
Apart-Hotel Halle | 1
Citystation Hostel | 5
DJH Halle | 2
Rotes Ross | 4

to be an important industrial and commercial centre, and forms a large part of a regional concentration of industrial plants and cities called the *Chemiedreieck* (Chemical Triangle). Even if its industrial heyday is long gone and its population – some 232,000 – is waning by some two thousand each year, Halle remains the state's largest city in its most urbanized region.

Halle's Martin Luther University, founded in 1694 and long a principal seat of Protestant learning, particularly flourished during the German Enlightenment when Christian Wolff and Christian Thomasius both resided here. Today, the university continues to add a youthful energy to this important regional transport hub. The best time to visit is during the **Händel Festival** (⊕haendelfestspiele.halle .de) in early June.

The Marktplatz

Halle's focal point is its large **Marktplatz** from which many Altstadt streets radiate, including Leipziger Strasse, the main shopping street. Casting broad shadows across the **Marktplatz** from its southern edge, the **Roter Turm** has become the city's symbol. Started in 1418, the 84m tower took a staggering 88 years to complete and it wasn't until 1999 that its final touch was added: one of the world's largest Glockenspiels, involving 76 bells. The tower is also notable for a **Roland statue** (see box, p.208) on its eastern side, an eighteenth-century version of the twelfth-century original. Also gracing Halle's Marktplatz is a bronze of the town's most famous son, composer George Frideric Handel.

THE KNIGHT ROLAND

Immortalized in the twelfth-century epic French poem *Song of Roland*, Roland was a knight in Charlemagne's forces, possibly even the king's nephew, who conquered much of Europe in the eighth century. His most famous hour came at the end of a rare military failure against the Moors in Spain in 778, when Charlemagne's forces retreated over the Pyrenees and their rearguard, which Roland commanded, was ambushed and Roland killed – largely, it seems, because he was too proud to blow his horn for reinforcements until it was too late, when the effort caused "blood to flow from his mouth and burst from his forehead".

The knight came to symbolize bravery, determination and steadfastness and by the late Middle Ages around fifty independent-minded German towns had erected giant statues of him in their marketplaces – equipped with horn and an unbreakable sword of justice – as a defiant symbol of their rights, prosperity and above all their self-determination and independence from local nobility. Around twenty Rolands survive or have been rebuilt today – including in Halle, Magdeburg and Quedlinburg – though the most famous stands in Bremen.

3

Unser Lieben Frauen

Marktplatz 12 • Jan & Feb Mon–Sat noon–5pm, Sun 3–5pm; March–Dec Mon–Sat 10am–5pm, Sun 3–5pm • Free, death mask €2, Hausmannstürme €2.50

The Roter Turm is actually the freestanding belfry of the Late Gothic market church behind, the **Unser Lieben Frauen** or **St Marien**, another curious construction, since it's the result of a conversion job that levelled the bodies of two existent churches in 1529, then incorporated their two pairs of towers into a large, flamboyant Catholic church designed to spearhead a local Counter-Reformation; eventually the church became Protestant. Martin Luther himself preached here on three occasions and his body was briefly stored here on its way from Eisleben to Wittenberg; a death mask is considered one of its great treasures. The **Hausmannstürme**, the pair of rounded towers connected by a bridge, can be climbed for good town views.

The Beatles Museum

Alter Markt 12 • Daily 10am–8pm • €5 • ⓦ beatlesmuseum.net

Though there's no connection between the Fab Four and Halle, its **Beatles Museum** is huge and exceptional. The 2500-item collection was begun privately in the 1960s, then toured Europe for decades before settling here in 2007. The plethora of music and video clips and various bits of Sixties nostalgia make it easy to spend several hours here.

The Moritzkirche

An der Moritzkirche 8 • Tues–Fri 11am–noon & 3–5pm, Sat 11am–noon & 1–5pm, Sun 1–5pm • Free

Just west of the Beatles Museum lies the stocky, Late Gothic, late fourteenth-century **Moritzkirche**, with its respectable little collection of wood carvings and sculptures. Particularly noteworthy are the early fifteenth-century works by Conrad von Einbeck, the church's master builder. These include the pious-looking *Holy Mauritius*, and, unusually, a self-portrait. The church organ is also considered one of Germany's best-sounding – check its website for free concerts, of which a series are held in a mid-September organ festival.

The Händel-Haus

Grosse Nikolaistr. 5 • April–Oct Tues–Sun 10am–6pm; Nov–March Tues–Sun 10am–5pm • €4 • ⓦ haendel-in-halle.de

The life of **George Frideric Handel** (born Georg Friedrich Händel) is documented in some detail at the **Händel-Haus**, the Baroque mansion where he was born. The best touch in the rather dry exhibition is the opportunity to listen to some of his work, including the famous *Messiah*. Also rewarding is the collection of around seven hundred musical instruments, many from Handel's time.

Kunstmuseum Moritzburg

Friedemann-Bach-Platz 5 • Mon & Wed–Sun 10am–6pm, Tues 10am–7pm • €7 • ⓦ kunstmuseum-moritzburg.de

A couple of minutes' walk northwest of the Händel-Haus, the stocky **Moritzburg** citadel dates back to the fifteenth century, though since it was pretty comprehensively destroyed by Swedes and fire during the Thirty Years' War, most of it is a late nineteenth-century rebuild. Now it's home to **Kunstmuseum Moritzburg**, a gigantic art collection. Various movements from Late Gothic up to GDR art are well represented in both painting and sculpture, but one strong point is art from the turn of the twentieth century, including the socially critical art of Max Leibermann and his contemporaries. Worth a particular look are two paintings actually painted in one of the castle's towers by Bauhaus member **Lyonel Feininger** between 1929 and 1931. Known as the *Halle-Bilder*, they are displayed alongside several pieces by other Bauhaus artists including Paul Klee, Hans Reichel and Fritz Winter.

The Franckesche Stiftung

Franckeplatz 1 • Tues–Sun 10am–5pm • €6 • ⓦ francke-halle.de

Just south of the Altstadt lies the **Franckesche Stiftung**, an early eighteenth-century complex that was once almost a town in itself, with its own school, orphanage, workshops, impressive public library, and three-thousand-strong population. Set up by theologian and scholar August Hermann Francke as an educational institution, it then developed under its own steam. The life of Francke and the complex's history are explored in the museum at its hub, the **Historisches Waisenhaus** (Historic Orphanage). More entertaining is the **Kunst- und Naturalienkammer** (Art and Natural History Chamber), a treasure-trove of all things that occupied the eighteenth-century scholastic mind, with a mock-up of the cosmic system and a pharmacists' workshop among a miscellany of curios from every corner of the globe.

Technisches Halloren- und Salinemuseum

Mansfelder Str. 52 • Tues–Sun 10am–5pm • €3.80 • ⓦ salinemuseum.de

A tall brick chimney poking from a gathering of half-timbered buildings just west of the Altstadt announces the presence of the city's old salt factory which now houses the **Technisches Halloren- und Salinemuseum**. On Sundays when the machinery is fired up you can view the salt-making process that effectively made Halle; the salt produced is sold in the shop.

Landesmuseum für Vorgeschichte

Richard-Wagner-Str. 9 • Tues–Fri 9am–5pm, Sat & Sun 10am–6pm • €8 • ⓦ lda-lsa.de • Tram #7, direction Kröllwitz

The **Landesmuseum für Vorgeschichte** (Museum of Prehistory) has an extraordinary one million prehistoric, Stone and Bronze Age artefacts, many of which are carefully accompanied by diagrams and illustrations to help portray life in ancient times. The most memorable exhibits are some 125,000-year-old elephant skeletons, though the museum's greatest treasure is probably the *Himmelsscheibe von Nebra*, a 3600-year-old Bronze Age metal plate made of bronze on which gold reliefs represent astronomical phenomena and mysterious religious symbols. Yet for all those heavyweight exhibits, the museum is perhaps best known for its superb temporary exhibitions.

Burg Giebichenstein

Seebener Str. 1 • Mid-April to Oct Tues–Fri 10am–6pm, Sat & Sun 10am–7pm • €4 • ☎0345 523 38 57 • Tram #7 or #8

The former residence of the bishop of Magdeburg, **Burg Giebichenstein** in fact constitutes two castles, both destroyed in the Thirty Years' War. The overgrown and ruined twelfth-century **Oberburg** offers sweeping views of the meandering Saale and is open to the public. The fifteenth-century **Unterburg** was built on the site of a tenth-century fort, was extensively rebuilt in the Baroque period, and survived as a prison; it's now partly occupied by an art college and closed to the public.

ARRIVAL AND INFORMATION

By plane Leipzig-Halle Airport (ⓦleipzig-halle-airport. de) is located 20km southeast of Halle and is connected by trains (frequent; 13min).

By train The Hauptbahnhof lies a fifteen-minute walk east of the Marktplatz.

Destinations Dessau (frequent; 55min); Eisleben (frequent; 35min); Leipzig (frequent; 25min); Naumburg (hourly; 40min); Quedlinburg (12 daily; 1hr 30min); Wittenberg (hourly; 1hr).

By tram Trams #2, #5, #7 and #9 run from the Hauptbahnhof to the Marktplatz. Rides cost €2, or €4.50 for a day-ticket.

Tourist office Marktplatz 13 (May–Oct Mon–Fri 9am–7pm, Sat & Sun 10am–4pm; Nov–April Mon–Fri 9am–6pm, Sat 10am–3pm; ☎0345 122 99 84, ⓦstadtmarketing-halle.de). The tourist office can help book private rooms (from €55).

ACCOMMODATION

HOTELS

Ankerhof Ankerstr. 2a ☎0345 232 32 00, ⓦankerhofhotel.de. Smart hotel in a stylishly converted nineteenth-century warehouse. The general ambience, as well as its sauna and fitness facilities, make it a bit of a bargain. With wi-fi. **€84**

★**Apart-Hotel Halle** Kohlschütter Str. 5–6 ☎0345 525 90, ⓦapart-halle.de. Jugendstil place, around 2km north of the centre, with themed rooms, mainly based on German cultural figures. Facilities include a sauna, solarium and whirlpool and a very good breakfast buffet. **€101**

Rotes Ross Leipziger Str. 76 ☎0345 23 34 30, ⓦdormero-hotel-rotes-ross.de. Elegant hotel with fairly regal-looking rooms and all the usual trappings of a

five-star place, including a sizeable fitness centre (€12 extra) as well as great online rates. **€83**

HOSTELS

Citystation Hostel Raffinerie Str. 16a ☎0345 315 4413, ⓦhostel-halle.de. Cheerful independent hostel by the train station with communal kitchen and bike rentals (€3 per day). Dorms sleep between two and six people, and extra charges are levied for linen (€3 per stay) and breakfast (€4). Dorms **€16**, doubles **€48**

DJH Halle August-Bebel-Str. 48a ☎0345 202 47 16, ⓦhalle.djh-sachsen-anhalt.de. Halle's DJH hostel sports a Jugendstil villa exterior, institutional 1970s interior and lies a 15min walk north of the centre, just north of the University district. Linen €3.50 extra. Dorms **€18.50**, doubles **€47**

EATING AND DRINKING

CAFÉS, BARS AND CHEAP EATS

Café Nöö Grosse Klausstr. 11 ☎0345 202 16 51. Grungy but cheerful and sociable bohemian place with a good menu – salads and pastas around €7 – and a small terrace, plus regular live music. Studenty, so breakfasts are served until 3pm. Mon–Fri 9am–3am, Sat & Sun 10am–3am.

Hallesches Brauhaus Grosse Nikolaistr. 2 ☎0345 21 25 70, ⓦbrauhaushalle.de. The only microbrewery in the old town, with a good line of its own *Hallsch* beers and various hearty traditional favourites – the goulash with dumplings and dark-beer sauce (€10) is excellent. Daily 11am–midnight.

★**Halloren Café** Marktplatz 13 ☎0345 299 76 79. Excellent café, which shares its entrance with the tourist office, and has two hundred years of tradition behind its splendid cakes and handmade pralines – its chocolate and

cream Halloren Kugeln are as locally famous as Mozart Kugeln are in Austria. Mon–Sat 9am–7pm, Sun 10am–6pm.

Kaffeeschuppen Kleine Ulrichstr. 11 ☎0345 208 08 03, ⓦkaffeeschuppen.de. Hip café with excellent breakfasts (€5–9), and a good selection of inexpensive soups, salads and mains like noodles and curries. There's often live jazz in the evenings, making it also a good place to start a bar crawl down Kleine Ulrichstrasse. Mon–Thurs 9am–1am, Fri 9am–2am, Sat 10am–2am, Sun 10am–1am.

★**Ökoase** Kleine Ulrichstr. 27 ☎0345 290 16 04. Veggie place with moderately priced canteen lunches – soups €3, mains from around €6. Among the more expensive and complex dishes are the pumpkin-seed *Rösti* with pears and Roquefort (€8.50) and the fried tofu with lemongrass in lime basmati rice (€9.50). Mon–Sat 8.30am–7pm.

RESTAURANTS

La Gondola Rathaus Str. 14 ☎0345 68 27 87 75. Friendly Italian with atmospherically dim lights beneath low arches and all the usual options as well as an excellent line in fresh fish. Mains are around €20. Mon–Sat 11am–3pm & 6–11pm.

Zum Schad Kleine Klausstr. 3 ☎0345 684 53 22, ⓦzum-schad.de. Good central choice for heavy but delicious giant portions of traditional German food: pork knuckle, goulash, *Schnitzel* and the like (most mains around €14). Quite a few horse-meat dishes including steaks, too. Daily 11am–11pm.

NIGHTLIFE

Flower Power Moritzburgring 1 ☎0345 688 88 88. Popular club with a good atmosphere that's always full of people keen to shake a leg, to a mix of chart, dance and party-classics. No cover, but drinks prices are a little steep. Daily 7pm–5am.

Objekt 5 Seebener Str. 5 ☎0345 47 82 33 67, ⓦobjekt5 .de. Popular offbeat venue with regular live music and packed dancefloors on weekend nights. Also has a fantastic

beer garden and good pub food (mains €6 to €11), making it a good stop after a visit to Burg Giebichenstein (see opposite) next door. Daily 10am–late.

Turm Friedemann-Bach-Platz 5 ⓦturm-halle.de. Atmospheric venue in the Moritzburg with a couple of dancefloors where there's usually something going on; often great for techno and hip-hop. The crowd tends to be early 20s. Cover around €5. Tues, Wed, Fri & Sat 10pm–late.

Naumburg and around

With lanes of tidy half-timbered houses fanning out from a central Marktplatz, **NAUMBURG** is a modest and attractive market town that would certainly be worth a visit even without the spectacle of the four-spired **Naumburger Dom**, which rears up on the town's northwestern side. On the last weekend of June Naumburg's usual sleepy peace is broken by the **Kirschfest** – a parade, fireworks and a fair. With Naumburg's attractions quickly enjoyed, the nearby wine-growing town of **Freyburg** makes a good side-trip (see p.213).

The Naumburger Dom

Domplatz 16 • March–Oct Mon–Sat 9am–6pm, Sun 11am–6pm; Nov–Feb Mon–Sat 10am–4pm, Sun noon–4pm • €6.50 including audio-guide in English • ⓦnaumburger-dom.de

With sturdy, pale-green towers rising high above the Altstadt, the giant **Naumburger Dom** is doubtless one of Germany's finest Gothic structures. It dates back to 1213, when work on its oldest parts – including the east choir, transept and main body – began in the late Romanesque style. These, and substantial sections of the rest, were thrown up in an impressively short fifty years, though the northeast towers date from the fifteenth century, and the southwest towers from 1894 during the Romantic movement's celebration of Gothic.

The choirs

The sheer size of the place is overwhelming and engrossing enough, but the leaflet and audio-guide are useful in drawing your attention to the extraordinary workmanship. The most impressive examples reside in the cathedral's **two choirs**. The **western** – completed in 1260 – is the more rewarding, thanks to the extraordinary work of the **Master of Naumburg**, a sculptor about whom little is known. His **rood screen** of the Passion bursts with character and gesture and even includes some of the earliest botanically accurate depictions of plants and flowers. But it's the **Founders' Statues** for which the Master is justifiably famous. These benefactors for the cathedral's construction may have been long dead by the time their statues were begun, yet the tender characterization of each is thoroughly captivating and they feature many Renaissance touches – putting the work a good century ahead of its time. Two statues in particular have captured the German imagination: that of **Margrave Ekkehard II** and his serenely beautiful wife **Uta**, who've become an idealized medieval couple that belong to the same chivalrous past as the *Nibelungenlied* saga (see p.527). The **eastern choir** is less interesting but don't miss the banisters leading up to its main body, which were carved with all sorts of fantastical creatures in the 1980s by Magdeburg artist Heinrich Apel.

The Altstadt

Naumburg's **Altstadt**, though pretty, takes little longer than the Dom to explore. The five-minute walk southeast along Steinweg brings you to the Markt, encircled by Gothic townhouses, a town hall and a parish church. The Gothic **Rathaus** with its many Renaissance touches is the most striking building. A sculpture on the capital of its northeastern corner shows two dogs fighting over a bone: a metaphor for tensions between the town and its ruling prince-bishops. Also on the square at no. 18 is the **Hohe Lilie** (daily 10am–5pm; €2.50; ⊛mvnaumburg.de), the town history museum, whose odds-and-ends include an unusual fourteenth-century drinking horn and a *Prunkstube*, an elegant living room from 1526. Other attractions in town include the **Marientor** (1455–56), a gate in what were clearly formidable town fortifications, a five-minute walk northeast of the Markt. In summer a puppet theatre regularly occupies its courtyard.

Wenzelskirche

Topfmarkt • Daily: April & Oct 1–3pm; May–Sept 10am–5pm • Church free, tower €1.50

Towering over the Markt from the south is the **Wenzelskirche**, which boasts two paintings by Lucas Cranach the Elder and an eighteenth-century organ once played and much praised by Johann Sebastian Bach. The church tower provides superb views of the Dom and Altstadt.

Nietzsche-Haus

Weingarten 18 • Tues–Fri 2–5pm, Sat & Sun 10am–5pm • €3 • ⊛mv-naumburg.de

About a five-minute walk southeast of the Markt lies the **Nietzsche-Haus**, where philosopher Friedrich Nietzsche spent much of his childhood. Though packed with biographical information, the museum is a bit dry and rather cowardly on the more interesting issues, particularly his appeal to the Nazis.

ARRIVAL AND INFORMATION   NAUMBURG

By train Naumburg's Hauptbahnhof, with regular connections to Halle (every 30min; 35min), is 1km northwest of the Dom and connected to the Altstadt (stop "Marientor") by an enjoyable 1892-era tram (daily 6am–8pm; every 30min) or bus #3 to stop "Dom".

Tourist office Markt 12 (April–Oct Mon–Fri 9am–6pm, Sat 9am–4pm, Sun 10am–1pm; Nov–March Mon–Fri 9am–6pm, Sat 9am–1pm; ☎03445 27 31 25, ⊛naumburg.de).

GETTING AROUND

Bike rental Rent bikes at Radhaus Steinmeyer, Bahnhofstr. 26 (☎03445 20 31 19, ⊛radhaus-naumburg .de), who charge €12 per day and can provide maps of the quiet, marked cycle routes to Freyburg; you can also take a bike on the boat to Freyburg (€2).

Boat trips Boat trips aboard the MS *Fröhliche Dörte* run up the Unstrut to Freyburg (daily: May–Sept 11am, 1.30pm & 4pm; 1hr 10min one-way; €14 return; ☎03445 20 28 30, ⊛froehliche-doerte.de), departing from *Camping Blütengrund* (see opposite).

ACCOMMODATION

HOTELS AND PENSIONS

Hotel Stadt Aachen Markt 11 ☎03445 24 70, ⊛hotel -stadt-aachen.de. Vine-covered place on the Markt with a venerable feel born out of dark-wood antique furniture and floral touches. Friendly and with bike hire and a good hotel restaurant. **€79**

Hotel Toscana Topfmarkt 16 ☎03445 289 20,

⊛hotel-toscana-naumburg.eu. Central place tucked just behind the market square with comfortable, fairly standard rooms, though some of those on the upper storeys boast attractive exposed beams. Good breakfast buffet. **€85**

Pension Hentschel Lindenhof 16 ☎03445 20 12 30, ⊛pension-hentschel-naumburg.de. Small, inexpensive and very friendly, if dated, pension in an excellent location just south of the Dom. Rates include a fairly basic breakfast and there's plenty of convenient free parking. **€50**

CAMPSITES AND HOSTELS

Camping Blütengrund Brückenstr. 1 ☎ 03445 26 11 44, ⓦ campingplatz-naumburg.de. Large and spacious riverside place 1.5km northeast of town, located conveniently beside a lido, close to tennis courts and a golf course and with canoe rental. Showers cost extra. Pitch **€3.50**, plus **€4.95** per person

DJH Naumburg Am Tennisplatz 9 ☎ 03445 70 34 22, ⓦ jugendherberge-naumburg.de. Large, well-organized, but institutional youth hostel, a fairly stiff 1.5km walk uphill south of town. All rooms are en suite and the hostel also offers half- and full board for an extra €4.50/€9 respectively. Dorms **€18**, doubles **€56**

EATING AND DRINKING

Firenze Markt 4 ☎ 03445 20 60 60. Standard Italian on the Markt, with very good pizzas and pastas for around €7. Since many places in town close fairly early, this is often the best place to eat later on. If you're keen on all things Italian, note that there's also a first-rate ice cream parlour on the Markt as well. Daily noon–midnight.

Mohrencafé am Dom Steinweg 16 ☎ 03445 230 10. Little café close to the Dom entrance with a small but delicious lunch menu: most dishes (around €9 each) are served with red cabbage and dumplings – but since they include the likes of rabbit and duck, they're by no means run of the mill. Daily 11am–4pm.

Sancho Pancha Domplatz 12a ☎ 03445 26 11 10. Mexican place with a pleasant terrace on which to sip a margarita and enjoy the setting sun on the nearby Dom. Dishes go well beyond the usual Tex-Mex taco-and-burrito fare; mains average €8. Tues–Sat 5–10pm.

Toscana Topfmarkt 16 ☎ 03445 289 20, ⓦ hotel-toscana-naumburg.eu. Though the name suggests Italian, German standards are served here, including a good local variation, the *Naumburger Rahmtöpfchen* (€10.50), a pork chop smothered in creamy onion sauce and served with potatoes and salad. Daily noon–3pm & 5–10pm.

Freyburg

At the centre of Europe's most northerly wine district, the tiny town of **FREYBURG**, 11km north of Naumburg and best reached via pleasant bike trails or by boat along the Unstrut, is known for its sparkling wine and fine castle. The second week in September, during its **wine festival**, is the best time to be in town.

Above all Freyburg is known as the home of **Rotkäppchen**, Sektkellereistr. 5 (hour-long tours: Mon–Fri 11am & 2pm, Sat & Sun 11am, 12.30pm, 2pm & 3.30pm; €5; ☎ 034464 340, ⓦ rotkaeppchen.de), a leading brand of German *Sekt*, which flourished throughout the GDR era and is now enjoying an *Ostalgie*-inspired revival. Tours include a glass of the tipple. Another great place for sparkling wine is the **Winzervereinigung** (Vintners' Union; Mon–Fri 7am–6pm, Sat 10am–6pm, Sun 10am–4pm; ⓦ winzervereinigung-freyburg.de), who run a shop on Querfurter Strasse on the northern edge of town, and are happy to open any bottle in stock for a free taste.

Wine, in the form of a wine museum, is also a big part of the town's other attraction, **Schloss Neuenburg** (April–Oct daily 10am–6pm; Nov–March Tues–Sun 10am–5pm; €6; ⓦ schloss-neuenburg.de), a brooding eleventh-century castle that looks down upon the riverside town from the southeast.

ARRIVAL AND INFORMATION
FREYBURG

By train Regular trains (every 1hr; 9min) link Freyburg to Naumburg.

By boat Boats run up the Unstrut from Naumburg in summer (see p.212).

Bike rental Radhaus Steinmeyer in Naumburg (see p.212) rents bikes and can provide a map of the cycle route between Naumburg and Freyburg.

Tourist office On the small Marktplatz (May–Oct Mon–Thurs 9am–5pm, Fri 9am–6pm, Sat 8am–2pm; Nov–April Mon–Fri 9am–5pm, Sat 8am–noon; ☎ 034464 272 60, ⓦ freyburg-tourismus.de).

EATING AND DRINKING

Gaststätte Zur Haldecke Brückenstr. 6 ☎ 034464 272 66, ⓦ haldecke.de. Just south of the town centre close to the Unstrut, this place serves full, traditional German meals (mains average €9) and a good selection of local wines. Tues–Sun noon–3pm & 5–9.30pm.

Lutherstadt Eisleben

"My fatherland was Eisleben" – is, like many things Luther said of his own life, not quite true. The reformer was certainly born and also died here, but spent precious little time in the place in between. Nevertheless the small yet sprawling and fairly plain little town is absolutely focused on him. It invented itself as a place of pilgrimage as early as 1689 when it started preserving its Luther-related landmarks and finally renamed itself **LUTHERSTADT EISLEBEN** in 1946. The **Eisleber Wiesenmarkt** (ⓦwiesenmarkt.de), a giant Volksfest, takes place at the start of September and is the liveliest annual event.

Luthers Geburtshaus

Lutherstr. 15 • April–Oct daily 10am–6pm; Nov–March Tues–Sun 10am–5pm • €4 • ☎ 03475 714 78 14

Though easily the town's most worthwhile attraction, **Luthers Geburtshaus** is not what it claims. Yes, the reformer was born on this spot, but the actual house he came into the world in burned down in 1689; the building in its place stems from 1693. Nevertheless, the museum has plenty of interesting content on the era and region into which Luther was born, and on the Reformation. This is done not only with displays of valuable old Bibles and retables, but also by reconstructing the medieval kitchen of Luther's parents. The museum also puts high-tech gadgets to good use, for example using Cranach the Elder's portraits of Luther's elderly parents to reconstruct how they might have looked at the time of his birth.

Modern audiovisual technology is also used well in an off-topic, but engrossing collection of **epitaph paintings** hauled from the Eisleben crypts of local worthies. At great expense they had themselves painted into biblical scenes, the significance and symbolism of which is expertly explained by touch-screen databases – in English as well as German. Another area of the museum focuses on baptism, a topic of great importance to Luther.

St Petri-Pauli Kirche

Petrikirchplatz 22 • May–Oct Mon–Fri 10am–noon & 2–4pm, Sat & Sun 11am–4pm • €1 • ⓦzentrum-taufe-eisleben.de

Luther was baptized at the fourteenth-century **St Petri-Pauli Kirche**, practically next door to the Luthers Geburtshaus. This has inspired various exhibitions on baptism inside this graceful Gothic church, which has dubbed itself "Zentrum Taufe", or the Baptism Centre.

The Markt and around

At the centre of Eisleben's compact **Altstadt**, with its tenth-century roots, lies the **Marktplatz**, where, predictably, a large bronze of Luther stands on a plinth decorated with scenes from his life. Part of the Marktplatz's backdrop are the towers of the austere, Gothic **St Andreaskirche** (May–Oct Mon–Sat 10am–4pm, Sun 11.30am–4pm; €1), where Luther delivered his last four sermons, from a pulpit that's been well preserved. Also in the church are the elaborate epitaphs to his family and an elegant high altar from the Nürnberg workshop.

Luthers Sterbehaus

Luthers Sterbehaus Andreaskirchplatz 7 • April–Oct daily 10am–6pm; Nov–March Tues–Sun 10am–5pm • €4 combined ticket with Regionalgeschichtliches Museum • ☎ 03475 60 21 24 • **Regionalgeschichtliches Museum** Münzgasse 7 • Same hours and ticket

Opposite the southern side of St Andreaskirche lies **Luthers Sterbehaus**, where Luther was long thought to have died. It's now known that he actually passed away down the road in what's now the *Graf von Mansfeld* hotel (see opposite), where he was lodging temporarily while he settled a legal dispute regarding the family copper works. Even so, the Sterbehaus has a reconstruction of Luther's last quarters, and a copy of his death mask and last testimony. The admission ticket also gets you into the **Regionalgeschichtliches Museum**, a local history museum a few metres down the road, whose exhibits include a Bronze Age boat.

ARRIVAL AND INFORMATION
LUTHERSTADT EISLEBEN

By train Eisleben's train station lies about 1km south of the town's market square and centre.

Destinations Halle (every 30min; 40min); Magdeburg (frequent; 2hr).

Tourist office Bahnhofstr. 36 (Mon, Wed, Thurs & Fri 10am–5pm, Tues 10am–6pm, Sat 10am–2pm; ☎ 03475 60 21 24, ⓦ eisleben-tourist.de).

ACCOMMODATION AND EATING

★ **Graf von Mansfeld** Markt 56 ☎ 03475 25 07 22, ⓦ hotel-eisleben.de. This luxurious option at the centre of the action exudes elegance and history – four-poster beds and the like – for less money than usual. Its restaurant is one of the town's best and offers modern international food that includes dishes based around steaks, octopus or herring (mains average €12). It has also cornered the local café market with its delicious home-made cakes. Restaurant daily 8am–11pm. **€95**

Lutherschenke Eisleben Lutherstr. 19 ☎ 03475 61 47 75, ⓦ lutherschenke-eisleben.de. Near the Geburtshaus and unusual for trying to provide meals to complement the sights, with dishes from medieval times. Hearty and

meaty, the menu includes deer, turkey (an exotic new food then) and pork liver, with mains around €11; lunch specials €7. Daily 11am–late.

Parkhotel Bahnhofstr. 12 ☎ 03475 540. Family-run place with few facilities and dated decor, but it's clean, friendly and central, making it the town's best budget accommodation choice. Wi-fi costs €3.50/day extra. **€60**

Schäfers Markt 12 ☎ 03475 68 00 73. Basic canteen at the back of a bakery on the marketplace, perfect for a quick, filling and very inexpensive bite (meals €3.50). Dishes change daily, and the selection is small – expect items like goulash and thick soups. Mon–Fri 7am–6pm, Sat 6.30am–11am.

Quedlinburg

If Disney were to mock up a small, medieval German town, it would surely resemble **QUEDLINBURG**, which straddles the Bode River in the gently rolling Harz foothills, 59km southwest of Magdeburg. With well over a thousand crooked half-timbered houses crowding cobblestone streets, and most of its medieval fortifications and churches well preserved, the town is deservedly popular and often bustles with visitors, but it's still large enough to escape the strolling masses at even the busiest times.

Quedlinburg's foundation dates back to a fortress built by Henry I (the Fowler) in 922, after which it quickly became a favourite residence of Saxon emperors; in 968 Otto I founded an imperial abbey there. The town flourished in the Middle Ages as a Hanseatic League member and centre for dyes, paper production and engineering.

The Schlossberg and around

Schlossberg Daily 6am–10pm • Free • **Stiftskirche** May–Oct Tues–Sat 10am–5.30pm, Sun noon–5.30pm; Nov–March Tues–Sat 10am–3.30pm, Sun noon–3.30pm • €4.50 • ☎ 03946 70 99 00 • **Schlossmuseum** Schlossberg 1 • Mon–Thurs, Sat & Sun 10am–6pm • €4.50 • ☎ 03946 90 56 81

Perched on the **Schlossberg**, a knuckle of rock on the southern side of the centre, the sixteenth-century castle of the same name looms over the town. Built on the site of an old fortress, the hub of the Schloss is the Romanesque **Stiftskirche St Servatius**, a former abbey church built between the tenth and twelfth centuries, chock-full of aged treasures such as early Bibles and valuable reliquaries in its **Schatzkammer**.

More treasures are on show just below the Schloss, in the **Schlossmuseum**, which displays a glut of local treasures from as far back as the Stone and Bronze ages, as well as a grisly array of torture instruments. Equally as chilling is an intriguing multimedia exhibition on the Nazi use of the site for propaganda purposes.

The Klopstockhaus

Schlossberg 12 · April–Oct Wed–Sun 10am–5pm · €3.50 · ☏ 03946 26 10

In the Alstadt, below the Schlossberg and curving around its base is a street of half-timbered houses that includes the **Klopstockhaus,** birthplace of the eighteenth-century poet Friedrich Gottlieb Klopstock. It's now devoted to the man who styled himself as the German Homer and whose work received recognition in Gustav Mahler's symphonies.

Lyonel-Feininger-Galerie

Schlossberg 11 · Daily: April–Oct 10am–6pm; Nov–March 10am–5pm · €6 · ☏ 03946 22 38 · ⓦ feininger-galerie.de

Behind the Klopstockhaus, in a robust turn-of-the-twentieth-century building, the **Lyonel-Feininger-Galerie** houses a number of drawings, woodcuts, lithographs and watercolours by the key Bauhaus protagonist Lyonel Feininger (1871–1956). All his work was banned under the Nazis but this collection was carefully hidden and saved by a Bauhaus scholar from Quedlinburg.

The Markt and around

Quedlinburg's colourful Markt is overlooked by a mix of buildings and styles, including several sixteenth-century guildhouses and a Renaissance **Rathaus** from 1320 that's fronted by a Roland statue (see box, p.208) dating from 1426. Look out too for cobbles in the Markt laid out to represent the city's coat of arms and its protectorate dog, Quedel. The lanes around the Markt are best explored at random, but try seeking out the **Gildehaus zur Rose**, Breite Str. 39, a textbook of Renaissance carving, and the courtyard **Schuhhof**, Breite Str. 51–52, where cobblers displayed their wares in ground-floor workshops, above which they lived.

Fachwerkmuseum

Wordgasse 3 · Daily except Thurs: April–Oct 10am–5pm; Nov–March 10am–4pm · €3 · ☏ 03946 38 28

Just south of the Markt lies the grandfather of Quedlinburg buildings. Its timbers date from 1310 making them Germany's oldest, and rendering it a suitable venue for the **Fachwerkmuseum** (Half-Timber Museum), which explains half-timbered construction techniques.

By bus and train The stations lie adjacent, a 10min walk southeast of the Markt. There are regular trains to Thale (hourly; 12min).

Tourist office Markt 4 (May–Oct Mon–Thurs 9am–6.30pm, Fri 9.30am–8.30pm, Sat 9.30am–4pm & 7–8.30pm, Sun 9.30am–3pm; Nov–April Mon–Fri 9.30am–5pm, Sat 9.30am–2pm; ☏03946 90 56 20, ⓦquedlinburg.de). Private rooms (from €50) are best booked through the tourist office.

ACCOMMODATION

HOTELS

Hotel Garni Am Dippeplatz Breite Str. 16 ☏ 03946 771 40, ⓦhotel-amdippeplatz.de. Pretty forgettable central option – the pine-furnished rooms are a bit dated and the breakfast buffet pretty average – but the location on a quiet central street is great, as are the prices. **€75**

Schlossmühle Kaiser-Otto-Str. 28 ☏ 03946 78 70, ⓦschlossmuehle.de. Smart hotel with superb castle views from many rooms, and free wi-fi. Rooms have exposed beams, but are otherwise pretty standard. **€109**

★**Theophano** Markt 13–14 ☏ 03946 963 00, ⓦhoteltheophano.de. Traditional place in a heavyweight half-timbered building with rustic charm and an unbeatable central location; many rooms have canopied beds and there's an atmospheric cellar bar to enjoy local beers and wines too. **€125**

Zum Bär Markt 8–9 ☏ 03946 77 70, ⓦhotelzumbaer .de. With a hotel here in the thick of things on the Markt for some 250 years, there's a sense of time-honoured tradition, as well as airy, pastel-furnished rooms. **€98**

Zum Brauhaus Carl-Ritter-Str. 1 ☏ 03946 90 14 81, ⓦhotel-brauhaus-luedde.de. Atmospheric lodgings in a restored half-timbered house where many rooms have exposed beams but furnishings are modern. Also offers good-value half-board deals in tandem with its brewery restaurant, *Brauhaus Lüdde* (see below). **€89**

HOSTELS
DJH Quedlinburg Neuendorf 28 ☏ 03946 81 17 03, ⓦ jugendherberge-quedlinburg.de. Housed in a half-timbered former warehouse that dates back to 1661, Quedlinburg's hostel is small, quiet, central but frequently full. Breakfast is included in rates and half- and full board are also available. Dorms **€18.50**, doubles **€52**

EATING AND DRINKING

CAFÉS AND BARS
Brauhaus Lüdde Blasiistr. 14 ☏ 03946 70 52 06, ⓦ hotel-brauhaus-luedde.de. Barn-sized microbrewery with a range of its own beers – *Pils*, *Alt* and seasonal beers – to wash down a range of heavy traditional meals, as well as a bustling beer garden. Mains €10–16.50. Mon–Sat noon–midnight, Sun noon–10pm.

Café Kaiser Finkenherd 8 ☏ 03946 51 55 52, ⓦ cafe-restaurant-kaiser.de. Rustic café a little off the main tourist drag, with a terrace and a penchant for chicken dishes, plus inexpensive omelettes and salads (all around €7) and home-made cakes. The eggs used come from its own chickens around the back. Tues–Sun 10am–7pm.

RESTAURANTS
Kartoffelhaus No 1 Breite Str. 37 ☏ 03946 70 83 34. Popular spot for filling up on all manner of potato dishes – in soups, baked, fried, roasted – served with various grilled meats; the *Sauerfleish* – marinated meat with crispy fried potatoes – is particularly good. Huge portions, with mains averaging €10. Daily 11am–midnight.

Schlosskrug Am Dom Schlossberg 1 ☏ 03946 28 38. Well-priced regional cuisine such as *Schnitzel* and game (most mains around €9) in three historic houses within the Schloss walls. The summertime outdoor seating offers great views over town. Tues–Sun noon–8pm.

Schlossmühle Kaiser-Otto-Str. 28 ☏ 03946 78 70, ⓦ schlossmuehle.de. One of Quedlinburg's finest restaurants, with mains – made from fresh local ingredients – from around €17. The menu changes daily, but it often includes Mediterranean choices and some lighter takes on German cuisine. There's a good wine list, and a few of the tables enjoy a pleasant courtyard location. Daily 6–10pm.

Theophano Markt 13–14 ☏ 03946 963 00, ⓦ hoteltheophano.de. Modern regional cuisine served in the cellar of a 360-year-old half-timbered house. Dishes include cod on a gherkin-dill risotto with fried tomatoes, or veal in a chervil-root sauce. The handmade truffles make an exquisite end to a meal. There's a great Gothic wine-cellar at the same address. Daily 11.30am–10pm.

The Harz mountains

Virtually unknown outside the country, but a mini-Black Forest to northern Germans, the **Harz** mountains lie where Saxony-Anhalt, Thuringia and Lower Saxony meet and cover an area about 100km long and 30km wide. Soaring peaks may be absent, but the region is blessed with thickly wooded rolling hills, low peaks and snug valleys in which small villages and modest resort towns nestle, offering pleasant base-camps for a variety of outdoor activities. The key points of interest are **Thale** for its location at the mouth of the Bode Valley, an attractive hiking destination; the **Brocken**, the Harz's highest peak, which lies at the heart of the heavily wooded **Nationalpark Harz** and has captivating associations with the pagan festival Walpurgisnacht; and the low-key ski resort town of **Braunlage**. Towns in the foothills such as Quedlinburg (see p.215) and Goslar (see p.224) are also possible gateways for forays into the hills, but if you're reliant on public transport you'll need to rise early; though offering vital shuttle services to hikers, bus connections around

THE HARZCARD
Staying in most towns entitles you to a **Gästekarte**, a discount card supplied by your accommodation, which will reduce the cost of various sights and activities. An even better source of discounts and free entry is the €29 **HarzCard** (ⓦ harzcard.info), which includes entry to around a hundred regional attractions for 48 hours. Pay €59 to get the same for four calendar days, which can be non-consecutive. Both cards also include use of the public transport network, and can be bought online or at most tourist offices in the region.

the Harz take time. Trains are a bit faster and – as part of a network of narrow-gauge railways with **steam trains** – the journeys are a delight in themselves.

Thale

Upstream along the Bode River, 10km southeast of Quedlinburg, the Harz mountains rear up beside the modest steel-making town of **THALE** in scenery which awed both Goethe and Heine. In particular, two rugged outcrops – the **Hexentanzplatz** and the **Rosstrappe** – capture the imagination, partly for their mythical associations. Both are accessible by chairlift, while the lush **Bode Valley** between them is home to the **Hexenstieg** (see p.220), an easy **day-hike** that's one of the Harz's most idyllic hiking routes. With a further 100km of marked trails in the vicinity, Thale also makes for a superb base for longer walking holidays.

Hexentanzplatz

Chairlift Easter–Oct daily 9.30am–6pm; Nov–Easter Sat & Sun 10am–4.30pm • €5.90 return • ⓦ seilbahnen-thale.de • **Walpurgishalle** May–Oct daily 10am–6pm • €1.50

Hexentanzplatz ("witches' dance place"), once the site of a Celtic fortress, is full of supernatural and pagan associations and is where the crones are said to have limbered up for Walpurgisnacht on the Brocken (see p.221), but there's little mystical atmosphere here at what has become a crowded coach park lined with souvenir shops. But you can feed your imagination at the **Walpurgishalle**, a museum devoted to explaining pagan worship, with many vivid drawings and

HEALTHY HARZ HOLIDAYS

As northern Germany's green lung and main range of proper hills, the Harz has been well-developed for all the most common outdoor activities. And some first-class spa and sauna complexes provide the perfect counterbalance.

HIKING

The rolling hills, low peaks and dark valleys of the Harz offer easy terrain for a huge network of well-signposted trails. **Maps** are readily available. Recommended are the inexpensive waterproof and tear-proof ones published by Publicpress – with a logo of a sun wearing sunglasses – which cover a number of areas of the Harz at different scales; the 1:50,000 ones are most useful for hiking. With navigation very straightforward and terrain relatively undemanding, it's easy to forget that the Harz is a highly changeable mountain environment, so be prepared for storms and sharp temperature changes.

With good trails everywhere there's no single **best base** for hiking the Harz, though Thale by the Bode Valley, and Schierke on the slopes of the Brocken, are particular hotspots.

CYCLING AND MOUNTAIN BIKING

Cycling the Harz is a pleasure if you're reasonably fit, though many of the roads have tight corners and fast traffic, so it's worth planning routes along the many even and fairly smooth forestry trails that crisscross the range. Again, these are well marked on Publicpress maps, though Publicpress also have a range of cycling maps at a more useful smaller scale. **Mountain-bikers** will find the network – expertly documented in the book *Der Harz für Mountainbiker* (€14.20; available from most tourist offices) – a bit tame, so adventurous riders should try visiting the main ski areas in summer for their ski-lift-accessed trails. Best are Braunlage (see p.222) and Hahnenklee (ⓦerlebnisbocksberg.de), 16km southeast of Goslar; Thale's Rosstrappe also has a single reasonable trail (see p.220).

WINTER SPORTS

When snowfall cooperates, **skiing and snowboarding** are possible throughout the Harz and many towns are geared up for winter sports, making equipment rental easy and inexpensive. **Tobogganing** is very popular, with special runs in many places, and the **cross-country-skiing** trail network well developed.

The main **downhill centres** are at Braunlage and St Andreasberg in the central Harz and Hahnenklee in the north, but there are half a dozen smaller spots too. Braunlage often has the best conditions and offers a good selection of runs to keep most skiers and boarders happy for a long weekend. Check ⓦharz-ski.de for conditions throughout the range.

Braunlage is also home to the **ice hockey** team Harzer Falken (ⓦharzer-falken.de), a reasonably talented and fairly rabidly supported outfit who play in the stadium in the centre of town. Catching a game can be good fun for the atmosphere and chants alone.

SPAS

The finest spas and saunas in the Harz are in some of its smallest towns, where good signposting generally means they're easy to find; enquire at a local tourist office for bus connections if you don't have your own transport.

Bodetal Therme Parkstr. 4, Thale ☎0170 528 55 66, ⓦbodetal-therme.info. The newest spa in the Harz, with a lovely selection of saunas and steam rooms and the crowning glory of some terrific views. 4hr €18.50. Mon–Wed & Sun 10am–10pm, Thurs–Sat 10am–11pm.

Heisser Brocken Karl-Reinecke-Weg 35, Altenau ☎05328 91 15 70, ⓦkristalltherme-altenau.de. Relatively new and well-designed sauna complex 20km northwest of Braunlage, with excellent views over wooded hills from several outdoor pools (one with a waterfall). 3hr €11.70. Mon–Thurs & Sun 9am–10pm,

Fri & Sat 9am–11pm.

Sole-Therme Nordhäuser Str. 2a, Bad Harzburg ☎05322 753 60, ⓦsole-therme-bad-harzburg.de. Rambling pool and sauna complex with many different heated outdoor pools, saunas and steam rooms, including one in which you rub salt into your body. Day-ticket €12.50. Mon–Sat 8am–9pm, Sun 8am–7pm.

Vitamar Masttal 1, Bad Lauterberg ☎05524 85 06 65, ⓦvitamar.de. Large family-friendly pool and small, swanky sauna complex, 18km southwest of Braunlage. 3hr €10.60. Mon–Sat 9am–10pm, Sun 9am–9pm.

3

THE HARZER SCHMALSPURBAHN

Among railway buffs the Harz is famous for having Europe's largest narrow-gauge railway network: the **Harzer Schmalspurbahn** (☎ 03943 55 80, ⓦ hsb-wr.de). Its 140km of track is plied largely by steam trains, and seeing the antique technology in action is as much part of the pleasure as the scenic terrain that's negotiated by steep gradients and tight corners. It all adds up to an interesting and unusual way to see some attractive, out-of-the-way places without doing the legwork yourself. **Tickets** can be bought for single journeys, or as a pass to the entire network (available at the main stations): €70 for three days, or €105 for five; children travel half-price, while a €88 family card covers two adults and three children for a day.

The network divides into three lines. The **Brockenbahn** climbs steeply from the Schierke up the Brocken to a height of 1125m, scenically at its best in winter when the peaceful heights are blanketed in snow. The **Harzquerbahn** is a 60km route that twists all the way across the Harz in seventy bends between Wernigerode in the north and Nordhausen in the south; at its highest point, Drei Annen Hohne, you can transfer onto the Brockenbahn. The **Skeletbahn**, beginning in Quedlinburg, runs to the Eisfelder Tal, where you can change onto the Harzquerbahn. The steam trains along this route are real antiques – the oldest is from 1887.

the ghoulish ancient sacrificial stone used at the Hexentanzplatz; exhibit labels are in German only.

The Rosstrappe

Chairlift Easter–Oct daily 9.30am–6pm; Nov–Easter Sat & Sun 10–4.30pm • €3.80 return

The **Rosstrappe**, opposite the Hexentanzplatz to the north of Thale, can also be reached by chairlift and was named for a legend in which Princess Brunhilde fled her unappealing husband-to-be Prince Bodo through the Harz on a mighty steed (or *Ross*), leaping the gorge from the Hexentanzplatz to leave a huge hoof imprint on the rock of the Rosstrappe. Meanwhile, in pursuit with more mortal skills, Bodo plunged into the valley, creating an indentation in the river and becoming a hell-hound that guarded the valley.

The Bode Valley and the Hexenstieg

Arguably the finest local walk is the **Hexenstieg** along the Bode Valley (marked with blue triangles), which takes in spectacular scenery and rich flora, including gnarled trees hundreds of years old. It is best done by taking bus #18 (5 daily; 30min) from Thale to the village of **TRESEBURG**, then walking the 10km back downstream, which should take between two and three hours. For a longer walk, take the chairlift to Hexentanzplatz (see p.218), then walk the 10km trail (marked by red dots) to Treseburg, stop for lunch at one of a number of inns, then return to Thale via the Hexenstieg – a total walk of around four or five hours.

ARRIVAL AND INFORMATION   THALE

By train The train and bus station lie at the base of the Rosstrappe. Regular trains run to and from Quedlinburg throughout the day (hourly; 12min).

Tourist office In the park at Bahnhofstr. 1 (Mon–Fri 9am–5pm, Sat & Sun 9am–3pm; ☎ 03947 776 80 00, ⓦ bodetal.de). The office can help with accommodation, including private rooms (€45), which are only hard to get around Walpurgisnacht at the end of April.

ACCOMMODATION AND EATING

Berghotel Hexentanzplatz Hexentanzplatz ☎ 03947 47 30, ⓦ berghotel-hexentanzplatz.de. On the mountain beside the Hexentanzplatz, serving traditional food (mains around €9–14), with the option of dining on an outdoor terrace with good views. Simple but clean and comfortable hotel rooms. Restaurant

daily 8am–9pm. **€80**

DJH Thale Bodetal-Waldkater ☎ 03947 28 81, ⓦ jugendherberge-thale.de. Close by the tourist office and beautifully situated in the Bode Valley. Offers lunch and dinner packages for €5 each. The one-off charge for sheets is €3.50. Dorms **€18.50**, doubles **€63**

Ferienpark Bodetal Hubertusstr. 9–11 ☎03947 776 60, ⓦferienpark-bodetal.de. Smart apartment complex with an outdoor pool, sauna and bike rental. Also has a beer garden and a reasonable restaurant with contemporary German food (mains around €14). Look out for well-priced hiking, biking, horseriding and spa packages on the hotel website. Restaurant daily 8am–10pm. **€95**

Kleiner Waldkater Kleiner Waldkater 1 ☎03947 28 26, ⓦkleiner-waldkater.de. Half-timbered house offering basic wood-clad rooms with cheerful dated decor in a riverside location deep in the woods around Thale. Does basic food, with *Schnitzels* around €10. Kitchen 11.30am–8.30pm. **€56**

The Rübeland caves

Blankenburger Str. 35, Rübeland • Daily: Feb–June, Sept & Oct 9am–4.30pm; July & Aug 9am–5.30pm; Nov–Jan 9am–3.30pm • €8 • ☎039454 491 32, ⓦharzer-hoehlen.de • Bus to Rübeland via Blankenburg from Thale (1hr) or Quedlinburg (1hr 30min)

The severe little town of **RÜBELAND**, strung out along the Bode River 15km from Thale, has been on the tourist map ever since the 600,000-year-old **Baumannshöhle** cave was discovered by a fifteenth-century miner. Goethe toured the cave three times, as did Heine, treading in the footsteps of Stone Age inhabitants and Ice Age bears, some of whose skeletons are on display. The neighbouring **Hermannshöhle** is more modest, but its stalagmites and stalactites are more impressive. The two sets of caves tend to open on alternate days; call in advance to find out.

Schierke and the Brocken

The large village of **SCHIERKE** gathers at the foot of the **Brocken** (1142m), the Harz's highest peak, 15km west of Rübeland, and is the last stop for the narrow-gauge Brockenbahn. Hiking up the **Brocken** is the obvious attraction, but there are many other good **rock-climbing**, **biking** and **hiking** routes in the area, including two enjoyable shorter walks to jagged rock formations: the Feuersteinklippen are just thirty minutes' walk away, the Scharcherklippen ninety minutes. Pick up free maps at the tourist office. In winter there's first-class **snowshoeing** and **cross-country skiing** on a 70km-long trail network.

The Brocken

Given its mystical reputation (see box below), and as the highest peak in the Harz, the ascent of the **Brocken** is for many a vital part of a Harz itinerary. So if you're after peace look elsewhere. Options to ascend it include the **Brockenbahn** railway (see box opposite;

3

WALPURGISNACHT

According to legend, every year on April 30 – **Walpurgisnacht** – witches and warlocks descend on the Harz to fly up the Brocken on broomsticks and goats. Here they gather to exchange tall tales of recent evil deeds as foreplay to a Bacchanalian frenzy of fornication, including with the devil himself. The event was so vividly embellished that for centuries local peasants lived in fear of meetings with stray witches. By hanging crosses and herbs on house and barn doors they tried to protect themselves and their animals; church bells would toll and the most superstitious would crack whips to deter evil forces.

At some point this night became combined with age-old local festivals: the Celts celebrated this as the devil's final fling before spring triumphs over winter in festivals similar to those in other Celtic lands, including Scotland's Beltane, while Germanic tribes celebrated the wedding of the gods Wodan and Freyen. The name Walpurgisnacht probably comes from Waldborg, the pagan goddess of fertility. Over the centuries, as Christianity frowned on these celebrations, they became a highlight of the black-magic calendar: Goethe's Faust joined a "whirling mob" of witches on the Brocken's summit.

Today, gatherings by New Age pagans and revellers occur all over the Harz on Walpurgisnacht, but the most popular places are at the Hexentanzplatz in Thale (see p.218), where 35,000 arrive for an organized celebration; and the trek up the Brocken from Schierke, in which similar numbers come together for a more rough-and-ready experience that lasts until dawn.

€18 one-way), **horse-drawn wagon** – or **sleigh** in winter (both around €20 return; contact the tourist office in Schierke) – or on foot. From Schierke, the sealed but traffic-free **Brockenstrasse** is a straightforward 12km hike, but probably makes a better descent, leaving you to take the more interesting and scenic 7km route via Eckerloch up. The **Brockenhaus** (daily 9.30am–5pm; €4; ⓦnationalpark-brockenhaus.de) by the railway terminus near the summit has exhibits about geology and the mountain's mythology, but says little about the GDR era, when the Brocken was a military no-go area for Germans. The easy 2.5km path around the summit offers good views over the blanket of trees that covers the Harz and some of the settlements in the foothills.

ARRIVAL AND INFORMATION SCHIERKE

By bus Schierke is connected by direct bus to Braunlage (bus #257: 10 daily; 16min), and reachable in about two hours from Quedlinburg with a change at Wernigrode.
Tourist office Kurverwaltung, Brockenstr. 10 (May–Oct Mon–Fri 9am–6pm, Sat 10am–4pm, Sun 10am–3pm; Nov–April Mon–Fri 9am–5pm, Sat 10am–4pm, Sun 10am–3pm; ☏039455 86 80, ⓦschierke-am-brocken.de). The office lies in Schierke's upper town along the main road to the Brocken, and shares its address with the Nationalparkhaus.

Nationalparkhaus The national park visitor centre is in the same building as the tourist office, Kurverwaltung, Brockenstr. 10 (May–Oct Mon–Fri 9am–6pm, Sat 10am–4pm, Sun 10am–3pm; Nov–April Mon–Fri 9am–5pm, Sat 10am–4pm, Sun 10am–3pm; ☏039455 814 44, ⓦnationalpark-harz.de), and is the best place for local info on outdoor activities.

ACCOMMODATION AND EATING

DJH Schierke Brockenstr. 48 ☏039455 510 66, ⓦschierke.djh-sachsen-anhalt.de. Large, institutional-looking youth hostel in the upper town, but with billiards, table tennis and even a bowling alley. There's a one-off €3.50 charge for sheets, and lunch and dinner are available for another €4.50 each. Dorms **€19**
Pension Schmidt Brockenstrasse 13 ☏039455 333, ⓦpension-schmidt.de. Central family-run guesthouse, close to the tourist office, with homely fittings, a sauna and free wi-fi. Offers some well-priced packages that include a ride on the railway up the Brocken. **€70**
Waldschlösschen Herman-Löns-Weg 1 ☏039455 86 70. Standard, family-run hotel a block from the main road in central Schierke, with compact modern rooms and impressive views over to Braunlage. Facilities include a pool and sauna. Serves good German food in its Art Nouveau restaurant, particularly its local venison, trout and wines. The local schnapps, *Schierker Feuerstein*, is the traditional end to meals here. Restaurant daily 7am–10pm. **€80**

Braunlage

The rather nondescript little town of **BRAUNLAGE** sits in a beautiful location in a cradle of hills that includes the **Wurmberg** (971m), the Harz's second-highest peak, whose regular snow has made the town a reasonable small **ski resort**. It's often offputtingly busy at weekends, however, and, in marginal winters, often slushy around its base. At these times, the better option is to repair to the excellent network of **cross-country-skiing** trails on the rolling hills about town, or mess around on a **toboggan**: there are good runs both on the Wurmberg and in town for this – look for signs to the Rodelbahn. Gear for all these winter activities is readily available in town: expect to pay around €22 for a ski or snowboard setup.

Braunlage is also a popular summer base for **hikers** and **bikers** – who can both use its cable car (daily 9.45am–5.30pm; summer one-way €6.50, ski day-ticket €28; ⓦwurmberg-seilbahn.de) – and the tourist office publishes useful free brochures on the local trail network.

ARRIVAL AND INFORMATION BRAUNLAGE

By bus If you're coming by bus, alight at the "Eisstadion" stop for the centre of town.
Destinations Bad Harzburg (hourly; 40min); Schierke (9 daily; 32min).

Tourist office Elbingröder Str. 17 (Mon–Fri 9am–12.30pm & 2–5pm, Sat 9.30am–12.30pm; ☏05520 930 70, ⓦbraunlage.de). The office will book private rooms (€39).

ACCOMMODATION

DJH Hostel Von-Langen-Str. 28 ☎ 05520 22 38, ⊛ djh -niedersachsen.de/jh/braunlage. Sparklingly clean DJH hostel at the edge of town in an attractive wood by a network of hiking and skiing trails. You can have lunch or dinner for €6 at its bistro. Dorms €22, doubles €60

Hotel Harz-Wald Karl-Röhrig-Str. 5a ☎ 05520 80 70, ⊛ relexa-hotel.de. Mid-sized modern hotel with wi-fi and extensive fitness facilities, which include a swimming pool, sauna and steam room. There's mountain-bike rental too, for guests and non-guests. €93

Pension Parkblick Elbingeröde Str. 13 ☎ 05520 12 37,

⊛ pension-parkblick.com. Friendly guesthouse in a solid red-brick townhouse with dated fittings, but clean, well-priced rooms in a central location. Also has a few single rooms. €45

Residenz Hohenzollern-Victoria-Luise Doktor-Barner-Str. 10–11 ☎ 05520 932 10, ⊛ residenz -hohenzollern.de. Extremely smart hotel on the sunny southern side of the Wurmberg with town views, a first-class spa and a superb restaurant, *Restaurant Braunlage* (see below). The airy rooms come with a Mediterranean feel or more traditional hardwood floors and furnishings. €155

EATING

Omas Kaffeestube Elbingröder Str. 2 ☎ 05520 23 90. Braunlage's best address for an afternoon slice of cake is this old-fashioned café whose various fortified coffees go down a treat in winter. Daily 11am–5pm.

Puppe Brotzeit Am Brunnen 2 ☎ 05520 487, ⊛ puppe-braunlage.de. For a quick sandwich try this deli, which specializes in local ingredients and will pack things up for your hiking trip or picnic, and also has space to eat in. Mon–Sat 10am–9pm, Sun 11am–9pm.

Restaurant Braunlage At the Residenz Hohenzollern-Victoria-Luise hotel, Doktor-Barner-Str. 10–11 ☎ 05520

932 10, ⊛ restaurant-braunlage.de. The town's premium hotel also has its finest restaurant: a superb gourmet affair serving all sorts of imaginative creations using local ingredients (five-course set menu €47). The outdoor terrace with its expansive views of Braunlage is a big selling point. Tues–Sun 6–9.30pm.

Rialto Herzog-Wilhelm-Str. 27 ☎ 05520 34 94, ⊛ rialto -braunlage.de. Long-standing Italian restaurant – here for more than 25 years – with lots of loyal local customers. Serves mainly Italian standards, such as pizzas, *lasagne* and tortellini from around €8. Daily 11.30am–11pm.

3

Bad Harzburg

The smart and sleepy spa resort of **BAD HARZBURG** lies only 9km southeast of Goslar in the Harz foothills, but offers good access to hikes in the mountains via a cable car. Bad Harzburg's other great attractions are its **spas**: the Sole-Therme (see box, p.219) is the best and lies conveniently at the base of the cable car.

Burgberg Seilbahn

Daily: April–Oct 9am–6pm; Nov–April 10am–4pm • €3 return • ☎ 05322 753 70

The **Burgberg Seilbahn** cable-car climbs the Grosser Burgberg where Heinrich IV's eleventh-century castle has crumbled to its foundations. Excellent views remain though, and a network of hiking trails fans out from here. The most straightforward trails return to town, but there are others to several mountain huts with restaurants: a board at the cable-car terminus shows which are open.

ARRIVAL AND INFORMATION   BAD HARZBURG

By bus and train From Goslar frequent buses (#810: hourly; 27min) and trains (every 30min; 12min) drop passengers at the Bahnhof, a 5min walk north of town and a 20min walk through the centre to the Seilbahn (or bus #810 or #873 to "Burgbergbahn").

Tourist office Beside the Seilbahn, Nordhäuser Str. 4 (Mon–Fri 8am–6pm, Sat & Sun 10am–4pm; ☎ 05322 753 30, ⊛ bad-harzburg.de). The office has full accommodation listings.

ACCOMMODATION AND EATING

Braunschweiger Hof Herzog-Wilhelm-Str. 54 ☎ 05322 78 82 70, ⊛ hotel-braunschweiger-hof.de. One of the nicest places to stay is this comfortable hotel with 4-star mod cons, but an easy-going rural feel. It also has one of the best restaurants in town, with mains like

lobster, salmon and steak for around €14. Restaurant daily 11.30am–10pm. €140

Palmen-Café Rudolf-Huch-Str. 21 ☎ 05322 48 05, ⊛ palmen-cafe.de. Atmospheric and inexpensive café in the Neoclassical Trinkhalle of the Kurpark, where spa-goers took the waters a century ago. Serves dishes like salmon in wine sauce or beef roulade with apple and red cabbage (mains from around €10). Tues–Sun 11am–5.30pm. **Tannenhof-Solehotel** Nordhäuser Str. 6–8 ☎ 05322

968 80, ⓦ solehotels.de. Friendly and comfortable mid-sized hotel beside the tourist office and Sole Therme spa, use of which is included in rates. Also offers bike rental; hiking paths strike out right behind the hotel. **€67**

Goslar

With an imperial past, palatial European Romanesque architecture and an Altstadt of medieval timber-framed beauties, **GOSLAR** is one of Germany's treasures. A town of just 48,000 people in the Harz foothills, perhaps, but a rich one figuratively and at one time literally. The area around the **Markt** is the town's showpiece and from it a main street, **Hoher Weg**, drives south to the **Kaiserpfalz**. Also south of town is the **Rammelsberg** mine, which produced ores until relatively recently and now offers tours. But the set pieces are only part of Goslar's attraction: simply wandering its huddled Altstadt streets and its many small but diverting museums is a pleasure in itself.

Brief history

In the tenth century the discovery of silver transformed this hamlet into one of northern Europe's leading medieval towns, whose deep coffers were loved by emperors and coveted by popes. By the mid-eleventh century, less than a hundred years after the first miners shouldered their picks, an imperial Diet (conference) of the Holy Roman Empire was held in the **Kaiserpfalz**, Goslar's new Romanesque palace. For over three hundred years the "treasury of German Emperors" ruled Germany's loose confederation of states as the seat of the Holy Roman Emperor and the city spent its wealth on finery becoming of a free imperial city (from 1342). Even a collective belt-tightening after the duke of Braunschweig-Wolfenbüttel snatched the mine in 1532 had its virtues: as funds dried up, so too did new building schemes, preserving the Altstadt. As a POW camp Goslar was also spared World War II bombing.

The Markt

Goslar's showpiece **Markt**, a gorgeous huddle of buildings – in sombre slate, zingy tangerine and clotted cream – is best admired crowd-free, so steer clear of 9am, noon, 3pm and 6pm when crowds gather for a parade of mining history which spins from a **Glockenspiel** at the top of its old treasury building. Atop a 1230 fountain is Goslar's icon – an imperial eagle, which looks more like a hybrid pigeon caught mid-lay.

The Rathaus

Marktplatz • Tours daily: April–Oct Mon–Fri 11am–3pm, Sat & Sun 10am–4pm • €3.50

The neat row of gables, arches and Gothic windows behind the Markt's central fountain belong to Goslar's fifteenth-century **Rathaus**. They look spectacular illuminated at night, but the building's real treasure is inside: on the wall and ceiling panels of its Huldigungssaal council chamber is a spectacular display of Renaissance fireworks by a mystery painter.

The Kaiserworth Hotel and the Marktkirche

Beside the Rathaus, the **Kaiserworth Hotel** is in the old fifteenth-century guildhall of cloth merchants and cutters. It's decorated with lively corbels and a sculpture of a naked **Dukatenmännchen** who strains to excrete a ducat in a bizarre parable about the fate of debtors. The backdrop to this ensemble piece is the Romanesque **Marktkirche**; look for a baptismal font (1573) of Rammelsberg copper which a local craftsman cast into a pictorial bible; and a thirteenth-century glass of patron saints Cosmas and Damian stained with ochre, azurite and verdigris dug from the mine.

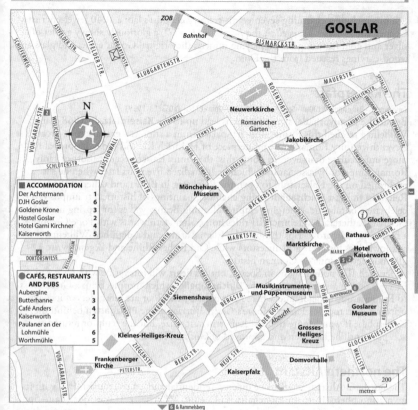

▼ 6 & Rammelsberg

Hoher Weg

Behind the Marktkirche, **Hoher Weg** heads south. At Hoher Weg 1, cherubs cavort, medieval ladies joust on cockerels and a saucy dairymaid hoists her dress as she churns butter on the 1526 **Brusttuch house**; it's now a hotel, so nip in for a look at the spectacular dining room. Its wealthy owner is said to have gone into debt during the building, explaining the two monkeys who squabble over coins on the gable end. The bakers on the opposite side of the street were far more prosaic with their 1557 **guildhouse**: look for a gold pretzel and gingerbread on its facade.

To the south the cluttered **Musikinstrumente- und Puppen-Museum**, Hoher Weg 5 (daily 11am–5pm; €3; ☎05321 269 45), features a medieval hurdy-gurdy it claims is Germany's oldest instrument. Continuing south over the Abzucht stream, past the architectural asceticism of the thirteenth-century hospice, **Grosses-Heiliges-Kreuz**, where a 1500s Christ with human hair now watches over craftsmen, you reach the **Domvorhalle** (daily 11am–5pm; free). This relic vestibule belonged to the imperial Dom of St Simon and St Judas, and contains the Kaiserstuhl (1060), the imperial stone throne.

The Goslarer Museum

Königsstr. 1 • April–Oct Tues–Sun 10am–5pm; Nov–March Tues–Sun 10am–4pm • €4 • ☎05321 433 94

From the Musikinstrumente- und Puppen-Museum, a path threads alongside the Abzucht stream and a waterwheel to the **Goslarer Museum** of local history, whose exhibits include a charming seventeenth-century chemist's lab; a 1240 jewel-encrusted Gospel, the *Goslarer Evangeliar*; the *Bergkanne* (1477), a gloriously showy goblet of silver and gold featuring music-playing miners; the original Goslar eagle; and glass and wood-carvings rescued from the Dom.

The Kaiserpfalz

Kaiserbleek 6 • Daily: April–Oct 10am–5pm; Nov–March 10am–4pm • €7.50 • ☎ 05321 311 96 93

Beside the Domvorhalle, sweeping lawns lead up to the **Kaiserpfalz**. In 1868 Kaiser Wilhelm I rescued this former imperial palace from a stint as a granary to re-create the eleventh-century Romanesque masterpiece of Heinrich III, and today it's probably more immaculate than ever. In doing this, the canny Kaiser became a sort of Holy Roman Emperor by association, which he formalized five years later when he sat enthroned on the Kaiserstuhl to open the Reichstag in Berlin and usher in the Second Reich. In the vast **Reichsaal** debating chamber, paintings of historical triumphs (1897) celebrate a bombastic, emerging empire: Sleeping Beauty wakes for "spring in the new German Fatherland"; Heinrich III rides home after stern words with Pope Gregory VI; a crusading Barbarossa rips through the Islamic army; and a dignified Wilhelm acknowledges his peers and ancestors while Old Father Rhine and Legend write a glorious new chapter in German history.

Heinrich III's body may be in Speyer, but his heart will forever be with his creation, in a gilt box in a sarcophagus in the **Ulrichskapelle**, which morphs from a Greek cross to Romanesque octagon and where floor bolts by the door are reminders of its days as a prison. Look, too, for Henry Moore's *Goslar Warrior* in the **Pfalzgarten** behind the Kaiserpfalz; it won Moore the first Kaiserring art prize, but the sculptor refused to accept it until he had seen and approved of Goslar. He did.

The northern Altstadt

The northern Altstadt tends to be quieter, residential and off the tourist trail, with its own atmosphere. Here the **Mönchehaus Museum**, Mönchestr. 1 (Tues–Sat 10am–5pm, Sun 10am–1pm; €5; ⓦ moenchehaus.de), holds a high-octane dose of modern painting and sculpture, including De Kooning, Ernst and Beuys. Meanwhile the **Neuwerkkirche**, Rosentorstr. 27 (March–Oct Mon–Sat 10am–noon & 2.30–4.30pm, Sun 2.30–4.30pm; free), a former Romanesque collegiate church, is uncharacteristic for its frippery: strikingly lavish outside, with polygonal towers punctuated by windows and an artistic apse, and with a contemporary rood screen and rich frescoes inside.

Frankenbergerviertel

Towards the western edge of the Altstadt lies the **Frankenbergerviertel** miners' parish. Here, the Baroque **Siemenshaus**, Schreiberstr. 12 (Tues & Thurs 9am–noon; free), was the mid-nineteenth-century home of the Siemens family who founded what became today's global corporation. Understandably it is a world away from the humble houses of the miners on **Peterstrasse** at the southwestern edge of the district. Their parish church, the **Frankenberger Kirche**, has a fantastical Baroque altar.

Bergbaumuseum Rammelsberg

Bergtal 19 • Daily 9am–6pm • Museum only €7, museum & tour €13 • ⓦ rammelsberg.de • Bus #803 from the train station (frequent; 10min)

The Rammelsberg silver mine, some 2km south of the Markt, was the backbone of Goslar's economic clout for a millennium, and only ceased production in 1998. Now the **Bergbaumuseum**, or **mining museum**, chronicles this history, explaining the processes and, best of all, allows you to don overalls and a miner's helmet and access two-hundred-year-old underground shafts.

ARRIVAL AND INFORMATION GOSLAR

By train The train station lies at the northern edge of town, an easy 5min walk from the centre.
Destinations Hannover (hourly; 1hr); Magdeburg (hourly; 2hr); Quedlinburg (every 30min; 1hr 30min).
By bus Regional services depart from the train station, where the office of Regionalbus Braunschweig (☎05321 194 49, ⓦrbb-bus.de) has timetables and network maps.

Destinations Bad Harzburg (every 30min; 12min); Braunlage (every 30min; 55min); Schierke (hourly; 2hr).
Tourist office Markt 7 (April–Oct Mon–Fri 9.15am–6pm, Sat 9.30am–4pm, Sun 9.30am–2pm; Nov–March Mon–Fri 9.15am–5pm, Sat 9.30am–2pm; ☎05321 780 60, ⓦwww.goslar.de). The office can book private rooms (from €45).

ACCOMMODATION

HOTELS

Der Achtermann Rosentorstr. 20 ☎05321 700 00, ⓦder-achtermann.de. By the Bahnhof, Goslar's smartest address is good value and has all the understated elegance and 4-star mod cons you could want, as well as an airy swimming pool and sauna complex. Free wi-fi. **€100**

★**Goldene Krone** Breite Str. 46 ☎05321 344 90, ⓦgoldene-krone-goslar.de. Well-run, simple and homely three-hundred-year-old inn in easy walking distance of the centre of town, with sparkling modern hotel rooms and parking. The huge breakfast buffet is excellent. **€94**

Hotel Garni Kirchner Doktorswiese 7 ☎05321 349 50, ⓦhotel-garni-kirchner.de. One of the more keenly priced options, a 10min walk from the centre but close to the train station. Rooms are airy and modern, though there's a vague mismatched chintziness throughout. Good breakfast buffet included. **€73**

Kaiserworth Markt 3 ☎05321 70 90, ⓦkaiserworth .de. Extravagant lodgings in a fifteenth-century former guildhall beside Goslar's showpiece Markt. Rooms are decorated in a range of styles from simple and modern to rustic, Neoclassical or Baroque. There's also a cosy wine-cellar and excellent restaurant, *Die Worth* (see p.227). **€127**

HOSTELS

DJH Goslar Rammelsberger Str. 25 ☎05321 222 40, ⓦjugendherberge.de/jh/goslar; bus #803 to "Theresienhof". Attractive, well-kept hostel close to the mining museum and easily reached from the train station. Also offers half- and full-board deals for €5/€10 respectively. Dorms **€23**, doubles **€46**

Hostel Goslar Wislicenusstr. 15 ☎017663 36 54 89, ⓦhostelgoslar.de. Hostel in an old villa full of a real hotchpotch of dated furnishings, but with a friendly atmosphere. Free bike hire and a shared kitchen. Dorms **€16**, doubles **€48**

EATING AND DRINKING

Aubergine Marktstr. 4 ☎05321 421 36, ⓦaubergine -goslar.de. Luxury restaurant with French and Italian food, tasteful floral decor, and great attention to detail in everything. Particularly good for fresh fish, though the lamb is excellent and the mocha-mousse desert a delicious house speciality. Mains €13–20. Daily noon–3pm & 5.30–11pm.

Butterhanne Marktkirchhof 3 ☎05321 228 86, ⓦbutterhanne.de. The food is pretty standard German favourites (mains average €9), but the outdoor seating is a boon and on weekend nights it's the place to be after about 10pm. Daily 8.30am–midnight.

Café Anders Hoher Weg 4 ☎05321 238 14, ⓦbarockcafe-anders.de. The smells alone make this a great address for afternoon coffee and cake. The room upstairs is dizzy with Baroque decor, while the terrace has great Harz views. Daily 8.30am–6pm.

Paulaner an der Lohmühle Gemeindehof 3–5 ☎05321 260 70. Bavarian chain, but with Harz specials

and a setting in a cosy inn next to the Abzucht stream. Prices are keen, with many mains around €9, and there's a good selection of Bavarian draught beers to wash it all down. Mon–Fri noon–midnight, Sat & Sun 11am–midnight.

Die Worth At the Kaiserworth hotel, Markt 3 ☎05321 70 90, ⓦrestaurant-goslar-worth.de. Excellent international restaurant under vaulted ceilings and stained-glass windows. The menu often has good game choices with local wild mushrooms (mains €15–35), though for an unusual experience try the *Harzer Blaubeer Schmandschnitzel*, a pork chop served with a creamy blueberry sauce. Daily 11.30am–10pm.

Worthmühle Worthstr. 4 ☎05321 434 02, ⓦworthmuehle.de. Regional accents abound in this Harz speciality restaurant: in the decor, in the good-value dishes such as wild boar and trout (mains average €15), and in the fruity local *Goslarer Gosebier*. Mon–Fri 5–11pm, Sat & Sun noon–2.30pm & 5–11pm.

3

Thuringia

FRESCOED CEILING, THE WARTBURG

Thuringia

Culturally as much as geographically Thuringia (Thüringen) is the heartland of Germany. When the Iron Curtain pulled back, West Germans were relieved to find the nation's "green heart" was spared the social realism of which the GDR was so fond. It remains the sort of place Germans have in mind when they talk of *früher*, a time past when things were less complicated – a tranquil state where slow travel rules, and no city is over 200,000 people. The surprise, then, is that were there a competition to decide Germany's cultural big-hitter, flyweight Thuringia would be a finalist. This is a state of Martin Luther, Bach, Schiller and, more than anyone else, Goethe. With nowhere more than a couple of hours' drive away, Thuringia is touring country par excellence. Factor in scenic backroads that slalom through valleys and you have a bucolic state that is all about a finger on the steering wheel, sunshine-sounds on the stereo and the gentle art of pottering about, whether in small towns or on trails. Slow travel has never been so much fun.

4

As ever, the reason Thuringia punches far above its weight is historical. As the ruling Saxon House of Wettin bequeathed land equally between male heirs, an area that was far from large to begin with fragmented into a mosaic of small duchies – Saxe-Weimar and Saxe-Gotha, for example, or Saxe-Coburg, better known in Britain as the House of Windsor. An upshot of these tin-pot fiefdoms was an arts race that saw the area's dukes woo the finest musicians, painters, poets and philosophers to their courts as testament to their learning and magnificence.

Nowhere expresses this better than **Weimar**, a Thuringia-in-microcosm that lobbed the intellectual atom-bomb of the German Enlightenment, whose shockwaves were felt throughout Europe. Most cities would struggle to make such an impact, let alone a small, courtly town. Adjacent **Jena** has maintained its academic tradition and the student nightlife that goes with it, while **Gotha** and especially **Eisenach** have a cultural weight far above their modest size. The state capital is **Erfurt**, Luther's university city and perhaps the most underrated capital in Germany thanks to its marriage of historic looks and university dynamism.

The **Thuringian Forest** to the south could not be more different. This is the state's rural core, whose sleepy villages are tucked into the folds of an upland blessed by good walking and cycling trails. You can lose a happy week crisscrossing the area by bike on labelled routes, or journey through its heart on the well-marked 168km **Rennsteig**, which traverses it. The state's many green landscapes also include the **Saale Valley** at the eastern fringe of the forest region, and the **Kyffhäuser** uplands to the north, site of the sixteenth-century Peasants' War sparked in the overlooked historic town of **Mülhausen**.

SCHILLERHAUS, WEIMAR

Highlights

❶ **Erfurt** The underrated Land capital may be cultured, and it is certainly charming, but it's the presence of a university that brings energy – and bars – to the historic streetscape. **See p.232**

❷ **Weimar** An erudite town steeped in three centuries of cultural prowess whose former residents read like a who's who of German arts. Don't worry – it's pretty, too. **See p.241**

❸ **Gotha** Spend the morning in a multifaceted museum, and the afternoon in the Thuringian Forest, reached on a historic tram. **See p.259**

❹ **Eisenach** A provincial backwater that just happens to be home to the Wartburg, as

potent an icon of German identity as you could wish for, where Luther hid and whose gloriously over-the-top halls inspired Wagner. **See p.261**

❺ **The Thuringian Forest** With your own transport there are cosy villages to find, castles to explore and pocket-sized ducal capitals to stroll in, in a region that offers slow travel at its best. **See p.266**

❻ **Rennsteig** On two legs or two wheels, "Der Runst" remains the track that any self-respecting trail-junkie must tick off. **See p.267**

HIGHLIGHTS ARE MARKED ON THE MAP ON P.232

Erfurt

Erfurt is a honeypot. A town would have to stand here even if the city had just been razed to the ground.

Martin Luther

So mused the most famous resident of Thuringia's state capital. While the father of the Reformation could also have acclaimed it as a fine little city bursting with character, ever the pragmatist, he got to the nub because a location at the heart of Germany – and Europe – was the making of **ERFURT**. While profits from woad helped fill coffers, its drip-feeds of finance were trade routes east–west from Paris to Russian city Novgorod, and north–south from the Baltic to Italy. Such was its wealth that the medieval city was hailed as "Efurtia turrita" because of its ninety spires.

With the merchants came progressive ideas and liberal attitudes. Luther's free thinking was nurtured at Erfurt's prestigious **university**, renowned as a cradle of

HIGHLIGHTS

1. Erfurt
2. Weimar
3. Gotha
4. Eisenach
5. The Thuringian Forest
6. Rennsteig

humanism. Centuries later, in 1970, open-minded Erfurt hosted ice-breaker *Ostpolitik* talks between West and East Germany. Though the largest city in Thuringia, Erfurt is pocket-sized, its easygoing **Altstadt** a traditional German townscape of the sort largely obliterated elsewhere by bombs and developers, and with a dynamo university that adds a sheen of modern style and passable nightlife. Put the two together and what's not to like? Few honeypots taste sweeter.

Erfurt has few set pieces; it's as an ensemble that the city impresses, with any street in the centre worth exploring, especially as you can walk from one side of the city to the other in about twenty minutes. The axes of Erfurt's central Altstadt are the Episcopal powerbase **Domplatz**; **Fischmarkt**, the civic heart; and **Anger**, a broad plaza at the head of the shopping streets. North of the centre in the studenty **Andreasviertel** and around the **Augustinerkloster** are especially photogenic quarters. Drop the map and explore by instinct.

Domplatz

The open space of **Domplatz** seems too handsome to be a child of war. French and Prussian forces met here in 1813 and the residential strip along its north fringe went up in smoke, leaving just the narrow half-timbered buildings that jostle for space on its east and south. The ashes were swept away, Domplatz expanded into the vacuum and now only its stones recall the travesty – cobbles demarcate the original Domplatz, flagstones indicate the rest.

Dom

Domplatz • **Dom** Mon–Sat 9.30am–6pm, Sun from 1–6pm • Free • **Tower tours** April–Oct Thurs & Fri pm hourly • €2.50

The High Gothic choir of the **Dom** looms over the square like the bows of a cruise-liner, perched atop a massive medieval substructure that expands the top of a previous Romanesque cathedral. A monumental staircase – a superb stage for evening spectaculars during summer's Domstufen-Festspiele – sweeps up to a triangular porch tacked on the north side, while a large tracery arrow at its portal follows Gothic's guiding dictum to direct eyes up to heaven.

The lofty cathedral within exudes the mysticism of the early church. Some of Germany's finest medieval stained-glass fills the slender lancet windows that stretch full-length in the choir, while in the south transept are a number of artworks from the original Dom, noticeably the twelfth-century "Wolfram" candelabrum – a bearded figure who sprouts from dragons as a symbol of the light of Christianity. Nearby are the tombstone of Count von Gleichen, a thirteenth-century bigamist pictured with his two wives, and a Romanesque stucco altar of an enthroned Madonna ablaze with stars. Medieval altarpieces wrapped around the columns catch the eye – as does eastern Germany's largest mural of St John the Baptist, Gothic sea-monsters swimming around his legs – but the finest artwork is a sumptuous Cranach altarpiece in a north-aisle chapel that depicts the Madonna and saints Catherine and Barbara with the simple intimacy of a family snapshot.

Tours ascend the **tower** to view the world's largest free-swinging medieval bell, the 2.5m-high *Gloriosa*, whose deep toll sounds far beyond the town centre on religious high days, though there are no views.

Severikirche

Domplatz • Daily noon–6pm • Free

Smaller than the Dom, the adjacent **Severikirche**, with a crown of three spires, refuses to be overshadowed. Near the entrance of a spacious five-aisled hall church lies the fourteenth-century sarcophagus of St Severi, its sheer bulk softened through its pink sandstone and a beautifully rendered life-story of the saint whose remains arrived in Erfurt in 836 AD. Other eye-catchers are the St Michael who spears one of the most vivid medieval devils you'll ever see, and a font covered by an extravagant fifteen-metre Gothic trellis.

ERFURT

0 — 200 metres

● RESTAURANTS

Clara	6
Il Cortile	1
Faustfood	9
Palais Wachsberg	7
Schildchen	3
Wirsthaus Christoffel	4
Zum Goldenen Schwan	8

CAFÉS & BARS

Double B	2
Goldhelm	5
Glashütte	11
Hemingway	10
SiJu	13
Steinhaus	12
Übersee	14
Weinstein Le Bar	15

NIGHTLIFE

Centrum-Club	4
Engelsburg	2
HsD & Museumskeller	1
Jazzclub	3
Presseklub	5
Stadtgarten	6

■ ACCOMMODATION

Am Kaisersaal	5
Augustinerkloster	1
IBB	4
Nikolai	3
Opera Hostel	8
Pullman Erfurt am Dom	6
Rad Hof	2
Re_4 Hostel	9
Victor's	10
Zumnorde	7

Museum für Thüringer Volkskunde

Haus zum Stockfisch

Kaufmannskirche

Angermuseum

Reglerkirche

Hauptbahnhof

Kaisersaal

Schottenkirche

Krämerbrücke

Aegidienkirche

Kleine Synagogue

Neue Mühle

Bartholomäusturm

Johanneskirche

Augustinerkloster

Collegium Maius

Michaeliskirche

Alte Synagogue

Rathaus

Predigerkirche

Barfüsserkirche

Staatskanzlei

Zum Breiten Herd

Zum Roten Ochsen (Kunsthalle Erfurt)

River Gera

DOMPLATZ

Severikirche

Dom

River Gera

Alte Oper Erfurt

Zitadelle Petersberg

Peterskirche (Forum Konkrete Kunst)

Kommandanthaus

Brühler Garten

Theater Erfurt

STAUFFENBERGALLEE

JURI-GAGARIN-RING

ANDREASTR.

LANGE BRÜCKE

LÖBERSTR.

BAHNHOFSTR.

THEATERSTR.

N

Zitadelle Petersberg

Forum Konkrete Kunst Wed–Sun: May–Oct 10am–6pm; Nov–April 10am–4pm • Free • ⓦ forum-konkrete-kunst-erfurt.de • **Tunnel tours** May–Oct Fri & Sat 7pm; book through tourist office • €9

Why the **Zitadelle Petersberg** above Domplatz is not a major attraction is a mystery. The only complete Baroque town fortress in central Europe is protected in statute but overlooked by the city and visitors alike despite its illustrious history. Emperor Frederick Barbarossa, Germany's real-life King Arthur, summoned nobles for five imperial Diets in the **Peterskirche** – one of the oldest buildings in the citadel – during the twelfth century, one of which saw Saxon duke Henry the Lion, the founder of Munich and ruler of most of present-day Lower Saxony and Schleswig-Holstein, humbled for refusing to back a disastrous escapade in Italy. Mainz archbishops took a similarly tough stance after city riots in 1664 – they consulted the latest French military ideas to create the massive Baroque citadel that recycles stone from the city's churches, one reason why Erfurt is no longer the "city of spires" medieval visitors acclaimed.

Today its architecture is an atmospheric jumble of former military buildings. As good a reason to visit as any is the panorama from its massive bastions. **Tours** venture into the labyrinth of **tunnels** beneath the fortifications and take in the Kommandanthaus, with its displays of uniforms and weaponry and models of the citadel's development. The barn-like Romanesque Peterskirche houses the **Forum Konkrete Kunst**, which contains changing exhibitions of modern international sculpture.

Fischmarkt and around

Running from Domplatz to Fischmarkt, **Marktstrasse** tracks the trade route that linked Russia to the Rhine. Side roads hold a couple of diversions: the fine Renaissance portal of Haus zum Sonneborn (now the registry office) on Grosse Arche; and former Renaissance breweries at Allerheiligenstr. 6 and 7, where portholes were stuffed with straw to announce a fresh beer had matured.

A hundred metres from the Domplatz but a world away in atmosphere, **Fischmarkt** is the centre-stage of Erfurt's civic life, crowded by colourful Baroque and Renaissance townhouses, among them **Zum Breiten Herd** (1584), decorated with a frieze of the five senses.

Zum Roten Ochsen and the Kunsthalle Erfurt

Fischmarkt • Tues–Sun 11am–6pm • €6 • ⓦ kunsthalle-erfurt.de

On the west flank of Fischmarkt, a fine facade graces **Zum Roten Ochsen** (1562); a frieze depicts the days of the week and Greek muses along with the beaming Red Ox of its name. The modern interior contains the **Kunsthalle Erfurt**, which stages exhibitions, usually of modern art and photography. The identity of the pot-bellied statue of the Roman soldier in front of it is a mystery; one theory suggests the Renaissance figure is a symbolic assertion of civic independence similar to the statues of Roland erected by Germany's Free Imperial cities. Another theory is that he is Erfurt's patron, St Martin.

Rathaus

Fischmarkt • Mon, Tues & Thurs 10am–6pm, Wed 10am–4pm, Fri 8am–2pm, Sat & Sun 10am–5pm • Free

Opposite Zum Roten Ochsen, the Festsaal in the tubby neo-Gothic **Rathaus** is painted with late Romantic, faux-medieval images of Tannhäuser and Faust legends alongside images of local hero Martin Luther.

Kleine Synagoge and the Alte Synagoge

Kleine Synagoge Tues–Sun 11am–6pm • Free • **Alte Synagoge** Tues–Sun 10am–6pm • €8 including audio-guide • ⓦ alte-synagoge.erfurt.de

Behind the Rathaus, hanging over the river, the **Kleine Synagoge** contains a small museum on Erfurt's Jewish community in a house that was consecrated for worship from 1840 to 1884. Its predecessor north of Fischmarkt at Waagegasse 8, is the medieval **Alte Synagoge**. One of Europe's earliest synagogues of what was one of the continent's richest and most powerful Jewish communities, the beautifully restored, early Gothic shell houses a 28-kilo haul of fourteenth-century gold bullion, tableware and ostentatious jewellery, notably a large Jewish wedding ring like a miniature building engraved with the Hebrew words *Mazel tov* (good luck). Historians suggest the buried treasure's owner converted the synagogue into a warehouse after the 1349 pogrom, which was triggered by a plague epidemic blamed on the town's Jews.

Predigerkirche

Predigerstrasse • May–Sept Tues–Sat 11am–4pm, Sun noon–4pm • Free

Just off Fischmarkt is the **Predigerkirche**, medieval church of the Dominican "preacher" order; Germany's most famous mystic, Master Eckhart, a thirteenth-century friar cited by Schopenhauer, was around for its construction. The highlight of its understated interior is a carved-stone choir screen.

North of Fischmarkt

Former university quarter, the **Andreasviertel** north of Fischmarkt, is one of the Altstadt's backwaters, albeit a lively one at weekends due to its small bar district. Most places are on main street Michaelisstrasse, the student centre during the heyday of Erfurt's old university. Opened in 1392, the fifth native-language university in Germany blossomed into the largest centre of learning in central Europe. Its **Collegium Maius** midway along Allerheiligenstrasse was recently restored from war damage. Opposite, the Gothic university church **Michaeliskirche** is where a former philosophy student named Martin Luther preached in 1522. If open, the Dreifaltigkeitskapelle reached from a lovely courtyard is worth a look for an unusual oriel window.

The Augustinerkloster

Augustinerstr. 10 • **Church and courtyard** Daily 9am–6pm • Free • **Tours** April–Oct Mon–Sat 9.30am, 11am, 12.30pm, 2pm, 3.30pm & 5pm, Sun 11am & noon; Nov–March Mon–Fri 9.30am, 11am, 12.30pm, 2pm & 3.30pm, Sat 9.30am, 11am, 12.30pm & 2pm, Sun 11am • €7.50 • ⓦ augustinerkloster.de

Quieter still than Michaelisstrasse is the photogenic nest of streets on the River Gera's eastern banks, not least postcard-pretty Kirchgasse. It's located at the back of the fourteenth-century **Augustinerkloster**, where Luther was a monk from 1505 to 1511. The story goes that he signed up in gratitude for the monastery's hospitality when he was caught out by a storm and it was here that the Reformer divined the presence of a merciful (as opposed to vengeful) God. "One difficult sentence was sufficient to occupy my thoughts for the whole day," he wrote of his time here, an intensity he probably never matched during four previous years as a student in Erfurt. On tours of the Augustinian monastery you can see a half-timbered nook similar to that in which the father of the Reformation studied as a novice – monastic rules of poverty forbid monks from owning their own cell – and there is a small ecclesiastical museum that belies the monastery's more recent glass-skinned extensions. However, Luther's church remains as he would have known it: suitably spartan in response to his condemnation of visual distractions and pepped up only with medieval stained-glass in the choir.

Krämerbrücke

Stiftung Krämerbrücke museum Daily 10am–6pm • Free • **Aegidienkirche tower** Tues–Sun 11am–5pm • €1.50

If the Dom has the majesty, Erfurt's second landmark has all the charm. It doesn't stretch the imagination too far to visualize medieval traders in floppy hats trundling carts across the **Krämerbrücke** (Merchants' Bridge) east of Fischmarkt. This is the longest inhabited bridge in Europe and the only one north of the Alps – Erfurt is quick to point out that its bridge existed before that of its southern counterpart, Florence's Ponte Vecchio. It thrived almost as soon as burghers tired of rebuilding wooden footbridges over the River Gera and erected this stone span in 1325. Merchants hawked luxury spices, medicines, dyes, silk and paper in 64 toy-town houses. The number has halved, but the trade remains high-end stuff, including touristy antiques, crafts, jewellery and products coloured blue with local woad.

The house at no. 31 is open as a small museum run by the **Stiftung Krämerbrücke**, where you can nose into the medieval cellars overlooking the river below and peruse displays about the bridge. The picture-postcard view of the bridge is from the tower of the **Aegidienkirche**.

Haus zum Stockfisch and around

Johannesstrasse, at the end of Futterstrasse, is lined by Renaissance mansions that were erected by flush woad merchants, none more eye-catching than **Haus zum Stockfisch** (1607); its "dried cod" mark is depicted absurdly as a *Jaws* look-alike. It now contains the **Stadtmuseum** (Tues–Sun 10am–6pm; €6; ⓦ stadtmuseum-erfurt.de), a missable plod through the city's history. More enjoyable is the homespun world of traditional Thuringian lifestyles in the **Museum für Thüringer Volkskunde** (Tues–Sun 10am–6pm; €6; ⓦ volkskundemuseum-erfurt.de), one block to the east at Juri-Gagarin-Ring 140a. Mask makers, glassblowers and woad printers are represented in its re-created workshops, and there are rooms of folk costume, tools and furnishings.

Anger

South of the civic centre of the Altstadt, spacious **Anger** square has long been Erfurt's commercial heart – once as a market for wool, wheat, woad and wine, today as the main square of the commercial shopping district.

The Angermuseum

Anger 18 • Tues–Sun 10am–6pm • €6 • ⓦ angermuseum.de

An impressive Baroque mansion at the corner of Anger with Bahnhofstrasse houses the **Angermuseum**, exhibiting Erfurt's decorative and fine art collections. Medieval religious art rescued from the Augustinerkloster and Barfüsserkirche occupies a room off the ground-floor atrium – notably an early Renaissance *Creation of Man* that depicts a unicorn among God's creations. Above there's art – second-division German Romantics, premier-league Impressionists like Max Beckmann, Lovis Corinth and Max Liebermann, and modern artists of the Leipzig scene – plus the usual applied arts, from fine porcelain and medieval guilds' tankards to interior design.

The Staatskanzlei

A few hundred metres west on Anger past the Bartholomäusturm, a surviving spire of a medieval church, the **Staatskanzlei** (State Chancellery) backs a spacious square. The Baroque palace hosted one of German history's most celebrated meetings in 1808, between Emperor Napoleon and Johann Wolfgang von Goethe. The breakfasting emperor saluted Goethe, "*Vous êtes un homme!*" and confessed he had read *The Sorrows of Young Werther* seven times. Come to Paris, Napoleon promised, and the German polymath would find a subject worthy of his skill, most likely the emperor's achievements, which he believed ranked alongside those of Roman rulers. Goethe never took up the offer, but found space in his study for a bust of the emperor thereafter.

4

Egapark

Egapark Daily: March, April & mid-Sept to Oct 9am–6pm; May to mid-Sept 9am–8pm (show pavilions till 6pm); Nov–Feb 10am–4pm • ⓦ egapark-erfurt.de • **Gartenbaumuseum** March–Oct Tues–Sun 10am–6pm; July–Sept also Mon • €6 • ⓦ gartenbaumuseum.de • Tram #2 from Anger to "Egapark"

Redressing the relative dearth of central green spaces are the kaleidoscopic gardens of **Egapark**, 2.5km southwest of the centre in the grounds of the **Cyriaksburg** castle. Visit in spring for the largest ornamental flowerbed in Europe (6000 square metres), plus rose, water and Japanese gardens to explore along with a tropical butterfly house (among other show pavilions) and cafés. The slab-sided fortification itself has been handed over as gardening museum, the **Gartenbaumuseum**.

ARRIVAL AND DEPARTURE   ERFURT

By plane The airport (ⓦ flughafen-erfurt.de) is 3km west of the centre. Tram #4 travels direct from the terminus to Domplatz and Anger. Alternatively, a taxi from the airport will cost around €15.

By train The Hauptbahnhof lies at the southeast edge of the Altstadt, a 10min walk from the centre.

Destinations Eisenach (every 30min; 30–50min); Gotha (every 30min; 15–25min); Ilmenau (hourly; 55min); Jena (hourly; 30min); Leipzig (hourly; 1hr 10min); Meiningen (10 daily; 1hr 30min–1hr 50min); Mülhausen (hourly; 50min–1hr 15min); Weimar (every 20–30min; 15min).

GETTING AROUND

By public transport Domplatz and Anger are the two hubs around which the public transport network revolves; a single ticket costs €1.70, a day-ticket €4.70.

By bike You can rent bikes at Radhaus am Dom, Andreasstr. 28 (☏ 0361 602 06 40, ⓦ radhausamdom .fahrradshop-thueringen.de).

By taxi There are ranks at the Hauptbahnhof and main square Domplatz, among other places. To book a cab call Taxigenossenschaft Erfurt ☏ 0361 66 66 66.

By car Avis, Weimarische Str. 37b ☏ 0361 262 92 00; Europcar, Weimarische Str. 32a ☏ 0361 77 81 30; Hertz, Reisezentrum, Hauptbahnhof ☏ 0361 34 08 50. All three outfits also have desks at the airport.

INFORMATION

Tourist office Behind the Rathaus at Benediktsplatz 1 (Mon–Sat 10am–6pm, Sun 10am–2pm; Jan–March closes 4pm on Sat; general ☏ 0361 664 00, accommodation ☏ 0361 66 40 110, ⓦ erfurt-tourismus.de). Most local tours are in German, but you can rent an English audio-

guide tour for €7.50.

Discount card The ErfurtCard (48hr €14.90) is valid for public transport, free entry to the municipal museums and a city tour, plus the usual discounts on scattered sights.

ACCOMMODATION

HOTELS

Am Kaisersaal Futterstr. 8 ☏ 0361 65 85 60, ⓦ hotel -am-kaisersaal.de. A fine mid-range choice in the centre, this well-appointed small hotel is set amid the café culture at the end of the Krämerbrücke. Though on the small side, rooms are comfortable. **€91**

Augustinerkloster Augustinerstr. 10 ☏ 0361 664 01 10, ⓦ augustinerkloster.de. A spiritual retreat rather than a hotel, the guest accommodation in the monastery where Luther studied has a sense of serenity engendered by the separate world of the monastery. Rooms divide between the monastery itself and the modern Waidhaus, both on a historic courtyard. **€87**

IBB Gotthardtstr. 27 ☏ 0361 674 00, ⓦ ibbhotels.com. Arguably the best location in Erfurt, beside the Krämerbrücke. Decor ranges from designer minimalism to classic modern, plus country-style suites in an incorporated medieval inn. Front rooms have views of the river. **€118**

Nikolai Augustinerstr. 30 ☏ 0361 59 81 70, ⓦ gaestehaus-nikolai.de. A nicely old-fashioned stay affiliated to the nearby *Augustinerkloster*. The pleasant guesthouse provides a friendly welcome, and rooms have homely touches and reproduction antiques. The location is another plus: a quiet corner of the Altstadt yet close to the bars on Michaelsstrasse. **€88**

Pullman Erfurt am Dom Am Theaterplatz 2 ☏ 0361 644 50, ⓦ pullmanhotels.com. Part of the Accor chain, this is a designer-modern business hotel with a neutral palette of coffee and cream located a 5min walk from the Dom. Facilities include a day-spa. **€89**

Rad Hof Kirchgasse 1b ☏ 0361 602 77 61, ⓦ rad-hof .de. Interesting little place directly behind the *Augustinerkloster* and catering to the post-backpacker market and especially welcoming to cyclists. Its six crisply styled, colourful en suites feature natural materials – call ahead to ensure the owner is around. **€66**

Victor's Hässlerstr. 17 ☎ 0361 653 30, ⓦ victors.de. Within a modern block hides a smart four-star from this international chain, styled in the usual classic-modern Italianesque style and with a fine restaurant. Located south of the Hauptbahnhof, about a 15min walk from the centre. €115

Zumnorde Anger 50–51 (enter on Weitergasse) ☎ 0361 568 00, ⓦ hotel-zumnorde.de. Efficient hotel in the heart of Erfurt whose classic-modern bedrooms are clean and spacious if not particularly big on character. The restored townhouse is lifted by splashes of Art Deco and has a modern extension. €99

HOSTELS AND CAMPSITES

Freizeitpark Stausee Hohenfelden ☎ 036450 420 81, ⓦ stausee-hohenfelden.de; bus #155. The nearest campsite, the state's largest, compensates for a location 16km southeast with a lakeside setting. It's a good option if you have kids in tow due to an adjacent woodland adventure playground plus an indoor fun-pool with slides and beach on the opposite shore. Other facilities include a lakeside restaurant. Pitch €2.50, plus €6 per person

★ **Opera** Walkmühlstr. 13 ☎ 0361 60 13 13 60, ⓦ opera-hostel.de; tram #1 or #2 to "Brühler Garten". A cut above the usual hostel in its funky design leanings, and friendly and spacious throughout, with en-suite rooms as well as three- to seven-bed dorms. Well located about a 15min walk south of Domplatz. The only downside is traffic noise at the front. Dorms €13, doubles €52

Re4 Hostel Puschkinstr. 21 ☎ 0361 600 01 10, ⓦ re4hostel.com; tram #5. Located south of the centre, about 1km west of the Hauptbahnhof, this great hostel is created from a former police station – room 13 retains its cell bars. Dorms are bright, cheerful and all bunk-bed-free; some rooms are hotel-standard en suites with a TV. Dorms €14, doubles €56

EATING AND DRINKING

Erfurt brings the energy of a federal capital and style sense of a university city to its historic buildings to good effect with its **restaurant** scene. There's also an abundance of **café** and **bar** culture: the former is strong at Wenigemarkt at the east end of the Krämerbrücke, the latter is focused on Michaelisstrasse in the student quarter.

CAFÉS AND BARS

Double B Marbacher Gasse 10 ☎ 0361 211 51 22, ⓦ doubleb-erfurt.de. Lazy paced bar in a quiet backstreet that attracts an older student clientele. There are six beers on tap, plus all-day breakfasts and cheap bar food, all best enjoyed in the beer garden. Mon–Fri 8am–late, Sat & Sun 9am–late.

Glashütte Petersberg 11 ☎ 0361 601 50 94, ⓦ glashuette-petersberg.de. The "glass hut" is an elevated lounge bar-café on top of the fortress walls that offers outstanding views over Erfurt's roofs and spires, plus a terrace for alfresco drinking on warm evenings. Nice spot for breakfast, too. Daily 10am–1am.

Goldhelm Kreuzgasse 5 ☎ 0361 660 98 51, ⓦ goldhelm-schokolade.de. Excellent, exotic ice cream flavours – think gin tonic cucumber or summer chai – and home-made chocolate pralines, right next to the Krämerbrücke – and with a tiny outlet on the bridge too. Daily noon–6pm.

Hemingway Michaelisstr. 45 ☎ 0361 551 99 44, ⓦ hemingway-erfurt.de. A more than usually atmospheric member of the whisky and cocktail chain, thanks to a low-lit backroom that features a chunk of the building's medieval fabric. While not great for wine, over 187 varieties of rum are on the drinks menu and there's a smoking lounge with cigars on sale – the bearded scribbler would be proud. Mon–Thurs & Sun 6pm–1am, Fri & Sat 6pm–3am.

SiJu Fischmarkt 1 ☎ 0361 655 22 95, ⓦ si-ju-erfurt.de. A good choice within the glass-walled arcades of the Rathaus, that segues from daytime café to evening bar. The terrace is perfect for people-watching and light lunches. Mon–Fri 11am–1am, Sat 9am–7pm.

Steinhaus Allerheiligenstr. 20–21 ☎ 0361 24 47 71 12, ⓦ eburg.de. An enjoyable bar for students (and those who never quite stopped feeling young) that rambles over several rooms of a medieval house. The beer garden – a lovely courtyard of half-timbering – is the real selling point, alongside cheap beer and low-priced passable food. Daily noon–late.

Übersee Kürschnergasse 8 ☎ 0361 644 76 07, ⓦ uebersee-erfurt.de. This relaxed club-styled café-bar is quietly hip without ever trying too hard and has one of the best river terraces in town – a great spot for weekend "DIY" breakfasts priced by item. An attached bar-restaurant is more maximalist glam. Mon–Sat 9am–1am, Sun 10.30am–1am.

Weinstein Le Bar Kleine Arche 1 ☎ 0361 43 03 91 05. Stylish and rather bohemian wine and cocktail bar that specializes in German wines and is nicely sited in a quiet lane that's central yet feels far from the crowds on Fischmarkt. A good choice for more sophisticated drinking in the Altstadt. Tues–Sun 7pm–midnight.

RESTAURANTS

Clara Futterstr. 15–16 ☎ 0361 568 82 07, ⓦ restaurant-clara.de. Erfurt's finest creative modern-German cuisine is cooked up by the young Maria Gross and her team; always seasonal, often regional, beautifully presented... and good enough for Erfurt's first Michelin star in 2014. The wine list is excellent, too. Tues–Sat 6.30pm–midnight.

Faustfood Waagegasse 1 ☎0361 786 99 69, ⓦfaustfood.de. Thuringia-style fast-food served in a half-timbered barn with a large grill at the entrance: local *Bratwurst* (€2), ribs and burgers (from €5), all washed down with cheap beer. Mon–Sat noon–3pm & 5.30pm–midnight, Sun 5.30–11pm.

Il Cortile Johannesstr. 150 ☎0361 56 64 41, ⓦilcortile .de. The most elegant Italian restaurant in Erfurt yet one which retains a relaxed ambience in the dining room thanks to rush-seat chairs, old beams and charming service. Mains such as halibut or rack of lamb cost around €22, while pastas in decent portion sizes come in at around €13. Tues–Sat noon–2pm & 6–11pm.

Palais Wachsberg Futterstr. 13 ☎0361 654 77 99, ⓦpalaiswachsberg.de. A restored Baroque manor house with three options under one roof: international cuisine in a slick modern restaurant; updated Thuringian favourites such as pork goulash in the *Wirtshaus*; and tapas and antipasti in a *Vinothek*. Mon–Sat 11.30am–midnight.

Schildchen Schildgasse 3–4 ☎0361 540 22 90, ⓦwirtshaus-schildchen.de. In a quiet corner of the old town, this cosy locals' *Gaststätte* appeals for its laidback atmosphere as much as its above-average cooking and good-value dishes: expect the likes of goulash with bread or steak with green asparagus and sherry cream. Daily 10am–1am.

Wirtshaus Christoffel Michaelisstr. 41 ☎0361 262 69 43, ⓦwirtshaus-christoffel-erfurt.de. Good solid stuff – duck with red cabbage and *Klösse* dumplings (€14.30) or Thuringian sausages served by the panful and priced in *Taler* on the scroll menu – in an idiosyncratic Middle Ages-themed restaurant with rough bench seating. All good fun. Daily 11am–midnight.

Zum Goldenen Schwan Michaelisstr. 9 ☎0361 262 37 42, ⓦzum-goldenen-schwan.de. A room to suit every mood – a tavern downstairs, a bistro behind and a courtyard space – and hearty regional dishes such as pork steak with fried chanterelle mushrooms with potato croquets (€15), washed down with unfiltered beers brewed on-site. Jan & Feb Mon–Fri 5pm–1am, Sat & Sun 11am–1am; March–Dec daily 11am–1am.

NIGHTLIFE AND ENTERTAINMENT

The tourist office's *Erfurtmagazin* (ⓦerfurt-magazin.info) is the best source of monthly cultural **listings**; free magazines *Blitz!* and *Fritz* cover gigs, clubs and cinemas – the tourist office sells **tickets** for all events.

CLUBS AND LIVE MUSIC

Centrum-Club Am Anger 7 ⓦcentrum-club.de. The biggest club in town offers five floors of nightlife till dawn at weekends, from chart sounds to dark wave, techno and drum'n'bass nights plus the occasional midweek and Sunday gig – check the website before a visit. Fri & Sat 10pm–5am.

Engelsburg Allerheiligenstr. 20–21 ☎0361 24 47 70, ⓦeburg.de. A student all-rounder in the Altstadt that rocks to indie-electro clubnights and hosts live rock and metal bands in a warren of cellars. Also screens repertory cinema. Start the night with food and a beer in the attached *Steinhaus* bar (see p.239). Clubnights Thurs–Sat 10pm–late.

HsD & Museumskeller Juri-Gagarin-Ring 140a ☎0361 562 49 94, ⓦmuseumskeller.de. Two venues in one location: the former a bit like a school hall, the latter an intimate stone cellar. Together they offer one of Erfurt's most consistent venues for interesting indie, alt-folk, blues, jazz and rock acts, with gigs several times a week, often from touring international acts. Also has a beer garden for a summer drink. Primarily open weekends with occasional midweek gigs. Fri & Sat 9pm–3am.

Jazzclub Fischmarkt 13–16 ⓦjazzclub-erfurt.de. "Keep swinging" is the motto of Erfurt's only dedicated jazz venue, an intimate cellar bar where the band almost plays in the audience – expect modern trios and quartets, often touring acts. Fri & Sat 8pm–late.

Presseklub Dalbergsweg 1 ☎0361 789 45 65, ⓦpresseklub.net. Favoured by a young crowd, this bar-club hosts regular midweek salsa and Sun sessions of jazzy funk sounds alongside unpretentious nights of karaoke or house and party classics. It's located bang on Karl-Marx-Platz whatever the address suggests. Opening times vary by clubnight. Tues–Sun 8 or 9.30pm–3am.

Stadtgarten Dalbergsweg 2 ☎0361 653 199 88, ⓦstadtgarten-erfurt.de. Grungy (sub)cultural centre just south of the Altstadt that hosts rock gigs – from death metal to soul, many by touring international artists – and alternative clubnights, usually with a couple of events in midweek, as well as screening major Bundesliga games on a big-screen TV. Opening days and times vary – check the website.

ERFURT FESTIVALS

Highlight of Erfurt's festival calendar is the **Krämerbrückenfest** towards the end of June, when food and beer stalls and performers in medieval costume engulf Erfurt's favourite bridge. The cathedral steps double as a stage for music and theatre during the **Domstufen-Festspiele** in July and August.

THEATRE, DANCE AND CLASSICAL MUSIC
Alte Oper Erfurt Theaterstr. 1 ☎0361 55 11 66, ⓦalteopererfurt.de. Musicals, *Travestie* shows, puppet theatre, cabaret and comedy plus the occasional hypnosis act or old-time rock all staged at weekends only, in a traditional theatre that feels far more intimate than its 970-capacity might suggest.
Kaisersaal Futterstr. 15–16 ☎0361 568 80, ⓦkaisersaal.de. A small cultural centre in the heart of the Altstadt which carries into the auditorium the Baroque elegance of its buildings – there are galleries, chandeliers and occasionally cabaret-style tables on the main floor. It generally programmes classical concerts and recitals.
Theater Erfurt Theaterplatz ☎0361 223 31 55, ⓦwww.theater-erfurt.de. Modern multi-stage venue with an eclectic taste in opera, operettas and occasional classical music concerts; expect classics like *Die Fledermaus* or *The Magic Flute* as well as evenings of *chanson*. As the leading dance and theatre stage, it also programmes ballet.

Weimar

Though modest in size, **WEIMAR** is the spiritual capital of German culture. A young Robert Schumann noted in his diary, "Germans are powerfully drawn to Weimar", and like those to Stratford in England they are not idle tourists so much as aesthete pilgrims come to revere a pantheon of intellectual and artistic saints. Saxe-Weimar dukes were patrons of Lucas Cranach and Johann Sebastian Bach as an overture to the town's finest hour in the late eighteenth century. During the rule of aesthete duke Carl August (1757–1828), the court capital was an intellectual hothouse of rare talents such as dramatist Friedrich Schiller, poet Christoph-Martin Wieland, theologian Johann Gottfried Herder and, more than anyone else, Johann Wolfgang von Goethe. The city flowered as the home of the German Enlightenment whose beauty and ideas astounded Europe. Later names in the roll call of honour include Franz Liszt, Richard Strauss, Friedrich Nietzsche and Bauhaus founders Walter Gropius, Paul Klee and Wassily Kandinsky. The town's name is also synonymous with the ill-fated Weimar Republic of post-imperial Germany.

Weimar is the charming museum city par excellence whose every street is steeped in a revered past. Definitively small-scale, notwithstanding the odd gallery and the handsome **Park an der Ilm** to the south, almost everything worth seeing lies within a ten-minute radius of the **Markt** in the lattice of streets bound to the north by **Graben**, the medieval moat, and to the south by **Steubenstrasse**.

The Markt

Site of a weekday market, the tourist office and two deservedly popular *Bratwurst* stands, the **Markt** is as good an introduction to Weimar as any, ringed by a pleasing jumble of buildings. If the monuments of the ducal town's Baroque flowering lie elsewhere, this is the wellspring of its early roots, as evidenced by a pair of handsome Renaissance mansions on the east side – the **Stadthaus**, a trade-turned-festivities centre picked out in green tracery, and adjacent **Cranachhaus** where Lucas Cranach the Elder worked as court painter for his final year in 1552; he followed erstwhile Elector Johann Friedrich of Saxony to Weimar having stuck with him through five years of captivity by his vanquisher, Emperor Karl V, and the Cranach winged-snake coat of arms is above one window arch.

The "anteroom for Weimar's living Valhalla", Austrian poet Franz Grillparzer decided, was hotel **Elephant** (see p.248) on the south side of the Markt. Acclaimed even in Goethe's day, author Thomas Mann set his novel *Lotte in Weimar*, which imagines Goethe's painfully polite reunion with an old flame, in the hotel. Johann Sebastian **Bach** composed cantatas in an adjacent house while court organist then concert master from 1708. In 1718 the son of the orchestra leader stepped into his father's shoes and the ambitious Bach, furious at being passed over, stomped off to Köthen, although not before the duke imprisoned him for four weeks to prevent his departure.

4

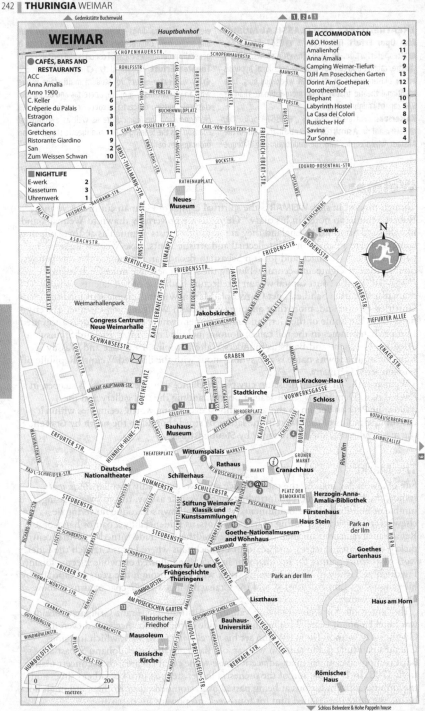

WEIMAR

Gedenkstätte Buchenwald

Hauptbahnhof

ACCOMMODATION

A&O Hostel	2
Amalienhof	11
Anna Amalia	7
Camping Weimar-Tiefurt	9
DJH Am Poseckschen Garten	13
Dorint Am Goethepark	12
Dorotheenhof	1
Elephant	10
Labyrinth Hostel	5
La Casa dei Colori	8
Russischer Hof	6
Savina	3
Zur Sonne	4

CAFÉS, BARS AND RESTAURANTS

ACC	4
Anna Amalia	7
Anno 1900	1
C. Keller	6
Crêperie du Palais	5
Estragon	3
Giancarlo	8
Gretchens	11
Ristorante Giardino	9
San	2
Zum Weissen Schwan	10

NIGHTLIFE

E-werk	2
Kasseturm	3
Uhrenwerk	1

Neues Museum

E-werk

Weimarhallenpark

Congress Centrum Neue Weimarhalle

Jakobskirche

Kirms-Krackow-Haus

Stadtkirche

Schloss

Bauhaus-Museum

Wittumspalais

Rathaus

Cranachhaus

Deutsches Nationaltheater

Schillerhaus

Herzogin-Anna-Amalia-Bibliothek

Stiftung Weimarer Klassik und Kunstsammlungen

Fürstenhaus

Haus Stein

Goethe-Nationalmuseum and Wohnhaus

Park an der Ilm

Goethes Gartenhaus

Museum für Ur- und Frühgeschichte Thüringens

Park an der Ilm

Liszthaus

Haus am Horn

Historischer Friedhof

Bauhaus-Universität

Mausoleum

Russische Kirche

Römisches Haus

0   200
metres

Schloss Belvedere & Hohe Pappeln house

Platz der Demokratie

Off the Markt's southeast corner, aristocratic **Platz der Demokratie** is boxed in by Baroque palaces, finest being the Fürstenhaus (prince's house), a butterscotch ducal mansion that holds the **Hochschule für Musik Franz Liszt** (Franz Liszt Music School). Its origins were as an early residence for then-prince Carl August, whose equestrian statue stands at the square's centre; that it is modelled on the memorial to Emperor Marcus Aurelius in Rome's Capitol speaks volumes about the swagger of the miniature state in the late 1700s.

Herzogin-Anna-Amalia-Bibliothek

Platz der Demokratie 1 • Tues–Sun 9.30am–2.30pm • €6.50 including English audio-guide • ⓦ klassik-stiftung.de

The misnamed Grünes Schloss encloses the east side of the elongated Platz der Demokratie. Here Goethe managed the library of Duchess Anna Amalia, the **Herzogin-Anna-Amalia-Bibliothek**, the wife of Carl August whose aesthetic leanings helped to pilot Weimar's ascent into the intellectual stratosphere. Restored after a severe fire in 2004 that destroyed fifty thousand tomes, the Rococo library is once more an exquisitely sensuous *Gesamtkunstwerk* (complete work of art) where busts of scholars stand on a gilt-trimmed gallery that houses one of the world's finest collection of German Enlightenment manuscripts. Entrance is limited to 250 people per day, so it's worth buying tickets early.

Haus Stein

Goethe pilgrims should head around the corner from the Grünes Schloss to **Haus Stein**, the former ducal stables, and home to Goethe's first great love, Charlotte Stein. That she was already married to the head stableman did not prevent him from sending 1700 adoring letters.

The Schloss

Burgplatz 4 • Tues–Sun: April–Oct 9.30am–6pm; Nov–March 9.30am–4pm • €7.50 • ⓦ klassik-stiftung.de

The ducal **Schloss** lies discreetly away from the east edge of the Altstadt at the head of Park an der Ilm. An absurdly ostentatious pile for what was a town of only six thousand people, the U-shaped palace was erected after a 1774 fire all but erased its predecessor – only the Renaissance gateway of the original remains, facing the Altstadt. Goethe proffered advice for the new plans and is honoured for his trouble in a corridor of sumptuous first-floor chambers that also salute Weimar's contemporary cultural heroes, Friedrich Schiller, poet Christoph-Martin Wieland and poet-pastor Johann Gottfried Herder. The Festsaal in the other wing is a paean to sober Neoclassicism.

Galleries

Impressive though the architecture is, the main reason to visit is the gallery of old masters. It kicks off on the ground floor with the heavy hitters of the German Renaissance, notably works by **Lucas Cranach the Elder** (1472–1553). Among the highlights are wedding portraits of sylph-eyed beauty Princess Sybille von Cleve and Johann Friedrich and two images of his friend Martin Luther – bearded when in hiding as Junker Jörg (Squire George) in the Wartburg, Eisenach, and clean-shaven twenty years later (see box, p.263). A couple of works by his contemporary Dürer introduce a cabinet of Renaissance curios next door, whose fripperies are an evocative testament to ducal decadence. Westphalian master Konrad von Soest stands out among the medieval artwork and Russian icons in the other wing, while works hung in the period rooms above fast-forward through the Enlightenment into Impressionism: star for the French is Monet's *Rouen Cathedral* caught in early morning, while for the Germans it's Max Beckmann and Pre-Raphaelite-inspired Christian Rohlfs.

Herderplatz

The heart of the medieval town was **Herderplatz**, west of the Schloss. Its name and that of the much-remodelled **Stadtkirche** dedicated to St Peter and Paul, usually known simply as the Herderkirche (Mon–Fri 10am–6pm, Sat 10am–noon & 2–4pm, Sun 11am–4pm; free), are a homage to town pastor Johann Gottfried Herder (1776–1803), a poet-theologian remembered with much affection. Complementing the artworks in the Schloss is the church's **Crucifixion triptych**, Cranach's swan song, completed by his son Lucas Cranach the Younger in 1555. A spurt of holy blood rains divine mercy onto the head of the snowy-bearded artist who stands beside Luther pointing to his doctrine. On the left wing are Johann Friedrich and his wife Sybille, now thirty years older than the young suitors Cranach pictured earlier. They died shortly afterwards – their flamboyant double-height tomb in the choir upstages the painter's tomb, shifted from the churchyard to the left of his creation, and which depicts the artist as a portly gent holding, presumably, an easel.

Kirms-Krackow-Haus

Jakobstr. 10 • April–Oct Fri 1.30–5pm, Sat & Sun 10am–5pm • €1.50 • Ⓦ thueringerschloesser.de

Just up from the church on Jakobstrasse is **Kirms-Krackow-Haus**. One of the oldest townhouses in Weimar, the galleried Renaissance courtyard residence preserves intact a bourgeois residence of eighteenth-century Weimar. Notwithstanding the richly patterned wallpaper, its joy is as an ensemble piece that retains the personal effects of its owners.

Neues Museum

Neues Museum Weimarplatz 5 • Daily except Tues: April–Oct 10am–6pm; Nov–March 10am–4pm • €4 • Ⓦ klassik-stiftung.de •
E-werk Am Kirschberg 7 • April–Oct Sat & Sun 10am–6pm • Free • Ⓦ ewerkweimar.info

When Weimar's erudite aspic cloys, head to the **Neues Museum** on Weimarplatz ten minutes' walk north of Herderplatz. The melted bronze figure outside is a taster of its refreshingly irreverent international art from the last four centuries, collated by a Cologne gallery owner, Paul Maenz, who clearly had a soft spot for minimal and conceptual work. Its building is no mean piece of architecture itself. Erected in 1869 as a ducal museum, it was rethought by the Nazis as the Halle der Volksgemeinschaft (People's Community Hall); in a characteristic piece of posturing, they obliterated surrounding streets, so it would stand at the head of a monumental space named Adolf-Hitler-Platz.

An adjunct to the museum is Rebecca Horn's *Konzert für Buchenwald* installation in tram-depot-turned-cultural-centre **E-werk**, east of the museum. Created as a memorial to victims of the Nazi concentration camp north of the city for Weimar's year as European Capital of Culture in 1999, it consists of a 40m-long wall of ashes behind glass.

Schillerhaus

Schillerstr. 12 • Daily except Tues: April–Oct 9.30am–6pm; Nov–March 9.30am–4pm • €5 • Ⓦ klassik-stiftung.de

Schillerstrasse arcs off Frauenplan southwest of the Markt as a leafy esplanade named for Friedrich Schiller (1759–1805). One of the founding fathers of Weimar Classicism, the itinerant poet and dramatist spent the last three years of his life at **Schillerhaus** and penned *The Bride from Messina* and *William Tell* in its attic study. That the eighteenth-century playwright had to find 4200 taler for his house helps explain its humble looks compared to Goethe's residence (see opposite). A modern museum, tacked behind, guides visitors around his life and works – it's expected to reopen after renovations in 2015.

Theaterplatz

Weimar's awesome twosome, Goethe and Schiller, share a plinth on **Theaterplatz**. One of the great cultural icons of Germany (and Weimar's landmark), the bronze of the pair with the laurel wreath of destiny is known to every schoolchild, and copies stand in Cleveland, San Francisco and, bizarrely, Shanghai. The square is named after the rebuilt court theatre in which the 1919 National Assembly ratified the ill-fated Weimar Republic that fumbled with democracy and raging inflation until Hitler wrested power with low politicking in 1933.

The Wittumspalais

Am Palais 3 • Tues–Sun: April–Oct 10am–6pm; Nov–March 10am–4pm • €6 • Ⓦ klassik-stiftung.de

Opposite the theatre is the **Wittumspalais** where widowed Duchess Anna Amalia hosted intellectual gatherings in classical Weimar. At a symbolic round table, the arts patron surrounded herself with noble and bourgeois aesthetes – indeed, Weimar's intellectual flowering was largely due to this unique dialogue between nobility and the middle classes. The Neoclassical interiors are Weimar's most graceful.

The Bauhaus-Museum

Theaterplatz 1 • Daily except Tues: April–Oct 10am–6pm; Nov–March 10am–4pm • €4 • Ⓦ klassik-stiftung.de

Weimar followed up the German Enlightenment by pioneering **Jugendstil** – Germany's Art Nouveau – and its successor **Bauhaus** a century later. Jugendstil was nurtured in the city by Belgian architect and painter Henry van de Velde after he was encouraged to set up an Arts and Crafts school here in 1902. The **Bauhaus-Museum** on Theaterplatz has a room of his work as context for its displays of furnishings from the Bauhaus design school, founded in Weimar in 1919 by Walter Gropius. A brand-new Bauhaus museum is under construction next to the Neues Museum (see opposite), due to open in 2019 to coincide with the anniversary of the design school's foundation.

Goethe-Nationalmuseum and Wohnhaus

Frauenplan 1 • Tues–Sun: April–Oct 9am–6pm; Nov–March 9am–4pm • €12 • Ⓦ klassik-stiftung.de

If Weimar is the temple of German culture, **Goethes Wohnhaus** is its holy of holies. Within the townhouse on Frauenplan, southwest of the Markt, the nation's cultural colossus created masterpieces for fifty years until his death in 1832, including his crowning achievement, *Faust*. He was given the house by Duke Carl August in 1792, and wrote to his benefactor in 1806 that he hoped he had "proven worthy of your gift, not having used it for a frivolous existence but to disseminate the knowledge of art and science". The garden was a botanical experiment for "pleasant and educational entertainment". Yet the house is as homely as it is erudite, best seen as an insight into the polymath's mind. The paintings, Italian busts and objets d'art Goethe picked up as holiday souvenirs are *in situ* in rooms whose colours he chose for their mood-altering "sensual-moral effects" – an upshot of his colour studies (see box, p.246). The staircase is modelled on those of Renaissance villas he had admired on Italian travels, and in the Juno room where his guests retired after dinner is the piano on which Mendelssohn showcased works in progress. Look, too, in the study where he dictated his works – Goethe only lifted a pen for poetry – for a bust of Napoleon that was placed there after the pair met in Erfurt to mutual declarations of admiration.

The house is entered via the adjacent **Goethe-Nationalmuseum**, recently overhauled and modernized, which presents an intriguing collection of texts, pictures and objects (colour wheels, botanical specimens, erotic art, his travel writing set) that place our hero's achievements into context. The treasure room at the end holds original copies of *Faust*.

JOHANN WOLFGANG VON GOETHE

No figure commands German culture like **Johann Wolfgang von Goethe** (1748–1832). A lazy comparison is often made to Shakespeare, which underplays the achievements of the last great Renaissance man of European culture. Not content with producing some of the most insightful drama in the German language, Goethe penned poetry, novels, travelogues and short stories, as well as philosophical essays and treatises on theology, humanism and science. His influence on German philosophy is incalculable. Indeed, he didn't see himself as a writer, and proposed near his death that he would be remembered for his *Theory of Colours* treatise. "As to what I have done as a poet … I take no pride in it," he said, "but that in my century I am the only person who knows the truth in the difficult science of colours – of that I am not a little proud." As it turned out his pride was misguided: his hypothesis suggested that darkness is not an absence of light but a polar opposite that interacts with it, with colour arising where the two flow together. Modern science has rebuffed his theory, but the idea was popular with artists such as Turner and Kandinsky.

The Frankfurt-born son of a wealthy family, Goethe trained as a lawyer but found fame in 1774 as the 26-year-old novelist of **The Sorrows of Young Werther**. Its semi-autobiographical tale of obsessive love not only became the best seller of the proto-Romantic Sturm und Drang movement, it so wowed 18-year-old Carl August that the Grand Duke of Saxe-Weimar-Eisenach took on Goethe as a court adviser in 1775. Goethe would remain there until his death, though paradoxically he was so wrapped up in official duties and science that literature went onto the back burner for that first decade. It was an Italian holiday from 1786 that rekindled his creative spark (and also sent countless young Germans mooning around Italy, having read his *Italian Journey*). On his return two years later he teamed up with Schiller to continue his major prose achievement, **Wilhelm Meister**, a six-novel cycle. He also began the work on the two-part lyric drama, **Faust**, which he would tinker with until his death. Ostensibly a narrative of the classic legend, his dramatic masterpiece strives to lay bare the soul of Western society.

Museum für Ur- und Frühgeschichte Thüringens

Humboldtstr. 11 · Tues 9am–6pm, Wed–Fri 9am–5pm, Sat & Sun 10am–5pm · €3.50

South of Frauenplan on Humboldtstrasse the **Museum für Ur- und Frühgeschichte Thüringens** (Museum of Pre- and Early Thuringian History) has excellent though overlooked displays of regional archeology from the dawn of man to the Romans and early medieval Frankish tribes.

Historischer Friedhof

Am Poseckschen Garten · Cemetery daily except Tues: April–Oct 10am–6pm; Nov–March 10am–4pm · Ducal mausoleum €4, church free

In the **Historischer Friedhof** cemetery one block behind the Museum für Ur- und Frühgeschichte Thüringens, the Fürstengruft was created as the ducal **mausoleum** for the House of Saxony-Weimar but also serves as the resting place for Goethe and Schiller after Carl August announced that he wanted to lie in state alongside the two brightest stars in Weimar's cultural firmament. Beside its severe Neoclassicism an **Orthodox Russian church** behind appears unexpectedly exotic. It was built in the 1860s for a daughter of the Tsar, Grand Duchess Maria Pavlovna.

Liszthaus

Marienstr. 17 · Daily except Tues: April–Oct 10am–6pm; Nov–March 10am–4pm · €4 · ⊛ klassik-stiftung.de

South of Frauenplan stands **Liszthaus**, the cottage of the court gardener where the composer spent summers surrounded by adoring students from 1869–86, inadvertently laying the ground for the music college that bears his name. An audio-guide with texts and music takes you around the upper four rooms that are still kept in the modest style Liszt favoured. Almost opposite Liszthaus on Geschwister-Scholl-Strasse is the Henry van der Velde-designed wing of the Bauhaus-Universität, wellspring of Walter Gropius's stylistic movement and still a university.

Park an der Ilm and Goethes Gartenhaus

Goethes Gartenhaus Daily except Tues: April–Oct 10am–6pm; Nov–March 10am–4pm • €6 • Ⓦ klassik-stiftung.de • **Romisches Haus** • April–Oct daily except Tues 10am–6pm • €4 • Ⓦ klassik-stiftung.de

The prize of southern Weimar is the **Park an der Ilm**. So expansive is the greenery that extends away from the Altstadt that Romantic author Adolf Stahr quipped, "Weimar is a park with a town inside." Goethe had a hand in its landscaping in English style, conceived as "a series of aesthetic pictures" in the manner of a Romantic landscape. In a canny bid to keep the writer in Weimar, Duke Carl August rewarded his garden plans in 1776 with the riverside **Goethes Gartenhaus**, his residence for six years before he moved to Frauenplan, and thereafter his favourite escape. Presumably it was more enchanting before most of the furnishings were stripped to preserve them from the happy hordes who visit.

Within view of the Goethes Gartenhaus – glinting white among the leaves south – is **Römisches Haus**, a mock-Roman temple where Duke Carl August lived out summers. His muralled study and bedrooms have been restored to their full lustre to serve as a backdrop for a so-so exhibit on the park.

Hohe Pappeln and Haus am Horn

Jugendstil pioneer **Henry van de Velde** declared his stylistic manifesto on Weimar's streets: his **Hohe Pappeln** house in the southern suburb of Ehringsdorf, where he lived with his family, was a key meeting point for the "New Weimar" school. The house, at Belvederer Allee 58, still contains a small display of his furnishings (April–Oct Tues–Sun 1–5pm; €3; bus #1 or #12 to Papiergraben). Van de Velde also designed houses at Cranachstr. 15 and 47.

The first Bauhaus edifice ever constructed – and the only one erected in its birthplace – is UNESCO-listed **Haus am Horn**, a severe, minimalist box created as a show home in 1923 by the movement's youngest designer, Georg Muche. A university exhibition space, it lies just east of Park an der Ilm at Am Horn 61.

Schloss Belvedere

April–Oct Tues–Sun 10am–6pm • €6 • Ⓦ klassik-stiftung.de • Bus #12

Lack of space in the town centre limited the ambitions of Weimar's early eighteenth-century duke, Ernst August. In **Schloss Belvedere** at the far edge of Weimar he found room for an airy summer palace suitable for a ruler who nurtured self-delusions about being a Thuringian "Sun King", even if its playful Baroque and canary-yellow paint job seem a touch jolly for an absolutist. Duke Carl August used it as a summertime pleasure house and hunting lodge, and much of his porcelain, glassware and furniture is displayed inside. Goethe supervised the garden's change from strict symmetrical landscape into today's naturalistic park for botany studies.

Gedenkstätte Buchenwald

Tues–Sun: April–Oct 10am–6pm; Nov–March 10am–4pm • Free • Ⓦ buchenwald.de • Bus #6 from Goetheplatz or the Hauptbahnhof to "Buchenwald"

In the wooded heights 10km northwest of central Weimar is the **Gedenkstätte Buchenwald**. Over the eight years from its opening in 1937 to hold "undesirables" and opponents of the Nazi regime, to its liberation through a prisoner uprising in April 1945 after the SS guards fled as the Allies approached, more than 250,000 people were held captive in the concentration camp. Over 55,000 died, most of the daily two hundred death toll due to disease or exhaustion from forced labour in the armaments factories, although some were killed through the torture and medical experiments of the SS. Wrought into the gate and visible from the muster ground, the inscription "*Jedem das Seine*" (roughly "to each his own") betrays the Nazi mentality that inmates were to blame for their incarceration.

A large quota of leading Communist and Social Democrat political inmates were executed here, making the camp a propaganda tool for the GDR authorities. It was only after the *Wende* in 1990 that mass graves were discovered with the remains of around seven thousand pro-fascist sympathizers and GDR opponents – they had been worked to death here when the former Nazi concentration camp became the communists' **Special Camp No. 2**.

While most of the buildings were razed to create a memorial to antifascist resistance in 1951, the large depot in which inmates' effects were sorted holds an **exhibition centre** that screens a thirty-minute documentary film (English subtitles) several times a day. The prisoners' canteen, detention cells in the gatehouse, crematorium and pathology department can also be visited.

ARRIVAL AND INFORMATION | WEIMAR

By train The Hauptbahnhof is a 15min walk north of the centre; several buses run to Goetheplatz at the western edge of the Altstadt.

Destinations Erfurt (every 30min; 15min); Jena (every 30min; 15–25min).

Tourist office Markt 10 (April–Oct Mon–Sat 9.30am–7pm, Sun 9.30am–3pm; Nov–March Mon–Fri 9.30am–6pm, Sat & Sun 9.30am–2pm; ☎03643 74 50, ⓦweimar.de). English-language audio-guide city tours are available (€7).

Within the tourist office are separate desks for the Buchenwald concentration camp memorial site and an information point of Weimar cultural administrator Klassic Stiftung Weimar (ⓦklassik-stiftung.de), which sells museum tickets and books and provides the usual flyers; the latter's website is the portal for all sights in Weimar.

Discount card The Weimar Card (48hr €27.50) provides twenty percent discounts on the major museums and free entry to lesser attractions, plus free public transport.

ACCOMMODATION

HOTELS AND PENSIONS

Amalienhof Amalienstr. 2 ☎03643 54 90, ⓦamalienhof-weimar.de. This small, church-affiliated hotel offers spacious, comfortable rooms with Neoclassical-style furnishings. The big breakfast buffet lasts till mid-morning – just one of the thoughtful touches that make this a comfy stay. **€80**

Anna Amalia Geleitstr. 8–12 ☎03643 495 60, ⓦhotel-anna-amalia.de. Popular, family-owned, mid-range place that is located right in the heart of the Altstadt. Modern accommodation in the form of pleasant pastel-shaded rooms is spread across three buildings in the town centre, one of which contains apartments. **€82**

Dorint Am Goethepark Beethovenplatz 1–2 ☎03643 87 20, ⓦhotel-weimar.dorint.com; bus #7 from the Hauptbahnhof. Four-star accommodation in a modern hotel that's more relaxed in style than some in this upmarket business chain. "Executive" rooms overlook the park, while furnishings in larger "Deluxe" level nod to Weimar's Art Nouveau and Bauhaus heritage. Also has good spa facilities. **€124**

Dorotheenhof Dorotheenhof 1, Schöndorf ☎03643 45 90, ⓦdorotheenhof.com. For country charm within easy striking distance of the sights, escape to this charming hotel 4km north of central Weimar, sympathetically created from the manor estate of a cavalry captain and set in its own grounds, with a new spa and gourmet restaurant. **€105**

Elephant Markt 19 ☎03643 80 20, ⓦhotelelephantweimar.com. Superbly sited and timelessly elegant in its Art Deco styling, Weimar's prestige address has been a rendezvous for every artist, poet, intellectual and statesman since the sixteenth century. Immaculate classic-modern rooms overlook the Markt or a garden. **€135**

La Casa dei Colori Eisfeld 1 ☎03643 48 96 40, ⓦcasa-colori.de. Modern Italianate decor in a pretty pension in the Altstadt – think floral fabrics, colourful walls and wood floors in rooms, all with large windows, plus terracotta-tiled bathrooms. **€90**

Russischer Hof Goetheplatz 2 ☎03643 77 40, ⓦrussischerhof.com. Part of the Best Western chain, the *Russischer Hof* retains some of the ambience of the grand hotel that hosted Liszt and Schumann in its public areas. Notwithstanding expensive "Historic" rooms, "Standard" rooms are fairly average. **€119**

Savina Meyerstr. 60 ☎03643 866 90, ⓦpension-savina .de. Largest of the town's pensions and fairly forgettable in its decor. Nevertheless its rooms are all en suite and comfortable and the price is one of the best in town outside the hostels. €60

Zur Sonne Rollplatz 2 ☎03643 862 90, ⓦ hotelzursonne-weimar.de. A proper little hotel in feel despite its location above a restaurant; its relative simplicity and old-fashioned formality is all part of the appeal. The price is certainly appealing – good value for its location on a central square. €67

HOSTELS AND CAMPSITES

A&O Hostel Buttelstedter Str. 27c ☎030 809 47 51 10, ⓦ aohostels.com. When the central hostels are full, walk five minutes north of the Hauptbahnhof for this large new hostel, with its spacious, clean accommodation. Dorms €16, doubles €51

Camping Weimar-Tiefurt Hauptstr 2, Weimar-Tiefurt ☎03643 85 01 21, ⓦ camping-weimar-tiefurt.de. The closest campsite to Weimar is this leafy place 4km from the centre, in the grounds of a former ducal palace beside the river, and with fresh eggs for sale (site chickens willing). The Ilmtal-Radweg riverside cycle path passes behind the site; without a bike, follow Tierfurter Allee behind the Schloss then continue ahead over the river on Robert-Blum-Str. Pitch €3, plus €6.50 per person

DJH Am Poseckschen Garten Humboldtstr. 17 ☎03643 85 07 92, ⓦ djh-thueringen.de. Near the Historiches Friedhof, this is the most central of Weimar's four official youth hostels and is popular with school groups; book early. Dorms €27, doubles €54

★ **Labyrinth Hostel** Goetheplatz 6 ☎03643 81 18 22, ⓦ weimar-hostel.com. Excellent friendly hostel in the centre whose rooms, individually styled by regional artists, have an appealingly quirky eye for decor and a touch of thrift-shop chic. Good dorms, roof terrace and a small kitchen. Dorms €13, doubles €40

EATING AND DRINKING

★ **ACC** Burgplatz 1 ☎03643 85 11 61, ⓦ acc-cafe.de. From walls featuring absurd panorama photos to an incorporated gallery, there's a cool arty vibe to this bar and café, not to mention tasty modern-European cooking and cheap daily specials on the menu. Mon–Fri noon–6pm, Sat & Sun noon–8pm.

Anna Amalia At *Hotel Elephant*, Markt 19 ☎03643 80 20, ⓦ restaurant-anna-amalia.com. Regularly hailed the gourmet address of the state thanks to Italian master chef Marcello Fabbri. Expect fine modern-European dishes served in an atmosphere of understated luxury or in a lovely garden in summer. Tues–Sat 6.30–11.30pm.

Anno 1900 Geleitstr. 12a ☎03643 90 35 71, ⓦ anno1900-weimar.de. Quietly elegant Art Nouveau-styled brasserie in a conservatory that is soundtracked by live piano jazz once a week. Modern European dishes such as salmon in thyme and lemon sauce lean towards Italian and the terrace is a lovely spot for breakfasts (until noon). Mon–Fri 11am–midnight, Sat & Sun 9am–midnight.

C. Keller & Galerie Markt 21 ☎03643 50 27 55, ⓦ c-keller.de. Two nicely scruffy student bars above and behind affiliated *Roxanne* café on the Markt: the former is an artfully shabby café-gallery with occasional art exhibitions; the latter is a grungy cellar bar steeped in decades of boozing. C. Keller daily 9pm–late; Galerie daily noon–1am.

Crêperie du Palais Am Palais 1 ☎03643 40 15 81, ⓦ creperie-weimar.de. An institution of Weimar eating for decades, this sweet simple café in a cobbled backstreet is run by a French and German couple, which means authentic *galettes*, crêpes (sweet from €4, hearty from €6), couscous, *Flammkuchen*, French cheeses and sausages, all washed down with a wide choice of Breton ciders and French wine. Mon–Fri 11am–11pm, Sat & Sun 10am–11pm.

Estragon Herderplatz 3 ☎03643 90 85 99, ⓦ estragon-suppenbar.de. The soup bar of organic supermarket Rosmarin is a great spot for a cheap central pit-stop: recipes change daily but expect fine home-made options (from €3) that change with the seasons, such as chorizo and *Knockwurst* or salmon and lemon. Mon–Fri 10am–7pm, Sat 10am–4pm.

Giancarlo Schillerstr. 11 ☎03643 80 47 90, ⓦ giancarlo-weimar.de. Old-fashioned Italian ice cream parlour on one of Weimar's nicest boulevards whose *raison d'être* is its home-made *gelati*: there are dozens of flavours to sample, from subtle melon or mango to rich house-special bitter chocolate. That said, the €1.20 coffee-and-croissant breakfast (9–11am) is a bargain. Daily 8am–midnight.

Gretchens Seifengasse 8 ☎03643 457 98 77, ⓦ gretchens-weimar.de. The rooftop terrace of this family-run restaurant and pension is a fabulous place for a summer lunch (set menu €7.50, including salad buffet) or dinner. Mediterranean-inspired dishes include Moroccan lentil stew and duck with saffron risotto (€17). Daily noon–1am.

Ristorante Giardino Seifengasse ☎0151 5066 5437, ⓦ giardino-weimar.de. This Italian restaurant in the romantic Oppelscher Garten has seating on the grass and under gazebos and a decent menu of pasta, pizza, meat and fish dishes priced around €10–15. April–Sept daily 9am–11pm.

San Eisfeld 4 ☎03643 25 89 42, ⓦ sanrestaurant.de. Serving small but authentic portions of Korean classics such as veg or meat *bibimbap* (fried rice, from €7), this restaurant doubles as a shop for lovely Korean ceramics. Cosy, with a

4

fireplace in winter. Tues–Sat noon–4&5-10pm–10pm.
Zum Weissen Schwan Frauentorstr. 23 ☎03643 90 87 51, ⓦhotelelephantweimar.com. Quality regional fare such as *Sauerbraten* (marinated beef) with *Klösse*

dumplings, plus Goethe's favourite dish – boiled beef in green herb sauce – in the poet's local inn. Touristy and inevitably modernized, but without sacrificing character. Tues–Sat noon–10pm.

NIGHTLIFE AND ENTERTAINMENT

CLUBS AND LIVE MUSIC

E-werk Am Kirschberg 4 ☎03643 74 88 68, ⓦewerkweimar.info. Grungy alternative cultural centre north of the centre that hosts very occasional live gigs alongside cutting-edge art exhibitions and regular rep cinema in venues created from a former tram depot. Regular cinema aside, dates are irregular, so check the website.

Kasseturm Goetheplatz 1 ⓦkasseturm.de. Weimar's last good student bar, in a former defence tower, programming a varied repertoire of student rock groups, jazz and crowd-friendly clubnights – think oldies, indie classics, charts plus the odd electro night – plus the occasional film night. Times vary by night, generally Thurs–Sat 8 or 9pm till late.

Uhrenwerk Am Alten Speicher 11 ⓦuhren-werk.de. A short walk north of the train station, a modern space inside a former watch factory hosts DJs and themed party nights at weekends. Fri & Sat from 10pm.

THEATRE AND CONCERTS

Congress Centrum Neue Weimarhalle Unesco-Platz 1 ☎03643 74 51 00, ⓦweimarhalle.de. Symphony concerts, rock gigs, even post-work parties – this two-space venue, one large, one small, programmes a mixed bag of largely mainstream musical entertainment within a streamlined modern venue in a gleaming glass box. Its large lakefront area is sometimes used for summer concerts.

Deutsches Nationaltheater Theaterplatz 2 ☎03643 75 53 34, ⓦnationaltheater-weimar.de. Such is its fame in the formation of the Weimar Republic, most visitors forget that this elegant Neoclassical theatre is also the town's mainstay of dramatic high culture, with classics of the operatic and theatrical canons, plus some contemporary works.

Jena

JENA, the next stop east from Weimar, is another university town that hothoused Classicism under Goethe and Schiller; thereafter, the similarities end. If Weimar is all about arts and culture, Jena is a centre of **science** nurtured over a long history of university research – the town has 23,000 students and one in four of the population is connected with the university. Jena is also less precious about its looks than Weimar – the Altstadt was pounded by the Allies, then GDR urban-planners embarked on some architectural vandalism of their own. Restoration has returned pockets of charm, and the setting in a bowl of wooded hills appeals, but neither is the point. Anyone of a scientific mindset will enjoy its museums while the **nightlife** is only bettered in Thuringia by Erfurt. All Jena's sights are within easy walking distance from the centre. To attempt the lot in a day, however, you're best off renting bikes.

The highlight of city **festivals** is open-air music beano Kulturarena (ⓦkulturarena.de), which attracts home-grown and international rock, folk, jazz and world acts from mid-July to late August.

The JenTower

Leutragraben 1 • Viewing platform daily 11am–11pm • €3 • ⓦjentower.de

The best navigation mark in Jena is the **JenTower** (previously known as the Intershop Tower), the tall silver tube marking the city centre. The GDR regime ignored protests in 1972 to construct this bold skyscraper for a bold communist future – never mind that that meant bulldozing one of the city's medieval squares, **Eichplatz**. The 120m tower proved spectacularly unsuitable for its intended use as a research institute, so was given to the university, then in the 1990s given its current mirrored sheen as a corporate headquarters. Far from lovable, it has become a city icon nevertheless, helped by its restaurant (see p.253) and viewing platform.

The Anatomieturm and Collegium Jenense

What did survive GDR redevelopment is a section of medieval city defences to the north of the JenTower and, to its south, octagonal defence bastion the **Anatomieturm**, so-called because anatomy lectures were held there – Goethe discovered the human central jawbone here. Goethe's five years in Jena were spent at the adjacent **Collegium Jenense**, the original university building housed in a Dominican abbey since 1548 – it was slated for demolition until the GDR succumbed to protests. Unpromising from outside, the building's cobbled courtyard off Kollegienstrasse features a swaggering portal bearing the coat of arms of founder patron Prince Johann Friedrich "the Magnanimous". The foyer is usually open to peruse displays of university memorabilia, such as Renaissance beer tankards and a desiccated human foot and arm studied by anatomy classes.

The Markt and around

East of Eichplatz, the picturesque **Markt** retains some of the atmosphere of medieval Jena. The twin-peaked **Rathaus** at its corner straddles both squares, mounted on the Markt side with a Baroque tower that houses an astronomical clock. On the hour, devil-figure *Schnapphans* ("Snatching Hans") attempts to grab a golden sphere dangled by a pilgrim – it was acclaimed one of the "seven wonders of Jena" in years past, but don't get too excited. A portly statue of the magnanimous Johann Friedrich I stands in all his regal pomp at the centre of the square.

The Stadtmuseum Göhre

Markt 7 • Tues, Wed & Fri 10am–5pm, Thurs 3–10pm, Sat & Sun 11am–6pm • €4 • ⓦ stadtmuseum.jena.de

At the back of the square rises one of the few historic houses in Jena, a Late Gothic construction with windows like theatre curtains beneath a half-timbered upper. It spins through town history as the **Stadtmuseum Göhre**, pinpointing the "seven wonders of Jena", and hosts art exhibitions. There's also a café at the top (same times; free access).

Stadtkirche St Michael

Kirchplatz • Mon noon–4pm, Tues–Sun 11am–4pm • Free

The defining edifice one block north of the Markt is the town church, **Stadtkirche St Michael**. The lofty interior and streamlined pillars within give no hint that the entire chancel rests on a Gothic passageway – the most acclaimed of Jena's wonders and probably the most impressive if only for resilience. The church's greater claim to fame is for a bronze relief of Martin Luther, who preached from its pulpit.

Botanischer Garten and around

Fürstengraben 26 **Botanischer Garten** • Daily: April–Oct 10am–7pm; Nov–March 10am–6pm • €3 • ⓦ spezbot.uni-jena.de • **Goethe-Gedenkstätte** • April–Oct Wed–Sun 11am–3pm • €1 • ⓦ uni-jena.de

When not pushing at anatomy's boundaries or rechannelling the River Saale, Goethe pottered in "seclusion in the flower and plant mountains" of the **Botanischer Garten**, opposite the Pulverturm on Fürstengraben. He is said to have planted the ginkgo near the Inspecktorhaus in which he lived for most of his five years in Jena between 1817 and 1822, a respite from the daily grind as a Weimar state minister that gave him the time to pen *Meister Wilhelm* and *Faust* as well as indulge scientific pursuits such as his theory of colours (see box, p.246). The scientific legacy of Goethe's studies in Jena is on display in the Inspektorhaus as the **Goethe-Gedenkstätte**.

Zeiss Planetarium

Am Planetarium 5 • Tues–Sun times vary by event • €8 • ⓦ planetarium-jena.de

At the eastern fringe of the Botanischer Garten lies the **Zeiss Planetarium**, the world's

---

JENA: A GLASS ACT

The Zeiss Planetarium's name doffs a cap to the original lenses of Zeiss, the global precision optic manufacturer founded in Jena in 1846 by **Carl Zeiss**. He teamed up with physicist and optic pioneer Ernst Abbe to produce the world's first scientific high-performance microscopes in 1866. **Otto Schott**, a doctor and physicist who developed heat- and chemical-resistant glass, joined the duo in 1891 to found Jenaer Glaswerk Schott & Genossen – today's global glass corporation Schott – and cement Jena's reputation as an optics centre. Small wonder it now markets itself a Lichtstadt ("light town").

---

oldest public planetarium, opened in 1926. It now also shows psychedelic three-dimensional laser animations soundtracked by Pink Floyd or Queen in between the standard space explorations.

Optisches Museum

Carl-Zeiss-Platz 12 • Tues–Fri 10am–4.30pm, Sat 11am–5pm (factory tour times at ticket desk) • €5 • ⓦ optischesmuseum.de

The narratives of Jena's glass pioneers Carl Zeiss and Otto Schott (see box above) are told in rather didactic fashion with a mock-up of the first factory in the **Optisches Museum** on Carl-Zeiss-Platz. More fun are the displays of optic curios such as the peepshows that preceded film. Carl-Zeiss-Platz is accessed most easily via glass-roofed mall Goethe Galerie off Leutragraben, which itself has a small free exhibition around a 193-lens star projector. Incidentally, the octagonal temple outside the museum, the **Ernst-Abbe-Denkmal**, studded with bronze reliefs of industry, is the work of Belgian Art Nouveau pioneer Henry van de Velde.

Schillers Gartenhaus

Schillergässchen 2 • Tues–Sun 11am–5pm; closed Sun Nov–March • €2.50

Heading south on Leutragraben, it's a fifteen-minute walk via Schillerstrasse to **Schillers Gartenhaus**, a surprisingly bucolic corner in the city centre where the poet Friedrich Schiller spent a decade as university professor during the 1790s. The area's then rural tranquillity outside the town walls clearly appealed to the dramatist poet – he settled longest here during an itinerant life in Thuringia and knuckled down to write *Wallenstein* and *Mary Stuart*. The ground floor has an exhibit about his Jena years, while upstairs his living quarters have been re-created.

ARRIVAL AND DEPARTURE
JENA

By train The most useful of Jena's three train stations is Jena-Paradies south of the centre. Most trains on the Berlin–Munich line stop here en route to larger Jena-Saalbahnhof north of the town centre. Those from Erfurt and Weimar stop at Jena-West southwest of the centre, a 10min walk west of Paradies.

Destinations Erfurt (hourly; 30min); Rudolstadt (hourly; 30min); Saalfeld (every 30min; 25–40min); Weimar (2 hourly; 20min).

INFORMATION

Tourist office Markt 16 (Jan–March Mon–Fri 10am–6pm, Sat 10am–3pm; April–Dec Mon–Fri 10am–7pm, Sat 10am–4pm; ☎ 03641 49 80 50, ⓦ jenatourismus.de).

Discount card The JenaCard (€11.90), available at the tourist office, provides 48 hours' free travel on public transport, entry to all municipal museums and reductions for most others.

Bike rental Fahrradhaus Kemter, at Löbdergraben 24, beside the Markt (☎ 03641 44 15 33).

ACCOMMODATION

Alpha One Lassallestr. 8 ☎ 03641 59 78 97, ⓦ hostel-jena.de. Although Jena's only private hostel is a mite bland due to its position in former offices, it is well located a few blocks west of the bars on Wagnergasse. Dorms come in

two- to six-bed varieties. Dorms €15, doubles €40
Camping Jena Am Erikönig ☎03641 66 66 88, ⓦjenacamping.de; tram #2 or #4. A small, pretty campsite 2km east of the centre off Karl-Liebknecht-Strasse (A7), which makes up in laidback vibe what it lacks in mod cons – a shower block in a prefab may not appeal to all. Reception is in the old tram carriage. €8 per person

Ibis Hotel City am Holzmarkt Teichgraben 1 ☎03641 81 30, ⓦibishotel.com. The usual identikit rooms from the modern chain, and on the snug side to boot, but keenly priced for the location just south of the city centre. Free internet in lobby (wi-fi in some rooms), breakfast till noon and parking available. €74

Steigenberger Esplanade Carl-Zeiss-Platz 4 ☎03641 80 00, ⓦsteigenberger.com. The city's address for visiting executives is a brisk, efficient hotel of the Steigenberger chain, well-placed a block west of the InterMarkt in the city centre and arranged around a high central atrium. Bland but inoffensive in decor and as comfortable as you'd expect of a four-star. €119

Zur Noll Oberlaungasse 20 ☎03641 597 70, ⓦzur-noll.de. One of the nicest stays in Jena, this family-owned place above a restaurant benefits from the characterful architectural features of its conjoined half-timbered houses and has an excellent location in the heart of the Altstadt. €75

EATING AND DRINKING

Alt Jena Markt 9 ☎03641 44 33 66. Historic pub on the Markt which prepares a large menu of solid traditional fare, including a decent variety of fish dishes, with prices almost as low as the ceilings upstairs. Weekday lunch is just €4, including a drink. A reliable choice. Mon–Wed & Sun 10am–11pm, Thurs–Sat 10am–1am.

Café Grünowski Schillergässchen 5 ☎03641 44 66 20, ⓦgruenowski.de. Stripped-down scruffy student café and bar in a garden villa just south of Schiller Gartenhaus, with an alternative artistic vibe. It's usually buzzing on summer evenings. Daily noon–late.

Café Stilbruch Wagnergasse 1–2 ☎03641 82 71 71, ⓦstilbruch-jena.de. One of the most popular bar-bistros on Jena's "Kniepemeile" (pub mile) is this cosy place styled with Art Nouveau leanings. A wide-ranging menu makes it a popular choice for weekend brunch; otherwise it offers light Italianate bistro fare plus a few Thuringian specials, all cooked to order, so service can be slow. Mon–Thurs 8.30am–2am, Fri 8.30am–3am, Sat 9am–3am, Sun 9am–2am.

Cleanicum Wagnergasse 11 ☎03641 63 88 84, ⓦcleanicum-jena.de. Sup a beer or cocktail while you wait for your laundry to finish in a bright candy-coloured bar-cum-laundrette on Jena's bar strip – a handy stop

for travellers that's also popular with students for its bistro food, made from all-organic ingredients and sourced from local providers where possible. Daily 11am–11.30pm.

Scala Leutragraben 1, in the JenTower ☎03641 35 66 66, ⓦscala-jena.de. Fine international cuisine in Jena comes with superb views from floor-to-ceiling windows that wrap about the 28th storey of the landmark JenTower. Expect experimental modern-European flavours such as lobster with green gazpacho, or wild shrimp and sea bass with green asparagus in a carrot-ginger cream. Mon–Sat 7am–11pm, Sun 8am–11pm.

Zum Roter Hirsch Holzmarkt 10 ☎03641 44 32 21, ⓦjembo.de. A fine choice for atmospheric eating on the cheap is this traditional inn, whose cocoon of snug panelled rooms dates back five centuries to its founding in 1509. The large menu of meaty dishes is just as reassuringly traditional and comes at student prices (€5–9). Mon–Sat 9am–midnight, Sun 10am–11pm.

Zur Noll Oberlaungasse 20 ☎03641 597 70, ⓦzur-noll .de. Low-lit restaurant furnished in a sort of charming modern-rustic style that updates regional cooking with international flavours. Dining comes in various ambiences, from historic rooms of wood panels or whitewashed Gothic vaults to a rear garden. Daily 10.30am–1am.

NIGHTLIFE

F-Haus Johannisplatz 14 ☎03641 558 10, ⓦf-haus .de. A university-affiliated place with cheap crowd-pleaser nights of Nineties and chart tunes a couple of times a week plus rock and metal gigs. Though times are a mite erratic it is generally open Wed & Sat, plus Thurs & Fri a few times a month. Clubnights 11pm–late; gigs 8pm–late.

Kassablanca Felsenkellerstr. 13a ☎03641 28 26 12 ⓦkassablanca.de; tram #1 or #3. A former train depot near Bahnhof Jena-West now serves as a grungy graffiti-covered countercultural centre. Expect clubnights coming

from left field – indie, reggae, hip-hop and techno – at weekends, plus usually one midweek. Fri & Sat 10 or 11pm–late.

Rosenkeller Johannisstr. 13 ☎03641 93 11 91, ⓦrosenkeller.org. A passage opposite the JenTower leads to a bastion of student boozing in cellars, with a wide roster of clubnights and varied programme of live bands that take in everything from afrobeat to anvil-metal via psych-rock. Wed–Sat: gigs 8pm–late, clubs 10pm–late.

The Saale Valley

Steep wooded slopes channel the meadows of the **Saale Valley**, which runs to the cultured, former ducal town of **Rudolstadt**, 37km southwest of Jena. That it's largely flat makes this one of the easiest sections of the long-distance **Saale Cycle Route** (ⓦsaale-radwanderweg.de), which slaloms along the valley for 200km from Kaatschen-Weichau to Sparnberg on the border of Bavaria. The E3 long-distance hiking route also traverses the area, taking in the **Schwarza Valley**. Slower but more adventurous is to **canoe** the lazy meanders of the thickly wooded river valley: tourism booklet *Wasserwandern auf der Saale* gives itineraries of the trip – the full route will take around ten days – plus details of boat hire, slipways and campsites en route.

Trains run from Jena to Rudolstadt and **Saalfeld**. The valley is covered by the regional tourism board of the Thuringian Forest (see p.266), even though it lies outside the official boundaries.

Rudolstadt

The post-World War I dissolution of Germany's petty ducal fiefdoms may have done for the princes of Schwarzburg-Rudolstadt, but their legacy lives on here. Only Weimar trumps **RUDOLSTADT** for the lingering sense of a Residenzstadt of the tin-pot duchies that had hitherto fragmented Thuringia. The same eighteenth-century inter-court arts race that elevated Weimar to cultural capital of the German Enlightenment also saw Rudolstadt flourish. Goethe and Schiller shook hands here for the first time in 1788, and the town's **theatre** at Anger 1 (ⓣ03672 42 27 66, ⓦtheater-rudolstadt.com) was renowned as the most prestigious stage in the area – and still is, for that matter.

Schloss Heidecksburg

Daily: April–Oct 10am–6pm; Nov–March 10am–5pm • Collections and tour €7, collections only €5, Rococo en Miniature €1.50 • ⓦheidecksburg.de

Commanding the town from its hill top, the princely residence **Schloss Heidecksburg** is not so much a palace as a statement of power. This is palace as self-aggrandizement, from the flamboyant Rococo building that replaced an earlier Renaissance number after a fire – an older portal is on the left as you enter the courtyard – to the fabulous interiors. You get a taste by viewing the various collections on your own: the princes' porcelain and art collections, the latter with Caspar David Friedrich's *Morning Mist in the Mountains*; an armoury; a pleasingly stuffy natural-history room of the late 1800s; and a missable town museum. But it's worth taking a **tour** to see the living quarters and the highlight, the **Festsaal**, a marbled pastel confection surmounted by a ceiling fresco of Olympus that is arguably the most theatrical ballroom in Thuringia. The chinoiserie of the Bänderzimmer also charms.

The last piece of frippery within the Schloss is "**Rococo en Miniature**" – precision 1:50 models of state palaces and contemporary life that are so intricate visitors are given magnifying glasses. Outside it is a display of leaf-styled Rococo sleighs fit for a fairy-tale prince, and there are good views over the Altstadt from the castle belvedere.

Stadtkirche St Andreas

It's worth detouring on the way down from the Schloss to take in the **Stadtkirche St Andreas**, between the Schloss and the Altstadt main square. Outwardly a rather frumpy church, within it is a time capsule of princely grandiloquence. Much of the revamp is Baroque – that it came soon after the conclusion of the Thirty Years' War may explain the exuberance of the princes' loft that traces a family tree from floor to ceiling, the host of angels that flutter in the vaults, or a pulpit on which a resurrected Christ dances a jig. Among the Renaissance eye-candy is a life-size funeral sculpture of a noble family by the pulpit.

Schillerhaus

Schillerstr. 25 • Daily: April–Oct 10am–6pm; Nov–March 10am–5pm • €5 • ⓦ schillerhaus-rudolstadt.de

Poet Friedrich Schiller lived briefly in Rudolstadt in 1787 as the personal tutor to burghers' daughters Charlotte von Lengefeld and Caroline von Beulwitz. Indeed, the dashing 28-year-old poet made such an impression on his charges that gossips speculated about a ménage à trois, a subject covered in the **Schillerhaus** museum on contemporary Rudolstadt and his time there. Schiller was also introduced to Goethe in the Baroque residence, a fateful meeting that took him to Weimar within a year.

Heinrich-Heine-Park and the Thüringer Bauernhäuser

Beyond the Altstadt, gathered around a spacious Markt, you can cross the River Saale to the **Heinrich-Heine-Park**. At its centre are the **Thüringer Bauernhäuser** (April–Oct daily 11am–6pm; €2.50), two traditional farmhouses plucked from the surrounding countryside and reassembled with original folksy furnishings, together with an apothecary.

ARRIVAL AND INFORMATION   RUDOLSTADT

By train The Hauptbahnhof is beside the river – walk straight ahead on Bahnhofgasse to reach the Markt. The hourly trains to and from Jena take 30min.

Tourist office Markt 5 (Mon–Fri 9am–6pm, Sat 9am–1pm; ☎ 03672 48 64 40, ⓦ rudolstadt.de).

ACCOMMODATION AND EATING

Adler Markt 17 ☎ 03672 44 03, ⓦ hotel-adler-rudolstadt.de. This central former inn dating from 1512 was Goethe's bunkdown in the early 1800s. Fortunately it has been sensitively modernized to provide a tasteful comfortable stay. €87

Marienturm Rudolstadt-Cumbach ☎ 03672 432 70, ⓦ hotel-marienturm.de. With your own transport, this place 2km south of Rudolstadt is an appealing option, offering 4-star mod cons and wonderful views across to the

town from its hilltop position. Locals recommend its country-styled restaurant too. €112

Schiller! Schillerstr. 25 ☎ 03672 48 64 75. By far the nicest eating in town is in the café and restaurant of the Schillerhaus museum. Its decor blends old-world elegance and pretty modern style, while the kitchen rustles up dishes such as *Zander* with wild rice or beef roulade with Burgundy sauce. Nice garden for summer, too. Tues–Sat 2–11pm, Sun 11am–6pm; Nov–Feb closed Tues.

Saalfeld

Having put its medieval mining past behind long ago, **SAALFELD**, 10km south of Rudolstadt, contents itself as a pleasant if anonymous market town in the Upper Saale Valley. Its enduring appeal for a day-trip is its location in the foothills of the **Thüringer Schiefergebirge** (Slate Mountains) which hump up south of the Schwarza Valley; its **show caves** lend Saalfeld the mawkish title "Feengrottenstadt" (Fairy Grottoes Town).

The Altstadt

In the **Altstadt** life revolves around the **Markt**, whose Rathaus is textbook German Renaissance: stolid in stature beneath turrets and cascading gables, and with the requisite oriel windows and octagonal tower. Towering over the Markt to the north are the twin spires of the **Johanneskirche**, whose size says much about Saalfeld's medieval wealth and whose astonishing interior is said to be a medieval representation of Christ's blood drenching the faithful.

Divert left en route to the Johanniskirche, up Brudergasse and you reach a former Franciscan friary, now the **Stadtmuseum** (Tues–Sun 10am–5pm; €5), with displays on local mining and folkcrafts. For a stroll, turn left at the end of Brudergasse on to Obere Torgasse along the former town walls, then left at the triangular fork with Hinter der Mauer, to reach the ruins of **Schloss Hoher Schwarm** (daily 9am–5/6pm; free), medieval seat of the Schwarzburg princes with a garden perfect for a picnic.

CANOEING AND BIKING IN THE UPPER SAALE VALLEY

The **Upper Saale Valley** that twists through pine-covered hills southeast of Saalfeld is a popular destination for **canoeing** and **mountain biking** along the Stausee Hohenwarte, a placid dammed waterway nicknamed the Thuringian Sea. Campsite *Bike & Boot-Camp Saalfeld*, at Am Weidig 3 (☎03671 45 62 90, ⓦbikeundbootcamp-saalfeld.de), rents bikes by the half-day, and kayaks and Canadian canoes by the day to explore. Canoe rental includes transfers to an inlet off the broadest section of the waterway: it narrows as you head upstream.

Feengrotten

Feengrotten Tours every 30min: May–Oct daily 9.30am–5pm; Nov–April daily 10.30am–3.30pm • €11 • **Feenweltchen and Grottoneum** May–Oct 9.30am–6pm • €6.60 each • ⓦ feengrotten.de • Bus #A from the Markt

What makes Saalfeld one of the premier destinations in the Thuringian Forest are the **Feengrotten**, just beyond the southwest suburbs at the woods' fringe. The "fairy grottoes" cave system was exploited in the sixteenth century as an alum-slate mine, then reopened in 1914 as show caverns that attracted seventeen million visitors in a year. By the 1920s a newly discovered mineral spring lured speleologists deeper to reveal caverns whose drip-water-features had been oxidized into a kaleidoscope of colours. In 1993 the *Guinness Book of Records* declared them the most colourful on the planet – as far as ochre, rust, cream and grey with the odd flash of green can be deemed colourful. The system's highlight is the "fairy dome", its carefully lit stalagmite citadels much like the Wagnerian stage-set they inspired in the composer's son for a production of *Tannhäuser*, though the Muzak schmaltz played here is faintly hilarious. The former mine's heritage is celebrated in a museum, the **Grottoneum**, while outside is children's attraction the **Feenweltchen**, a "little fairy world" of buildings in the woods.

ARRIVAL AND INFORMATION   SAALFELD

By train The Bahnhof is on the Saale's east bank, a 15min walk from the centre; follow Bahnhofstrasse then left up Saalstrasse to reach the Markt. Trains to and from Jena take 25–40min (every 30min).

Tourist office Markt 6 (Mon–Fri 9am–6pm, Sat 9am–1pm; ☎03671 52 21 81, ⓦsaalfeld.de). The office can provide information on accommodation upon the unlikely event you choose to stay.

EATING

Thüringer Stuben Am Markt 25–26 ☎03671 59 91 03. The traditional restaurant of the *Anker* hotel prepares regional dishes with *Klosse* potato dumplings and has a terrace in prime people-watching position on the Markt.

Sister restaurant *Güldene Gans* (Tues–Sun 6pm–10pm) prepares creative fusion cooking in a historic cellar setting. Daily 11am–10pm.

Altenburg

Few towns in Thuringia have suffered from reunification like **ALTENBURG** at Thuringia's eastern limits. Once drip-fed by GDR finances, the town has slipped into stagnation as its population and wealth is sucked out by West Saxony's dynamic duo Leipzig and Zwickau. Only the architecture and art attest to its former status as the once-glorious Residenzstadt of the Saxe-Altenburg duchy. Today a visit to Altenburg is really about its two museums: the ducal Schloss, and an art museum.

The Markt

While much of Altenburg is shabby, the elongated **Markt** hints at former glories, boxed in by tall handsome townhouses and the Renaissance **Rathaus** with an impressive portal and bulging corner oriel. It's at its best when filled by a market on Wednesday and Saturday. The **Brüderkirche** closes the west end of the Markt, borrowing freely from earlier styles and nodding to its own era (1901) with a Jugendstil mosaic of a sermonizing Christ.

The Bartholomäikirche and Skat fountain

A block north of the Markt is the **Bartholomäikirche**, where Martin Luther defended his propositions against the papal envoy in 1519; a Gothic child of the Reformation, it preserves a Romanesque core in the crypt. On a small square to the right of the church a bronze fountain of brawling card-players honours Altenburg's cherished pursuit, the card game **Skat** (see box below). Local lore claims cards baptized in its waters are lucky – die-hard players can buy cards and book an official *Kartentaufe* (card baptism) via tourist information.

The Schloss

Tues–Sun 9.30am–5pm • €3.50, combined ticket with Lindenau-Museum €9 • ⓦ residenzschloss-altenburg.de

"Even an emperor need not feel ashamed of such a building," Martin Luther is said to have said upon seeing the walls and towers of the ducal **Schloss**, east of the centre via Burgstrasse and Theaterplatz. The courtyard is romantic Germany writ large in its splendid jumble of architecture: a dumpy Romanesque keep, the Flasche, just predates the slender Hausmannsturm, a round Gothic watchtower fit for Rapunzel; and there is a graceful arcaded Renaissance gallery. Within a Baroque corps de logis, the castle's rooms – a backdrop for its exhibitions – are similarly eclectic: the **Festsaal** is a swaggering revival synthesis crowned by a bright fresco of the marriage of Amor and Psyche by Munich's Karl Mossdorf; the **Sibyllen-cabinet** is a wonderfully florid Baroque nook to display porcelain and glass; the **Bachsaal** alludes to the Renaissance; and the **Schlosskirche**, where Bach played the organ, is in rich Baroque. The Schloss's south wing houses the **Schloss- und Spielkartenmuseum** of Meissen china, weaponry and – what else? – playing cards.

The Lindenau-Museum

Gabelentzstr. 5 • Tues–Fri noon–6pm, Sat & Sun 10am–6pm • €6, combined ticket with Schloss €9 • ⓦ lindenau-museum.de

A palazzo in the far reaches of the Schlosspark behind the Schloss contains the **Lindenau-Museum**, the private collections of Bernhard von Lindenau, an eighteenth-century statesman who prepared the ground for the state of Saxony. He had exquisite taste. As well as superb antique Roman and Greek ceramics, and German art from Romantic to Expressionist, there is an excellent gallery of early Italian art. Most of the 180 pieces in the collection are early Renaissance works from Florence and Siena: Perugino's *St Helen* is lost in holy reverie; Botticelli produces a swooning portrait of *St Catherine* as a young woman; and there are exquisite small works by Masaccio and Lorenzo Monaco.

SKAT!

It was during Altenburg's golden age as the Residenzstadt of the Saxe-Altenburg duchy that it achieved its fame as the cradle of **Skat**, Germany's favourite **card game**, whose rules were honed by court intellectuals in the early 1800s. "My five months' stay in Altenburg gave me more mental and social experience than that gained by many a human being during the whole span of life," one F.A. Brockhaus exclaimed, though he also enthused about editing dictionaries. Today Altenburg is the home of the **Skatgericht**, court of arbitration on all things Skat, and Germany's largest manufacturer of playing cards, ASS Altenburger.

By plane A national airport 5km east is served by buses coordinated with flight times.

By train The Hauptbahnhof is a 10min walk north of the centre.

Destinations Erfurt (six daily; 1hr 50min); Leipzig (hourly;

50min–1hr); Zwickau (hourly; 40min).

Tourist office Markt 17 (Mon–Fri 9am–6pm, Sat 9am–4pm, Sun 10am–4pm; Oct–March closed Sun; ☎ 03447 51 28 00, ⊛ altenburg-tourismus.de).

EATING AND DRINKING

Kulisse Theaterplatz 18 ☎ 03447 50 09 39, ⊛ kulisse -abg.de. A relaxed *Kneipe* just downhill from the Schloss that is decorated with publicity shots from the adjacent theatre. The menu is typical modern bistro fare: pastas and contemporary German cooking. Daily 5pm–midnight, Fri & Sat 5pm–1am.

Ratskeller Markt 1 ☎ 03447 31 12 26, ⊛ ratskeller -altenburg.de. Traditional Thuringian plates for €9–15 plus a few international dishes in the venerable *Ratskeller*, a popular option for lunch, especially in summer when tables are set on the Markt rather than beneath the Renaissance vaults. Mon–Sat 10am–midnight, Sun 11am–11pm.

Gotha

Vintage travel books acclaim **GOTHA** as the richest and most attractive town in Thuringia. Leaving aside the question of whether their authors had visited Weimar or nearby Erfurt, it remains a handsome if low-key small town whose looks were buffed in the eighteenth century as the courtly residence of the House of Saxe-Coburg, the dynasty better known in Britain as the House of Windsor – the British royals sensed the public mood during war with Germany and rebranded itself in 1917. The legacy of that glorious heyday is **Schloss Friedenstein**, the main reason to visit just as it was for Voltaire or Goethe and their pals during the Enlightenment, its collections just as erudite. However, the town also serves as a handy gateway to the Thuringian Forest – and if first impressions count there are few better ways to arrive at the forest than by historic tram, the Thüringerwaldbahn (see p.267), which departs from Gotha's Bahnhof.

4

Hauptmarkt

Compact Gotha is easily strollable. Figuratively and geographically, the **Altstadt** is very much in the shadow of the Schloss. **Hauptmarkt**, its elongated core, sweeps up to the hilltop castle in a gesture of subservience. As befits a courtly Residenzstadt, the so-called Wasserkunst, the town's water system, was prettified with belvederes and fountains which gush from grottoes – not Baroque for all its looks but conscious antiquarianism of the late 1800s. Incidentally, court painter Lucas Cranach lived at Hauptmarkt 17, its lintel bearing his snake coat of arms. Hauptmarkt flattens into a small square by a tubby Renaissance **Rathaus**. Its tower (daily: April–Oct 11am–6pm; Nov–March 11am–4pm; €0.50) offers an elevated view up the Hauptmarkt's cobbled slope to the Schloss framed by houses.

Schloss Friedenstein

Tues–Sun: May–Oct 10am–5pm; Nov–April 10am–4pm • All collections €10, Ekhof-Theater only €5, Schlosspark free; audio-guide €2.50 • ⊛ stiftungfriedenstein.de

There's no doubt about who rules in Gotha. **Schloss Friedenstein** not only takes up half of the town centre, it commands the Altstadt beneath as the largest early-Baroque palace in Germany: 100m by 140m and cornered by massive square bastions that seem to be a response to its being built just after the Thirty Years' War in the 1640s. Its sober looks owe much to the religion of Ernst I, a Protestant nicknamed "the Pious", who chose austere symmetry instead of the flamboyance preferred by his Catholic peers and gave over all but a handful of private quarters to his administration.

Schlossmuseum

Set aside a morning for the **Schlossmuseum**, and its ducal collections and period rooms. Kicking off on the ground floor is an excellent gallery, notably a room of works from Cranach the Elder; highlights are *Fall and Salvation of Man* and *Judith at the Table of Holofernes*, her death already foretold in the background that is enlarged as the subsequent *Death of Holofernes*. Cranach himself looks on at the action from a shrub in the left-hand side of the former. The gallery's star work is *Gotha Lovers* (*Gothaer Liebespaar*), a sumptuous piece by an anonymous master of the 1480s whose foppish beau and coquettish belle epitomize the courtly love of the time. Following rooms shift towards humanism with Dürer prints and Conrad Meit's outstanding statuettes of *Adam and Eve*.

Period rooms above fast-forward through decorative styles, none packing more punch than the **Festsaal**, its ceiling an impasto of sculpted stucco figures and garlands, and its table set with the Wedgwood china used at a banquet for King Friedrich III in 1768. Its swagger extends to a stucco portal of Zeus who straddles the family crest mounted on weaponry. The ducal **Kunstkammer** also warrants investigation for its curio cabinet of fancies that caught ducal eyes, and its fine Egyptian and Roman antiquities collected by a court scientist during his Middle East travels in 1809.

Ekhof-Theater and the Museum für Regionalgeschichte

The far tower houses exhibits of regional culture and archeology as the **Museum für Regionalgeschichte und Volkskunde** and also a lovely, perfectly preserved court theatre, the **Ekhof-Theater**. One of the oldest and last Baroque theatres in Europe – many went up in smoke thanks to the era's use of candlelight and pyrotechnics – it preserves the under-stage pulleys that whisked scenery on to the stage. The venue is as much of an attraction as the drama during Gotha's Ekhof-Festival (ⓦekhof-festival.de) in July and August. The **Schlosskirche** in the northeast wing is worth a look as well, and you can also ask about tours of a 300m section of the castle's subterranean **fortifications** that date from the Schloss's construction, when the Turkish Ottoman steamroller was crushing all opposition east of here.

The Schlosspark

A trim **Rosengarten** behind the palace and the pretty, original **Orangerie** and **Teeschlösschen** folly to its east are the only manicured parts of a **Schlosspark** that spreads luxuriantly as a mature parkland of English-style naturalistic planting. Leaflets from the Schloss ticket desk pinpoint the requisite Romantic temples. However, after the heavy cultural stuff before, it's pleasant simply to amble around the Grosser Parkteich boating lake; its small island holds the tomb of Duke Ernst II. Go clockwise around the lake to find Thuringia's Neoclassical Merkurtempel.

ARRIVAL AND INFORMATION	GOTHA

By train The Bahnhof is on the Erfurt line and the terminus for the dinky Thüringerwaldbahn to Friedrichroda in the Thuringian Forest (see p.267). It's sited a 15min walk south of the centre, but you can cut through the Schlosspark at the junction with Parkallee or take tram #3 (€1.50) to Arnoldiplatz, a high street east of Hauptmarkt.

Destinations Eisenach (hourly; 20min); Erfurt (every 15–30min; 15min); Friedrichroda (every 30min; 1hr); Mülhausen (10 daily; 20min).

Tourist office Hauptmarkt 33 (Mon–Fri 9am–6pm, Sat 10am–3pm, Sun 10am–2pm; Oct–April closed Sun; ☎03621 507 85 70, ⓦkultourstadt.de). The office stocks brochures on the Thuringing Forest and walking maps of the Rennsteig (see box, p.267).

ACCOMMODATION

Am Schloss Bergalle 3a ☎03621 85 32 06, ⓦpas-gotha.de. One of the best of the many cheap pensions scattered around Gotha, this is a traditional homely place located in a residential district close to the front of the Schloss. The cheapest rooms share amenities. Nice garden, too. €50

Am Schlosspark Lindenauallee 20 ☎03621 44 20, ⓦhotel-am-schlosspark.de. This pleasant four-star hotel with a beauty spa is sited on the west side of the Schlosspark. The best rooms have views of the greenery and decor in all rooms is a cut above the usual bland classic-modern hotel. **€114**

Herberge Augustinerkloster Jüdenstr. 27 ☎ 03621 30 29 10, ⓦ augustinerkloster-gotha.de. A 750-year-old monastery, two blocks west of the Hauptmarkt, offers basic, modern, en-suite rooms, some with views over the beautiful cloister. There are no radios, TVs or phones, so you can detox from modern life. The excellent on-site café serves light meals for around €7. Café Mon–Fri 11am–5pm. **€64**

EATING AND DRINKING

Brauhaus Valentino Brühl 7 ☎ 03621 22 64 41, ⓦ valentino-brauhaus.de. This microbrewery is an ever-popular option for a relaxed beer – freshly brewed *Pils*, *Schwarzbier* and a seasonal special – plus pizza, pasta (€6) and Italian mains. Daily 11.30–midnight.

Pagenhaus Parkallee 1 ☎ 03621 40 36 12. A traditional option beside the Schloss's entry gate, with a late-nineteenth-century dining room and a rear garden. It offers regional cuisine plus German favourites such as lamb with a tomato crust, plus mid-afternoon coffee and cake.

Tues–Sat 11am–10pm; mid-May to mid-Sept also Sun 11am–10pm.

Weinschänke Gartenstr. 28, corner of Lutherstrasse ☎ 03621 30 10 09, ⓦ restaurant-weinschaenke.de. A block north of the Markt you'll find this snug cocoon of dark wood panelling, a 1903-vintage wine bar that's one of Gotha's oldest. It serves the best cuisine in the centre of town, specifically regional with a few international dishes; *Thüringer Rostbrätel* is €9. Tues–Sat 11.30am–2.30pm & 6–11pm, Sun 11.30am–2.30pm.

Eisenach

Small in stature, **EISENACH**, 30km west of Gotha, abounds with the big hitters of German culture. It is the birthplace of Johann Sebastian Bach and the refuge from which Martin Luther shaped German Protestantism. Goethe and – with a bit of poetic licence – Wagner get a look in, too, thanks to the **Wartburg**, not just a UNESCO-listed castle whose thirteenth-century court inspired an opera, *Tannhäuser*, but a cradle of culture that's hard-wired into the national psyche. Indeed, such is the heavyweight punch of the small town that everyone rather overlooks the fact that Eisenach is also an amiable place that wears its cultural legacy lightly, not to mention a good launch-pad from which to explore the Thuringian Forest just south. Its compact **Altstadt** is best enjoyed at walking pace – and as the town is on every coach-tour itinerary in Thuringia you may not have any choice about it.

The Wartburg

Daily: April–Oct 8.30am–8pm; Nov–March 9am–5pm • Castle complex free • ⓦ wartburg-eisenach.de • Bus #10 runs from the Hauptbahnhof via the Markt; tourist mini-trains ascend from the Markt April–Oct

Few German cities possess so potent an icon as the UNESCO-listed **Wartburg**, which commands a hilltop south of the Altstadt. The story goes that founder Ludwig der Springer, impressed by the landscape on a hunt, cried, "Wait, mountain [Wart' Burg!], you shall have my castle!", a good yarn that overlooks an early watchtower (Warte). First mentioned in 1080, the castle was beefed up after Landgrave Ludwig II married into the family of mighty Holy Roman Emperor Frederick Barbarossa, and was then tinkered with by members of the dynasty thereafter. Consequently it peels back along its ridge like a picture-book composite of German castles, best appreciated from a lookout uphill from the Torhaus gatehouse. Laid over this architectural encyclopedia is the revivalist fetishizing of the past in vogue during its renovation in the 1840s. Indeed, it is only Goethe's perception that the site was significant to German identity that stopped the complex being left to collapse.

You're free to wander about the twin courtyards or ascend the **Südturm**, the only watchtower preserved from the medieval castle, for views over the complex and the Thuringian Forest beyond. It's a stiff forty-minute walk from the Altstadt to the Wartburg, much of it uphill: the most direct route is southeast of the Predigerkirche,

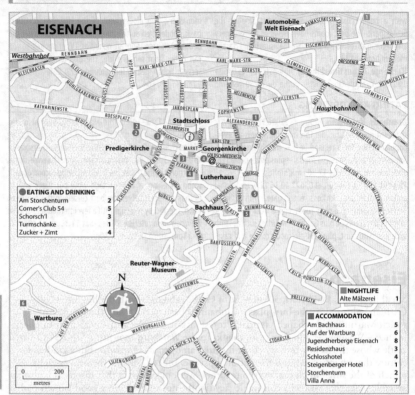

the most atmospheric is a woodland path off Reuterweg, near the Reuter-Wagner-Museum. And word of warning: crowds are heavy on high-summer weekends.

The Palas

Tours daily: April–Oct 8.30am–5pm; Nov–March 9am–3.30pm; English tour at 1.30pm, or notes on request • Tours €9, museum €5 or free with tours

The **Palas**, the oldest and most architecturally impressive building of the Wartburg, is accessed on tours. Its early Romanesque rooms are canopied by vaults that umbrella from a single column capped with inventive (if reproduction) capitals. Those that most catch the eye are the quarters that have been rather zealously restored as a paean to medieval roots: former women's quarters the **Elisabeth Room**, which shimmers in a skin of faux-Byzantine mosaics (1902), or the **Elisabeth Gallery** and **Hall of Minstrels** that inspired Wagner, both frescoed with rich medieval-esque images by Romantic painter Moritz von Schwind. Then there's the gloriously over-the-top **Festsaal**, the venue in which student fraternities laid down a gauntlet to the ruling elite in 1817 (see box opposite). So impressed was "Mad" Bavarian king Ludwig II by this coffered banqueting hall that he commissioned a replica for Schloss Neuschwanstein.

Museum

It was Goethe's idea to turn the Schloss into a museum of medieval exhibits at a time when Germany was rediscovering its heritage. Today the small museum in the women's quarters, the **Neu Kemenate**, displays a small hoard of Wartburg treasure

THE WARTBURG: CRADLE OF CULTURE

The Wartburg dominates German culture as much as it commands Eisenach's skyline. It has its own saint for a start, **St Elisabeth**, a thirteenth-century Hungarian princess, betrothed to Landgrave Ludwig IV, who renounced courtly splendour to pursue an ascetic life caring for the sick. It was some court to snub, too. At the time Wartburg was considered to be one of the richest arts centres in Europe. The finest troubadour of his generation, Walther von der Vogelweide, clashed with *Parsifal* author Wolfram von Eschenbach in the celebrated **Contest of Minstrels** sing-offs; the winner of the six-strong Battle of the Bards met with princely favour, the loser the hangman's noose.

Arguably, the most significant moment in the Wartburg's history, though, was the arrival of **Martin Luther** in May 1521. Excommunicated and declared a heretic for refusing to renounce his doctrine at the Diet of Worms, the renegade priest was kidnapped by order of Saxony Elector Frederick the Wise and protected within the Wartburg's mighty walls. The former cleanly shaven, tonsured monk remained incognito as bearded, tousle-haired **Junker Jörg** (Squire George) while he toiled for fourteen months over the first translation of the New Testament from Greek into the vernacular. For German Protestants that makes the Wartburg a holy of holies. For everyone else, Luther simultaneously propelled German into a modern language.

On October 18, 1817, five hundred students from eleven German universities met to celebrate a **Wartburgfest**. The jollies morphed into a rallying call for unity delivered to a nation of petty fiefdoms, and the first demand for democratic rights delivered to its ducal rulers. And when students of Jena university hoisted their fraternity flag above the fireplace, Germany found the black, red and gold colours for its future **national flag**. A darker upshot was that the Nazis cited as an inspiration their book-burning of Napoleonic works.

4

and Reformation-era art, notably portraits by Lucas Cranach, including one of Martin Luther, and a cabinet carved with intricate scenes inspired by the prints of Albrecht Dürer.

The Lutherstube

From the museum, tours continue to the **Lutherstube**. It was in this simple room that Martin Luther, then excommunicated and in hiding as squire Junker Jörg, toiled over a German translation of the New Testament (see box above). They say he hurled his inkpot at a devil that appeared to prevent his labours, which is why there is a patch of bare masonry in one corner – the wood panels have been chipped away by centuries of souvenir-hunters.

The central Altstadt

After the glory (and popularity) of the Wartburg, Eisenach's cobbled old town is an amiable, low-key place. It is also compact, with no sight except the motor museum and Wagner's villa more than a ten-minute walk from the Altstadt centre. Incidentally, a detour to Johannisstrasse west of the Markt will reveal **Schamels Haus** at no. 9, claimed to be the narrowest inhabited half-timbered house in Germany at just 2m wide.

The Georgenkirche

Markt • Mon–Sat 10am–12.30pm & 2–5/7pm, Sun 11.30am–12.30pm & 2–5pm • Free

The obvious place to begin a tour of Eisenach Town is the spacious **Markt** that is closed on one side by the pastel-peach Baroque box of the **Georgenkirche**. Former choirboy Martin Luther returned here as an outlaw following his excommunication at the Diet of Worms to preach a sermon in 1521, and the organist's son, Johann Sebastian Bach, was baptized in the Gothic stone font in March 1685. The choir at the other end is ringed by epitaphs of the Ludowinger Landgraves who lorded it over Eisenach from Wartburg; founder Ludwig I – known as Ludwig "der Springer" after a jump from a prison window – is behind the altar on the right with a model of the town's first church; Ludwig II who beefed up the castle into a medieval fortress is the bruiser in chain mail.

The Stadtschloss

Markt 24 • Wed–Sun 11am–5pm • €2

The palatial pile that faces the church is the **Stadtschloss**, a minor residence of the Saxony-Weimar dynasty that doubles as the tourist information centre and the Thüringer Museum. The latter holds regional decorative arts, notably displays of Baroque porcelain.

Predigerkirche

Predigerplatz 2 • Tues–Sun 11am–5pm • €4

The **Predigerkirche**, west of the Markt, is a one-time Dominican church erected to honour the canonization of Eisenach's thirteenth-century saint, Princess Elisabeth, which now houses two rooms of Thuringian religious art. Highlights include a sculpture of Heinrich Raspe, the brother-in-law of Elisabeth and benefactor who stumped up the cash for the church, and a willowy *Mourning John* from a southern Harz monastery. Of less artistic merit but enjoyable nonetheless is an altarpiece of the *Holy Family* (1500) composed like a group snapshot, while burghers, one in a Jewish hat, mug behind. A second room holds art exhibitions.

Lutherhaus

Lutherplatz • Daily 10am–5pm • €6 • ⓦ lutherhaus-eisenach.de

Just uphill from the Georgenkirche, **Lutherhaus** is something of a misnomer for a residence in which Martin Luther bunked down while a schoolboy with the Cotta family – a wealthy family, too, if their Gothic townhouse is a guide. Small wonder Luther later referred to Eisenach as *"meine liebe Stadt"* ("my dear town"). As well as reconstructions of the quarters of the fêted lodger, who spent two stints here between 1498 and 1501, interactive displays in English and archive reproductions attempt to pin down the man and his doctrine in the context of his time. The museum is currently being renovated, and is due to reopen in mid-2015.

Bachhaus

Frauenplan 21 • Daily 10am–6pm • €7.50 • ⓦ bachhaus.de

No less groundbreaking than Luther in his sphere, Johann Sebastian Bach is the subject of the museum five minutes' walk uphill from Lutherhaus along Lutherstrasse on Frauenplan. **Bachhaus** was not the great composer's 1642 birthplace as was supposed when the museum was founded in 1906 – that honour goes to the house opposite at the top of Lutherstrasse, marked by a plaque – but that does not distract from the house's representation of the interiors of Bach's era, which act as a backcloth to the narration of his life story, from Weimar schoolboy to the notoriously tetchy composer who harrumphed between courts in Thuringia and nearby Leipzig. Indeed, the displays are as revealing as a portrait of the petty courts that dictated life in the state.

Bach, however, is all about the music and the highlights are a room of iPods with explanations of the music in English, and **concerts** of his works performed hourly on historic instruments. The **statue** of Bach outside is also worth a look. Originally erected in the Markt, it was forged in 1884 as an idealized image of the great composer based on the best of the wildly varying portraits painted in his lifetime. So hot was the debate that civic authorities in Leipzig exhumed his skeleton a decade later to settle the issue. Modern academics suggest the composer was rather fleshier in the face.

Reuter-Wagner-Museum

Reuterweg 2 • Fri–Sun 11am–5pm • €4

Ten minutes' walk south of Bachhaus on Marienstrasse, Eisenach relaxes into small-town mode as you approach Reuter-Villa. Its accreditation as the **Reuter-Wagner-Museum** derives from the villa's twin status as a former home of the nineteenth-century writer Fritz Reuter and the home of a huge array of Wagner memorabilia in its period rooms, including his death mask. The composer set his opera *Tannhäuser* in the Wartburg after a visit to Eisenach in 1842.

Automobile Welt Eisenach

Friedrich-Naumann-Str. 10 • Tues–Sun 11am–5pm • €5 • W awe-stiftung.de

Not all Eisenach's heavyweights are cultural. **Automobile Welt Eisenach** (known as **AWE**), in a 1930s factory north of the centre, celebrates the motors that were manufactured here from 1898 onwards. Worth a look for petrolheads are the carriage-like first Wartburg, which rolled off the production line in 1899, and the Wartburg 311 sports coupés – a racy GDR-era marque caught somewhere between Austen Healey and Mercedes, it gets overlooked in the wave of nostalgia for Trabant kitsch. There's also a dinky 1920s Dixi that was destined to be rebranded as a BMW after the Bavarian giant acquired the company moulds in 1929.

ARRIVAL AND INFORMATION   EISENACH

By train Eisenach's Hauptbahnhof lies a short walk east of the Altstadt's edge.

Destinations Erfurt (three hourly; 30–50min); Gotha (hourly; 20min); Meiningen (hourly; 1hr).

Tourist office Markt 24 (Mon–Fri 10am–6pm, Sat & Sun 10am–5pm; ☎ 03691 792 30, W eisenach.info). The office can book accommodation and concert or theatre tickets – keep an eye open for summer concerts in the Wartburg's

Festsaal, renowned for its superb acoustics.

Discount card The Eisenach Classic Card (valid 24hr for €16, 72hr for €36), available from the tourist office, gives free public transport and entry to the museums and the Wartburg.

Bike rental Bikes can be rented from Zweirad Hennig, Schmelzerstr. 4–6, west of the Markt (☎ 03691 78 47 38); electric bikes are available from Cycle Service, Bahnhofstr. 33, next to the station (☎ 03691 73 28 31).

ACCOMMODATION

Am Bachhaus Marienstr. 7 ☎ 03691 204 70, W hotel-am-bachhaus.de. Renovated in 2014, this family-run hotel with a restaurant now has fresh, modern rooms in an excellent location on a quiet central square in the Altstadt. **€86**

Auf der Wartburg Auf der Wartburg 2 ☎ 03691 79 70, W wartburghotel.de. A 100-year-old luxury pile adjoining the Wartburg with equally fabulous views. While perhaps overpriced due to the prestige of its location, it nevertheless exudes country-manor elegance in public areas – individually furnished rooms defer to more modern comforts. **€249**

Jugendherberge Eisenach Mariental 24 ☎ 03691 74 32 59, W eisenach.jugendherberge.de; bus #3 or #10 to "Unterhalb der Herberge". The official youth hostel is popular with all ages and no wonder – its spacious Jugendstil pile drops hints of its original grandeur. The location at the foot of the Wartburg hill means a 1km walk to the centre, however. Dorms **€23**, doubles **€46**

Residenzhaus Auf der Esplanade ☎ 03691 21 41 33, W residenzhaus-eisenach.de. The place to live out Rapunzel fantasies is this medieval watchtower behind the

Georgenkirche: you ascend a spiral staircase to modern hostel-style rooms, including one en suite and one with waterbeds. Simple certainly, but great value for the location. **€50**

Schlosshotel Markt 10 ☎ 03691 70 20 00, W schlosshotel-eisenach.de. Located beside the Lutherhaus in the centre of town, this is a modern courtyard hotel – fairly bland in decor but highly comfy due to four-star standards and with an excellent central location. "Komfort" rooms are worth the extra €10 for their extra space. **€107**

Steigenberger Hotel Karlsplatz 11 ☎ 03691 280, W steigenberger.com/eisenach. Though not as elegant as its vintage building suggests from outside, this is a bright, stylish member of the Steigenberger chain nonetheless. Its bar-bistro prepares healthy modern cuisine plus tapas plates at respectable prices. **€97**

Storchenturm Georgenstr. 43a ☎ 03691 73 32 63, W gasthof-am-storchenturm.de. Hugely popular hostel-pension on a quiet courtyard a short walk from the Markt. Spotless and modern(ish) throughout, it retains the occasional beam from the original medieval barn. Cheap three- to six-bed rooms are available for groups. **€46**

4

Villa Anna Fritz-Koch-Str. 12 ☎ 03691 239 50, ⓦ hotel-villa-anna.de. The design-hotel tag is somewhat misleading for a rather dated purple-and-grey colour scheme. Once past that, this modernized Art Nouveau villa is spotless, comfortable and welcoming. One warning: without a car it's a long walk back from the centre. **€110**

EATING, DRINKING AND NIGHTLIFE

Alte Mälzerei Palmental 1 ☎ 036920 84 10, ⓦ jazzclub-eisenach.de. Jazz and blues at weekends in the basement of a converted malthouse northeast of the centre – continue across two streams to what feels like the town limits. Not cheap at around €10–15 a ticket, mind, and erratic – check the website before a visit. Generally open weekends with an occasional midweek gig. Fri & Sat 8.30pm– late.

Am Storchenturm Georgenstr. 43a ☎ 03691 73 32 63, ⓦ gasthof-am-storchenturm.de. Big portions of regional specialities – *Bratwurst* for €8.50, rump steak €16.50 – in this *Gasthof* that's a pocket of rural idyll in the centre: the lofty interior is furnished with rustic knick-kacks, the beer garden shaded by fruit trees. All in all a pleasant spot for lazy eating and drinking in summer. Daily 11am–11pm.

Corner's Club 54 Wartburgallee 54 ☎ 03691 88 65 00. Wine and cocktails in a small modern bar whose leather loungers and dark-wood floors take decor cues from American city style. Friendly and popular with older drinkers, it also hosts the occasional jazz concert. Wed–Sat 7pm–late.

Schorsch'l Georgenstr. 19 ⓦ schorschl.de. By far the most atmospheric drinking den in the centre is this candlelit pub on a corner 100m from the Markt, frequented by a relaxed twenty- to forty-something crowd. It also hosts the occasional acoustic gig of the folk/singer-songwriter/rockabilly variety. Daily 7pm–late.

Turmschänke Karlsplatz 28 ☎ 03691 21 35 33, ⓦ turmschaenke-eisenach.de. The town's fine-dining address, acclaimed by Gault Milau and Michelin critics, with dishes that lean towards modern French and Mediterranean – grilled shrimp with strawberry gazpacho for example, or lamb with Hainich beans and feta cheese. The dining room in a medieval defence tower, however, is very traditional. Menus from €30. Mon–Sat 6pm–midnight.

Zucker + Zimt Markt 2 ☎ 03691 74 11 41, ⓦ zucker-zimt-eisenach.de. A Mediterranean café and restaurant with a summer terrace overlooking the action on the main square. The ingredients of the food – for example baked sweet potato with avocado cream – are often regional, organic or fair-trade. Mon–Fri 9am–11pm, Sat & Sun 10am–11pm.

Thuringian Forest

Much of Thuringia's acclaim as the green heart of Germany is due to the **THURINGIAN FOREST** (Thüringer Wald). Around two-thirds of the upland region of the state's southwest – 135km from Eisenach west to the A9 east, 35km north to south and 982m at its highest point – is thickly cloaked in pines interspersed with mixed forest or highland meadow, and irrigated by countless streams. Germans have celebrated its landscapes at least since Goethe rambled around **Ilmenau**, and its romantic villages with cottage workshops do little to dispel the illusion of an area that's a timewarp back a few decades. Indeed, the ambience is more of a draw than sights in the few towns: modest spa-town **Friedrichroda**, sleepy **Schmalkalden**, its Altstadt a fairy-tale of half-timbered buildings, or former courtly town **Meiningen**, repository of the area's high culture, such as it is.

With your own transport this is touring country, a place to potter around pretty villages. Without, getting around is best by the **Süd Thüringen Bahn** (ⓦ sued-thueringen-bahn.de), which loops from Eisenach to Erfurt via Meiningen, with a branch line to Schmalkaden. However, the region is superb to explore by foot and bike. With five or six days spare you could take to one of Germany's most famous long-distance paths, the **Rennsteig** (see box opposite), along the highlands' spine. At weekends, four "RennsteigShuttle" trains a day connect Erfurt and Ilmenau to Bahnhof Rennsteig in the middle of the forest, a good starting point for a hike. Regional tourism website ⓦ thueringer-wald.com is handy for planning if your German's up to it.

The Hainich National Park

Baumkronenpfad Daily: April–Oct 10am–7pm; Nov–March 10am–4pm • €8.50 • ⓦ nationalpark-hainich.de

Though most of its pine woods cloak the area south of Eisenach, the Thuringian

---

IF YOU GO DOWN TO THE WOODS: THE RENNSTEIG AND OTHER ACTIVITIES

Germany's most popular trail is the **Rennsteig** ridgeway (ⓦrennsteig.de) that slices west–east through the Thuringian Forest. Its 168km path along the region's uplands, from **Hörschel** near Eisenach to **Blankenstein** on the River Saale, was a messenger route in the Middle Ages, and in the nineteenth century acquired a cachet as a symbol of national unity because it both formed the border of, and ran through, patchwork of petty principalities. It still forms a border of sorts – Thuringians argue over whether the state's best sausages are produced north or south of it.

If fit, you could do "Der Runst", as the Rennsteig is colloquially known, in five days' **hiking**, stopping at villages overnight and dodging the wild boar that root in the woods. It's more enjoyable if you take six. Sections of it make good day-hikes – the route ascends over Grosser Inselberg near Friedrichroda – and the 30km and 15km at either end, with the greatest altitude differences, are favoured by cyclists on a parallel mountain-bike trail. Kompass's 1:50,000 *Rennsteig* map (no. 118) covers both routes and is available from tourist offices throughout the region. An alternative if cycling is to follow part of the north–south 300km **Werratal-Radweg** (ⓦwerratal.de) that tracks the Werra River west of Eisenach to Meiningen and beyond.

The area usually receives a good dump of snow in winter. The focus for **skiing** is a 2km piste on Grosser Inselberg. For ski rental and lessons go to Sport Hellmann at Lauchagrundstr. 13, Tabarz (☏036259 508 52, ⓦsport-hellmann.de). In the east Thuringian Forest, skiing is at Steinach at the Skiarena Silbersattel (ⓦsilbersattel.de). In summer, this renames itself **Bikepark** (May–Oct Sat 10.30am–5pm, Sun 11am–4pm; 4hr €15, day-card €18) and reinvents the pistes as downhill cycle trails for kamikaze mountain-bikers.

4

Forest's boundaries also incorporate the mixed **Hainich National Park** to the northeast. The main attraction of its 75-square-kilometre area of ancient beech forest is the **Baumkronenpfad**, Europe's first canopy-walk, which circles up to a 44m lookout. Access is on the C-road west of Bad Langensalza.

Friedrichroda

Notwithstanding the Goethe trail from Ilmenau (see p.271), **FRIEDRICHRODA** is the most accessible starting point for day-hikes in the Thuringian Forest. A popular resort in GDR days, when the monstrous *Berghotel* blighted a hill top, it has since returned to its incarnation of the late 1800s as a quiet spa resort cradled in wooded hills. You can fill up bottles with mineral spring water from a fountain pavilion on Marktstrasse. The **Thüringerwaldbahn** tram (day-ticket €9.10; ⓦwaldbahn-gotha.de) trundles from Gotha (see p.260) through the countryside to Friedrichroda twice an hour, continuing on to a couple of sights west of town: the Marienglashöhle and the Grosser Inselsberg.

Marienglashöhle

Daily: April–Oct 9am–5pm; Nov–March 9am–4pm • €6 • Thüringerwaldbahn tram from Gotha or Friedrichroda

Aside from natural cures, the time-honoured attraction of Friedrichroda is Europe's largest crystal cave, **Marienglashöhle**, 1.5km west of the centre. The showcave's name refers to the gypsum crystal harvested for glitter on statues of the Virgin.

Grosser Inselberg

Bus #42 Mon–Fri 10am, Sat & Sun 10.15am & 2.45pm, get off at Kleiner Inselsberg; return only Sat & Sun at 1pm • ⓦkvg-eisenach.de • Bus #856 Mon–Fri 11.32am & 4.42pm, Sat & Sun 11.32am, 1.32pm, 2.22pm & 5.32pm • ⓦbahn.de

The Thüringerwaldbahn terminates at **Tabarz**, a ski and walking base. From here you can board bus #42 to the **Grosser Inselsberg**. At 916m this is not the highest summit in the Thuringian Forest, and it's far from the most photogenic due to an ugly telecoms tower, but its sweeping panorama across wooded hills is unrivalled. From here you could hike along the Rennsteig ridgeway path (see box, p.267) east over the lesser summits of Trockenberg and Grosser Jagdberg to *Heuberghaus* (around 4km; 2hr) to hook up with bus #856 back to Friedrichroda station; double-check times before you set off.

ARRIVAL AND INFORMATION   FRIEDRICHRODA

By train Tram #4 (aka the Thüringerwaldbahn) runs every 30min from Gotha to central Friedrichroda, the Marienglashöhle and Tabarz (day-ticket €9.10; ⓦ waldbahn-gotha.de).

Tourist office Marktstr. 15 (Mon–Thurs 9am–5pm, Fri 9am–6pm, Sat 9am–noon; ☎ 03623 332 00; ⓦ friedrichroda.de). The office can provide maps and current timetables of the Inselberg-Express.

ACCOMMODATION AND EATING

Brauhaus Friedrichroda Bachstrasse 14 ☎ 03623 30 42 59, ⓦ brauhaus-friedrichroda.de. As traditional a house-brewery as you could ask for, with waitresses in traditional costume and regional platters such as game stew with *Klösse* dumplings plus the likes of salmon in lemon sauce. Choose from a traditional beer hall or a small garden. It also offers simple rooms. Daily 11am–2pm & 6pm–midnight. €52

Schmalkalden

Once you're past its underwhelming outskirts, **SCHMALKALDEN** is a picture-postcard Thuringian Forest classic with an Altstadt of jostling half-timbered buildings. It's hard to believe today, but the sleepy, small town played a central role in the Reformation. The Schmalkaldic League of Lutheran princes coalesced here as an independent power bloc that opposed the centralization of Catholic Emperor Charles V. Even if the League lost the battles of 1546–47, they ultimately won the war after Charles, weary from years of warfare and recognizing the intractable Protestant hard core within Central Europe, agreed to the Peace of Augsburg in 1555, thereby permitting German states freedom to choose their religion.

The Altmarkt

No history lessons are needed to appreciate **Altmarkt**, its colourful heart fronted as ever by the Gothic **Rathaus** (Mon–Fri 8.30am–4pm, Thurs till 6pm; free) in which the Schmalkaldic League plotted strategies. The fire of revolution had been sparked by the sermons of Martin Luther preached in 1537 in the adjacent **Stadtkirche St Georg**, built of blushing-pink sandstone and worth a look for the net of stellar vaulting thrown across its chancel. Death scythes down a young girl as a memento mori on its clock tower as the hour strikes.

Lutherhaus and around

Mohrengasse leads from Altmarkt via pretty Salzbrücke and Steingasse to Lutherplatz and **Lutherhaus**, the chunky sixteenth-century house in which the renegade preacher stayed – identifiable from its red-painted beams and a Baroque plaque bearing the white rose of the Reformation. Fellow firebrand Philipp Melanchthon stayed at Steingasse 11, today a chemist's.

The Martin-Luther-Weg

Lutherplatz represents the start of the **Martin-Luther-Weg**, marked by a green "L", a 17km trail that tracks Luther's footsteps on the day the Schmalkalden Articles laid down the gauntlet to Charles's Holy Roman Empire in 1537. It makes an enjoyable, easy five-hour trail that ascends meadows to a 742m high-point en route to the village of **Tambach-Dietharz**. Tradition demands walkers drink from the Lutherbrunnen (Luther Well) on the outskirts of the village. Bus #851 makes the return journey a couple of times a day; check times with the tourist office.

Schloss Wilhelmsburg

Schlossberg 9 • April–Oct daily 10am–6pm; Nov–March Tues–Sun 10am–4pm • €3.50 • ⓦ museumwilhelmsburg.de

Thirty years after the Peace of Augsburg deal, Hessen Landgrave Wilhelm IV began work on a courtyard hunting lodge and summer residence on the hill top above Lutherhaus. **Schloss Wilhelmsburg** impresses most as a perfectly preserved slice of the Renaissance, with its displays about the Hessen dynasty and the Schmalkalden Articles taking second billing. The **Riesensaal** state room in the east wing with a painted coffered ceiling and murals of the duke among Old Testament and mythological heroes exudes ducal swagger. The Schloss's highlight though, is the galleried **Schlosskirche**. Finished with snow-white stucco decoration, it is one of the first chapels to follow Luther's dictates to elevate the Word above religious eye-candy – the pulpit is strategically placed as a focus above the altar. The organ tucked away above is a pearl of the Renaissance, the oldest playable instrument in Central Europe, with a light flutey tone from its wooden pipes; it features in monthly concerts in summer.

A northeast tower screens a twenty-minute 3D film *Ritter der Tafelrunde*, which animates **murals** of the Arthurian legend discovered in the cellar of an Altstadt house. Before you go in check out the reproductions of the thirteenth-century murals – said to be the oldest secular murals in Central Europe – in a basement room accessed off the castle courtyard.

ARRIVAL AND INFORMATION   SCHMALKALDEN

By train Schmalkalden's Hauptbahnhof is a 10min walk west of the centre; coming by train from Erfurt requires a change at Zella-Mehlis.
Destinations Eisenach (hourly Mon–Fri, five daily Sat & Sun; 55min).

Tourist office Corner of Altmarkt at Mohrengasse 1a (April–Oct Mon–Fri 10am–6pm, Sat & Sun 10am–3pm; Nov–March Mon–Fri 10am–5pm, Sat 10am–1pm; ☏ 03683 40 31 82, ⓦ schmalkalden.de).

ACCOMMODATION

Patrizier Weidebrunner Gasse 9 ☏ 03683 60 45 14, ⓦ stadthotel-patrizier.de. Old-fashioned and all the more charming for it, this is a traditional country hotel in a half-timbered building. Personal service, flowery wallpaper and antique-styled furnishings, plus a good location in the heart of the Altstadt. **€89**

Pension Barbara Auer Gasse 5–7 ☏ 03683 60 08 27, ⓦ pensionbarbara.com. Two half-timbered houses that have been divided into four modernized apartments sleeping one to five people: a great location just off historic Altmarkt, and a good base from which to explore the region. **€54**

Meiningen

MEININGEN, 20km south of Schmalkalden, is a surprise in a region fond of half-timbering. There's a touch of aristocratic swagger to this small town huddled on the River Werra. It blossomed as a Residenzstadt of the dukes of Saxe-Meiningen, notably nineteenth-century culture-vulture Georg II. Under the tenure of this friend of Brahms, the town acquired fame Europe-wide for its theatre and orchestra. Enter from the north on boulevard Bernhard Strasse and you're greeted by the duke's city-sized **theatre**, whose massive portico acclaims his noble gift to "the people to befriend and elevate". Adjacent to the portico at Bernhardstr. 3 is the municipal gallery **Galerie Ada** (Wed–Sun 3–8pm; free), with exhibitions of modern and regional works, with the landscaped **Englischer Garten** behind.

Schloss Elisabethenburg

Schlossplatz 1 • Tues–Sun 10am–6pm • €4, combined ticket with Theater Museum €5.50 • ⓦ meiningermuseen.de

The heart of ducal culture is **Schloss Elisabethenburg** at the end of Bernhard Strasse. It's an edifice of the most austere Baroque, with a traditional U-shape closed by an odd round wing. Once past an ancestral gallery and a room of Thuringian religious art, a series of faintly shabby rooms hang second-division Old Masters and one premier-league work, a sexually charged encounter between Lot and his daughter by Caravaggio-inspired Spaniard Jusepe de Ribera. A Baroque tapestry of Alexander's triumphant entry into Babylon is another highlight. Displays on the second floor furnished in the revival style favoured by Georg II honour the town's musical tradition. Don't miss the lovely Biedermeier **café** (free) at the top, too.

Baumbachhaus

To the left of the Schloss on Burgstrasse, the **Baumbachhaus** (same times & ticket) houses a small display of literary figures associated with the court, among them Enlightenment dramatist and poet Friedrich Schiller, who sojourned in Meiningen during his tour of Thuringian courts.

Theater Museum

Schlossplatz 2 • Tours Tues–Sun 10am, noon, 2pm & 4pm • €3.50, combined ticket with Schloss €5.50 • ⓦ meiningermuseen.de

The former equestrian hall on the right side of the Schloss, in which Duke Georg II practised dressage, was the only space able to take the huge painted backcloths that star in the **Theater Museum**. The "theatre duke" tasked two artists to actualize the "lofty, magnificent images of nature… required by poetry" that he saw in his mind's-eye and they excelled themselves in those designed for productions of *Hamlet*.

The Premiumwanderweg

The best of the many footpaths that explore the adjacent Werra Valley is the **Premiumwanderweg**, which makes a 12km circuit from the Schloss via neo-Gothic hotel *Schloss Landsberg* (see below) and the ruins of a thirteenth-century fort, **Habichtsburg**, on a wooded hill top. It begins off Burgstrasse on the left-hand side of the castle and in theory is signposted throughout – check at the tourist office.

Dampflokwerk Meiningen

Am Flutgraben 2 • Tours in German at 10am on 1st and 3rd Sat of the month, July & Aug every Sat • €5 • ⓦ dampflokwerk.de

Western Europe's last steam locomotive works, **Dampflokwerk Meiningen**, lies a fifteen-minute walk north from the station. Locomotives and historical rail vehicles from across Europe are brought here for maintenance and repairs. Tours start off with a short film, and pass through the locomotive hall, heating house and boiler shop before ending with a coal-grilled *Bratwurst*. You're left relatively (and un-Germanly) free to wander around the huge hall with its half-dissembled steam trains and wagons. The annual Steam Locomotive Days take place here in the first weekend of September.

ARRIVAL AND INFORMATION
MEININGEN

By train and bus The Bahnhof is at the back of the Englischer Garten, north of the centre.
Destinations Eisenach (hourly; 1hr); Erfurt (every 2hr; 1hr 35min).

Tourist office Markt 14, behind the church (Mon–Fri 10am–6pm, Sat 10am–3pm, Sun 10am–3pm; Oct–April closed Sun; ☎ 03693 446 50, ⓦ meiningen.de /tourismus).

ACCOMMODATION AND EATING

Altes Knasthaus Fronveste An der Oberen Mauer 1–3 ☎ 03693 881 90, ⓦ meininger-hotels-mit-flair.de. On the west of the Altstadt beyond the Markt in a modernized former prison, *Altes Knasthaus Fronveste* is Meiningen's modest design hotel, styled in a sort of relaxed minimalism: think pine furnishings and crisp white walls. **€80**
Sächsischer Hof Georgstr. 1 ☎ 03693 45 70,

ⓦ saechsischerhof.com. Brahms was a fan of what remains the finest hotel in the Thuringian Forest: elegant Biedermeier-style furnishings and spacious dimensions reflect its early 1800s vintage as a former coaching inn. There are two excellent restaurants: the *Kutscherstube* prepares high-quality regional home-cooking in a traditional-styled inn; *Die Posthalterei* is Meiningen's relaxed fine-dining venue, with Mediterranean and Asian accents to its modern German cuisine. *Kutscherstube* daily 11am–2pm & 5pm–midnight; *Die Posthalterei* Wed–Sat 5.30pm–midnight. **€92**

Schloss Landsberg ☎03693 881 90, ⓦmeininger-hotels-mit-flair.de. This neo-Gothic pile was erected after a Meiningen duke visited his sister, Princess Adelheid, at Windsor Castle. Standard rooms don't quite live up to the promise, but this is still the place for baronial romance. **€140**

Schlundhaus Schlundgasse 4 ☎03693 813 838, ⓦmeininger-hotels-mit-flair.de. *Klösse* potato dumplings are the house special of this traditional inn located in a side street off the Markt – it claims a former chef invented the Thuringian side-dish. Rooms above the restaurant are styled in a modern take on traditional country style: laminate flooring and colour-wash furniture. Restaurant Mon–Thurs 11.30am–2pm & 5.30–10pm, Fri & Sat 11.30am–10.30pm, Sun 11.30am–9.30pm. **€88**

ENTERTAINMENT

Meiningen Theater Bernhardstr. 5 ☎03693 45 12 22, ⓦdas-meininger-theater.de. Heavyweights of theatre, opera and ballet plus classical music concerts in a beautiful Neoclassical hall.

Ilmenau

"I was always happy to spend time here," wrote Goethe of **ILMENAU**, a somnambulant university town on the River Ilm. Ilmenau returns the complement with a museum of daily life as Goethe knew it in the Baroque **Amtshaus** on the main square (Tues–Sun 10am–5pm; €3). You can't miss it – a celebrated bronze monument of Goethe sits on a bench outside.

Goethewanderweg

Notwithstanding the charms of the pastel-tinted core, the main reason to visit Ilmenau is to tread "**auf Goethes Spurren**" (in Goethe's footsteps) on the **Goethewanderweg** day-hike. The 20km trail's appeal is the variety of scenery en route – you'll need six to eight hours to complete it and come mentally prepared for the occasional stiff uphill section.

The trail begins on the Markt at the **Amtshaus** with a primer on Goethe's activities in the area as a court official of Weimar-based duke Carl August. From here a trail of signposts directs you west via the peaks of Schwalbenstein – inspired by the view, Goethe knocked off the fourth act of his reworking of Greek tragedy *Iphigenie in Tauris* in a day on its summit – and Emmasteinfelsen to Manebach village. From here it's a long, steady ascent up the Kickelhahn (861m), also reached on a short cut by road south of Ilmenau. At its summit are a faux-watchtower lookout and a replica of the hut in which Goethe penned his celebrated *Wayfarer's Night Song*, inscribed in sixteen languages within. The ubiquitous hilltop restaurant is a good spot to pause for lunch. Ten minutes along the trail are displays on Goethe's scientific work in former hunting-lodge **Jagdhaus Gabelbach** (Tues–Sun: April–Oct 10am–5pm; Nov–March 10am–4pm; €3), then it's an easy romp 5km south to the trail terminus at Stützerbach village. Should you wish to return by bus from Stützerbach take #300 – double-check timetables first at the Ilmenau tourist office.

ARRIVAL AND INFORMATION   ILMENAU

By train Ilmenau is on a branch line from Erfurt, or reached from Meiningen with a change at Arnstadt.

Tourist office Amtshaus Markt 1 (Mon–Fri 9am–6pm, Sat & Sun 10am–5pm; ☎03677 60 03 00, ⓦilmenau.de).

ACCOMMODATION

Jugendherberge Ilmenau Am Stollen 49 ☎03677 88 46 81, ⓦilmenau.jugendherberge.de; tram #A, #B or #C from the train station to "Jugendherberge". The youth hostel is in a modern block 2km southeast of the centre and has two- and four-bed rooms, all of which are en suite. Dorms **€23**, doubles **€46**

Lindenhof Lindenstr. 3 ☎03677 680 00, ⓦhotel-lindenhof.de. A central, comfortable Altstadt hotel whose facilities, such as a sauna, make it ideal to recuperate after a hard day's walk. It has classic-modern rooms and a decent restaurant with a terrace for a slap-up post-walk dinner. **€100**

4

Mühlhausen

Greatness nipped in the bud characterizes **MÜHLHAUSEN**. A former medieval free imperial city visited by kings and emperors, it is now bypassed by tourists on a pilgrimage to the Eisenach–Erfurt–Weimar holy trinity, although a lack of visitors only adds to the atmosphere of the Altstadt, an oval maze of cobbled alleys ringed by one of the few remaining medieval city walls in Germany.

The town walls and the Historische Wehranlage

Historische Wehranlage April–Oct Tues–Sun 10am–5pm • €3 • ⓦ muehlhaeuser-museen.de

There's no finer introduction to Mühlhausen than the medieval **town walls** which wrap a 3km belt around the town, studded intermittently with watchtowers. A 375m section of the ramparts is open at the west end of the Altstadt as the **Historische Wehranlage**, accessed from the Inneres Frauentor, a former gateway that commanded the principal route into the town, and whose bastions house dry displays of town history.

The Marienkirche

Bei der Marienkirche • Tues–Sun 10am–5pm • €3 • ⓦ muehlhaeuser-museen.de

Holzstrasse curls away from the Inneres Frauentor to the **Marienkirche**, in which Thomas Müntzer (see box below) delivered his final sermon beneath the rainbow banner of his "Eternal League of God". The church houses a memorial to its former firebrand as the **Müntzergedenkstätte** – pick up English notes as you enter – although its displays are less impressive than the five-nave hall church itself, the second-largest in Thuringia after Erfurt's Dom and crowned by a soaring nineteenth-century spire. Look, too, at the southern portal near the entrance, where statues of late fourteenth-century Emperor Karl IV, his wife, and a lord and lady of court peer over the balustrade at a street used for processions during Mühlhausen's imperial Diets.

The Rathaus

Ratsstr. 20 • Mon–Thurs 10am–4pm, Fri 10am–1pm; tours in German Mon–Fri 11am • Free; tours €2.50

Ratsstrasse, at the far end of the Marienkirche, leads to the **Rathaus**. Added to over the centuries, so that it now straddles the street, the complex has as its core the Grosse Ratsstube, a barrel-vaulted, muralled council chamber in which Thomas Müntzer ruled the town during the three-month tenure of his revolutionary league. Its typically oversized painting from the GDR era depicts him in full oratorical flight.

THOMAS MÜNTZER OF MÜHLHAUSEN

Its place in history books is as the hotbed of the Peasants' War of 1525, sparked by its renegade priest **Thomas Müntzer**. A social radical who despised Lutheran doctrine with the same passion as Catholicism, he led eight thousand farmers into battle against the princes at Frankenhausen with the rallying cry that God was on their side. Apparently not. Utterly defeated then tortured, Müntzer was decapitated in his home town, something which saw him held up as a proto-Marxist hero by GDR authorities and placed on the 5 Mark note. They conveniently overlooked the fact that Müntzer interpreted the defeat as God's judgement on an unworthy populace. Mühlhausen may have quietly dropped the "Thomas-Müntzer-Stadt" label, but its early hero remains the star.

The Bauernkriegsmuseum

Kornmarkt • Tues–Sun 10am–5pm • €5 • ⓦ muehlhaeuser-museen.de

Continue south from the Rathaus and you emerge at pretty Kornmarkt and the **Kornmarktkirche** housing the **Bauernkriegsmuseum**, which fleshes out the tale of Thomas Müntzer with a narrative of the ill-fated Peasants' War; a large model of the battlefield with a running commentary of events is all good fun. Among a small gallery of twentieth-century artwork inspired by the war, are four characteristically dark works by Expressionist Käthe Kollwitz.

Untermarkt

Any of the alleys south from Kornmarkt will take you to spacious **Untermarkt** and the **Divi-Blasii-Kirche**, an early Gothic church founded by the Teutonic Order and famous as the office of Johann Sebastian Bach during his tenure as organist in 1709, when he was a precocious 24-year-old.

Off the corner of Untermarkt, behind the church at Kristanplatz 7, the **Kulturhistorisches Museum** (Tues–Sun 10am–5pm; €2; ⓦ muehlhaeuser-museen .de) has silver and Biedermeier furniture plus exhibitions on regional art and other themes.

ARRIVAL AND INFORMATION   MÜHLHAUSEN

By train The Bahnhof is 400m east of the Altstadt, which is reached by Karl-Marx-Strasse.

Destinations Erfurt (hourly; 1hr); Gotha (every 2hr; 20min).

Tourist office Ratsstr. 20, opposite the Rathaus (Mon–Fri 9am–5pm, Sat & Sun 10am–4pm; Nov–April Mon–Fri 9am–5pm, Sat 10am–2pm; ☏03601 40 47 70, ⓦ muehlhausen.de).

ACCOMMODATION AND EATING

DJH Mühlhausen Auf dem Tonberg 1 ☏03601 81 33 18, ⓦdjh-thueringen.de; bus #5 or #6 to "Blobach" from where it's a 500m walk. This youth hostel, 2km northwest of the centre, is typical of the breed, with modern(ish) dorms of up to four beds with a washbasin; bathrooms are shared. Often block-booked by school and sports groups. Dorms **€20.50**, doubles **€41**

Mühlhäuser Hof Steinweg 65 ☏03601 88 86 70, ⓦmuehlhaeuser-hof.de. The most modern rooms in the Altstadt are those in this *hotel garni* a short walk from the centre – it provides rather snug en-suite rooms with modern blonde-wood and accent walls. It also has a popular Italian restaurant, *Il Piano*, and a bar, *Cubano*. Restaurant daily 11.30am–2.30pm & 5.30–10pm; bar daily 7pm–late. **€89**

Wirtshaus Antonius Mühle Am Frauentor 7 ☏03601 40 38 50, ⓦantoniusmuehle.de. The finest food in the Altstadt is prepared in this historic garden mill, which has been modernized without sacrificing character, and whose house special is an *elle* (a 58cm medieval cloth measurement) of *Bratwurst* – good luck. Tues–Fri 5.30pm–midnight, Sat & Sun 11.30am–2pm & 5.30pm–midnight.

Zum Löwen Felchtaer Str. 3 ☏03601 47 10, ⓦbrauhaus-zum-loewen.de. Traditional country-style place in the heart of the Altstadt with bright and modern(ish) yet dated accommodation. Reception is in the half-timbered microbrewery restaurant, which rustles up regional fare. Restaurant daily 7am–1am. **€89**

The Kyffhäuser

Thuringia heaps up unexpectedly in its northern reaches as the **Kyffhäuser**. While it requires an optimist to describe these wooded sandstone uplands as mountains – no peak in the sixty-square-kilometre extension of the Harz range is above 480m – their low-lying nature and lack of development make for pleasant walking country. The range also holds a special place in the nation's psyche as the resting place of **Emperor Frederick Barbarossa**. Possibly. Fact – or at least historical chronicles – record that the mighty twelfth-century German king and Holy Roman Emperor challenged papal authority to establish German predominance in Western Europe before he drowned in the Holy Land in 1190. Legend, however, counters that "Red Beard" slumbers deep within a Kyffhäuser mountain and will one day awaken to lead the united German people to victory against their enemies. It is, as the marketing board never tires of saying, the land where Barbarossa dreams. In more recent history Thomas Müntzer's peasants' revolution (see box, p.272) was swatted aside on the flanks of the Kyffhäuser in 1525.

Bad Frankenhausen and around

The most convenient base to ascend into the range is well-aired little spa town, **BAD FRANKENHAUSEN**. It's at its best on main square Anger, though the leaning tower of the **Oberkirche** – 4.22m off vertical – to the east via Frauenweg is one for the photo album.

The Panorama Museum

Am Schlachtberg 9 • Tues–Sun: April–Oct 10am–6pm; Nov–March 10am–5pm; July & Aug also Mon 1–6pm • €5 • ⓦ panorama-museum.de

A kilometre uphill from the town a large rotunda crowns the Schlachtberg (Battle Hill) with the **Panorama Museum**. Thomas Müntzer's peasants' war army, the first organized people's rebellion in Germany, was crushed here, making the hill a site of secular martyrdom for GDR authorities. In 1989 they unveiled what is claimed as the largest painting in the world – 123m by 14m – titled *The Early People's Revolution in Germany* to celebrate the regime's fortieth birthday – one of its swan-song acts as it turned out. What could have been another piece of clunking GDR propaganda is salvaged by artist Werner Tübke, the University of Leipzig professor's original plan for a battle-scene morphed into a more ambitious project inspired by the allegorical works of medieval masters Peter Bruegel the Elder and Hieronymus Bosch. Audio-guides (available in English) sift through the layers of secular and sacred symbolism in Tübke's epic, five years in the making and whose cast of thousands spans from the fifteenth century to his age. Critics hated it, of course, and derided its artistry and politics alike after the *Wende*. No quibbles with its visual impact, though.

Kyffhäuser-Denkmal

13km north of Bad Frankenhausen • Daily: April–Oct 9.30am–6pm; Nov–March 10am–5pm • €6 • ⓦ kyffhaeuser-denkmal.de • VGS bus #494 from Bad Frankenhausen Busbahnhof, southeast of the centre on Esperstedter Strasse, runs to the Kyffhäuser-Denkmal at weekends (mid-April to Oct 4 daily; ⓦ vgs-suedharzlinie.de), but only on demand; call ☎ 0391 536 31 80 2hr in advance

From the Panorama Museum you can continue uphill on the Kyffhäuserweg trail (17km; 4–5hr), which ascends via Rathsfeld and Tilleda to the **Kyffhäuser-Denkmal**, jutting above the trees on the hills' brow at 457m. A fabulously absurd piece of imperial pomp, it was unveiled in 1896 as a war veterans' memorial to Wilhelm I who had died a decade previously. The father-figure of Germany's Second Reich, Wilhelm quashed rival fiefdoms to forge a united nation, and in doing so inherited the mantle of Frederick Barbarossa. The monstrous equestrian statue of Wilhelm rides out between war god Thor and History with a pen and laurel wreath, while Barbarossa awakens on his throne beneath like a spare prop from *Lord of the Rings*. Small wonder Hitler paid several visits in the hope the stardust would rub off. Moscow rejected local apparatchiks' offer to dynamite the symbol after the war on the grounds that Germany had to learn from its history. There's a small museum of the memorial within the hollow core of the walloping monument and superb views of the Kyffhäuser from the crown 81m up.

Much of the memorial's pink stone was mined from the **Reichsburg** behind, a fortification that Barbarossa had bolstered into the stronghold of his Hohenstaufen empire. Upper defence the Oberburg has vanished except for a clumsily patched-up tower and what is claimed as the world's deepest well (176m), leaving the Unterburg (free) beneath the monument as the only reference of former scale. It's a lovely picnic spot, too: Goethe and Saxe-Weimar duke Carl August were ticked off by a forest warden for the mess theirs created – you have been warned.

ARRIVAL AND INFORMATION   BAD FRANKENHAUSEN

By train Bad Frankenhausen's Bahnhof lies south of the Altstadt. It's on a branch line, so requires a change at Sömmerda from Erfurt.

Tourist office Anger 14 (April–Oct Mon–Fri 9.30am–6pm, Sat 9.30am–12.30pm, Sun 9.30–11.30am;

Nov–March Mon–Fri 10am–5pm, Sat 10am–noon; ☎034671 717 16, ⓦkyffhaeuser-tourismus.de). The office supplies sketch maps of walks, plus details of a three-day 37km circuit of the Kyffhäuser; it can also confirm the Kyffhäuser bus for you.

ACCOMMODATION AND EATING

Alte Hämmelei Bornstr. 33 ☎034671 51 20, ⓦalte-haemmelei.de. Hotel rooms plus a hostel in the eaves, where old-fashioned decor adds to the charm: think checked fabrics and pine furnishings. The sausage house beneath serves cheap regional dishes in a historic dining room or small rear beer garden. It is located a few blocks east of the Markt. Restaurant daily 5–11.30pm & Fri–

Sun 11am–3pm. Dorms €25, doubles €64

Thüringer Hof Anger 15 ☎034671 510 10, ⓦthueringer-hof.com. Solid regional food has been served at *Thüringer Hof* since the sixteenth century. It's just north of the Markt, and there's a nice front terrace in summer. Daily 11am–10pm.

4

Northern Bavaria: Franconia

TREPPENHAUS, THE RESIDENZ, WÜRZBURG

5

Northern Bavaria: Franconia

Entering Franconia (Franken) from the north or west can be a disorientating experience for anyone expecting Alps, blue-and-white flags and *Weisswurst* – Bavaria's northernmost region is not at all the Bavaria of popular cliché. Red and white are the colours of Franconia, the sausage of choice is *Bratwurst* and the unspoilt wooded uplands which cover much of the region rarely rise to mountainous heights, or feature on the itineraries of foreign tourists. In many respects, it has more in common with Thuringia or Hesse than it does with the "real" Bavaria to the south.

Franconia isn't historically Bavarian at all. It owes its name to the Frankish tribes whose territory it originally was, and from the Middle Ages until the early nineteenth century it was highly fragmented. In Lower Franconia and Bamberg, ecclesiastical rule predominated, and the archbishops of Mainz in Aschaffenburg and the prince-bishops of Würzburg and Bamberg ruled their modest fiefdoms in some style, leaving behind the architectural splendour to prove it. Protestantism took root in the north and east, specifically in Hohenzollern-ruled Brandenburg-Bayreuth and Wettin-ruled Saxe-Coburg and Gotha, whose territories spanned the boundary between Franconia and Thuringia and whose judicious marriage policy ensured its familial links included many of the royal houses of Europe. Outshining all – until its decline at the end of the sixteenth century – was the free imperial city of Nuremberg, seat of the Holy Roman Empire's imperial Diet and one of Europe's great medieval manufacturing and trading centres. Free, too, were the little city-states of Rothenburg ob der Tauber and Dinkelsbühl, though political diversity ended when Napoleon incorporated Franconia into the newly upgraded Kingdom of Bavaria – previously a mere duchy – in 1806.

Yet it remains a fantastically diverse place to visit. In **Oberfranken** (Upper Franconia), the Protestant religion and beer predominate. Here, the cultural and historical associations are with **Wagner** in **Bayreuth** and with **Luther** and the British royal family in **Coburg**; everywhere there's a sense of the proximity of the lands of central Germany to the north. **Bamberg** remains a splendid exception, a beer town through and through, but opulently Catholic in an otherwise Lutheran region, and one of Germany's most beautiful cities.

Unterfranken (Lower Franconia), centred on **Würzburg**, is wine-growing country, with a feel of the sunny south; it is also the starting point for the **Romantic Road**, a tourist route linking many of Bavaria's most beautiful (if scarcely undiscovered) towns, including the perfectly preserved medieval gems of **Rothenburg ob der Tauber** and **Dinkelsbühl**, both in **Mittelfranken** (Middle Franconia). Also in Mittelfranken is **Nuremberg**, unmissable for its fascinating and occasionally uneasy blend of medieval splendour and Nazi bombast.

Highlights

❶ Nuremberg Franconia's greatest city is a reminder of the triumphs and tragedies of German history, set against a splendid medieval backdrop. **See p.280**

❷ Opera in Bayreuth Plan years in advance if you want to experience Wagner at the world-famous Festspiele. **See p.295**

❸ Vierzehnheiligen church This fabulous place of pilgrimage is a vision of heaven, if heaven's designers were masters of the Rococo. **See p.301**

❹ Bamberg Lost-in-time beauty and a distinctive beer culture make Bamberg a Franconian must-see. **See p.302**

❺ The Residenz, Würzburg Balthasar Neumann's Baroque masterpiece is as magnificent a palace as any in Europe. **See p.311**

❻ The walled towns of the Romantic Road Take a trip back in time to the magical medieval towns of Rothenburg ob der Tauber, Dinkelsbühl and Nördlingen. **See p.318, p.323 & p.325**

❼ Cycling in the Taubertal Slow right down to get the most out of this gentle wine-growing country at the start of the Romantic Road. **See p.322**

HIGHLIGHTS ARE MARKED ON THE MAP ON P.280

5

Though the towns and cities are the major attractions, Franconia's wooded hills and national parks offer tempting opportunities to escape the crowds.

While long-distance **hiking** and **cycle** trails cross the region, the bigger cities have fast main-line **rail** connections and many smaller towns still have a rail link – though the trains serving them can be slow.

Nuremberg (Nürnberg)

Nowhere in Germany gives such a powerful impression of the highs and lows of German history as the former free imperial city of **NUREMBERG**. Despite terrible destruction during World War II, much of the city remains convincingly medieval in appearance, and when touring the forbidding **Kaiserburg** or exploring surviving lanes of half-timbered houses in the city's **Altstadt**, which is still encircled by its medieval city walls, it's easy to imagine how the Nuremberg of Albrecht Dürer, Veit Stoss or the Meistersingers might have looked. Not surprisingly the museums – from the intimate **Albrecht-Dürer-Haus** to the encyclopedic **Germanisches Nationalmuseum** – are compelling.

The city has a bewildering array of **festivals** throughout the year, including Classic Open Air – a series of alfresco classical concerts by the city's two orchestras at the Luitpoldhain park in July and August – and the somewhat Oktoberfest-like Altstadtfest in September.

Brief history

From 1050 to 1571 – when the custom died out – Nuremberg was the nearest thing the **Holy Roman Empire** had to a capital, for it was here that newly chosen emperors

HIGHLIGHTS

① Nuremberg
② Opera in Bayreuth
③ Vierzehnheiligen church
④ Bamberg
⑤ The Residenz, Würzburg
⑥ The walled towns of the Romantic Road
⑦ Cycling in the Taubertal

NORTHERN BAVARIA: FRANCONIA

held their imperial Diet or Reichstag. At the same time, commercial acumen and artisan skills – above all in metalworking – made the city one of the wealthiest and most important **trading centres** in Europe, despite the poverty of its rural hinterland and the lack of a navigable river. And then – happily for today's visitors – it fell into a long decline, which spared its medieval monuments from ruinous "improvement" or replacement.

As for a historical low point, what's remarkable is how much is still recognizable from Leni Riefenstahl's hypnotic film images of the 1930s Nazi party rallies, not least at the **Zeppelintribüne** where Hitler addressed the massed, uniformed crowds. The dictator purloined the medieval credentials of this most German of all German cities in order to lend credibility to his regime; as a consequence no other city is more closely associated with the Nazi movement – certainly not Munich, where it was actually born.

Nuremberg today

The introduction of driverless trains on the Nuremberg U-Bahn in 2008 prompted the quip that things run better without a Führer – *Führer* also being the German for driver – but the city of the Nuremberg rallies, Nuremberg laws and postwar Nuremberg trials can never be entirely rid of the Nazi association. It's greatly to the city's credit that it handles this sensitive legacy with such honesty, and a visit to one or more of Nuremberg's Nazi monuments south and west of the city is an essential counterpoint to the Altstadt's medieval glories. Away from the centre much of Nuremberg is surprisingly industrial and working class, which helps make it a rare stronghold of the left-of-centre SPD party in conservative Bavaria.

Hauptmarkt and around

It was the Bohemian king and Holy Roman Emperor Charles IV who gave Nuremberg's city fathers permission to expel the inhabitants of its Jewish ghetto in 1349 in order to establish a market. His decision unleashed a pogrom in which at least 562 Jews were burnt to death. For all its gory origins, **Hauptmarkt** remains the focus of the Altstadt and the scene of the world-famous annual **Christkindlesmarkt** or Christmas market. Most of the buildings fringing the square are postwar, but reconstruction from wartime damage was tactful and a few key monuments survive.

Schöner Brunnen

In the northwest corner of the Hauptmarkt stands a multicoloured nineteenth-century copy of the aptly named **Schöner Brunnen**, a flamboyant Gothic skyrocket of a fountain, erected at the start of the twentieth century to replace the weathered fourteenth-century original, the remains of which are in the Germanisches Nationalmuseum (see p.287). The forty figures on it depict Moses, the four Apostles and the seven electors of the Holy Roman Empire, among others.

CHRISTKINDLESMARKT

Nuremberg's most famous annual event is the **Christkindlesmarkt** (Ⓦchristkindlesmarkt .de), perhaps the world's most famous Christmas market, which animates the Hauptmarkt from the end of November until Christmas Eve, with 180 wooden stalls selling everything from *Lebkuchen* to Christmas decorations and traditional wooden toys. The market dates back to the sixteenth century and its history mirrors that of Nuremberg itself, having gradually dwindled in importance from the early years of the twentieth century until the Nazis returned it to the centre of the city they described as the "Reich's treasure chest". Despite the Altstadt's destruction in World War II, the market was re-established as early as 1948.

5

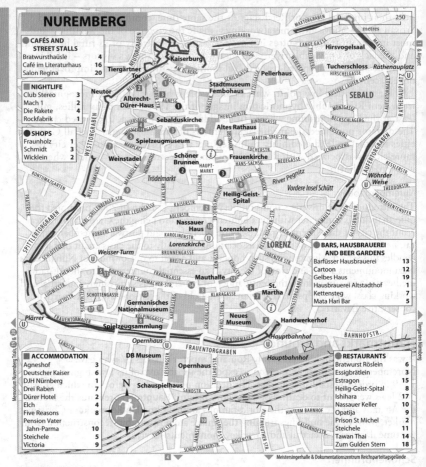

NUREMBERG

● **CAFÉS AND STREET STALLS**
Bratwursthäusle 4
Café im Literaturhaus 16
Salon Regina 20

■ **NIGHTLIFE**
Club Stereo 3
Mach 1 2
Die Rakete 4
Rockfabrik 1

● **SHOPS**
Fraunholz 1
Schmidt 3
Wicklein 2

■ **ACCOMMODATION**
Agneshof 3
Deutscher Kaiser 6
DJH Nürnberg 1
Drei Raben 7
Dürer Hotel 2
Elch 4
Five Reasons 8
Pension Vater
Jahn-Parma 10
Steichele 5
Victoria 9

■ **BARS, HAUSBRAUEREI AND BEER GARDENS**
Barfüsser Hausbrauerei 13
Cartoon 12
Gelbes Haus 19
Hausbrauerei Altstadthof 1
Kettensteg 7
Mata Hari Bar 5

■ **RESTAURANTS**
Bratwurst Röslein 6
Essigbrätlein 3
Estragon 15
Heilig-Geist-Spital 8
Ishihara 17
Nassauer Keller 10
Opatija 9
Prison St Michel 2
Steichele 11
Tawan Thai 14
Zum Gulden Stern 18

The Frauenkirche

Hauptmarkt 14 • Mon & Thurs 8am–6pm, Tues & Fri 9am–6pm, Wed 8am–7pm, Sat 9.30am–6.30pm, Sun 12.30–7pm • Free • ⓦ frauenkirche-nuernberg.de

Presiding over Hauptmarkt on its eastern side is the **Frauenkirche**, the rather stubby Gothic church which Charles IV decreed should be built on the site of the destroyed synagogue and dedicated to the Virgin Mary. The result – the work of Peter Parler, the architect of Prague's St Vitus cathedral – was the first Gothic hall church in Franconia. In World War II, the church was intended to serve as the storage place for the imperial crown jewels and its holy relics, but something – probably security concerns – led to the plans being altered, and they were taken instead to Karlstein castle near Prague. The Frauenkirche was reduced to a shell by World War II bombs, but restoration was deft, and the place retains a feeling of antiquity along with fragments of the *Kaiserfenster*, or Emperor's Window, the oldest stained glass in the city. Foremost among the Frauenkirche's various treasures – which survived the hail of bombs by being stored underground – is the expressive *Tucher Altar*, the city's greatest pre-Dürer work of art.

On the west front of the church, a Glockenspiel dating from 1509 re-enacts Charles's **Golden Bull** decree of 1536, which formalized the status of the seven electors who would choose an emperor, and enshrined in statute the role of the Kaiserburg (see p.284) as the venue for the imperial Diet.

Altes Rathaus

Lochgefängnisse guided tours March–Oct & during Christkindlesmarkt daily 10am–4.30pm; Nov Mon–Fri 10am–4.30pm; Jan & Feb by appointment only • €3.50

North from Hauptmarkt, Burgstrasse climbs towards the Kaiserburg, with the steep roofs of the fifteenth-century **Kaiserstallung** – built as a grain warehouse but used during imperial Diets as a stable – looming over it. The right-hand side of Burgstrasse is dominated by the splendid Renaissance facade of the **Altes Rathaus**, built between 1616 and 1622 by Jakob Wolff the Younger in the style of an Italian palazzo. Splendid as it is, it screens much older parts of the building, including the **Historischer Rathaussaal** (1332–40), rebuilt after wartime destruction, which was the setting in 1649 for the peace banquet that celebrated the end of the Thirty Years' War.

Little of the Rathaus is open to general view, but you can visit the creepy **Lochgefängnisse**, a medieval jail complex and torture chamber.

The Sebalduskirche

Albrecht-Dürer-Platz 1 • Daily: Jan–March 9.30am–4pm; April, May & mid-Sept to Dec 9.30am–6pm; June to mid-Sept 9.30am–8pm • Free • **Ⓦ** sebalduskirche.de

Opposite the Rathaus rises the twin-spired **Sebalduskirche**, the city's oldest parish church. It dates from the early thirteenth century and has been Protestant since 1525. Unusually large and magnificent for a mere parish church, its style is transitional between Romanesque and Gothic, and the interior has a rich array of artistic treasures. The most eye-catching is the tomb of **St Sebald**, in which the casket of the city's patron saint is sheltered by an incredibly delicate Gothic canopy, the work of Peter Vischer the Elder and his sons, who laboured from 1508 to 1519 to complete it. In the east choir there is a Crucifixion group by **Veit Stoss**, the city's most celebrated sculptor. The figures of Mary and St John were created in 1507–08 for the Frauenkirche. Photo plaques in the east choir show the extent of war damage to the church, along with a **Cross of Nails** from Coventry Cathedral.

The Fembohaus: Stadtmuseum

Burgstr. 15 • Tues–Fri 10am–5pm, Sat & Sun 10am–6pm; also Mon 10am–5pm during Christkindlesmarkt • €5 including audio-guide • **Ⓦ** museen.nuernberg.de

The best surviving Renaissance house in the city is the **Fembohaus**, further up Burgstrasse, which houses the **Stadtmuseum**. Take the lift to the top of the house for the **Tönendes Stadtmodell**, an audiovisual presentation and large-scale model representing the Altstadt in 1939, on the eve of its destruction. The museum's displays on Nuremberg's trading and artistic prowess are all the more compelling for being accommodated in this splendid house, built for the Dutch trader Philipp van Orl in 1591–96. The Baroque vestibule on the second floor has a wonderful stucco ceiling from 1674 by Carlo Moretti Brentano, the Italian who was also responsible for the stuccowork in Munich's Theatinerkirche.

The Stadtmuseum incorporates the richly decorated **Schönes Zimmer** (Beautiful Room) which came from the **Pellerhaus**, a magnificent Renaissance house built for Martin Peller (1559–1629), the city's richest merchant in his day. The house was largely destroyed during World War II, but the Stadtmuseum has a model, and you can see what survives on **Egidienplatz** east of Burgstrasse; bizarrely, the remains of the Renaissance courtyard were incorporated into the 1950s-style Stadtbibliothek, though a more thorough restoration is slowly progressing.

5

The Museum Tucherschloss

Hirschelgasse 9–11 • Guided tours Mon 10am–3pm, Thurs 1–5pm & Sun 10am–5pm • €5 • ⓦ museen.nuernberg.de

The northeastern corner of the Altstadt is the part of town that least resembles its pre-bombing self, and there's a lot of soulless postwar development. One exception to the dreary rule is the **Museum Tucherschloss**, in the summer residence of the patrician Tucher family, built between 1533 and 1544 in an eclectic style blending Gothic, Italian Renaissance and French influences. Its restored interiors reflect the lifestyle of a rich merchant family of the period, and the exhibits include a Renaissance double goblet by Nuremberg silversmith **Wenzel Jamnitzer**. In the garden you can visit the **Hirsvogelsaal**, a splendid Renaissance hall which dates from 1534 and originally formed part of the now-destroyed Hirsvogel mansion.

The Kaiserburg

Daily: April–Sept 9am–6pm; Oct–March 10am–4pm; Tiefer Brunner guided tours run every 30min 9.30am–5.30pm • Combined ticket Palas, museum, Tiefer Brunnen & Sinwellturm €7; Palas & museum €5.50; Sinwellturm & Tiefer Brunnen €3.50; audio-guide €2 • ⓦ kaiserburg-nuernberg.de

Simultaneously medieval Germany's parliament and its treasure chest, the **Kaiserburg** lords it over the rooftops of the northern Altstadt. The approach up Burgstrasse takes you past the Kaiserstallung and left past the **Sinwellturm** into the Ausserer Burghof; the **museum** and **Palas** are grouped around the Innerer Burghof beyond. Spared the attentions of Renaissance or Baroque builders who might have prettified or domesticated it, the Kaiserburg is a tough-looking fortress, every inch the medieval strongroom. It grew over the centuries from the original eleventh-century castle erected by the Frankish Salian kings; of their complex, only the **Fünfeckturm** on the west side of the Kaiserstallung survives.

The Palas and the museum

Though the **Palas** represents the Kaiserburg at its most domestic, its staterooms lack any real warmth, for it was never actually a private home, and never at any stage possessed its own furniture. Rather, it was a sort of medieval congress centre, whose rooms were only furnished – with items loaned by the patrician families of the city – when they were in use. Highlight of the Palas is undoubtedly the Romanesque **Doppelkapelle** of 1180, whose double-height design is deeply symbolic of the social hierarchy of the day, with the emperor at eye level with Christ, lording it physically over his fellow monarchs in the upper chapel, and with lesser fry relegated to the crypt-like lower level. The emperor's balcony is decorated with the Habsburg double eagle.

Admittance to the Palas also allows entry to the **museum**, whose armoury displays and models of the fortress as it was in 1100 and 1300 will pass the time if you're waiting for one of the regular guided tours of the Tiefer Brunnen.

The Tiefer Brunnen and Sinwellturm

The unassuming half-timbered building that houses the **Tiefer Brunnen**, the castle's 47m well, can only be visited as part of a guided tour (every 30min 9.30am–5.30pm). Its very existence was a state secret lest it be tainted by throwing an animal carcass down the shaft. Tour leaders demonstrate its impressive depth by lowering a tray of candles to the bottom and by dropping a carafe of water into it and asking you to count the seconds until the splash – it takes around five seconds. Your ticket is also valid for an ascent of the circular **Sinwellturm**, worth the climb for the most panoramic of all views of the city. Afterwards, stroll west through the leafy **Burggarten** to descend to the Altstadt, which you reach at the **Neutor**.

NUREMBERG'S CELLAR TOURS

The *Hausbrauerei Altstadthof* on Bergstrasse (see p.292) is the meeting and ticket point for tours of the **Nürnberger Felsengänge** (W historische-felsengaenge.de), a warren of passageways and chambers hollowed out of the castle hill and used since the Middle Ages to store beer. The existence of such passageways proved invaluable during World War II, when the city's art treasures were hidden underground out of harm's way in the **Historischer Kunstbunker**, which can also be visited. At the start of the war, prudent officials equipped this former beer cellar with air conditioning, moisture-proof storage cells and guardrooms so it could perform its new function. In the summer months you can also tour the unique Renaissance **casemates** and fresh water conduits carved out of the rock beneath the Kaiserburg.

TOURS

Nürnberger Felsengänge Mon–Fri 11am, 1pm, 3pm & 5pm, Sat & Sun hourly 11am–5pm; €5 including audio-guide.

Historischer Kunstbunker Daily 2.30pm & Sat 5.30pm; €5.

Casemates April–Oct daily 3.15pm; €6.

The Albrecht-Dürer-Haus

Albrecht-Dürer Str. 39 • Tues, Wed & Fri 10am–5pm, Thurs 10am–8pm, Sat & Sun 10am–6pm; also Mon 10am–5pm July–Sept & during Christkindlmarkt; English-language guided tour Sat 2pm • €5 including English audio-guide, guided tour in English €2.50 • W museen.nuernberg.de

Among the most photographed of all Nuremberg views is the one east across the little square by **Tiergärtner Tor**, fringed with atmospheric pubs and with the Kaiserburg towering above. On the west side of this open space is the **Albrecht-Dürer-Haus**, the fifteenth-century half-timbered house that was the home of the artist from 1509 until his death in 1528. The self-guided tour – supposedly narrated by his wife Agnes – steers you through the details of Dürer's domestic arrangements as well as visiting a mock-up of his studio on the second floor, complete with copper plates and tools used for copperplate engraving. A "digital Dürer" media station shows 43 selected works; on the third floor the **Graphische Kabinett** displays graphic works by Dürer, his contemporaries and others; while the **Dürer Saal**, which opened in 2012, displays high-quality copies of his most famous works.

The Spielzeugmuseum

Karlstr. 13–15 • Tues–Fri 10am–5pm, Sat & Sun 10am–6pm; also Mon 10am–5pm during Christkindlmarkt • €5 • W museen.nuernberg.de

From the Nurnberger Felsengänge, a turn down Schmiedegasse towards the Sebalduskirche brings you to the **Spielzeugmuseum**, which presents the history of toys from antiquity to Lego and Barbie. Nuremberg was long a renowned toy-making centre, and the museum greets visitors with an array of wooden toys before progressing to tin toys, dolls and dolls' houses and a model railway.

From the museum, head west along Weinmarkt and Irrerstrasse to reach **Weissger-bergasse**, the most photogenic and perfectly preserved street of half-timbered houses in the city.

Along the River Pegnitz

Though it cuts right through the centre of the city, the banks of the **River Pegnitz** are among the most tranquil spots in Nuremberg. At the western end of the Altstadt the city walls leap across the river in a mighty stone arch; in its shadow, the little **Kettensteg** chain bridge dates from 1824 and is one of the oldest surviving chain bridges in Europe. The next bridge to the east is **Maxbrücke**, which offers lovely views of another of

5

Nuremberg's great medieval set-pieces: the vast, half-timbered **Weinstadel** – built between 1446 and 1448 as a lepers' hospital before later becoming a wine store and finally, after World War II, a student hall of residence – and the **Henkersteg**, a covered wooden bridge originally built in 1595 and which got its name – "Hangman's Bridge" – because it led to the **tower** in which the town's hangmen lived from the sixteenth to the nineteenth centuries. As if this architectural ensemble were not picturesque enough, willows hanging low over the water add the final, camera-friendly *pièce de résistance*.

Trödelmarkt
Charming, small-scale **Trödelmarkt** – "junk market" – on an island in the middle of the river (and itself connected by bridge to both the north and south banks) proves that postwar German shopping developments can be sympathetic to their surroundings.

The Fleischbrücke and Museumsbrücke
East of the Trödelmarkt is the **Fleischbrücke** of 1596, modelled on the Rialto bridge in Venice. A good view of it can be had from the neighbouring **Museumsbrücke**, which also looks east towards the **Heilig-Geist-Spital**, a medieval hospice that was extended on two shallow arches over the River Pegnitz in the sixteenth century. It's now one of the city's best-known traditional restaurants (see p.291).

The southern Altstadt
The commercial realities of modern life intrude south of the River Pegnitz, for it's here that Nuremberg's busiest shopping streets are found, along with a startlingly upfront red-light district in and around Frauentormauer. Along with the commercial brashness comes a certain amount of uninspired modern architecture, yet the southern half of the Altstadt has its share of historic and artistic riches too.

Lorenzkirche
Mon–Sat 9am–5pm, Sun 1–4pm • Free (€1 voluntary donation requested)

The Catholic **Lorenzkirche** is the southern Altstadt's counterblast to the Sebalduskirche north of the river. In silhouette the two are startlingly similar, but the Lorenzkirche is the later of the two, consisting of a three-aisled basilica with a decorative west front and a Late Gothic hall-choir which dates from 1439 to 1477. Like the Sebalduskirche, the Lorenzkirche lost its roof in World War II, but again restoration has been deft and its artworks are exceptional – in particular the beautiful *Annunciation* (1517–18) by Veit Stoss, suspended in midair like a burst of joy in elegantly carved wooden form. There's also an impressively tall, elegant Gothic tabernacle, with a wonderfully lifelike self-portrait by its creator, Adam Kraft, at its base.

Opposite the church is the tall **Nassauer Haus**, a well-preserved, medieval patrician tower house; the lower parts of it date from the early thirteenth century, while the upper level with its eye-catching corner towers was built between 1422 and 1433.

Mauthalle
South of the Lorenzkirche along Königstrasse, the **Mauthalle** is another mammoth medieval survivor, built between 1498 and 1502 as a grain warehouse and with five storeys of attics rising above its stone walls. From 1572 onwards it was also the city's weigh- and customs house. The cellar is now a *Hausbrauerei* (see p.291).

St Martha
On the east side of Königstrasse is the inconspicuous church of **St Martha**, remarkable chiefly as the place where the guild of **Meistersingers of Nuremberg** – the artisan folk singers immortalized by Richard Wagner – performed and practised from 1578 to 1620, the church having been secularized during the Reformation. The Meistersingers

composed verses based on strict formulae of medieval melody and rhyme; the most famous of them all was Hans Sachs (1494–1576). The church was extensively damaged by fire in June 2014 and at the time of writing is closed to visitors.

Handwerkerhof
Am Königstor • Mid-March to Dec Mon–Fri 10am–6.30pm, Sat 10am–4pm, also open Sun during Christkindlesmarkt • ⓦ handwerkerhof.de

Nestling in the shade of the mighty Königstor at the southern entrance to the Altstadt is the twee **Handwerkerhof**, an artisan village whose handicrafts are something of a disappointment given Nuremberg's illustrious tradition – there's some good stuff, but also a lot of "Nürnberger Tand", the historic expression for pretty things of little real worth.

The Neues Museum
Luitpoldstr. 5 • Tues, Wed & Fri–Sun 10am–6pm, Thurs 10am–8pm • €4 • ⓦ nmn.de

Lurking behind the Handwerkerhof and as sleekly incongruous as a digital watch in a costume drama, the **Neues Museum** is Nuremberg's elegant glass-fronted museum of contemporary art and design. The contemporary art collection – only a fraction of which is on view at any one time – is particularly strong on international abstraction and the work of Eastern European artists, while the design section presents works of contemporary applied art and design in collaboration with Munich's Neue Sammlung (see p.346). Excellent temporary exhibitions ensure the experience remains fresh and thought-provoking.

Germanisches Nationalmuseum
Kartäusergasse 1 • Tues–Sun 10am–6pm, Wed until 9pm • €8, English audio-guide €2 (ID required) • ⓦ gnm.de

The giant among Nuremberg's museums – and the largest museum of its kind in Germany – the **Germanisches Nationalmuseum** was founded in 1852 by a Franconian nobleman, Hans Freiherr von und zu Aufsess. The impetus for its establishment was to provide cultural affirmation of the liberal ideal of the nation-state at a time when Germany was still a mass of competing kingdoms, dukedoms and landgraviates. The architectural core of the complex is an old Carthusian monastery and its cloisters, but what first strikes visitors is the crisp modernity of the 1993 Museumsforum and the monumental *Street of Human Rights*, a row of white concrete columns inscribed in various languages, by Israeli artist Dani Karavan.

The collections
The sheer scale of the museum can be daunting: the medieval collections and fine art aside, there's a hangar-like room full of historic musical instruments and entire farmhouse interiors have been reconstructed in the folk art section. It pays, therefore, to be selective. Among the highlights of the prehistoric section is the gorgeously delicate, wafer-thin **Ezelsdorf-Buch Gold Cone**, which dates from between 1100 and 900 BC. Highlights of the medieval collections include sculptures by **Veit Stoss** and the Thuringian-born but Würzburg-based **Tilman Riemenschneider**, while the star among the scientific instruments is undoubtedly the **Behaim Globe**, which dates from 1491–93 and is the oldest existing representation of the Earth as a sphere. The glory of Nuremberg's metalworking tradition is admirably demonstrated by the splendidly ornamental **Schlüsselfelder Schiff**, a table centrepiece of a sailing ship from 1503, while its greatest artist, **Albrecht Dürer**, is represented by a dedicated gallery. Twentieth-century paintings include an Expressionist self-portrait by **Ernst Ludwig Kirchner**.

The DB Museum
Lessingstr. 6 • Tues–Fri 9am–5pm, Sat & Sun 10am–6pm • €5 • ⓦ dbmuseum.de

Brave the pounding traffic along Frauentorgraben to reach the **DB Museum**, with an additional open-air display area around the corner in Sandstrasse. It's Deutsche Bahn's

5

house museum, and tells the story of the railway from its origins in Britain to the thrusting modernity of the ICE high-speed expresses and beyond, with a "holodeck"-style glimpse into the future. Highlights include a replica of the **Adler**, the very first German train, which ushered in the age of rail in 1835 when it travelled from Nuremberg to nearby Fürth. You can also see **Ludwig II's royal train** and the saloon coach used by **Bismarck**. The darker side of German railway history is not ignored, with a section on the role of the railway in the Holocaust.

The Dokumentationszentrum Reichsparteitagsgelände

Bayernstr. 110 • Mon–Fri 9am–6pm, Sat & Sun 10am–6pm • €5 including audio-guide • ⓦ museen.nuernberg.de • Tram #9 from Hauptbahnhof

If you're even vaguely curious about the role Nuremberg played in the iconography of the Nazi movement, you shouldn't miss a journey out to the **Luitpoldhain** park in the south of the city to see the **Dokumentationszentrum Reichsparteitagsgelände** (Documentation Centre Nazi Party Rally Grounds). Housed in an ultramodern museum that pierces the side of the **Kongresshalle** – a typically gargantuan piece of Nazi architectural bombast, planned to seat 50,000 but never completed – the permanent exhibition **Fazination und Gewalt** (Fascination and Force) charts the rise of the Nazis with a focus on Nuremberg's role. At the start, skateboarding youths guide you through a short introductory film that juxtaposes the modern city with clips from Leni Riefenstahl's party-rally film *Triumph of the Will*, scenes of war and the Holocaust and the ghastly ruins of Nuremberg in 1945. Further sections of the exhibition deal with the Führer cult, the ritual and organization of the party rallies and the experience of attending them, and the history of the Reichsparteigelände post-1945; there's also a chilling section on anti-Semitism.

The party rally ground

A circular **walk** signposted in German and English takes you from the Kongresshalle along the 2km **Grosse Strasse**, the main axis of the complex, deliberately oriented towards the distant Kaiserburg. Still recognizable from old film footage, the **Zeppelintribüne** on the opposite side of the Dutzendteich lake from the Kongresshalle

---

THE NUREMBERG RALLIES

The Nazis held their **Reichsparteitag**, or party rallies, in Nuremberg in 1927 and 1929 for both political and practical reasons: the city's illustrious past and glorious medieval monuments lent Hitler's posturing a spurious air of historical legitimacy, but the Mittelfranken region in which Nuremberg stands was already a Nazi power-base. Silent film footage from this time portrays SA men marching through the Altstadt. Violence associated with the rallies led the city council to ban them, but local Gauleiter (party chief) Julius Streicher – who gained particular notoriety as the publisher of the deranged anti-Semitic newspaper *Der Stürmer* – could already count on the support of the local police chief.

After the *Machtergreifung* (Nazi seizure of power) in 1933, the party rallies became an annual ritual, attracting massive numbers of participants and hangers-on. A vast, self-glorifying **Parteitagsgelände** (party rally ground) was therefore planned, and though much of it – including the colossal **Deutsches Stadion**, which would have accommodated 400,000 spectators – was never built, what survives gives a powerful impression of the gigantism that was designed, in part, to shrink the role of the individual into insignificance and to create an overwhelming experience for the participants that appealed to the emotions, not to reason.

The rallies had a wider audience too, for during the 1930s many foreign newspapers sent reporters to cover the event. **Leni Riefenstahl** (the regime's favoured documentary-maker) used a crew of 170 and some ground-breaking camera techniques to record the 1934 rally for her film *Triumph of the Will*; the crowning event of the 1935 rally was the special session of the Reichstag convened in Nuremberg to pass the anti-Semitic Nuremberg Laws.

5

is where Hitler would address the rally – you can climb to the podium where he stood, though the terraced structure is a bit crumbly nowadays – and where Hitler's chief architect, Albert Speer, created his famous **Lichtdom**, or light cathedral, using hundreds of searchlights; the glow was so powerful it could be seen in Prague.

Memorium Nuremberg Trials

Bärenschanzstr. 72 • Daily except Tues 10am–6pm; admission to Courtroom 600 only when court not in session • €5 including English audio-guide • Ⓦ museen.nuernberg.de • U-Bahn Bärenschanze

The Nuremberg Trials of Nazi leaders for the newly created crimes against peace, war crimes and crimes against humanity took place from November 20, 1945, to October 1, 1946, in the specially reconstructed **Courtroom 600** (Schwurgerichtssaal 600) of Nuremberg's war-damaged Justizpalast, now the **Landgericht Nürnberg-Fürth**. A fascinating exhibition, the **Memorium Nuremberg Trials**, tells the story of the trials in the wider context of international law, from the foundation of the Red Cross and the Geneva Conventions of 1864 and 1906 – which were supposed to "civilize" war – to the origin of the concept of war crimes and the trial itself. It's still a working court today and still quite closely resembles the 1940s newsreel footage; if the court isn't in session, it is also possible to visit the courtroom itself.

Tiergarten Nürnberg

Am Tiergarten 30 • Daily: April–Sept 8am–7.30pm; Oct–March 9am–5pm • €13.50 • Ⓦ tiergarten.nuernberg.de • Tram #5 or bus #65

Light relief from the weight of historical events is at hand at the city's zoo, the **Tiergarten Nürnberg**, which moved to its present site in 1939 when it was evicted from its previous home by the Dutzendteich to make way for more of Albert Speer's architectural megalomania. Still, the move was the zoo's gain as it's an unusually beautiful place, lushly wooded and dotted with small lakes. The zoo has more than three hundred species, from lions and zebras to polar bears; its lakes provide a home for sea lions, penguins and otters, and there's also a dolphin lagoon.

ARRIVAL AND DEPARTURE NUREMBERG

By plane Nuremberg's airport (Ⓣ 0911 937 00, Ⓦ airport -nuernberg.de) is on the northern edge of the city at Flughafenstr. 100; it's linked to the city's Hauptbahnhof by U-Bahn line #2.

By train Nuremberg's Hauptbahnhof is directly opposite the main southern entrance to the Altstadt.

Destinations Augsburg (every 30min–1hr 30min; 1hr 10min); Bad Staffelstein (for Vierzehnheiligen: every 1hr;

1hr 5min); Bamberg (4 per hour; 30min–1hr); Bayreuth (every 2hr; 1hr); Berlin (every 30min–1hr 30min; 5hr); Coburg (hourly; 1hr 40min–2hr); Dinkelsbühl (via Ansbach, then bus: hourly; 1hr 45min); Frankfurt (every 30min–1hr; 2hr 5min); Ingolstadt (1–2 per hour; 30–45min); Munich (2–3 per hour; 1hr 15min–1hr 40min); Regensburg (hourly; 1hr); Würzburg (2–4 per hour; 1hr).

GETTING AROUND

By public transport Nuremberg's public transport system (Ⓦ vgn.de) includes trams, U-Bahn and buses. Single tickets cost €2.50, a one-day *TagesTicket* €5.30 and a strip of five single tickets €11.90.

Bike rental Nuremberg has a public bike hire network,

NorisBike (Ⓦ norisbike.de), with more than seventy hire points across the city (€1 for 30min or €9 for 24hr). You can register as a user and pay by credit card at the hire station, online or at the tourist information office.

INFORMATION

Tourist offices The main office is opposite the Hauptbahnhof at Königstr. 93 (Mon–Sat 9am–7pm, Sun 10am–4pm; Ⓣ 0911 233 60, Ⓦ tourismus.nuernberg.de), with a second one at Hauptmarkt 18 (Mon–Sat 9am–6pm; May–Oct also Sun 10am–4pm; during Christkindlesmarkt Mon–Sat

9am–7pm, Sun 10am–7pm; same telephone number).

Discount card Either tourist office can sell you a €21 Nürnberg Card, valid for two days and offering free use of the city's public transport system and free entry to museums and attractions.

5

ACCOMMODATION

You can search and book **accommodation** through the tourist office website. There are plenty of hotels in the southern Altstadt and near the Hauptbahnhof, with a scattering on the north side of the Pegnitz in the most atmospheric corner of the Altstadt. The prize for the most evocative location in the city, however, for once goes to the youth hostel, right next to the Kaiserburg.

HOTELS AND PENSIONS

★**Agneshof** Agnesgasse 10 ☎0911 21 44 40, ⓦagneshof-nuernberg.de. Smart and welcoming *hotel garni* tucked into a quiet lane in the northwest Altstadt, with 74 rooms, all with bath or shower and WC and some with balcony. On-site facilities include sauna and jacuzzi. Advance online rates for double rooms can be up to twenty percent lower. **€94**

Deutscher Kaiser Königsstr. 55 ☎0911 24 26 60, ⓦdeutscher-kaiser-hotel.de. Neo-Gothic architecture and a few turn-of-the-century decorative trappings add a note of class to this central and comfortable 3-star hotel. There's free wireless internet; parking is available at extra cost. **€108**

Drei Raben Königsstr. 63 ☎0911 27 43 80, ⓦhoteldreiraben.de. Very stylish modern hotel in a central location close to the Neues Museum and with a groovy bar on the ground floor. Rooms have themed decor, with some boasting free-standing bathtubs; a/c rooms have flat-screen TV, DVD, CD sound system and iPod connection. **€150**

Dürer Hotel Neutormauer 32 ☎0911 214 66 50, ⓦduerer-hotel.de. The peaceful and central location – close to the Albrecht-Dürer-Haus and in the shadow of the city walls – is the x-factor here. Rooms have free wi-fi, en-suite bathroom, minibar and flat-screen TV, and there's an underground car park. **€99**

Elch Irrerstr. 9 ☎0911 249 29 80, ⓦhotel-elch.com. Superbly located family-run hotel in a fourteenth-century half-timbered house in the northern Altstadt. Modern comforts include shower and WC, minibar and free wi-fi. Pets and families are welcome and there's a restaurant, *Schnitzelria*, on the ground floor. **€89**

Pension Vater Jahn-Parma Jahnstr. 13 ☎0911 44 45 07, ⓦhotel-vaterjahn-parma.de. Immaculate and friendly guesthouse just south of the Opernhaus on the other side of the railway tracks, close to the Hauptbahnhof and Altstadt. The cheapest rooms share bathrooms; rooms with shower and WC cost from €65. **€47**

Steichele Knorrstr. 2–8 ☎0911 20 22 80, ⓦsteichele .de. The modern hotel extension doesn't have quite the same timeless charm as the lovely original *Weinrestaurant* next door, but nevertheless this is a good, central option, with good advance rates online. Rooms have shower and WC, free internet and cable TV; there are 28 singles. **€85**

Victoria Königsstr. 80 ☎0911 240 50, ⓦhotelvictoria .de. A pleasant mix of tradition and modernity behind a listed nineteenth-century facade right next to the Handwerkerhof and close to the Hauptbahnhof. Rooms have minibar and wi-fi, and hypoallergenic bedding is available on request. Non-smoking. **€118**

HOSTELS

DJH Nürnberg Burg 2 ☎0911 230 93 60, ⓦnuernberg .jugendherberge.de; U-Bahn #1 or #11 to Rathenauplatz, then 10min walk. This recently refurbished HI hostel has a wonderful location in the 15th-century imperial stables next to the Kaiserburg, overlooking the Altstadt. Dorms **€29.90**, doubles **€74**

Five Reasons Frauentormauer 42 ☎0911 992 86625, ⓦfive-reasons.de. Stylishly revamped independent hostel on the fringe of the red-light district, a short walk from the Hauptbahnhof. It offers free wi-fi, a guest kitchen and an iPad for guest use. Reception open 24 hours. Dorms **€18**, doubles **€49**

NUREMBERG'S SWEET AND SAVOURY SPECIALITIES

Slim, char-grilled **Nürnberger Bratwürste** are Nuremberg's savoury speciality, and though the little sausages are served in high style in quite fancy restaurants, they're never more delicious than when eaten hot from a street stall *Drei im Weckla* – three in a bun. One of the best places to try them is ★*Bratwursthäusle* by the Sebalduskirche (Mon–Sat 10am–10pm; *3 im Weckla* €2.50). More substantial savoury dishes are often served with **Nürnberger Klösse** (potato dumplings), which are good fuel on a wintery day and excellent for soaking up meaty sauces.

You can buy Nuremberg's famous sweetly-spiced **Lebkuchen** gingerbread – originally a Christmas treat, but now available all year around – at *Wicklein* at Hauptmarkt 7 (Mon–Fri 9.30am–6.30pm, Sat 9.30am–4pm) or from Schmidt at Plobenhofstr. 6 (Mon–Fri 9am–6.30pm, Sat 9am–4pm; ⓦlebkuchen-schmidt.com). You can get gluten-free and diabetic versions from Fraunholz at Bergstr. 1 (Mon–Fri 9am–6.30pm, Sat 11am–4pm, Sun 10.30am–6pm).

5

EATING AND DRINKING

Nuremberg has many excellent German restaurants, but it has plenty of good ethnic choices too. There's no particular concentration of places to **eat** or **drink**, with good options scattered throughout the Altstadt. The same goes for **bars**, though in addition to the Altstadt's offerings there are one or two places worth venturing beyond the city walls for.

CAFÉS

★ **Café im Literaturhaus** Luitpoldstr. 6 ☎ 0911 234 26 58, ⓦ restaurant-im-literaturhaus.de. Excellent, spacious 1950s-style café with red leatherette seats, good cake (from €2.70) and a civilized ambiance. *Flammkuchen* from €4; hot main courses from around €9. Breakfast served 9am–3pm. Mon–Sat 9am–midnight, Sun 9am–10pm.

Salon Regina Fürther Str. 64 ☎ 0911 929 17 99, ⓦ salonregina.de. Trendy former *Konditorei* in the hip Gostenhof neighbourhood west of the Alstadt, now a café-bar but still preserving its wonderful early Sixties decor and very handy for the Memorium Nuremberg Trials. Lunch specials €6.30 up. Mon–Thurs 10am–midnight, Fri & Sat 10am–1am, Sun 10am–10pm.

RESTAURANTS

Bratwurst Röslein Rathausplatz 6 ☎ 0911 21 48 60, ⓦ bratwurst-roeslein.de. Big, buzzing, shamelessly tourist-oriented place serving Franconian specialities including – of course – *Bratwurst* (6 for €7.20) as well as a wider range of meaty main courses from around €8 and a two-course lunch menu for €9.99. Daily 10am–midnight.

Essigbrätlein Weinmarkt 3 ☎ 0911 22 51 31. Yves Ollech's innovative "spice cuisine" has earned this old-established Nuremberg restaurant two Michelin stars, for dishes such as sea trout with cucumber and yoghurt ice cream with radish and cucumber. There's a three-course lunch for €72, with four courses in the evening for €119. Tues–Sat noon–1.30pm & 7–9.15pm.

Estragon Jakobstr. 19 ☎ 0911 241 80 30, ⓦ estragon -nuernberg.de. Stylish, gay-friendly restaurant with reasonably priced pasta, salad and veggie dishes from around €8.50, plus more substantial meaty dishes for around €14.50 on the weekly changing menu. It has a policy of employing people with disabilities. Tues–Fri 11am–11pm, Sat & Sun 5–11pm.

Heilig-Geist-Spital Spitalgasse 16 ☎ 0911 22 17 61, ⓦ heilig-geist-spital.de. *Bratwurst* and affordable Franconian specialities are served with plenty of atmosphere in the historic surroundings of the former medieval hospice, and there's Franconian wine to wash it all down. Six *Bratwürste* €6.70; *Krustenschäufele* with *Kloss* (dumplings) and *Sauerkraut* €13.90. There's also a pretty, sheltered inner courtyard. Daily 11.30am–11pm.

Ishihara Schottengasse 3 ☎ 0911 22 63 95, ⓦ ishihara .de. Esteemed (and rather elegant) Japanese restaurant in the southern Altstadt, with *teppanyaki*, noodle dishes, soups and salads at lunchtime, plus set menus at €35, €38 and €49. Mon–Sat noon–2.30pm & 6–10pm.

Nassauer Keller Karolinenstr. 2–4 ☎ 0911 22 59 67, ⓦ nassauerkeller.de. The cellar of the medieval Nassauer Haus is an atmospheric place to enjoy *Bratwürste* (€7.20 for six) or pork shoulder with potato *Klösse* (€14.90), but first you have to negotiate the extraordinarily low doorway and steep medieval stairs. Mon–Sat 11am–11pm; kitchen closes 10pm.

Opatija Unschlittplatz 7 ☎ 0911 22 71 96, ⓦ opatija -restaurant.de. Elegant restaurant in the *Merian* hotel, with plenty of fish, plus Italian and Balkan influences, on the cosmopolitan menu. Main courses €16–26; simpler grills including *cevapcici* from around €10. Daily 11.30am–2.30pm & 6–11pm.

Prison St Michel Irrerstr. 2 ☎ 0911 22 11 91. Quirky French restaurant that serves up *brochettes de fruits de mer* followed by *mousse au chocolat* to Francophiles who've tired of *Bratwurst*. €18.90 set menu. Daily 7pm–1am.

Steichele Knorrstr. 2–8 ☎ 0911 20 22 80, ⓦ steichele .de. Gorgeous late-Baroque *Weinrestaurant* in the southern Altstadt with a dark wood interior and a menu that displays Italian and German influences. Daily specials from around €8. Mon–Sat 11am–2pm & 5.30–10pm.

Tawan Thai Kornmarkt 4 ☎ 0911 236 96 90, ⓦ tawanthai-nuernberg.de. Good Thai food a stone's throw from the Germanisches Nationalmuseum, with meat and fish mains from around €15.50 and a few veggie options from around €9.50. Lunch specials from €5. Mon–Fri 11.30am–3pm & 5.30–11pm, Sat 11.30am–11pm.

Zum Gulden Stern Zirkelschmiedsgasse 26 ☎ 0911 205 92 88, ⓦ bratwurstkueche.de. The most atmospheric of all the *Bratwurst* restaurants, in an exceptionally picturesque half-timbered building on the fringe of the red-light district. They stick to what they know here, so expect a short and *Bratwurst*-dominated menu; six *Bratwürste* from the open beechwood grill €7.20. Daily 11am–10pm.

BARS, HAUSBRAUEREI AND BEER GARDENS

Barfüsser Hausbrauerei Hallplatz 2 ☎ 0911 20 42 42, ⓦ barfuesser-nuernberg.de. Vast *Hausbrauerei* in the cellar of the Mauthalle, with own-brew blonde and black beers and affordable German food from around €8. Beer costs €2.60 for 0.3 litre, or €33 for a five-litre barrel to share at the table. Daily 11am–midnight.

5

Cartoon An der Sparkasse 6 ☎0911 22 71 70, ⊛cafe -cartoon.de. Spacious lesbian and gay café-bar in the southern Altstadt, with a small additional basement bar that's open Fri and Sat evenings only. Cocktails from €6.70, pasta dishes €6.80. Mon–Thurs 11am–1/2am, Fri & Sat 11am–3/5am, Sun 2pm–1/2am.

★ **Gelbes Haus** Troststr. 10 ☎0911 26 22 74, ⊛gelbes -haus.de. Classy cocktail bar in the trendy Gostenhof neighbourhood west of the Altstadt, with a big selection of whiskies and cocktails, from the tried-and-tested juleps and pisco sours to more inventive options, from around €7. They also do delicious non-alcoholic cocktails and light food. Mon–Sat 8pm–late.

Hausbrauerei Altstadthof Bergstr. 19 ☎0911 244 98 59, ⊛hausbrauerei-altstadthof.de. *Hausbrauerei* close to Tiergärtner Tor and the Albrecht-Dürer-Haus, producing five varieties of beer, including a Nuremberg *Rotbier* and a

seasonal (and strong) *Maibock*, plus organic whiskies and *Bierbrand* – Schnapps made from beer. *Rotbier* €3.10 for 0.4 litre. Daily 11am–midnight; *Biergarten* Mon–Sat 11am–8pm, Sun 11am–3pm.

Kettensteg Maxplatz 35 ☎0911 22 10 81. In the summer months there's no more alluring a *Biergarten* in Nuremberg than this, right on the river by the bridge of the same name, at the point where the city walls cross the River Pegnitz. Half-litre of beer €3.30; the food includes big salads for €7.80 as well as more substantial meaty fare. Daily 11am–11pm.

Mata Hari Bar Weissgerbergasse 31 ☎0911 19 49 500, ⊛mataharibar.de. One of a cluster of lounge-style bars in and around Weissgerbergasse, *Mata Hari* is tiny but cool, with a music policy that ranges from indie to rockabilly and a drinks list that is particularly strong on whiskies. Occasional live gigs. Wed & Thurs 8pm–2am, Fri & Sat 8pm–4am.

NIGHTLIFE AND ENTERTAINMENT

CLUBS AND LIVE MUSIC

Pick up a copy of *Plärrer* (€2) for what's-on information in German.

Club Stereo Klaragasse 8 ☎0911 211 04 55, ⊛club -stereo.net. Hip Altstadt club, with live bands and eclectic DJ nights embracing everything from indie bands to electro and hip-hop. Occasional live gigs from 8pm; DJ nights Thurs–Sat 11pm–late.

Mach 1 Kaiserstr. 1–9 T0911 240 66 02, ⊛mach1-club .de. Smart and stylish city-centre club with a main dancefloor pumping house and hip-hop sounds, a more intimate second dancefloor and a lounge area. Fri & Sat 10pm–5am.

Die Rakete Vogelweiherstr. 64 ☎0911 801 53 15, ⊛dierakete.com; U-Bahn Frankenstrasse. Live venue and dance club in the industrial southern suburbs, with a regularly changing line-up of events but an emphasis on techno. Fri & Sat 11pm–late, Sun afterparty from 6am.

Rockfabrik Klingenhofstr. 56 ☎0911 56 50 56, ⊛rockfabrik.de; U-Bahn Herrnhütte. Alternative rock venue in an industrial zone northeast of the Altstadt, with regular live gigs plus DJ nights spinning anything from nu metal to goth and electro. Concerts generally from 7pm; DJ nights from 9pm.

THEATRE, OPERA AND CLASSICAL MUSIC

Meistersingerhalle Münchener Str. 21 ☎0911 231 80 00, ⊛meistersingerhalle.nuernberg.de. Conference venue and concert hall that is the setting for performances by the Nuremberg Symphony Orchestra and others.

Staatstheater Nürnberg Richard-Wagner-Platz 2–10 ☎0180 523 16 00 (ticket hotline), ⊛staatstheater -nuernberg.de. Opera and ballet are staged at the historic, grandiose Opernhaus; the smaller Kammerspiele and the city's main drama stage – the Schauspielhaus – are in the recently renovated, modernist extensions. Also home to the Staatsphilharmonie Nürnberg orchestra.

Bayreuth

Richard Wagner casts a long shadow over **BAYREUTH**. For most of the world Bayreuth and Wagner are synonymous, as though outside the social and musical spectacle of the **Festspiele** no other Bayreuth existed. Yet the town you see owes more to the passions of another remarkable individual, the Markgräfin Wilhelmine (see box opposite), who in the eighteenth century transformed it into a graceful Baroque Residenzstadt. Her **Baroque quarter** wraps itself around the eastern and southern sides of the **Altstadt** – both compact enough to be explored easily on foot. The leafy **Hofgarten** stretches east from her **Neues Schloss** to Wagner's **Villa Wahnfried**, while his **Festspielhaus** is on high ground north of the centre. It's also worth venturing out to Wilhelmine's summer palace, **Eremitage**. Quite the paparazzi hotspot during the Festspiele, Bayreuth is a quiet, stolidly respectable place the rest of the time, though Wilhelmine's magic ensures it's worth a stay of a day or two.

WILHELMINE AND BAYREUTH

The eldest daughter of Friedrich Wilhelm I of Prussia and the sister of Frederick the Great, **Wilhelmine** (1709–58) was groomed by her Hanoverian mother for marriage into the British royal family. But the plans were thwarted by her father, who – partly for political reasons, partly out of loathing for his wife's British relatives – married her off instead to a minor royal and distant relative, **Friedrich von Brandenburg-Bayreuth**, the future margrave of the insignificant Franconian microstate of the same name. Despite its unpromising start, the marriage was a happy one, and with her aspirations to enter the glittering world of the London court thwarted, the intelligent and educated Wilhelmine decided instead to bring worldly sophistication to Bayreuth, embarking on an extravagant **building programme** whose fruits still grace the town today.

Markgräfliches Opernhaus

Opernstr. 14 • Exhibition open daily: April–Sept 9am–6pm; Oct–March 10am–4pm • €2.50 • ⓦ schloesser-bayern.de

Wagner's Festspielhaus may have superb acoustics, but it's notoriously spartan; Wilhelmine's **Markgräfliches Opernhaus**, on the other hand, is a Baroque gem. Wilhelmine's cultural ambitions were nurtured with more than a backward glance at her beloved brother's court in Berlin. If Frederick the Great entertained Voltaire, then so must she, and if Berlin had an opera house then so, too, must Bayreuth. Only the best would do: Wilhelmine commissioned the renowned Italian theatre designer Giuseppe Galli Bibiena and his son, Carlo, for the job. The results let Bayreuth look Berlin in the eye, for the Markgräfliches Opernhaus is commonly regarded as one of the most beautiful Baroque theatres in Europe; the handsome but relatively restrained exterior gives no hint of the opulence within.

The Opernhaus was inspected – and rejected – by Wagner, but it is nevertheless still a functioning opera house. Though it's closed for restoration work until 2017, it's still possible to get a glimpse of the Fürstenloge (royal box) and there's an exhibition on the building's history.

The Schlosskirche

Opernstrasse • Schlossturm €1 by prior arrangement; enquire at tourist office

Close by the opera house, court architect, Frenchman Joseph Saint-Pierre, built the **Schlosskirche**, or court chapel, from 1753 to 1758. Wilhelmine died the year it was completed and is buried in a vault in the church's delicate Rococo interior, along with her husband and daughter, Friederike, Duchess of Württemberg. The octagonal **Schlossturm** attached to the church dates from 1565 and offers good views across the town to the Fichtelgebirge from the top.

Alongside the church is the **Altes Schloss**, a fine seventeenth-century Baroque pile whose partial destruction by fire in 1753 gave Wilhelmine the impetus to commission its splendid replacement, the Neues Schloss, a short walk to the south along Ludwigstrasse.

The Neues Schloss

Ludwigstr. 21 • April–Sept daily 9am–6pm; Oct–March Tues–Sun 10am–4pm • €5.50 • ⓦ schloesser-bayern.de

The job of building the Neues Schloss was entrusted to the court architect, Frenchman Joseph Saint-Pierre; construction began in 1753. The long, low facade is gracious enough, but is on a scale sympathetic to the town, and it gives no clue to the heights of Rococo refinement within, which reach a peak of inventiveness and flair in rooms such as the **Spiegelscherbenkabinett**, where seemingly random fragments of mirror adorn a chinoiserie design – look out for Wilhelmine herself, portrayed as a tea-drinking Chinese woman receiving documents from a servant. A gold ceiling and stuccoed mussel shells adorn the grotto-like neighbouring room where Wilhelmine would retire to read;

Wilhelmine once again puts in an appearance in Oriental guise in the ceiling of the graceful **Japanisches Zimmer**. Most inventive of all is perhaps the stunning **Palmenzimmer**, where gilded and carved palm trees sprout from the walnut-panelled walls.

The ground floor contains an exhibition on **Wilhelmine's Bayreuth**, a collection of **Bayreuth faïence** and a branch of the Bavarian state **art** collection, displaying seventeenth- and eighteenth-century works including some from the Dutch "golden age". Tickets also allow you to join a tour of the summery rooms of the **Italiänisches Schlösschen**, with charming stuccowork in ice-cream colours that dates from after Wilhelmine's death.

Friedrichstrasse

West of the Neues Schloss at Jean-Paul-Platz, Ludwigstrasse intersects with **Friedrichstrasse**, the most elegant street in Bayreuth, full of noble stone houses, one of which houses the renowned **Steingraeber** piano company, whose graceful premises are frequently a venue for classical music concerts.

The Hofgarten

Behind the Neues Schloss, the **Hofgarten** (free access) was planned in classic Baroque style with parterres, pergolas and a canal as a central axis. It was later redesigned in informal English style, but it still preserves the canal with its right turn and central islands, and the parterre in front of the south wing of the Schloss was restored in 1990.

Villa Wahnfried: the Richard Wagner Museum

Richard Wagner Str. 48 • ⓦ wagnermuseum.de

It's just a short stroll through the Hofgarten to the **Villa Wahnfried**, Richard Wagner's imposing, if not especially big, villa. It was sponsored by his patron, "mad" King Ludwig II of Bavaria, and designed largely by Wagner himself. This was his principal home from 1874 until his death in 1883, though he spent long periods away from it, particularly in Italy, where he died. An inscription on the street facade proclaims: "Here, where my delusions have found peace, let this place be named Wahnfried". Badly damaged in the closing weeks of World War II, when the side facing the Hofgarten was demolished, it was restored to its original appearance in the 1970s. Wagner is buried, along with his wife Cosima and his favourite dog, in the back garden.

The villa houses the **Richard Wagner Museum**, which at the time of writing was closed for renovation and extension. It should be open again by mid-2015, with a long, low, new museum building alongside the villa; hopefully, this will rectify the museum's hitherto rather dry, mausoleum-like character.

Franz Liszt Museum

Wahnfriedstr. 9 • Daily: July & Aug 10am–5pm; Sept–June 10am–noon & 2–5pm • €2

Cosima Wagner's father was the composer and piano virtuoso **Franz Liszt**, and there's a small museum to his memory in the house neighbouring Villa Wahnfried, where he died on 31 July 1886, having come to Bayreuth for the Festspiele although he was already seriously ill. The exhibits include pianos, portraits and a diary Liszt kept as a young man, and the composer's music accompanies your visit thanks to a high-quality audio system.

The Altstadt and around

After the Baroque grace of Wilhelmine's Bayreuth and the *Sturm und Drang* of Wagner's life, the charm of Bayreuth's **Altstadt** lies in its modesty. Narrow lanes huddle around the **Stadtkirche** (or the Stadtkirche Heilig-Dreifaltigkeit to give it its full name), the town's

Lutheran parish church, rebuilt after a disastrous town fire in 1605. Surprisingly, the builder, Michael Mebart, chose to rebuild in the original Gothic rather than in a more contemporary style. Extensive restoration work in recent years has meant access to the church has been restricted, but the church should be open to visitors again in 2015.

Just to the north of the Altstadt is **Maximilianstrasse**, Bayreuth's main shopping street.

Historisches Museum

Kirchplatz 4 • July & Aug daily 10am–5pm; Sept–June Tues–Sun 10am–5pm • €2 • ⓦ historischesmuseum-bayreuth.de

On the north side of the Stadtkirche is Bayreuth's local history museum, the **Historisches Museum**, housed in a seventeenth-century schoolhouse. Exhibits include Bayreuth faïence and a display on Hitler's bizarre plans for the town, which as the home of his beloved Wagner and the Festspiele, was highly favoured by the regime.

Kunstmuseum Bayreuth

Maximilianstr. 33 • Tues–Sun 10am–5pm; July & Aug also Mon 10am–5pm • €2 • ⓦ kunstmuseum-bayreuth.de

In the Renaissance **Altes Rathaus**, the **Kunstmuseum Bayreuth** shows a changing selection of the municipal art collection, which is particularly strong on twentieth-century works. It shares the premises with the **Tabakhistorische Sammlung der British American Tobacco** (British American Tobacco Historical Tobacco Collection), tobacco production being an important local industry.

Further west along Maximilianstrasse, it's worth quickly visiting the small but exceptionally pretty **Spitalkirche**, the work of Wilhelmine's court architect Joseph Saint-Pierre – though it is undergoing restoration.

Maisel's Brauerei- und Büttnerei Museum

Kulmbacher Str. 40 • Tours daily 2pm • €5 • ⓦ maisel.com/museum

A few minutes' walk from the Altstadt, you can tour a handsome nineteenth-century brewery and cooperage at **Maisel's Brauerei- und Büttnerei Museum**; in addition to the original brewing equipment, there's a vast selection of beer glasses and enamel advertisements. The ninety-minute tour ends with a glass of Maisel's *Weissbier*.

The Festspielhaus

Festspielhügel 1–2 • Tours May, Sept & Oct daily 10am, 11am, 2pm & 3pm; Nov–April daily 2pm; no tours June–Aug during rehearsals and Festspiele • €7 • ⓦ bayreuther-festspiele.de • Bus #305 from ZOH (central bus station) or Luitpoldplatz

Richard Wagner first considered Bayreuth as a candidate for the site of his **Festspiele** because of the unusually large stage at the Markgräfliches Opernhaus, but he rejected it as unsuitable after a visit in April 1871. He was, however, taken with the

---

FESTSPIELE AND OTHER BAYREUTH FESTIVALS

Tickets for the **Festspiele** (☎ 0921 78 78 780, ⓦ bayreuther-festspiele.de) in late July and August are famously hard to come by: you must book through the website or write (no emails or faxes) to Kartenbüro, Postfach 100262, D-95402 Bayreuth, by October of the previous year, and in practice it will be several years before you stand any chance of actually getting them, since the event is hugely oversubscribed. During the festival itself, any returns are available on the day at the box office from 1.30pm to 4pm; performances start at 4pm because of the great length of Wagner's operas.

OTHER FESTIVALS

Bayreuth's other festivals include **Musica Bayreuth** (ⓦ musica-bayreuth.de) in May, which takes place at various historic venues around town; the **Bayreuther Klavierfestival** (Bayreuth Piano Festival; ⓦ steingraeber.de) in July, with a second part in late September and October; and the **Bayreuther Volksvest** folk festival at Whitsun, with fairground rides, beer and live music.

5

town itself, and so decided to make his home in Bayreuth and to build a festival theatre here. Proposals already existed by Gottfried Semper – architect of the Dresden opera house and of the Burgtheater in Vienna – for a grandiose opera house in Munich, but in the event a far more spartan design was selected for the **Festspielhaus**, which stands on a low hill north of the town centre. Wagner – who intended the building to be provisional – was the driving force behind the concept, and his own notes on the blueprints declared "away with the ornaments". True to his word, the builders produced an auditorium with magnificent acoustics but no creature comforts: the orchestra is concealed to preserve sight lines, and to preserve the unique acoustic, the audience sit on wooden benches – thus ensuring that they, too, suffer for Wagner's art.

Eremitage

Altes Schloss guided tours daily: April–Sept 9am–6pm; first two weeks Oct 10am–4pm • €4.50 • ⓦ schloesser-bayern.de • Bus #302 from ZOH

East of town, Margrave Georg Wilhelm – Friedrich's uncle – laid out a park and Schloss known as the **Eremitage** (or Hermitage) from 1715 onwards as a place where he and his court could live a simple life, dressing in monks' habits, sleeping in cells and eating soup from brown earthenware bowls. When Friedrich acceded as Margrave in 1735 he gifted this house, now known as the **Altes Schloss**, to Wilhelmine. She immediately set about having the Schloss extended, creating a series of magnificent Rococo rooms that eschewed Georg Wilhelm's original austerity without actually eradicating it. From around 1750, Wilhelmine set about replanning the park (free access), building a crescent-shaped Orangerie as a centrepiece, now known as the **Neues Schloss**, focal point of which is the domed, circular Sonnentempel, topped with a gilded representation of Apollo's chariot – with the clear intention of glorifying Friedrich as the Apollo of his day. Trick fountains in the Obere Grotte play hourly on the hour from May to October, and fifteen minutes later in the Untere Grotte.

ARRIVAL AND GETTING AROUND · BAYREUTH

By train Trains from Nuremberg take around 1hr to reach Bayreuth's Hauptbahnhof, north of the town centre.
Destinations Bad Staffelstein (for Vierzehnheiligen: every 2hr; 1hr); Bamberg (every 2hr; 1hr 20min); Coburg (hourly; 1hr 30min); Nuremberg (every 30min–2hr; 50min–1hr 10min).

By public transport Municipal buses (ⓦ bvb-bayreuth .de) depart from the ZOH between Hohenzollernring and Maximilianstrasse on the north side of the Altstadt.
Bike rental Movelo electric bikes (ⓦ movelo.com) are available to rent from the tourist information office.

INFORMATION

Tourist office Opernstr. 22, close to the Markgräfliches Opernhaus (Mon–Fri 9am–7pm, Sat 9am–4pm; May–Oct also Sun 10am–2pm; ☏ 0921 885 88, ⓦ bayreuth -tourismus.de). You can book accommodation through the tourist office website, or they'll happily book it for you.
Discount cards The three-day Bayreuth Card (€12.90)

grants free museum entry, reduced-price entry to the Neues Schloss and Eremitage as well as use of the town's buses. It's available at the tourist office.
Guides You can rent an iGuide (3hr €8) from the tourist office, which takes you on a self-guided tour of the town.

ACCOMMODATION

HOTELS AND PENSIONS

Bayreuther Hof Rathenaustr. 28 ☏ 0921 50 70 45 60, ⓦ bayreuther-hof.de. Twelve good-value, modern double rooms above a *Gaststätte* west of the Hofgarten, with en-suite bath or shower, WC, flat-screen TV and soundproofed windows. Prices are higher during the Festspiele. Check-in from 4.30pm. €72

Eremitage Eremitage 6 ☏ 0921 79 99 70, ⓦ eremitage -bayreuth.de. Individually styled rooms at this elegant restaurant in the grounds of Schloss Eremitage, east of town, with views into the park. Prices rise during the Festspiele. €95

★**Goldener Anker** Opernstr. 6 ☏ 0921 787 77 40, ⓦ anker-bayreuth.de. Very handsome, classy and central hotel, family-run since 1753, with spacious, individually styled rooms, period furnishings and bathrooms and an attractive Art Deco restaurant. Note that the hotel is a scheduled historic monument, and there's no lift. **€168**

Goldener Hirsch Bahnhofstr. 13 ☎0921 15 04 40 00, ⓦbayreuth-goldener-hirsch.de. Independently run 3-star place, comfortable if slightly bland, in a convenient location between the town centre and Festspielhaus, and with some singles. Rooms have shower or bath and TV, and there's secure parking. **€85**

Lohmühle Badstr. 37 ☎0921 530 60, ⓦhotel -lohmuehle.de. Housed in an old half-timbered watermill a short walk east of the town centre, this is a

comfortable, traditional choice, with a good restaurant. The solar panels on the roof add a surprising contemporary touch. Note that prices are considerably higher during the Festspiele. **€109**

HOSTELS
DJH Bayreuth Universitätsstr. 28 ☎0921 76 43 80, ⓦbayreuth.jugendherberge.de. Modern hostel a short distance southeast of the Hofgarten and close to the university. There are four single and four twin rooms, some of them en suite; accommodation is otherwise mostly in four- or six-bed dorms. Breakfast and linen included. Dorms **€23.40**; family rooms (per person) **€28.90**

EATING AND DRINKING

Good places to **eat** and **drink** are scattered about the centre of Bayreuth, with some of the best restaurants being located in the hotels. The town's rather modest **nightlife** scene clusters in the lanes around the Stadtkirche on the western fringe of the Altstadt.

Café Müller an der Oper Opernstr. 16. ☎0921 507 14 21. Elegant coffee-and-cake haunt next to the Markgräfliches Opernhaus that also serves savoury dishes: penne in puttanesca sauce €8.20, fried *Schupfnudel* with ratatouille €8.50. Mon & Wed–Sat 10am–6pm, Sun noon–6pm; open Tues during Festspiele.

Engins Ponte am Canale Grande Opernstr. 24 ☎0921 871 05 03, ⓦengins-ponte.de. Large, modern café-bar with a sunny terrace right on the Canale Grande – a rather modest millstream of which the locals are rather fond. There's a versatile menu of salads, fish, meat, pasta and pizza (main courses around €7 upwards). Breakfast (from €2.90) is served until 2pm on weekdays, and on Sun there's a €14.90 breakfast buffet. Mon–Sat 8am–2am, Sun 9am–2am.

Goldener Anker Opernstr. 6 ☎0921 787 77 40, ⓦanker-bayreuth.de. The *Goldener Anker's* smart,

Art-Deco French restaurant serves the likes of fillet beef with balsamic jus and braised peppers, or poached butterflied salmon with Riesling sauce; three courses cost €45, four courses €59. There's also a bistro offering simpler, cheaper fare from 11am daily. Daily 6–10pm.

Plaka Sophienstr. 18 ☎0921 533 03, ⓦplaka-bayreuth .de. Buzzy, urbane Greek restaurant in the Altstadt, with a terrace at the front and a *Biergarten* for alfresco dining, and a menu replete with salads, fish and grilled meats. Main courses around €11 up. Mon & Sun 11.30am–2.30pm & 5.30–10pm, Tues–Sat 11.30am–2.30pm & 5.30–11pm.

Porsch Maximilianstr. 63 ☎0921 646 49. Unpretentious, friendly, wood-panelled traditional *Gaststätte* with Stöckel beer and affordable Franconian staples such as *Schäufele* or *Krustenbraten* with tables fronting Maximilianstrasse in fine weather. Mains from €7.90. Mon–Sat 10am–late, Sun 11am–late; kitchen closes 8pm.

Coburg

With the Thüringer Wald just to the north, Protestant **COBURG** scarcely feels Bavarian at all. Until the end of World War I it was capital of the diminutive duchy of Saxe-Coburg and Gotha, which famously supplied Queen Victoria with her Prince Consort, Albert, and the opportunity to rediscover Britain's forgotten dynastic link with Germany is one very compelling reason to visit. That aside, Coburg is a particularly handsome specimen of a Residenzstadt, with a small but perfectly preserved **Altstadt** – barely 500m across – fringed by some fine examples of Jugendstil. **Schloss Ehrenburg** – the town residence of Coburg's dukes until 1918 – is on Coburg's eastern fringe facing **Schlossplatz**, from where it's a stiff 1km walk uphill to **Veste Coburg**, the town's major attraction and one of the largest medieval castles in Germany. Further afield, you might wish to venture east of town to see **Schloss Rosenau**, birthplace of Prince Albert.

Somewhat improbably, Coburg hosts Europe's biggest samba **festival** in July (ⓦsamba-festival.de).

5

Brief history

The history of Coburg is intimately bound up with that of its ducal family, a branch of the Wettin dynasty whose most distinguished member was Elector **Friedrich the Wise**, champion and protector of **Martin Luther**. Excommunicated and outlawed in the Holy Roman Empire, Luther stayed at the Veste Coburg fortress above the town for six months during the Diet of Augsburg in 1530, under the protection of Friedrich's brother and successor, Johann the Steadfast. Though he was banned from attending, Luther used messengers to stay in touch with the Diet's negotiations on the fate of the Reformation, which led to the Augsburg Confession, a foundation stone of the Protestant Church.

Their loyalty to the Protestant cause cost the Wettins their Electoral status; as mere dukes they thereafter ruled a modest territory from Coburg, extended to include the Saxon duchy of Gotha in 1826, after which they were known as dukes of Saxe-Coburg and Gotha. Modest though their domain was, they pursued a highly successful "marriage offensive", marrying their offspring into the great royal houses of Europe, including those of Belgium, Portugal, Bulgaria and Sweden. The most famous marriage of all was that of **Prince Albert**, younger son of Duke Ernst I, to his cousin **Queen Victoria** in 1840. Though its historic links to Thuringia and Saxony are strong, Coburg's inhabitants voted against union with Thuringia after World War I, and the town became Bavarian.

The Altstadt

Three of the original town gates – the **Spitaltor**, **Judentor** and **Ketschentor** – still guard the entrance to Coburg's compact Altstadt. The Altstadt's centrepiece is the spacious marketplace, **Markt**, with a statue of Prince Albert in the centre and, on the north side, the **Stadthaus**, a late Renaissance chancery built under Duke Johann Casimir from 1597 to 1601 and with richly coloured *Coburger Erker* – two-storeyed oriel windows; look out also for the carved heads on the corner facing Herrngasse. On the south side of the square, the stately **Rathaus** cloaks its Renaissance pedigree behind playful Rococo ornament that dates from a 1750 rebuild, but a characteristic *Erker* window remains; its neighbour, the **Sparkasse**, is frothily Rococo. On the east side of the square, the **Hofapotheke**, or court pharmacy, dates from before 1500 and still performs its original function.

The Münzenmeisterhaus, Casimirianum and St Moriz

Just to the south of Markt, the fifteenth-century **Münzenmeisterhaus** on Ketschengasse is the oldest and most impressive half-timbered house in Coburg. To the east of here, the splendid Renaissance gable of the **Casimirianum** – a grammar school founded in 1605 – faces the west front of **St Moriz**, Coburg's main Protestant church, a slightly lopsided affair with one tower shorter than the other. Luther preached here during his stay at the Veste Coburg; the interior was given a rather bleak Baroque makeover in the eighteenth century.

Schlossplatz

On the eastern side of the Altstadt at the foot of the Hofgarten – the park that leads up to the Veste Coburg – is the dignified **Schlossplatz**. On its north side, the neo-Renaissance **Palais Edinburgh** is so named because it was the home of Alfred, Duke of Edinburgh – a son of Queen Victoria – until he inherited the title of Duke of Saxe-Coburg and Gotha from his childless uncle Ernst II in 1893. Next to it stands the elegant **Landestheater**, which dates from 1840; a statue of **Duke Ernst I** – Prince Albert's father – presides over the square's pretty, central garden. In summer, Schlossplatz is the venue for **open-air concerts** by big-name acts.

Schloss Ehrenburg

Schlossplatz • Guided tours hourly Tues–Sun: April–Sept 9am–6pm; Oct–March 10am–4pm • €4.50, combined ticket with Schloss Rosenau €7, combined ticket with Veste Coburg, Schloss Rosenau & glass museum €12 • ⓦ schloesser-bayern.de

Coburg's dynastic link with Britain is mirrored in the neo-Tudor appearance of **Schloss Ehrenburg**, which dominates the south side of Schlossplatz. The facade is the work of Germany's greatest nineteenth-century architect, Karl Friedrich Schinkel, but it conceals a much older structure, commissioned in 1543 on the site of a defunct Franciscan monastery by Duke Johann Ernst and dubbed Ehrenburg – "castle of honour" – by the Emperor Charles V because it was completed without compulsory labour; it was subsequently extended under Duke Johann Casimir.

The interior

Traces of the Renaissance Schloss survive in the south facade, but a catastrophic fire in 1690 swept away much of the rest, and Duke Albrecht commissioned Italian artists to create sumptuous interiors, of which the **Schlosskapelle** and ornate **Festsaal** survive. The latter is known as the **Riesensaal**, or "giants' hall" on account of the 28 Atlas figures who seem to shore up the immense weight of its heavy stucco ceiling. In contrast, the **Thronsaal** – a copy of Napoleon's throne room at the Tuileries Palace – and the private apartments date from the nineteenth century and are in French Empire style. Queen Victoria was a frequent guest, and the tour visits the room in which she stayed.

The Veste Coburg

Kunstammlungen der Veste Coburg April–Oct daily 9.30am–5pm; Nov–March Tues–Sun 1–4pm • €6, combined ticket with Schloss Ehrenburg, Schloss Rosenau & glass museum €12, audio-guide €1.50 • ⓦ kunstsammlungen-coburg.de • Bus #5 from the town centre, or take the Geckobahn tourist train from the Altstadt (ⓦ geckobahn.de)

On the east side of Schlossplatz, steps lead up the stone-built **Arkaden** into the spacious **Hofgarten**, through which it's a pleasant – but increasingly steep – twenty-minute walk up to the **Veste Coburg**, the massive fortress that dominates the town; the latter part of the walk is up long flights of steps.

The "Coberg", or site of the castle, is first mentioned in 1065, and it passed into Wettin hands in 1353. The oldest surviving part of the complex is the slate-roofed, onion-domed thirteenth-century **Blauer Turm**; of the massive stone buildings that form the castle's inner core, the **Hohes Haus**, which dates from the fourteenth and fifteenth centuries, is the oldest. The bastions and towers visible from the exterior create a sombre and forbidding impression, but once you're in the castle precincts its residential function is more readily apparent, and the stonework is softened by trees and greenery.

The Kunstsammlungen der Veste Coburg: Fürstenbau

The Veste's interior houses the ducal art collection, the **Kunstsammlungen der Veste Coburg**. You enter via the **Fürstenbau**, which contains the so-called **historic rooms**, apartments created in the early years of the twentieth century for the English-born Carl Eduard, last Duke of Saxe-Coburg and Gotha, who lost his English titles as a result of fighting on the German side in World War I and later became a committed Nazi. The objects on display here include Prince Albert's baby clothes; on the second floor, the wood-panelled **Cranachzimmer** contains a number of paintings by Lucas Cranach the Elder.

Steinerne Kemenate

The next building, the **Steinerne Kemenate** (Stone Bower), is accessed directly from the Fürstenbau and is the highlight of the museum. On its second floor is the **Jagdintarsienzimmer** (Hunting Marquetery Room), a *tour de force* of richly ornamented late-Renaissance woodcarving, commissioned by Duke Johann Casimir in 1632 and

5

with sixty inlaid panels depicting hunting scenes. The **Georg Schäfer collection** of medieval German art is displayed on this floor, and includes Matthias Grünewald's *Last Supper*, Lucas Cranach the Elder's *St Mary Magdalene and St Elizabeth* from 1515 and Hans Holbein the Younger's *Portrait of Lady Rich*. Among the sculptures, the so-called *Coburg Pietà* (1360–70) is of either Franconian or Thuringian origin.

On the first floor is the **Grosse Hofstube**, or banqueting hall, built between 1501 and 1504 and displaying elaborate suits of armour, as well as the **Lutherzimmer** – the rooms in which Martin Luther lived and worked from April to October 1530. In the **Lutherstube**, you can see a portrait of Luther from the workshop of Lucas Cranach the Elder.

Carl-Eduard-Bau and Herzoginbau

The adjacent **Carl-Eduard-Bau** contains the museum's print and glass collections: the former including works by the anonymous Master of the Coburg Roundels, the latter everything from sixteenth-century Venetian glass to beautifully decorative Art Nouveau items. Beyond it, the sixteenth-century **Herzoginbau** houses suits of armour beneath its spectacular rafters and, on its lower floors, hunting rifles and an impressive array of carriages and sledges, including a pair of sixteenth-century wedding carriages and a coach that may have belonged to Queen Victoria.

Schloss Rosenau and the Europäisches Museum für Modernes Glas

Schloss Rosenau Guided tours hourly Tues–Sun: April–Sept 9am–6pm; Oct–March 10am–4pm • €4.50, combined ticket with Schloss Ehrenburg €7, combined ticket with Schloss Ehrenburg, Veste Coburg & glass museum €12 • W schloesser-bayern.de • **Glass museum** Rosenau 10 • April–Oct daily 9.30am–1pm & 1.30–5pm; Nov–March Tues–Sun 1–4pm • €4, combined ticket with Schloss Ehrenburg, Veste Coburg & Schloss Rosenau €12 • W kunstsammlungen-coburg.de • Train to Rödental, then bus #3

Set in an English-style landscaped park east of Coburg, **Schloss Rosenau** was a ruin when it was acquired by the ducal family in 1805. Rebuilt between 1808 and 1817 in a pretty neo-Gothic style inspired by the young Schinkel, it was here that Prince Albert was born in 1819. In 1845 he returned with his wife, Queen Victoria, who was so enchanted by the picturesque Schloss that she wrote in her diary, "If I were not who I am, my real home would be here."

Also at Rosenau is the **Europäisches Museum für Modernes Glas**, which displays the Veste Coburg's superb collection of contemporary fine-art glassware in a parkland setting.

ARRIVAL AND INFORMATION   COBURG

By train Coburg's Hauptbahnhof is about a 10min walk northwest of the Altstadt.
Destinations Bad Staffelstein (for Vierzehnheiligen: hourly; 30min); Bamberg (hourly; 40min); Bayreuth (hourly; 1hr 30min); Nuremberg (hourly; 1hr 40min).

Tourist office Off Markt at Herrngasse 4 (April–Oct Mon–Fri 9am–6pm, Sat 10am–4pm; Nov–March Mon–Fri 9am–5pm, Sat 10am–2pm; ☎ 09561 89 80 00, W coburg -tourist.de).

ACCOMMODATION

Goldener Anker Rosengasse 14 ☎ 09561 557 00, W goldener-anker.de. Altstadt hotel with spacious and comfortable, if slightly characterless, rooms with bath or shower, WC, TV and wi-fi, close to the Rathaus. **€109**
Goldene Traube Am Viktoriabrunnen 2 ☎ 09561 87 60, W goldenetraube.com. Coburg's "grand hotel", with attractive, individually styled rooms in three categories, behind a handsome nineteenth-century facade on the edge of the Altstadt; the hotel also has a brace of good restaurants. **€125**

Münchner Hofbräu Kleine Johannisgasse 8 ☎ 09561 23 49 23, W coburg-muenchnerhofbraeu.de. Bright, attractive but simply furnished rooms above a pub in the heart of the Altstadt, with singles, doubles and a solitary apartment. Doubles **€85**, apartment **€105**
Ringhotel Stadt Coburg Lossaustr. 12 ☎ 09561 87 40, W hotel-stadt-coburg.de. Comfortable 3-star hotel handy for the Hauptbahnhof, with a sauna and guest parking. Singles, doubles and suites have cable TV and wi-fi. **€108**

EATING AND DRINKING

Coburg's Altstadt has its fair share of good places to **eat** and **drink**, with some atmospheric traditional options alongside more international offerings. Coburg's *Bratwürste* – traditionally char-grilled over pine cones, though health and safety legislation threatens that – are particularly fine; there's usually a stall selling them on Markt.

Bratwurstglöckle Kleine Johannisgasse 5 ☎09561 752 70. Atmospheric, traditional *Gaststätte*, with painted, vaulted ceilings and a huge menu offering everything from salad to *Schnitzel* (€9.80). Tues–Sun 11am–2pm & 5–10.30pm.

Esszimmer At the Goldene Traube, Am Viktoriabrunnen 2 ☎09561 87 60, ⓦgoldenetraube.com. Intimate and luxurious gourmet restaurant serving molecular and traditional *haute cuisine*, with the likes of lamb served with chickpeas, aubergine, quinoa and miso. Set menus cost €72–115, à la carte mains €49. There's also a more informal steak and seafood restaurant, *Victoria Grill*, in the same hotel. Tues–Sat 6–9.30pm.

Goldenes Kreuz Herrngasse 1 ☎09561 51 34 07, ⓦgoldenes-kreuz-coburg.de. A classy, dark-wood-panelled interior and a menu of Franconian and seasonal dishes including fish and veggie options, next to the Stadthaus. Daily specials €8.50; meaty main courses around €12.50. Mon & Wed–Sat 11.30am–2pm & 5.30pm–midnight, Sun 11.30am–2pm; kitchen closes 10pm Mon & Wed–Sat.

Konditorei-Café Feyler Rosengasse 6–8 ☎09561 804 80, ⓦfeyler-lebkuchen.de. Grand, old café and confectioner – a former *Hoflieferant* to the Coburg court – particularly known for its Coburger *Schmätzchen*, honey-flavoured biscuits sold in a variety of elaborately packaged guises, from €4. Mon–Fri 8am–6pm, Sat 8am–2pm.

ENTERTAINMENT

Landestheater Schlossplatz 6 ☎09561 89 89 89, ⓦlandestheater-coburg.de. The imposing nineteenth-century Landestheater is the place in Coburg to see opera, operetta, ballet and drama, with a programme of events for children too. The season lasts from September to mid-July.

Vierzehnheiligen and Kloster Banz

Lonely and proud on its hilltop site overlooking the Main Valley on the northwestern edge of Fränkische Schweiz, the pilgrimage church of **Vierzehnheiligen** is one of the masterpieces of southern-German late Baroque and Rococo. Facing Vierzehnheiligen across the valley is **Kloster Banz**, built from the same honey-coloured stone on a similarly commanding site high above the valley. Though it's undoubtedly a fine piece of architecture, Banz doesn't dazzle the visitor in quite the way Vierzehnheiligen does, but if you're visiting Vierzehnheiligen with your own transport it's certainly worth a look.

Vierzehnheiligen

Near Bad Staffelstein, 24km south of Coburg • Daily: May–Sept 6.30am–8pm; Oct–April 7.30am–5pm • ⓦvierzehnheiligen.de

Standing on the pilgrims' route to Santiago de Compostela, the church of **Vierzehnheiligen** replaced an earlier structure at the place where, during 1445 and 1446, Hermann Leicht, a shepherd at the Cistercian abbey of Langheim near Lichtenfels, had visions of a crying child. The third time the child appeared to him, it was accompanied by the fourteen Holy Helpers – a group of saints whose intercession is often invoked in Catholicism – who told Leicht they wanted a chapel to be built on the site. Soon afterwards the first miracle was reported and the site became a place of pilgrimage.

Vierzehnheiligen was designed by **Balthasar Neumann**, the architect of Würzburg's Residenz. Construction began in 1723 but the church was not consecrated until 1772, nineteen years after Neumann's death. His plans were nevertheless adhered to, and the results impress long before you reach the twin-towered church, for it can be seen from a distance as you ascend from the valley.

5

The interior

Vierzehnheiligen is built of a particularly warm, gold-coloured stone, but even so the noble exterior is no preparation for the dazzling Rococo vision within, a symphony of white, gold and grey that is sure to lift your spirits, whatever your feelings about the legend that created it. The church is of cathedral-like proportions, its interior focused on Johann Michael Feichtmayr's central **Gnadenaltar**, built on the site of Hermann Leicht's vision and with statues of the fourteen helpers, some eye-catchingly gory: **St Denis**, patron saint of those with headaches, is portrayed with his head tucked under his arm; **St Pantaleon**, with his hands nailed to his head.

Kloster Banz

5km north of Bad Staffelstein • Museum Daily: April–Oct 10am–5pm; March & Nov 10am–4pm; Dec–Feb by prior arrangement only • €2.50 • ☎ 09573 33 77 44

The former Benedictine monastery of **Kloster Banz** was designed by Leonhard Dientzenhofer to replace the previous abbey, wrecked by Swedish troops during the Thirty Years' War. The **church** was consecrated in 1719, and its interior surprises because it is based on a series of ellipses; it's usually open as far as the grille. There's a **museum** of fossils and Oriental artefacts at the abbey entrance; when this is open **tours** of the abbey's historic rooms are available, albeit at somewhat irregular hours.

ARRIVAL AND DEPARTURE

VIERZEHNHEILIGEN AND KLOSTER BANZ

By train and bus Trains link Coburg (30min) and Bamberg (10–20min) with Bad Staffelstein, from where buses run once a week from April to October to both Vierzehnheiligen (Tues: departs 1.50pm, returns 4.15pm; 15min) and Kloster Banz (Thurs: departs 1pm, returns at 4.50pm).

By car There's a large car park halfway up the hill to Vierzehnheiligen church, though at off-peak times you should be able to park in the smaller car park by the church itself. There's also a car park opposite the Kloster Banz.

EATING AND DRINKING

Klosterbrauerei Trunk Vierzehnheiligen ☎ 09571 34 88. At the *Klosterbrauerei Trunk* just uphill from the church you can tuck into simple, rustic food – salami and ham platters cost €4.50–5.70 – washed down with dark or lager-style *Nothelfer* ("Holy Helper") beer, at €2.10 per half-litre. Daily 10am–8pm.

Klosterschänke Kloster Banz ☎ 09573 331 51 91, ⓦ klosterschaenke-banz.de. Strategically sited *Gaststätte* at the entrance to the abbey, with a sunny *Biergarten* and the likes of *Sauerbraten* with *Kloss* (dumplings) and red cabbage from around €9.80; fish dishes start around €9, and there are gluten-free and vegetarian options too. Daily 10am–10pm.

Bamberg

History has twice been kind to beautiful **BAMBERG**, for centuries until secularization in 1802, capital of an independent Catholic prince-bishopric within the Holy Roman Empire. Occupied twice by the Swedes during the Thirty Years' War, it was spared the wholesale destruction visited on so many German cities by that conflict. By some

BAMBERG ORIENTATION

Bamberg is split neatly into three by the parallel courses of the River Regnitz – a short tributary of the Main – and the Main–Donau canal, both of which run southeast to northwest through the city. The **Gärtnerstadt** in the east is of relatively little interest to visitors; **Inselstadt** between the canal and river is the handsome, secular city centre; while for centuries spiritual and temporal power in Bamberg had its seat in the **Bergstadt** – built, like Rome, on seven hills – on the west bank of the Regnitz. Within easy reach of the city, **Schloss Seehof** and **Schloss Weissenstein** are a couple of Baroque palaces associated with the prince-bishops which make for pleasant half-day excursions.

BAMBERG

NIGHTLIFE

Jazz Club Bamberg	1
Live-Club	2

ACCOMMODATION

Alt-Bamberg	5
Brudermühle	6
DJH Am Kaulberg	7
Messerschmitt	4
National	1
Nepomuk	8
Spezial	2
Wilde Rose	3

●CAFÉS AND RESTAURANTS		●BARS AND BRAUEREIGASTSTÄTTEN	
Brudermühle	10	Fässla Stub'n	2
Café Müller	4	Greifenklau	12
Calimeros	6	Klosterbräu	11
DaCaBo	3	Schlenkerla	8
Graupner	5	Spezial	1
Hofbräu	9	Stilbruch	7

miracle, it came through World War II with barely a scratch too. It thus preserves a wonderfully complete historic townscape, notable not just for its highlights – the four-spired **Dom**, the Baroque **Residenz** and the picturesque old **Rathaus** on an island in the river – but also for its quaint corners and quiet, narrow lanes, worth exploring for their lost-in-time charm and traditional brewery-owned *Gaststätten*. No wonder UNESCO put Bamberg's entire historic centre on its World Heritage list in 1993. Compact enough to be explored in a few days, Bamberg is a tempting place to linger, thanks to its unique atmosphere and history, hilly views, and distinctive *Rauchbier* (smoked beer).

The Altes Rathaus

If a competition had been held to design the most picturesque building in Germany, it might have been won by Bamberg's **Altes Rathaus**, an enchanting combination of Baroque *Lüftmalerei* and half-timbered quaintness wedged onto an artificial islet in the Regnitz, bracketed on either side by the stone arches of the **Obere Brücke**. Yet picturesque effect wasn't the reason for the curious site: depending which version you prefer, it was either built mid-river by stubborn burghers after the prince-bishop refused to donate any land for its construction, or to mark the division between the sacred and profane parts of the city and thus demonstrate the independent-mindedness of the burghers.

The half-timbered **Rottmeisterhäuschen** of 1668, which teeters over the rushing waters on the south side of the islet, is the only part of the Altes Rathaus to preserve its original appearance, but it's not the oldest part of the complex, for the main body of the Rathaus preserves a fifteenth-century core beneath an exuberant Baroque and Rococo makeover, which dates from 1744 to 1756. **Johann Anwanders'** lush allegorical paintings on the flanks of the building have startling depth – watch out for the chubby angel's leg that really *does* jut out, on the side facing Inselstadt.

Sammlung Ludwig
Tues–Sun 9.30am–4.30pm • €4.50 • ⓦ museum.bamberg.de

The Altes Rathaus houses the **Sammlung Ludwig**, a visual feast of Strasbourg faïence and Sèvres and Meissen porcelain, including Johann Joachim Kendler's **Monkey Orchestra** of 1753 – a caricature of human virtues and vices in porcelain form. The ticket also includes entrance into the elegant Rococo Room, which dates from 1750 and has an attractive stucco ceiling by Franz Jakob Vogel.

Schloss Geyerswörth

To the south of the Altes Rathaus, the course of the Regnitz is a cat's cradle of little bridges and islets. On the largest of these, close to the tourist office, **Schloss Geyerswörth** was originally a medieval patrician residence, before being rebuilt in 1580 to 1587 as a bishop's palace.

The Inselstadt

Cross the narrow, picturesque **Alter Kanal** by the footbridge behind the Schloss to **Inselstadt**, the historic heart of the secular city. Its main thoroughfare, Grüner Markt, is presided over by the massive Baroque **Pfarrkirche St Martin**. The work of brothers Georg and Leonhard Dientzenhofer, and completed in 1693, the church has a shallow, *trompe l'oeil* dome. Grüner Markt leads into spacious **Maxplatz** (or Maximilianplatz to give it its official name), dominated by the imposing former seminary, built between 1732 and 1737 by Balthasar Neumann and now functioning as the city's **Neues Rathaus**. Maxplatz is the focus for numerous events, including Bamberg's **Christmas market**.

The Naturkundemuseum
Fleischstr. 2 • Tues–Sun: April–Sept 9am–5pm; Oct–March 10am–4pm • €3.50 • ⓦ naturkundemuseum-bamberg.de

Tucked behind the Pfarrkirche St Martin on Fleischstrasse is the **Naturkundemuseum**, the city's natural history museum. Its chief glory is the **Vogelsaal**, in which stuffed birds are still exhibited in the original Neoclassical eighteenth-century display cases. The museum also boasts a modern multimedia show, *Biosphäre*.

E.T.A. Hoffmann-Haus
Schillerplatz 26 • May–Oct Tues–Fri 3–5pm, Sat & Sun 10am–noon • €2

From Grüner Markt, a pleasant stroll along Habergasse and Zinkenwörth brings you to the modest but pretty eighteenth-century **E.T.A. Hoffmann-Haus**, where the composer, critic and author of the eponymous *Tales* lived from 1808 to 1813. The house contains an imaginatively presented exhibition which chronicles his life, work and the opera, *Undine*.

The Inselstadt riverside: Am Kranen and Klein Venedig

There's a studenty vibe to some of the streets between Maxplatz and the river. Follow Heumarkt into Stangstrasse, before heading south down Kapuzinerstrasse to **Am Kranen**, on the banks of the Regnitz where a couple of historic cranes mark the site of the city's main quay from the fourteenth century until 1912; barges sailed downstream from here along the Main and Rhine to the Netherlands and, after 1846, upstream along the Main–Donau canal too. The eighteenth-century slaughterhouse on the riverside – identifiable by a stone effigy of an ox on its gable – dumped its waste and blood directly into the river. The riverside north from here is a particularly picturesque jumble of medieval fishermen's houses, with jetties for gardens and steep red-tiled roofs hanging low over the river. Known as **Klein Venedig**, or Little Venice, it's seen to best effect from the Bergstadt side of the river.

The Bergstadt

Crossing the River Regnitz by either the **Obere Brücke** or the **Untere Brücke** just to the north, you enter the lower reaches of the **Bergstadt**, an atmospheric hotchpotch of antique shops, antiquarian booksellers and ancient *Brauereigaststätten*. South of the bridges along Judenstrasse and Concordiastrasse are two of Bamberg's most imposing Baroque houses, the outrageously florid **Böttingerhaus** (1707–13), built for the privy councillor and elector Johann Ignaz Tobias Böttinger, and the more dignified **Wasserschloss Concordia** on the riverside, built for the same client by Johann Dientzenhofer between 1717 and 1722. The Wasserschloss Concordia houses the **Internationales Künstlerhaus** (Ⓦ villa-concordia.de), and can be visited when art exhibitions are on.

Obere Pfarre

Frauenplatz • Daily 9am–5pm • Free • Ⓦ obere-pfarre-bamberg.de

Just uphill from the Böttingerhaus on Untere Kaulberg is the **Obere Pfarre** or Pfarrkirche zu Unserer Lieben Frau, Bamberg's only purely Gothic church. Built in the fourteenth century, it has a particularly lovely tabernacle in the ambulatory, while its treasures include Tintoretto's *Assumption*. At the time of writing it was currently undergoing lengthy restoration, so parts of the church may be subject to closure.

Kaiserdom

Domplatz • Daily: April–Oct 9am–6pm; Nov–March 9am–5pm • Free • Ⓦ bamberger-dom.de

The distinctive four-spired silhouette of Bamberg's **Kaiserdom**, or imperial cathedral, dominates **Domplatz**, one of the most splendid urban spaces in southern Germany and for centuries the nexus of spiritual and temporal power in Bamberg. Bamberg's bishopric was established by the Emperor Heinrich II in 1007, but the present cathedral was completed in 1237 in a style that blends late Romanesque and early Gothic elements, and which was influenced by the design of the hilltop cathedral in Laon, France. **Heinrich II** and his consort **Kunigunde** are buried in a fabulously elaborate marble tomb between the east and west choirs, carved by Tilman Riemenschneider between 1499 and 1513.

Not to be missed is Veit Stoss's **Christmas Altar** in the south transept – the Nuremberg carver's last great work, it dates from 1523. The cathedral's most famous monument is the **Bamberger Reiter** of 1235, a stone sculpture of a fine-featured, beardless nobleman on horseback, which has over the centuries been regarded as the embodiment of medieval chivalry. The artist is unknown, and it's not known for certain who the subject was either, though the crowning canopy in the form of a city suggests a saint and thus King Stephen I of Hungary, who completed the task of converting his country to Christianity and was later canonized.

Diözesanmuseum

Domplatz 5 • Tues–Sun 10am–5pm • €5 • Ⓦ dioesesanmuseum-bamberg.de

The cathedral cloisters house the **Diözesanmuseum** (Diocese Museum), whose prize exhibits are its unique collection of eleventh-century vestments, including Heinrich II's stunning blue-and-gold *Sternmantel*, made in Regensburg around 1020.

5

Ratsstube: the Historisches Museum

Domplatz 7 • May–Oct Wed–Sun 9am–5pm; Nov–April temporary exhibitions only • €5 • ⓦ museum.bamberg.de

On the east side of Domplatz, the elaborate Renaissance **Ratsstube** houses the **Historisches Museum**, whose rich and varied collection documents the history of Bamberg and the surrounding area. Its treasures include paintings by Lucas Cranach the Elder and Pieter Bruegel as well as an early view of Bamberg – and one of the earliest-ever painted depictions of a German city – in *The Apostles' Farewell* by Wolfgang Katzheimer the Elder. The innovative "Lebensader Regnitz" section tells the story of Bamberg in relation to its river, and during Advent the museum hosts an exhibition of nativity scenes.

Behind the Ratsstube is the **Alte Hofhaltung**, a meandering complex of fifteenth-century half-timbered buildings that formerly housed the prince-bishops' household.

Neue Residenz

Domplatz 8 • Guided tours daily: April–Sept 9am–6pm; Oct–March 10am–4pm • €4.50, combined ticket with Schloss Seehof €7 • ⓦ schloesser-bayern.de

Zigzagging across the north side of Domplatz is the impressive Baroque **Neue Residenz**, begun in 1613 but extended to its present magnificence under prince-bishop Lothar von Schönborn between 1697 and 1703. The work of Leonhard Dientzenhofer, it has more than forty state rooms, the most impressive of which is the **Kaisersaal**, decorated with sixteen larger-than-life-size portraits of Holy Roman Emperors by Melchior Steidl and with a subtly *trompe l'oeil* ceiling – much shallower than it appears. More intimate but touching are the apartments once occupied by **Otto of Greece**, a member of the Bavarian Wittelsbach royal family who became King of Greece in 1832 but who as a devout Catholic refused to convert to the Orthodox faith and was ultimately forced to abdicate in 1862. He lived out the remainder of his years in Bamberg.

After the tour, you can enjoy the paintings of the **Gemäldegalerie** – including works by Lucas Cranach the Elder and Michael Wolgemut – at your leisure.

The rose garden

The **rose garden** behind the Residenz is absolutely lovely, and boasts sweeping views over the rooftops of the town and up to the Michaelsberg monastery. The garden is the setting in summer for the **Rosengarten Serenaden** chamber music concerts (ⓦ rosengarten-serenaden.com), while its lovely little Baroque café – closed for renovation at the time of writing – is one of the best places in Bamberg to unwind over a drink.

The Michaelsberg and monastery of St Michael

Michaelsberg 10f • Fränkisches Brauereimuseum April–Oct Wed–Fri 1–5pm, Sat & Sun 11am–5pm • €3.50 • ⓦ brauereimuseum.de

An idyllic (if steep) walk from Aufsessstrasse below Domplatz leads through terraced orchards to the former Benedictine monastery of **St Michael** atop the Michaelsberg hill, with wonderful views over the city. It was founded in 1015 under Heinrich II, but was reconstructed following a catastrophic fire in 1610; the church was complete – in a curious hybrid Gothic style – by 1617. The surrounding Baroque abbey buildings were built by Leonhard Dientzenhofer from 1696 onwards. The church cannot currently be visited, but you can visit the **Fränkisches Brauereimuseum**, in which Bamberg's own distinguished brewing tradition takes centre stage.

Schlosspark Seehof

Memmelsdorf • April–Oct Tues–Sun 9am–6pm; Wasserspiele May–Sept hourly 10am–5pm • €4, combined ticket with Neue Residenz €7 • ⓦ schloesser-bayern.de • Bus #907 from Bamberg bus station

Six kilometres of Bamberg at Memmelsdorf, the delightful summer palace of **Schloss Seehof** is evidence of the prince-bishops' lavish ways. Constructed to plans by

5

Antonio Petrini from 1686 onwards, it fell into disrepair after the secularization of the prince-bishopric and today most of it houses the Bavarian organization responsible for the care and maintenance of historic buildings. Its nine state rooms, however, have been restored, and include the Weisse Saal with magnificent ceiling paintings by Giuseppe Appiani. The eighteenth-century Rococo **water gardens** with their restored **Wasserspiele** (fountains and cascade) were once famous throughout Germany.

Schloss Weissenstein

96178 Pommersfelden • Entry by guided tour only: daily on the hour April–Oct 10am–4pm; English tours on special request (book in advance) • €7 • W schloss-weissenstein.de • No public transport

While Schlosspark Seehof (see p.306) was the prince-bishops' "official" summer residence, the immense **Schloss Weissenstein** at Pommersfelden, 20km south of the city, was and remains the private home of the Schönborn family, and when they are in residence they fly a standard, just like the British royal family. The Schloss was commissioned by prince-bishop Lothar Franz von Schönborn and built to designs by his court architect, Johann Dientzenhofer, and Johann Lukas von Hildebrandt, the celebrated Austrian Baroque architect and designer of Vienna's Belvedere.

The results are magnificent, particularly in Hildebrandt's graceful ceremonial **Treppenhaus**, or staircase, which inspired the still more magnificent example at Würzburg built nine years later. The principal state room, the **Marmorsaal** or marble hall, rises through two storeys and was a tour de force of structural ingenuity in its day, its weighty marble floor resting on the wooden arches of the grotto-like Gartensaal beneath. Schloss Weissenstein is also home to an impressive private **art collection**, including works by Titian, Van Dyck, Rubens and Brueghel.

ARRIVAL AND GETTING AROUND   BAMBERG

By train Bamberg's Hauptbahnhof is in Gärtnerstadt, a good 15min walk from the centre of the Altstadt.
Destinations Bad Staffelstein (for Vierzehnheiligen; 2–3 per hour; 10–20min); Bayreuth (every 2hr; 1hr 15min); Coburg (hourly; 45min); Nuremberg (2–4 per hour; 35min–1hr); Würzburg (2 per hour; 55min–1hr 10min).
By bus The central bus station is on Promenadestrasse in

Inselstadt, connected by numerous buses (5min) to the train station.
Bike rental Radl-Dran, Weidendamm 5 (☎ 0176 38 08 05 30, W radl-dran.de); Fahrradhaus Griesmann (electric bikes), Obere Königstrasse 42 (☎ 0951 229 67, W fahrradhaus-griesmann.de).

INFORMATION

Tourist office From the Inselstadt it's a short walk to the tourist office on an island in the Regnitz at Geyerswörthstr. 5 (Mon–Fri 9.30am–6pm, Sat 9.30am–4pm, Sun 9.30am–2.30pm; ☎ 0951 297 62 00, W bamberg.info). You can book somewhere to stay through their website and the

office also has a list of private rooms.
Discount card The tourist office can sell you a three-day Bamberg Card (€12), which entitles you to free travel on city buses, free entry to seven museums and a free guided tour of the city.

ACCOMMODATION

HOTELS AND PENSIONS

Alt-Bamberg Habergasse 11 ☎ 0951 98 61 50, W hotel-alt-bamberg.de. Plain but attractive rooms above a restaurant in a half-timbered house very centrally located close to the Regnitz. Rooms have phone and TV, cyclists are welcome and parking is available. There is also one triple and one four-bed apartment. **€65**
Brudermühle Schranne 1 ☎ 0951 95 52 20, W brudermuehle.de. Traditionally styled family hotel in an enviable location on the Bergstadt riverside just metres from the Altes Rathaus, with an atmospheric riverside

restaurant (see opposite). There's free wi-fi, rooms have safes and you can hire bikes. **€125**
Messerschmitt Lange Str. 41 ☎ 0951 29 78 00, W hotel-messerschmitt.de. The unintentionally comic name aside – it means simply "cutler" in German – this is a lovely, upmarket Inselstadt hotel in an attractive and historic *Weinhaus*, with masses of mellow wood and a well-regarded restaurant. Facilities include a/c, wi-fi, sauna and whirlpool bath, and they have rooms suitable for allergy sufferers. **€145**
★ **National** Luitpoldstr. 37 ☎ 0951 50 99 80, W hotel-national-bamberg.de. Friendly and comfortable 3-star

hotel in an attractive nineteenth-century building in the Gärtnerstadt, handy for the Hauptbahnhof and with some singles. There's free wi-fi and limited car parking on site. **€79**

★**Nepomuk** Obere Mühlbrücke 9 ☎0951 984 20, ⊕hotel-nepomuk.de. Stylish, 4-star hotel built out over the river, with a glass bridge linking the Bergstadt and mid-river wings. Rooms are contemporary in style; the suite has views downriver to the Altes Rathaus. Facilities include safes in rooms, bicycle hire and wi-fi. **€130**

Spezial Obere Königstr. 10 ☎0951 243 04, ⊕brauerei-spezial.de. Simple but comfortable single and double rooms, most with shower and WC, above an atmospheric half-timbered Gärtnerstadt *Brauereigaststätte* (see p.310).

It's cyclist- and pet-friendly, and there's car parking available. **€50**

Wilde Rose Kesslerstr. 7 ☎0951 98 18 20, ⊕hotel-wilde-rose.de. Good, very central mid-range option in a former brewery in Inselstadt, with a restaurant serving Franconian cuisine and the in-house *Wilde Rose Bier*. Rooms have shower, WC and internet. **€103**

HOSTELS

DJH Am Kaulberg Untere Kaulberg 30 ☎0951 29 95 28 90, ⊕bamberg.jugendherberge.de. Five minutes on foot from the Dom and city centre, with accommodation in doubles, four- and six-bed dorms or family rooms. Renovated in 2011, it has secure bike storage. Dorms **€25.50**

EATING AND DRINKING

Bamberg's Altstadt has plenty of good places to **eat** and **drink**, including the atmospheric *Gaststätten* associated with its many breweries (known as *Brauereigaststätten*). Obere Sandstrasse in the lower Bergstadt has the liveliest concentration of places to drink or to hear **live music**.

CAFÉS AND CHEAP EATS

Café Müller Austr. 23 ☎0951 20 29 43. Classic all-day café-bar with bentwood chairs, a jazzy soundtrack and white wood-panelled walls. Breakfast (from €3.60) is served until 4pm; pasta and specials cost from around €6.30, salads from €7.20. Mon–Thurs & Sun 9am–1am, Fri & Sat 9am–2am.

Calimeros Lange Str. 8 ☎0951 20 11 72, ⊕calimeros.de. Slick Tex-Mex bar/diner near the Altes Rathaus, and something of an Anglo-American hangout, with generous portions of quesadillas, burritos and burgers and regular weekly deals: all-you-can-eat spare ribs on Tues (€11.80), all-you-can-eat tacos on Wed (€9.90). Mon–Wed 6pm–1am, Thurs & Fri 6pm–3am, Sat 11am–3am, Sun 10am–1am.

★**DaCaBo** Am Heumarkt 7 ☎0951 297 18 68, ⊕dacabo-bamberg.de. Pleasant, modern café-bar on a tranquil cobbled square in Inselstadt, with a terrace shaded by plane trees and a big selection of juices, teas and coffees, breakfasts (from €4.30) until 2pm, plus delicious, healthy daily specials for around €6.80. Mon–Sat 9am–10pm, Sun 9am–7pm.

Graupner Lange Str. 5 ☎0951 98 04 00, ⊕graupner-patisserie.de. Classy and reasonably priced Inselstadt *Konditorei* and chocolatier. It's much the best traditional *Kaffee und Kuchen* stop in Bamberg, with cakes at €2.50 per portion. It also serves breakfasts from €2.80 and lunchtime pasta or noodle specials from €5.50. Mon–Sat 9am–6pm, Sun 10am–5pm.

RESTAURANTS

Brudermühle Schranne 1 ☎0951 955 20, ⊕brudermuehle.de. Cosy, rather traditional riverside restaurant in the hotel of the same name, close to the Altes

Rathaus, and serving hearty fare such as Franconian *Schäufele* in *Rauchbier* sauce, beef roulade or *Wildschweinbraten*. They also serve *Kaffee und Kuchen* in the afternoon. Meaty mains from around €12. Daily 7am–midnight.

Hofbräu Karolinenstr. 7 ☎0951 533 21, ⊕hofbraeu-bamberg.de. Despite the name, this elegant but informal place on the Bergstadt side of the Regnitz is more restaurant than bar, with a few French and Italian touches alongside the Franconian dishes and contemporary art on the walls. Mains from around €16.50. Live piano Mon nights. Daily 10am–1am.

BARS AND BRAUEREIGASTSTÄTTEN

Fässla Stub'n Kleberstr. 9 ☎0951 265 16. Friendly, studenty bar in Inselstadt with daily changing drinks specials and great music. Excellent draught Fässla beer €1.90, snacks from €3.20 and what they claim is the strongest *Bockbier* in Bamberg. Mon–Thurs & Sun 8pm–2am, Fri & Sat 8pm–4am.

★**Greifenklau** Laurenziplatz 20 ☎0951 532 19, ⊕greifenklau.de. Cosy, atmospheric wood-panelled Bergstadt *Brauereigaststätte* that's well worth the treck uphill, serving delicious *Bock* and *Weizen* beers as well as its excellent regular *Greifenklau* brew (half-litre €2.60). They have simple meals for around €7, and the *Biergarten* at the back has lovely views of the Altenburg. Tues–Sat 10.30am–11.30pm, Sun 10.30am–2pm.

Klosterbräu Obere Mühlbrücke 1–3 ☎0951 522 65, ⊕klosterbraeu.de. Bamberg's oldest *Brauereigaststätte* is a rambling collection of picturesque buildings on the Bergstadt side of the Regnitz; its *Braunbier* (€3.10/half-litre) dates back to its origins as the prince-bishops' own brewery, and there's filling, affordable Franconian food

5

(mains from around €9). Mon–Fri 10.30am–11pm, Sat 10am–11pm, Sun 10am–10pm.

★**Schlenkerla** Dominikanerstr. 6 ☎0951 560 60, ⓦschlenkerla.de. The classic place to try smoky Bamberg *Rauchbier* (€2.60/half litre) is this venerable half-timbered Bergstadt pub. Though very touristy it's entirely authentic and certainly looks the part, with a wonderfully historic, beamed interior. They serve simple Franconian food too, though; service is occasionally grumpy. Daily 9.30am–11.30pm.

★**Spezial** Obere Königstr. 10 ☎0951 243 04, ⓦbrauerei-spezial.de. Rustic, traditional *Brauereigaststätte* in an attractive corner of Gärtnerstadt, serving an own-brew

Rauchbier that's milder than the smokier *Schlenkerla* variety, as well as a *Weissbier*; there's also simple food (from €5.40) to soak up the beer. The Spezial brewery was founded in 1536, and the place also offers rooms (see p.309). Mon–Fri & Sun 9am–11pm, Sat 9am–2pm.

Stilbruch Obere Sandstr. 18 ☎0951 519 00 02, ⓦstilbruch-bamberg.de. The most "alternative" of the Bergstadt bars, still fabulously beamy and old but with a laidback and more youthful atmosphere, good music selection and *Spezial Rauchbier* (€2.60/half-litre). There's also simple food including burgers (€5.90) and the cellar houses the old-established *Jazz Club Bamberg* (see below). Mon–Thurs & Sun 11am–2am, Fri & Sat 11am–4am.

NIGHTLIFE AND ENTERTAINMENT

CLUBS AND LIVE MUSIC

★**Jazz Club Bamberg** Obere Sandstr. 18 ☎0951 537 40, ⓦjcbamberg.de. *Jazz Club Bamberg* has an eclectic programme of regular jazz and cabaret gigs in the vaulted cellar of an Inselstadt pub, and organizes outdoor events in summer. Concerts generally start at 8 or 9pm.

Live-Club Obere Sandstr. 7 ☎0951 533 04, ⓦlive-club.de. The *Live-Club* opposite *Stilbruch* in Bergstadt's liveliest street is the best place to hear live bands in Bamberg, with gigs and DJ nights most Mondays, Fridays and Saturdays and a music policy that ranges from indie to jazz, rock, soul and blues. Gigs generally start at 8.30 or 9pm.

THEATRE AND CLASSICAL MUSIC

E.T.A. Hoffmann Theater E.T.A.-Hoffmann-Platz 1 ☎0951 87 30 30, ⓦtheater-bamberg.de. Highbrow cultural tastes are catered to by the E.T.A. Hoffmann Theatre, which presents everything from classic and contemporary drama to poetry slams and ballet. The season runs from October to July.

Konzerthalle Bamberg Mussstr. 1, on the banks of the Regnitz ☎0951 964 71 00, ⓦbamberger-symphoniker.de. Home base of the Bamberger Symphoniker orchestra, founded in 1946 by refugee German musicians from Czechoslovakia and currently led by Briton Jonathan Nott. A busy programme of concerts both in Bamberg and internationally, and a repertoire that includes much modern music.

THE ROMANTIC ROAD

Though there are tourist roads that crisscross Germany for everything from wine to fairy tales and half-timbered houses, the **Romantic Road** (ⓦromanticroad.de) remains by far the best-known internationally. The "Romantic" name is something of a catch-all, but the route does encompass much that is most traditionally – and charmingly – German, from walled medieval towns to fairy-tale castles and richly decorated Rococo churches, and it's precisely this combination of historic sights and lost-in-time-charm that makes the journey worthwhile.

Created in the 1950s to boost tourism, it threads its way south from the River Main to the Alps as the landscape progressively changes from gentle, rolling agricultural country to the fringes of the mountains. Along the way, it passes by some of Germany's most remarkable and famous visitor attractions: the Residenz in **Würzburg** (see opposite), the perfectly preserved medieval towns of **Rothenburg ob der Tauber** (see p.318) and **Dinkelsbühl** (see p.323), the UNESCO World Heritage Site of the **Wieskirche** (see p.388) and "Mad" King Ludwig II's Wagnerian fantasy castle of **Neuschwanstein** (see p.386).

GETTING AROUND

By bus Much the easiest way to travel the Romantic Road is, of course, by car, but if you don't have your own transport the Eurolines-affiliated Europabus (ⓦeurolines.de/en/national-bus/romantische-strasse) travels the road once daily in each direction from mid-April to October between Frankfurt, Würzburg, Munich and Füssen, with special offers for hikers and cyclists and facilities to transport bikes

(spaces must be booked in advance); you can book tickets online.

By bike and on foot There's a 440km cycle route, most of it fairly gentle and characterized by well-made local tracks or quiet local roads, or you can follow the route on foot; the GPS data for the entire walk can be downloaded from the Romantic Road website, ⓦromanticroad.de.

Würzburg

Vine-covered hills form the backdrop to **WÜRZBURG**, a visible reminder that you're no longer in beer country. The city marks the start of the **Romantic Road** (see box opposite), which leads south to the Alps from here, and with its picturesque setting, artistic and architectural treasures and fine wines, Würzburg makes a fitting start to Germany's most famous road trip. Most of the sights are concentrated in the compact, walkable area between the Residenz and **River Main**, but you'll need to cross the Alte Mainbrücke to get the classic view of the Altstadt's pinnacled skyline. Also not to be missed is the **Marienberg fortress**, rising above vineyards on the opposite side of the river.

Brief history

The centre of the Franconian wine industry was for centuries dominated by the bishopric founded by the English missionary St Boniface in 742 AD and, as in Bamberg, its prince-bishops wielded both spiritual and temporal power. In the late fifteenth and early sixteenth centuries the city nurtured the talent – while ultimately spurning the revolutionary politics – of the master woodcarver Tilman Riemenschneider. In the eighteenth century two prince-bishops of the luxury-loving Schörnborn dynasty were responsible for commissioning the city's greatest monument – and Bavaria's most magnificent palace – the **Residenz**, now a UNESCO World Heritage Site. Horrendous damage was visited on Würzburg by Britain's Royal Air Force on March 16, 1945, when the city was subjected to an ordeal by firestorm that consumed the Altstadt and killed five thousand people; destruction was so severe the city was afterwards dubbed "The Grave on the Main". Justification for the raid derived supposedly from the city's rail junction, though it had long been on a list of cities earmarked for attack for no specific reason other than their size. After the war, Würzburg recovered with remarkable success, and its war-damaged monuments were slowly and painstakingly restored or rebuilt.

The Residenz

Residenz Daily: April–Oct 9am–6pm; Nov–March 10am–4.30pm; guided tours in English daily at 11am & 3pm, also at 4.30pm April–Oct • €7.50 • ⓦ residenz-wuerzburg.de • **Martin von Wagner Museum** Gemäldegalerie Tues–Sat 10am–1.30pm, Sun 10am–1.30pm; Graphische Sammlung by appointment; Antikensammlung Tues–Sat 1.30–5pm, Sun 10am–1.30pm • Free • ⓦ museum.uni-wuerzburg.de • **Hofgarten** Daily until dusk or 8pm, whichever is earlier • Free

Dominating the Altstadt's eastern flank, the **Residenz** is an eighteenth-century status symbol that puts Würzburg firmly into the architectural super league, as it was fully intended to do. Johann Philipp Franz von Schönborn, prince-bishop of Würzburg from 1719 to 1724, transferred his court from the Marienberg to the town, but was not at all satisfied with the modest little Schloss on the site of the present Residenz, and so commissioned Balthasar Neumann to design something more appropriate to his princely status. The proceeds of a lawsuit provided the necessary funds, and Schloss Weissenstein at Pommersfelden – recently completed for the bishop's uncle, Lothar Franz von Schönborn – provided the blueprint. Other architects of the day, including the Viennese Baroque master Lucas von Hildebrandt, provided some of the inspiration. The bishop never lived to inhabit his creation and his immediate successor stopped building work, but it restarted under his brother Friedrich Carl and thus the palace is the coherent creation of a relatively short period of construction. The results are breathtaking: impressively wide, the Residenz faces a paved *Hof* on three sides. After visiting the interior, stroll in the formal **Hofgarten** afterwards to see the Residenz's southern and eastern facades.

The Haupträume (principal rooms) and the North Wing

Inside, the highly theatrical **Treppenhaus**, or staircase, stretches across five bays and is topped by a mammoth unsupported vault – a structurally audacious design of which

5

WÜRZBURG

NIGHTLIFE
Posthalle 1

CAFÉS, BARS AND PUBS
Alter Kranen 2
Café Konditorei Michel 5
Joe's Cantina y Bar 3
Schönborn 7

RESTAURANTS
Alte Mainmühle 8
Ratskeller 9

WEINSTUBEN
Bürgerspital 4
Weinstuben Juliusspital 1
Zum Stachel 6

ACCOMMODATION
Babelfish 1
Best Western Premier
  Hotel Rebstock 6
Central Hotel Garni 4
DJH Würzburg 7
Hotel am
  Congress-Centrum 2
Sankt Josef 5
Zur Stadt Mainz 3

Neumann was so confident he offered to fire a battery of artillery at it to prove its strength. His confidence was vindicated in 1945, when the ceiling withstood the aerial bombardment of the city – which wrecked the north and south wings of the Schloss but left the Treppenhaus intact. The staircase rises through a series of half-landings, their walls richly ornamented with stucco, but everything is merely a setting for **Giovanni Battista Tiepolo**'s magnificent allegorical ceiling fresco, which measures thirteen by eighteen metres and is the largest ever created. It depicts the four continents of Asia, Africa, America and Europe, with the Würzburg court depicted as the centre of the arts in Europe.

At the top of the stairs, the white and pale grey **Weisser Saal** is decorated with tasteful stuccowork by Materno Bossi. Completed in 1745, the room provides an entirely deliberate aesthetic breathing-space between the Treppenhaus and the most extravagant of the state rooms, the giddily opulent **Kaisersaal**. With its twenty red marble columns, large oval dome and Tiepolo frescoes celebrating Würzburg's position in the Holy Roman Empire, the richly coloured Kaisersaal provides a memorable setting for classical music concerts. To either side, long processions of rooms lead into the north and south wings. In the north, the delicate stucco ceilings had to be re-created after wartime damage; the **Grünlackiertes Zimmer**, or Green Lacquered Room, is the highlight.

5

The Southern Imperial Apartments, Hofkirche and Martin von Wagner Museum

The **Southern Imperial Apartments** can only be visited on a free guided tour – enquire in the Weisser Saal – but are well worth seeing for the **Spiegelkabinett**, a riot of painted mirror panels and gold leaf that was re-created after wartime destruction using old photographs and surviving shards of glass as a guide. Afterwards, visit the **Hofkirche** on the south side of the complex, the religious counterpart to the Residenz's secular pomp, again with frescoes by Tiepolo. The south wing is also the venue for interesting temporary exhibitions, and contains the **Martin von Wagner Museum**, the university's collections of antiquities and art, exhibited in the Gemäldegalerie, Graphische Sammlung and Antikensammlung. Art highlights include works by Tilman Riemenschneider and Tiepolo.

The Dom and around

Domstr. 43 • Free • ⓦ dom-wuerzburg.de

From the Residenz, Hofstrasse leads west to the heart of the bishops' city. The twin-towered **Dom St Kilian** was built in the eleventh and twelfth centuries and is one of the largest surviving Romanesque cathedrals in Germany. Its exterior has a pleasing austerity; inside, surviving examples of early eighteenth-century stuccowork are balanced by the simplicity of the postwar restoration. Balthasar Neumann's gorgeous **Schönbornkapelle**, built onto the northern transept from 1721 to 1736, competes with the main body of the cathedral for monumental effect and nearly wins: it's a suitably imposing memorial to the self-important Schönborn bishops.

Museum am Dom

Kiliansplatz • April–Oct Tues–Sun 10am–6pm; Nov–March Tues–Sun 10am–5pm • €3.50, combined ticket with Domschatz €4.50 • ⓦ museum-am-dom.de

On the north side of the Dom opposite the Schönbornkapelle is the **Museum am Dom**, which houses the diocesan art collection. The exhibits are hung conceptually, and the result is very far from a dusty collection of religious relics: in addition to sculptures by Tilman Riemenschneider you can see works by Otto Dix and Käthe Kollwitz and art from the former GDR.

Domschatz

Plattnerstrasse • Tues–Sun 2–5pm • €2, combined ticket with Museum am Dom €4.50 • ⓦ domschatz.bistum-wuerzburg.de

A short walk south of the Dom is the **Domschatz**, an intensely dark treasury where the highlights include an impressive eleventh-century lion-head door knocker originally from the Dom, and some well-preserved items from the graves of Würzburg's bishops.

The Neumünster

Schönbornstrasse • Mon–Sat 6am–7pm, Sun 7am–7pm • Free • ⓦ neumuenster-wuerzburg.de

North of the Dom along Schönbornstrasse is the **Neumünster**, whose elegant Baroque facade conceals an eleventh-century Romanesque basilica. The church is built on the site of the graves of the Irish missionary St Kilian and his associates St Kolonat and St Totnan, who were murdered in Würzburg in 689 AD.

Marktplatz and around

Bustling **Marktplatz** is the heart of secular Würzburg, with an eclectic selection of buildings from the medieval to the stylishly modern ranged around its irregular fringes. Much the prettiest of the Markplatz buildings is the **Falkenhaus** on the north side, once a *Gasthaus* and now housing the tourist office and municipal library; its sugary external stucco decoration dates from 1751 and looks almost good enough to eat.

5

Marienkapelle

Looming alongside the Falkenhaus is the **Marienkapelle**, a lofty, Late Gothic hall church founded in 1377 on the site of the town's synagogue, which was destroyed in a pogrom in 1349. Tilman Riemenschneider was responsible for much of the church's sculpture; the famous figures of *Adam and Eve* are copies, the originals now being in the Mainfränkisches Museum in the Marienberg (see opposite), but the tomb of Konrad von Schaumberg is original.

The Rathaus

Just west of Marktplatz, the oldest part of the **Rathaus**, the **Grafeneckart**, with its slender Romanesque tower, was originally the seat of episcopal officials, but has served as the city's Rathaus since 1316. Its northern extension, the late Renaissance **Rote Bau**, was reduced to a shell in 1945 but has been carefully restored. A small exhibition on the ground floor tells the story – with text in German and English – of Würzburg's wartime destruction; the photographs are gripping enough, but the scale model of the destroyed Altstadt is truly shocking.

Alte Mainbrücke and riverside

Just beyond the Rathaus, the fifteenth-century **Alte Mainbrücke** crosses the river, lined on either side with Baroque statues of saints – among them St John Nepomuk, who was martyred by being pushed into Prague's Vltava River. Whatever compromises Würzburg's postwar builders made when they reconstructed the city, from the centre of the bridge the illusion of timelessness is perfect, and the skyline of the Altstadt is a festive huddle of spires and cupolas. North of the bridge, the **Alter Kranen** is a pair of eighteenth-century riverside cranes, the work of Balthasar Neumann's son Franz Ignaz Michael.

The Museum im Kulturspeicher

Oskar-Laredo-Platz 1 • Tues 1–6pm, Wed & Fri–Sun 11am–6pm, Thurs 11am–7pm • €3.50 • ⓦ kulturspeicher.de • Bus #9 from Residenz

North of the Altstadt, a converted dockside warehouse is now the **Museum im Kulturspeicher**, which houses the municipal collection of art from the nineteenth century to the present day, including works from the Romantic, Biedermeier, Impressionist and Expressionist periods. In addition, the museum houses the Peter C. Ruppert collection of post-1945 Concrete Art, with works by Victor Vasarely, among others.

Röntgen-Gedächtnisstätte

Röntgenring 8 • Mon–Fri 8am–8pm, Sat 8am–6pm • Free • ⓦ wilhelmconradroentgen.de

To the east from the Museum im Kulturspeicher along Röntgenring is the **Röntgen-Gedächtnisstätte**, the laboratory in which Wilhelm Röntgen discovered x-rays, by accident, in 1895. The very first x-ray was of Röntgen's wife's hand: "I have seen my death!" she exclaimed when she saw it. Exhibits in the museum include some of the apparatus Röntgen used in his experiments.

Marienberg fortress and the Kappele

Mainfränkisches Museum Tues–Sun: April–Oct 10am–5pm; Nov–March 10am–4pm • €4 • Fürstenbau Museum Mid-March to Oct Tues–Sun 9am–6pm • €4.50, combined ticket with castle guided tour (mid-March to Oct in English at 3pm) €6 • ⓦ mainfraenkisches -museum.de • From Easter to Oct bus #9 shuttles between the Residenz, Kulturspeicher and Marienberg; the rest of the year trams #2 and #4 will get you most of the way there from Juliuspromenade

Looming above the city on the high west bank of the Main is the **Festung Marienberg**, which was the seat of the prince-bishops from 1253 until Johann Philipp Franz von Schönborn moved his court down into the city in 1719. Part medieval fortress, part Renaissance palace and with later Baroque extensions, the sheer scale of the Marienberg is impressive. The walk up through vineyards from the west bank of the river is lovely; otherwise, you can take the bus, or there's ample car parking west of the fortress.

Mainfränkisches Museum Würzburg

The Baroque Zeughaus, or arsenal, has been home since 1947 to the **Mainfränkisches Museum Würzburg**, which in addition to its sprawling permanent collection mounts engrossing temporary exhibitions. The undoubted highlight is the room devoted to **Tilman Riemenschneider**, the best-known sculptor of the late German Gothic. Born in Thuringia around 1460, he established a flourishing workshop in Würzburg by 1485 which he ran until his death in 1531. The Mainfränkisches Museum has the largest collection of his expressive works anywhere, and it's particularly rewarding to see them up close, rather than at a distance as they might usually be seen in a church. Highlights include his *Mary in Mourning* from Acholshausen, the *Adam and Eve* figures from the Marienkapelle (see opposite) and the two so-called *Candlestick Angels* from 1505. Successful as an artist, Riemenschneider also rose to prominence in politics, becoming mayor of Würzburg in 1520, before falling from grace when the city council formed an alliance with the peasants during the Peasants' War of 1524–25.

Fürstenbau Museum

Beyond the Zeughaus, the Kernberg – the core of the fortress – contains the **Fürstenbau Museum**, whose Brussels tapestries, clerical vestments and religious silver are less engrossing than the chance to see the interior of the building itself; despite being badly damaged by fire in 1945, it retains traces of its original painted decoration. The models of Würzburg as it was in 1525 and 1945 make a fascinating comparison. Afterwards, be sure not to miss the panoramic views of the city from the **Fürstengarten**.

The Kappele

On a neighbouring hillside to the south of the Festung Marienberg stands Balthasar Neumann's **Kappele**, a sweetly picturesque pilgrimage church built between 1748 and 1752, whose interior is a riot of Rococo ornament.

Schloss Veitshöchheim and around

Schloss Echterstr. 10, Veitshöchheim • Mid-April to Oct Tues–Sun 9am–6pm • €4.50, Hofgarten free • ⓦ schloesser-bayern.de • **Boat trips** Depart from Alter Kranen May–Sept daily 10am–4pm; limited service in April & Oct • One-way €8, return €10 • ⓦ schiffstouristik .de or ⓦ vpsherbert.de

One very popular summer excursion from Würzburg is the 45-minute **boat trip** from Alter Kranen to the neat village of **Veitshöchheim**, where Würzburg's prince-bishops had their summer residence, **Schloss Veitshöchheim**. Originally built as a hunting lodge in the late seventeenth century, the Schloss was transformed into a Baroque summer residence by Balthasar Neumann in 1753; inside, there are fine stucco ceilings by Antonio Bossi. The furnishing reflects the era of the prince-bishops and of the Grand Duke Ferdinand of Tuscany, who ruled Würzburg in the brief period between secularization and the city's incorporation into Bavaria in 1814. The Schloss's chief glory, however, is the splendid Rococo **Hofgarten**, which is graced by more than two hundred allegorical sandstone statues and a number of pavilions and follies, including the shell-encrusted Grottenhaus, topped with a belvedere.

Jüdisches Kulturmuseum

Thüngersheimerstr. 17, Veitshöchheim • March–Oct Thurs 3–6pm & Sun 2–5pm • €2 • ⓦ jkm.veitshoechheim.de

In the centre of Veitshöchheim, the village's Baroque **synagogue** dates from 1730 and forms part of a museum chronicling three centuries of rural Jewish life in Franconia. Defiled on Kristallnacht and later converted into a fire station, the synagogue was restored, using its original fittings, between 1986 and 1994.

5

ARRIVAL AND GETTING AROUND   WÜRZBURG

By train Würzburg's Hauptbahnhof is on the northern edge of the Altstadt, from where Kaiserstrasse leads into the centre.
Destinations Aschaffenburg (hourly; 40min); Bamberg (every 30min; 55min–1hr 10min); Frankfurt (every 30min–1hr; 1hr 10min); Nuremberg (every 15–30min; 55min–1hr 10min); Rothenburg ob der Tauber (via Steinach; hourly; 1hr 10min).

By public transport Würzburg is compact, but you might want to use public transport (W wvv.de) to reach the Marienberg fortress. A *Kurzstrecke* ticket for up to four stops costs €1.25, a single €2.45 and a one-day *Tageskarte* €4.75.
Bike rental Ludwig Körner, Bronnbachergasse 3 (☎0931 523 40), and Radsport Schuster, Raiffeisenstr 3 (☎0931 123 38), both offer bike rental.

INFORMATION

Tourist office In the Falkenhaus on Markt (Jan–March Mon–Fri 10am–4pm, Sat 10am–2pm; April, Nov & Dec Mon–Fri 10am–6pm, Sat 10am–2pm; May–July Mon–Fri 10am–6pm, Sat & Sun 10am–2pm; Aug–Oct Mon–Fri 10am–6pm, Sat 10am–3pm, Sun 10am–2pm; ☎0931 37 23 98, W wuerzburg.de). You can hire an English-language

iGuide (€7.50 3hr) at the office. The office can also make accommodation bookings.
Discount card The Würzburg Welcome Card (€3), available from the tourist office, is valid for one week and entitles you to reductions on museum entry, boat trips to Veitshöchheim and in various restaurants and *Weinstuben*.

ACCOMMODATION

HOTELS AND PENSIONS

Best Western Premier Hotel Rebstock Neubaustr. 7 ☎0931 309 30, W rebstock.com. Behind a prettily Rococo facade, this is one of the classiest addresses in town, with individually designed rooms and suites, all with bath or shower and wi-fi. There's also a fitness studio and sauna and the hotel has a gourmet restaurant, *Kuno 1408*. **€212**
Central Hotel Garni Koellikerstr. 1 ☎0931 460 88 40, W centralhotel-wuerzburg.de. Good-value if slightly bland a/c rooms in a very central, privately run hotel opposite the Juliusspital, with underground parking, one three-bed room and a family room that sleeps up to four. **€82**
Hotel am Congress-Centrum Pleichertorstr. 26 ☎0931 230 79 70, W hotel-am-congress-centrum.de. Much prettier than its dreary name suggests, this 4-star hotel is close to the river on the northern fringe of the Altstadt. Smoking and a/c rooms are available. **€100**
Sankt Josef Semmelstr. 28 ☎0931 30 86 80, W hotel -st-josef.de. Small, cyclist-friendly hotel, plain but very well kept and handy for the Altstadt's sights. Rooms have

wireless internet, safe and shower, and there's a choice of smoking or nonsmoking. **€89**
Zur Stadt Mainz Semmelstr. 39 ☎0931 531 55, W hotel -stadtmainz.de. Fifteen comfortable rooms with shower, WC and TV, above an atmospheric restaurant on the east side of the Altstadt. There's also a honeymoon suite. **€100**

HOSTELS

Babelfish Haugerring. 2 ☎0931 304 04 30, W babelfish-hostel.de. Hostel opposite the Hauptbahnhof with accommodation in simple but modern four- to ten-bed dorms, single and double rooms, plus bar and roof terrace, free wi-fi and lockers, and luggage storage. Dorms **€17**, doubles **€62**
DJH Würzburg Fred-Joseph-Platz 2 ☎0931 46 77 860, W wuerzburg.jugendherberge.de. In a superb location beneath the Marienberg fortress by the river, with accommodation mostly in two- to six-bed rooms. Also has bike hire. Reception 7am–1am. Breakfast and linen included. Dorms **€25.90**

EATING AND DRINKING

CAFÉS

★**Café Konditorei Michel** Marktplatz 11 ☎0931 53 776, W cafe-michel.de. The top spot for coffee and cakes in Würzburg, with a tempting display of cakes at the front, wood-panelled cosiness within, and delicious sweet or savoury strudels from €3.20. They serve breakfast until 4pm. Mon–Fri 8am–6pm, Sat 7.30am–6pm, Sun 10am–6pm.
Schönborn Marktplatz 30 ☎0931 404 48 18, W cafe -schoenborn.de. Bustling modern café on Markt, serving breakfast until 4pm, as well as *Flammkuchen* (from €6.40), pasta salads and light dishes, and with great views over the buzzing marketplace from its tables upstairs. Breakfasts

from €2.40, meaty mains €9 up. Mon–Sat 8.30am–1am, Sun 9.30am–midnight.

RESTAURANTS

Alte Mainmühle Mainkai 1 ☎0931 167 77, W alte-mainmuehle.de. Convivial and classy wood-panelled restaurant in an old watermill right on the Alte Mainbrücke, with a few cosmopolitan touches on the lengthy, Franconian menu. Main courses around €16–21. Daily 9.30am–midnight.
★**Ratskeller** In the Rathaus, Langgasse 1 ☎0931 130 21, W ratskeller-wuerzburg.de. Franconian specialities, *Schnitzels* and steaks are on the menu in a wonderful

FRANCONIAN WINE

Grown on the slopes above the meandering River Main, Franconia's wines are fuller bodied and often drier than other German wines, their distinctiveness arising in part from the climate, which is less kind than that of the wine-growing regions further west. Summers are warm and dry, but winters are cold, rainfall is high and frosts come early, so slow-ripening varieties like Riesling are less important here. Müller-Thurgau – which is also known as Rivaner – and Silvaner are the significant **white wine** grape varieties, with new crosses such as Bacchus also coming to the fore. **Red wines** are grown in the west of the region, around Aschaffenburg, while Würzburg's Stein vineyard has given rise to the generic name **Steinwein**, which is sometimes used to describe all Franconian wines. Most distinctive of all is the squat, rounded **Bocksbeutel** in which Franconian wines are bottled – very different from the tall, slim-necked bottles used by most German wine-makers.

WINE TASTING IN WÜRZBURG

Much the easiest way to experience Franconian wine in Würzburg is in one of its traditional *Weinstuben* (see below). You can also tour the impressive **Staatlicher Hofkeller cellars** by the Residenz, where the €7 price of the tour (March–Dec Fri at 4.30 & 5.30pm, Sat hourly 10am–noon & 2–5pm, Sun hourly 10am–noon & 2–4pm) includes a small glass of wine.

The city has a busy programme of **wine festivals** throughout the summer months, culminating with the alfresco Weinparade on Marktplatz in September; the tourist office has details.

---

vaulted space beneath the Rathaus, with Würzburg wines to wash them down. In fine weather you can dine in the very pretty courtyard of the Rote Bau. Main courses from around €11. Daily 10am–midnight; kitchen closes 10pm.

BARS AND PUBS

★**Alter Kranen** Kranenkai 1 ☎0931 99 13 15 45, ⓦalterkranen.de. Vast *Brauerei-Gasthof* on the riverside by the Alter Kranen, with a huge beer garden in summer, superb views of the Marienberg fortress and hearty traditional fare to anchor down the local *Würzburger Hofbräu* beers; main courses from around €9.50. Mon–Sat 11am–1am, Sun 10am–late.

Joe's Cantina y Bar Juliuspromenade 1 ☎0931 57 12 38, ⓦjoes-wuerzburg.de. Lively Mexican bar/restaurant popular with a young crowd and with DJs on Fri and Sat nights. There's burrito and enchilada-type food from around €10, and a 5–8pm happy hour, when cocktails cost €4.20. Mon–Thurs & Sun 5pm–1am, Fri & Sat 5pm–2am.

WEINSTUBEN

Bürgerspital Theaterstr. 19 ☎0931 35 28 80, ⓦbuergerspital-weinstuben.de. Sample the wines

from this seven-hundred-year-old hospital's own vineyard in its rambling and atmospheric old *Weinstube* – you can sit outside in the eighteenth-century *Innenhof* in fine weather. The menu embraces inexpensive Franconian specialities (from around €7) to more sophisticated, occasionally Mediterranean-influenced main courses: veal meatballs with seared *Speckknödel* and chanterelle mushrooms €14.90. Daily 10am–midnight.

Weinstuben Juliusspital Juliuspromenade 19, corner of Barbarossaplatz ☎0931 540 80, ⓦjuliusspital-weinstuben.de. Like the *Bürgerspital*, this is a *Weinstube* associated with a hospital, though in this case an enormous Baroque one; there's a wide selection of Franconian wines – including the *Juliusspital's* own – and steaks and Franconian specialities on the menu (around €13–27). Daily 10am–midnight.

★**Zum Stachel** Gressengasse 1 ☎0931 527 70, ⓦweinhaus-stachel.de. Absolutely gorgeous old *Weinstube* in a building which in part dates back to around 1200, with refined Franconian cooking – such as veal *Tafelspitz* in horseradish sauce with tagliatelle and cranberry – and local wines. Main courses €11–20. Tues–Sat 11.30am–midnight, Sun 11.20am–4pm.

NIGHTLIFE AND ENTERTAINMENT

CLUBS AND LIVE MUSIC

Posthalle Bahnhofplatz 2 ☎0931 99 17 78 90, ⓦposthalle.de. Vast club and music venue close to the Hauptbahnhof, with everything from Nineties nights to gay dance parties and live rock bands. There's a smaller venue, *Immerhin*, in the basement. Gigs generally from 8pm, clubnights from 10 or 11pm.

THEATRE

Mainfranken Theater Würzburg Theaterstr. 21 ☎0931 390 81 24, ⓦtheaterwuerzburg.de. The city's main venue for drama, opera and classical concerts, with large and small auditoria. Performances generally begin at 7.30 or 8pm.

Rothenburg ob der Tauber

The jewel-like hilltop town of **ROTHENBURG OB DER TAUBER** has reason to be grateful for the Peasants' War of 1525 – in which it allied itself with the rebels – and the Thirty Years' War that swept across Central Europe to such catastrophic effect a century afterwards. A former free imperial city that had been thriving and prosperous, Rothenburg dwindled to insignificance after these events, its wealth lost to plunder and reparations and its population halved. As a result of this reverse in its fortune, development came to a standstill, leaving the town with the miraculous legacy of perfectly preserved medieval and Renaissance buildings with which it charms visitors today. The twentieth century's greatest conflict wasn't so kind: aerial bombardment in March 1945 damaged Rothenburg to an extent that would surprise present-day visitors. After the war, the town's numerous fans – including many from abroad – rallied round to ensure its reconstruction was swift and successful, and to all but the most hawk-eyed observers there is little visual evidence of the destruction.

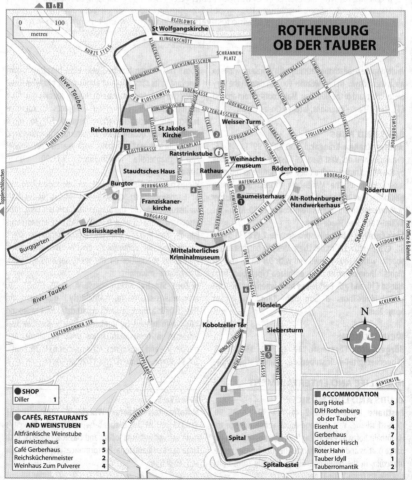

ROTHENBURG OB DER TAUBER

0 — 100 metres

St Wolfgangskirche

Reichsstadtmuseum
St Jakobs Kirche
Weisser Turm
Ratstrinkstube
Staudtsches Haus
Rathaus
Weihnachtsmuseum
Röderbogen
Burgtor
Franziskaner-kirche
Baumeisterhaus
Alt-Rothenburger Handwerkerhaus
Röderturm
Blasiuskapelle
Mittelalterliches Kriminalmuseum
Plönlein
Kobolzeller Tor
Sieberturm
Spital
Spitalbastei

SHOP
Diller — 1

CAFÉS, RESTAURANTS AND WEINSTUBEN
Altfränkische Weinstube — 1
Baumeisterhaus — 3
Café Gerberhaus — 5
Reichsküchenmeister — 2
Weinhaus Zum Pulverer — 4

ACCOMMODATION
Burg Hotel — 3
DJH Rothenburg ob der Tauber — 8
Eisenhut — 4
Gerberhaus — 7
Goldener Hirsch — 6
Roter Hahn — 5
Tauber Idyll — 1
Tauberromantik — 2

> ## ROTHENBURG OB DER TAUBER ORIENTATION
>
> Finding your way around this relatively small town is simple. Rothenburg's layout is a variation on the classic cross-shaped medieval street plan, with east–west and north–south streets crossing in the centre at Marktplatz. The River Tauber snakes along the western side of the Altstadt buried in its verdant valley, while the near-complete medieval defences still encircle the town, peppered with picturesque towers.

Rothenburg lies on the **Romantic Road** (see box, p.310), accessible by rail and close to the Ulm–Würzburg stretch of the A7 Autobahn. As such, it's something of a day-tripper magnet, and the crowds can be oppressive – not only in summer, for the town has an undeniable magic in the weeks leading up to Christmas, too. Yet this is no mere tourist trap: Rothenburg's beauty is undeniable, its restaurants often cosily inviting and its hotels frequently charming. Perhaps the best way to enjoy it is to simply stay overnight, to experience the calm that descends when the shops are closed, the bus tours depart and the crowds have finally thinned.

Foremost among Rothenburg's festivals is the **Meistertrunk Festspiel** (ⓦmeistertrunk .de), performed with much attendant parading and music over the Whitsun weekend.

Röderturm and the eastern Altstadt

The easternmost of the town's towers – and the first you'll see as you approach from the Bahnhof – is the tall **Röderturm** (March–Nov daily 10am–5pm weather permitting; €1.50), which you can climb to get your bearings. There's also an exhibition here about the World War II destruction of Rothenburg. Afterwards, an enjoyable way to while away an hour or two is to complete the circuit of the walls; much of the walkway is under cover.

The eastern side of Rothenburg's Altstadt bore the brunt of destruction in 1945, and it's here that the sharp-eyed visitor might spot a few traces of the restorer's art. Yet even here, Rothenburg can be exceptionally picturesque, notably around the quaint **Röderbogen** gateway at the eastern end of Hafengasse, which dates from around 1200. Just before the Röderbogen, turn left into Alter Stadtgraben to reach the **Alt-Rothenburger Handwerkerhaus** at no. 26 (Easter–Oct Mon–Fri 11am–5pm, Sat & Sun 10am–5pm; during Advent daily 2–4pm; €3), an evocative thirteenth-century house stuffed full of peasant-style furniture and craftsmen's tools.

The Rathaus

Marktplatz • Tower April–Oct daily 9.30am–12.30pm & 1–5pm; Nov & Jan–March Sat & Sun noon–3pm; during Advent Mon–Thurs & Sun 10.30am–2pm & 2.30–6pm, Fri & Sat 10.30am–2pm & 2.30– 8pm • €2

The gulf between Rothenburg's modest present-day status and its former glory is eloquently demonstrated by the magnificence of its **Rathaus**. The splendid Renaissance structure facing Marktplatz dates from 1572 to 1578 and is the work of local architect Leonhard Weidemann; the older Gothic structure behind the Rathaus was built between 1250 and 1400 and is topped by the spindly **Rathausturm**, which offers stunning vistas over the town's huddled red rooftops. Be warned, however, the way up gets progressively steeper and narrower and the observation platform feels precarious if you're at all prone to vertigo.

Historiengewölbe

Marktplatz 1, entrance is from the covered alley at the back • Daily: March noon–4pm; April 10am–4pm; May–Oct 9.30am–5.30pm; Nov Mon–Fri 1–4pm, Sat & Sun 10am–4pm; Advent Mon–Fri 1–4pm, Sat & Sun 10am–7pm; closed Jan & Feb • €2.50

The engagingly theatrical **Historiengewölbe** (Historic Vaults), tucked beneath the Rathaus off Herrngasse, illustrates aspects of the town's history – including its Jewish history, and the Meistertrunk (see box, p.320) – in a kitsch but accessible style; the visit culminates with a look at the grisly dungeons, complete with cells, pillory and rack.

5

> ## GENERAL TILLY'S MASTER DRAUGHT
>
> The gabled **Ratstrinkstube** on the north side of Marktplatz was the scene of the most celebrated – if probably apocryphal – episode of the Thirty Years' War in Rothenburg, the so-called **Meistertrunk** or Master Draught of 1631. The feared Catholic general Tilly, whose troops were occupying Rothenburg ob der Tauber, promised to spare Protestant Rothenburg destruction if a councillor managed to empty an enormous tankard containing 3.25 litres of wine in a single draught. The former mayor Georg Nusch managed the feat, and Rothenburg was saved. Each year at Whitsun, a festival commemorates the event.

St Jakobs Kirche

Klostergasse 15 • Daily: Jan–March & Nov 10am–noon & 2–4pm; April–Oct 9am–5.15pm; during Christmas market 10am–4.45pm • €2

Immediately to the north of the Rathaus rises the Protestant parish church of **St Jakob**, begun in 1311 but not consecrated until 1485. Its chief glory is the extraordinary **Heilig-Blut-Altar** (1499–1505), so named for the relic it contains – supposedly three drops of Christ's blood – which turned Rothenburg into a major place of pilgrimage in the Middle Ages. The sinuous, delicate Gothic structure created by local cabinet-maker Erhard Harschner provides a memorable setting for Tilman Riemenschneider's characteristically expressive figures. Centre-point of the altar is his depiction of the Last Supper. Also notable is the richly colourful **Zwölfbotenaltar** or Twelve Apostles' Altar, decorated with fifteenth-century paintings by Nördlingen artist Friedrich Herlin, including one that depicts Rothenburg's Rathaus as it was before fire destroyed the original Gothic building facing Marktplatz.

West along Herrngasse

Leading west from Marktplatz, stately **Herrngasse** lives up to its name – Lords' Lane – with some of the finest surviving patrician houses in Rothenburg, though at the Marktplatz end it is dominated by the year-round Christmassy commercialism of the Käthe Wohlfahrt store and its associated **Deutsches Weihnachtsmuseum**, Herrngasse 1 (German Christmas Museum: April–Christmas daily 10am–5.30pm; 1–6 Jan daily 10am–5pm; 10 Jan–March restricted opening; €4; ⊛ weihnachtsmuseum.de), filled with historic Christmas decorations. Things calm down further west at the austere **Franziskanerkirche** (Mon–Sat 10am–noon & 2–4pm, Sun 2–4pm; free), worth a look for Tilman Riemenschneider's early **St Francis Altar**, which dates from around 1490. At the western end of Herrngasse rises the soaring fourteenth-century **Burgtor**, the highest tower in the town walls.

The Burggarten

West of the Burgtor is the **Burggarten**, a park on the former site of Rothenburg's fortress, destroyed by an earthquake in 1356. From here you get good views of the **Doppelbrücke**, or double bridge, spanning the Tauber to the south, which despite its fourteenth-century design rather resembles a Roman aqueduct.

Topplerschlösschen

Taubertalweg 98 • Fri–Sun 1–4pm; closed Nov • €1.50

A thirty-minute stroll down through the Burggarten and along the Taubertalweg brings you to the very odd **Topplerschlösschen**, a retreat built in 1388 for Heinrich Toppler, the most famous and powerful of Rothenburg's mayors and resembling a small medieval house inexplicably perched atop a stone tower.

The Reichsstadtmuseum

Klosterhof 5 • Daily: April–Oct 9.30am–5.30pm; Nov–March 1–4pm • €4.50 • ⊛ reichsstadtmuseum.info

North of Herrngasse, a former Dominican convent houses the **Reichsstadtmuseum**. Founded in 1258, the convent closed in 1554 after the last nun died; it passed to the control of the city council and was used as a widows' home. It exhibits a mixed bunch of artefacts of local interest: the original Renaissance stone figures from the Baumeisterhaus (see below), which depict the seven virtues and – altogether more enjoyably – the seven vices, were moved here to protect them from decay in 1936. You can also see the cycle of twelve medieval paintings of the Rothenburger Passion from the Franziskanerkirche's rood screen, once thought to be the work of Dürer but now generally believed to be by Martinus Schwarz. Not to be missed is the convent's well-preserved medieval kitchen; there's also a section on Rothenburg's medieval Jewish community.

St Wolfgangskirche

Beim Klingentor • Daily except Tues: April–Sept 10am–1pm & 1.30–4.30pm; Oct 10am–3.30pm; also open Sat & Sun 11am–3pm during Advent • €1.50 • ⓦ schaefertanzrothenburg.de

A stroll north from the Reichsstadtmuseum along Klingengasse brings you to the Klingentor gate and the curious, late fifteenth-century **St Wolfgangskirche**, a fortress church with ramparts in the church loft and casemates down below.

Mittelalterliches Kriminalmuseum

Burggasse 3–5 • Daily: Jan, Feb & Nov 2–4pm; March & Dec 1–4pm; April 11am–5pm; May–Oct 10am–6pm • €5 • ⓦ kriminalmuseum.rothenburg.de

At the end of Hofbronnengasse, the **Mittelalterliches Kriminalmuseum** (Medieval Crime Museum) is a dark affair, with exhibits relating to crime and punishment from the Middle Ages to the ninteenth century. These include an executioner's mask, and instruments of torture including an iron maiden and a witch's chair.

The southern Alstadt

Head south from Marktplatz down Schmiedgasse past the imposing Renaissance **Baumeisterhaus** of 1596 to reach the southern part of the Altstadt. The tourist crowds and souvenir shops are particularly thick on the ground here, as most visitors want to see the absurdly picturesque **Plönlein**, a happily informal little square formed by the intersection of streets from the **Siebersturm** – which leads into the southern Altstadt – and the **Kobolzeller Tor**, beyond which a road winds down to the Doppelbrücke. It's one of the most-photographed views in Germany. The very southern tip of the Altstadt is marked by the formidable defensive complex of the **Spitalbastei**, built in the seventeenth century with two inner courtyards, seven gates and an upper walkway with embrasures.

ARRIVAL AND INFORMATION ROTHENBURG OB DER TAUBER

By train Rothenburg's Bahnhof is a short walk to the east of the Altstadt. Regular trains run to Würzburg (via Steinach: hourly; 1hr 10min).

Tourist office Next to the Rathaus in the fifteenth-century Ratstrinkstube (City Councillors' Tavern) at Marktplatz 2 (May–Oct & during Advent Mon–Fri 9am–6pm, Sat & Sun 10am–5pm; Nov–April Mon–Fri 9am–5pm, Sat 10am–1pm; ☎09861 40 48 00, ⓦ tourismus.othenburg.de). From Easter to October and during Advent the tourist office organizes daily English-language tours at 2pm (€7; 90min); alternatively, you can hire a hand-held audiovisual CityTour (€7.50) year-round.

ACCOMMODATION

HOTELS AND INNS

★ **Burg Hotel** Klostergasse 1–3 ☎09861 948 90, ⓦ burghotel.eu. Charming 3-star hotel in an idyllic location right on the town ramparts, with just 15 rooms and furnished in a simple but attractive country style; there are four-poster beds in some rooms and the hotel has a

pretty garden. €125

Eisenhut Herrngasse 3–5/7 ☎09861 70 50, ⓦ eisenhut .com. Rothenburg's classiest hotel oozes restrained good taste, from its handsome lobby to its 78 individually styled rooms, which boast period furnishings and modern amenities, including minibar, free wi-fi and flat-screen TV. €124

5

CYCLING THE TAUBERTAL

One very attractive way to get around is to slow the pace right down and explore the gently beautiful Franconian wine-growing countryside by bicycle along the **Liebliches Taubertal Radweg**. The 100km route follows the course of the Tauber from Rothenburg northwest to Wertheim; a tougher route completes the circuit by returning southwest towards Rothenburg along the heights of the Taubertal through Königsheim and Boxberg west of the Tauber. Along the way, there are stunning Tilman Riemenschneider altars at **Detwang** and **Creglingen**, a Schloss and museum of the Teutonic Knights at **Bad Mergentheim** and a Matthias Grünewald *Madonna* at **Stuppach**. Not to be missed is the Schloss at **Weikersheim** (ⓦ schloss-weikersheim.de), with its splendid Renaissance Rittersaal (Knights' Hall) and beautiful Baroque gardens.

The route follows forest or farm tracks for much of the way; from May to October the **regional trains** on the west bank of the Tauber between Freudenberg, Wertheim and Schrozberg – 22km west of Rothenburg – carry special luggage vans to cope with cycles, so you don't have to cycle both ways if you don't want to. There's also a baggage service to which some hoteliers sign up, so that you don't need to haul everything with you. There are **cycle repair and rental** facilities in several of the villages along the route. For more **information**, contact Liebliches Taubertal e.V, c/o Landratsamt Main-Tauber-Kreis, Gartnerstr. 1, Tauberbischofsheim (ⓣ 09341 82 58 06, ⓦ liebliches-taubertal.de).

Gerberhaus Spitalgasse 25 ⓣ 09861 949 00, ⓦ gerberhaus.rothenburg.de. Very attractive cyclist-friendly small hotel with twenty prettily rustic, refurbished en-suite rooms above a café; there's also a lovely garden – in the shade of the medieval fortifications – and free internet. **€84**

Goldener Hirsch Untere Schmiedgasse 16 ⓣ 09861 87 49 90, ⓦ hotel-goldener-hirsch.de. Elegant and spacious hotel in the southern Altstadt, with period furnishings and views over the Taubertal. Rooms have satellite TV, safe and phone, shower or bath and WC. **€99**

Roter Hahn Obere Schmiedgasse 21 ⓣ 09861 97 40, ⓦ roterhahn.com. Good-value, pretty rooms in an atmospheric inn dating from 1380 which claims to be one of Germany's oldest. Rooms have shower or bath and WC; there's satellite TV and a restaurant. **€89**

HOSTELS AND CAMPSITES

DJH Rothenburg ob der Tauber Mühlacker 1 ⓣ 09861 941 60, ⓦ rothenburg.jugendherberge.de. Located in two historic buildings – the Rossmühle and Spitalhof – in a great location at the southern tip of the Altstadt, with accommodation in four- to eight-bed dorms plus some doubles. Breakfast included. Dorms **€24.90**, doubles (per person) **€27.90**

Tauber Idyll Detwang 28 ⓣ 09861 31 77, ⓦ rothenburg.de/tauberidyll. Campsite in the Tauber Valley 1.5km from Rothenburg, next to the Taubertal cycle route (see box above), with laundry facilities, free wi-fi and a children's play area. Open from the week before Easter until Oct. Pitch **€6**, plus **€5.50** per person

Tauberromantik Detwang 39 ⓣ 09861 61 91, ⓦ camping-tauberromantik.de. Campsite in the Tauber Valley just 1km from the Altstadt, with on-site shop, bicycle hire, free hot showers and around 120 pitches. There's a ten percent discount if you stay six nights or longer. Open mid-March to early Nov and during Advent. Pitch **€6**, plus **€6** per person

EATING AND DRINKING

Rothenburg is full of attractive places to **eat** and **drink**. Franconian **wine** – including local Taubertal wines – is the drink of choice. The local sweet treats are *Schneeballen* – literally snowballs, balled-up masses of biscuit dough which though not light, do have a pleasant, home-baked flavour. Buy them at the Diller bakery, which has three branches in town including one at Obere Schmiedgasse 7.

Altfränkische Weinstube Klosterhof 7 ⓣ 09861 64 04, ⓦ altfraenkische-weinstube.de. Rothenburg has many snug and cosy old *Weinstuben*, but this twee, rustic and pretty example close to the Reichstadtmuseum probably takes the prize. The food – including the likes of pork loin with herb butter, peppers and courgettes, and *Nürnberger Bratwürste* – is not expensive (around €8–12), and there's a roaring fire if the weather demands. Daily 6–10.30pm

Baumeisterhaus Obere Schmiedgasse 3 ⓣ 09861 947 00, ⓦ das-baumeisterhaus.de. Coffee, cakes and a short menu of hot main courses from around €9 are served in evocative surroundings in this Renaissance house, with elaborate wall paintings, vaulted ceilings and a spectacular half-timbered *Hof*. Daily 10am–8pm.

Café Gerberhaus Spitalgasse 25 ⓣ 09861 949 00,

wgerberhaus.rothenburg.de. Ice cream, *Kaffee und Kuchen* and *Bratwurst* with *Sauerkraut* in classy but informal surroundings in the southern part of the Altstadt. There's also a beer garden. Franconian wines from €3.80 a glass, beer from €2.50. Tues–Sun 1–11pm.

Reichsküchenmeister Kirchplatz 8 ☎ 09861 97 00, wreichskuechenmeister.com. Salads, *Flammkuchen* and Franconian regional specialities from €12–15, beneath the splendidly saggy wooden ceiling of this buzzy hotel restaurant. There's also a more informal *Weinstube*, *Löchle*, with bottles hanging up outside. Daily 11am–10pm.

★ **Weinhaus Zum Pulverer** Herrngasse 31 ☎ 09861 97 61 82. Simple, inexpensive dishes – *Maultaschen* with salad, *Käsespätze* with roast onions – are served alongside more sophisticated fare in the beautiful wood-panelled dining room of this *Weinstube* close to the Burgtor. Simpler fare costs from €7.50, more substantial main courses €12–13. Wed–Fri 5pm–late, Sat & Sun noon–late.

Dinkelsbühl

DINKELSBÜHL, 48km south of Rothenburg ob der Tauber along the Romantic Road, is another medieval gem. Though it lacks the sparkle of Rothenburg's hilly setting, making do with the placid River Wörnitz, some parkland and a few large ponds to set off its perfectly preserved medieval fortifications, it boasts an Altstadt which is, if anything, even more flawless, having escaped damage in World War II. It's also less overwhelmed by tourism. Like Rothenburg, Dinkelsbühl was once a free imperial city; it changed hands eight times in the Thirty Years' War, but after it was occupied by the Swedes in 1632 it was largely spared further damage.

The **Altstadt** measures just 1km from northwest to southeast, and is barely 500m wide from Segringer Tor in the west to Wörnitz Tor in the east. A walk around the outside of the medieval walls is therefore not only instructive but enjoyable. Once within the walls, there's hardly anything to disturb the illusion of medieval perfection.

The medieval walls

Heading south from the **Wörnitz Tor**, fourteenth century but for its sixteenth-century gabled bell tower, you pass the picturesque, half-timbered **Bäuerlinsturm** before reaching the southern tip of the Altstadt at the **Nördlinger Tor**. West of Nördlinger Tor, the **Alte Promenade** passes a parade of austere, unadorned medieval towers before reaching the **Segringer Tor**, one landmark that was damaged by the occupying Swedes; it was rebuilt in 1655 in Baroque style. Here, the fortifications turn north, reaching the lovely ensemble of the **Faulturm** and **Rothenburger Tor** before swinging southeast again to Wörnitz Tor.

The Museum 3.Dimension

Nördlinger Tor • April–June, Sept, Oct & Christmas–New Year daily 11am–5pm; July & Aug daily 10am–6pm; Nov–March Sat & Sun 11am–5pm • €10 • w3d-museum.de

Next to the Nördlinger Tor, the impregnable-looking fourteenth-century Stadtmühle houses the **Museum 3.Dimension**, an offbeat but enjoyable museum dedicated to

---

KINDERZECHE FESTIVAL

Dinkelsbühl's most celebrated festival is the **Kinderzeche** (wkinderzeche.de), an annual children's and folklore festival that takes place in July. It has its origins in the Thirty Years' War: the story goes that in 1632 a deputation of local children dissuaded the commander of the besieging Swedish forces from ransacking the town by singing. Children in historic costume still form an important element in the festival parades, with music provided by the Knabenkapelle, a famous boys' band.

5

three-dimensional imagery, with everything from stereoscopic art and holographs to a rare collection of Viewmasters, the colour-slide viewing devices that were once a firm favourite as a Christmas gift or holiday souvenir.

Haus der Geschichte Dinkelsbühl

Altrathausplatz 14 • May–Oct Mon–Fri 9am–6pm, Sat & Sun 10am–5pm; Nov–April daily 10am–5pm • €4

It's just a short walk from Wörnitz Tor to the **Altes Rathaus**, the oldest parts of which date back to 1361. It now houses the **Haus der Geschichte Dinkelsbühl**, which presents the history of the town in war and peace over four floors. In addition to artefacts from Dinkelsbühl's imperial heyday, the museum has a gallery showing works that chart the rediscovery of the town by artists in the nineteenth century and later, including a view painted by the Expressionist Karl Schmidt-Rottluff.

The Münster St Georg

Marktplatz 1 • **Church** Daily: summer 9am–noon & 2–7pm; winter 9am–noon & 2–5pm • Free **Tower** May–Oct Fri–Sun 2–5pm • €1.50

Just to the north of the Rathaus, the **Münster St Georg** looms over the centre of the Altstadt. The lofty Late Gothic hall church was built between 1488 and 1499 to the plans of Nikolaus Eseler, and it's generally reckoned to be one of the most beautiful of its era in southern Germany; the tower is Romanesque, and dates from 1220 to 1230. In summer you can climb it in fine weather for views over the Altstadt's steep, red-tiled rooftops.

Facing the church across **Weinmarkt** is a stately parade of five tall, gabled houses, dating from around 1600, the most magnificent being the **Schranne**, a former grain warehouse, and the **Deutsches Haus**, which has a richly decorated, late Renaissance facade – the figures include a representation of Bacchus, the god of wine.

ARRIVAL AND INFORMATION
DINKELSBÜHL

By public transport Getting to Dinkelsbühl is a bit of a headache out of season if you don't have your own transport. Journeys from Rothenburg involve switching from train to bus or bus to bus; there are direct buses from Nördlingen to the south (#501; 35–45min). Things are easier from mid-April to Oct when a Eurolines bus (weurolines.de/en/national-bus/romantische-strasse)

links the various stops along the Romantic Road (see box, p.310).

Tourist office In the Haus der Geschichte Dinkelsbühl at Altrathausplatz 14 (May–Oct Mon–Fri 9am–6pm, Sat & Sun 10am–5pm; Nov–April daily 10am–5pm; ☎09851 90 24 40, wdinkelsbuehl.de).

ACCOMMODATION AND EATING

Dinkelsbühl's hotels and Gasthöfe are generally small, family-run and traditional in style; the tourist office also has lists of holiday flats and private rooms. The town's youth hostel was closed for refurbishment at the time of writing, but due to reopen during 2015.

DCC-Campingpark Romantische Strasse Kobeltsmuehle 6 ☎09851 78 17, wcampingplatz -dinkelsbuehl.de. Large, 4-star campsite on the shores of a lake northeast of the Altstadt along Dürrwanger Strasse, open all year round and with minigolf, bathing, fishing and a restaurant and Biergarten. Pitch **€9.30**, plus **€4.40** per adult

Deutsches Haus Weinmarkt 3 ☎09851 60 58, wdeutsches-haus-dkb.de. Atmospheric and central hotel in the most beautiful of Dinkelsbühl's tall patrician houses, dating from 1440. There are just two single rooms,

eleven double rooms and a brace of suites; decor is a blend of contemporary touches and period furniture, including some four-poster beds. The restaurant serves refined regional cooking in a lovely, atmospheric dining room with painted ceilings; in summer there's also a terrace out front. Mains range from veal fillet with spring vegetables and morel foam (€25.80) to venison shoulder with spicy bread crust & cranberry crêpes (€28.50); simpler meaty mains cost around €13.50. Restaurant daily noon–2pm & 6–10pm. **€129**

Goldenes Lamm Lange Gasse 26–28 ☎09851 22 67,

ⓦgoldenes.de. This cyclist-friendly hotel occupies a pair of gabled houses to the south of Weinmarkt, with plenty of beams, a pretty garden terrace and parking. All rooms have shower or bath, WC and TV, and in addition to the singles and doubles there are larger rooms that sleep three or four.

The menu at the restaurant features both meat and vegetarian dishes, with *Schweinebraten* for €8.50, *Tafelspitz* with horseradish for €9.80 and meat-free *Quarkknödel* or *Käsespätzle*. Restaurant daily except Wed 11am–1.30pm and 5–9pm. **€84**

Nördlingen

Fifteen million years ago a meteorite slammed into the Alb plateau close to the site of present-day **NÖRDLINGEN**, southeast of Dinkelsbühl on the boundary with Baden-Württemberg. Hitting the earth at a speed of 70,000km per hour, the impact of the meteorite was sufficient to form a crater 25km wide, known today as the **Ries**, and reputedly the best-preserved impact crater on the planet. Geology isn't the only reason to visit the town however, for Nördlingen is another of the **Romantic Road**'s perfectly preserved medieval gems, a beautiful former imperial free city like Rothenburg ob der Tauber and Dinkelsbühl, but less touristy than either.

The medieval walls

Nördlingen retains its complete circuit of **medieval walls**, and it's well worth making the 2.7km circuit of them while you're here – they're the most complete and, arguably, even more impressive than those in either Rothenburg ob der Tauber or Dinkelsbühl.

Along the way you can visit the **Stadtmauermuseum** (City Walls Museum: April–Oct Tues–Sun 10am–4.30pm; €2) in the fourteenth-century **Löpsinger Torturm**. Its exhibits include a massive diorama of the 1634 Battle of Nördlingen during the Thirty Years' War.

St Georgskirche and the Daniel

Church Mon–Fri 9.30am–12.30pm & 2–5pm, Sat 9.30am–5pm, Sun 11am–5pm • Free • **Tower** Daily: Jan, Feb & Nov 10am–4pm; March, April & Oct 10am–5pm; May, June & Sept 9am–6pm; July & Aug 9am–7pm; Dec 9am–5pm • €3

St Georgskirche, which was built between 1427 and 1505, is one of the largest and most beautiful Late Gothic hall churches in southern Germany, with an airy interior of slender columns and graceful vaulting. Nördlingen's medieval church-builders were thoughtful enough to make the church's tower – known as the **Daniel** – tall enough to make it the dominant landmark for miles around; it's a climb of no less than 90m, but energetic visitors are rewarded with superb views of the almost perfectly circular Altstadt and the landscape of the Ries beyond.

> ### SO, G'SELL, SO – THE TREACHERY OF THE NÖRDLINGEN TOWN GUARDS
>
> Every half-hour between 10pm and midnight the **tower watchman** atop the Daniel issues the traditional cry "So G'sell, so" (roughly "ah, so that's how it is, lads"). The "official" explanation for this strange custom is that one evening in 1440 the town guards left the town gate open, having been bribed by Count Hans of Oettingen, who wanted to storm the town. Their treachery was discovered by a woman passing the Löpsinger Gate; her appalled reaction is echoed to this day in the watchman's cry. It's not certain how accurate the story is, but it is a matter of record that two guards were charged with treason that year and executed.

5

The Tanzhaus and the Rathaus

Close by St Georgskirche, the impressive half-timbered **Tanzhaus** was built as a cloth exchange and ballroom during the period 1442 to 1444 and features a statue of the Emperor Maximilian I, dating from 1513. Directly opposite, Nördlingen's **Rathaus** has been in continuous use as a town hall since 1382; the most beautiful part of the complex is the elegant Renaissance **Freitreppe** (open staircase), built in 1618 by Wolfgang Walberger.

The Heilig-Geist-Spital: the Stadtmuseum

Vorderer Gerbergasse 1 • March–Nov Tues–Sun 1.30–4.30pm • €4 • ⓦ stadtmuseum-noerdlingen.de

To the north along Baldingerstrasse is the **Heilig-Geist-Spital**, a medieval hospital that now houses Nördlingen's local history museum, the **Stadtmuseum**, whose typically eclectic collection focuses on the settlement history of the Ries region, the Thirty Years' War and the history of the former imperial free city itself.

Rieskrater-Museum

Eugene-Shoemaker-Platz 1 • Tues–Sun: May–Oct 10am–4.30pm; Nov–April 10am–noon & 1.30–4.30pm • €4

Just opposite the Stadtmuseum is the **Rieskrater-Museum**, occupying six rooms in the Holzhof – a sixteenth-century barn. Its displays on the formation of craters in general and the Ries in particular are partly annotated in English, and there are samples of rocks, meteorites and fossils.

ARRIVAL AND DEPARTURE   NÖRDLINGEN

By train To reach Nördlingen by train from Augsburg or Ingolstadt you have to change at Donauwörth. The Bahnhof is on the eastern edge of the Altstadt, from where it's a short walk to the tourist information office.

Destinations Augsburg (via Donauwörth: approx hourly; 1hr 12min); Ingolstadt (via Donauwörth: hourly, 1hr 35min).

By bus Buses from Dinkelsbühl (7 daily; 35–50min) drop you at the bus station in Bürgermeister-Reiger-Strasse, between the Bahnhof and Altstadt.

INFORMATION

Tourist office Opposite the Rathaus at Marktplatz 2 (Easter–Oct Mon–Thurs 9.30am–6pm, Fri 9.30am–4.30pm, Sat & Sun 10am–2pm; Nov–Easter Mon–Thurs 9.30am–5pm, Fri 9.30am–3.30pm; ☏ 09081 841 16, ⓦ noerdlingen.de).

Geopark Ries Info-Zentrum Eugene-Shoemaker-Platz 3 (Tues–Sun 10am–4.30pm). This information centre for the Ries crater is located between the Stadtmuseum and the Rieskrater-Museum.

Discount card The tourist office can sell you a three-day TouristCard (€9.95 single, €19.95 family) which entitles you to free entrance to the museums, the Daniel, and local fitness, sauna and swimming facilities.

ACCOMMODATION AND EATING

Kaiserhof Hotel Sonne Marktplatz 3 ☏ 09081 50 67, ⓦ kaiserhof-hotel-sonne.de. Located right across from the Daniel, in an attractive historic building. Rooms are pleasant, some with peasant-style furniture, and have bath or shower, WC, wireless internet and phone; there are some singles. Has a restaurant too. **€80**

Kirchenwirt am Daniel Marktplatz 12 ☏ 09081 29 01 20, ⓦ gasthof-kirchenwirt.eu. Traditional-style *Gasthof* directly opposite the Daniel, with a restaurant serving good-value dishes – *Maultaschen*, *Schnitzel* and the like – from around €8. All rooms have shower, WC and TV. **€58**

Meyer's Keller Marienhöhe 8 ☏ 09081 44 93, ⓦ meyerskeller.de. Michelin-starred restaurant in a suburban setting a short distance southwest of the Altstadt. Chef Joachim Kaiser offers two styles of cooking: a highly creative one with a seven-course tasting menu for €99 (matched wines €59.50); and a simpler one based on regional and seasonal produce, for which there's a €35 three-course menu. Wed–Sun 11.30am–2pm & 5.30–10pm.

Roter Ochse Baldinger Str. 17 ☏ 09081 34 84, ⓦ www .rochse.de. Classic regional fare in a historic gabled house in the Altstadt, with a menu that draws on local produce from the Ries in dishes like wild boar medallions with creamed mushrooms and *Semmelknödel*. Main courses are around €10–18, including a few meat-free options. Daily 10am–10pm.

Aschaffenburg

ASCHAFFENBURG is a last taste – or first glimpse – of Bavaria for travellers between the Free State and neighbouring Hesse, tucked into the westernmost corner of Franconia at the foot of the wooded Spessart hills. Closer to Frankfurt than to Würzburg, from the tenth century it belonged to the archbishopric of Mainz, and was the capital of the largest of several scattered parcels of territory known as the Oberes Erzstift (Upper Archdiocese). It was the archbishops' second residence until the archbishopric's dissolution in 1803; the town passed to Bavaria in 1814. Aschaffenburg was once dubbed the "Bavarian Nice" for its mild climate, and though that comparison is a little far-fetched, it is an attractive town, which recovered well from grievous damage in the last weeks of World War II and has enough sights to justify an overnight stop.

Schloss Johanissburg

Schlossplatz • Tues–Sun: April–Sept 9am–6pm; Oct–March 10am–4pm • €5.50, combined ticket with Pompejanum €9 • ⓦ schloesser-bayern.de

The vast red-sandstone Renaissance **Schloss Johanissburg** was built between 1605 and 1614 under Archbishop Johann Schweikart von Kronberg after its predecessor was destroyed by the troops of the Hohenzollern Margrave Albrecht Alcibidades in 1552. With its four corner towers creating a distinctive and impressive silhouette high on the banks of the River Main, the Schloss is the symbol of Aschaffenburg, instantly recognizable even to drivers rushing past on the A3 Autobahn.

Schlossmuseum

Reduced to a shell by the fighting in the spring of 1945, the Schloss has been immaculately restored and now houses the eclectic collection of the **Schlossmuseum**. A display at the start of the visit explains the history of the Schloss with the aid of models and shocking photographs of its desolate post-1945 state. Happily, most of the Schloss's contents were stored for safekeeping during the war, and thus it was possible to re-install Archbishop Friedrich Carl von Erthal's restrained, Neoclassical eighteenth-century **apartments** afterwards, one storey higher than their original position. His **art collection** is also on display, and includes Jacob Jordaens' *Allegory on the teaching work of St Augustine* and Rembrandt's *St John the Evangelist* as well as works by Van Dyck, Lucas Cranach the Elder and Hans Baldung Grien.

The museum also has a series of remarkable **cork models** of the monuments of ancient Rome, created by the court confectioner and his son between 1792 and 1854. There's also a local history section, with a model of the Altstadt as it was in 1800 and interesting displays on local industries.

The Pompejanum

Pompejanumstr. 5 • April to mid-Oct Tues–Sun 9am–6pm • €5.50, combined ticket with Schlossmuseum €9

A pleasant stroll through the Schlossgarten high above the Main brings you to the remarkable **Pompejanum**, an idealized replica of a Roman villa built for King Ludwig I between 1840 and 1848 by Friedrich von Gärtner, with rooms laid out around a peristyle in Roman fashion, though the central court has a glazed roof in concession to the German winter. The villa provides an authentic setting for antiquities from the state collection, and hosts temporary exhibitions on archeological themes.

Jesuitenkirche

Entrance on Pfaffengasse • Tues 2–8pm, Wed–Sun 10am–5pm • €4 • ⓦ museen-aschaffenburg.de

Opposite the Schloss Johanissburg, on the south side of **Schlossplatz** – the focus of

5

Aschaffenburg's modest but pleasant Altstadt – the deconsecrated **Jesuitenkirche** is the venue for an interesting array of temporary art exhibitions, with a slight bias towards classic twentieth-century modernism.

The Stiftskirche

Stiftsgasse 5 • **Church** Daily: summer 8am–6pm; winter 9am–5pm • Free • **Cloisters** Sat, Sun & public holidays: winter 1–5pm; summer 8am–6pm • €1

To the south of Schlossplatz lies the imposing **Stiftskirche**. Founded in the tenth century, it's an eclectic mishmash of Gothic, Romanesque and Baroque, though the interior is predominantly Romanesque and plain to the point of austerity. It has a noteworthy art collection, however, including Matthias Grünewald's moving *Lamentation*, painted in 1525, and the *Maria Schnee Altar* in the elegant Gothic chapel of the same name; it contains a copy of Grünewald's *Stuppach Madonna*, which was originally painted for the Stiftskirche. You can also visit the church's Romanesque cloisters, which preserve some fifteenth-century frescoes.

Stiftsmuseum

Stiftsplatz 1a • Tues–Sun 11am–5pm • €2.50 • ⓦ museen-aschaffenburg.de

Next to the Stiftskirche is the **Stiftsmuseum**, whose collections encompass archeology, Romanesque and Gothic sculpture, and Renaissance and Baroque art. Prize exhibits include the *St Magdalene Altar* from the studio of Lucas Cranach; the *Aschaffenburger Tafel*, one of the oldest surviving retables of its kind in Germany and originally from the Stiftskirche; and fragments of an altar by Tilman Riemenschneider.

Park Schöntal and Park Schönbusch

Aschaffenburg also has a brace of attractive parks. **Park Schöntal** lies on the eastern fringe of the Altstadt and centres on the picturesque ruins of a church that had a brief existence – built in 1544, it was destroyed less than a decade later. To the west of the town on the opposite side of the Main, **Park Schönbusch** is one of the oldest surviving English-style parks in Germany. Its centrepiece is the archbishops' pretty little Neoclassical summer **Schloss** (April–Sept: guided tours Tues–Sun 9am–6pm; exhibition Sat, Sun and public holidays 11am–6pm; €3.50), furnished in Louis XVI style. The ticket also gives admission to an exhibition on the history of the park in the kitchen rooms.

ARRIVAL AND INFORMATION ASCHAFFENBURG

By train Aschaffenburg's Bahnhof, which has high-speed connections with both Würzburg and Frankfurt, is around a 10min walk north of the Altstadt on Ludwigstrasse; alternatively, frequent buses #6, #10 and #12 connect the station to the Stadthalle next to the tourist office. Destinations Frankfurt (2 per hour; 30–40min);

Nuremberg (hourly; 1hr 35min); Würzburg (hourly; 40min).
Tourist office In the heart of the Altstadt at Schlossplatz 2 (April–Sept Mon–Fri 9am–6pm, Sat 9am–1pm, Sun 11am–3pm; Oct–March Mon–Fri 9am–5pm, Sat 10am–1pm; ☎ 06021 39 58 00, ⓦ info-aschaffenburg.de).

ACCOMMODATION

Goldener Karpfen Löherstr. 20 ☎ 06021 45 90 90, ⓦ hotels-aschaffenburg.de. The simple but comfortable *Goldener Karpfen* occupies an attractive half-timbered building across the street from its sister hotel *Wilder Mann*, which has the reception, breakfast room and restaurant facilities for both. Rooms come with bath or shower, and there are also single rooms with en-suite facilities. **€79**

Wilder Mann Löherstr. 51 ☎ 06021 30 20, ⓦ hotels-aschaffenburg.de. The classy, historic and reasonably priced *Wilder Mann* is the prestige choice in Aschaffenburg's Altstadt, with a restaurant, sauna and wireless internet. It's also very cyclist friendly and offers cycle hire to residents. Also has two-person apartments with kitchen. Apartments **€172**, doubles **€102**

EATING AND DRINKING

Gastwirtschaft Schlappeseppel Schlossgasse 28 ☎ 06021 255 31, ⓦ schlappeseppel-ab.de. Close to the Jesuitenkirche and Schloss, the splendidly named *Schlappeseppel* is a classic, old-fashioned family-owned beer hall, with dark wood-panelled walls, a tiled oven and long benches in the street outside. There's standard *Brauhaus* fare, with main courses from around €7, and the beer comes from the Faust brewery in nearby Militenberg. Daily 10am–1am.

Schlossgass 16 Schlossgasse 16 ☎ 06021 123 13, ⓦ schlossgass16.de. Half-timbered inn with a very pretty beamed interior, serving traditional Frankfurt and Franconian dishes including lighter options such as *Handkäs mit musik* (cheese marinated in oil and vinegar with onions). Main courses from around €10. Mon–Fri 11am–2pm & 4–11pm, Sat 11am–late, Sun 11am–11pm.

Wirtshaus Zum Fegerer Schlossgasse 14 ☎ 06021 156 46, ⓦ fegerer.de. Classy and atmospheric place, with a slightly more refined menu than its neighbour, *Schlossgass 16* (see above), serving up the likes of grilled pike-perch with fennel salad or boiled beef tongue with herb and mustard vinaigrette. Main courses from around €11. There's a sheltered courtyard garden at the back. Daily 11.30am–2.30pm & 5pm–late.

NIGHTLIFE AND ENTERTAINMENT

Colos-Saal Rossmarkt 19 ☎ 06021 272 39, ⓦ colos-saal.de. Excellent music venue close to Park Schöntal, with live bands of all kinds – from jazz to heavy rock – playing every night of the week; the line-up includes the occasional big-name act from Britain, Canada, Ireland or the US. Gigs generally start at 8 or 9pm; DJ nights Fri & Sat 11.30pm–late.

Stadthalle Schlossplatz Schlossplatz 1 ☎ 06021 330 1888, ⓦ stadttheater-aschaffenburg.de. Fronting Aschaffenburg's main square, this modern concert hall is the town's principal venue for classical music, ballet, opera and operetta, and occasionally hosts musicals too. There are large and small auditoria.

Stadttheater Schlossgasse 8 ☎ 06021 330 18 88, ⓦ stadttheater-aschaffenburg.de. Aschaffenburg's main venue for drama is the elegant Neoclassical Stadttheater, rescued after World War II damage by a citizens' initiative and refurbished in 2011/12. Performances generally start 8pm.

Munich
and central
Bavaria

THE MUSEUM BRANDHORST, MUNICH

Munich and central Bavaria

6

"Laptop and Lederhosen" is the expression Germans use to explain the Bavarian paradox: the unlikely combination of social conservatism and business acumen that has made it a powerhouse of the European economy. Nowhere is the contrast sharper than in its capital. Munich is much loved by the cashmere-clad *Schickies* (yuppies) for whom it is, self-evidently, the "northernmost city in Italy". Yet to detractors it's also the beer- and sausage-obsessed *Millionendorf* – a village with a million inhabitants. Beyond Munich, the urbanized and industrialized heartlands of Bavarian Swabia and Upper Bavaria display similar contrasts, with perfectly preserved old towns alongside world-beating manufacturing industries. This is not yet the Bavaria of popular cliché: there aren't even any mountains.

It is, above all, a region of urban glories. As capital of the Duchy that Napoleon expanded and raised to the status of a kingdom, **Munich** has the air – and cultural clout – of a capital city to this day, though its heyday as capital of the kingdom of Bavaria lasted little more than a century. To the west, the Swabian city of **Augsburg** has far older claims to urban greatness, which have left their mark in the city's splendid Renaissance core. In the north, **Ingolstadt** balances respect for its history with pride in its industrial prowess, notably as the home of the car manufacturer Audi. Smaller towns too retain memories of past glories, from the picture-book Residenzstadt of **Neuburg an der Donau** to the little ecclesiastical city of **Eichstätt**. Only south of Munich does the landscape come to the fore, in the rolling lakeland of the **Fünf-Seen-Land**, where the Alps are at last a discernible presence, if only on the horizon. Yet even in the south, **Landsberg am Lech** provides a glorious urban counterpoint to the approaching mountains.

Getting around this densely populated part of Bavaria is relatively straightforward, with Munich's suburban rail system extending far out into the surrounding countryside and the other major population centres linked to it by Autobahn and rail. Moreover, Munich's airport – Germany's second busiest after Frankfurt – ensures it couldn't be easier to get into, or out of, the region. Yet even here, the Bavarian paradox holds true; the efficient modern airport is named after one of postwar Germany's most controversial and reactionary politicians, the long-time Bavarian premier and leader of the conservative CSU party, Franz Josef Strauss.

Munich

If there's such a thing as the German dream, **MUNICH** (München) embodies it. Germany's third – and favourite – city often tops surveys to find the world's most liveable city, and it's easy to see why, with lakes and mountains on its doorstep, a fine roster of historic and

OKTOBERFEST, MUNICH

Highlights

❶ **Lenbachhaus** Masterpieces from Munich's very own artistic avant-garde, with paintings by Kandinsky, Jawlensky, Klee, Franz Marc and August Macke. **See p.347**

❷ **Amalienburg** The Rococo style reaches silvery perfection in this beautiful little hunting lodge built for the Bavarian Wittelsbach dynasty. **See p.351**

❸ **Oktoberfest** Lederhosen, dirndls and impossibly vast quantities of beer characterize the world's most alcoholic folk festival. **See p.357**

❹ **KZ Dachau** A visit to the former Nazi concentration camp on Munich's northern outskirts is a sombre but thought-provoking experience. **See p.359**

❺ **Kloster Andechs** *Carmina Burana* and Benedictine beer make a winning combination on the shores of the Ammersee. **See p.362**

❻ **Neuburg an der Donau** The stately burghers' houses of Neuburg's old town provide the backdrop for a magnificent Renaissance Schloss on the Danube. **See p.365**

❼ **Augsburg's Altstadt** Renaissance architecture meets racy nightlife in Augsburg's beautiful old town, whose splendour is testament to the city's past wealth. **See p.370**

HIGHLIGHTS ARE MARKED ON THE MAP ON P.334

cultural sights, glittering shops and the air of confidence that comes from being the home of BMW and Siemens. For all Bavaria's conservatism, it's also relatively liberal. If there's a fault, it's in the very lack of a flaw: with little grunge to offset it, Munich's well-groomed bourgeois perfection can at times seem a little relentless.

Brief history

Founded in 1158, Munich became the seat of the Wittelsbach dynasty in 1255, but for much of its history it was outclassed by the wealth and success of Augsburg and Nuremberg. Finally, as capital of a fully-fledged Kingdom of Bavaria, established by Napoleon in 1806, it witnessed a surge of construction as Ludwig I and his architect Leo von Klenze endowed it with the Neoclassical monuments commensurate with its status. The turn of the twentieth century brought intellectual kudos: the Blaue Reiter group of artists flourished, and a young Thomas Mann completed *Buddenbrooks* in the bohemian district of **Schwabing**. War changed everything, and in the chaos after World War I the city gave birth to the Nazi movement, which ultimately brought disaster upon it.

Post-World War II

After World War II, Munich assumed Berlin's role as Germany's international metropolis, the haunt of VIPs, celebrities and the leisured rich. Much of the Federal Republic's film output emerged from the Geiselgasteig studios; Wim Wenders graduated from film school here and Rainer Werner Fassbinder held court at the

MUNICH & CENTRAL BAVARIA

HIGHLIGHTS
1. Lenbachhaus
2. Amalienburg
3. Oktoberfest
4. KZ Dachau
5. Kloster Andechs
6. Neuburg an der Donau
7. Augsburg's Altstadt

6

MUNICH ORIENTATION

Despite being a city of 1.44 million, Munich is easy to get to grips with. A line of boulevards follows the course of the medieval defences to define the **Altstadt**, which still preserves three of its medieval city gates: at **Karlsplatz** (also known as **Stachus**), **Sendlinger Tor** and **Isartor Platz**. The city's hub is **Marienplatz**; immediately north of it is the **Residenz**, the Wittelsbach dynasty's palace, fringing **Odeonsplatz**. Beyond it is the **Maxvorstadt** – an urbane neighbourhood which contains many of the most important museums – and the formerly bohemian (and now comfortably middle-class) district of **Schwabing**, which fringes the famous **Englischer Garten**. West of Schwabing is the **Olympiapark**, site of the 1972 Olympic Games. To the south of the Altstadt, the trendy **Gärtnerplatzviertal** and **Glockenbachviertel** – known collectively as the **Isarvorstadt** – line the north bank of the **Isar**. Across the river is **Haidhausen**, similarly urbane if rather less trendy. Further afield are the Baroque palace at **Nymphenburg**, **Hellabrunn Zoo** and the **Bavaria Filmstadt**, plus the striking **Allianz Arena** stadium.

Deutsche Eiche. More surprisingly, Munich was a cradle of the disco movement too, as producers like Giorgio Moroder fused strings, synthesizers and soulful vocals to massively commercial effect, though the acts – notably Donna Summer – were often American and sang in English, so the music's "Germanness" went unnoticed. The 1972 Olympic Games should have crowned this golden age, but the murder of eleven members of the Israeli team shocked the world and overshadowed all other events.

Munich today

Berlin reasserted its old role post-reunification, but Munich has not rested on its laurels: the **Museum Brandhorst**, **Pinakothek der Moderne** and **Allianz-Arena** have all added lustre to the city in recent years. And, of course, there's always the beer: whether in a historic *Bierkeller*, shady *Biergarten* or in a vast tent at the **Oktoberfest**, Munich's tipple of choice is a world-beater.

Marienplatz and around

When Munich has something to celebrate – from Christmas markets to Christopher Street Day – the focus of the festivities is **Marienplatz**, the small and irregularly shaped piazza at the heart of the Altstadt. As public squares go, it's an amorphous space, with historic buildings scattered around in no particular order, though the gilded *Madonna and Child* atop the **Mariensäule** column, erected in 1638 by the Elector Maximilian I in thanks for the sparing of the city by its Swedish occupiers during the Thirty Years' War, provides a central focus. Munich's main pedestrian shopping area stretches west from Marienplatz along Kaufingerstrasse, lined with the usual German chainstores.

Neues Rathaus

Marienplatz 8 • **Glockenspiel mechanical dancers** Daily: Nov–Feb 11am & noon; March–Oct 11am, noon & 5pm • Free • **Tower** May–Oct Mon–Fri & hols 10am–7pm; Nov–April Mon–Fri 10am–5pm • €2.50

Marienplatz's monumentality comes courtesy of the immense **Neues Rathaus**, a sooty pile in Flemish Gothic style that has dominated the square since the late nineteenth century. Its **Glockenspiel** draws crowds for the mechanical dancers that perform to musical accompaniment: jerky musicians and jousting knights celebrate the 1568 marriage of Wilhelm V and Renata von Lothringen while coopers dance to celebrate the passing of the plague in 1517. You can climb the Rathaus **tower** for views of the city.

Altes Rathaus: the Spielzeugmuseum

Marienplatz 15 • Daily 10am–5.30pm • €4

Immediately to the east of the Neues Rathaus, the tall gate tower and Gothic hall of the **Altes Rathaus** originally date from 1470 to 1480, but were largely destroyed by

6

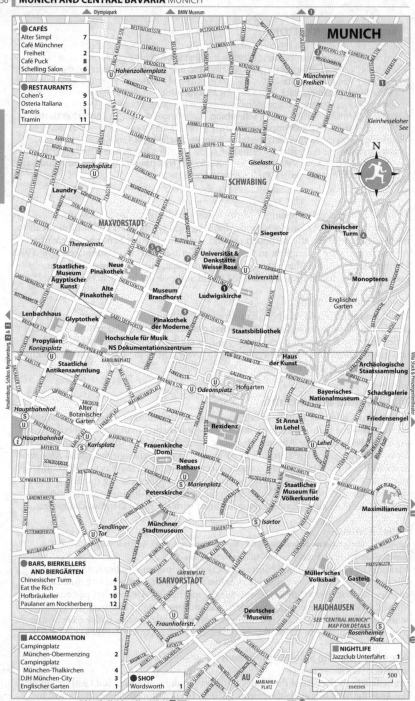

MUNICH

● CAFÉS
Alter Simpl	7
Café Münchner Freiheit	2
Café Puck	8
Schelling Salon	6

● RESTAURANTS
Cohen's	9
Osteria Italiana	5
Tantris	1
Tramin	11

● BARS, BIERKELLERS AND BIERGÄRTEN
Chinesischer Turm	4
Eat the Rich	3
Hofbräukeller	10
Paulaner am Nockherberg	12

■ ACCOMMODATION
Campingplatz München-Obermenzing	2
Campingplatz München-Thalkirchen	4
DJH München-City	3
Englischer Garten	1

● SHOP
Wordsworth	1

■ NIGHTLIFE
Jazzclub Unterfahrt	1

bombs during World War II and not fully rebuilt until the 1970s. The Altes Rathaus now houses the **Spielzeugmuseum**, with a charming collection of old-fashioned dolls' houses, model trains and teddy bears.

St Peter

Rindermarkt 1 · Tower Summer Mon–Fri 9am–6.30pm, Sat & Sun 10am–6.30pm; winter Mon–Sat 9am–5.30pm, Sat & Sun 10am–5.30pm · €2

Overlooking Marienplatz from the south is central Munich's oldest church, **St Peter**, popularly known as the Peterskirche or Alter Peter. The oldest parts of the church date from 1368, though much of its present appearance is the result of a later Baroque rebuild, including the altar which provides an elaborate setting for the Late Gothic, seated figure of *St Peter* by Erasmus Grasser (1492). Its **tower** offers better views than the Neues Rathaus tower – not least because you can see the Rathaus itself.

St Peter's near neighbour, the **Heilig-Geist-Kirche**, hides its Gothic origins behind an even more radical Baroque remodelling, the high point of which is a giddily ornamental interior by the Asam brothers, Munich's greatest practitioners of religious Baroque.

Northeast of the Altes Rathaus

The warren of narrow streets northeast of the Altes Rathaus preserves something of the atmosphere of medieval Munich, though much restored and rebuilt. Notable buildings include the **Stadtschreiberhaus** at Burgstr. 5, Munich's oldest private residence, which dates from 1550 and has lovely Renaissance paintings by Hans Mielich on its facade; and the nearby **Alter Hof**, Burgstr. 8, a thirteenth-century complex that was the Wittelsbachs' first castle and which now houses the **Infopoint Museen & Schlösser Bayern** (Mon–Sat 10am–6pm; ⓦinfopoint-museen-bayern.de), a useful information office for historic buildings in Bavaria. Just to the north of the Alter Hof, the **Alte Münze** or Old Mint, at Hofgraben 4, hides a lovely sixteenth-century Italian Renaissance arcaded courtyard behind its later facades.

The Hofbräuhaus

Platzl 9 · Daily 9am–11.30pm · ☎ 089 290 13 61 00, ⓦ hofbraeuhaus.de

Probably the most famous monument in Munich's Altstadt is the much-mythologized **Hofbräuhaus** (see p.356), one block east of the Old Mint, which dubs itself "the most famous tavern in the world", and is immortalized in the song *In München Steht ein Hofbräuhau*, written, incidentally, by a Berliner. More ominously, it was here on February 24, 1920, that Hitler proclaimed the 25 theses of the nascent Nazi party at its first big rally. That dubious claim to fame aside, it's a typically big, brassy and bustling Munich beer hall, with a history that stretches back to 1589; the current building dates from 1896.

The Bier & Oktoberfest Museum

Sterneckerstr. 2 · Tues–Sat 1–6pm · €4 · ⓦ bier-und-oktoberfestmuseum.de

Tucked into a narrow lane off Tal, southeast of Marienplatz, the **Bier & Oktoberfest Museum** occupies a fine old burgher's house built, like the nearby Isartor, after the great city fire of 1327. The exhibits chart the 5000-year history of beer production as well as explaining the origins of the Oktoberfest in the festivities surrounding the marriage of Crown Prince Ludwig with Therese of Sachsen-Hildburghausen. On the ground floor you can sample various beers in the **Museumsstüberl**, which also serves food.

Viktualienmarkt

Mon–Sat from around 7/8am to 6pm, though individual stall opening times vary

South of the Heilig-Geist-Kirche sprawls the **Viktualienmarkt**, the city's famous open-air food market, built on ground cleared of charitable buildings belonging to the

6

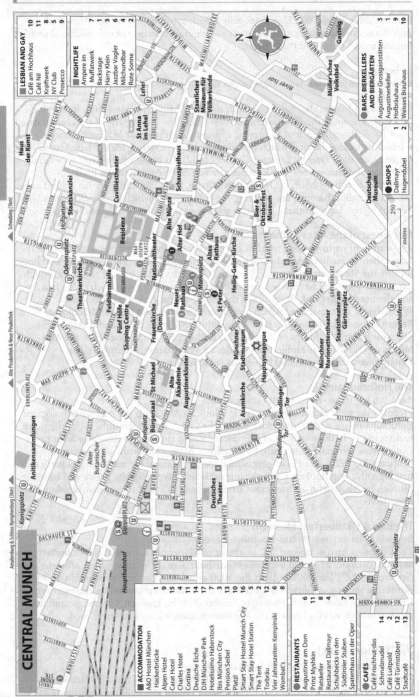

CENTRAL MUNICH

LESBIAN AND GAY
Café am Hochhaus 10
Café Nil 11
Kraftwerk 8
NY Club 5
Prosecco 9

NIGHTLIFE
Ampere im 7
Muffatwerk 1
Backstage 3
Harry Klein 6
Jazzbar Vogler 4
Milchundbar 2
Rote Sonne

BARS, BIERKELLERS AND BIERGÄRTEN
Augustiner Grossgaststätten 5
Augustinerkeller 1
Hofbräuhaus 9
Weisses Brauhaus 10

SHOPS
Dallmayr 1
Hugendubel 2

ACCOMMODATION
A&O Hostel München 1
Hackerbrücke 9
Alpen Hotel 15
Carat Hotel 4
Charles Hotel 11
Cortina 14
Deutsche Eiche 17
DJH München-Park 3
Hotelissimo Haberstock 7
Ibis München City 13
Pension Seibel 16
Platzl 5
Smart Stay Hostel Munich City 2
Smart Stay Hotel Station 12
The Tent 6
Torbräu 12
Vier Jahreszeiten Kempinski 8

RESTAURANTS
Augustiner am Dom 6
Prinz Myshkin 11
Ratskeller 8
Restaurant Dallmayr 4
Schuhbecks in den 7
Südtiroler Stuben
Spatenhaus an der Oper 3

CAFÉS
Café Frischhut-das 14
Schmalznudel
Café Luitpold 2
Café Turmstüberl 12
Stadtcafé 13

Church by decree of Maximilian I in 1807. It's much the best place to get a cheap meal in Munich if you don't mind standing up – the various butchers and snack stalls sell hot slices of *Leberkäse* – literally liver cheese, a type of meatloaf – and delicious, lemony veal *Weisswurst* – Munich's sausage speciality, traditionally eaten only before midday. As well as Bavarian specialities and fruit-and-vegetable displays, the market has some quite fancy stalls selling wine, cheese and imported delicacies.

The Münchner Stadtmuseum

St-Jakobs-Platz 1 • Tues–Sun 10am–6pm • €7 including temporary exhibitions, otherwise €4 • ⓦ muenchner-stadtmuseum.de

Close to Viktualienmarkt, the **Münchner Stadtmuseum** occupies a rambling complex of buildings, the oldest part of which – the medieval Zeughaus or armoury – dates back to 1491–93. Centrepiece of the museum is the permanent exhibition **Typisch München** (Typically Munich), which provides an overview of the city's history, including a reappraisal of how the city spun its own myths at the time of the museum's foundation in 1888. There's also a section dealing with Munich's role as "secret capital" of West Germany during the Cold War, with a "Chill Out Loden Lounge" in which images of football stadiums and beer tents, laptops and Lederhosen are projected. The darker side of Munich's history is dealt with by a section on its role as the "Hauptstadt der Bewegung" – the capital city of the Nazi movement.

Hauptsynagoge

St-Jakobs-Platz • Guided tours Mon–Thurs noon, 4.30pm & 6pm, Sun noon, 2pm & 4pm • €5 • Book in advance on ☎ 089 202 40 01 00 • ⓦ juedischeszentrumjakobsplatz.de

Facing the Stadtmuseum across St-Jakobs-Platz is the striking **Hauptsynagoge**, a starkly elegant, modern stone-and-mesh cube that opened in 2006 as a fitting replacement for the grandiose old synagogue destroyed in the summer of 1938 – several months before Kristallnacht. It's one of the largest – as well as the most visually striking – new synagogues in Europe, and serves a community of 9500, the second largest in Germany after Berlin.

Jüdisches Museum

St-Jakobs-Platz 16 • Tues–Sun 10am–6pm • €6 • ⓦ juedisches-museum-muenchen.de

Next to the Hauptsynagoge is the **Jüdisches Museum** (Jewish Museum), which houses a permanent exhibition on the history of Jewish Munich and on the Jewish faith, and often has fascinating temporary exhibitions on topics as diverse as contemporary Jewish art or the influx of Jewish migrants from the former Soviet Union, often with a distinctly Munich – or at least Bavarian – focus.

Asamkirche

Sendlinger Str. 62 • Daily except Fri 9am–6pm, Fri 1–6pm • Free

A short stroll west of the Jüdisches Museum along Sendlinger Strasse is the **Asamkirche**, officially the church of St John Nepomuk, but universally known by the name of its creators, the Asam brothers, who between 1733 and 1746 created the most gaudily theatrical – if by no means the biggest – church interior in Munich, a riot of Rococo opulence just 28m long and 9m wide. The design of the little church was influenced by both Bohemian and Italian Baroque, and it was intended as their own family chapel, which explains its opulence – without a client, all restraints were off. Sendlinger Strasse leads to the tough-looking fourteenth-century city gate, **Sendlinger Tor**.

Frauenkirche

Frauenplatz 1 • Mon–Wed & Sat 7am–7pm, Thurs 7am–8.30pm, Fri 7am–6pm • Tower closed until 2016 for restoration

Just west of Marienplatz, the 98m-high twin pepperpot towers (1524–45) of the **Frauenkirche** soar above the surrounding buildings and are the visual symbols of the city; the southern tower, which offers views over the city, was closed for restoration as this book went to press. Dating from 1468 to 1488, the Frauenkirche was the last big Gothic hall church to be built in the Wittelsbachs' domains, and its austere brick elevations and whitewashed interior – much simplified since its postwar restoration – are pleasingly coherent and simple in a city where fussy Baroque ornament is the usual ecclesiastical style. The onion domes atop the twin towers were intended as a reference to the Dome of the Rock in Jerusalem – actually a mosque, but believed at the time to be King Solomon's Temple. Inside, a mysterious black footprint in the floor beneath the towers is said to have been left by the Devil, stamping in rage after architect Jörg von Halsbach won a wager with him to build a church without visible windows – by pointing out a spot where pillars hid every one.

St Michael

Neuhauser Str. 6 • Fürstengruft Mon–Fri 9.30am–4.30pm, Sat 9.30am–2.30pm • €2

West of the Frauenkirche, dominating the eastern end of Neuhauser Strasse, is the Jesuit church of **St Michael**, built under the auspices of Duke Wilhelm V between 1583 and 1597 to replace an earlier church – the first Jesuit church north of the Alps, based on the order's mother church of Il Gesù in Rome – whose tower collapsed before it could even be consecrated. This was the cue to build an even larger and more splendid church, whose financing bankrupted the state and forced Wilhelm to abdicate upon completion. Inside, the 20m-wide, stucco-ornamented, barrel-vaulted roof dominates; stylistically it was the prototype for scores of churches built later in southern Germany, though postwar restoration was not entirely accurate. The **Fürstengruft**, or crypt, contains the graves of Wilhelm and another extravagant Wittelsbach, "Mad" King Ludwig II, who commissioned the fairytale castle of Neuschwanstein (see p.386), the mock Versailles of Herrenchiemsee (see p.400) and the more modest Schloss Linderhof (see p.390).

The northern Altstadt

North from Marienplatz you enter Munich's most exclusive shopping district, its modern face represented by the slick **Fünf Höfe** mall subtly inserted into the townscape west of Theatinerstrasse. Its more traditional elegance, by contrast, is epitomized by the grand **Dallmayr** delicatessen in Diener Strasse and by the stately facades (and international designer names) of **Maximilianstrasse**, spiritual home of Munich flaneurs. It's dominated at its eastern end by the **Maximilianeum**, the terracotta-clad building high on the opposite bank of the river Isar that houses the Bavarian Land parliament. Like the street itself, it is named after King Maximilian II, during whose reign construction began. At the western end of Maximilianstrasse, the Neoclassical **Nationaltheater** – reconstructed to the original plans after being gutted during World War II – presides over **Max-Joseph-Platz**.

The Residenz

Residenzmuseum and Schatzkammer Entrance on Max-Joseph-Platz • Daily: April to mid-Oct 9am–6pm; mid-Oct to March 10am–5pm; last admission 1hr before closing • €7 for single entry to either Residenzmuseum or Schatzkammer, €11 combined, €13 including Cuvilliés-Theater; English audio-guide included in price • **Cuvilliés-Theater** Entrance on Residenzstrasse • April–July & mid-Sept to mid-Oct Mon–Sat 2–6pm, Sun 9am–6pm; Aug to early Sept daily 9am–6pm; mid-Oct to March Mon–Sat 2–5pm, Sun 10am–5pm; last admission 1hr before closing • €3.50 • **Hofgarten** Free • ⓦ residenz-muenchen.de

The Residenz, the enormous royal palace complex of Bavaria's ruling Wittelsbach dynasty who resided here right up until 1918, has its origins in a small fourteenth-century castle, the Neuveste, of which nothing remains. Over the centuries it was gradually transformed into a considerable palace complex by the Wittelsbachs, first as dukes, then from 1623 as electors and finally from 1806 as kings of Bavaria. What survives today is the result of several phases of construction and of post-1945 reconstruction after extensive damage during World War II. The oldest surviving Renaissance part dates from the reign of Albrecht V (1550–79) and was the work of Jacopo Strada and Simon Zwitzel, elaborated and extended from 1581 onwards by the Dutch architect Friedrich Sustris. Baroque and Rococo extensions followed, notably in the eighteenth century under court architect François Cuvilliés – the diminutive Walloon who also designed Schloss Augustusburg at Brühl. A final major round of construction took place under Leo von Klenze during the reign of King Ludwig I; the additions made by Ludwig II – which included a rooftop winter garden complete with a royal barge on an indoor lake – have not survived.

Along the north facade of the Residenz is the formal **Hofgarten**, the former palace garden, whose geometric design dates from the reign of Maximilian I (1610–20).

The Residenzmuseum

Much of the Residenz palace interior is open to the public as the **Residenzmuseum**. The most spectacular room you see is also the oldest, the **Antiquarium**, originally built to house Duke Albrecht's collection of antiquities but remodelled under his successors, Wilhelm V and Maximilian I, as a banqueting hall. The results are remarkable: the 66m-long vaulted hall is claimed to be the largest and most lavish Renaissance interior north of the Alps, richly decorated with frescoes, with allegories of Fame and Virtue by court painter Peter Candid covering the ceiling, while the vaults above the windows and the window jambs are covered with images of the towns, markets and palaces of Bavaria. The **Ahnengalerie**, which was commissioned by the Elector Karl on his accession in 1726, incorporates more than a hundred portraits of members of the Wittelsbach family. It was intended to draw attention to the elector's credentials as a potential emperor – and appears to have done the trick as he was crowned Emperor Karl VII in Frankfurt in 1742. François Cuvilliés' inspired hand is evident in the aptly named **Reiche Zimmer**, or Ornate Rooms, in which everything from the gilded rocailles on the stucco walls and ceilings to the furniture received the master's attention. The rooms were created between 1730 and 1733. Leo von Klenze's more restrained nineteenth-century **Königsbau** rooms were off limits to visitors at the time of writing due to restoration work.

The Schatzkammer

The collection on display in the **Schatzkammer** (Treasury) on the ground floor of the Königsbau was initiated by Albrecht V and is one of the largest royal treasure-houses in Europe; highlights include the ninth-century ciborium of King Arnulf of Carinthia and a dazzling statuette of St George created between 1586 and 1597. The royal insignia of the Kingdom of Bavaria are also on display.

Cuvilliés-Theater

You'll need to re-enter the Residenz complex by the middle entrance on Residenzstrasse and cross the Brunnenhof courtyard to reach the exquisite **Cuvilliés-Theater**, built from 1751 to 1755 as a court theatre under Elector Max III Joseph. Cuvilliés' extravagance survives only because the elaborately carved tiers of boxes were removed from their original location in the Alte Residenztheater building – between the Nationaltheater and Residenz – for safekeeping during World War II. This building was completely destroyed by wartime bombs and replaced by the modern Residenztheater (see p.358) that now stands on the site, but the boxes were re-erected after the war in their present location. It's still used as a theatre.

"Shirkers' Alley"

Directly opposite the entrance to the Cuvilliés-Theater on Residenzstrasse, little **Viscardigasse** was known colloquially during the Nazi years as "Drückebergergasse" or "Shirkers' Alley", because it was a short cut that could be used to avoid passing the SS honour guard stationed day and night on the Feldherrnhalle on nearby Odeonsplatz – and thus to avoid having to give the compulsory "German greeting" or Nazi salute. A **bronze trail** set into the cobbles now recalls those who preferred to "shirk".

Odeonsplatz and the Hofgarten

Whatever its historical associations, **Odeonsplatz** is one of Munich's most handsome squares. Modelled on the Loggia dei Lanzi next to the Palazzo Vecchio in Florence and designed by Friedrich von Gärtner, the **Feldherrnhalle** on the south side of the square was built in 1841 to 1844 to shelter statues of two celebrated Bavarian generals: General Tilly (of Rothenburg Meistertrunk fame; see p.320); and Prince Wrede, who helped Napoleon to victory at Wagram before Bavaria switched sides in time to participate in the Congress of Vienna.

Theatinerkirche St Kajetan

Odeonsplatz • Free

On the west side of the square, the buttercup-yellow exterior of the **Theatinerkirche St Kajetan** hides an airy white interior. The work of three architects – Agostino Barelli, Enrico Zuccalli and François Cuvilliés – it was modelled on St Andrea della Valle in Rome. Construction began in 1663 but was not completed until a century later, so the church spans the transition from Baroque to Rococo. Like St Michael, it has a crypt full of Wittelsbachs.

Haus der Kunst

Prinzregentenstr. 1 • Daily 10am–8pm, Thurs until 10pm • €10 *Tagesticket* gives admission to all exhibitions for 1 day • ⓦ hausderkunst.de

Northeast of the Hofgarten on broad, straight Prinzregentenstrasse is the **Haus der Kunst**, a stripped Classical pile commissioned by Hitler, and completed in 1937 as a showcase for the sort of art of which he approved. Its architect, Paul Ludwig Troost, made his name designing the interiors of ocean liners, but missed the mark here, for what was obviously meant to be an imposing building is too squat to have the desired effect: rather than a finished building, it looks more like the plinth for something much bigger. These days it's used for temporary exhibitions of the sort of modern art, design and photography the Nazis would have regarded as "degenerate".

Bayerisches Nationalmuseum

Prinzregentenstr. 3 • Tues–Sun 10am–5pm, Thurs until 8pm • €5, €7 including temporary exhibitions • ⓦ bayerisches-nationalmuseum.de

The sprawling **Bayerisches Nationalmuseum** (Bavarian National Museum) is one of the big hitters among Munich's museums, with a dizzying array of fine and applied arts from late antiquity to the early twentieth century, much of it stemming from the Wittelsbachs' own collections. The ground floor is devoted to works of the Romanesque, Gothic and Renaissance, from suits of armour to winged altarpieces and carvings by Tilman Riemenschneider. The basement houses the world's largest collection of Nativity cribs, with examples from the Alps and Southern Italy, plus Bavarian furniture of the eighteenth and nineteenth centuries, often decorated with paintings on religious themes. Upstairs, musical instruments from the Wittelsbachs' court, silver table services and antique board games add a luxuriously domestic note, and there's Nymphenburg porcelain and Rococo sculpture by Johann Baptist Straub and Ignaz Günther. The museum's Baroque collections were scheduled to transfer to the newly-renovated west wing by the end of 2014. Another wing of the museum houses the **Sammlung Bollert** collection, with southern German carvings from the Gothic to the Renaissance, including more work by Riemenschneider.

Schack-Galerie

Prinzregentenstr. 9 • Wed–Sun 10am–6pm • €4 or €12 *Tagesticket* with the Pinakothek museums (see p.344) & Museum Brandhorst (see p.344) • ⓦ schack-galerie.de

The Bayerisches Nationalmuseum's near neighbour, the **Schack-Galerie**, houses the art collection built up by Adolf Friedrich Graf von Schack (1815–94), a diplomat who in later life devoted himself entirely to his literary and intellectual pursuits. As an art collector he favoured young and little-known artists, in the process building up a collection of works by artists who were to number among the most important in nineteenth-century Germany, including Anselm Feuerbach and Arnold Böcklin. To this day the collection reflects Count Schack's personal tastes since – with the exception of a handful of losses during World War II – it remains largely intact.

Villa Stuck

Prinzregentenstr. 60 • Tues–Sun 11am–6pm, plus 1st Fri of month 6–10pm • Historical rooms €4, historical rooms plus exhibitions €9, free on 1st Fri of month 6–10pm • ⓦ villastuck.de

On the eastern side of the River Isar, the last in Prinzregentenstrasse's line-up of art attractions is the **Villa Stuck**, the former home of Franz von Stuck (1863–1928), one of the founders of the Munich Secession and a tutor of Paul Klee and Wassily Kandinsky. The house was conceived as a *Gesamtkunstwerk* – a total work of art unifying life, work, art and architecture, music, theatre and a dash of narcissism. An eclectic mix of Jugendstil and other styles current at the time, the villa provides a suitably lush setting for Stuck's own work as well as a venue for temporary exhibitions on his artistic contemporaries.

Ludwigstrasse and the Maxvorstadt

North from Odeonsplatz stretches arrow-straight **Ludwigstrasse**, lined with early nineteenth-century Neoclassical buildings created during Ludwig I's reign by Leo von Klenze and Friedrich von Gärtner. The street terminates at its north end with the **Siegestor**, a triumphal arch based on the Arch of Constantine in Rome. Badly damaged during World War II, the arch was restored in such a way as to leave the extent of the damage visible. Long, handsome and dignified, Ludwigstrasse was a self-conscious attempt to create a Whitehall or Unter den Linden for Munich, though it's not exactly the liveliest of streets, only really becoming animated near the Ludwig-Maximilians-Universität at Geschwister-Scholl-Platz. The district laid out on a grid pattern west of Ludwigstrasse is known as the **Maxvorstadt** and is one of the most urbane in Munich; its rich mix of antiquarian bookshops, antique shops and cafés repays browsing.

Ludwig-Maximilians-Universität and the DenkStätte

Geschwister-Scholl-Platz 1 • DenkStätte Mon–Fri 10am–4pm, Sat noon–3pm • Free

A touching and innovative memorial in front of the **Ludwig-Maximilians-Universität** recalls the bravery and martyrdom of the anti-Nazi student group, Weisse Rose (see box, p.344): plaques resembling the doomed students' antifascist leaflets are set into the cobbles almost at random, as though they had just fluttered to earth. In the university atrium where Hans and Sophie scattered their leaflets, the small **DenkStätte** is an exhibition about the Weisse Rose movement.

6

THE WEISSE ROSE

Though nowadays it looms large in the mythology of anti-Nazi resistance, the **Weisse Rose** (White Rose) was from beginning to end a modest affair, the initiative of a small group of students – most of whom were studying medicine – and others from their wider circle of friends; the only older member of the group was the Swiss-born philosophy professor **Kurt Huber**. The core of the group, which came together in 1942, consisted of the devoutly Christian **Hans Scholl** – a former Hitler Youth group leader who had become vehemently opposed to Nazi ideology – and the Russian-born medical student **Alexander Schmorell**; Hans's sister **Sophie** also subsequently became involved. At night, the group daubed walls with slogans such as "Hitler, mass murderer" or "Freedom", but it is for the six leaflets it produced and distributed – including one that made public the murder of the Jews – that the Weisse Rose is remembered. The last of these proved fateful. On February 18, 1943, Hans and Sophie deposited copies in the atrium of the university, but were spotted by the janitor and subsequently arrested by the Gestapo. Hans and Sophie were tried before the notorious Nazi judge Roland Freisler; they, along with other members of the group, were sentenced to death by guillotine.

The Museum Brandhorst

Theresienstr. 35a • Tues–Sun 9am–6pm, Thurs until 8pm • €7, *Tageskarte* with Pinakothek museums (see below) & Schack-Galerie (see p.343) €12, English audio-guide €3 • ⓦ museum-brandhorst.de

The **Museum Brandhorst** – an eye-catching structure clad with 36,000 polychromatic ceramic rods – was designed by Berlin architects Sauerbruch Hutton and opened in 2009 to house the collection of German and international modern art built up by Udo and Anette Brandhorst in a setting of restrained, spacious modernism. The exhibits – which rotate on a regular basis – include works by such international figures as Andy Warhol, Jeff Koons and Picasso, as well as by major contemporary German artists such as Gerhard Richter and Georg Baselitz. The room specially designed to house Cy Twombly's vibrant *Lepanto* canvasses is a particular delight.

The Staatliches Museum Ägyptischer Kunst

Gabelsbergerstr. 35 • Tues 10am–8pm, Wed–Sun 10am–6pm • €7, €1 on Sun; prices are higher during special exhibitions • ⓦ smaek.de

Visitors enter Munich's impressive new **Staatliches Museum Ägyptischer Kunst** (Egyptian Museum) via a grand descent reminiscent of the entrance to a Pharoah's tomb. Opened in 2013 to house artefacts formerly housed in the Residenz, the museum has a collection which spans 5000 years of Egyptian history. Particularly fascinating are the sections dealing with the Ptolemaic and Roman periods, which illustrate how cultural influences crossed and re-crossed the Mediterranean.

The Pinakothek museums

Reason enough for a visit to Munich is provided by the royal flush of Pinakothek art galleries, each of which is dedicated to a different era in art history. The **Alte Pinakothek** contains one of the greatest collections of Old Masters in the world, the **Neue Pinakothek** is particularly strong on nineteenth-century German art, while the **Pinakothek der Moderne** houses modern and contemporary art and has seen record-breaking visitor numbers since its debut in 2002.

The Alte Pinakothek

Barer Str. 27 • Tues 10am–8pm, Wed–Sun 10am–6pm • €4, €1 on Sun, *Tageskarte* with Schack-Galerie (see p.343), Museum Brandhorst (see above) & other Pinakothek museums €12 • ⓦ pinakothek.de

The scars of war are visible on the broken facade of Leo von Klenze's **Alte Pinakothek**, at the time of its construction in 1826 to 1836 the largest art gallery in the world. Even today, it can be an overwhelming experience: the collections, which are based on the royal collection of the Wittelsbach dynasty over five hundred years, are arranged geographically and chronologically, encompassing German, Dutch, Flemish, Spanish, French and Italian art, with a timespan from the Middle Ages to the eighteenth century. The museum is undergoing long-term renovation which will continue until 2017; during this time certain galleries will be subject to closure for lengthy periods and entry prices have been reduced.

Ground floor

Things kick off on the west side of the ground floor with **German painting** from the fifteenth and sixteenth centuries. Outstanding works here include Michael Pacher's *Kirchenväteraltar*, created for the Augustine abbey of Neustift in the South Tyrol, Lucas Cranach the Elder's *Adam and Eve* and the same artist's *Golden Age* of 1530, which depicts man's lost earthly paradise. Also on display on the ground floor is Pieter Bruegel the Elder's richly comic *The Land of Cockayne*, which depicts the vices of idleness, gluttony and sloth by showing three prostrate figures evidently sleeping off a good lunch.

First floor

The main exhibition space is upstairs, beginning with more **medieval painting**: Hans Memling's *The Seven Joys of Mary* (1435–40) is an entire narrative in one painting, with the story of the Three Magi as its centrepiece; startlingly modern by comparison is Albrecht Dürer's innovative *Self Portrait with a Fur Trimmed Coat* from 1500, which depicts the artist at the age of 28 with flowing locks and aquiline nose – every inch the confident Renaissance man.

Italian art is represented by, among others, Botticelli's vivid *Pietà* of 1490 and an intriguing *Christ with Mary and Martha* by Tintoretto from 1580; but the centrepiece of the Alte Pinakothek's collection is the Rubenssaal, which was intended as the heart of the museum to reflect the importance of the Wittelsbachs' collection of works by Peter Paul Rubens. The room is dominated by the 6m-high *Last Judgement* of 1617. One of the largest canvases ever painted, it depicts 65 figures, most of them naked, as graves open and the dead are separated into the blessed and the damned. Commissioned for the high altar of the Jesuit church at Neuburg an der Donau, it offended contemporary sensibilities and spent much of its short time at Neuburg draped – though it was the nudity, rather than the depiction of death and damnation, that caused offence. Among **Spanish works** in the collection, El Greco's *Christ Stripped of his Garments*, painted in 1606 to 1608 for Toledo cathedral, is notable for also having caused a scandal. Not only does it depict a scene of humiliation almost never painted in Western art, but it also includes Mary Magdalene and the Virgin Mary as onlookers, with the implication that they will at any moment witness Christ's disrobing.

The Neue Pinakothek

Barer Str. 29 • Mon & Thurs–Sun 10am–6pm, Wed 10am–8pm • €7, €1 on Sun, *Tageskarte* with Schack-Galerie (see p.343), Museum Brandhorst (see opposite) & other Pinakothek museums €12 • ⓦ pinakothek.de

Facing the Alte Pinakothek across Theresienstrasse, the **Neue Pinakothek** picks up where the older museum leaves off, concentrating on art from the nineteenth century to Jugendstil. Like the Alte Pinakothek, it was founded under the auspices of King Ludwig I, but unlike its sister museum its destroyed buildings were not resurrected after World War II. Instead, a modern building was opened to house the collection in 1981.

The tour begins with art from around **1800**, prominent among which are a number of canvases by Goya, before progressing to English painting of the era, including Gainsborough's lovely *Portrait of Mrs Thomas Hibbert*, Constable's *View of Dedham Vale from East Bergholt* of 1815 and Turner's *Ostend* of 1844. Much of the rest of the museum is given over to German art, including works by artists active at Ludwig's court, such as a view of the Acropolis by Leo von Klenze. Another architect, Karl Friedrich Schinkel, is represented by a copy of his fantastical *Cathedral Towering Over a*

Town of 1830. More contemplative in tone are Caspar David Friedrich's sensual *Summer* of 1807. Later works include Adolph von Menzel's *Living Room with the Artist's Sister* of 1847, which shows that the great self-taught Prussian painter was as at home with intimate, domestic scenes as he was with his big, official works.

French **Impressionist** and **Post-Impressionist** works include Monet's *Seine Bridge at Argenteuil* and Manet's *Monet Painting on His Studio Boat* of 1874, as well as one of Van Gogh's *Sunflowers*. There are also several canvases by Cézanne and starkly contrasting works by the Austrians Klimt and Schiele.

The Pinakothek der Moderne

Barer Str. 40 • Tues, Wed & Fri–Sun 10am–6pm, Thurs 10am–8pm • €10, €1 on Sun, *Tageskarte* with Schack-Galerie (see p.343), Museum Brandhorst (see p.344) & other Pinakothek museums €12 • ⓦ pinakothek.de

The third of the Pinakothek museums, the **Pinakothek der Moderne**, gathers its somewhat disparate collections of classic modern and contemporary art, design and architecture around a striking central rotunda. Stephan Braunfels' clean modern architecture won much praise at the time of the museum's debut, though the building isn't perhaps quite as pleasing as the earlier Kunstmuseum in Bonn, and the layout's complexity means you'll need to hang on to your floorplan if you're to navigate the museum successfully.

All the same, it's a rewarding place to visit. Make a beeline for the **Modern Art Collection** on the first floor, where the top-lit rooms are divided by the central rotunda. Only a small selection of the 3000-strong permanent collection is on show, and considerable space is devoted to temporary exhibitions. On the west side of the building are works representing the last century's key artistic movements, from Cubism, through Weimar-era Neue Sachlichkeit to Surrealism and beyond. Prominence is given to Max Beckmann, a key figure in the development of representational art in the twentieth century, to Paul Klee and to Joseph Beuys; the museum has one of the most extensive collections by the *enfant terrible* of postwar German art. The east wing is devoted to **contemporary art**, including room installations by Dan Flavin and Fred Sandback as well as works by Georg Baselitz, Gerhard Richter and Blinky Palermo. The museum's ground floor is devoted to architecture and to a rotating selection of the graphic works of the **Staatliche Graphische Sammlung**. The basement, meanwhile, is a temple to the **Neue Sammlung**'s collections of applied **design**, with everything from a streamlined 1930s Tatra car to an Audi "design wall", computer design, classic bentwood chairs and – in the rotunda – a permanent display of classic modern jewellery.

Königsplatz and around

Nowhere expresses Ludwig I's desire to erect an Athens-on-the-Isar better than **Königsplatz**, a short walk to the southwest of the Pinakothek museums. It's a stiff but proper set-piece of Neoclassical architecture, presided over by Leo von Klenze's **Propyläen** gateway of 1846 to 1862, decorated with friezes depicting Greek warriors, and flanked by non-identical twin temples to the arts of antiquity – the Glyptothek on the north side, another of Klenze's works, and the Staatliche Antikensammlung on the south side. Close by is the **Lenbachhaus**, which houses an important collection of classic modern art by the Munich-based Blaue Reiter group.

Glyptothek

Königsplatz 3 • Tues, Wed & Fri–Sun 10am–5pm, Thurs 10am–8pm • €6 combined ticket with Staatliche Antikensammlung (see opposite), €1 on Sun • ⓦ antike-am-koenigsplatz.mwn.de

Wartime destruction did a great aesthetic favour to the **Glyptothek**, for it allowed the museum's curators to strip away Leo von Klenze's fussy and much-criticized interiors and instead present the museum's beautiful collection of antique statuary in surroundings of exquisite austerity. The collection starts as it means to go on with a roomful of early depictions of Greek youths, including a large, rust-coloured **grave statue** of a youth from Attica, dated around 540 or 530 BC. The most famous single sculpture in the museum is the **Barberini Faun**, a remarkable depiction of a sleeping satyr, languid yet athletic, which was probably originally erected in the open space of a Greek sanctuary dedicated to Dionysos. Dated around 200 BC, the sculpture's route to Munich was via the Palazzo Barberini in Rome, from which it acquired its popular name. The largest single collection of sculptures in the museum is the superb group of pediment sculptures from the **Sanctuary of Aphaia** on the island of Aegina, which date from around 500 BC. The Glyptothek also has a fascinating selection of **Roman** sculptures from the period of the late Republic, when – in contrast to the aesthetic ideal always depicted in Greek sculptures – there was an attempt to produce genuine likenesses.

Staatliche Antikensammlung

Königsplatz 1 • Tues–Sun 10am–5pm, Wed until 8pm • €6 combined ticket with Glypothek (see opposite), €1 on Sun • W antike-am-koenigsplatz.mwn.de

The essential counterpoint to the Glypothek's statuary is provided by the more fragile artworks of the **Staatliche Antikensammlung**. Here, you can feast your eyes on astonishingly delicate jewellery in the basement, including many very beautiful Etruscan earrings, a solid-gold diadem from the Greek Black Sea colony of Pantikapeion in what is now Ukraine, dated 300 BC, and a splendid gold funerary wreath from Armento in Italy, dated to 370–360 BC. The ground floor of the museum is devoted to Greek pottery in all its varieties, variously decorated with mythological themes or with scenes from everyday life.

The Lenbachhaus

Luisenstr. 33 • Tues 10am–9pm, Wed–Sun 10am–6pm • €10 including English audio-guide • W lenbachhaus.de

On the northwestern side of the Propyläen gateway, the **Lenbachhaus** museum marks the continuation of Brienner Strasse. Reopened in 2013 with a new extension by Foster + Partners, the museum has at its core the richly-decorated historic rooms of the Italian-style villa that belonged to the nineteenth-century Munich painter Franz von Lenbach. The collection encompasses romantic landscape paintings of the nineteenth-century Munich school, works by Lovis Corinth, Max Slevogt, the Weimar-era Neue Sachlichkeit and Joseph Beuys, whose installations *Show your wound* and *Before departing from camp I* are displayed in one wing. The museum is best known, however, for the world's largest collection of works by the **Blaue Reiter** (see box below), displayed on the top floor. The ravishing selection of canvasses highlights the individual style as well as the collective spirit of the group, from Franz Marc's harnessing of Italian Futurist techniques to convey movement in his famous images of animals, to Kandinsky's epoch-making progression towards abstraction.

BLAUE REITER

One of the most significant groupings of modern artists in Germany at the start of the twentieth century, the **Blaue Reiter** emerged in Munich and Murnau in the years before World War I. Taking its name from a 1911 image of a rider on horseback produced by group member Wassily Kandinsky, Blaue Reiter was characterized by its colourful, expressive and partly abstract style. Alongside the Russians Kandinsky and Jawlensky and Kandinsky's long-time partner Gabriele Münter, the cosmopolitan group included the Swiss German Paul Klee, Bavarian Franz Marc and Rhinelanders August Macke and Heinrich Campendonk. World War I obliterated the Blaue Reiter; the non-Germans in the group fled the country, while Macke and Marc were drafted and later killed in action.

6

The Party Forum and NS-Dokumentationszentrum

Something about Königsplatz's bleak Classical splendour appealed to Hitler, for not only did the Nazis designate it a **Party Forum** and turn it into a parade ground, they also located the party's institutions in various buildings on its eastern side. Most prominent of these were the twin structures flanking Brienner Strasse, which still survive – the one on the north side is the so-called **Führerbau**, where Hitler had his Munich office and where the Munich agreement to dismember Czechoslovakia was signed in 1938; it's now a school of music and drama. On the site of the former Nazi party headquarters at the junction of Brienner Strasse and Arcisstrasse – the so-called "Brown House" – the stark, cuboid **NS-Dokumentationszentrum München** (⊚ns-dokumentationszentrum-muenchen.de) opens in April 2015 to provide a central focus for visitors wishing to learn more about Munich's pivotal role in the birth and development of the Nazi terror.

Along the River Isar

South of the Viktualienmarkt, the graceful but densely packed, nineteenth-century apartment blocks of the **Gärtnerplatzviertel** – whose streets radiate out from pretty, circular Gärtnerplatz – and the similar but more amorphous **Glockenbachviertel**, to the west, constitute some of the most sought-after addresses for young professionals in the city, including a high proportion who are lesbian and gay. Though there are few real sights, these districts – collectively known as the **Isarvorstadt** or Isar suburb – offer a strollable mix of quirky boutiques and inviting neighbourhood cafés and bars. On the opposite bank of the Isar, the **Müller'sches Volksbad** (Mon 7.30am–5pm, Tues–Sun 7.30am–11pm; sauna daily 9am–11pm; swim €4.20) is worth a visit as much for its wonderful Jugendstil architecture as for a swim.

Deutsches Museum

Deutsches Museum Museumsinsel 1 • Daily 9am–5pm • €8.50, combined ticket with Verkehrszentrum & Flugwerft Schleissheim (see p.360) €15 • **Verkehrszentrum** Am Bavariapark 5 • Daily 9am–5pm • €6, combined ticket with Deutsches Museum & Flugwerft Schleissheim (see p.360) €15 • ⊚ deutsches-museum.de • U-Bahn #4 or #5 to Schwanthalerhöhe

On a narrow island mid-river stands the **Deutsches Museum**, Munich's sprawling museum of science and technology, which houses one of the world's largest collections of its kind, constantly updated and with plenty of interactive exhibits. It honours not just the achievements of science, but the scientists themselves: the **Ehrensaal** on the first floor contains busts of such familiar names as Karl Benz, Rudolf Diesel and Albert Einstein.

The rolling programme of renovation and updating the exhibits means sections of the museum are subject to temporary closure.

The core of the museum's collection was formed by the mathematical and physical instruments of the **Bavarian Academy of Sciences**. With around fifty separate sections, from a **planetarium** to an **aviation section** whose exhibits include an early Me262 jet fighter, there's something here to please most tastes and age groups. Younger visitors will enjoy the dedicated **Kids' Kingdom**, with its wave-bouncing weir, building blocks and computers aimed at 3–8-year-olds, while in the **Centre for New Technology** there's a laboratory where visitors can perform their own experiments. There are also sections on mathematics, pharmaceuticals, chronometry and physics, and the beauty of some of the older scientific instruments ensures it's not just one for the nerds.

The Deutsches Museum also has an outstation, the **Verkehrszentrum**, above the Theresienwiese, which accommodates its collection of **historic vehicles** and another, the Flugwerft Schleissheim, at Oberschleissheim (see p.360) that houses its **aircraft collection**.

The Englischer Garten

In 1789 the American Sir Benjamin Thompson – later ennobled as Lord Rumford, which explains the origins of Rumfordstrasse in the Isarvorstadt – suggested that a 5km marshy strip along the River Isar be landscaped in English style, and it's thanks to his advice that the people of Munich can enjoy one of the largest city parks in Europe, the **Englischer Garten**. It stretches north from the Haus der Kunst on Prinzregentenstrasse, beside which surfers ride the waves on the **Eisbach** stream when spring meltwater makes the "surf" high enough; in summer nude sunbathers stretch out behind the Haus der Kunst and at the **Schwabinger Bucht**. The landmark **Chinesischer Turm** in the centre of the park – which has a huge *Biergarten* at its base – was modelled on the pagoda at Kew Gardens in London. The Englischer Garten's better-known English connection, however, is that it was here in September 1939 that Unity Mitford, the Hitler-obsessed sister of Diana Mosley and the writer Nancy Mitford, shot herself, unable to bear the thought that England and Germany were at war. She failed to kill herself, however, and was shipped home via Switzerland to Britain, where she died shortly after the war, the bullet never having been dislodged from her brain.

6

Schwabing

At the north end of the Englischer Garten, the placid Kleinhesseloher See boating lake borders **Schwabing**, the once bohemian but now safely middle-class neighbourhood where Thomas Mann wrote *Buddenbrooks*. Lenin and the poet Rainer Maria Rilke are among the other famous figures associated with Schwabing. Its literary and artistic heyday ended with World War I, and though the district became a centre of student radicalism in the 1960s it's not these days the sort of place you'd associate with slogans, except perhaps the kind written by advertising copywriters. Nevertheless, it's a pleasant and lively part of town, with some attractive Jugendstil architecture and plenty of café life.

The Olympiapark

Olympiastadion Daily: March to mid-April 9am–4pm; mid-April to mid-Sept 9am–8pm; mid-Sept to early Nov daily 9am–6pm; mid-Nov to end Nov, Jan & Feb 11am–4pm; closed Dec • €3, roof tour €41 **Olympiaturm** Daily 9am–midnight • €5.50 Sea Life Mon–Fri 10am–5/7pm according to season, Sat & Sun 10am–7pm • €16.50 or €9.50 online • ⓦ olympiapark.de • U-Bahn #3 or #8, stop "Olympia-Zentrum"

Built on the collected rubble from the bomb-devastated ruins of World War II and thus rising quite literally out of the ashes of the old Munich, the tent-like structures of the **Olympiapark** north of the centre were supposed to set the seal on Munich's status as an international metropolis of the first rank. Certainly, Günther Behnisch's amorphous acrylic roofscapes look as fresh and futuristic today as they did in 1972, but the Munich Olympics are inevitably remembered for reasons other than their architecture or, indeed, the achievements of swimmer Mark Spitz or gymnast Olga

---

THE MUNICH OLYMPIC MASSACRE OF 1972

Ten days into the **1972 Olympic Games** in the early morning of September 5, Palestinian gunmen belonging to the **Black September** group took eleven members of the Israeli team hostage in their quarters in the Olympic Village. Two were rapidly killed for resisting their captors; within the hour the police and Olympic Committee were informed and for the rest of the day the events played out live in the world's media. An ill-conceived attempt by the police to ambush the terrorists at **Fürstenfeldbruck military airbase** as they transferred their hostages from helicopters to a plane to flee the country ended in disaster shortly after midnight on September 6, as one of the Palestinians threw a grenade into one helicopter while the other was raked with gunfire. All the hostages died, yet, incredibly, the games continued. Security has been far tighter at subsequent Olympic Games, though not tight enough to prevent a further terrorist attack in Atlanta, where a bomb killed two people. The excellent documentary *One Day in September* charts the events from initial kidnapping to botched rescue attempts, while the Israeli authorities' determination to track down surviving members of the Black September team behind the hostage-taking was the subject of Steven Spielberg's 2005 film, *Munich*.

6

Korbutt, all totally overshadowed by the murder of eleven members of the Israeli team (see box, p.349).

Inevitably, the Olympiapark has to some extent the air of a place from which events have moved on, though on architectural grounds alone it's worth a visit, and there's usually something going on – the pool and ice rink keep things lively, and the Olympiahalle is the venue for concerts by big-name rock acts. You can visit the **Olympiastadion** itself (more adventurous souls can take an escorted walk across the undulating roof), and afterwards ascend the 291m-high **Olympiaturm** TV tower for views over the Olympic complex, city and beyond, or visit the **Sea Life** complex with its 400,000-litre ocean aquarium.

The BMW Museum

Am Olympiapark 2 • **Museum** Tues–Sun 10am–6pm • €9 • **Factory** Mon–Fri 9am–4.30pm • €8 • Book in advance on ☎ 089 1250 160 01, ⓦ bmw-welt.com

Just across the Mittlerer Ring highway from the Olympiapark is the **BMW Museum**. The exhibition is divided into seven separate sections: the obligatory worshipping of the BMW brand aside, it does contain some beautiful specimens of the company's output over the past ninety years or so – including both cars and motorcycles. Alongside it is BMW Welt, a glossy combination of showroom and delivery centre for BMW customers. If you're still not sated, you can tour the **factory** behind the complex.

Schloss Nymphenburg

Daily: April to mid-Oct 9am–6pm; mid-Oct to March 10am–4pm; Amalienburg and Schlosspark pavilions closed mid-Oct to March • Steinerner Saal & Schönheitsgalerie €6, Marstallmuseum & Museum Nymphenburger Porzellan €4.50, Amalienburg & Schlosspark pavilions €4.50, combined ticket for all Nymphenburg attractions €11.50 (€8.50 mid-Oct to March) • ⓦ schloss-nymphenburg.de • Tram #12 to Romanplatz or #17 to Schloss Nymphenburg

Munich's western suburbs are the setting for **Schloss Nymphenburg**, the summer palace of the Bavarian electors. It has its origins in the simple cube-shaped building commissioned by the Elector Ferdinand Maria and his consort Henrietta Adelaide to celebrate the birth of their son, which was designed by Agostino Barelli and begun in 1664. The building was subsequently enlarged by that son – Max Emanuel – to plans by Enrico Zuccalli and Joseph Effner to create the substantial palace you see today. For the full monumental effect of its immensely wide frontage, approach it along the arrow-straight Auffahrtsallee, which straddles the ornamental canal aligned with the centre of the facade.

Steinerner Saal

The massive **Steinerner Saal**, or Great Hall, in the central pavilion is a riot of Rococo stuccowork by Johann Baptist Zimmermann, created under the aegis of François Cuvilliés in 1755 and producing an effect that is at once festive and monumental. The room preserves its original Rococo form – since it was completed in 1758, work has been limited to dusting, filling cracks and light retouching.

Schönheitsgalerie

The most famous room in the rest of the Schloss is the **Schönheitsgalerie**, or Gallery of Beauties, lined with portraits of famous beauties of the day painted for Ludwig I in the 1830s by Joseph Stieler. Among the women portrayed is the dancer Lola Montez – the Elector's infatuation with her pushed Munich to the brink of rebellion, and Ludwig abdicated shortly afterwards.

Marstallmuseum and the Museum Nymphenburger Porzellan

In the south wing of the Schloss, the **Marstallmuseum** houses a collection of historic state coaches, including a predictably magnificent selection belonging to

Ludwig II. Upstairs, the **Museum Nymphenburger Porzellan** displays porcelain from the Nymphenburg factory from its foundation by Elector Max III in 1747 until around 1920.

The Amalienburg and the Schlosspark pavilions

The decorative highlight of Nymphenburg is not in the main palace at all, but in the English-style park at the back of the Schloss, which is where you'll find the graceful little **Amalienburg**, a hunting lodge created between 1734 and 1739 for the Electress Amalia by François Cuvilliés. Its ethereal **Spiegelsaal** is one of the pinnacles of the Rococo style: silver, not gold, is the dominant colour and the delicate stuccowork is again the work of Johann Baptist Zimmermann, with themes relating to Diana, Amphitrite, Ceres and Bacchus. The room was used for banquets, balls, concerts and relaxation after the hunt, and it's hard to imagine a more ravishing setting for a party. Three other charming eighteenth-century pavilions in the **Schlosspark** – the **Badenburg**, **Pagodenburg** and **Magdalenenklause** – can also be visited.

6

Hellabrunn Zoo

Tierparkstr. 30 • Daily: April–Sept 9am–6pm; Oct–March 9am–5pm • €12 • ⓦ tierpark-hellabrunn.de • U-Bahn #3 to Thalkirchen, or bus #52 from Marienplatz

Set within the landscape conservation area of the river Isar to the south of the city centre, **Hellabrunn Zoo** aims to present animals in a more naturalistic setting than in most city zoos, with relatively large enclosures. Established in 1911, its attractions include the Orang-Utan Paradies, and the polar bear compound.

Bavaria Filmstadt

Bavariafilmplatz 7 • Daily: mid-April to early Nov 9am–4.30pm (last entry); mid-Nov to mid-April 10am–3.30pm (last entry) • Guided tour €13, entire site €27.50 • ⓦ filmstadt.de • Tram #25 to Bavariafilmplatz

The studio tour at the famous Geiselgasteig's **Bavaria Filmstadt** is more for fans of cinematic thrills and spills than for dedicated film-buffs, though this is the place where **Das Boot** was made and you do get to see the sets from the film, as well as effects from the children's film fantasy, **The Neverending Story**. There's also a humorous interactive section, **Bullyversum**, and a 4D motion simulation cinema. The studio is sandwiched between the River Isar and the Perlacher Forst to the south of the city centre.

The Allianz-Arena

Werner Heisenberg Allee 25 • Daily: 10am–6pm; tours at 11am, 1pm, 3pm & 4.30pm; English-language tour at 1pm • €10 • Advance booking only ☎ 089 699 31 222, ⓦ allianz-arena.de • U-Bahn #6 to Fröttmaning

The giant **Allianz-Arena** on the northeastern edge of the city alongside the A99 ring road is worth the trek for lovers of architecture as much as for football fans, for it's a spectacular building. Designed by Swiss team Herzog & de Meuron – who also designed London's Tate Modern – and completed in 2005, the 70,000-seat stadium resembles an enormous tyre laid alongside the Autobahn thanks to its air-cushioned facade, which can be illuminated white for the national squad or in the colours of the two soccer teams that play there – red for **Bayern München**, blue for **TSV 1860**.

ARRIVAL AND DEPARTURE	MUNICH

By plane Munich's airport (☎ 089 975 00, ⓦ munich -airport.de), one of Germany's biggest and most modern, is 28.5km northeast of the city centre. Lufthansa-operated buses (€10.50 one-way, €17 return) depart every 20min for the Hauptbahnhof. S-Bahn trains on lines #1 and #8 link the airport to the city centre; of the two, #S8, which routes via the Ostbahnhof, is quicker to both Marienplatz and the Hauptbahnhof. A taxi to the centre should cost upwards of €60 or so, though there is no fixed tariff for the airport run except to the Messe (trade fair grounds: €59).

6

By train Munich's Hauptbahnhof is a short distance west of the Altstadt.

Destinations Augsburg (every 10–20min; 29–47min); Berchtesgaden (via Freilassing; hourly; 2hr 42min); Berlin (1–2 per hour; 6hr 5min–6hr 46min); Dachau (every 10–20min; 20min); Frankfurt (every 45min–2hr; 3hr–3hr 52min); Füssen (every 2hr; 2hr); Garmisch-Partenkirchen (hourly; 1hr 22min); Herrsching (every 20min; 49min); Ingolstadt (2–3 per hour; 43min–1hr 2min); Landsberg am Lech (via Kaufering: every 30min; 47–53min); Mittenwald (hourly; 1hr 51min); Nuremberg (2 per hour; 1hr 10–1hr 20min); Oberammergau (via Murnau: hourly; 1hr 43min); Oberschleissheim (every 20min; 21min); Passau (hourly; 2hr 14min); Regensburg (hourly; 1hr 27min); Starnberg (every 30min; 17–33min); Tegernsee (2 per hour; 1hr 4min); Ulm (2 per hour; 1hr 14min–1hr 59min); Würzburg (2 per hour; 2hr 6min–2hr 22min).

By car There's central parking at Marienplatz Garage, Rindermarkt 16; Pschorr-Hochgarage, Altheimer Eck 16; City Parkhaus am Färbergraben, Färbergraben 10; Königshof, Karlsplatz 25.

GETTING AROUND

By public transport The city's public transport system includes the S-Bahn, the U-Bahn, trams and buses (Ⓦ mvv-muenchen.de). Single tickets for the central zone (which covers most of the places you'll probably want to visit with the exception of the airport and some outlying sights such as Dachau) cost €2.60 cash, €2.50 if you pay using 10-journey stripe tickets; a one-day *Tageskarte* for the same zone costs €6. Tickets must be validated in the blue machines at stations before you travel unless you've bought a pre-validated ticket from Deutsche Bahn.

Bike rental Mike's Bike Rentals, corner Hochbrückenstr. and Bräuhausstr. (Ⓣ 089 25 54 39 87 or Ⓣ 089 25 54 39 87, Ⓦ mikesbiketours.com); Radius Bikes by platform 32 of Hauptbahnhof (Ⓣ 089 54 34 87 77 40, Ⓦ radiustours.com).

By taxi IsarFunk Taxizentrale (Ⓣ 089 45 05 40, Ⓦ isarfunk .de); Taxi München (Ⓣ 089 216 10, Ⓦ taxi-muenchen. com).

By car The following all have rental outlets at the airport: Avis Ⓣ 089 97 59 76 00; Europcar Ⓣ 089 973 50 20; Hertz Ⓣ 089 978 86 14; SIXT Ⓣ 01806 25 25 25.

Sightseeing tours Gray Line (Ⓣ 089 5490 7560, Ⓦ grayline.com/munich); Mike's Bike Tours (Ⓣ 089 25 54 39 87, Ⓦ mikesbiketours.com); Weis(er) Stadtvogel (Ⓦ stadtvogel.de).

INFORMATION

Tourist offices At the Hauptbahnhof (Mon–Sat 9am–8pm, Sun 10am–6pm; Ⓣ 089 23 39 65 00, Ⓦ muenchen.de) and in the Neues Rathaus, Marienplatz 8 (Mon–Fri 9am–7pm, Sat 9am–4pm, Sun 10am–5pm). Both offices stock city maps (€0.40).

Discount cards The tourist offices sell the CityTour Card (1 day €10.90, 3 days €20.90), which offers unlimited use of the city's public transport system and reductions on various attractions and tours – though as these don't include the major museums, whether the card represents good value or not depends on how much you expect to use public transport.

ACCOMMODATION

Munich is stronger on stylish and luxurious **hotels** than it is on budget offerings, with many of the latter clustering in the slightly seedy streets near the Hauptbahnhof, which is also where you'll find most of the **backpacker hostels**. **Youth hostels** and **campsites** are, however, in the suburbs. You can book accommodation through the **tourist office** – by phone, on its website or in person – and they won't charge you for their assistance (Ⓣ 089 23 39 65 55, Ⓦ muenchen.de). There's incredibly heavy demand for hotels during **Oktoberfest**, and if you find anything at all, chances are it will be much more expensive than usual.

HOTELS AND PENSIONS

Alpen Hotel Adolf Kolping Str. 14 Ⓣ 089 55 93 30, Ⓦ alpenhotel-muenchen.de; map p.338. Very pleasant 4-star hotel that's a cut above the average for the area around the Hauptbahnhof, and on one of the area's quieter side-streets. **€148**

★**Carat Hotel** Lindwurmstr. 13 Ⓣ 089 23 03 80, Ⓦ carat-hotel-muenchen.de; map p.338. Pleasant 3-star hotel close to Sendlinger Tor. It's part of a small chain, and the comfortable if slightly bland rooms boast showers and WC, wi-fi, minibar and TV. **€111**

Charles Hotel Sophienstr. 28 Ⓣ 089 544 55 50, Ⓦ thecharleshotel.com; map p.338. Polished, luxurious modern outpost of the exclusive Rocco Forte Collection. Even the standard rooms are an impressive 40m square, with individually controlled a/c, minibar, safe and interactive TV; most have views over the old botanical gardens. **€440**

Cortiina Ledererstr. 8 Ⓣ 089 242 24 90, Ⓦ cortiina .com; map p.338. The doyen of Munich's designer hotels: super-chic, modest in size and right in the heart of the Altstadt. Rooms have lots of natural oak and local Jura stone, and are equipped with wi-fi and iPod stations. **€179**

6

Deutsche Eiche Reichenbachstr. 13 ☎089 231 16 60, ⓦdeutsche-eiche.com; map p.338. Comfortable and stylish modern rooms with en-suite showers and wi-fi, located above Munich's most famous gay *Gasthaus*, where Rainer Werner Fassbinder and Freddie Mercury were once customers; most hotel guests are gay or lesbian. **€139**

Englischer Garten Liebergesellstr. 8 ☎089 383 94 10, ⓦhotelenglischergarten.de; map p.336. Homely and attractive Schwabing pension in a quiet, leafy setting close to the Englischer Garten; most rooms have en-suite facilities, and there are some good-value single rooms and also apartments in a nearby annexe, rented out by the month. **€132**

Hotelissimo Haberstock Schillerstr. 4 ☎089 55 78 55, ⓦhotelissimo.com; map p.338. One of the better of the mid-range options by the Hauptbahnhof, offering good value for the standard of accommodation, with singles, doubles and the possibility of a third bed; weekend rates are particularly keen. **€98**

Ibis München City Dachauer Str. 21 ☎089 55 19 30, ⓦibishotel.com; map p.338. Comfortable and affordable outpost of the budget chain, close to the Hauptbahnhof. Rooms are small but have a/c, en-suite shower, TV and WC, plus high-speed internet. Secure parking is available. **€94**

Pension Seibel Reichenbachstr. 8 ☎089 231 91 80, ⓦseibel-hotels-munich.de; map p.338. Very central, simple pension in the Isarvorstadt, within walking distance of the Viktualienmarkt, Marienplatz and Hofbräuhaus. Decor is basic and Bavarian in style, and the guests a diverse bunch, including many lesbian and gay visitors. **€89**

Platzl Sparkassenstr. 10 ☎089 23 70 30, ⓦplatzl.de; map p.338. Tastefully decorated, upmarket hotel in the Altstadt, with traditionally styled rooms with a/c, flat-screen TV and safes; there's also a splendid wood-panelled Bavarian suite in rustic style. **€195**

Smart Stay Hotel Station Schützenstr. 7 ☎089 552 52 10, ⓦsmart-stay.de; map p.338. Basic rooms without en-suite facilities or more comfortable en-suite rooms, plus dorms, in this vibrant budget option in a convenient, central location close to the Hauptbahnhof. There's a sister hostel close to the Theresienwiese. Dorms **€14.90**, doubles **€130**

Torbräu Tal 41 ☎089 24 23 40, ⓦtorbraeu.de; map p.338. Elegant, long-established, family-run 4-star hotel right next to the Isartor. The a/c rooms blend traditional and more contemporary styles, and there are singles and some triple rooms. Free wireless internet and mineral water. **€209**

Vier Jahreszeiten Kempinski Maximilianstr. 17 ☎089 21 25 27 99, ⓦkempinski.com/vierjahreszeiten; map p.338. In a prime position on Munich's most elegant shopping avenue, the *Vier Jahreszeiten* is the city's grandest hotel. Standard rooms are decorated in elegantly restrained contemporary style and have flat-screen TVs; some have artworks on the ceiling. **€320**

HOSTELS

A&O Hostel München Hackerbrücke Arnulfstr. 102 ☎089 45 23 59 58 00, ⓦaohostels.com; tram #17; map p.338. Bright, decent, if slightly institutional modern hostel five stops west of the Hauptbahnhof. Dorms have private facilities, and there are also en-suite singles and doubles. Bedding €3 extra. Dorms **€24**, doubles **€88**

DJH München-City Wendl-Dietrich-Str. 20 ☎089 20 24 44 90, ⓦmuenchen-city.jugendherberge.de; map p.336. Cyclist-friendly youth hostel a short distance from Rotkreuzplatz U-Bahn in the west of the city, close to Nymphenburg; accommodation is mostly in four- to six-bed dorms. Breakfast included. Dorms **€28.40**, doubles **€56.80**

DJH München-Park Miesingstr. 4 ☎089 78 57 67 70, ⓦmuenchen-park.de; map p.338. This hostel is in the south of the city, close to Hellabrunn Zoo and Thalkirchen U-Bahn station, from where it's five stops to Sendlinger Tor. Recently revamped, the place has a cafeteria, bistro, recreation facilities and free wi-fi. Accommodation is in single, two-, three-, four- and six-bed rooms. Dorms **€24**, doubles **€72**

Smart Stay Hostel Munich City Mozartstr. 4 ☎089 558 79 70, ⓦsmart-stay.de; map p.338. Cheerful hostel close to the Theresienwiese (and thus handy for the Oktoberfest), with a bar/lobby area, 24hr reception and accommodation in dorms; single and doubles also available. Dorms **€19.90**, doubles **€89**

Wombat's Senefelderstr. 1 ☎089 59 98 91 80, ⓦwombats-hostels.com; map p.338. Funky modern Munich outpost of the well-known Austrian chain, close to the Hauptbahnhof. Though breakfast is extra (€3.90), there's free wi-fi, lockers and laundry facilities, as well as a glass-roofed patio and bar. Bedding included. Open 24hr. Dorms **€26**, doubles **€76**

CAMPSITES

Campingplatz München-Obermenzing Lochhausener Str. 59 ☎089 811 22 35, ⓦwww.campingplatz-muenchen.de; S-Bahn line #2 to Untermenzing, then #164 bus; map p.336. Close to the end of the A8 Stuttgart Autobahn in the west of the city; they usually have space for tents here even during Oktoberfest. Open mid-March to Oct. Pitch **€4.50**, plus **€5** per car and **€5.50** per adult

Campingplatz München-Thalkirchen Zentralländstr. 49 ☎089 723 17 07, ⓦcamping-muenchen.de; U-Bahn #3 to Thalkirchen/bus #135; map p.336. South of the centre close to Hellabrunn Zoo, with a shop and snack bar, hot showers, razor and electric points, laundry, TV and games lounge. Open mid-March to Oct. Two-person pitch **€4.50**, plus **€9.10** per person in high season

The Tent In den Kirschen 30 ☎089 141 43 00, ⓦthe
-tent.com; tram #17 to Botanischer Garten; map
p.338. Low-cost, not-for-profit campsite north of
Nymphenburg, a 500m walk from Botanischer Garten;
facilities include free wi-fi, bike rental and a *Biergarten*,
and you can pitch your own tent or sleep in a cheap dorm
tent. Open June to early Oct. Dorm tent €7.50; pitch
€5.50, plus €5.50 per person

EATING AND DRINKING

Munich is a splendid place to **eat** or **drink**, whether your tastes run to traditional Bavarian *Schweinshaxe* – roasted pig's
trotter – or to the latest in fusion cuisine. At the top end of the market the city can boast some genuinely impressive
gastronomic temples. The stalwarts of the city's culinary scene are, however, its brewery-affiliated restaurants and
Bierkellers, where in addition to hearty Bavarian specialities you can sample the famous **beer**: well-known brands include
Augustiner, Paulaner, Franziskaner and Löwenbräu (among which the latter two belong to the Spaten brewery); the
Erdinger and Schneider brands are also popular, though they are brewed outside the city. The classic Munich beer is a
Weissbier or *Weizenbier* – a cloudy, sharp and refreshing wheat beer, served in half-litre measures in dark (*dunkles*) or light
(*helles*) varieties.

CAFÉS

Alter Simpl Türkenstr. 57 ☎089 272 30 83,
ⓦeggerlokale.de; map p.336. Lovely wood-panelled
café-bar whose name derives from the famous satirical
magazine *Simplicissimus*, many of whose writers or
cartoonists were once regulars here. Affordable food
includes salads, burgers and meat mains, much of it under
€10. The kitchen is open until well after midnight, though
as the evening wears on it becomes more bar-like. Mon–
Fri 11am–3am, Sat & Sun 11am–4am.

Café Frischhut das Schmalznudel Prälat-Zistl-Str. 8
☎089 26 82 37; map p.338. A Munich legend for its
heavy, doughnut-like *Schmalznudeln*, this little café near
the Viktualienmarkt is equally beloved by early risers and
night owls heading home. Mon–Sat 8am–6pm.

Café Luitpold Brienner Str. 11 ☎089 242 87 50,
ⓦcafe-luitpold.de; map p.338. Munich is rather thin on
grand old *Kaffee und Kuchen* places, but the *Luitpold* –
where Thomas Mann and Henrik Ibsen were once
customers – is one of the better offerings, with daily lunch
specials from around €12. Tues–Sat 8am–11pm, Sun
8am–7pm.

Café Münchner Freiheit Münchner Freiheit 20 ☎089
330 07 99 0, ⓦmuenchner-freiheit.de; map p.336.
Spacious, versatile café/*Konditorei* on Schwabing's main
drag, laid out over several floors, with breakfasts (until
2pm) from €3.30, omelettes (€7.50) and a few hot dishes,
as well as the inevitable tempting cakes and ice cream.
Daily: summer 7am–9pm; winter 7am–7pm.

★**Café Puck** Türkenstr. 33 ☎089 280 22 80,
ⓦcafepuck.de; map p.336. Relaxed, vaguely Art Deco
café with jazzy music, leather sofas and an eclectic
selection of affordable eats, from falafel to pasta (from
€6.80) and burgers. The breakfast selection (from €4) –
available until 6pm on weekdays and until 8pm at
weekends – is massive. Daily 9am–1am.

★**Café Türmstüberl** In the Valentin-Karlstadt-
Musäum, Isartorplatz ☎089 29 37 62, ⓦValentin
-musaeum.de; map p.338. Cluttered, eccentric café at the
top of one of the city's medieval gates; you have to pay the
€2.99 entrance charge to the museum downstairs to gain
admission. Generous portions of *Obazda* with onions for
€6.90; home-made cakes from €3.40. Mon, Tues & Thurs
11am–5.30pm, Fri & Sat 11am–6pm, Sun 10am–6pm.

Schelling Salon Schellingstr. 54 ☎089 272 07 88,
ⓦschelling-salon.de; map p.336. Huge, atmospheric old
café on a corner site in the Maxvorstadt, with various
games including billiard tables, table tennis and chess, plus
cheap hot food from around €6.30. Mon & Thurs–Sun
10am–1am.

★**Stadtcafé** In the Stadtmuseum, St-Jakobs-Platz
☎089 26 69 49, ⓦstadtcafe-muenchen.de; map p.338.
Buzzy café serving good breakfasts and delectable cakes;
the airy interior has cheerful red leather seating and there
are alfresco tables in the Stadtmuseum's *Hof* in summer.
Mon–Thurs & Sun 10am–midnight, Fri & Sat
10am–1am.

RESTAURANTS

Augustiner am Dom Frauenplatz 8 ☎089 23 23 84 80,
ⓦaugustineramdom.de; map p.338. Hearty dishes of
roast duck with red cabbage or *Bratwürste* with *Sauerkraut*
are washed down with Augustiner beers, all at moderate
prices, right opposite the Frauenkirche. Main courses €11–
19, *Flammkuchen* €9.90. Daily 10am–midnight.

Cohen's Theresienstr. 31 ☎089 280 95 45, ⓦcohens
.de; map p.336. Family-run place serving traditional
Eastern-European Jewish cooking, including *Königsberger
Klopse*, and *borscht* alongside Sephardic Mediterranean-
style dishes. Main courses €12–18. Mon–Sat noon–3pm
& 6–10.30pm.

Osteria Italiana Schellingstr. 62 ☎089 272 07 17,
ⓦosteria.de; map p.336. Italian food like mamma used
to make in lovely, traditional surroundings at this very
long-established restaurant – it was here in the 1930s that
Unity Mitford stalked Hitler over lunch. There's a more
informal *Bar dell'Osteria* next door. Main courses around
€24. Mon–Sat noon–2.30pm & 6.30–11pm.

6

6

Prinz Myshkin Hackenstr. 2 ☏089 26 55 96, ⓦprinzmyshkin.com; map p.338. Smart and long-established veggie restaurant and café/bar, with affordable pasta and curries, big salads from €10.90 and lunch specials from €7.50. More elaborate main courses have refined Asian and Mediterranean touches such as truffle and tempura. Daily 9.30am–12.30am.

★**Ratskeller** Neues Rathaus, Marienplatz 8 ☏089 219 98 90, ⓦratskeller.com; map p.338. The labyrinthine cellar of the Neues Rathaus is always full – by no means just with tourists. Serving everything from *Bratwurst* with *Sauerkraut* to elegant seasonal dishes including game, the food is hearty and good. Main courses from around €11. Daily 10am–midnight.

Restaurant Dallmayr Dienerstr. 14–15 ☏089 213 51 00, ⓦdallmayr.com; map p.338. This is the restaurant of Munich's celebrated Dallmayr delicatessen: the quality of the produce is unsurprisingly superb, while the creativity of the cooking has helped it win two Michelin stars. Five-course menus start at €130; there's also a cheaper, but still classy, café/bistro plus a champagne bar, *Lukullusbar*. Tues–Fri 7–11pm, Sat noon–1.20pm & 7–11pm.

Schuhbecks in den Südtiroler Stuben Platzl 8 ☏089 216 69 00, ⓦschuhbeck.de; map p.338. One of Munich's gastronomic temples: proprietor Alfons Schuhbeck is a TV chef and celebrity, who fuses Bavarian and cosmopolitan influences using seasonal produce; the setting is conservative but elegant. Set menus start at €78 for three courses. The more informal and cheaper – but beautiful – *Orlando* next door is run by the same team. Mon 6–11pm, Tues–Sat noon–2.30pm & 6–11pm.

Spatenhaus an der Oper Residenzstr. 12 ☏089 290 70 60, ⓦkuffler.de; map p.338. The elegantly Alpine decor matches the refined Bavarian cooking at this restaurant opposite the opera. Main courses in the informal downstairs restaurant range from €13.50 to €28; expect to pay a little more in the classier upstairs dining room. Daily: ground floor 9.30am–12.30am; upstairs 11.30am–1am.

Tantris Johann-Fichte-Str. 7 ☏089 361 95 90, ⓦtantris .de; map p.336. Munich's most renowned restaurant is the place where Bavarians were first introduced to *nouvelle cuisine*. Expect classic 1970s decor and a modern gourmet menu: the four-course Sat lunch costs €130 with wine, after which things start getting seriously expensive. Tues–Sat noon–3pm & 6.30pm–1am.

Tramin Lothringerstr. 7 ☏089 44 45 40 90, ⓦtramin -restaurant.de; map p.336. Elegant Haidhausen restaurant with neutral, contemporary decor and a four-course fixed price €60 menu that blends German and modern European elements. The wine list emphasizes German and Austrian producers. Tues–Sat 6pm–1am.

BARS, BIERKELLERS AND BIERGÄRTEN

Augustiner Grossgaststätten Neuhauser Str. 27 ☏089 23 18 32 57, ⓦaugustiner-restaurant.com; map p.338. The Augustiner brewery's city-centre flagship is right in the main pedestrian shopping zone, in a very attractive, late nineteenth-century building with atmospheric interiors and a garden out back. There's a substantial food menu, including daily specials from around €7.95. Daily 10am–midnight.

Augustinerkeller Arnulfstr. 52 ☏089 59 43 93, ⓦaugustinerkeller.de; map p.338. Vast beer garden under leafy chestnut trees, located west of the Hauptbahnhof and very popular with the locals. There's draught Augustiner *Edelstoff* beer and simple food – sausages, grilled fish, chicken – with mains around €15. Daily: beer garden 11.30am–midnight; restaurant 10am–1am.

Chinesischer Turm Englischer Garten 3 ☏089 383 87 30, ⓦchinaturm.de; map p.336. Vast *Biergarten* at the foot of the eponymous Chinese-style pagoda in the heart of the Englischer Garten, serving Hofbräu beers, with food stalls dishing up typically rustic fare and an elegant restaurant nearby serving a set-price €26/€33 lunch. Daily 10am–11pm.

Eat the Rich Hessstr. 90, Maxvorstadt ☏089 18 59 82, ⓦeattherich.de; map p.336. An institution on the Munich nightlife scene; the cocktails (from €7.90) are served in half-litre measures at this packed, studenty party locale near the university, which at least eases pressure on the bar. Tues–Sat 7pm–3am.

Hofbräuhaus Platzl 9 ☏089 290 13 61 00, ⓦhofbraeuhaus.de; map p.336. The "most famous pub in the world" is overrun with tourists, but a visit is a Munich "must". If the noise and crowds inside are too raucous, push through to the peaceful *Biergarten*, shaded by chestnut trees. A *Mass* (litre) of beer costs €8. Daily 9am–11.30pm.

Hofbräukeller Innere Wiener Str. 19 ☏089 459 92 50, ⓦhofbraeukeller.de; map p.336. Imposing neo-Renaissance place in Haidhausen, attracting a wide range of customers including politicians from the nearby Maximilianeum. The Hofbräu beer aside, there's also a wide range of hearty food, from around €9, plus a *Biergarten* out back. Daily 10am–midnight.

Paulaner am Nockherberg Hochstr. 77, Giesing ☏089 459 91 30, ⓦnockherberg.com; map p.336. Naturally cloudy *Nockherberger* beer – which is only available here – plus typical specialities like *Obazda* (soft cheese) and *Leberkäse* – a type of meatloaf – are among the charms of this *Biergarten* attached to a modern beer hall. Daily 10am–1am.

Weisses Brauhaus Tal 7 ☏089 290 13 80, ⓦweisses -brauhaus.de; map p.338. Handsome old *Brauhaus* belonging to the Schneider brewery, once Munich-based but since 1944 based in Kelheim and known particularly for its Schneider Weisse wheat beer and for the *Weisswurst* sausages it serves. A half-litre of *Weissbier* costs €3.95. Daily 8am–12.30am.

6

OKTOBERFEST AND THE REST

The Munich **festival** season kicks off with the annual pre-Lent carnival, known here as **Fasching**; immediately afterwards, the **Starkbierzeit**, or festival of strong beer, starts and lasts for around four weeks, making the Lenten fast more bearable. In April or early May, the **Frühlingfest**, or spring festival, brings beer tents and fairground rides to the Theresienwiese. In July the Olympiapark is the venue for the **Tollwood Sommerfestival** of music, theatre and cabaret (W tollwood.de), which attracts big-name live acts; while the July **Opernfestspiele** includes free live broadcasts of opera performances on a big screen in front of the Nationaltheater. The biggest of all Munich festivals is, of course, **Oktoberfest**.

OKTOBERFEST

The single most important thing to know about **Oktoberfest** (W oktoberfest.de) – Munich's legendary festival of beer and bonhomie – is that it's all over after the first Sunday in the month it's named after. The bulk of the Fest, which lasts sixteen days, therefore generally takes place during the last two weeks in September, depending on when the first weekend in October falls. The first Oktoberfest was indeed held in October – in 1810, to celebrate the marriage of Crown Prince Ludwig to Princess Theresa von Sachsen-Hildburghausen, but over the years, as the festival got longer, the dates were pulled forward into September. The first draught **Mass** (1 litre stein) of **Oktoberfestbier** is always pulled with much (televised) ceremony, after which Bavarian television keeps up a regular live feed from the Theresienwiese, the rather bleak open space named after Ludwig's bride that is the venue for the annual rites. The Oktoberfest is quite a celebrity magnet, with the unlikeliest B-listers donning traditional attire to make their appearance before the cameras – Paris Hilton in a dirndl being one memorable example.

To have any chance of joining them in the biggest tents, you'll need to reserve your spaces in advance. You can't do this on the Oktoberfest website, but it does have information on the individual tents, and you can book through the tents' own websites. There are fourteen **big tents**, including some familiar names – Löwenbräu (W loewenbraeuzelt.de), Augustiner (W festhalle-augustiner.com), Hofbräu (W hb-festzelt.de) – and some with particular culinary specialities, such as the Ochsenbraterei (beef; W ochsenbraterei.com) and Fischer Vroni (fish; W fischer-vroni.de). Many of the **smaller tents** also have a strong food focus, from chicken and Wurst to game and even *Kaffee und Kuchen*. Without a **reservation**, you might still squeeze into one of the smaller, more intimate tents, which – particularly as the evening wears on and the atmosphere becomes more raucous – can be easier for Oktoberfest newbies to enjoy anyway.

Since its inception at the bicentennial Oktoberfest in 2010, a parallel attraction at the southern end of the Theresienwiese is the **Oide Wiesn**, which aims to re-create a more traditional Oktoberfest atmosphere with a focus on Bavarian costume and folklore; there's a modest admission fee.

Not surprisingly, widespread drunkenness is a regular phenomenon at Oktoberfest – which doesn't stop the drinkers from visiting the enormous **funfair** that takes up around half the Theresienwiese's vast acreage. There's simple food – roast chicken, giant pretzels, *Obazda* and the like – to soak up the beer; one additional annual ritual is the intake of breath at the **price** of a *Mass* of beer – at €9.70–10.10 a litre (2014 prices), it may be good, but carousing Oktoberfest-style doesn't come cheap. To reach the Theresienwiese take U-Bahn #4 or #5 to "Theresienwiese".

NIGHTLIFE AND ENTERTAINMENT

Munich has a chic and sophisticated **nightlife** scene, with everything from glitzy cocktail bars to noisy techno clubs. The city is also a heavyweight on the international classical music scene: the orchestra at the **Bayerische Staatsoper**, principally at the Nationaltheater, is under the direction of the Russian Kirill Petrenko, while since 2012 Lorin Maazel occupies the role of chief conductor of the **Münchner Philharmoniker** (W mphil.de). Additional orchestras include the **Symphonieorchester des Bayerischen Rundfunks** (W br.de) and its sister orchestra, the **Münchner Rundfunkorchester**. For **what's on** information, pick up a free copy of *In München* magazine from cafés, bars and venues or check the listings on W muenchen.de.

CLUBS

Ampere im Muffatwerk Zellstr. 4, Haidhausen ☏ 089 45 87 50 10, W muffatwerk.de; map p.338. Hip club in the Muffatwerk cultural complex on the Haidhausen side of the Isar, a historic former power station. Eclectic music policy with live bands and DJs, and decor that blends

6

industrial and modern. Clubnights generally start at 10pm.

Harry Klein Sonnenstr. 8 ☎089 40 28 74 00, ⓦharrykleinclub.de; map p.338. Music synchs with avant-garde visuals projected onto the walls of this esteemed and innovative temple to electronic dance music. Wed–Sat 11pm–6am, occasionally also Sun.

Milchundbar Sonnenstr. 12 ☎089 450 28 80, ⓦmilchundbar.de; map p.338. Cult club for hardcore night owls who want to party through into the next morning, recently relocated to the city centre and with an eclectic soundtrack of 1980s and 1990s hits, house, electro and funk. Mon–Thurs 10pm–7am, Fri & Sat 11pm–9am.

Rote Sonne Maximilianplatz 5 ☎089 55 26 33 30, ⓦrote-sonne.com; map p.338. DJ sets from big names on the international techno and electro circuit are the main draw at this intimate, trendy city-centre dance club. The same complex houses an outpost of the famed Spanish *Pacha* club. Wed–Sat 11pm–6am.

LIVE MUSIC VENUES

Backstage Reitknechtstr. 6 ☎089 126 61 00, ⓦbackstage.eu; tram #17; map p.338. Bar, club and live venue west of the Hauptbahnhof along Arnulfstr., with a varied programme of live bands, DJ nights from rock to reggae plus cinema and big-screen soccer. Clubnights Fri & Sat 11pm–late (and occasionally Thurs from 10pm); live gig starting times vary, but most commonly around 8pm.

Jazzbar Vogler Rumfordstr. 17 ☎089 29 46 62, ⓦjazzbar-vogler.com; map p.338. Jazz club, bar and restaurant in the Gärtnerplatzviertel, with an eclectic programme of live music including jam sessions (Mon), piano bar (Tues–Thurs) and live latin, jazz or soul bands (Fri & Sat). Venue opens 7pm, concerts start 8.30pm.

Jazzclub Unterfahrt Einsteinstr. 42, Haidhausen ☎089 448 27 94, ⓦunterfahrt.de; map p.336. The big names of the international jazz circuit alternate with new discoveries at this renowned Haidhausen jazz club, where there are also regularly-changing temporary exhibitions of modern art. Daily 7.30pm–1am.

Muffatwerk Zellstr. 4, Haidhausen ☎089 45 87 50 10, ⓦmuffatwerk.de; map p.338. International arts venue presenting a busy programme of live gigs in both the main Muffathalle (a former turbine hall) and the more intimate *Ampere* club and *Café Muffathalle*. Gigs generally begin at 8.30pm or 9pm.

THEATRE, OPERA AND CLASSICAL MUSIC VENUES

Cuvilliés-Theater Residenzstr. 1 ☎089 21 85 01; map p.338. Beautiful Rococo auditorium whose opulent fittings were spared World War II destruction. It's now used as a stage for drama productions by the Bayerisches Staatsschauspiel.

Deutsches Theater Schwanthalerstr 13 ☎089 55 23 44 44, ⓦdeutsches-theater.de; map p.338 . Imposing, recently refurbished, nineteenth-century theatre that's currently Munich's main venue for big-budget international musicals.

Gasteig Rosenheimerstr. 5 ☎089 48 09 80, ⓦgasteig .de; map p.338. Modern convention centre in Haidhausen that is also Munich's main concert venue, with everything from classical concerts by the Münchner Philharmoniker or Symphonieorchester des Bayerischen Rundfunks to pop, rock and jazz.

Nationaltheater Max-Joseph-Platz 2 ☎089 21 85 19 20, ⓦstaatsoper.de; map p.338. The beautiful Neoclassical Nationaltheater next to the Residenz is the city's principal stage for opera and ballet; it's the home venue for the Bayerische Staatsoper and its orchestra, the Staatsorchester.

Prinzregententheater Prinzregentenplatz 12 ☎089 21 85 02, ⓦprinzregententheater.de; map p.336. With a design based on the Bayreuth Festspielhaus – but more opulent and with higher levels of comfort – this restored theatre is home to the innovative and highly respected Münchner Kammerorchester (ⓦm-k-o.eu) and a venue for classical, jazz and world music as well as drama.

Residenztheater Max-Joseph-Platz 1 ☎089 21 85 19 40, ⓦresidenztheater.de; map p.338. Modern theatre sandwiched between the Nationaltheater and Residenz; it's the principal stage of the Bayerisches Staatsschauspiel, the city's leading drama company, which also performs at the Cuvilliés-Theater and the nearby Marstall.

Schauspielhaus Maximilianstr. 26–28 ☎089 23 39 66 00, ⓦmuenchner-kammerspiele.de; map p.338. One of the best-preserved Jugendstil theatres in Germany, this is the principal venue for the Münchner Kammerspiele's productions of serious drama, from Shakespeare to Kafka. The programme includes occasional adaptations of art-house cinema classics by the likes of Fellini and Fassbinder.

Staatstheater am Gärtnerplatz Gärtnerplatz 3 ☎089 20 24 11, ⓦstaatstheater-am-gaertnerplatz.de; map p.338. Opera, operetta, jazz, dance and musicals are all in the repertoire of this beautifully refurbished nineteenth-century theatre south of Viktualienmarkt.

THE LESBIAN AND GAY SCENE

Munich's **lesbian and gay scene** is one of the biggest and most diverse in Germany after Berlin and Cologne, and is conveniently concentrated in the hip Gärtnerplatzviertel and equally trendy neighbouring Glockenbachviertel, stretching roughly from Viktualienmarkt to Sendlinger Tor. Though neither district is by any means a gay "ghetto", the gay presence is upfront and the atmosphere relaxed. The annual **Christopher Street Day** festivities take place in July (ⓦ csd-munich.de) and are great fun, not least for the opportunity to see exotic plumage and traditional Lederhosen on parade in roughly equal measure. For bar listings and information on accommodation, shopping and health advice (in German), pick up the free *Rosa München* guide, regularly updated and available in bars and cafés. Clubbing in Munich tends to revolve around one-nighters rather than fixed venues.

Café am Hochhaus Blumenstr. 29 ☎ 089 89 05 81 52, Ⓦ cafeamhochhaus.de; map p.338. More DJ bar than café, this former dance hall and café-*Konditorei* has been reworked to attract a young, hip, mixed crowd to a prominent site opposite Munich's only Weimar-era skyscraper. Cocktails from €7.50. Daily 8pm–late.

Café Nil Hans-Sachs-Str. 2 ☎ 089 23 88 95 95, Ⓦ cafenil .com; map p.338. Slick, smart café/bar with mock-Egyptian decor, packed with a good-looking crowd of mainly twenty- to forty-something gay men at weekends. One of the oldest-established gay bars in the city, it's undergoing a real Renaissance these days. Daily 3pm–3am.

Kraftwerk Thalkirchner Str. 4 ☎ 089 21 58 88 81; map p.338. Relaxed and recently rechristened Glockenbachviertel café-bar that is one of the lynchpins of the Munich lesbian and gay scene, with good-value food – main courses around €7 – and a diverse crowd. Mon– Thurs & Sun 10am–1am, Fri & Sat 10am–3am.

NY Club Sonnenstr. 25 ☎ 089 59 10 56, Ⓦ nyclub.de; map p.338. Munich's only exclusively gay and lesbian disco, with slick modern decor, Fri night "Luxuspop" party and Raw Riot on Sat featuring big-name DJs spinning progressive, tribal and vocal house. Fri & Sat 11pm–late.

★ **Prosecco** Theklastr. 1 ☎ 089 23 03 23 29, Ⓦ prosecco-munich.de; map p.338. Tiny, camp bar that blends Alpine kitsch with every other variety of decorative excess. The music is a mix of German *Schlager* (schmaltzy German pop) and addictive made-in-Munich Eurodisco hits. There isn't room to dance, but everyone does; you'll queue to get in. Thurs–Sat 10pm–late.

DIRECTORY

Bookshops Wordsworth, Schellingstr. 3, is an English-language bookshop; Hugendubel, Marienplatz 22, has a large English-language section.

Consulates UK, Möhlstr. 5 ☎ 089 21 10 90; US, Königinstr. 5 ☎ 089 288 80.

Emergency numbers Police ☎ 110; fire & medical ☎ 112; dental ☎ 089 723 30 93; women and rape ☎ 089 76 37 37; AIDS ☎ 089 5446 470.

Laundry Der Wunderbare Waschsalon, Görresstr. 12; Kingsgard, at the Hauptbahnhof, offers 3hr dry cleaning.

Left luggage There are coin-operated lockers and a left luggage office at the Hauptbahnhof.

Pharmacies For information on the city's out-of-hours service, see Ⓦ lak-bayern.notdienst-portal.de.

Post office Bahnhofplatz 1 (Mon–Fri 8am–8pm, Sat 9am–4pm).

Around Munich

Munich's efficient public transport network stretches far into the surrounding countryside, making day-trips relatively straightforward. By far the most sombre, but also the best-known destination in the city's hinterland is the former Nazi concentration camp at **Dachau**, north of the city. Also to the north, but altogether more light-hearted, is **Oberschleissheim**, with its palaces and aviation museum. To the south of the city, the lakes of the **Fünf-Seen-Land** are an obvious lure in summer, given added lustre by the monastery of **Kloster Andechs** and by a remarkable art collection at **Bernried** on **Starnberger See**.

KZ-Gedenkstätte Dachau

Daily 9am–5pm; documentary film at the visitor centre in English 10am, 11.30am, 12.30pm, 2pm & 3pm • Free, English audio-guide €3.50 • Ⓦ kz-gedenkstaette-dachau.de • Dachau's S-Bahn station is on line S2 from Munich; from the S-Bahn take bus #726 to the KZ-Gedenkstätte (Mon–Fri & peak time Sat every 20min, Sun every 40min). There is parking (€3 March–Oct) a short, well-signposted walk from the camp

Lieber Gott, mach mich stumm, dass ich nicht nach Dachau kumm.
Please God, make me dumb, so I don't wind up in Dachau.

Popular saying

In contrast to the Nazis' extermination camps in Poland, the former concentration camp at **Dachau**, now the **KZ-Gedenkstätte Dachau**, was no secret. Established on the site of a redundant munitions works in March 1933 and a model for all subsequent camps, it was highly publicized, the better to keep the Third Reich's malcontents in line. In its twelve-year existence more than 200,000 people were imprisoned here, of whom 43,000 died. It was finally liberated by US troops on April 29, 1945.

You enter the camp through an iron **gate** into which is set the Nazis' bitter joke against its victims – the slogan *Arbeit Macht Frei* ("work makes you free"); here, as in so many other camps, hard work was no guarantee even of survival. Much of the camp compound now consists of the empty foundations of the old barrack blocks, but two have been reconstructed to give an idea of what conditions were like, and how they deteriorated during the course of the war as the camp became more overcrowded. The SS guards used any infringement of the barracks' rigid cleanliness regime as an excuse to administer harsh discipline; nevertheless, when the camp was finally liberated, typhus was rife.

A place of remembrance as well as a museum, the site is peppered with memorials: there are Jewish, Orthodox, Protestant and Catholic memorials at the fringes of the camp, and an expressive **international memorial** in front of the maintenance building.

The maintenance building

An **exhibition** in the former camp **maintenance building** describes the full horror of Dachau, including a graphic colour film shot at liberation and grisly details of the medical experiments conducted on prisoners, including hypothermia and altitude experiments conducted on fit young male prisoners in order to determine how long downed Luftwaffe pilots might survive in extreme circumstances, as well as others in which inmates were deliberately infected with malaria or tuberculosis.

The camp prison (Bunker)

Behind the maintenance building, the camp **prison** (known as the Bunker) contained cells for important prisoners who were kept separate from the rest of the inmates; these included Georg Elser, who tried to assassinate Hitler with a bomb at the *Bürgerbräukeller* in Munich on November 8, 1939, and Richard Stevens, one of the two British secret agents kidnapped and smuggled across the border from the Netherlands the following day in the notorious Venlo incident.

The gas chamber

Though it wasn't an extermination camp Dachau did have a **gas chamber**, screened by trees and located outside the camp perimeter. A crematorium was built in the summer of 1940 because of the rapidly rising numbers of prisoner deaths; in 1942–43 a larger one was built, and this incorporated a gas chamber. Though it was never used for systematic extermination, former prisoners testify that it was used to murder small groups of prisoners. As in other camps, the fiction of it being a shower room was maintained. A plaque in the crematorium commemorates four women agents of the British SOE murdered here on September 12, 1944.

Oberschleissheim

The small town of **Oberschleissheim**, just outside Munich, is home to the **Schleissheim palace complex**, comprised of the splendid Baroque Neues Schloss, the Schloss Lustheim hunting lodge and the Renaissance Altes Schloss. A short signposted walk from the Altes Schloss is the Deutsches Museum's **Flugwerft Schleissheim** (daily 9am–5pm; €6; ⓦ deutsches-museum.de), which houses the museum's collection of historic aircraft.

Schleissheim Palace and Park

Tues–Sun: April–Sept 9am–6pm; Oct–March 10am–4pm • Neues Schloss €4.50, Schloss Lustheim €3.50, Altes Schloss €3, combined ticket €8 • ⓦ schloesser-schleissheim.de • S-Bahn #1, direction Freising, from Munich

The splendid Baroque **Neues Schloss**, designed by Enrico Zuccalli, began construction in 1701 under Elector Max Emanuel, but the intervention of the War of the Spanish Succession left the palace an incomplete shell and work was only finally completed in 1719; of the four wings originally planned, only one was built. This, however, is quite imposing enough, with a glorious sequence of **ceremonial rooms** united by the theme of Max Emanuel's fame. An international team of artists laboured to create the interiors; the beautiful stuccowork by Johann Baptist Zimmermann and lovely ceiling frescoes by Cosmas Damian Asam and Jacopo Amigoni are the highlights of the visit. The palace's 57m-long **Grosse Galerie** houses a collection of Flemish and Italian Baroque painting, including works by Rubens.

The magnificent Baroque **Hofgarten** stretching away from the east front of the Neues Schloss has never been substantially remodelled and thus is rare in preserving its original Baroque form. At the eastern end of the garden, the little hunting lodge of **Schloss Lustheim** houses a collection of Meissen porcelain.

Immediately to the west of the Neues Schloss stands the much smaller Renaissance **Altes Schloss**, which contains two museums, one comprising images of private piety and public religious festivals from around the world, and another cataloguing the vanished culture of the former Prussian provinces of East and West Prussia, now mainly part of Poland, whose German-speaking inhabitants fled or were expelled as the Red Army swept across Europe in 1945.

Starnberger See

To the south of Munich, the region known as the **Fünf-Seen-Land** provides a tantalizing glimpse of Alpine beauty as well as wide open waters for recreation right on the city's doorstep. Of the two large lakes, **Starnberger See** is known as the Princes' Lake and has the opulent real-estate to prove it; it was on the shores of this lake that "Mad" King Ludwig II and his doctor met their mysterious deaths one night in June 1886. The other large lake, **Ammersee**, is known as the Farmers' Lake, which reflects its somewhat simpler style.

Starnberg

The region's natural centre is **STARNBERG** on Starnberger See. The town, which is on S-Bahn line #6 from Munich, is one of the wealthiest communities in Germany, and the lakeshore is lined with expensive villas. The town itself has a rather suburban feel, albeit with a stunning setting at the north end of the lake, and a backdrop of distant Alps.

Sammlung Buchheim

Am Hirschgarten 1, Bernried • Tues–Sun: April–Oct 10am–6pm; Nov–March 10am–5pm • €8.50 • ⓦ buchheimmuseum.de • Boat or S-Bahn #6 to Tutzing/Regionalbahn to Bernried and bus #9614 from either; there's also plenty of car parking at the museum

Housed in a beautiful lakeside building designed by Günther Behnisch, the **Sammlung Buchheim** or **Museum der Phantasie** in Bernried looks from the outside more like a luxurious spa than a museum. It houses the varied collections of the artist and writer Lothar-Günther Buchheim, best known as the author of the book on which the hit film *Das Boot* was based. The museum is built along a central axis, which allows the various departments to branch off independently – a clever solution to the problem of displaying a collection whose constituent parts never

---

STARNBERG BOAT CRUISES

Starnberg makes a handy departure-point for **cruises** (Easter to mid-Oct; cruises €9.50–17 depending on itinerary; ⓦ seenschifffahrt.de) on the lake by the boats of **Bayerische Seenschifffahrt**. The longer Grand Tour departs four times daily in high season; two of its sailings stop at Bernried at the southern end of the lake for the Sammlung Buchheim.

6

> ### THE CARL ORFF-FESTSPIELE
>
> **Carl Orff** (1897–1982), composer of *Carmina Burana*, is buried at Kloster Andechs, and in the summer months the monastery is the venue for the **Carl Orff-Festspiele** festival of the composer's work. The festival website Ⓦ carl-orff-festspiele.de has details.

really make a coherent whole: roomfuls of applied art and unlabelled ethnographic objects feature, along with a good deal of Buchheim's own work, but the core of the collection is a stunning selection of classic twentieth-century German art. Lovis Corinth is represented by his *Dancing Dervish* of 1904, Max Liebermann by some of his lovely drawings, while a few very early works by Max Beckmann contrast with his more familiar, later style. There's a caustic Otto Dix portrait, *Leonie*, as well as works by the Expressionists Ernst Ludwig Kirchner, Karl Schmidt-Rottluff and Alexei von Jawlensky.

Kloster Andechs

Church Daily 9am–7pm • Free, guided tours in English €5.50 (Mon–Fri; advance booking required) • **Brewery** Tours €5.50 (Mon–Wed; advance booking required) • **Bräustüberl** Daily 10am–8pm • ☎ 08152 37 62 53, Ⓦ andechs.de • S-Bahn #8 to Herrsching or #6 to Starnberg Nord, from either of which the infrequent bus #951 will get you to the abbey

Where art presides at the southern end of the Starnberger See, beer and religion reign supreme on **Ammersee**, where the Benedictine monastery of **Kloster Andechs** crowns a hilltop on the north side of the village of Erling. The monastery has for centuries attracted pilgrims to see the relics supposedly brought to Andechs by Rasso, an ancestor of the counts of Andechs, in the tenth century. These days it's just as famous for its brewery – which can be visited – and for its Benedictine **beers**, which can be sampled in the adjacent *Bräustüberl* restaurant. The abbey **church**, which is not at all as big as its mighty onion-domed tower might lead you to think, makes up for its modest size with the exuberance of its Rococo decoration by the ever-industrious Johann Baptist Zimmermann. Buried beneath the Rococo swirls are traces of the fifteenth-century Gothic church, which was struck by lightning and largely destroyed in the seventeenth century; the Heilige Kapelle still retains its Gothic appearance.

Ingolstadt

With a strategic location on the Danube midway between Nuremberg and Munich, for centuries **INGOLSTADT** was a formidable fortress and from 1392 to 1447 the capital of the Duchy of Bayern-Ingolstadt. Yet despite a rich legacy of historic monuments it's a bustling and remarkably down-to-earth place, with none of the preserved-in-aspic feel that sometimes plagues smaller, more tourist-dominated Bavarian towns. Its streets are tidy and handsome, but the feeling is of solid prosperity rather than overt wealth, with an economy buttressed by oil refineries and by the town's status as the home of the Audi car plant.

Ingolstadt's Altstadt – entirely surrounded by greenery on the site of its former defences – is an enjoyable place to spend a day, while beyond the centre are the contrasting delights of the Audi Forum and the Ingolstadt Village outlet mall.

The Altstadt

The towers of the **Moritzkirche** and its near neighbour the **Pfeifturm** (guided visits April–Oct Sun 10.30am & 11.30am; assemble on Rathausplatz in front of the Altes Rathaus; €3.50), the former city watchtower, make a central point of reference in the heart of the Altstadt, close to **Schliffelmarkt** where the main east–west and north–south streets cross. From Schliffelmarkt, Ingolstadt's main shopping street, Ludwigstrasse, heads east to Paradeplatz.

The Bayerisches Armeemuseum

Paradeplatz 4 • Tues–Fri 9am–5.30pm, Sat & Sun 10am–5.30pm • €3.50, combined ticket with Reduit Tilly & Turm Triva (see p.364) €7 • ⓦ armeemuseum.de

The impressive whitewashed **Neues Schloss** was begun in the first half of the fifteenth century by Duke Ludwig the Bearded and completed under the dukes of Landshut after the Ingolstadt line of the Wittelsbachs died out. Since 1972 it has housed the **Bayerisches Armeemuseum** (Bavarian Army Museum), with more than 35 rooms displaying artefacts from half a millennium of military history, alongside older archeological finds. The exhibits include uniforms of the Bavarian kings, plus booty from the wars against the Turks in the seventeenth and eighteenth centuries, including a beautiful embroidered Turkish tent.

Liebfrauenmünster

Kreuzstr. 1 • Free

A short walk west of Schliffelmarkt along Theresienstrasse brings you to the Late Gothic **Liebfrauenmünster**, Ingolstadt's largest church, whose red-brick flanks soar impressively above the modest-sized surrounding houses. The largest Late Gothic hall church in Bavaria, it's notable mainly for its unusual towers, set at an oblique angle to the west end of the church, and for its vast, steep roof, which conceals seven attic storeys for which 3800 tree trunks were needed.

Maria de Victoria

Neubaustr. 1 • March, April & Oct Tues–Sun 9am–noon & 1–5pm; May–Sept daily 9am–noon & 1–5pm; Nov–Feb Tues–Sun 1–4pm • €2

To the north of Liebfrauenmünster, the Asam brothers' Baroque church of **Maria de Victoria** could scarcely be more different. Built between 1732 and 1736 for the Marian student congregation and lacking either forecourt or towers, the church nevertheless startles with the icing-sugar delicacy of its external decoration.

Inside, the eye is drawn irresistibly to Cosmas Damian Asam's ceiling **fresco** on the theme of the Incarnation – the world's largest fresco on a flat surface, it measures 42 by 16 metres. The church's other treasure is the **Lepanto Monstrance** of 1708, which depicts the Christians' naval victory over the Turks at the Battle of Lepanto in 1571 – the last naval battle to be fought between ships driven by oars.

On the corner opposite the Maria de Victoria church, the gabled **Tillyhaus** at Neubaustr. 2 is where the feared Catholic commander in the Thirty Years' War, Count von Tilly, died of his battle wounds in 1632.

Deutsches Medizinhistorisches Museum

Anatomiestr. 18–20 • Tues–Sun 10am–5pm • €5

On the western fringe of the Altstadt, the **Deutsches Medizinhistorisches Museum** occupies the Baroque building of the Alte Anatomie (Old Anatomical Institute). Its medical-historical displays include ancient Greek, Roman and Egyptian artefacts as well as a selection of amputation saws, cauterizing irons and bloodletting knives that may not be for the fainthearted.

The Kavalier Hepp museums

Auf der Schanz 45 • Tues–Fri 9am–5pm • Combined ticket for Stadtmuseum and Spielzeugmuseum €3

A little to the north beyond the brick Gothic Kreuztor, the mid-nineteenth-century fort of **Kavalier Hepp** houses two museums: the **Stadtmuseum**, Ingolstadt's local history museum, with relics from an early Celtic settlement and a model of the city as it was in 1571; and the **Spielzeugmuseum** (Toy Museum), complete with working model railways, tin soldiers and dolls.

The Museum für Konkrete Kunst

Tränktorstr. 6–8 • Tues–Sun 10am–5pm • €3

Close to the river, the **Museum für Konkrete Kunst** is Germany's only museum dedicated to Concrete Art – an abstract art movement that rose to prominence in the 1940s and flourished until the 1960s – and houses the Gomringer Collection which was acquired by the city in 1981. Artists featured include Josef Albers and Victor Vasarely, and there's a sculpture garden outside the museum.

The Reduit Tilly and Turm Triva

Klenzepark • Both Tues–Fri 9am–5.30pm, Sat & Sun 10am–5.30pm • €3.50 each, combined ticket with Bayerisches Armeemuseum €7 • ⓦ armeemuseum.de

Two outposts of the Bayerisches Armeemuseum (see p.363) face the Altstadt across the river. The **Reduit Tilly** is the surviving portion of the mighty new fortress built between 1828 and 1848 to replace the old Ingolstadt fortress, destroyed in 1800. Its facade was designed by the Bavarian court architect, Leo von Klenze. The complex now houses a wide-ranging exhibition on Germany's experience in World War I, focusing not just on life in the trenches but on the home front and the changing role of women.

The **Turm Triva** houses the **Bayerisches Polizeimuseum**, with exhibits on the unrest at the end of World War I to the policing of the old Iron Curtain and the protests against the Wackersdorf nuclear reprocessing plant in the 1980s.

The Audi Forum

Factory tour Mon–Fri 8am–5.30pm • €7 • ☎ 0800 283 44 44 (call in advance to reserve) • Audi Museum Mobile Daily 9am–6pm • €2 • After Work Jazz Lounge Thurs 6.30pm • ⓦ audi.de/foren • Bus #11 or #15 from centre

As glassy and ultramodern as you'd expect, the **Audi Forum Ingolstadt**, north of the Altstadt along Ettinger Strasse, offers everything from an **After Work Jazz Lounge** with regular live music to the opportunity to take a **factory tour**. Housed in an eye-catching circular building, the **Audi Museum Mobile** is the company museum, with old and new cars and prototypes on view.

ARRIVAL AND INFORMATION INGOLSTADT

By train The Hauptbahnhof is approximately 2km south of the Altstadt on the far side of the Danube; frequent buses (ⓦ invg.de) take around 5min to connect it with the centre. Destinations Augsburg (hourly; 57min); Eichstätt Stadt (via Eichstätt Bahnhof; hourly; 42min); Munich (2–3 per hour; 36min–1hr 12min); Neuburg an der Donau (hourly; 15–22min); Nuremberg (2 per hour; 29–43min); Regensburg (hourly; 1hr 5min).

Tourist office In the Altes Rathaus at Rathausplatz 2 (April–Oct Mon–Fri 9am–6pm, Sat & Sun 10am–2pm; Nov–March Mon–Fri 9.30am–4.30pm, Sat 10am–1pm; ☎ 0841 305 30 30, ⓦ ingolstadt-tourismus.de).

ACCOMMODATION

HOTELS

Adler Theresienstr. 22 ☎ 0841 351 07, ⓦ hotel-adler -ingolstadt.de. Traditional, family-run 3-star hotel in a very central location close to the Liebfrauenmünster; some parts of the interior date from the fifteenth century and all rooms have either bath or shower plus WC. **€109**

Bayerischer Hof Münzbergstr. 12 ☎ 0841 93 40 60, ⓦ bayerischer-hof-ingolstadt.de. In the quiet southwest corner of the Altstadt, this is a comfortable 3-star option with tasteful decor in simplified modern Bavarian style, with heavy wood furniture. Singles, doubles and some stylish modern apartments available. **€87**

Rappensberger Harderstr. 3 ☎ 0841 31 40, ⓦ rappensberger-hotel.de. A stylish blend of modernity and tradition, with 75 rooms in various categories, from standard singles to "Tradition" rooms with historical features, to a 43-square-metre suite. There's also an Italian restaurant, *Il Castello*, plus wi-fi and limited parking. **€97**

CAMPSITES AND HOSTELS

Azur Campingpark ☎ 0841 961 16 16, ⓦ azur -camping.de. A lakeside campsite on the eastern outskirts of town at Auwaldsee, with fishing, minigolf, laundry facilities, a sunbathing meadow by the lake and a children's

play area. Open all year round. Pitch €8.50, plus €8.50 per person
DJH Ingolstadt Friedhofstr. 4 1/2 ☎0841 305 12 80, ⓦingolstadt.jugendherberge.de. A historic bastion on the fringe of the Altstadt makes an atmospheric location for this cyclist-friendly youth hostel. Accommodation is in family rooms or eight- or twelve-bed dorms. Rates include breakfast. Dorms & family rooms €19.20

EATING AND DRINKING

Gaststätte Daniel Roseneckstr. 1 ☎0841 352 72. Traditional Bavarian cooking and *Herrnbräubier* in Ingolstadt's oldest *Gaststätte*, which dates from 1471; choose between the snug and cosy interior or the summer *Biergarten*. Main courses from around €8. Tues–Sun 9am–1am.

★**Kuchlbauer Biermuseum** Schäffbräu Str. 11a ☎0841 355 12, ⓦbiermuseum-ingolstadt.de. Atmospheric *Gaststätte* with beers from the small Kuchlbauer brewery, an array of historic brewing-related paraphernalia and everything from salads to ox in *Starkbier* sauce; there's also a beer garden at the rear. Main courses from €11. Daily 11am–3pm & 5pm–1am.

Das Mo Bergbräustr. 7 ☎0841 339 60, ⓦmo-sigis .de. Splendid walled *Biergarten* in the shadow of chestnut trees and the Liebfrauenmünster, with Herrnbräu beer, waitresses in traditional garb and a chalked-up selection of light meals (from €6.50) to supplement the main menu's more substantial fare. Mid-April to mid-Oct daily 10.30am–late; mid-Oct to April Mon–Fri 4.30pm–late, Sat from 2pm & Sun from 11am–late.

SHOPPING

Ingolstadt Village Otto-Han-Str. 1 ⓦingolstadtvillage .com; bus #20 from Rathausplatz. On the eastern side of Ingolstadt close to exit 61 of the A9 Autobahn, Ingolstadt Village is a designer outlet mall done in tasteful, small-town architectural style: beneath its postmodern oriels and gables you can browse through more than a hundred boutiques, including big names such as Calvin Klein, Hugo Boss, Levi's and Roberto Cavalli. Mon–Sat 10am–8pm.

Neuburg an der Donau

Despite its name, which means "new castle on the Danube", the delightful little town of **NEUBURG AN DER DONAU**, 21km west of Ingolstadt, is scarcely new, though it was only after the foundation of the principality of Pfalz-Neuburg in 1505 that it really gained any importance. The "official" quarter on a bluff high above the river has a dolls'-house prettiness, with stately seventeenth- and eighteenth-century gabled houses lining the main street, **Amalienstrasse**, and the principal civic buildings – including the late Renaissance **Hofkirche** – grouped around a handsome central square, **Karlsplatz**. The town is utterly dominated by its impressive Renaissance **Schloss**, which is the main reason for a visit. If you're in Neuburg in the spring be sure to try the locally grown Schrobenhausen asparagus, which is considered a great delicacy.

The Schloss

Tues–Sun: April–Sept 9am–6pm; Oct–March 10am–4pm • €5.50, combined ticket with Stadtmuseum €6.50, chapel free • ⓦ schloesser-bayern.de

Neuburg's magnificent Renaissance **Schloss** was constructed from 1530 onwards for Pfalzgraf (Count Palatine) Ottheinrich, the principality's first ruler; the splendid arcaded courtyard is decorated with elaborate sgraffito, while the **chapel** was the first purpose-built Protestant church in Germany and has beautiful frescoes by Hans Bocksberger dating from 1543. Highlights of the Schloss's interior include the **Rittersaal** (Knights' Hall) in the north wing, with its mighty columns and wooden ceiling. A Baroque east wing was added in 1665 to 1670, complete with two round towers that dominate the river and town. The Schloss's west wing contains the **Bayerische Staatsgalerie Flämische Barockmalerei**, with 120 works of Flemish art by masters including Rubens, Van Dyck and Bruegel.

The Stadtmuseum

Weveldhaus, Amalienstrasse • Mid-March to Dec Tues–Sun 10am–6pm • €3, combined ticket with Schloss €6.50 • ⓦ stadtmuseum-neuburg.de

Just off Karlsplatz the Weveldhaus – a sixteenth-century nobleman's mansion – houses Neuburg's modestly engrossing local history museum, the **Stadtmuseum**, with displays ranging from fishing on the Danube to the town's complex religious and political history, and nineteenth-century bourgeois life. Next door, the early Rococo **Provinzialbibliothek** (tours May–Oct Wed 2.30pm; €2.50) dates from 1731–32; the splendid Baroque library on the upper floor has elegant carved bookcases from the former imperial monastery of Kaisheim.

ARRIVAL AND INFORMATION   NEUBURG AN DER DONAU

By train Trains from Ingolstadt arrive at Neuburg's Bahnhof, a short walk south of the Altstadt.
Destinations Ingolstadt (hourly; 17–21min).
Tourist office Close to the Schloss on Ottheinrichplatz

(Easter–Oct daily 9am–6pm; Nov–Easter Mon–Thurs 9am–noon & 2–4pm, Fri 9am–1pm; ☎08431 552 40, ⓦ neuburg-donau.de).

ACCOMMODATION AND EATING

Gasthaus zur Blauen Traube Amalienstr. 49 ☎ 08431 83 92, ⓦ zur-blauen-traube.de. Very central and atmospheric hotel in the historic upper part of the town, close to the Schloss, with a restaurant serving light meals and savoury platters from around €6. Restaurant daily 10.30am–3pm & 5.30pm–midnight. **€45**

Kate Café am Theater Residenzstr. A66 ☎ 08431 647 89 99. Situated halfway between the tourist office and the Schloss, this excellent café has pretty decor and serves breakfasts (from €4.90) and delicious cakes (from €2.80),

as well as local beers, wine by the glass and cappuccinos. Tues–Sun 9am–6pm.
Neuwirt Färberstr. 88 ☎ 08431 20 78, ⓦ neuwirt -neuburg.de. This *Brauerei-Gasthof* in the lower part of town has a range of rooms, including stylish refurbished and budget options with shared bath and WC. The restaurant serves Bavarian food, with organic beef a speciality; main courses cost €7 and up. Restaurant daily except Tues 10am–2.30pm & 5pm–midnight. **€59**

Eichstätt

Few places illustrate more graphically the contrast between the capital-city airs and country-town scale of a minor German Residenzstadt than **EICHSTÄTT**, tucked into a loop in the Altmühl River in the region known as the Franconian Jura, south of Nuremberg. Even today, the little cathedral and university city is no bigger than a small market town, with a population of barely 14,000. Yet for five centuries, from 1305 until secularization at the beginning of the nineteenth century, its prince-bishops held spiritual and temporal power over a diminutive territory on Franconia's southern fringe. A Catholic stronghold during the Thirty Years' War, it paid for its piety when it was sacked by the Swedes on February 12, 1634. The Baroque reconstruction by the Italians Giacomo Angelini, Mauritio Pedetti and Gabriel de Gabrieli created the capital-city-in-miniature that delights visitors today.

The Dom

Guided tours of Dom and Residenz (see opposite) mid-April to May & Oct Mon, Wed & Fri at 11am; June–Sept Tues, Thurs & Fri at 11am • Book though tourist office • Tours €3

The focus of Eichstätt's "official" quarter is the **Dom**, largely fourteenth-century Gothic, though you'd scarcely know it, so completely do the later Baroque accretions wrap around it on all but the north side facing Domplatz, creating the slightly odd effect of a large ecclesiastical building with no real main facade. Inside, the most notable artwork is the richly carved 11m-high limestone **Pappenheim Altar**, a gift in 1489 from Kaspar Marschall von Pappenheim in thanks for his safe return from a pilgrimage to the Holy Land.

A door between the south tower and the Sakramentskapelle leads to the **Mortuarium**, though anything less like a mortuary than this lovely twin-aisled Late Gothic hall with its graceful vaulting and stately central pillars is hard to imagine. It forms the western side of the cathedral's cloisters.

Domschatz und Diözesanmuseum
April–Oct Wed–Fri 10.30am–5pm, Sat & Sun 10am–5pm • €3

Housed in twelve rooms above the cloisters, the **Domschatz und Diözesanmuseum** (cathedral treasury and museum) displays treasures including the supposed vestments of St Willibald, the Anglo-Saxon who was appointed first bishop of Eichstätt by St Boniface in 740 AD.

The Residenz
Guided tours of Residenz April–Oct Sat & Sun at 10.15am, 11am, 11.45am, 2pm, 2.45pm & 3.30pm • Book through tourist office • €1 •
Guided tours of Residenz and Dom combined Mid-April to May & Oct Mon, Wed & Fri at 11am; June–Sept Tues, Thurs & Fri at 11am •
Book through tourist office • €3

The Baroque **Residenzplatz** curves in spectacular fashion around the south and west sides of the Dom. It is a wonderfully uniform urban space, its elegant crescent of houses echoing the style of the bishops' palace – the **Residenz** – opposite. The Residenz was built in three phases from 1700 to 1777 by Jakob Engel, Gabriel de Gabrieli and Mauritio Pedetti respectively. High points of the tour around the building are Pedetti's impressive staircase and the Spiegelsaal, or Hall of Mirrors, on the second floor.

Willibaldsburg
Bastiongarten Mid-April to mid-Oct Tues–Sun 9am–6pm • Free • **Jura Museum & Museum für Ur- und Frühgeschichte** April–Sept
Tues–Sun 9am–6pm; Oct–March Tues–Sun 10am–4pm • €4.50 • ⓦ schloesser.bayern.de

Dominating the town from its site high above the Altmühl to the west is the massive **Willibaldsburg**, former seat of the prince-bishops. The castle was established in 1355 by Bishop Berthold von Zollern but owes its present appearance to Elias Holl – architect of Augsburg's Rathaus – who extended it for prince-bishop Konrad von Gemmingen between 1595 and 1612. The bishop established a celebrated botanical garden within the castle walls. Destroyed during the Thirty Years' War, in recent years it has been re-established as the **Bastiongarten**.

NATURPARK ALTMÜHLTAL

The meandering valley of the River Altmühl threads its way from west to east across the three-thousand-square-kilometre **Naturpark Altmühltal (ⓦ** naturpark-altmuehltal.de), one of Germany's largest nature reserves. Its Jurassic geology not only yields the remarkable fossils that are on display in the Willibaldsburg's Jura Museum (see p.367), but also produces fascinating, sculpted landforms, such as the **Zwölf Apostel** at **Solnhofen** west of Eichstätt.

The region's blend of scenic and cultural attractions makes it a popular destination for hikers and cyclists alike, and it is crisscrossed with hiking trails and cycle paths. The classic walk is the 200km-long **Altmühltal Panoramaweg**, which follows the course of the river, linking Gunzenhausen on the edge of the Altmühlsee in the west with Solnhofen, Eichstätt and Kelheim in the east. The gentle 166km-long **Altmühltal Radweg** for cyclists follows a similar route from Gunzenhausen to Kelheim. From May to October Freizeitbus services with bike trailers cover the region between Eichstätt and Regensburg; Freizeitbus #2 (day-ticket with bike €11; day-ticket without bike €8) follows the central sections of the Panoramaweg and Radweg.

Altmühl itself is one of the slowest-flowing rivers in Bavaria and consequently highly popular with canoeists: Johann Gegg in Dollnstein, 16km west of Eichstätt, rents out **canoes** by the day (from €25; ☎ 084 226 91, ⓦ kanuvermietung-altmuehltal.de).

For more information on activities and accommodation in the Naturpark, contact the information centre in Eichstätt (see p.368).

The castle contains two museums: the **Jura Museum**, which displays fossils from the region's unusually rich Jurassic limestone deposits, including a rare fossil of an *Archaeopteryx*, a type of prehistoric bird; and the **Museum für Ur- und Frühgeschichte**, which catalogues the region's history from the Stone Age to the early Middle Ages.

ARRIVAL AND INFORMATION EICHSTÄTT

By train Eichstätt's Bahnhof is on the Nuremberg–Munich line some distance from town, with shuttle trains completing the last 5km to the Eichstätt-Stadt Bahnhof close to the Altstadt.
Destinations Ingolstadt (hourly; 40 min).
Tourist office Domplatz 8 (April–Oct Mon–Sat 9am–6pm, Sun 10am–1pm; Nov–March Mon–Thurs 10am–noon &

2–4pm, Fri 10am–noon; ☎08421 600 14 00, ⊛eichstaett.de).
Naturpark Altmühltal information centre In the Baroque church of Notre Dame de Sacre Coeur (Easter–Oct Mon–Fri 9am–5pm, Sat & Sun 10am–5pm, closes 6pm from Whitsun until mid-Sept; Nov–Easter Mon–Thurs 9am–noon & 2–4pm, Fri 9am–noon; ☎08421 987 60, ⊛naturpark-altmuehltal.de).

ACCOMMODATION AND EATING

Braugasthof Trompete Ostenstr. 3 ☎08421 981 70, ⊛braugasthof-trompete.de. Just east of the Altstadt, the *Braugasthof Trompete* serves the local Hofmühl beer along with Bavarian and Italian food. Pasta from around €6.20; traditional meaty main courses like *Bierkümmelbraten* from around €7.90 and up. Mon–Fri 7am–1am, Sat & Sun 7.30am–1am.
DJH Eichstätt Reichenaustr. 15 ☎08421 98 04 10, ⊛eichstaett.jugendherberge.de. Located below the Willibaldsburg, with facilities for cyclists including tools and safe storage. Accommodation is mainly in six-bed dorms with a few single and double rooms. Dorms **€24.90**, doubles **€49.80**
Gasthaus Krone Domplatz 3 ☎08421 44 06, ⊛krone-eichstaett.de. Attractive, traditional *Gasthaus* opposite the Dom, with a menu that specializes in local Altmühltal

lamb. Prices are reasonable, with hearty main courses from around €12 and *Schnitzels*, salads or *Käsespätzen* (cheese noodles) for less. Mon, Tues & Thurs–Sun 10am–2pm & 5pm–midnight.
Hotel Adler Marktplatz 22 ☎08421 67 67, ⊛adler-eichstaett.de. Behind a fine Baroque facade on the main market square, the *Adler* offers comfortable, recently renovated rooms in several categories, including one suite; there's an Italian restaurant on the ground floor. All rooms have bath or shower, WC, minibar and cable TV. **€90**
Ratskeller ☎08421 90 12 58, ⊛ratskeller-eichstaett .de. Simple but attractive accommodation in the same former abbey complex as the Altmühltal information centre; it also serves food and has a *Biergarten*. Rooms have shower, WC and radio; some also have cable TV and phone. **€68**

Augsburg

Proud **AUGSBURG** may only be Bavaria's third-largest city, but it's the state's oldest, tracing its origins to the Roman fort of Augusta Vindelicum founded in the first century AD. The largest city of Bavarian Swabia – a western region linguistically, and historically quite distinct from Bavaria proper – it was one of the wealthiest financial centres in Europe during the Middle Ages, helped by its position on the route south to Italy. Its traders and financiers – the Fuggers and Welsers – were the Rothschilds or Vanderbilts of their day, with business connections across Europe and beyond. Augsburg was renowned for its craftsmanship, above all in metalwork, and it also produced the father-and-son artists Hans Holbein the Elder and Younger. The city reached a peak of magnificence during the Renaissance, from when much of the city's most impressive architecture dates, notably the splendid **Rathaus** by Elias Holl, who was the municipal architect.

> ## AUGSBURG ORIENTATION
>
> Finding your bearings in Augsburg is simple enough. The Altstadt runs north–south along the axis of Maximilianstrasse–Karolinenstrasse–Hoher Weg–Frauentorstrasse, with a busy east–west traffic route cutting it into unequal halves. The northern Altstadt is smaller and quieter, centred on the **Dom**; the southern Altstadt, with its magnificent **Rathaus** and the stately mansions of **Maximilianstrasse**, is the hub of the city's shopping and nightlife.

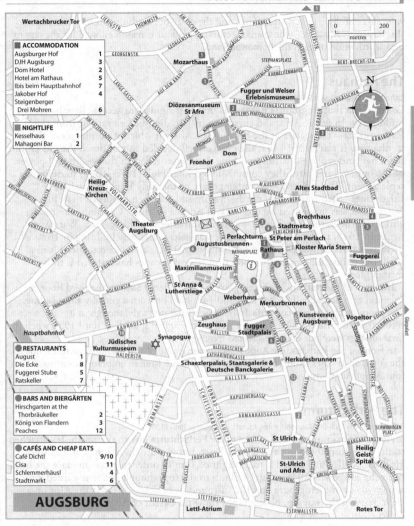

AUGSBURG

ACCOMMODATION

Augsburger Hof	1
DJH Augsburg	3
Dom Hotel	2
Hotel am Rathaus	5
Ibis beim Hauptbahnhof	7
Jakober Hof	4
Steigenberger Drei Mohren	6

NIGHTLIFE

Kesselhaus	1
Mahagoni Bar	2

RESTAURANTS

August	1
Die Ecke	8
Fuggerei Stube	5
Ratskeller	7

BARS AND BIERGÄRTEN

Hirschgarten at the Thorbräukeller	2
König von Flandern	3
Peaches	12

CAFÉS AND CHEAP EATS

Café Dichtl	9/10
Cisa	11
Schlemmerhäusl	4
Stadtmarkt	6

Brief history

An imperial free city, Augsburg took centre stage in the religious controversies of the sixteenth century. The city, though with a Catholic bishopric, nevertheless strongly favoured Luther. In 1530 the **Augsburg Confession** – one of the founding documents of the Lutheran faith – was formulated here and presented to the Emperor Charles V at an Imperial Diet. At a subsequent Diet, in 1555, the Peace of Augsburg initiated peaceful coexistence between the religions, in imperial free cities at least, though Ferdinand II attempted to overturn it with his Edict of Restitution in 1629 in the thick of the Thirty Years' War. This had the effect of reversing the power balance between Catholic and Protestant in Augsburg, and the city remains largely – but not overwhelmingly – Catholic today. Augsburg became Bavarian in 1806, and in the following century grew into an important industrial centre. Firms such as MAN and Messerschmitt ensured it attracted Allied air raids during World War II, yet the scars were successfully repaired afterwards, and the glory of Augsburg's history is evident to this day in its **Altstadt** – whose architectural splendour is reason enough for the city to be a worthwhile stop on the **Romantic Road**.

The Rathaus

Rathausplatz · Goldener Saal daily 10am–6pm · €2.50

Locals claim that Augsburg's **Rathaus** is the most significant secular Renaissance building north of the Alps, and surveying its tall, dignified elevations from the Rathausplatz – the square at the heart of the Altstadt which it dominates – it's hard to disagree. It was in 1614 that the city council decided to tear down the old Gothic town hall and replace it with something that better reflected the wealth and power of the imperial free city. They commissioned Elias Holl (1573–1646) to design its replacement. The architect – a contemporary of the early English classicist Inigo Jones – had travelled to northern Italy and it's often supposed that, like Jones, Holl was influenced by the work of Andrea Palladio. Certainly, the results anticipate the Baroque style that was to bloom after the Thirty Years' War. Work began in 1615; the first council meeting was held in the new building in 1620. A little over three centuries later, on February 26, 1944, an air raid reduced it to a shell, but painstaking reconstruction over several decades has restored it to its former glory.

The peak of the Rathaus's restored glory is the **Goldener Saal** on the third floor, a splendid ceremonial hall 32.5m long and 14m high beneath a gilded walnut ceiling. The room fulfils the city council's 1614 design brief perfectly, though in its reconstructed form it wasn't fully restored to its original splendour until 1996 when the final touches were put on its re-created frescoes.

In front of the Rathaus, the **Augustusbrunnen** is one of three handsome fountains in the Altstadt. It dates from 1588–94 and honours the Roman emperor Augustus, founder of Augsburg.

The Perlachturm

Rathausplatz · Daily April–Oct 10am–6pm; during Advent Fri, Sat & Sun 1–7pm · €1.50

Stylistic companion to the Rathaus is the **Perlachturm** just to the north. It's attached to the little Romanesque church of St Peter, but it quite dwarfs the church, since Holl remodelled and raised it to a height of 70m in order to accommodate the bells from the old town hall. It's quite a climb to the top, though you're rewarded with superb views over Augsburg and the surrounding region – as far as the Alps on a clear day. On the way up, photographs show the extent of Augsburg's 1944 destruction.

Brechthaus

Auf dem Rain 7 · Tues–Sun 10am–5pm · €2.50

Poet and playwright Bertolt Brecht was born on February 10, 1898, just to the east of Augsburg's Rathaus at Auf dem Rain 7, now the **Brechthaus**. He didn't stay long – the family upped sticks the same year. The building now houses an exhibition on the writer's life and work. Brecht's relationship with Augsburg was a scratchy one, and it was only from the mid-1960s on, as the Cold War began to thaw a little, that the city fathers considered him worthy of recognition. Close by, Elias Holl's splendid **Stadtmetzg** (Butchers' Guild House; 1606–09) guards the way back to Rathausplatz.

The Maximilianmuseum

Fuggerplatz 1 • Tues –Sun 10am–5pm • €7 • ⓦ kunstsammlungen-museen.augsburg.de

A little to the west of Rathausplatz along Philippine-Welser-Strasse, the sixteenth-century **Welserhaus**, with its eighteenth-century Classical facade, and the gabled house of the patrician **Köpf** family, which dates from 1578, provide suitable neighbours for the beautiful **Maximilianmuseum**, a sixteenth-century merchant's house which now houses the city's principal historical and applied art collections. The highlight is the section dedicated to the fabulously skilled silver- and goldsmiths whose work brought Augsburg international renown. The museum also regularly hosts temporary exhibitions on themes related to Augsburg and applied art.

St Anna

Entered from Annastrasse via Im Annahof • May–Oct Mon noon–6pm, Tues–Sat 10am–12.30pm & 3–6pm, Sun 10am–12.30pm & 3–5pm; Nov–April closes 1hr earlier • Free

The church of **St Anna**, close by the Maximilianmuseum, was originally a Carmelite monastery but has been Protestant since 1525. The Late Gothic **Goldschmiedekapelle** (Goldsmiths' Chapel) is dedicated to St Helen and decorated with beautiful frescoes; at the west end of the church, the showy Renaissance **Fuggerkapelle**, commissioned by Jakob Fugger the Rich for himself and his brothers and built between 1509 and 1512, quite upstages the nave of the church. St Anna is closely associated with Martin Luther, who stayed here in 1518; there's a small museum (free), the **Lutherstiege**, on the subject.

A little way to the south on Zeugplatz, the impressive **Zeughaus** or city arsenal by Elias Holl dates from 1602 to 1607.

Maximilianstrasse

Running south from Rathausplatz, stately **Maximilianstrasse** is, in its entirety, the clearest possible expression of Augsburg's Renaissance wealth, lined with the town palaces of the wealthy. Nowadays the "Maximilian" referred to in the street's name is the Habsburg Emperor Maximilian I, whose fondness for the city led to him being dubbed "Mayor of Augsburg", but it previously referred to another, less popular "Max" – the Bavarian Elector Maximilian Joseph. Its historical importance aside, Maximilianstrasse is a visually impressive link between the Rathaus and the church of St Ulrich und Afra in the south – and it's also the centre of Augsburg's nightlife.

The Weberhaus

The second of Augsburg's trio of splendid Renaissance fountains, the **Merkurbrunnen**, stands opposite the fourteenth-century **Weberhaus** (Weavers' Guild House), at Moritzplatz, a little way south of the Rathaus. The richly coloured paintings on its facade were originally done by Johann Matthias Kager in 1605 but were renewed after World War II. They depict the history of the cloth trade – once very important in Augsburg – and the Battle of Lechfeld in 955 AD, in which the German King Otto held back the Magyar advance into Western Europe south of the city.

Fugger Stadtpalais

Just south of the Weberhaus, the 68m-long sgraffito facade of the **Fugger Stadtpalais** dominates the midsection of Maximilianstrasse. Originally built in 1512 to 1515 as a town palace for Jakob Fugger the Rich, the complex was badly damaged during World War II and rebuilt in simplified form afterwards. During business hours, you can view the lovely Italian Renaissance-style **Damenhof**, or Ladies' Court, through the doors at the back of the Rieger & Kranzfelder bookshop.

The Schaezlerpalais: Deutsche Barockgalerie and Staatsgalerie

Maximilianstr. 46 • Tues–Sun 10am–5pm • €7 • ⓦ kunstsammlungen-museen.augsburg.de

Adrian de Vries' 1602 Herkulesbrunnen – the third of Augsburg's Renaissance fountains – stands in front of the most imposing Rococo building in the city, the **Schaezlerpalais**. Built in 1765 as a town palace for Baron Adam Liebert von Liebenhofen, it now houses the paintings of the **Deutsche Barockgalerie**, including works by Angelika Kauffmann, Rubens and Tiepolo. High point of the visit, however, is the beautiful Rococo Festsaal, or ballroom, which is used as a concert venue in the summer months – it can't be heated, so it isn't used during the winter.

The same ticket also admits you to the adjacent **Staatsgalerie**, whose collection of older works includes a 1520 Dürer portrait of Jakob Fugger the Rich. Don't miss the delightful garden afterwards.

St Ulrich und Afra

Maximilianstrasse is brought to a visual stop by the impressive onion-domed bulk of **St Ulrich und Afra**, in size only the second largest church in Augsburg but in terms of its place in the townscape, of massively more importance than the Dom. The interior is a really splendid work of Late Gothic architecture; begun in 1474, construction continued until 1603, completion of the choir and tower being delayed by the turmoil of the Reformation. The church contains the tombs of St Ulrich – the prince-bishop who defended the city against the Magyars – and of St Afra, while beautiful painted vaulting dating from 1492 to 1496 crowns the chapel of **St Simpert**, burial place of the eponymous saint, who is said to have been a nephew of Charlemagne. In front of St Ulrich und Afra, the pretty little Protestant church of **St Ulrich** represents in built form the workable coexistence Augsburg's Protestants and Catholics reached after the religious turmoil of the sixteenth and seventeenth centuries.

The eastern Altstadt

Augsburg's eastern Altstadt lacks the formal grandeur of Maximilianstrasse but repays exploration for its quiet lanes, watercourses and one really outstanding attraction, the **Fuggerei**. The small-scale lanes and waterways of the **Handwerkerviertel** (Artisans' Quarter), have undeniable charm, though the area was quite badly affected by World War II bombs; one of the houses lost was the birthplace of **Hans Holbein the Younger** at Vorderer Lech 20. The building now on the site is home to the **Kunstverein Augsburg** (Tues & Thurs–Sun 11am–5pm, Wed 11am–8pm; free; ⓦkunstverein-augsburg.de), which mounts temporary exhibitions of modern art.

Fuggerei

Jakoberstr. 26 • Daily: April–Sept 8am–8pm; Oct–March 9am–6pm • €4 • ⓦ fugger.de

The remarkable **Fuggerei** was established for the virtuous poor of Augsburg by Jakob Fugger the Rich and his brothers in 1521 and is generally regarded as the world's oldest social-housing scheme. Residents must be Catholic and must say three prayers a day for the founder and the Fugger family; that duty aside, they pay a nominal rent – excluding heating – of €0.88 a year. The Fuggerei's eight lanes of simple, ochre-washed houses constitute a city within a city, complete with seven gates and a church of its own, and it's a charming place simply to wander. An informative **museum** on **Mittlere Gasse** tells the story of the Fuggers in English and German and includes a visit to a house furnished as it would have been historically; you can also visit a modernized show apartment at **Ochsengasse 51** to gain an insight into living conditions at the Fuggerei today. In the former **air raid shelter** nearby, an exhibition tells the tale of the destruction of much of the Fuggerei on the night of February 25–26, 1944, as USAF bombers targeted the Messerschmitt aircraft factory, and of the rapid reconstruction after the war.

The northern Altstadt

The east–west thoroughfare of Leonhardsberg was punched through the Altstadt during postwar reconstruction, and its snarling traffic has the effect of separating the peaceful northern Altstadt – which is dominated by the **Dom** – from the rest of the city. A new museum, the **Fugger und Welser Erlebnismuseum** (Ⓦfugger-und -welser-museum.com), was scheduled to open in the Renaissance Wiesel Haus in Aussere Pfaffengässchen as this book went to press. It will chart the influence of Augsburg's powerful merchant class on the historical development of the city.

Dom

Daily 7am–6pm • Free

Architecturally, Augsburg's cathedral is an utter hotchpotch: entirely lacking the sublime clarity of St Ulrich und Afra's design, it's more of a picturesque jumble than a coherent building. The spires date from 1150, but much of the rest of the building was rebuilt in Gothic style in the fourteenth century, and it's from this time that the north and south portals – built by sculptors of the Parler School – date. On the south side of the nave, the five **Prophetenfenster** depicting Moses, David, Hosea, Daniel and Jonas, date from 1065 and are the oldest figurative stained-glass windows in existence. Older still is the bishop's throne or **Cathedra**, which dates from around 1000 AD.

Diözesanmuseum St Afra

Kornhausgasse 3–5 • Tues–Sat 10am–5pm, Sun noon–6pm • €5

On the north side of the cathedral, the **Diözesanmuseum St Afra** contains the cathedral's art treasures. Pride of place goes to the magnificent eleventh-century bronze cathedral doors, which consist of 35 bronze plates illustrating scenes from the Old Testament and allegories of good and evil. There's also some splendid Augsburg silver on display.

Mozarthaus

Frauentorstr. 20 • Tues–Sun 10am–5pm • €3.50 • Ⓦ kunstsammlungen-museen.augsburg.de

A short walk to the north from the Diözesanmuseum St Afra, Augsburg makes the most of its tenuous Mozart connection with the rather enjoyable **Mozarthaus**, an imaginatively presented exhibition in the house in which Mozart's father Leopold was born in 1719. The museum is quite engrossing for the light it casts on Leopold's role in the nurturing of his son's talent, and there's English labelling alongside the German.

The Jüdisches Kulturmuseum Augsburg Schwaben

Halderstr. 6–8 • Tues, Wed & Thurs 9am–6pm, Fri 9am–4pm, Sun 10am–5pm • €4 • Ⓦ jkmas.de

West of the Altstadt, midway between Königsplatz and the Hauptbahnhof, Augsburg's synagogue houses the **Jüdisches Kulturmuseum Augsburg Schwaben**, an engrossing exhibition on the history of Jewish settlement not just in Augsburg itself, but also in the surrounding districts where – thanks to the region's complex political position as an outlier of the Habsburg lands – Jewish communities grew up in quite small rural districts. In the margravate of Burgau as many as a third of the inhabitants of some villages were Jewish. The Augsburg community was extinguished by the Nazis, and the postwar community was dwindling in size as recently as the 1980s, but subsequent immigration from the former Soviet Union has boosted its numbers to 1600 – larger than it was before the Holocaust. The exhibition ends with a glimpse into the synagogue itself, a darkly beautiful blend of Jugendstil and Byzantine influences with a shallow dome picked out in gold.

The Glaspalast

H2 Zentrum für Gegenwartkunst Tues–Sun 10am–5pm • €7 • **Kunstmuseum Walter** Fri, Sat & Sun 11am–6pm • €6 •
ⓦ glaspalast-augsburg.de

East of the Altstadt on Amagasakiallee, the **Glaspalast**, an imposing iron-and-glass former textile mill, houses the **H2 Zentrum für Gegenwartkunst**, Augsburg's municipal gallery of contemporary art, which exhibits temporary installations. The same ticket admits you to the **Staatsgalerie**, a branch gallery of Munich's Pinakothek der Moderne, which concentrates on post-1945 representations of the human form. The Glaspalast also houses the **Kunstmuseum Walter**, a private collection of classical modern and contemporary art, including 118 works in glass by Egidio Costantini.

ARRIVAL AND DEPARTURE

AUGSBURG

By train Augsburg's Hauptbahnhof – Germany's oldest still in everyday use, built between 1843 and 1846 – is just west of the Altstadt at the western end of Bahnhofstrasse. Destinations Füssen (hourly; 1hr 39min–1hr 52min); Ingolstadt (hourly; 1hr); Landsberg am Lech (hourly; 52min); Munich (approx every 15–35min; 29–47min); Nördlingen (via Donauwörth: hourly; 1hr 8min); Nuremberg (approx every 30min–1hr 30min; 1hr 8min); Stuttgart (1—2 per hour; 1hr 44min).

GETTING AROUND

By public transport Almost everything you're likely to want to see is within the Altstadt, which is walkable; public transport including buses and trams radiates from both the Hauptbahnhof and Königsplatz just west of the Altstadt (single €1.30, *Tageskarte* day-ticket €5.80).

Bike rental Augsburg has a bike rental network, Nextbike (ⓣ 030 69 20 50 46, ⓦ nextbike.de,) with a dozen hire points around the city including one close to the Hauptbahnhof, behind the BohusCenter on Halderstrasse. You rent bikes by app, phone or SMS (€1 for 30min or €9 per day).

INFORMATION

Tourist office Rathausplatz 1 (April to mid-Oct Mon–Fri 9am–6pm, Sat 10am–5pm, Sun 10am–3pm; mid-Oct to March Mon–Fri 9am–5pm, Sat 10am–5pm, Sun 10am–3pm; ⓣ 0821 50 20 70, ⓦ augsburg-tourismus.de).

ACCOMMODATION

HOTELS AND PENSIONS

Augsburger Hof Auf dem Kreuz 2 ⓣ 0821 34 30 50, ⓦ augsburger-hof.de. Attractively furnished rooms, including some with a few traditional Bavarian touches, in an old house in the northern Altstadt. There's free wireless and a guest internet terminal, and the hotel has an attractive restaurant and bar. €99

Dom Hotel Frauentorstr. 8 ⓣ 0821 34 39 30, ⓦ domhotel-augsburg.de. In a central but peaceful location in the northern Altstadt, with a swimming pool and, in summer, breakfast on the patio outside. Rooms range from the blandly modern to the beamy and atmospheric. €104

Hotel am Rathaus Am Hinteren Perlachberg 1 ⓣ 0821 34 64 90, ⓦ hotel-am-rathaus-augsburg.de. You couldn't be more central than in this discreetly smart hideaway, tucked down a quiet lane behind the Rathaus and with all rooms equipped with bath or shower and WC. There's underground parking plus free wi-fi in the public areas. €105

Ibis beim Hauptbahnhof Halderstr. 25 ⓣ 0821 501 61 50, ⓦ ibishotel.com. Close to the Hauptbahnhof and convenient for the Altstadt, this is the more central of two outposts of the budget chain in Augsburg, with comfortable, if bland, en-suite rooms, and keen rates if you book in advance. €56

★**Jakober Hof** Jakoberstr. 41 ⓣ 0821 51 00 30, ⓦ jakoberhof.de. Attractive, family-run budget option close to the Fuggerei, with good-value rooms with shared facilities and reasonably priced en suites. All rooms have wi-fi; decor is simple but modern. Shared facilities €49; en suite €89

Steigenberger Drei Mohren Maximilianstr. 40 ⓣ 0821 503 60, ⓦ steigenberger.com. Traditionally the best address in town, the *Drei Mohren* occupies a prime position on the city's most elegant street and was completely refurbished in 2012. The 131 a/c rooms and suites are decorated with restrained contemporary elegance, and there are some low-allergen rooms for allergy sufferers. €119

HOSTELS

DJH Augsburg Unterer Graben 6 ⓣ 0821 780 88 90, ⓦ augsburg-jugendherberge.de. Bright, modern hostel on the fringe of the northern Altstadt, with accommodation in four-bed rooms as well as 35 en-suite doubles. There's an attractive café/bar area at the front. Breakfast included. Dorms €21.90, doubles €51

AUGSBURG FESTIVALS

Augsburg's biggest folk festival is **Plärrer** (Ⓦ augsburgerplaerrer.de), a combination of funfair and beer tents held twice each year, in spring and autumn. From mid-July to mid-August the **Internationaler Augsburger Jazz Sommer** (Ⓦ augsburger-jazzsommer.de) brings a varied line-up of international jazz acts to the city. Augsburg's annual Christmas market, the **Augsburger Christkindlesmarkt**, takes place in front of the Rathaus from late November until Christmas Eve (Ⓦ augsburgerchristkindlesmarkt.com).

EATING AND DRINKING

CAFÉS AND CHEAP EATS

Café Dichtl Bahnhofstr. corner of Schrannenstr; and at Maximilianstr. 18 ☎ 0821 52 50 30, Ⓦ dichtl.de. This big café-*Konditorei* is about the best bet for *Kaffee und Kuchen* in Augsburg, with impressive cakes, chocolates and inexpensive hot meals from around €7. Both branches Mon–Fri 8am–6.30pm, Sat 8am–6pm, Sun 9.30am–6pm.

Cisa Antoniushof, Maximilianstr. 57 ☎ 0821 608 44 91, Ⓦ cisa-augsburg.de. Very stylish, modern café-bar and bistro that also serves breakfast (10am–2pm, from €5.90) and full meals; daily specials from around €7. There are seats outside in the pretty frescoed *Hof* in fine weather. Tues–Sat 10am–midnight, Sun 9am–5pm.

Schlemmerhäusl Karolinenstr. 2, entrance on Am Perlachberg. Tiny delicatessen close to the Perlachturm that serves wholesome, bargain-priced hot meals (from €5.95) at lunchtime for little more than the price of a burger. Mon–Fri 8.30am–7pm, Sat 9am–4pm.

★**Stadtmarkt** Between Fuggerstr. & Annastr. Ⓦ stadtmarktaugsburg.de. The covered hall of Augsburg's market is a wonderful place for a cheap lunch if you don't mind eating at a counter, with everything from *Bratwurst* to Italian and specialities from Germany's lost eastern territories, from around €5. The queues build up fast, though. Mon–Fri 7am–6pm, Sat 7am–2pm.

RESTAURANTS

August Frauentorstr. 27 ☎ 0821 352 79. Classy, modern gourmet restaurant in the northern Altstadt, with two Michelin stars and the likes of Pata Negra ham with broad beans, Japanese garlic and beetroot curry to tempt the palate. Five-course menu €149; six courses €159. Wed–Sat 7pm–1am.

Die Ecke Elias-Holl-Platz 2 ☎ 0821 51 06 00, Ⓦ restaurant-die-ecke.de. Snug, intimate and long-established gourmet restaurant just behind the Rathaus, with refined cooking that embraces German and other influences in dishes like beef roulade with macademia

pesto and Szechuan pepper; main courses from €30. Daily 11am–2pm & 5.30pm–1am.

Fuggerei Stube Jakoberstr. 26 ☎ 0821 308 70, Ⓦ fuggerei-stube.de. Charmingly old-fashioned place at the front of the Fuggerei, serving *Schnitzel*, pork medallions with wild mushrooms and the like from around €12 beneath its vaulted ceilings and stone capitals. They also do salads. Tues–Sat 11.30am–2pm & 6–11pm, Sun 11.30am–3pm.

Ratskeller Rathausplatz 2 ☎ 0821 31 98 82 38, Ⓦ ratskeller-augsburg.de. Despite its historic setting in the cavernous undercroft of the Rathaus there's a surprisingly bustling, contemporary feel here. It serves a sprawling, versatile menu of salads (from around €6), *Flammkuchen* (€6.90) and Bavarian-style tapas, plus meaty mains (from around €8) and cocktails or Riegele beer to wash it down. Daily 11am–1am, Fri & Sat 11am–2am.

BARS AND BIERGÄRTEN

Hirschgarten at the Thorbräukeller Heilig Kreuz Strasse 20 ☎ 0821 51 19 91, Ⓦ thorbraeu-keller.de. Lovely *Biergarten* in a quiet corner of the peaceful northern Altstadt, not far from the Thorbräu brewery, whose beers it sells. There's also food, from *Rösti* or *Flammkuchen* (from around €6) to heartier main courses. Mon–Thurs & Sun 5pm–midnight, Fri & Sat 5pm–1am.

★**König von Flandern** Karolinenstr. 12 ☎ 0821 15 80 50, Ⓦ koenigvonflandern.de. Lively, atmospheric *Gasthausbrauerei* in a historic cellar brewing its own *Helles*, *Dunkel* and *Weissbier*; there's also hearty Bavarian food, from *Weisswurst* (€1.80 each) to salads (from €7.50) and hearty main courses from around €12. Daily 11am–1am.

Peaches Maximilianstr. 73 Ⓦ peaches-augsburg.de. Perennially popular cocktail bar on Maximilianstrasse's main nightlife strip, with a menu that embraces sours, daiquiris and fizzes, a 7–10pm happy hour and cocktails from €4.30. Mon–Thurs & Sun 7pm–2am, Fri & Sat 7pm–3am.

NIGHTLIFE AND ENTERTAINMENT

The city's surprisingly extensive **nightlife** is mostly of the cocktails-and-dance-music variety, concentrated on the southern end of Maximilianstrasse and the surrounding streets, though there are options scattered elsewhere in the city too.

6

CLUBS

Kesselhaus Riedingerstr. 26 ⓦkesselhaus-augsburg .de. Stripped, postindustrial surroundings, high ceilings and a range of party nights from cheesy *Schlager* hits to hip-hop and oldies at this big club in the north of the city, which also hosts live gigs. Fri & Sat 11pm–late, plus occasional Sun 10pm–late.

Mahagoni Bar Ulrichsplatz 3 ☎0821 51 72 05. Hip dance club and live music venue with an eclectic music policy embracing everything from drum 'n' bass, deep house and electro to hip-hop, Balkan beats and indie. Fri & Sat 10pm–late, plus occasional Wed.

THEATRES

Puppenkiste Spitalgasse 15 ☎0821 450 34 50, ⓦdiekiste.net. Augsburg's celebrated puppet theatre puts on shows of particular appeal to children and is housed in the Heilig-Geist-Spital, a protected historic building in the southern Altstadt.

Theater Augsburg Kennedyplatz 1 ☎0821 324 49 00, ⓦtheater-augsburg.de. The grandiose Theater Augsburg – one of the city's major nineteeth-century architectural landmarks – is the home of drama, opera, ballet and classical music. It also hosts an annual Viennese-style opera ball in late January or early February.

Landsberg am Lech

South of Augsburg on the Romantic Road, the handsome little town of Landsberg am Lech makes a worthwhile stopover on the way to the Alps. It has gone down in history as the place where Adolf Hitler wrote *Mein Kampf*, during his absurdly short stretch in prison following the 1923 Beer Hall Putsch. The prison – which after 1945 held high-ranking war criminals – still serves its original purpose.

For much of its history Landsberg was a border town on Bavaria's western fringes, which helps explain the sheer size of its surviving medieval fortifications, including a number of impressive gate towers. Mightiest of all the town's fortifications is the Late Gothic **Bayertor** (May–Oct daily 10am–noon & 2–5pm; €1), which dates from 1425 and is worth the steep climb up Alte Bergstrasse for its almost cathedral-like architecture and for the **view** it offers over the Altstadt, River Lech and distant Alps. The chief focus of the Altstadt is the broad central square, **Hauptplatz**, with Joseph Streiter's 1783 *Madonna* gracing the **Marienbrunnen** fountain in the centre.

The Historisches Rathaus

Hauptplatz 152 • May–Oct Mon–Fri 9am–12.30pm & 1.30–6pm, Sat & Sun 10am–5pm; Nov–April Mon–Thurs 9am–noon & 2–5pm, Fri 9am–12.30pm • €2, combined ticket with Neues Stadtmuseum & Herkomer Museum €6

Hauptplatz's real show-stopper – and the most visible emblem of Landsberg's civic pride – is its town hall, the **Historisches Rathaus**, with a magnificent stucco facade by Dominikus Zimmermann, the Rococo church architect who collaborated on the Wieskirche in Steingaden (see p.388) with his brother Johann Baptist. The Rathaus facade dates from 1719–21 and conceals an equally rich interior. You can visit the **Sitzungssaal** on the second floor with its stucco ceiling by Dominikus Zimmermann and the frescoed **Festsaal** above it.

There's another work by Dominikus Zimmermann a short walk north on Vorderer Anger: the diminutive **Johanniskirche**, with a dazzling Rococo altar that quite outshines the modesty of the church's proportions.

The Neues Stadtmuseum

Von Helfenstein Gasse 426 • Tues–Fri 2–5pm, Sat & Sun 10am–5pm • €3.50, combined ticket with Historisches Rathaus & Herkomer Museum €6

Midway between Hauptplatz and the Bayertor, Landsberg's local history museum occupies an impressive seventeenth-century building erected by the Jesuits in the style of an Italian palazzo. Its displays span the area's history, from archeological finds to the lives of Landsberg's burghers and the interior of a nineteenth-century pharmacy.

Herkomer Museum and Mutterturm

Von Kühlmann Str. 2 • Herkomer Museum Tues–Fri 2–5pm, Sat & Sun 11am–5pm, Mutterturm Sun noon–5pm • €3.50, combined ticket with Historisches Rathaus & Neues Stadtmuseum €6

The **Herkomer Museum** and adjacent nineteenth-century **Mutterturm** on the west bank of the Lech together commemorate the life and work of the Anglo-German portrait painter Sir Hubert von Herkomer RA, whose studio the tower was. The museum has been undergoing renovation and is subject to closure during 2015.

ARRIVAL AND INFORMATION

By train Landsberg am Lech's Bahnhof is on the west side of the River Lech, a short walk from the Altstadt.
Destinations Augsburg (hourly; 53min); Munich (via Kaufering: every 30 min; 55min).

Tourist office Rathaus, Hauptplatz 152 (May–Oct Mon–Fri 9am–12.30pm & 1.30–6pm, Sat & Sun 10am–5pm; Nov–April Mon–Thurs 9am–noon & 2–5pm, Fri 9am–12.30pm; ☎ 08191 12 82 46, ⓦ landsberg.de).

ACCOMMODATION AND EATING

There are plenty of informal café stops for ice cream, cakes, snacks and simple meals in Landsberg's **Altstadt**, but nothing of any great culinary ambition, though there are several Italian places. You'll need to take a steep hike uphill to find the most interesting options.

Hotel Goggl Hubert von Kerkomer Str. 19–20 ☎ 08191 32 40, ⓦ hotelgoggl.de. Pleasant and very central family-run 3-star hotel just off Hauptplatz, with comfortable rooms with en-suite bath or shower and pretty junior suites with four-poster beds in rustic Bavarian style. There's also a sauna and on-site parking. €89

Gasthaus Süssbräu Alte Bergstr. 453 ☎ 08191 391 92, ⓦ suessbraeu.de. Family-owned for almost a century, this very traditional *Gasthof* close to the Bayertor serves rustic meaty dishes like calf's tongue with mushrooms, plus home-made cakes. Main courses from around €8. Mon–Thurs & Sat 8.30am–late, Sun 2pm–late.

Neu Landsberg Alte Bergstr. 436 ☎ 08191 305 98 49, ⓦ neu-landsberg.de. Innovative cooking with the likes of octopus and mango salad, or tandoori pork *sous vide* with black lentils, at this restaurant and bar close to the Bayertor. Set menu €35, mains from €13. Restaurant Tues–Fri 5pm–late, Sat & Sun from 11.30am–midnight; bar Thurs–Sat 10pm–3am.

Schafbräu Hinterer Anger 338 ☎ 08191 49 20, ⓦ schafbrau.de. Plain but spacious renovated rooms above a pizzeria in the Altstadt, with off-street parking and secure storage for bicycles and motorbikes. Breakfast is included, and in addition to the restaurant there's a beer garden in fine weather. €75

The Alps and eastern Bavaria

KLOSTER WELTENBURG

The Alps and eastern Bavaria

All the images that foreigners think most typically Bavarian accumulate in profusion in the region south of Munich, where "Mad" King Ludwig's palaces preside over dramatically scenic Alpine settings. Here, onion-domed church towers rise above brilliant green meadows, impossibly blue lakes fringe dark forests and the sparkling snow-capped peaks of the Bavarian Alps define the southern horizon. Villages are tourist-brochure quaint, while traditional *Tracht* is by no means the fancy dress it can sometimes seem in Munich. Politically and socially, this is Bavaria at its most Catholic and conservative, though sheer numbers of visitors nowadays add a certain cosmopolitan sheen, particularly to major resorts such as Füssen or Garmisch-Partenkirchen – Germany's highest, and most famous ski centre. A themed tourist road, the Deutsche Alpenstrasse (wdeutsche-alpenstrasse.de) links many of the region's most famous sights.

Eastern Bavaria could scarcely be more different: in place of a wall of mountains, it is defined by one of the great cultural and trading thoroughfares of Central Europe, the River Danube. Consequently its ancient cities – notably the perfectly preserved, former imperial free city of **Regensburg** and the prince-bishopric of **Passau** – bear the legacy of Rome and the influence of Italy with considerable grace, while even relatively modest towns such as **Straubing** and **Landshut** preserve architectural wonders from their distant golden ages.

Getting around the region is remarkably easy: Regensburg, Passau, Garmisch-Partenkirchen and the Berchtesgadener Land are all linked into the Autobahn network, while train services connect Munich with the major towns and reach into the Alps as far as Füssen, Garmisch-Partenkirchen and Berchtesgaden. Where train services end, buses take over, with services linking at least the most important tourist sites relatively frequently.

Füssen

The first – or last – stop on the Romantic Road (see box, p.310) is **FÜSSEN**, in a beautiful setting on the River Lech at the southwest end of the broad Forggensee hard by the Austrian border. The town is dominated by its Late-Gothic Schloss and by the impressive buildings of the former Benedictine abbey of St Mang, and is much the liveliest place in the district, with a compact Altstadt that fizzes with activity at any time of year. No mere tourist spot, Füssen is also a garrison town, home to a couple of battalions of the German army's mountain troops. With a direct rail connection from Munich, moreover, it's the most practical base from which to explore the royal castles at Hohenschwangau and other sights of the eastern Allgäu region, which straddles the modern Baden-Württemberg–Bavaria border. It likewise makes an ideal base for hikers and cyclists, with an extensive network of **walking and bike trails** fanning out into the surrounding district, including some that cross the border into Austria.

Tourist discount cards p.383	Gäubodenfest p.412
"Mad" King Ludwig II p.386	Regensburg orientation p.414
Outdoor activities in Chiemsee p.399	The Landshuter Hochzeit p.422
Danube boat trips p.409	

EAGLE'S NEST, BERCHTESGADEN

Highlights

❶ Mad Ludwig's palaces Enter the extravagant fantasy world of "Mad" King Ludwig II with a visit to his fairytale castle at Neuschwanstein, his Alpine villa at Linderhof or his sad, unfinished tribute to the Sun King, Herrenchiemsee. **See p.386, p.390 & p.400**

❷ The Wieskirche A vision of heaven inspired by a tearful statue of Christ, the Wieskirche is a masterpiece of Bavarian Rococo. **See p.388**

❸ Skiing at Garmisch-Partenkirchen Whether enjoying the views from the Zugspitze's high-altitude pistes or cutting a dash on the Kandahar run, skiing at Germany's biggest winter resort is a memorable experience. **See p.392**

❹ The Eagle's Nest, Berchtesgaden Hitler hardly used it, but you're sure to enjoy the breathtaking views from his famous mountain eyrie. **See p.406**

❺ Regensburg Gothic tower-houses are the distinctive feature of one of Central Europe's best-preserved medieval cities. **See p.414**

❻ The Donaudurchbruch at Kelheim Glorious scenery, impressive architecture and delicious beer on an exceptional stretch of the Danube. See **p.420**

HIGHLIGHTS ARE MARKED ON THE MAP ON P.382

Hohes Schloss

April–Oct Tues–Sun 11am–5pm; Nov–March Fri–Sun 1–4pm • €6, combined ticket with Museum der Stadt Füssen €7

Perched just high enough above Füssen's lively **Altstadt** to dominate the town from every angle, the white-walled, red-roofed, Late Gothic **Hohes Schloss** was rebuilt around 1500 as a summer residence for the bishops of Augsburg and the result is one of the most important Late Gothic castle complexes in Germany, with delightful Lüftmalerei wall paintings on the facades of the Innenhof, including numerous "oriel windows" which can be uncannily convincing when viewed from certain angles. There are also splendid views over the Altstadt.

The Schloss houses the **Staatsgalerie** – an outpost of the Bavarian state art collection showing fifteenth- and sixteenth-century paintings from Swabia and the Allgäu – and the **Städtische Galerie**, which concentrates on the turn-of-the-twentieth-century Munich School and the graphic works of the nineteenth-century artist Franz Graf von Pocci. Highlight of the interior is the Rittersaal, or Knights' Hall, with its magnificent coffered wooden ceiling; as part of your visit you can climb the castle clock tower for the views.

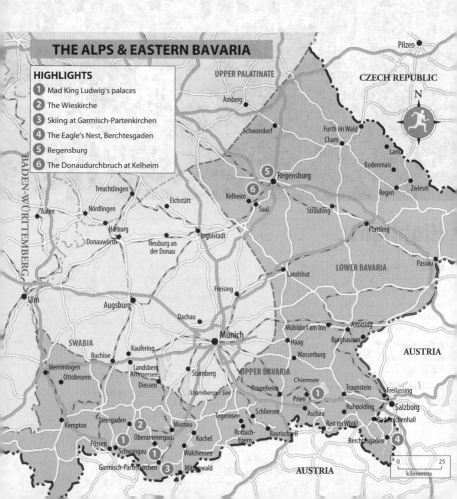

TOURIST DISCOUNT CARDS

If you're intending to visit many tourist attractions in the region south of Munich it may be worth considering the **Oberbayern card** (W oberbayern-card.eu), which for €29.90 for 48 hours, €41 for three selected days in a fourteen-day period or €59.90 for six days in a year, offers free or reduced-price entry to museums and spa facilities plus free (but not unlimited) travel on certain cable cars and lake steamers. You can buy it at tourist offices or at some of the participating museums or cable car stations, though note that it's not valid in the Allgäu region to which Füssen belongs.

If you stay with a participating hotel in Füssen or the neighbouring village of Schwangau you'll receive a similar card free of charge, the **Königscard** (W koenigscard.com), whose benefits extend across the border into Austria.

Museum der Stadt Füssen

April–Oct Tues–Sun 11am–5pm; Nov–March Fri–Sun 1–4pm • €6, combined ticket with Hohes Schloss €7

Competing with the Hohes Schloss for dominance, high above the River Lech, the Baroque buildings of the former Benedictine abbey of **Kloster St Mang** now house the **Museum der Stadt Füssen** in a series of rooms in high Bavarian Baroque style; particular highlights are the Kaisersaal (Emperors' Hall) and the abbey library. The museum's exhibits include numerous lutes and violins, which reflect Füssen's historic importance as a centre for the manufacture of musical instruments – a guild of lute-makers was founded here in the sixteenth century. The Baroque **Annakapelle** features the **Füssener Totentanz** (Dance of Death) mural, completed in 1602 at a time when the plague was raging in the district. The Baroque basilica of **St Mang** itself – now the town's parish church – rests on much older foundations, with tenth-century frescoes in the east crypt.

Tegelbergbahn

Daily 9am–5pm • €12.20 one-way, €19 return; ski day-pass €27 • W tegelbergbahn.de

A short distance to the east of town above Schwangau, the **Tegelbergbahn** cable car serves a long red **ski run** which in winter descends to the valley from the 1720m Tegelberg; there's also a ski school (see below). In summer the cable car gives access to extensive **hiking** and **climbing** in Bavaria's largest nature reserve, the **Ammergebirge**, as well as being a popular launch spot for **hang-gliding** and **paragliding** (see below).

ARRIVAL AND INFORMATION · FÜSSEN

By train Füssen's Bahnhof is just to the northwest of the Altstadt.

Destinations Augsburg (hourly; 1hr 50min); Munich (every 2hr; 2hr).

Tourist office Kaiser-Maximilian-Platz 1 (Mon–Fri 9am–5pm, Sat 10am–2pm; ☎ 08362 938 50, W fuessen .de). It can advise on walks in the area and will help with finding somewhere to stay, or you can search and book through its website.

Discount card The Füssen card is issued free to visitors staying within the town, and gives free use of local buses and of certain trains, reductions on entry to Füssen's museums and to Neuschwanstein and Hohenschwangau, and various other reductions on attractions and activities.

ACTIVITIES

Hang-gliding and paragliding Three hang-gliding and paragliding schools operate on the Tegelburg mountain: Flugschule Tegelberg (W abschweb.net); Flugschule Aktiv (W flugschule-aktiv.de); and Erste DAeC Gleitschirm Schule (W erste-daec-gleitschirm-schule.de). Courses start from around €250.

Ice-skating The Bundesleistungszentrum für Eishockey (Federal Ice Hockey Training Centre), west of the Altstadt along Kemptener Strasse, offers indoor public skating (daily 1.30–5pm; closed June & early July; €3.80) and disco skating (Mon 7–9pm; €4). National and junior teams use the centre for training, and the centre also hosts ice-hockey matches.

Skiing A ski school, Skischule-tegelberg (W skischule -tegelberg.de), offers lessons in downhill and Nordic skiing and snowboarding. Group courses cost €30/person/day; one-on-one tuition is €30/hour.

ACCOMMODATION

Camping Hopfensee Fischerbichl 17 ☎ 08362 91 77 10, ⓦ camping-hopfensee.com. The nearest campsite to Füssen is this well-equipped five-star site on the shores of a small lake to the north of the town. Pitch €14, plus €10.10 per adult

DJH Füssen Mariahilferstr. 5 ☎ 08362 77 54, ⓦ fuessen.jugendherberge.de. A 10min walk west of the Bahnhof, this hostel has accommodation in two- to six-bed rooms. Breakfast and linen are included and there is secure storage for bikes. Dorms €25.40

Hotel Hirsch Kaiser-Maximilian-Platz 7 ☎ 08362 939 80, ⓦ hotelfuessen.de. Very central, on the edge of the Altstadt and with lots of character, from the individually

designed rooms, some with quirky themes, to the restaurant and Bavarian-style *Bierstube*. €128

Old Kings Franziskanergasse 2 ☎ 08362 883 73 85, ⓦ oldkingshostel.com. Funky "design hostel" in the heart of the Altstadt, with three individually-themed doubles and two eight-bed dorms with shared shower and WC. There's also free wi-fi. Dorms €22, doubles €52

Via Hotel Sonne Prinzregentenplatz 1 ☎ 08362 80 00, ⓦ hotel-fuessen.de. Swanky and central, with stylish modern decor throughout and several categories of themed rooms, from small to very large, with en-suite facilities and internet access; some also have balconies. €135

EATING AND DRINKING

Eisenschmidt Augsburger Str. 4 ☎ 08362 94 14 55. Café/bar just north of the Altstadt, with Paulaner, König Ludwig and Thurn & Taxis beers plus a long menu of Italian and regional fare, plus salads. Pizza from €5.90. Mon–Fri

10am–2pm & 5pm–midnight, Sat 11am–2am, Sun 3pm–1am.

Gasthof Woaze Schrannenplatz 10 ☎ 08362 63 12, ⓦ woaze.de. Simple but hearty and affordable Bavarian

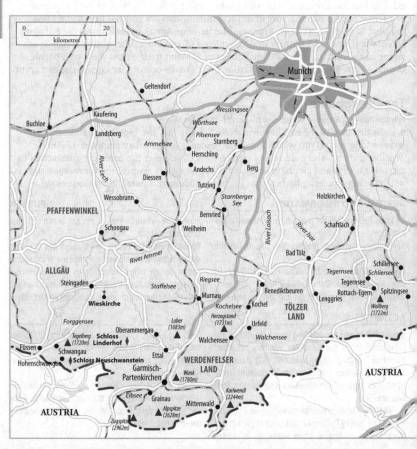

dishes – *Leberkäse, Schnitzel* and the like – plus Brauhaus Füssen beers in a rustic setting in the Altstadt. There's a *Biergarten* in the *Hof*, and a terrace out front in fine weather. Light snacks €5.90 and up, meaty mains from €12.90. Daily except Tues 10am–11pm.

Il Pescatore Franziskanergasse 13 ☎08362 92 43 43, ⓦilpescatore-fuessen.de. Traditional Italian restaurant in the Altstadt, with good-value home-made, fresh pasta and pizza from around €6–7, plus fish specialities. Daily except Wed 11.30am–2.30pm & 5.30–11.30pm.

Weisses Zimmer Kaiser-Maximilian-Platz 7 ☎08362 939 80, ⓦhotelfuessen.de. The *Hotel Hirsch*'s pretty, Alpine-style restaurant serves regional Allgäu cuisine, with simple fare like *Allgäuer Kässspatzen* with salad from €10 and venison goulash with home-made *Spätzle* for €14.90. There's also a €31.90 three-course seasonal menu. Daily 11.30am–2pm & 6–9.30pm.

Neuschwanstein and Hohenschwangau

The vision of the pinnacled and turreted castle of **Neuschwanstein**, perched high on its crag and rising above the mist, is perhaps the most reproduced of all tourist images of Germany, a Disney-like fantasy amid a setting of breathtaking Alpine beauty. Neuschwanstein is not the only royal castle at Hohenschwangau: if it weren't literally and figuratively overshadowed by Neuschwanstein, **Schloss Hohenschwangau**, in the valley below Ludwig's castle at the southern end of the village, might be more widely

7

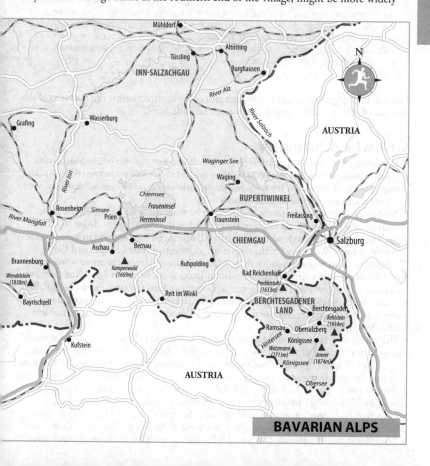

BAVARIAN ALPS

7

"MAD" KING LUDWIG II

For someone who was so shy and reclusive in life, **King Ludwig II** has achieved remarkable and lasting popularity in death. Born at Schloss Nymphenburg in 1845, he had spirited good looks not unlike those of his cousin, the Austrian Empress Elisabeth, and cut quite a dash when he came to the Bavarian throne in 1864 at the age of 18. Ludwig was fascinated with the French royal dynasty, the Bourbons, to which his own family was related. This developed into a fixation with the most illustrious of the Bourbons, Louis XIV, whose absolute power contrasted so starkly with the relative powerlessness of the Bavarian monarchy after its defeat alongside Austria in the 1866 war against Prussia. Seemingly overcompensating for this political impotence, the king retreated increasingly into an extravagant fantasy world, becoming steadily more eccentric and – towards the end of his life – rather corpulent.

He was a patron of Richard Wagner, whose fantastical operas fired the king's own vivid imagination, and though he disapproved of Wagner's anti-Semitism he continued to support the composer financially, even planning a lavish festival theatre to host the composer's operas in Munich, which was to remain unbuilt. A political reactionary but at the same time a romantic, Ludwig devoted his attention to fabulous but ruinously expensive projects to realize his fantasies in built form: a castle straight from the age of chivalry at **Neuschwanstein** (see below), a homage to the Sun King at **Herrenchiemsee** (see p.400) and an eclectic but breathtakingly opulent "villa" at **Linderhof** (see p.391). Eventually his spending caught up with him, as foreign banks threatened to foreclose. Ludwig's refusal to react to this crisis in rational fashion prompted the Bavarian government to act unconstitutionally, declaring him insane and removing him from the throne. He was interned at the castle of Berg on Starnberger See, where he and his doctor were discovered drowned in mysterious circumstances on June 13, 1886. Very shortly afterwards his palaces – which had been intensely private places during his life – were opened to the paying public.

---

famous. Completing Hohenschwangau's trio of royal attractions is the **Museum of the Bavarian Kings**, recently opened in a former lakeside hotel.

Schloss Neuschwanstein

Neuschwansteinstr. 20, Schwangau • Daily: April to mid-Oct 9am–6pm; mid-Oct to March 10am–4pm • €12, combined ticket with Schloss Hohenschwangau €23, combined ticket with Schloss Hohenschwangau & Museum of the Bavarian Kings €29.50; tickets can only be bought at the ticket centre at Alpseestr. 12 in Hohenschwangau village (ticket centre closes 5pm in summer, 3pm in winter); note that the ticket is for an obligatory guided tour • ⓦ neuschwanstein.de

If **Schloss Neuschwanstein** seems too good to be true, that's no surprise. The most theatrical of all "Mad" King Ludwig II's castles has its origins in his desire to rebuild an existing ruin in the style of the German Middle Ages. Ludwig was inspired by the recently restored Wartburg in Thuringia; his architects, Eduard Riedel and Georg Dollmann – who would go on to design Linderhof and Herrenchiemsee – worked from drawings by theatre designer Christian Jank. Work began in 1869, the castle was "topped out" in 1880 and the king was able to move into the (still unfinished) Pallas, or castle keep, in 1884. Ludwig chopped and changed the plans as he went along, incorporating a huge throne room that required modern steel-framed construction methods to make it viable.

The exterior of Neuschwanstein, in a sort of exaggerated Romanesque, is theatrical enough, but the real flights of fancy begin inside, where the decorative schemes are inspired by Wagner's operas *Tannhäuser* and *Lohengrin*. The Byzantine-style **Thronsaal** (Throne Room), inspired by the church of Hagia Sophia in Istanbul, was intended to represent the Grail Hall from *Parsifal* and was completed in the year of Ludwig's death, 1886. Ludwig's **bedroom** is in a heightened Gothic style, with the king's four-poster bed more closely resembling some fifteenth-century church altar than a place in which to sleep. The highlight – and peak of the king's Wagnerian obsession – however, is the **Sängersaal** (Singers' Hall), which occupies the entire fourth floor and was inspired by the famous hall at the Wartburg that was the scene of the Singers' Contest from *Tannhäuser*.

If you've not seen it on your way from the bus, it's worth strolling uphill to the **Marienbrücke** after the tour finishes for the dramatic views down into the Pöllat gorge and across to the castle.

Schloss Hohenschwangau

Alpseestr. 30, Schwangau • Daily: April to mid-Oct 8am–5.30pm; mid-Oct to March 9am–3.30pm • €12, combined ticket with Schloss Neuschwanstein €23, combined ticket with Schloss Neuschwanstein & Museum of the Bavarian Kings €29.50; tickets can only be bought at the ticket centre at Alpseestr. 12 in Hohenschwangau village (ticket centre closes 5pm in summer, 3pm in winter); note that the ticket is for an obligatory guided tour • ⓦ hohenschwangau.de

Standing on a low wooded hill above Alpsee, **Schloss Hohenschwangau** was a ruin when Ludwig's father, Maximilian II, bought it in 1832 while still crown prince, and had it rebuilt in a prettily romantic neo-Gothic style. Ludwig II spent much of his childhood here, and it was here that he first encountered the legend of *Lohengrin*, the Swan Knight; the Schloss is decorated with frescoes on the theme by Michael Neher and Lorenz Quaglio. Schloss Hohenschwangau still belongs to a Wittelsbach trust, not to the state of Bavaria, and part of its charm is that it feels altogether more homely than its showy neighbour.

Museum of the Bavarian Kings

Alpseestr. 27, Schwangau • Daily: April–Sept 9am–7pm; Oct–March 10am–4pm • €9.50, combined ticket with Schloss Neuschwanstein & Schloss Hohenschwangau €29.50; tickets can only be bought at the ticket centre at Alpseestr. 12 in Hohenschwangau village (ticket centre closes 5pm in summer, 3pm in winter) • ⓦ hohenschwangau.de

Occupying a former hotel on the edge of Alpsee, the **Museum of the Bavarian Kings** tells the story of the Wittelsbach dynasty – Bavaria's royal family – with particular focus on Maximilian II and his son Ludwig II, the builders respectively of Schloss Hohenschwangau and Schloss Neuschwanstein. You get to see Ludwig's unrealized plans for the Hohenschwangau area, and there's a section on the end of the monarchy in Bavaria and the fate of the ruling family in post-1945 West Germany.

ARRIVAL AND DEPARTURE

NEUSCHWANSTEIN AND HOHENSCHWANGAU

By bus The frequent OVG buses #73 or #78 connect Füssen's train station with Hohenschwangau village (8min); in summer, it is also served by the Europa Bus that travels the length of the Romantic Road in both directions (see p.310).

By car Arriving by car or motorbike, you'll get no further than Hohenschwangau village, where you'll have to pay for parking (€5/2 respectively).

From the village to Neuschwanstein If you don't fancy the stiff 30min uphill walk to Neuschwanstein, you can take the shuttle bus from *Schlosshotel Lisl* (€1.80 uphill, €1 down, €2.60 return) or go by horse-drawn carriage (€6 uphill, €3 down); the bus drops you by the Jugend lookout point by the Marienbrücke, from which it's a 600m walk downhill to the Schloss – a lot easier than the ascent on foot, but still scarcely suitable for anyone with limited mobility.

EATING

Schlossrestaurant Neuschwanstein Neuschwansteinstr. 17 ☎ 08362 811 10, ⓦ schlossrestaurant -neuschwanstein.de. Attractively situated high above the village, just down from the castle gates, this place serves pizza (from €7.10), light snacks (from around €6) and Bavarian regional specialities, with mains from around €10. You can also just stop by for coffee. Daily: summer 9am–6pm; winter 10am–5pm.

Steingaden

The Romantic Road reaches one of its highlights at **STEINGADEN**, which stands in rolling countryside 21km northeast of Füssen in the placid rural district known as the Pfaffenwinkel, or Clerics' Corner – so called because of its numerous churches and monasteries. In most respects it's a fairly modest country town, clustering around the **Welfenmünster** (daily: summer 8am–7pm; winter 8am–4pm; free), a handsome former abbey church that preserves its Romanesque exterior appearance and cloister but is otherwise flamboyantly Baroque. Fine though the Welfenmünster is, this is not the church that brings visitors from across the world to Steingaden. They come instead to see the **Wieskirche**, 5km southeast of town.

The Wieskirche

Wies, 5km from Steingaden • Daily: summer 8am–8pm; winter 8am–5pm • Free • ⓦ wieskirche.de

The **Wieskirche**, or meadow church, lies in the tiny hamlet of **Wies**. In 1738 farmer's wife Maria Lory spotted tears coming from the eyes of an abandoned figure of a scourged Christ; the site became a place of pilgrimage, and two years later a tiny chapel was built to accommodate the flow of pilgrims. Sheer visitor numbers soon overwhelmed it, however, and so the present church was begun in 1745 to the designs of Dominikus Zimmermann. It was consecrated in 1754.

Though the exterior is handsome enough, nothing prepares you for the overwhelming grace and beauty of the interior – a vision of a Rococo heaven in pastel shades, with ceiling frescoes by Dominikus's elder brother Johann Baptist, whose work also graces the monastery of Kloster Andechs and the Wittelsbachs' summer palace at Nymphenburg. The church is generally regarded as one of the pinnacles of the Rococo style, and it was added to UNESCO's World Heritage list in 1983. The church is busy with tour groups in summer, but it's a magical (if freezing cold) experience to visit in midwinter, when you might just have the place to yourself. In the summer months it is also the venue for evening concerts.

ARRIVAL AND INFORMATION

STEINGADEN

By bus Bus #9606 connects Füssen's train station with Steingaden (45min), before continuing to the Wieskirche and on to Oberammergau and Garmisch-Partenkirchen; in summer, the Wieskirche is also served by the Europa Bus service along the Romantic Road (see p.310).

On foot There are a couple of footpaths joining Steingaden to the Wieskirche, 5km away – the tourist office has details.

The round trip takes around 3hr on foot.

By bike You can rent mountain bikes and electric bikes from Ahornstr. 2 (ⓣ 08862 93196; from €8.50/half day).

Tourist office In the Rathaus at Krankenhausstr. 1 (Mon–Thurs 8am–noon & 2–5pm, Fri 8am–noon; during summer holidays also Fri 3–5pm & Sat 10am–noon; ⓣ 08862 200, ⓦ steingaden.de).

ACCOMMODATION AND EATING

There's a cluster of places to eat and drink around the Wieskirche, but little else; it makes more sense to stay in Steingaden at one of the hotel restaurants there.

Gasthof Graf Schongauer Str. 15 ⓣ 08862 246, ⓦ gasthof-graf.de. Rustic, traditional *Gasthof* with single, double, triple and four-bed guest rooms, a restaurant serving regional produce and a beer garden. **€60**

Gasthof zur Post Marktplatz 1 ⓣ 08862 203,

ⓦ zurpost.steingaden.de. Long-established, inexpensive *Gasthof* in the centre of Steingaden; rooms have shared facilities. The restaurant specializes in game and fish: there's a €14.50 set menu and simple fare like *Leberkäs* from around €6.50 – plus there's a beer garden. Breakfast included. **€46**

Oberammergau

Nestling at the foot of the Ammergauer Alpen between the distinctive peaks of **Kofel** (1342m) and **Laber** (1684m), the highly photogenic village of **OBERAMMERGAU** has achieved international fame thanks to the **Passion Play**, which depicts the life of Jesus and is performed by local people every ten years in a purpose-built theatre; it will be performed again in 2020. It has its origins in a promise by the villagers in the seventeenth century to perform a play if God would spare them the effects of the plague, which was then ravaging the region. For the nine years in each decade between passion plays Oberammergau is busy with visitors who come to see its elaborately **frescoed houses** and to buy the **woodcarvings** in which its craftsmen specialize.

Passionstheater

Theaterstr. 16a • April–Oct Tues–Sun 10am–5pm • €6 combined ticket with Worlds behind Glass exhibition in the Pilatushaus & Oberammergau Museum • ⓦ passionstheater.de

You can visit the **Passionstheater** where the play is staged on a guided tour; in addition to seeing the impressive open-air stage, you'll get to see costumes and props from the last time the play was performed. The theatre doesn't sit empty between passion plays, but hosts drama and concerts.

The Pilatushaus

Ludwig-Thoma-Str. 10 • April–Oct Tues–Sun 1–6pm • Craft workshop free; Worlds behind Glass exhibition €6 combined ticket with Passionstheater & Oberammergau Museum

The artform of **Lüftmalerei**, or *trompe l'oeil* facade-painting, reaches a particularly refined level on the facade of the **Pilatushaus**, which was built between 1774 and 1775 and painted by Franz Seraph Zwinck. His work here is considered one of the masterpieces of South German *Lüftmalerei*. The ground floor houses a crafts workshop, while upstairs is **Welten hinter Glas** (Worlds behind Glass), an exhibition of glass paintings.

Oberammergau Museum

Dorfstr. 8 • April–Oct Tues–Sun 10am–5pm; mid-Feb to March Sat & Sun 10am–5pm • €6 combined ticket with Passionstheater & Pilatushaus • ⓦ lebende-werkstatt.de

Diagonally opposite the Pilatushaus is the **Oberammergau Museum**, where you can see more specimens of local woodcarving up close; the nine rooms on the first floor represent a "museum within a museum", reflecting how the museum appeared when it opened in 1910. The museum also hosts regular temporary exhibitions on themes of local artistic or historical interest.

Kolben Sesselbahn

Daily: hours vary with season, but summer generally Mon–Fri 10am–4.45pm, Sat & Sun 9am–5.45pm; winter 9am–4.30pm • €6.50 one-way, €10 return; ski day-pass €27; toboggan run €10 • ⓦ kolbensattel.de

Once you've drunk in the twee prettiness of Oberammergau's painted houses, the obvious thing to do is to don walking boots and ascend the **Kolben Sesselbahn**, a chairlift that ascends to 1276m immediately west of the village and gives access to the **Königssteig** hiking trail, which heads east below the ridge for roughly 5km towards the Kofel before descending to the valley south of Oberammergau, though there's also an easier path that descends to the valley from the **Kolbensattelhütte** at the top of the chairlift. There's also a summer **toboggan run**, which at 2.6km claims to be the world's longest. In winter, the downhill route becomes a long blue (easy) **ski** run.

Laber Bergbahn

Daily: winter 9am–4.30pm; summer 9am–5pm (June–Aug Thurs until 10pm) • €9 one-way, €14.50 return; ski day-pass €23 • ⓦ laber-bergbahn.de

On the eastern side of Oberammergau, the **Laber Bergbahn** ascends the 1684m Laber, from the summit of which a rugged trail descends rapidly to the eastern edge of

7

Oberammergau (about 7km); a somewhat easier but longer route meanders down via a small lake, **Soilasee** (about 11km). In winter, a black **ski** run – one of the steepest in Germany – takes the short route back down to Oberammergau.

ARRIVAL AND INFORMATION OBERAMMERGAU

By bus Direct bus #9606 links Garmisch-Partenkirchen with Oberammergau in around 40min. The same bus takes around 1hr 35 min to reach Oberammergau from Füssen.

By train If you're coming by train from Garmisch-Partenkirchen (1hr 14min), you'll need to change at Murnau.

Tourist office Eugen-Papst-Str. 9a (July to mid-Sept Mon–Fri 9am–6pm, Sat & Sun 9am–1pm; mid-Sept to Oct & mid-Dec to June Mon–Fri 9am–6pm, Sat 9am–noon; Nov to mid-Dec Mon–Fri 9am–6pm; hours vary during Advent; ☎08822 92 27 40, ⓦ ammergauer-alpen.de /oberammergau).

ACCOMMODATION AND EATING

DJH Oberammergau Malensteinweg 10 ☎08822 41 14, ⓦ oberammergau.jugendherberge.de. Oberammergau's newly-refurbished youth hostel is on the southwestern edge of the village, beneath the Kofel; accommodation is mainly in four- to six-bed dorms and facilities include a disco, table tennis and ski store room. Dorms **€24.90**

Hotel Alte Post Dorfstr. 19 ☎08822 91 00, ⓦ altepost .com. Long-established hotel in the centre of Oberammergau, with *Lüftmalerei* on the facade and wireless internet and satellite TV alongside the traditional charm. Its restaurant serves snacks, Allgäu specialities and meaty mains, with a good-value €13.50 three-course set menu of pasta, meat and daily fish specials; pasta and lighter dishes from around €6. Restaurant daily 11am–9pm. **€95**

Hotel Maximilian Ettaler Str. 5 ☎08822 94 87 40, ⓦ maximilian-oberammergau.de. Plush, family-run five-star hotel that mixes slick modernity with a few rustic Alpine touches. There's also an award-winning microbrewery, *Ammgergauer Maxbräu*, on the premises, with home-brewed beer, light "*Brotzeit*" snacks from €0.50 and meaty main courses for around €13 and up; decor is stylish and faux-rustic, and there's also a beer garden. Restaurant daily 11am–11pm; kitchen closes 10pm. **€203**

Theater Café Othmar-Weis-Str. 3 ☎08822 15 15, ⓦ theatercafe-oberammergau.de. Pretty restaurant, café and *Konditorei* close to the Passionstheater, open from breakfast but also serving full meals, including Bavarian and Italian specialities, with main courses from around €8.50; there's Bavarian beer and wine from the South Tyrol. Tues–Sun 10am–6pm.

Ettal and Schloss Linderhof

Slotted into a narrow gap in the mountains between Oberammergau and Oberau and, if possible, even more improbably pretty than Oberammergau, the tiny village of **ETTAL** is utterly dominated by its magnificent Benedictine abbey, **Kloster Ettal**. Tucked even further into the mountains midway between Ettal and the Austrian border is Ludwig II's opulent **Schloss Linderhof**.

Kloster Ettal

Ettal • Daily: summer 8am–7.45pm; winter 8am–6pm • Free • ⓦ abtei.kloster-ettal.de • Buses #9662 or #9606 take 10–20min to reach Ettal from Oberammergau

Originally founded in 1330, **Kloster Ettal** was rebuilt in its present, showily Baroque form between 1744 and 1753 by Joseph Schmuzer, who was required to replace the still-incomplete work of his fellow architect Enrico Zuccalli after the abbey and abbey church were devastated by fire in 1744. Despite the overwhelmingly Baroque appearance of his work, bits of the old church were incorporated into the present structure – you pass through a fourteenth-century Gothic portal on your way into the church. The domed interior is quite breathtaking, with frescoes by the Tyroleans Johann Jakob Zeiller and Martin Knoller. After you've admired the church, you can head to the abbey shop to stock up on carvings, candles, Ettaler beer and herbal Ettaler Kloster Liqueur.

Schloss Linderhof

Daily: April to mid-Oct 9am–6pm; mid-Oct to March 10am–4pm; park closed mid-Oct to March • €8.50 April to mid-Oct, €7.50 mid-Oct to March • ⓦ linderhof.de • Bus #9622 from Oberammergau takes around 30min

Tucked into a narrow valley some 11.5km west of Ettal, Ludwig II's **Schloss Linderhof** was originally a hunting lodge belonging to Ludwig's father Maximilian II. The palace was enlarged and re-clad between 1870 and 1878 by Georg Dollmann, who was later to design Schloss Herrenchiemsee. Unlike that palace, Linderhof was actually completed during Ludwig's lifetime. It looks relatively modest from the outside, but the elaborate neo-Rococo interiors are anything but: the riot of gold leaf reaches a crescendo in the king's staggeringly ornate bedroom, which is the largest room in the house.

The **park** surrounding the Schloss is delightful, and is particularly known for its **fountains**, which perform every half-hour from April to mid-October. There are several highly theatrical follies in the grounds, including the **Maurische Kiosk** (Moorish kiosk) and the spectacular **Venus-Grotte**, an artificial cave with a lake, fake stalactites and stalagmites, and a golden barge with Cupid as a figurehead – all inspired by Wagner's opera, *Tannhäuser*.

7

Garmisch-Partenkirchen and around

As the hyphen in its name suggests, the chic skiing resort of **GARMISCH-PARTENKIRCHEN** was originally not one Alpine village but two, which faced each other across the Partnach stream and were united in a shotgun wedding in time for the 1936 Winter Olympics. The Games were an enormous success – so much so that the town was slated to host the 1940 Winter Games after the Japanese city of Sapporo withdrew. In the event, of course, war intervened and the 1940 Games didn't take place, but Garmisch-Partenkirchen has been on the international winter-sports map ever since, which gives the resort a relatively cosmopolitan air. Though any clear distinction between Garmisch and Partenkirchen has long since vanished, the two halves of the town do have sharply contrasting characters: Garmisch is lively and international, while Partenkirchen better preserves its original Alpine charm. Looming over them both is the **Zugspitze**, at 2962m Germany's highest mountain. In summer, the town's mountainous setting attracts hikers and climbers.

Garmisch

Curving around the southern side of its neat **Kurpark**, the centre of **Garmisch** has the bustling air of an international resort, with plenty of places to eat and drink and a **casino** at Am Kurpark 10 (Mon–Thurs & Sun 3pm–2am, Fri & Sat 3pm–3am; French and American roulette from €1, blackjack from €5). The old part of the village clusters around the onion-domed eighteenth-century parish church of **St Martin** west of the Kurpark. It has a Rococo pulpit by the Tyrolean artist Franz Hosp. To the north across the Loisach stream is the **Museum Aschenbrenner**, Loisachstr. 44 (Tues–Sun 11am–5pm; €3.50), a collection of dolls, French and German porcelain and nativity scenes.

Garmisch is also home to the **Olympia Eissportzentrum**, at the southern end of Olympiastrasse at Am Eisstadion 1 (Olympic Ice Sport Centre: early July to April daily 11am–4pm & 8–10pm; €4.50). In addition to staging ice-hockey tournaments, concerts and the like, it has indoor and outdoor skating rinks.

Partenkirchen

Partenkirchen is less lively than Garmisch but better preserves a sense of history, with an attractive main street, Ludwigstrasse, along which you'll see some eye-catching examples of *Lüftmalerei*. Opposite the parish church is the **Werdenfels Museum**, Ludwigstr. 47 (Tues–Sun 10am–5pm; €2.50), a folk museum with some beautiful examples of religious and folk art, from crucifixion scenes to paintings on glass and furniture. One room is devoted to the local Fastnacht, or Shrovetide customs. Nearby is the **Richard Strauss Institut**, Schnitzschulstr. 19 (Mon–Fri 10am–4pm; €3.50), with a multimedia exhibition devoted to the composer who lived in Garmisch-Partenkirchen and who died here in 1949.

Olympia-Skistadion and Skisprungschanze

Guided tours of Skisprungschanze Wed 6pm & Sat 3pm • €10

At the southern end of Partenkirchen is the **Olympia-Skistadion**, a U-shaped stadium in characteristically self-important Nazi style, rebuilt in this more bombastic form after the 1936 Games, and focused on the **Skisprungschanze** or ski jump, which in 2007 replaced the one from which the traditional New Year's Ski Jump had taken place. The new jump is illuminated at night and is much the most dramatic and impressive landmark in town.

The Partnachklamm

Daily: May, June & Oct 8am–6pm; July–Sept 8am–7pm; Nov–April 9am–6pm • €3.50 • ⓦ partnachklamm.eu

Close by the Olympia-Skistadion is the **Partnackklamm**, a narrow 700m-long Alpine gorge with waterfalls and wild rapids. It's particularly spectacular in winter, when the waterfalls freeze into bizarre shapes. The gorge is a 25-minute walk from the Olympia-Skistadion car park, or you can hitch a ride in a horse-drawn carriage.

The Zugspitze massif

Zugspitzbahn Daily 8.15am–2.15pm; every 1hr • **Eibseeseilbahn** Daily 8am–4.45pm; every 30min • **Gletscherbahn** Operates when Zugspitzbahn and Eibseeseilbahn are running • Zugspitze combined ticket €29.50 one-way, €51 return; Zugspitzplatt ski day-pass including ascent €41.50 • ⓦ zugspitze.de • **Tiroler Zugspitzbahn** Daily 8.40am–4.40pm • €39 return • ⓦ zugspitze.at

To get to the top of the **Zugspitze**, Germany's highest peak (2962m), take the **Zugspitzbahn** cogwheel railway from the Bahnhof Zugspitzbahn alongside Garmisch-Partenkirchen's Hauptbahnhof at least as far as **Eibsee**, where you can either stay on the cog railway, or else transfer to the dramatic (and much faster) **Eibseeseilbahn** cable car, which ascends nearly 2000m to the summit in ten minutes. If you stick with the train, you're deposited on the Schneefern glacier on the **Zugspitzplatt** plateau below the peak, from where you complete the journey to the summit on the ultramodern **Gletscherbahn** cable car. At the summit, there's a second cable car station – the top of the **Tiroler Zugspitzbahn**, which ascends from the Austrian side.

From November to April the Zugspitzplatt offers Germany's highest **skiing**, with powder snow, a range of red and blue runs and spectacular views, extending in clear weather as far as Italy and Switzerland. For a brief period in midwinter you can also stay in an **igloo hotel** (see opposite). In summer, there is a limited selection of short **hikes**, including one which crosses the glacier to the Windloch observation point, from which you have good views of Ehrwald in Tyrol, 2000m below. The descent on foot to Garmisch-Partenkirchen is only for the fit, and takes seven to ten hours, though many choose to break the journey overnight at the *Reintalangerhütte* refuge operated by the German Alpine Association (ⓣ00821 708 97 43, ⓦreintal.de; dorms €12, doubles €25 per person, half-board €20 per person).

The Garmisch Classic

Alpspitzbahn Daily: March–June 8.30am–5pm; July–Sept 8am–5.30pm; Oct–Feb 8.30am–4.30pm • **Kreuzeckbahn** Daily: March–June 8.30am–4.30pm; July–Sept 8.30am–5.30pm; Oct 8.30am–5pm; Nov–Feb 8.30am–4.15pm • **Hausbergbahn** Ski season only: Daily: Nov–Feb 8.30am–4.15pm; March 8.30am–4.30pm • Garmisch Classic combined ticket €25 round trip; one-day ski pass €38.50 • ⓦ zugspitze.de

Three cable cars – the **Alpspitzbahn**, **Kreuzeckbahn** and **Hausbergbahn** – give access to a more extensive skiing area than the Zugspitze, the **Garmisch Classic** below the 2050m

Osterfelderkopf. Black and red runs predominate, including the famous **Kandahar** run, used for World Cup downhill races. In summer the Garmisch Classic is hiking and mountaineering terrain, with two challenging climbers' routes – the Ferrata trail and Nordwandsteig – ascending the 2628m **Alpspitze** from the Osterfelderkopf. An even tougher route, the Mauerläufersteig, was opened in 2009.

The Königshaus on the Schachen

Early June to early Oct daily guided tours 11am, 1pm, 2pm & 3pm • €4.50

The most remote and dramatically situated of all Ludwig II's residences is the little wooden **Königshaus** high on the **Schachenalpe** south of Garmisch-Partenkirchen close to the Austrian border. Built of wood in the style of a Swiss chalet, its modest exterior gives no clue to the *Thousand and One Nights* extravaganza of the opulent **Türkische Saal** (Turkish Hall) on the upper floor, though for once much of the rest of the living accommodation could actually be described as simple, with local *Zirbelholz* (Swiss pine) used for some of the furnishings.

The Königshaus can only be reached after a long and strenuous walk; the easiest approach is along the well-signposted 10km **Königsweg** from the car park by **Schloss Elmau**, midway between Garmisch-Partenkirchen and Mittenwald, though even this has steep stretches and ascends 850m. It is passable by mountain bike. A more strenuous 9km route ascends via the **Partnachklamm** gorge (see opposite) south of the Olympic ski stadium.

ARRIVAL AND INFORMATION
GARMISCH-PARTENKIRCHEN

By train Trains from Munich (hourly; 1hr 25min) arrive at Garmisch-Partenkirchen's Hauptbahnhof, which is slightly closer to the centre of Garmisch than it is to Partenkirchen, though both are within walking distance.

Tourist office Next to the Kongresshaus in Garmisch at Richard-Strauss-Platz 2 (mid-May to mid-Oct Mon–Sat 8am–6pm, Sun 10am–noon; mid-Oct to mid-May Mon–

Fri 9am–5pm, Sat 9am–3pm; ☎08821 18 07 00, ⍟gapa .de); there's a second office at Rathausplatz 1 in Partenkirchen (Mon–Wed & Fri 8am–1pm, Thurs 8am–1pm & 2–5pm). They can provide information on walks, sell you walking maps, and have comprehensive lists of holiday flats and a number of bed-and-breakfast places. They can also direct you to several bike rental places.

ACCOMMODATION

Atlas Grand Hotel Ludwigstr. 49 ☎08821 936 30, ⍟www.atlas-grandhotel.com. Very handsome and historic 4-star hotel on Partenkirchen's main street, with 59 rooms and junior suites, a *Lüftmalerei* facade and public spaces in a traditional style that lives up to the "grand" in the name. **€91**

DJH Garmisch-Partenkirchen Jochstr. 10 ☎08821 96 70 50, ⍟garmisch.jugendherberge.de. Garmisch's youth hostel is 3km north of town on the edge of the village of Burgrain, with accommodation in four- and six-bed dorms, and facilities for cyclists. Breakfast included. Dorms **€28.90**

★ **Gasthof Fraundorfer** Ludwigstr. 24 ☎08821 92 70, ⍟gasthof-fraundorfer.de. Very attractive, traditional *Gasthof* in Partenkirchen, with spectacular *Lüftmalerei* on the facade and pretty Alpine-style furniture in its cosy

rooms. There's also a restaurant serving Bavarian food. **€98**
Iglu Dorf Zugspitze ☎041 612 27 28, ⍟iglu-dorf.com. In the winter months you can stay in an igloo hotel high up on the Zugspitze; warm sleeping bags are provided, plus an evening meal and a whirlpool bath. **€109** per person

Riessersee Hotel Am Riess 5 ☎08821 75 80, ⍟riessersee.com. Swanky resort hotel in an idyllic location on a small lake 2km from town, with spa and fitness facilities, pool and well-equipped, comfortable rooms, including some suites. **€182**

Schachenhaus ☎0172 876 88 68, ⍟schachenhaus.de. Simple mountain guesthouse ideal for hikers and mountain bikers visiting the Königshaus (see above), though it's a three-and-a-half-hour trek from the road. There's also hearty, inexpensive food. Open June to mid-Oct. Dorms **€15**, doubles **€30**

EATING AND DRINKING

Garmisch is packed with places to eat and drink, from fast-food joints to proper **restaurants** and a superfluity of plush *Kaffee und Kuchen* stops; Partenkirchen's rustic **Gasthöfe** are less showy but arguably more charming. Many of the hotels also have good restaurants that are open to non-residents.

7

Alpenhof Am Kurpark 10 ☎08821 590 55, ⓦ restaurant-alpenhof.de. Bustling but snug and very central Garmisch steakhouse with a carnivore-friendly menu: rump steaks €19.50, T-bone €23.50, plus a few fish dishes. Three-course set menu €22.90. Daily 11am–11pm; kitchen closes 10pm.

Gasthof Fraundorfer Ludwigstr. 24 ☎08821 92 70, ⓦ gasthof-fraundorfer.de. *Schnitzels* from €12.90, plus Bavarian staples like *Schweinshaxen* and *Weisswurst* in the homely, rustic surroundings of one of Partenkirchen's most charming inns. Mon & Thurs–Sun 7am–midnight, Wed 5pm–midnight.

★**Konditorei Krönner** Achenfeldstr. 1 ☎08821 30 07, ⓦ kroenner.com. Garmisch's plushest café-*Konditorei*, with a chandelier-lit interior and a short menu of hot dishes including *Flammkuchen* and *Schnitzel* alongside the luscious cakes and coffee. They also serve breakfast (from €3.40). Mon–Sat 9am–6.30pm, Sun 9.30am–6.30pm.

Pavillon Café Richard-Strauss-Platz ☎08821 31 79, ⓦ adlwaerth.de. Bright, glassy café and restaurant at the entrance to the Kurpark, with a full and eclectic food menu of steaks, salads, *bruschette* and pasta; mains €8.50 and upwards. Daily 9am–9pm.

Peaches Marienplatz 17 ☎08821 187 27, ⓦ peaches.de. Brash, lively cocktail bar in the old part of Garmisch, in a complex which also includes a sports bar, pizzeria and the *Music Café* disco (€3 entry). Peaches Mon–Thurs & Sun 7pm–1am, Fri & Sat 7pm–3am; Sports Bar daily 10am–3am; Music Café Fri & Sat from 10pm.

Poststube Marienplatz 12 ☎08821 70 90, ⓦ atlas-posthotel.com. The snug, wood-panelled restaurant of the *Atlas Posthotel* is one of the loveliest settings for a meal in Garmisch. It serves Bavarian specialities from around €16.50, with cheaper pasta dishes from around €7 and steaks from €18.50, and there's a glazed terrace running the full width of the front of the building. Daily 11.30am–10pm.

Mittenwald and around

Goethe considered the sweetly pretty mountain resort of **MITTENWALD** to be a "living picturebook", and one look at the magnificent *Lüftmalerei* on Obermarkt's houses and the church tower and you're likely to agree. The town is famous for violin making, a trade brought here by local boy Matthias Klotz (1653–1743), who learned it on the other side of the Alps in Italy. The intriguing **Geigenbaumuseum Mittenwald**, Ballenhausgasse 3 (Tues–Sun 10/11am–4/5pm; €4.50), has many splendid examples of the local craftsmen's handiwork, from the Baroque to the present day.

The mountains around Mittewald offer skiing in winter and wonderful hiking in summer; a popular walk around Mittenwald is into the so-called **Leutschacher Geisterklamm**, a narrow gorge which lies largely within Austrian territory.

Karwendel

Karwendelbahn Daily: summer 9am–4.30pm; ski season (Dec–April) 9am–3.45pm • €24.50 return; ski pass €35 • ⓦ karwendelbahn.de

The 2244m **Karwendel** towers over Mittenwald and can be ascended via the dramatic **Karwendelbahn** cable car; at the top, there is an easy one-hour **Panoramarundweg**, a circular path around the summit, but the other trails are for experienced – and properly kitted out – hikers and climbers; for information on mountain guides contact the Mittenwalder Bergführer at Im Gries 16 (☎08823 926 96 66, ⓦ bergfuehrer-mittenwald .de). Most of the **Karwendelgebirge** massif actually lies across the border in the Austrian Tyrol. In winter, the Panoramarundweg remains open, and experienced skiers can enjoy the unprepared powder snow of the 7km **Dammkar Skiroute** – Germany's longest downhill ski run.

Skiparadies Kranzberg

Chairlift daily 9am–4.30pm • €8 return; ski pass €26.50 • ⓦ skiparadies-kranzberg.de

West of the town on the 1391m Hoher Kranzberg, the **Skiparadies Kranzberg** offers less challenging skiing than at the Dammkar: there are blue and red runs and just one black. The same lift gives access to the mountain for hikers in summer.

ARRIVAL AND INFORMATION

By train Frequent buses (30min) and hourly trains (21min) connect Garmisch-Partenkirchen to Mittenwald.

Tourist office Dammkarstr. 3 (summer Mon–Fri 8.30am–6pm, Sat 9am–noon, Sun 10am–noon; spring & autumn Mon–Fri 8.30am–5pm, Sat 9am–noon; winter

MITTENWALD

Mon–Fri 8.30am–5pm, Sat 9am–noon, Sun 10am–noon; ☎ 08823 339 81, ⓦ alpenwelt-karwendel.de), and can help find accommodation, which you can also search for and book through the tourist office website.

ACCOMMODATION

Alpenrose Obermarkt 1 ☎ 08823 927 00, ⓦ alpenrose -mittenwald.de. Prettily rustic, rather atmospheric *Gasthof* with lovely *Lüftmalerei* paintings on the facade, reasonably priced en-suite double rooms and some singles, triples and four-bed rooms. There's also a restaurant serving traditional Bavarian food. **€89**

DJH Mittenwald Buckelwiesen 7 ☎ 08823 17 01, ⓦ mittenwald.jugendherberge.de. Mittenwald's youth hostel lies 4km north of the village in a nature reserve, and has a climbing wall, bike store and sauna. Note that there's only one double room available, though there are family rooms with larger capacities. Breakfast included. Dorms or family rooms (per person) **€24.49**

Hotel Post Karwendelstr. 14 ☎ 08823 938 23 33, ⓦ posthotel-mittenwald.de. Rambling 4-star hotel with a choice of room styles from Jugendstil to country house or rustic; all have en-suite bath or shower and WC, and internet (for which there is a charge), and most have a balcony. There are three restaurants serving Bavarian fare. **€115**

Naturcampingplatz Isarhorn Am Horn 4 ☎ 08823 52 16, ⓦ camping-isarhorn.de. Mittenwald's campsite is 3km north of the village, with laundry facilities, a beer garden and in winter a drying room and ski storage. There's an 11m climbing tower on site. Open all year. Pitch **€9.50**, plus **€6.50** per person

EATING AND DRINKING

Haller Café Hochstr. 16 ☎ 08823 15 69, ⓦ cafe-haller .de. One of several *Kaffee und Kuchen* options, open for breakfasts, light snacks (from around €3.50) and a few heartier mains, as well as for cakes and ice cream; there's an outside terrace in summer. Daily 10am–6pm, or 10pm in fine weather June–Sept.

Markt Restaurant Dekan-Karl-Platz 21

☎ 08823 926 95 95, ⓦ das-marktrestaurant.de. Stylish gourmet restaurant with a rustic seventeenth-century stone cellar and, in summer, an outside terrace. The refined cooking includes dishes such as trout with green asparagus and lemon purée or pink-roast veal with celery cream, salt plums and broccoli. Mains €16–23. Tues–Sun noon– 2.30pm & 6–10pm.

Walchensee and Kochelsee

North of Mittenwald, the unequal twin lakes of **Walchensee and Kochelsee** are connected by a twisting, scenic pass across the narrow ridge of the **Kocheler Berge**. The 300m difference in altitude between the two has been used to generate electricity since 1924, and there's a visitor centre at the hydroelectric power station, **Erlebniskraftwerk Walchensee** (daily: May–Oct 9am–5pm; Nov–April 10am–4pm; free).

Walchensee

Walchensee is the bigger and higher of the two lakes, ringed by wooded mountains and with enough wind to ensure it's a popular spot for windsurfing and dinghy sailing in summer. At the northern end of Walchensee village, the **Herzogstandbahn** cable car (summer Mon–Fri 9am–5.15pm, Sat & Sun 9am–5.45pm; winter Sat & Sun 9am–4pm; €6.70 one-way, €11.50 return; ski day-pass €16.50; ⓦ herzogstandbahn.de) ascends the 1600m **Fahrenberg**, offering breathtaking lake and mountain vistas and access in summer to hiking trails and, in winter, to the red and black ski runs of the **Skigebiet Herzogstand**.

At the northern end of Walchensee, at Urfeld, the **Walchensee Museum** (June–Sept Thurs–Sun 10.30am–4.30pm; €6; ⓦ walchenseemuseum.de) exhibits three hundred graphic works by the German Impressionist Lovis Corinth, who lived and worked here between 1918 and 1925. There are also sections relating to the traditional culture of the Walchensee area.

Kochelsee

Kochelsee is altogether less wild than Walchensee, the mountains on its southern shore giving way to a gentle, pastoral landscape to the north. At the village of Kochel am See, the **Franz Marc Museum** (Tues–Sun: April–Oct 10am–6pm; Nov–March 10am–5pm; €8.50; ☏08851 92 48 80, ⓦfranz-marc-museum.de) houses a substantial collection of works by Franz Marc (1880–1916), a celebrated member of the Blaue Reiter group (see box, p.347), along with works by his contemporaries Paul Klee, August Macke, Wassily Kandinsky and Alexei von Jawlensky from the Etta and Otto Stangl collection, plus postwar German abstracts. The collection is regularly rotated, and there are temporary exhibitions. The museum restaurant, *Zum Blauen Reiter*, has views over the lake from its terrace.

Benediktbeuern

Guided tours April–June Tues, Thurs & Sat at 2.30pm, Sun 1pm & 2.30pm; July–Sept Mon–Sat 2.30pm, Sat & Sun 1pm & 2.30pm; Oct Tues, Thurs, Sat & Sun 2.30pm; Nov–March Sat & Sun 2.30pm • €4 • ⓦ kloster-benediktbeuern.de

The gentle terrain north of Kochelsee is the setting for the onion-domed Baroque abbey of **Benediktbeuern**. Founded in 725 AD, the abbey was rebuilt in its present form in the late seventeenth century. The *Carmina Burana* manuscripts – a series of thirteenth-century verses – were discovered in the library here when the abbey was secularized in 1803.

ARRIVAL AND INFORMATION WALCHENSEE AND KOCHELSEE

By train Regular trains run from Munich to Kochel am See (1hr 9min).

By bus Bus #9608 links Garmisch and Mittenwald with Walchensee and Kochelsee.

Tourist office The Walchensee office is at Ringstr. 1 (May, June, Sept & Oct Mon–Fri 9am–noon & 1–5pm; July & Aug Mon–Fri 9am–noon & 1–5pm, Sat 9am–noon; Nov–April

Mon–Thurs 9am–noon & 1–4pm, Fri 9am–noon; ☏08858 411, ⓦwalchensee.de). The Kochel am See office is at Bahnhofstr. 23 (May, June & mid-Sept to Oct Mon–Fri 8.30am–noon & 1–5pm; July to mid-Sept Mon–Fri 8.30am–noon & 1–6pm, Sat 8.30am–noon; Nov–April Mon–Thurs 8.30am–noon & 1–4pm, Fri 8.30am–noon; ☏08851 338, ⓦkochel.de).

ACCOMMODATION AND EATING

Hotel-Gasthof Zur Post Schmied-von-Kochel-Platz 6, Kochel am See ☏08851 924 10, ⓦposthotel-kochel.de. Traditional, family-run *Gasthof* in the centre of Kochel, with *Lüftmalerei* on the facade, a rustic interior and a restaurant specializing in fish and game. Rooms have shower or bath and WC; most have balcony and some are wheelchair accessible. **€94**

Seehotel-Gasthof Einsiedl Einsiedl 1 ☏08858 90 10, ⓦhotelamwalchensee.de. In an idyllic setting on the southern shore of Walchensee; rooms have balcony, bath and WC, and the restaurant serves Bavarian dishes with a few Mediterranean touches. You can hire boats and bikes nearby. Closed Nov–March. Restaurant daily except Tues 11.30am–9pm. **€90**

Tegernsee

With its crystal waters dotted with boats, beautiful mountain backdrop and neat lakeside villages, **TEGERNSEE** – the terminus of a direct rail link with Munich – is a classic Alpine lake resort, with the obligatory cable car, the **Wallbergbahn** (summer daily 8.45am–5pm; winter 8.45am–4.30pm; one-way €10, return €18; ⓦwallbergbahn.de) ascending a handy mountain for views over the lake. It's a chic spot, its upmarket status buttressed by smart hotels and a brace of 18-hole **golf courses**, though it's also popular for **cycling**, with an annual mountain-biking festival in the late spring and a number of biking trails in the surrounding mountains.

The lake's obvious focus is the village of **Tegernsee** itself, which stretches along the eastern shore. Pride of place on the lakefront is taken by the **Strandbad Tegernsee**, a modern bathing complex that includes a beach, café, spa and sauna (Mon–Thurs

10am–11pm, Fri & Sat 10am–midnight, Sun 10am–9pm; from €13; ⑩monte-mare .de/tegernsee). There's also a more informal white-sand beach a ten-minute walk south of the village centre. **Boat hire** (€5 per person for 30min) is available from Rixner by the *Schloss-Café*, or you can take a **lake cruise** with the Schifffahrt Tegernsee, Seestr. 70a (Jan–March Sat & Sun 10am–5.30pm; April, Nov & Dec daily 10am–5.30pm; May–Oct daily 10am–7pm; various itineraries; departures approx. every 30min–1hr; €13.50; ⑩seenschifffahrt.de).

A little way back from the shore is **Schloss Tegernsee**, a former Benedictine abbey which is now the seat of the ducal line of the Wittelsbach dynasty; you can visit the former abbey church of **St Quirinus**, whose airy Baroque interior is enriched with frescoes by Georg Asam.

Olaf Gulbransson Museum

Im Kurgarten 5 • Tues–Sun 10am–5pm • €6 • ⑩ olaf-gulbransson-museum.de

Fringing Tegernsee's small **Kurgarten** is the delightful **Olaf Gulbransson Museum**, which displays graphic works by the Norwegian cartoonist of the same name, illustrator of the Munich magazine *Simplicissimus*. Gulbransson lived at Tegernsee from the 1920s until his death in 1958. The museum also mounts temporary exhibitions on cartoonists of international standing.

ARRIVAL AND INFORMATION   TEGERNSEE

By train Regular trains run from Munich to Tegernsee Bahnhof (every 30 min; 1hr 4min).

Tourist office Hauptstr. 2, Tegernsee (May–Oct Mon–Fri

8am–6pm, Sat & Sun 9am–2pm; Nov–April Mon–Fri 9am–5pm, Sat & Sun 10am–1pm & 2–4pm; ☎08022 18 01 40, ⑩tegernsee.de).

ACCOMMODATION AND EATING

DJH Kreuth-Scharling Hauptstr. 91, Kreuth am Tegernsee ☎08029 99 560, ⑩kreuth.jugendherberge .de; bus #9556 from Tegernsee Bahnhof. Tegernsee's renovated, family-oriented youth hostel is south of the lake between Rottach-Egern and Kreuth; accommodation is mainly in six-bed dorms. Breakfast included. Reception 8am–noon & 5–7pm. Dorms **€23.90**

Herzogliches Bräustüberl Tegernsee Schlossplatz 1 ☎08022 41 41, ⑩braustuberl.de. Bustling *Brauhaus* in the Schloss, with classic beer-hall food from pretzels or *Obatzda* (around €6) to *Schweinshaxen*, all at reasonable prices and all washed down with half-litres of the local Tegernsee beers. Mon–Thurs & Sun 9am–11.30pm, Fri

& Sat 9am–midnight.

Kreutzkamm am See Hauptstr. 45 ☎08022 271 92 78, ⑩shop.kreutzkamm.de. Posh lakefront outpost of the well-known Munich café and *Konditorei*, with luscious cakes, a few hot main courses (from around €9) at lunchtime and a Sun breakfast buffet for €14.50. Tues–Sun 9am–6pm.

Seehotel Luitpold Hauptstr. 42 ☎08022 187 79 70, ⑩seehotel-luitpold.de. Elegant boutique-style hotel in a renovated historic building on Tegernsee's lakefront. Rooms are furnished in a tasteful blend of traditional and modern styles, with Philippe Starck bathrooms and lake views; some rooms have four-poster beds. There's also a restaurant and bar. **€190**

Schliersee

Smaller and less developed than its neighbour, **Schliersee** has a similarly sublime mountain backdrop and clear waters, but where Tegernsee has a sophisticated air, in Schliersee cows graze in the centre of the village. Dominating the lakefront is the big, modern **Vitalwelt spa complex** (daily 10am–8pm; pool €5 for 2hr, *Tageskarte* €8; sauna from €12), which contains a pool, sauna, solarium, whirlpool and water slides. **Boats** of the Schlierseeschifffahrt depart the nearby landing stage for 45-minute cruises to the island of Wörth in the centre of the lake (May–Sept daily 11am–5pm; hourly; €6; ⑩schlierseeschifffahrt.de). On the eastern side of the village a **cable car** (daily: 8.30am–10pm; €5 one-way, €8 return) ascends to the 1061m **Schliersbergalm** for panoramic views over the lake; there's also minigolf and a summer toboggan run.

ARRIVAL AND INFORMATION

By bus Regular buses run from Tegernsee (7 daily; 36min).
By train Regular trains run from Munich (hourly; 50 min).
Tourist office In Vitalwelt at Perfallstr. 4 (Mon–Fri 8.30am–6pm, Sat & Sun 9am–1pm; ☎08026 606 50, ⓦschliersee.de). Accommodation – mostly in the form of holiday apartments – can be booked through the website.

EATING AND DRINKING

Hofhaus am See Mesnergasse 2 ☎08026 944 99, ⓦhofhaus-am-see.de. Traditional place just back from the lake shore, with Bavarian staples including lighter, snacky fare and fresh fish from the lake (from around €9); there's a pretty beer garden too. The 3-course *Tagesmenü* costs €14.95. Daily 9am–11pm; kitchen closes 9pm.

Wirtshaus im See Insel Wörth 1 ☎08026 929 95 88, ⓦwirtshaus-im-see.de. In an idyllic setting on an island in the lake, with a sunny terrace and a menu of baked potatoes (from €7.50), *Schnitzel*, fish and the like from €11–12, plus a €17.90 brunch menu on Sun. Daily Aug, otherwise opening times vary; closed Jan & Feb.

Bayrischzell

Nestling at the foot of the towering, 1838m Wendelstein, **Bayrischzell** is a modest huddle of wooden balconies and *Lüftmalerei* in a setting of breathtaking natural beauty. Though it feels wonderfully pristine and remote, it's easy enough to reach, since it's the terminus of the rail line from Schliersee.

The Wendelstein

Cable car May & Oct and late Nov to end April daily 9.15am–4pm; June–Sept 9.15am–5pm; closed Nov • €21 return, combined ticket with rack railway €30; ski day-pass €32 • **Rack railway** Daily 9am–3pm; closed Nov to mid-Dec; every 1hr • €31 return • **Cave** Daily May–Nov depending on weather • €2 • ⓦwendelsteinbahn.de

In the summer months the main visitor focus is the **Wendelstein** itself: you can ascend by cable car and descend by rack railway or vice versa, from Brannenburg, 20km northeast of Bayrischzell; a bus service links the two valley stations. At the top there's a radio station, observatory and a twenty-minute walk to the summit; once you've enjoyed the views you can visit Germany's highest consecrated church and its highest show cave. In the winter there's **skiing** on the Wendelstein, with a 5km red run descending to the cable-car station in the valley and a lengthy black run to the east.

Sudelfeld

Ski lifts Dec to early April daily 8.30am–4.30pm • Ski day-pass €29 • ⓦsudelfeld.de

Five kilometres from Bayrischzell and reached by free shuttle bus, **Sudelfeld** offers extensive **skiing**, with 21 lifts giving access to 31km of prepared pistes, mainly blue and red, but with four black runs. In summer, Sudelfeld is prime hiking country.

ARRIVAL AND INFORMATION

By bus Buses run from Schliersee (4 daily; 35min) and Tegernsee (4 daily; 1hr 15min).
By train Regular trains run from Munich (every 30min–1hr; 1hr 18min) and Schliersee (every 30min–1hr; 24min).
Tourist office Kirchplatz 2 (Mon–Fri 8am–noon & 1–5pm, Sat 8am–noon; ☎08023 648, ⓦbayrischzell.de).

ACCOMMODATION AND EATING

Alpenrose Schlierseer Str. 6 ☎08023 819 70 70, ⓦbayrischzell-alpenrose.de. Prettily traditional in style, with thirty individually-styled rooms, each with bath or shower and WC; some rooms have mountain views. The restaurant serves *Schnitzel*, fish and the like from around €9, and there are two outdoor terraces in summer. **€75**

DJH Bayrischzell-Sudelfeld Unteres Sudelfeld 9 ☎08023 675, ⓦsudelfeld.jugendherberge.de. Bayrischzell's youth hostel is in a fabulously scenic location close to the ski runs at Sudelfeld, with football and volleyball in the extensive grounds and, in winter, snow shoe and sledge hire. Breakfast included. There's a small supplement for guests over the age of 27. Dorms **€20.90**

Chiemsee and around

A shimmering expanse of silvery waters with a backdrop of distant Alps, **Chiemsee** is often referred to as the Bavarian Sea. Sheer size alone would justify the claim, for the lake covers eighty square kilometres and is tidal, but its origins also make the tag appropriate, for Chiemsee is a remnant of the primeval Thetis Sea which once covered half of Europe. In summer, it's a magnet for active tourism, notably sailing; in winter, much of the lake freezes over, particularly at the placid southern end. The lake's most famous attraction is Ludwig II's Schloss on the island of **Herrenchiemsee**, an extravagant (and unfinished) attempt to re-create the palace of Versailles in a Bavarian setting. The best place to stay for exploring Chiemsee is the spirited lakeside town of **Prien**; it's connected by rail to the mountain resort of **Aschau im Chiemgau** to the south, which makes an excellent base for hiking across the border into Austria.

Prien am Chiemsee

The liveliest town on the lake and its main transport hub, **PRIEN AM CHIEMSEE** is the obvious base from which to explore Chiemsee. The town itself is pleasant enough, if not of any great architectural interest. Its church has a prettily Baroque interior and the pastel pink, onion-domed Lourdes Grotte next to it, which serves as the town's war memorial, is a perfect Bavarian church in miniature. There's a very fancy beach, pool and sauna complex, **Prienavera**, right on the lakefront at Seestr. 120 (beach May–Sept daily 9am–8pm; pool Mon–Fri 10am–10pm, Sat & Sun 9am–10pm; pool from €9; ☎08051 60 95 70, ⓦprienavera.de).

ARRIVAL AND INFORMATION

PRIEN AM CHIEMSEE

By train Prien's Bahnhof is right in the centre of the town. A narrow-gauge steam railway, the Chiemseebahn (mid-May to early Sept daily; approx hourly; €3.70 return), links the town centre with Prien-Stock on the lakeshore.

By boat From the lakeshore you can embark on a lake steamer of the Chiemsee Schifffahrt (€8.50 return; ☎08051 60 90, ⓦchiemsee-schifffahrt.de), which connects Prien with Herreninsel all year round, though in winter sailings can be halted by ice on the lake.

Tourist office At Alte Rathausstr. 11 (May–Sept Mon–Fri 8.30am–6pm, Sat 8.30am–4pm; Oct–April Mon–Fri 8.30am–5pm; ☎08051 690 50, ⓦtourismus.prien.de).

OUTDOOR ACTIVITIES IN CHIEMSEE

The real reason to come to Prien is to get away from it, with plenty of options for exploring the lake area. Prien's tourist office also has information on many other **activities** in the region, from ballooning over the lake to Nordic walking, paragliding, rafting and canyoning.

CYCLING

From Prien, a cycle route – the **Chiemsee Uferweg** – circuits the lakeshore for 70km, sticking close to the shore and in many places passing suitable **bathing** spots. You can **rent bikes** from Radlverleih Chiemsee at Seestr. 104 (☎08051 96 47 89) or Fahrradhaus Prien, Hallwanger Str. 22 (☎08051 59 34). Numerous other cycle routes radiate from the shore of the lake into the surrounding countryside. From early June to early October, a hikers' and cyclists' bus (#9586) circuits the lake daily with a trailer to take bikes.

HIKING

A route for hikers, the **Priental-Weg**, links Prien with Aschau, and there's another relatively short hiking trail, the **Uferweg Chiemsee**, hugging the western shore of the lake to the north and south of Prien.

SAILING

If you want to learn to **sail**, head for the Segelschule Prien am Chiemsee, Noderwiechs 27a, Bruckmühl (☎08062 809 801, ⓦsegelschule-prien.de), which offers practical and theoretical sailing and motorboat courses, with prices starting at €95.

ACCOMMODATION AND EATING

Bayerischer Hof Bernauer Str. 3 ☎08051 60 30, ⓦbayerischerhof-prien.de. Comfortable 3-star hotel in the centre of Prien with rooms in three categories, each with bath or shower and free wireless internet, and some with balconies or terraces. Also has restaurant serving hearty Bavarian cooking. **€100**

Camping Hofbauer Bernauer Str. 110 ☎08051 41 36, ⓦcamping-prien-chiemsee.de. Campsite on the southern outskirts of town on the road to Bernau, with a snack bar and children's play area. Open April–Oct. **€13** per person

Fischer am See Harrasser Str. 145 ☎08051 907 60, ⓦfischeramsee.de. Regarded as one of the best fish restaurants in Germany, this elegantly traditional restaurant serves fish fresh from the lake and has its own smokehouse. Main courses cost from around €13. Daily 8.30am–11.30pm; closed Mon Oct–April.

König Ludwig Stub'n Seestr. 95 ☎08051 48 02. The Alpine-style *König Ludwig Stub'n*, 150m from the lakeside in Prien-Stock, has rustic, farmhouse-style rooms including some that sleep three or four, each with bath or shower and WC. Ground-floor rooms are wheelchair accessible, and there's a restaurant with traditional Bavarian dishes. **€116**

Kurcafé Heider Marktplatz 6 ⓦcafe-heider.de. You can stock up on cake, coffee and calories at *Kurcafé Heider*, close to the church, with a glassy winter garden and, in summer, an outside terrace. Tues–Sat 8am–6pm, Sun 8.30am–6pm; also Mon 11am–6pm in July & Aug.

Panoramacamping Harras Harrasser Str. 135 ☎08051 90 46 13, ⓦcamping-harras.de. Four-star campsite on a peninsula jutting into the lake, with restaurant and *Biergarten*, baby changing room and disabled-accessible washing facilities. Open April to early Nov. Pitch **€4.60**, plus **€5.90** per person

Herreninsel and Schloss Herrenchiemsee

Daily: April–Oct 9am–6pm, last tour 5pm; Nov–March 10am–4.45pm, last tour 3.40pm • €8, includes admission to König Ludwig II Museum & Augustiner Chorherrenstift; buy tickets at the cash desk close to the Herreninsel landing stage; note that the ticket is for an obligatory guided tour • Chiemsee Schifffahrt lake steamer from Prien (daily; €8.50 return; ☎08051 60 90, ⓦchiemsee-schifffahrt.de), then 20min walk from the landing stage or horse-drawn carriages (€3) in summer • ⓦherrenchiemsee.de

The largest of Chiemsee's islands, **HERRENINSEL** is also its greatest visitor magnet thanks to "Mad" King Ludwig II's splendidly deranged attempt to build a copy of the palace of Versailles on it. The result of Ludwig II's efforts is **Schloss Herrenchiemsee**. Construction began in 1878 to the plans of Georg Dollmann, but the Schloss was still unfinished upon the king's death in 1886, when construction abruptly stopped. The result is a tragi-comic testament to Ludwig's obsession with the French "Sun King" Louis XIV, whose image and fleur-de-lys motif are repeated in the Schloss's decor. The tour begins with bare brick, progresses through unimaginable opulence – including, of course, a 100m-long copy of the Hall of Mirrors – and encounters bare brick again on an unfinished staircase, the minimalist *yin* to the lavish main staircase's chandeliered *yang*. Ludwig only spent ten days here, and though the interiors have a festive look this was scarcely a festive place when he stayed. Famously misanthropic, the king was also afraid of the dark, and would stay awake by candlelight, retiring to bed during the day. Highlights of the tour include Ludwig's beautiful but ludicrous 60,000-litre bath, which took hours to fill.

The exhibits of the **König Ludwig II Museum** (same ticket) include a model of Gottfried Semper's theatre for Richard Wagner – which was never built – and fascinating images of the winter garden Ludwig had built atop the Residenz in Munich, complete with a lake on which floated a royal barge. At the end, it's hard to escape the conclusion that "Extravagant" would have been a more accurate description of him than "Mad".

Augustiner Chorherrenstift

Daily: April–Oct 9am–6pm; Nov–March 10am–4.45pm; art gallery closed Nov–March

Your ticket to the Schloss also admits you to the Baroque **Augustiner Chorherrenstift**, which boasts a splendid Kaisersaal with *trompe l'oeil* frescoes and a museum documenting the building's history, including a section on the meeting that laid the basis for West Germany's postwar constitution, which took place here in 1948. There's also an **art gallery** devoted to the works of the Munich Secessionist Julius Exter.

Fraueninsel

Lake steamers continue northeast from Herreninsel the short distance to the second largest of Chiemsee's islands, **FRAUENINSEL**. Much smaller and more built-up than its neighbour – it measures just twelve hectares yet has 250 inhabitants – its attractions are also more low-key. Dominating the island is the onion-domed campanile of the Benedictine nunnery of **Frauenwörth** (☎08054 90 70, ⌨frauenwoerth.de). Founded in the eighth century, the abbey can only be visited on guided tours booked in advance, though you can visit its shop, which sells liqueurs, *Lebkuchen* and marzipan. The island's **fishing village** is known for its smoked fish; more than any specific attraction, however, Fraueninsel appeals for its lake views and its traffic-free peace and quiet. From Fraueninsel, the lake steamers continue to **Gstadt** on the "mainland", which is less likely than Prien to be ice-bound in winter.

Aschau im Chiemgau

South of Prien, the land swiftly assumes an Alpine character as you approach **ASCHAU IM CHIEMGAU**, a large but rather scattered village that is a starting point for numerous **hiking trails** up the 1669m **Kampenwand** and beyond it to the 1813m Geigenstein to the south and across the border into Austria.

Kampenwandbahn

Daily: May, June & mid-Sept to Nov 9am–5pm; July to mid-Sept 9am–6pm; Christmas–April 9am–5pm • High season from €17.50 return, low season from €16 return; ski pass €27 • ⌨ kampenwand.de

A cable car, the **Kampenwandbahn**, ascends from the southern part of the village to the high-level trails and superb views over Chiemsee; in winter, the same cable car gives access to a limited network of blue, red and black **ski runs** and chairlifts which together offer the possibility of skiing all the way back down to the valley.

Schloss Hohenaschau

Schloss Hohenaschau Guided tours May–Oct Tues, Thurs & Sun 1.30pm & 3pm, Wed & Fri 10am & 11.30am • €5 • **Falconry demonstrations** Tues–Sun: April–Oct 3pm; July & Aug also 11am • €7

Opposite the valley station of the Kampenwandbahn, the impressive bulk of **Schloss Hohenaschau** crowns a small wooded hill. The former seat of the aristocratic Freyberg and Preysing families and of the Cramer-Klett industrial dynasty, the Schloss has been extensively restored in recent years. From April to October there are regular **falconry** demonstrations here.

ARRIVAL AND INFORMATION

ASCHAU IM CHIEMGAU

By train Trains run approximately hourly from Prien along the Chiemgaubahn branch line, taking just 15min to reach Aschau's Bahnhof.

Tourist office A short walk from the Bahnhof along Kampenwandstrasse at no. 38 (mid-May to mid-Oct Mon–Fri 8am–6pm, Sat 9am–noon; mid-Oct to mid-May Mon–Fri 8am–noon & 1.30–5pm; ☎08052 90 49 37, ⌨aschau .de). The office can help with finding rooms.

ACCOMMODATION AND EATING

Burghotel Aschau Kampenwandstr. 94 ☎08052 90 80, ⌨burghotel-aschau.de. Three-star hotel in a picturesque setting in the shadow of the Schloss. Rooms have bath, WC, cable TV, free wi-fi and minibar; many also have terrace or balcony. There's a restaurant, too. **€100**

Gasthof zum Baumbach Kampenwandstr. 75 ☎08052 14 81, ⌨zum-baumbach.de. Long-established and family-run *Gasthof* and restaurant at the foot of the Kampenwand. All of the rooms have shower and WC and some have balconies, for which you'll pay extra. Note that to get the best rates you'll need to stay three nights or more. Restaurant Tues–Sun 9am–midnight. **€68**

Residenz Heinz Winkler Kirchplatz 1 ☎08052 179 90, ⌨residenz-heinz-winkler.de. For a truly memorable meal, head for the *Residenz Heinz Winkler*, a renowned gourmet destination, with two Michelin stars and a menu of luxurious modern-European dishes with the occasional Asian influence. A five-course evening meal costs €155. Daily noon–2pm & 6.30–10pm.

7

Reit im Winkl

In a broad valley fringed by mountains and meadows that blaze with wild flowers in the spring, Reit im Winkl exudes wholesome Alpine charm, with a compact but picturesque centre of chalet-style buildings. Hard by the Austrian border, it's very much a centre for active holidays, from mountain biking, hiking or Nordic walking in summer to skiing in winter, when it has one of the best snow records in Germany.

Skimuseum

Schulweg 1 • Summer Tues & Thurs 3-6pm; winter Tues, Wed & Fri 2–5pm • Free

The first people to ski in the district some hundred years ago were foresters and Norwegian students; the **Skimuseum** takes up the story, with exhibits from the dawn of skiing history and skis from sporting "greats" including local Olympic heroine Rosi Mittermeier and the Austrian Toni Sailer.

Skigebiet Winklmoosalm

Winklmoosalm Late Nov to early April daily 8.30am–4.30pm • Ski day-pass for Winklmoosalm €26, with Steinplatte €43 • ⓦ winklmoosalm.de • Free buses from Reit im Winkl every 30min • **Chairlift** Summer daily in fine weather 9.30am–4pm • €12 return

The present-day focus for skiing is the **Skigebiet Winklmoosalm** to the east of town. The skiing is mostly blue or red, and descends from the 1860m Steinplatte on the Austrian side of the border; there's a gondola up from Waidring on the Austrian side. The area is prime walking country in summer; an old-fashioned chairlift from the Winklmoosalm ascends the Dürrnbachhorn on the German side, or you can ascend via the gondola on the Austrian side.

ARRIVAL AND INFORMATION

REIT IM WINKL

By bus From Prien (approx. hourly; 55min).

Tourist office Dorfstr. 38 (Mon–Fri 9am–noon & 2–5pm,

Sat & Sun 9am–noon; closes 6pm Mon–Fri July–Sept & at lunchtime in low season; ☏ 08640 800 27, ⓦ reitimwinkl.de).

ACCOMMODATION AND EATING

Alpengasthof-Hotel Winklmoosalm Dürrnbachhornweg 6 ☏ 08640 974 40, ⓦ winklmoosalm.com. In the thick of the hiking and skiing country, on a high plateau 1160m up. Rooms have balcony, bath or shower, minibar and safe, and singles are available; there's also a restaurant, with tables outside on a terrace in summer. Winter half-board only. **€72**

Unterwirt Kirchplatz 2 ☏ 08640 80 10, ⓦ unterwirt.de. Upmarket chalet-style hotel in the centre of the village, with decor that blends chic modernity with Alpine character. The en-suite rooms are comfortable, and there's a swimming pool, whirlpool, sauna and a restaurant using meat from the hotel's own butcher, with hot food from around €10. Daily 11.30am–2pm & 6–9pm. **€142**

Berchtesgadener Land

Shaped like a figure of eight and pushing south deep into Austria's Salzburger Land, the compact territory of **Berchtesgadener Land** contains some of Germany's loveliest Alpine scenery and, in the south, its third highest mountain, the 2713m **Watzmann**. Reached most easily via Austria and almost walled in by its mountains, the rugged southern part of the Land has the feel of a separate little country. For much of its history it was an independent bishopric growing fat on its precious salt deposits, in many ways a smaller version of its eastern neighbour, Salzburg; their ways only diverged after the 1803 secularization, with Salzburg ultimately passing to Austria and Berchtesgaden to Bavaria. The region attracted notoriety in the 1930s and 1940s as the preferred holiday-home (and putative last redoubt) of Adolf Hitler, whose "**Eagle's Nest**" has since become one of its most popular attractions.

In the summer months, the **Nationalpark Berchtesgaden** is a paradise for hikers and day-trippers alike; in winter, there's skiing on the **Jenner**, at **Rossfeld** and on the **Hirschkaser** west of Berchtesgaden, though at times the region's scenic beauty can be wreathed in dense, icy fog. The little town of **Berchtesgaden** is the natural focus of the Land; a second centre for visitors is the prim spa-town of **Bad Reichenhall** to the north.

Berchtesgaden

Capital of Berchtesgadener Land is the small town of **BERCHTESGADEN** itself, also known as Markt Berchtesgaden to distinguish it from the wider Land; deep eaves, chalet-style architecture and elaborate *Lüftmalerei* images give it a quaintly Alpine look, reinforced by the exhilarating mountain views available from much of the town. There's a pool and sauna complex, the **Watzmann Therme**, at Bergwerkstr. 54 (daily 10am–10pm; €10.50; Ⓦwatzmann-therme.de).

The Schloss

Schlossplatz 2 • Guided tours mid-May to mid-Oct Mon–Fri & Sun 10am–noon & 2–5pm; mid-Oct to mid-May Mon–Fri 11am & 2pm • €9.50 • Ⓦ schloss-berchtesgaden.de

Berchtesgaden's prevailing aura of twee rusticity is countered by the pink but imposing facade of its **Schloss**. Built on the site of an Augustinian monastery whose Romanesque cloisters it incorporates, the Schloss was for centuries the seat of Berchtesgaden's ecclesiastical rulers; after secularization it passed to the Bavarian royal family, the Wittelsbachs, whose residence it remains. The splendid Gotische Halle, which dates from around 1400, was once the monks' refectory and contains an outstanding collection of medieval sculpture, including altarpieces by Tilman Riemenschneider. There are also rooms in Renaissance, Empire and Biedermeier styles, in which artworks contemporary with the styles of the rooms are displayed.

The Stiftskirche and Arkadenbau

Next to the Schloss stands the twin-towered former Augustinian church, now the **Stiftskirche**, which was built between 1283 and 1303. Facing the church and Schloss across Schlossplatz is the long, arcaded **Arkadenbau**, whose facade paintings by Josef Hengge are the town's war memorial and include a very rare depiction in public of soldiers in the uniform of the old Wehrmacht.

The Salzbergwerk Berchtesgaden

Bergwerkstr. 83 **Salzzeitreise** Daily: May–Oct 9am–5pm; Nov–April 11.30am–3pm • €16 • Ⓦ salzzeitreise.de • **Salzheilstollen** Daily: office hours Mon–Fri 8.30am–4.30pm, Sat & Sun 30min before admission • €28 • ☎ 08652 97 95 35, Ⓦ salzheilstollen.com

To the northeast of the Schloss on the banks of the Berchtesgadener Ache is the **Salzbergwerk Berchtesgaden**, the salt mine that was the source of the town's wealth, now open to visitors as the **Salzzeitreise** ("Salt Time Journey"). The visit commences with a change into protective gear before you journey by train into the mountain; you then slide down a traditional miner's slide into the so-called salt cathedral before being ferried across an underground lake. There's also an underground saline **spa** facility, the **Salzheilstollen**.

The Haus der Berge

Hanielstr. 7 • Daily 9am–5pm • €4 • Ⓦ haus-der-berge.bayern.de

Opened in 2013 to replace the old National Park information centre, the **Haus der Berge** ("House of the Mountains") is a striking rust-coloured structure on Berchtesgaden's southwestern fringe. It incorporates a cinema, restaurant, library and education centre, but the primary attraction is the exhibition "Vertikale Wildnis", during which you ascend through the various ecosystems of the Bavarian Alps, from the depths of Königsee through woods and Alpine meadows to the Alpine peaks

7

themselves. The literal high point of the exhibition is a twelve-minute nature film projected onto a giant 11m by 15m screen.

ARRIVAL AND DEPARTURE BERCHTESGADEN

By train Berchtesgaden's oversized Hauptbahnhof – it dates from when this was a major resort for Nazi bigwigs – is in the valley below the Altstadt. From Munich change at Freilassing on the Austrian border (approx hourly; 2hr 42min), or at Salzburg onto bus #840 (hourly; 2hr 46min).

By bus Regular buses run from Bad Reichenhall (hourly; 40min).

INFORMATION

Regional tourist office Opposite the station at Königseer Str. 2 (June to mid-Oct Mon–Fri 8am–6pm, Sat 9am–5pm, Sun 9am–3pm; mid-Oct to May Mon–Fri 8.30am–5pm, Sat 9am–noon; ☎08652 96 70, ⓦberchtesgaden.com).

Municipal tourist office In the Kongresshaus, Maximilianstr. 9 (May–Oct & mid-Dec to end Jan Mon–Sat 9am–6pm, Sun 10am–1pm & 2–6pm; Nov to mid-Dec & Feb–April Mon–Fri 9am–5pm; ☎08652 944 53 00, ⓦberchtesgaden.de).

ACCOMMODATION

Berchtesgaden has been a resort for a long time, so there's plenty of accommodation, both in the town and scattered throughout the district. As well as hotels there are plenty of holiday apartments. Note that in Berchtesgaden you'll pay a small supplementary *Kurtaxe* in addition to the advertised room rate.

HOTELS AND APARTMENTS

Haus am Berg Am Brandholz 9 ☎08652 949 20, ⓦpension-hausamberg.de. Holiday apartments in a chalet-style house with mountain views on a hillside a 15min walk from the centre of town. All rooms have either terrace or balcony. Apartments **€55**

Hotel Wittelsbach Maximilianstr. 16 ☎08652 963 80, ⓦhotel-wittelsbach.com. Pleasant, rather old-fashioned 3-star hotel with elegant turn-of-the-twentieth-century resort-style architecture and spacious en-suite rooms, each with TV and minibar; some also have balconies. **€94**

InterContinental Berchtesgaden Resort Hintereck 1 ☎08652 975 50, ⓦberchtesgaden.intercontinental .com. Luxurious – and controversial – modern resort hotel in a spectacular location on the site of Göring's Obersalzberg holiday home, complete with on-site spa and a wide range of restaurants and bars. **€329**

Vier Jahreszeiten Maximilianstr. 20 ☎08652 95 20, ⓦhotel-vierjahreszeiten-berchtesgaden.de. Sprawling, atmospheric 3-star hotel close to the town centre. It has been in the hands of the same family since 1876, and the modern wings are more extensive than the compact central building. Spacious rooms are in an Alpine, but not over-rustic style. **€96**

CAMPSITES AND HOSTELS

DJH Berchtesgaden Struberberg 6 ☎08652 943 70, ⓦberchtesgaden.jugendherberge.de. Stylish and cyclist-friendly revamped hostel in the district of Strub west of the town centre, with a playing field, climbing wall and views of the Watzmann massif. Breakfast included. Dorms **€25.40**

Familiencamping Allweglehen Allweggasse 4 ☎08652 23 96, ⓦallweglehen.de. Five-star campsite with wi-fi, restaurant, swimming pool and mountain views. It stays open for caravans and camper vans in winter. Pitch **€10.95**, plus **€8.85** per adult

EATING AND DRINKING

Bier-Adam Marktplatz 22 ☎08652 23 90, ⓦbier -adam.de. There's a modern interpretation of *Lüftmalerei* on the outside, and affordable simple meals – *Leberkäse* (meatloaf) with fried egg, *Bratwurst* with potato salad – on the menu, alongside a few more elaborate dishes. From around €7. Daily 9am–11.30pm.

★ **Bräustüberl** Bräuhausstr. 13 ☎08652 97 67 24, ⓦbraeustueberl-berchtesgaden.de. Jolly, atmospheric place next to the Berchtesgadener Hofbräuhaus brewery downhill from the Altstadt, with light snacks and reasonably priced fish dishes, and Bavarian and Austrian specialities to accompany the excellent local beer. Light snacks from €2.40, mains from around €8. Open daily 11am–midnight.

Goldener Bär Weihnachtsschützenplatz 4 ☎08652 25 90, ⓦgasthof-goldener-baer.de. Old-established and rustic *Gaststätte* in the Altstadt, with quite an extensive menu, including breakfasts (until 11.30am), salads, snacks and more substantial *Schweinebraten* and *Zwiebelrostbraten*, from around €9. There are terraces front and back in fine weather. Daily 8am–10pm.

Martin Kruis Hofbäckerei Rathausplatz 2 ☎08652 20 04. Gourmet bakery and *Kaffee und Kuchen* spot, a little to the north of the Schloss and right opposite the Rathaus; they also sell home-made ice cream. Cakes from €2.35. Mon–Fri 6am–6.15pm, Sat 6am–12.15pm.

Königsee and around

Bayerische Seen-Schifffahrt boat trips late June to mid-Sept daily 8am–5.15pm; hours otherwise vary according to season • €13.90 return to St Bartholomä, €16.90 return to Salet • ⓦ seenschifffahrt.de • Bus #841 or #842 from Berchtesgaden

Around 4km south of Berchtesgaden, the scattered community of **SCHÖNAU AM KÖNIGSEE** is home to one of Germany's most dramatically beautiful (and most photographed) lakes, the eight-kilometre-long, fjord-like **Königsee**, whose wonderfully still, 190m-deep waters are the result of glacial action during the last Ice Age and are dominated by the sheer east wall of the **Watzmann** peak. Buses drop you at the car park a short way back from the north end of the lake, and you have to run the gauntlet of a rather tacky cluster of souvenir shops and snack stops to reach the landing stage, but once you board the electric-powered **boats** of the Bayerische Seen-Schifffahrt all thoughts of commercialism are left behind as the majestic scenery unfolds before you.

The most popular stopoff is the little onion-domed pilgrimage chapel of **St Bartholomä**, nestling on a peninsula at the foot of the Watzmann and reachable only by boat. It's an undeniably picturesque juxtaposition that is among the most photographed views in Germany. The former hunting lodge next door is now a *Gaststätte* (mains from around €10; ☎08652 96 49 37) serving *Schnitzels*, Bavarian specialities and fresh fish from the lake.

At **Salet** at the southern end of the lake a popular and relatively short walk brings you to a second, smaller lake, **Obersee**, beyond which is Germany's highest waterfall, the 400m **Röthbach-Wasserfall**.

Jenner

Jennerbahn Daily: June–Sept 9am–5pm; Oct–May 9am–4.30pm • €21.40 return to peak, €16.40 return to mid-station; ski pass €30.70 • ⓦ jennerbahn.de

If the Watzmann seems forbidding from the vantage point of the Königsee, the 1874m **Jenner** is altogether more approachable thanks to the **Jennerbahn** cable car at the eastern end of Jennerbahnstrasse. Located a short walk east of the bus stop and lake car-park, it gives access to high-level hiking trails in summer, and in winter to red and blue ski runs that allow you to ski all the way back down to the valley.

Obersalzberg and the Eagle's Nest

Though its mountain panoramas are as breathtaking as any in the German Alps, Nazi associations hang over **OBERSALZBERG** like an evil spell from some Grimm tale. Hitler knew and loved the scattered settlement 3km east of Berchtesgaden long before he came to power; after 1933 the new regime expropriated locals to turn the entire mountainside into a sprawling private fiefdom for Nazi bigwigs, many of whom had their holiday homes here. The most notable of these was Hitler's **Berghof**, bought and extended with the royalties from sales of *Mein Kampf*; the dictator invited diplomatic guests here – including British prime minister Neville Chamberlain at the time of the Sudetenland crisis in 1938 – to be overawed by the scenic setting and the magnificent panorama from its famous picture-window. As war progressed and Allied air raids on German cities underlined the vulnerability of the site to air attack, a vast system of bunkers was built beneath the mountainside, but in the event the feared "last stand" of the SS never happened here. British bombers destroyed much of the complex in 1945; afterwards, the ruins were largely demolished.

Dokumentation Obersalzberg

April–Oct daily 9am–5pm; Nov–March Tues–Sun 10am–3pm • €3 • ⓦ obersalzberg.de • Bus #838 from Berchtesgaden

Close to the site of the Berghof stands the **Dokumentation Obersalzberg**, a fascinating exhibition on the rise, fall and crimes of the Nazi movement, its mythology and its association with Obersalzberg. As you reach the latter stages of the exhibition, you descend into a decidedly spooky preserved section of the bunker complex, which was built from 1943 onwards.

7

The Eagle's Nest

Buses mid-May to Oct daily 7.40am–4pm • €16.10 return

Frequent buses depart from the terminus on the far side of the car park by the Dokumentation Obersalzberg, climbing the spectacular 6.5km **Kehlsteinstrasse** in the first stage of the ascent to Hitler's celebrated teahouse, the **Kehlsteinhaus**, or **Eagle's Nest** as it is known in English, which is preserved in more or less its original condition. The ascent is very much part of the experience: the narrow, twisting cobbled road – blasted from solid rock in just thirteen months in 1937 and 1938 – ascends 700m and passes through five tunnels. The buses make the journey at a cracking pace, so anyone prone to vertigo may want to sit on the side of the bus away from the view. You alight next to the tunnel leading to the lift which ascends through solid rock to the teahouse; before you enter, you have to decide which bus you're going to return on and get your ticket stamped accordingly.

The teahouse

Once you reach the teahouse itself – now a restaurant – how long you stay depends on the weather conditions: if it's clear, the views are genuinely breathtaking and it's worth wandering across the narrow summit for the views back to the building; if not, a quick glance at the photographic exhibition will suffice. The Kehlsteinstrasse and teahouse were commissioned by Martin Bormann as the Nazi party's fiftieth birthday present to Hitler using funds donated to the party by industrialists, but after an initial rush of enthusiasm in 1938 Hitler rarely visited, fearing lightning strikes and attack from the air. Eva Braun used it more frequently: since she didn't officially exist, she had to make herself scarce during diplomatic visits to the Berghof, and would come here to sunbathe.

The Obersalzberg cable car and the Carl-von-Linde Weg

Obersalzbergbahn Daily: summer 9am–5.30pm; winter 9.30am–4pm • €10 return • ⓦ obersalzbergbahn.de

If you seek a less historically troubling encounter with Obersalzberg's stunning panoramas, take the **Obersalzbergbahn** cable car from Berchtesgaden to the **Carl-von-Linde Weg**, a gentle 5.4km hiking trail that offers impressive views of Berchtesgaden, the Watzmann and the 1973m Untersberg on the border with Austria. You can follow the trail northeast from the cable car to reach the Dokumentation Obersalzberg.

The Rossfeld Panoramastrasse

Rossfeld Panoramastrasse Car and driver €5, each additional adult €2, child €1.30, motorbikes €4 • **Ski runs** Ski day-pass €18 • ⓦ rossfeldpanoramastrasse.de

Though the Kehlsteinstrasse up to the Eagle's Nest is open to buses only, you can take your own car or motorbike 1600m above sea level along the **Rossfeld Panoramastrasse**, a toll road which begins just east of the Obersalzberg bus station and is open all year round. Mountain views aside, the road offers a starting point for **hikes** to the 1692m Purtscheller Haus and to the Eagle's Nest; in winter, it gives access to Rossfeld's blue and red **ski** runs.

Bad Reichenhall

North of Berchtesgaden at the point where the Munich–Salzburg Autobahn crosses the narrow neck of Berchtesgadener Land is the conservative spa-town of **BAD REICHENHALL** with a neat, traffic-free centre and a diminutive old town tucked well away from the main tourist drag. The imposing old royal saltworks, the **Alte Saline** (May–Oct daily 10–11.30am & 2–4pm; Nov–April Tues–Fri 10am–11.30am & 2–4pm; 1st Sun in month 2–4pm; €8), is at the southern end of town, with a museum and mine workings to visit.

The Kurgarten

Kurgarten Daily: April–Oct 7am–10pm; Nov–March 7am–6pm • **Wandelhalle** April–Oct 7am–9.30pm; Nov–March 7am–5.30pm • Free

In comparison with the scenic splendour of its setting Bad Reichenhall's attractions can seem a little tame, but there's genuine turn-of-the-twentieth-century charm and elegance to be found in the diminutive **Kurgarten**, notably in the Jugendstil **Wandelhalle** with its free newspapers, saline spring and outsize chess boards, and in the bizarre **Gradierhaus**, a sort of giant, outdoor wooden air-filter or *Inhalatorium*.

The Rupertus Therme

Friedrich-Ebert-Allee 21 • Daily 9am–10pm • Day-ticket (pools) €21, sauna €28 • ⓦ rupertustherme.de

Bad Reichenhall's modern **spa complex** is on the north side of town close to the River Saalach, and has indoor and outdoor pools and saunas, steam baths, various health and beauty treatments, a restaurant, bar and café and a gym.

The Predigstuhl

Südtiroler Platz 1 • Daily: March–Oct 9am–5pm; Nov–Feb 9am–4pm • €21 return • ⓦ predigstuhlbahn.de

At the southern end of town, the **Predigstuhlbahn** ascends 1150m to the top of the 1614m **Predigstuhl**. The cable car dates from 1928 and is the world's oldest still in its original condition. At the top, there are impressive **views** north over Bad Reichenhall, and hiking trails head south into the **Lattengebirge** massif, a biosphere reserve.

ARRIVAL AND INFORMATION   BAD REICHENHALL

By bus Regular buses run from Berchtesgaden (hourly; 43min).

By train Regular trains run from Berchtesgaden (hourly; 28min).

Tourist office In the Kurgastzentrum on Wittelsbacher Strasse, a short walk from the Hauptbahnhof (April–Oct Mon–Fri 8.30am–5pm, Sat 9am–noon; Nov–March Mon–Fri 8.30am–4.30pm, Sat 9am–noon; ☎08651 60 60, ⓦ bad-reichenhall.de). The office can advise on accommodation, though there's no compelling reason to stay here rather than in Berchtesgaden.

EATING

Café Reber Ludwigstr. 10 ☎08651 600 30, ⓦ reber .com. *Café Reber* is famous for its *Genuine Reber Mozartkugeln* – a sort of chocolate-coated marzipan treat – much to the annoyance of confectioners across the border in Mozart's home town of Salzburg. There is also a big selection of coffees and cakes (from €2.70), and breakfasts from €3.95. Mon–Sat 9am–6pm, Sun 2–6pm.

★**Café Spieldiener** Salzburger Str. 5 ☎08651 3006. The best option for *Kaffee und Kuchen* in Bad Reichhall is this spacious and upmarket café-*Konditorei* opposite the Kurgarten. It also serves ice cream and light savoury dishes, with pasta or *Maultaschen* from €7.70. Mon–Wed & Fri–Sun 9.30am–6pm.

Along the Danube

Topography has determined the character of Eastern Bavaria every bit as much as the Alps have shaped the south of the state. A vast, uninterrupted belt of forested upland – the **Bayerischer Wald** or Bavarian Forest – guards Bavaria's eastern flank on the border with the Czech Republic. It's a sparsely populated and – compared with much of the rest of Bavaria – still relatively little-visited tract, which was for decades a sort of rural cul-de-sac running northwest to southeast along the Iron Curtain. In contrast, immediately to the west of the Bayerischer Wald, the valley of the Danube runs parallel to the border, and is one of the great natural trade routes of Central Europe. Strung out along it is a series of attractive small cities, each of which has known some glory in its past: **Regensburg**, the largest of them, is a former free imperial city with one of the best-preserved medieval cityscapes in Central Europe;

in the south, **Passau** is a former prince-bishopric with more than a touch of Italy in its monuments. Between the two, **Straubing** looks back to a distant golden age as the capital of a strange medieval duchy that straddled Bavaria and the Netherlands. Not to be forgotten is **Landshut** on the River Isar, the ancestral seat of the Wittelsbach dynasty.

Passau

With a memorable – and flood-prone – location on the Austrian border at the confluence of the rivers Inn, Ilz and Danube, **PASSAU** has a lively, cosmopolitan feel that quite belies its modest size. A city of just 50,000 inhabitants, it has nevertheless long been an important place. There was a Roman fort on the site from around 80 AD, a bishopric was founded here in 739 AD and this was raised to the status of an independent prince-bishopric in 1217, a status it retained for centuries until, secularized and annexed, it shared the fate of the other Bavarian prince-bishoprics at the start of the nineteenth century. Passau also rates a mention in the *Nibelungenlied* (see box, p.527), the epic poem that formed the basis for Wagner's *Ring*, as the heroine Kriemhild is welcomed to the city by her uncle Bishop Pilgrim. In June 2013 the city experienced its worst floods since 1501, but is bouncing back with vigour.

The Altstadt

Passau's long history of independence has left it with an impressive array of monuments gracing its **Altstadt**, which occupies a narrow wedge of land between the Inn and the Danube. There's a blend of Central European and Italian Baroque architectural influences similar to that other great ecclesiastical city-state, Salzburg, though here the ice-cream colours add a sunny, southern glow that not even Salzburg can match. Add to that a mighty, photogenic fortress and the buzz created by its university and the cruise ships that depart its **quays** for Vienna, Bratislava and Budapest, and Passau is well worth an overnight stop.

The most distinctive feature of Passau's Altstadt is its location on a tapering peninsula at the point where the Danube and Inn meet, and the best place to experience the drama of its situation is in the little park at the eastern tip of the peninsula – the **Dreiflüsseeck**. Almost tucked out of sight behind the fifteenth-century **Veste Niederhaus** – the lower part of Passau's massive medieval fortress complex – is the Ilz, very much the junior of the three rivers, which flows into the Danube from the north just before its confluence with the Inn.

Museum Moderner Kunst

Bräugasse 17 • Tues–Sun 10am–6pm • €5 • ⓦ mmk-passau.de

Tucked into a quiet street close to the Dreiflüsseeck, Passau's **Museum Moderner Kunst** is laid out over three floors of one of the Altstadt's most beautiful Gothic houses, and has a small permanent collection of works by the artist Georg Philipp Wörlen (1886–1954) and his circle, though this is often not on view as the museum also hosts surprisingly big-name international touring exhibitions of modern and contemporary art.

DANUBE BOAT TRIPS

In the summer months, the **tourist boats** of Wurm & Köck, Höllgasse 26 (☏ 0851 92 92 92, ⓦ donauschifffahrt.de), depart Passau's Danube quays on a variety of excursions long and short, from 45min sightseeing trips around the confluence of the three rivers to lengthier cruises downstream to Linz. The more luxurious Danube **cruise ships**, however, tend to be booked through travel agents.

Rathaus

Schrottgasse • Rathaussäle March–Oct & Dec daily 10am–4pm • €2

Passau's **Rathaus** fronts an open square facing the Danube, with the high-water mark from various catastrophic floods marked at the base of its neo-Gothic tower. A plaque commemorates the future Empress Elisabeth of Austria's last stop on Bavarian soil as she made her journey to marry Franz Josef of Austria; known as Sissi, she was born a Wittelsbach. The Rathaus itself is an amalgam of eight buildings of various ages that were united to form a more-or-less coherent whole in the nineteenth century, with the Saalbau on the eastern side dating from around 1400. It was one of many victims of a fire that devoured much of Passau in 1662. Among the results of the rebuilding work afterwards are the **Rathaussäle**, a pair of grand Baroque halls on the first floor that are reached via the entrance on Schrottgasse. The larger of the two is decorated with Ferdinand Wagner's 1890 paintings showing the triumphant entry of a rather plump, plain Kriemhild into the city.

Glasmuseum Passau

Rathausplatz 2 • Daily 9am–6pm • €7 • ⓦ glasmuseum.de

Incongruously housed in the *Wilder Mann Hotel* immediately to the west of the Rathaus is the **Glasmuseum Passau**, well worth visiting for its dizzying array of historic glass from ancient times to Jugendstil, Art Deco and beyond. There's a particular emphasis on the glassware of the Central European regions of Silesia and Bohemia.

Neue Residenz: the Domschatz und Diözesan-Museum

Residenzplatz • May–Oct Mon–Sat 10am–4pm • €2

A short stroll up Schrottgasse and into Schustergasse brings you to Residenzplatz, a small square dominated by the **Neue Residenz**, the residence of the prince-bishops, whose wide, early eighteenth-century Baroque facade is the work of Italian architects and conceals a beautiful Rococo staircase. The palace houses the ecclesiastical treasures of the **Domschatz und Diözesan-Museum** (Cathedral Treasury and Diocesan Museum).

Dom Sankt Stephan

Domplatz • Daily: summer 6.30am–7pm; winter 6.30am–6pm • Free

Immediately to the west of the Neue Residenz, the splendid copper-domed **Dom Sankt Stephan** stands on high ground at the centre of the Altstadt, its twin-towered west front dominating the patrician houses of **Domplatz** and betraying quite plainly the Italian origins of its design by Carlo Lurago. The cathedral owes its present appearance to the same 1662 fire that wrecked the Rathaus, though Lurago's design did incorporate surviving fragments of its Gothic predecessor. The interior is a fabulously opulent essay in rich Italian stuccowork by Giovanni Battista Carlone, with frescoed ceilings by Carpoforo Tencalla. It also boasts the largest cathedral organ in the world; there are regular organ recitals from May to October and again during the Advent season.

The square in front of the cathedral is the venue in December for one of southern Germany's classiest **Christmas markets** (ⓦ passauer-christkindlmarkt.de).

The Veste Oberhaus

Oberhaus 125 • Mid-March to mid-Nov Mon–Fri 9am–5pm, Sat & Sun 10am–6pm; Christmas–6 Jan daily 10am–4pm • €5 • Ascend the steps opposite the north end of the Luitpoldbrücke or take the shuttle bus from Rathausplatz, which departs every 30min

Dominating Passau from its hilltop site high above the north bank of the Danube, the **Veste Oberhaus** is one of the largest surviving medieval fortress complexes in Europe, begun shortly after Passau was raised to the status of a prince-bishopric in 1217 but considerably extended and modernized in the second half of the sixteenth century. It now houses the city's local history museum, divided into themed sections: **Faszination Mittelalter** ("Fascinating Middle Ages") delves into the medieval life of the castle; **Geheimnis der Bruderschaft** deals with the craftsmen's guilds; and the exhibition

Passau: Mythos und Geschichte ("Passau: Myth and History") explores the history of the city and surrounding region. The castle is also the venue for temporary exhibitions on themes relating to Passau. From the Veste Oberhaus's **Batterie Linde** there are stunning views over the Altstadt.

ARRIVAL AND INFORMATION   PASSAU

By train Passau's Hauptbahnhof is just west of the Altstadt on Bahnhofstrasse.

Destinations Munich (hourly; 2hr 20min); Regensburg (every 2hr; 1hr 3min).

Tourist offices Passau has two tourist offices (☎0851 95 59 80, ⓦtourismus.passau.de): one is directly opposite the train station at Bahnhofstr. 28 (Easter–Sept Mon–Fri 9am–noon & 12.30–5pm, Sat & Sun 10.30am–3.30pm; Oct–Easter Mon–Thurs 9am–noon & 12.30–5pm, Fri 9am–noon & 12.30–4pm, Sat & Sun 10.30am–3.30pm); and a second is at Rathausplatz 3 (Easter–Sept Mon–Fri 8.30am–6pm, Sat &

Sun 9am–4pm; Oct–Easter Mon–Thurs 8.30am–5pm, Fri 8.30am–4pm, Sat & Sun 10am–3pm).

Discount card The tourist offices sell the PassauCard (24hr €16, 48hr €25, 3 days €30; ⓦpassaucard.de), which includes free use of local buses, free entry to museums and reductions on attractions in the surrounding area and across the border in Upper Austria and the southern Czech Republic.

Bike rental Bikehaus Rent a Bike is at the Hauptbahnhof (March–Oct daily 9am–12.30pm & 3–6pm; ☎0151 12 83 42 24).

ACCOMMODATION

HOTELS AND PENSIONS

Altstadt Hotel Bräugasse 23–29 ☎0851 33 70, ⓦaltstadt-hotel.de. Right on the banks of the Danube in a quiet part of the Altstadt, with slick, modern public areas and 36 en-suite rooms with TV and minibar – many with a Danube view. **€80**

Deutscher Kaiser Bahnhofstr. 30 ☎0851 955 66 15, ⓦdeutscher-kaiser-passau.de. Comfortable and reasonably priced hotel *Garni* opposite the Hauptbahnhof and a short walk from the Altstadt, with parking for cars and bicycles. All rooms have cable TV; cheaper rooms share bathroom facilities. **€68**

★**Hotel Schloss Ort** Im Ort 11 ☎0851 340 72, ⓦhotel-schloss-ort.de. Romantically pretty rooms with four-poster or iron-framed beds and a wonderfully atmospheric location at the meeting of the Inn and Danube rivers make this a real charmer among Passau's hotels. **€97**

Pension Rössner Bräugasse 19 ☎0851 93 13 50, ⓦpension-roessner.de. Plain but comfortable en-suite rooms in a small pension in a quiet part of the Altstadt, close to the Museum Moderner Kunst, with a fitness room and breakfast on a veranda overlooking the Danube. **€60**

Weisser Hase Heiliggeistgasse 1 ☎0851 921 10,

ⓦweisser-hase.de. Plush, historic 4-star hotel in a great location at the western edge of the Altstadt. Rooms have bath or shower and WC, flat-screen TV and internet, though the style is rather bland and business-oriented. **€119**

Wilder Mann Am Rathausturm ☎0851 350 71, ⓦwilder-mann.com. Pretty, traditional painted furniture graces some of the en-suite rooms of this historic hotel close to the Danube riverfront, whose past guests include the Empress Elisabeth of Austria. **€88**

CAMPSITES AND HOSTELS

DJH Passau Veste Oberhaus 125 ☎0851 49 37 80, ⓦpassau.jugendherberge.de. In a very atmospheric location within the Veste Oberhaus fortress complex, high above the city; the hostel occupies the castle's former tavern. Accommodation is in four- to twelve-bed dorms, some of which have en-suite facilities. Breakfast included. Dorms **€23.40**

Zeltplatz Ilzstadt Halser Str. 34 ☎0851 414 57; bus #1, #2 or #4. The nearest campsite to town, a 15min walk from the Altstadt on the banks of the Ilz; no mobile homes allowed. Open April–Oct. **€9** per person

EATING AND DRINKING

Altes Bräuhaus Bräugasse 5 ☎0851 490 52 52, ⓦaltes-braeuhaus.de. Warren-like *Bierhaus* with vaulted ceilings, Austrian wines from Styria and the Wachau, and local Arcobräu beer, plus a menu of rustic, simple Bavarian food including lighter *Brotzeit* options – Bratwurst, Leberkäse with egg – from around €5. Daily 11am–1am.

Café Bar am Theater Untere Sand 2 ☎0851 25 90, ⓦcafe-aquarium.eu. Spacious café/bar next to the theatre, with breakfasts from €6.80, home-made cakes, panini from €4.20 and *Flammkuchen*. They also have

regular jazz nights. Daily 10am–late.

★**Café Museum** Bräugasse 17 ☎0851 966 68 88, ⓦcafe-museum.de. Classy café/bar in the vaulted space under the Museum Moderner Kunst, offering light food, home-made cakes, Austrian wines and a regular programme of live jazz. Tues & Sun 11am–6pm, Wed–Sat 11am–11pm.

Eiscafé La Veneziana Theresienstr. 4 ☎0851 317 73. Family-run Italian-style ice cream parlour serving the most delicious home-made ice cream in the Altstadt, plus coffee and cake. Two scoops in a cone €2. Feb–Oct Mon–Fri 9am–10pm, Sun 10am–10pm.

★**Heilig Geist Stiftsschenke** Heiliggeistgasse 4 ☎0851 26 07, ⓦstiftskeller-passau.de. Wood-panelled, Gothic-vaulted and very atmospheric old *Weinhaus*, with award-winning Bavarian cooking that includes the likes of *Tafelspitz* (boiled meat), *Schnitzel* or trout, with mains from around €10. Daily except Wed 10am–1am.

Ristorante Zi'Teresa Theresienstr. 26 ☎0851 21 38, ⓦzi-teresa.de. Affordable Italian restaurant in a pretty, vaulted setting. Pizzas from €6.70, a massive choice of pasta dishes from €6.30, plus steaks, salads and a €29 set menu. Mon–Thurs & Sun 11.30am–11.30pm, Fri & Sat 11.30am–midnight.

Scharfrichterhaus Milchgasse 2 ☎0851 359 00, ⓦscharfrichter-haus.de. Café and wine bar attached to an art-house cinema, with meat and veggie food (around €11), Austrian wines and regular jazz and cabaret, plus a pretty *Innenhof* for alfresco dining. Thurs–Sat 5pm–late.

ENTERTAINMENT

Theater im Fürstbischöfliche Opernhaus Gottfried-Schäffer-Str. 2–4 ☎0851 929 19 13, ⓦlandestheater-niederbayern.de. Passau's most prestigious venue for drama, classical music and opera.

Straubing

STRAUBING stands at the heart of the Gäuboden, a rich grain-producing district that stretches along the Danube midway between Passau and Regensburg. The Lower Bavarian town experienced a relatively brief but glorious heyday between 1353 and 1425 as the capital of the lesser, Bavarian portion of the eccentric independent Duchy of Straubing-Holland, the greater portion of whose territories lay in the present-day Netherlands. The architectural monuments of this period still preside over Neustadt, the planned medieval "new town" that replaced Straubing's original Altstadt as the main focus of the town.

Neustadt

The **Neustadt** is laid out on a grid pattern, with a broad east–west central square that reaches from one side to the other. At its western end it's known as Theresienplatz and is graced by a particularly fine Baroque column, the **Dreifaltigkeitssäule**, or Holy Trinity Column, erected in 1709 during the War of the Spanish Succession. The eastern half is known as **Ludwigsplatz**. The two halves meet at the **Stadtturm**, a 68m fire- and watchtower begun in 1316 and topped out with five copper-clad pinnacles in the sixteenth century. Next to it stands the step-gabled **Rathaus**, a Gothic trading hall bought by the town in 1382 and which still has its historic council chambers behind the present, neo-Gothic facade.

St Jakob

Looming over the Straubing skyline to the north is **St Jakob**, the most imposing of the town's medieval churches. The tall, brick Gothic hall-church was begun around 1395 and is regarded as a masterpiece of southern German, Gothic church architecture. It was the work of Hans von Burghausen, and there are similarities to St Martin in Landshut – also partly his work – including a soaring, slender brick tower and a relatively simple layout. Inside, there's a beautiful, Late Gothic high-altar, and an over-the-top Rococo pulpit that dates from 1752–53 and is the work of Wenzel Myrowsky and Mathias Obermayr.

GÄUBODENFEST

Straubing's biggest **festival** is the **Gäubodenfest** (ⓦvolksfest-straubing.de), which takes place over ten days in August and is Bavaria's second-biggest folk festival after the Oktoberfest, complete with beer tents, funfair rides and cultural events. It kicks off with a **procession**, in which brass brands and traditional peasant costume are much in evidence. Local hotels book out months in advance, so you'll need to plan ahead if you want to stay.

Gäubodenmuseum

Fraunhoferstrasse • Tues–Sun 10am–4pm • €4

In the northeast of Neustadt, the **Gäubodenmuseum** is Straubing's local history museum, the most remarkable part of which is the section housing the Roman treasures found during excavations in 1950. This is the most important find of Roman ceremonial armour anywhere; the horde includes pieces of armour for men and horses, and reflects Straubing's ancient status as the Roman military frontier outpost of Sorviodurum.

The Karmelitenkirche, Ursulinenkirche and Herzogsschloss

In the northeast corner of Neustadt two historic abbeys and their churches straddle Burggasse. The **Karmelitenkirche** is the work of Hans von Burghausen, but its Late Gothic exterior hides an exuberant Baroque interior by a member of the Dientzenhofer architectural dynasty. The far smaller **Ursulinenkirche** is more theatrical still, its compact interior the last joint work of the Asam brothers, completed in 1741 on the cusp of the transition from Baroque to Rococo. At the north end of Burggasse, the **Herzogsschloss** (Ducal Castle) dates from Straubing's fourteenth-century glory days and is impressive in its size and monumentality, though these days it's the home of various local government offices and has a rather institutional feel.

Alstadt

Straubing's original centre, **Altstadt**, is a short distance to the east of Neustadt, and is nowadays an odd mix of suburban blandness interspersed with historic monuments. Nevertheless, it's worth a visit to see the basilica and beautiful churchyard of **St Peter** at the eastern end of Petersgasse. The twin-towered Romanesque basilica is austerely handsome, and is set in a stunningly beautiful medieval graveyard, in which stand three imposing, Late Gothic **chapels**. One contains a red-sandstone monument to Agnes Bernauer, sweetheart of the future Duke Albrecht III, drowned in the Danube in 1435 on the orders of Albrecht's father Ernst, who did not consider the match suitable. Another contains eighteenth-century frescoes of the **Totentanz** (Dance of Death), by the Straubing artist Felix Hölzl.

ARRIVAL AND INFORMATION   STRAUBING

By train Direct trains from Passau reach Straubing's Bahnhof in just 45min, though it's usually necessary to change at Plattling, in which case journey time is around an hour. The station is a short walk south of Neustadt.

Tourist office Theresienplatz 2 (Mon–Wed & Fri 9am–5pm, Thurs 9am–6pm, Sat 10am–noon; ☎ 09421 94 43 07, ⓦ straubing.de) in the Rathaus.

ACCOMMODATION AND EATING

Campingplatz der Stadt Straubing Wundermühlweg 9 ☎ 09421 897 94, ⓦ campingplatzstraubing.de. Municipal campsite, on an island in the river north of Neustadt, with 74 pitches, a playing field and beer garden. Car, tent and two people €18.50

DJH Straubing Friedhofstr. 12 ☎ 09421 804 36, ⓦ jugendherberge.de. Straubing's youth hostel is a 15min walk east of Neustadt. Aside from a solitary double and two three-bed rooms, accommodation is in four- to eight-bed dorms. Facilities include table tennis and barbecue. Breakfast included; €4 supplement for over-27s. Open March–Oct. Dorms €17.20

Hotel Seethaler Theresienplatz 9 ☎ 09421 939 50, ⓦ hotel-seethaler.de. Comfortable, long-established and family-run 3-star hotel in the heart of Neustadt. Rooms have minibar, safe and cable TV. The

traditional-style restaurant serves GM-free versions of the Bavarian classics, with main courses around €12–14 and lighter fare including Bratwurst, Weisswurst and Leberkäse from around €4.40. Restaurant Tues–Sat 11.30am–2pm & 6–9.30pm. €105

Hotel Theresientor Theresienplatz 51 ☎ 09421 84 90, ⓦ hotel-theresientor.de. Striking, modern 4-star hotel on the edge of Neustadt's pedestrian zone, with a/c rooms with bath or shower, cable TV and free internet. There's underground parking adjacent to the hotel. €112

Wirtshaus Zum Geiss Theresienplatz 49 ☎ 09421 30 09 37. Good, hearty regional cooking in a historic step-gabled inn at the western end of Neustadt, with a few more sophisticated options alongside the Bratwurst and Schweinebraten; mains from around €8. Daily 11am–2pm & 5–10pm.

7

Regensburg and around

Spared from devastation in the twentieth century's wars, timeless **REGENSBURG** (Ratisbon in English, though the name is nowadays little used) preserves the appearance of an important medieval trading-city better than just about anywhere else in Central Europe. It's the only major medieval city in Germany to remain intact, and to a remarkable extent the Regensburg you see today preserves its fourteenth-century street layout and much of the architecture – secular and religious – that reflects how it must have looked during its medieval zenith. Straddling routes to Italy, Bohemia, Russia and Byzantium, Regensburg had trading links that stretched as far as the Silk Road. Trade brought cultural interchange too, and the mighty tower-houses of the city's medieval merchants – so reminiscent of Italy – are found nowhere else north of the Alps. No wonder UNESCO added the city to its list of World Heritage Sites in 2006.

Glorious though its architectural heritage may be, this vibrant city is no museum piece: its thousand or so historic monuments act as a backdrop for the thoroughly contemporary tastes and concerns of its modern citizens, who include large numbers of students. For visitors, Regensburg is a surprisingly multifaceted place, well worth a stay of a few days or so.

Brief history

Remarkably, the city is actually even older than it looks. The Romans founded a fort here as part of the empire's Limes, or military frontier, in the then-uninhabited region of Donaubogen in 80 AD; it was destroyed in an attack by Marcomanni tribes in 167 AD, only to be re-established as a legion fortress under the name Castra Regina on the site of the present-day Altstadt. As the western Roman Empire died in the fifth century AD, the Roman inhabitants were gradually replaced by Germanic settlers. Regensburg became a bishopric from 739 AD, and then a free imperial city in 1245.

The Dom

Domplatz 1 • Daily: April, May & Oct 6.30am–6pm; June–Sept 6.30am–7pm; Nov–March 6.30am–5pm • Free; guided tours daily at 2.30pm (also at 10.30am Mon–Sat April–Oct) • €4

The history of Regensburg's **Dom** is a familiar German tale of medieval artistic ambition thwarted, with the builders' original vision only fully realized after centuries of delay. Construction of the cathedral began in 1273 after fire ravaged its predecessor, of which the **Eselturm** or Ass's Tower on the north side survives. After 1285, an essentially French high-Gothic style was adopted. The three choirs were completed by around 1320, but apart from the cloisters, construction came to a halt around 1500 with the building incomplete, the twin west towers still lacking their spires. Baroque accretions of the seventeenth century were removed between 1828 and 1841 on the orders of Ludwig I; between 1859 and 1872 the medieval vision was finally completed with the addition of the spires – which somewhat resemble those of Cologne – transept gable and crossing flèche.

Despite its six-hundred-year construction history, the result is coherent and graceful, with ribbed vaulting soaring 32m above the nave. Among the artworks, the

---

REGENSBURG ORIENTATION

Finding your bearings in Regensburg is relatively simple. The **Altstadt** runs east–west along the south bank of the **Danube**. Within the Altstadt, the **mercantile** quarters of the medieval city are largely to the west of the **Dom**, while the **eastern** side of the Altstadt is both quieter and more ecclesiastical. The distinction between episcopal and mercantile Regensburg is remarkably sharp even to this day, and where the eastern Altstadt is placid to the point of colourlessness, the streets of the western Altstadt are bustling day and night. **Schloss St Emmeram** is on the south side of the Altstadt, beyond which a belt of parkland separates the old town from the **Hauptbahnhof**. To the north of the Alstadt, and linked by the **Steinerne Brücke**, is the **Stadtamhof** district on an island.

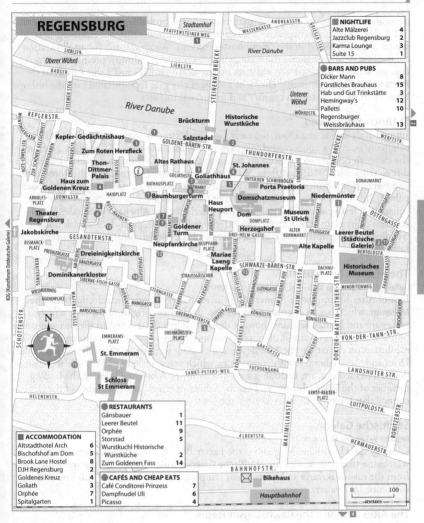

REGENSBURG

■ **NIGHTLIFE**
Alte Mälzerei	4
Jazzclub Regensburg	2
Karma Lounge	3
Suite 15	1

● **BARS AND PUBS**
Dicker Mann	8
Fürstliches Brauhaus	15
Hab und Gut Trinkstätte	3
Hemingway's	12
Palletti	10
Regensburger Weissbräuhaus	13

■ **ACCOMMODATION**
Altstadthotel Arch	6
Bischofshof am Dom	5
Brook Lane Hostel	8
DJH Regensburg	2
Goldenes Kreuz	4
Goliath	3
Orphée	7
Spitalgarten	1

● **RESTAURANTS**
Gänsbauer	1
Leerer Beutel	11
Orphée	9
Storstad	5
Wurstkuchl Historische Wurstküche	2
Zum Goldenen Fass	14

● **CAFÉS AND CHEAP EATS**
Café Conditorei Prinzess	7
Dampfnudel Uli	6
Picasso	4

0 — 100 metres

Annunciation Group on the west piers of the crossing stands out. It dates from around 1280 and is the work of the anonymous "Master of St Erminold"; the so-called **Smiling Angel** depicts Gabriel conveying the good news to Mary. Also of note are the five distinctive canopied Gothic altars, while the silver high-altar is a splendid example of Augsburg craftsmanship. Outside, the **west front** is richly decorated with **sculptures**, many of which relate to St Peter, to whom the cathedral is dedicated. The Dom's boys' choir, the famous **Domspatzen** or "Cathedral Sparrows", traces its origins to the school founded by Bishop Wolfgang in 975 AD.

Domschatzmuseum

Krauterermarkt 3 • Early Jan–March Fri & Sat 11am–5pm, Sun noon–5pm; April to early Jan Tues–Sat 11am–5pm, Sun noon–5pm • €3

Exit the Dom via the north transept to reach the **Domschatzmuseum** (Treasury Museum), whose star attraction is the **Emailkästchen**, a glittering reliquary chest decorated with enamel images of mythical creatures, probably made in France around 1400. The museum incorporates the beautiful sixteenth-century Schaumburg altar, which originally stood in the **Obermünster** convent. Watch out too for an illustration on the first floor that shows the cathedral's towers in their stumpy, pre-nineteenth-century state. If you leave the museum on the north side, it's just a short stroll to the **Porta Praetoria**, a substantial chunk of a Roman city gate incorporated into the bishops' brewery in the seventeenth century and uncovered in 1885.

St Ulrich and around

Immediately east of the Dom, the early Gothic thirteenth-century church of **St Ulrich**, originally built as a court chapel, displays a millennium's worth of Christian art from the eleventh century to the present; closed at the time of writing for refurbishment, it is due to reopen in 2016. East from St Ulrich fronting Alter Kornmarkt, the **Römerturm** and **Herzogshof**, built around 1200, are surviving parts of a Romanesque Wittelsbach palace. This is the site of the Roman fort of Castra Regina. On the south side of the square, the festive white-and-gold Rococo interior of the **Alte Kapelle** is a delightful contrast to its plain-Jane Carolingian exterior; unsurprisingly, it does a brisk trade in weddings. To the north, the Baroque interior of the **Niedermünster** is, in contrast, rather glum.

The Historisches Museum

Dachauplatz 2–4 • Tues–Sun 10am–4pm, • €5, free on 1st Sun of month

East of Alter Kornmarkt, a former Minorite monastery houses the eclectic **Historiches Museum**, which has an engrossing section on the Roman origins of the city; scorched tableware and human remains showing signs of violent death attest to the precariousness of life in this distant outpost of empire. The monastery's cloisters and church house an exhibition on the city in the Middle Ages, including sections on the construction of the Dom and the medieval Jewish community, which was expelled in 1519. The top floor is devoted to medieval art, including a room devoted to Albrecht Altdorfer, the leading member of the sixteenth-century Danube School of artists, and a member of the city council that took the decision to expel the Jews.

Städtische Galerie

Bertoldstr. 9 • Tues–Sun 10am–4pm • €5

Close by the Historiches Museum is the Leerer Beutel, a fifteenth-century grain warehouse that now houses the **Städtische Galerie**, which focuses on the work of artists from the east of Bavaria and hosts major temporary exhibitions. The building is also the venue for live jazz concerts.

The Altes Rathaus: the Reichstagsmuseum

Rathausplatz 1 • Reichstagsmuseum guided tours in English daily: April–Oct 3pm; Nov, Dec & March 2pm. In German daily: April–Oct every 30min 9.30am–noon & 1.30–4pm; Nov, Dec & March 10am, 11.30am, 1.30pm, 3pm & 3.30pm; Jan & Feb10am, 11.30am, 1.30pm, 3pm • €7.50

A secular counterweight to the Dom, the **Altes Rathaus** is the dominant landmark of the western, mercantile part of the Altstadt. The oldest part of the building is its 55m tower, but the most historically significant is the magnificent fourteenth-century Gothic Reichssaal, which was, from 1663 to 1806, the fixed venue for the imperial Diet or Reichstag; it can now be visited as part of the **Reichstagsmuseum**. There's also a prison and torture chamber in the basement.

The Goliathhaus and Goldener Turm

The western Altstadt is the liveliest and most rewarding part of the city in which to get creatively lost, though the area isn't wanting for landmarks either, with some particularly splendid medieval **tower houses**. The most impressive of these medieval skyscrapers is the **Goliathhaus**, built in the thirteenth century for the Thundorfer family but deriving its name for the much-retouched sixteenth-century fresco of the eponymous giant that looms over Goliathstrasse. Magnificent as it is, the Goliathhaus isn't the tallest of the towers: that honour goes to the nine-storey **Goldener Turm** on Wahlenstrasse.

Neupfarrplatz and around

Just south of the Goliathhaus is **Neupfarrplatz**, where the **Neupfarrkirche** replaced the destroyed medieval synagogue; immediately to the west, the white **Ort der Begegnung** (Place of Encounter) by Israeli artist Dani Karavan stands on the actual site of the synagogue, rediscovered in 1995. It outlines the shape of the synagogue, complete with low columns. On the north side of the Neupfarrkirche is the entrance to the subterranean **document Neupfarrplatz** (guided tours Thurs–Sat 2.30pm; July & Aug also Sun & Mon 2.30pm; €5), a slice of archeological life that embraces the remains of Roman officers' quarters, traces of the medieval Jewish quarter and a World War II air-raid bunker.

To the west of Neupfarrplatz on the corner of Am Ölberg and Gesandtenstrasse, the Lutheran **Dreieinigkeitskirche** has a simple but charming wooden balconied interior and a tall **tower** (April–Oct daily noon–6pm, longer hours during festivals; €2), worth the rather scary climb for the fine views over the city from the top.

The banks of the Danube

Picture-postcard views of the Altstadt are available from the twelfth-century **Steinerne Brücke** at the north end of Brückstrasse; it links the Altstadt to the district of **Stadtamhof** on an island on the north bank of the Danube. Before crossing the river it's worth stopping by the **Brückturm** (April–Oct daily 10am–7pm; €2), the last survivor of the bridge's watchtowers, which you can climb for yet more views. Before reaching Stadtamhof, the Steinerne Brücke crosses the narrow neck of the island of **Unterer Wöhrd** and the **Jahninsel**, which is the narrow, easternmost tip of the island of **Oberer Wöhrd**. Stadtamhof itself is pretty, with something of the air of a separate town, which is not altogether surprising, since for much of its history that's precisely what it was.

Back on the Altstadt side of the river at Keplerstr. 5, the **Kepler Gedächtnishaus** (Sat & Sun 10.30am–4pm; €2.20) commemorates Johannes Kepler (1571–1630), the celebrated astronomer and contemporary of Galileo, who died here.

Schloss St Emmeram

Emmeramsplatz 3 • **Interior and cloisters** Guided tours: April–Oct 90min tour daily at 10.30am, 12.30pm, 2.30pm & 4.30pm; shorter (55min) tour daily at 11.30am, 1.30pm and 3.30pm; Nov, Dec & Jan–March 90min tour Sat & Sun 10.30am, 1.30pm & 3.30pm; 55min tour Sat & Sun 11.30am & 2.30pm; Nov also Mon–Fri 90min tour at 2pm, 55min tour at 3.30pm; English audio-guide available • €13.50 for 90min tour, €10 for 55min tour • **Fürstliche Schatzkammer** April–Oct Mon–Fri 11am–5pm, Sat & Sun 10am–5pm; Nov–March Sat & Sun 10am–5pm • €4.50 • ⓦ thurnundtaxis.de

Occupying a former Benedictine monastery and sprawling like a city within a city on the southern edge of the Altstadt is **Schloss St Emmeram**, home of the **Thurn und Taxis** dynasty. The family, whose origins are in northern Italy, held the office of imperial Postmaster General from 1595 and retained it for more than 350 years. The family transferred its court from Frankfurt to Regensburg in 1748, and Schloss St Emmeram has been its home since 1812. You can visit the **interior**, which incorporates Rococo elements from the old Thurn und Taxis palace in Frankfurt, on a guided tour, which also takes in the abbey's impressive medieval cloisters. The ancient abbey church of **St Emmeram** itself can be visited without joining a tour; its joyful Baroque interior was the work of the Munich-based Asam brothers. The fabulous wealth of the Thurn und Taxis dynasty is eloquently demonstrated by the richness of the collections in the **Fürstliche Schatzkammer** (Princely Treasury), where the exhibits range from furniture to porcelain and an impressive collection of snuff boxes.

KOG – the Kunstforum Ostdeutsche Galerie

Dr-Johann-Maier-Str. 5 • Tues, Wed & Fri–Sun 10am–5pm, Thurs 10am–8pm • €6 • ⓦ kunstforum.net

Just to the west of the Altstadt, the **KOG – Kunstforum Ostdeutsche Galerie** (Art Forum East German Gallery) focuses on German art in Eastern Europe from the Romantic period to the present, with works by Lovis Corinth and Käthe Kollwitz among others. It also stages exhibitions of contemporary art from Eastern Europe.

Walhalla

Donaustauf, 10km from Regensburg • Daily: April–Sept 9am–5.45pm; Oct 9am–4.45pm; Nov–March 10–11.45am & 1–3.45pm • €4 • ⓦ walhalla-regensburg.de • RVV bus #5 from Regensburg to stop "Kriegerdenkmal"

High on a hill overlooking the Danube 10km east of Regensburg in the village of Donaustauf, **Walhalla** is impossible to miss, for it dominates the surrounding countryside. Built by Ludwig I's court architect Leo von Klenze in purest Grecian classical style, this Teutonic Parthenon was a pet project of the future king as far back as 1807, while his father was still an ally of Napoleon. The aim was to house sculptures of "laudable and distinguished" Germans in a building of suitable architectural dignity, and although Ludwig could not finance the building while still crown prince, he commissioned the busts from a number of famous sculptors at a time when German troops were marching with Napoleon's army to Moscow. Sixty busts were complete by the time Ludwig became king; they included figures of Swiss, Dutch, Austrian and Anglo-Saxon origin – "Germanic" in its widest definition. The building itself was completed by 1842; its name derives from that of the resting place of fallen heroes in Nordic myth.

The interior

The figures honoured in its spacious interior include monarchs such as Frederick Barbarossa and Catherine the Great of Russia (born in the then-German port of Stettin, now in Poland) and military men such as Blücher, hero of Waterloo, and Radetzky, the Austrian field marshal after whom the Strauss march is named. Writers, artists and thinkers are rather under-represented, but range from Mozart and Goethe to Immanuel Kant and Albrecht Dürer. New figures continue to be added, with Heinrich Heine, the great German-Jewish poet, one of the most recent. There are still relatively few women and there are some surprising omissions from recent history: you'll look in vain for Count von Stauffenberg, Heinrich Böll or Willy Brandt, for instance. Presiding over them all, of course, is Ludwig himself. Quite apart from its architectural and historical interest, Walhalla offers lovely views over the expansive Danube plain below.

ARRIVAL AND GETTING AROUND   REGENSBURG

By train From Regensburg's Hauptbahnhof it's a few minutes' walk along Maxmilianstrasse into the Altstadt.
Destinations Ingolstadt (hourly; 1hr 6min); Landshut (1–2 per hour; 37–49min); Munich (hourly; 1hr 33min); Nuremberg (hourly; 1hr 8min); Passau (every 2hr; 1hr 6min); Saal an der Donau (for Donaudurchbruch: hourly; 22min); Straubing (hourly; 25min).
By bus You may need to use the local RVV buses

(ⓦ rvv.de) if you're heading out to Walhalla (#5), which is on the edge of fare zone 2 (€2.90); a one-day *TagesTicket* for zones 1 and 2 costs €4.80. If you're just exploring the Altstadt, however, the best way to do so is on foot.
By bike Bikehaus, at Bahnhofstr. 18 (ⓣ 0941 599 88 08), is on the left as you leave the Hauptbahnhof on the northern (Altstadt) side.

INFORMATION

Tourist office In the Altes Rathaus at Rathausplatz 4 (April–Oct Mon–Fri 9am–6pm, Sat 9am–4pm, Sun 9.30am–4pm; Nov–March Mon–Fri 9am–6pm, Sat 9am–4pm, Sun 9.30am–2.30pm; ⓣ 0941 507 44 10, ⓦ regensburg.de). The tourist office is often extremely busy. You can rent an English-language audio-guide (3hr €8) here, and you can book accommodation through the

tourist website or by calling ⓣ 0941 507 44 12.
Discount card The tourist office can sell you a Regensburg Card (24hr €9; 48hr €17) with various discounts on attractions plus free use of public transport. Note that the 24hr card only allows travel on zones 1 and 2 of the local public transport network, whereas the 48hr card covers up to zone 5 – enough for a visit to Kelheim (see p.420).

ACCOMMODATION

HOTELS

Altstadthotel Arch Haidplatz 2–4 ☎0941 586 60, ⓦaltstadthotelarch.de. Atmospheric 4-star hotel in a twelfth-century patrician house in the Altstadt, with a modern, air-conditioned extension. Prices include breakfast and free wireless internet, and reduced-price parking is available nearby. €122

Bischofshof am Dom Krauterermarkt 3 ☎0941 584 60, ⓦhotel-bischofshof.de. A stylish mix of tradition and modernity with rooms fronting a courtyard or quiet lane in the heart of the Altstadt. The setting – in the shadow of the cathedral – is historic and beautiful. All rooms have flat-screen TV, minibar and internet. €150

★**Goldenes Kreuz** Haidplatz 7 ☎0941 558 12, ⓦhotel-goldeneskreuz.de. In a stunning former imperial lodging-house with a five-hundred-year history, complete with beautiful frescoes and plenty of beams. Tastefully decorated rooms have en-suite facilities and internet. €105

★**Goliath** Goliathstr. 10 ☎0941 200 09 00, ⓦhotel-goliath.de. Exceptional boutique-style hotel in the heart of the Altstadt, with stylish decor, individually styled, a/c rooms and suites. There's a sauna, fitness room and beauty treatments, plus a wonderful roof terrace. €155

★**Orphée** Untere Bachgasse 8 ☎0941 59 60 20, ⓦhotel-orphee.de. Baroque details vie with structural beams and four-poster beds for attention in the rooms of this lovely Altstadt hotel above a classy French bistro, with two annexes: one in nearby Wahlenstrasse and another in Stadtamhof across the river. Main building and Stadtamhof annexe €135, Wahlenstrasse annexe €100

Spitalgarten St Katharinenplatz 1 ☎0941 847 74, ⓦspitalgarten.de. Simple but comfortable rooms with shared facilities, next to a shady beer garden just across the Steinerne Brücke from the Altstadt, directly on the Danube bike trail and with views of the bridge and cathedral. Parking is available. €60

HOSTELS

Brook Lane Hostel Obere Bachgasse 21 ☎0941 696 55 21, ⓦhostel-regensburg.de. Independently run hostel in the Altstadt, with accommodation in snug dorms or spartan singles and doubles furnished in a bland but modern style; shower and WC facilities are shared and there's a guest kitchen. Open 24hr. Dorms €16, doubles €60

DJH Regensburg Wöhrdstr. 60 ☎0941 466 28 30, ⓦregensburg.jugendherberge.de. On an island in the Danube, within easy walking distance of the Altstadt and with a lockable cycle store, table tennis and a children's playground. Breakfast included. Dorms €23.90

EATING AND DRINKING

CAFÉS AND CHEAP EATS

★**Café Conditorei Prinzess** Rathausplatz 2 ☎0941 59 53 10, ⓦcafe-prinzess.de. Regensburg's classic *Kaffee und Kuchen* option: pass the mouthwatering displays of pralines in the window to enter Germany's oldest coffee house, opened in 1686. The café is on the first floor and there's a *salon de thé* on the second. Coffee from €0.20. Daily 9am–6.30pm.

Dampfnudel Uli Watmarkt 4 ☎0941 532 97, ⓦdampfnudel-uli.de. One of the most popular places in Regensburg for hearty Bavarian food, including meaty mains and the eponymous (and surprisingly light) sweet dumplings with custard (€6.40). Tiny, atmospheric and inexpensive. Wed–Fri 10am–6pm, Sat 10am–3pm.

Picasso Unter den Schwibbögen 1 ☎0941 536 57, ⓦcafe-picasso-regensburg.de. Informal café/bar in the spectacular setting of the former Salvatorkapelle, which dates from 1476; open for breakfast (from €3.20) from 10am, with inexpensive pasta, salads and light dishes later. Mon–Thurs & Sun 10am–2am, Fri & Sat 10am–3am.

RESTAURANTS

Gänsbauer Keplerstr. 10 ☎0941 578 58, ⓦgaensbauer.de. Extremely pretty restaurant with a refined menu that mixes German and wider European influences, including dishes such as tartar of Angus fillet beef with roast pumpernickel, or black Angus fillet steak with Calvados sauce. The set menu is €41.50. Mon–Sat 6pm–1am.

Leerer Beutel Berdoldstr. 9 ☎0941 589 97, ⓦleerer-beutel.de. "Slow food" restaurant in the atmospheric setting of a medieval warehouse, with main courses such as pork with a nut crust and pink peppercorn sauce or veal *Tafelspitz* with bouillon from around €16. Mon 6pm–1am, Tues–Sat 11am–1am, Sun 11am–3pm.

Orphée Untere Bachgasse 8 ☎0941 52 977, ⓦhotel-orphee.de. Classy, convivial French bistro, *salon de thé* and patisserie, with the likes of *coquilles St-Jacques* and *coq au vin* on the menu and main courses from around €17. Breakfast from €3.80; crêpes from €5.80. Daily 8am–1am.

Storstad Watmarkt 5 ☎0941 59 99 30 00, ⓦstorstad.de. Slick new fusion-cuisine restaurant with austere modern Scandinavian decor, a €35 business lunch and a highly creative €95 five-course menu in the evening. Tues–Sat noon–2pm & 6–10pm; bar open until 1am.

Wurstkuchl Historische Wurstküche Thundorferstr. 3 ☎0941 46 62 10, ⓦwurstkuchl.de. Located right next to the Steinerne Brücke and looking like somewhere a hobbit might grill sausages. The smells issuing from this tiny, rustic and historic sausage restaurant – which dates back to the seventeenth century – are nevertheless mouthwatering. €8.40 for six *Bratwürste* with *Sauerkraut*. Daily 8am–7pm.

7

Zum Goldenen Fass Spiegelgasse 10 ☎0941 20 91 44 49, ⍟augustiner-goldenes-fass.de. In one of the quieter corners of the southern Altstadt, a traditional *Wirtshaus* in lovely old premises with plenty of beams, wood and stone. The food is rustic – dark beer goulash and the like – and there's Augustiner beer, and a *Biergarten* to enjoy it in. Lunch specials from €5.50. Tues–Sat 11am–midnight, Sun 11am–10pm.

BARS AND PUBS

Dicker Mann Krebsgasse 6 ☎0941 573 70, ⍟dicker -mann.de. Atmospheric fourteenth-century *Gasthof* that claims to be one of the oldest pubs in Germany, with a *Biergarten* in the *Innenhof*. There's a full food menu and the specials are particularly good value – with prices from €5.40 – though it's hardly undiscovered. Daily 9am–1am; kitchen closes 11pm.

Fürstliches Brauhaus Waffnergasse 6–8 ☎0941 280 43 30, ⍟fuerstlichesbrauhaus.de. The *Brauhaus* of the Thurn und Taxis family (see p.417), with a copper microbrewery behind the bar, a shady beer garden and own-brew *Original*, *Marstall Dunkell* and *Braumeister Weisse* beers. There's also classic *Brauhaus* fare, with light meals from €5 and mains from around €8, plus a "Bavarian buffet" every second Wed. Mon–Fri 11am–midnight, Sat

& Sun 10am–midnight.

Hab und Gut Trinkstätte Keplerstr. 3 ☎0941 56 06 35, ⍟habundgutbar.de. One of the classier cocktail bars close to the Altstadt's riverside, with Asian bar food (*pho*, *yakitori* chicken) from around €6, a good selection of spirits and a young, studenty crowd. Tues–Sat 6pm–late.

Hemingway's Obere Bachgasse 3–5 ☎0941 56 15 06, ⍟hemingway.de. Big, vaguely Art Deco-style café and cocktail bar, serving breakfast until 2pm; there's everything from Thai food to *Schnitzel* and pasta on the affordable food menu, and an emphasis on rum-based cocktails at the bar. Mon–Thurs & Sun 9am–1am, Fri & Sat 9am–2am.

Palletti In the Pustetpassage, Gesandtenstr. 6 ☎0941 515 93. Attracting an older but rather bohemian crowd, this arty café/bar is a lovely place to stop for an espresso or glass of wine and is frequently packed in the evenings. There's a daily changing, cosmopolitan menu too. Mon–Sat 8pm–1am, Sun 4pm–2am.

Regensburger Weissbräuhaus Schwarze-Bären-Str. 6 ☎0941 599 77 03, ⍟regensburger-weissbräuhaus .de. The gleaming copper microbrewery is the focus of this *Hausbrauerei*, with its own-brew light and dark beers. Main courses – including veggie food – from around €9 and lighter options from around €7. Daily 10am–late.

NIGHTLIFE AND ENTERTAINMENT

CLUBS

Karma Lounge Obermünsterstr. 14 ☎0941 465 91 93, ⍟karmalounge.de. Hip bar and club spinning mainstream dance music to a mixed trendy/studenty crowd, with reduced-price entry for students and a variety of themed nights. Tues–Sat 11pm–3/4am.

Suite 15 Adolph Kolping Str. 5 ☎0941 504 12 07, ⍟suite15.de. Cult club with an eclectic programme that straddles mainstream and alternative tastes, with everything from soul and Sixties music to indy, electro and rock. Tues–Sun 11pm–2am; until 4am Fri & Sat.

LIVE MUSIC

Alte Mälzerei Galgenbergstr. 20 ☎0941 78 88 10, ⍟alte-maelzerei.de. Multifunctional arts centre hosting live bands, with everything from reggae to death trash

metal, psychedelic rock and African world music. The centre also hosts cabaret and comedy performances and disco nights. Disco nights from 11/11.30pm.

Jazzclub Regensburg At the Leerer Beutel, Bertoldstr. 9 ☎0941 56 33 75, ⍟jazzclub-regensburg.de. Regensburg's jazz club hosts gigs at a variety of locations but its home base is the Leerer Beutel arts centre.

THEATRE

Theater Regensburg Bismarckplatz 7 ☎0941 507 24 24, ⍟theater-regensburg.de. This is the main venue for drama, operetta and opera in Regensburg, though its programme of classical music concerts is staged at a number of different locations across the city. Box office open Mon–Fri 10am–6pm, Sat 10am–2pm.

Kelheim

A little over 27km southwest of Regensburg, **KELHEIM** is the jumping-off point for visits to Ludwig I's **Befreiungshalle** and to the scenically situated **Kloster Weltenburg**, the latter best reached by boat along the **Donaudurchbruch**, a narrow, cliff-rimmed stretch of the Danube to the west of the Kelheim that's one of the region's most beloved excursions. In Kelheim itself, the **Schneider brewery**, on the eastern side of the modestly pretty Altstadt, offers tours (Tues 2pm; April–Oct also Thurs 2pm; €8.50).

The Befreiungshalle

Daily: mid-March to Oct 9am–6pm; Nov to mid-Feb 9am–4pm • €3.50 • ⓦ befreiungshalle.org • A footpath ascends to the Befreiungshalle from Kelheim, or there's ample (paid) car parking

Perched on a romantic bluff high above the river, the **Befreiungshalle** (Liberation Hall) was Ludwig's monument to the wars of liberation against Napoleon and to the idea of German unity. It was begun in 1842 by Friedrich von Gärtner but completed after Gärtner's death by Leo von Klenze. From the outside, the drum-shaped building looks a little like a Neoclassical gasometer fashioned from painted stucco; the spectacular interior is ringed by 34 winged goddesses of victory with the names of Austrian, Prussian and Bavarian generals picked out in gold above them. A narrow staircase ascends to an internal gallery from which you can better admire the sheer spaciousness of the hall; beyond it, a stone staircase leads to an exterior gallery, well worth the climb for the views over Kelheim and the Donaudurchbruch.

Kloster Weltenburg

Abbey Daily 8am–7pm • ⓦ kloster-weltenburg.de • **Boat from Kelheim** Mid-March to Oct daily 8–11am & noon–5pm; every 30min on summer weekends; the journey upstream to Weltenburg takes 40min, the return leg 20min • €5.40 one-way, €9.70 return • ⓦ schifffahrt-kelheim.de • **Weltenburg ferry** Daily mid-March to end Oct 8–11am & noon–5pm • €1

The Donaudurchbruch ends at **Kloster Weltenburg**, wedged scenically between the river and cliffs. The Baroque abbey church is the work of the Asam brothers, but Weltenburg is altogether more famous for its brewery, which claims to be the world's oldest abbey brewery and produces the excellent *Barock Dunkel* beer. You can sample it at the *Klosterschenke* in the main courtyard (see below). The most popular way to reach Weltenburg is on a boat trip from Kelheim, but two-hour hiking trails through the gorge allow a more leisured appreciation of the exceptional landscape, which forms the **Weltenburger Enge** nature reserve. The closest route to the gorge follows the north bank; there's a simple ferry across the river to the abbey at Weltenburg itself.

ARRIVAL AND DEPARTURE   KELHEIM AND AROUND

By train and bus Trains take 22min to reach Saal an der Donau from Regensburg; from Saal it's a short bus ride into the centre of Kelheim.

EATING AND DRINKING

Klosterschenke Weltenburg Asamstr. 32 ☎09441 675 70, ⓦklosterschenke-weltenburg.de. The abbey's own *Brauhaus* is the best place to sample Weltenburg's abbey beers – including the delicious *Barock Dunkel* dark beer – on draught, with a menu of stout Bavarian staples from around €9.50 to soak up the ale. Daily 8am–7pm; closed Mon & Tues in winter.

Weisses Brauhaus Emil-Ott-Str. 3, Kelheim ☎09441 34 80, ⓦweisses-brauhaus-kelheim.de. If you want to eat or drink in Kelheim's Altstadt, the obvious place to head for is the *Gaststätte* and *Biergarten* of the Schneider brewery, with salads and veggie options (from €7.90) as well as hearty Bavarian dishes (from around €9) to help anchor down the *Schneider Weisse* beer. Jan–March Wed–Sun 10am–midnight; April–Dec daily 10am–midnight.

Landshut

Capital of Lower Bavaria for the past eight hundred years and for a brief period in the thirteenth century Munich's predecessor as the Wittelsbachs' main seat, **LANDSHUT** has architectural splendours that quite outshine its present status as a bustling but essentially provincial town. Its glory days came under the so-called "rich dukes" between 1393 and 1503, when it was the seat of government for the Duchy of Bayern-Landshut. The 1475 wedding of one of the dukes, Georg, to Jadwiga (Hedwig in German) – daughter of the Polish king – was one of the most lavish celebrations of the late Middle Ages, and it provides a template for the town's most celebrated festival – the **Landshuter Hochzeit** or Landshut Wedding (see box, p.422) – to this day.

THE LANDSHUTER HOCHZEIT

The **Landshuter Hochzeit** takes place every four years in June and July, and features medieval-costumed revelries including jousting tournaments, falconry and medieval music (next event: June 28–July 12, 2017; ⊛ landshuter-hochzeit.de).

Laid out along the south bank of the River Isar, Landshut's Altstadt is a grid, defined by two broad, parallel main streets – known confusingly as **Altstadt** and **Neustadt** – and by the shorter, narrower side-streets that link the two. Altstadt is lined on either side with stately gabled houses five storeys high, while Neustadt is scarcely less imposing.

St Martin

Kirchgasse 232 • April–Sept daily 7.30am–6.30pm; Oct–March Mon–Fri 7.30–5pm, closed lunchtimes Mon & Fri • Free

Dominating everything is the Late Gothic hall church of **St Martin** on the Altstadt, begun in 1392 and with an austerely graceful, airy interior. The most remarkable feature of the church is, however, its slender brick skyrocket of a tower, which looms over the Altstadt and was completed around 1500. It climbs to a height of 130m and is thus the tallest brick structure in the world.

The Rathaus

The nineteenth-century neo-Gothic facade of the **Rathaus** hides a much older structure, parts of which date from the end of the fourteenth century; the richly ornamented neo-Gothic **Prunksaal**, or main hall (Mon–Fri 2–3pm; free), contains the wall paintings depicting the 1475 Landshuter Hochzeit that prompted the establishment of the festival that re-enacts it (see box above). The room is the venue for live concerts.

The Stadtresidenz

Altstadt 79 • Guided tours Tues–Sun: April–Sept 9am–6pm; Oct–March 10am–4pm • €3.50, more during temporary exhibitions, combined ticket with Burg Trausnitz €8

Facing the Rathaus across the Altstadt is the **Stadtresidenz**, a town palace commissioned by Duke Ludwig X in 1536 but chiefly remarkable for the lovely Italienischer Bau, or Italian building, which fringes the central courtyard and postdates the duke's travels to Italy. Inspired by the Palazzo Te in Mantua, the duke hired Italian architects to build an addition to his palace and the result was the first palace in the Italian Renaissance style on German soil. The **Innenhof**, or palace courtyard, is a lovely, arcaded Renaissance work – a piece of sixteenth-century Italy, with soft, warm Mediterranean colours. High point of the interior is the **Italienischer Saal**, or Italian Hall, with its coffered stucco ceilings enriched with frescoes on humanist themes by Hans Bocksberger.

Burg Trausnitz

Burg Trausnitz 168 • Guided tours daily: April–Sept 9am–6pm; Oct–March 10am–4pm • €5.50, combined ticket with Stadtresidenz €8

High above the Altstadt and reached via a steep ascent up Alte Bergstrasse is **Burg Trausnitz**, a mighty fortress begun under Duke Ludwig I in 1204. The ancestral castle of the Wittelsbach dynasty, it preserves much of its medieval fabric, including the impressive fortifications, the tall Wittelsbach tower and the castle chapel. The arcaded courtyard, the state rooms with their tapestries and tiled stoves and the famous **Narrentreppe**, or Fools' Stair, with its frescoes of Commedia dell'Arte buffoons, all date from the time of the Renaissance. The **Damenstock** (Ladies' Apartments) contain the **Kunst und Wunderkammer**, or Chamber of Arts and Curiosities, in the characteristically eclectic style of museum collections of the Renaissance, with 750 exhibits spanning natural history, science, and European and Oriental art.

| ARRIVAL AND INFORMATION | LANDSHUT |

By train Trains take around 40–50min to reach Landshut's Hauptbahnhof from Regensburg. The station is north of the Altstadt on the north side of the River Isar; to reach the centre of town, walk down Luitpoldstrasse and cross the bridge or take a Stadtlinie bus – most of which link the station with either Altstadt proper or Ländtorplatz close by. Destinations Munich (1–2 per hour; 46–58min); Nuremberg (every 2hr; 1hr 55min); Passau (hourly; 1hr 30min); Regensburg (hourly; 40min).

Tourist office In the Rathaus at Altstadt 315 (March–Oct Mon–Fri 9am–6pm, Sat 10am–4pm; Nov–Feb Mon–Fri 9am–5pm, Sat 10am–2pm; ☎0871 92 20 50, ⓦlandshut.de).

ACCOMMODATION AND EATING

DJH Landshut Richard-Schirrmann-Weg 6 ☎0871 234 49, ⓦlandshut.jugendherberge.de. The youth hostel is between the Altstadt and Burg Trausnitz, with accommodation in dorms or in two-, four- or six-bed rooms; double rooms have shower and WC. Breakfast included. Dorms **€17.90**

Gasthof zum Freischütz Neustadt 446 ☎0871 430 37 79. Inexpensive, atmospheric and old-fashioned *Gasthof* serving rustic Bavarian fare including *Milzwurst* and *Saures Lüngerl* (calves' lungs and other offal in a tart sauce). Lunchtime specials from €6.90. Daily 9am–midnight.

Goldene Sonne Neustadt 520 ☎0871 925 30, ⓦgoldenesonne.de. Behind a tall, historic gabled facade, this smart, traditional and family-run 4-star hotel has sixty comfortable rooms with shower, cable TV, minibar and internet; some of them have beams. **€139**

Stadthotel Herzog Ludwig Neustadt 519 ☎0871 97 40 50, ⓦstadthotel-herzog-ludwig.de. Tucked behind a gabled facade on Neustadt, the *Herzog Ludwig* offers plenty of character and high levels of comfort, including partial a/c, soundproofing, TV, wireless internet and minibar. Parking is available nearby. **€110**

Stegfellner Altstadt 71 ☎0871 280 15, ⓦstegfellner-landshut.de. Bustling restaurant above a wonderful Gothic-vaulted butcher's shop and dairy close to the Rathaus, with a chalked-up selection of daily specials plus the likes of Bavarian lamb, *Schweinebraten* or fresh fish. Main courses from around €13. There's also a wine bar in the moodily-lit cellar. Mon & Tues 8am–6.30pm, Wed–Fri 8am–9.30pm, Sat 7am–5pm & 6–9.30pm.

7

Baden-Württemberg

SCHLOSS, HEIDELBERG

Baden-Württemberg

Baden-Württemberg is the result of combining the states of Baden, Hohenzollern and Württemberg after World War II, yet it feels coherent thanks to the strong Swabian identity of most of its people. The rest of Germany caricatures Swabians as hardworking, frugal and rather boring, but their industriousness and inventiveness has made the region one of Europe's wealthiest. This industrial prowess makes up a big part of the Swabian identity, as does its regional food – a pasta-based cuisine that famously includes *Spätzle*; a love of good local wine; and a quirky regional accent. Baden-Württemberg is also influenced by its proximity to Switzerland and France, with which it shares much history.

Stuttgart and its environs are the industrial heartland of an otherwise fairly rural Baden-Württemberg. As the headquarters of industrial heavyweights that include Mercedes-Benz, Porsche and electronics giant Bosch, Stuttgart predictably oozes self-confidence and reeks of wealth. However, surprises lurk here too, in the form of an attractive setting between a series of hills, down which vineyards run right to the city's edges. Abundant city parks, thermal baths and Renaissance palaces all help make the compact, business-orientated town a likeable destination for a weekend or so. The car industry museums are particularly good and the city also has the region's best restaurant and nightlife scene. As a significant regional transport hub, it is also a good place from which to launch day-trips, the most obvious being **Ludwigsburg**, with its excessive Baroque palace and, at the other end of the hedonism scale, the old monastery at **Maulbronn**, whose buildings tell a story of a simple, long-forgotten monastic life. Both are brilliant, well-preserved and very different snapshots of Germany's past.

Stuttgart is also well-connected to the thriving nearby university town of **Tübingen** and the upbeat city of **Ulm** with its giant minster. Both cities lie at the foot of an upland plateau known as the **Swabian Alb**. This thinly-populated agricultural region, with its strong local dialect and identity, rises as a steep escarpment some 50km south of Stuttgart, and runs southwest to all but join the southern Black Forest. Its wonderful limestone scenery offers interesting hiking, and a rash of romantic castles built at strategic overlooks make equally good day-trips. A short journey south of the Swabian Alb lies the vast **Bodensee**, where a huge body of water and Germany's best weather combine to form a popular holiday destination. **Konstanz** is the largest and most engaging of several attractive lakeside settlements. West of here the hills rise and darken with the Black Forest, Baden-Württemberg's most famous asset – covered in Chapter 9.

Meanwhile, in the far north of the state, the towns of **Heidelberg** and **Karlsruhe** stick out as two lively university cities which offer appealing stop-offs for visitors travelling

MERCEDES-BENZ-MUSEUM, STUTTGART

Highlights

❶ **Mercedes-Benz-Museum** Pay tribute to Swabian hard work and inventiveness at this magnificent automotive museum. **See p.436**

❷ **Tübingen** Punt or paddle the languid waters of this relaxed and venerable university town. **See p.443**

❸ **Maultaschen** These Swabian ravioli were once poor food but are now often the yardstick for many regional restaurants; those at the *Hotel am Schloss* in Tübingen are hard to beat. **See p.446**

❹ **Ulm** Climb the world's tallest church spire, for giddying old-town views and vistas of the distant Alps. **See p.449**

❺ **Beuron** Let the dulcet Gregorian chants wash over you at this Baroque monastery. **See p.454**

❻ **Friedrichshafen** Float high above the Bodensee in a Zeppelin, or, if your budget won't stretch to that, explore reconstructions and the airship's history at the Zeppelin Museum. **See p.457**

❼ **ZKM, Karlsruhe** Button-push your way into the future at this world-class interactive multimedia museum. **See p.470**

❽ **Heidelberg** Soak up the atmosphere of Germany's most celebrated semi-derelict castle. **See p.471**

HIGHLIGHTS ARE MARKED ON THE MAP ON P.428

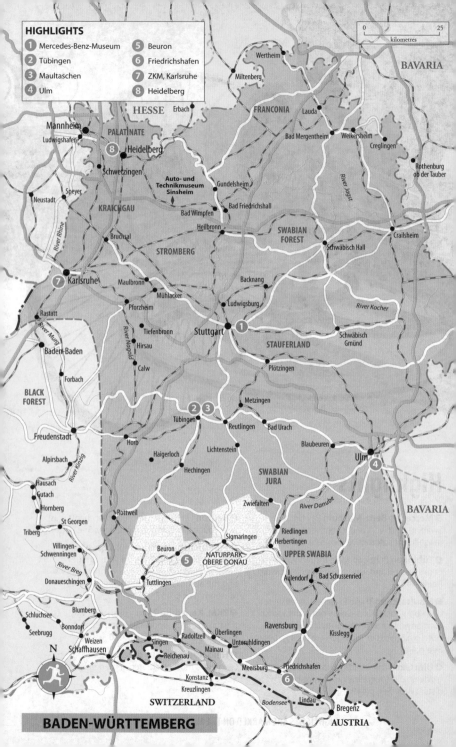

between the Rhineland and the Black Forest. Though Karlsruhe is known for, and centred around, a palace, its Rhine-side location has given it an industrial base and a modern dynamism reflected in its world-class contemporary art and technology museum, the ZKM. Heidelberg is more removed from modernity and is a major tourist honeypot, thanks to an attractive valley setting and a mighty ruined castle. It's particularly popular with Americans who like to follow in the steps of Mark Twain's own enchantment with the city. A short hop distant, the workaday town of **Mannheim** is worth visiting for its Jugendstil architecture.

Stuttgart is the main **regional transport** hub, but the whole state – with the exception of the Swabian Alb – is easy to navigate by public transport. Getting to remote places is of course easiest with your own wheels – and given the importance of the motor industry in the state, this is a part of Germany where roads are kept in premium condition and you can really let rip on the Autobahn.

Stuttgart

World-leading car city it may be, but **STUTTGART** is certainly no Detroit. Instead the Baden-Württemberg capital is surprisingly small (population 600,000), laidback, leafy and very wealthy. Its idyllic setting in the palm of a valley – where vineyards thrive – and its multitude of parks often seem to shape it more than the presence of industrial giants.

Stuttgart's industrial prowess was punished in World War II when bombs rained on the Altstadt, and the rebuilt city feels rather bereft of history, though there's no shortage of high culture in its heavyweight museums, particularly the **Staatsgalerie**'s art collections and the archeological treasures of **Landesmuseum Württemberg**. Many of the city's best sights, however, are spread across and beyond the hills that surround the city, where you can find good hikes among **vineyards** and between Stuttgart's celebrated rustic wine bars: *Weinstuben*.

The attractions on Stuttgart's southern fringes include the **Zahnradbahn**, an antique rack-railway, while the eighteenth-century **Schloss Solitude**, one of the city's most popular day-trips, is just west of the city. Stuttgart's northern end is defined by **Bad Cannstatt**, an old spa town it absorbed in 1905, but which still feels distinct. Though traditionally known for its mineral baths, these days it's as famous as the birthplace of the car and **Mercedes**, which has a terrific museum here. An ex-employee of that company spawned Porsche nearby, and the achievements of that brand are celebrated in the **Porsche Museum**, 9km to the north of Stuttgart's centre. All out-of-town attractions are readily reachable on Stuttgart's excellent public transport system.

Brief history

The town – and its name – has its origins in a stud farm, or "Stutengarten" established in 950 AD, and a black stallion still graces the city's heraldic crest. It developed as a trade centre and in 1311 became the seat of the Württemberg family. However, the city only really took regional control once Napoleon made Württemberg a kingdom and Stuttgart its capital in 1805. Eighty years later Daimler and Benz mapped out Stuttgart's future as a motor city, inadvertently helping to make the town a target for Allied bombing in World War II, which changed the town's appearance forever.

STUTTGART ORIENTATION

The city's main hub is its main public square, **Schlossplatz**, from which the sizeable parkland of the Schlossgarten extends north, running parallel to **Königstrasse**, the busy, bland, but spotless main commercial chain-store strip leading northeast to the **Hauptbahnhof**. Königstrasse also extends southwest of Schlossplatz, leading to what is left of the prewar city and the **Altstadt**.

8

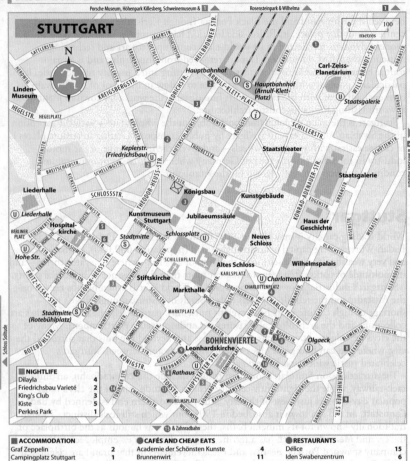

STUTTGART

■ **NIGHTLIFE**

Dilayla	4
Friedrichsbau Varieté	2
King's Club	3
Kiste	5
Perkins Park	1

■ **ACCOMMODATION**		● **CAFÉS AND CHEAP EATS**		● **RESTAURANTS**	
Graf Zeppelin	2	Academie der Schönsten Kunste	4	Délice	15
Campingplatz Stuttgart	1	Brunnenwirt	11	Iden Swabenzentrum	6
DJH Stuttgart	4	Café Königsbau	3	Nirvan	12
Hostel Alex 30	8			Tauberquelle	13
Hotel Centro	6	● **MICROBREWERIES AND**		TÜ8	14
Schwabennest	5	**BEER GARDENS**		Der Zauberlehrling	8
Unger	3	Biergarten im Schlossgarten.	1	● **WEINSTUBEN**	
Wörtz zur Weinsteige	9	Calwer-Eck-Bräu	5	Kachelofen	9
Der Zauberlehrling	7	Palast der Republik	2	Schnellenturm	10
				Stetter	7

The Aussichtsplattform

Arnulf-Klett-Platz • Daily 10am–6pm, Thurs until 8pm • Free

The ideal place to orientate yourself and start exploring Stuttgart is the **Aussichtsplattform**, at the top of a tower that rises from the **Hauptbahnhof**, crowned by a revolving Mercedes logo. Lower down the Aussichtsplattform tower you might like to pop in and have a look at the models and map projections for a project known as Stuttgart 21. It involves a very controversial and expensive ongoing initiative to re-route local railway lines in a more efficient manner that will involve destroying part of Stuttgart's nineteenth-century train station and many trees in the nearby Schlossgarten park. Perhaps unsurprisingly, the project has caused huge demonstrations and ongoing politicking. Costing a whopping €4.5 billion, it's due for completion in 2021.

The Schlossgarten

East of the Hauptbahnhof a finger of parkland, the **Schlossgarten**, runs alongside the railway tracks to the 3km-distant Neckar River. Lazy paths weave around a well-used strip populated by sunbathers, strollers and roller-bladers at the first hint of sunshine. Particular points of interest include the excellent *Biergarten im Schlossgarten* (see p.439) and the glass pyramid of **Carl-Zeiss-Planetarium** (show times vary, generally Tues–Fri 10am, 3pm & 8pm, Sat 2pm, 3pm, 4pm, 6pm & 7.15pm, Sun 2pm, 3pm, 4pm & 6pm; €6; ⓦ carl-zeiss-planetarium.de), with its superb virtual stargazing. The Schlossgarten also offers a peaceful alternative route to the city centre from the Hauptbahnhof to the central Schlossplatz, passing well-tended lawns and the Staatstheater, a grandiose 1912 opera house.

Schlossplatz

Of all Stuttgart's green spaces, **Schlossplatz** is by far the busiest and most noble. Schlossplatz's grand centrepiece is the **Jubiläumssäule**, which commemorates the 25th anniversary of King Wilhelm I's accession to the Württemberg throne, and features him enthroned and lauded by fawning nobles in a bombastic relief on the base. Flanking it on either side are capacious Neoclassical fountains with frolicking cherubs.

Neues Schloss

Schlossplatz 4 • Römisches Lapidarium Sat & Sun 10am–5pm • Free

The state culture and finance ministries occupy the Baroque **Neues Schloss** built by Friedrich I between 1746 and 1806. It swaggers on the eastern side of the square, its roof lined with allegorical statues and the heraldic stag of the dukes and kings of Württemberg prances atop its gate. Inside, the basement of the south wing houses the **Römisches Lapidarium**, an overflow of the Landesmuseum (see p.432), which brings together regional Roman reliefs, sculptures and fragments. Closed for renovations, the Lapidarium will reopen in July 2015.

Königsbau

King Wilhelm I of Württemberg's Neoclassical **Königsbau** rears up opposite the Neues Schloss, built in the 1850s for court events and stock-market traders in the Börse (stock exchange), who only moved to a more modern dealing-floor in 1991. Today the **Königsbau Passagen**, an upmarket shopping mall strong on interior-design shops, occupies the building.

Kunstgebäude

Schlossplatz 2 • Tues & Thurs–Sun 11am–6pm, Wed 11am–8pm • €5 • ⓦ wkv-stuttgart.de

A golden Württemberg stag crowns the dome of the **Kunstgebäude** on the north side of the square. Here temporary displays of big-name artists (past masters include Otto Dix, Munch and Man Ray) and up-and-coming talent hang in spacious exhibition halls.

Kunstmuseum Stuttgart

Kleiner Schlossplatz 1 • Tues–Thurs, Sat & Sun 10am–6pm, Fri 10am–9pm • €6 • ⓦ kunstmuseum-stuttgart.de

The exhibitions in the eye-catching glass box of the **Kunstmuseum Stuttgart** are all temporary, but usually revolve around modern or contemporary art; the mobile in front of the building is by Alexander Calder and purchased for the equivalent of €500,000, causing a stir among frugal Swabians when the city bought it in 1981.

Schillerplatz

One block south of Schlossplatz lies the remaining part of prewar Stuttgart's **Altstadt**, centred on **Schillerplatz**, where a romantic statue of the eponymous hero shows him in an open shirt with his cloak draped casually over a shoulder. The eighteenth-century dramatist and lyric poet enrolled to train as an army doctor at the Hohe Karlsschule for seven unhappy years.

The north side of the square is boxed in by the **Alte Kanzlei**, a Renaissance office-block of the Chancellery; the adjacent **Princenbau** claims the honour of welcoming Stuttgart's last king, Wilhelm II, into the world on February 25, 1848.

Stiftskirche

Stiftsstr. 12 • Mon–Thurs 10am–7pm, Fri & Sat 10am–4pm, Sun noon–6pm • Free • ⓦ stiftskirche.de

Flanking Schillerplatz, the renovated **Stiftskirche** is an airy modern space with arty floor-to-ceiling glass strips that might have surprised its municipal Late Gothic architects Hänslin and Aberlin Jörg. Yet somehow it's all in keeping with the church's history, which began in 1436, when the father-and-son duo was commissioned to unite an existing hotchpotch of styles. They melded old and new beautifully, particularly the twelfth-century Romanesque square tower, which morphs into an octagonal bell-tower.

The interior

In the choir, Sem Schlör's **ancestral gallery** of the Württemberg dukes – from city patron Count Ulrich who erected the first stone Schloss in 1265 (far right) to Heinrich of Mömpelgard (1519; far left) – is an absorbing German Renaissance masterpiece. Each family member has been imaginatively characterized, and family squabbles recounted. Hand on hip in the centre, Ulrich IV argues his case to his father Eberhard I rather than debate with the impressively bearded Eberhard II beside him. The brothers' co-rule of Stuttgart between 1333 and 1362 exploded into a furious spat about land division. Ulrich IV stepped down in disgust, earning Eberhard II the nickname "Der Greiner" ("the Quarreller"). Look, too, for a Late Gothic pulpit on which the Four Evangelists work on their gospels, and a beautiful carving of Christ who shelters all society beneath his shroud in the baptistery.

Markthalle

Dorotheenstr. 4 • Mon–Fri 7.30am–6.30pm, Sat 7am–5pm • Free • ⓦ markthalle-stuttgart.de

Just southeast off Schillerplatz lies the attractive frescoed Jugendstil **Markthalle**, an indoor market where stalls are laden with smoked Schwarzwald (Black Forest) hams, doughy *Spätzle*, twee pots of home-made jam and marmalade, a bewildering number of varieties of *Wurst*, German breads and all sorts of strange cheeses to sample. It's all a bit overwhelming but also an ideal place to assemble a Schlossgarten picnic. Diagonally opposite the Markthalle, spacious **Karlsplatz** hosts a small, but worthwhile, Saturday flea market.

The Altes Schloss

The stolid **Altes Schloss** on the east flank of Schillerplatz is where Stuttgart started. Some two centuries after the original stud farm was established here in 950 AD, a moated stone castle was built to protect it; a stocky corner tower is all that remains of its fourteenth-century replacement. Until Duke Carl Eugen despaired of its "prison-like" conditions and left for Ludwigsburg (see p.441), the Württemberg dukes resided here in the sixteenth-century Schloss, which received a Renaissance makeover courtesy of court architect Aberlin Tretsch. Tretsch excelled in the graceful galleried courtyard that proved too elegant for the intended jousting tournaments, and is more fitting for today's inexpensive summer-evening classical concerts. Tretsch also added a Reittreppe, or riding ramp, which allowed his master to make a flamboyant entrance into the Rittersaal (Knight's Hall) at full gallop.

The Landesmuseum Württemberg

Schillerplatz 6 • Tues–Sun 10am–5pm • €5 • ⓦ landesmuseum-stuttgart.de

The Altes Schloss now houses the rewardingly eclectic **Landesmuseum Württemberg**. Don't miss the chance to examine its Swabian devotional sculptures: a brightly coloured Ulm Passion cycle (1520) catches the eye, but far finer are a pair of carvings by Germany's Late-Gothic supremo Tilman Riemenschneider, whose finesse and expression need no gaudy make-up. Other treasures include Europe's oldest pack of playing cards (1430) which reveal the era's obsessions in suits of falcons and hounds, ducks and stags; the state jewellery box includes a necklace with a large 22-carat diamond and a silver filigree tiara fit for a fairy-tale princess.

The **archeology** section also has much of local interest, with its finest piece probably the large chariot complete with harnesses and finely worked jewellery – from a sixth-century-BC Celtic burial mound near Ludwigsburg. Also here is a Bronze Age lion head sculpted from a chunk of mammoth tusk, one of the world's oldest pieces of art.

The Landesmuseum ticket is also valid for the **Musikinstrumenten Sammlung**, in the modernized sixteenth-century wine warehouse and granary, the Fruchtkasten, on Schillerplatz. Occasional concerts bring some of its prodigious collection alive.

The Bohnenviertel

An underpass allows you to avoid the furious traffic along Konrad-Adenauer-Strasse to walk east from the centre into the **Bohnenviertel** (Bean Quarter), the traditional blue-collar district that occupies the city blocks between Charlottenstrasse and Pfarrstrasse. Founded in the fourteenth century and largely spared wartime bombs, its cobbled lanes convey a more distant history, and have settled happily into gentrification. The former houses of market gardeners and wine growers are highly prized by jewellers, galleries and antique shops as well as several cosy *Weinstuben* – while a modest red-light district occupies the south.

Haus der Geschichte Baden-Württemberg

Konrad-Adenauer-Str. 16 • Tues, Wed & Fri–Sun 10am–6pm, Thurs 10am–9pm • €4 • ⓦ hdgbw.de

Curious perspex boxes containing "found objects" blare with videos and music at the **Haus der Geschichte Baden-Württemberg**, a frequently conceptual, occasionally baffling fast-forward through the history of Baden-Württemberg. Its "Wirtschafts-Wunder" section salutes regional heroes of industry – including Stuttgarter Robert Bosch, now synonymous with power tools – and, far more fun, the "Kunststück Schwarzwald" section documents the Black Forest's blossoming from rustic backwater to darling of German tourism (blame nineteenth-century Romantics) in photos and tacky souvenirs.

The Staatsgalerie

Konrad-Adenauer-Str. 30–32 • Tues, Wed & Fri–Sun 10am–6pm, Thurs 10am–9pm • €5, free Wed • ⓦ staatsgalerie.de

The striking curved glass facade by British architect James Stirling at the northern end of Konrad-Adenauer-Strasse announces the **Staatsgalerie**, a superlative art collection and local cultural highlight. Based on the collection of the Württemberg dukes, the gallery begins with early German masters and a pair of exquisite Cranachs, and includes Italian Baroque painters such as Annibale Carracci, and leading lights of the French Impressionist movement – including Monet – as well as the vivid expressionism of Kandinsky, Kirchner, Nolde, Kokoschka and Schiele. The collection goes right into the twentieth century and is particularly strong on Picasso: two rooms chronicle his early works from the Blue Period (*Mother and Child* and, on its reverse, *Crouching Woman*) to iconic Cubism such as the louche *Breakfast in the Open Air* and the most important of his late sculptures, *Bathers*, which is reminiscent of African tribal sculpture. Lastly, don't miss the Graphische Sammlung's alternating treasury of graphic arts, from Dürer to twentieth-century greats.

8

The Zahnradbahn and Fernsehturm

From the Hauptbahnhof it's six quick stops south on the U-Bahn to Marienplatz, starting point of the **Zahnradbahn**, a rack railway. Affably known as the "Zacke", the train has been climbing to the suburb of Degerloch since 1884. It's Stuttgart's big public transport oddity and included on passes for the entire network, though using it alone just requires a *Kurzstrecke* ticket. From the summit Nägelestrasse station it's a five-minute walk east to the **Fernsehturm** (TV tower; ⓦ fernsehturmstuttgart.com), which hails from 1956, making it the earliest example of this much-imitated olive-on-a-toothpick design. In 2013 the Fernsehturm was closed to the public for safety reasons, but there are moves afoot to repair and reopen it in the summer of 2015.

Schloss Solitude

Solitude 1 • Guided tours (in German) every 45min April–Oct Tues–Sat 10am–noon & 1.30–5pm, Sun 10am–5pm; Nov–March Tues–Sat 1.30–4pm, Sun 10am–4pm • €4 • ⓦ schloss-solitude.de • Bus #92 from Hauptbahnhof

A ridge on the western side of Stuttgart, 7km from the centre, is home to the 1760s **Schloss Solitude**, which was the main summer residence of the Württemberg court for twenty years or so. It's one of Stuttgart's most popular days out, though palace rooms can only be visited by guided tours in German.

Duke Carl Eugen, who built so feverishly in Ludwigsburg (see p.441), commissioned Philippe de La Guêpière to design the palace. The Parisian architect drew a masterpiece, an exquisite oval palace that tempers the final flickers of Rococo with emergent Neoclassicism. Inevitably, despite a ruler-straight 15km road from Ludwigsburg, the swaggering aristocrat bored of his pleasure palace barely six years after its 1769 completion and it was only ever used for rare courtly high-jinks with visiting dignitaries. A 30-year-old Johann Wolfgang von Goethe on a hunting jaunt with the Duke of Weimar in 1779 marvelled at its festive hall, the **Weisser Saal**, which claims centre stage and has a boastful allegorical fresco about the peaceful good government of Carl Eugen. In one wing are the elegant rooms of his official apartment – the marble Marmorsaal and Palmenzimmer. Like courtiers and visitors, the duke resided in the outbuilding **Kavalierbau** at the rear, a mirror-image of the administrative Officenbau, which today houses a gourmet restaurant.

Höhenpark Killesberg

Lying 2.5km due north of the city centre, **Höhenpark Killesberg** was the product of a Nazi work-creation scheme, which transformed a disused quarry to host a flower show in 1939. Replanted after the war and jewelled with sparkling water cascades and fountains, Stuttgart's highest park now affords sweeping panoramas over the city from the **Killesberg Turm**, a 43m-high lookout of winding staircases like an aluminium DNA strand. There are also outdoor pools, children's zoos and restaurants, and a shamelessly twee tourist-train.

Weissenhofsiedlung

Weissenhofmuseum Rathenaustr. 1 • Tues–Fri 11am–6pm, Sat & Sun 11am–6pm • €5 • ⓦ weissenhofmuseum.de

The 1950s Messe (trade fair) buildings at Hohenpark Killesberg's southern fringe help locate the **Weissenhofsiedlung**. In 1927, Stuttgart invited the cutting edge of European architecture to erect show houses for guild show "Die Wohnung". They might have frowned at patchy postwar restoration, but Mies van der Rohe, Le Corbusier, Walter Gropius, Hans Scharoun and the other modernist architects involved at the time would be delighted that their clean-lined Bauhäuser still provide homes. Today you can walk around the **Weissenhofmuseum**, a small museum in the house designed by Le Corbusier, that tells the story of the architecture show.

Rosensteinpark and around

From the eastern end of Höhenpark Killesberg, Brünner Steg crosses a bundle of
S-Bahn lines on a footbridge that leads to the copses of mature trees of **Rosensteinpark**.
Here, natural history is thoroughly explored, from its paleontological beginnings in the
Museum am Löwentor to the fine botanic garden and zoo.

Wilhelma

Daily 8.15am–dusk • €14 • ⓦ wilhelma.de • U-Bahn Wilhelma

Wilhelm I spent a decade from 1852 seeding botanical gardens here, which have since
grown into heavyweight zoo and botanic gardens, **Wilhelma**. Romantic Moorish
fantasies are dotted around the zoo's gardens, which feature Europe's largest magnolia
grove and four thousand orchids – a perfect backdrop for its nine thousand animals.

Schloss Rosenstein

Tues–Fri 9am–5pm, Sat & Sun 10am–6pm • Schloss Rosenstein and Museum am Löwentor €4 each, combined ticket €5 •
ⓦ naturkundemuseum-bw.de • U-Bahn Mineralbäder

Wilhelma botanic gardens were once simply the gardens of **Schloss Rosenstein**, the
Neoclassical hilltop retreat by Giovanni Salucci in the southeastern corner of the park.
Today this contains the dreary stuffed menagerie of the Museum für Naturkunde.
Thankfully, an extra €1 buys you a combination ticket that includes the modern and
very good **Museum am Löwentor** further west, a paleontologist's dream of impressive
fossils and dinosaur skeletons.

Mineral-Bad-Berg and Mineral-Bad-Leuze

Mineral-Bad-Berg Am Schwanenplatz 9 • April–Sept Mon–Fri 7am–8pm, Sun 7am–5pm; Oct–March Mon–Sat 8am–8pm, Sun
8am–5pm • €7.60 day entry • **Mineral-Bad-Leuze** Am Leuzebad 2 • Daily 6am–9pm • 2hr €8.10 • ⓦ stuttgart.de/baeder • U-Bahn
Mineralbäder

Just beyond the southern edge of Rosensteinpark lie two large mineral baths beside the
Neckar where you can sample the local curative waters: **Mineral-Bad-Berg**, a mineral
pool and sauna where two of Stuttgart's nineteen springs bubble up and pensioners
brave winter to swim dutiful lengths in an outdoor pool; and **Mineral-Bad-Leuze** next
door, which is slightly more boisterous.

Bad Cannstatt

During its early years, **Bad Cannstatt**, 3km northeast of central Stuttgart, competed
squarely with Stuttgart, especially with its – now faded – riverfront grandeur and its
attractive Marktplatz and Altstadt streets. The town was treasured above all for the
curative powers of the 22-million-litre torrent that gushed from seventeen springs each
day, and in the mid-nineteenth century it duly became a fashionable spa town. Stroll
north of the town centre and Wilhelm I of Württemberg on horseback fronts his
Neoclassical **Kurhaus**, still a spa for rheumatism, while on its left the **Mineral-Bad-
Cannstatt** caters to a full range of watery pursuits, from frolics to fitness (daily
9am–9.30pm; 2hr 30min €7.90; ⓦ stuttgart.de/baeder). Behind the Kurhaus lies the
lovely Kurpark.

The Gottlieb-Daimler-Gedächtnisstätte

Taubenheimstr. 13 • Tues–Fri 2–5pm, Sat & Sun 11am–5pm • Free

Take the path right of the Kurhaus and you'll pass the **Gottlieb-Daimler-
Gedächtnisstätte**, a curious shed-cum-greenhouse that served as the workshop of
Gottlieb Daimler (see box, p.436) and apprentice Wilhelm Maybach. Though
World War II bombs destroyed the adjoining villa, the shed escaped unharmed,
even if the workshop – with its workbench tidily laid-out with well-oiled spanners,

---

BADEN-WÜRTTEMBERG'S AUTO PIONEERS

Mechanical engineer **Gottlieb Daimler** left formal employment in 1880, and started tinkering in his Bad Cannstatt workshop in 1882. His quest to produce a light, fast, internal combustion engine was done so secretively that police raided his workshop for money-counterfeiting on the tip-off of a gardener. In 1883, his single-cylinder four-stroke shattered the repose of Kurhaus spa-goers and by 1885 his patented 264cc "Grandfather Clock" powered a motorbike. A year later the world's first motorboat, the *Neckar*, chugged upriver and his motorized carriage terrorized horses. Daimler moved to a factory on Seelberg in July 1887.

Meanwhile, unaware of the goings-on in Daimler's shed, **Karl Benz** in Mannheim was blazing his own motor trail to found Benz & Cie in 1883, the same year as Daimler. The world's two oldest motor manufacturers eventually united in June 1926 as Daimler-Benz long after Daimler had died and Benz retired. The Mercedes name was introduced in 1902 to honour the daughter of early Austrian dealer Emil Jellinek.

---

screwdrivers, vices and drills – now seems a little too humble to be the cradle of the world-changing automobile. Models of the first designs put into context the amazing achievements since.

Mercedes-Benz-Museum

Mercedesstr. 100 • Tues–Sun 9am–6pm • €8 • ⓦ mercedes-benz.com/museum • 5min walk south of S-Bahn Gottlieb-Daimler-Stadion

Housed in a futuristic landmark building on the banks of the Neckar, 4km northeast of the city centre, the **Mercedes-Benz-Museum** is chock-full of 110 years of immaculate motors. It starts with Daimler's pioneering motorbike – a wooden bone-shaker with a horse's saddle – and beside it is the one-cylinder motor-tricycle Motorwagen and motorized carriage Motorkutsche; Benz and Daimler created them independently in 1886, both capable of a not-so-giddy 16kmph. Benz just pipped Daimler to produce the world's first car.

Another trail-blazer is the robust **Benz Vélo**, the world's first production car, for which twelve hundred of the moneyed elite parted with 20,000 gold Marks. A racy 500K Special Roadster in preening pillarbox red begs for a Hollywood Thirties starlet, but it's the racers that truly quicken the pulse, no more so than the legendary **Silver Arrows** of the 1920s and 1930s; a cinema shows the sleek machines in action. Just as eye-catching are a pair of experimental record-breakers that look far more futuristic than their dates suggest: in the **W125**, Rudolf Caracciola clocked up 432.7km per hour on the Frankfurt–Darmstadt Autobahn in 1938 (no one's been faster on a public highway since); and six-wheeler sci-fi vision **T80** was powered by an aeroplane engine to 650km per hour in 1939, though World War II killed the project.

Porsche Museum

Porscheplatz 1 • Tues–Sun 9am–6pm • €8, including English-language audio-guide • ⓦ porsche.com/museum • S-Bahn Neuwirtshaus

As if two motor-car pioneers weren't enough, Stuttgart also lays claim to Ferdinand Porsche, Daimler's 1920s technical director, who left the company in 1938 to produce sleek racing machines of his own – until Hitler demanded he create the Volkswagen. He returned to racing cars later, and the company's badge honours the debt to Stuttgart with a rearing horse. The **Porsche Museum**, 9km north of the city centre, is a crash course in Porsche's designs. Dozens of priceless, highly polished examples of engineering at its finest are interpreted by an intelligent audio-guide and touch-screen monitors. Racing-driver video testimonials help bring the vehicles to life, as do recordings of engine noises. The success of the brand is underlined by a display of some of Porsche's 28,000 trophies.

The Schweinemuseum

Schlachthofstr 2a · Daily 11am–7.30pm · €5.90 · ⊕ schweinemuseum.de · U-Schlachthof

The **Schweinemuseum** (Pig Museum), some 3.5km east of Stuttgart's centre, bills itself as being about "Kunst, Kultur und Kitsch": art, culture and kitsch. And yes, a little of all this is here, but more than anything the enterprise is a testament to what single-minded collecting can achieve. The museum's collection is the work of one Erika Wilhelmer, a former pub landlady who was given a model pig for her birthday in the 1980s. Smitten with the cute porcine, quickly her collection grew. By 1989 there was more than enough for a museum; in 1991 the collection earned her a *Guinness Book of Records* entry; and in 2010 she moved the collection – valued at around €1.5 million – into the perfect venue: an old slaughterhouse on Stuttgart's fringes.

Inside are 50,000 pig images and models and scores of facts about them, organized thematically. We learn that the average German eats about 56kg of pork per year – that's forty pigs during the average life; that all of today's pigs are genealogically

STUTTGART WEINSTUBEN

Cradled in a valley of five hundred **vineyards** – some of which spill right into the city – Stuttgart naturally enjoys its wine. Local vintners produce a number of whites, including an elegant Riesling, as well as the popular, full-bodied red Trollinger. Don't be surprised if you haven't heard of Stuttgart's wines though: wine consumption here is twice the national average so local supplies only just meet the demand and few wines leave the valley. So, while Frankfurt has its cider taverns and Munich its beer halls, Stuttgart's unique drinking dens are its **Weinstuben** or **wine bars** – a few of which are listed below.

Weinstuben tend to open evenings only, rarely on a Sunday, and are usually unpretentious rustic places. All serve solid and inexpensive Swabian dishes, which invariably include doughy *Spätzle* (noodles) and *Maultaschen*, the local oversized ravioli. More homely still are **Besenwirtschaften**, temporary wine-bars that appear in the front rooms of people's houses to serve the season's vintage with home-cooking, including potato soup (*Kartoffelsuppe*), noodle and beef stew (*Gaisburger Marsch*) or a *Schlachtplatte*, a meat feast served with vegetables. These places traditionally announce themselves with a broom hung outside and their locations vary from year to year. They're all listed in the guide *Stuttgarter Weine*, available from the tourist office, which is also a good place to pick up information on the *Stuttgart Weinwanderweg* (⊕ stuttgarter-weinwanderweg.de), the **hiking routes** that circle through local vineyards and past many *Besenwirtschaften*.

Stuttgart's other great wine-initiative is the **Stuttgarter Weindorf** (⊕ stuttgarter-weindorf .de), held during the last weekend in August, when the Marktplatz and Schillerplatz fill with wine buffs sampling hundreds of regional tipples. The year's vintages are on sale, and it's a great chance to pick up rarer wines. A similar event is the **Fellbacher Herbst** on the second weekend in October, in Fellback, just east of Bad Cannstatt.

WEINSTUBEN

Kachelofen Eberhardstr. 10 ☎ 0711 24 23 78. A bastion of beams and lacy tablecloths among the hip bars of Hans-im-Gluck south of Marktplatz, this is the *Weinstube* favoured by Stuttgart's smarter set. It serves hearty regional food as four-course set meals (€33–43). Mon–Thurs noon–midnight, Fri & Sat noon–1am.

Klösterle Marktstr. 71, Bad Cannstatt ☎ 0711 56 89 62. Swabian specials, including delicious sausage salad and good *Maultaschen* (mains €10–20), in the rustic interior of a wonky half-timbered building from 1463, which looks like an incongruous film-set among the modern flats. Mon–Fri 5pm–midnight, Sat & Sun 11.30am–midnight.

Schnellenturm Weberstr. 72 ☎ 0711 236 48 88, ⊕ weinstube-schellenturm.de. Duke Christopher's 1564 defence tower transformed into a cosy half-timbered nest. Quality and prices are a little above the average *Weinstube* fare – mains such as *Schwäbischer Sauerbraten* in a rich sauce average about €15. Mon–Sat 5pm–midnight.

★ **Stetter** Rosenstr. 32 ☎ 0711 24 01 63, ⊕ weinhaus-stetter.de. A wine connoisseurs' heaven – at the last count, over 575 wines, nearly 200 regional, were on the list of this family-run place though, just locals exchanging news and tucking into spicy bean soup or rich beef goulash. Mains average €10. Mon–Fri 3–11pm, Sat 11am–3pm.

8

Chinese; and that Denmark is the only country with more pigs than people. Pigs appear on belt buckles, pin cushions, ashtrays, piggy banks, toys, games, in books and in sayings, and the collection culminates in a huge tower of stuffed toy pigs in the attic. Throughout your visit you're likely to catch the smell of pork wafting up from below, since there is a good restaurant as well as a beer garden with a canteen attached.

ARRIVAL AND DEPARTURE   STUTTGART

By plane Stuttgart's international airport (STR; ☎01805 94 84 44, ⓦflughafen-stuttgart.de) lies 15km south of the city centre. S-Bahn lines S2 and S3 run to the Hauptbahnhof in around 30min (daily 5am–12.30pm; €3.50). Expect to pay €26 for a taxi.

By train The Hauptbahnhof is on the northeastern edge of

the town centre.

Destinations Frankfurt (every 30min; 1hr 30min); Friedrichshafen (hourly; 2hr 10min); Heidelberg (hourly; 40min); Karlsruhe (hourly; 45min); Konstanz (8 daily; 2hr 40min); Ludwigsburg (frequent; 10min); Munich (frequent; 2hr 20min); Tübingen (frequent; 1hr); Ulm (frequent; 1hr).

GETTING AROUND

By public transport Verkehrs- und Tarifverbund Stuttgart (ⓦvvs.de) run a public transport network, with the Hauptbahnhof its main hub. From here the U-Bahn rumbles city-wide and commuter lines of the S-Bahn rail network zip to outer suburbs. A single ticket in zone 1 costs €2.20; a day-pass for two zones – which will get you to the Mercedes and Porsche museums – costs €6.50 per person, or €11.30 for a group ticket for up to five people.

By car Major international players share an office on platform 16 of the Hauptbahnhof and most big outfits have a desk at the airport.

By bike Deutsche Bahn operates its public bike-sharing Call-a-bikes scheme in Stuttgart (see p.34).

On foot The city centre is easily walkable, and parks – such as the Schlossgarten – make even longer walks north to Bad Cannstatt a pleasure.

INFORMATION

Tourist offices The main office is at Königstr. 1a, opposite the Hauptbahnhof (Mon–Fri 9am–8pm, Sat 9am–6pm, Sun 11am–6pm; ☎0711 222 82 53, ⓦstuttgart-tourist .de). They can book accommodation and they sell the StuttCard. There's another branch in the airport in the terminal 3 arrivals area (Mon–Fri 8am–7pm, Sat

9am–1pm & 1.45–6.30pm, Sun 10am–1pm & 1.45–5.30pm; ☎071178 28 58 31).

Discount cards The StuttCard (1–3 days; €23–45) includes public transport within city boundaries and free entry to most museums, plus sightseeing tours, entertainment and discounts in some shops and restaurants.

ACCOMMODATION

Stuttgart's many business hotels often lower their rates by as much as a third at weekends, but in general budget options are scarce, so it's almost always easiest to let the tourist office book for you, or use its online booking engine.

HOTELS AND PENSIONS

★**Graf Zeppelin** Arnulf-Klett-Platz 7 ☎0711 204 80, ⓦsteigenberger.com. Five-star place opposite the Hauptbahnhof with *fin-de-siècle* elegance. Rooms come in different styles, some classical, some with clean avant-garde lines. The hotel has its own pool, sauna, gym, bar and three extremely good restaurants: one gourmet, another a steak specialist and a more informal regional restaurant. **€157**

Hotel Centro Büchsenstr. 24 ☎0711 585 33 15, ⓦhotelcentro.de. Bare-bones hotel, but clean and only a couple of minutes' walk from the pedestrianized centre and U- and S-Bahn Stuttgart Stadtmitte. There are also some bargain singles, if you don't mind sharing a bathroom. **€97**

Schwabennest Hospitalstr. 9 ☎0711 29 68 10, ⓦschwabennest.de. Spotless guesthouse with dated furnishings above a budget bistro with daily specials around the €8 mark. One of the few central accommodation

bargains. Some rooms en suite, others share bathrooms. Breakfast €8.50 extra. **€57**

Unger Kronenstr. 17 ☎0711 209 90, ⓦhotel-unger.de. Classy, modern 4-star business-hotel in the Altstadt. The breakfast buffet is excellent and there's a fitness studio too. Rates are reduced by about a third on Fri, Sat and Sun nights. Broadband internet included. **€143**

Wörtz zur Weinsteige Hohenheimer Str. 30 ☎0711 236 70 00, ⓦzur-weinsteige.de; U-Bahn Dobelstrasse. Traditional family-run hotel southeast of the centre where heavy dark-wood furniture provides a bit of time-honoured style; some suites even have Baroque themes. Also has a gourmet restaurant on site. With free wi-fi. **€130**

Der Zauberlehrling Rosenstr. 38 ☎0711 237 77 70, ⓦzauberlehrling.de. Suave, family-run, boutique hotel with a hip Bohnenviertel location and extravagant themed decor in every room. This ranges from Japanese minimalism to faded nineteenth-century glamour, but all of it manages to be airy and tasteful. The breakfast buffet costs €19, and there's a good upmarket restaurant here too (see below). **€150**

CAMPSITES AND HOSTELS
Campingplatz Stuttgart Mercedesstr. 40 ☏0711 55 66 96, ⊛campingplatz-stuttgart.de; S-Bahn Bad Cannstatt. Campground with riverside pitches 4km from the city centre in Bad Cannstatt. It's 1km southeast of the S-Bahn and there's another similar campground nearby. Pitch **€4.50**, plus **€7** per person

DJH Stuttgart Hausmannstr. 27 ☏0711 664 74 70, ⊛jugendherberge-stuttgart.de; bus #42 or tram #15 to "Eugensplatz". Large, well-organized and generally spotless hostel whose dorms and en-suite two-bed rooms have fantastic views over Stuttgart. If you're walking, it's 15min southeast of the Hauptbahnhof. Dorms **€27**, doubles **€65**

★ **Hostel Alex 30** Alexanderstr. 30 ☏0711 838 89 50, ⊛alex30-hostel.de; U-Bahn to Olgaeck. Cheerful independent hostel a 20min walk southeast of the Hauptbahnhof, close to the Bohnenviertel. It has a bar, café, kitchen, tiny terrace and free wi-fi. Private rooms are simple and spacious. Dorms **€24**, doubles **€58**

EATING AND DRINKING

As a wealthy business centre Stuttgart has plenty of good restaurants. Stylish places gather at the southern end of **Königstrasse** around **Eberhardstrasse**, where many have outdoor seating. For something earthy and traditional try the Bohnenviertel – particularly **Rosenstrasse** and **Pfarrstrasse**. Several of Stuttgart's hotels also have good restaurants (see opposite).

CAFÉS AND CHEAP EATS
Academie der Schönsten Kunste Charlottenstr. 5 ☏0711 24 24 36, ⊛academie-der-schoensten-kuenste. de. Marvellous café a 5min walk south of the Staatsgalerie. Its quirky mix of 1930s decor and modern painting is a hit with Stuttgart's arty set, who tuck in to healthy sandwiches and salads or weekend brunches – eggs served direct in the pan are delicious – with frothy bowls of cappuccino. Mon–Sat 8am–midnight, Sun 8am–8pm.

★ **Brunnenwirt** Leonhardsplatz 25 ☏0711 24 56 21. Simple sausage kiosk that's become a local institution, legendary in particular for *Currywurst* (€2.70) and *Rote Wurst* (€2.40) – a salty and heavily spiced local *Bratwurst* – and for offering perfect french fries or *pommes frites*. Daily 11am–late (usually around 2am).

Café Königsbau Königstr. 28 ☏0711 29 07 87, ⊛cafe-koenigsbau.de. Excellent café with all the right ingredients in place: the cakes are home-made, including some particularly fine fruit-based offerings; there's seating outside for people-watching on Schlossplatz; and indoors there's a traditional coffee-house atmosphere to enjoy. Mon–Sat 9am–7pm, Sun 11am–7pm.

RESTAURANTS
★ **Délice** Hauptstätter Str. 61 ☏0711 640 32 22, ⊛restaurant-delice.de. Intimate, six-table city-centre gourmet restaurant. Master chef Friedrich Gutscher conjures exquisite international flavours and his €98 five-course *Gastrosophisches Menü* is fresh, international and relatively good value given the quality and inventiveness. The wine list is first-class and the sommelier's expertise seamless. Mon–Fri 6.30pm–midnight.

Iden Swabenzentrum Eberhardstr. 1 ☏0711 23 59 89, ⊛iden-stuttgart.de. Pay-by-weight veggie place, offering a buffet of local and organic produce; lots of salads and juices and great home-made soup and cake too. The ingredients are of the highest quality, but prices correspondingly high – expect to pay at least €10 for a mid-sized plate of food. Mon–Fri 11am–6pm, Sat 11am–5pm.

Nirvan Eberhardstr. 73 ☏0711 24 05 61, ⊛nirvan-stuttgart.de. Persian basement restaurant with excellent grilled lamb, poultry and veal (mains around €13). Authentic decor lends atmosphere, as does the belly-dancing on Fridays. And there are even a few Persian wines to complete the experience. Mon–Fri & Sun 11am–11pm, Sat 11am–midnight.

Tauberquelle Torstr. 19 ☏0711 553 29 33, ⊛tauberquelle-stuttgart.de. All the Swabian favourites – several varieties of *Maultaschen*, *Kasespätzle*, *Gaisburger Marsch* and *Rostbraten* – are good value (mains €6.50–14.50) and done to perfection at this central restaurant. Also has a quiet beer garden – ideal if you need to step away from the city-centre bustle. Mon–Sat 11.30am–midnight.

TÜ8 Tübinger Str. 8 ☏0711 223 78 88. Complex housing three restaurants that share the great beers of the resident microbrewery. All three tend towards formulaic themes, but are inexpensive and dependable: *Mäxle* serves Swabian classics; *Spaghettissimo*, vast portions of inexpensive Italian food; and *Hacienda*, Tex-Mex favourites. Mäxle daily 11.30am–midnight; Spaghettissimo Mon–Thurs & Sun 11am–midnight, Fri & Sat 11am–2am; Hacienda daily 5pm–3am.

Der Zauberlehrling Rosenstr. 38 ☏0711 237 77 70, ⊛zauberlehrling.de. Relaxed restaurant of a boutique hotel (see opposite), serving excellent upmarket German and international cuisine and a good-value €30 three-course regional menu. Mon–Fri 6pm–late.

MICROBREWERIES AND BEER GARDENS
Biergarten im Schlossgarten Canstatter Str. 18. ☏0711 226 12 74, ⊛biergarten-schlossgarten.de. Large, summer-only beer garden in the Schlossgarten near the

8

Hauptbahnhof. Offers solid traditional canteen food, an array of drinks and a convivial atmosphere with regular live music – which spans the easily digested likes of country, rock 'n' roll, *Schlager* and Italian pop. Summer daily 10.30am–1am.

Calwer-Eck-Bräu Calwer Str. 31 ☎ 0711 22 24 94 40, ⓦ brauhaus-calwereck.de. Stuttgart's oldest microbrewery with several good standard brews – some organic – and interesting seasonal offerings. The cosy, cheerful atmosphere can be further savoured with a menu of good local offerings:

the *Maultaschen* soup (€4.80) is excellent and daily lunch specials (around €7) include a beer. Mon–Thurs 11am–midnight, Fri & Sat 11am–1am, Sun 10am–1am.

Palast der Republik Friedrichstr. 27 ☎ 0711 22 64 88. Offbeat cult place – a former public loo that's now a beer kiosk – where when the sun shines, the unconventional hang out in droves, with many ending up lounging around on the pavement in summer. Mon–Wed 11am–2pm, Thurs–Sat 11am–3pm, Sun 2pm–1am.

NIGHTLIFE AND ENTERTAINMENT

For its size Stuttgart has a nightlife scene it can be proud of, with plenty of busy downtown **clubs**, particularly along Theodor-Heuss-Strasse, three blocks west of Königstrasse. Stuttgart's wealthy burghers also stimulate a prodigious amount of high culture. Look out for concerts of the **Internationale Bachakademie Stuttgart** (ⓦ bachakademie.de) under director Professor Helmuth Rilling, and check the **Stiftskirche** for choral concerts: Stuttgart has one of Germany's densest concentration of top-class choirs. The free **listings magazine** *Moritz* (ⓦ moritz.de), available from the tourist office and local bars, provides a rudimentary what's-on rundown; for detailed information pick up *Lift Stuttgart* (ⓦ lift-online.de), the city's what's-on bible, or *Prinz* (ⓦ prinz.de/stuttgart). The tourist office sells **tickets** to most events.

CLUBS AND VENUES

Dilayla Eberhardstr. 49 ☎ 0711 236 95 27, ⓦ dilayla.de. Dimly lit basement that bustles with a broad spectrum of generally half-cut people dancing to a broad range of Seventies and Eighties hits or lounging on couches on the last stop of the night; note that it only gets busy after midnight. Mon–Thurs & Sun 9pm–4am, Fri & Sat 9pm–6am.

Friedrichsbau Varieté Friedrichstr. 24 ☎ 0711 225 70 70, ⓦ friedrichsbau.de; U-Bahn Friedrichsbau Börse. Good old-fashioned variety shows and cabaret showcasing a broad variety of acrobatic and comedic talents; tickets start at €20. Full bar and good finger-food available. Hours vary, generally shows start Wed–Sat 8pm, Sun 6pm.

King's Club Calwer Str. 21, entry on Gymnasiumstrasse ☎ 0711 226 45 58, ⓦ kingsclub-stuttgart.de. Pivotal local gay and lesbian basement club that's been on the go since the late 1970s, catering to diverse musical tastes and hosting regular theme nights. Only busy after midnight except on Thurs, which is karaoke night. Thurs 9pm–late, Fri & Sat 10pm–late, Sun 10pm–6am.

★ **Kiste** Hauptstätter Str. 35 ☎ 0711 553 28 05, ⓦ kiste-stuttgart.de. Venerable and generally packed dive that's one of the few places with regular live music in Stuttgart. The range of acts is incredibly broad, going all

the way from classical to punk, but a particular strong point is jazz. Mon–Thurs 6pm–1am, Fri & Sat 6pm–2am.

Perkins Park Stresemannstr. 39 ☎ 0711 256 00 62, ⓦ perkins-park.de. Popular with twenty- and thirty-somethings, this club's been spinning records for two decades, making it a local classic. The hippest local DJs play here, and the music can go in virtually any direction. Cover around €10. Wed 8pm–late, Fri & Sat 9pm–late, Sun 10pm–late.

THEATRES AND CONCERT HALLS

Liederhalle Berliner-Platz 1–3 ☎ 0711 202 77 10, ⓦ liederhalle-stuttgart.de. One of Germany's finest classical outfits, the Radio-Sinfonieorchester, perform concerts here, as do the Stuttgarter Philharmoniker, and the renowned chamber orchestra, Stuttgarter Kammerorchester, under American conductor Dennis Russell Davies. Also a venue for occasional musicals.

Staatstheater Oberer Schlossgarten 6 ☎ 0711 20 20 90, ⓦ staatstheater-stuttgart.de. The main address for opera, theatre and productions by world-acclaimed Stuttgart Ballet Company (ⓦ stuttgart-ballet.de); tickets come at bargain prices (from €9) and its restored 1909–12 Opernhaus is worth a visit for its galleried hall alone.

STUTTGART FESTIVALS

Stuttgart really livens up in April, during the three-week **Stuttgarter Frühlingsfest** (ⓦ stuttgarter-fruehlingsfest.de), which salutes spring with beer and grilled sausages; in August, when the open-air **Sommerfest** (ⓦ stuttgarter-sommerfest.de) takes over the Schlossplatz with live music; and during the **Stuttgarter Weindorf** (see box, p.437) later in the same month. Stuttgart also hosts Germany's largest **Christmas Market** in December, but the town's really big event is the late-September, sixteen-day **Cannstatter Volksfest** (ⓦ cannstatter-volksfest.de), a sizeable local equivalent to Munich's Oktoberfest, that's as yet undiscovered by invading armies of tourists.

DIRECTORY

Hospital Katharinenhospital, Kriegsbergstr. 60 ☎0711 27 80.

Laundry Waschsalon Trieb Königstr. 1b (daily 5am–midnight).

Pharmacy Apotheke im Hauptbahnhof (Mon–Fri 6.30am–8.30pm, Sat 8am–6pm, Sun 10am–5pm), in the main train station.

Police Hahnemannstr. 1 ☎0711 899 00.

Post office Königsbaupassagen, northwest of Schlossplatz (Mon–Fri 10am–8pm, Sat 9am–4pm); there's a branch in the Hauptbahnhof too.

Ludwigsburg

For a heady century the small town of **LUDWIGSBURG** was adorned with grandeur as the seat of the Württemberg dukes and Germany's largest Baroque **palace**. During that time a planned town developed on the basis of free land and building materials, and a fifteen-year tax exemption. The elegant Marktplatz at its centre suggests these planned origins, with its perfectly balanced streets radiating from a statue of palace founder, Eberhard Ludwig, flouncing on a fountain.

When Friedrich I's Neues Schloss rose in Stuttgart, 14km to the south, Ludwigsburg suddenly reverted to provincial obscurity, although its Versailles-inspired palace continues to draw visitors and delight lovers of Baroque. The town returns the compliment by theming as much as it can in this style, including its **Christmas market**. Other seasonal high-points include the mid-May **Pferdemarkt**, a traditional horse festival, with much clip-clopping around town; the **Schlossfestspiele** (June to mid-Sept; ⓦschlossfestspiele.de), a classical music, opera, dance and theatre festival; and, in early September, the Venetian-style costume **Carnevale**.

Schloss Ludwigsburg

Schlossstr. 30 • 1hr 30min guided tours in English daily: mid-March to mid-Nov Mon–Fri 1.30pm, Sat & Sun 11am, 1.30pm & 3.15pm; mid-Nov to mid-March daily 1.30pm • €7 • ⓦschloss-ludwigsburg.de

Schloss Ludwigsburg was born out of Duke Eberhard Ludwig's envy of palaces admired on military campaigns abroad. French troops, who in 1697 reduced the ducal hunting lodge here to ashes, provided the required excuse to build a replacement; a Baroque palace was duly begun in 1706. Just before its completion, the duke demanded two further wings, in part to lodge his mistress. The court was furious at his extravagance, yet a second, far larger Corps de Logis rose to close the square.

However, Eberhard Ludwig was almost modest compared with his successor Duke Carl Eugen. Upon ascending to the duchy throne in 1744, the 16-year-old ruler declared the Residenzschloss his home and established the most vibrant court in Europe, where the finest opera, ballet and French comedy was offered, and extramarital dalliances were part of the menu: the Duke forbade ladies from wearing blue shoes at court except "those who would ... devote their honour to him ... (and who should) never appear without this distinguishing mark," notes a 1756 court report. Small wonder his wife stomped back to her parents after eight years of marriage.

The interior

Of the sixty-odd rooms on show of the palace's 452 across eighteen buildings, the older ones are perhaps the most extravagant: a gorgeous allegorical fresco of the arts and sciences for Eberhard Ludwig in the **Ahnensaal** (Ancestors' Hall) leads to Carl Eugen's charming **Schlosstheater**, which entertained Mozart, Casanova and Goethe and where classical music is still staged in the summer. Eberhard Ludwig's **Schlosskapelle** spurns Protestant piety to show off ritzy Baroque. The east wing's **Satyrkabinett** features cherubs above moustachioed Turkish prisoners of war who lament Eberhard Ludwig's success in the field, and *trompe l'oeil* frescoes play tricks on the ceiling of the **Ordenshalle**, the festive hall of the

8

ducal hunting order. The new **Corps de Logis** is largely dressed in opulent early Neoclassicism that ranks among Germany's finest, a makeover for Frederick I's summer retreat; the Stuttgart king became so bloated through gluttony that he had to be hoisted by block and tackle on to his mount until one could be trained to kneel camel-fashion. The palace entry ticket also covers small palace museums of theatre and court dress, and a shop retails the hand-painted china of a factory established in 1758 by Carl Eugen.

The Blühendes Barok

Daily 7.30am–8.30pm • €8.50 • ⓦ blueba.de

To the rear of Schloss Ludwigsburg lies the **Blühendes Barok**, the palace's landscaped gardens, which provide a natural breather from the head-spinning opulence inside. Largely landscaped in naturalistic style, punctuated with a castle folly, a Japanese garden, an aviary and a whimsical fairy-tale garden – complete with kitsch sound effects – they're a relaxing spot to lounge and picnic.

ARRIVAL AND INFORMATION   LUDWIGSBURG

By train Frequent S-Bahn (lines S4 & S5) and mainline trains zip from Stuttgart to Ludwigsburg's Bahnhof, a 5min walk northwest to the Marktplatz, another 5min to the Schloss.

By boat From mid-May to Oct the *Neckar Käpt'n* (☎ 0711 54 99 70 60, ⓦ neckar-kaeptn.de) offers relaxed 2hr cruises

from Bad Cannstatt to Ludwigsburg-Hoheneck, a 25min walk east of the Residenzschloss – or a quick journey on bus #427.

Tourist office MIK, Eberhardstr. 1 (Mon–Sun 10am–6pm; ☎ 07141 910 22 52, ⓦ ludwigsburg.de).

ACCOMMODATION AND EATING

Alte Sonne Bei der Katholischen Kirche 3 ☎ 07141 92 52 31, ⓦ altesonne-durst.de. Smart, central restaurant with high-quality innovative international dishes, such as Pinot Noir risotto or Breton-style lamb with Provence goulash. Mains are in the €24–40 price range, while fixed-price menus are €84–109. A less formal and less expensive brasserie shares the same address, with simple high-quality fish and meat dishes for around €13–20. Wed–Sun noon–2pm & 6–10pm.

Hotel Favorit Gartenstr. 18 ☎ 07141 97 67 70, ⓦ hotel-favorit.de. The cheerful rooms at this Best Western business hotel have pastel walls and pine furniture

and come in three comfort categories. Amenities include a sauna, free wi-fi and an extensive breakfast buffet which is included in the rates. **€99**

Nestor Hotel Stuttgarter Str. 35/2 ☎ 07141 96 70, ⓦ nestor-hotels.de. This excellent, modern 179-room hotel has given the old red-brick garrison building beside the Schloss a new lease of life. The a/c rooms have a bright, boutique feel, and occasional original features such as pillars or exposed beams add charm. There's also wi-fi (only free in the lobby) and a sauna, and the included buffet breakfast is first-class. **€80**

Kloster Maulbronn

Klosterhof 5 • March–Oct daily 9am–5.30pm; Nov–Feb Tues–Sun 9.30am–5pm • Church and refectory €7, audio-guide €2 • ⓦ kloster-maulbronn.de

Nestled in a relatively isolated valley, 33km northwest of Stuttgart, the small town of **MAULBRONN** is famous for the well-preserved medieval **Kloster Maulbronn**. Founded as a Cistercian monastery in 1140, it was dissolved during the sixteenth century, after which it became a Protestant school: fans of former pupil Hermann Hesse may recognize it as the semi-fictional Mariabronn in his book *Narziss und Goldmund*. Parts still serve as a school for around fifty pupils.

Initially the most striking feature of the monastery is the wall that encircles it and other defensive fortifications, dating from an era when the region was wild and fairly lawless. Within the compound a tidy collection of Gothic half-timbered buildings reveal themselves, looking much as they would have done five hundred years ago.

You can wander the compound free of charge, and there's a useful information board showing the layout and original uses of the buildings outside the **visitor centre**, which sells entry tickets to the church and refectory, and rents out moderately useful audio-guides.

The Klosterkirche

The **Klosterkirche** is a typically Cistercian bare-bones affair with no tower and little decoration, though over time works of art and decorations were commissioned to brighten the place up. If anything, decoration was more important in the **refectory** where it was part of a conscious attempt to help distract the mind from the paltriness of meals. Some of the frescoes here were the work of Jerg Ratgeb, who also adorned the ceilings of the **well-house** in the courtyard where monks washed before each meal. Here he depicts events from the monastery's history, as well as a severe self-portrait; he left the work unfinished to become embroiled in the early sixteenth-century Peasants' War, and was quartered in Pforzheim's marketplace for his trouble.

The rest of the monastery

No other buildings are open to the public, but you can walk around the complex. Look out for the **Faustturm**, the residence of Dr Faust, a magician who claimed to be able to make gold, and was given a job by an unscrupulous abbot. Faust was a celebrity in his time and the subject of fables in the 1587 *Faustbuch*, published half a century after his death. Contemporary intellectuals certainly took him seriously, and much later various German literary giants – particularly Lessing, Goethe and Thomas Mann – dwelt on him in their exploration of power and absolute knowledge. Another striking building is the turreted, Renaissance-era **Jagdschloss**, built by the dukes of Württemberg as a hunting lodge but now part of the school. As you wander between these buildings look out for remnants of a complicated **irrigation system**, which distributed water around the compound and supplied a series of fish ponds.

8

ARRIVAL AND INFORMATION
KLOSTER MAULBRONN

By train and bus The journey from Stuttgart (or Karlsruhe, also around 30km away) to Maulbronn is tricky and generally requires taking a train to Bretten or Mühlacker and then a bus to the monastery. Connections from both are frequent and take about an hour; you can get all the exact connections at ⓦbahn.de or from any railway station.

Tourist office In the Rathaus at Klosterhof 31 (Mon, Tues, Thurs & Fri 8am–noon, Wed 9am–1pm & 2–6pm; ☎07043 10 30, ⓦmaulbronn.de). The office can help with accommodation; there are plenty of places along the main road with "Zimmer Frei" signs.

ACCOMMODATION AND EATING

Hotel Klosterpost Frankfurter Str. 2 ☎07043 10 80, ⓦhotel-klosterpost.de. Good, traditional inn that's snagged itself the status of UNESCO World Heritage Site thanks to its half-timbered exterior from 1201. Inside are bright, modern rooms and a good regional restaurant (mains average €12); one of its specialities is *Maultaschen*, which are also sold bagged up for you to take away.

Restaurant daily 11.30am–4pm & 5.30pm– late. **€89**
Klosterkatz Klosterhof 21 ☎07043 87 38, ⓦkloster-katz.de. Solid, everyday Italian food served in the atmospheric courtyard of the monastery. Prices for its excellent thin-crust pizzas come in around €8; look out for similarly-priced daily fresh pasta specials which are usually very good. Daily except Tues 11am–late.

Tübingen

TÜBINGEN, 40km south of Stuttgart, first appears in the history books in 1078, but the town didn't really blossom until four hundred years later when Württemberg Count Eberhard established its university. Much of the medieval city that grew out of this initiative remains, with half-timbered houses on twisting cobbled lanes gathering around two focal squares – **Holzmarkt** and the **Markt** – below a fortress, **Schloss Hohentübingen**.

But what really marks the place out is still the **university**, one of Germany's best. It injects this venerable city with modern and youthful energy; one-in-four of the town's 70,000 population is directly connected with it, and a local quip runs that the town doesn't have a university – it is one. Its celebrity scholars include Philipp Melanchthon, who taught here before moving to Wittenberg; Goethe, who published his first works here; the philosopher Hegel; astronomer Johannes Keppler; and psychiatrist Alois Alzheimer. More recently Joseph Ratzinger – once Pope Benedict XVI – taught theology here and had a famously hard-line against 1960s student radicalism. A scholarly atmosphere persists around town, but that doesn't mean the students don't let their hair down – the bar scene is happening and punting on the Neckar good fun – and everything's much less touristy than in regional rival Heidelberg.

The Eberhardsbrücke and the Hölderlinturm

No view better captures idyllic Tübingen, muse of poets and writers, than that from the Eberhardsbrücke, which overlooks the **Platanenallee**, a leafy boulevard on a narrow man-made island. Punts pass serenely by and a row of pink-, mustard- and cream-coloured houses that prop each other up on the opposite riverbank look on. One of these is the **Hölderlinturm**, at Bursagasse 6 (Tues–Fri 10am–noon & 3–5pm, Sat & Sun 2–5pm; €2.50; ⊛hoelderlin-gesellschaft.de), once part of the town's medieval fortifications. Named for acclaimed poet Friedrich Hölderlin, who spent his last 36 years here, it houses memorabilia of his life and of the carpenter's family who nursed him. Much of his most original and complex work was produced here, when he was on the brink of madness. He moved to the tower from Tübingen's first hospital, the Burse on Bursagasse, the road behind, which is now student halls.

The Holzmarkt and around

The Holzmarkt, one of Tübingen's principal squares, lies just north of the river. The main attraction here is the splendid Stiftskirche St Georg, but the square also has links to a couple of the town's literary luminaries: **Hermann Hesse** worked as a bookbinder and seller in the Buchhandlung Heckenhauser on the north side of Holzmarkt before he nurtured his own literary genius; and **Goethe** lodged here for three nights with his publisher Johann Friedrich Cotta in September 1797, as a plaque on Cottahaus, opposite the church's main entrance, remembers (not that it was all literary business – a plaque on the adjacent student dormitory replies scurrilously, "Hier kotzte Goethe", or "Goethe puked here").

Just west of the square at Münzgasse 20 lies the old prison, the **Karzer** (20min tours Sat & Sun 2pm; €1), where in earlier days delinquent students might have found themselves on bread and water. Now tourists inspect the graffiti-and-soot silhouettes they created to while away the hours during their incarceration.

Stiftskirche St Georg

Clinicumsgasse • Daily 9am–4pm • Choir and tower €1 • ⊛stiftskirche-tuebingen.de

Holzmarkt is dominated by Count Eberhard's Gothic, late fifteenth-century **Stiftskirche St Georg**. Magnificent star vaulting spreads across nave and aisle roofs, and

---

PUNTING THE NECKAR

Tübingen's stretch of willow-lined **Neckar** is too shallow for commerce – one factor in the town's lack of industrialization – but has also formed the basis for one of the quintessential Tübingen activities: poling a *Stocherkahn*, or **punt**, up and down the river.

The big event on the river is the annual **Tübingen punt race** – in May or June – when student fraternities battle it out in front of thousands of spectators. At other times in summer punting down the river with a group of friends, a picnic or crate of beer, seems as popular a student activity as any. Join them by renting a rowing boat, pedalo or canoe – from €9 per hour – from Bootsvermietung Märkle, Eberhardsbrücke 1 (mid-April to Oct; ☎07071 315 29, ⊛bootsvermietung-tuebingen.de), by the tourist office. Or let them do the work by renting the traditional twelve-seater *Stocherkahn* with a guide for €48 per hour.

a pulpit buds from a single stem into carvings of Mary, Pope Gregory and early Christian fathers. In a choir dappled by beautiful stained glass, university founder Count Eberhard is upstaged by the mausoleum of Countess Mechthild (the work of Ulm's Hans Multscher), one of thirteen members of the House of Württemberg buried here. For two hundred years the dynasty made the town their second residence, and they hid their tombs from prying eyes behind a graceful Gothic rood-screen. Albrecht Dürer's pupil Hans Schäufelein created its centrepiece altar. The entrance ticket to the choir also provides admission to the church **tower** for views over the Holzmarkt and the roofscape of this part of the Altstadt.

The Markt

From the Holzmarkt, half-timbered Kirchgasse leads west in an attractive preamble to Tübingen's extraordinary **Markt**. The town's heart and main hangout is liveliest during its Monday, Wednesday and Friday markets, when traders' stalls gather around the series of jolly cherubs and women who depict the seasons on the **Neptunenbrunnen**. Competing for attention behind is the Gothic **Rathaus** (1433) with its neo-Renaissance frescoes of local heroes painted to celebrate the university's four-hundredth birthday in 1877. The real Renaissance is represented here in the form of an astronomical clock (1510), above a Baroque balcony that juts out like an opera box.

Stadtmuseum

Kornhausstr. 10 • Tues–Sun 10am–5pm • €2.50 • ☏ 07071 204 17 11

Marktgasse on the lower side of the Markt runs into a network of old streets, lanes and passages that once served as a wine-growing neighbourhood. These bygone days are the subject of the **Stadtmuseum**, at the end of the Marktgasse, which carefully documents nine hundred years of city history.

Schloss Hohentübingen

Burgsteige 11 • Museum Wed–Sun 10am–5pm, Thurs until 8pm • €5 • ☏ 07071 297 73 84

From the Markt, the walk uphill naturally leads to Burgsteige, a handsome street where antique shops encourage loitering en route to **Schloss Hohentübingen**, the Renaissance successor to an eleventh-century castle. The Württemberg dukes' coat of arms on its 1604 triumphal gateway lets you know who was responsible for the structure and a couple of viewpoints on the outer perimeter offer fine views over the red-roofed Altstadt.

Inside, much of the Schloss houses university departments, but one wing contains a **Museum of Archeology and Egyptology**, which is a bit disappointing, despite having one of the world's earliest sculptures: a horse carved from a mammoth tusk by an Upper-Paleolithic sculptor.

ARRIVAL AND INFORMATION
TÜBINGEN

By bus and train Tübingen's bus and train stations are adjacent, 5min from the Altstadt via the Eberhardsbrücke.

Tourist office An der Neckarbrücke 1 (Nov–Sept Mon–Fri 9am–7pm, Sat 10am–4pm; May–Sept also Sun 11am–4pm; ☏ 07071 913 60, ⊛ tuebingen-info.de). Located at the southern end of the bridge, the office also has an accommodation booking service, which is particularly helpful for finding private rooms (from €50).

ACCOMMODATION

HOTELS

Hotel am Bad Uferweg Freibad 2 ☏ 07071 797 40, ⊛ hotel-am-bad.de. Good mid-range choice, in a quiet and leafy spot beside the river and lido, a 2km walk from the centre. With clean, simple modern rooms, wi-fi, an extensive breakfast buffet and plenty of parking. **€109**

Hotel am Schloss Burgsteige 18 ☏ 07071 929 40, ⊛ hotelamschloss.de. Half-timbered place with overstuffed window boxes just below the Schloss and with fine views over town. Comes with oodles of traditional charm and a great regional restaurant (see p.446). **€118**

Hotel Hospiz Neckarhalde 2 ☎07071 92 40, ⓦhotel-hospiz.de. Standard mid-priced hotel whose trump card is its location a mere block from Marktplatz, which means the modern, pine-furnished en-suite rooms are fairly snug. Has internet access and prices include a breakfast buffet. **€148**

Hotel Krone Uhlandstr. 1 ☎07071 133 10, ⓦkrone-tuebingen.de. Prestigious riverside address by the Eberhardsbrücke where bright modern rooms are dotted with the occasional antique. Has its own sophisticated gourmet restaurant with regional specialities, a separate urbane café-bar and free parking. **€165**

Hotel Meteora Weizsäckerstr. 1 ☎07071 970 90 20, ⓦhotel-meteora.de. Cheerful basic rooms in a spotless mid-priced hotel a 10min walk northeast of town with free on-street parking. Not all rooms are en suite, but single rooms are particularly good value from €33. Also has a good Greek restaurant on the premises with mains for around €11. **€89**

CAMPSITES AND HOSTELS

DJH Tübingen Gartenstr. 22/2 ☎07071 230 02, ⓦtuebingen.jugendherberge-bw.de; bus #22 from the Hauptbahnhof. Fairly institutional riverside hostel a 5min walk east of the Altstadt where rates include a good buffet breakfast and sheets. Reception is open 8am–10pm. Dorms **€24**

Neckar Camping Tübingen Rappenberghalde 61 ☎07071 431 45, ⓦneckarcamping.de; bus #20. Shaded spots on the banks of the Neckar around 1.5km west of the Altstadt. Amenities include table tennis and wi-fi. Open April–Oct. Pitch **€5.80**, plus **€6.50** per person

Viktor-Renner-Haus Frondsbergstr. 55 ☎07071 55 90 20; bus #13, #14, #18 or #19 to "Tübingen Breiter Weg". Basic lodgings 1km north of the Altstadt run by the Internationaler Bund, a youth and social-work organization, which offers no-frills singles (from €33) and doubles, but no breakfast. Rooms have internet connections and good views. **€55**

EATING AND DRINKING

CAFÉS, BARS AND BEER GARDENS

Marktschenke Am Markt 11 ☎07071 220 35, ⓦtangente-marktschenke.de. Pleasant little bar on the marketplace that's popular mainly for its location: it spills out onto the square and is a good place to start a night out. Mon–Wed 9am–midnight, Thurs–Sat 9am–1am, Sun 10am–midnight.

★**Neckarmüller** Gartenstr. 4 ☎07071 278 48. Far and away the best, and usually heaving, beer garden in town, attached to a microbrewery. Also does good basic dishes, particularly bargain lunches, veggie choices and good *Maultaschen*. Mains average €10. Daily 10am–1am, food until 11pm.

Tangente Jour Münzgasse 17 ☎07071 245 72, ⓦtangente-marktschenke.de. Café near the Stiftskirche with great Altstadt atmosphere, and specializing in breakfast and light meals – excellent bagels and seasonal salads – but also serves several local beers until late. Daily 8am–1am.

RESTAURANTS

★**Hotel am Schloss** Burgsteige 18 ☎07071 929 40, ⓦhotelamschloss.de. Great regional restaurant that many claim serves the best *Maultaschen* in the Land. There's certainly an excellent selection of these regional giant ravioli, with 23 varieties – including veggie options

– on the menu. Many are seasonal, like the trout or asparagus, but all are under €10, and there are fine views from the outdoor terrace too. Daily 11.30am–3pm & 5.30pm–midnight.

Ratskeller Haagasse 4 ☎07071 213 91, ⓦratskeller-tuebingen.de. Upmarket traditional dishes served behind, rather than in, the Rathaus. Great for meat dishes, such as the excellent pork medallion in a Cognac cream sauce, but also known for its giant pancakes. Daily 11.30am–2.30pm & 5.30–11pm.

Weinstube Forelle Kronenstr. 8 ☎07071 240 94, ⓦweinstube-forelle.de. Traditional wine bar and local favourite which oozes old-world charm; its walls are painted with cherubs, vines and heraldic crests. Known for its regional ingredients and cooking, the trout (*Forelle*) in almond butter is particularly good, as is the game. There's also a good selection of salads and some good local wines. Tues–Sun 11.30am–3pm & 5.30–10pm.

Die Würstkuche Am Lustnauer Tor 8 ☎07071 927 50, ⓦwurstkueche.com. No-nonsense roasts and doughy Swabian noodles are on the menu in this country-style restaurant in the west of town. Sensational *Maultaschen* too. Inexpensive (mains average €8) and very popular, though it's spread over two floors, so getting a seat is rarely a problem. Daily 11am–midnight.

NIGHTLIFE AND ENTERTAINMENT

CLUBS AND LIVE MUSIC

Blauer Turm Lounge Friedrichstr. 21 ☎07071 36 03 90, ⓦblauer-turm.de. Easy-going basement lounge with relaxed leather sofas and ambient house music until around 11pm when DJs start playing sets, the tempo picks

up and the dancefloor gradually fills. Entry rarely exceeds €3. Thurs & Sun 8pm–3am, Fri 9pm–5am, Sat 9pm–6am.

Jazzkeller Haagasse 15 ☎07071 55 09 06, ⓦjazz-keller.eu. Sociable upstairs bar whose basement regularly

sees a variety of DJs and bands pack out a small dancefloor. There's often jazz but the music is generally quite varied and the excellent Thurs hip-hop nights the stuff of local legend. Mon 7pm–1am, Tues–Thurs 7pm–2am, Fri & Sat 7pm–3am.

Tangente Night Pfleghofstr. 10 ☎ 07071 230 07, ⓦ tangente-night.com. Studeny place in the centre that's built for hard partying and heavy drinking and legendary for its raucous karaoke (Mon–Thurs) and Sun night *Kölsch* specials. DJs occasionally play Sat nights. Mon–Wed & Sun 6pm–3am, Thurs 6pm–4am, Fri & Sat 6pm–5am.

Zoo Tübingen Schleifmühleweg 86 ☎ 07071 97 73 00, ⓦ zoo-tuebingen.de. Popular pub, beer garden and

disco, about 1km west of the Altstadt. Has a very provincial atmosphere and many teenagers in the crowd, but the vibe is generally upbeat and the venue is often good for techno acts. Cover around €5. Wed–Sun 9am–late.

THEATRE

Landestheater Eberhardstr. 6 ☎ 07071 159 29, ⓦ landestheater-tuebingen.de. Always worth a look for its good mixed programme of modern and classic plays and Theatersport events – a kind of improv comedy theatre that has a local cult following, but needs very good German to appreciate. Hours vary, generally daily from 8pm.

Around Tübingen

Tübingen lies within view of the northwestern edge of the Swabian Alb, where sections of limestone have resisted erosion better than the surrounding land, leaving steep escarpments and craggy outcrops. Many cry out for fortresses and castles to be built on them, and over the centuries, that's exactly what happened. The most impressive today are the Gothic palaces built by the Romantic movement for pure show – and in that sense are no more authentic than Disney palaces – but their impressive locations are undeniable and many come with some interesting history of their own.

Schloss Lichtenstein

Feb, March & Nov Sat & Sun 10am–4pm; April–Oct daily 9am–5.30pm • Entry to courtyard €2, 30min tour €6 • ⓦ schloss-lichtenstein .de • Train services from Tübingen take you to Reutlingen (frequent; 10min), for buses (#400: hourly; 25min) to the village of Lichtenstein, from which the castle is a 30min walk

From its high-peak vantage point, photogenic **Schloss Lichtenstein** lies on an escarpment at the edge of the Swabian Alb where views of the flat river-valley below and the ready visibility of the plains around Tübingen, 32km away, provide a feeling that you are on the edge of a mountain range. The many-gabled and -turreted Schloss itself was constructed in the 1840s, with its design based largely on the exaggerated literary descriptions of an earlier fortress on the site, provided by fairy-tale writer Wilhelm Hauff. Grand views aside, the castle's most impressive feature is its armoury.

Burg Hohenzollern

Daily: mid-March to Oct 10am–5.30pm; Nov to mid-March 10am–4.30pm; tours every 20min • €5, tours €10 • ⓦ burg-hohenzollern.de • Trains link Tübingen (frequent; 20min) with the town of Hechingen, 4km south of the castle, from where two daily shuttle buses depart at 11.22am and 1.22pm

Rising dramatically from an isolated crag 31km southwest of Tübingen, **Burg Hohenzollern** is one of Germany's finest fairy-tale castles. Yet its medieval-looking battlements and towers are deceiving, since they were built between 1846 and 1867 by Friedrich August Stüler (a pupil of Schinkel), though he incorporated details of a fortress that had existed here since the eleventh century. Only the St-Michael-Kapelle, a chapel with ornate stained glass, survives from the original. The castle still belongs to the Hohenzollern family who reigned over a united Germany between 1871 and 1918; and the crown of Emperor Wilhelm II is the pride of the castle treasury. Also among the family artefacts are several snuff boxes from Frederick the Great's immense collection.

Ulm

ULM lies just south of the Swabian Alb, some 95km southeast of Stuttgart and 85km east of Tübingen, but it's the city's location on the Danube that shaped it most. In the Middle Ages it enabled Ulm to build great wealth from trading, boat building and textile manufacture. Ulm became an imperial city in 1376 and then leader of the Swabian League of cities, which it used to throw its weight about on the European stage. Over time though, corruption, wars and epidemics whittled away at the city's greatness; then, in just thirty minutes in December 1944 its glorious **Altstadt** disappeared beneath 2450 tonnes of explosive. Luckily its giant Münster came out relatively unscathed, and parts of the Altstadt have been reconstructed, but Ulm has also used the opportunity to experiment with some bold modern buildings. This sets the scene for a city that is as forward-looking as it is nostalgic and one that celebrates its **festivals** (see box, p.452) with an almost Latin passion. The best place to appreciate Ulm's skyline is on the eastern side of the Danube in the modern and uninteresting **Neu Ulm** – a city in its own right and in Bavaria.

The Münster

Münsterplatz **Church** Daily: Jan & Feb 9am–4.45pm; March & Oct 9am–5.45pm; April–July & Sept 9am–6.45pm; Aug 9am–7.45pm •
Free • **Tower** Daily: Jan & Feb 9am–3.45pm; March & Oct 9am–4.45pm; April–June & Sept 9am–5.45pm; July & Aug 9am–6.45pm • €4 •
Organ concert Mon–Sat noon, Sun 11.30am • €3.50 • ⓦ muenster-ulm.de

Quickly commissioned and begun in 1377, the year after Ulm received its independence, its flamboyant Gothic **Münster** reflected the city's incredible ambitions.

8

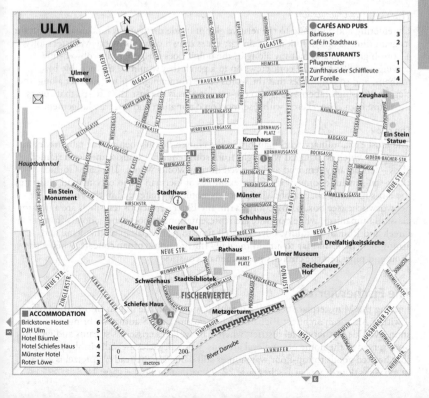

ULM ORIENTATION

The vast sweep of **Münsterplatz** provides Ulm with its focal point, and when there's not some sort of event taking place here (see box, p.452) it provides space for Wednesday- and Saturday-morning markets. The dimensions of the square are matched by the gigantic **Münster** beside, which protrudes from town like a Gothic rocket and provides an easy orientation point wherever you are. The streets south of the Münster contain the **Fischerviertel**, Ulm's most immediately attractive old quarter, where fisher-folk once lived. Ulm's **Rathaus** and two best **museums** lie just south of here.

Though only a parish church, it was designed for a standing congregation of twenty thousand – more than twice the population of the city at the time – and plans included far and away the world's tallest spire.

The tower

From any angle the dimensions of the powerful openwork **spire** impress. Following the guiding principle of Gothic church architecture to draw the observer's eyes to the heavens, medieval architect Matthäus Böblinger exaggerated the principle a little too much for the workmanship of the day, for in 1492 stones rained from the tower mid-build onto a Sunday congregation. Böblinger fled Ulm in disgrace and his spire was fudged until nineteenth-century Romantics rediscovered the medieval plans and applied their superior know-how: it finally reached 161.6m in 1890. Views of the Black Forest and, on clear days, the Alps, are possible, framed by stone filigree as you gasp up 768 lung-busting steps to a height of 143m.

The interior

On entering and adjusting to the relative gloom inside the church, it takes a moment for its giant dimensions to sink in. Again, the eye is drawn upwards by the Münster's lofty 41.6m-high nave, and halfway along it, the **pulpit** does this too: in its cobweb-fine carving a smaller staircase corkscrews up to a perch that would be unreachable by humans, and so symbolizes that the words come from a higher place. Further along, the elegant 26m-high **tabernacle** is also eye-catching, as is the vast 1471 fresco that covers the entire high chancel arch with a sermon on damnation and the Last Judgement.

The choir

The most extraordinary workmanship in the church lies just behind the tabernacle, in the **choir**, which is spangled with light from some equally exquisite medieval stained-glass – temporarily removed and so saved during World War II. The Late Gothic choir-stalls include some of the finest examples of German wood carving and illustrate the city's medieval charter of civil rights – symbolically reiterated in the annual Schwörwoche (see box, p.452). Jörg Syrlin the Elder's vivacious ten sibyls are a nod to classical humanism, while opposite are representations of poets and scholars from Greek and Roman antiquity. Give yourself time to really soak in all the detail and atmosphere here, and try to attend the daily thirty-minute **organ concert**, when eight thousand pipes test the church's phenomenal acoustics.

The Fischerviertel

Leaving the Münsterplatz behind, a downhill walk from the tourist information office – within American architect Richard Meier's Postmodern Stadthaus – brings you to the snug riverside **Fischerviertel** district, where narrow lanes crisscross streams and which once served as the home of medieval artisans, whose legacies are still visible: pulleys that hoisted goods to top-floor warehouses still dangle at the ready; a pretzel is carved in a baker's door-frame at Fischergasse 22, a boatman at Fischergasse 18.

The quirkiest and most time-worn place of all is the 1443 **Schiefes Haus** (now a hotel – see p.452), which slumps into the stream on its piles, every bit the crooked house of its name. Moments north is the **Schwörhaus** (Oath House), where Ulm residents gather on Schwörmontag (see box, p.452) to hear their mayor pledge a 1397 city oath "to be the same man to rich and poor, without reservation, in all common and honourable matters". Just south of the Schiefes Haus you can climb onto the 1480 riverside defence wall and walk downstream to another crooked building: the fourteenth-century defensive tower of the **Metzgerturm**, the "Leaning Tower of Ulm", which is 2m off the vertical.

The Rathaus

Münsterplatz 50 • Mon–Fri 9am–6pm, Sat 9am–4pm, Sun 11am–3pm

From the Metzgerturm it's a brief uphill walk to the sixteenth-century **Rathaus**, with its decorative frescoes that salute Ulm's medieval heyday as an imperial merchant: tubby Danube merchant-ships gather beneath the crests of trading partners; vices and virtues are caricatured; and tributes are paid to emperors and electors. Inside hangs a replica of Albrecht Ludwig Berblinger's hang-glider (see box below).

Catching the eye nearby is the all-glass pyramid of the **Stadtbibliotek** (City Library), designed by Gottfried Böhm and completed in 2004. Opposite lies Jörg Syrlin the Elder's startling *Fischkastenbrunnen* (Fish-crate Fountain), which depicts three saints dressed as knights, and in which fishmongers once kept their produce fresh.

Kunsthalle Weishaupt

Hans-und-Sophie-Scholl-Platz 1 • Tues–Sun 11am–5pm, Thurs until 8pm • €6, combined ticket with Ulmer Museum €10 • ⓦ kunsthalle-weishaupt.de

The square on the north side of the Rathaus is named after Hans and Sophie Scholl, two local students who organized anti-Nazi resistance by overtly distributing flyers, for which they were executed. Overlooking it is the striking modern building of **Kunsthalle Weishaupt**, which is most extraordinary at night when its illuminations make it resemble a giant ice-cube. Inside, it's equally striking, its giant, bright, clear rooms containing the vivid colours of vast modern and Pop Art canvases: Warhol, Klee, Macke, Kandinsky and Picasso are among those represented.

Ulmer Museum

Marktplatz 9 • Tues–Sun 11am–5pm, Thurs until 8pm • €5, free Fri, combined ticket with Kunsthalle Weishaupt €10 • ⓦ museum.ulm.de

The **Ulmer Museum**, the town history museum, is joined by bridge to the Kunsthalle. Much of the museum is a crash course in Ulm and Swabian arts from the Middle Ages to the present, with particular reference to the Renaissance. Illustrations depict a powerful city dominated by a stumpy Münster and enclosed within river fortifications. Among the archeological exhibits, don't miss the stunningly old and atavistic *Löwenmensch*, a 28cm-tall carving of a human form with a lion's head from 30,000 BC.

> **THE TAILOR OF ULM**
>
> Albrecht Ludwig Berblinger, aka the "**Tailor of Ulm**", crash-landed his home-made hang-glider into the Danube in 1811, eighty years before his pioneering countryman Otto Lilienthal took to the air. Ulm has since warmed to its tailor as an eccentric hero – a plaque on Herdbrücke marks the spot where he took off – but in his day Berblinger was mocked mercilessly. Worn down by ceaseless jibes, his business in tatters, he died bankrupt in 1825, a drunkard and gambler. Ironically, his design has since proved to be workable, and only the lack of thermals on the day caused failure and ruin.

8

EINSTEIN IN ULM

One connection Ulm likes to celebrate, in memorials and merchandise, is its link to **Albert Einstein**, born here on March 14, 1879. Never mind that the great Jewish physicist lived here for only fifteen months and that he refused the town's 70th birthday gift of honorary citizenship; an Einstein Monument now marks his **birthplace** on Bahnhofstrasse (later obliterated by bombs). More striking is Jürgen Gortz's wacky bronze of the physicist with his tongue out, which lies a 750m walk northeast of the Münster in front of the Zeughaus.

ARRIVAL AND DEPARTURE   ULM

By train Ulm's Hauptbahnhof lies just west of the centre, a 5min walk from the focal Münsterplatz.

Destinations Freiburg (frequent; 3hr); Munich (frequent;

1hr 20min); Stuttgart (frequent; 1hr); Tübingen (hourly; 1hr 30min).

INFORMATION AND ACTIVITIES

Tourist office Münsterplatz 50 (Jan–March Mon–Fri 9am–6pm, Sat 9am–4pm; April–Dec Mon–Fri 9am–6pm, Sat 9am–4pm, Sun 11am–3pm; ☎0731 161 28 30, ⓦ tourismus.ulm.de). Offers an accommodation reservation service.

Discount cards The tourist office sells the Ulm Museum Card (€12), which gives entry to eight city museums, including all those detailed in this book.

Canoe tours Sportiv Touren (☎0731 970 92 90, ⓦwww .sportivtouren.de) offer 2hr 30min canoe tours for €22.

ACCOMMODATION

HOTELS

Hotel Bäumle Kohlgasse 6 ☎0731 622 87, ⓦhotel-baeumle.de. Renovated five-hundred-year-old building in the shadow of the Münster, with good-value standard hotel rooms. Free broadband and parking. Also has a rustic wood-panelled restaurant. **€103**

★ **Hotel Schiefes Haus** Schwörhausgasse 6 ☎0731 96 79 30, ⓦhotelschiefeshausulm.de. Famously wonky, half-timbered place from 1443 with wood-beam ceilings and floors that are so crooked that the bed legs are different lengths. Relatively recent renovations have preserved the property's rustic nature, while adding plush touches such

as modern bathrooms with spacious tubs. Wi-fi and bike hire as well. **€148**

Münster Hotel Münsterplatz 14 ☎0731 641 62, ⓦmuenster-hotel.de. Cheerful, great-value and very central, if basic, hotel: not all its clean and tidy rooms are en suite, but some have Münster views. Extensive breakfast buffet included but the hotel will only take cash. **€74**

Roter Löwe Ulmer Gasse 8 ☎0731 14 08 90, ⓦhotel -roter-loewe.de. Modern hotel located in the pedestrian streets between the Hauptbahnhof and Münster and with its own swimming pool, sauna and

ULM FESTIVALS

Few summer weekends go by when there's not something going on in Ulm, and particularly on its central Münsterplatz which hosts the June **Stadtfest** and a famously grand **Christmas market** in December. But the city's biggest annual bash is **Schwörwoche** (Oath Week) in late July, which centres on the Danube, and celebrates an annual mayoral address in which a pledge to honour the town's 1397 constitution is reiterated. This rather solemn affair takes place at 11am on Schwörmontag – the penultimate Monday in July – but is bookended by a couple of livelier celebrations. The enchanting **Lichtserenade** (Light Serenade) in which candle-lit lanterns are floated down the Danube takes place on the previous Saturday, and the big event, **Nabada**, starts at 3pm on Schwörmontag when all manner of vessels and raucous crew navigate their way a couple of kilometres downstream to a fairground. Water pistols feature heavily in the celebrations – and local department stores discount them on the day.

The Danube is also the focus of other traditional frolics whose origins go back to the fifteenth century and are held every four years (next in 2017 and 2021): **Fischerstechen** (Fishermen's Jousting; ⓦfischerstechen-ulm.de) takes place on the river on the second and third Saturday in July; and a **Bindertanz** (Coopers' Dance) is held on a pair of July Fridays the same year. Finally, the banks of the Danube also host a biannual July event, **Donaufest** (held on even years), which celebrates the music and culture of the communities along the river's length; Austrians, Hungarians, Serbians and Romanians arrive to sing, dance, and sell snacks and handicrafts.

solarium and extensive breakfast buffet. Free wi-fi and underground parking for cars and bikes. **€125**

HOSTELS

Brickstone Hostel Schützenstr. 42 ☎0731 602 62 00, ⓦbrickstone-hostel.de; bus #7 from Hauptbahnhof, direction Willy-Brandt-Platz, stop "Schützenstrasse". Friendly, clean and independent hostel, over the river in Neu Ulm, with six rooms on two floors with between two and four beds each and common kitchen facilities. Free wi-fi. Dorms **€18**, doubles **€44**

DJH Ulm Grimmelfinger Weg 45 ☎0731 38 44 55, ⓦjugendherberge-ulm.de; bus #4 to stop "Schulzentrum". Good, clean and well-organized hostel – with large social areas – in wooded surroundings on the edge of town, 3.5km southwest of the Hauptbahnhof. Dorms **€45.40**

EATING AND DRINKING

The Fischerviertel and streets just north of Münsterplatz are both ideal for finding somewhere to eat and bar-hopping. For events, pick up the monthly **listings magazine** *Spazz* at the tourist office, which also sells tickets.

CAFÉS AND PUBS

Barfüsser Lautenberg 1 ☎0731 602 11 10, ⓦbarfuesser-brauhaus.de. Ulm's best beer-hall and microbrewery, with a range of beers that includes a delicious, tangy *Schwarzbier*. Big portions of traditional pub food (mains €7–13) complement the beers, or simply have an excellent home-made pretzel. Mon–Thurs & Sun 10am–1am, Fri & Sat 10am–2am.

Café in Stadthaus Münsterplatz 50 ☎0731 600 93, ⓦcafe-restaurant-stadthaus.de. Stylish, modern café with outdoor seating, great Münster views and good light meals for €8–16, but best of all are its excellent home-made cakes and apple strudel. Popular, so service can be slow. Mon–Thurs 8am–midnight, Fri & Sat 8am–1am, Sun 9am–midnight.

RESTAURANTS

★ **Pflugmerzler** Pfluggasse 6 ☎0731 602 70 44, ⓦpflugmerzler.de. The full menu of Swabian cooking, all excellently prepared, in a cosy restaurant hidden on an alley off Hafenbad north of the Münster. Also offers top-quality organic steaks, and there's an incredible range of German wines to choose from. Mon–Sat 6–11pm.

Zunfthaus der Schiffleute Fischergasse 31 ☎0731 644 11, ⓦzunfthaus-ulm.de. An old fifteenth-century guildhouse for fishermen, this half-timbered house with its stone floors and timeless, heavy wooden furniture houses one of Ulm's oldest restaurants. Traditional Swabian food is done to perfection here, with home-made *Spätzle* coming in many forms; often, though, the most interesting choices are seasonal, such as asparagus, chanterelle mushrooms or venison. Also a good selection of local beers and a fantastic vanilla ice cream with hot figs as dessert. Daily 11am–midnight.

Zur Forelle Fischergasse 25 ☎0731 639 24, ⓦforelle-ulm.de. One of Ulm's smartest and most charming dining options. This snug 1626 Fischerviertel house – which has a Napoleonic cannonball lodged in one wall – is a place where the tall have to stoop. An Ulm dish worth trying is the spicy herb and salmon soup with garlic. Among the mains (average €15) try the *Gaisburger Marsch* (a hearty beef, potato and *Spätzle* stew) or the trout (*Forelle*) speciality. Einstein and Karajan both dined here on their visits to Ulm, and it's popular enough to merit booking ahead. Mon–Fri 11am–3pm & 5pm–midnight, Sat & Sun 11am–midnight.

8

Upper Danube Valley

On its southeastern side, the Swabian Alb tends to fall away more gradually than in the west, but in many places the Danube has cut a tremendous gorge through the rock, producing steep cliffs and spectacular scenery, particularly in the **Upper Danube Valley**. Much of this is protected as the **Naturpark Obere Donau** (ⓦnaturpark-obere-donau.de), which is centred on this forested and steep-sided limestone valley and is particularly colourful in both spring, when wildflowers bloom, and during its magnificent autumn foliage – all best appreciated on hikes that head up to the many viewpoints above the valley.

With a railway along much of its length, the quiet region is very accessible for day-trips from Ulm. However, it also has plenty of inexpensive accommodation, encouraging longer exploration, particularly by bike following the Donauradweg (**Danube cycle path**) that begins at the source of the Danube in the unassuming provincial town of Donaueschingen and follows the Danube for 199km to Ulm. There's plenty of smaller **wildlife** to watch along the route, particularly on the marshy right bank of the Danube between Ehingen and Ulm, which teems with waterfowl.

Blaubeuren

BLAUBEUREN, 20km west of Ulm, is not in the Danube Valley but rather the source of the tributary Blau River, which joins the Danube in Ulm's Fischerviertel. Nevertheless it's a good first-stop on a journey to the higher reaches of the Danube, and a good day-trip from Ulm, particularly if you have time to **hike** the rocky hills cradling the town. Key sights are a half-timbered former **monastery** that was used for only 25 years before the Reformation and beside it the **Blautopf**, the source of the Blau. The rich blue waters of this 20m-deep pool are transformed into green then yellowy brown by rain. Beside it lies the **Hammer-schmiede**, a mid-eighteenth-century mill and smithy at the trailhead of a number of hikes.

ARRIVAL AND INFORMATION   BLAUBEUREN

By train Trains from Ulm (hourly; 11min) pull into the Bahnhof, on the southern edge of town.

Tourist office Kirchplatz 10 (Tues–Sun: mid-March to Nov

10am–5pm; Dec to mid-March 2–5pm; ☎07344 966 90, ⓦ blaubeuren.de), a 5min signposted walk from the Bahnhof, with good information on local hikes.

Schloss Sigmaringen

Sigmaringen • Tours daily: April–Oct 9am–6pm; Nov–March 10am–4pm • €9 • ⓦ schloss-sigmaringen.de

The small Danube town of **SIGMARINGEN** is known for and entirely dominated by the vast Gothic **Schloss Sigmaringen**, among the best of the Romantic-era castles. Built as a medieval fortress, it was brutally sacked in the Thirty Years' War, then subject to a fire in the late nineteenth century, so today only two original towers remain. Owned by a branch of the Hohenzollern family, the Schloss provided a useful foothold during the Prussian unification of Germany in the nineteenth century. Its impressive armoury is testament to the military might that underpinned this, and the grizzly highlight of the castle tours.

ARRIVAL AND INFORMATION   SIGMARINGEN

By train The Bahnhof lies on the eastern side of the town centre.

Destinations Friedrichshafen (hourly; 1hr 15min); Lindau (hourly; 1hr 40min); Stuttgart (frequent; 1hr); Tübingen (hourly; 1hr 30min).

Tourist office Schwabstr. 1 (April–Sept Mon–Fri

10am–1pm & 4–6pm, Sat & Sun 10am–1pm; Oct–March Mon–Fri 10am–1pm & 2–4pm; ☎07571 10 62 24, ⓦ sigmaringen.de). Located in a huddle of houses in the Altstadt below the Schloss, an easy 5min walk from the train station.

ACCOMMODATION

Traube Fürst-Wilhelm-Str. 19 ☎07571 645 10, ⓦ hotel-traube-sigmaringen.de. Old-fashioned half-timbered place with cheerful modern rooms. Its reliable,

inexpensive regional restaurant has a particularly good line in salads and is very strong on seasonal offerings like asparagus and chanterelles (mains around €12). **€80**

Beuron

Some of the most dramatic sections of the Upper Danube Valley lie around the village of **BEURON**, 28km west of Sigmaringen. The town gathers around an enormous Baroque **monastery**, which is of scant interest but for the chance to attend a **service** at the monastery church (Mon–Sat 11.15am & 6pm, Sun 10am & 3pm; ⓦ erzabtei-beuron.de) and hear monks who are world famous for their **Gregorian chanting**. Beuron is also at the centre of some great **hiking** territory. Rewarding destinations include the **Knopfmacherfelsen**, a viewpoint 6km from town, and the youth hostel at **Burg Wildenstein** (see opposite).

ARRIVAL AND INFORMATION   BEURON

By train Beuron is connected by regular trains to Konstanz (8 daily; 1hr 24min), Sigmaringen (frequent; 20min) and Ulm (8 daily; 1hr 35min).

Tourist office Kirchstrasse 18 (Mon–Fri 9am–noon & 1–4pm; ☎07579 921 00, ⓦ beuron.de). A very modest affair, but has some hiking information. More useful is the large map on a board in the car park opposite.

ACCOMMODATION

★**DJH Burg Wildenstein** ☎07466 411, ⓦjugendherberge-burg-wildenstein.de. Burg Wildenstein, an eleventh-century stronghold in a precarious spot above the Danube, now houses one of Germany's most atmospheric youth hostels. Breakfast is included in the price of a dorm bed, and half- and full-board (€6/10 extra respectively) are also possible – useful since there are no restaurants or other services in the vicinity. Dorms €21.20, doubles €53.40

The Bodensee

As a giant body of water with a balmy dry climate, the **Bodensee**, or **Lake Constance**, has long been Germany's Riviera. It hugs the country's southwest border with Austria and Switzerland where the Alps rear up to form a fine backdrop. Most German towns along the lake dot the north shore and include the idyllic island-town of **Lindau**, the transport hub of **Friedrichshafen** and the archetypal medieval lakeside settlement, **Meersburg**. The upbeat city of **Konstanz** on its southern shore is the most cosmopolitan place on the lake, and easily the best base with its regular ferry services across the lake and to nearby **islands**.

Given its good weather, the Bodensee region is known for **outdoor activities**, particularly hiking and cycling on trails that connect small lakeside towns, vineyards, orchards and beaches. Watersports are also popular, but most visitors simply sunbathe, swim and mess around in the water, which averages a pleasant 20°C in the summer, providing a respite from the humidity. Summer is the most popular holiday season, but popularity brings congested roads and booked-up hotels, making spring a better time to visit, when fruit trees blossom; autumn, meanwhile, is prime time for those interested in the wine harvest.

8

GETTING AROUND THE BODENSEE

With a circumference of 273km the Bodensee is a respectable body of water that can produce truly sea-like conditions – waves pound the shores in poor weather and shipwrecks litter the lake bed. But these days, travelling around the Bodensee is invariably safe and most visits to the region will – indeed should – involve catching a ferry or two, as sailing the lake is part of the experience.

FERRY SERVICES

The lake's lifeline service is the **car ferry** between Konstanz and Meersburg, a fifteen-minute crossing, 24 hours a day (every 15min 5.30am–9pm; every 30min 9pm–midnight; hourly midnight–5am; car with driver €7.90 one-way; ☎07531 80 30, ⓦfaehre.konstanz.de). Another useful service is the fifty-minute foot passenger crossing on **Der Katamaran** between Konstanz and Friedrichshafen (hourly: Mon–Fri 6am–8pm, Sat & Sun 8am–8pm; €10.20 one-way; ☎07541 971 09 00, ⓦder-katamaran.de). Otherwise the network of services between lakeside towns is organized by a number of companies, particularly **BSB** (ⓦbsb-online.com). The website ⓦbodenseeschiffahrt.de provides a good independent overview of all the various services.

FERRY TICKETS AND PASSES

Thankfully things are simplified by **Euregio Bodensee**, a regional public transport system of ferries, buses and trains in Germany, Austria and Switzerland. Various **day-tickets** (ⓦeuregiokarte.com) are offered for a network that's divided into zones: a €31 day-pass covers the entire system and is sold at tourist offices, train stations and ferry terminals. Use of the network is also included in the price of the main **Bodensee Erlebniskarte** (ⓦbodensee.eu), which provides admission or substantial discounts to a range of regional attractions. It's available from tourist and ferry offices between April and October and costs €72 for three days, €95 for seven or €133 for fourteen.

CYCLE PATHS

The 268km-long **Bodensee-Radweg** (ⓦbodensee-radweg.com) is a network of cycle paths around the lake; bikes are allowed on most ferries and trains – allowing for adaptable itineraries if the weather turns or you get tired.

Lindau

Bavaria begins – and the German shore of the Bodensee ends – at the idyllic resort of **LINDAU**, on the Austrian border with the town of Bregenz clearly visible across the lake. Though modern Lindau sprawls for several kilometres along the mainland shore, the focal point is the picture-postcard medieval Altstadt on an island in the lake. With a sunny, south-facing harbour, mild climate and luxuriant vegetation it's a complete tourist honeypot. Crowded it may be, but it's sweet for all that, with barely an eyesore in sight.

The harbour

Smart hotels and café terraces line Lindau's **harbour**, which is busy with yachts and excursion boats in summer and whose entrance is guarded by a tall lighthouse and an outsized Bavarian lion, placed there in the mid-nineteenth century. Beyond it, a spectacular backdrop of snow-capped Alps rises above the far shore. On the quay, the thirteenth-century **Mangturm** – the predecessor to the present lighthouse – has an almost Venetian look, complete with its colourful tiled roof.

The Rathaus and Maximilianstrasse

A little way back from the harbour stands the fourteenth-century **Rathaus**, the splendour of its stepped gables a reflection of Lindau's medieval importance as a trading centre and former free imperial city, though the colourful frescoes on the exterior – which depict the imperial Diet held here in 1496 – date from the nineteenth century. On the north side of the Rathaus, Maximilianstrasse – Lindau's main thoroughfare – runs roughly east–west across the island and is lined with tall, gabled houses, their oriel windows and Gothic arcades hinting at their antiquity.

Haus zum Cavazzen: the Stadtmuseum

Marktplatz 6 • April–Aug daily 11am–5pm; Sept to late Oct Tues–Fri & Sun 11am–5pm, Sat 2–5pm • €3 • ☏ 08382 94 40 73

The elegant Baroque **Haus zum Cavazzen**, built in 1729, now houses the charming **Stadtmuseum**, whose collection of religious paintings includes extraordinary *Spottbilder* – satirical Reformation-era works. The museum also has glass painting, toys, furniture from the Rococo, Biedermeier and Jugendstil periods, and a couple of rooms full of prettily painted peasant furniture and spinning wheels.

Peterskirche and Diebsturm

The most interesting of Lindau's churches is the unassuming little eleventh-century **Peterskirche**, on Schrannenplatz one block northeast of Maximilianstrasse. As well as serving as the town's war memorial it also contains the *Lindauer Passion* – the only known surviving wall frescoes by Hans Holbein the Elder. Opposite the church the absurdly picturesque fourteenth-century **Diebsturm**, thanks to glittering multicoloured roof tiles, belies its former function as a jail and part of the town's defences.

ARRIVAL AND INFORMATION | **LINDAU**

By ferry Lindau's main passenger ferry harbour lies beside its Hauptbahnhof. There are regular services throughout the day run by BSB (ⓦ bsb-online.com) and other companies. See the box on p.455 for details of tickets.

Destinations Friedrichshafen (hourly; 1hr 30min); Konstanz (hourly; 3hr); Meersburg (hourly; 2hr 30min); Unteruhldingen (4 daily; 3hr).

By train Lindau's old town is linked to the mainland by rail and road causeways, with the charmingly old-fashioned Hauptbahnhof close to the harbour.

By car Vast car parks dot the north shore of the island.

Tourist office Alfred-Nobel-Platz 1 (Jan–March & mid-Oct to Dec Mon–Fri 10am–noon & 2–5pm; April to mid-Oct Mon–Sat 10am–6pm, Sun 10am–1pm; ☏ 08382 26 00 30, ⓦ lindau-tourismus.de). The office has details of many relatively inexpensive apartments and private rooms around town.

ACCOMMODATION

Bayerischer Hof Seepromenade ☎08382 91 50, ⓦbayerischerhof-lindau.de. Luxury hotel in an 1854 Neoclassical building in prime lakefront position beside the focal harbour. The spacious rooms sport nineteenth-century-style furnishings while the hotel boasts excellent modern fitness and spa facilities, among them a pool and sauna. €194

DJH Lindau Herbergsweg 11 ☎08382 967 10, ⓦlindau.jugendherberge.de; bus #1 or #2 from Altstadt to ZUP, then bus #3, direction Zech, stop "Jugendherberge". Standard, comfortable but somewhat institutional youth hostel with games room and cafeteria serving three daily meals. On the mainland in the district of Reutlin. Prices include breakfast. Dorms €26.40

Park Camping Fraunhoferstr. 20 ☎08283 722 36, ⓦpark-camping.de. Attractive, well-run, leafy campground hard on the Austrian border, with separate areas for motorhomes and tents. Facilities include wi-fi and an indoor lounge and games room. Open late March to early Nov. Tent with one person €11.50, plus €8 per extra person

Reutemann Seepromenade ☎08382 91 50, ⓦreutemann-lindau.de. A little more informal than its sister hotel, the *Bayerischer Hof*, but still stylish and with arguably the better, more central location on the harbour with fine Alpine views. A good restaurant, too (see below). €194

Spiegel-Garni In der Grub 1 ☎08382 949 30, ⓦhotel-spiegel-garni.de. Very pleasant hotel in the Altstadt, with rooms that range from the simple to the extravagantly Alpine in style, with wood-clad interiors, iron stoves and a forest of floral drapes. Prices include breakfast and parking is available at extra cost. €70

EATING AND DRINKING

Alte Post Fischergasse 3 ☎08382 934 60, ⓦalte-post-lindau.de. The pretty dining room of this dark-wood inn serves *Schnitzels*, Austrian *Tafelspitz* (boiled beef), home-made *Maultaschen* and the like, with mains averaging €16. The cobbled terrace is a lovely summer spot. Daily 11am–2.30pm & 5–10pm.

Reutemann Seepromenade ☎08382 91 50, ⓦreutemann-lindau.de. The elegant terrace at this hotel is a prime lakefront spot for *Kaffee und Kuchen* and more substantial dishes such as fresh Bodensee fish. Meat options are also excellent, and include veal in a Calvados cream sauce and lamb in a thyme and garlic crust (€18).

Daily 7am–11pm.

Treibgut Vordere Metzgergasse 17 ☎08382 274 44 39. This spacious bar has some good organic beers, various games and occasional live music and Rockabilly events. The work of local photographers graces the walls. Daily 5pm–late.

Zum Sünfzen Maximilianstr. 1 ☎08382 58 65. Lindau's most atmospheric and traditional place to eat is this fourteenth-century, wood-clad place. Food is moderately priced (mains €10–25) and fresh Bodensee fish is a speciality, though the venison is also excellent. Daily 11am–10.30pm.

ENTERTAINMENT

Lindauer Marionettenoper im Stadttheater Fischergasse 37 ☎08382 94 24 46, ⓦmarionettenoper .de. Inventive perfomances of classic operas are put on here using puppets. Pieces are polished, entertaining and have been produced with an eye for detail, so not as kitsch as it sounds. Popular pieces include *The Magic Flute*, *The Barber of Seville*, *Carmen* and *La Traviata*. Tickets €21–29. Usually Tues, Wed & Thurs and every other Sat & Sun.

Friedrichshafen

Overlooking the lake's widest point and with the longest promenade of any Bodensee town, **FRIEDRICHSHAFEN**, 22km west of Lindau, has the feel of a seaside resort, but as the lake's only industrial town, the place leads a double life. It was thanks to its **aviation industry** that it was bombed to smithereens during World War II, but this industry also made it the setting for one of the world's most intriguing aeronautical events: it was here that **Count Ferdinand von Zeppelin** manufactured and launched his cigar-shaped airships. On July 2, 1900, his first *LZ1* drifted over the lake and three decades later, Friedrichshafen became a hub for long-distance international travel (see box, p.458).

Dornier Museum

Claude-Dornier-Platz 1 • May–Oct daily 9am–5pm; Nov–April Tues–Sun 10am–5pm • €8 • ⓦdorniermuseum.de

A silvery and architecturally eye-catching hangar at Friechrichshafen's airport contains the **Dornier Museum**, which celebrates the company and work of aviation pioneer

LOOK, NO WINGS!

In the late nineteenth century **Count Ferdinand von Zeppelin**, a maverick with an impressive walrus moustache and military honours, turned his attention – and most of his wealth – to airships. His pioneering *LZ1* drifted above the Bodensee in 1900, to great enthusiasm and jubilation. Later the Zeppelins acquired their first real use as World War I bombers and scouts.

In 1928 the pride of the fleet, *Graf Zeppelin*, hummed across the Atlantic in four days, fifteen hours and 44 minutes; a year later she circumnavigated the globe in just twelve days' air-time: the golden age of **luxurious airships** had arrived. Once times improved to well under two days, a scheduled service to New York was set up, with passengers paying around 1200 Reichsmarks for a return ticket – around seven months' the average wage of the time. Airships made scheduled flights to Stockholm, Rome, Cairo and Leningrad, and the truly rich could leave Friedrichshafen to step off at Rio de Janeiro after twelve days in the clouds.

No matter that she had made 590 flights, 114 of them ocean-going, the *Graf Zeppelin*'s days were numbered as soon as the 245m sister-ship **Hindenburg** erupted into a fireball in New Jersey on May 6, 1937, killing 36 passengers and crew (61 survived). Later analysis suggests that a static spark from earthed mooring-lines ignited the varnish on the linen skin, causing a blaze which quickly spread to the airship's hydrogen tanks. Ironically the airship had been designed for inert and non-combustible helium, but the US had refused permission to use this fuel.

The disaster, along with progress elsewhere in the aviation industry, put Zeppelins out of favour for a long time, although there has been a good deal of research and development since and they're now often seen over the Bodensee. Run by the **Zeppelin NT**, these airships are non-rigid, filled with helium and only a tenth of the size of the originals; they climb to 2000m to take twelve well-heeled passengers for jaunts above the Bodensee (from €200/30min; ☎07541 590 00, ⓦzeppelinflug.de).

Claude Dornier. Engineering-whizz Dornier was instrumental in designing the first all-metal aircraft shells and was later celebrated for his unique propeller configurations in aircraft engines. Inside are some dozen Dornier planes and a series of elegant exhibits on everything from Dornier's flying boats to the company's continuing role in NASA's space programme. The good café has fine views of the airport and incoming Zeppelin NTs (see box above) – which seems fitting since it was on Zeppelins that Dornier cut his aeronautical engineering teeth.

The Zeppelin Museum

Seestr. 22 • May–Oct daily 9am–5pm; Nov–April Tues–Sun 10am–5pm • €8, English audio-guide €3 • ⓦ zeppelin-museum.de

Friedrichshafen's most celebrated association has produced its chief site: the **Zeppelin Museum**. Located on the promenade on the eastern side of the town centre, the collection celebrates Friedrichshafen's quirky entry into the annals of aviation history, with the advent and production of giant gas-powered rigid airships. With most museum signage in German, the English-language audio-guide is extremely useful.

The museum's centrepiece is a 33m section of the **Hindenburg** where you can nose around a Bauhaus-style lounge in which a pianist would play as the clouds slid by, and peek into one of its 25 tiny cabins. Also on view are the remains of the *Graf Zeppelin* engine, battered from storage. Spare a thought for the engineers cocooned in its bubble for three-hour stints to nurse a constant 50°C temperature. More fascinating is archive film of the Zeppelin era showing the enthusiastic reception they received wherever they appeared and revealing how hundreds of people were needed to land the things. The exhibition also commemorates the *Hindenburg* disaster with various relics: the charred jacket of radio operator Willy Speck; simple ribbons from families; bombastic requiems from the Nazis who hijacked memorial services to make its victims Third Reich martyrs; and a clock stripped to bare metal, forever stuck at 7.25.

Oddly, the top floor of the museum is devoted to **regional art** from Gothic to modern. Otto Dix, who moved to lakeside village Hemmenhofen in 1936, provides bite among whimsical canvases and is in withering form in *Vanity*, an update of the old-masters' favourite with a brassy nude shadowed by a bent crone.

The Uferpromenade

Friedrichshafen's 1km-long **Uferpromenade**, or harbour promenade, begins by the Zeppelin Museum and is a lively place for a summer stroll, watching ferries come and go, and fishermen unloading crates of *Felchen* – a Bodensee delicacy somewhere between salmon and trout – all in front of a backdrop of the white-capped Swiss Alps. It's especially scenic at sunset, when the snow glows in the dusk. The 22m-high **Moleturm** tower on a breakwater provides an elevated view of the action, and **boats** – rowing, motor and pedaloes – are available for rent (from €5/hour). Midway along the promenade is the **Zeppelindenkmal**, a bronze obelisk in a park which also contains the mawkish **Zeppelinbrunnen**, a copy of a 1909 fountain depicting a naked child cradling a blimp atop the world.

Schlosskirche

Schlossstr. 2• Daily mid-April to Oct 9am–6pm • Free

At Uferpromenade's western end, beside a neo-Renaissance pier, is the Schloss of the Württemberg dukes, fashioned from a Benedictine priory in 1654, still in the family's hands and strictly private. Behind it are the landmark onion-domes of Christian Thumb's Baroque **Schlosskirche**, with a stucco garden on its roof which was re-created during postwar restoration.

ARRIVAL AND DEPARTURE   FRIEDRICHSHAFEN | 8

By ferry Friedrichshafen's main passenger ferry harbour is beside the Zeppelin Museum. Regular services – including a high-speed catamaran to Konstanz – leave throughout the day and are run by BSB (@bsb-online.com) and other companies. See the box on p.455 for more information on travelling the Bodensee by boat.

Destinations Konstanz (hourly; 30min by catamaran, 1hr by ferry); Lindau (hourly; 1hr 30min); Meersburg (hourly; 1hr); Unteruhldingen (hourly; 30min).

By air Bodensee Airport (@fly-away.de) has regular flights to Berlin, Cologne and Frankfurt, as well as London Heathrow and Gatwick.

By train Some trains stop at Hafenbahnhof beside the Zeppelin Museum and port; all pull in at the central Stadtbahnhof on the west side of the town centre.

Destinations Freiburg (frequent; 3hr); Lindau (hourly; 22min); Stuttgart (every 30min; 2hr 14min); Ulm (frequent; 1hr).

INFORMATION

Tourist office Bahnhofplatz 2 (April & Oct Mon–Thurs 9am–noon & 2–5pm, Fri 9am–noon; May, June & Sept Mon–Fri 9am–noon & 1–6pm, Sat 9am–1pm; July & Aug

Mon–Fri 9am–6pm, Sat 9am–1pm; Nov–March Mon–Thurs 9am–noon & 2–4pm, Fri 9am–noon; ☎07541 300 10, @friedrichshafen.info).

ACCOMMODATION

★**Buchhorner Hof** Friedrichstr. 33 ☎07541 20 50, @buchhorn.de. Bright rooms with views over the Bodensee in the best address in town: a century-old traditional place, but with the modern conveniences of a sauna, steam room and whirlpool. The freshest fish is prepared in an acclaimed restaurant (mains around €20) and there's a charming *Weinkeller* for an aperitif. €180

CAP Rotach Lindauer Str. 2 ☎07541 734 21, @cap-rotach.de; bus #7587, direction Kressbronn, stop "Jugendherberge". Small campsite on the lakefront, 2km east of the Hafenbahnhof. Also offers some clean, modern and pine-furnished pension rooms with internet connection. Doubles €68; pitch €4.50, plus €6.50 per person

City-Krone Schanzstr. 7 ☎07541 70 50, @hotel-city-krone.de. Bright and very central 4-star place where terracotta tones and rattan furnishings add warmth to modern styles. Also has a small swimming pool, sauna and a restaurant with a good international menu. €159

DJH Friedrichshafen Lindauer Str. 3 ☎07541 724 04, @jugendherberge-friedrichshafen.de; bus #7587, direction Kressbronn, stop "Jugendherberge". Popular, large and sociable hostel opposite the *CAP Rotach* campsite, with all the usual facilities. Almost always fully booked so advance reservation is recommended. Also has some twin rooms, and rates include breakfast. Dorms €24, doubles €59

Maier Poststr. 1–3 ☎07541 40 40, @hotel-maier.de. Rustic and elegant family-run hotel in Fischbach, a sleepy district at the western edge of town, about 5km from the centre. Rooms are of the bold boutique variety and have satellite TV and free wireless internet, while the excellent

facilities include a Finnish sauna, steam sauna and a solarium. Its restaurant is first class for game, herring and pike-perch (mains €12–23). **€100**

EATING AND DRINKING

For picnic items try the Saturday **farmers' market** on Adenauerplatz, with all sorts of home-made sausages and cheeses and fresh regional fruit. Many of the best places for a sit-down meal are along the **seafront**, although most of the better hotels have excellent restaurants too (see p.459).

Glückler Olgastr. 23 ☎07541 221 64, ⓦweinstube -gluckler.de. Small *Weinstube* where *Zander*, Bodensee *Felchen* and trout are on the menu along with a baffling variety of the house-special Breton *galettes*, from simple butter to a feast of cheese, ham, onions, tomato and Roquefort liberally laced with garlic. Prices are moderate, with mains averaging €11. Daily 5pm–1am; kitchen closes 11pm.

Lammgarten Uferstr. 27 ☎07541 2 46 08. Inexpensive restaurant where €8 will buy you fresh *Felchen* plucked

from the Bodensee, and *Schnitzel*, served in a leafy beer garden behind the yacht marina. With plenty of tables and quick service. Daily 11am–11pm.

Museums-Restaurant Seestr. 22 ☎07541 333 06, ⓦzeppelinmuseum-restaurant.de. You'll need patience to claim a table on the Zeppelin Museum's terrace above the harbour's comings and goings. The menu here is internationally eclectic, ranging from Swabian specials to Norwegian salmon, with lunch specials priced around €8. Mon & Sun 10am–3pm, Tues–Sat 10am–9.30pm.

Meersburg

With a wonderfully ramshackle castle looming over a narrow lakefront strip of half-timbered houses, **MEERSBURG**, 17km west of Friedrichshafen, is something of a living snapshot of a fairy-tale Germany. Small wonder then that in peak season, coach parties and day-trippers crush in. But arrive early or linger till dusk and you'll certainly appreciate the magic. Good local festivals include the **Winzerfest** on the first weekend in July, and the **Bodensee Weinfest**, on the second weekend in September, when you can sample the latest vintage.

Entered from the modern town and main road via the medieval **Obertor** gate, almost all Meersburg's Altstadt is pedestrianized. A short way downhill from the gate is the small **Marktplatz**, from where Steigstrasse runs down past rows of touristy shops to the lakefront and pleasant **Seepromenade**. Meanwhile a lane parallel to Steigstrasse leads to the **Altes Schloss** and **Neues Schloss** that dominate the upper town.

The Altes Schloss

Schlossplatz 10 • Daily: March–Oct 9am–6.30pm; Nov–Feb 10am–6pm • €9.50 • ⓦ burg-meersburg.de

The origins of the austere **Altes Schloss** date back to Merovingian king Dagobert I in 628 AD, putting it among Germany's oldest castles. It's certainly archetypal: moats, dungeons, a great hall, manifold turrets, old armour and weaponry, portraits of glowering ancestors and a general heavy atmosphere are all present. The public can visit thirty furnished rooms decorated in the style of various eras, right up to the cheery and flowery Biedermeier quarters of **Annette von Droste-Hülshoff** (1797–1848). Arguably Germany's greatest female poet, she lived here when the castle belonged to her brother-in-law, Baron Joseph von Lassberg, finding inspiration for her Romantic angst-racked verses in the castle's severity. The bedroom where she died on May 24, 1848, and her study, are both treated with shrine-like reverence.

The Neues Schloss

Schlossplatz 12 • Gallery April–Oct daily 9am–6.30pm • €5 • ⓦ neues-schloss-meersburg.de

The general cheerlessness of the Altes Schloss finally inspired the powerful prince-bishops of Konstanz – who'd had it as their summer residence since 1268 – to build a more civilized palace next door in the eighteenth century. Baroque supremo Balthasar Neumann was drafted in for the purpose and the **Neues Schloss** was the pastel-pink result. It only saw fifty years' service until secularization in 1802, but the views from gardens over roofs to the shimmering Bodensee continue to enchant, and are openly accessible. They tend to top the municipal gallery inside, though its exhibits on local flying-boat pioneer Claude Dornier may interest aeronautical fans. There's also an elegant café here with a scenic terrace overlooking the lake.

ARRIVAL AND INFORMATION MEERSBURG

By ferry Meersburg's car ferry leaves from a harbour just north of town; passenger services leave from the southern end of town throughout the day and are run by BSB (wbsb-online.com) and other companies. See the box on p.455 for more information on travelling the Bodensee by boat.
Destinations Friedrichshafen (hourly; 1hr); Konstanz (hourly; 30min); Lindau (hourly; 2hr 30min); Unteruhldingen (hourly; 30min).

By bus Meersburg doesn't have a train station, but bus #7395 from Friedrichshafen (every 30min; 40min) drops passengers above the Altstadt and at the ferry terminal just to the west.
Tourist office Kirchstr. 4, by the Obertor (Mon–Fri 9am–12.30pm & 2–6pm, Sat & Sun 10am–2pm; ☎ 07532 44 04 00, wmeersburg.de). The tourist office has full accommodation listings including a number of private rooms, the only budget option.

ACCOMMODATION

★ **Gasthof zum Bären** Marktplatz 11 ☎ 07532 432 20, wbaeren-meersburg.de. Window boxes are overstuffed with geraniums at this romantic old place which harks back to the thirteenth century. Rooms are good value considering they're in the heart of the Altstadt, even if they're a little snug. **€88**
Hotel Löwen Marktplatz 2 ☎ 07532 430 40, whotel -loewen-meersburg.de. Half-timbered, family-run place with cosy wood-clad interiors, a good restaurant and snug wine-bar. Some rooms have been modernized, but most are pretty cramped. **€110**

Seehotel Off Uferpromenade 51 ☎ 07532 447 40, wseehotel-off.de. Lakeside option beside vineyards, which is run on feng shui and eco-friendly principles. Most rooms have a private balcony and lake views. The on-site health centre offers aromatherapy, Reiki and the like. **€112**
Seehotel zur Münz Seestr. 7 ☎ 07532 435 90, wseehotel-zur-muenz.de. Hotel on the lakefront with fairly standard but very well kept rooms, of which many have balconies and overlook the lake. Rates include a reasonable buffet breakfast; parking costs a little extra. **€120**

EATING AND DRINKING

★ **Café Gross** Unterstadtstr. 22. ☎ 07532 60 55. Worth seeking out for the best home-made cakes in town, which often include renditions of classics like the Sacher Torte or the Schwarzwalderkirschtorte (Black Forest cherry cake). The portions are large, the coffee freshly ground and the hot chocolate excellent. Daily 11am–6pm.
Gutsschänke Seminarstr. 4 ☎ 07532 80 76 30, wgutsschaenke-meersburg.de. Patience and quick feet will win you a table on the terrace for idyllic views and a

summer lunch of light bites – try the rich home-made Leberwurst (liver sausage). Mains, like the excellent Flammkuchen, average €10. Daily 11am–11pm.
Zum Becher Höllgasse 4 ☎ 07532 90 09. Cosy, rustic and cheerfully cluttered wine-bar serving excellent traditional food such as Rostbraten with Spätzle (€17), and an array of local fish dishes. A big wine list complements the food and makes it a good place for just a drink too. Tues–Sun 10am–2pm & 5pm–midnight; closed in Jan.

Uhldingen-Mühlhofen

There's not much to the unassuming town of **Uhldingen-Mühlhofen**, 9km northwest of Meersburg, but it does have a train station and is the vague hub for three attractions, each around 2km away. The pleasant lakefront district of **Unteruhldingen** is best known for its museum of prehistoric dwellings, but also in the area are an extravagant Baroque church and a fine monkey sanctuary.

The Pfahlbauten Museum

Strandpromenade 6, Uhldingen-Mühlhofen • Tours April–Sept daily 9am–7pm; Oct daily 9am–5pm; Nov Sat & Sun 9am–5pm • €9 • w pfahlbauten.de • Bus #7395 from Friedrichshafen

The heavily advertised **Pfahlbauten Museum** features open-air reconstructions of Stone and Iron Age dwellings, whose forms are based on archeological remains found here. Jolly and obligatory German-only tours take you round the structures, which are famously supported on huge stakes driven into the lake. Sadly, they're not quite true to life though, since lake levels were lower back then, putting these structures firmly on dry land.

Basilika Birnau

Birnau-Maurach 5, Uhldingen-Mühlhofen • Daily: May–Sept Wed 7.30am–7pm; Oct–April 7.30am–5.30pm • Free • ⓦ birnau.de • Bus #7395 between Friedrichshafen and Überlingen

A twenty-minute uphill walk through vineyards from the Pfahlbauten Museum takes you to the fine Rococo **Basilika Birnau**, designed by Peter Thumb, painter Gottfried Bernhard Göz and sculptor Josef Anton Feichtmayr, among others. The furiously lurid interior is a riot of optical illusions, including a mirror in the cupola. One curious altar to the right of the main one is dedicated to St Bernard of Clairvaux, whose words were said to be sweet as honey. A cherub, sucking a finger he's dipped in a bees' nest, illustrates this.

Affenberg Salem

Mendlishauser Hof, Salem • Mid-March to Oct daily 9am–6pm • €8.50 • ⓦ affenberg-salem.de • Frequent shuttle bus (late April to late Oct) from the Pfahlbauten and Uhldingen-Mühlhofen train station

As a monkey sanctuary where you can wander among and even feed the animals, **Affenberg Salem** is a sure-fire hit with kids. But it's also a pleasant spot for some two hundred North African Barbary macaques from Morocco and Algeria to thrive. Listed as an endangered species, the park has done good work in not only providing a suitable home in a similar climate, but also supporting reintroduction projects. Park visitors can enter their vast enclosure and watch everyday monkey activities: feeding, grooming, snoozing, playing and fighting. But the highlight is being able to interact with them at close quarters, by feeding them popcorn supplied by the park. Park rangers are on hand to provide a great deal of knowledgeable information, and at regularly scheduled feeding times they'll explain fascinating details about the family dynamics within groups – in German, though most will explain things in English too. The park's other animals are a minor sideshow in comparison, but include deer, and storks whose huge nests grace several admin buildings beside the reasonable café and bistro.

Konstanz

Straddling the Swiss border on the southern side of the lake, the likeable university town of **KONSTANZ** came out of the war almost unscathed – it was deemed too close to neutral Switzerland to be bombed – ensuring its **Altstadt** is well preserved. Though with Roman origins, it's largely medieval, dating back to when the town thrived as a free imperial city, gaining fame particularly between 1414 and 1418 when the Council of Konstanz met here to heal the Great Schism in the Catholic Church in a restructuring that replaced three popes with one. Altstadt sightseeing aside, Konstanz also makes a good base for **day-trips** to nearby islands, particularly **Mainau** and **Reichenau**. With one in seven of its population students, Konstanz is a bustling town, and the **restaurant and bar scene** unusually lively in this otherwise staid region.

The town's biggest annual festival is **Seenachtsfest** in August when the lake mirrors a firework bonanza.

The waterfront

Straddling the Rhine and overlooking the Bodensee, Konstanz's **waterfront** is one of its major assets, on which it capitalizes with a pleasant **promenade** that links aged buildings, attractive greenery and eye-catching statues. It starts beside the train stations and yacht harbour and heads north towards the Rhine where some old town fortifications survive.

The harbour and Sealife

The southern end of the promenade is defined by the clattering sails of the yacht **harbour** and several old warehouses that have been stylishly converted into a small, upbeat restaurant district. Beside all this lies the **Sealife** aquarium, Hafenstr. 9 (daily 10am–5pm; €16.50, sizeable discounts online; ⓦvisitsealife.com), part of the international chain, which showcases the rather lacklustre sea creatures of the Rhine and Bodensee, and is largely geared to kids.

The Konzilgebäude and Imperia

Beside an underpass to the Markstätte and the Altstadt, lies the waterfront's most striking building, the **Konzilgebäude**, a conference and concert hall which dates back to a 1388 granary and warehouse, but gets its name as the probable site where the Council of Konstanz convened to elect Pope Martin V in 1417. Also recalling the Council is **Imperia**, the imposing 9m-high rotating statue of a voluptuous woman, erected at the end of the pier in 1993. It's based on a prostitute vividly described in a Balzac novel about the days of the Council of Konstanz, though in truth the infamously powerful lady lived in a later time.

The Insel

Near the beginning of the pier another statue commemorates airship-inventor Count Ferdinand von Zeppelin (see box, p.458), who was born on a tiny island, simply called the **Insel**, just north of the leafy **Stadtgarten** park at the end of this section of promenade. The Insel was long the seat of a Dominican priory – Jan Hus spent time incarcerated in its cellars – but is now occupied by the five-star *Inselhotel* (see p.465).

8

The Rheintorturm

A short walk north of the Insel, the **Rheintorturm**, a fifteenth-century defensive tower with a conical red-tile roof, and the adjacent **Rheinbrücke**, mark where the Rhine and the Bodensee meet. The bridge leads north over the Rhine to a row of handsome Art Nouveau villas, the Archäologisches Landesmuseum (see p.464) and a promenade to Strandbad Horn (see p.465).

The Altstadt

Just southeast of the confluence of the Rhine and Bodensee, lies the oldest part of the **Altstadt**, which retains a snug atmosphere in its twisting network of tight alleys, dotted with local shops, wine bars and restaurants. It's an easy place to enjoy at an ambling pace, ducking in and out of appealing lanes, which grow progressively broader to the south of the focal **Münsterplatz**. From here various old pedestrianized lanes snake south and east providing several options to loop back to the waterfront, though the busiest route goes south along Wessenbergstrasse, which becomes Hussenstrasse, then east along Konzilstrasse to the **Markstätte**, the large, elongated marketplace and commercial hub of town. There's plenty of bustle and atmosphere along the way, but few real attractions.

Münsterplatz and the Kulturzentrum am Münster

Romans laid the foundation stones in the old part of town and their work can be viewed through a glass panel in the midst of **Münsterplatz**, the square that surrounds the Münster. The rest of the Münsterplatz is surrounded by fine old townhouses from as far back as the fifteenth century, so it comes as a surprise to see them reflected in the glass of the alarmingly modernist **Kulturzentrum am Münster**, Wessenbergstr. 43 (Tues–Fri 10am–6pm, Sat & Sun 10am–5pm; €3), in which the Städtische Wessenberg-Galerie puts on often engaging temporary exhibitions on regional art and history.

JAN HUS (1370–1415)

If ever there was a man before his time it was Bohemian religious reformer, **Jan Hus**. He made his name attacking ecclesiastical abuses, and starting a **Hussite** religious movement that was similar to the Protestantism which emerged a century later. Excommunicated in 1410, Hus continued to preach throughout Bohemia, vocally supporting the religious writings of Englishman John Wycliffe, calling for church reform and protesting against the sale of indulgences. His following quickly grew into substantial numbers, which led to his invitation to the Council of Konstanz in 1414 to explain his position. This came with a promise of a safe passage home, but in the event the councillors decided to defy his imperial protection, incarcerate him, place him on trial and burn him at the stake for heresy. This helped make Hus the same sort of national figurehead for Czechs as Martin Luther is for Germans.

The Münster

Münsterplatz **Church** Mon–Sat 10am–6pm, Sun 10am–6pm • Free • **Tower** Mon–Sat 10am–5pm, Sun 12.30–5pm • €2

Konstanz's main church is the elegant Romanesque and Gothic **Münster**, built of soft local sandstone. Its fine oak **main doors** deserve a closer look for the well-preserved medieval carvings of New Testament scenes. Inside, the oldest part is the Carolingian crypt, but most of the Romanesque structure dates from between the twelfth and fifteenth centuries, though the vaulted Gothic side-aisles and main choir-stalls are clearly a later vintage, as are the glittering Baroque high-altar and nineteenth-century neo-Gothic spires, one of which can be climbed for a fine view over town. One unusual thing to look out for is the "**Schnegg**" – which gets its name from an old-fashioned slang word for snail – a late fifteenth-century spiral staircase in the northern transept that's ablaze with decoration. The church was the main meeting-place of the Council of Konstanz, and was where **Jan Hus** (see box above) stood trial – he's thought to have stood in the central isle at about row 24 to hear his judgement.

Hus-Museum

Hussenstr. 64 • April–Sept Tues–Sun 11am–5pm; Oct–March Tues–Sun 11am–4pm • Free

The **Hus-Museum**, at the southern end of Hussenstrasse, occupies the house where the would-be reformer Jan Hus (see box above) stayed prior to his imprisonment in 1414. Events that took place over a hundred years later in Wittenberg showed he was a man well before his time, and, just as Luther became a figurehead of German nationhood, so too did Hus become vital to Czech identity – hence the museum is run by a Czech Jan Hus society, though its exhibition is a bit thin.

Rosgartenmuseum

Rosgartenstr. 3 • Tues–Fri 10am–6pm, Sat & Sun 10am–5pm • €3, free on 1st Sun of month & after 2pm Wed • ⓦ rosgartenmuseum-konstanz.de

A town history museum in an old butchers', grocers' and pharmacists' guildhall, the **Rosgartenmuseum** contains an eclectic collection of regional art, maps and models which help bring medieval Konstanz alive. Its greatest treasure by far is Ulrich Richental's *Chronicle of the Council of Konstanz*, a beautifully illustrated work of the great event, which of course includes a lurid burning of Jan Hus (see box above).

The Archäologisches Landesmuseum

Benediktinerplatz 5 • Tues–Sun 10am–6pm • €4, free on 1st Sat of month • ⓦ konstanz.alm-bw.de

Over on the north side of the Rhine, a former convent on Benediktinerplatz houses the **Archäologisches Landesmuseum**, the state's archeological collection, which neatly arranges finds by era. Many of the most impressive exhibits are Roman, particularly some wonderful second-century bronzes from Lopodunum – today's Ladenburg, between Heidelberg and Mannheim. Among them are proud lion-heads, deities and fantastical creatures such as sea leopards. The collection also contains items of local

8

interest, particularly details of some of the many Bodensee shipwrecks, remnants of a local fifteenth-century merchant ship and some canoes from 650–750 AD. There's also some information on Pfahlbauten and the culture that built them, more accurately but less vividly presented than over the lake near Meersburg (see p.460).

Strandbad Horn and around

From the Rheinbrücke, Seestrasse, Konstanz's finest promenade, heads east out of town to a peninsula of forest and beaches. It's nowhere near as busy as the promenade in the centre, and a particular pleasure on a bike. A network of paths combine to head around the peninsula and up to the ferry terminal at Staad and on to the island of Mainau. En route are many good places to **swim** and **sunbathe** including the private beach **Strandbad Horn** at the eastern end of Eichhornstrasse (bus #5 from town centre), the most popular beach at the tip of the peninsula. Entry is free (parking charges operate) and there are all the usual changing facilities you'd expect, including cafés and sausage kiosks (with great fries).

ARRIVAL AND DEPARTURE

KONSTANZ

By ferry Small passenger-only ferries – and the catamaran – dock at the waterfront, while car ferries from Meersburg arrive 4km northwest in the suburb of Staad, from where bus #1 runs to the city centre. See the box on p.455 for more information on travelling the Bodensee by boat.
Destinations Friedrichshafen (hourly; 30min by catamaran, 1hr by ferry); Lindau (hourly; 3hr); Meersburg (hourly; 30min).

By train Konstanz has two train stations, which lie almost beside one another between the harbour and Altstadt: the Deutscher Bahnhof is the southern terminus of the Schwarzwaldbahn, from Offenburg via Triberg; the Schweizer Bahnhof has connections to Swiss destinations.
Destinations Basel (frequent; 2hr 20min); Freiburg (frequent; 2hr 30min); Stuttgart (hourly; 3hr); Triberg (hourly; 1hr 40min); Zurich (hourly; 1hr 20min).

GETTING AROUND

By bus The hub of the local public bus system (🚌 sw .konstanz.de) is the railway station; single tickets cost €2.30, day-passes €4.30, or you can travel free with a *Gästekarte*, which your local host will provide if you stay for two nights or more.

By bike Kultur-Rädle, Bahnhofplatz 29 (Mon–Fri 9am–12.30pm & 2.30–6pm, Sat 10am–4pm; Easter–Oct also Sun 10am–12.30pm; €12 per day; ☎07531 273 10, 🌐 kultur-raedle.de).

INFORMATION

Tourist office Beside the Deutscher Bahnhof at Bahnhofplatz 43 (April–Oct Mon–Fri 9am–6.30pm, Sat

9am–4pm, Sun 10am–1pm; Nov–March Mon–Fri 9am–6pm; ☎07531 13 30 30, 🌐 konstanz-tourismus.de).

ACCOMMODATION

Most of Konstanz's central hotels occupy atmospheric old buildings, so expect things to be a bit cramped and pricey. Cheaper options, like campsites, the hostel and most private rooms – bookable via the tourist office – are well outside the centre.

HOTELS AND PENSIONS

Barbarossa Overmarkt 8–12 ☎07531 220 21, 🌐 barbarossa-hotel.com. Central mid-range place, with some real time-honoured class – frescoes adorn the outside walls and Kaiser Friedrich I signed a peace treaty with the Italians here in 1183 – but bathrooms are cramped. **€97**

Graf Wisenstr. 2 ☎07531 128 68 90, 🌐 hotel-pension-graf.de. Nonsmoking family-run pension near the station and central Konstanz. Rooms are simple, clean and airy but not all are en suite. Also offers singles for €49, triples for €99 and four-bed rooms for €135. Free wi-fi. **€75**

Hotel-Sonnenhof Otto-Raggenbass-Str. 3 ☎07531 222 57, 🌐 hotel-sonnenhof-konstanz.de. Basic but

well-priced hotel in a quiet residential street just yards from the Swiss border at the southern end of town. Rooms have dated, 1970s-era furnishings and orange walls. Also has singles (€65) and triples (€125). With parking. **€89**

Steigenberger Inselhotel Auf der Insel 1 ☎07531 12 50, 🌐 steigenberger.com. Prestigious five-star place in an old thirteenth-century Dominican monastery on its own tiny island that overlooks the Bodensee. With all the trimmings, including a fitness centre, sauna and 24hr room service. **€289**

CAMPSITES AND HOSTELS

Campingplatz Bruderhofer Fohrenbühlweg 45 ☎07531 313 88, 🌐 campingplatz-konstanz.de; bus #1 and then walk to Tannenhof. One of two pleasant neighbouring campgrounds on the lakeshore, 3km northeast of the centre and 1km from the car ferry. Getting here can be a bit awkward without your own transport, but lakeshore cycle paths make it ideal if you've a bike. Pitch €7.50, plus €6.50 per person

DJH Konstanz Zur Allmannshöhe 18 ☎07531 322 60, ⓦjugendherberge-konstanz.de; bus #4 to "Jugendherberge". Excellent hostel uniquely located in an old water tower, but a fair way out of town and even a good walk from the car ferry docks. Thankfully it has its own good bistro. Breakfast included. Dorms €24

EATING AND DRINKING

Konstanz has some great **cafés** and small **restaurants** tucked away in pedestrian streets south of the Münster, but in summer you'll likely be drawn to all the activity at the harbour, where there's first-class people-watching and often a bit of oompah music in lakefront **beer gardens** too.

Brauhaus Johann-Albrecht Konradigasse 2 ☎07531 250 45, ⓦbrauhaus-joh-albrecht.de. Atmospheric little microbrewery that's a bit of a local institution and worth seeking out for its good array of beers and well-priced pub food such as *Schnitzel* (the daily special on Thurs) and *Flammkuchen* (most mains around €13). Daily 11.30am–1am.

★**Hafenhalle** Hafenstr. 10 ☎07531 211 26, ⓦhafenhalle.com. The biggest of the harbourside restaurants, with good local fish and game on the menu of the fairly smart restaurant and with simple canteen food in its beer garden. Great for breakfast, particularly on Sun when there's live Dixieland and jazz. Daily 10am–1am.

Niederburg Weinstube Niederburggasse 7 ☎07531 297 47. Tiny, rustic and very sociable backstreet wine bar hidden in an alley and serving hundreds of regional wines.

Attracts a broad spectrum of customers, united by their love of wine. Basic dishes like sausage salad are offered. Daily 11am–midnight.

Staader Fährhaus Fischerstr. 30 ☎07531 361 67 63. A bit off the beaten track, beside the ferry terminal in the suburb of Staad, but worth the trek if you're after creative and excellent local fish dishes (priced around the €13 mark). Other light cuisine includes an unusually good selection of vegetarian food, and most ingredients are local and organic. Mon & Tues 11am–11pm, Thurs 6–11pm, Fri–Sun 11am–11pm.

Steg 4 Hafenstr. 8 ☎07531 174 28, ⓦsteg4.de. Restaurant with excellent stone-oven-baked, thin-crust pizzas (most around €8) in an old warehouse by the ferry harbour. Not exactly an adventurous option but great for convivial harbourfront atmosphere. Daily 10am–1am.

NIGHTLIFE AND ENTERTAINMENT

As a student town, there's a fair bit going on in Konstanz, with the best source of listings the German-only website, ⓦparty-news.de. **Rock Am See** (ⓦrock-am-see.de) is a big open-air outdoor music festival in late June. Rivalling it, but playing to a very different crowd, are a number of classical music festivals throughout the summer, particularly the **Bodensee Festival** (ⓦbodenseefestival.de) in May.

CLUBS, CASINO AND LIVE MUSIC

★**Das Boot** Am Hafen ⓦdasboot.de. For something unique and local, check out the events and clubnights on this old ferry. These are generally on Sat nights and don't occur more than a handful of times every year – making them the hot ticket when they are on.

K9 Hieronymusgasse 3 ☎07531 167 13, ⓦk9 -kulturzentrum.de. Venue with an incredibly eclectic range of events and musical performances. World music is a particular strongpoint, but the programme also often includes the likes of jazz, dance nights, over-30s discos, cabaret and indie rock. Cover €5–13. Hours vary, though generally Wed, Fri–Sun 9pm–late; café daily 10pm–1am.

Konstanz Casino Seestr. 12 ☎07531 815 70,

ⓦcasino-konstanz.de. Draws the crowds with all the usual table games: slots, roulette, poker, black jack. There's a €3 cover, a jacket-and-tie dress code. Over-21s only – ID required. Daily 11am–2am.

THEATRE

Stadttheater Konstanz Konzilstr. 11 ☎07531 90 01 50, ⓦtheaterkonstanz.de. Germany's oldest active theatre – since 1607 – with dependably good productions ranging from the likes of *Faust* to contemporary pieces about terrorist attacks, plus occasional live music. Also organizes the programmes of two other venues – the Spiegelhalle for experimental theatre, and the Werkstatt which focuses on puppet theatre.

The Bodensee islands

The two most obvious jaunts from Konstanz are to the islands of **Mainau** and **Reichenau**, both of which are connected to the mainland by causeway and linked to

Konstanz by well-marked cycle paths and ferry. Both have also flourished thanks to rich soils and the near-tropical climate hereabouts that comes from the warm *Foehn* winds blowing off the Alps. Mainau is the smaller and busier of the two, and little more than an elaborate landscaped garden. The sedate market-garden haven of Reichenau, with several small hamlets, ancient monastic churches and a contagious laidback pace, has far more to explore. Its lovely little fish restaurant, *Riebel* (see p.468), alone makes the trip here worthwhile and you can combine a stop-off on Reichenau with a cruise around the surrounding Zeller See using services from the harbour in Konstanz.

Mainau
Daily dawn–dusk • €18 • ⓦ mainau.de

With its thriving palm groves, orange orchards and flower gardens, the tiny island of **MAINAU**, 6km north of Konstanz, has a Mediterranean feel, which, combined with Alpine views, make it as idyllic and romantic as it is popular. Over two million people visit per year, which can easily be a bit much; try to come early or late in the day to avoid the worst crowds. Other good times include the **Count's Island Festival**, around the last weekend of May, and an outdoor music festival in July.

The gardens
For five hundred years Mainau was owned by the Teutonic Knights during which time they erected a Baroque Schloss and Schlosskirche. The crowd-pleasing **gardens** didn't arrive until 1853, courtesy of new owner Grand Duke Friedrich I of Baden. His current descendant, Count Bernadotte, an aristocratic Swede, continues the tradition with a dazzling year-round horticultural spread: in spring the island is carpeted in tulips, on the eastern slopes rhododendrons and azaleas erupt into colour; in summer the Italian rose-garden hits peak form and opulent fuchsias bloom; and in autumn there's a riot of dahlias. Whatever the season, tropical butterflies flit in a vast butterfly house while banana trees and bamboos fill the lush tropical garden.

ARRIVAL AND DEPARTURE — MAINAU

By bike Mainau is easily reached by bike from Konstanz along well-signposted paths – though bikes are not allowed on the island (there are cycle racks at the entrance bridge).

By bus #4 from the Stadtbahnhof (frequent; 14min).
By boat Various boats and ferries to Meersburg and elsewhere from Konstanz's harbour stop at Mainau.

EATING

Schwedenschenke ☎07531 30 31 56. Among the several bistros and cafés on Mainau it's worth seeking out this good-value restaurant – renowned for its Swedish meatballs – by day; at night it transforms into an elegant flagship of *haute cuisine* and is excellent for fresh local perch and trout in a romantic setting. Daily: late May to early Nov 11am–11pm; early Nov to Dec 11.30am–3pm.

Reichenau
Though the causeway that joins **REICHENAU** to the mainland is only 2km long, the island's sleepy atmosphere makes it feel a world apart from Konstanz only 8km west. It was this sense of remoteness coupled with a very forgiving climate and easy vegetable cultivation that encouraged Benedictines to found a monastery here in 724 AD. It grew to become one of Europe's premier places of learning in the tenth century and was particularly famous for its massive library and scriptorium, where monks would sit in rows patiently producing extraordinarily intricate and beautiful manuscripts.

Museum Reichenau
Mittelzell • April–June, Sept & Oct Tues–Sun 10.30am–4.30pm; July & Aug Tues–Sun 10.30am–5.30pm; Nov–March Sat & Sun 2–5pm • €3 • Take a regional train to Reichenau station (hourly; 8min), then change to bus #7372 to "Mittelzell" (frequent; 20min)

Original medieval manuscripts can be seen, and copies purchased, in the **Museum Reichenau** in the central village of Mittelzell. The museum also has an excellent section on the island's history – in English too – which provides the best introduction to the island's three surviving tenth-century monastic churches. The most impressive is the **Münster** around the corner from the museum.

ARRIVAL AND INFORMATION
REICHENAU

By bike and ferry Reichenau measures only 4.5km by 1.5km and is fairly flat and traffic free, which makes it ideal to explore by bike. One good idea is to rent a bike in Konstanz and ride the 10km to the island along well-marked cycle paths, explore its quiet roads, then take one of the frequent ferries back to Konstanz from the southwestern side of the island.

By train and bus From Konstanz, regional trains run to Reichenau station (hourly; 8min), where frequent buses leave for the island.

Tourist office Pirminstr. 145 (April & Oct Mon–Fri 9am–12.30pm & 1.30–5pm; May–Sept Mon–Fri 9am–6pm, Sat 10am–2pm; Nov–March 9am–12.30pm & 1.30–4pm; ☎07534 920 70, ⓦreichenau.de). Located close to Museum Reichenau.

EATING

★**Riebel** Seestr. 13 ☎07534 76 63, ⓦreichenau er-fischhandlung.de; bus #7372 from Reichenau station. The hot tip for fresh fish is owned and run by fishermen and does a brisk trade in simple but superb grilled fish, served with salads (dishes around €12; excellent fish soup only €4)

to eager locals gathered at long communal tables overlooking the lake. The restaurant lies on the northeastern side of the island – the first road on your right once you've come off the causeway. Varies with weather and season but usually April–Oct daily 11.30am–5pm.

Karlsruhe

Only 15km from France, bright and busy **KARLSRUHE** is one of Germany's youngest cities: "Karl's rest" was created in 1715 by Margrave Karl Wilhelm of Baden as a place to escape his dull wife and spend time with his mistresses. It grew as capital of Baden from 1771 and developed as a liberal town where art and science flourished, as did the university that still gives the town a lively feel. After the war it lost out to Stuttgart as regional capital, but as seat of Germany's two highest courts it still plays a significant national role and is also an important industrial base. Karlsruhe's premier attractions are its excellent **museums**, particularly the **ZKM** with its contemporary art and high-tech installations. The city also lies within a well-priced regional public transport network, which puts it within easy reach of the Northern Black Forest and Baden-Baden (see p.484). One unusual event in town to look out for is the **Trachten and Folklorefest**, when folk groups from all over Europe converge in the June of even-numbered years.

The Schloss: Badisches Landesmuseum

Schlossbezirk 10 • Tues–Thurs 10am–5pm, Fri–Sun 10am–6pm • €4, free after 2pm on Fri • ⓦlandesmuseum.de

At the town's centre stands Karlsruhe's **Schloss**, now home to the **Badisches Landesmuseum**. The palace was originally designed in the 1750s Francophile Baroque style, but was destroyed during World War II then rebuilt with Neoclassical additions. The formal palace is surrounded by more relaxed **gardens** – including a botanical one – which are a popular hangout with students from the university campus just to the southeast.

Inside the Schloss, the **Badisches Landesmuseum** is effectively the vault of Baden's royal family. Along with their jewelled crown, sword and sceptre, there's a bevy of medieval art and sculpture and a prodigious number of war trophies from Ludwig Wilhelm's seventeenth-century Ottoman campaigns. Known as the *Türtenbeute* (Turkish spoils), these are testament to the sophistication of the Ottomans: the embroidery, books, jewellery, leather and wood crafts are exquisitely made and the hoard of grim and powerful weapons suggest what an impressive feat victory over the Turks was. Of more local interest is the museum's strong collection of regional archeology: finds include Assyrian ivory carvings and impressive Roman sculptures, with two standout nautical gods.

A trip up the **Schloss tower** best reveals Karlsruhe's unusual circular road layout: from the centre, roads radiate out in an attempt to resemble a fan – the work of local architect Friedrich Weinbrenner, though postwar rebuilding has made the design less obvious.

The Staatliche Kunsthalle

Hans-Thoma-Str. 2–6 • Tues–Sun 10am–6pm • €8 • ⓦ kunsthalle-karlsruhe.de

Immediately southwest of the Schloss, one of Germany's finest art galleries, Karlsruhe's **Staatliche Kunsthalle**, is strong on Late Gothic masters such as Cranach the Elder, Dürer, Burgkmair and Baldung as well as Matthias Grünewald, whose emotional *Crucifixion* gets centre stage. Equally accomplished are the Dutch, Flemish and French sections – the latter features Delacroix and Courbet as well as Impressionists Degas, Manet, Monet, Pissarro, Renoir and Sisley. Local talent is represented by a glut of nineteenth-century work by Black Forest native Hans Thoma who was gallery director for twenty years, while members of the Blaue Reiter group (see box, p.347) also get a look in, particularly Marc.

The Marktplatz and Kaiserstrasse

The **Marktplatz**, two blocks south of the Schloss, remains another key focal point, and was similarly the vision of Friedrich Weinbrenner, whose work was deeply influenced by Roman styles, as the Neoclassical forms around the Marktplatz attest. On Marktplatz's northern side, the **Museum beim Markt** (Tues–Thurs 11am–5pm, Fri–Sun 10am–6pm; €2, free after 2pm on Fri; ⓦ landesmuseum.de) is worth a look if you're a fan of twentieth-century industrial art and design for its collection of elegant and accomplished Art Nouveau, Art Deco and Bauhaus pieces. Stretching west of here is the main commercial street, **Kaiserstrasse**.

The Stadtmuseum

Karlstr. 10 • Tues & Fri 10am–6pm, Thurs 10am–7pm, Sat 2–6pm, Sun 11am–6pm • Free

Once nationally important as the residence of the last chancellor of the Second Reich, who announced the abdication of the Kaiser and paved the way for the Weimar Republic, the **Prinz-Max-Palais** is now of purely local interest as Karlsruhe's **Stadtmuseum**. It's the best place to see the city as it was originally intended in 1834 via a splendid collection of prints and maps. Also here is the Daisienne, the 1818 work of a local inventor, probably the world's first bicycle.

The ZKM

Lorenzstr. 19 • Wed–Fri 10am–6pm, Sat & Sun 11am–6pm • Medienmuseum €6, Museum für Neue Kunst €6, combined ticket €10; both free on Fri after 2pm • ⓦ zkm.de • Tram #2E from Hauptbahnhof

The hulking detached building 2km southwest of Karlsruhe's Schloss was once a munitions factory, but like so many defunct industrial buildings it has leant itself superbly to becoming an exhibition space. The Zentrum für Kunst und Medientechnologie, or **ZKM**, occupies the building's vast airy halls, and includes cafés, restaurants and space for regular and dependably great temporary exhibitions, as well as two excellent museums.

Medienmuseum

Art and gadgetry collide in the **Medienmuseum** which is chock-full of entertaining electronic gimmicks that synthesize various elements of music, film, photography and design into creative and interactive art installations which can easily take all day to explore. Activities include using electronic dice to create a pastiche of a waltz by irreverently cobbling together bars of Mozart; using a vast image library to create collages; and shooting small movies using geometric shapes. All this is of course based on computer technology, so as a tribute you can see the maze of tubes and cables of the world's oldest operable computer (1941). Look out also for the 1950s- and 1960s-vintage optical illusions of the **Neuer Tendenzen**, or Nouvelles Tendances, an avant-garde school of art that pioneered this style. If all this hasn't left you fuzzy headed enough, the top floor of the museum is replete with various playable video games from every era.

Museum für Neue Kunst

After the Medienmuseum, the **Museum für Neue Kunst** (Museum for Contemporary Art) could easily be an anticlimax, but its thoughtful exhibits are engaging. They include 1960s Pop Art, but are usually dominated by contemporary art that reflects on aspects of modern-day Germany.

Städtische Galerie

Lorenzstr. 27 • Wed–Fri 10am–6pm, Sat & Sun 11am–6pm • €3, free on Fri after 2pm • ⓦ staedtische-galerie.de

At the end of the ZKM, and accessed by a separate entrance, is the **Städtische Galerie**, the most staid – if still accomplished – of the trio of museums here. It focuses on local and postwar German art, but is usually most worthwhile for its temporary exhibitions, which try for broad popular appeal – such as exhibitions of graphic novels.

ARRIVAL AND GETTING AROUND KARLSRUHE

By train The Hauptbahnhof lies 3km southwest of the Marktplatz, joined by tram #3.
Destinations Baden-Baden (frequent; 20min); Freiburg (frequent; 1hr).
By public transport A tram-cum-light-rail service is the hub of a system (ⓦ vbk.info) that extends all the way to

Baden-Baden and Bruchsal (single ticket €1.80, 24hr €6 or €9.50 for groups of up to five people; regional day-tickets €10.50 or €18 for up to five).
By bike Deutsche Bahn maintains a fleet of Call-a-bikes in Karlsruhe (see p.34).

INFORMATION

Tourist office At Hauptbahnhof, Bahnhofplatz 6 (Mon–Fri 8.30am–6pm, Sat 9am–1pm, Sun 10am–1pm; ☎0721 37 20 53 83, ⓦ karlsruhe-tourismus.de). Stocks the listings magazine *Karlsruhe Extra*, sells tickets to local events and

rents out audio tours for the town (€7.50).
Discount cards Karlsruhe WelcomeCard (24hr €6.50; 48hr €12.50, 72hr €17.50) includes public transport and discounted museum entry. Available from the tourist office.

ACCOMMODATION

Avisa Am Stadtgarten 5 ☎0721 349 77, ⓦ hotel-avisa .de. Dependable if unexciting hotel two blocks northeast of the train station with clean and tidy, if small and somewhat

dated rooms and a reasonable breakfast buffet. Singles start at €87. Free wi-fi. **€120**
DJH Karlsruhe Moltkestr. 24 ☎0721 282 48,

ⓦjugendherberge-karlsruhe.de; tram #2 (direction Siemensalle), #3 (direction Heide) or #4 (direction Waldstadt) from Marktplatz to stop "Europaplatz". Multistorey hostel with en-suite dorms an easy 5min walk northwest of the centre. Dorms **€22.70**; twins **€56.40**
Eden Bahnhofstr. 15–19 ☎0721 181 80, ⓦeden-ka .de. Large hotel beside the large, leafy Stadtgarten, midway between Hauptbahnhof and the centre (a 10min walk from

either). The modern rooms are sizeable and reasonable value, the breakfast buffet large and varied. **€77**
★**Hotelwelt Kübler** Bismarckstr. 37–43 ☎0721 14 40, ⓦhotel-kuebler.de. Hotel complex with a variety of rooms from standard mid-range affairs to the eccentric themed rooms in the *Allvitalis Traumhotel*. The complex also includes a spa and the *Badisches Brauhaus*, a microbrewery with an evening buffet. **€83**

EATING AND DRINKING

CAFÉS AND BARS

Café Brenner Karlstr. 61a ☎0721 35 67 89, ⓦcafe -brenner.de. A coffee house since 1896 but with more of a 1950s or 1960s feel to it, and a good place for that mid-afternoon sugar rush from its selection of great cakes; very popular with local pensioners. Mon & Wed–Sat 8.30am–6pm, Sun 10am–6pm.
★**Der Saftladen** Waldstr. 54 ☎0721 151 93 77, ⓦdersaftladen.de. Bohemian place on Waldstrasse that has the cheerful interiors you find in a doll's house. First-class smoothies and coffees, and good for a bowl of muesli early in the day too. Basic breakfasts are well-priced at around €5. Mon–Fri 7.15am–6pm (May–Oct to 7pm), Sat 9am–5pm.
Stövchen Waldstr. 54 ☎0721 292 41, ⓦstoevchen.com. Cheerful pub with sociable beer garden and a low-budget menu – which has daily specials with salad and dessert for as little as €5 and hence attracts students in droves. Also great for *Schnitzel*, *Käsespätzle* and *Flammkuchen*. Mon–Thurs & Sun 9am–1am, Fri & Sat 9am–3am.

RESTAURANTS AND WEINSTUBEN

Casa Aposto Ludwigsplatz ☎0721 160 77 73, ⓦaposto .eu. Good Italian restaurant with €5 lunch specials as well as good pizzas, pastas and salads. The home-made Italian ice cream is also first class and the outdoor seating on a convivial square makes it a place to linger. Mon–Thurs 9.30am–1am,

Fri & Sat 9.30am–2am, Sun 10.30am–1am.
El Taquito Waldstr. 22–24 ☎0721 238 81, ⓦel-taquito.de. All the usual Tex-Mex favourites are here, averaging an inexpensive €6 per dish and served indoors or outside in a quiet courtyard. Also offers a reasonable Sat brunch (noon–3pm; €8.50). Mon–Thurs & Sun 11am–1pm, Fri & Sat 11am–2am.
Lehner's Wirtshaus Karlstr. 21 ☎0721 249 57 20, ⓦlehners-wirtshaus.de. Hip place but still good for its range of inexpensive traditional favourites; set lunches are good value at €5.90, as is the crispy *Flammkuchen* at €8. A good place for breakfast too. Mon–Fri 11am–1am, Sat & Sun 10am–1am.
★**Oberländer Weinstube** Akademiestr. 7 ☎0721 250 66, ⓦoberlaender-weinstube.de. Venerable wine bar and bistro with eight hundred wines and a small seasonal gourmet menu to match – most mains cost around €20, but reckon on around €50 per person, which makes the €26.80 lunch menu a bargain. Strong on seafood and game. Tues–Sat noon–3pm & 6pm–midnight.
Viva Rathaus-Passage, Lammstr. 7 ☎0721 232 93, ⓦviva-restaurant.de. Laudable self-service vegetarian place, with excellent salads and several hot options too. Pay by the weight of your plate, so if you pile it high, you're in for a shock. Mon–Fri 11am–8.30pm, Sat 11am–5pm, Sun 11am–3am.

NIGHTLIFE AND ENTERTAINMENT

CLUBS

Club le Carambolage Kaiserstr. 21 ☎0721 37 32 27, ⓦclub-carambolage.de. Wacky club with truly experimental decor – everything from stuffed mountain goats to antique wheelchairs – opposite the university campus, so fairly studenty but with plenty of thirty-somethings too. Organizes lots of themed nights which pack out the dancefloor. Also has billiards. Daily until at least 3am.

THEATRE

Badisches Staatstheater Baumeisterstr. 11 ☎0721 355 74 50, ⓦstaatstheater.karlsruhe.de. Regionally known for dependable theatre productions, opera and classical concerts. Expect the likes of Verdi, Strauss and Liszt here, though the range is quite broad and there's been a recent campaign to attract families, with many more productions for kids.

Heidelberg

Nestled in a wooded gorge on the River Neckar, the university town of **HEIDELBERG** boasts a roster of sights that has inspired many great men: Goethe waxed lyrical about its beauty; Turner was so bewitched he captured it for posterity; and Benjamin Disraeli fell for its "exceeding loveliness", for here "the romantic ruggedness of the German

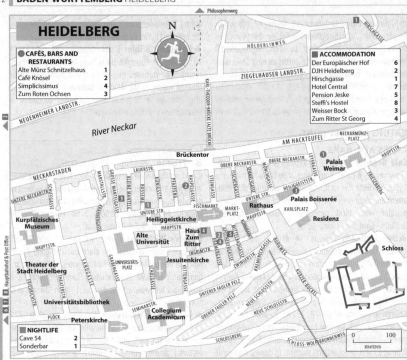

HEIDELBERG

● **CAFÉS, BARS AND RESTAURANTS**
Alte Münz Schnitzelhaus	1
Café Knösel	2
Simplicissimus	4
Zum Roten Ochsen	3

■ **ACCOMMODATION**
Der Europäischer Hof	6
DJH Heidelberg	2
Hirschgasse	1
Hotel Central	7
Pension Jeske	5
Steffi's Hostel	8
Weisser Bock	3
Zum Ritter St Georg	4

■ **NIGHTLIFE**
Cave 54	2
Sonderbar	1

landscape unites in perfect harmony with the delicate beauty of Italy". So effective was all this PR, that today three million tourists a year arrive, and for many Heidelberg remains the must-see of a Grand European Tour, just as it was for the nineteenth-century Romantics. Ironically, they had stumbled upon a town down on its luck. French troops had ravaged Heidelberg in 1688 and even more devastatingly in 1693 when writer Nicolas Boileau suggested the Académie Française be informed that "Heidelberger deleta". To cap its tale of woe, Palatinate elector Charles Philip left in favour of Mannheim in 1721 after the Protestant stronghold refused to embrace Catholicism, so demoting ravaged Heidelberg to just another provincial town.

Heidelberg's devastation proved its salvation: to Romantic eyes, the mighty red **Schloss** sited magnificently on a bluff and mailed in ivy was not simply a ruin but a wistful embodiment of melancholy and decay. Even that scurrilous wit Mark Twain described it as "deserted, discrowned, beaten by the storms, but royal still, and beautiful". The war was kind to Heidelberg too: it was one of very few German cities to suffer next to no bomb damage. This, and a decision by US authorities to develop a base here, helped the town blossom and become even more cosmopolitan.

The Schloss

Schloss Daily 8am–6pm • €6, courtyard and terrace free 6pm–dusk • ⓦ schloss-heidelberg.de • **Bergbahn** Daily: mid-April to Sept 9am–8pm; Oct to mid-April 9am–5.30pm • Lower portion including Schloss entrance €6, return trip to upper viewpoint €12 • ⓦ bergbahn-heidelberg.de

The semi-derelict **Schloss** is Heidelberg's pride. It is reached by a steep staircase or via the Bergbahn funicular from the Kornmarkt, but far better is to take adjacent

Burgweg and marvel at the massive towers. The Dicker Turm (Fat Tower), blasted by French explosives despite 7m-thick walls, is impressive, but the southeast Pulverturm is the darling of romantics past and present. French sappers split in two the mighty bulwark, the cleaved section slid into the moat and the powder tower became the **Gesprengter Turm** (Exploded Tower). It's best admired from the Grosser Altan terrace (see below).

The Schlosshof

Impressive though they are, the Schloss fortifications are only a warm-up act for the **Schlosshof**, the central courtyard, reached via the Torturm gatehouse, the only building to survive explosives. Look for a crack in the left-hand door's iron ring – the bite of a witch after Ludwig V pledged his new castle to anyone able to chomp the ring in two – then enter the courtyard, which is surrounded by impressive Gothic and Renaissance buildings.

Ruprechtsbau

Tours 4–6 daily • €4

The Gothic **Ruprechtsbau** has an angelic keystone, said to be a memorial to the master builder's late sons, and fancy Renaissance fireplaces and castle models. Springs from the Königstuhl hill behind fed the 16m-deep well in the Brunnenhaus loggia opposite. Its marble pillars were swiped from Charlemagne's Ingelheim castle, although the Holy Roman Emperor had himself snatched them from a Roman palace.

Ottheinrichsbau

Deutsches Apotheken Museum April–Oct daily 10am–6pm; Nov–March 10am–5.30pm • Same ticket as Schloss

The magnificent shell of the Renaissance **Ottheinrichsbau** (1559) has a four-tier chorus of allegorical sculptures, including planetary deities, Old Testament heroes and the Virtues. The basement contains the quirky and charmingly cluttered **Deutsches Apotheken Museum**, with eighteenth- and nineteenth-century dispensaries from the area.

Friedrichsbau

Tours 4–6 daily • €4

The **Glässener-Saal-Bau** (Hall of Mirrors), a Romanesque take on cutting-edge Renaissance, links the Ottheinrichsbau to the show-piece **Friedrichsbau**, where the ancestral gallery of swaggering sculptures traces the House of Wittelsbach from a highly dubious claim on Charlemagne to its builder Frederick V, a lineage legitimized in the centre by Justice. Join a tour to see the original statues, a beautiful, Late Gothic Schlosskapelle and rooms re-created in period style.

Fassbau

The **Fassbau** contains the **Grosses Fass** (1751), a cottage-sized wine cask; around 130 oak tree trunks created this 221,725-litre whim of Elector Karl Theodor, and many a quadrille was danced atop its platform. Before it stands a statue of the ruler's court jester, keeper of the vat and legendary boozer Clemens Perkeo. He was named, they say, for his response to offers of wine – "Perche no?" ("Why not?").

Grosser Altan

The **Grosser Altan** terrace once bloomed with Frederick V's Hortus Palatinus ornamental gardens (1616), the wonder of their age, but today are most spectacular for their views over the Altstadt's roofs. Visit at night to sympathize with Mark Twain's dazzled assessment of the town's after-dark splendour: "One thinks

---

THE WINTER KING

The Wittelsbach ruler, **Frederick V**, commissioned his ornamental gardens (see p.473) to charm his uppity English bride, 19-year-old Elizabeth Stuart, daughter of James I, and to surprise her, says local lore, he erected overnight the **Elisabethentor** (1615) to the west of the Schloss terrace. Poor **Frederick**. Few of his attempts to impress succeeded. Four years later, against better advice, the impetuous 24-year-old was crowned **King of Bohemia** and so declared a threat by the mighty Habsburg dynasty. The clash proved a disaster, both for him – his forces were routed by Emperor Ferdinand II, and the "Winter King" was stripped of all titles – and for Europe, by igniting the Thirty Years' War.

Heidelberg by day the last possibility of the beautiful, but when he sees Heidelberg by night, a fallen Milky Way … he requires time to consider the verdict."

Marktplatz and Karlsplatz

With public executions and stocks long gone, crowds linger over beer and coffee instead at the focal **Marktplatz**. At its centre, the Gothic **Heiliggeistkirche** with a Baroque mansard roof upholds a medieval tradition once common country-wide with traders' stalls snuggled between its buttresses. Founder Ruprecht III is entombed in the north aisle, and scraps of medieval frescoes hint at the riches which were stripped from here in a 1693 orgy of French looting, when the only house left standing was **Haus Zum Ritter** opposite, with its flamboyant Renaissance facade, an uncharacteristic extravagance by a Calvinist cloth merchant.

Just to the east, **Karlsplatz** is flanked by a pair of Baroque palaces: a grandiose ducal number by Rémy de la Fosse; and the Palais Boisserée, home of flamboyant French art collectors Sulpiz and Melchior, who twice hosted Goethe during his forty-year love affair with Heidelberg.

The Alte Brücke and the Philosophenweg

North of Marktplatz, the **Brückentor** gateway topped by jaunty Baroque helmets guards the graceful **Alte Brücke**. Goethe hailed the bridge of "such beauty as is perhaps not to be equalled by any other in the world", and it certainly provides a classic vista of the Altstadt. The view is only trumped by the panorama from **Philosophenweg**, a north-bank hillside path named after the university's debating students; it's a ten-minute walk above the river. At sundown you can watch the Schloss blush in a play of light Turner captured beautifully in *Heidelberg Sunset*.

The University

Universitätsmuseum and Alte Aula Universitätsplatz • April–Oct Tues–Sun 10am–6pm; Nov–March Tues–Sat 10am–4pm • €3 combined ticket with Studentenkarzer • **Studentkarzer** Augustinergasse • April–Oct daily 10am–6pm; Nov–March Mon–Sat 10am–4pm • €3 combined ticket with Universitätsmuseum and and Alte Aula • **Universitätsbibliothek** Plöck 107–109 • Daily 10am–6pm • Free

The Baroque **Alte Universität** on Universitätsplatz is the ritziest building of Germany's oldest university, founded in 1386 by Ruprecht III, and a palace compared with the modern Neue Universität in the same square. One ticket admits you into the small **Universitätsmuseum**, a grand nineteenth-century assembly hall, **Alte Aula**, and the **Studentkarzer** (Student Prison; entrance on Augustinergasse). Pranks – drunkenness, extinguishing street lamps, chasing pigs – earned students up to two weeks inside the university jail, but breaking the law could spell up to four weeks. Since it could be taken at the miscreant's convenience (and even then, offenders were bailed for exams), small wonder a stint inside was *de rigueur* for all self-respecting graduates, many of whom have left their marks in graffiti and candle-soot silhouettes.

South along Grabengasse the **Universitätsbibliothek**, a blur of students in term-time, houses scholarly exhibitions. To the east on Schulgasse the **Jesuitenkirche**'s spacious hall features restrained Rococo stucco.

The Kurpfälzisches Museum

Hauptstr. 97 • Tues–Sun 10am–6pm • €3 • ⓦ museum-heidelberg.de

The **Kurpfälzisches Museum**, a regional history museum in a Baroque mansion on Hauptstrasse, contains as its highlight Tilman Riemenschneider's *Altar of the Twelve Apostles*, which has shed its suffocating polychrome coat to emerge as an expressive Late Gothic masterpiece.

ARRIVAL AND GETTING AROUND   HEIDELBERG

By train The Hauptbahnhof is a 20min walk west of the Altstadt, or a 10min ride on tram #5 or #21.

Destinations Karlsruhe (frequent; 45min); Mannheim (frequent; 14min); Stuttgart (hourly; 40min).

By bus and tram Heidelberg is small, but the bus and tram system is handy. Single trip €2.40, 24hr ticket €6.20.

INFORMATION

Tourist office Outside the Hauptbahnhof at Willy-Brandt-Platz 1 (Mon–Sat: April–Oct 9am–7pm; Nov–March 9am–6pm; ☎ 06221 194 33, ⓦ tourism-heidelberg.com).

Discount card The HeidelbergBeWelcomeCARD (1 day €11; 2 days €13; 4 days €16) provides free entrance to some sights, including the Schloss, and transport.

ACCOMMODATION

Finding accommodation in Heidelberg can be difficult, so try to reserve well ahead – and don't expect assistance from the overworked tourist office. If all else fails, consider staying in Mannheim (see p.477), a 15min hop away by train.

HOTELS AND PENSIONS

Der Europäischer Hof Friedrich-Ebert-Anlage 1 ☎ 06221 51 50, ⓦ europaeischerhof.com. Individually decorated rooms, suites furnished with antiques and gourmet restaurant *Die Kurfürstenstube* combine to create the premier address in town. The hotel also has a couple of other quality restaurants and a bar. **€208**

Hirschgasse Hirschgasse 3 ☎ 06221 45 50, ⓦ hirschgasse.de. The connoisseur's choice counts Mark Twain and Count Otto von Bismarck among past guests. The style is luxury country – four-posters and Laura Ashley – and its north-bank location is spared summer hordes; prices can vary greatly from day to day. **€185**

Hotel Central Kaiserstr. 75 ☎ 06221 206 41, ⓦ hotel-central-heidelberg.de. Sparkling and airy, but rather bland modern hotel near the train station. It's one of the best-value places in town that's likely to have a bed, even if the rooms are a bit snug. An extensive breakfast buffet is included. **€75**

Pension Jeske Mittelbadgasse 2 ☎ 06221 237 33, ⓦ pension-jeske-heidelberg.de. Bright and central Altstadt place, cheerfully decorated and usually full – and generally unwilling to take reservations so turn up early on the day. It has some cheap triples and singles too, but not all rooms are en suite. Breakfast not included. **€40**

Weisser Bock Grosse Mantelgasse 24 ☎ 06221 900 00, ⓦ weisserbock.de. Small but comfortable rooms high in atmosphere in a backstreet charmer with a lovely dining room. Rooms have hardwood floors and furnishings and a timeless style, and there's an upper-end restaurant on site too, specializing in modern interpretations of regional dishes. **€120**

★ Zum Ritter St Georg Hauptstr. 178 ☎ 06221 13 50, ⓦ ritter-heidelberg.de. Nostalgic charm in Heidelberg's most magnificent late-Renaissance patrician mansion near the Marktplatz. Rooms aren't quite as exciting though; some are not even en suite. **€170**

HOSTELS

DJH Heidelberg Tiergartenstr. 5 ☎ 06221 65 11 90, ⓦ jugendherberge-heidelberg.de; bus #32 from Hauptbahnhof to stop "Jugendherberge". Big busy hostel a 3km walk west of the centre on the other side of the Neckar River. Often overwhelmed with school groups, but somehow spotless nonetheless. Dorms **€27**; twins **€65**

Steffi's Hostel Alte Eppelheimer Str. 50 ☎ 6221 778 27 72, ⓦ hostelheidelberg.de. Giant independent hostel in a former brick factory a short walk from the train station, with a guest lounge, kitchen, free wi-fi and bike rental. The breakfast buffet is a €4 bargain. Dorms **€18**, doubles **€56**

8

EATING AND DRINKING

Alte Münz Schnitzelhaus Alte Münz Neckarmünzgasse 10 ☎ 06221 43 46 43. There's a mind-blowing selection of some hundred *Schnitzels* on the menu at this traditional place, which range from classic Viennese style to exotic concoctions with spicy chocolate sauce; portions are large and many *Schnitzels* cost around €10. Nice summer beer garden with river views. Mon–Thurs 5–10.30pm, Fri 5–11pm, Sat & Sun 11am–11pm.

Café Knösel Haspelgasse 20 ☎ 06221 223 45. Old-world chocolatier which has been selling its *Studentenkuss* (Student's Kiss), a chocolate praline filled with praline and nougat (€2), since 1830. *Kaffee und Kuchen* doesn't come much more stylish than at its café just up the street on the corner of Untere Strasse. Daily 8am–11pm.

Simplicissimus Ingrimstr. 16 ☎ 06221 18 33 36, ⓦ simplicissimus-restaurant.de. A good gourmet option in Heidelberg, with quietly elegant decor and superb French cuisine. A four- or five-course *Tagesmenü* is offered (€68/78); otherwise mains are €24–34 and include imaginative beef, veal or seafood concoctions. Tues–Sat 6–11pm.

★ **Zum Roten Ochsen** Hauptstr. 217 ☎ 06221 209 77, ⓦ roterochsen.de. Student haunt since the 1630s with much of this history of revelry preserved in bric-a-brac and sepia fraternity photos. Still atmospheric and used by fraternities, even if most patrons are tourists. Food is the hearty traditional German kind, and mains priced around €12. May–Oct Mon–Sat 11.30am–2pm & 5pm–late; Nov–April Mon–Sat 5pm–late.

NIGHTLIFE

Cave 54 Krämergasse 1 ☎ 06221 278 40, ⓦ cave54.de. Last stop for many after a night of carousing in central Heidelberg, this basement club is often packed with a very broad crowd and offers a wide range of music from hip-hop on Mon to live rock on Fri and Sat (covers around €5) to jazz on Sun. Daily 8pm–late.

Sonderbar Untere Str. 13 ☎ 06221 252 00. One of several hip, young, tightly packed drinking spots along this alley, and with a local cult status. An extensive drinks and absinthe menu and an alt-rock-flavoured playlist attract a very mixed and very sociable young crowd. Mon–Fri 2pm–2am, Sat & Sun 2pm–3am.

Auto- und Technikmuseum Sinsheim

Am Technik Museum 1, Sinsheim • Mon–Fri 9am–6pm, Sat & Sun 9am–7pm • €14, with IMAX €19 • ⓦ technik-museum.de • Bus #564 (frequent; 15min) from Speyer (see p.520); S-Bahn 5 from Heidelberg (frequent; 46min)

Vast museum flags and the unmistakeable silhouette of a Concord plane beside the A6 motorway announce the gigantic **Auto- und Technikmuseum Sinsheim**. It's the main claim to fame of the ancient but dull little town of Sinsheim, and lies some 33km southeast of Heidelberg and 40km east of Speyer, with whose Technik Museum (see p.522) it has links.

Despite its giant size – 3000 exhibits in 50,000 square metres of warehouse – the museum still retains the slightly jumbled feel of a personal collection, which is no bad thing since it provides a sense of discovery as you make your way through. It should appeal to anyone who's ever had more than the slightest passing interest in anything mechanical, and for those interested in twentieth-century history, it's a chance to see some of the vehicles, particularly military ones, that helped shape it.

The collection's 1000 **vehicles** range from 1890s prototypes (motorized unicycles, steam-powered cars), though tractors, steam ploughs, trains, Formula 1 cars, 1950s Cadillacs, motorbikes, 1930s Mercedes, amphibious cars and dragsters to a victorious Tour de France bicycle (Jan Ullrich, 1997). The **military** section is particularly expansive: tanks galore guard dozens of rare uniforms – the German Afrika Korps and the SS included – and a full range of military vehicles and planes; there's even the remains of a crashed World War II plane retrieved from the bottom of the Mediterranean.

The two headline acts are a **Concorde** and the Soviet equivalent, the **Tupolev Tu-144**, which offered the first ultrasonic passenger flights and was brought here from Moscow on a somewhat ironic 34-day-long odyssey. In both planes the insanely complicated cockpits couldn't contrast more with the compact minimalism of the cabins. The Tupolev is the more engaging, mostly for the unmistakeably Soviet flavour of its interior oranges, squared-off detailing and instrument panels.

Much of the above will delight most kids, who'll also love the chance to slide down from the hold of a plane on sacks, race mini-karts and experience Germany's largest **IMAX cinema**. It's easy to spend the best part of a day here, which is one reason there's a large restaurant on site – the rest of Sinsheim is an industrial area away.

Mannheim

Presiding over the confluence of the Rhine and Neckar 19km from Heidelberg, **MANNHEIM** has a big-city feel quite unlike its bookish neighbour. It gained urban status in 1607 under Elector Friedrich IV of the Palatinate, its glory days coming a century later when Elector Carl Philipp transferred his capital from Heidelberg. The industrial revolution affected the city profoundly: Karl Benz founded his motor company in Mannheim in 1883, and three years later he tested the world's first real car here. Mannheim lost much to World War II bombs, but the major landmarks were later restored, the museums are excellent and it remains a good place to see Jugendstil (Art Nouveau). Nowadays it's one of Germany's most cosmopolitan cities – as reflected by the multiethnic make-up of platinum-selling local R&B group Söhne Mannheims (Sons of Mannheim).

The Barockschloss

Bismarckstrasse • Tues–Sun 10am–5pm • €6 including English audio-guide • ⓦ schloss-mannheim.de

The enormous **Barockschloss** was commissioned by Elector Carl Philipp in 1720; the architect was Louis Rémy de la Fosse, who also designed Darmstadt's **Residenzschloss** (p.574). Grievously damaged by air raids in 1943, it was later restored to house the university, and its 440m-long facade dominates the city's southern flank with absolutist swagger. The **Prunkräume**, or principal state rooms, include the lofty white-stucco ceremonial staircase and the impressive central **Rittersaal** (Knights' Hall), whose ceiling frescoes, originally by Bavarian Baroque master Cosmas Damian Asam, have been re-created. Loveliest of all is the delicate Rococo **Bibliothekskabinett** or private library of the Electress Elisabeth Augusta, on the ground floor and only visible through a glass door. It was the only one of the palace's five hundred rooms to escape significant wartime damage.

The Reiss-Engelhorn museums

Museum Zeughaus C5, Museum Weltkulturen D5, Museum Schillerhaus B5, 7 • Tues–Sun 11am–6pm • €2.50 per museum • ⓦ rem-mannheim.de

Facing each other across a piazza several blocks north of the Schloss are the main buildings of the **Reiss-Engelhorn museums**. Occupying the dignified eighteenth-century Neoclassical armoury, the **Museum Zeughaus** focuses on fine and applied arts and Mannheim's history. The modern building opposite houses the archeological, natural history and ethnographic collections of the **Museum Weltkulturen**, in which Africa and the South Sea islands are well represented. In a Baroque house south of the

---

MANNHEIM ORIENTATION

Mannheim's map betrays it as a planned city: it has a rigid central grid of streets within a circular ring, and an unusual but logical system of addresses, with numbered and lettered blocks replacing conventional street names. Exceptions to this rule include Planken – the main shopping street – and Kurpfalz Strasse, which has the Schloss at its southern tip. East of the centre is the Jugendstil **Friedrichsplatz** – the modern city's real hub – and beyond it **Oststadt**, where there's more Art Nouveau architecture and a lavish park.

Zeughaus, the **Museum Schillerhaus** is dedicated to the Mannheim days (1783–85) of dramatist Friedrich Schiller; it was here that his first play, *Die Räuber* ("The Robbers"), premiered.

Friedrichsplatz

Grouped around the fountains and gardens of Friedrichsplatz is one of Germany's best surviving ensembles of **Jugendstil** architecture. Particularly fetching are the rich red sandstone and melodramatic sculptural groups of Bruno Schmitz's **Rosengarten**, built from 1899 to 1903 and still the city's main concert and exhibition venue. The focus of the square is the 1886 **Wasserturm**, built to store drinking water. Its monumental appearance has helped make it the city's symbol.

The Kunsthalle Mannheim

Friedrichsplatz 4 • Tues & Thur–Sun 11am–6pm, Wed 11am–8pm • €9 • ⓦ kunsthalle-mannheim.com

Mannheim's wonderful Jugendstil art gallery, **Kunsthalle Mannheim**, faces onto a minor street, robbing Hermann Billing's daring 1907 building of the prominence it deserves. The collection is strong on French and German Impressionism, German Expressionism and Weimar-era art. Notable paintings include Manet's *Execution of Emperor Maximilian*, Cézanne's *Man With a Pipe*, George Grosz's portrait of the writer Max Herrmann-Neisse and Franz Marc's 1912 *Dog, Cat, Fox*. The latter was scorned by Nazis but saved from confiscation because a veterans' organization objected to the classification of the World War I hero Marc as "degenerate". The Kunsthalle's post-1945 collection includes work by Francis Bacon and Hans Hartung, and there is sculpture by Wilhelm Lehmbruck, Barbara Hepworth and Henry Moore.

The Luisenpark and around

Luisenpark Daily 9am–dusk • March–Oct €6, €1.50 after 6pm; Nov–Feb €3; gondola cruise €4 • ⓦ luisenpark.de • **Fernmeldeturm** Daily 10am–midnight • €5 • ⓦ skyline-mannheim.de • **Technomuseum** Daily 9am–5pm • €6 • ⓦ technoseum.de • Tram #6 and bus #64 from the Hauptbahnhof

East of Friedrichsplatz is **Oststadt**, Mannheim's most elegant district. Here, the 42-hectare **Luisenpark** is named after Kaiser Wilhelm I's daughter and was laid out between 1892 and 1903. There's a lake on which you can take a gondola cruise, a Chinese garden and teahouse, a chill-out zone or "sound oasis" and hothouses with tropical and subtropical zones. The park is also known for its storks.

On its north side, the 212m-high, 1970s-built **Fernmeldeturm** has an observation platform offering spectacular views, plus a revolving restaurant. To the south of the park, the **Technomuseum** celebrates the region's industrial and technological past with permanent displays that include a paper mill, railway station, eighteenth-century astronomical instruments and a giant steam engine.

ARRIVAL AND GETTING AROUND   MANNHEIM

By train Mannheim's Hauptbahnhof is four blocks from Friedrichsplatz at Willy-Brandt-Platz.
Destinations Darmstadt (frequent; 45min–1hr 25min); Frankfurt am Main (frequent; 40min); Heidelberg (frequent; 14min); Karlsruhe (frequent; 30min); Neustadt an der Weinstrasse (via Ludwigshafen: frequent; 20–35min); Speyer (frequent; 30min); Worms (frequent; 15–30min).
Public transport A €6.20 Ticket24 is valid for 24hr (ⓦ vrn.de).

INFORMATION

Tourist office Next to the Hauptbahnhof at Willy-Brandt-Platz 5 (Mon–Fri 9am–7pm, Sat 10am–1pm; ☎ 0621 293 8700, ⓦ tourist-mannheim.de). You can rent an English audio-guide here (3hr €7.50, all day €10).

Discount card The MannheimCard (1 day €8.50, 3 days €13.50), available from the tourist office, includes use of public transport and reductions on entry to museums and attractions.

ACCOMMODATION

Am Bismarck Bismarckplatz 9–11 ☎ 0621 40 04 19 60, ⓦ hotel-am-bismarck.de. Popular mid-range hotel near the Hauptbahnhof, with clean, a/c rooms with WC and bath or shower, wireless internet and minibar. Good breakfast buffet with home-made jam and a bar that serves *Flammkuchen* until 3am. **€80**

DJH Mannheim Rheinpromenade 21 ☎ 0621 82 27 18, ⓦ jugendherberge-mannheim.de. Mannheim's 102-bed youth hostel has few communal facilities but lies in a leafy riverside setting a 10min walk from the Hauptbahnhof. Follow signs to Lindenhof and then Victoria-Turm to follow tram tracks on Rennshoferstrasse. Dorms **€27.40**

Hotel Garni Haase Werftstr. 37 ☎ 0621 156 66 65, ⓦ hotel-haase.com. Spartan but reasonably cheerful and bright single-, double- and triple-bed pine-furnished rooms with WC, shower and TV, in a family-run hotel about 1km northeast of the centre. Wi-fi and free parking available. **€60**

Maritim Parkhotel Mannheim Friedrichsplatz 2 ☎ 0621 158 80, ⓦ maritim.de. The *Parkhotel* dates from 1900 and occupies a prime position facing Friedrichsplatz. Pillars and chandeliers create a "grand hotel" ambiance; rooms are tasteful, with a/c, private bath, TV and safe. **€96**

EATING AND DRINKING

Andechser N2, 10 ☎ 0621 10 16 18, ⓦ andechser -mannheim.de. Draught beer from the famous abbey brewery with hearty Bavarian food (most mains around €10), live music and a summer *Biergarten* full of jovial groups living it up. At just over the €4 mark, beers are a little expensive, but the quality and selection is good. Daily 10.30am–11pm.

C Five Restaurant C5 ☎ 0621 122 95 50, ⓦ c-five.de. Stylish restaurant, café and bar in a pavilion behind the Zeughaus, with French- and Italian-influenced dishes such as calf's liver with confit shallots; mains from €19. Cheaper pasta or salad dishes are served in the bar. Restaurant daily noon–2.30pm & 6–9.30pm.

Café Prag E4, 17 ☎ 0621 76 05 98 76. A former tobacconists' shop is the setting for this wonderful little café, where there's occasional live jazz to supplement the coffee, hot chocolate and wine, and selection of free newspapers. Mon–Sat 10am–6.30pm, Sun 1–5.30pm.

Konditorei Herrdegen E2, 8 ☎ 0621 201 85, ⓦ cafe -herrdegen.de. Classic *Kaffee und Kuchen* place in one of the city's few surviving eighteenth-century Baroque houses, with a mouthwatering display of cakes (from around €3 per slice) that it supplies to many local cafés including *Café Prag*. Mon–Fri 9am–6pm, Sat 8.30am–5.30pm.

NIGHTLIFE AND ENTERTAINMENT

CLUBS AND VENUES

Alte Feuerwache, Brückenstr. 2 ☎ 0621 293 92 81, ⓦ altefeuerwache.com. Arts centre just north of the centre in a converted fire station, hosting live music and DJs, from jazz to world music and rock. Also has a bustling bar and café serving good salads and *Flammkuchen*, and a sociable beer garden. Mon–Thurs & Sun 10am–1am, Fri & Sat 10am–3am.

★ **Capitol** Waldhofstr. 2 ☎ 0621 336 73 33, ⓦ capitol-mannheim.de. Impressive 1920s cinema that's now a cult venue for live bands, stand-up, theatre and diverse theme nights. Many shows are sold as packages with three-course meals, for which the setting is linen-table-cloth elegant. Hours vary, generally weekend nights from 6.30pm.

MS Connexion Angelstr. 33 ☎ 0621 854 41 44, ⓦ msconnexion.com. Sprawling factory complex south of the city centre, which was for many years one of Germany's biggest gay clubs. Nowadays it attracts a mixed gay/ straight crowd and some top DJs from all over the world. Hours vary, generally Fri & Sat 11pm–late.

THEATRE

Nationaltheater Mannheim Goetheplatz ☎ 0621 168 01 50, ⓦ nationaltheater-mannheim.de. The city's big, prestige venue, operating here since 1779. Divides into three stages: the largest for opera and ballet, a slightly smaller one for chamber music and theatre; and a children's theatre. Also the venue for a Friedrich Schiller festival in early June. Hours vary, generally Wed–Sun 7pm–late.

8

The Black Forest

LIFE-SIZED CUCKOO CLOCK, KINZIG VALLEY

9

The Black Forest

As the setting of countless Grimm Brothers' fairy tales, the Black Forest happily plays up to its image as a land of cuckoo clocks, cherry gâteaux, outlandish traditional garb, hefty half-timbered farmhouses and hill upon hill of dark evergreen forest. But even brief exploration soon reveals more of the character of a region that's part of the state of Baden-Württemburg (see p.424) but was shaped as much by its history as a long-disputed borderland between Germany, France and Switzerland – and where something of each is in evidence. Relative to its fame, the Black Forest region is not terribly big – about 150km long and maybe 50km wide – and so is easily explored by car in just a few days, though of course that rather misses the chance to drop down a gear in one of Germany's most treasured regions, where good scenery is matched by many time-honoured traditions.

Since Roman times this series of rounded granite summits, which topographically forms a counterpart to France's Vosges on the other, western, side of the Rhine Valley, has been a border region. The Romans found it harsh and rather impenetrable and the region took centuries to populate – and even then was considered an oddly backward part of Germany. Inevitably the Black Forest first rose to commercial prominence for its timber, and forestry naturally spawned woodwork – giving farmers something to do in the winter – and so the famous cuckoo-clock industry, the associated precision engineering, and the manufacture of musical instruments followed. All these continue to provide jobs, though the regional mainstay is now tourism, which continues year-round thanks to skiing and spa facilities. So you won't find yourself alone exploring this attractive region, but escaping the crowds at the various hotspots is easy, particularly if you're keen to explore on foot or by bike.

Dozens of attractive slow-paced small towns and villages make touring a delight, but perhaps the best way to explore is to base yourself in one of the two largest towns and strike out from there. The most genteel base is **Baden-Baden**, a grand old nineteenth-century spa town in the north that specializes in dignified recuperation and pampering. Bad Wildbad is another smaller, less expensive alternative in the **Northern Black Forest**, which is otherwise known for its attractive marked drives, particularly the scenic **Schwarzwaldhochstrasse**, and the **Badische Weinstrasse**, which travels the range's foothills through wine country. Both drives can be used to access the attractive **Kinzig Valley** which, along with the adjoining **Gutach Valley**, is considered the most quintessential and traditional Black Forest area. South of here, the attractive and upbeat university town of **Freiburg** dominates. Exploring its usually sun-soaked narrow streets is fun, but its main attraction is as a handy base

SCHWARZWÄLDER FREILICHTMUSEUM

Highlights

❶ Baden-Baden Avoid losing your head in the elite company of Baden-Baden's casino, and then let the town's elegant spas rejuvenate you. **See p.484**

❷ Europa-Park Germany's biggest amusement park offers countless rides to keep the kids entertained. **See p.496**

❸ The Schwarzwälder Freilichtmuseum Peep into the region's rustic past in this open-air museum. **See p.499**

❹ Triberg Home to the world's largest cuckoo clock, and a good place to buy your own piece of timeless Black Forest kitsch. **See p.499**

❺ Freiburg Ascend the Schauinsland cable car for incredible views over the Black Forest, Rhine Valley and France's Vosges, then walk or mountain-bike back to Freiburg on fine woodland trails. **See p.504**

❻ Todtnau Ski, mountain-bike or rattle down a summer bobsleigh track at this all-season resort. **See p.508**

❼ Wutachschlucht Hike in the deep, dark and attractively lush gorge that tourist brochures dub "Germany's Grand Canyon". **See p.513**

HIGHLIGHTS ARE MARKED ON THE MAP ON P.484

9

from which to explore the entire **Southern Black Forest**, where deep valleys are flanked by rounded peaks like the **Feldberg** that tops out at 1493m, and include many minor ski and lake resorts.

Baden-Baden

The smart and dignified *grande dame* of German spas, **BADEN-BADEN** lies cradled in the palm of idyllic and gentle wooded hills, 42km south of Karlsruhe. In the

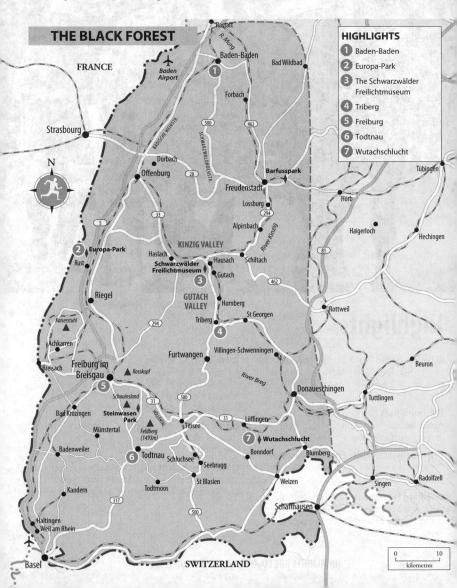

THE BLACK FOREST

HIGHLIGHTS

1. Baden-Baden
2. Europa-Park
3. The Schwarzwälder Freilichtmuseum
4. Triberg
5. Freiburg
6. Todtnau
7. Wutachschlucht

9

BLACK FOREST DISCOUNT CARDS

Staying overnight in most hotels and pensions in the Black Forest entitles you to a **Gästekarte**, which offers a number of reductions at various local attractions. Those with a "Konus" logo also include free public transport in the region. Another money-saving option, particularly if you plan a busy itinerary, is the three-day **SchwarzwaldCard**, which includes free admission to over 150 regional attractions, including museums, cable cars, boat trips, spas and pools; the full list of partners is at ⓦ blackforest-tourism.com. Available at most of the region's tourist offices, the adult pass costs €35, or €60.50 for a version that includes a day at Europa-Park (see p.496), and there are also kids' (€25/50.50) and family versions (€107/209); the family pass covers two adults and three children.

nineteenth century this was the St Tropez of high society and something of this era's privilege survives in the dusty elegance of its villas, hotels and boutiques and in the manicured gardens where well-groomed socialites promenaded. The absence of any heavyweight sights, moreover, helps make it a near perfect setting for a recuperative weekend.

Brief history

Baden margraves built today's thermal baths in 1810 around the same springs that once lured Roman bathers – in particular Emperor Caracalla – nearly two millennia earlier. The baths were a hit in nineteenth-century Germany, so architect Friedrich Weinbrenner designed a complementary Neoclassical spa quarter. Some thirty years later, dapper Parisian impresario Jacques Bénazet added a casino, catapulting Baden-Baden to an elite playground that lured an international who's-who to play, promenade and soothe their rheumatic joints: Tolstoy, Strauss, Queen Victoria, Kaiser Wilhelm I, Dostoyevsky, Bismarck, Tchaikovsky, Brahms and the Vanderbilts all visited. More recent visitors have included Bill Clinton, Barack Obama and Victoria Beckham. Mark Twain came too, but had mixed feelings, describing it as "an inane town, filled with sham and petty fraud and snobbery". The town emerged unscathed from World War II and now effortlessly blends its halcyon days with modern-day pampering.

The Trinkhalle

Kaiserallee 3 • Mon–Thurs & Sun 10am–2am, Fri & Sat 10am–3am • Free

Set amid parkland on the west bank of the Oos, the **Trinkhalle** (Drinking Hall) is home to the tourist office and the natural place to start exploring. Fronted by a sixteen-column parade, the **Trinkhalle** features a 90m portico that shelters fourteen nineteenth-century frescoes depicting local legends. Mark Twain fumed at the "tranquil contemptuousness" of the young female clerks who served spa waters to nineteenth-century spa-goers; you needn't negotiate them today for a drink from the tap in the centre of the hall – plastic cups for the purpose are available from the adjoining café for a small charge.

BADEN-BADEN ORIENTATION

Baden-Baden is split in two by the north–south-flowing Oos. On its **west bank** gather all the grand nineteenth-century buildings and follies that were built as social centres and as points between which to promenade. The rest of the town centre is grouped on the right bank of the Oos, home to the relatively modern **Altstadt** and all the commercial areas, as well as the famous **baths**. Behind them sloping meadows and forests rise up, surrounding **Burg Hohenbaden** above town.

9

Stourdza-Kapelle

Stourdzastrasse • By appointment: daily 10am–6pm • Free • ☎ 07221 285 74

Behind the Trinkhalle, paths idle up to the **Stourdza-Kapelle** amid redwoods and rhododendrons. Michael Stourdza, having settled in Baden-Baden after his exile as last ruler of Moldovia, commissioned Munich master architect Leo von Klenze to build this requiem for his 17-year-old son, killed in a Paris duel in 1863. Pathos in the dignified marble interior comes from frescoes of the dead prince and his parents.

The Kurhaus and casino

Kurhaus Kaiserallee 1 • Tours daily every 30min April–Oct 9.30am–noon; Nov–March 10am–noon • €5 • ⓦ kurhauscasino.de • **Casino** Daily noon–late • €1–5 depending on games; ID required • ⓦ casino-baden-baden.de

Nowhere better captures Baden-Baden's aristocratic pretensions than the **Kurhaus**,

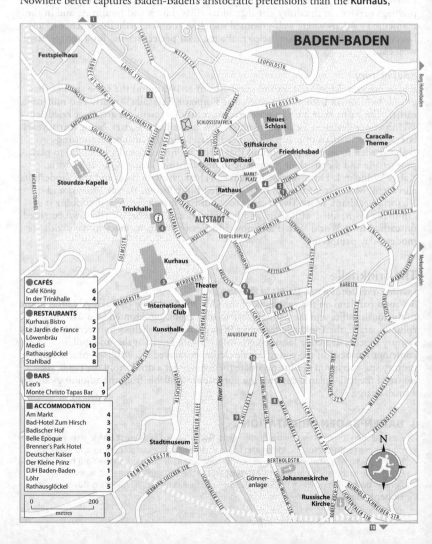

BADEN-BADEN

● CAFÉS	
Café König	6
In der Trinkhalle	4

● RESTAURANTS	
Kurhaus Bistro	5
Le Jardin de France	7
Löwenbräu	3
Medici	10
Rathausglöckel	2
Stahlbad	8

● BARS	
Leo's	1
Monte Christo Tapas Bar	9

■ ACCOMMODATION	
Am Markt	4
Bad-Hotel Zum Hirsch	3
Badischer Hof	2
Belle Epoque	8
Brenner's Park Hotel	9
Deutscher Kaiser	10
Der Kleine Prinz	7
DJH Baden-Baden	1
Löhr	6
Rathausglöckel	5

which almost single-handedly made the town what it is today. Weinbrenner's 1820s centrepiece for his fledgling spa resort is an exercise in restraint, dignity and poise: strictly Neoclassical in style, it is guarded by eight Corinthian columns and set behind a manicured lawn with cheerful flowerbeds.

The Kurhaus **interior** is far less solemn. In 1855, Edouard Bénazet commissioned Parisian craftsmen to spice up the **casino** he inherited from his father Jacques – the portrait of that first *roi de Bade* takes pride of place in the casino lobby – fusing Versailles opulence and *belle époque* glamour in an attempt to outdo both. In its **Wintergarten**, Second Empire-style fountains shimmer in gilt mosaic, Hsien-Feng porcelain vases line the walls and a gold-trimmed roulette table winks seductively in the light. The adjacent **Roter Saal**, modelled on Versailles, is just as striking, ablaze with strawberry silk wall-coverings from Lyon and a riot of gilt trim, while the Renaissance-style **Florentinesaal** drips crystal from chandeliers and once rang to concerts by Brahms and Clara Schumann. Small wonder Marlene Dietrich whistled that it was the most beautiful casino in the world.

The casino

You can marvel at the shameless opulence on twenty-minute tours of the Kurhaus, but far better to drink in the Bond-movie glamour during the evening shuffle of cards and clatter of roulette balls. For women, dresses or skirts are obligatory, while men need a jacket and tie (€8 and €3 respectively to rent), and while smart jeans are permitted, sports shoes certainly aren't. Minimum stakes begin at €5, but night owls can watch Saudi sheiks play the final hand of baccarat around 3am, when all stake limits (usually €25,000) are waived. Needless to say, there's an ATM inside, but beware: an aide to Tsar Nicolas II arrived in 1902 with twenty million roubles' worth of booty swiped from royal treasure chests and left penniless a week later; Dostoyevsky also lost heavily here, which helped inspire him to write *The Gambler* to pay off his gambling debts.

The bandstand

The small **bandstand** in front of the Kurhaus was once the stage for concerts by Strauss and Brahms. Nowadays, however, it usually plays host to light jazz to entertain summer strollers following in the footsteps of the fashionable spa-goers who once shamelessly posed along the adjacent avenue of chestnut trees, now lined by expensive boutiques.

Lichtentaler Allee and around

A 2.5km-long parkland avenue south of the Kurhaus and beside the Oos, **Lichtentaler Allee** has long been Baden-Baden's key place to stroll, lounge, saunter and promenade – and to be seen doing so. And it's still so well-kept that it's not hard to imagine the click of ebony walking-canes on cobbles and the swish of silk dresses. It took its present form in 1860 at the instigation of Edouard Bénazet, who transformed a simple avenue of oaks to an English-style garden of global specimen trees. Queen Victoria took the air here and even Mark Twain grudgingly admired its "handsome pleasure grounds, shaded by noble trees and adorned with sparkling fountain jets". Today, perfectly clipped grass is carpeted with crocuses in March and dotted with rhododendrons, azaleas, roses and busts of luminary former-guests while palatial villas in elegant shades of cream look on. A heavyweight contemporary art museum, the town museum and an elegant rose garden, add interest to the bucolic riverside walk to the suburb of Lichtental; you'd never guess the traffic of the B500 thunders in a tunnel beneath your feet.

The Theater Baden-Baden and International Club

Goetheplatz 1 • ☎ 07221 93 27 51, ⓦ theater-baden-baden.de

The first notable building on Lichtentaler Allee, the neo-Baroque **Theater Baden-Baden**, modelled on the Paris Opera House, opened in 1863 for the premiere of Berlioz's *Béatrice*

9

> ## WHEN TO CHOOSE YOUR HAT CAREFULLY
>
> Baden-Baden's social highlight of the year is the August **Iffezheim races**, Germany's Ascot, which has been going strong since 1858 and encompasses two events: the **Frühjahrsmeeting** over the last week of May; and the grander **Grosse Woche** in the last week in August, when the country's elite dress to the nines and don flamboyant hats.

et Bénédict conducted by the French composer. Beside it, Weinbrenner's 1820 summer palace for Queen Friederike of Sweden has been claimed by the **International Club** as headquarters for the social event of the year, the Iffezheim horse races (see box above).

The Kunsthalle and Sammlung Frieder Burda

Lichtentaler Allee 8a • Tues–Sun 10am–6pm • €12 • ⊛ kunsthalle-baden-baden.de, ⊛ museum-frieder-burda.de

The **Kunsthalle** is home to dependably high-profile international contemporary art exhibits. Its bold, modern concrete-and-glass annexe, by Richard Meier, is the **Sammlung Frieder Burda**, one of Germany's most extensive private modern-art collections: a high-octane display of German Expressionism, Cubist Picassos and Abstract Expressionists such as Pollock and De Kooning.

The Stadtmuseum

Lichtentaler Allee 10 • Tues–Sun 11am–6pm • €5 • ☎ 07221 93 22 72

At the southern end of the most formal part of the park, the **Stadtmuseum** skips through the town's Roman roots to dwell on the vintage roulette wheels and spa cures that made Baden-Baden a glamorous nineteenth-century playground.

The Gönneranlage

Beside the Stadtmuseum, the arterial Bertholdstrasse crosses the park and a five-minute stroll beyond, across the Oos on a neat footbridge, lies the **Gönneranlage**, a secret garden behind thick beech hedges where over four hundred varieties of rose thrive in the benevolent microclimate to create a heady perfume. Pergolas, statues and fountains add structure.

Russische Kirche

Lichtentaler Str. 76 • Feb–Nov daily 10am–6pm • €0.50

The area known as the Südstadt was the traditional expat quarter, and one of the outstanding mementos of this era is the Byzantine-style **Russische Kirche**, which lies two blocks east of the Gönneranlage. Crowned by a gold onion-dome, the church was built in the 1880s for a then sizeable population of expatriate Russian diplomats, nobles and writers. Its heavily frescoed interior is the work of Grigor Grigorijevitsch Gagarin, painter to the tsars.

Lichtental

A half-hour walk – or bus #201 – from the Gönneranlage through parkland paths beside the Oos brings you to the southern suburb of **Lichtental**, with its tranquil abbey and a house that was once home to the composer Brahms. Those with sturdy legs can stroll 3km further on Geroldsauer Strasse to the idyllic **waterfalls** snuggled in the woods (see box, p.491).

Kloster Lichtental

Hauptstr. 40 • **Fürstenkapelle** Tours Wed, Sat & Sun 3pm • €4 • **Shop** Mon–Sat 10am–5.30pm, Sun 1–5pm • ⊛ abtei-lichtenthal.de

The thirteenth-century **Kloster Lichtental** huddles in peaceful contemplation around a triangular courtyard of gnarled trees, screened off from the world by a high wall. The thirty nuns in residence here are famous both for their religious handicrafts and for a powerful spirit distilled in the convent – both are on sale in a small shop – while the prize of their Cistercian abbey founded in 1245 is the **Fürstenkapelle**, chapel of the Baden margraves until 1372.

Brahmshaus

Maximilianstr. 85 • Mon, Wed & Fri 3–5pm, Sun 10am–1pm • €3 • ⓦ brahms-baden-baden.de

A five-minute walk from the abbey, the tiny rooms of the **Brahmshaus** are much as the German composer knew them during his 1865–74 sojourn here, when he sweated over his first and second symphonies and wrestled with his monumental *Deutsches Requiem*.

The Altstadt

On the eastern bank of the Oos and gathered around the Rathaus, lies the **Altstadt**, which is none too old, thanks to the actions of one General Duras. Leading the French troops in the Palatinate War of Succession, he swooped upon Baden-Baden in 1689 – while Margrave Ludwig Wilhelm commanded forces in Hungary – and reduced it to ashes, executing Louis XIV's order to turn disputed borderlands into a *glacis*, or wasteland. Ludwig Wilhelm deserted his ravaged town for Rastatt in 1705 and Baden-Baden began a century-long rebuild. Though its layout is far older, most of the Altstadt buildings are a product of this rebuild – as their cream, coffee and pink facades attest.

Above this network of bustling streets, the **Marktplatz** has a forgotten feel, its shuttered villas lining up like a stage set for an Italian operetta. The square's **Rathaus** started life as a seventeenth-century Jesuit college and quietly glosses over its fourteen years as a casino and restaurant from 1810 before the Kurhaus opened for business.

Stiftskirche Liebfrauen

Marktplatz • Daily 8am–6pm • Free

Opposite the Rathaus is the **Stiftskirche Liebfrauen**, whose landmark spire is a crash course in its history: a Romanesque square tower sprouts an octagonal Gothic cap, then buds into Baroque cupolas. Inside, lurking in the gloom, is a superb Late Gothic (1467) 5.6m **crucifix** sculpted from a single block of sandstone, the masterpiece of Nikolaus Gerhaert von Leyden, an influential Dutch sculptor who pioneered an expressive realism. Crudely showing off before it in styles from Renaissance to Rococo are the **tombs** of Baden-Baden margraves. The finest is a swaggering apotheosis of Ludwig Wilhelm: marshal's baton in hand, he is lauded by Courage (left), Justice (right) and Wisdom (above) and stands above the apparatus of war with which he routed Turkish forces to earn his nickname, "Turkenlouis". Don't overlook an intricate **tabernacle** to the left of the choir – carved two decades after Gerhaert's work, it hides polychrome saints among knotted vines and twisted branches, and its anonymous sculptor signs his work on the base with a self-portrait holding set-square and compasses.

Altes Dampfbad

Marktplatz 13 • Tues–Fri 3–6pm, Sat & Sun 11am–5pm • Free • ⓦ gfjk.de

Behind the Stiftskirche Liebfrauen, occasional wisps of steam from grilles in the adjacent Friedrichsbad drift over the cobbles in front of the Tuscan-styled **Altes**

THE HIGH LIFE: HOT-AIR BALLOONING IN BADEN-BADEN

As a premier magnet for the well-heeled, it's maybe no surprise that Baden-Baden has Europe's largest fleet of **hot-air balloons**. So if you've struck it lucky at the casino, you might like to splurge on a two-hour champagne breakfast flight along the Rhine Valley between the Black Forest and the Vosges for €253 per person with Ballooning 2000 (☎ 07223 600 02, ⓦ ballooning2000.de).

9

Dampfbad. From 1848, spa-goers gasped for air in its steam baths; now its lofty rooms host temporary contemporary art exhibitions, many with a local theme.

Neues Schloss

To the left of the Altes Dampfbad the Schlossstaffeln stairway zigzags up to the **Neues Schloss**. The Baden margraves claimed the highest point in town for a more central seat to replace Burg Hohenbaden from 1479 until they fled to Ratstatt. Snapped up by the Al-Hassawi group in 2003, there's been no public access to the Renaissance palace or the fine views from its gardens since, though there will be, once renovation work – which will create a five-star hotel – is complete.

The Bäderviertel

The narrow alleys at the northeastern end of the Altstadt open up to reveal the large buildings and parkland of the **Bäderviertel** (Bath Quarter). The Romans were bathing here some 2000 years ago, as ruins reveal, but today's visitors have the choice of two complexes: the venerable old Friedrichsbad and the more sociable and modern Caracalla.

Friedrichsbad

Römerplatz 1 • Daily 9am–10pm, last entry 8pm • 3hr €23, 3hr 30min including a brush massage €35 • ⓦ roemisch-irisches-bad.de

Friedrichsbad is the undisputed queen of German spas. By happy coincidence the wraps came off the splendid neo-Renaissance bathing hall five years after Kaiser Wilhelm I outlawed gambling in 1872, and the baths cashed in on the casino's temporary halt. And just as Bénazet had brought opulence to local gambling, so Grand Duke Friedrich I's spa elevated bathing. Outside, the Friedrichsbad looks like a minor palace, fronted by busts of Baden-Baden spa heroes including Friedrich I crowned with green copper cupolas; inside it is a paean to a golden age of antiquity, a colonnaded beauty of elegant arches and columns in tones of terracotta and stone.

Speciality of the house is the **Roman-Irish bath**, a three-hour-long course of showers, baths, steam rooms and saunas of ever-decreasing temperatures. By stage ten, you drift dazed in a pool, watched by a ring of cherubs on an ornamented cupola; at stage sixteen you collapse, prune-like and dozy, in a resting area for a snooze. As Twain noted, "Here at the Friedrichsbad you lose track of time within ten minutes and the world within twenty." Leave your inhibitions at the door, however – bathing is mixed (except Mon & Thurs when sexes are segregated) and nude. Children under 14 are not allowed, those over only with parents.

The Römische Badruinen

Römerplatz 1 • Mid-March to mid-Nov daily 11am–noon & 3–4pm • €2.50 • ⓦ badruinen.de

Baths were first established by the Romans around 75 AD, for their town Aquae Aureliae, as local spring waters were thought to ease aching joints. The ruins of their structures, the **Römische Badruinen**, now lie in the basement of the Friedrichsbad, where computer animations help make sense of crumbling walls.

Caracalla Therme

Römerplatz 1 • Daily 8am–10pm, last entry 8pm • 2hr €15, 3hr €18, 4hr €21 • ⓦ caracalla.de

Across the square from the Friedrichsbad is the modern **Caracalla Therme**, named after the Roman emperor who nurtured Baden-Baden's bathing culture. It contains modern pools (one outdoor) between 18°C and 38°C as well as steam baths and saunas (the only nude area in the complex). The three springs – the Friedrichsquelle, Fettquelle and Murquelle – that spout from fountains in the upstairs foyer can be viewed without admission, and many people simply come here to knock back a glass of the curative warm and salty water; it's a taste that's not forgotten in a hurry though.

WALKS AROUND BADEN-BADEN

The 43km-long **Panoramaweg** hiking trail encircles Baden-Baden and is generally split into five legs, all accessible by bus; the tourist office can supply maps. One short, easy and popular part of the circuit is the 3km return trip to the **Geroldsauer waterfalls** from a trailhead 6km south of town; it's best in June when the rhododendrons are in bloom. A café at the falls provides sustenance for the return journey.

Another good walk from Baden-Baden is accessed via the **Merkurbergbahn** (daily 10am–10pm; €4 one-way; ⓦstadtwerke-baden-baden.de; bus #204 or #205 from Leopoldsplatz), a funicular which runs to the top of the Merkur (668m), just east of the centre. Take the trail back towards the base station, then turn off north along the marked **Panoramaweg** and follow that back into the centre of Baden-Baden for a 5km, mostly downhill hike.

Burg Hohenbaden

Alter Schlossweg 10 • May–Sept 11am–10pm • Free • ⓦschloss-hohenbaden.de • Bus #215 from Augustaplatz or the Caracalla Spa

Aloof and magnificent on a bluff 3km north of the town centre, the ruins of **Burg Hohenbaden** (also called the Altes Schloss) has long been a favourite destination for a stroll. It's a 45-minute walk from central Baden-Baden: from the Neues Schloss (see opposite), take the meandering path uphill through meadows and deciduous woods. The eleventh-to-fifteenth-century seat of the Baden margraves, it was ruined by fires in 1584 and 1597. Its keep perches on a knuckle of rock to the rear, guarded in front by the fourteenth-century Unterburg. There are vast cellar vaults to explore; mantelpieces that cling surreally halfway up walls; and stairways that spiral to long-crumbled towers. Sweeping views over the Black Forest and Rhine plains also make the climb worth all the effort, and a **restaurant** (daily 11am–10pm, closed Oct–April; ☎07221 269 48) rustles up inexpensive German staples and pastas. Behind the castle a path clambers through protected woods to **Battert** (Battery), a cliff popular with local climbers.

ARRIVAL AND GETTING AROUND

BADEN-BADEN

By plane Karlsruhe-Baden airport (FKB; ☎07221 66 20 00, ⓦbadenairpark.de) lies 15km west of Baden-Baden and is connected by hourly buses (Mon–Fri 6.52am–8.26pm; 26min). Taxis cost around €30.

By train The station is located 4km northwest in the suburb of Oos; bus #201 goes to the centre, "Leopoldsplatz".

Destinations Freiburg (hourly; 1hr); Heidelberg (every 30min; 1hr 10min); Karlsruhe (frequent; 20min); Konstanz (hourly; 2hr 45min); Strasbourg (every 30min; 1hr).

Public transport Baden-Baden is very walkable, and promenading is *de rigueur*, but there's also a good bus system run by Stadtwerke Baden-Baden (☎07221 27 71, ⓦstadtwerke-baden-baden.de), whose two-zone, €2.30 ticket covers all city destinations; the €10.50 day-ticket extends to Karlsruhe.

INFORMATION

Tourist office In the Trinkhalle on Kaiserallee (Mon–Sat 10am–5pm, Sun 2–5pm; ☎07221 27 52 00, ⓦbaden-baden.de). The office can book accommodation in private rooms (from €68).

ACCOMMODATION

HOTELS

★**Am Markt** Marktplatz 18 ☎07221 270 40, ⓦhotel-am-markt-baden.de. Friendly, family-run pension on the charming Marktplatz – ask for a room with a view. Fairly basic, but rooms are bright and modern and it's hands-down the town's best budget choice in the centre. €95

Bad-Hotel Zum Hirsch Hirschstr. 1 ☎07221 93 90, ⓦheliopark-hirsch.de. Thermal spring water flows from the taps in antique-furnished rooms at this historic hotel in the central Altstadt. Its fine public rooms include an especially splendid ballroom. €142

Badischer Hof Lange Str. 47 ☎07221 93 40, ⓦhotel-badischerhof-badenbaden.de. Landmark place that was long the social centre of the rich and famous and whose thermal pools, steam baths and saunas make it the luxury historic hotel of choice for spa-goers – some rooms even have thermal spa water on tap. €144

9

Belle Epoque Maria-Viktoria-Str. 2c ☎07221 30 06 60, ⓦhotelbelleepoque.de. An 1870s villa every inch the retreat of Second Empire aristocrats. Sixteen luxurious rooms are furnished top to bottom in rich antiques while cleverly hiding all their mod cons from view. Rooms are themed: you can choose between the styles of Empire, Louis XV, Biedermeier, Victorian, Louis Philippe and Louis XVI. Book early – advance reservations are a must. **€195**

Brenner's Park Hotel Schillerstr. 4–6 ☎07221 90 00, ⓦbrenners.com. The queen of Baden-Baden addresses, located in its own park opposite Lichtentaler Allee, has all the effortless elegance of the town's heyday and remains world class. Lounges are furnished in Second Reich antiques, rooms have flowery fabrics and chandeliers and there's also an excellent modern spa and gym complex. The *Park-Restaurant*, meanwhile, is a gourmet address. You can pay as much as €1700 for a suite in high season. **€345**

Deutscher Kaiser Hauptstr. 35 ☎07221 721 52, ⓦhoteldk.de; bus #201 to "Eckerlestrasse." Pleasant, family-run place 2km from the centre in the lovely suburb of Lichtental. Not all the clean and simply furnished rooms are en suite, but it's a great budget choice all the same. **€65**

★Der Kleine Prinz Lichtentaler Str. 36 ☎07221 34 63, ⓦderkleineprinz.de. Occupying two elegant city mansions, this sister hotel to the *Belle Epoque* has an upmarket rustic air and is decorated with prints of Antoine de Saint-Exupéry's charming hero. Every room has a special feature – whirlpool, fireplace, balcony, tower – and the quality of the service and its restaurant are both outstanding. **€140**

Löhr Lichtentaler Str. 19 ☎07221 30 60, ⓦhotel-loehr.com. Central hotel, with clean but very standard mid-range en-suite rooms; rates include a continental breakfast served in the hotel's bistro, a popular locals' hangout later in the day. Has wi-fi as well. **€120**

Rathausglöckel Steinstr. 7 ☎07221 906 10, ⓦrathausgloeckel.de. Family-run hotel in a sixteenth-century house with neat and small pine-furnished en-suite rooms with the occasional nineteenth-century touch. Some have views over the town's roofs. Wi-fi included. **€147**

HOSTELS

DJH Baden-Baden Hardbergstr. 34 ☎07221 522 23, ⓦjugendherberge-baden-baden.de; bus #201 to "Grosse-Dollenstrasse". A signposted 10min climb from the bus stop, this uninspiring HI hostel is located between the train station and the centre. It does, however, have barbecue areas and gardens. Breakfast included. Reception open 5–10pm. Dorms **€22.70**; twins **€28.20**

EATING AND DRINKING

CAFÉS

Café König Lichtentaler Str. 12 ☎07221 235 73, ⓦchocolatier.de. The place for *Kaffee und Kuchen* and a throwback to the elegant days pictured on the black-and-white prints on its walls. The delicate *Schwarzwälder Kirschtorte* (Black Forest gâteau) is the finest you'll eat and there's quiche, soups and salads for lunch. Daily 8.30am–6.30pm.

In der Trinkhalle Kaiserallee 3 ☎07221 05 30 29, ⓦin-der-trinkhalle.de. Idyllic café in a wing of the Trinkhalle that's perfect for a lazy cappuccino or light lunch on either the suntrap terrace or a leather Chesterfield inside. Daily 10am–2am.

RESTAURANTS

Kurhaus Bistro Kaiserallee 1 ☎07221 90 70, ⓦkurhausrestaurant.de. Attached to the Kurhaus (see p.486) and so a cut above the usual bistro, its walls covered by signed photos of dignitaries who have sampled its seasonally geared, international menu. Mains €19–24. Daily noon–2pm & 6–10pm.

★Le Jardin de France Lichtentaler Str. 13 ☎07221 300 78 60, ⓦlejardindefrance.de. Baden-Baden's elegant gourmet restaurant is in a courtyard off Lichtental Strasse, with a decor of antiques and flowers that's every bit as exquisite as the creative, modern dishes (mains €30–40), which use inventive and unusual ingredients such as pak choi, morels, turbot or Alsatian pigeon. The service is immaculate, too. Reservations required. Tues–Sat noon–2pm & 7–9.30pm.

Löwenbräu Gernsbacher Str. 9 ☎07221 223 11, ⓦloewenbraeu-baden-baden.de. If you're sick of Swabian fare, head to *Löwenbräu* and eat like a Bavarian (mains average €17). There's also a boisterous summer beer garden, with a traditional breakfast (*Weisswurst, Brezn* and beer) for €6. Daily 10am–11pm.

Medici Augustaplatz 8 ☎07221 20 06, ⓦmedici.de. *Belle époque*-style restaurant which has welcomed Bill Clinton and Nelson Mandela yet serves moderately priced mains (€9–17) such as *Zander* filet with pancetta, tomato and aubergine torte and, the house special, a Thai chicken curry. *Medici*'s bar is the most fashionable in town and a great place to people-watch. Daily 6pm–late.

Rathausglöckel Steinstr. 7 ☎07221 906 10, ⓦrathausgloeckel.de. Inexpensive traditional favourites like venison goulash (€9.50) are served in this cosy sixteenth-century hotel on a side street off the Marktplatz. The wine soup is an odd speciality worth trying. Mon–Sat 6–11pm, Sun noon–3pm & 6–10pm.

Stahlbad Augustaplatz 2 ☎07221 245 69, ⓦstahlbad.com. An aristocrat among local restaurants, this place elevates traditional Black Forest dishes like trout, goose or venison steak to new heights with the addition of exquisite French flavours. In the right season, look out too for the first-class fettuccini Alfredo with white truffles. Some of the best specialities are goose liver broiled with a champagne *Sauerkraut*, and breast of quail with grapes. Most mains are in the €15–30 range. Mon–Fri noon–2.30pm & 6–10.30pm, Sat & Sun noon–11pm.

BARS

Leo's Luisenstr. 8–10 ☎07221 380 81, ⓦleos-baden-baden.de. Heaving bistro and wine bar that's

Baden-Baden's hippest hangout; the restaurant – all dark woods and black-and-white photos – serves international dishes (average €16) in wonderful sauces flavoured with such ingredients as Dijon mustard and rosemary. Mon–Thurs & Sun 10am–1am, Fri & Sat 10am–2am.

★ **Monte Christo Tapas Bar** Eichstr. 5, Baden-Baden ☎07221 39 34 34. Huge selection of tasty tapas (most €5–11) – which include superb meatballs and a seafood skillet – served in a central location with a lovely courtyard. Ingredients are top-notch and the wine selection superb. Mon–Sat 6pm–1am.

NIGHTLIFE AND ENTERTAINMENT

There are places to find a bit of nightlife in Baden-Baden, particularly in the hotels: try the *Jockey Bar* in *Badischer Hof*, or the *Oleander Bar* in *Brenner's*, but dress up. Aside from its **casino** (see p.487), Baden-Baden is also excellent for high culture. Every summer the tourist office organizes free classical and jazz **concerts** in the gardens around the Kurhaus, and their box office in the Trinkhalle (daily 10am–6.30pm; ☎07221 93 27 00) sells tickets to everything else that's listed in the what's-on booklet *Baden-Baden Aktuell*.

Festspielhaus Beim Alten Bahnhof 2 ☎07221 301 31 01, ⓦfestspielhaus.de. This 2500-seat concert hall hosts the distinguished Baden-Badener Philharmonie (ⓦphilharmonie.baden-baden.de) and often welcomes international stars such as the London or Berlin philharmonics. It also stages ballet and opera.
Kurhaus Kaiserallee 1 ☎07221 35 32 07, ⓦkurhaus-baden-baden.de. The casino building provides a venue for

smaller classical concerts and often jazz.
Theater Baden-Baden Goetheplatz 1 ☎07221 93 27 51, ⓦtheater-baden-baden.de. Grandiose theatre modelled on Paris's Opéra National, with performances for a broad range of tastes, from musicals to Shakespeare. Tickets €22–40. Performances Sat & Sun and occasional weekdays.

The Northern Black Forest

Though plenty of small towns and villages dot the Northern Black Forest, most are of little specific interest, though the spa town of **Bad Wildbad** does offer an alternative base to Baden-Baden. Instead this region is best known for its scenic drives, including the **Badische Weinstrasse**, which travels through the strip of vineyards that line the Rhine Valley and is home to **Europa-Park**, Germany's largest amusement-park. Just east, above the valley, another waymarked drive, the **Schwarzwaldhochstrasse** is considered *the* classic scenic drive in the Black Forest.

Bad Wildbad

If the snootiness of Baden-Baden turns you off, you might prefer the more relaxed spa town of **Bad Wildbad**, a 41km drive east – and close enough to Stuttgart to make it an easy day-trip. It's an attractive place too, with its own venerable baths, and a wonderful funicular, which climbs steeply out of a town centre that's strung out along the base of the narrow Enz Valley. The railway summits at the **Sommerberg**, where hiking and **mountain biking** awaits. Some of the latter is of the white-knuckle downhill variety that requires body-armour, and injects a good dose of youthful adrenaline into the town.

Bad Wilbad itself is quickly explored: be sure to look around the elegant **Haus des Gastes**, König-Karl-Str. 1 (daily 8am–midnight; free), a grand spa building built in 1889 which serves as a venue for town events, and wander around the stately and relatively wild **Kurpark**, just to the west, where you can picnic, feed ducks and perambulate.

9

SOMMERBERG TO KALTENBRONN WALK

A good circular walk from the summit of the Sommerbergbahn funicular above Bad Wildbad is to the small resort town of **Kaltenbronn**, 7km away. En route, the *Grünhütte* inn offers refreshments, and beyond it the trail passes the **Wildsee**, one of an attractive series of moorland lakes, before dropping into Kaltenbronn via boardwalks. From Kaltenbronn, bus #7780 (hourly until 5.30pm; 20min) travels back to Bad Wildbad – or if you're doing the walk in reverse, you can take the funicular back into Bad Wildbad.

The Sommerbergbahn

Sommerbergbahn Uhlandplatz • Mon–Wed 8.45am–8.45pm, Thurs–Sun 8.45am–10.15pm • €3.50 one-way • ⓦ sommerbergbahn.de • **Mountain-bike routes** April–Oct Wed–Sun 10am–6pm • Day-pass €24 • ⓦ bikepark-bad-wildbad.de

Though the venerable old funicular **Sommerbergbahn** dates back to 1908, since 2011 flash new carriages have climbed the 300m up the **Sommerberg** on new tracks. The group of buildings at the summit includes a café, a bike shop and a ski shop, as well as signs to half a dozen marked **hiking routes** of varying lengths from and around the top (see box above).

The **downhill mountain-bike** routes are managed by Bikestation, the bike shop at the top of the funicular. In winter there are opportunities for downhill **skiing** both on the Sommerberg and in the more extensive Kaltenbronn, as well as access to a 45km-network of cross-country skiing tracks.

The baths

Palais Thermal Kernerstr. 1 • Mon–Fri noon–10pm, Sat & Sun 10am–10pm • 4hr €19 • ⓦ palais-thermal.de •
Vital Therme Bätznerstr. 85 • Mon, Wed, Sat & Sun 9am–7pm, Tues, Thurs & Fri 9am–9pm; saunas open 1pm on weekdays and are women-only on Wed • €10 • ⓦ vitaltherme-wildbad.de

One of Europe's oldest bathhouses, the **Palais Thermal** dates back to 1847 and comprises an original building full of elegant neo-Byzantine touches and tilework with a myriad of pools, a lovely atrium in which to lounge, a restaurant with inexpensive specials and a new section with several saunas, steam rooms and outdoor areas. Don't worry about signs to the men's and women's baths; bathing is, as usual, naked and mixed, though the showers are separate, and if you're shy you can don a bathrobe (available for rent) and find your own private pool among the many on hand. It's too quiet and adult to be much fun for kids, for whom a better option is the town's other spa, the **Vital Therme**, on the hill behind the Haus des Gastes, which also has a selection of saunas and pools – one of which is outdoors.

ARRIVAL AND INFORMATION   BAD WILDBAD

By train The station lies at the northern end of town, an easy walk from the centre.
Destinations Stuttgart (hourly; 1hr 10min).
Tourist office In the centre of town at König-Karl-Str. 5 (Mon–Fri 9am–6pm, Sat 10am–noon, Sun 11am–1pm; ☎07081 102 80, ⓦ badwildbad.de).

Bike rental Bikestation, Peter-Liebig-Weg 10 (Wed–Sun 10am–6pm; ☎07081 38 01 20, ⓦ bikepark-bad-wildbad.de), rent out heavyweight downhill bikes for €55 per day, and cross-country bikes for €15. They also offer body-armour rentals for €38 per day.

ACCOMMODATION AND EATING

If you're keen to visit the baths, look out for **package deals** on the tourist office website – prices start from €65 per person for 3-star accommodation and two day-tickets to the baths. A couple of the town's eating places offer basic **private rooms**.

Café Winkler König-Karl-Str. 11 ☎07081 25 82. Old-fashioned *Konditorei* with delicious cakes and handmade chocolates, plus fresh croissants, soups and quiches. Also

has simple private rooms with twin beds and en-suite facilities. Café Tues–Sat 9am–6pm, Sun 1–6pm. €44
Hotel Alte Linde Wilhelmstr. 74 ☎07081 92 62 00,

ⓦhotelaltelinde.de. Central, mid-range choice with bright and airy modern rooms, some with balconies. Big continental breakfast buffet included. With wi-fi, bike rental, parking garage and even a bowling alley. **€82**

Melange Kuranlagenallee 8 ☎07081 93 94 50. Modern German restaurant with views over the Kurgarten and pleasant outdoor seating. Mains average €13 and include tasty items such as the filling Swabian platter: a steak, a chop, *Maultaschen* and *Spätzle* – all home-made. Also a nice place for tapas and cocktails later on. Mon–Thurs 5pm–midnight, Fri 5pm–1am, Sat & Sun 11am–midnight.

Mokni's Palais Kurplatz 4–6 ☎07081 30 10, ⓦhotelbaeren-badwildbad.de. Bad Wildbad's poshest digs are this pair of hotels: the *Badhotel* is a gathering of dignified Neoclassical buildings surrounding an attractive central courtyard; the *Rossini* is where the eponymous Italian composer lodged and allegedly gained inspiration. Both are extremely elegant, share an excellent gourmet restaurant and include entrance to the Palais Thermal in their rates. **€150**

Wildbader Hof König-Karl-Str. 43 ☎07081 24 76, ⓦwildbaderhof.de. Friendly, rustic German place with large portions of Swabian specialities including a good pot roast (€15) and several dishes with local wild-mushroom sauces. Also has the interesting feature of herbs growing on its outdoor tables to allow for some last-minute seasoning. Extremely child-friendly, with crayons and toys available. Also offers basic rooms without en-suite facilities. Restaurant daily except Tues 10am–late. **€34**

The Badische Weinstrasse

The **Badische Weinstrasse** (Badische Wine Road), a 160km-long waymarked route that winds through the foothills of the Black Forest, cuts through vineyards and past ruined castles on its way from Baden-Baden to Freiburg. It's an attractive alternative to the motorway corridor along the Rhine Valley for north- or south-bound travellers with time on their hands, and particularly those with an interest in sampling and buying fine wines.

Durbach

The tiny town of **Durbach**, some 50km south of Baden-Baden, set amid rolling vineyards and overlooked by the impressive Schloss Staufenberg, is a perfect stop along the Badische Weinstrasse, and of particular interest to **wine** lovers for its excellent **Durbacher Winzergenossenschaft** (Wine Co-operative: Mon–Fri 9am–6pm, Sat 9am–1pm), a shop with a great selection of distinguished and well-priced local wines that's liberal with its samples. It's signposted and just off the main road at the centre of Durbach.

Schloss Staufenberg

April–Oct daily 11am–9pm; Nov–March Wed–Sun 11am–6pm • ⓦschloss-staufenberg.de

On the opposite side, **Schloss Staufenberg** looms over town from its perch on a vineyard-draped hill. Of eleventh-century origin, the castle's been in the wine trade since 1391, and though it's not open for tours, you can roam around its inner courtyard and sample wines in its earthy wine bar or on an outdoor terrace with stunning valley views. You can drive up here, but the hike is more rewarding and can form part of one of six waymarked routes that visit various attractive viewpoints and vineyards in the valley; pick up a map from the tourist office.

INFORMATION
DURBACH

Tourist office On the main road at Tal 36 (Mon–Fri 9am–noon & 2–5pm, Sat 10am–noon; ☎0781 421 53, ⓦdurbach-info.de). The office has details of a large and wide-ranging number of accommodation options, with private rooms starting at €40.

ACCOMMODATION AND EATING

Hotel Ritter Tal 1 ☎0781 932 30, ⓦritter-durbach.de. Family-run boutique hotel in central Durbach, with tasteful contemporary decor, great fitness and spa facilities and a Michelin-starred restaurant with regional *nouvelle cuisine* (four courses €98). The hotel also has a less formal wine cellar (mains average €18), with high-end versions of simple dishes, including *Flammkuchen*. Restaurant Tues–Sat 6pm–10pm; cellar until 11pm. **€160**

9

Europa-Park

Europa-Park-Str. 2, Rust • Daily: early April to early Nov 9am–6pm; late Nov to early Jan 11am–7pm • €41 • ⓦ europapark.de • Train to Ringsheim and then shuttle bus to park

Though not really famous beyond Germany's borders, the **Europa-Park** is one of Europe's premier theme-parks and a sure-fire kid-pleaser. Some fifty rides are dotted around an area the size of eighty football pitches and alongside a number of villages themed by European country. Located 35km north of Frieburg near the village of Rust, it's particularly handy for drivers heading between Strasbourg or Karlsruhe and the Swiss Alps.

The Schwarzwaldhochstrasse

There are various routes from Baden-Baden into the heart of the Black Forest, but the most attractive is probably the magnificent **Schwarzwaldhochstrasse** – the Black Forest Highway, or B500 – which climbs from Baden-Baden through an idyllic combination of pines and meadows, valleys and peaks to Freudenstadt. The route may only be 60km long but it's worth taking at least half a day over the drive, allowing for time to break the journey at the various car parks, viewpoints and belvederes which dot the route to take in fine views of the Upper Rhine Valley and France's Vosges. Allow time too for a couple of short worthwhile **hikes**, particularly the easy 1.5km loop around the touristy but pretty **Mummelsee**, and the twenty-minute walk to an attractive waterfall from the **Klosterruine Allerheiligen**, an impressive ruin of a Gothic Premonstratensian monastery; it's signposted off the B500 6km to the south of Mummelsee.

Freudenstadt and around

Freudenstadt is not a place to make for deliberately, but you're likely to end up there if you're driving the Schwarzwaldhochstrasse, or getting around by train, since it's a major rail intersection. Nevertheless, it's pleasant enough for an overnight stop. Built on a high plateau, this planned town was commissioned by Duke Friedrich I in 1599 and designed around the structure of a Roman camp, to make it fit to be the capital of Württemberg. The plans never bore fruit, but the town's giant **Marktplatz** – Germany's biggest – tells of the scale of the project. The palace intended to fill much of it was never built, and instead it's the town's major traffic intersection, although reasonably quiet for all that and fringed by Italianate arcades harbouring everyday shops.

Stadtkirche

Marktplatz 36 • Daily 10am–5pm • Free • ⓦ ev-kirche-fds.de

The Marktplatz's most imposing buildings are its Rathaus and the unusual **Stadtkirche**, diagonally opposite one another. The plain church was given its odd "L" shape in an attempt to segregate men and women and keep their minds on the sermon. Its centrepiece is a magnificent, early twelfth-century Romanesque baptismal font (c.1100), on which dragons breathe fire, deer run and horses canter. The painted wooded lectern behind is from the same era and designed to look as if it is being carried by the Four Evangelists.

The Barfusspark

Mühlweg, Dornstetten • Late April to mid-Oct daily 9am–6pm • Free; donation requested • ⓦ barfusspark.de

For all the hype of the local tourist office, there's not really much to do in Freudenstadt, so you might consider an excursion 9km east to the small neighbouring town of Dornstetten, for the oddity of exploring its **Barfusspark**, or Barefoot Park. Here shoes are exchanged for the therapy of feeling different surfaces on the soles of your feet. A 1km beginners' loop takes around thirty minutes, the 2km advanced route twice that.

| ARRIVAL AND INFORMATION | FREUDENSTADT AND AROUND |

By train Freudenstadt lies at a railway intersection, with frequent trains to cities in neighbouring Baden-Württemberg and locations along the Kinzig and Gutach valleys. Destinations Alpirsbach (hourly; 16min); Karlsruhe (hourly; 1hr 55min); Schiltach (hourly; 27min); Stuttgart (hourly; 1hr 23min).

Tourist office Marktplatz 64 (May–Sept Mon–Fri 9am–6pm, Sat & Sun 10am–3pm; Oct–April Mon–Fri 10am–5pm, Sat 10am–1pm, Sun 11am–1pm; ☏ 07441 86 40, ⓦ ferien-in-freudenstadt.de).

ACCOMMODATION AND EATING

Bären Lange Str. 33 ☏ 07441 27 29, ⓦ hotel-baeren-freudenstadt.de. Friendly 3-star place a block east of the Marktplatz where clean rooms, some with balcony, have a dated, vaguely 1950s feel. Internet available. The inn also serves solid traditional food. Restaurant daily 6–10pm. **€97**

★ **Traube Tonbach** Tonbachstr. 237 ☏ 07442 4920, ⓦ traube-tonbach.de. One of Germany's finest hotels, 12km north of Freudenstadt, with lovely Black Forest views and countless international awards to its name. Amenities include extensive spa facilities and three truly top-class restaurants that are always full of gourmet surprises (fixed-price menus €35–170). Restaurant Wed 7–9pm, Thurs–Sun noon–2pm & 7–9pm. **€285**

The Kinzig and Gutach valleys

The Kinzig and Gutach valleys are quintessential Black Forest landscapes; they're also the birthplace of many of its most eccentric folk costumes, and cuckoo clocks are sold here by the tonne. From Baden-Baden the region is most attractively accessed along the twisty and scenic Schwarzwaldhochstrasse (see opposite), which leads to the northeastern end of the steep-sided and densely forested **Kinzig Valley**, the horseshoe-shaped hub of the Black Forest's largest valley system, dotted with a series of picturesque small towns. Particularly appealing are the monastery and brewery town of **Alpirsbach**, and the quaint gathering of half-timbered houses at **Schiltach**. For generations this remote valley made its money logging and farming, and its modest and fairly sleepy communities celebrate this heritage with various evocative museums, including the open-air **Schwarzwälder Freilichtmuseum**, one of the region's premier sights, just up the feeder valley of the River Gutach.

This small stream is responsible for the broad 25km-long **Gutach Valley**, famous for its *Bollenhut*, a black hat with red pompoms worn as a traditional folk costume by women and reproduced in tourist literature throughout the region. Close to the head of the valley lies **Triberg**, the Black Forest's most touristy town, packed with cuckoo-clock shops and coach parties and probably worth avoiding unless you're after a chirping time-piece – in which case you'll certainly want to visit the excellent nearby clock museum, the **Deutsches Uhrenmuseum**, too.

| GETTING AROUND | THE KINZIG AND GUTACH VALLEYS |

By train and bus Train lines run along much of the Kinzig and Gutach valleys, and are supplemented by a bus network, making getting around the valleys easy; expect hourly connections. From Freudenstadt bus SEV travels to Shiltach (hourly; 39min) and Hausach (hourly; 1hr 10min), where you can change onto a train to Triberg (hourly; 20min). From Freiburg, bus #1066 travels (Mon–Fri 1 daily; 2hr 15min) to Haslach and Schiltach.

By bike Following the 91.5km Kinzigtalradweg – a marked cycle route from Offenburg to Lossburg – is one-way to absorb some of this region at the pace it deserves.

Alpirsbach

Kloster Alpirsbach Mid-March to Oct Mon–Sat 10am–5.30pm, Sun 11am–5.30pm; Nov to mid-March Thurs, Sat & Sun 1–3pm • €4 • **Dormitory** 1hr tours (in German): mid-March to Oct Mon–Sat 11am, noon, 1.30pm, 2.30pm & 3.30pm, Sun hourly 12.30–3.30pm; Nov to mid-March Thurs, Sat & Sun 1.30pm • €9 • ⓦ kloster-alpirsbach.de • **Brewery museum** Tours (in German) daily 2.30pm • €7 • ⓦ alpirsbacher.de

Strung out along a road in a tight valley, the small town of **ALPIRSBACH**, some 69km south of Baden-Baden, lacks any real heart, but is an attractive enough place

9

thanks to a medieval golden age which left it with the Romanesque Benedictine monastery, **Kloster Alpirsbach**. The hulking Klosterkirche, built of regional red sandstone in the eleventh century, has an empty interior, but is worth a look for its nave capitals, a tribute to the early Christian fixation with good and evil. Its museum includes various items from the sixteenth century, including the clothes of former pupils, who studied here once the monastery had been dissolved. The monks' chilly Dormitorium and a Calefectorium can be visited on tours in German, as can the brewery museum of the adjacent **Alpirsbacher Klosterbräu**, in which a variety of local beer is introduced.

INFORMATION	ALPIRSBACH
Tourist office Krähenbadstr. 2 (Mon 9am–noon & 2–6pm, Tues & Thurs 9am–noon & 2–5pm, Wed 9am–noon, Fri 9am–1pm & 2–5pm, Sat 10am–noon; Sept–May closed Sat; ☎ 07444 951 62 81, ⊛ stadt-alpirsbach.de).	Located opposite the brewery museum in the centre of town. The office has plenty of hiking and cycling information, plus accommodation listings.

ACCOMMODATION AND EATING

Zur Löwen-Post Marktplatz 12 ☎ 07444 955 95, ⊛ loewen-post.de. Hearty traditional place that loves to cook with beer, using roasted brewers malt to garnish salads, and local beers to batter pork chops (most mains around €10). A full selection of local beers is available, with six offered as a beer taster. It also has sleek guestrooms with polished wooden floors and smart modern bathrooms. Restaurant Tues 11.30am–2pm, Mon & Wed–Sun 11.30am–2pm & 5.30–11.30pm; kitchen closes 9pm, 8pm on Sun. **€76**

Schiltach

From Alpirsbach, the River Kinzig flows 9km southwest to the tiny, postcard-perfect town of **SCHILTACH**. It's a quiet place, gathered around the gurgling river where an old lumber mill has been reconstructed for the **Schüttesägemuseum** (Sawmill Museum; late March to Oct daily 11am–5pm; Nov & Dec Sat & Sun 11am–5pm; free) in the centre of town, where black-and-white photos of loggers illustrate the region's history. The town's focus, the steeply sloping **Marktplatz** a couple of minutes' walk upstream, is encircled by half-timbered buildings dating no earlier than the mid-sixteenth century. Murals on its Rathaus explain why: look out for the witch who was allegedly responsible for a conflagration which reduced the town to ashes in 1533.

INFORMATION	SCHILTACH
Tourist office Marktplatz 6 (May–Sept Mon–Fri 9am–noon & 2–5pm, Sat 10am–2pm; ☎ 07836 58 50, ⊛ schiltach.de).	They have the usual accommodation listings and can point you in the direction of a couple of good local walks.

ACCOMMODATION AND EATING

Zum Weyssen Rössle Schenkenzeller Str. 42 ☎ 07836 387, ⊛ weysses-roessle.de. Good old-fashioned hotel a couple of minutes' walk east of the Marktplatz, with country-style rooms with floral decor, wi-fi and a good continental breakfast buffet included in the rates. Its restaurant (mains €10–21) features German cooking that's far more adventurous than the rustic decor would suggest. Restaurant Tues–Sun 6–10pm. **€76**

Haslach

The Kinzig Valley starts to widen 21km downstream of Schiltach around the idyllic little Black Forest town of **HASLACH**. The dense cluster of half-timbered houses in its small pedestrianized Altstadt were funded by a medieval silver-mining boom and are worth a wander, but the main sight is the **Schwarzwälder Trachtenmuseum**, Museum Klosterstr. 1 (Museum of Black Forest Costumes: April to mid-Oct Tues–Sat 10am–12.30pm & 1.30–5pm; mid-Oct to end Dec, plus Feb & March Tues–Sat

10am–12.30pm & 1.30–6pm; €2; ⓦtrachtenmuseum-haslach.de.vu). Its comprehensive collection of local costumes showcases some of the more outlandish Black Forest folk garbs, among them the famous *Bollenhut* – a bonnet clustered with pompoms and worn by the women of the Gutach Valley. The eye-catching red pompoms are reserved for the unmarried; wives have to make do with black. Look out too for some of the wild and disturbing carnival costumes.

ACCOMMODATION AND EATING
HASLACH

★**Hotel Storchen** Hauptstr. 35 ☎07832 97 97 97, ⓦhotel-storchen.de. Half-timbered, traditional guesthouse in the pedestrian centre of Haslach, whose exterior suggests nothing of the madness within: rooms are all themed, with concepts including oriental, aquatic, barn, desert island and even hot-air balloon. The inn's satisfying food is much more conventional; the menu spans from pizza and pasta to venison goulash (most mains €7–9) with home-made *Spätzle*. Restaurant daily 5–11pm. **€98**

The Schwarzwälder Freilichtmuseum

Vogtsbauernhof 1, Gutach • Late March to early Nov daily 9am–6pm; closes 7pm in Aug • €8 • ⓦ vogtsbauernhof.org

Just over 1km south of the River Gutach's confluence with the River Kinzig lies the **Schwarzwälder Freilichtmuseum**, an open-air museum focused on an old farm – the Vogtsbauernhof – that's been here since 1570. Its huge roof is typical of the local traditional building style and the sort of place that caused Jerome K. Jerome to comment: "The great charm about a Black Forest house is its sociability: the cows are in the next room, the horses are upstairs, the geese and ducks in the kitchen, while the pigs, children and chickens live all over the place."

The 26 other buildings in the complex – which include a sawmill, granary, bakery, distillery, smithy and chapel – have been moved here from elsewhere to create a rather phoney little village. But great effort has gone into authentically furnishing them all and costumed guides doing craft demonstrations help bring the place alive and broaden the appeal.

Triberg and around

From where it meets the Kinzig Valley, the Gutach Valley progressively narrows then climbs to a point some 1000m above sea level after 20km, where the air is so pure it once made the town of **TRIBERG** a health resort. But this was long ago, and today the town is obsessed with only one thing: the **cuckoo clock** (see box, p.500). Thousands are on sale here, and the tourist traffic the industry spawns can be nightmarish, but if you embrace the kitsch and are in the market for a clock, it can be fun.

The long, thin **Marktplatz** that follows the main road through town is Triberg's natural focus, with a large pilgrimage church, or Wallfahrtskirche, looming over it decked out in florid Baroque. The busiest end of town is uphill from here at a bend in the main road, where **clock shops** are squeezed together. They're an attraction in themselves, and certainly as well visited as the town's two other main attractions – the Schwarzwaldmuseum and the waterfall – nearby. For a less commercial look at clocks travel to the Deutsches Uhrenmuseum, 16km to the south in Furtwangen.

Schwarzwaldmuseum

Wallfahrtstr. 4 • April–Sept daily 10am–6pm; Oct–March Tues–Sun 10am–5pm • €5 • ⓦ schwarzwaldmuseum.de

The better of the town's two attractions is the **Schwarzwaldmuseum**, a cache of local curios. Of course clock-making apparatus is here in force, but so too are various other mechanical instruments including what claims to be Europe's largest barrel-organ collection and a model Schwarzwaldbahn. As interesting is the collection of local folk costumes (including, of course, the *Bollenhut*), and there are sections on mining and winter sports, both traditionally a major part of life hereabouts.

9

THE CUCKOO CLOCK

The origins of the **cuckoo clock** are uncertain. Though the first known description comes from Saxony in the mid-sixteenth century, it's thought they were probably first made in Bohemia. Certainly it was only about a hundred years later – in the 1730s – that cuckoo clocks began to be made in the Black Forest, with Schönwald near Triberg being the site of the earliest workshops. The quality of the craftsmanship and engineering quickly captured the imagination and the European market, and the cuckoo clock has roosted here ever since.

Local shops sell a bewildering array, but as the over-eager shop assistants will inform you, it all boils down to three designs: the **chalet**, the **hunting theme** and the simple **carved cuckoo**. The technology in each clock is much the same: clocks with small pine cones dangling below them require daily winding, while those with larger cones need only weekly attention. There's more labour-saving on hand, thanks to the digital revolution which hasn't been allowed to bypass this traditional craft: some models are battery- and quartz-driven, and play recordings of an actual cuckoo on the hour; others are even light sensitive so both you and the bird can get some sleep. **Prices** vary according to the size of the clock: good-sized clocks can be bought for under €100, but for a real talking-piece you'll need to pay almost twice that – and some creations fetch thousands. The choice is overwhelming, competition keen and almost all shops offer shipping services.

SHOPS

Uhren-Park Schonachbach 27 ⓦuhren-park.de. One shop you might want to visit is this place on the main road 2.7km south of Triberg, which charges a €2 fee to see what it claims is the largest cuckoo clock in the world – though there's a rival claimant on the other side of town. Easter to Oct Mon–Sat 9am–6pm, Sun 10am–6pm; Nov to Easter Mon–Sat 9am–5.30pm, Sun 11am–5pm.

The Triberger Wasserfälle

March to early Nov (closed in winter except between Christmas and New Year) • €3.50

Accessed from a trailhead at the bend in the main road above the Marktplatz, Triberg's **waterfall** is a bit of a disappointment, even though it calls itself Germany's longest waterfall. In reality it is a series of seven smaller falls over a distance of 163m, and its natural beauty is completely compromised by the presence of strolling masses on the wide pavements alongside.

Deutsches Uhrenmuseum

Robert-Gerwig-Platz 1, Furtwangen, 16km south of Triberg • Daily: April–Oct 9am–6pm; Nov–March 10am–5pm • €5 • ⓦdeutsches-uhrenmuseum.de

For a non-commercialized insight into the world of clocks head 16km south of Triberg to the town of **Furtwangen**, where the excellent **Deutsches Uhrenmuseum** has an inspiring glut of timepieces in a myriad of styles from just about every era, from sun dials through early mechanical timepieces to the mass-produced items of an industry that aimed to put a clock in every room and a watch on every wrist. Naturally though, the museum highlight is the section on cuckoo clocks, and its collection includes many elaborate and aged examples with painted faces, elaborate carvings and swaying pendulums.

ARRIVAL AND INFORMATION

TRIBERG

By train Despite being remote, Triberg is well integrated into the rail system and is on the Schwarzwaldbahn rail line between Offenburg and Konstanz. The station lies a 15min walk downhill from its centre, but is connected by local buses stopping at the Marktplatz.

Destinations Konstanz (hourly; 1hr 30min); Offenburg (hourly; 40min).

By bus The bus station is located next to the train station.

Tourist office Wahlfahrtstr. 4 (daily 9am–5pm; ☎07722 86 64 90, ⓦtriberg.de). The helpful tourist office has English-language information on the area and accommodation listings which include a good number of traditional farmhouse bed-and-breakfasts (from €40), much the best local option if you have your own transport; they announce themselves with "*Zimmer frei*" signs along country roads.

ACCOMMODATION AND EATING

★**Adler** Hauptstr. 52 ☎07722 45 74, ⓦhotel-cafe-adler.de. Hotel and café with easily some of the best cakes in the region, which can be enjoyed in a little courtyard away from the main road. The rooms are spacious and well turned out, and the breakfast buffet tremendous. Restaurant daily except Tues 10am–5.30pm. **€74**

DJH Triberg Rohrbacher Str. 35 ☎07722 41 10, ⓦjugendherberge-triberg.de. Somewhat institutional but comfortable hostel on a ridge at the southeastern edge of town, a 3km walk from the Bahnhof. Dorms **€21.20**

Gästehaus Maria Spitz Weihermatte 5, Schonach ☎07722 54 34. Hillside farmhouse 3.7km west of Triberg where cattle graze beneath your bedroom window and you

can enjoy freshly baked bread for breakfast, and milk and eggs direct from the barn. **€36**

Parkhotel Wehrle Gartenstr. 24 ☎07222 860 20, ⓦparkhotel-wehrle.de. Triberg's most prestigious lodging, where Hemingway once stayed on a fishing trip. As well as the old-fashioned charm of a house built in the 1600s and individually decorated rooms with rustic frills, there's a health centre with a pool and a garden. The restaurant's one of the best in the area, with its local fish and game dishes (mains around €21) and good regional food, which includes *Schwarzwälder Schäfele*, a shoulder of smoked pork, traditionally reserved for special occasions. Restaurant daily noon–2pm & 7–10pm. **€159**

Freiburg

Blessed with one of Germany's warmest and sunniest climates and wooded hills that virtually rise out of a picture-postcard Altstadt, **FREIBURG** – officially Freiburg im Breisgau – is immediately likeable. Its accessible size makes it easy to explore and the sizeable university helps make it an upbeat, lively place. Though the town centre is quickly covered, the city's role as a regional transport hub makes Freiburg a good base for a few days' exploration of the hills around the town and the Southern Black Forest, putting the town's good cafés, restaurants and nightlife at your disposal after a day in the mountains.

Freiburg's **Altstadt** was founded in 1091 and – despite suffering twenty minutes of bombardment in the war in which over eighty percent of the town was levelled – still preserves a quaint and historic feel. The Altstadt fans out around a magnificent **Münster** and focuses on a series of squares, which don't take much more than a morning to explore. This allows plenty of time for relaxing in Freiburg's cafés or exploring the great outdoors on its doorstep – at the very least try to take a trip up to the **Schlossberg** or **Rosskopf** via the funicular railway, or better still, take the cable car up **Schauinsland** peak and walk or bike back to town.

The Münster

Münsterplatz • Church Mon–Sat 10am–5pm, Sun 1–7.30pm; Tower Mon–Sat 10am–16.45pm, Sun 1–5pm • €2

Built from the region's signature dark-red sandstone, Freiburg's magnificent Gothic **Münster** was lucky to come out of the war almost unscathed. Work on the church began in around 1200 when Freiburg's population was around four thousand, its giant dimensions saying a lot about local civic ambitions of the time, particularly since it wasn't a bishopric so all funding had to come from local coffers. One of the first parts of the church to be built was the **west porch**, now the most magnificent entrance, with impressive rows of carvings that produce something of a poor-man's Bible, but include no less than 125 images of Maria, to whom the church is devoted.

FREIBURG'S BÄCHLE

One curious feature of Freiburg is its *Bächle*: little streams sunken into the pavement which originally provided water for animals and firemen. Today they're largely decorative, though plenty of people use them to cool their heels on a summer's day. Fall into one and, according to local wisdom, you'll marry a Freiburger.

9

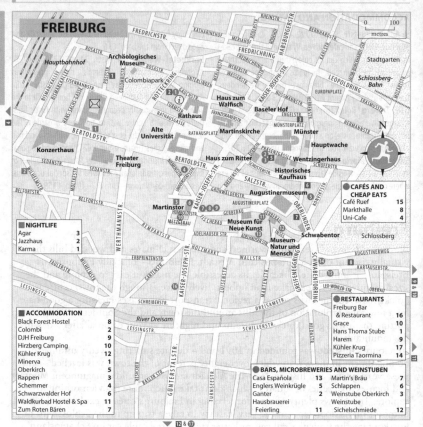

FREIBURG

The interior

Within, the gloominess of the church interior serves to enhance the dazzling effect of the incredible **stained glass**: note the forerunner of today's banner advertising in the panes at the base of the windows – the boots of the cobblers' guild and the pretzels of the bakers show exactly who sponsored the church. This reliance on local funding was one reason why the Münster took four hundred years to build, which resulted in a medley of styles. The earliest sections – easily identifiable by small windows and thick walls – are Romanesque and copy elements of Basel's Münster, while later Gothic sections belong to a period when local architects looked to copy Strasbourg for inspiration and built with huge arches and giant windows.

Of the many pieces of ecclesiastical art dotting the church, those in the **ambulatory** are particularly noteworthy. Recesses here are lined with the altarpieces of rich church patrons – look out for one by Hans Holbein the Younger – while at their centre is the exquisite **high altar** painted between 1512 and 1516 by Hans Baldung Grien, a pupil of Albrecht Dürer.

The tower

Rising high above all this is the Münster's 116m-high **tower**, with an octagonal summit. At this height it was seen to metaphorically reach out to God, while its filigree stonework, completed in 1330, makes it Germany's first openwork spire, its carvings inspired by mysticism. The workmanship can be admired while climbing it en route to views over town, the surrounding hills and all the way to France.

Münsterplatz

Surrounding Freiburg's chief church, the **Münsterplatz** is home to a bustling daily market but is largely the work of modern builders, since much was levelled during World War II and not rebuilt in the original style. One notable exception is the blood-red **Historisches Kaufhaus** on the southern side, a 1530 trading hall. Three of the four Habsburg emperors decorating the facade visited Freiburg, back in the days when the town gave itself to them for protection, making it a part of the Austrian empire.

Wentzingerhaus: the Museum für Stadtgeschichte

Münsterplatz • Tues–Sun 10am–5pm • €3, combined ticket with all municipal museums €6 • ⓦ museen.freiburg.de

Of the two Baroque palaces either side of the Kaufhaus the **Wentzingerhaus** (1761) to the east is the more remarkable. Once the townhouse of sculptor Christian Wentzinger, it now houses the **Museum für Stadtgeschichte**, which offers a few interesting insights into Freiburg's history. As impressive are the mansion's elaborate frescoes and fine Rococo staircase railings; Wentzinger also left lovingly crafted allegorical statues of the Four Seasons in the back garden.

Augustinerplatz and around

Alleys between buildings on the southern side of Münsterplatz lead through to **Schusterstrasse**, one of Freiburg's best-preserved – or rather reconstructed – medieval streets, where pavement mosaics announce tradesmen and shops. The next street south, Salzstrasse, is a broader thoroughfare and flanked by **Augustinerplatz**, a relaxed square around which lie three reasonable museums.

The Augustinermuseum

Augustinerplatz • Tues–Sun 10am–5pm • €6, includes entry to all municipal museums (see box below) • ⓦ museen.freiburg.de

The **Augustinermuseum** shows off the extensive medieval art collection of a former monastery and has in its ecclesiastical art collection several old masters, including paintings by Cranach the Elder and Hans Baldung Grien. Also worth a look is the exceptional stained-glass collection, which includes some of the earliest of the Münster windows, placed here for preservation while copies are in situ. A section on folklore is also of interest if you are about to explore the Black Forest.

Museum für Neue Kunst

Marienstr. 10 • Tues–Sun 10am–5pm • €3, combined ticket with all municipal museums €6 • ⓦ museen.freiburg.de

Regional culture influences the Expressionist and Abstract art of the **Museum für Neue Kunst**, just southeast of Augustinerplatz. The museum is particularly strong on German Expressionism and its counterpoint the New Objectivity. Some 200m east of the museum the thirteenth-century **Schwabentor**, one of Freiburg's main town gates, is worth a look.

FREIBURG'S MUSEUM TICKET

Freiburg has five municipal museums (ⓦ museen.freiburg.de): the Museum für Stadtgeschichte, the Augustinermuseum, Museum für Neue Kunst, Museum Natur und Mensch and the Archäologisches Museum Colombischlössle. The **Tageskarte**, a day-pass to all of them, costs just €6 and is available to buy at any of them; at the Augustinermuseum this is the only ticket option.

9

Museum Natur und Mensch

Gerberau 32 • Tues–Sun 10am–5pm • €3 • ⓦ museen.freiburg.de

The natural history collection of the **Naturmuseum** explores the Earth's geological history and its various habitats, but the museum is most fascinating for its truly global ethnographic collection, which is showcased in oft-changing temporary exhibitions.

The university district

From Augustinerplatz, the old tannery street Gerberau leads west to one of the town's surviving main gates, the **Martinstor**, which marks the beginning of a network of streets that spreads west into a **university district**. The arterial Kaiser-Joseph-Strasse, which passes through the gate and runs north through town, is little more than a strip of chain and department stores, and better passed over in favour of walking the parallel Universitätstrasse to the west. There are no real set-piece sights here, but the bustling atmosphere and pavement cafés make it a pleasant place to linger.

Rathausplatz and around

At its northern end Universitätstrasse empties into Rathausplatz, where the Renaissance **Neues Rathaus** – whose carillon plays daily at noon – is linked to the 1559 Altes Rathaus. Looming over both is the **Martinskirche**, a former Franciscan monastery church that was badly battered in World War II, but meticulously rebuilt.

West of the Rathausplatz, lively, narrow Rathaussgasse leads to the edge of the Altstadt, where things quickly open up around the **Columbiapark**, Freiburg's most central park. Here the Colombischlössle villa houses the **Archäologisches Museum**, Rotteckring 5 (Tues–Sun 10am–5pm; €4, combined ticket with all municipal museums €6; ⓦ museen.freiburg.de), which has a collection of Stone Age, Celtic and Roman remains, and is hardly unmissable, but deserving of a quick look.

The Schlossberg-Bahn and Rosskopf

Stadtgarten • Mon & Wed–Sun 9am–10pm, Tues 9am–6pm • €3 one-way • ⓦ schlossberg-bahn.de

The **Schlossberg-Bahn**, a funicular that leaves from the Stadtgarten just northwest of the Altstadt, advertises that you'll be in the Black Forest in three minutes. That's not far from the truth, as the Schlossberg and the adjoining Rosskopf peak form a microcosm of the region. A network of signposted **trails** crisscrosses the entire ridge, travelling from the gourmet restaurant *Dattler* (daily except Tues 9am–late; mains around €20) at the railway's end, through dense woodland past twelfth-century castle ruins and even vineyards, to a lookout tower at the top of the **Rosskopf**, where fantastic views of the entire region await; allow around three hours for the walk to the summit and back to Freiburg. If you're on a bike, it's best to ride out to the *DJH Hostel* (see p.506) and start the climb from there, leaving you a lovely long descent back into the city.

The Schauinslandbahn

Im Bohrer 63, Horben • Daily: Jan–June 9am–5pm; July–Sept 9am–6pm; Oct–Dec 9am–5pm • €12 return, €8.50 one-way • ⓦ bergwelt-schauinsland.de • Tram #2 to its Günterstal terminus, then bus #21

Translating as "look at the land", the 1286m mountain of **Schauinsland**, 7km south of Freiburg's Altstadt, is true to its name, lying as it does on the edge of the Black Forest range. The stellar views are also easily reached, thanks to the **Schauinslandbahn**, a cable car that makes the lengthy journey up there quick and easy. From its terminus a five-minute walk down a trail brings you to the lookout tower and the start of several well-marked trails. These offer first-class **hiking** and **mountain biking** – partly because almost the entire 14km journey back to Freiburg is downhill – with great views along the way. Despite good signposting a map is useful, since many trails crisscross the mountain; pick this up at the tourist office or a bookshop before you strike out. Alternatively, you can rent an off-road **scooter** from the top cable-car station and rattle down dirt-roads back to the base (€22 per run; ⓦ rollerstrecke.de).

Steinwasen Park

Steinwasen 1, Oberried • Daily: April–June & mid-Sept to Oct 10am–4.45pm; July to mid-Sept 9am–5.45pm • €23 • ⓦ steinwasen-park .de • Train to Kirchzarten (hourly; 13min) then connecting bus #7215 (hourly; 15min)

An essential stop for those with kids in tow, **Steinwasen Park**, 25km southeast of Freiburg, successfully mixes a sense of nature with a sense of fun. Attractions include a spectacular 218m-long hanging bridge and four rides, including a water ride and a summer luge. Meanwhile woodland trails connect spacious animal enclosures with some thirty species of local and Alpine animals, such as marmot, deer and lynx.

ARRIVAL AND DEPARTURE   FREIBURG

By plane Basel's EuroAirport (ⓦ euroairport.com), 74km to the south, is connected to Freiburg by the hourly Freiburger Airportbus (55min; €20; ☎ 0761 50 05 00, ⓦ freiburger-reisedienst.de), from the bus station.

By train The Hauptbahnhof is on the Altstadt's western edge.

Destinations Feldberg-Bärental (hourly; 45min);

Freudenstadt (hourly; 2hr 15min); Karlsruhe (frequent; 1hr); Konstanz (frequent; 2hr 30min); Schluchsee (hourly; 1hr); Stuttgart (hourly; 2hr); Titisee (frequent; 40min); Triberg (hourly; 1hr 30min).

By bus The bus station is on the southern side of the train station.

Destinations Todtnau (frequent; 1hr 15min).

GETTING AROUND

By bus and tram Though walking is the best way to explore, Freiburg's bus and tram service run by VAG (ⓦ vag-freiburg.de) is excellent.

By bike Freiburg Bikes, at the Hauptbahnhof (☎ 0761 202 34 26, ⓦ freiburgbikes.de), have bikes from €13 per day.

INFORMATION AND TOURS

Tourist office Rathausplatz 2–4 (June–Sept Mon–Fri 8am–8pm, Sat 9.30am–5pm, Sun 10am–3.30pm; Oct– May Mon–Fri 8am–6pm, Sat 9.30am–2.30pm, Sun 10am–noon; ☎ 0761 388 18 80, ⓦ freiburg.de). Located an easy 5min walk west of the Münster.

Walking tours Kultour run informative English-language walking tours of Freiburg (Sat 11.30am; 90min; €9; ☎ 0761 290 74 47, ⓦ freiburg-kultour.com), departing from the tourist office. The same outfit offer many more tours in German.

ACCOMMODATION

Freiburg has the full range of **accommodation** choices, from a pleasant campground and hostels on the edge of town to luxurious central options. However, competition for beds can be keen, so if you're having trouble head straight for the tourist office and get them to do the legwork for a €3 fee.

HOTELS AND INNS

Colombi Am Colombi Park ☎ 0761 210 60, ⓦ colombi .de. Tradition, taste and luxury combine in this *grande dame* of Freiburg hotels, with its central yet quiet park-side location. Amenities include a pool, steam baths, sauna and free wi-fi. Its *Hans Thoma Stube* is one of Freiburg's premier gourmet restaurants (see p.506). Daily noon–3pm and 7–11pm. **€268**

Kühler Krug Torplatz 1, Freiburg-Günterstal ☎ 0761 291 03, ⓦ kuehlerkrug.de; tram #2 to Günterstal terminus. Old-fashioned family-run inn, 2km from the centre of Freiburg, with cosy antique-laden rooms and a superb restaurant (see p.507); if staying, you can book a

three-course dinner for just €18. **€98**

Minerva Poststr. 8 ☎ 0761 38 64 90, ⓦ minerva-freiburg.de. Hotel in an elegant Art Nouveau building a 5min walk from the Altstadt. Rooms are spotless and modern, and there's a sauna, free wi-fi and an extensive breakfast buffet. The rooms facing away from the main road are the better bet for a quiet night's sleep. **€130**

Oberkirch Münsterplatz 22 ☎ 0761 202 68 68, ⓦ hotel-oberkirch.de. Open the curtains to Münster views in this traditional family-run place. Its rooms – including some well-priced singles – have a rustic feel, and the German restaurant (see p.507) is classy. **€175**

9

Rappen Münsterplatz 13 ☎0761 313 53, ⌨hotelrappen.de. Old-fashioned place in the thick of things with its own *Weinstube* and café on Münsterplatz and with a dash of Black Forest cosiness inside. Rooms are straightforward but some have fine Münster views. Free wi-fi. €85

Schemmer Eschholzstr. 63 ☎0761 20 74 90, ⌨hotel-schemmer.de. Tidy little hotel in a townhouse a short walk from the Hauptbahnhof. It's the cheapest central deal, though not all the modest rooms have their own bathroom. Wi-fi & breakfast included. €65

Schwarzwalder Hof Herrenstr. 43 ☎0761 380 30, ⌨shof.de. Small and smart hotel a stone's throw from Münsterplatz. Rooms all have solid wood flooring, minimalist elegance and free internet connections. €99

★**Zum Roten Bären** Oberlinden 12 ☎0761 878 70, ⌨roter-baeren.de. Germany's oldest hotel, inside the 1250 Schwabentor (one of Freiburg's two preserved medieval city gates – the other is the Martinstor), welcomed its first guests in 1120, 200 years before the Münster's spire was sketched on to parchment. Scattered antiques continue to give it a venerable feel, while all facilities have been brought up to date. €178

HOSTELS AND CAMPSITES

★**Black Forest Hostel** Kartäuserstr. 33 ☎0761 881 78 70, ⌨blackforest-hostel.de. Laidback bohemian place with a sociable vibe and large communal areas – which include a guest kitchen and dining area and lounge with ping-pong – as well as internet and bike rental. Dorms €17, doubles €58

DJH Freiburg Kartäuserstr. 151 ☎0761 676 56, ⌨jugendherberge-freiburg.de; tram #1 to "Römerhof". Massive and hugely popular hostel that's often packed with school groups despite a rather inconvenient location beyond the eastern fringes of town, 3km from the Altstadt. Follow signs from Römerhof station for the 10min walk to the hostel. Dorms €27, doubles €65

Hirzberg Camping Kartäuserstr. 99 ☎0761 350 54, ⌨freiburg-camping.de; tram #1 to "Stadthalle". Well-organized and leafy – if tightly packed – campground where you can also rent tents. It's located 1.5km east of the Altstadt. Tent rental €12; pitch €4, plus €7.50 per person

Waldkurbad Hostel & Spa Waldseestr. 77 ☎0761 775 70, ⌨waldkurbad.de. Relaxing hostel set beside quiet woods at the edge of town, that's superb and unusual for having its own spa: included in the rates are three saunas, a pool, a relaxation yurt and women-only area (the whole spa is nude-only). Wi-fi and parking also included. Breakfast (poor) costs €5.50, but there's a traditional German restaurant close by for other meals; other eating options and a shopping mall are a 15min walk away along Möslestrasse and Waldseestrasse by the "Musikhochschule" stop of tram #1. Bike hire available. Dorms €26, doubles €66

EATING AND DRINKING

As befits a place with students and fine weather, there are lots of relaxed **cafés** with pavement seating for lazing around in and cheerful bars with beer gardens in which to unwind. The **restaurant** scene is a shade less vibrant. Some of the best high-end options are outside the Altstadt.

CAFÉS AND CHEAP EATS

★**Café Ruef** Kartäuserstr. 2 ☎0761 336 63, ⌨ruef.de. A second living-room for many local students who chill out in the well-worn armchairs, eat cheap, delicious pies and cakes and sometimes enjoy live music. Popular place to hit for a fresh, warm croissant after clubbing. Daily 6am–late.

★**Markthalle** Martinsgässle 235 & Grünewalderstr. 4 ⌨markthalle-freiburg.de. Bustling food court with quality regional Swabian, Mexican, Indian, Asian, French and Italian dishes. It's standing only, so hardly a place for a relaxed bite, but the food is good-value and service quick. The entrance can be tricky to find: the side entrance lies at the end of an alley just east of the Martinstor, the main entrance is barely more obvious and off Grünewalderstrasse. Mon–Thurs 8am–8pm, Fri & Sat 8am–midnight.

Uni-Cafe Niemensstr. 7 ☎0761 38 33 55. Cult see-and-be-seen place, one of a cluster of cafés on this pedestrianized corner of the university district, with some very good *Flammkuchen*. Daily 10am–2am.

RESTAURANTS

★**Freiburg Bar & Restaurant** Kaiser-Joseph-Str. 278 ☎0761 704 86 18, ⌨freiburg-bar.net. Universally popular restaurant and bar that attracts all ages and walks of life. Its salad, pasta, steak and Thai stir-fry menu (mains average €10) is hardly adventurous, but the food is excellent and daily specials are always worth a try. Transforms into a popular bar after 10pm, with smoking lounge and DJs; always a good vibe. Daily 6pm–late; meals until 10pm, tapas always available

Grace Humboldtstr. 2 ☎0761 20 88 99 30, ⌨grace-freiburg.de. Smart resto-bar serving attractively presented dishes from an eclectic and inventive changing menu that can include pretty much anything from *Schnitzels* to tapas to curries. Daily lunch specials are good value at €9; dinner mains cost not much more. Also good for breakfast at weekends. Mon–Thurs noon–midnight, Fri & Sat 10am–1am.

Hans Thoma Stube Am Colombi Park ☎0761 210 60, ⌨colombi.de. One of Freiburg's premier gourmet restaurants, in the venerable *Columbi Hotel* (see p.505) – a place of tiled stoves, antique wood panelling and regional delicacies, with mains in the €35–45 range. Daily noon–3pm and 7–11pm.

Harem Gerberau 7 ☎ 0761 225 33, ⓦ harem-restaurant .de. Great little Turkish place with well-priced (€6–9) versions of the usual suspects: *börek, pide, döner,* lamb kebabs and *baklava* sweets. Be sure to try the superb *saç,* a Turkish stir-fry, named after the pan it's made on – several versions are vegetarian. Daily 11.30am–midnight.

Kühler Krug Torplatz 1, Freiburg-Günterstal ☎ 0761 291 03, ⓦ kuehlerkrug.de; tram #2 to Günterstal terminus. Classic regional dishes get modern twists at this traditional inn, 2km from the centre. Fish is served with creative sauces such as saffron on salmon; game dishes, like wild rabbit, in a hazelnut sauce (mains around €13). Daily except Wed 11am–midnight.

★ **Pizzeria Taormina** Schwabentorring 4 ☎ 0761 341 60, ⓦ pizzeriataorminafreiburg.de. Modest pizzeria serving the best pizzas in Freiburg and at very reasonable prices – most dishes around €7. Daily 11.30am–2.30pm & 5.30pm–midnight.

BARS, MICROBREWERIES AND WEINSTUBEN

Casa Española Adelhauser Str. 9 ☎ 0761 202 30 40, ⓦ casaespanola.de. Fairly basic tapas bar of the sort found everywhere in Spain but rarely abroad. The tapas are top-notch – the clay dishes of fat prawns in sizzling garlic oil are a particular treat – and there's an extensive Iberian wine selection. Mon–Sat 11am–1am.

Englers Weinkrügle Konvikstr. 12 ☎ 0761 38 31 15. Cosy wood-panelled *Weinstube* with very good and reasonably priced regional food (mains average €11). Look out for the Black Forest dessert: cherries in hot liqueur, served with vanilla ice cream. Tues–Sun 11am–2pm & 5.30pm–midnight.

Ganter Münsterplatz 18 ☎ 0761 343 67, ⓦ ganter-brauereiausschank.de. Belonging to the town's largest brewery with a commanding location on the Münsterplatz. There's a good range of beers, including an unfiltered *Urtrunk,* and also hearty meals, though they're nothing special. Daily 10am–midnight.

Hausbrauerei Feierling Gerberau 46 ☎ 0761 24 34 80, ⓦ feierling.de. Cheerful microbrewery with a wood-and-copper interior and Freiburg's best beer garden. Serves a good range of pub food – mains average €10 and include giant *Schnitzels* as well as a handful of veggie options. Its sour *Patrizier-Bräu* beer has a bit of a cult following, but is an acquired taste. Mon–Thurs & Sun 11am–midnight, Fri & Sat 11am–1am.

Martin's Bräu Kaiser-Joseph-Str. 237 ☎ 0761 387 00 18, ⓦ mbfr.de. Cosy cellar microbrewery, with a great selection of beers, including several wheat beers and a tasty smoky *Rauchbier.* The basic pub-grub is filling but forgettable (mains average €10), but at least the kitchen closes late. Mon–Thurs & Sun 11am–midnight, Fri & Sat 11am–2am; kitchen closes 11pm.

★ **Schlappen** Löwenstr. 2 ☎ 0761 334 94, ⓦ schlappen .com. Laidback studenty pub with jazz-themed decor, known for its huge range of absinthe and whiskies. Also reasonable for simple food like *Flammkuchen* – done here to perfection – with dishes in the €5–10 range. Mon–Thurs 11am–1am, Fri & Sat 11am–3am, Sun 3pm–1am.

Weinstube Oberkirch Münsterplatz 22 ☎ 0761 202 68 68, ⓦ hotel-oberkirch.de. Excellent traditional place with outdoor seating on the Münsterplatz. Food is of a traditional regional variety, served in large portions and running from ox with *Späztle* (€15) to good poultry dishes, particularly pheasant. Mon–Sat 7am–midnight; kitchen noon–2pm & 6.30–9.30pm.

Weinstube Sichelschmiede Insel 1 ☎ 0761 350 37. A quirky delight in one of the loveliest corners of Freiburg. There are lots of nooks full of country clutter to nestle into and its food is a triumph of good-value home-cooking; delicious suckling pig €12. Daily noon–late.

NIGHTLIFE AND ENTERTAINMENT

There's plenty going on in Freiburg and the nightlife tends to morph out of some of the more popular and late-opening cafés and bars (see opposite and above), making it best to just investigate one or two and go with the flow. To see what's on, pick up **listings magazine**, *Freiburg Aktuell*. **Tickets** to most events are sold by BZ-Kartenservice, Bertholdstr. 7 (☎ 0761 496 88 88, ⓦ freiburg-tickets.de).

FREIBURG FESTIVALS

Freiburg plays host to several lively festivals. **Fastnet** is celebrated with various fire rituals and particular gusto on the eve of Shrove Tuesday, and preceded by a jester parade the day before. In May the city has a big ten-day **Volksfest** as part of the **Frühlingsfest**. Other celebrations fill the summer, with the **Internationales Zeltmusikfest** (late June/early July) hosting many musical genres, but particularly jazz, and the **Weintagen** (late July) and **Weincost** (mid-Aug) both celebrating local wines. Towards the end of the year there's the **Herbstfest** (Oct).

9

Agar Löwenstr. 8 ⓣ 0761 38 06 50, ⓦ agar-disco.de. One of Freiburg's longest-standing clubs, with three bars and a large dancefloor. Theme nights are a regular feature and the place is particularly busy on Sun nights. Cover €6. Tues & Thurs–Sun usually 11pm–4am.

★**Jazzhaus** Schnewlinstr. ⓣ 0761 292 34 46, ⓦ jazzhaus.de. Club in an old wine cellar that attracts a range of ages and hosts all manner of musical events, from world music concerts, blues, jazz, rock and hip-hop, to busy, fairly mainstream weekend clubnights. Big names occasionally play here, when tickets run to around €10–30; otherwise the cover is about €7. Open until at least 3am most nights.

Karma Bertoldstr. 51–53 ⓣ 0761 207 45 18, ⓦ karma-freiburg.de. Popular and diverse complex with a stylish café-bar (daily till 3am), a bistro (closed Sun) with weekday lunch specials for around €6, and a club in the cellar playing funk and house. Fri & Sat 11pm–5am.

Konzerthaus Konrad-Adenauer-Platz 1 ⓣ 0761 388 15 52, ⓦ konzerthaus.freiburg.de. Modern concert hall and arts venue, home to regular performances by the Freiburger Barockorchester (ⓦ barockorchester.de), but also one of Freiburg's bigger venues for a variety of other music and live performances.

The Southern Black Forest

South of Freiburg the Southern Black Forest gradually rises into a series of rounded and densely forested mountains that begins with the Schauinsland peak (see p.504) and includes the ski resorts of **Todtnau** and **Feldberg**. Only smaller settlements dot their slopes or huddle at the valley bottoms. The more densely wooded hills just south of here are also thinly populated, with the modest lakeside resort towns of **Titisee** and **Schluchsee** and the small spa resort of **St Blasien** among the few exceptions. To the east, on the fringes of the Black Forest, lies the **Wutachschlucht**, a deep overgrown gorge that's popular for hiking; while to the west, where the land flattens around the Rhine and the French border, the prim spa-town of **Badenweiler** is a draw, as is the idyllic cluster of vineyard-draped hills called the **Kaiserstuhl**, sticking out in what's an otherwise clear run up to the impressive Vosges mountains on the horizon.

GETTING AROUND — THE SOUTHERN BLACK FOREST

By train and bus Travel to outlying towns from Freiburg by public transport is straightforward, though you may have to change services en route; all are frequent enough, however, so as not to make this a problem. Services are coordinated by RVF (ⓣ 0761 20 72 80, ⓦ rvf.de).

Travel passes The €11 REGIO24 ticket is a useful day-pass that covers all the places detailed in the rest of this chapter except Todtnau, St Blasien and Bonndorf. The group version of the ticket covers up to five people travelling together for €21 per day. Note that if staying in the region you'll be given a *Gästekarte* at your accommodation which should include use of the local bus network.

Todtnau

The quiet little mountain town of **TODTNAU**, 32km southeast of Freiburg and 25km beyond the Schauinslandbahn, bustles with activity in winter when it becomes a gateway to a network of **ski** lifts around the Feldberg (see p.510). Aside from skiing, Todtnau's other great draw is a 97m-tall **waterfall** that cascades over several craggy rocks on the opposite (northern) side of the valley. To get there from town, hike the signposted 2km trail from the church at the centre of Todtnau, or simply follow the much shorter trail from the car park on the hairpin of the L126 en route to Freiburg and Kirchzarten. The falls freeze in the winter to magical effect, but beware the slippery trails.

The Hasenhorn

Hasenhorn Daily 10am–4.30pm • Half-day ticket €17, toboggan rental €5, bobsleigh ride €9.50 • ⓦ hasenhorn-rodelbahn.de • **Bikepark Todtnau** Fri–Sun 9.30am–5.30pm • Bike, helmet and pads €85/day • ⓦ bikepark-todtnau.de

A ski lift up the Hasenhorn carries **toboggans** in winter and continues to attract a steady trickle of visitors in summer thanks to the presence of a 2.9km roller-coaster-cum-**bobsleigh-track** and a couple of excellent downhill **mountain-bike** trails aimed at experienced riders who can buy or rent any equipment they need at the base-station Bikepark Todtnau shop.

ARRIVAL AND DEPARTURE · TODTNAU

By bus Without your own transport you'll need to take a bus to get to Todtnau from Freiburg. Change at Kirchzarten or Titisee (see below); either way the scenic journey will take around an hour.

Höllental

From Freiburg the Black Forest rises rapidly to the southeast, an accelerating wildness best appreciated along the deep, dark canyon of the 9km-long **Höllental**. Its raw, jagged and shaded cliffs begin 15km east of Freiburg and are followed by both the B31 and the **Höllentalbahn**, a train line that winds through a creative network of tunnels and viaducts; when it was built in 1887 much of the engineering involved was groundbreaking. Some of this can be viewed from the path at the top of the gorge, which forms part of an excellent four-hour **mountain-bike** ride back to Freiburg from the train station at Titisee (see below) – the local tourist office has details. Trains from Freiburg to Titisee (hourly; 45min) will transport bikes, though space is limited.

Titisee

The relaxed but rather touristy lake-resort of **TITISEE** lies 29km from Freiburg, via the Höllentalbahn or the B31, and offers a quick way into the mountains. There are plenty of well-marked hiking, cycling and cross-country-skiing routes in the area, making it easy to leave the crowds and lakefront souvenir shops behind, and there's always the option of messing around on the quiet, scenic lake, with short **cruises** offered (hourly; 25min; €5; ⓦboote-titisee.de) and rowing boats for rent (€20 per hour). The most obvious **walk** is the easy 6km hike around the lake past several good bathing spots and the 1192m Hochfirst; only the most basic of maps are needed to tackle this – you can pick them up for free from the tourist office. Otherwise **swimming** and lounging are the main summer attractions. In winter, Titisee offers one of the best **cross-country-skiing** networks in the region, including a 3km floodlit track for night skiing.

Schwarzwald Badeparadies

Early July to mid-Sept Mon–Thurs, Sat & Sun 9am–10pm, Fri 10am–11pm; mid-Sept to early July Mon–Thurs 10am–10pm, Sat 10am–11pm, Sun 9am–10pm; Galaxy Schwarzwald closed weekday mornings · Day-pass €19–26 · ⓦ badeparadies-schwarzwald.de

The popularity of the lake for swimming is rivalled by the state-of-the-art **Schwarzwald Badeparadies**, a huge pool complex which includes Galaxy Schwarzwald, a children's dream with eighteen water slides. The complex also has pools and lagoons surrounded by 180 palm trees and four different saunas.

ARRIVAL AND INFORMATION · TITISEE

By train The train station lies a 5min signposted walk from Titisee's lakefront.
Destinations Freiburg (hourly; 45min); Konstanz (hourly; 1hr 48min).
Tourist office Strandbadstr. 4 (Mon–Fri 9am–6pm, Sat & Sun 10am–1pm; ☎07651 12 06 81 20, ⓦtitisee-neustadt .de). Located on the lakefront at the western edge of the town centre.

Ski equipment and bike rental Ski-Hirt (Titiseestr. 26, Neustadt; ☎07651 922 80, ⓦski-hirt.de) rents out skis, snowboards, cross-country gear and snowshoes as well as mountain bikes (€15 per day). It's located on the main road in Titisee-Neustadt, some 6km from the lake, and a single stop on the train.

ACCOMMODATION AND EATING

DJH Hinterzarten/Titisee Bruderhalde 27 ☎07651 238, ⓦjugendherberge-titisee-veltishof.de; bus #7300, direction "Zell/Todtnau". Hostel in a dignified seventeenth-century Black Forest house located 2km south of the tourist office. If you don't fancy the bus, it's a 30min walk from the Kurhaus. There's a games room and bistro, and rates include a packed lunch. Dorms **€26.70**, doubles **€64.40**

Gästehaus Wiesler Bruderhalde 8 ☎ 07652 16 18, ⓦ gaestehaus-wiesler.de. Well-priced, family-run lodgings in a romantic spot a 10min walk southwest of town and close to the lake, with dated but spotless wood-clad rooms. The breakfast buffet is extensive and very good. **€69**

Parkhotel Waldeck Parkstr. 4–6 ☎ 07651 80 90, ⓦ parkhotelwaldeck.de. Central option with small colourful rooms and a great spa which encompasses a pool,

hot tubs and saunas, and make the rates reasonably good value. Also runs a cheaper guesthouse a very short walk away. Rates include wi-fi and a good buffet breakfast served in its quality regional restaurant. **€150**

Treschers Schwarzwaldhotel Seestr. 10 ☎ 07651 80 50, ⓦ schwarzwaldhotel-trescher.de. Swank and sprawling lakeside place with commanding lake views, first-class amenities and a good regional restaurant, with starters including melon with Black Forest ham, and mains such as the excellent broiled trout with parsley potatoes (mains €20–37); reservations recommended. Restaurant daily 8am–11pm. **€150**

Feldberg

At 1493m the **Feldberg** is the Black Forest's highest summit, but it's hardly a soaring peak. Instead its huge bulk rears into a bald, rather flat, treeless dome. Nevertheless, the area is protected as a **nature reserve**, where wild flowers flourish, as do unusual fauna like mountain hens and goat-like chamois. The scattered presence of traditional Black Forest farmhouses and the occasional alpine hut add to the charm. But most villages in the area exist to provide for the major regional **downhill-skiing** centre. The most convenient is the slope-side village of **FELDBERG**, little more than a group of roadside houses on a 1234m-high pass, but given its general lack of services and nightlife you might prefer to stay in the more well rounded village of **Altglashütten**, in the valley 8km away.

Haus der Natur

Dr.-Pilet-Spur 4 • Daily 10am–5pm; closed Mon Nov–May

In summer the main focus on the Feldberg is on the **Haus der Natur** visitor centre, which has various displays on natural history in German and is the start point for various **hikes**, including the **Feldberg-Steig**, a highly recommended 12km loop that links five alpine huts around the upper reaches of the Feldberg. Much of it passes over open ground, offering open vistas which many other Black Forest hikes lack. In winter a good portion of this and other local trails form popular **cross-country-skiing** routes.

Feldbergbahn

Daily 9am–4.30pm • €9.50 return in summer; ski day-pass €30 • ⓦ feldbergbahn.de (summer), ⓦ liftverbund-feldberg.de (winter)

A short walk from the Haus der Natur lies the **Feldbergbahn** which, in winter, is part of a network of 28 ski lifts and covered by a day-pass. In summer it offers the chance of great views over the Alps without any legwork.

ARRIVAL AND INFORMATION   FELDBERG

By train and bus The nearest train station to Feldberg is Feldberg-Bärental on the branch line from Titisee. Buses provide a frequent service for the final 6km to Feldberg village. Altglashütten is on the railway network and linked to Freiburg (hourly; 51min).

Destinations Titisee (every 30min; 30min).

Tourist office In Feldberg information is provided by the Haus der Natur visitor centre, Dr.-Pilet-Spur 4 (daily

10am–5pm; closed Mon Nov–May); in Altglashütten, the tourist office is in the Rathaus, Kirchgasse 1 (Mon–Fri 8.30am–5.30pm; ☎ 07655 80 19, ⓦ feldberg-schwarzwald .de).

Ski equipment rental For skis, try Skiverleih Schubnell, Bärentalerstr. 1, Altglashütten (☎ 07676 560, ⓦ skiverleih-feldberg.de), who offer skis, boots and poles for €20/day. The Haus der Natur rents out snowshoes for €10/day.

ACCOMMODATION AND EATING

DJH hostel Passhöhe 14, Feldberg ☎ 07676 211, ⓦ jugendherberge-feldberg.de; bus #7300 from Feldberg-Bärental train station to Hebelhof (hourly;

10min). Spotless modern hostel in a chalet right in the thick of the skiing action at the top of the 1234m-high Feldberg pass. Most rooms are en suite and the hostel is otherwise well equipped with ski storage and even a gym. Dorms **€25.30**

Haus Waldvogel Köpfleweg 25, Feldberg ☎07676 480, ⓦ cafe-waldvogel.de. Traditional-looking Black Forest house with plush modern rooms on a sunny spot on the Feldberg pass. Excellent home-made cakes in its café,

and a reasonable restaurant. Rates include access to the spa facilities of a nearby hotel. **€99**

Sonneck Hotel Schwarzenbachweg 5, Altglashütten ☎07676 211, ⓦ sonneck-feldberg.de. Chalet with modern rooms in the centre of Altglashütten opposite the tourist office, with a good, inexpensive regional restaurant. **€105**

Schluchsee

A far larger body of water than the Titisee, and further off the beaten track, is the more relaxed **Schluchsee**. Located 10km to the south, it's a quiet, calm and clean lake with several communities basking in the peace and quiet along its eastern shore. The largest, also called **SCHLUCHSEE**, has a reasonable beach, managed as **Aqua Fun** (June to mid-Sept daily 9am–7pm; €4; ☎07656 77 31), the most popular place to swim on the lake. Schluchsee is also the local hub for sailing and windsurfing, and the departure point for the **boat trips** of Thomas Toth; boats circle the lake at hourly intervals (May to late Oct 10am–5pm; €9.50; ☎07656 92 30, ⓦ seerundfahrten.de), stopping at various points where you can hop on and off.

For a bird's-eye view of the lake, the easy two-hour walk up to the **Riesenbühlturm** (1097m) begins off Dresselbacher Strasse just northeast of town and continues up a forestry track just to the right of a sports centre; maps of this and other local walks are available from the tourist office.

Heimethus am Scheffelbach

Mattenweg 1 • Tues–Sat: April–Sept 1–6pm; Oct–March 1–5pm • €3 • ⓦ perlentasche.de

In town, consider popping in at the **Heimethus am Scheffelbach**, the workshop of Helga Reichenbach, which crafts all manner of traditional Black Forest costume and handicrafts; you can pick up a mini-*Bollenhut*, or more usefully some *Finken* – woven Black Forest slippers.

ARRIVAL AND INFORMATION SCHLUCHSEE

By train Trains travelling the branch line from Titisee (hourly; 22min) arrive at the lakefront, a short signed walk from the tourist office.

Tourist office Fischbacher Str. 7 (Mon–Fri 9am–5pm, Sat 10am–noon; ☎07656 12 06 85 00, ⓦ schluchsee.de). Located on the town's central square, with several reading rooms and free wi-fi.

ACCOMMODATION AND EATING

DJH Schluchsee-Wolfsgrund Im Wolfsgrund 28 ☎07656 329, ⓦ jugendherberge-schluchsee-wolfsgrund.de. Very popular with groups for its great location on a peninsula jutting into the lake, a 10min walk west along the shore from the Schluchsee train station. With games room, canoe hire and bistro. Dorms **€23.80**

Landhaus Mühle Unterer Mühlenweg 13 ☎07656 209, ⓦ landhaus-muehle.de. A picture-book traditional Black Forest house nestled among pine trees to the west of town, but whose simple rooms feature modern comforts. Balconies brim with blooms and the restaurant is a picture of rusticity. There's no menu, only a daily three- or four-course meal using local ingredients from around €35; reservations are essential. The breakfast buffet is also excellent. **€146**

★**Parkhotel Flora** Sonnhalde 22 ☎07656 974 20, ⓦ parkhotel-flora.de. Sprawling but charming 4-star

family-run hotel where personal touches abound. It has a country-style elegance and lake views as well as a pool and sauna, and breakfasts are first class. **€166**

Schiff Kirchplatz 7 ☎07656 975 70, ⓦ hotel schiffschluchsee.com. Traditional hotel in the centre of Schluchsee with modest and old-fashioned but perfectly comfortable rooms, and a lakeside terrace attached to its restaurant which serves good regional food; mains from €12. Restaurant daily 6pm–late. **€110**

★**Seehotel Hubertus** Seebrugg 16 ☎07656 524, ⓦ hubertus-schluchsee.de. Friendly family-run hotel with a superb spa, lovely lakeside location, free wi-fi and excellent breakfast buffet. The restaurant also serves dinner and specializes in meat and game dishes such as wild boar; its Chateaubriand steak is phenomenal (mains average €13). Restaurant daily 6–10pm. **€150**

9

St Blasien

Nestled in a tight, forested valley, the small spa town of **ST BLASIEN**, 15km south of Schluchsee, is odd for being dominated by the grandiose **Dom St Blasien**, a church that's well out of proportion with the rest of the mountain town. Wandering St Blasien's handful of central streets doesn't take long, though admiring its various wooden sculptures – product of the town's annual woodcarving festival – adds a few minutes. Another place to dwell is **Museum St Blasien** (Tues–Sun 2.30–5pm; €1.60; ⍵museum-st-blasien.de), the town's oddball local history museum above the tourist office.

The town forms a good **hiking** and **skiing** base (the tourist office has a good stock of outdoor sports information), though much of this action is 9km away in the incorporated village of **Menzenschwand**. Menzenschwand is also the location of the **Radon Revital Bad** (daily 10am–9pm; 4hr €9; ⍵radonrevitalbad.de), a smart spa and sauna complex offering watery bliss.

The Monastery and Dom

Am Kurgarten 13 • **Dom** Daily: May–Sept 8am–6.30pm; Oct–April 8.30am–5pm • Free • ⍵dom-st-blasien.de • **Concerts** July & Aug Tues & Sat 8.15pm • Free, though donations expected • ⍵domkonzerte-stblasien.de

St Blasien first found itself on maps in the ninth century when a Benedictine **monastery** was founded here, but its golden hour came in the eighteenth century when **Dom St Blasien** was built under powerful prince-abbot Martin Gerbert. Modelled on St Peter's in Rome, much of its Italian-inspired design was brought here by French architect Michel d'Ixnard who effectively introduced monumental Neoclassicism to Germany. Its standout feature is its huge cupola, which at 36m wide is Europe's third largest, but inside it's not the twenty powerful supporting Corinthian pillars that overwhelm as much as the dazzlingly white interior. Light floods in through the cupola, reflecting off the light stonework and brilliant stucco to give an impression of white marble; only close examination proves otherwise. The church also has superb acoustics, which are best appreciated during its classical music **concerts**. The rest of the monastery is now a Jesuit-run boarding school and one of Germany's top private schools.

ARRIVAL AND INFORMATION

ST BLASIEN

By bus St Blasien is linked to Seebrugg, the southernmost settlement on the Schluchsee, by bus #7319 (hourly; 20min).

Tourist information The St Blasien tourist office is in the Haus des Gästes at Am Kurgarten 1–3 (Mon–Fri 9am–noon & 2–5pm; ☏07672 414 30, ⍵st-blasien.de), beside a small park in the shadow of the Dom. It can help with booking private rooms (from €34) in the area, some of which are very smart indeed. In Menzenschwand, Sport Gfrörer, Hinterdorfstr. 8 (Mon, Tues, Thurs & Fri 9am–noon & 3–6pm, Wed & Sat 9am–noon; ☏07675 92 38 10, ⍵sport-gfroerer.de), provides local tourist and trail **information**.

Ski equipment and bike rental Sport Gfrörer in Menzenschwand (see above) rents out ski gear in winter and **bikes** in summer.

ACCOMMODATION AND EATING

ST BLASIEN

Dom Hotel Hauptstr. 4, St Blasien ☏07672 22 12, ⍵dom-hotel-st-blasien.de. Great deal on the doorstep of the Dom that offers smart, simple and spotless rooms. The restaurant below serves Black Forest specialities like fresh trout, game and home-made cherry cake. A good regional wine list too. Mains average €9. Restaurant daily 11pm–10pm. **€50**

Hotel Klostermeisterhaus Im Süssen Winkel 2, St Blasien ☏07672 848, ⍵klostermeisterhaus.de. Slick choice in an early nineteenth-century villa around the back of the Dom, where rooms are sleekly furnished with bare wood. Its stylish restaurant serves modern European cuisine: try grilled *Zander* with spinach or roast beef and a risotto with red lentils (mains €10–25). Restaurant Wed–Sun 11.30am–1.30pm & 6pm–late. **€98**

MENZENSCHWAND

DJH St Blasien-Menzenschwand Vorderdorfstr. 10, Menzenschwand ☏07675 326, ⍵jugendherberge-menzenschwand.de; bus #7321 from St Blasien. Friendly hostel in an idyllic old wooden farmhouse in a quiet valley. Has a games room and bistro, but otherwise relatively modest facilities. Dorms **€21.20**, doubles **€53.40**

> **MUSHING IN TODTMOOS**
>
> Little more than an idyllic gathering of traditional Black Forest houses in a remote valley, the small town of **Todtmoos**, 14km west of St Blasien, is best known as the venue for a large **international dog-sled race** in late January, which shouldn't be missed if you're in the area at the time. The event attracts hundreds of mushers and huskies and thousands of spectators, particularly for the torch-lit night races. The Todtmoos tourist office (**ⓦ** todtmoos.de) has accommodation listings.

The Wutachschlucht

On the southeastern fringes of the Black Forest and hidden from view in the rolling landscape of farms and pastures lies the 33km-long **Wutachschlucht**, a deep gorge that's been fed and shaped by the waters of the Titisee. The thickly forested and overgrown chasm with its stretches of craggy cliffs, churning waters and unspoilt, ancient forests has become a popular **hike**.

Several communities act as gateways to the valley, with the most practical being **Löffingen** to the north of the Wutachschlucht, and **Bonndorf** to the south. The gorge walk is too long to do in a day, but local buses pick up and drop off hikers along the gorge route for a flat rate of €3.20 per day. A popular quick taster of the canyon landscape is the feeder valley of the **Lotenbachklamm**, along which an easy and attractive hour-long, round-trip walk runs to the **Schattenmühle**, an old watermill and inn in the Wutach Valley. The *Schattenmühle* is also the ideal place to start a hike of the most stunning stretch of the Wutachschlucht: take bus #7259 from Löffingen or #7344 from Bonndorf, to the *Schattenmühle*, or park there, then walk five hours east along the gorge to Wutachmühle, and take bus #7344 back to the start (9am–6pm hourly; 25min) or on to Bonndorf.

ARRIVAL AND INFORMATION

THE WUTACHSCHLUCHT

To Bonndorf An easy bus ride from Titisee on bus #7258 (hourly; 38min).

To Löffingen Connected to Freiburg by regular trains (hourly; 1hr).

Tourist offices In Bonndorf at Martinstr. 5 (May–Oct Mon–Fri 9am–noon & 2–6pm, Sat 10am–noon; Nov–April Mon, Tues, Thurs & Fri 9am–noon & 2–5pm, Wed 9am–noon; **ⓣ** 07703 76 07, **ⓦ** bonndorf.de); in Löffingen at Rathausplatz 14 (Mon–Fri 9am–noon & 2–5.30pm; **ⓣ** 07652 12 06 83 50, **ⓦ** hochschwarzwald.de); both offer maps and bus timetables.

ACCOMMODATION AND EATING

BONNDORF

Germania Martinstr. 66, Bonndorf **ⓣ** 07703 281, **ⓦ** germania-bonndorf.de. Traditional inn with bright, clean rooms and an atmospheric restaurant offering excellent steaks and game and some interesting, delicious *Zander* dumplings, on a seasonal menu (mains average €12). Restaurant daily 5–10pm. **€64**

Kranz Martinstr. 6, Bonndorf **ⓣ** 07703 938 30, **ⓦ** kranz-bonndorf.de. Solid portions of inexpensive (mains average €8) rib-sticking traditional food – *Schnitzels*, steaks and goulash in large portions – all washed down with a foaming beer in an unpretentious *Gaststätte*. Just the ticket after a long walk. Daily except Tues 8am–9.30am, 11.30am–2pm & 5.30–9pm.

Schwarzwald-Hotel Rothausstr. 7, Bonndorf **ⓣ** 07703 932 10, **ⓦ** schwarzwaldhotel.com. Bonndorf's finest restaurant and hotel. Dishes rely on regional produce and an excellent lunchtime buffet is laid out most days. Rooms are colourful and modern and there's a sauna, steam room and pool on site. Free wi-fi. Restaurant daily 11am–late. **€128**

LÖFFINGEN

Hotel Restaurant Hexenschopf Obere Hauptstr. 9a, Löffingen **ⓣ** 07654 80 60 30, **ⓦ** hexenschopf.de. Good place for pizza or pasta (average €7), with a genuine trattoria feel thanks to exposed brick and tiles. Also offers bright, modern guest rooms. Restaurant daily 11am–2pm & 5pm–midnight. **€78**

Badenweiler

A classic little Black Forest spa town, **BADENWEILER** is the closest really good spa to Freiburg, 35km away to the north. As a tiny, southern version of Baden-Baden, it has much the same credentials: the Romans first developed the baths here, and the

9

foundations of their complex from 75 AD are still well preserved in the town centre as the **Römische Baderunie** (daily: April–Oct 10am–7pm; Nov–March 10am–5pm; €1.50). This lies beside today's **Cassiopeia Therme**, Ernst-Eisenlohr-Str. 1 (daily 9am–10pm; €13.50–23.50 depending on areas visited; ⓦbadenweiler.de), which includes three thermal pools, a collection of saunas and a Roman–Irish bath (a course of baths and saunas and a massage). More than a century after Chekhov railed at the town's lack of charisma (see box above), Badenweiler still has a rather dull if thoroughly recuperative air. The gardens are nice for a wander, with some half-dozen cafés serving delicious cakes; the nearby Hochblauen peak invites more strenuous activity.

Hochblauen

The 7km trail from Badenweiler up the **Hochblauen** (1165m) through thick evergreen forest is a popular three-hour return **hike**, but it's also one of the few rewarding Black Forest summits up which you can coax a car, and its location at the point where the Black Forest gives way to the rolling slopes of the Upper Rhine Valley ensures good views in every direction. A viewing tower, restaurant and sausage kiosk ensure you should want for nothing.

ARRIVAL AND INFORMATION — BADENWEILER

By train and bus The nearest railway station is at the town of Mühlheim, where passengers from Freiburg need to change onto bus #111. The whole journey takes about 45min, with the last connection back at around 8pm in the evening.

Tourist office Opposite the Cassiopeia Therme at Ernst-Eisenlohr-Str. 4 (April–Oct Mon–Fri 9am–5pm, Sat 10am–1pm; Nov–March Mon–Fri 9am–1pm & 2–5pm; ☎07632 79 93 00, ⓦbadenweiler.de). The tourist office has extensive private-room listings (from €42) and its website has a useful online booking tool.

ACCOMMODATION AND EATING

Hotel Römerbad Schlossplatz 1 ☎07632 700, ⓦhotel-roemerbad.de. Elaborate and historic full-service spa hotel with opera-house grandeur and a list of former guests that includes Nietzsche, Thomas Mann and Andy Warhol. €179

Hotel Zur Sonne Moltkestr. 4 ☎07632 750 80, ⓦzur-sonne.de. Old-fashioned upmarket hotel, with elegant pastel rooms and a first-class restaurant with wood-panelled charm and inventive international cuisine. Menu items might include carpaccio of veal, braised guinea fowl, fresh fish or lobster ravioli (mains average €21). Restaurant daily noon–2pm and 6–9pm. €138

Villa Martha Friedrichstr. 8 ☎07632 51 04, ⓦvilla-martha.com. Central, late nineteenth-century villa with cheerful, country-style rooms, several with balconies overlooking its extensive leafy gardens. Open April–Oct. €60

Wappen von Baden Ernst-Eisenlohr-Str. 14 ☎07632 82 49 37. Smart regional restaurant in an old central inn. Mains average €13 and include a good range of standard regional meat and fish specialities, as well as a daily menu based on seasonal ingredients such as chanterelles or asparagus, and an extensive list of *Vespers*, or light meals. Good selection of regional wines. Mon–Thurs 5.30–9.30pm, Fri–Sun 11am–2pm.

The Kaiserstuhl

The **Kaiserstuhl** (ⓦnaturgarten-kaiserstuhl.de) is something of a geological oddity: a small group of hills of volcanic origin on an otherwise flat plain around the Rhine, 25km northwest of Freiburg. Their isolated position has made them ripe for local legend: Frederick Barbarossa supposedly died here en route to the Holy Land, and the Kaiserstuhl is said to be shaped to seat him on his second coming. Until that happens the land offers great **hiking** and **biking** along with splendid views of the Black Forest region and the Rhine Valley framed by France's Vosges mountains. Thanks to its volcanic soil and clement microclimate, an array of fruit **orchards** – striking when blooming in spring – and **vineyards** thrives here, with the area noted for *Spätburgunder* (Pinot Noir) and *Grauburgunder* (Pinot Gris). Many of the steep local slopes are densely terraced and several rustic wine-bars tempt for a tipple.

GETTING AROUND   THE KAISERSTUHL

By train An easy way to explore is to take the Kaiserstuhlbahn, a rail loop of the hills, picked up at the town of Riegel am Kaiserstuhl, itself a fifteen-minute hop from Freiburg by train.

On foot Riegel is the start of the 15km Winzerweg, a hiking trail which travels southwest across the Kaiserstuhl, through a series of vineyards and past several taverns to the bus station at the small town of Achkarren.

By bike The 64km Kaiserstuhltour, a loop of the region, makes a good day out for reasonably fit cyclists and is signposted from Breisach, a regional town on the French border 27km west of Freiburg. The tourist office in Breisach, Marktplatz 16 (Jan–March 9am–12.30pm & 1.30–5pm; April–Dec Mon–Fri 9am–12.30pm & 1.30pm–6pm, Sat 10am–1pm; ☎ 07667 94 01 55, ⓦbreisach.de), can provide a list of local bike rental places.

Rhineland-Palatinate and Saarland

BURG RHEINSTEIN, THE ROMANTIC RHINE

Rhineland-Palatinate and Saarland

10

The Rhine and its tributaries have almost single-handedly shaped both the Rhineland-Palatinate (Rheinland-Pfalz) and the Saarland in just about every way. While large portions of both states are rural and remote, their three main waterways – the Rhine, Mosel and Saar – have bustled with traffic and commerce for generations. Vital as trade routes, the Rhine and Mosel have been studded by strategically placed fortifications and towns since Roman times. Many have been repeatedly destroyed and rebuilt in competition for the land, particularly with the French, who have at one time or another held most of the region and left their mark on its culture and food. Viticulture along all three rivers is hugely important and the region's wines are of international quality.

Travelling down the Rhine, as it works its way north and west along the eastern border of the region, the first places of any significance are a trio of imperial cathedral cities: **Speyer**, **Worms** and **Mainz**, which grow in magnitude and importance as you move downstream.

West beyond them the Rhine passes the foothills of the Taunus mountains where the attractive **Rheingau** wine region harbours the touristy town of **Rüdesheim**. Then, some 40km west of Mainz, the Rhine squeezes its way through its famous Gorge, on a stretch nicknamed the **Romantic Rhine** for its many dramatic fairy-tale castles. These feel hugely evocative of earlier times, even though most were built by eighteenth-century aristocrats. This 65km leg of the Rhine ends at the sprawling, semi-industrial city of **Koblenz**, where it meets the Mosel as it finishes its own journey from the southwest. The most scenic portion of the Mosel Valley, dubbed the **Mosel Weinstrasse**, is a Romantic Rhine-in-miniature with yet more atmospheric castles, fine wines, meandering river scenery and absorbing, half-timbered old towns. Here, however, the scale is more intimate, the towns slower-paced and the setting more rural.

South along the Mosel the steep sides of the valley fade away around the Luxembourg border and the venerable city of **Trier**, with its glut of Roman remains. Due south of here, the Mosel meets the **Saar**, leaving the landscape of castles and wines to travel through what in the early twentieth century was one of Europe's leading industrial regions. These days most of that lies closed, decaying and rusting, but at least the **Völklinger Hütte** ironworks has been recognized and preserved as a fascinating snapshot of a bygone era. The big city on its doorstep, **Saarbrücken**, has some good museums and a little international flair thanks to its proximity to the French border.

In general **roads** and **trains** follow the main rivers around the region, so getting between the main cities and points of interest is straightforward. There's plenty off the beaten track too, and all three rivers have marked **cycle routes**. If that seems too much like hard work, you can always hop on and off the many **boats** that cruise up and down the Rhine and Mosel, with or without a bike in tow.

Tourist discount cards p.521
The Nibelungenlied p.527
The Gutenberg press p.530

Cruising the Romantic Rhine p.535
Frankfurt-Hahn Airport p.543
Green Hell: The Nürburgring p.546

KAISERTHERMEN, TRIER

Highlights

❶ Worms The tales of the *Nibelungenlied* are the star attraction in this handsome town with a fascinating museum on the subject. **See p.527**

❷ Mainz Dirty your hands with printer's ink as you get to grips with early printing technology in the town where it was invented. **See p.528**

❸ The Romantic Rhine The classic castle-hopping route along the Rhine Gorge. **See p.534**

❹ Vierseenblick Clamber up a series of chains and ladders or take a laidback 1950s chairlift to this classic Rhine viewpoint. **See p.539**

❺ The Nürburgring Zip around one of the world's most infamous motor-racing circuits. **See p.546**

❻ Bernkastel-Kues Cosy up in a half-timbered *Weinstube* and try some of the Mosel's fine wines. **See p.547**

❼ Trier Wander Europe's most impressive Roman remains – complete with baths and amphitheatre. **See p.548**

❽ Völklinger Hütte The rusting carcass of the Saarland's steel industry has been preserved as a fascinating monument to the region's industrial heritage. **See p.554**

HIGHLIGHTS ARE MARKED ON THE MAP ON P.520

Speyer and around

The pleasant market-town of **SPEYER**, 25km southwest of Heidelberg (see p.471), is a quiet place these days, but things were very different in the Middle Ages when it regularly hosted imperial parliaments and was a key player in the Holy Roman Empire – as the presence of a giant Romanesque **Dom** suggests. From the cathedral the pedestrianized **Maximilianstrasse** cuts through the small Baroque Altstadt and is lined by most of its cafés and shops, while on its other sides the Dom is surrounded

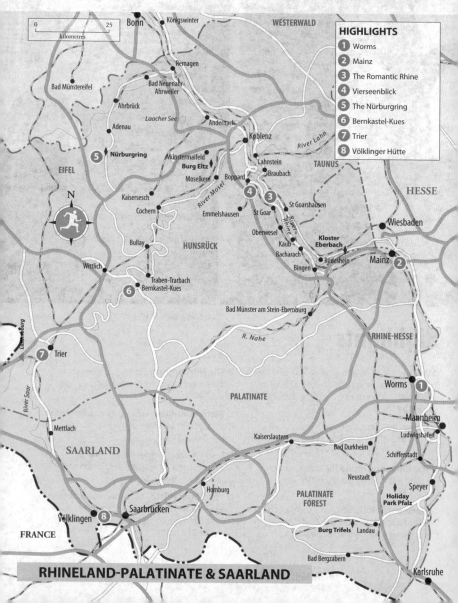

WESTERWALD

HIGHLIGHTS

1. Worms
2. Mainz
3. The Romantic Rhine
4. Vierseenblick
5. The Nürburgring
6. Bernkastel-Kues
7. Trier
8. Völklinger Hütte

Bonn
Königswinter
Remagen
Bad Münstereifel
Bad Neuenahr-Ahrweiler
Ahrbrück
Laacher See
Andernach
Adenau
Koblenz
River Lahn
⑤ Nürburgring
Münstermaifeld
Lahnstein
TAUNUS
Burg Eltz
Moselkern
Boppard
Braubach
EIFEL
Kaisersesch
④ ③ St Goarshausen
HESSE
Cochem
St Goar
Wiesbaden
Emmelshausen
Oberwesel
Kloster
Eberbach
Bullay
HUNSRÜCK
Kaub
Wittlich
Bacharach
Rüdesheim
Traben-Trarbach
Bingen
Mainz ②
⑥ Bernkastel-Kues

Bad Münster am Stein-Ebernburg

R. Nahe
RHINE-HESSE

⑦ Trier

River Saar

Worms ①

PALATINATE

Mannheim

Mettlach
Ludwigshafen
Kaiserslautern
Bad Dürkheim
Schifferstadt
SAARLAND
Neustadt
Speyer
Homburg
Holiday Park Pfalz
PALATINATE
FOREST
Saarbrücken
Völklingen ⑧
Burg Trifels Landau
FRANCE
Bad Bergzabern
Karlsruhe

kilometres 0 — 25

RHINELAND-PALATINATE & SAARLAND

> **TOURIST DISCOUNT CARDS**
>
> If you're doing anything more than just passing through the Rhineland region, consider the **FreizeitCARD** (April–Oct; 24hr €14, 3 days €41.50, 6 days €66; ⓦ freizeitcard.info), which offers free entry and often sizeable discounts to some two hundred regional attractions – in the Rhineland, Saarland, Luxembourg and neighbouring portions of Belgium and France – and is sold at most tourist offices. Some public transport use is included, but otherwise bear in mind the superb-value **Rheinland-Pfalz-Ticket** (€23, or €39 for groups of up to five), which allows you to use any local trains and buses for the day and is sold at train stations.

by gardens which separate it from the Rhine and the **Technik Museum**, a first-class transport museum a kilometre from the centre.

The Kaiserdom

Domplatz • Daily: April–Oct 9am–7pm; Nov–March 9am–5pm • Free • ⓦ dom-speyer.de

With its square towers and copper dome soaring above town, Speyer's vast and dignified **Kaiserdom** (Imperial Cathedral) is the world's best-preserved Romanesque church. The project began in 1030, though it took until 1858 to get it to its present form. Over the years the building has witnessed a good deal of drama: in 1689, locals stacked their furniture in the church for safekeeping as French troops bore down on the town, though to no avail. The soldiers broke in and torched the lot anyway and the heat effectively destroyed the western end of the church. During the French Revolution there was more chaos as locals ran riot inside the church. Unsurprisingly, then, the interior is almost devoid of furnishings, which helps emphasize the building's mighty proportions – though the pieces that are there are rather mediocre and nineteenth century. This dearth of furniture makes the beautiful **crypt** a highlight, its rows of elegant tombs of Salian emperors, kings and queens helping to explain the scale of the church.

Maximilianstrasse

Along **Maximilianstrasse** Speyer's two-thousand-year pedigree and Roman origins are most evident. The unusually broad and straight road was built with triumphalist parades of Roman troops in mind and was later used for the same purpose by medieval emperors. However, the backdrop would have looked very different then, and up until the Middle Ages at least; in 1689 marauding French troops fairly comprehensively destroyed the Altstadt. What's on view today is a pastel Baroque rebuild.

The Altpörtel

Maximilianstrasse • April–Oct Mon–Fri 10am–noon & 2–4pm, Sat & Sun 10am–5pm • €1.50

At its western end, Maximilianstrasse terminates in the 55m-high **Altpörtel**, a twelfth-century city gate that was once one of 68 towers in town, but is now alone in crowning what remains of Speyer's fortifications. It offers good views of Speyer's roofscape through arrow slits on its western side.

Historisches Museum der Pfalz

Maximilianstrasse • Tues–Sun 10am–6pm • €7 • ⓦ museum.speyer.de

Facing the Dom on the corner of Maximilianstrasse is the small but superb **Historisches Museum der Pfalz**, which is famous for its outstanding *Goldener Hut von Schifferstadt*, a piece of odd, conical Bronze Age headwear, and, in its little wine museum, a jellied **third-century wine**, thought to be the world's oldest. Various sparkling Domschatz (Cathedral Treasury) treasures also call the museum home.

10

The Technik Museum

Am Technik Museum 1 • Mon–Fri 9am–6pm, Sat & Sun 9am–7pm • €14, with IMAX €19, with Auto & Technik Museum Sinsheim (see p.476) €35 • ⓦ technik-museum.de

From the Dom, an attractive, signed 1km walk through its gardens leads to the **Technik Museum**, Speyer's other big draw. The museum's glut of vintage vehicles and other minor transport engineering marvels are completely overshadowed by the many **aeroplanes** perched on pedestals around the museum. Most are open for you to clamber around, including a Boeing 747 (a video inside shows how complicated it was to mount here) and many curious Eastern Bloc designs. By far the most spectacular is the Soviet **space shuttle** – or rather the prototype for its Buran spacecraft – the only Russian shuttle ever to have been launched into space. A piece of moon-rock and some life-sized models of a moon buggy and space suits help complete this part of the exhibition. Elsewhere there's a rare chance to poke around the claustrophobic confines of a submarine, plus an IMAX cinema and a playground.

Holiday Park Pfalz

Holiday-Park-Str. 1-5, D-67454 Hassloch • Mid-April to early Nov, hours vary but usually at least 10am–5.30pm • €24.50 • ⓦ plopsa.be • Suburban train to Hasloch, then bus #518; combined transport and park tickets sold at train stations

If you love roller-coasters, and feel half-a-million annual visitors can't be wrong, then head to **Holiday Park Pfalz**, 12km east of Speyer. This large amusement park prides itself on its cutting-edge rides: its Free Fall Tower was the first of its kind in Europe; the Expedition GeForce roller-coaster features near-vertical drops combined with equally abrupt, stomach-churning twists; and the Sky Scream coaster hits speeds of 100km/hr. Many other attractions, including water-ski shows, ensure there's something for everyone.

ARRIVAL AND INFORMATION
SPEYER

By train and bus Speyer's Hauptbahnhof and adjacent bus station lie about 1km north of the centre along Bahnhofstrasse. Destinations Heidelberg (frequent; 45min); Stuttgart (hourly; 1hr 10min); Worms (hourly; 1hr).

Tourist office Maximilianstr. 13 (April–Oct Mon–Fri 9am–5pm, Sat 10am–3pm, Sun 10am–2pm; Nov–March Mon–Fri 9am–5pm, Sat 10am–noon; ☎ 06232 14 23 92, ⓦ speyer.de).

ACCOMMODATION

DJH Speyer Geibstr. 5 ☎ 06232 615 97, ⓦ jugendherberge.de. Modern hostel a short walk from the Technik Museum beside the Rhine and a large public pool. All twin rooms have private bathrooms and there's a bistro and café on site as well as several common rooms and various games including table football and board games; prices include breakfast. Dorms **€22.50**, doubles **€56**

★**Domhof** Im Bauhof 3 ☎ 06232 132 90, ⓦ domhof. de. Venerable ivy-clad hotel in the shadow of the Dom with classy, spacious and bright antique-studded rooms overlooking a cobbled courtyard, where in summer you can sit and enjoy a top-class breakfast buffet. Rates drop substantially on Sun evenings. **€120**

Hotel am Technik Museum Am Technik Museum 1 ☎ 06232 671 00, ⓦ hotel-am-technik-museum.de. Motel-style rooms and a campsite for campervans and tents close to a large, modern pool and the Technik Museum, a 10min walk from the town centre. Prices include a fairly minimal continental breakfast. Pitches **€22**, doubles **€107**

Trutzpfaff Webergasse 5 ☎ 06232 29 25 29, ⓦ trutzpfaff-hotel.de. Centrally located hotel on a quiet street a block south of the tourist office, with straightforward, bright and simple rooms, and a *Weinstube* (see opposite). **€95**

EATING AND DRINKING

★**Backmulde** Karmeliterstr. 11–13 ☎ 06232 715 77, ⓦ back-mul.de. Probably the finest restaurant in town, located a block south of the Altpörtel. Specializes in French dishes, seafood and gourmet versions of regional recipes using local ingredients. Menu items might include quail stuffed with lamb or oysters in champagne for around €25–30; the daily three-course menu's a more reasonable €40 and the wine list is huge. Tues–Sat 5.30–midnight, Sun noon–2.30pm & 5.30pm–midnight.

Domhof Brauerei Grosse Himelsgasse 6 ☎ 06232 740 55, ⓦ domhof.de. Local microbrewery, close to the Dom, with Speyer's best beer garden. The food is hearty, local and inexpensive, with most mains around €10. Mon 11.30am–11pm, Tues–Fri 11.30am–midnight, Sat 11am–midnight, Sun 11am–11pm.

Trutzpfaff Webergasse 5 ☎ 06232 29 25 29, ⓦ trutzpfaff-hotel.de. Well-priced mains average €10 at this hotel's *Weinstube*. The local speciality, *Saumagen* (pig's stomach stuffed with meat, potatoes and herbs then

boiled, sliced and fried) – though sufficiently gory-sounding to turn you towards the good selection of veggie dishes – is excellent. Daily 5–10pm.

★ **Zum Alten Engel** Mühlturmstr. 1a ☎ 06232 709 14, ⓦ zumaltenengel.de. Cosy and convivial restaurant in an atmospheric, antique-furnished and vaulted cellar. Its outstanding regional dishes use local ingredients whenever possible and are mostly meaty, such as the liver dumplings and *Sauerbraten*; mains €9–23. Popular, so reserve in advance if you can. Daily 6pm–late.

10

The Deutsche Weinstrasse

Established in 1935 as a way to boost local wine sales, the 85km-long **Deutsche Weinstrasse** (German Wine Route) meanders almost due north from the French border at Schweigen-Rechtenbach, connecting picturesque wine-growing villages that dot wooded hills of the Pfälzer Wald and the broad, flat Rhine Valley. Not surprisingly, wine is the main attraction; much of it dry, white and made with Riesling grapes, though reds made with Pinot Noir are increasingly attracting praise. Alongside the lively and attractive "capital", **Neustadt an der Weinstrasse**, the neat spa-town of **Bad Dürkheim** is the main urban focus, though the region's real charm is in its villages: alongside viticulture, a refined culinary scene has emerged in places like **Deidesheim** and the little walled town of **Freinsheim**. Hugely popular with Germans and also attracting many French and Dutch, the Route gets going in March, when the almond trees blossom.

Burg Trifels

Annweiler • Daily: Jan–March, Oct & Nov 9am–5pm; April–Sept 9am–6pm; closed Dec • €3

Castles dot the Wine Route's skyline – often romantically ruined, since the French laid waste to this part of Germany during the War of the Palatine Succession. Most eye-catching is **Burg Trifels**, a much-restored Salian fortress high above the former imperial free city of Annweiler. The imperial crown jewels were once stored here, as was Richard the Lionheart as a prisoner in 1193.

Hambacher Schloss

Neustadt an der Weinstrasse • Daily: April–Oct 10am–6pm; Nov–March 11am–5pm • €4.50 • ⓦ hambacher-schloss.de

The **Hambacher Schloss** overlooks **Neustadt an der Weinstrasse** and, in 1832, was the scene of the Hambacher Fest, one of Germany's first mass pro-democracy demonstrations. An English leaflet available at the entrance deciphers the German-only exhibition.

GETTING AROUND

By train From Neustadt's Hauptbahnhof – connected by frequent trains to Ludwigshafen (25min) and Mannheim (25min) – trains run to towns and villages along the northern Wine Route including Bad Dürkheim, Deidesheim, Freinsheim, Maikammer and Edenkoben. To reach Annweiler (for Trifels) change at Landau.

By bike A cycle route, the Radweg Deutsche Weinstrasse, parallels the Wine Route road.

On foot There's a choice of hiking trails: the 153km Pfälzer Weinsteg, which sometimes follows the wooded heights, and the more direct, 96km Wanderweg Deutsche Weinstrasse.

INFORMATION   THE DEUTSCHE WEINSTRASSE

Tourist office Neustadt's tourist office is opposite the Hauptbahnhof at Hetzelplatz 1 (April–Oct Mon–Fri 9.30am–6pm, Sat 9.30am–4pm; Nov–March Mon–Fri

9.30am–5pm; ☎ 06321 926 80, ⓦ neustadt.pfalz.com).
Website ⓦ deutsche-weinstrasse.de.

10

ACCOMMODATION

Deidesheimer Hof Am Marktplatz 1, Deidesheim ☏ 06326 40 09 68 70, ⊛ deidesheimerhof.de. Lovely, rambling old five-star hotel in the heart of one of the Weinstrasse's most popular – and chic – villages, with two excellent restaurants (see below). **€365**

DJH Neustadt Hans-Geiger-Str. 27, Neustadt ☏ 06321 22 89, ⊛ diejugendherbergen.de; bus #501 from the Hauptbahnhof. Cheerful, modern hostel by Neustadt's Hambacher Schloss, where all rooms are en suite and have between two and four beds. Rates include breakfast. If you don't fancy the bus, the hostel is reachable via a 15min walk over the bridge that crosses the tracks and up Alter Viehberg. Dorms **€22.50**, twins **€56**

St Martiner Castell Maikammererstr. 2, St Martin ☏ 06323 95 10, ⊛ hotelcastell.de. Attractive hotel in an old castle on the edge of the Pfälzer Wald above one of the most attractive wine-road villages west of Maikammer, with good-value rooms and a restaurant, where regional main courses are priced in the region of €10–22. **€108**

Weingut Mugler Peter-Koch-Str. 50, Gimmeldingen ☏ 06321 660 62, ⊛ weingut-mugler.de. Three stylish modern rooms in a winery north of Neustadt, with an attached *Weinstube* (see below). **€99**

EATING AND DRINKING

Whether it's the rustic likes of *Saumagen* (stuffed pig's stomach) or haute cuisine, the Wine Route is a good place to **eat** well, usually in an atmospheric setting. Most towns and villages on the route have at least a couple of options. No visit to the region is complete without a visit to a *Weingut* (**winery**) to taste and buy the local product. Many publish visitor opening times, but even so it's often worth calling ahead. Look out for VDP-affiliated producers – the Verband Deutscher Prädikatsweingüter – a sign of quality.

RESTAURANTS

Deidesheimer Hof Am Marktplatz 1, Deidesheim ☏ 06326 40 09 68 70, ⊛ deidesheimerhof.de. The two restaurants in this five-star hotel are first class: *Restaurant St Urban* was a favourite of former chancellor Helmut Kohl, for its regional specialities like *Saumagen* (mains around €17); *Schwarzer Hahn* is the hotel's more expensive gourmet restaurant, where fixed-price menus go from €90 to €180. Daily 6pm–late.

Freinsheimer Hof Breite Str. 7, Freinsheim ☏ 06353 508 04 10, ⊛ restaurant-freinsheimer-hof.de. Beautiful restaurant in an old *Weingut* that's the place to feast on wild salmon strudel with ginger lentils or spring *Saumagen* with asparagus and herb sauce. Mains average €25. Mon, Tues, Fri & Sat 6pm–midnight, Sun noon–3pm & 6pm–midnight.

Luther Hauptstr. 29, Freinsheim ☏ 06353 934 80. Regionally renowned restaurant, Michelin-starred since the early 1980s and serving the likes of duck liver parfait with papaya relish or veal fillet in pancetta (menu €87). It lies in the centre of Freinsheim, where other top-notch gastronomic options abound. Daily 6pm–late.

WINERIES

August Ziegler Bahnhofstr. 5, Maikammer ☏ 06321 957 80, ⊛ august-ziegler.de. The Ziegler family's winery has been awarded German "winemaker of the year" three times, and produces a variety of wines including Riesling, *Weissburgunder* (Pinot Blanc) and *Spätburgunder* (Pinot Noir). Mon–Fri 8am–6pm, Sat 9am–3pm.

Reichstrat von Buhl Weinstr. 16, Deidesheim ☏ 06326 965 00, ⊛ reichsrat-von-buhl.de. Patrician *Sekt* (champagne) maker in grandiose premises close to the *Deidesheimer Hof* (see left). Still owned by the same family who founded it in 1849, it's been among Germany's most celebrated wineries for decades. Mon–Fri 9am–noon & 1–6pm, Sat, Sun & public holidays 10am–noon & 1–5pm; closed Sun in Jan.

Weingut Mugler Peter-Koch-Str. 50, Gimmeldingen ☏ 06321 660 62, ⊛ weingut-mugler.de. This VDP producer does, among other things, a very creditable Pinot Noir. You can sample the estate's wines in its *Weinstube*, which serves specialities from the Palatinate priced between €9 and €25. Tues–Sat 5pm–late, Sun noon–late.

Worms

Midway between Speyer and Mainz – both 50km away – **WORMS** is one of Germany's oldest cities, famous as the fifth-century home of the Burgundian kingdom, as celebrated in the great epic poem, the **Nibelungenlied** (see box, p.527), on the subject of which Worms has an excellent multimedia **museum**. But the city has also flourished in several eras since, first under Charlemagne, who made it his winter residence, and particularly during the Salian dynasty (1024–1125) when the city's grand Romanesque **Dom** was built. Worms also occasionally served as a seat for the imperial parliament, most famously when it sat in judgement on Martin Luther in 1521.

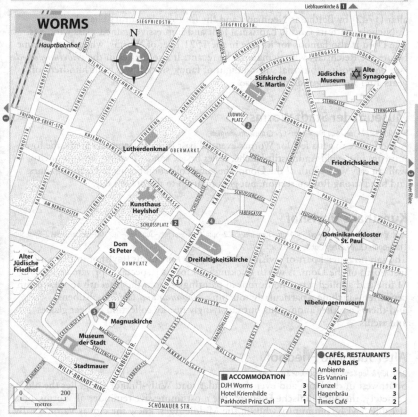

For many centuries Worms was also home to a powerful **Jewish community**, which began to grow prodigiously in the eleventh century to become – along with Mainz and Speyer – one of the foremost in Germany. It survived the fifteenth century when many other cities expelled their Jews, only to be virtually eradicated by the Third Reich. Nevertheless important reminders remain, above all in its Jewish **graveyard** and rebuilt **synagogue**. All this is fairly quickly explored, leaving you to wander Worms' pedestrianized Altstadt, which was attractively rebuilt following almost total destruction in World War II. The old town always has a reasonable bustle about it, but is best during the mid-August **Nibelungen Festspiele**, a two-week theatre festival based on the epic, and the Backfischfest, a wine festival that follows, when fried fish is the accompaniment of choice.

Dom St Peter

Daily: April–Oct 9am–6pm; Nov–March 10am–5pm • Free • ⓦ wormser-dom.de

Rearing up high enough to offer a handy orientation point from anywhere in the city and even far beyond, **Dom St Peter** is the pride of Worms' Altstadt. Largely built in the eleventh century in late Romanesque style, many of its walls are unusual in being flat on one side and curved on the other. The earliest exterior walls are like this, but it's easiest to see this design inside in the east choir, the church's oldest part. Highlights to look out for include the impressively large and opulent high altar (1742) by Balthasar Neumann and the fourteenth-century chapel of St Nichola, with its Gothic baptismal font and impressive stained-glass windows. The Dom is also famous for its role in the 1521 Diet of Worms, when Luther came before the Reichstag, who demanded he recant. It also figures in the *Nibelungenlied* (see box opposite), but that's just a flight of fancy, since it was built hundreds of years after the Burgundians' demise.

10 Museum der Stadt Worms

Wecklingplatz 7 • Tues–Sun 10am–6pm • €2 • ⓦ museum.worms.de

A good place to get a feel for Worms' eventful past is the **Museum der Stadt**, the town museum in the old Andreastift Kirche. It lies beside some surviving sections of city wall, an easy walk south of the Dom. The good collection begins in Neolithic times and has a strong Roman section, but goes right up to the present day.

Kunsthaus Heylshof

Stephansgasse 9 • Mid-Feb to April Sun 11am–5pm, Tues–Sat 2–5pm; May–Sept Tues–Sun 11am–5pm; Oct–Dec Tues–Sat 2–5pm, Sun 11am–5pm • €3.50 • ⓦ heylshof.de

Though no crucial part of a visit to Worms, the **Kunsthaus Heylshof** in the park just north of the Dom, is worth ducking into for its respectable private collection of fine and applied arts. The European paintings – from the fifteenth to nineteenth centuries – include a particularly touching *Madonna and Child* by Rubens and there's a rather anomalous but satisfyingly quirky collection of beer glasses and steins.

Alter Jüdische Friedhof

Daily: July & Aug 8am–8pm; Sept–June 8am–dusk

Southwest of the Dom and over the circular road Willy-Brandt-Ring, lies the old cemetery, the **Alter Jüdische Friedhof**, the most impressive reminder of Worms' once sizeable Jewish community who, in the Middle Ages, knew the city as Varmaiza. By 1933 the community exceeded a thousand; now the figure is around a hundred, with most being more recent settlers from former Soviet territories. The graveyard opened for business in 1076 and has the unkempt look typical of most traditional Jewish graveyards.

Among the crooked **headstones**, a few stand out for their larger piles of memorial pebbles and messages: one belongs to Rabbi Meir of Rothenburg who died in 1293, imprisoned for trying to lead a group of persecuted Jews to Palestine. His captor, Rudolf of Habsburg, was the first of the dynasty on the German throne. Rothenburg's is the only stone in the graveyard to point to Jerusalem in the customary fashion, though why the others don't is unknown.

Alte Synagoge

Synagogenplatz • Daily: April–Oct 10am–12.30pm & 1.30–5pm; Nov–March 10am–noon & 2–4pm • Free

Most of Worms' Jewish community would have spent much of their lives in the Jewish ghetto on the northeast edge of the Altstadt, which was centred on **Judengasse**, a ten-minute walk from the cemetery along Lutherring – where a large statue celebrates the reformer and his associates. Little of the ghetto's history is evident around Judengasse, except for the **Alte Synagoge**, a 1961 replacement for an eleventh-century one destroyed by Nazis. Around the side, the twelfth-century *mikveh*, used for ritual bathing, survived more or less intact.

Jüdisches Museum

Hintere Judengasse 6 • Tues–Sun: April–Oct 10am–12.30pm & 1.30–5pm; Nov–March 10am–12.30pm & 1.30–4.30pm • €1.50 • ☎ 06241 853 47 07

Alongside the Alte Synagoge, the Raschi Haus, named for the renowned rabbi-scholar who studied in Worms, houses the **Jüdisches Museum**, a modest enterprise with some general information about Jewish customs and beliefs along with a few exhibits about local Jews.

10

The Nibelungenmuseum

Fischerpförtchen 10 • Tues–Fri 10am–5pm, Sat & Sun 10am–6pm • €5.50 • ⓦ nibelungenmuseum.de

Dedicated to the *Nibelungenlied*, the great German epic poem (see box below), the **Nibelungenmuseum**, a five-minute walk east of the Dom, is easily Worms' most engaging and satisfying attraction. Occupying a chunk of the town's extant medieval fortifications – two towers and a portion of wall – it uses the building to good effect to recount the story behind the epic. A first-class multilingual audio-guide is the most important of a number of audiovisual tools that recount the *Nibelungenlied*; others include excerpts from Fritz Lang's film and music from Wagner's opera. But the museum goes well beyond simply narrating the tale, by trying to put it into context – exploring myths of medieval honour and valour and the way in which the tale was twisted into emotive Nazi propaganda that portrayed Germans as a Nordic race – and their enemies as barbarians from the east. There's also a good view over the surrounding landscape from the top of one tower.

ARRIVAL AND INFORMATION   WORMS

By train and bus The train and adjacent bus stations are 5min walk northwest of the Dom.
Destinations Frankfurt (frequent; 1hr); Heidelberg (frequent; 1hr); Speyer (hourly; 30min); Stuttgart (hourly; 1hr 15min).

Tourist office Neumarkt 14 (April–Oct Mon–Fri 9am–6pm, Sat & Sun 10am–2pm; Nov–March Mon–Fri 9am–5pm; ☎ 06241 250 45, ⓦ worms.de). Offers a useful free English-language walking-tour brochure.

THE NIBELUNGENLIED

Written at the end of the twelfth century, the *Nibelungenlied* is *the* German epic tale, based on legends surrounding the destruction of the Burgundian kingdom: Roman allies who ran Worms for about twenty years in the fifth century AD before being driven out by the Huns. It's a captivating tale with a glut of mythic beings like dragons and giants, and much drama in the form of love, hate, riches, treachery, revenge and lots of death.

Nibelung himself was the mythical king of Nibelungenland (Norway), who, with twelve giants, guarded a hoard of treasure. **Siegfried**, prince of the Netherlands and hero of the first part of the poem, kills Nibelung and his giants and pinches the hoard as a dowry for his new wife **Kriemhild** of Burgundy. Siegfried then helps Kriemhild's brother, **Gunther**, King of Burgundy, to gain the hand of **Brunhild** of Iceland. This is no mean feat since the immensely powerful Brunhild will only marry a man who can beat her at the javelin, shot put and long jump. Siegfried helps Gunther to cheat – using his rather handy cloak of invisibility – and win Brunhild over. After the marriage, Kriemhild indiscreetly lets Brunhild know how she'd been tricked, which infuriates her so much that she arranges for Gunther's aide, **Hagan** (the poem's chief villain), to murder Siegfried, grab the treasure, and toss it in the Rhine. The plan is to recover it later, but by the end of the poem everyone's dead, so the treasure's lost.

The second part of the poem tells of Kriemhild's subsequent marriage to Attila the Hun (called **Etzel** in the poem). Kriemhild invites the Burgundians to the Hunnish court, where Hagan lets rip once again and ends up killing Etzel's son. Aghast, Kriemhild decapitates Gunther and Hagan with her own hands, only to be killed herself.

ACCOMMODATION

DJH Worms Dechaneigasse 1 ☎06241 257 80, ⓦjugendherberge.de; bus #1a or #1b from Hauptbahnhof. Modern hostel whose rooms are nearly all en suite. Has an on-site café and bistro and various common rooms and is close to a big public swimming pool. Dorms €21.50, doubles €54

Hotel Kriemhilde Hofgasse 2–4 ☎06241 911 50, ⓦhotel-kriemhilde.de. Modest central inn in a modern building with verdant window boxes. Its en-suite singles and doubles are straightforward and uncluttered, if fairly

small. Also has a *Weinstube* where you can sample good local wines, and a reasonable restaurant that prides itself on its *Matjes*, a soused herring offered in mains for around €10. €78

★**Parkhotel Prinz Carl** Prinz-Carl-Anlage 10–14 ☎06241 30 80, ⓦparkhotel-prinzcarl.de. Swish hotel in a former nineteenth-century barracks just north of the town centre, with spacious and cheerful rooms. The breakfast buffet is excellent and there's free wi-fi. Also has a good bistro, bar and gourmet restaurant on site. €98

EATING AND DRINKING

Ambiente Weckerlingplatz 6 ☎06241 304 98 88, ⓦambiente-worms.de. Quality Italian, with hardwood floors and modern decor, that is as good for a quick pizza (€6–12) as for more imaginative dishes like the venison-and-chestnut tortellini (€12). But be sure to leave room for the excellent tiramisu or the many different flavours of Italian ice cream. Daily 9am–midnight.

★**Eis Vannini** Am Marktplatz ☎06241 230 51, ⓦvannini.de. Marktplatz kiosk close to the Dom and the central pedestrianized district with outdoor seating and a bewildering array of delicious Italian ice cream flavours; an essential stop on any summer trip to Worms. Daily 10am–11pm.

Funzel Güterhallenstr. 53 ☎06241 556 09, ⓦdie-funzel.de. Happening alternative bar tucked behind the railway station and with regular events and some snacks such as salads and sandwiches. Sunday night is "Black

Night" with Cuban and African-American music and Cuba Libre specials. Mon–Thurs & Sun 6pm–1am, Fri & Sat 6pm–3am.

Hagenbräu Am Rhein 3 ☎06241 92 11 00, ⓦhagenbraeu.de. For microbrewery beer and inexpensive hearty German food (most mains around €10) head down to this Rhine-side locale a 5min walk from the centre. Daily lunch specials are particularly well priced at around €7 considering they include the fancy likes of veal in red wine sauce. Mon–Fri 10am–11pm, Sat & Sun 9am–11pm.

Times Café Ludwigsplatz 1 ☎06241 84 97 00. Sympathetically cosy and dependably busy café with good breakfasts, quick items like burgers, *Flammkuchen* and salads (each around €9) and daily lunch specials for around €7. Also good for cakes and cocktails later on. Mon–Sat 8.30am–late, Sun 10.30am–late.

Mainz

As the largest town and capital of Rhineland-Palatinate and with rapid transport links to Frankfurt 42km to the northeast, **MAINZ** has a very different, more urban feel, to the rest of the state. The city has also made a heavyweight contribution to German history: starting as a strategically important settlement at the confluence of the Main and Rhine, by the eighth century it had developed into the main ecclesiastical centre north of the Alps, and its archbishop was one of the most powerful Holy Roman electors. The city also entered the history books when Mainz resident **Johannes Gutenberg** made their mass production possible with the invention of the printing press in the fifteenth century.

Like much of the Rhineland, Mainz had a spell in French hands as the city of Mayence (1792–93 and 1798–1814), which it survived quite well. It was less fortunate during World War II when bombers pounded a good portion of the city into submission. Nevertheless enough of the half-timbered **Altstadt** and the **Dom**, around which the main sights are centred, survived or was rebuilt to make its compact centre attractive to explore. The bustling adjacent **Marktplatz** is home to the **Gutenberg Museum**, while the only attractions outside the immediate centre are relatively minor draws, appealing most to those interested in Roman history: the **Landesmuseum** and the **Museum für Antike Schiffahrt**.

Mainz's many **Weinstuben** offer a good place to refresh your palate and rest your legs at the end of the day, while the liveliest time to be in town is during the Carnival – on

the Monday and Tuesday before Ash Wednesday – which Mainz celebrates with gusto; and during the late-June **Mainzer Johannisnacht**, when half a million revellers come to a giant Volksfest.

The Dom

Dom March–Oct Mon–Fri 9am– 6.30pm; Sat 9am–4pm, Sun 12.45–3pm & 4–6.30pm; Nov–Feb Mon–Fri & Sun till 5pm • Free • W mainz-dom.de • **Dommuseum** Tues–Fri 10am–5pm, Sat & Sun 11am–6pm • €5 • W dommuseum-mainz.de

Mainz's majestic six-towered Romanesque **Dom** isn't the first cathedral on the site, but a twelfth-century replacement for one that burnt down in 1066, a day before its consecration. Outside, one notable feature is the unusual way in which many of its red sandstone walls adjoin surrounding houses – which tends to make the church look bigger. Inside, the church is rather spartan and gloomy and, though some of the tombstones of archbishops and other notables are interesting enough, most of the real treasures are tucked away in the **Dommuseum**, accessed from adjoining cloisters. Its treasures include sparkling reliquaries and some intricate fifteenth- and sixteenth-century tapestries, but most of the cathedral's artwork is stored in the adjacent **Gewölbehallen**. The highlights here are a thirteenth-century rood screen from the Master of Naumburg, which vividly depicts sin and salvation, an early fourteenth-century pewter baptismal font and some Rococo choir stalls from an impressive collection of more church furnishings.

The Gutenburg Museum

Liebfrauenplatz 5 • **Museum** Tues–Sat 9am–5pm, Sun 11am–5pm • €5 • **Druckladen** Mon–Fri 9am–5pm, Sat 10am–3pm • Free • W gutenberg-museum.de

The highlight of a visit to Mainz is the **Gutenburg Museum**, which celebrates the work of the city's most famous son, Johannes Gutenberg, whose printing press was one of

10

> ## THE GUTENBERG PRESS
>
> It was in the early fifteenth century that goldsmith **Johannes Gutenberg** began developing a printing press. Working in secret he effectively pioneered several technologies simultaneously: moveable metal type; the moulds to produce it; oil-based inks that would take to the type and then the page; and the technology of the actual printing press, which adapted designs used in wine presses.
>
> It's fair to say that the results changed the world forever, enabling information to spread more quickly and be controlled less easily, and making literacy important to all levels of society. The results proved remarkably democratizing and one of the earliest unforeseen consequences was to smooth the passage of the Protestant Reformation, with the knock-on effects of popularizing written German and galvanizing the development of a Germanic identity.

the most important inventions of all time (see box above). The museum itself is mainly a tribute to the technology, but it goes far beyond Gutenberg and the historical presses of the time, with displays encompassing earlier Asian printing and some hand-copied manuscripts, which became a dying art. But the museum's greatest single showpiece is a copy of Gutenberg's first major work, the 1455 **forty-two-line Bible**, named for the number of lines on each page.

Druckladen

The hands-on extension of the Gutenberg Museum – and beside it – is the **Druckladen** (Printing Shop), where you can hand-set type to make posters, cards and the like. It's a fun setup, with a relaxed atmosphere and enthusiastic staff, who'll encourage you to get stuck in and happily guide you through the process. If that doesn't appeal, or sounds too messy (aprons are provided), at least browse the quirky hand-printed items on sale.

Landesmuseum Mainz

Grosse Bleiche 49–51 • Tues 10am–8pm, Wed–Sun 10am–5pm • €6 • ⓦ landesmuseum-mainz.de

Based at the site of a Roman military camp from 12 BC, and an easy five-minute walk north of the Altstadt, Mainz's **Landesmuseum** covers local and regional history quite broadly, but is strongest on Roman history. This includes first-century tombstones of soldiers and civilians and the strikingly ornate **Jupitersäule**, a triumphal column from Nero's time.

Museum für Antike Schiffarht

Neutorstr. 2b • Tues–Sun 10am–6pm • Free • ☎ 06131 28 66 30

The **Museum für Antike Schiffahrt** lies at the southern edge of central Mainz, a fifteen-minute walk from the Dom. Its exhibits are based around a find of five wooden ships used by Roman Rhine patrols; impressive full-sized replicas provide a wonderful insight into the past.

ARRIVAL AND DEPARTURE

MAINZ

By train The station is a 15min walk northwest of the centre, down Bahnhofstrasse; or take a tram or bus to Höffchen. Destinations Frankfurt (frequent; 35min); Koblenz (frequent; 1hr); Saarbrücken (frequent; 2hr 15min); Speyer (hourly; 1hr); Stuttgart (hourly; 1hr 30min); Trier (hourly; 2hr 30min); Worms (frequent; 40min).

INFORMATION AND TOURS

Tourist office Brückenturm am Rathaus (Mon–Fri 9am–5pm, Sat 10am–4pm; ☎06131 24 28 88, ⓦ touristik-mainz.de); it can be tricky to find with its isolated position above the street beside a pedestrian bridge. Offers a free room-booking service, with rooms from €54.

Discount card The tourist office sells the MainzCard (€10), which provides two days of discounts to town attractions and unlimited public transport use.

Tours English-language tours (May–Oct Mon, Wed, Fri, Sat & Sun 2pm; Nov–April Sat 2pm; €7) leave from the tourist office.

ACCOMMODATION

HOTELS

★ **Hof Ehrenfels** Grebenstr. 5–7 ☎ 06131 971 23 40, ⓦ hof-ehrenfels.de. Half-timbered, fifteenth-century convent with Dom views that's long since been converted into a smart hotel gathered around a leafy cobbled courtyard, though with modest rooms and a nice *Weinstube* that serves rustic local dishes – with mains averaging €12. **€100**

Hotel Hammer Bahnhofplatz 6 ☎ 06131 96 52 80, ⓦ hotel-hammer.com. One of the best of the hotels around the Hauptbahnhof: an elegant, well-managed modern place with business-level facilities which include wi-fi and a sauna. Though without any traditional rustic ambience, the glitzy hotel bar has some good local wines. **€99**

Hyatt Regency Mainz Malakoff-Terrasse 1 ☎ 06131 73 12 34, ⓦ mainz.regency.hyatt.com. Sophisticated five-star hotel in a striking modern building a 10min walk southeast of the Dom. Amenities include a busy beer garden, pool and fitness centre. Some units look out onto the Rhine. **€116**

Ibis Mainz Holzhofstrasse 2 ☎ 06131 24 70, ⓦ ibishotel.com. Clean and economical branch of this international hotel chain, with small functional rooms on the edge of the Altstadt. Online deals can undercut rack rates substantially, but in any case the value for money is hard to beat. Free wi-fi. **€68**

Schwan Liebfrauenplatz 7 ☎ 06131 14 49 20, ⓦ mainz-hotel-schwan.de. Family-run hotel in a sixteenth-century Altstadt building with some really pleasant rooms: they're all spacious and a Baroque touch gives them a bit of style. Its *Weinstube* claims to be the oldest in the region. **€98**

Stadt Coblenz Rheinstr. 49 ☎ 06131 629 04 44, ⓦ stadt-coblenz.com. A central, old inn with plain, modern rooms at bargain prices near the Dom, though most are pretty cramped and some suffer from street noise. Breakfast is included, but don't expect much given the budget rates. Free wi-fi as well. **€67**

HOSTELS

DJH Mainz Otto-Brunfels-Schneise 4 ☎ 06131 853 32, ⓦ diejugendherbergen.de; bus #62 & #63 from the Hauptbahnhof to stop "Am Viktorstift Jugendherberge" within 400m of it. Modern hostel, with single, twin and four-bed rooms, in the wooded heights of Weisenau. Dorms **€22.50**, twins **€56**

EATING AND DRINKING

In some corners of Mainz's Altstadt the **Weinstuben** sit cheek by jowl, making them an essential part of the Mainz experience and great for a glass or two of local wine – perfect accompanied by *Spundekäse*, a cheese, onion and cream dip with crusty bread. In general *Weinstuben* are also the local first choice for traditional meals.

RESTAURANTS

★ **El Chico** Kötherhofstr. 1 ☎ 06131 23 84 40, ⓦ elchicomainz.weebly.com. Small, informal bistro specializing in perfect steaks, making reservations a near necessity. Has some good local choices on the short wine list, but don't expect too much from the side salads. Daily 6–11pm.

Heiliggeist Rentengasse 2 ☎ 06131 22 57 57, ⓦ heiliggeist-mainz.de. The Gothic vaults of a fifteenth-century hospital have been turned into this attractive and inexpensive bistro whose mains (average €9) are international but include several Italian options. Mon–Fri 4pm–1am, Sat & Sun 9am–2am.

L'Angolo Augustinerstr. 8. ☎ 06131 23 17 37, ⓦ l-angolo.de. Authentic and oft-packed trattoria with superb pizza and pasta (€8–12) and a few meat dishes. Look out for well-priced specials and bear in mind that takeaways attract a 25 percent discount. Mon–Sat 11am–midnight, Sun noon–midnight.

Zur Kanzel Grebenstr. 4 ☎ 06131 23 71 37, ⓦ zurkanzel.de. Delightful restaurant with debonair service and candlelit seating in a courtyard. The French and regional cuisine is hardly experimental, but of high quality with mains priced around €18. Mon–Fri 5pm–1am, Sat noon–4pm & 6pm–1am.

PUBS AND WEINSTUBEN

★ **Geberts Weinstuben** Frauenlobstr. 94 ☎ 06131 61 16 19, ⓦ geberts-weinstuben.de. Simple and traditional wine-tavern in one of Mainz's oldest buildings, hugely popular for its local dishes, particularly fish but also game (mains around €26), and with a fine choice of wines. Tues–Fri & Sun 11.30am–2.30pm & 6pm–midnight, Sat 8pm–midnight.

Haus des Deutschen Weines Gutenbergplatz 3 ☎ 06131 22 13 00, ⓦ hdw-gaststaetten.de. While living up to its name, with hundreds of wines from all over Germany, there's also good-quality and inexpensive food here (most mains around €10). Recommended is the fresh or marinated salmon, a traditional Rhine dish, and the

venison, but many items on the menu are local and seasonal. Daily 10am–midnight.
Irish Pub Mainz Weissliliengasse 5 ☎06131 23 14 30, ⓦirish-pub-mainz.de. Convivial pub with live music almost every night and so always busy. Mon–Thurs 6pm–1am, Fri 6pm–2am, Sat 3pm–2am, Sun 3pm–1am.

NIGHTLIFE AND ENTERTAINMENT

Though Frankfurt is within striking distance for a night out, there's a surprising amount going on in Mainz. For **listings**, check free local monthlies *Fritz* (ⓦfrizz-online.de) and *Mainzer* (ⓦdermainzer.net); the tourist office sells **tickets** to most bigger events.

LIVE MUSIC
Frankfurter Hof Augustinerstr. 55 ☎06131 22 04 38, ⓦfrankfurter-hof-mainz.de. Good venue for trendier, low-key and diverse performances – jazz, folk, pop and classical – and organizer of many big-name gigs, listed on their website. Hours vary though generally Tues–Sun 8pm–late.
Kuz Dagobertstr. 20b ☎06131 28 68 60, ⓦkuz.de. Mainz's most dependably happening venue for twenty- and thirty-somethings, with a sociable beer garden and a

busy events schedule which often features gigs, particularly world music. Cover around €8. Hours vary though generally Wed–Sun 8pm–late.

THEATRE AND OPERA
Staatstheater Gutenbergplatz 7 ☎06131 285 12 22, ⓦstaatstheater-mainz.de. The town's premier venue for opera and drama. Expect classics like *Romeo and Juliet*, Mozart's *Idomeneo*, Wagner and Tennessee Williams plays. Hours vary though generally Thurs–Sun 7pm–late.

The Rheingau

West of Mainz, on the gently sloping north bank of the Rhine, lies the **Rheingau** (ⓦrheingau.de), one of Germany's most prestigious wine-growing regions, known for its Riesling and *Spätburgunder* or Pinot Noir. The English term *Hock* for German wines derives from Hochheim near Wiesbaden, whose wines found favour with Queen Victoria. It's a region of photogenic, vine-clad hillsides and pretty villages, and one unmissable attraction: the hauntingly beautiful Gothic monastery of **Kloster Eberbach**. At the western end of the region, the day-tripper magnet of **Rüdesheim** balances brash commercialism with a range of fine- and wet-weather attractions.

Separate but broadly parallel, three **wine routes** – the **Rheingauer-Riesling Route** for cars, the **Riesling Radwanderweg** for cyclists and the **Rieslingpfad** for hikers – meander west from Wiesbaden (see p.581) to Rüdesheim past vineyards, villages and historic landmarks, with plenty of spots to stop and sample local wines along the way, including seasonal wine-maker-run *Strausswirtschaften*. The cyclists' route stays closest to the river while the hikers' route hugs the higher and more scenic ground on the fringe of the Taunus, but all three thread their way through wine-growing villages – **Eltville**, **Kiedrich**, **Oestrich-Winkel** among them – and pass Kloster Eberbach.

The Rheingau has a busy programme of **wine-related festivals** all year round, from a gourmet festival in early March to Kiedrich's Rieslingfest in June and the Riesling Gala at Kloster Eberbach in November. Tourist offices have details.

Kloster Eberbach

16km northeast of Rüdesheim • Abbey Daily: April–Oct 10am–6pm; Nov–March 11am–5pm; Wine shop daily 10am–6pm • €7.50, English audio-guide €3.50 • ⓦkloster-eberbach.de • Bus #172 (hourly; 20min) links Kloster Eberbach with the rail network at Eltville, on the line from Rüdesheim (every 30min; 18min)

Tucked discreetly into the narrow Kisselbach Valley above the Kiedrich–Hattenheim road, **Kloster Eberbach** was established as a Cistercian abbey in 1136. The first monks from Burgundy brought with them the wine-making expertise for which the abbey is still famed – the expression *Kabinett* or cabinet, which refers to high-quality German wines, derives from the abbey's *Cabinetkeller* or cellar, and there's a **wine shop** in the old hospital. The abbey's well-preserved medieval interior is compelling; a left turn as you reach the cloister takes you to the star-vaulted chapter house with its single central pillar and thence into the memorably austere church. Antique wine-presses fill the immense, damp, lay refectory on the west side, but it's the 72m-long monks' **dormitory** on the east side – which dates from 1250–70 and is one of the most splendid, secular, early Gothic rooms in Europe – that is the highlight. Interior scenes of the big-screen version of Umberto Eco's *The Name of the Rose* were filmed at Eberbach.

Rüdesheim

10

After the beauty and tranquillity of the Rheingau landscape, first impressions of **RÜDESHEIM** can come as a shock, above all the noisy, crowded **Drosselgasse**, a narrow lane leading up from the river into which tour groups are funnelled for an over-amplified facsimile of German joviality. Having suffered wartime bombardment, Rüdesheim's not even consistently pretty. Yet beneath the veneer of plastic oompah lurks a genuine wine-growing village with quaint and peaceful corners worth exploring, including at the uphill end of Drosselgasse on **Oberstrasse** where the half-timbered **Brömserhof** at no. 29 dates from 1542 and now houses **Siegfried's Mechanisches Musikkabinett** (March–Dec daily 10am–6pm; €6.50; ⊛siegfrieds-musikkabinett.de), a quirky collection of musical automata. Another saggy half-timbered beauty worth seeking out is the early sixteenth-century **Klunkhardshof**, in a narrow lane off Markt two blocks east of Drosselgasse. Meanwhile, at the eastern edge of town – a twenty-minute walk from the centre – you can watch a short presentation and buy a variety of local brandies from the Asbach distillery at the **Asbach Besucher Center**, Ingelheimer Str. 4 (March–Dec Tues–Sat 9am–5pm; free; ⊛asbach.de).

The Seilbahn Rüdesheim, Niederwald Denkmal and Assmannshausen

Oberstr. 37 • March–Nov daily 9.30am– 5/7pm; also during Christmas market • €7 return, or €13 for a "Ringtrip" which includes a return boat from Assmannshausen • ⊛ seilbahn-ruedesheim.de

For great views over the town and the Rhine Valley that stretches away to Mainz, take Rüdesheim's antique 1950s chairlift, the **Seilbahn Rüdesheim**, from Oberstrasse to the **Niederwald Denkmal**, a vast, bellicose monument celebrating the 1871 foundation of the German Reich. You can also reach the monument on foot along a track that begins next to the Romanesque Boosenburg tower close to the Rheingauer Weinmuseum (see below).

From the monument a hiking trail passes several fine viewpoints before snaking through vineyards into Rüdesheim's sister settlement of **Assmannshausen** – a walk of around two hours. Here the picturesque ruins of medieval **Burg Ehrenfels** face the equally romantic **Mäuseturm**, originally used to collect river tolls from an islet in the river before being wrecked by the French in 1688. From Assmannshausen you can catch a boat back to Rüdesheim.

Rheingauer Weinmuseum

Rheinstr. 2 • Daily: mid-March to Oct 10am–6pm • €5 including English audio-guide • ⊛ rheingauer-weinmuseum.de

At the western end of Rüdesheim, the twelfth-century Brömserburg castle provides an atmospheric setting for the **Rheingauer Weinmuseum**. The exhibition begins with a huge collection of old wine presses before progressing through viticulture's origins in the ancient world and its arrival in the Rhineland. There are amphorae from the eastern Mediterranean, old brandy stills and antique goblets, punch bowls and Jugendstil wine coolers, while the vertigo-inducing battlements offer grand views of the vineyards around town.

ARRIVAL AND INFORMATION	RÜDESHEIM
By train The station is at the western end of the village; walk along the riverfront Rheinstrasse.	Destinations Cologne (hourly; 2hr); Frankfurt (hourly; 1hr 12min); Koblenz (hourly; 1hr); Mainz (hourly; 55min).

10

Tourist office Geisenheimer Strasse (Jan–March, Nov & Dec Mon–Fri 9am–4.30pm; April–Oct Mon–Fri 8.30am–6.30pm, Sat & Sun 10am–4pm; ☏06722 90 61 50, ⊛ruedesheim.de).

ACCOMMODATION AND EATING

Burg Schwarzenstein Rosengasse 32, Johannisberg ☏06722 995 00, ⊛burg-schwarzenstein.de. For a special meal, head 5km east out of Rüdesheim to this Michelin-starred gourmet restaurant where the views of the Rhine Valley are as memorable as the French-influenced cuisine; menus from €50. Wed–Sat 6.30–10pm, Sun noon–2.30pm & 6.30–10pm.

DJH Rüdesheim Jugendherberge 1 ☏06722 27 11, ⊛djh-hessen.de. In a scenic setting above town with excellent views and walks through the vineyards. Hostel has modern dorm rooms, a canteen, and table tennis and table football in its communal areas. Breakfast included; half- or full-board packages available for not much more. Dorms **€20.50**, twins **€56**

Zum Grünen Kranz Oberstr. 42–44 ☏06722 483 36, ⊛gruenerkranz.com. Bright, modern rooms in the thick of things above a historic restaurant and *Weinstube* where you can eat and drink local food and wines (mains around €10). With pleasant outdoor seating in a courtyard in summer. **€80**

The Romantic Rhine

Upstream of Rüdesheim, the banks of the Rhine gradually rear up into a deep and winding 65km-long gorge that's dubbed the **Romantic Rhine** for its many quaint towns, steep vineyards and bewildering number of castles, all of which have helped make it a UNESCO World Heritage Site. Much of this romance is, of course, pure fabrication, first by nineteenth-century German Romantics, who rebuilt most of the castles, and subsequently, by the tourist and wine industries. Coach parties are very much part of the scenery, but don't be put off: many castles are certainly worth a look, as are the many *Weinstuben* for their excellent local vintages. The annual **Rhine in Flames** festival – which also takes place in Koblenz (see p.541) – is another draw, with spectacular fireworks filling September skies above the village of St Goar.

This stretch of the Rhine offers the full range of **transport** options: you can drive, follow cycle paths or take trains up either side of the river, while car ferries cross the river in several places. But probably the most relaxing way to travel and appreciate the scenery is by **boat** (see box opposite); many conveniently begin in Mainz, Rüdesheim or Koblenz, and several companies offer hop-on, hop-off services. If you're pressed for time a day-trip is all you'll need to get a feel for the place, but if you're keen to explore some of the castles, you'll need an extra day or two.

Brief history

Geologically, the gorge is made of a type of slate sedimentary rock, folds in which produced the Hunsrück mountains to the west and the Taunus mountains to the east, while the Rhine carved a passage between the two, creating steep, 200m-high walls, and its own sheltered, sun-trap microclimate. Many of the riverbank's slopes were terraced for agriculture from an early age, the south-facing ones in particular providing near-perfect conditions for **viticulture**. This, together with booming trade along the river, brought wealth to the string of small riverside settlements whose many rulers built **castles** to protect interests and levy tolls. This racket was lucrative enough to make this area an important region in the Holy Roman Empire and a focus for much of the **Thirty Years' War**. The latter ruined many castles, as did campaigns that briefly claimed this region for France in the early nineteenth century until Prussia turned things around, reinventing the place as a sort of quintessential Germany, rebuilding legendary castles and featuring it in much of the art of the time. Wagner, for example, uses this stretch of the Rhine as the setting for his powerful *Götterdämmerung*.

CRUISING THE ROMANTIC RHINE

There's little to choose between the half-dozen or so operators who offer **boat cruises** along the Romantic Rhine, so the convenience of their hub will tend to be the deciding factor. Most also take bikes and allow you to hop on and off, making it possible to create your own itinerary. The price of a round trip between Koblenz and Bingen/Rüdesheim – the entire Romantic Rhine – comes in at around €35 and takes three hours and thirty minutes in each direction. Virtually all services stop at every dock along the way, but double-check if you have particular destinations in mind – look too at the frequency of services, which becomes important if you want to make short stops at various places along the way.

Bingen-Rüdesheimer ☎ 06721 141 40, ⊕ bingen-ruedesheimer.com. Offers trips from Bingen and Rüdesheim as far as St Goar – so covering the eastern half of the gorge. Feb to late Dec.

Hebel Line ☎ 06742 24 20, ⊕ hebel-linie.de. Based in Boppard, with daily sailings to Rüdesheim and Koblenz and most points of interest between.

Köln-Düsseldorfer ☎ 0221 208 83 18, ⊕ k-d.com. The big player, with several daily sailings between Koblenz and Rüdesheim, with some continuing to, or starting in, Mainz too. Bikes welcome.

Loreley-Line ☎ 06773 341, ⊕ loreley-linie.com. Boppard-based company with six daily sailings to the Loreley and back for just €15 return.

Bingen to Bacharach

From the towns of **Rüdesheim** and **Bingen**, which watch each other from opposite banks of the Rhine and are connected by a car ferry (May–Oct 6am–midnight; Nov–April 6am–10pm; ⊕ bingen-ruedesheimer.com/rheinfaehren) some 30km west of Mainz, the Rhine Gorge starts to emerge and its first sentinels come into view: three castles worth a visit on the 17km journey to **Bacharach**, the next settlement of any size. All lie on the south, or left, bank of the river.

Burg Rheinstein

Mid-March to Oct daily 9.30am–6pm; Nov to mid-March Sat & Sun 10am–5pm • €5 • ⊕ burg-rheinstein.de

Burg Rheinstein, a compact pile with blackened towers, was given a complete makeover in 1820 to transform it into a neo-Gothic summer residence – setting a trend for the rest of the valley. The pastel and rather twee interior rooms feel as though they belong in a very different building. Various boats stop below the castle, or you can follow a signed thirty-minute walk from the train station at the village of **Trechtingshausen**, 2km west.

Burg Reichenstein

Mid-March to mid-Nov Tues–Sun 10am–6pm • €5 • ⊕ burg-reichenstein.de

A short walk from the village of Trechtingshausen leads up to the landmark Rhineland **Burg Reichenstein**, whose brooding form looms above the village. The atmospheric interior is appropriately cluttered with hunting trophies, armour and timeworn furnishings.

Burg Sooneck

Tues–Sun: Jan–March, Oct & Nov 9am–5pm; April–Sept 9am–6pm • €4 • ⊕ burgen-rlp.de

Some 6km east of Bacharach sits the fairly obviously nineteenth-century **Burg Sooneck**, mainly of interest for its Biedermeier furniture and paintings. Many boats stop just below the Burg, otherwise the nearest train station is Niederheimbach, a signposted thirty-minute walk away.

Bacharach

Pretty, half-timbered **BACHARACH**, 15km from Bingen, huddles behind a fourteenth-century wall which can be walked for a fine overview of the town. The town's streets radiate from the **Peterskirche** (daily: April–Oct 10am–6pm; Nov–March 10am–5pm), whose bawdy capitals are worth a look: serpents suck at the breasts of a guilty woman to warn against adultery. From here any of the centre's alleyways are good for a wander, full of quirky buildings such as the celebrated **Altes Haus** at Oberstr. 61, which is so wonky it seems to lean in all directions at once. Many of them house *Weinstuben*, where you should try local favourite *Hahnenhof* Riesling. If your legs are up to it afterwards, take a short walk up to **Burg Stahleck**, a twelfth-century castle reached via a path beside the Peterskirche. It once served as the seat of the Count Palatine of the Rhine, but now provides fabulous hostel accommodation (see below).

10

INFORMATION

BACHARACH

Tourist office Oberstr. 45 (April–Oct Mon–Fri 9am–5pm, Sat & Sun 10am–3pm; Nov–March Mon–Fri 9am–noon; ☎06743 91 93 03, ⊕rhein-nahe-touristik.de).

Located beside the Peterskirche and close to most local accommodation.

ACCOMMODATION

Campingplatz Sonnenstrand Strandbadweg 9 ☎06743 17 52, ⊕camping-sonnenstrand.de. Pleasant campground with dated facilities 500m south of town beside the main road and Rhine. Open April–Oct. Also has a basic restaurant serving *Schnitzel*, steaks and the like (mains €8–14). Restaurant daily 9am–10am, noon–2pm & 6–9pm. Pitch **€3**, plus **€5.50** per adult

★**DJH Bacharach** ☎06743 12 66, ⊕diejugend herbergen.de. Wonderfully atmospheric hostel in the medieval Burg Stahleck, with grand views over the Rhine and surrounding vineyards. Rooms sleep one to six and are almost

all en suite. Breakfast included; well-priced half- and full-board deals available. Dorms **€21.50**, doubles **€54**

Im Malerwinkel Blücherstr. 41 ☎06743 12 39, ⊕im-malerwinkel.de. Best budget choice is this lovely half-timbered house built into the old town wall; all rooms are en suite and there's a guest kitchen and a private terrace and rose garden in which to kick back. **€68**

Rhein Hotel Langstr. 50 ☎06743 12 43, ⊕rhein-hotel-bacharach.de. Excellent family-run, half-timbered hotel with spotless rooms, located alongside the town's ramparts. **€98**

EATING AND DRINKING

★**Altes Haus** Oberstr. 61 ☎06743 12 09. One of the Rhine region's most famously attractive buildings, where trout and salads are good for a light bite, but the hungry should choose the *Wildschwein* (wild boar) in a *Spätburgunder* and rosemary sauce; most mains are around €13. Daily noon–4pm & 6pm–midnight.

Kurpfälzische Münze Oberstr. 72 ☎06743 13 75. Worthwhile old favourite with a snug interior that bursts with character. The *Münzteller* (€12) – a large plate of hams, cheeses and breads – is a summer treat, particularly when washed down with Bacharacher Reisling. Daily noon–10pm.

Rhein Hotel Langstr. 50 ☎06743 12 43, ⊕rhein-hotel-bacharach.de. Good regional food, including *Rieslingbräten* – a pot roast, marinated for days in Riesling wine and mustard, then served with *Spätzle* (mains average €13). Daily except Tues 5–9.15pm.

Zum Grünen Baum Oberstr. 63 ☎06743 12 08, ⊕insel-riesling.de. Perfect, atmospheric half-timbered old *Weinstube*, with some outdoor seating, where you can enjoy a sampler of fifteen wines for €14. Uniquely, one wine comes from a family-run vineyard on an island in the Rhine. Daily noon–late.

Kaub

KAUB, 4km from Bacharach but on the opposite bank of the Rhine – and linked by a car ferry that runs in all but high-water conditions (daily, hours vary but at least 8am–7pm; ⊕faehre-kaub.de) – is famed for the unusual **Burg Pfalzgrafenstein**. The chief claim to fame of Kaub itself, meanwhile, is as the site where Prussian general Blücher constructed a vital pontoon bridge in a Napoleonic campaign. The general later became famous for his timely intervention that won the day at Waterloo. The townhouse he used as his headquarters is now the **Blüchermuseum**, Metzgergasse 6 (April–Oct Tues–Sun 11am–5pm; Nov Sat & Sun 10am–4pm; ⊕bluechermuseum-kaub.de), where much military clutter evokes the time.

Burg Pfalzgrafenstein

Jan, Feb & Nov Sat & Sun 10am–5pm; March Tues–Sun 10am–5pm; April–Oct Tues–Sun 10am–6pm • €5 including ferry from Kaub (every 30min) • ⊕burg-pfalzgrafenstein.de

Victor Hugo memorably described this castle as "A ship of stone, eternally afloat upon the Rhine, and eternally lying at anchor …" Indeed, it does appear to be "moored" on an islet, where it was built by Ludwig the Bavarian in 1325 to levy tolls on Rhine shipping. The gun bastions and lookouts are seventeenth-century additions.

Oberwesel

Some 5km north of Kaub, and back on the left bank, the charming wine-town of **OBERWESEL** boasts the best-preserved medieval fortifications in the region. A 3km-long medieval wall, dotted with guard towers, surrounds most of the Altstadt and would be picture-perfect, were it not for the railway lines that clumsily separate the town from the river.

Stadtmuseum

Rathausstr. 23 • April–Oct Tues–Fri 10am–5pm, Sat & Sun 2–5pm; Nov–March Tues–Fri 10am–2pm • €2.50 • ⓦ kulturhaus-oberwesel.de

The Altstadt is quickly explored, but its local history museum, the **Stadtmuseum**, is worth a closer look. It's within the Kulturhaus cultural complex and is known for a collection of nineteenth-century engravings that romanticized this stretch of Rhine. Also intriguing are a series of photos that depict a quirky local tradition: every April since the 1940s a local lady has been crowned a *Weinhexe* – a good witch who protects the wine harvest.

INFORMATION

OBERWESEL

Tourist office Rathausstr. 3 (April & May Mon–Thurs 9am–1pm & 2–5pm, Fri 9am–1pm & 2–6pm; June–Oct Mon–Thurs 9am–1pm & 2–5pm, Fri 9am–1pm & 2–6pm, Sat 9am–1pm; Nov–March Mon–Thurs 9am–1pm & 2–5pm, Fri 9am–1pm; ☎06744 71 06 24, ⓦoberwesel .de).

ACCOMMODATION AND EATING

★ **Burghotel Auf Schönburg** Auf Schönburg ☎06744 939 30, ⓦburghotel-schoenburg.de. Rooms in a Rhine castle from 1914, tacked onto ruins that date as far back as the tenth century, and with a glamorous *fin-de-siècle* feel. Closed Feb. **€250**

Hotel Römerkrug Marktplatz 1 ☎06744 81 76, ⓦ hotel-roemerkrug.rhinecastles.com. Dignified half-timbered place with old-fashioned rooms with wooden beams and four-poster beds, as well as all the usual modern amenities. The restaurant has much the same atmosphere and a predictable range of German favourites, most around €15. Restaurant Thurs–Tues 6–10pm. **€80**

St Goar

Some 7km downstream of Oberwesel lies the smaller but far more popular town of **ST GOAR**. Much of this bustle is thanks to the presence of St Goarshausen and the Loreley (see p.538) on the opposite riverbank and linked by a **car ferry** (Mon–Fri 5.30am–midnight, Sat & Sun 6.30am–midnight; ⓦfaehre-loreley.de). However, its own sprawling, ruined **Burg Rheinfels** is equally worthwhile. In the town itself, the **Heimatmuseum** (May–Oct daily 10am–12.30pm & 1–5.30pm; free) is worth a look for early models of the castle.

Burg Rheinfels

Mid-March to early Nov daily 9am–6pm • €4 • ☎06741 383 • A steep 20min uphill walk from its riverside car park, or a short trip on the Burgexpress shuttle (April–Oct every 20min; €3)

Burg Rheinfels is one of the most evocative Rhine castles, with an under-siege history. In 1255 the then-new building survived a fourteen-month siege by the nine thousand troops of the Rhineland City League, and under the Hesse Landgraves it blossomed into a magnificent Renaissance fortress which frustrated 28,000 troops of Louis XIV during the 1692 War of Palatinate Succession. Ironically, it fell in 1794 without a shot being fired. Seduced by the promise of "Liberté, égalité, fraternité!" commandant

10

General von Resius yielded to French troops and was later executed for his naïveté. No wonder, because the French immediately demolished the only castle they were unable to take by force in the war, to leave spectacular, labyrinthine ruins.

INFORMATION   ST GOAR

Tourist office Heerstr. 86, a couple of minutes' walk downstream of the car ferry (April & Oct Mon–Fri 9am–12.30pm & 1.30–5pm; May–Sept Mon–Fri 9am–6pm, Sat 10am–1pm; Nov–March Mon–Thurs 9am–12.30pm & 1.30–5pm, Fri 9am–2pm; ☎ 06741 383, ⓦ st-goar.de).

ACCOMMODATION AND EATING

Hotel Schloss Rheinfels Schlossberg 47 ☎ 0641 80 20, ⓦ schloss-rheinfels.de. Elegant lodgings in the wing of an otherwise ruined Rhine castle with wonderful views of the Loreley from individually furnished rooms. Its top-notch gourmet restaurant likes to serve game from the nearby Hünsrück highlands; try the smoked venison with celery and mango salad. Four courses €70. Restaurant Tues–Sat 6.30pm–late. **€190**

Hotel zur Loreley Heerstr. 87 ☎ 06741 16 14, ⓦ hotel-zur-loreley.de. Central hotel with bright and spotless standard rooms and a good regional restaurant with a vast local wine selection and mains for around €13. Also has a good little shop selling local wines at fair prices. Restaurant Mon–Fri 5pm–late, Sat & Sun 11.30am–late. **€76**

Zum Goldenen Löwen Heerstr. 82 ☎ 06741 28 52. Best local bet for food, serving traditional top-notch German cuisine (mains average €14). There's lots of fish – meaty Zander, or light Felchen from the Bodensee – but true culinary adventurers should try the regional delicacy Pfälzer Saumagen (pig's stomach stuffed with cabbage) or Braten vom Spanferkal (roasted suckling pig). Also rents spotless standard rooms with mismatched furniture. Daily 11am–11pm. **€79**

St Goarshausen and the Loreley

Across the Rhine from St Goar, **ST GOARSHAUSEN** is famous above all for the **Loreley**, a giant rock outcrop above town. Legends claim an alluring siren sat on the Loreley, combing her blonde locks and bewitching sailors with her beauty and plaintive song. Then, distracted from their job, the sailors would be lured to their deaths in the awkward currents along this stretch of the Rhine – as it thins to its narrowest point between Switzerland and the North Sea. The maiden is portrayed in bronze at river level, but more impressive is the view from the outcrop. If you can't face the thirty-minute climb, drive or take a shuttle bus (April–Oct hourly; €2.50) from the tourist office. At the summit, the **Loreley Besucherzentrum** visitors' centre (April–Oct daily 10am–6pm; €2.50; ☎ 06771 59 90 93, ⓦ loreley-besucherzentrum.de) has engaging displays on the region's geography and natural history and the history of Rhine Valley tourism.

Burg Katz and Burg Maus

Above St Goarshausen is the thirteenth-century customs castle **Burg Katz** (closed to the public), which the counts of Katzenelnbogen built to trump the Archbishop of Trier's castle then known as Burg Peterseck, 3km downstream above Wellmich. The latter became nicknamed **Burg Maus** as a play on the cat-and-mouse game being played. The castle is occasionally open for tours – enquire and buy tickets at the tourist office in St Goarshausen.

INFORMATION   ST GOARSHAUSEN

Tourist office Bahnhofstr. 8, by the train station (April–Oct Mon–Fri 9am–5pm, Sat 10am–noon; Nov–March Mon–Thurs 9am–12.30pm & 2–5pm, Fri 9am–1pm; ☎ 06771 91 00, ⓦ loreley-touristik.de).

ACCOMMODATION AND EATING

Berghotel auf der Loreley Auf der Loreley ☎ 06771 809 20, ⓦ berghotel-loreley.de. Modern place with small rooms and a good German restaurant (mains €8–19) with a fine outdoor terrace and great setting on the Loreley. Restaurant daily 11.30am–8pm. **€75**

Campingplatz auf der Loreley Auf der Loreley 5

☎ 06771 80 26 97. The best local campsite is this family-run place which has plenty of well-shaded sites, and great Rhine views from its bistro to boot. Showers are included. **€9.50** per person

★**Loreley Weinstuben** Bahnhofstr. 16 ☎ 06771 70 68, ⓦ loreleyweinstuebchen.de. Snug, unpretentious restaurant with all sorts of fresh fish, an excellent wine-laced *Rieslingschnitzel* (€8) and a surprising selection of exotic meats such as kangaroo and crocodile. Also offers

tiny, bright, modern rooms. Restaurant daily 11am–11pm. **€60**

Rheingold Professor-Müller-Str. 2 ☎ 06771 450, ⓦ rheingold-kaiser.de. Good riverfront restaurant which does a great *Rheinischer Börsetopf* – a rich meatball-and-vegetable stew (€12) – and has fine views of Burg Rheinfels from an upstairs terrace that's preferable to its shamelessly chintzy dining-room. Daily 11am–10pm.

Boppard

Strung along the outside of a horseshoe bend in the Rhine, 21km south of Koblenz and 14km upstream of St Goar, **BOPPARD** is a sizeable and attractive place, which is reasonably touristy, despite having few real sights. Its great assets are its riverfront **promenade** and a chairlift that takes visitors to the **Vierseenblick**, an attractive viewpoint above town.

The place centres on its right-angled Marktplatz, home to a Friday-morning market and the late Romanesque **Severuskirche**, in which tender medieval frescoes venerate its patron saint. The square south of the church is the busiest and adjoins main shopping street Oberstrasse. Crossing it is Kirchgasse, which leads to the **Römer-Kastell**, a preserved part of Boppard's fourth-century Roman walls. Of the 28 watchtowers that once graced the military camp, four have been preserved and illustrations on information boards here help conjure up the past.

Karmelitenkirche

Two minutes' walk west of Marktplatz along Oberstrasse lies Karmeliterstrasse, named after a Carmelite monastery that once stood here. Its church, the **Karmelitenkirche**, is noteworthy for particularly egalitarian carvings on its Gothic choir which celebrate farmers alongside monks and prophets. Local farmers have taken this to heart, and for as long as anyone can recall have placed the season's first ripe grapes in a niche outside alongside the **Traubenmadonna**, or Grape Madonna, to receive her blessing. It seems to work, as Boppard is known for excellent Rieslings. The Rhine is just north of here, and a leafy riverfront promenade leads east back towards the town centre.

The Alter Burg: Museum der Stadt Boppard

Burgplatz • April–Oct Tues–Sun 10am–12.30pm & 1.30–5pm • Free • ⓦ museum-boppard.de

Rearing up a little beyond the Marktplatz, the **Alter Burg** is easily the most impressive building on Boppard's riverfront. Built in 1340 as a stronghold and tollhouse for the Elector Balduin of Trier, it now houses the **Museum der Stadt Boppard**. This local history collection makes much of local cabinetmaker Michael Thonet (1796–1871), who invented **bentwood furniture**. By soaking layered strips of veneer in hot glue then bending them into shape in metal moulds, he created elegantly curved furniture that became all the rage in the mid-nineteenth century. His curved-frame chairs – effectively two hoops joined together – are the best known, having graced thousands of European cafés since then.

Gedeonseck and the Vierseenblick

Chairlift daily: April–Oct 10am–6pm; Nov–March 10am–5pm • €7 return, mountain bike day-pass €12

The 1950s chairlift at Boppard's northern end, **Sesselbahn Boppard**, makes its unhurried journey to two premier viewpoints, each with attendant restaurant and attractive terrace. **Gedeonseck**, near the summit of the chairlift, affords perfect views of the Rhine's hairpin curve; while a five-minute walk further on, the famous **Vierseenblick**, or Four Lakes View, is so-called because the four visible sections of the Rhine look disconnected.

10

The pleasant wooded terrain around here is home to a few good **hikes**, the most rewarding and adventurous of which is the **Klettersteig** – a clamber up precipitous rock faces with the aid of chains and ladders set into the rock. It's best climbed rather than descended – a perfect three-hour loop for the reasonably fit, starting from the base of the chairlift, which you can use to get back down if your legs give out. It's also possible to drive or cycle up to the Vierseenblick, and locals have built a pretty hairy **mountain-bike trail** from the summit.

10

INFORMATION AND TOURS   BOPPARD

Tourist office Marktplatz (May–Sept Mon–Fri 9am–6.30pm, Sat 10am–2pm; Oct–April Mon–Fri 9am–5pm; ☎ 06742 38 88, ⓦ boppard-tourismus.de).

Wine-tasting tours The tourist office organizes wine tastings (April–Oct; €5) at local vineyards.

ACCOMMODATION AND EATING

Bellevue Rheinallee 41 ☎ 06742 10 20, ⓦ bellevue-boppard.de. Luxurious waterfront lodgings, which still exude 1887 grandeur and where the choicest antique-decorated rooms overlook the Rhine. Gourmet meals in its elegant *Chopin* restaurant, one of several here, are served to piano music (mains around €18). Restaurant Mon & Thurs–Sun 6pm–late. **€195**

★ **Severusstube** Untere Marktstr. 7 ☎ 06742 37 18, ⓦ severus-stube.de. For hearty food and low prices try this snug, wood-beamed inn where dishes including the rack of lamb or half-kilo *Schweinehaxe* should satisfy the largest of appetites. Mains run €8–13. Mon, Tues & Fri–Sun 11.30am–2pm & 5pm–late, Wed 5pm–late; kitchen closes 10pm.

Weinhaus Heilig Grab Zelkesgasse 12 ☎ 06742 23 71, ⓦ heiliggrab.de. Two-hundred-year-old wine bar opposite the Hauptbahnhof whose lovely shady garden is the ideal place to sip local wine; there's nothing much of note on the menu but the *Flammkuchen* (€8) is an excellent accompaniment. Also offers smart little rooms. Restaurant daily except Tues 3pm–late. **€63**

Braubach and the Marksburg

Castle tours daily: late March to Oct 10am–5pm, tours in English 1pm & 4pm; Nov to late March 11am–4pm • €6 • ⓦ marksburg.de • 12min train journey from Koblenz's Hauptbahnhof to Braubach, then follow one of three signed walking routes uphill (approx 20min)

BRAUBACH, just two tight horseshoe bends downstream of Boppard but on the opposite bank, is a half-timbered delight that's best known for its magnificent **Marksburg**, one of the Rhine Gorge's most impressive castles with as fine a hilltop setting as any. It's also one of the few castles never to have been destroyed, making its huddle of towers and turrets authentically medieval. Tour highlights include an atmospheric Gothic grand hall and an armoury that bristles with weapons and grisly torture instruments.

Schloss Stolzenfels

Tues–Sun: Jan–March, Oct & Nov 10am–5pm; April–Sept 9am–6pm • €4 • ⓦ schloss-stolzenfels.de • Bus #650 from Koblenz Hauptbahnhof to "Stolzenfels-Schlossweg", a signed 15 min walk from the castle gates

Over the river and 3km upstream of the Marksburg castle and 5km upstream of Koblenz, a series of set-square-perfect crenellated battlements belong to **Schloss Stolzenfels**, a Prussian rebuild of a thirteenth-century castle that French troops reduced to rubble in 1689. The ruins were given to Friedrich Wilhelm IV who entrusted the task of rebuilding the structure as a summer residence to celebrated architect Karl Friedrich Schinkel, who used original plans and local styles but added touches from elsewhere, particularly Moorish architecture. The results almost caricature mid-nineteenth-century Romanticism: an oversized toy castle where medieval fantasies were played out in lavish neo-Gothic living quarters where Queen Victoria once stayed.

Koblenz

Founded as the Roman settlement Confluentes at the confluence of the Rhine and Mosel in 10 BC, **KOBLENZ**, some 90km downstream of Mainz, marks the transition from the Rhine Gorge to the gentler landscapes of the Middle Rhine, which continue down to Bonn 70km away. Its strategic location has meant it has been fought over and conquered several times, most notably by the Swedes in the Thirty Years' War, the French in 1794 and the Russians in 1814, and turned over to Prussia in 1822 only to be comprehensively destroyed by British Lancaster bombers towards the end of World War II. In its rebuilt form – a mix of old-looking and modern – it's a relaxed if unexciting town with few sights. But, as the northern gateway to the Romantic Rhine – several cruises down both the Rhine (see box, p.535) and Mosel (see p.543) start here – and with a good collection of bars and restaurants in a likeable pedestrian centre, it makes a good base. The best time to be in town is during the annual **Rhein in Flammen** (Rhine in Flames; ⓦrhein-in-flammen.de) festival in August, a firework bonanza, best appreciated from **Festung Ehrenbreitstein** fortress above town or on one of a convoy of boats on the river.

10

The Deutsches Eck and around

Exploration of Koblenz is best started at the point where it was founded, on a promontory adjacent to the Rhine–Mosel confluence called the **Deutsches Eck** (bus #1 from the Hauptbahnhof). A large statue of Kaiser Wilhelm I on horseback presides over it and behind him there's yet more Germanic pedigree in the form of the **Deutschherrenhaus**, once the thirteenth-century headquarters of the Teutonic Knights, and today home to the **Ludwig Museum** of modern and contemporary art (Tues–Sat 10.30am–5pm, Sat 11am–6pm; €5; ⓦludwigmuseum.org). The collection is primarily focused on postwar French art, though the temporary exhibitions are far more eclectic.

South of the Deutschherrenhaus, the **Rheinpromenade** is a pleasant promenade that stretches for around 3km along the banks of the Rhine, and is worth strolling for its riverside views, though the heart of town lies west.

The Altstadt

The picturesque and brightly painted **Altstadt** centres on a series of small squares of which the **Florinsmarkt** is the closest to the Mosel, just a block in from its southern bank. Its **Florinskirche** is known above all for the *Augenroller*, a figure below its clock who rolls its eyes and sticks its tongue out every half-hour (June–Aug daily 11am–5pm).

Liebfrauenkirche

An der Liebfrauenkirche 16 • Daily 8.30am–6pm

Alleys from the Florinsmarkt lead south to the **Liebfrauenkirche**, Koblenz's main church which, despite its Baroque onion-domed towers, is of Romanesque origin. Inside, the Gothic choir and chancel stand out. The Liebfrauenkirche is surrounded by a square where restaurants and cafés have attractive outdoor seating.

Am Plan

Am Plan lies just south of the Liebfrauenkirche and is accessed by an alley. This civic space has had a particularly bloody past, with a spell as a butcher's market and as the town's main place for executions and medieval tournaments. At its southwestern corner, at the crossroads of two main shopping streets, lie the **Vier Türme**: four seventeenth-century buildings celebrated for their ornate facades.

Forum Confluentes and the Mittelrhein-Museum

Zentralplatz 1 • Tues–Sun 10am–6pm • €6 • ⓦ mittelrhein-museum.de

Gracing the southern edge of Koblenz's Altstadt with its elegant glassy presence, the state-of-the-art **Forum Confluentes** building incorporates the city library, the tourist information office (see below) and the **Mittelrhein-Museum**, a regional history museum. The museum is particularly interesting for its collection of nineteenth-century paintings that helped romanticize this stretch of the Rhine. Also of interest are works of leading Rococo painter Januarius Zick, who lived in Koblenz. The complementary adjacent building encloses a large, top-notch shopping mall.

10

Festung Ehrenbreitstein

Festung Ehrenbreitstein Daily 10am–midnight • €6 including Landesmuseum, free after 6pm • **Landesmuseum** Mid-April to late Oct daily 10am–5pm; late Oct to mid-April Sat & Sun 10am–5pm • €6 • ⓦ landesmuseumkoblenz.de • From Koblenz take the passenger ferry (Easter to mid-Nov Mon–Fri 8am–6.55pm, Sat & Sun 8.30am–6.55pm; €1.50), from the Rheinpromenade, then a chairlift (daily: late April, May & Oct 10am–6.30pm; June–Sept 10am–10pm; €9 return, combined ticket with Landesmuseum €11.80), or bus #9 or #10 to "Obertal" and walk 10min

Watching over Koblenz's Altstadt on the east bank of the Rhine, the gigantic fortress **Festung Ehrenbreitstein** has a commanding position over everything. So mighty was it that it proved impregnable until 1801 when Napoleonic troops comprehensively destroyed it. Today's version is an impressive 1832 Prussian rebuild that houses various enterprises, including a hostel, restaurants and the **Landesmuseum**, which mainly explores the region from the point of view of the industries that shaped it: trade, tobacco, wine, photography and automobiles – the latter a tribute to August Horch, the founder of Audi who hailed from Winningen, 10km upstream along the Mosel.

ARRIVAL AND INFORMATION   KOBLENZ

By train Koblenz's Hauptbahnhof lies a little over 1km southwest of the Altstadt.
Destinations Frankfurt (hourly; 1hr 30min); Saarbrücken (hourly; 2hr 30min); Speyer (hourly; 2hr); Trier (hourly; 1hr 30min); Worms (hourly; 1hr 45min).
Tourist office The main branch is at central Zentralplatz 1

(daily 10am–6pm; ☎0261 313 04, ⓦ koblenz-touristik .de); another branch is at the Rhine-front Konrad-Adenauer-Ufer (April–Oct Fri 1–4pm, Sat & Sun 10am–4pm). The tourist office accommodation booking service can be useful since the town is a hub for large coach parties and hotels can fill quickly.

ACCOMMODATION

HOTELS
Diehl's Hotel Rheinsteigufer ☎0261 19 70 70, ⓦ diehls-hotel.de. A bit dated maybe, but the riverside location, views of the Rhine and good facilities, which include a pool and sauna, make up for it. Rooms are smart, modern and bright and there are some pretty luxurious suites to choose from too. **€99**
Hotel Brenner Rizzastr. 20–22 ☎0261 91 57 80, ⓦ hotel-brenner.de. Elegant, friendly and great-value hotel a 5min walk south of the Altstadt, with spotless, if dated, rooms and a garden. Free wi-fi. The extensive breakfast spread includes home-made jams and a variety of fresh coffees. **€101**
Hotel Jan van Werth Von-Werth-Str. 9 ☎0261 365 00, ⓦ hoteljanvanwerth.de. Great little budget family-run bed and breakfast, located midway between the Hauptbahnhof and Altstadt, with bright, pine-furnished rooms, some of which share a bathroom. **€66**
Kleiner Riesen Kaiserin-Augusta-Anlagen 18 ☎0261 30 34 60, ⓦ hotel-kleinerriesen.de. Traditional place

southeast of the town centre and one of the few places to stay that fronts the Rhine. The rooms are a bit chintzy, but there are several public rooms and the atmosphere is relaxed. Free wi-fi. **€95**

HOSTELS AND CAMPSITES
Campingplatz Rhein-Mosel Schartwiesenweg 6 ☎0261 827 19, ⓦ camping-rhein-mosel.de. Spacious campground opposite the Deutsches Eck and Festung Ehrenbreitstein and with good views of both. A passenger ferry across the Mosel gives campers a convenient way to get to the Altstadt. Pitch **€11**, plus **€8.50** per person
DJH Koblenz Festung Ehrenbreitstein ☎0261 97 28 70, ⓦ diejugendherbergen.de. One of Germany's most remarkable hostels, deep inside the Festung Ehrenbreitstein citadel, yet with modern facilities and incredible views from its terrace over the Rhine, Mosel and Koblenz, particularly when there's a good sunset. Many rooms are en suite. Guests get discounts on the chairlift and free entry to Festung Ehrenbreitstein. Dorms **€22.50**, doubles **€56**

EATING AND DRINKING

CAFÉS, BARS AND WEINSTUBEN

★**Affenclub** Münzstr. 16 ☎0261 921 79 24. One-time gay and lesbian bar that's long since become popular across the board, and is always packed to the gunnels until the early hours, sometimes till 6am. As for the monkeys (*Affen*) – they're soft toys dangling all over the place amid plenty of greenery. Daily 5pm–late.

Cafe Miljöö Gemüsegasse 12 ☎261 142 37, ⓦcafe-miljoeoe.de. Stylish traditional café with fresh flowers, greenery and a sophisticated feel which help make it a good spot to come for breakfast, salad lunches or home-made cakes later on. Great coffee. Mon–Thurs & Sun 9am–1am, Fri 9am–2am, Sat 8am–2am.

Irish Pub Koblenz Burgstr. 7 ☎0261 973 77 97, ⓦirishpubkoblenz.de. Convivial pub with regular live music on weekend nights; a favourite with local English-speakers. Cheerful bar staff and a large range of drinks – and not just from the Emerald Isle. Mon–Thurs 4pm–1am, Fri 4pm–2am, Sat 3pm–2am, Sun 3pm–1am.

Weindorf Julius-Wegeler-Str. 2 ☎0261 133 71 90, ⓦweindorf-koblenz.de. A small group of wine taverns around a mock village square off the Rheinpromenade: touristy but fun for standard German food like *Schnitzels* and wine (mains €7–18). The beer garden can be good fun late in the day. Daily 11am–late.

Weinhaus Hubertus Florinsmarkt 6 ☎0261 311 77, ⓦweinhaus-hubertus.de. Lovely 1696 Altstadt wine tavern opposite the Old Rathaus with an excellent local wine selection and good seasonal menu with items like pumpkin-flavoured rack of lamb: almost always has an excellent grilled *Zander* (a local perch). Mains €13–22. Mon–Thurs 3pm–late, Fri–Sun noon–late.

RESTAURANTS

Guarida An der Liebfrauenkirche 19 ☎0261 91 46 98 00, ⓦguaridakoblenz.de. Spanish place with plenty of outdoor seating in the shadows of the Liebfrauenkirche. The tapas (most around €5) menu is lengthy and dependable, and includes larger items like salads and omelettes. Daily 10am–midnight.

Los Gauchos Am Plan 7 ☎0261 140 06, ⓦlos-gauchos .de. Great Argentinean steakhouse, with several dishes (average €13) that are flambéed at your table with much showmanship. The Mexican bean salad is an excellent side dish. Daily 11am–11pm.

Pizzeria La Mamma Am Plan 7 ☎0261 177 60. Good Italian place with candle-lit outdoor seating on one of Koblenz's main squares. Great for pizzas (€6–10), of course, but also a range of other dishes including some excellent mussels in white wine sauce in the winter months. Daily noon–midnight.

10

The Mosel Weinstrasse

Along its final 195km-long stretch between Koblenz and Trier the Mosel cuts a sinuous and attractive deep gorge, home to some of Germany's steepest vineyards and best full-bodied wines. The route that follows the banks of the river is known as the **Mosel Weinstrasse**, or Mosel Wine Road. Beautiful vistas await at every bend in the river, from the picture-perfect hilltop castle perched above Cochem, to vineyard-cloaked hills that plunge steeply down to the river, but the highlights of the route are the faultless medieval castle **Burg Eltz**, **Traben-Trarbach** with its attractive Jugendstil villas, and **Bernkastel-Kues**, the Weinstrasse's most colourful town.

GETTING AROUND   THE MOSEL WEINSTRASSE

By train and bus The northern half of the river, as far as the town of Bullay, is served by rail; the southern portion, to Trier, is covered by frequent Moselbahn buses (☎0651 968 00, ⓦmoselbahn.de).

By boat Three companies run boat trips along the Mosel: Köln-Düsseldorfer (ⓦk-d.com) cover the northern leg between Cochem and Koblenz; Mosel-Schiffs-Touristik (ⓦmoselpersonenschifffahrt .de) concentrate on the middle leg around Traben-Trarbach and Bernkastel-Kues; and Personenschifffarht Gebrüder Kolb (ⓦmoselfahrplan.de) sails from Trier to Bernkastel-Kues.

FRANKFURT-HAHN AIRPORT

Popular with budget carriers like Ryanair, Frankfurt-Hahn Airport (HHN) (☎06543 50 92 00, ⓦhahn-airport.de), may be hopelessly inconvenient for Frankfurt, but is an ideal hub for the Rhine and Mosel valleys. Buses from the airport go to Koblenz (6 daily; 1hr 5min), Mainz (14 daily; 1hr 10min) and Trier (20 daily; 1hr), and there are five car-rental companies to choose from.

By bike and on foot The extensive combination of train, bus and boat links make it easy to explore sections of long-distance hiking and cycling routes as day-trips: the Moselhöhenweg hiking trail runs along the top of both valley sides; the Mosel-Radweg cycle route goes all the way to Metz in France, but is most popular along the 210km stretch from Koblenz to Trier. All forms of transport take bikes.

Burg Eltz

April–Oct 9.30am–5.30pm • €8 • ⓦ burg-eltz.de • Burg Eltz's car park, signposted from the village of Münstermaifeld, is an 800m walk from the castle (shuttle bus €2). A more attractive approach is via the riverside town of Moselkern (regular trains from Koblenz and Trier, or passenger boat); follow signs to the *Ringelsteiner Mühle*, an inn with a car park 2km behind Moselkern along the Eltztal road, from which a 45min trail follows the valley to the castle

Tucked in a hidden valley, 29km southwest of Koblenz, **Burg Eltz** is a hot contender for the title of Germany's finest castle. The setting is absolutely perfect, with the fortification standing on a seemingly purpose-built knuckle of rock at the centre of a wooded and otherwise deserted small valley, and the structure itself is an archetypal Romantic castle. Its first stones were laid in the twelfth century, and though there have been plenty of later additions, with the greatest portion built between the mid-fifteenth and mid-sixteenth centuries, the compact turreted pile has never been destroyed or rebuilt. But it did have its share of close shaves: it was under siege for two years in the early fourteenth century and during the general regional destruction by the French in 1689 it was only saved by the good fortune of having a family member in the French army. After the attractive setting and exterior, tours of the well-preserved **interior** are a bit anticlimactic, but its **treasury** contains some well-crafted gold and silver among the family booty, and its armoury some painful and unwieldy-looking items.

Traben-Trarbach

The twin town of **TRABEN-TRARBACH**, straddling the Mosel 55km south of Koblenz, is notable for its attractive collection of Jugendstil villas. Though lacking any kind of heart, a couple of appealing promenades follow both banks of the broad river, which is sometimes used for speedboat and waterskiing competitions, but more frequently by the boats of the Mosel-Schiffs-Touristik (May to mid-July Sat & Sun; mid-July to Oct daily; €14 one-way; ☎06531 82 22, ⓦmoselpersonenschifffahrt.de), which sail five times a day to Bernkastel-Kues, giving you the option of taking the boat one-way, then returning on a reasonably strenuous scenic 8km walk back.

Traben

The town itself doesn't take long to look around: **Traben**, on the north side of the Mosel, where the tourist office, bus and train station are, is more workmanlike, though fans of Jugendstil design will want to look at the riverside **Hotel Bellevue**. It was Berlin architect Bruno Möhring who gave it its hallmark turret, domed tower gables and high-pitched roof as well as elaborate timberwork and oak lobby. Step inside to admire the stained glass. There's another chance to admire his work while crossing the bridge to Trarbach where **Brückentor**, which he designed, acts as a sentinel at the bridge's end.

Trarbach

Trarbach, on the southern bank of the Mosel, has a couple of pretty but unspectacular pedestrian streets, which are quickly seen en route to its Marktplatz. From the Marktplatz a steep footpath leads up to the **Grevenburg**, the ruined fourteenth-century castle that watches over town. There's not much left of it, but considering it was laid siege to six times and destroyed seven, that even two walls remain is a small wonder.

10

GREEN HELL: THE NÜRBURGRING

The Eifel, the tranquil region immediately northwest of the Mosel Valley, is known for sleepy villages, gentle hills and bare heathland, but famous for the incongruous **Nürburgring** (☎02691 30 26 30, ⓦnuerburgring.de), a racetrack that's one of motorsport's most hallowed pieces of tarmac.

Among aficionados, its **Nordschleife** (north loop), completed in 1927, is widely considered the world's toughest, most dangerous and most demanding purpose-built racetrack. With 73 curves along its 22.8km length it proved so difficult that over the years it's claimed dozens of lives, including those of four Formula One drivers. Jackie Stewart dubbed it "The Green Hell", though he chalked up three wins here, including one of his finest ever in the rain and fog of 1968. Some eight years later Niki Lauda's near-fatal crash caused race organizers to move things to Mannheim's Hockenheimring in 1977, though the building of the **Südschleife** in 1984 brought Formula One back and it now alternates with the Hockenheimring as the venue for the annual German Grand Prix.

DRIVING THE NÜRBURGRING

Other motorsports and novelty events, such as old-timer races, regularly use the track, but when these aren't on it's possible to **drive the Nordschleife** (generally daily 9am–dusk, but check online first; €27). Despite common misconceptions to the contrary, German road law applies: speed limits exist, though not everywhere, and passing on the right is prohibited.

For an inside view of the real deal and speeds of up to 320kmph, book a passenger seat in the **BMW Ring-Taxi** (March–Nov Mon–Fri 10am–noon; ☎02691 93 20 20, ⓦbmw-motorsport .com/ms_en), who charge €225 for up to three people (anyone over 150cm tall). It's popular and often booked up months in advance, though last-minute cancellations are not unheard of.

THE RINGWERK

Otherwise visit the excellent visitor centre **Ringwerk** (hours vary, generally late March to Oct & late Dec daily 10am–5pm; €16.90), with its many white-knuckle high-tech racing simulators, films and exhibits, which will keep kids busy for hours.

GETTING THERE

The Nürburgring lies 46km west of Koblenz and is tricky to get to using public transport: look online under ⓦbahn.de for train and bus connections from your nearest town to "Nürburgring welcome center". The nearest train station is Mayen; buses also arrive from Adenau.

From their vantage point you can make out a spot on the opposite bank that has seen similar activity: Louis XIV built a fortress here in the late seventeenth century, which only survived a few decades before its dismantling.

ARRIVAL AND INFORMATION

By train The station, with regular connections to Koblenz (12 daily; 1hr 15min), lies beside the tourist office.
Tourist office Am Bahnhof 5 (May–Oct Mon–Fri

TRABEN-TRARBACH

10am–5pm, Sat 11am–3pm; Nov–April Mon–Fri 10am–4pm; ⓦtraben-trarbach.de). Organizes local wine tours and will book accommodation.

ACCOMMODATION AND EATING

Brücken-Schenke Brückentor ☎06541 81 84 35, ⓦaltstadtcafe-trarbach.de. Good place to eat in interesting surroundings, with a menu of standard German dishes and fine river views; most mains are around the €10 mark and there's an excellent selection of desserts and cakes. Daily 11am–10pm.
Central Hotel Bahnstr. 43 ☎06541 62 38, ⓦcentral -hotel-traben.de. Truly central, modern and solid family-run mid-market option. Also has a restaurant and beer garden where you can enjoy wines from the family vineyard. Good-value half- or full-board packages offered. **€70**

DJH Traben-Trarbach Hirtenpfad 6 ☎06541 92 78, ⓦdiejugendherbergen.de. Large, modern hostel located a signed 1.2km walk from the station. All rooms are en suite and there's a bistro, as well as wi-fi and a games room. Breakfast is included and full- or half-board is available for €7–10. Dorms **€21.50**; twins **€54**
Hotel Bellevue Am Moselufer ☎06541 70 30, ⓦbellevue-hotel.de. The town's top place to stay with classy antique-furnished rooms, a fitness centre, spa, sauna, pool and free bike rental. Its restaurant will delight gourmands with regional and international dishes (mains average €21). Free wi-fi. Restaurant daily noon–10.30pm. **€165**

Bernkastel-Kues

The twin town of **BERNKASTEL-KUES** nestles by a serpentine bend in the Mosel, some 8km on foot through woods and steep vineyards from Traben-Trarbach, but the terrain is such that the road takes 17km to link the two and the river an even twistier 24km. Against this scenic backdrop, Bernkastel-Kues is a half-timbered gem. Predictably, it's touristy, but with some of the wonkiest houses you'll ever see and wall-to-wall with wine taverns to help distort their dimensions even more, it's a place that shouldn't be passed up. There's always a cheerful buzz about town, but things are liveliest on the first September weekend when gallons of the local *Bernkastelr Doctor* wine are downed with spirited results – even the Marktplatz fountain flows with wine.

10

Bernkastel

Easily the more attractive part of town, tiny **Bernkastel**, on the east bank of the Mosel, gathers behind the **Pfarrkirche St Michael**, a fourteenth-century church that once formed part of the town's defence. A short walk behind, the tiny focal **Marktplatz** is surrounded by half-timbered houses with decorative gables and is so well preserved that if it weren't for the other visitors and souvenir shops, you'd think you'd walked into a medieval street scene – even the ring on the Rathaus onto which miscreants were chained is intact. Just uphill from here is the faintly absurd **Spitzhäuschen**, a tiny, precarious-looking, top-heavy house that's Bernkastel at its most extreme.

Burg Landshut

Castle Open access • Free • **Shuttle bus** April–Oct hourly 10am–6pm • €7 return

From the Marktplatz, the main Mandatstrasse brings you to the back of town and becomes Burgstrasse as far as signs for the 3km hiking trail to **Burg Landshut**, the ruined eleventh- to thirteenth-century castle that surveys this stretch of the Mosel. It served the archbishops of Trier and provides tremendous views of cascading valley hillsides streaked by green vines. The steep hike on easy woodland paths takes about 45 minutes, or hop aboard a shuttle bus from the tourist office.

The St-Nikolaus Hospital and Mosel-Weinmuseum

St-Nikolaus Hospital Cusanusstr. 2 • Mon–Fri & Sun 9am–6pm, Sat 9am–3pm; guided tours in German April–Oct Tues 10.30am, Fri 3pm • Free, tours €5 • ⓦ cusanus.de • **Mosel-Weinmuseum** Daily: mid-April to Oct 10am–5pm; Nov to mid-April 2–5pm • €5 • ⓦ moselweinmuseum.de

In comparison to Bernkastel, the far larger town of **Kues** is rather workaday, though it does have one sight that justifies crossing the river: the **St-Nikolaus Hospital**, a poorhouse founded in 1458 by theologian Nikolaus Cusanus, a local who rose to great ecclesiastical heights as a cardinal in Rome. There's a Gothic chapel and cloister to explore and its library is of interest for Cusanus's extraordinary collection of thousand-year-old manuscripts, though it's only accessible on a guided tour. Also here, in the cellars, is the **Mosel-Weinmuseum**, which has a wine bar where you can taste as many local wines as you like for €15.

ARRIVAL AND INFORMATION

BERNKASTEL-KUES

By bus and train Though not on the rail network, Bernkastel-Kues is efficiently served by buses from Wittlich train station 16km away.

Tourist office Am Gestade 6, by the bridge in Bernkastel (April–Oct Mon–Fri 9am–5pm, Sat 9.30am–5pm, Sun 10am–1pm; Nov–April Mon–Fri 9.30am–4pm; ☎06531 50 01 90, ⓦ bernkastel.de). The tourist office has a hotel reservations board with a free phone – handy since the town is often near-full.

ACCOMMODATION AND EATING

Campingplatz Kueser Werth Am Hafen 2 ☎06531 82 00, ⓦ camping-kueser-werth.de. Lies on a grassy peninsula that juts into the Mosel 2km upstream of Bernkastle and by Kues' yacht harbour. The nicest sites are

10

on the river banks. Pitch €6, plus €6 per person
DJH Bernkastel-Kues Jugendherbergstr. 1 ☎06531
23 95, ⊛diejugendherbergen.de. Basic hostel with
games room beside Burg Landshut on the Bernkastel
side. Great views of the Mosel Valley from the terrace, but
otherwise things are pretty standard. Half- or full-board
packages (an extra €6–8) available. Dorms €17, twins €46
Doctor Weinstuben Hebegasse 5 ☎06531 996 50,
⊛doctor-weinstube-bernkastel.de. Atmospheric, half-
timbered seventeenth-century place with many

woodcarvings and small bright rooms. Its *Weinstube* is
great for traditional German food (mains average €15) and
local wines. Also has bike rental and free wi-fi. Restaurant
daily 7.30am–10.30am, noon–2.30pm & 6–9pm. €143
Zur Post Gestade 17 ☎06531 967 00, ⊛hotel-zur-
post-bernkastel.de. Elegant lodgings with small, bright,
modern pastel rooms and sauna. Also with a good rustic
restaurant serving the usual spread of German mains
(€14–28) and a superb four-course game menu in the
autumn (€39). Daily 11.30pm–late. €110

Trier

South of Bernkastel-Kues the landscape around the Mosel gradually opens up, so that
TRIER, 50km downstream, sits among gentle hills. The city is best known for having
northern Europe's greatest assemblage of **Roman remains**, but Trier is not a place that
lives entirely on its past, and the **vineyards** around the city, along with a large student
population, help liven things up, while the proximity to Luxembourg and France
provides a cosmopolitan feel that makes it an immediately likeable and easy-going
place. It's also a good base for day-trips, not just along the Mosel Valley but also to
Völklinger Hütte (see p.554) and Saarbrücken (see p.553). And if you're driving don't
forget to nip over to Luxembourg for the cheap fuel – price differences have spawned a
minor industry just over the border.

Brief history

Founded as Augusta Treverorum in 15 BC, Trier grew to become capital of the western
Roman Empire by the third century AD. As Rome declined, Trier fell into the hands of
various tribes, including the Huns under Attila, until the Franks eventually asserted
themselves at the end of the fifth century, ushering in a period of relative stability
which saw the city gain independence from Ostfrankenreich in 1212 and become an
archbishopric in 1364. This sparked a second golden age when its archbishops became
prince-electors and vital imperial power-brokers.

The Porta Nigra

Porta Nigra Daily: March & Oct 9am–5pm; April–Sept 9am–6pm; Nov–Feb 9am–4pm • €3 • **Stadtmuseum** Simeonstr. 60 • Tues–Sun
10am–5pm • €5.50 • ⊛museum-trier.de

Incredibly, Trier's northern city gate, the **Porta Nigra**, dates back to the second century.
Its name – Black Gate – comes from its blackening by the passage of time, but it's more
remarkable for its ingenious design, with the entire structure supported by just its own
weight and a few iron rods. In the eleventh century the gate was converted into a
church – St Simeonkirche – and named in honour of a resident Greek hermit. A
monastery, the **Simeonstift**, was attached to the church, but now houses the
Stadtmuseum, a well-above-average local history museum with not only a good Roman
section, but also some fine textiles and East Asian sculptures.

Simeonstrasse and the Hauptmarkt

Simeonstrasse is the broad, straight pedestrian road that leads south from the Porta
Nigra to the **Hauptmarkt** at the Altstadt's centre. At Simeonstr. 19 is the
Dreikönigenhaus, an unusual thirteenth-century Gothic townhouse whose original
entrance was on the first floor at the top of a staircase that could be withdrawn in times
of trouble. The bustling **Hauptmarkt**, home to a market most days, is focused on the

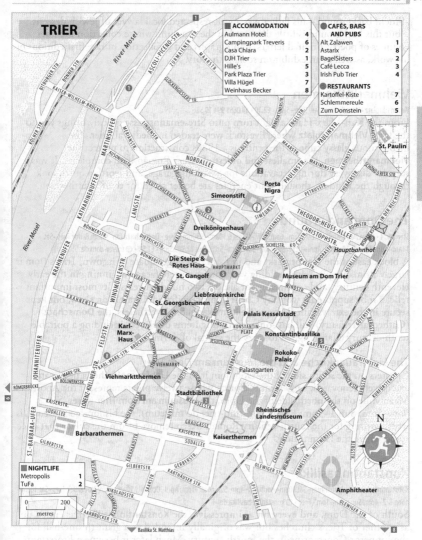

brightly coloured **Petrusbrunnen** fountain, and encircled by grand houses. Among these are the vivid **Rotes Haus** and the eye-catching **Steipe**, a one-time banqueting hall and now a **Spielzeugmuseum** (Toy Museum), a cheerful collection of miniature trains and dolls (Jan–March Tues–Sun 11am–5pm; April–Dec Tues–Sun 11am–6pm; €4.50; ⊕ spielzeugmuseum-trier.de).

The Karl-Marx-Haus

Brückenstr. 10 • April–Oct daily 10am–6pm; Nov–March Mon 2–5pm, Tues–Sun 11am–5pm • €4 • ⊕ fes.de/Karl-Marx-Haus/

From the western corner of the Hauptmarkt, Fleischstrasse leads south into a dense network of Altstadt lanes and directly to the **Karl-Marx-Haus**, where the political philosopher (1818–83) was born and grew up. The bourgeois mansion attests to Marx's affluent background – his father was a well-respected local lawyer of Jewish descent – but this background is little discussed in the museum, whose collection includes volumes of poetry, original letters, photographs and a collection of rare first editions of his work, as well as an exhibit on socialist history.

Viehmarktthermen

Viehmarktplatz • Usually Tues–Sun 9am–5pm • €2.10 • ☎ 0651 994 10 57

From the Karl-Marx-Haus a right turn onto Stresemannstrasse quickly brings you to the large **Viehmarktplatz** where livestock were traded in medieval Trier. The incongruous glassy cube at the centre is a 1980s construction to protect the **Viehmarktthermen**, the smallest and oldest of Trier's Roman bath complexes. It was a surprise discovery during excavations for a parking garage, and worth a quick look through the window, though your energies are better saved for the Kaiserthermen.

The Dom and around

Sternstr. 4 • **Dom** Daily: April–Oct 6.30am–6pm; Nov–March 6.30am–5.30pm • Free • **Domschatz** Jan–March & Nov Tues–Sat 11am–4pm, Sun 12.30–4pm; April–Oct & Dec Mon–Sat 10am–5pm, Sun 12.30–5pm • €1.50 • ⓦ trierer-dom.de

A block east of the Hauptmarkt and in front of a large square of its own, Trier's **Dom** is largely Romanesque, with building work on its austere facade beginning in the early eleventh century (and continuing for almost two hundred years). Its most important relic, a robe supposedly worn by Christ at his crucifixion, is rarely on show, but kept secure in the extravagant Baroque **Heiltumskapelle**. Nevertheless, the **Domschatz** (Cathedral Treasury) still has some interesting items displayed, including a portable tenth-century altar designed to carry the sandal of St Andrew.

The Liebfrauenkirche and the Museum am Dom Trier

Cloisters on the south side of the Dom join it to the **Liebfrauenkirche**, a newly and extensively renovated, early Gothic church whose twelve pillars represent the Apostles. Meanwhile on the north side of the Dom, the **Museum am Dom Trier** (Tues–Sat 9am–5pm, Sun 1–5pm; €3.50; ⓦ bistum-trier.de/museum), the bishopric's museum, is worth visiting for the fourth-century Roman fresco removed from the palace that once stood where the Dom is now.

Konstantinbasilika

Konstantinplatz • Jan–March Tues–Sat 10am–noon & 3–4pm, Sun noon–1pm; April–Oct daily 10am–6pm; Nov & Dec Tues–Sat 10am–noon & 2–4pm, Sun noon–1pm • Free • ⓦ konstantin-basilika.de

South of the Dom, and every bit as impressive, the **Konstantinbasilika** has ended up as another of Trier's churches but was originally intended as a giant throne-hall for the Emperor Constantine in the fourth century. Much later it became a Protestant church for use by prince-electors residing in the neighbouring **Rokoko-Palais** (closed to the public), a garish, pink, Baroque affair that couldn't contrast more with the sombre church.

Rheinisches Landesmuseum

Weimarer Allee 1 • Tues–Sun 10am–5pm • €6 • ⓦ landesmuseum-trier.de

South of the suitably formal gardens of the Rokoko-Palais, lies the **Rheinisches Landesmuseum**, a Roman archeology museum par excellence, with an engrossing scale-model of fourth-century Trier which puts what survives in context, and a well-presented hoard of glassware, coins, tombstones and mosaics. Prize exhibit is the *Neumagener Weinschiff*, a Roman sculpture of a wine ship.

The Kaiserthermen

Weimarer Allee 2 • Daily: March & Oct 9am–5pm; April–Sept 9am–6pm; Nov–Feb 9am–4pm • €3

Adjacent to the Landesmuseum, Trier's **Kaiserthermen** (Imperial Thermal Baths) were not only the largest of several in town, but also the largest in the Roman world. Little of the buildings remain, but their foundations and underground heating system are intact. As you wander around, information panels help you to visualize the scale of this fourth-century complex, which is impressively large even today.

10

Amphitheater

Bergstr. 45 • Daily: March & Oct 9am–5pm; April–Sept 9am–6pm; Nov–Feb 9am–4pm • €3 • ☎ 0651 730 10

Trier's **Amphitheater** – a ten-minute walk southeast along Olewiger Strasse from the underpass southeast of the Kaiserthermen – is as impressive for its scale as its antiquity. This 20,000-capacity arena was built around 100 AD – making it Trier's oldest Roman structure – for gladiatorial and animal fights. It is so well preserved that it's easy to imagine its dank cellars hanging heavy with tension and the stench of sweat and blood as participants waited to be brought to baying crowds.

The Barbarathermen and the Römerbrücke

If you still have the time and interest after a day of sightseeing, then a couple of secondary Roman sights along Olewiger Strasse, which becomes Südallee, are worth exploring. Alongside the road and readily visible are the **Barbarathermen**, a second-century Roman bath now under renovation, while close to the end of the road, the **Römerbrücke** is a bridge which is still supported by five Roman-era pylons.

ARRIVAL AND DEPARTURE   TRIER

By train The station is a 5min walk west of the Porta Nigra. Destinations Frankfurt (hourly; 3hr); Speyer (hourly; 3hr); Stuttgart (hourly; 4hr); Völklingen (hourly; 1hr); Worms (hourly; 3hr 20min).

INFORMATION

Tourist office By the Porta Nigra (Jan & Feb Mon–Sat 10am–5pm, Sun 10am–1pm; March, April, Nov & Dec Mon–Sat 9am–6pm, Sun 10am–3pm; May–Oct Mon–Sat 9am–6pm, Sun 10am–5pm; ☎ 0651 97 80 80, ⊛ trier-info .de). The tourist office can help with booking accommodation (hotline ☎ 0651 978 08 16) in Trier, where it's a little pricier than usual and regularly booked up.

Discount cards The tourist office sells the three-day TrierCard (€9.90; family €21 for two adults and three children), which, among other things, includes free public transport and a 25 percent discount to all its Roman sights.

The AntikenCard (€9) gives free entrance to the Rheinische Landesmuseum and two of the four big Roman attractions: the Porta Nigra, Kaiserthermen, Amphitheater and Barbarathermen. The Premium version of the card (€14) gives free entry to all of them; cards can be bought at any of them.

Guided tours Trier's tourist office is the starting point for 75-minute English-language walking tours of the city (May–Oct Sat 1.30pm; €6). It also has a schedule of wine tours by local vintners.

Bike rental The tourist office offers bike rental (€12/day).

ACCOMMODATION

HOTELS AND PENSIONS

Aulmann Hotel Fleischstr. 47–48 ☎ 0651 976 70, ⊛ hotel-aulmann.de. Good 3-star place in the pedestrianized centre with very clean, straightforward rooms which are relatively quiet at night and handy for the sights. A standard continental breakfast is included; wi-fi is extra. **€130**

Casa Chiara Engelstr. 8 ☎ 0651 27 07 30, ⊛ casa -chiara.de. Friendly, family-run place, with scrupulously clean rooms and good breakfasts, a couple of minutes' walk

from the Porta Nigra – some rooms even have views of it. Parking costs an extra €6 per night. **€105**

Park Plaza Trier Nikolaus-Koch-Platz 1 ☎ 0651 999 30, ⊛ parkplaza-trier.de. Big, central chain hotel, with predictable and spotless 4-star comforts and service. There's a Roman-themed pool and sauna area, which costs extra, as does breakfast; package deals including both are around €116. **€99**

Villa Hügel Bernhardstr. 14 ☎ 0651 93 71 00, ⊛ hotel-villa-huegel.de. Upscale Art-Nouveau villa,

10

highly recommended for its cheerful rooms and facilities which include a pool, sauna and a sun terrace with lovely valley views. **€148**

Weinhaus Becker Olewiger Str. 206 ☎0651 93 80 80, ⓦ weinhaus-becker.de. Stylish pension in the wine-producing suburb of Olewig, 2km from the centre, but an easy walk from the amphitheatre. There's a decent restaurant, and the pension can usually organize wine-tasting tours. **€110**

HOSTELS AND CAMPSITES

Campingpark Treveris Luxemburger Str. 81 ☎0651 820 09 11, ⓦ camping-treviris.de. Pleasant family-run campground with shaded sites on the banks of the Mosel

around 2km southwest of town. With beer garden. Open April–Oct. Pitch **€5**, plus **€5.80** per person

DJH Trier An der Jugendherberge 4 ☎0651 14 66 20, ⓦ diejugendherbergen.de; bus #12 from the Hauptbahnhof. Spotless riverside hostel, 1km northeast of the centre. All the bright and cheerful rooms have their own bathroom and no more than six beds. Dorms **€22.50**, doubles **€56**

Hille's Gartenfeldstr. 7 ☎0651 710 27 85, ⓦ hilles-hostel-trier.de. Homely, clean and sociable independent hostel with a decidedly 1970s vibe, a 10min walk south of the station. Reception open daily July–Oct 2–8pm; Nov–June 4–6pm. Sheets included; breakfast and bike rental available. Dorms **€15**, doubles **€50**

EATING AND DRINKING

Many Altstadt restaurants are touristy yet Trier's students ensure a circuit of good, lively and inexpensive places to eat. Also note the presence of wine bars in the basements of many of the best restaurants. They usually share a kitchen and are excellent for regional wines.

CAFÉS, BARS AND PUBS

Alt Zalawen Zurlaubener Ufer 79 ☎0651 286 45. Traditional tavern, with outdoor seating overlooking the Mosel. It does a fine meat platter (€7) and is an excellent place to try out local cider, Viez, if you're tired of wine. Mon–Fri 3pm–1am, Sat 6pm–1am.

Astarix Karl-Marx-Str. 11 ☎0651 722 39, ⓦ astarix-trier.de. Large laidback student bar with good inexpensive pizzas and casseroles for around €5. The portions are big, the place always lively, but the service a little slow. Look for the entrance down an alley. Mon–Sat 11.30am–late, Sun 1pm–late.

★**BagelSisters** Pferdemarkt 8 ☎0651 430 00, ⓦ bagelsisters.de. Fun café with not just great bagels and muffins but also quirky breakfasts, including the "hangover" – a bottle of beer and an aspirin – which sets the tone of the place. Also superb daily soups (€4.50). Wed–Fri 8am–5pm & Sat 9am–4pm.

Café Lecca Bahnhofsplatz 7 ☎0651 994 98 30, ⓦ cafelecca.de. Stylish café close to the Hauptbahnhof that's great for breakfast and cakes. Renowned for its fantastic Sunday brunch buffet (€10.50), cocktails and live Budesliga games. With free wi-fi too. Mon–Fri 9am–late, Sat & Sun 9am–late.

Irish Pub Trier Jakobstr. 10 ☎0651 495 39, ⓦ irishpub-trier.de. Cosy pub and a favourite with local Anglophones – including American soldiers from nearby bases – and those keen on watching the English premier league.

Regular live music. Mon–Thurs & Sun noon–1am, Fri & Sat noon–2am.

RESTAURANTS

Kartoffel-Kiste Fahrstr. 13–14 ☎0651 979 00 66, ⓦ kiste-trier.de. Dependable, solid German food at reasonable prices served in a place that prides itself on its fairly encyclopedic collection of potato-based dishes (most mains around €9). Daily 11am–midnight; kitchen closes 10pm.

Schlemmereule Domfreihof 1 ☎0651 736 16, ⓦ schlemmereule.de. Gourmet place tucked away in Trier's Altstadt offering delicious creations off a small international and oft-changing menu. The €49 three-course menu is usually the way to go; two-course lunches cost just €19. The service and wine-list are equally first-class. Reservations recommended. Mon–Sat noon–2.30pm & 6–10.30pm.

Zum Domstein Hauptmarkt 5 ☎0651 744 90, ⓦ domstein.de. Innovative place with both standard regional dishes (three courses €16–35) – such as trout in a Riesling sauce – as well as quirky choices in the basement *Römischer Weinkeller* where Roman dishes are served. The recipes – which almost all involve very rich sauces – are those of the court cook for the Emperor Tiberius. This is also a good place for a spot of wine tasting: three different glasses together cost only €7.50. Daily 8.30am–midnight.

NIGHTLIFE AND ENTERTAINMENT

Metropolis Hindenburgstr. 4 ⓦ metropolis-trier.de. Club that starts to pack with twenty-somethings after midnight for latin, house, hip-hop and occasional gigs. Wed–Sat 10pm–late.

TuFa Wechselstr. 4–6 ☎0651 718 24 14, ⓦ tufa-trier.de. Former towel factory that's now a venue for both conventional and off-beat music, drama and dance. Daily shows. Hours vary, usually Wed–Sun 7pm–late for events.

Saarbrücken and around

Modern **SAARBRÜCKEN** is not a place to go out of your way for, but is nevertheless a lively university city whose closeness to France comes across in attitudes and food. This background is the subject of the city's local history museum, **Historisches Museum Saar**, Saarbrücken's most rewarding museum, though the **Museum für Vor- und Frühgeschichte** with its hoard of Celtic treasures, comes close. The city centres on **Sankt Johanner Markt**, hub for a series of lively restaurants and cafés. From here Bahnhofstrasse, the main shopping street, heads north to the Hauptbahnhof, paralleling a promenade along the River Saar over which lies an area known as **Alt-Saarbrücken**. Most of Saarbrücken's few real sights are clustered here, including the remains of an eighteenth-century **Schloss**, built during the city's heyday under Prince Wilhelm Heinrich (1718–68) and designed by court architect Friedrich Joachim Stengel, who was also behind several nearby Baroque townhouses and churches. Ten kilometres outside the city, the rusty **Völklinger Hütte** ironworks make a fascinating day-trip.

St Johann

A town in its own right from 1353, **St Johann** became part of Saarbrücken under the Prussians in 1815, but its focus remains the long, elongated square, **Sankt-Johanner-Markt**, where the city's oldest buildings surround an ornate Stengel-designed fountain. At no. 24, the Stadtgalerie (Tues–Fri noon–6pm, Sat & Sun 11am–6pm; free; ⓦstadtgalerie.de) is often worth a look for its quirky contemporary art.

Saarland Museum

Bismarckstr. 11–15 • Tues & Thurs–Sun 10am–6pm, Wed 10am–6pm • €5 • ⓦ kulturbesitz.de

A large collection of modern art is to be found at the **Moderne Galerie**, within the **Saarland Museum**, a fifteen-minute walk southeast from Sankt-Johanner-Markt through residential streets. The German Impressionist section – Liebermann and the like – is strong and neatly contextualised by the work of French contemporaries. It's also good on Expressionism, with Kirchner's *Bathers in a Room* one of its most celebrated paintings.

Alt-Saarbrücken

From Sankt-Johanner-Markt it's an easy five-minute walk southwest along the pedestrian Saarstrasse and the Alte Brücke footbridge over the Saar to **Alt-Saarbrücken**.

Schlosskirche

Am Schlossberg 6 • Tues & Thurs–Sun 10am–6pm, Wed 10am–10pm • €5 • ⓦ kulturbesitz.de

Beyond the thundering and unsightly A620 Autobahn, the generally Baroque quarter begins with a Gothic **Schlosskirche**, which is worth a look. It had its stained glass blown out in the war, to be replaced by obviously 1950s panes, and now holds a museum of religious art from the thirteenth century onwards, which includes some noteworthy fifteenth-century pieces. Behind the church is the heart of Alt-Saarbrücken's residential quarter; its fine pastel townhouses are some of Stengel's best work.

Saarbrücker Schloss: the Historisches Museum Saar

Schlossplatz 15 • Tues, Wed, Fri & Sun 10am–6pm, Thurs 10am–8pm, Sat noon–6pm • €5 • ⓦ historisches-museum.org

A short walk uphill from the Schlosskirche, the grand **Schlossplatz** provides a rather lifeless forecourt for the **Saarbrücker Schloss**, a largely Renaissance and Baroque edifice designed by Stengel, with a glass extension – by Gottfried Böhm

10

– that looks every inch the 1980s addition that it is. Inside, the excellent **Historisches Museum Saar** specializes in exhibitions about the region and its turbulent twentieth-century history.

Museum für Vor- und Frühgeschichte and the Alte Sammlung

Schlossplatz 16 • Tues & Thurs–Sun 10am–6pm, Wed 10am–10pm • Free • ⓦ kulturbesitz.de

Located adjacent to the Saarbrucker Schloss, the **Museum für Vor- und Frühgeschichte** is of particular interest for the hoard of Celtic jewellery found in a princess's grave from around 400 BC on what's now the French border 25km southeast of Saarbrücken. At the same address is the Saarlandmuseum's collection of fine and applied art, the **Alte Sammlung**, which includes pieces that date back to the eleventh century but is strongest on medieval pieces and on sixteenth- to nineteenth-century portraiture. Of particular regional interest is its tapestry collection – including many fine examples from Alsace, Lorraine and Luxembourg.

Ludwigskirche

Ludwigsplatz • Jan–March Tues noon–5pm, Wed–Sat 10am–5pm; April–Sept Tues–Sun 10am–6pm • Free • ⓦ ludwigskirche.de

Saarbrücken's de facto city symbol, the **Ludwigskirche**, is arguably Stengel's finest building in the city but also one of Germany's most important Protestant churches. It's at the centre of a grand eponymous square surrounded by noble townhouses which were all part of the master urban plan hatched in the 1760s. Much was levelled in World War II, but the church has since been rebuilt pretty true to its original form. This is highly unusual, not only for being a rare Baroque Protestant church, but also for having its altar, pulpit and organ placed upon each other at the centre of the church – amid all the frenzied stucco.

Völklinger Hütte

Rathausstr. 75–79, Völklingen • Daily: April–Oct 10am–7pm; Nov–March 10am–6pm • €15, free on Tues after 3pm • ⓦ voelklinger-huette.org • Frequent trains from Saarbrücken to Völklingen (7min), then 5min signposted walk

The town of **VÖLKLINGEN**, 10km downstream along the Saar from Saarbrücken, is one of those one-time industrial powerhouses – and now a picture of industrial malaise and decline – that most people would usually make a wide berth around when they can. However, its huge and rusty old ironworks, **Völklinger Hütte**, a couple of minutes' walk from the Hauptbahnhof, have become so celebrated that UNESCO have even made it a World Heritage Site. It's preserved as one of the last of a generation; a quiet reminder of a grimy and fast-disappearing period of European history. Opened in 1873, the ironworks' huge size and complexity are what immediately impress most. By its mid-1960s heyday the workforce peaked at around 17,000, before slowly decreasing until production finally ceased in 1986.

It's now hard to imagine the place at full throttle with all the noise, dust and dirt involved, but the excellent multilingual audio-guide and useful signs (in English too) do their best to bring all this alive, while a candid exhibition on the lives and health problems of former workers sets the tone for an honest appraisal of the site's history. Numerous spaces in the ironworks serve as temporary exhibition **galleries** for photography and art, with the raw backdrop often adding an unexpected poignancy to pieces. **Concerts** also take place here, with jazz a regular feature of Friday nights.

ARRIVAL AND INFORMATION
SAARBRÜCKEN AND AROUND

By train To get into the centre from the Hauptbahnhof, follow Reichstrasse south to Bahnhofstrasse.

Destinations Frankfurt (hourly; 2hr 10min); Speyer (frequent; 2hr); Stuttgart (hourly; 2hr 10min); Trier (frequent; 1hr 10min); Völklingen (frequent; 10min); Worms (frequent; 2hr 10min).

Tourist office Just east off the southern end of Bahnhofstrasse in the town's Rathaus (Mon–Fri 9am–6pm,

Sat 10am–4.30pm; ☎01805 72 27 27, ⓦdie-region-saarbruecken.de). Getting here and around the compact centre is generally easy enough on foot. As always the tourist office can help with private rooms (from €50); given that Saarbrücken attracts few casual visitors, most accommodation is geared to business travel.

ACCOMMODATION

Am Triller Trilerweg 57 ☎0681 58 00 00, ⓦhotel-am-triller.de. Swish modern hotel in a quiet corner of Alt-Saarbrücken with a mix of well-kept nondescript rooms and some more imaginative designer digs. Excellent facilities include a pool, sauna and fitness centre and wi-fi. Free parking. **€79**

DJH Saarbrücken Meerwiesertalweg 31 ☎0681 330 40, ⓦdiejugendherbergen.de; tram S1 to Johanneskirche and then bus #101 to stop "Jugendherberge". Sparkling modern hostel in the university district northeast of the centre and on the green edges of town. Rooms have only two or four beds and all are en suite. Dorms **€22.50**

★**Madeleine** Cecilienstr. 5 ☎0681 322 28, ⓦhotel-madeleine.de. Family-run, mid-range choice with small bright rooms in a great central location opposite the Rathaus. Free bike rental and organic breakfasts sweeten what's already a good deal and rates even drop a little during the week. **€69**

Schlosskrug Schmollerstr. 14 ☎0681 367 35, ⓦhotel-schlosskrug.de. Bland but clean and well-run budget option a 5min walk east of the centre. Not all of the rooms have their own bathroom, but at €31 the singles are real bargains. **€55**

EATING, DRINKING AND ENTERTAINMENT

CAFÉS, BARS AND PUBS

★**Café Kostbar** Nauwieserstr. 19 ☎0681 37 43 60, ⓦcafekostbar.de. Courtyard place with a laidback feel and good inexpensive food for around €6, including many veggie dishes such as fried potatoes with *tsatziki*, salad and bread. Particularly good for breakfast or Sun brunch (€12). Most of the food is organic and local. Daily 10am–1am.

Karateklub Meier Nassauerstr. 11 ☎0681 329 29. Laidback and sociable pub – one of a couple on the block – with spartan furnishings, loud rock and the constant flicker of silent films on the wall. Occasional live music too. Daily 8pm–late.

Kulturcafé Sankt-Johanner-Markt 24 ☎0681 379 92 00, ⓦkulturcafe-saarbruecken.de. Part of the Stadtgalerie, as art-lined café walls remind, and with outdoor seating in premium people-watching position; but both will have to compete for your attention with the excellent cakes. Daily 8.30am–late.

Tempelier Kappenstr. 9 ☎0681 910 42 67. Belgian pub with first-rate *frites* – served with mayo and fried onions – as well as excellent *Flammkuchen* and dozens of malty beers. Has some pleasant outdoor seating too but can get very busy. Mon–Thurs & Sun noon–midnight, Fri & Sat noon–3am.

Zum Stiefel Am Stiefel 2 ☎0681 93 64 50, ⓦstiefelgastronomie.de. Oldest house (1702) in town with a *Brauhaus* atmosphere, popular beer garden and hearty portions of local food – such as *Dibbelabbes*, a leek, meat and potato casserole and *Hoorishe*, potato rissoles – all easily washed down with *Bruch-Bier*. Mon–Sat 11.45am–11pm.

RESTAURANTS

★**Hashimoto** Cecilienstr. 7 ☎0681 39 80 34, ⓦhashimoto-saar.de. Near-gourmet Japanese restaurant with friendly and attentive service and a good range of dishes including first-class sushi. Three courses begin at €22; prices are lower at lunch. Tues–Fri & Sun noon–2.30pm & 6.30–10.30pm, Sat 6.30–10.30pm.

Krua Thai Mainzer Str. 71 ☎0681 646 95, ⓦkruathai-sb.de. Excellent Thai place with extravagant floral arrangements and authentic, MSG-free mains for around €13. Look out for daily specials and be sure to try the papaya and riceball salad when it's offered. Tues–Fri & Sun noon–2pm & 6.30–10.30pm, Sat 6.30–10.30pm.

La Bastille Kronenstr. 1b ☎0681 310 64. Small, cosy French restaurant on a side street by the Markt that's been a local fixture for some 35 years. The seasonal menu is reasonably priced with mains from around €10. *Dibbelabbes* is a house speciality. Mon–Fri noon–3pm & 5–11pm, Sat noon–midnight, Sun 5pm–midnight.

NIGHTLIFE AND ENTERTAINMENT

Staatstheater Schillerplatz 1 ☎0681 30 920, ⓦtheater-saarbruecken.de. Grand Neoclassical venue for high culture with regular ballet, drama, opera, musicals and concerts. Nightly from 7.30pm.

Völklinger Hütte A novel option is to hop on a train to Völklingen (frequent; 7min) and attend an event at the old ironworks (see opposite). These are very varied, but jazz and swing tend to be strong points. Hours vary, usually Fri & Sat from 7pm.

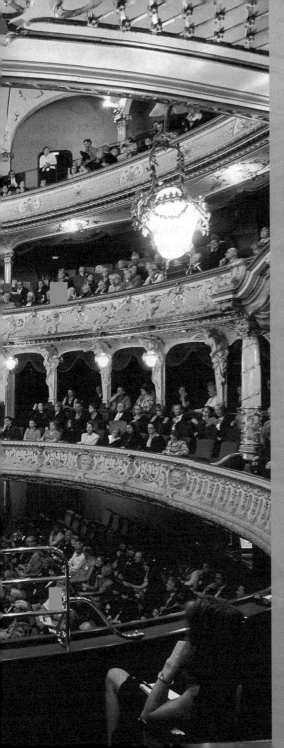

Hesse

HESSISCHES STAATSTHEATER, WIESBADEN

Hesse

For many visitors – particularly those arriving at Frankfurt airport – Hesse is their first taste of Germany. It can be a disconcerting experience, for at first sight there's little about Frankfurt's steel-and-glass modernity or its easy internationalism to summon up childhood notions of a Hansel-and-Gretel Germany. Yet dig a little deeper and you'll find reminders of the world-famous German figures who were either born here, made their home in Hesse or passed this way: of Goethe in Frankfurt; of the Brothers Grimm in Marburg and Kassel; and of St Boniface – the English bishop who became the patron saint of Germany – in Fritzlar and Fulda. In Darmstadt, meanwhile, there are reminders of Germany's complex relationship to the British royal family.

The modern Land of Hesse was created by the occupying Americans after World War II, who joined the Prussian province of Hesse-Nassau – itself an amalgamation of the old Electorate of Hesse-Kassel, the comic-opera statelet of Hesse-Homburg and the Duchy of Nassau – to the former Grand Duchy of Hesse-Darmstadt. Confusing? Perhaps. But the complexity of its history helps explain the richness and diversity of Hesse's attractions. If it's big-city buzz that you crave, then **Frankfurt** – Germany's fifth largest city and the financial capital of the Eurozone – has much to offer, from heavyweight museums to evocative reminders of its literary, imperial and Jewish pasts. In the south, laidback **Darmstadt** is unmissable for fans of Jugendstil, and also a base for visiting a brace of UNESCO World Heritage sites – the **Messel** fossil site and the monastery at **Lorsch**. The genteel spa-towns of **Wiesbaden** and **Bad Homburg** make the perfect antidote to Frankfurt's urban stress. Away from the Rhine–Main region, Hesse is archetypal Germany, with a rolling and often forested landscape that reaches near-mountainous heights in the **Taunus** and **Rhön**. Other than Frankfurt, the towns are mostly small, but they're an appealing bunch, from picture-book cathedral towns such as **Fritzlar**, **Limburg an der Lahn** and **Wetzlar** to the proud university town of **Marburg** or the handsome former prince-bishopric of **Fulda**. Smaller than them all, yet well worth a visit, is the tiny ducal seat of **Weilburg**. In the north, **Kassel** lures visitors for the **documenta** contemporary art fair, but then surprises with its exceptional Baroque gardens and excellent museums.

Frankfurt am Main

Thrusting, dynamic **FRANKFURT** is the beating heart of Germany's financial sector and home to the European Central Bank. It has an impressive skyline bristling with eye-catching skyscrapers, earning it the nickname Mainhattan, and business travellers flock here for the trade shows, which include the world's largest book fair. It's an

FRESHLY PRESSED *APFELWEIN*, FRANKFURT

Highlights

❶ **Apfelwein** Frankfurt's cider is best enjoyed on summer nights outside one of old Sachsenhausen's traditional wine taverns. **See p.571**

❷ **Mathildenhöhe, Darmstadt** The spirit of Jugendstil – the German form of Art Nouveau – lingers on at Darmstadt's remarkable artists' colony. **See p.576**

❸ **Hessisches Staatstheater, Wiesbaden** See grand opera at not-so-grand prices in the Viennese setting of Wiesbaden's beautiful turn-of-the-century theatre. **See p.582**

❹ **Cycling the Lahn Valley** Gentle inclines, cyclist-friendly hotels and beautiful towns and countryside make the Lahn Valley a cyclist's joy. **See p.589**

❺ **Rhön Biosphere Reserve** Hike, paraglide or simply enjoy the spectacular views in this pristine upland landscape. **See p.601**

❻ **Half-timbering** Hesse is the heartland of half-timbered architecture, from tiny village churches to the ancient townhouses of Limburg, Wetzlar, Marburg and Fritzlar. **See p.590, p.592, p.594 & p.601**

❼ **Wilhelmshöhe** Old masters and eighteenth-century water tricks in a remarkable garden landscape that's a monument to the extravagance – and vanity – of the Hesse-Kassel dynasty. **See p.606**

HIGHLIGHTS ARE MARKED ON THE MAP ON P.560

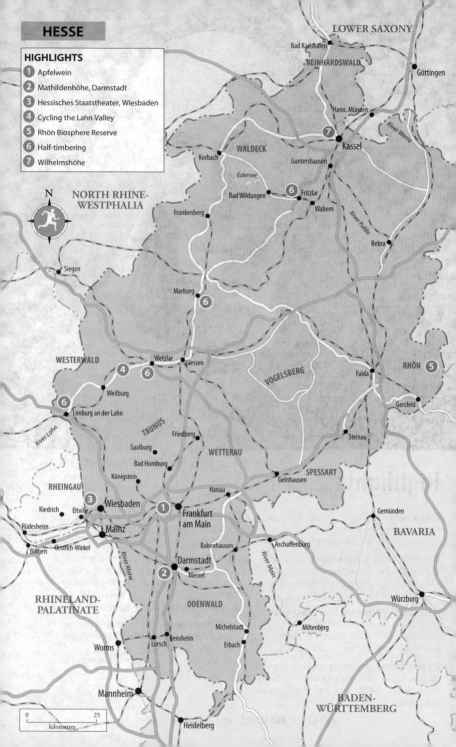

FRANKFURT ORIENTATION

The centre of Frankfurt is easily recognizable on a map, surrounded by a crescent of green spaces called Anlagen, which follow the course of the old fortifications. The major shopping streets intersect at the **Hauptwache**, while the skyscrapers of the financial district straddle the **Taunusanlage** and **Gallusanlage** to the west. Further west still is the **Bahnhofviertel** around the main train station, which is where many of the hotels are located. Frankfurt's major historic sites are close to the north bank of the River Main, where the carefully reconstructed **Römerberg** square provides the focus; across the river is **Sachsenhausen**, home to the city's celebrated *Apfelwein* taverns and to most of its museums.

---

important transport hub too, with Germany's busiest Autobahn intersection and its largest international airport, linked directly to the high-speed ICE rail network.

First impressions of limousines, office towers and briefcases can suggest Germany's fifth largest city is all work and no play, and among business travellers it sometimes commands more respect than affection. Yet Frankfurt's charms are real enough, from alfresco *Apfelwein*-imbibing in Sachsenhausen to museum-hopping on the Museumsufer or Ibiza-style DJ bars atop city-centre car parks. Spend time discovering them and you'll find this sophisticated, cosmopolitan city repays your investment with interest.

The Römerberg and around

Steep gables, half-timbered facades and the picturesque sixteenth-century **Gerechtigkeitsbrunnen**, or Justice Fountain, make spacious **Römerberg**, the old central square, the focal point of Frankfurt's Altstadt and the very image of a medieval town square. It's the perfect setting for the city's Christmas market, just as it has been the scene for major events since the Middle Ages. What you see is, however, in part an illusion. The old town went up in flames during an air raid on the night of March 22, 1944, and the much-photographed **half-timbered houses** on the east side are modern reconstructions. The one genuine half-timbered house on Römerberg is **Haus Wertheim** in the southwest corner, which dates from around 1600 and was spared destruction in the 1944 raid.

The Römer

Römerberg • Kaisersaal daily 10am–1pm & 2–5pm • €2

On the west side of Römerberg, the stately **Römer** – Frankfurt's Rathaus – is a genuine enough medieval survivor, though it was grievously damaged during the war and its three central gables were "improved" by the addition of neo-Gothic elements in the nineteenth century. Nevertheless, the oldest bits of the rambling complex date back to 1322.

Cross the main courtyard – accessed via Limpurgergasse on the south side – to visit the **Kaisersaal** on the first floor, with its 52 nineteenth-century portraits of kings and emperors of the Holy Roman Empire, from Charlemagne to Franz II. It was here that the Electors would hold their concluding banquet after the selection of a new emperor, and the reconstructed hall is still used for VIP receptions. It has a touch of postwar blandness about it, however, and the graceful Renaissance staircase you climb to reach it is rather more appealing.

Historisches Museum

Saalgasse 19 • Tues & Thurs–Sun 10am–5pm, Wed 10am–9pm • €7 • ⓦ www.historisches-museum.frankfurt.de

Behind the pretty little thirteenth-century Gothic Nikolaikirche – used as a spectator stand during imperial coronations – stands the **Historisches Museum Frankfurt**, a collection of buildings that houses the city's excellent local history museum. The

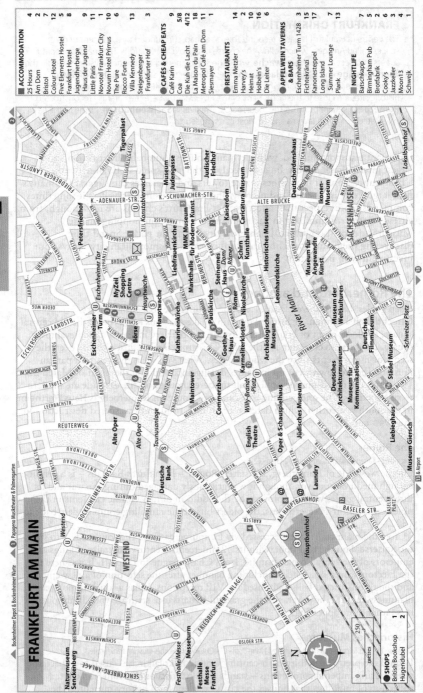

FRANKFURT AND GERMAN HISTORY

For all its high-octane modernity, Frankfurt has long played an often distinguished role in German history. In the **Middle Ages** it was a free imperial city, and even today its fierce civic pride echoes that doughty medieval independence. In 1562 it succeeded Aachen as the city in which **Holy Roman Emperors** were crowned, a role it retained until 1792, and in 1848 it was the setting for the first democratically elected **German national assembly**. A century later, it narrowly lost out to Bonn in the competition to become capital of the new Federal Republic of Germany. Frankfurt also has a proud **Jewish history**: the Rothschild banking dynasty originated here, and though the Jewish tradition was all but wiped out under the Nazis it has, of late, made a spirited comeback.

---

historic **Saalhof** incorporates a twelfth-century Romanesque **chapel** – originally a court chapel and the oldest building in Frankfurt – in whose cellar emperors stored the imperial crown jewels when they were in Frankfurt.

The museum's **permanent exhibitions** do a good job of tracing the city's history from 784 to the present day: there's a giant model of the Altstadt as it was before its destruction and a section focusing on twelve of the city's most historically significant art collections. There's also the chance to climb to the top of the fifteenth-century **Rententurm**, a surviving tower of the city's medieval defences. The museum is undergoing major refurbishment, including the construction of a new extension; from 2017 the permanent exhibitions will be re-curated. The museum also hosts interesting **temporary exhibitions** on Frankfurt-related themes.

Paulskirche
Paulsplatz 11 • Daily 10am–5pm • Free

Immediately to the north of the Römer the circular Neoclassical **Paulskirche** has a proud place in German history, for it was in this, the city's principal Lutheran church, that on May 18, 1848, the first democratically elected German national assembly met, only to collapse in little more than a year, its demise hastened by a wave of nationalist sentiment allied to the Schleswig-Holstein question and by the machinations of Prussia and Austria. The interior is very plain following postwar reconstruction, with bilingual panels to help explain its historical significance.

The eastern Altstadt

Away from the showpiece of the Römerberg, only isolated buildings were rebuilt after World War II. One is the **Steinernes Haus**, east of Römerberg at Markt 44. Built in 1464 for a patrician family from the Rhineland, it now houses the **Frankfurter Kunstverein** (Tues, Thurs & Fri 11am–7pm, Wed 11am–9pm, Sat & Sun 10am–7pm; €6; ⓦfkv.de), which hosts temporary art exhibitions. Between here and the Dom stood the hated **Technisches Rathaus**, a crass lump of 1970s concrete that trampled over the historic setting and scale of the Altstadt until torn down in 2010–11. Work is now underway to reinstate the medieval street pattern and to re-create fifteen of the lost historic houses accurately, with additional new buildings to complete the restored "Altstadt" setting in sympathetic style and scale. Known as the **Dom-Römer Projekt** (ⓦdomroemer.de), the scheme is scheduled for completion in 2016.

Schirn Kunsthalle
Römerberg • Tues & Fri–Sun 10am–7pm, Wed & Thurs 10am–10pm • Entry price depends on exhibition • ⓦ schirn.de

Facing the construction site of the "new" Altstadt on the site of the former Technisches Rathaus, the **Schirn Kunsthalle** ignores the scale of the old town just as blatantly, but is much more sympathetic in style. It's the city's main venue for large-scale touring exhibitions of fine and applied art.

Saalgasse

On the Schirn Kunsthalle's southern flank along **Saalgasse**, a row of tall, gabled houses in postmodern style cleverly reproduces the scale and feel of the Altstadt without aping medieval methods or materials. At the eastern end of Saalgasse on Weckmarkt, another medieval patrician house – the **Leinwandhaus** – is home to the **Caricatura Museum** of satirical and comic art (Tues & Thurs–Sun 10am–6pm, Wed 10am–9pm; €6; ⓦcaricatura-museum.de).

The Kaiserdom

Domplatz 1 **Kaiserdom** Mon–Thurs 8am–8pm, Fri 12.30–8pm, Sat & Sun 9am–8pm • Free • **Tower** Daily: April–Oct 9am–6pm; Nov–March 11am–5pm; closed Tues & Wed in winter • €3 • ⓦ domturm-frankfurt.de • **Dommuseum** Tues–Fri 10am–5pm, Sat & Sun 11am–5pm • €4 • ⓦ dommuseum-frankfurt.de

Dominating the eastern Altstadt is the west tower of the **Kaiserdom**, not a cathedral at all but the city's principal Catholic church, dedicated to St Bartholomew and the venue for ten imperial coronations between 1562 and 1792. Much of the church dates from the thirteenth and fourteenth centuries; the tower, built to the designs of Madern Gerthener between 1415 and 1513 but left incomplete for 350 years when its top was added, was for centuries the dominant feature of Frankfurt's skyline.

The interior

Inside, the tower hall contains a 1509 **Crucifixion** group by the Mainz sculptor Hans Backofen, while the Marienkapelle houses the lovely **Maria-Schlaf altar** from 1434. The **Wahlkapelle** where emperors were elected is surprisingly modest. It was used for this purpose from 1356, at a time when the coronations were still taking place in Aachen. You can climb the cathedral **tower** for a view over the city; there are three hundred steps to the 66m observation platform. The cathedral cloisters house the **Dommuseum**, which in addition to displaying seventh-century Merovingian grave goods and the cathedral's ecclesiastical treasure, also hosts interesting exhibitions of contemporary art.

MMK Museum für Moderne Kunst

Domstr. 10 • Tues & Thurs–Sun 10am–6pm, Wed 10am–8pm • €12, free on last Sat of month • ⓦ mmk-frankfurt.de

A little to the north of the Kaiserdom, the **MMK Museum für Moderne Kunst** houses the city's collection of modern and contemporary art in a striking postmodern building by the Austrian architect Hans Hollein, whose design owes something to the Expressionist architecture of the 1920s. The collection spans the period from the 1960s to the present day, from American Pop Art and Joseph Beuys to works by Gerhard Richter, Bruce Nauman and a younger generation of artists including Julian Schnabel.

Museum Judengasse

Kurt-Schuhmacher-Str. 10 • Tues & Thurs–Sun 10am–5pm, Wed 10am–8pm • €5, combined ticket with Jüdisches Museum €10 • ⓦ juedischesmuseum.de

A short walk east along Battonnstrasse brings you to the remarkable **Museum Judengasse**, an outpost of the Jüdisches Museum (see opposite) built over the excavated foundations of the cramped medieval ghetto. In 1560, around a thousand of Frankfurt's 12,000 inhabitants were Jewish; by 1600 the community had grown to 27,000. Shortly afterwards rioting citizens plundered Judengasse and expelled the Jews, but they were escorted back by imperial troops and afterwards the imperial crest was fixed to the ghetto gates as a sign of the Emperor's protection. The families who trace their roots to this street include the Rothschilds, whose name derived from a house called Rotes Schild. The museum was closed for renovation at the time of writing but scheduled to reopen late in 2015.

FRANKFURT'S JEWISH COMMUNITY: INTEGRATION AND PERSECUTION

In the early nineteenth century Frankfurt's professional classes played a key role in the birth of the **Jewish Reform movement**, which introduced preaching and prayers in German and organ accompaniment for choirs, as well as rescinding the strict separation of men and women. On the eve of the Nazi takeover, the city's Jewish community numbered 30,000, among them the young **Anne Frank**. In the years 1938 to 1942 more than seven hundred despairing Frankfurt Jews took their own lives; deportations of the rest to the ghettoes of Łódź, Minsk and Riga began late in 1941. The postwar community, founded in 1948, has grown in recent years and now has more than seven thousand members.

St Leonhardskirche

A short stroll west along the river from the Römerberg, the beautiful **St Leonhardskirche** escaped the worst of the wartime air raids and thus preserves the smell and feel of antiquity in a way that the other Altstadt churches don't. It's late Romanesque, with some lovely Late Gothic details, including a suspended vault depicting the Scourging of Christ. Nowadays it's the church for Frankfurt's English-speaking Catholic congregation; it was closed for renovation at the time of writing, but is scheduled to reopen by early 2016.

Karmelitenkloster

Institut für Stadtgeschichte Münzgasse 9 • Mon–Fri 10am–6pm, Sat & Sun 11am–6pm • Free • **Archäologisches Museum Frankfurt** Karmelitergasse 1 • Tues & Thurs–Sun 10am–6pm, Wed 10am–8pm • €7, free on last Sat of month • ⓦ archaeologisches-museum.frankfurt.de

Close to St Leonhardskirche on Karmelitergasse is the **Karmelitenkloster**, a thirteenth-century abbey complex whose refectory and cloisters contain wonderful wall paintings by the Swabian artist and revolutionary Jerg Ratgeb, portraying the Passion of Christ and the story of the Carmelites. Ratgeb was executed by quartering in Pforzheim in 1526 for his part in the Peasants' War. The Ratgeb paintings form part of the **Institut für Stadtgeschichte**, which also mounts interesting exhibitions on themes related to the city's history. The Karmelitenkloster also houses the **Archäologisches Museum Frankfurt**, which, in addition to its permanent collection of local, Classical and Oriental antiquities, hosts regular temporary exhibitions.

Jüdisches Museum

Untermainkai 14–15 • Tues & Thurs–Sun 10am–5pm, Wed 10am–8pm • €7, combined ticket with temporary exhibitions €9, combined ticket with temporary exhibitions and Jüdisches Museum €10; free entry last Sat of month • ⓦ juedischesmuseum.de

West along the Mainkai brings you to the **Jüdisches Museum**, which occupies a Neoclassical mansion that once belonged to the Rothschilds. Its displays on the history of Frankfurt's Jewish community are occasionally a little dry, but the English audio-guide helps make sense of it all and there are regular temporary exhibitions too. If you've already been to Judengasse (see opposite), look out for the large-scale model of the medieval ghetto.

Goethe-Haus

Grosser Hirschgraben 23–25 • Mon–Sat 10am–6pm, Sun 10am–5.30pm • €7, English PDA-guide €3 • ⓦ goethehaus-frankfurt.de

On the boundary between the Altstadt and the modern city centre, is the **Goethe-Haus** where Johann Wolfgang von Goethe – commonly regarded as Germany's greatest writer – was born on August 28, 1749. Even if you're not familiar with *Faust* or *The Sorrows of Young Werther* it's an engrossing museum, for it creates a powerful impression of bourgeois family life in eighteenth-century Frankfurt. Take a good look at the bottom four steps of the main staircase: following the destruction of the house by bombs in 1944 on the anniversary of Goethe's death, the ruins rose no higher than these. Postwar reconstruction was loving and astoundingly effective.

Your ticket includes admission to the adjacent Goethe-Museum, entered via the museum, which displays art from the eighteenth and nineteenth centuries. Proposals also exist for a new **Deutsche Romantik-Museum**, to be built on an adjacent site, with completion scheduled for 2018.

Goethestrasse, Zeil and around

Just to the north of the Goethe-Haus, the Baroque **Katharinenkirche**, where the Goethe family worshipped, overlooks the **Hauptwache**, a graceful little eighteenth-century guardhouse that now houses a café. West of the Hauptwache, chic **Goethestrasse** is lined with luxury boutiques, while to the east stretches **Zeil**, one of the busiest shopping streets in Germany and the scene of Baader-Meinhof's rather farcical debut in April 1968, when Andreas Baader, Gudrun Ensslin and others set fire to two department stores, only to be arrested shortly afterwards. Architecturally, Zeil is a mix of dull postwar buildings and attention-grabbing newer developments. The brash new **MyZeil** mall incorporates skyscrapers and – rather more improbably – a reconstruction of the destroyed Baroque **Thurn und Taxis Palais** around the corner on Grosse Eschenheimer Strasse.

At the end of Grosse Eschenheimer Strasse the pinnacled fifteenth-century **Eschenheimer Turm** looks too Disney-perfect to be true, but it's a perfectly genuine survivor of the city's medieval defences. Like the cathedral tower, it's partly the work of Madern Gerthener.

Mainhattan: the financial district

A giant illuminated Euro symbol stands at Willy-Brandt-Platz, its backdrop of banking towers marking the nexus of Frankfurt's **financial district** – though no longer of the European Union's monetary system, since the European Central Bank (ECB) was relocating to its new €1bn headquarters tower in the east of the city as this book went to press.

Commerzbank and Maintower

Commerzbank Tours on last Sat of month 10am–5pm, hourly • Free • ✉ hochhausfuehrungen@commerzbank.com • **Maintower viewing platform** Mon–Thurs & Sun 10am–9pm, Fri & Sat 10am–11pm; winter closes 2hr earlier • €6.50 • ⓦ maintower.de

For the full, canyon-like **Mainhattan** effect of towering skyscrapers, take a stroll up Neue Mainzer Strasse. Much the most interesting building architecturally is the 299m-high **Commerzbank** by British architect Norman Foster. Completed in 1997, it's the tallest office building in Europe and looks its best at night, when its pinnacles glow an unearthly yellow, creating a geometric lightshow. Tours of the Commerzbank take place on the last Saturday of the month and need to be booked well in advance; more easily accessible is the viewing platform of its neighbour, the 200m-high **Maintower**. The views are most magical at sunset, and there's a smart restaurant one floor down.

Alte Oper and the Börse

A few minutes' walk to the north of Maintower the handsome neo-Renaissance **Alte Oper** straddles the Taunusanlage at the western end of Grosse Bockenheimer Strasse. The opera house was a ruined shell for many years after World War II before finally being restored in the early 1980s. To the east on Börseplatz, bronzes of a bull and bear symbolize rising and falling markets in front of Germany's principal stock exchange, the **Börse** (introductory talks and visitors' gallery open Mon–Fri 10am, 11am & 2pm; free; pre-registration required; ⓦ deutsche-boerse.com).

The Westend

Skyscrapers pepper the western fringes of the Taunusanlage, but the **Westend** was originally a smart residential district. A stroll west from the Alte Oper along Kettenhofweg underlines the extent to which this is still a discreetly desirable – and wonderfully central – place to live.

Naturmuseum Senckenberg

Senckenberganlage 25 • Mon, Tues, Thurs & Fri 9am–5pm, Wed 9am–8pm, Sat & Sun 9am–6pm • €9, English audio-guides €3 • Ⓦ senckenberg.de

At Kettenhofweg's western end on Senckenberganlage is the **Naturmuseum Senckenberg**, whose dinosaur skeletons are a rainy-day godsend for parents with small children. The museum's natural history collection is remarkably comprehensive, and includes a section on the fossil finds from the Grube Messel (see p.579), worth seeing before you visit the site itself.

Palmengarten

11

Siesmayerstr. 61 • Daily: Feb–Oct 9am–6pm; Nov–Jan 9am–4pm • €7 • Ⓦ palmengarten.de

Providing a lush, green context for the Westend's affluent streets, the **Palmengarten** beyond Bockenheimer Warte is a splendid botanical garden of the old school, with prodigious flower beds and a series of hothouses accommodating plants of various habitats, from mangrove swamp to semi-desert and alpine.

Sachsenhausen

South of the river, the modest, winding lanes of **Alt-Sachsenhausen** perform the "Altstadt" task of providing inexpensive eating and easy bar-hopping between unpretentious *Apfelwein* taverns, though it all looks rather tacky by day. More appealing for daytime browsing is the area around **Brückenstrasse** and **Wallstrasse**, which is the focus for some of Frankfurt's most original and fashionable shopping. Sachsenhausen's chief draw, however, is the impressive riverside line-up of museums along the so-called **Museumsufer** or Museum Embankment.

Ikonen-Museum

Brückenstr. 3–7 • Tues & Thurs–Sun 10am–5pm, Wed 10am–8pm • €4 • Ⓦ ikonenmuseumfrankfurt.de

Gateway to Sachsenhausen's museum district is the Baroque **Deutschordenshaus**, a former monastery at the southern end of the Alte Brücke that now houses the **Ikonen-Museum**, whose permanent collection of Orthodox religious icons is supplemented by regular temporary exhibitions.

Museum für Angewandte Kunst

Schaumainkai 17 • Tues & Thurs–Sun 10am–6pm, Wed 10am–8pm • €9, free last Sat of month • Ⓦ museumangewandtekunst.de

The first attraction on the Museumsufer proper is the **Museum für Angewandte Kunst** (Museum of Applied Art), an airy white building by American architect Richard Meier. The collection was re-curated in 2013 to focus on a series of thematic temporary exhibition areas, which draw on the museum's own considerable collection as well as loan items to explore the interrelationships between design past, present and future. The adjacent Neoclassical **Villa Metzler** has nine period rooms that painstakingly re-create historic styles from Baroque to Jugendstil, while the "Elementary Parts" permanent exhibit displays the curators' favourites from the permanent collection, including works of East Asian and Islamic origin.

Museum der Weltkulturen

Schaumainkai 29–37 • Tues & Thurs–Sun 11am–6pm, Wed 11am–8pm • €7, free last Sat of month • Ⓦ weltkulturenmuseum.de

The **Museum der Weltkulturen** is the city's ethnological museum, with a collection of

67,000 artefacts from the Americas, Africa, Asia and Oceania, including the largest collection of contemporary African art in the German-speaking world. There are regular temporary exhibitions and the museum has a substantial photographic archive.

Deutsches Filmmuseum

Schaumainkai 41 • Tues & Thurs–Sun 10am–6pm, Wed 10am–8pm • Permanent exhibition €6, temporary exhibitions prices vary • Ⓦ deutsches-filmmuseum.de

Reopened in the autumn of 2011 after extensive reconstruction, the **Deutsches Filmmuseum** has a new permanent exhibition on two floors. The focus of the exhibits on the first floor is the development of the moving picture, starting with the eighteenth- and nineteenth-century predecessors of modern film, including early peep-show devices such as the Mutoscope and Magic Lantern before progressing to the pioneering work of the Lumière brothers. On the second floor, film-making techniques are explained. Temporary exhibitions explore the cultural side of cinema history, and there's also a small **art-house cinema** (see p.573), whose programme includes screenings of silent movie classics.

Deutsches Architekturmuseum

Schaumainkai 43 • Tues & Thurs–Sun 11am–6pm, Wed 11am–8pm • €9 • Ⓦ dam-online.de

The **Deutsches Architekturmuseum** next door to the Filmmuseum features a house-within-a-house used in the staging of temporary exhibitions. The permanent exhibition traces the development of building from the paleolithic hut to the skyscraper, and there's good labelling in English.

Museum für Kommunikation

Schaumainkai 53 • Tues–Fri 9am–6pm, Sat & Sun 11am–7pm • €3, English audio-guide €1.50 or pick up a free leaflet • Ⓦ mfk-frankfurt.de

The **Museum für Kommunikation** presents the history of post and telecommunications with real flair, from the horse-drawn mail coaches that switched from wheels to sleighs in winter to the vintage postal vans and buses, original telegrams from the *Titanic* and an amusing display of brick-like, early mobile phones.

Städel Museum

Schaumainkai 63 • Tues, Wed, Sat & Sun 10am–6pm, Thurs & Fri 10am–9pm • Tues–Fri €12, Sat & Sun €14 • Ⓦ staedelmuseum.de

The undoubted star of the Museumsufer is the **Städel Museum**, which has a world-class collection of fine art from seven centuries. Recently refurbished and extended with an airy, bright new gallery beneath the museum's garden for post-1945 art, the Städel has doubled its exhibition space. The original nineteenth-century museum building now exhibits the old masters and works of classic modernism. The Städel lost seven hundred works as a result of the Nazi campaign against "degenerate" modern art, and one of the most interesting features of the collection is the way in which works lost during the Third Reich have subsequently been re-acquired. Thus, you can see Franz Marc's *Dog Lying in the Snow*, painted in 1910–11 and acquired in 1919, confiscated in 1937 and repurchased in 1961, or Max Beckmann's *Still Life with Saxophones*, repurchased in 1955. Other modernist gems include Picasso's *Portrait of Fernande Olivier*, considered a definitive work of Cubism.

Works of European art from the Middle Ages to the Baroque include Tischbein's *Goethe in the Roman Campagna*, painted in 1787, which is the best-known likeness of the writer, while there is a heavyweight selection of early German painting, including Lucas Cranach the Elder's *Venus* and works by Stephan Lochner and Albrecht Dürer. Non-German masters include Tiepolo's *Saints of the Crotta Family* and Rembrandt's *Blinding of Samson*. The Städel also hosts big-name temporary exhibitions.

Liebieghaus

Schaumainkai 71 • Tues, Wed & Fri–Sun 10am–6pm, Thurs 10am–9pm • €7 • Ⓦ liebieghaus.de

Housed in a grandiose nineteenth-century villa, the sculpture collection of the **Liebieghaus** encompasses the art of classical antiquity along with splendid examples of the medieval

German "beautiful" style and works of the Renaissance, Mannerist and Baroque periods. Among the highlights are Hans Multscher's alabaster *Holy Trinity* of 1430 from Ulm and Matthias Steinl's gorgeously theatrical *Maria Immaculata* from Vienna, created in 1688. The museum regularly stages excellent themed exhibitions, while the villa's upper floors give an insight into the heavy historicist decor favoured by the city's nineteenth-century elite.

Museum Giersch

Schaumainkai 83 • Tues–Thurs noon–7pm, Fri–Sun 10am–6pm • €5 • ⓦ museum-giersch.de

The westernmost of the Museumsufer's museums, the **Museum Giersch**, showcases art from the Rhine–Main region, with two exhibitions each year focusing on the region's artistic output during the nineteenth and early twentieth centuries.

ARRIVAL AND DEPARTURE   FRANKFURT

By plane Frankfurt's airport (ⓣ 01805 372 46 36, ⓦ frankfurt-airport.com) is a short distance southwest of the city. S-Bahn trains from the Regionalbahnhof in Terminal One take just 11min to reach Frankfurt's Hauptbahnhof.

By train The Hauptbahnhof is a 10min walk west of the Hauptwache.

Destinations Aschaffenburg (2 per hour; 30–45min); Bad Homburg (2 per hour; 25min); Berlin (hourly; 4hr 5min–4hr 20min); Bonn (every 2hr; 2hr); Cologne (1–2 per hour; 1hr–2hr 23min); Darmstadt (2–3 hourly; 15–45min); Frankfurt airport (very frequent; 10–13min); Fulda (3 per hour; 53min–1hr 22min); Hamburg (1–2 per hour; 3hr 37min–4hr 37min); Heidelberg (hourly; 52min); Kassel-Wilhelmshöhe (2–4 per hour; 1hr 22min–2hr); Limburg an der Lahn (every 30min–1hr 30min; 1hr 10min); Mainz (4 per hour; 33–42min); Mannheim (3 per hour; 37min–1hr 6min); Marburg (2 per hour; 57min–1hr 23min); Munich (1–2 per hour; 3hr 21min–3hr 48min); Nuremberg (1–2 per hour; 2hr 6min); Rüdesheim (hourly; 1hr 11min); Stuttgart (1–2 per hour; 1hr 18min–1hr 34min); Wetzlar (1–2 per hour; 55min–1hr 18min); Wiesbaden (very frequent; 35–53min); Würzburg (1–2 per hour; 1hr 10min).

GETTING AROUND

By public transport Frankfurt's public transport is integrated with the rest of the Rhine–Main region as part of the RMV network (ⓦ rmv.de), which makes accessing the neighbouring cities of Wiesbaden, Darmstadt and Bad Homburg by S-Bahn easy. Within the city, buses, trams and U-Bahn make navigation straightforward, though frequency of service drops noticeably in the evening. Announcements on public transport are in both German and English.

Tickets If you're only travelling a kilometre or so you can buy a *Kurzstrecke* ticket (€1.60), otherwise single tickets cost €2.60 and a *Tageskarte* €6.60 – the latter is valid until

public transport shuts down for the night, and you can use it on night buses.

By car Major car rental agencies are represented at the airport. There are also the following desks at the Hauptbahnhof: Avis ⓣ 069 27 99 70 10; Europcar ⓣ 069 242 98 10; Hertz ⓣ 01805 33 35 35; SIXT ⓣ 01805 25 25 25.

By bike Bike rental is available through public bike-sharing initiatives Next Bike (ⓦ nextbike.de) and Call-a-bikes (operated by Deutsche Bahn; see p.34).

By taxi Ranks at the Hauptbahnhof and throughout the city centre, or call ⓣ 069 25 00 01 or ⓣ 069 23 00 01.

INFORMATION AND TOURS

Tourist office In the Hauptbahnhof's main reception hall (Mon–Fri 8am–9pm, Sat & Sun 9am–6pm; ⓣ 069 21 23 88 00, ⓦ frankfurt-tourismus.de); there's also a second office in the Altstadt at Römerberg 27 (Mon–Fri 9.30am–5.30pm, Sat & Sun 9.30am–4pm).

Discount cards Both tourist offices sell the Frankfurt Card (1 day €9.90, 2 days €14.50) which gives fifty percent discounts on museums plus unlimited, free use of the public transport system and discounts at various other venues, including theatres, restaurants, cafés and

bars. The Museumsufer Ticket, available at tourist information offices and the 34 participating museums, costs €18 for two days.

Self-guided sightseeing A self-guided tour with English commentary on iPod Touch from tourist offices costs €7.50 4hr/€10 all day.

Boat trips Frankfurter Personenschiffahrt (ⓣ 069 133 83 70, ⓦ primus-linie.de) runs 50min and 1hr 20min sightseeing cruises on the Main, plus longer excursions to Rüdesheim or Aschaffenburg.

ACCOMMODATION

You can book **accommodation** through the tourist office website or their accommodation hotline (ⓣ 069 21 23 08 08). Frankfurt's **hotels** are largely aimed at business travellers, though a new breed of more individual, smaller hotels is

11

challenging the expense-account blandness at all price levels. Room rates – which can be extremely high during the week and if there's a trade fair in Frankfurt – take a tumble at weekends, making this a good time to visit the city.

HOTELS

★**25 Hours** Niddastr. 58 ☏ 069 256 67 72 55, ⓦ 25hours-hotels.com. Hyper-trendy denim-themed hotel attached to the German headquarters of the Levi's jean company, close to the Hauptbahnhof, with free wi-fi throughout, a roof terrace and a practice room for budding rock stars. **€79**

Am Dom Kannengiessergasse 3 ☏ 069 28 21 41, ⓦ hotelamdom.de. Small, quiet family-run place with just 29 rooms – including 13 singles – in a very central location in the shadow of the Dom. All rooms have shower or bath, TV and wi-fi. **€120**

Bristol Ludwigstr. 15 ☏ 069 24 23 90, ⓦ bristol-hotel .de. Attractive, modern boutique-style hotel close to the Hauptbahnhof, with wi-fi, bar and breakfast in the garden in summer. Good value for the high standards it provides. Cheaper at weekends and with good advance rates online. **€72.25**

Colour Hotel Baseler Str. 52 ☏ 069 36 50 75 80, ⓦ colourhotel.de. Bright, basic, modern budget hotel whose funky design and vibrant colours make a virtue of its somewhat cell-like austerity. Single rooms are also available and there's free wi-fi throughout the hotel. **€63**

Little Paris Karlsruher Str. 8 ☏ 069 273 99 63, ⓦ little -paris-hotel.de. Comfortable budget option close to the Hauptbahnhof. All rooms are decorated in the colours of the tricolour and have shower, WC and flat-screen TV; some of the cheaper rooms have balconies, while more expensive ones are at the back of the hotel. **€79**

Novotel Frankfurt City Lisa-Meitner-Str. 2 ☏ 069 79 30 30, ⓦ novotel.com. Comfortable, contemporary 4-star outpost of the business-oriented chain, west of the centre and close to the Messe, with solarium, sauna and underground parking, and offering excellent weekend deals. **€59**

Novum Hotel Primus Grosse Rittergasse 19–21 ☏ 069 62 30 20, ⓦ novum-hotels.de. Comfortable if slightly bland 3-star hotel close to Alt-Sachsenhausen's *Apfelwein* taverns and the Museumsufer. Good-value soundproofed rooms have TV and free wi-fi and they have single rooms on request. **€89**

Rocco Forte Villa Kennedy Kennedyallee 70 ☏ 069 71 71 20, ⓦ villakennedy.com. Twice voted best business hotel in Europe, the city's plushest hotel is centred on a historic late nineteenth-century villa on the Sachsenhausen side of the river. **€233**

Steigenberger Frankfurter Hof Am Kaiserplatz ☏ 069 215 02, ⓦ steigenberger.com. Frankfurt's prime example of a traditional grand hotel, with imposing nineteenth-century architecture, a Michelin-starred restaurant and an excellent, central location. There are good deals on advance rates. **€169**

The Pure Niddastr. 86 ☏ 069 710 45 70, ⓦ the-pure.de. Minimalist all-white designer hotel north of the Hauptbahnhof, with flat-screen TV and parquet floors in rooms, free wi-fi, parking, and a sauna and steam room. Can be pricey during the week, but rates tumble at weekends. **€95**

HOSTELS

Five Elements Hostel Moselstr. 40 ☏ 069 24 00 58 85, ⓦ 5elementshostel.de. Bright and modern Bahnhofsviertel hostel with guest kitchen, free bedlinen and towels, free wi-fi and a 24hr bar and reception. Dorms hold 3–8 beds and there are also apartments sleeping 1–4. Dorms **€18**, doubles **€55**, apartment (per week) **€590**

Frankfurt Hostel Kaiser Str. 74 ☏ 069 247 51 30, ⓦ frankfurt-hostel.com. Bustling backpacker hostel on the upper floors of a nineteenth-century building close to the Hauptbahnhof, with a groovy ambience. There are en-suite singles and doubles, triple rooms and dorms sleeping 4–10, including women-only dorms. Dorms **€20**, doubles **€54**

Jugendherberge Haus der Jugend Deutschherrnufer 12 ☏ 069 610 01 50, ⓦ jugendherberge-frankfurt.de. Frankfurt's modern youth hostel is on the south side of the river to the east of the city centre, close to Alt-Sachsenhausen's *Apfelwein* taverns but with a 2am curfew. Accommodation is in singles, doubles, or four- to ten-bed dorms. Dorms **€23.50**, doubles **€64**

EATING AND DRINKING

What's left of Frankfurt's Altstadt – around Römerberg – doesn't really perform the culinary function that similar districts in Cologne or Düsseldorf do. You'll have more luck finding inexpensive places to eat and drink in **Sachsenhausen**, which is full of traditional **Apfelwein taverns**; more elegant and expensive **restaurants** cluster around the Börse, Alte Oper and Grosse Bockenheimer Strasse, also known as **Fressgass** or "Scoff Lane", and there are some good options further afield too.

CAFÉS & CHEAP EATS

★**Café Karin** Grosser Hirschgraben 28 ☏ 069 29 52 17, ⓦ cafekarin.de. Perennially popular café just around the corner from the Goethe-Haus. It serves a huge choice of breakfasts (from €3.20) until 6pm, and has plenty of outside seating in fine weather. Lunch main-courses from €8.50. Mon–Sat 9am–midnight, Sun 10am–7pm.

Coa Schillerstr. 4 ☏ 069 92 03 99 66, ⓦ coa.as.

EATING AND DRINKING, FRANKFURT STYLE

Frankfurt has its own, highly distinctive traditional food and drink culture. The *Apfelwein* taverns of Sachsenhausen are the ideal places to try **Handkäs mit Musik** – cheese marinated in oil and vinegar, which is absolutely delicious if done well – or **Frankfurter Grüne Sosse** – a refreshing, creamy sauce made with yoghurt or sour cream, eggs, and a bewildering variety of fresh green herbs, usually served with boiled meat. As for the **Apfelwein** itself – also known as *Ebbelwoi*, it's the tart Frankfurt version of cider, often served in blue jugs (*Bembel*) and drunk *Gespritzt* with the addition of mineral water.

Pan-Asian food including stir-fries (from €6.90), Thai curries (from €7.90), salads (from €.90) and noodle dishes in a minimalist setting close to the Börse, with plenty of veggie choices. There are branches at the airport and in the MyZeil shopping centre. Mon–Sat 11.30am–10pm, Sun 1–9pm.

★ **Die Kuh die Lacht** Schillerstr. 28 ☎ 069 27 29 01 71, ⊛ diekuhdielacht.com. The name means "the cow that laughs", and the friendly service and excellent burgers (from €6.95) – including veggie options – are sure to induce a smile. There's also a branch at Friedensstr. 2 close to the Euro sign. Mon–Sat 11am–11pm, Sun noon–10pm.

La Maison du Pain Schweizer Str. 63 ☎ 069 61 99 44 81, ⊛ lamaisondupain.de. Sachsenhausen's best breakfast place is a classy, overtly Francophile affair, with a terrace, accordion music on tape and prodigious pastries, cakes and breads, plus quiches, *tartines* and breakfasts from €4.90. Mon–Fri 7.30am–7pm, Sat & Sun 8am–7pm.

Metropol Café am Dom Weckmarkt 13–15 ☎ 069 28 82 87, ⊛ metropolcafe.de. This relaxed café in the shadow of the Dom is one of the best bets for a meal or snack in the Altstadt, with organic produce, good cakes (€2.70) and a pleasant outdoor terrace. Breakfast (from €4.70) is served until 4pm at weekends. Veggie, meat or pasta mains start at around €9.50. Tues–Sun 9am–1am.

★ **Siesmayer** Siesmayerstr. 59 ☎ 069 90 02 92 00, ⊛ palmengarten-gastronomie.de. Frankfurt's most alluring spot for *Kaffee und Kuchen*, on the fringe of the Palmengarten, with a sunny terrace fronting the park. It's also a great place for breakfasts – from €9.10, or cheaper à la carte – or an alfresco lunch (two courses €18.95). Daily 8am–7pm.

RESTAURANTS

Emma Metzler Im Metzlerpark, Schaumainkai 17 ☎ 069 6199 5909, ⊛ emma-metzler.com. Creative gourmet cooking at the Museum für Angewandte Kunst, with treats for veggies and omnivores alike: braised red onions with buffalo mozzarella and sweet potato bread, or lamb shoulder with pak choi, shiitake mushrooms and coconut curry foam. It's pricey à la carte, but two-course set lunches start from just €19.50. Tues–Sat noon-11pm, Sun noon-6pm.

Harvey's Bornheimer Landstr. 64 ☎ 069 48 00 48 78, ⊛ emeg.de. Stylishly revamped, high-ceilinged gay-friendly neighbourhood bar-restaurant between Nordend and Bornheim, with a versatile menu and plenty of seating outside. *Flammkuchen* €8.10, burgers from €10.50, breakfast from €5. Mon–Fri 10am–1am, Sat 10am–2am, Sun 10am–midnight.

Heimat Berliner Str. 70 ☎ 069 29 72 59 94, ⊛ heimat -frankfurt.com. An elegant 1950s pavilion on what is otherwise Frankfurt's ugliest street is the setting for this stylish and creative restaurant, serving modern European dishes such as black Angus beef with celery, chanterelles and fresh fig, or fried octopus with artichoke, aubergine and herb aïoli. Main courses €22–33. Daily 6pm–1am.

Holbein's Holbeinstr. 1 ☎ 069 66 05 66 66, ⊛ meyer -frankfurt.de. The Städel Museum's bistro is a classy, airy modern place, great as a culinary pitstop while pounding the Museumsufer and with a sunny terrace. Snacks and panini start at €10, and lunchtime main courses cost from around €15. They also serve coffee and cake. Mon 6pm–midnight, Tues–Sun 10am–midnight.

Die Leiter Kaiserhofstr. 11 ☎ 069 29 21 21, ⊛ dieleiter .de. Plush Franco-Italian restaurant just off Fressgass, full of debonair financial-sector types, with a pretty terrace in summer and creative dishes like fish casserole with coconut milk and lemongrass; main courses €19.50–29.50. Mon–Sat noon–1am.

APFELWEIN TAVERNS & BARS

Eschenheimer Turm 1428 Eschenheimer Turm ☎ 069 29 22 44, ⊛ eschenheimer.de. The location at the foot of "Frankfurt's oldest skyscraper" – a medieval city gate – makes this highly popular bar an easy one to find. There's a full food menu and a huge outdoor terrace in summer; cocktails start from around €8.50. Mon–Thurs noon–1am, Fri & Sat noon–3am.

Fichtekränzi Wallstr. 5 ☎ 069 61 27 78, ⊛ fichtekraenzi.de. One of the nicest of Sachsenhausen's *Apfelwein* taverns, with a wood-panelled interior, a spacious garden and a menu of Frankfurt specialities; *Handkäse mit Musik* €2.50, mains from around €9.80. Daily 5pm–late; garden closes around 1hr before the bar; kitchen closes 11.30pm.

11

Kanonesteppel Textorstr. 20 ☎069 66 56 64 66, ⓦ kanonesteppel.de. Low-key, traditional Sachsenhausen *Apfelwein* tavern with a simple interior and garden, serving *Grüne Sosse* and a meaty *Schlachtplatte* to anchor down the 0.3-litre *Gerippte* of *Apfelwein*; main courses from around €9. Mon–Sat 11am–midnight.

★**Long Island Summer Lounge** Parkdeck 7, Parkhaus Börse ☎0151 61 50 98 89, ⓦ longislandsummerlounge .de. Very stylish, summer-only "beach" bar atop a financial-district car park, with palms, pools, deckchairs and DJs plus a few nautical trappings. €5 cover charge. Mon–Fri 4pm–1am, Sat & Sun 2pm–1am.

Plank Elbestrasse 15, corner Müchener Str. ☎ 069 26 95 86 66, ⓦ barplank.de. Unassuming but hip café/bar in the Bahnhofviertel, with minimalist all-black decor, serving *Kaffee und Kuchen* by day but turning into a cult DJ bar at night. Mon–Thurs 11am–1am, Fri & Sat 11am–2am.

NIGHTLIFE AND ENTERTAINMENT

Some of Frankfurt's best **clubs** are found in the rejuvenated strip of docklands east of the Altstadt, while the **lesbian and gay scene** clusters in the streets north of Zeil – for lesbian and gay listings, pick up a free copy of *Gab* magazine from bars or cafés. Frankfurt's **arts** scene is lively and well patronized, with the Forsythe ballet company in particular enjoying an international reputation. For free monthly **listings** information (in German), pick up a copy of *Frizz, Journal Planer* or *Strandgut* – available from many cafés, bars and other venues. There's more listings info, plus restaurant and bar reviews, online at ⓦ prinz.de.

CLUBS AND LIVE MUSIC

Batschkapp Gwinner Str. 5, Seckbach ☎069 95 21 84 10, ⓦ batschkapp.de; U-Bahn #4 or #7 to "Gwinner Strasse". Long-established live venue for indie bands, recently relocated to newer and more spacious premises. Ticket prices vary according to who's playing.

Brotfabrik Bachmannstr. 2–4 ☎069 24 79 08 00, ⓦ brotfabrik.de. Independently-run arts and concert venue in a former bakery, with a varied programme of live gigs, clubnights and theatre, including Wed salsa night and a monthly tango *milonga*. Clubnights usually from 9 or 9.30pm.

Cooky's Am Salzhaus 4 ☎069 28 76 62, ⓦ cookys.de. Stylishly revamped black music club north of Berliner Strasse, hosting a variety of DJ nights from hip-hop and house to soul, plus occasional live acts. Cover varies: €5–10. Tues–Sat 10pm–8am.

Festhalle Messe Frankfurt Ludwig-Erhart-Anlage 1 ☎069 92 00 92 13, ⓦ messefrankfurt.com. The graceful old main hall of the trade-fair grounds is also the venue for big-name rock concerts – as well as ice shows, wrestling and other large-scale spectacles.

Jazzkeller Kleine Bockenheimer Str. 18a ☎069 28 85 37, ⓦ jazzkeller.com. Long-established jazz club that attracts an international line-up of live acts. It also has regular Wed jam sessions (€5), plus Latin dance nights on Fri (€6). Jam sessions Wed from 9pm; dance nights Fri 10pm–3am.

Moon13 Carl-Benz-Str. 21 ☎069 87 20 00 13, ⓦ moon13.de. New club in the spectacular space formerly occupied by techno star Sven Väth's superclub *Cocoon*, with five themed areas and a music policy that ranges from electronica to house. Entry prices vary, but there are often reduced prices for early arrival. Thurs–Sat 10pm–late.

GAY NIGHTLIFE

Birmingham Pub Battonnstr. 50 ☎069 28 74 71, ⓦ birmingham-pub.com. Smart, spacious and friendly gay bar that's named for Frankfurt's English twin town and stays open later than just about any other in the city centre. The decor's Anglo imagery is more London than Birmingham and there are Irish beers – Guinness and Kilkenny – on draught. Daily noon–6am.

Schwejk Schäfergasse 20 ☎069 29 31 66, ⓦ schwejk -frankfurt.de. Tacky and camp it may be, this small but incredibly popular gay bar is nevertheless enormous fun, spinning a cheesy mix of eurodisco and singalong *Schlager* hits. Tues–Thurs noon–1am, Fri & Sat noon–3am, Sun 6pm–1am.

THEATRES AND CINEMA

Alte Oper Opernplatz ☎069 134 04 00, ⓦ alteoper.de. Classical concerts by the HR-Sinfonieorchester, Frankfurter Opern-und Museumsorchester and others – including big-name touring orchestras – are the mainstay of the programme at the magnificently restored opera house.

FRANKFURT FESTIVALS

Frankfurt's major **festivals** include the spring and autumn **Dippemess** funfairs in the east of the city, and the traditional **Mainfest** funfair and **Museumsuferfest** cultural festival, both of which take place on the banks of the River Main in August; early September brings wine tasting to Fressgass in the form of the **Rheingauer Weinmarkt**. The city's **Christmas market** is one of Germany's most famous, with historic Römerberg as its setting.

Bockenheimer Depot Carlo-Schmid-Platz 1 ☎069 21 24 94 94, ⓦtheforsythecompany.com. The main local venue for performances by the internationally renowned ballet company under the aegis of American William Forsythe, which has home bases in Frankfurt and Dresden. Ticket prices from €27; also hosts opera and drama.

Deutsches Filminstitut Schaumainkai 41 ☎069 961 22 02 20, ⓦdeutsches-filminstitut.de. The Filmmuseum's modern art-house cinema frequently shows films with the original English soundtrack and German subtitles (OmU).

Oper Frankfurt Willy-Brandt-Platz 1 ☎069 21 24 94 94, ⓦoper-frankfurt.de. The classical opera repertoire, in a modern auditorium on Willy-Brandt-Platz opposite the Euro sign; the same building is also home to the Schauspiel Frankfurt (ⓦschauspielfrankfurt.de), the city's premiere company for serious drama.

Papageno Musiktheater In the Palmengarten ☎069 134 04 00, ⓦpapageno-theater.de. Operetta, opera and concert venue in the Palmengarten, with separate children's performances of classics such as The Nutcracker. Performances generally at 4pm, with evening performances on Sat at 7.30pm.

The English Theatre Gallusanlage 7 ☎069 24 23 16 20, ⓦenglish-theatre.de. The city's English-speaking theatre, well supported by the large Anglophone expat community, is reputedly continental Europe's largest, with a populist programme of musicals and established box-office favourites.

Tigerpalast Heiligkreuzgasse 16–20 ☎069 920 02 20, ⓦtigerpalast.de. Glossy, old-style variety shows, with everything from clowns and magicians to acrobats and tightrope walkers. Tickets from €59.75. There's also a restaurant, bar and bistro. Shows Tues–Thurs at 7 & 10pm, Fri & Sat at 7.30 & 10.30pm, Sun 4.30 & 8pm.

DIRECTORY

Bookshops British Bookshop, Börsenstr. 17 (ⓦbritish -bookshop.de), and Hugendubel, Steinweg 12, have good selections of English books.

Consulates Australia, Main Tower 28th floor, Neue Mainzer Str. 52–58 ☎069 90 55 80; UK honorary consul, Barclays Capital, Bockenheimer Landstr. 38–40 ☎069 71 67 53 45; US, Giessener Str. 30 ☎069 753 50.

Emergency Doctor or fire brigade ☎112, police ☎110, women's emergency number ☎08000 116 016.

Laundry Miele Wash World, Moselstr. 17 (Mon–Sat 6am–11pm).

Pharmacy Vivesco Apotheke im Hauptbahnhof on the lower (U-Bahn) concourse of the Hauptbahnhof (Mon–Fri 6.30am–9pm, Sat 8am–9pm, Sun 9am–8pm; ☎069 23 30 47).

Post office Zeil 90 (Mon–Sat 10am–8pm); Hauptbahnhof (Mon–Fri 7am–7pm, Sat 9am–4pm).

Darmstadt and around

Jugendstil, the German version of Art Nouveau, is the reason most people visit **DARMSTADT**, thanks to Grand Duke Ernst Ludwig (1868–1937), under whose aegis the remarkable **Mathildenhöhe** artistic colony flourished in the years before World War I. Nowadays it boasts of its scientific as well as its artistic credentials; students at the Technische Universität ensure an easy-going nightlife, while Darmstadt is popular with families downshifting from the hurly-burly of Frankfurt. The laidback ambience is infectious; in summer a day or two here is liable to induce a certain feel-good languor.

Darmstadt lost its Altstadt to a nightmarish 1944 air raid, and its bland central shopping streets can safely be skipped in favour of the cluster of monuments around the **Schloss** and **Herrngarten**. The most significant attraction, **Mathildenhöhe**, is to the east, while south of the centre there are more formal gardens in **Bessungen**. Away from the main sights, much of Darmstadt – particularly the districts fringing its parks – has a villagey charm.

Darmstadt is a good base for forays into the unspoilt southern-Hesse countryside. To the east, the city gives way to woodland and a remarkable archeological site, the **Grube Messel**. To the south, the Bergstrasse passes through one of Germany's mildest climate zones on its way to Heidelberg. Protected from easterly winds by the Odenwald uplands, the region produces almonds, cherries, peaches and apricots, and in spring is a profusion of blossom. The major attraction, however, is Charlemagne's abbey at **Lorsch**.

11

DARMSTADT

Map labels:
Grossherzoglich-Hessische Porzellansammlung
Prinz-Georgs-Garten
Prettlackisches Gartenhaus
Herrngarten
Hessisches Landesmuseum Darmstadt
Kollegiengebäude
Schloss
Ludwigsmonument
Weisser Turm
Altes Rathaus
Stadtkirche
Altstadtmuseum
Jugendstilbad
MATHILDENHÖHE
Ausstellungsgebäude
Hochzeitsturm
Russische Kapelle
Grosses Glückerthaus
Haus Behrens
Ernst-Ludwig-Haus
Haus Olbrich
Haus Deiters
Kleines Glückerthaus
Haus Habich
Grosser Woog

Streets: PALLASWIESENSTR., BECKERSTR., ECKHARDTSTR., KAUPTSTR., GARDISTENSTR., ARHEILGER STR., FUHRMANNSTR., HEINHEIMER STR., WENCKSTR., LICHTENBERGSTR., KRANICHSTEINER STR., GUTENBERGSTR., HOHLER WEG, KITTLERSTR., SPESSARTRING, DIEBURGER STR., LUKASWEG, OLBRICHWEG, ALEXANDRAWEG, PRINZ-CHRISTIANS-WEG, EUGEN-BRACHT-WEG, ERBACHER STR., LANDGRAF-GEORG-STR., FRANKFURTER STR., SCHLOSSGARTENSTR., ÖFFSTE., MÜLLERSTR., LAUTESCHLAGERSTR., HOCHSCHULSTR., MAGDALENENSTR., MAUERSTR., PÜTZERSTR., ALEXANDERSTR., FRAUNHOFER STR., RUNDETURMSTR., MERCKSTR., STIFTSTR., SCHLEIERMACHERSTR., LUISENSTR., ZEUGHAUSSTR., KAROLINENPLATZ, SCHLOSSGRABEN, RHEINSTR., MARKTPLATZ, WURTHWEG, SCHUCHARDSTR., ERNST-LUDWIG-STR., LUDWIGSTR., KIRCHSTR., PÄDAGOGSTR., RIEDLINGER STR., SÖDERSTR., TEICHHAUSSTR., MARTIN-BUBER-STR., WIENERSTR., DARMSTR., GERVINUSSTR., WILHELMINENSTR., SCHULSTR., ELISABETHENSTR., HÜGELSTR., KARLSTR., KIESSTR.

CAFÉS
3Klang — 2
Café Bormuth — 6

RESTAURANTS
Bockshaut — 7
Havana — 4
L'Oliva — 1
L'Orangerie — 8

BARS
Petri — 3
Ratskeller — 5

ACCOMMODATION
Bockshaut — 5
DJH Darmstadt — 4
friends — 1
Hotel Hornung — 3
Welcome Hotel — 2

NIGHTLIFE
Goldene Krone — 2
Jagdhofkeller — 3
Schlosskeller — 1

0 _____ 200
metres

Luisenplatz

Napoleon raised Darmstadt's Landgraves to the status of Grand Dukes of Hesse and Rhine in 1806. A Neoclassical column, the **Ludwigsmonument**, commemorates the first of them, Grand Duke Ludwig I. It dominates **Luisenplatz**, which with **Mathildenplatz** to the north still suggests the dignity of a capital city in miniature. The Baroque **Kollegiengebäude** on Luisenplatz is the former Hessian Ministry of the Interior.

The Schloss

Schlossmuseum • Marktplatz 15 • Visit by guided tour only every 90min Fri–Sun 10am–5pm • €4 • ⓦ schlossmuseum-darmstadt.de

East of Luisenplatz looms the red-sandstone **Residenzschloss**, a mishmash of ages and styles. In the eighteenth century, French architect Rémy de la Fosse was commissioned to design a Baroque replacement, but only two wings were built. One of these dominates the north side of Marktplatz. The older Renaissance wing houses the **Schlossmuseum**, whose paintings, furniture and objets d'art – including Jugendstil pieces from Mathildenhöhe – give an insight into life at the Darmstadt court.

DARMSTADT'S DYNASTIC WEB

Ernst Ludwig, Grand Duke of Hessen und bei Rhein (1868–1937), was a grandchild of Queen Victoria, as was his first wife Princess Victoria of Edinburgh, but the marriage was an unhappy one and ended in divorce. In In 1931, **Georg Donatus**, Ernst Ludwig's son by his second wife Eleonore, married **Cecilia of Greece**, a member through the maternal line of the Battenberg family, whose family seat, Schloss Heiligenberg, is just south of the city. Shortly after Ernst Ludwig's death in 1937, the young couple were killed in a plane crash en route to a wedding in London. But the connection to Britain lived on: the wedding – of Georg Donatus's brother **Ludwig** to **Margaret Geddes**, daughter of the British politician and businessman Auckland Geddes – went ahead; the bride wore black. After the war, Cecilia's brother Philip married the future Queen Elizabeth II, becoming **Duke of Edinburgh**. Philip's uncle **Louis Mountbatten** was the son of the German-born British admiral Prince Louis of Battenberg – who anglicized the family name during World War I – and of his wife Viktoria, Ernst Ludwig's sister.

THE RUSSIAN CONNECTION

The anglophile Hesse-Darmstadts remained close to the British royal family until Margaret's death in 1997. Yet the family's dynastic links were not only with Britain. Another of Ernst Ludwig's sisters married **Tsar Nicholas II** to become Tsarina Alexandra Fyodorovna, notorious for her friendship with Rasputin. The dynastic links between Darmstadt, London and Russia explain why, when the Russian royals' remains were rediscovered in Yekaterinburg in the early 1990s, a DNA sample from the Duke of Edinburgh helped to identify them.

11

The Altstadt

Facing the Schloss across Marktplatz, the Renaissance **Altes Rathaus** dates from 1598 and nowadays houses a *Hausbrauerei*; a little to the south, the fourteenth-century **Stadtkirche** (Mon 9am–noon, Tues–Fri 9am–4pm, Sat 9am–noon, free) is a rather bleak affair, heavily restored after wartime damage, but it's worth a visit for the magnificent 9m alabaster memorial to Magdalena zur Lippe, wife of Landgrave Georg I.

The streets hereabouts, which once constituted Darmstadt's old town, are now rather soulless. For a glimpse of what was lost cross the footbridge over Holzstrasse to reach the **Hinkelsturm**, a surviving tower of the old city walls, which houses the **Altstadtmuseum** (April–Oct Sat & Sun 2–4pm; €2), where you can see a video of the vanished Altstadt and a model of the city as it was in 1930. Close by, the handsome **Jugendstilbad** (daily 10am–10pm; €5.80) dates from 1909 and offers the chance to swim in grandiose surroundings.

Hessisches Landesmuseum Darmstadt

Friedensplatz 1 • Tues, Thurs & Fri 10am–6pm, Wed 10am–8pm, Sat & Sun 11am–5pm • €6 • ⓦ hlmd.de

Facing the Schloss across **Karolinenplatz** stand two stately nineteenth-century buildings: the Neoclassical court theatre, now the Hesse state archive, and the **Hessisches Landesmuseum Darmstadt**, which reopened in 2014 after a five-year refurbishment programme. Housed in a grandiose, early twentieth-century building by Alfred Messel – who also designed Berlin's Pergamon Museum – the Landesmuseum is one of Germany's largest museums, and its extensive collection embraces everything from fine art to Jugendstil and natural history, including fossils from the Grube Messel. There are paintings by Rubens and Breughel, Arnold Böcklin, August Macke and Gerhard Richter, a seven-room "Beuys Block" that assembles 290 pieces by the artist, and a print collection with works by Michelangelo, Rembrandt and Albrecht Dürer.

The Herrngarten and around

The informal, English-style **Herrngarten** leads north from Karolinenplatz and features a memorial to Goethe, who was a member of the literary circle known as the

Darmstädter Kreis. The streets fringing the Herrngarten have a sleepy charm, with half-timbered cottages and shuttered windows creating a village-like setting.

Prinz-Georg-Garten

Daily: March–Oct 7am–7pm; Nov–Feb 8am–5pm • Free

In the northeast corner of the Herrngarten is the Rococo **Prinz-Georg-Garten**, whose formal design dates from 1764 and combines ornament with practicality: courgettes and chillies grow amid sundials, flowerbeds and neatly pruned fruit trees. On the east side, the **Prettlack'sches Gartenhaus** dates from 1710 and has a prettily painted exterior.

Grossherzoglich-Hessische Porzellsammlung

Schlossgartenstr. 10 • April–Oct Fri–Sun 10am–5pm • €4 • ⓦ porzellanmuseum-darmstadt.de

On the north side of the Herrngarten, the Baroque **Prinz-Georg-Palais** provides a light-flooded setting for the **Grossherzoglich-Hessische Porzellansammlung**. The grand ducal porcelain collection includes Ludwig I's Sèvres dinner service and some delightful Meissen, as well as items from the local Hoechst, Frankenthal and Kelsterbach works and some intriguing English pieces.

Waldspirale

A kilometre or so to the north of Herrngarten across Rhönring stands the extraordinary **Waldspirale** apartment complex, a typical work of the eccentric Austrian architect Friedensreich Hundertwasser, who died in 2000. Trees grow on roofs, onion domes and majolica catch the light and – a Hundertwasser trademark – there isn't a straight line in sight.

Mathildenhöhe

From Karolinenplatz, a traffic-free promenade heads east to **Mathildenhöhe**, the artists' colony founded by the Grand Duke Ernst Ludwig in 1899 (see box below). A grove of clipped plane trees, the **Platanenhain**, stands at the entrance and provides shade for summer boules players. The first building is the tiny, richly decorated **Russische Kapelle** (Tues–Sat 10am–1pm & 2–4pm, Sun 2-4pm; donation requested) built for Ernst Ludwig's relatives, the Russian royal family.

THE MATHILDENHÖHE KÜNSTLERKOLONIE

The **Matildenhöhe** artists' colony in Darmstadt was founded by Grand Duke Ernst Ludwig with the aim of making the city a cultural centre unique in Germany. The artists who joined it built their own houses and lived and worked here, in a district that covered a cluster of streets. The Grand Duke was a passionate art lover, inspired by the English Arts and Crafts movement, one of whose members, Mackay Hugh Baillie Scott, refashioned two rooms of the Grand Duke's residence in 1898. Shortly afterwards, the Grand Duke's office was designed by the German Jugendstil artist Otto Eckmann, and **Jugendstil** – literally the "style of youth" – became the colony's trademark style. Of the seven founding members, the best known are the Austrian architect **Joseph Maria Olbrich**, who as leader of the colony was responsible for the concept of the first two big exhibitions, and the pioneering modernist **Peter Behrens**.

Four major exhibitions – in 1901, 1904, 1908 and 1914 – spread the fame of the colony and its innovative work, which embraced architecture, interior design, furniture and applied arts. Olbrich left for Düsseldorf in 1907, where he designed the Tietz department store (see p.654); he died shortly afterwards. His role as leader of the colony was taken by Albin Müller, but the 1914 exhibition was cut short by the outbreak of World War I, which brought the colony's brief heyday to an end.

The Hochzeitsturm
Tues–Sun 10am–6pm • €3

Behind the Platanenhain soars the 48.5m-high **Hochzeitsturm**, or Wedding Tower, designed by Joseph Maria Olbrich as the city's wedding present to the Grand Duke on the occasion of his second marriage in 1905 and completed in 1908. It remains the colony's most prominent landmark. It's an impressive work of architecture, reflecting the eclectic roots of the style: daringly modern for its time yet with copper-clad gables that recall North German brick Gothic.

Take the lift to the top to enjoy views which extend to Frankfurt and the Taunus on a clear day, then descend via two richly decorated rooms: the **Hochzeitszimmer** (Wedding Room) and the opulent **Fürstenzimmer**. The tower still functions as Darmstadt's registry office.

The Ausstellungsgebäude
Closed until 2016 for renovation • Ⓦ mathildenhoehe.eu

Alongside the Hochzeitsturm the **Ausstellungsgebäude** was built for the colony's 1908 exhibition and is now the venue for major touring exhibitions. It is closed until 2016 for restoration, which as well as modernizing its exhibition facilities will restore it to a closer approximation of its historical appearance.

Museum Künstlerkolonie
Olbrichweg 13a • Tues–Sun 11am–6pm • €5 • Ⓦ mathildenhoehe.eu

Much smaller than the Hochzeitsturm but more richly decorated, nearby **Ernst-Ludwig-Haus** was built for the colony's 1901 exhibition and functioned as the artists' ateliers. It now houses the **Museum Künstlerkolonie**, a fascinating exhibition on the history and work of the colony. There's a model of the area in the foyer, while the displays document the four great exhibitions and the work of individual members of the colony. Highlights include the dining room Peter Behrens created for the Berlin department store Wertheim in 1902.

The artists' villas
South of the main complex lie the **artists' villas**, many of which have been taken over for institutional purposes. Particularly noteworthy are the **Grosses Glückerthaus** at Alexandraweg 23, **Haus Olbrich** at no. 28 and **Haus Behrens** at no. 17.

Rosenhöhe and the Grosser Woog

A five-minute walk east of Mathildenhöhe, the Expressionist, brick-built 1924 **Löwentor** is topped by the lions from the 1914 exhibition and marks the entrance to **Rosenhöhe**, a former vineyard reworked as an English-style park in the early nineteenth century. The grounds are peppered with buildings, from the 1950s artists' ateliers to a pretty Biedermeier tea house and the Neoclassical mausoleum in which many of the Hesse-Darmstadts are buried. The highlight is the formal rose garden created for Ernst Ludwig.

West of Rosenhöhe on Landgraf-Georg-Strasse, the **Familienbad Grosser Woog** (mid-May to mid-Sept Mon, Sat & Sun 9am–8pm, Tues–Fri 8am–8pm; €3) offers open-air swimming at the lake of the same name.

Bessungen

The southern suburb of **Bessungen** (tram #3 from the centre) is home to more verdant delights, where splendid formal Baroque gardens stretch in front of Rémy de la Fosse's elegant 1721 **Orangerie**, which is occasionally used for concerts. Bessungen itself still has the air of a village, especially along Bessunger Strasse, where there's a pretty eleventh-century church and an eighteenth-century hunting lodge, the **Bessunger Jagdhof**. To the north of Bessunger Strasse is another park, the informal Prinz-Emils-Garten.

ARRIVAL AND INFORMATION   DARMSTADT

By train Fast trains from Frankfurt take 15min to reach Darmstadt's Jugendstil Hauptbahnhof, west of the centre. From the station, trams #2, #3 and #5 (€1.90) take around 5min to reach Luisenplatz.

Destinations Frankfurt (up to 5 per hour; 15–20min); Heidelberg (hourly; 35min–1hr 9min).

Tourist office Luisenplatz 5 (April–Sept Mon–Fri 10am–6pm, Sat 10am–4pm, Sun 10am–2pm; Oct–March Mon–Fri 10am–6pm, Sat 10am–4pm; ☎ 06151 13 45 13, ⊚ darmstadt-marketing.de). It can help with accommodation.

Discount card The Darmstadt Card (1 day €6/2 days €9), available from the tourist office, entitles you to free public transport and reduced-price entry to museums.

ACCOMMODATION

Bockshaut Kirchstr. 7–9 ☎ 06151 996 70, ⊚ bockshaut .de. Attractive, country-style rooms above a traditional inn next to the Stadtkirche, on the same site since the eighteenth century and originally a tannery – hence the name, which means buckskin. **€99**

DJH Darmstadt Landgraf-Georg-Str. 119 ☎ 06151 452 93, ⊚ djh-hessen.de. Modern hostel on the fringe of the Grosser Woog lake, a short walk from the Mathildenhöhe museums. Accommodation is in two-, four- or six-bed rooms, all of which are en suite. Prices include breakfast. Dorms **€25.50**

friends Spessartring 53 ☎ 06151 39 15 50, ⊚ hotelfriends.de. Stylish, revamped boutique-style hotel close to Mathildenhöhe that is a lot more attractive

than its rather brutalist external appearance suggests, with 22 individually decorated rooms with balcony and free wi-fi. Rates are cheapest at weekends. **€85**

Hotel Hornung Mornewegstr. 43 ☎ 06151 92 66, ⊚ hotel-darmstadt.com. Business-oriented hotel with big, bright rooms with minibar, TV and bath or shower, and a peaceful, if characterless location between the Hauptbahnhof and Herrngarten. Bargain rates at weekends. **€45**

Welcome Hotel Karolinenplatz 4 ☎ 06151 391 40, ⊚ welcome-hotel-darmstadt.de. Stylish, business-style hotel on a very central site fringing both Karolinenplatz and the Herrngarten. Air-conditioned rooms have flat-screen TVs and wi-fi, and there are cheap weekend rates and early booking deals. **€84.15**

EATING AND DRINKING

A cluster of places between the Schloss and Stadtkirche aside, the most promising area for places to **eat** and **drink** in Darmstadt is north and east of the Herrngarten in the Martinsviertel, with another scattering of good options in Bessungen.

CAFÉS

3Klang Riegerplatz 3 ☎ 06151 669 88 43, ⊚ 3klang-bar.de. Stylish, very popular café/bar in the Martinsviertel, serving breakfast (€5.80 up) until 3pm and a daily-changing menu of salads and pasta from around €8. Outdoor seating in summer. Mon 4pm–midnight, Tues–Thurs & Sun 9.30am–midnight, Fri & Sat 9.30am–1am.

Café Bormuth Marktplatz 5 ☎ 06151 170 90, ⊚ bormuth.de. Sumptuous cakes, a large selection of reasonably-priced breakfasts (from €2.45), pasta (€6.95 up), salads and savouries and a terrace with views of the Schloss and Altes Rathaus, though it's not quite as swanky as it was in its 1950s prime. Mon–Fri 7.30am–7pm, Sat 7.30am–6pm, Sun 10.30am–6pm.

RESTAURANTS

Bockshaut Kirchstr. 7–9 ☎ 06151 996 70, ⊚ bockshaut .de. Reasonably-priced regional cooking (main courses from €12) plus lighter choices, in an atmospheric, traditional-style *Gasthaus* close to the Stadtkirche and

Rathaus. There's a lovely shady garden terrace in summer. Mon–Thurs noon–2pm & 6–10pm, Fri & Sat noon–3pm & 6–10.30pm, Sun noon–3pm.

Havana Lauteschlägerstr. 42 ☎ 06151 71 04 59, ⊚ havana-da.de. Labyrinthine Cuban/Hispanic restaurant close to the Technische Universität, with a long menu, classic and Latin cocktails and a very pretty garden at the back. *Rollos* (filled flatbreads) from €9.10, tortillas from €7.30 and pizza from €6.30. Mon11am–1am, Tues–Thurs 5pm–1am, Fri 5pm–2am, Sat 11am–2am, Sun 11am–1am.

L'Oliva Pallaswiesenstr. 19 ☎ 06151 278 39 39, ⊚ loliva-darmstadt.de. Modern Italian restaurant with a €9.90 three-course set lunch, pasta from €7.50 and meat or fish main courses around €14–20. There's a very pleasant tree-shaded garden at the front. Mon–Fri 11.30am–2.30pm & 5.30–11.30pm, Sat 5.30–11.30pm.

L'Orangerie Bessungerstr. 44 ☎ 06151 396 64 46, ⊚ orangerie-darmstadt.de; tram #3. Michelin- and Gault-Millau-garlanded gourmet restaurant in Bessungen, with a cool, spacious dining room and Italian-influenced cooking. Set menus from €48, six-course dégustation menu €75. Daily noon–2pm & 6.30–10.30pm.

BARS

Petri Arheilger Str. 50 ☎06151 971 04 30, ⓦpetri-gaststaette.de. Relaxed, rather stylish neighbourhood bar near the Herrngarten, with a pleasant beer garden, simple food and *Apfelwein*. Chalked-up menu of *Flammkuchen*, salads, *Schnitzel* etc from around €7.60. Mon–Sat 6pm–late.

★**Ratskeller** Marktplatz 8 ☎06151 264 44, ⓦratskeller-darmstadt.de. *Hausbrauerei* in the old Rathaus, dominated by a copper microbrewery and serving its own-brew *Pils*, dark *Spezial*, *Bock* and *Hefe* beers (from €3.20 for 0.4l). There's traditional food – including *Leberkäse* and *Schnitzel* – from around €6. Daily 10am–1am.

NIGHTLIFE AND ENTERTAINMENT

The presence of the university ensures a smattering of studenty clubs and live venues in Darmstadt; these aside, the city tends rather more towards laidback drinking than late-night revelry. In July and Aug the **Darmstädter Residenzfestspiele** brings classical music to historic venues across the city, including the Orangerie, Kollegiengebäude and Mathildenhöhe.

CLUBS AND LIVE MUSIC

Goldene Krone Schustergasse 18 ☎06151 213 52, ⓦgoldene-krone.de. Disco, theatre and live bands in the Altstadt's only surviving seventeenth-century burgher's house. There's live music free of charge most days in the *Kneipe*, plus indie, trash and hip-hop discos (€4) Fri & Sat. Kneipe gigs start 7pm; discos generally from 10pm.

Jagdhofkeller Bessungerstr. 84 ☎06151 66 40 91, ⓦjagdhofkeller.com. Jazz, *chanson* and stand-up comedy in the gorgeous setting of the Jagdhof's stone-vaulted cellar, originally used to store game. There's a bar and a French restaurant, *Belleville*. Gigs generally begin at 8–9pm.

Schlosskeller In the Schloss ☎06151 16 31 17, ⓦschlosskeller-darmstadt.de. Student-run DJ bar and live-music venue in the cellars of the Schloss; there's also a *Biergarten* in one of the Schloss's courtyards and cinema shows in summer. Tues live gigs and cultural events 8pm; Thurs–Sat 10pm–late.

THEATRE

Staatstheater Darmstadt Georg-Büchner-Platz ☎06151 281 16 00, ⓦstaatstheater-darmstadt.de. The main venue for drama, concerts and opera in Darmstadt, with three auditoria, its own resident opera, drama companies and an orchestra, the Staatsorchester.

11

The Grube Messel

A few kilometres east of Darmstadt is the **GRUBE MESSEL**, a redundant oil-shale pit on the site of an ancient volcanic crater-lake which has yielded such rich fossil finds that it is now a UNESCO World Heritage Site. The fossils date from the Eocene period around 49 million years ago, when the climate in what is now Hesse was subtropical; the present-day descendants of many of the species found here – including opossum, anteaters, flightless birds and crocodiles – are now only found far from Germany.

The fossils are in exceptionally good condition, often preserving food residue in their stomachs: the macrocranion – a relative of the modern hedgehog – has been found with fish bones in its stomach, while the stomachs of the world's oldest-known bats preserve the scales of moths and butterflies. Messel is particularly famous for its fossils of ancient horses, which were tiny compared with their modern descendants.

Visitor centre

Rössdorfer Str. 108, Messel • Daily 10am–5pm; last entry one hour before closing • €10; fossil pit tours from €7; €20 surcharge per group for tours in English • ⓦgrube-messel.de • Train from Darmstadt to Messel (hourly; 10min), then bus (hourly; 2min) to the centre; by car, take the side turning off the road to Messel, just north of the junction with the Darmstadt–Dieburg road

The impressive modern **Besucherzentrum** (visitor centre) has displays relating to the origins and history of the site, from vulcanicity and the evolution of the landscape to its later industrial heritage. It also organizes regular daily **guided tours** of the pit itself; it's advisable to book in advance, since demand is heavy. The centre has a café.

Fossilien- und Heimatmuseum

Langgasse 2, Messel • April–Oct daily 11am–5pm, Nov–March Sat & Sun 11am–5pm • Free • ⓦ messelmuseum.de • Train from Darmstadt to Messel (hourly; 10min)

As well as seeing the pit itself, it's worth3 stopping by the small **Fossilien- und Heimatmusem Messel** in the old centre of Messel north of the train station, which has lots of fossils on display. The Senckenberg Museum (see p.567) in Frankfurt is also worth a visit.

Kloster Lorsch

Abbey grounds Tues–Sun 10am–5pm • Free • **Königshalle** Guided tours hourly March–Oct Tues–Sun 11am–4pm; Nov–Feb Sat & Sun 11am–4pm • €5 • **Lauresham** Tours April–Oct Tues–Sun at 11am, 1pm & 3pm • €5 • **Museumszentrum Lorsch** Nibelungenstr. 35 • Tues–Sun 10am–5pm • €3 • ⓦ kloster-lorsch.de

What it lacks in size, the mysterious **Königshalle** at the former Benedictine abbey of **Lorsch** – a UNESCO World Heritage Site – more than makes up for in beauty and historical significance. The royal abbey was built between 767 and 880 AD, and the Königshalle dates from the latter part of this period. With its well-preserved, festive red-and-white stone facade rising above three very Roman-looking arches, it certainly looks like a gatehouse, hence its popular name of Torhalle or "gatehouse", but it's actually not at all certain what the original function of the little building was. Archeological investigation suggests, however, that it stood within the main gate of the abbey, whose precincts covered a much greater area than that which you now see. The hall upstairs is a palimpsest of wall paintings, from two layers of Carolingian origin to traces of Romanesque and more substantial, later Gothic work.

The church, Wissensspeicher, Lauresham and Altmünster

Considerable work has been done in recent years to fully realize the visitor potential of the Lorsch site. The tough-looking twelfth-century abbey **church** behind the Königshalle is built on what remains of a much larger and older building; the grounds also contain a herb garden and an imposing medieval tithe-barn, refurbished during 2014 as the **Wissensspeicher** to house archeological displays (accessible during guided tours). **Lauresham**, a re-creation of a Carolingian agricultural settlement, was scheduled to open late in 2014; a suggested route for visitors unites it with the Königshalle and **Kloster Altmünster**, the site of the earliest abbey buildings. Along the way you pass a tobacco field; a further museum is planned in the former tobacco barn close to Kloster Altmünster.

Museumszentrum Lorsch

To visit the Königshalle's interior enquire at the **Museumszentrum Lorsch** across Nibelungenstrasse from the abbey. It has a recently enlarged section on the abbey's history plus well-curated displays on tobacco – a major crop in the area until the twentieth century – and an intriguing section on domestic life, with period interiors including a 1920s so-called Frankfurt Kitchen, regarded as the prototype of the fitted kitchen.

ARRIVAL AND DEPARTURE	KLOSTER LORSCH

By train To reach Lorsch by train from Darmstadt change at Bensheim onto the Worms line; the journey takes at least 40min. The abbey is within walking distance of the station.

EATING AND DRINKING

Café am Kloster Nibelungenstr. 39 ☎ 06251 554 11. Conveniently sited close to the abbey and museum, this café dispenses breakfasts (from €3.20), filled rolls (from €2) and light meals plus home-made ice cream and cakes. Daily 9am–midnight.

Raffaello Bahnhofstr. 5 ☎ 06251 987 025. Big, reliable traditional Italian a short stroll from the abbey and museum along Lorsch's main street, with good-value pasta (around €5.60) and pizza dishes, plus coffee and ice cream. Daily 11.30am–3.20pm & 5.30–11pm.

Wiesbaden

With its grand hotels, opulent villas and antique shops, few places in Germany exude the style of Kaisers Zeiten – the age of the Kaisers – quite as strongly as **WIESBADEN**, 40km west of Frankfurt. The Romans had a fort here, the hot springs have been popular for centuries and the city was capital of the Duchy of Nassau from 1815 until it was subsumed into Prussia after the 1866 Austro-Prussian war. But it was after German unification in 1871 that Wiesbaden experienced its fashionable heyday, favoured by Kaiser Wilhelm II himself, and it's from this period that its grandiose architecture dates. It came through two world wars in good shape, its status growing post-1945 as capital of the new Land of Hesse and as the European headquarters of the US Air Force: the Berlin airlift was coordinated from here. It's also a centre for the *Sekt* – or **German champagne** – industry.

Idyllically situated at the foot of the rolling Taunus and with lavish parks and greenery, Wiesbaden combines the attractions of a health resort with those of a city. The traffic-free **Altstadt** is easily explored on foot and is fringed to the east by **Wilhelmstrasse** – the kilometre-long avenue known as the "Rue" – with the **Kurhaus** on its eastern side. Within easy reach to the north, the **Neroberg** is popular for fresh air and views, while south of the centre the suburb of **Biebrich** boasts a Baroque Schloss and park. Offering everything from bracing walks and spa facilities to good restaurants,

11

WIESBADEN

CAFÉS AND CHEAP EATS
Café Maldaner	7
Feinkost Feickert	10
Fritz Kunder	11
Der Turm	1

RESTAURANTS
Ente	3
Il Delfino	5
Käfers	9
Lumen	4
Orangerie	3
Spital	2

BARS AND WEINSTUBEN
Andechser im Ratskeller	8
Weinhaus Kögler	6

ACCOMMODATION
DJH Wiesbaden	6
Drei Lilien	4
Hotel de France	1
Hotel Hansa	7
Hotel Klemm	2
Nassauer Hof	5
Town Hotel	3

NIGHTLIFE
Alibi	2
Park Café	3
Schlachthof	4
Thalhaus	1

0   200
metres

luxurious shopping and high culture – all of it overlaid with an atmosphere of faded glamour and genteel convalescence – the "Nice of the North" is unique among major German cities. The big annual cultural event is the **Maifestspiele** in May, Germany's second-oldest theatre festival after Bayreuth.

The Altstadt

Most of the sights of Wiesbaden's Altstadt cluster around Schlossplatz, where the modest, early seventeenth-century **Altes Rathaus** is the oldest building in the city, and its more imposing neighbours are testament to Wiesbaden's rapid rise during the nineteenth century.

Stadtschloss, Neues Rathaus and Marktkirche

The Neoclassical **Stadtschloss**, on the north side of Schlossplatz, was built in 1840 as a town residence for Duke Wilhelm of Nassau and was later a favourite residence of the Kaiser. It now houses the Hessischer Landtag – Hesse's state parliament. On the east side, the **Neues Rathaus** is an odd-looking affair, having lost much of its neo-Renaissance facade during World War II; the facade facing Dern'sches Gelände to the south is original. Next to the Neues Rathaus rise the red brick spires of the neo-Gothic **Marktkirche**, the city's main Lutheran church and a distinctive landmark. To the north and west of Schlossplatz, the maze of narrow lanes is enlivened in summer by café terraces, particularly along **Goldgasse**.

Kaiser Friedrich Therme and around

May–Aug daily 10am–10pm; Sept–April Mon–Thurs & Sun 10am–10pm, Fri & Sat 10am–midnight • Summer €4.50/hour, winter €6/hour • ⓦ wiesbaden.eu

On the Altstadt's western fringe stands the **Kaiser-Friedrich-Therme**, whose imposing Irish-Roman Bath – a Jugendstil pool and sauna richly ornamented with frescoes and ceramics – opened in 1913 on the site of a hot spring known to the Romans. The sauna is nudist.

Just south is the **Heidenmauer**, a fragment of a fourth-century defensive wall that is the most visible remnant of Wiesbaden's Roman past. To the north, steam issues from the pavilion housing the **Kochbrunnen** or boiling fountain – aptly named, as the water bubbles up at a piping 66°C. Grand hotels and former hotels surround the Kochbrunnenplatz on which the spring emerges.

The "Rue" and around

Wilhelmstrasse – the so-called "Rue" – runs north to south through the city, its western side a *flâneur*'s paradise of upmarket boutiques, elegant cafés and hotels, many of them long established behind florid, late nineteenth-century facades.

Hessisches Staatstheater

On the eastern side of Rue lies the **Hessisches Staatstheater**, a turn-of-the-twentieth-century pile built at the behest of Kaiser Wilhelm II by the renowned Viennese theatre architects Fellner and Helmer, and a rarity in a large German city for preserving its graceful auditorium in its original neo-Baroque style. The extravagant neo-Rococo foyer, built in 1902, now functions as a breathtakingly opulent bar. Even if you don't go to a performance, it's worth asking whether any of the tourist office's themed guided tours might be due to visit, though they were not doing so at the time of writing. The theatre's relatively inconspicuous main entrance is in the colonnaded group of buildings surrounding the **Bowling Green** to the north.

FROM TOP MUSEUM FÜR KOMMUNIKATION, FRANKFURT (P.568); PORTAL, ELISABETHKIRCHE, MARBURG (P.595) >

Kurhaus and Casino Wiesbaden

Casino Wiesbaden Kurhausplatz 1 • Daily: slot machines noon–4am, table games 2.45pm–3am (until 4am Fri & Sat) • Slot machines minimum stake 1 euro cent; table games area admission €2.50, minimum bet €1 • ⓦ casino-wiesbaden.de

Dominating the Bowling Green to the north of the Hessisches Staatstheater is the Neoclassical **Kurhaus**, built at the Kaiser's request between 1904 and 1907 and housing a splendid concert hall, the **Friedrich von Thiersch Saal**, as well as the plush **Casino Wiesbaden**, where you'll need proper attire; for men that means a jacket and preferably a tie, though neat jeans are acceptable and if your clothing fails to cut a dash, they have an emergency stock for hire. You'll also need photo ID.

Kurpark and Thermalbad Aukammtal

In summer, a broad café terrace sits on the edge of the English-style **Kurpark** at the back of the Kurhaus, where there's a boating lake (boat hire Wed–Fri from 3pm, Sat & Sun from 11am; from €7). A pleasant walk east from here through parkland brings you to the **Thermalbad Aukammtal**, Leibnizstr. 7 (pools Mon, Wed, Thurs & Sun 8am–10pm, Tues 6am–10pm, Fri & Sat 8am–midnight; €10), a modern spa with indoor and outdoor pools and extensive sauna facilities.

North from the Kurpark: Taunusstrasse and the Neroberg

Antique dealers and art galleries set the tone in discreetly luxurious **Taunusstrasse**, which begins at the Kurpark's northwestern corner and leads to another garden, the **Nerotal-Anlagen**. Fringed by villas, the little park contains a statue of **Bismarck** looking every inch the Prussian warrior-statesman, complete with spiked *Pickelhaube* helmet.

The Neroberg

Nerobergbahn April, Sept & Oct daily 10am–7pm; May–Aug daily 9am–8pm • One-way €2.50, return €3.30 • ⓦ eswe-verkehr.de/nerobergbahn/ • Opelbad May–Sept 7am–8pm • €8.20

At the far end of the Nerotal-Anlagen, a charmingly old-fashioned funicular railway, the **Nerobergbahn**, ascends the slopes of the 245m Neroberg – part of the wooded **Taunus** range (see p.587), which sweeps along Wiesbaden's northern boundary and is crisscrossed by hiking and cycling trails, a few of which depart from the base of the Nerobergbahn. A steep, zigzag path also gives access to the hill. There are wonderful views over the city from the little **Nerobergtempel** near the top, and there's also a beautiful Bauhaus-style lido, the **Opelbad**, whose open-air pool overlooks vineyards and has a café.

Russische Kirche and Russian cemetery

Russische Kirche Summer daily 10am–6pm; winter Sat & Sun10am–4.45pm • €2

From the Neroberg's summit, paths wind down through the woods to the gold-domed Orthodox **Russische Kirche**, built between 1848 and 1855 in memory of Elisabeth Michailovna, the young wife of the Duke of Nassau and niece of the Tsar, who died in childbirth in 1845, less than a year after arriving in Wiesbaden; her sarcophagus is inside. Nearby a lovely **Russian cemetery** contains the grave of the painter Alexei von Jawlensky and a who's who of the Baltic German aristocracy – members of the old ruling caste of Russian-dominated Estonia and Latvia who, while preserving their German identity, converted to the Orthodox faith.

South from the Kurpark: Warmer Damm

To the south of the Kurpark, grand villas fringe another large park, **Warmer Damm**, including the **Villa Söhnlein**, also known as the "Little White House", built in 1906 by the *Sekt* merchant Wilhelm Söhnlein for his American wife in imitation of the Washington original, and the Pompeian **Villa Clementine**, the scene of the forced repatriation in 1888 of the 12-year-old Crown Prince of Serbia, whose mother had settled in Wiesbaden after separating from the Serbian king, Milan I.

Gustav-Freytag-Strasse and Solmsschlösschen

From the southeast corner of Warmer Damm, a stroll uphill on **Gustav-Freytag-Strasse** underlines the opulence of nineteenth-century Wiesbaden, with villas in every conceivable style from Neoclassical to half-timbered and Jugendstil. The jumble of porticoes, shutters, castellated roofs and gables is more impressive the higher you climb: a right turn into Solmsstrasse brings you to one of the most imposing, the **Solmsschlösschen**, a neo-Gothic fantasy built in 1890 for Prince Albrecht zu Solms-Braunfels.

Museum Wiesbaden

Friedrich-Ebert-Allee 2 · Tues & Thurs 10am–8pm, Wed & Fri-Sun 10am–5pm · €6 · ⓦ museum-wiesbaden.de

The high point of the **Museum Wiesbaden** is the collection of paintings by the Russian-born but Wiesbaden-based Expressionist, **Alexei von Jawlensky** (1864–1941). Jawlensky was a key member of the Munich Blaue Reiter group (see box, p.347) in World War I and is best known for his richly coloured portraits of women, represented here by *Lady with a Fan* from 1909. There are also some late works by Karl Schmidt-Rottluff and paintings by Ernst Ludwig Kirchner, Emil Nolde and Max Beckmann. More contemporary art – including large-scale installations – is exhibited on the first floor. The museum's collection of old masters encompasses everything from Vermeer to religious art and landscapes; there's also an extensive natural history collection.

Biebrich

The riverside suburb of **Biebrich** (bus #4 or #14) feels like a separate town, graced by a Baroque **Schloss** that sprawls along the banks of the Rhine and was built between 1700 and 1750 for the Dukes of Nassau. It's not generally open to the public, but the lovely park behind it is worth a stroll. Biebrich is also a stopping-off point for **boat trips** of the KD line (ⓣ 0611 60 09 95, ⓦ k-d.com).

On the northern fringe of Biebrich is **Henkell**, the best-known – if not necessarily the most prestigious – German *Sekt* producer. By booking three weeks in advance you can tour its neo-Rococo **Sektkellerei** (Mon, Wed & Thurs 10am & 2pm, Tues & Fri 10am; 90min; €8/person includes free tastings; ⓣ 0611 632 09, ⓦ henkell.de; bus #4 or #14, stop "Landesdenkmal").

ARRIVAL AND GETTING AROUND   WIESBADEN

By train S-Bahn trains from Frankfurt take 42min to reach Wiesbaden's monumental Hauptbahnhof, south of the centre, from where buses (#4, #14) head north to Dern'sches Gelände. Destinations Frankfurt (very frequent; 33–47min); Mainz (3–4 per hour; 11–14min).

By bike You can rent bicycles from Der Radler at the Hauptbahnhof (Mon–Fri 8am–6pm; May–Sept also Sat 9am–1pm; ⓣ 0171 222 78 88).

INFORMATION

Tourist office Marktplatz 1 (Mon–Fri 10am–6pm, Sat 10am–3pm; April–Sept also Sun 11am–3pm; ⓣ 0611 1729 930, ⓦ wiesbaden.eu). It can help with accommodation.

Discount card The Wiesbaden Tourist Card (2 days €12.50), available from the tourist office, entitles you to free travel on public transport in Wiesbaden and to and from Frankfurt airport, plus cut-price entry to museums.

ACCOMMODATION

HOTELS

Drei Lilien Spiegelgasse 3 ⓣ 0611 99 17 80, ⓦ dreililien.com. Privately-run hotel in an attractive Jugendstil building close to the Kurhaus and theatre.

En-suite rooms have TV and free wi-fi. Room rates exclude breakfast. **€85**

Hotel de France Taunusstr. 49 ⓣ 0611 95 97 30, ⓦ hoteldefrance.de. Elegantly contemporary, modest-sized

11

boutique-style hotel on one of Wiesbaden's smartest shopping streets. Rooms have flat-screen TV, free wi-fi, bath or shower, and most have DVD and CD players. Good deals are available through the website. **€71.25**

Hotel Hansa Bahnhofstr. 23 ☎ 0611 90 12 40, ⓦ hotel-hansa-wiesbaden.de. Comfortable mid-range hotel dating from 1898, part of the Best Western network and close to the Museum Wiesbaden. Rooms have bath or shower, TV and fast internet. The hotel has a restaurant, and parking is available. **€84**

Hotel Klemm Kapellenstr. 9 ☎ 0611 58 20, ⓦ hotel-klemm.de. Family-run boutique hotel with nineteenth-century Jugendstil architecture, stylish, individually-designed non-smoking rooms and a quiet but central location just off Taunusstrasse and close to the Kochbrunnen. Rooms have shower, WC, wi-fi and flat-screen TV. **€72**

Nassauer Hof Kaiser-Friedrich-Platz 3–4 ☎ 0611 13 30, ⓦ nassauer-hof.de. The best hotel in town – a grand hotel of the old school with every conceivable luxury and a plum position close to the Kurhaus. Rooms have en-suite bath or shower, minibar, safe, TV and wireless internet and there's an extensive spa and fitness complex. A member of the Leading Hotels of the World. Room rates do not include breakfast. **€250**

Town Hotel Spiegelgasse 5 ☎ 0611 36 01 60, ⓦ townhotel.de. Bright, attractive hotel with crisp, modern decor and a very central yet relatively quiet location; rooms have hardwood floors, pale maple furniture, flat-screen TV, kettles and high-speed internet. **€69**

HOSTELS

DJH Wiesbaden Blücherstr. 66 ☎ 0611 44 90 81, ⓦ djh-hessen.de; bus #14 from Hauptbahnhof to "Gneisenaustrasse". Modern hostel to the west of the city centre, with renovated en-suite accommodation including large family rooms, a sports ground including a volleyball court and wireless internet. Breakfast included. Dorms and family rooms (per person) **€27.50**

EATING AND DRINKING

CAFÉS AND CHEAP EATS

Café Maldaner Marktstr. 34 ☎ 0611 30 52 14, ⓦ cafe-maldaner.de. Grand café and *Konditorei*, established in 1866 and the classic Wiesbaden *Kaffee und Kuchen* stop. Breakfasts from €4.50, baked potatoes €7.90, *Flammkuchen* – Alsace-style pizza – and *Schnitzels* from €8.90. Mon–Sat 8.30am–7pm, Sun 10am–6pm.

Feinkost Feickert Wilhelmstr. 14 ☎ 0611 990 75 13, ⓦ feinkost-feickert.de. Informal bistro attached to Wiesbaden's best delicatessen, with a terrace fronting the "Rue", and a short, cosmopolitan menu of light, daily-changing specials. Breakfast from €4, salads and mains from around €9. Mon–Fri 9am–6.30pm, Sat 9am–4pm.

★ Fritz Kunder Wilhelmstr. 12 ☎ 0611 30 15 98, ⓦ kunder-confiserie.de. Every spa town has its sweet treat to take away the taste of the waters; Wiesbaden's is the *Wiesbaden Törtchen*, a sophisticated affair of pineapple jelly and bitter dark chocolate, available from this elegant *Konditorei*. They also serve ice creams, coffee (from €1.70) and cakes (from €2.80). Mon–Fri 9am–6.30pm, Sat 9am–4pm.

Der Turm Auf dem Neroberg 1 ☎ 0611 959 09 87, ⓦ derturm.com. Strategically placed café atop the Neroberg, with a sunny terrace, cocktails, light snacks and full food menu including salads and *Flammkuchen* from €8.50. The tower itself is all that remains of a historic hotel that once stood on the site. Mon–Thurs & Sun noon–midnight, Fri & Sat noon–1am.

RESTAURANTS

Ente Kaiser-Friedrich-Platz 3–4 ☎ 0611 13 36 66, ⓦ nassauer-hof.de. Michelin-starred *haute cuisine* in the elegant surroundings of one of Germany's most long-established gourmet haunts, at the *Nassauer Hof* hotel (see above). Four-course set menu €98, five courses €115; main courses à la carte from around €44. There's also a more informal bistro. Tues–Fri 6.30–10pm, Sat noon–3pm & 6.30–10pm.

Il Delfino Goldgasse. 12 ☎ 0611 37 50 09. Good-value Italian with alfresco tables on lively Goldgasse, with a vast selection of pizza from €5 and an equally impressive selection of pasta dishes from €6.50, plus salads and chalked-up meat and fish specials. It stays open later than most, too. Daily 11am–midnight.

Käfers Kurhausplatz 1 ☎ 0611 53 62 00, ⓦ kurhaus-gastronomie.de. Classy without being stuffy, this elegant brasserie in the Kurhaus has bags of atmosphere and a beer garden in the Kurpark. Main courses from around €18.50; two-course business lunch €20, Sun brunch with live music €35. Mon–Thurs 11.30am–1am, Fri & Sat 11.30am–2am, Sun 11am–1am.

Lumen Marktplatz ☎ 0611 30 02 00, ⓦ lumen-wiesbaden.de. Huge, light-flooded restaurant, café & bar in the centre of Marktplatz, with a massive garden terrace in summer, a daily-changing menu and a fixed-price €13 lunch with mineral water and coffee. Mon–Thurs 9am–1am, Fri & Sat 9am–1am, Sun 10am–1am.

Orangerie Kaiser-Friedrich-Platz 3–4 ☎ 0611 13 36 33, ⓦ nassauer-hof.de. The *Nassauer Hof* hotel's German restaurant has a pretty winter garden and serves refined daily specials from around €24: char with white bean purée or Irish black Angus beef with herb butter, for instance – plus a €39 Sun-lunch buffet. Daily noon–11pm.

Spital Kochbrunnenplatz 3 ☎ 0611 52 88 30, ⓦ spital-wiesbaden.de. Trendy café/bar and restaurant close to the Kochbrunnen, with a stylish mix of historic and modern decor, DJs, outdoor terrace and food. There's a big choice of breakfasts (from €5.40) until 3pm; main courses from around €13. Mon–Fri 10am–1am, Sat & Sun 10am–2am.

BARS AND WEINSTUBEN

Andechser im Ratskeller Schlossplatz 6 ☎ 0611 30 00 23, ⓦderandechser-wiesbaden.de. Hearty Bavarian cooking – including *Schweinshaxe* for €9.80 – washed down with *Weissbier*, *Dunkel* or *Bergbock* from the famous Andechs monastery brewery in the spacious vaulted setting of the Neues Rathaus's *Bierkeller*. Mon–Sat 11am–midnight, Sun 11am–10pm.

Weinhaus Kögler Grabenstr. 18 ☎ 0611 37 67 37, ⓦweinhaus-koegler.de. Wiesbaden's oldest *Weinstube* is a charmingly traditional affair in the Altstadt, with good dry Rieslings to accompany the soups, cheese dishes (including *Handkäs mit Musik*) and more substantial mains (€13–17). Mon–Sat 5pm–1am.

NIGHTLIFE AND ENTERTAINMENT

CLUBS AND LIVE MUSIC

Alibi Taunussstr. 27 ☎ 061 123 45 67, ⓦalibi-club.de. Stylish, intimate dance club with revamped modern decor and a "dress to impress" door policy. Fri nights focus on house sounds, with a more varied programme – including live acts – on Sat. Fri & Sat 11pm–5am.

Park Café Wilhelmstr. 36 ☎ 0611 341 32 46, ⓦpcwi.de. Classy lounge bar and disco, with a long history – Elvis Presley and Frank Sinatra are among its many past VIP denizens – and a music policy embracing salsa, house, hip-hop and urban beats. Wed 8pm–late, Fri–Sun 10pm–late.

Schlachthof Murnaustr. 1 ☎ 0611 97 44 50, ⓦschlachthof-wiesbaden.de. Wiesbaden's foremost venue for live gigs, in a former slaughterhouse close to the Hauptbahnhof. On weekdays it hosts live gigs, film, food events and poetry slams; at weekends there are clubnights (including gay night Let's Go Queer), with DJs spinning anything from hip-hop to deep house. Gigs from 8pm; clubnights 11pm–late.

Thalhaus Nerotal 18 ☎ 0611 18 51 267, ⓦthalhaus.de. Intimate café and arts venue between Taunusstrasse and the Neroberg, with a hugely varied programme that includes everything from comedy to cabaret, live music and improvisation. It also hosts discos. Performances generally 5pm or 8pm.

THEATRES

Friedrich-von-Theirsch-Saal Kurhausplatz 1 ☎ 0611 172 92 90, ⓦwiesbaden.de. Opulent 1350-seat concert hall in the historic setting of the Kurhaus, the venue for orchestral and choral concerts and balls.

Hessisches Staatstheater Christian Zais Str. 3 ☎ 0611 13 23 25, ⓦstaatstheater-wiesbaden.de. Wiesbaden's gorgeous Viennese-style nineteenth-century theatre hosts classical and contemporary drama, opera and ballet, musicals and concerts. In addition to the main auditorium there's a smaller, modern one and an intimate, 89-seat studio.

11

The Taunus

North of Frankfurt, skyscrapers and Autobahns swiftly give way to the unspoilt, wooded hills of the **Taunus**. Tantalizingly close to the city, the Taunus range is never very high, but it offers a refreshing foretaste of what much of rural Hesse away from the Rhine–Main conurbation is like. The affluent spa-town of **Bad Homburg** – at the foot of the Taunus yet within sight of the Frankfurt skyline – is the region's gateway, with easy access to the heights of the **Hochtaunus range** and to the reconstructed Roman fort at **Saalburg**.

Bad Homburg

BAD HOMBURG disputes with Wiesbaden and Baden-Baden the dubious distinction of being the spa where Russian novelist Fyodor Dostoyevsky frittered away his fortune at the roulette wheel and thus found inspiration for *The Gambler*. Literary associations aside, the town has a certain genteel quality and a rather longer history than its Wilhelmine airs and graces would suggest: from 1622 to 1806 it was the seat of the Lilliputian landgraviate of Hesse-Homburg, and it has the Schloss to prove it. In the nineteenth century Kaiser Wilhelm II was a regular visitor and the Prince of Wales – the future British king Edward VII – popularized the Homburg hat. Long, straight Louisenstrasse links the **historic quarter** at the top of the hill with the **spa quarter** lower down.

The Landgrafenschloss

Schloss Guided tours hourly Tues–Sun: March–Oct 10am–4pm; Nov–Feb 10am–3pm • €4 • ⓦ schloesser-hessen.de • **Weisser Turm** March–Oct Tues–Sun 10am–4pm; Nov–Feb daily 10am–3pm • €1 • **Schlosspark** Daily until dusk • Free

The historic quarter centres on the **Landgrafenschloss**, a largely Baroque affair created in 1678 for the one-legged Landgrave Friedrich II, known as "Silver Leg" and the inspiration for Kleist's drama *The Prince of Homburg*. The Schloss apartments reflect not just the taste of the Landgraves but also that of the Hohenzollerns, for Bad Homburg was the imperial family's preferred summer residence before 1918. The **Englischer Flügel**, or English Wing, contains the collections of Elizabeth, daughter of the British king George III, who married Landgrave Friedrich VI in 1818. The **Königsflügel** or King's Wing of the Schloss was undergoing extensive renovation as this book went to press.

The slender, 48m **Weisser Turm** is the sole surviving part of the original medieval castle; you can climb it for views of the surrounding countryside. The attractive **Schlosspark** mixes formal beds with informal, English-style landscaping.

The Altstadt and Dorotheenstrasse

To the north of the Schloss, Bad Homburg's diminutive **Altstadt** is little more than a huddle of red roofs clustering around the surviving vestiges of the medieval defences; rather more impressive is the elegant quarter along Dorotheenstrasse east of the Schloss, where the restored Baroque **Sinclair Haus** (Tues 2–8pm, Wed–Fri 2–7pm, Sat & Sun 10am–6pm; €5, free on Wed) is the venue for temporary art exhibitions.

The Kurpark

Park Free access • **Kur-Royal Day Spa** Daily 10am–10pm • 2hr €25 • ⓦ kur-royal.de • **Seedammbad** Seedammweg 7 • Mon 1–9pm, Tues–Fri 7am–9pm, Sat & Sun 8am–8pm • €6/day • ⓦ stadtwerke-bad-homburg.de • **Taunus Therme** Seedammweg 10 • Mon, Tues, Thurs & Sun 9am–11pm, Wed & Fri 9am–midnight • 2hr Mon–Fri €14, Sat & Sun €16 • ⓦ taunus-therme.de

Bad Homburg's **spa quarter** centres on the verdant **Kurpark** one block north of Louisenstrasse; it was the creation of the nineteenth-century garden designer Peter Joseph Lenné and is one of Germany's largest town parks. At the entrance on Kaiser-Friedrich-Promenade, a bust of Friedrich III – Emperor of Germany for just 99 days in 1888 – faces his English consort Victoria, eldest daughter of Queen Victoria, across formal flowerbeds. The focal point of the park is the imposing copper-domed **Kaiser-Wilhelms-Bad**, built in 1887–90 and now home to the **Kur-Royal Day Spa**, which offers a variety of steam treatments, beauty therapies and massage.

Other attractions are the **Siamesischer Tempel**, donated in 1907 by King Chulalongkorn, and the **Russische Kirche**, whose opening was attended by the last Tsar of Russia and his Hesse-born wife. There are more **spa facilities** on the eastern side of the park including the **Seedammbad** with indoor and outdoor pools, sunbeds and a whirlpool bath, and the similar but more gimmicky **Taunus Therme**.

Casino Bad Homburg

Im Kurpark • Slot machines daily noon–4am, table games Mon–Thurs & Sun 2.30pm–3am, Fri & Sat 2.30pm–4am • Table games area admission €2.50, slot machine area free • ⓦ casino-bad-homburg.de

Alongside the Kaiser-Wilhelms-Bad stands the **Casino Bad Homburg**, modest looking from the outside but smart within; jeans and sports shoes aren't allowed and men are required to wear a jacket, though a polo shirt will suffice underneath. It was established by the French Blanc brothers in 1841, one of whom went on to establish the casino at Monte Carlo; the casino consequently styles itself "Mother of Monte Carlo".

ARRIVAL AND INFORMATION	**BAD HOMBURG**

By train S-Bahn trains take 25min to link Frankfurt to Bad Homburg's Bahnhof, which lies south of the Kurpark and shopping zone. From the station, head up Bahnhofstrasse to Louisenstrasse and turn left to reach the tourist office.

Tourist office In the Kurhaus, Louisenstr. 58 (Mon–Fri 10am–6pm, Sat 10am–2pm; ☎ 061721 178 37 10, ⓦ bad-homburg-tourismus.de).

ACCOMMODATION

DJH Bad Homburg Mühlweg 17 ☎ 06172 239 50, ⓦ djh-hessen.de. Bad Homburg's youth hostel is next to the Schlosspark, with a large outdoor area for sports and accommodation in two- to four-bed rooms with en-suite shower and WC. Breakfast included. Dorms €27.50

Steigenberger Kaiser-Friedrich-Promenade 69–75 ☎ 06172 18 10, ⓦ steigenberger.com. Bad Homburg's "grand hotel", with elegant decor including touches of Art Deco, plus a/c, wi-fi, a French-style bistro and a fitness complex with sauna, steam bath and solarium. Some keen rates are available through the website. €119

Villa am Kurpark Kaiser-Friedrich-Promenade 57 ☎ 06172 180 00, ⓦ villa-am-kurpark.de. An attractive Jugendstil villa opposite the Kurpark with a linked annexe. Airy rooms have bath or shower and TV, radio/CD player and minibar. €99

EATING AND DRINKING

La Vecchia Banca Ludwigstr. 12 ☎ 06172 681 68 83, ⓦ la-vecchia-banca.de. Refined, high-ceilinged Italian restaurant in a historic former bank building close to the Kurhaus, serving pasta dishes from around €12.50, classic *saltimbocca alla romana* for €19.50 and fish mains from around €19.50. Daily noon–2.30pm & 6–11pm.

Orangerie im Kurpark Augusta Allee 10 ☎ 01672 17 11 90, ⓦ huber-partyservice.de. Elegant restaurant and café in the Kurpark's mid-nineteenth-century orangerie, serving daily specials, *Schnitzels* (€18.90) and salads (from €9.50), plus ice cream and *Kaffee und Kuchen*. Tues noon–6pm, Wed–Sat noon–10pm, Sun 11am–10pm.

Schreinerei Pfeiffer Audenstr. 6 ☎ 06172 201 68, ⓦ schreinerei-badhomburg.de. Tucked behind an elaborate wood facade, this atmospheric former carpentry workshop is festooned with woodworking tools and serves reasonably priced *Schnitzels* (from €11.20), burgers (€5.50 up) and light meals. Mon–Fri 5.30pm–1am, Sat 11.30am–1am, Sun 11.30am–11pm.

Naturpark Hochtaunus

If you head north out of Bad Homburg along the B456 you're immediately into the **Naturpark Hochtaunus** (ⓦ naturpark-hochtaunus.de), the second-largest protected nature reserve in Hesse. The highest, conifer-clad peaks are along a ridge – the **Hochtaunusklamm** – which runs northeast to southwest for 40km; highest of all is the 879m **Grosser Feldberg**, which is climbed by a minor road that twists its way up from Oberursel, west of Bad Homburg, and is crowned by an observation tower. In winter the hills are busy with cross-country skiers when the somewhat unreliable snow allows; there's even a lift for downhill skiing on the **Pechberg**. In summer the entire Hochtaunusklamm is popular with hikers; the 591m **Herzberg** is car-free and close to Bad Homburg.

Saalburg Roman fort

March–Oct daily 9am–6pm; Nov–Feb Tues–Sun 9am–4pm · €5 · ⓦ saalburgmuseum.de · Bus #5 from Bad Homburg Bahnhof (Mon–Fri every 2hr, Sat & Sun hourly; 20 min)

For more than a hundred and fifty years from the first century AD, the Hochtaunusklamm formed part of the **Limes**, the military frontier separating the Roman Empire from the Germanic tribes to the north and east. There's a reconstructed **Roman fort** just off the B456 at **Saalburg**, where in addition to the usual archeological displays you'll get a vivid impression of what a lonely military outpost of the empire might have actually looked like to the five to six thousand troops stationed there. Saalburg is a stop on the **Deutsche Limes-Strasse** (ⓦ limesstrasse.de), which links up sites along the old frontier from Bad Hönningen near Koblenz to Regensburg.

Along the River Lahn

North of the Taunus and on Hesse's western border, the River Lahn – a tributary of the Rhine – meanders its way through a placid landscape of gentle upland beauty, threaded with historic and interesting small towns. The **Lahntalradweg** cycle route ensures the valley is deservedly popular with cyclists, and many hotels proclaim their cycle-friendliness, while the Lahn's waters are popular with canoeists. But the valley can be explored just as easily by car or train. Highlights along the way include the delightful small cathedral cities of **Limburg an der Lahn** and **Wetzlar**, and the diminutive but pristine Residenzstadt of **Weilburg**.

Limburg an der Lahn

Perched on a crag overlooking the River Lahn in full view of traffic speeding along the Frankfurt–Cologne Autobahn, **LIMBURG**'s impeccably picturesque Dom acts as a sort of billboard-in-stone for the charms of this beguiling little city. Deservedly popular with day-trippers, Limburg is also an inviting spot for an overnight stay.

The Dom

Domplatz • Daily 8am–7pm • Free, English info leaflet €0.50 • ⦿ dom.bistumlimburg.de

Count Konrad Kurzbold founded a collegiate chapter of eighteen canons in 910 AD on a superb defensive site high above the river, but the present **Dom** dates from the thirteenth century, its construction financed by the wealth accumulated by local merchants during the Crusades. Its seven spire-topped towers aside, what makes the Dom's appearance so singular is the fusion of late Rhenish Romanesque and early French Gothic details and its brick red-and-white colour scheme, the result of a 1960s project that restored the exterior to its original medieval colour scheme.

Colour is a feature of the interior too, subtly enlivened by original frescoes that are among the best preserved from the time in Germany. The depiction of Samson uprooting a tree is particularly prized. The baptismal font in the south aisle is a mass of Romanesque sculptural detail, while the figurative supports of Konrad Kurzbold's tomb in the north transept predate the Dom.

The Schloss

Tucked almost unnoticed behind the Dom is Limburg's **Schloss** (no public access to the inside), a jumble of half-timbered and stone buildings whose overall effect is more picturesque than martial; the oldest part dates from the early thirteenth century.

Diözesanmuseum

Domstr. 12 • April to 4th Sun in Advent Tues–Sat 10am–1pm & 2–5pm, Sun 11am–5pm • €3 • ⦿ staurothek.bistumlimburg.de

A short walk downhill from the Dom on Domstrasse brings you to the **Diözesanmuseum**, whose treasures include the *Staurothek*, a tenth-century Byzantine cross reliquary, and a reliquary of similar age from Trier said to contain a portion of St Peter's staff.

The Altstadt

Occupying the long slope down from the Dom to the fourteenth-century **Alte Lahnbrücke**, Limburg's **Altstadt** is a coherent mass of tall, gabled medieval houses, many of them half-timbered and sagging in an appealing fashion. There are splendid examples dating back to the thirteenth century, including the **Werner Senger Haus** at Rütsche 5, which dates from around 1250, and which houses a restaurant. Not everything is wood – a notable exception is the impressive, Gothic step-gabled **Steinernes Haus** at Fischmarkt 1, which dates from 1350 and is made of stone. The former **Rathaus** opposite has a Gothic vaulted cellar and a grand hall on the ground floor, nowadays home to the town's art collection (Mon 8.30am–noon, Tues 7am–noon, Wed 8.30am–2pm, Thurs 8.30am–noon & 2–6pm, Fri 8.30am–noon & 2–4pm, Sat & Sun 11am–5pm; €2). To enjoy the classic **view** of the Dom looming high above the river, stroll across the Alte Lahnbrücke.

ARRIVAL AND DEPARTURE

LIMBURG AN DER LAHN

By train Limburg's Bahnhof is in the modern part of the town centre, a couple of minutes' stroll from the Altstadt; there's also a station at Limburg-Süd on the high-speed Frankfurt–Cologne ICE line south of the town; the two stations are connected by bus.

Destinations Frankfurt (1–2 per hour; 1hr 3min–1hr 12 min); Weilburg (every 30min; 23–36min); Wetzlar (every 30min; 41min–1hr 11min).

INFORMATION AND TOURS

Tourist office Next to the Bahnhof at Bahnhofsplatz 2 (April–Oct Mon–Fri 9am–5pm, Sat 10am–noon; Nov–March Mon–Fri 9am–5pm; ☎ 06431 61 66, ⊛ limburg.de).
Cruises In summer the *Wappen von Limburg* cruises the Lahn, a short distance upriver to Dietkirchen and a longer route downriver across the Land boundary to Balduinstein in Rheinland Pfalz, passing through four locks along the way (April–Oct Tues–Sun; Dietkirchen €12, Balduinstein €16; ☎ 06431 39 84, ⊛ lahntalschiffahrt.de).

ACCOMMODATION

Campingplatz Limburg Schleusenweg 16 ☎ 06431 226 10, ⊛ lahncamping.de. Campsite on the riverbank opposite the Dom and Altstadt, with great views, a beer garden, children's play area, shop and table tennis. Open April–Oct. Pitch €8, plus €5.20 per person
DJH Limburg Auf dem Guckucksberg ☎ 06431 414 93, ⊛ djh-hessen.de. Limburg's youth hostel is a short distance southeast of the Altstadt, with plentiful outdoor space including two volleyball courts and a barbecue. Accommodation is mostly in four-bed dorms, with just one single and one double. Dorm and doubles (per person) €24.50

Dom Hotel Grabenstr. 57 ☎ 06431 90 10, ⊛ domhotellimburg.de. Upmarket hotel on the fringe of the Altstadt, with striking modern decor, wireless internet and 42 stylish, individually designed rooms. Non-smoking rooms on request. It also has a restaurant, *De Prusse* (see below). €111
Hotel Huss Bahnhofsplatz 3 ☎ 06431 933 50, ⊛ hotel-huss.de. Comfortable if slightly characterless hotel in an ugly modern building next to the Bahnhof and tourist office. Rooms have en-suite bath or shower, TV and wireless internet, and there's free parking for guests' use. €85

EATING AND DRINKING

Der Kleine Prins At the Nassauer Hof hotel, Brückengasse 1 ☎ 06431 99 60, ⊛ hotel-nassauerhof-limburg.de. Creative modern German cooking, with dishes such as chicken roulade with pesto filling, sage gnocchi and rabbit fillet with red lentils, plus a prime location right next to the Lahn. Mains €14–16. Tues–Sat 6–10pm, Sun noon–2.30pm & 6–10pm.
Kosmol Bischofsplatz 3 ☎ 06431 64 10. Busy *Café-Konditorei* serving breakfasts, salads and light lunch dishes from around €5.10 and cakes and ice creams from €3.50; *Baumkuchen* – "tree cake" – is the speciality. There's a terrace in the beautiful square at the front. Mon–Sat 7am–6pm, Sun 10.30am–6pm.
De Prusse Grabenstr. 57 ☎ 06431 90 10, ⊛ domhotellimburg.de. The *Dom Hotel*'s elegant restaurant serves the likes of veal chop with morel cream sauce or cod in beer batter with cucumber and potato salad and Frankfurter *Grüne Sosse*; main courses cost €18 up. Tues–Sat 6–9.30pm, Sun noon–2.30pm.

Weilburg

Even the landscape genuflects to the feudal authority of **WEILBURG**'s Schloss, for the River Lahn loops so tightly around the immaculate little town that its Altstadt is almost an island, with the massive Schloss at its heart. Its extraordinary setting aside, Weilburg's other great curiosity is the **Schiffstunnel**, a short-cut through the neck of the meander behind the Altstadt, cut between 1844 and 1847 and unique in Germany. In summer you can take a **boat trip** through it (May–Oct Sat & Sun at 2pm; €12.50; ⊛ flossfahrt-lahn.de).

The Schloss

Schloss Schlossplatz 3 • March–Oct Tues–Sun 10am–5pm; Nov–Feb Tues–Sun 10am–4pm; last tour 1hr before closing • €4 • ⊛ schloesser-hessen.de • **Schlosspark** Daily April–Sept 7am–dusk; Oct–March 8am–dusk • Free

Weilburg's **Schloss** presents very different faces according to your vantage point: stern and overbearing from the river, it appears gracious from its sunny-terraced Baroque

Schlosspark and prettily Renaissance once in the Hof or central courtyard. A castle has existed here since the tenth century, but the present Schloss was built between 1535 and 1575 for the counts of Nassau-Weilburg. A further phase of construction in the eighteenth century created the massive Marstall or stable block to the north, along with the formal layout of the **Marktplatz**. The latter is dominated by the Julius Ludwig Rothweil-designed **Stadtkirche**, with the town's Rathaus built onto it; it's regarded as the most important Baroque Protestant church in Hesse. Between June and early August, the Schloss's central courtyard, the Stadtkirche and the parterres by the orangery in the Schlosspark are the venues for the classical **Schlosskonzerte** (ⓦweilburger-schlosskonzerte.de).

The Bergbau- und Stadtmuseum

Schlossplatz 1 • April–Oct Tues–Fri 10am–noon & 2–5pm, Sat & Sun 10am–5pm; Nov–March Mon–Fri 10am–noon & 2–5pm • €3.50 • ⓦ museum-weilburg.de

Facing the main entrance to the Schloss on Schlossplatz is the **The Bergbau- und Stadtmuseum Weilburg**, which in addition to the more predictable local museum exhibits has a 200m reconstruction of an iron ore mine – an important industry in the area until the 1950s.

ARRIVAL AND INFORMATION

WEILBURG

By train Weilburg is on the Koblenz–Giessen line, with direct trains from Limburg. The Bahnhof is on the north side of the river a little to the east of the Altstadt: cross either of the two main bridges to reach the Altstadt.

Tourist office Mauerstr. 6–8 (April–Oct Mon–Fri 9am–6pm, Sat 10am–noon; Nov–March Mon–Wed 10am–4pm, Thurs 10am–6pm, Fri 10am–noon; ☎06471 314 67, ⓦweilburg.de).

ACCOMMODATION AND EATING

DJH Weilburg Am Steinbühl 1 ☎06471 71 16, ⓦdjh -hessen.de. Weilburg's youth hostel is west of the Altstadt in the suburb of Odersbach, with three four-bed rooms and the bulk of the accommodation in six- to eight-bed dorms. Sports facilities include a basketball hoop and table tennis, and there's plenty of outside space, plus a barbecue. Breakfast included. Dorms **€22.50**

Hotel Weilburg Frankfurter Str. 27 ☎06471 912 90, ⓦhotel-weilburg.de. Simple *hotel garni* a short distance east of the Altstadt, with single, twin or double rooms equipped with TV; all rooms have a shower and some have terraces. **€70**

Schlosshotel Weilburg Langgasse 25 ☎06471 509 00, ⓦschlosshotel-weilburg.de. Occupying the eighteenth-century Prinzessinbau on the north side of the Schloss, this is Weilburg's plushest hotel. Rooms have minibar, TV, phone and either bath or shower, and there's a restaurant. **€105**

Tommy's Mauerstr. 2 ☎06471 92 32 74, ⓦtommys-weilburg.de. Lively sports bar and café on the main route through the Altstadt, with a small but popular outside terrace and a versatile calamari-to-*Schnitzels* menu; salads cost €6.50 up, hot food from €7.80. Daily 10am–1am; kitchen closes 11pm.

Wetzlar

WETZLAR was once a place of some importance. In the mid-fourteenth century it rivalled Frankfurt in size, while from 1693 until its dissolution in 1806 it was the seat of the Reichskammergericht, the highest court of the Holy Roman Empire. This drew Goethe, who came here in 1772 as a legal trainee and it was here he developed an attachment to Lotte Buff, who was to inspire the character of Lotte in *The Sorrows of Young Werther*. The hilly **Altstadt** stands aloof from the rather tacky modern commercial quarter on the other side of the river. Though not without modern intrusions Wetzlar has, like Limburg, many impressive groups of half-timbered houses, including one at Kornmarkt 7 where Goethe lived in the summer of 1772.

The Dom

Domplatz • April–Sept 9am–7pm; Oct–March 10am–4.30pm • Free

Centred on Domplatz, the Altstadt is dominated by the eccentric **Dom**, which is, in effect, two churches in one, for not only is it shared by separate Protestant and Catholic congregations, but it combines two quite separate designs. As Wetzlar grew in size and prosperity during the thirteenth century, envious looks were cast at the splendid new churches in Limburg and Marburg, and plans were hatched for a new, more imposing building to replace the Romanesque Stiftskirche, barely forty years old at the time. But the project ground to a halt, and what should have been a soaring, twin-spired Gothic hall church was stopped in its tracks halfway, with one tower complete and the other barely begun. What makes the half-Romanesque, half-Gothic result odder still is that the older half is cold and grey, while the Gothic church is constructed in cheerful red sandstone.

The Reichskammergerichtsmuseum

Hofstatt 19 • Tues–Sun 10am–1pm & 2–5pm • €3, combined ticket for all Wetzlar museums except Viseum €4.50, combined ticket for all Wetzlar museums €6

The downhill extension of Domplatz is Fischmarkt: at no.13 is the much-rebuilt fourteenth-century **Rathaus** which served as the Holy Roman Empire's Reichskammergericht. A stroll south along Krämerstrasse and across Eisenmarkt brings you to Hofstatt and the **Reichskammergerichtsmuseum**, which chronicles Wetzlar's associations with the court. It's located in a house that, in the mid-eighteenth century, was known as Avemannsche Haus, and was let to court officials and their families.

Sammlung Lemmers-Danforth

Kornblumengasse 1 • Tues–Sun 10am–1pm & 2–5pm • €3, combined ticket for all Wetzlar museums except Viseum €4.50, combined ticket for all Wetzlar museums €6

Opposite the Reichskammergerichtsmuseum, another fine eighteenth-century house is occupied by the **Sammlung Lemmers-Danforth**, a collection of European furniture from the fifteenth to the eighteenth centuries, with paintings, clocks and ceramics.

Stadt- und Industriemuseum, Viseum and Lottehaus

Lottestr. 8–10 • All Tues–Sun 10am–1pm & 2–5pm • Stadt- und Industriemuseum €3, Lottehaus €3, Viseum €3.50, combined ticket for all Wetzlar museums except Viseum €4.50, combined ticket for all Wetzlar museums including Viseum €6

A short stroll from Domplatz, in a complex which once belonged to the Teutonic Knights, the **Stadt- und Industriemuseum** charts Wetzlar's history as a free imperial city and, later, a centre of ironworking, machine tools, vacuum technology and others. The same complex contains **Viseum**, a slick, modern exhibition on optics – still an important industry in Wetzlar, whose most famous brand name is the camera company Leica.

The half-timbered building next door is now the **Lottehaus**, furnished in period style and with a number of exhibits relating to Goethe's *The Sorrows of Young Werther*, including a first edition, translations and parodies.

ARRIVAL AND INFORMATION

WETZLAR

By train Wetzlar is on the Koblenz–Giessen line with frequent trains from Limburg and Weilburg. The Bahnhof is north of town by the Forum Wetzlar shopping mall on the far side of the B49 highway: cross under the highway and head down the traffic-free shopping precinct and cross the river to reach the Altstadt, or take the Citybus (Mon–Fri 10am–7pm, Sat 10am–3pm; €0.50), which shuttles every 30min between the Forum and Domplatz.

Tourist office The tourist office is at Domplatz 8 (May–Sept Mon–Fri 9am–6pm, Sat 10am–2pm, Sun 11am–3pm; Oct–April Mon–Fri 9am–5pm, Sat 10am–noon; ☎06441 99 77 55, ⓦwetzlar.de).

ACCOMMODATION

Bürgerhof Konrad-Adenauer-Promenade 20 ☎06441 90 30, ⓦbuergerhof-wetzlar.com. Rambling, traditional hotel a short walk from the Altstadt, with a cosy half-timbered restaurant, *Der Postreiter*. Rooms have bath or shower, TV, phone and wi-fi, and there's ample parking. **€92**
DJH Wetzlar Richard-Schirmann-Str. 3 ☎06441 679 050, ⓦdjh-hessen.de. Wetzlar's modern youth hostel is a complex of three buildings on the southern edge of the town, with views over it. Accommodation is in four- to eight-bed dorms; four-bed rooms have en-suite shower and WC. Breakfast included. Dorms **€22.50**
Pension Domblick Langgasse 64 ☎06441 901 60, ⓦdomblick.de. Attractive, cyclist-friendly pension on the west side of the Lahn. All rooms are en suite, simply

11

11

furnished with plenty of pine. Rooms for allergy sufferers are available on request. Pets are welcome. **€79**

Wetzlarer Hof Obertorstr. 3 ☎06441 90 80, ⓦwetzlarerhof.de. Pleasant, rather business-oriented modern hotel on the fringe of the Altstadt. Rooms have bath or shower and WC, TV and wireless internet; some also have balconies. Prices are slightly cheaper at weekends. **€97**

EATING AND DRINKING

Café am Dom Fischmarkt 13 ☎06441 322 88. Excellent *Café-Konditorei* in the former Reichskammergericht, with baked potatoes (€5.40), delicious filled rolls from around €2.50, breakfast from €3.70 up, and tempting cakes. A terrace offers views up to Domplatz. Mon–Fri 9am–6pm, Sat 8am–6pm, Sun 10am–6pm.

Der Postreiter Konrad Adenauer Promenade 20 ☎06441 903 44 44, ⓦbuergerhof-wetzlar.com. The *Bürgerhof* hotel's restaurant is a classy, half-timbered affair, with a three-course set menu for €33.90, or the likes of Frankfurter *Grüner Sosse* with eggs and potatoes, veal *Schnitzel* or Allgäu rump steak with herb butter and potato gratin. Main courses €12–21. Daily noon–2pm & 6–10pm.

Ristorante Wirt am Dom Domplatz 9 ☎06441 425 22, ⓦwirtamdom.de. Good-value Italian staples next to the tourist office, with pizza from €7.50, pasta dishes from €8.50 and a long, versatile menu of meaty main courses, fish and salad. There's a terrace with views of the Dom. Tues–Sun 11.30am–2.30pm & 5.30–11.30pm.

Marburg

"Other towns have a university; **MARBURG** *is* a university" – so runs the saying, and there's a grain of truth to it, for the prestigious Philipps University dominates the life of the town. It's the oldest Protestant university in the world, founded in 1527 by Landgrave Philipp the Magnanimous without imperial or papal recognition. Notable figures associated with it include Nobel Prize-winning physiologist Emil von Behring, the philosopher Martin Heidegger and the political theorist Hannah Arendt.

Physically, the town is dominated by the splendid hilltop **Landgrafenschloss**, a reminder of Marburg's former status as the seat of the Hessian Landgraves, visible from all over town and a handy navigation aid. Below, the perfectly preserved medieval **Oberstadt** (upper town), which centres on the steeply sloping Markt, tumbles downhill towards the River Lahn. The lower town, the **Unterstadt**, curves around Oberstadt following the course of the Lahn, its chief glory being the Gothic hall church dedicated to St Elisabeth of Hungary.

Landgrafenschloss

April–Oct Tues–Sun 10am–6pm; Nov–March Tues–Sun 10am–4pm • €4

From almost any vantage point, Marburg is dominated by the mighty **Landgrafenschloss** which is reached up the Schlosstreppe off the north end of Markt in Oberstadt and then up steep, cobbled Landgraf-Philipp-Strasse. Pause for breath on the way to admire the impressive gable of the **Landgräfliche Kanzlei**, built in 1573. There has been a fortress atop the Gisonenfelsen crags since 900 AD, though most of what you see today – the slate-hung Renaissance **Rentkammer** on the south front as you climb the hillside – is essentially Gothic, and the splendour of its proportions reflects its status as the residence, from 1292 onwards, of the first Landgraves of an independent Hesse. Nineteenth-century "restoration" robbed it of some of its original fabric – including its medieval roof timbers – but what survives is impressive enough.

The interior

You enter via the **Saalbau** on the north side of the Hof; upstairs is the **Fürstensaal**, one of the largest secular Gothic rooms in Germany, with an elaborately beautiful wooden Renaissance doorway by Nikolaus Hagenmüller dating from 1573. Equally impressive is the thirteenth-century **Schlosskapelle** (court chapel) on the south side, reached across an upstairs landing from the Saalbau and preserving a refined full-length fresco of St Christopher and the original (and beautiful) coloured floor tiles.

The east wing, or **Wilhelmsbau**, contains the **Museum für Kulturgeschichte** (same ticket) whose extensive collections of folk and religious art include Catholic and Protestant folk costumes or *Tracht*, still a common sight in Marburg as recently as the 1950s, though nowadays they're seen only on special occasions. To the west of the Schloss, the small but pretty **Schlosspark** is the venue for concerts and open-air film shows in summer.

The Oberstadt

Characterized by meandering lanes, elaborate roofscapes and plenty of steps, Oberstadt – the hilly "upper town" – focuses on elongated, lively **Markt**. Fringed by multistorey half-timbered houses that sag at giddy angles and with a step-gabled, early sixteenth-century stone **Rathaus** on the southern, downhill side, it's as lovely a town square as any in Germany, its café terraces buzzing contentedly in fine weather. Just off the northeast corner of Markt on Schlosssteig – which was called Judengasse (Jew Lane) until 1933 – are the glassed-in remains of the town's **medieval synagogue**, demolished in 1452 and excavated between 1993 and 1998.

To the west of Markt along Nikolaistrasse, the terrace in front of the Gothic Lutheran **Pfarrkirche** offers superb views over the huddled rooftops. The oldest parts of the church date from the thirteenth century, and it has a distinctive, twisted spire. To the south of Markt, the overbearing neo-Gothic mass of the **Alte Universität** dominates the lower approaches to Oberstadt. It was built in the late nineteenth century on the foundations of a thirteenth-century former Dominican monastery which the university had long since outgrown.

Haus der Romantik

Markt 16 • Tues–Sun 11am–1pm & 2–5pm • €2 • ⓦ romantikmuseum-marburg.de

At Markt 16, the **Haus der Romantik** commemorates the Marburger Romantikkreis group, whose members included the Brothers Grimm, and which met from 1800 to 1806 to discuss the political and philosophical trends of the day. The museum also presents changing exhibitions on the Romantics.

The Unterstadt

From Markt, one of Oberstadt's gentler inclines leads north down Wettergasse, Neustadt and Steinweg to the medieval core of **Unterstadt**. The twin **lifts** of the **Oberstadt Aufzug** (daily 7am–1.30am) also connect the upper and lower towns. The houses in Unterstadt are no less beautiful than in the upper town, but they're more modest in scale. On the east bank of the Lahn, you can rent a pedalo or rowing **boat** from Gischler at Auf dem Wehr 1a (April–Oct daily 9am–dusk; ☎06421 804 84 67, ⓦ bootsverleih-marburg.de).

The Elisabethkirche

Elisabethstr. 3 • Daily: Jan–March & Nov 10am–4pm; April–Oct 9am–5pm; Dec 10am–5pm • Choir and transepts €2.50, otherwise free • ⓦ elisabethkirche.de

There's nothing modest about the **Elisabethkirche**, the oldest pure-Gothic hall church in Germany. It was constructed in less than fifty years between 1235 and 1283, which explains the unusual purity and coherence of its twin-towered design. The church was built by the Teutonic Knights on the site of the grave of St Elisabeth of Hungary, the young widow of Landgrave Ludwig IV of Thuringia, who died in Italy on his way to the Crusades. After his death Elisabeth eschewed courtly life, founding a hospital and devoting herself single-mindedly to the care of the sick. Elisabeth also died young, and was rapidly canonized; the church built over her tomb became one of the most important places of pilgrimage in medieval Europe.

The interior
The rich furnishings include the brightly coloured **Französische Elisabeth** on the left side of the nave, which dates from 1470 and depicts a regal-looking Elisabeth holding a model of the church. A relief at the base of her **tomb** in the north transept depicts the grief-stricken sick and poor mourning her corpse. Somewhat incongruous among the gorgeously coloured monuments to medieval virtue is the austere tomb of **Paul von Hindenburg**, the last president of the Weimar Republic and the man who appointed Hitler – the man he had belittled as a "Bohemian corporal" – chancellor in 1933.

The Kornspeicher: Mineralogisches Museum
Firmaneiplatz 1 • Wed 10am–1pm & 3–6pm, Thurs & Fri 10am–1pm, Sat & Sun 11am–3pm • €2

The severe-looking buildings that cluster around the Elisabethkirche include the **Kornspeicher**, a grain store built by the Teutonic Knights in 1515. It now houses the **Mineralogisches Museum**, with a glittering array of crystals in glass cases.

Universitätsmuseum für Bildende Kunst
Biegenstr. 11 • Closed for renovation

The engrossing **Universitätsmuseum für Bildende Kunst** houses paintings by Tischbein and Winterhalter and a tiny Paul Klee etching, as well as works of local interest, including some by Otto Ubbelohde, illustrator of the Grimm fairy tales. There's also some rather *völkisch* art by Carl Bantzer, who was feted by the Nazis, though he maintained a certain distance from them. The museum was closed for restoration as this book went to press.

Kaiser Wilhelm Turm
Mon–Sat 1–7pm, Sun 11am–7pm; closes 6pm Nov–March • €1 • ⓦ www.spiegelslustturm.de • Bus #7, #11 or #16 to "Uni-Klinikum" then a 20min walk

You can enjoy Marburg's scenic setting by heading up to the **Kaiser Wilhelm Turm** high on the ridge of the Lahnberge east of town, where there are breathtaking views from the observation platform at the top. There's also a café.

ARRIVAL AND INFORMATION | MARBURG

By train The Hauptbahnhof is north of the centre on the opposite side of the Lahn; from here it's a good 10min stroll to the centre of town.

Tourist office In Unterstadt close to the Oberstadt Aufzug lifts at Pilgrimstein 26 (Mon–Fri 9am–6pm, Sat 10am–2pm; ☎ 06421 991 20, ⓦ marburg.de).

ACCOMMODATION

DJH Marburg Jahnstr. 1 ☎ 06421 234 61, ⓦ djh-hessen.de. The town's youth hostel is in a pretty and peaceful setting south of the centre on the riverside, right on the Lahn-Radweg. There's a games room with table football and table tennis, and you can hire bikes and canoes. Breakfast included. Dorm €21.50

Hostaria del Castello Markt 19 ☎ 06421 243 02, ⓦ del-castello.de. Pretty, good-value rooms, furnished in rustic, peasant style with shower, WC and TV, above an Italian restaurant in a half-timbered building in the heart of Oberstadt. €78

Hotel im Kornspeicher Molkereistr. 6 ☎ 06421 94 84 10, ⓦ hotel-kornspeicher.de. Tastefully decorated single and double rooms with bath or shower, wi-fi and satellite TV, plus a few suites and apartments, in a modern hotel south of the centre. €95

★**Marburger Hof** Elisabethstr. 12 ☎ 06421 59 07 50, ⓦ marburgerhof.de. Good-value, sprawling hotel between the Hauptbahnhof and town centre, with a wide choice of rooms and price levels from snug, comfortable budget-priced singles to handsomely renovated doubles and fancy suites. €63

EATING AND DRINKING

★**Elisabeth Gasthausbrauerei** Steinweg 45 ☎ 06421 183 05 44, ⓦ www.elisabethbraeu.de. Trendy

Hausbrauerei close to the Elisabethkirche, with a bistro serving food (mains €11.20 up), a *Bierkeller* and excellent own-brand light and dark beers. Restaurant daily 11am–2pm & 6–11pm; *Bierkeller* daily 6pm–2am.

Felix Barfüsserstr. 28 ☎ 06421 30 73 36, ⓦ felix-marburg .de. One of a number of modern café/bars in Oberstadt selling baked potatoes, burgers and salads at very student-friendly prices – burgers start at €5.50, salads from €5.50. There's a long cocktail list, too, from €4.90. Mon–Fri & Sun 10am–1am, Fri & Sat 10am–2am.

Hinkelstein Markt 18 ☎ 06421 242 10, ⓦ hinkelstein-marburg.de. Goth meets Gothic in this wonderfully atmospheric, smokey and noisy studenty rock bar in a medieval cellar in Oberstadt, with draught *Bosch Braunbier* and occasional live bands. Mon–Thurs 7pm–3am, Fri 7pm–5am, Sat 3pm–5am, Sun 7pm–3am.

KostBar Barfüsserstr. 7 ☎ 06421 16 11 70, ⓦ kostbar-marburg.de. Trendy café/bar and restaurant offering

salads, veggie and pasta dishes with a few inventive touches; main courses from around €9.40. They also serve organic breakfasts (from €3.90) until noon. Daily 10am–1am.

Taverne Korfu Ketzerbach 21 ☎ 06421 68 13 86, ⓦ korfu-marburg.de. Classy little Greek fish restaurant in Unterstadt, with white tablecloths and a daily-changing menu that might include mixed grilled calamari and octopus (€18.50), or seafood platter to share (€33.50/ person). There are also a few cheaper non-seafood options. Mon–Sat 11.30am–2.30pm & 5.30pm–midnight.

Weinlädele Schlosstreppe 1 ☎ 06421 142 44, ⓦ weinlädele.de. Regional wines and light, inexpensive food including *Flammkuchen* are served in this wine tavern's lovely, beamy interior or outside with views over Markt. Main courses start at around €9.50 and there's a big choice of wine by the glass. Daily 11.30am–midnight.

11

NIGHTLIFE AND ENTERTAINMENT

Cavete Steinweg 12 ☎ 06421 661 57, ⓦ cavete-marburg.de. Jazz club midway between Oberstadt and Unterstadt, with regular open stage jazz sessions, gigs, literary readings and – in summer – a *Biergarten*. Daily 9pm–1am.

Hessisches Landestheater Am Schwanhof 68–72 ☎ 06421 990 20, ⓦ theater-marburg.com. Marburg's

theatre presents a varied programme of classical and contemporary drama, from populist revivals to Brecht and children's theatre.

KFZ Schulstr. 6 ☎ 06421 138 98, ⓦ kfz-marburg.de. Cultural centre hosting a varied programme of cabaret, satire, kids' events, live bands and clubnights, including occasional lesbian and gay events.

Fulda and around

With the uplands of the Vogelsberg to the west and the impressive sweep of the ancient, volcanic Rhön mountains rising to over 900m in the east, there's a touch of wild grandeur to the spacious landscape around **FULDA**. And there's more than a hint of pomp about the old prince-bishops' Residenzstadt itself, with a stately official **Barockviertel** (Baroque quarter) crowning a low-rise hill, adding a stately flourish to the fringes of its attractive, walkable **Altstadt**. Relatively remote from Hesse's other major cities, Fulda has never grown especially large, but it has a bustling, self-sufficient air that makes it an enjoyable place to spend a few days. On the city's fringe, **Schloss Fasanerie**, the summer residence of the prince-bishops, makes a worthwhile excursion if you have your own transport, while further afield the beautiful uplands of the **Rhön Biosphere** reserve can be reached easily from Fulda by bus.

The Barockviertel

Fulda's **Barockviertel** was built in the early eighteenth century as the city recovered financially from the Thirty Years' War, and it lends Fulda the air of a comic-opera capital city, with all the necessary grandeur and dignity for the role, but on a human scale.

Dom

Domplatz 1 • April–Oct Mon–Fri 10am–6pm, Sat 10am–3pm, Sun 1–6pm; Nov–March Mon–Fri 10am–5pm, Sat 10am–3pm, Sun 1–6pm • Free • ⓦ bistum-fulda.de

The first of the Barockviertel's landmarks to be built was the **Dom**, which faces spacious, paved Domplatz. The work of the Bamberg architect Johann Dientzenhofer, it was constructed between 1704 and 1712 but still contains elements of its predecessor, the Ratgar Basilica, which was the largest Carolingian church north of the Alps. With its twin towers and central dome the cathedral looks more southern than central German; the airy, white stucco interior is relatively restrained by the standards of the style, though the high altar, which portrays the Assumption of the Madonna, provides a theatrical focal point, smothered in gold leaf. The crypt contains the tomb of St Boniface, the English-born apostle to the Germans and patron saint of Germany, who was murdered while proselytizing in Frisia in 754 AD.

Dommuseum

Domplatz 2 • April–Oct Tues–Sat 10am–5.30pm, Sun 12.30–5.30pm; Nov to mid-Jan & mid-Feb to March Tues–Sat 10am–12.30pm & 1.30–4pm, Sun 12.30–4pm • €2.10

The wealth and importance of Fulda's Catholic bishopric is vividly illustrated by a visit to the **Dommuseum**, where the sheer weight of eighteenth-century ecclesiastical bling is almost overwhelming. Amid the Baroque excess the Silver Chapel and its ghoulish skull reliquary of St Boniface stand out; there are also some lovely medieval woodcarvings, and a painting by Lucas Cranach the Elder, *Christ and the Adulteress*, dating from 1512.

Michaelskirche

Michaelsberg 1 • Daily: April–Oct 10am–6pm; Nov–March 10am–noon & 2–5pm • Free

Overlooking the Dom to the north is the simple but lovely **Michaelskirche**, the Carolingian burial chapel of Fulda's Benedictine abbey, parts of which date back to 822 AD; it was extended into a Roman cross form in the tenth and eleventh centuries. The rotunda is particularly beautiful.

Schlossgarten

Daily: April–Oct 7am–10.30pm; Nov–March 7am–9pm • Free

Fulda's most delightful secular Baroque monuments face each other across the beautiful **Schlossgarten** opposite Domplatz. The **Orangerie**, now part of the *Maritim Am Schlossgarten* hotel (see p.600), is perhaps the most elegant of all, a refined pleasure-palace designed by Maximilian von Welsch between 1722 and 1725. The **Apollosaal** in the centre of the building with its ceiling frescoes is impressive – nowadays it's the hotel's breakfast room, but if there's not an event on nobody minds too much if you take a look. The formal part of the Schlossgarten is planted with colourful borders in summer and centres on a fountain.

Stadtschloss

Schlossstr. 1 • Tues–Sun 10am–5pm; Schlossturm closed Nov–March • €3.50, combination ticket with Vonderau Museum €5.30

The **Stadtschloss** on the south side of the Schlossgarten is the work of Johann Dientzenhofer, who from 1706 to 1717 extended and rebuilt the existing Renaissance Schloss and incorporated the twelfth-century **Schlossturm**, which faces the Schlossgarten and can be climbed for an exhilarating view over the park, city and surrounding landscape.

Built as the prince-bishops' residence, the Schloss now functions as Fulda's Rathaus, but you can visit the **Historische Räume**, which preserve their Baroque appearance. The coolly elegant, stucco Kaisersaal on the ground floor opens onto the Schlossgarten and is decorated with portraits of Habsburg emperors; upstairs, a procession of rooms displaying eighteenth-century Fulda and Thuringian porcelain leads to the delightful **Spiegelkabinett**, or cabinet of mirrors; on the second floor is the **Fürstensaal**, a splendid reception room whose stucco ceiling is decorated with paintings on mythological themes by the Tyrolean artist Melchior Steidl. Opposite the Stadtschloss the **Hauptwache** is reminiscent of its Frankfurt namesake and now houses a café/bar.

The Altstadt

The charms of Fulda's largely traffic-free **Altstadt** are low key in comparison with the pomp of the Barockviertel, but it's an animated and interesting district to explore, with plenty of quaint corners, cobbled streets and civilized places to eat and drink. A stroll down Friedrichstrasse from the Stadtschloss brings you to the towering but rather dull Baroque **Stadtpfarrkirche**. Tucked behind it is the picturesque half-timbered **Altes Rathaus** (1500–31) with a galleried ground floor and a memorable roofline – the attic windows eschew the usual dormers for a series of look-at-me pinnacles.

Vonderau Museum

Jesuitenplatz 1 • Tues–Sun 10am–5pm • €3.50, combined ticket with Historische Räume €5.30; planetarium €4 • ⓦ museum-fulda.de

Just to the south of the Altes Rathaus, another Baroque pile – a former seminary – now houses the **Vonderau Museum**, Fulda's biggest museum and principal wet-weather refuge. The core of the museum is essentially a local history collection, whose curiosities include the reconstructed Drogerie zum Krokodil – a Jugendstil pharmacy – and the Fulda-Mobil, a curious bubble car that was built in Fulda in the 1950s and 1960s. There are also sections on natural history, a collection of paintings and sculptures and a **planetarium**, for which you'll have to reserve in advance.

Alte Universität and Hexenturm

Opposite the Vonderau Museum is Andreas Gallasini's 1733 **Alte Universität**. Founded by prince-bishop Adolph von Dalberg, the university was dissolved in 1805 after secularization brought the prince-bishops' rule to an end. The southern and western fringes of the Altstadt in particular preserve many half-timbered houses and here – in contrast to the banal shopping quarter north of the Alte Universität – restoration has been sensitive. In nearby Kanalstrasse, the 14m **Hexenturm** is a surviving remnant of the medieval city wall.

ARRIVAL AND INFORMATION

FULDA

By train Fast, frequent ICE trains connect Frankfurt with Fulda's Hauptbahnhof, on the eastern side of the Altstadt.
Destinations Frankfurt (2–3 per hour; 53min–1hr 20min); Kassel-Wilhelmshöhe (2 per hour; 30min).
Tourist office Palais Buttlar, Bonifatiusplatz 1 (Mon–Fri 8.30am–6pm, Sat & Sun 9.30am–4pm; ⓣ 0661 10 21 81 34, ⓦ tourismus-fulda.de). The office can rent you a handy English-language audio-guide (2hr €7) to take you on a 2hr guided walk through the city.
Discount card The tourist office can sell you a Museums Pass (€12), offering free entry to the major museums.

ACCOMMODATION

Altstadthotel Arte Doll 2–4 ⓣ 0661 25 02 98 80, ⓦ altstadthotel-arte.de. Modern, rather business-oriented hotel with a wide variety of room styles from Romantic to arty, and a prime location in the southern Altstadt; rooms have shower or bath, WC and hairdryers, and there's parking. **€99**

DJH Fulda Schirrmannstr. 31 ⓣ 0661 733 89, ⓦ djh-hessen.de. Youth hostel 2km southwest of the centre on the far side of the River Fulda, with plenty of outside space for sports; it's popular with visiting athletics clubs and football teams. Accommodation is in singles, doubles or dorms sleeping up to eight. Dorm price includes breakfast. Dorm **€24.50**, double **€57**

★**Goldener Karpfen** Simpliziusbrunnen 1 ⓣ 0661 868 00, ⓦ hotel-goldener-karpfen.de. Classy family-run

hotel on a pretty square in the southern Altstadt, with lovely, welcoming public areas, a restaurant (see p.600) – and Goethe for a former guest. Rooms vary in style quite widely, from traditional to minimalist. **€135**

Hotel am Schloss Habsburgergasse 5–11 ⓣ 0661 250 55 80, ⓦ hotel-am-schloss-fulda.de. Rambling, cyclist-friendly hotel in a historic half-timbered house. The location is peaceful but central, close to the Stadtschloss and Dom; rooms are compact but equipped with flat-screen TV, shower and WC. **€69**

Hotel Garni Hirsch Löherstr. 36 ⓣ 0661 90 01 18 85, ⓦ hotel-hirsch-fulda.de. One of Fulda's most central budget options, with simple but attractive rooms at bargain rates above a Turkish restaurant in an atmospheric half-timbered house, handy for the southern Altstadt's

11

nightlife scene. Reception Mon–Fri 11am–2pm & 5–11pm, Sat & Sun 5–11pm. **€63**

Maritim am Schlossgarten Pauluspromenade 2 ☎0661 28 20, ⓦmaritim.de. Smart, business-oriented

hotel in a quiet but very central location on the Schlossgarten, and incorporating the magnificent Baroque Orangerie. Rooms have en-suite bath or shower, some have balconies and there's an indoor pool, sauna & solarium. **€151**

EATING AND DRINKING

Fulda's lively Altstadt is liberally peppered with places to **eat** and **drink**, with the thickest cluster of bars around Karlstrasse and Kanalstrasse at the southern end of the Altstadt.

★**Café Palais** Bonifatiusplatz 1 ☎0661 250 92 63. Stylish, modern café/bar next to the tourist office, with a big terrace, modern art and generous portions; salads or *Flammkuchen* €6.90, massive tortillas €7.20. They serve a delicious breakfast buffet too (weekdays €7.50, weekends €9.80). Mon–Thurs 9am–7pm, Fri & Sat 9am–1am, Sun 9.30am–7pm.

Café Thiele Konditorei Mittelstr. 2 ☎0661 727 74, ⓦcafe-thiele.de. Founded in 1892, this is the cream of Fulda's *Kaffee und Kuchen* stops, with a big selection of coffee and hot chocolate, breakfasts from €4.20, light meals and cakes; the *Crème Giovanni*, with biscuit, fresh puréed strawberries and vanilla cream is the speciality. Tues–Sat 9am–6pm, Sun 10am–6pm.

Felsenkeller Leipzigerstr. 12 ☎0661 727 84, ⓦfelsenkeller-fulda.de. Friendly bar and *Biergarten* of the Hochstift brewery, on the brewery premises just north of the Barockviertel, with a menu of hearty *Schweinbraten* and *Schnitzel*; salads from €6.60, specials €13.80. Mon–Sat 11am–2pm & 5pm–late, Sun 11.30am–10pm; kitchen closes 10pm.

Goldener Karpfen Simpliziusbrunnen 1 ☎0661 868

00, ⓦhotel-goldener-karpfen.de. Elegant hotel restaurant serving a refined menu, such as cod with leaf spinach, lemon & vanilla sauce. There's a set lunch (€22 for two courses/€28 for three); evening à la carte main courses cost upwards of €20. Daily 11am–11pm.

Hohmanns Brauhaus Florengasse 3–5 ☎0661 250 296 86 00, ⓦhohmanns-brauhaus.de. Big *Gasthausbrauerei* in the southern Altstadt with splendid copper microbrewery, a menu of meaty dishes (main courses €11 up), and *Fuldaer Kellerbier* and *Hefeweizen* beers. Try the delicious, smooth *Bierbrand* – distilled from beer – too. Mon–Fri 6.30am–2pm & 5.30pm–late, Sat & Sun 6.30am–late.

★**Schwarzer Hahn** Friedrichstr. 18 ☎0661 24 03 12, ⓦschwarzerhahn-fulda.de. Delicious *Ehernberger Pilgerstoff* beer and good German food – including *Tafelspitz* (boiled beef) with superb *Frankfurter Grüne Sosse* – are served in pleasantly fussy surroundings here, and there's a terrace in summer. Veggie dishes from €7.80, *Schnitzel* from €8.50 and meaty main courses from around €11.50. Daily 11am–11pm.

NIGHTLIFE AND ENTERTAINMENT

Esperantohalle Esperantoplatz ☎0661 242 910, ⓦesperantohalle.de. Big congress centre and concert hall that is the main venue in Fulda for touring big-name rock and comedy acts, dance spectaculars, musicals and the like.

Schlosstheater Schlossstr. 5 ☎0661 102 14 83,

ⓦschlosstheater-fulda.de. Fulda's theatre is in the Stadtschloss complex, and offers a remarkably wide ranging programme, from classical and contemporary drama and music, to modern dance, operas, operetta and musicals.

Schloss Fasanerie

Guided tours on the hour April–Oct Tues–Sun 10am–5pm; porcelain collection tours at 3pm • €6, or €10 with porcelain collection • ⓦschloss-fasanerie.de • Bus #43 from Fulda ZOB

Seven kilometres south of Fulda is **Schloss Fasanerie**. A modest country house was built on the site in 1711, but in 1739 it was massively extended by the prince-bishops' architect Andreas Gallasini to create a magnificent Baroque summer residence. It has a chequered history: after the dissolution of the prince-bishopric it fell into a ruinous state before becoming the residence of the Elector Wilhelm II of Hesse-Kassel, whose architect Johann Conrad Bromeis rebuilt the interior in elegant Neoclassical style. The lofty **Kaisertreppe**, or main staircase, is decorated with portraits of Habsburg emperors; in summer, the splendid **Grosser Saal** – the largest room in the Schloss – is the venue for classical music concerts. The Schloss is also home to a collection of priceless **porcelain**, which includes the Electors' 1800-piece dinner service. The Schloss is still in the hands of the Hesse royal family.

The Rhön Biosphere Reserve

East of Fulda and accessible by bus, the 950m **Wasserkuppe** is the highest mountain of the Rhön and the highest point in Hesse. The Rhön region – which stretches into Thuringia and Bavaria – has been declared a UNESCO Biosphere Reserve to safeguard its pristine upland landscapes, so it comes as a surprise to find the grassy summit of the Wasserkuppe so cluttered with buildings. Amongst them is the **Deutsches Segelflugmuseum** (daily: April–Oct 9am–5pm; Nov–March10am–4.30pm; €5; ⊕segelflugmuseum.de), a small museum packed with full-sized and model gliders: the summit has been the main centre for gliding in Germany since the 1930s. Beyond the cluster of buildings you'll see paragliders launching themselves off the summit – there's a school (see below) should you want to join them.

ARRIVAL AND INFORMATION   RHÖN BIOSPHERE RESERVE

By bus and train Infrequent bus #35 (4 daily; 50min) connects Fulda's ZOB, on the eastern side of the Altstadt, with the Wasserkuppe. In summer (May–Oct) the RhönRadBus connects the Wasserkuppe with Gersfeld Bahnhof for trains to and from Fulda (Mon–Fri 5 daily, Sat & Sun 3–4 daily; ⊕hochrhoenbus.de), carrying bikes in a trailer.

Tourist information On the summit at Wasserkuppe 1 (daily 10am–4pm; ☎06654 918 340, ⊕rhoen.de).

ACTIVITIES

Hiking and biking The Rhön is splendid hiking country. A circular walk around the summit offers breathtaking views south over neighbouring peaks and west towards Fulda. The 89km Rhön Rennsteig Weg – which links the Rhön and Thüringer Wald – starts here, while the 180km Hochrhöner, which passes over the Wasserkuppe, is a sort of "greatest hits" of Rhön hiking, rated among Germany's most beautiful walks. Unsurprisingly, the Wasserkuppe is also a popular destination for bikers.

Paragliding There's a paragliding school on the summit (☎06654 75 48, ⊕wasserkuppe.com).

Skiing The Wasserkuppe has blue, red and black ski runs (⊕skilifte-wasserkuppe.de). You can rent ski gear on site and there's a ski and snowboarding school.

Tobogganing On the northwest side of the summit at Märchenwiesenhütte there's a summer toboggan run (€2.50).

Fritzlar and around

Half-timbered old towns aren't unusual in Hesse, yet even by the standards of the region, **FRITZLAR**'s **Altstadt** is magical, surrounded by its medieval defences and with a central **Marktplatz** of such theme-park quaintness you pinch yourself to believe that the houses – which are perfectly genuine – weren't built that way merely to attract tourists. The most eye-catching is the crooked **Gildehaus**, or Kaufhäuschen, which was built around 1475 and was the guildhouse of the Michaelsbruderschaft, one of the first German trade guilds, which survived into the mid-nineteenth century. An hour west of Fritzlar lies the beautiful **Edersee** reservoir, one of the targets of the World War II Dambuster raids.

Regionalmuseum and Grauer Turm

Fritzlar's most impressive house is the mammoth **Hochzeitshaus** a little to the west of Marktplatz. Built from 1580 to 1590, it's the largest half-timbered house in North Hesse and together with the neighbouring Patrizierhaus is home to the **Regionalmuseum** (Easter to Advent Tues–Fri 10am–noon & 3–5pm, Sat 10am–noon, Sun 3–5pm; €2; ⊕museum-fritzlar.de), whose eclectic local history displays embrace everything from geology and prehistory to folklore. Afterwards, climb the lofty **Grauer Turm** on the town walls at the end of Burggraben for views across the Altstadt's rooftops (April–Oct 9.30am–12.30pm & 2–5pm; €0.45).

Dom and Domschatz

Dom Mon–Fri 9am–5pm, Sat 9am–4pm, Sun noon–4pm • Free • Ⓦ www.katholische-kirche-fritzlar.de • **Crypt, cloisters and Domschatz** April–Oct Tues–Sat 10am–noon & 2–5pm, Sun 2–4.30pm; Nov–March Tues–Sun 2–4pm • €3

South of Marktplatz, Fritzlar's stone and slate-hung **Rathaus** dates from 1109 and is claimed to be the oldest in Germany still fulfilling its original function; facing it, the **Dom** is successor to the modest wooden church founded by St Boniface in 723 AD. It's a handsome blend of Romanesque and Gothic, nowhere more magical than in the Romanesque **crypt**, which contains the tomb of St Wigbert, a contemporary of St Boniface. The same ticket gives access to the fourteenth-century **cloisters**, the Dom's library and the **Domschatz**, whose treasures include the jewelled *Heinrichskreuz* from 1020.

ARRIVAL AND INFORMATION   FRITZLAR

By train Fritzlar is linked to Kassel's Wilhelmshöhe station by infrequent trains (1 daily; 35min) and buses; the Bahnhof is south of the Altstadt on the south side of the River Eder.
Tourist office In the crazily twisted Spitzchenhäuschen at Zwischen den Krämen 5, halfway between the Marktplatz and Dom (Mon 10am–6pm, Tues–Thurs 10am–5pm, Fri 10am–4pm, Sat 10am–2pm; ☎05622 98 86 43, Ⓦ fritzlar.de).

ACCOMMODATION AND EATING

Kaiserpfalz Giessener Str. 20 ☎05622 99 37 70, Ⓦ kaiserpfalz.com. Comfortable hotel in a restored historic building in the Altstadt, with eighteen single and double rooms, each with shower & TV; there's a lift, sauna and parking. The excellent restaurant is friendly and welcoming, serving salads from €8.80, steaks from around €22 and delicious fish; there's simpler fare available in the afternoons. Restaurant Mon–Sat 11.30am–2pm, 2.30–5pm & 5–10pm, Sun 11am–2pm & 2.30–5pm. **€82**
Das Nägel Marktplatz 12–14 ☎05622 790 6000, Ⓦ das-naegel.de. Classy and bustling Austrian restaurant/ bistro/bar on the main square, serving breakfast (from €2.20), *Schnitzels* from €9.80, pasta, meaty mains (from €13.90) and calorific sweet treats like *Kaiserschmarren*. Tues–Sun 9am–midnight.
Zur Spitze Marktplatz 25 ☎05622 18 22, Ⓦ zur-spitze .de. Freshly renovated single and double rooms in a pretty, half-timbered house right on the market square. Rooms have shower, WC, TV and phone, and there's a restaurant. **€65**

Edersee

Twenty kilometres west of Fritzlar is the **Edersee**, one of the Sauerland reservoirs whose **dams** were the targets of the famous World War II **Dambuster raids** in May 1943. Not that you'd know it today: the dam was rapidly repaired after the raid and looks as solid now as it must have done before the attack. You can stroll from one side to the other, or hire a boat (see box below); it's certainly a beautiful spot, on the fringe of the **Sauerland Nationalpark** and with the meandering lakeshore hugged by low, wooded hills. The dam is illuminated to impressive effect in the evening.

Sperrmauer Museum Edersee

Easter to early Nov daily 11am–5pm • €4 • Ⓦ dambusters.de

West of the dam, just off the road to Bringhausen, a bouncing bomb sits in front of the **Sperrmauer Museum Edersee**. The museum tells the story of the Edersee raid, though don't expect a straightforward tale of stiff-upper-lip British patriotism – the destructive

---

EDERSEE BOAT TRIPS

There are a number of places on the east side of the dam where you can hire **rowing** or **electric boats**, including Bootsverleih Edership (☎05623 16 66, Ⓦ edership.de), Monis Bootsverleih (☎05623 47 08) and Wassersportcenter Sun & Fun (☎0171 642 99 15, Ⓦ sun-fun .de). Alternatively, enjoy the lake in more sedate style aboard one of the **pleasure boats** of the Personenschifffahrt Edersee (April–Oct up to 8 departures daily from east and west sides of the dam; €7–15; ☎05623 54 15, Ⓦ personenschifffahrt-edersee.de).

(and deadly) effects of the raid and the use of slave labour to repair the dam are also covered. Plans exist for a new, bigger museum closer to the dam.

ARRIVAL AND INFORMATION

EDERSEE

By bus and train To reach the east side of the Edersee dam take a bus or train to Bad Wildungen, then change to the bus #510, direction "Medebach". The journey takes a little over an hour.

Tourist information There's a tourist information office on the dam itself (mid-April to Oct daily 11am–5pm; Christmas holidays daily noon–4pm; ☎ 05623 99 98 50, ⓦ edersee.com).

ACCOMMODATION AND EATING

Terrassen Hotel Randstr. 4 ☎ 05623 947 90, ⓦ terrassenhotel-edersee.de. Hotel-restaurant on the lakeside close to the eastern side of the dam. Spacious double rooms have TV, shower and WC; some have lake views. The cedar-built *Loghouse* restaurant, café and *Biergarten* serves *Schnitzels* from around €12.90, plus steaks and pike-perch fresh from the lake. **€116**

Kassel

11

KASSEL is the largest city in northern Hesse. Internationally, it's renowned for the **documenta** contemporary art exhibition (see box below), which rolls in every five years, taking over the city and leaving a legacy of public sculpture unique in Germany. Between times Kassel falls off the radar. True, the centre is dull – as single-mindedly devoted to shopping as any in Germany – but the city has some fine museums (including a new one devoted to the **Brothers Grimm**, who wrote their famous fairy tales here), its eighteenth-century **parks** are among the most extraordinary in Europe, and the setting, fringed by wooded hills, is lovely. For those who don't relish hanging out in shopping malls, the leafy, attractive **Vorderer Westen** quarter – between the city centre and Wilhelmshöhe – has all the elegant Jugendstil architecture and relaxed café life you could wish for.

For visitors, Kassel is a linear city, with most of the sights at either end of **Wilhelmshöher Allee**. In the east are the city centre's museums and a beautiful park, **Karlsaue**; in the west there's the exceptional landscape and art collection of **Wilhelmshöhe**, declared a UNESCO World Heritage Site in 2013. Hotels and places to eat and drink are scattered between the two.

The Altstadt

You'll look in vain for much that's old in Kassel's **Altstadt**, for what the RAF didn't obliterate in 1943 the planners swiftly eradicated afterwards, sparing a few isolated monuments: the fourteenth-century **Martinskirche** on Martinsplatz, whose towers and interior were rebuilt in a strangely inventive 1950s interpretation of Gothic; the sixteenth-century Weser Renaissance **Marstall**, rebuilt as a market hall (Thurs & Fri 7am–6pm, Sat 7am–2pm) and a great place to assemble a picnic; and the **Druselturm** on Druselplatz, a spindly thirteenth-century survivor from the medieval city defences.

DOCUMENTA

One of the world's most important exhibitions of contemporary art and often known as the "one hundred days museum", **documenta** (ⓦ documenta.de) was founded in 1955 by the artist and art educator Arnold Bode to reconcile the German public to international modernism after the Nazi years, when the official artistic policy had been reactionary and anti-modern. It became an unparalleled success, and takes place every five years under a new director, with the most recent one attracting 750,000 visitors. documenta 14 runs from 10 June to 17 September 2017.

11

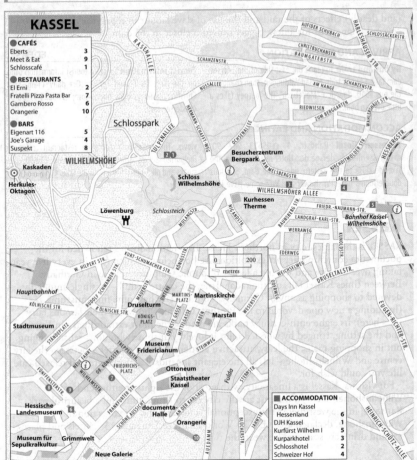

KASSEL

CAFÉS
Eberts	3
Meet & Eat	9
Schlosscafé	1

RESTAURANTS
El Erni	2
Fratelli Pizza Pasta Bar	7
Gambero Rosso	6
Orangerie	10

BARS
Eigenart 116	5
Joe's Garage	4
Suspekt	8

ACCOMMODATION
Days Inn Kassel Hessenland	6
DJH Kassel	1
Kurfürst Wilhelm I	5
Kurparkhotel	3
Schlosshotel	2
Schweizer Hof	4

West of the Altstadt, main shopping street **Obere Königsstrasse** preserves its handsome proportions, but little of its prewar architecture.

Museum Fridericianum

Friedrichsplatz 18 • Wed & Fri–Sun 11am–6pm, Thurs 11am–8pm • €5 • ⓦ fridericianum.org

Vast Friedrichsplatz is dominated by the Neoclassical portico of the **Museum Fridericianum**, which, in the late eighteenth century, was one of the first museums in Europe to display royal collections to the public – in this instance, those of Landgrave Friedrich II of Hesse-Kassel, whose statue stands in the centre of the square named after him. Nowadays the Fridericianum is a venue for documenta exhibitions and hosts touring exhibitions of contemporary art. Tucked into the rear of the building is the **Zwehrenturm**, a surviving medieval city gate, reworked as an observatory in the early eighteenth century.

The Ottoneum: Naturkundemuseum

Steinweg 2 • Tues & Thurs–Sat 10am–5pm, Wed 10am–8pm, Sun 10am–6pm • €3.50 • ⓦ naturkundemuseum-kassel.de

Brave roaring traffic to cross Steinweg from Friedrichsplatz to reach the **Ottoneum**,

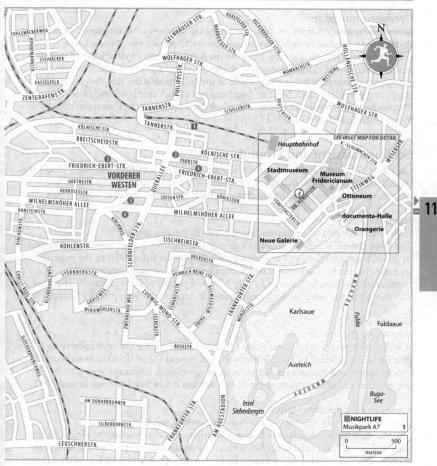

built between 1604 and 1607 as Germany's first theatre but now housing the **Naturkundemuseum**, whose natural history displays include the skeleton of an elephant from Friedrich II's menagerie and the Holzbibliothek – a library-like presentation of leaves, flowers and seeds. Nearby, the ultramodern **documenta-Halle** is a hive of activity during the documenta exhibitions.

The Karlsaue

From the documenta-Halle, steps lead down to the Karlsaue (free access), an eighteenth-century park on a vast scale. Its groomed lawns and well-drilled trees and water features stretch into the distance from the elegant, yellow-painted Orangerie, built in the early eighteenth century as a summer residence for Landgrave Karl. At the southern end of the park is the **Insel Siebenbergen** (April–Oct Tues–Sun 10am–6pm; €3), renowned for its flowering plants, including many tender species not often seen in Germany. The banks of the river Fulda – which separates the Karlsaue from the equally extensive Fuldaaue – are quite lovely, lined with rowing clubs and, in summer, dotted with beer gardens.

11

Orangerie museums

Astronomisch-Physikalisches Kabinett An der Karlsaue 20a • Tues, Wed & Fri–Sun 10am–5pm, Thurs 10am–8pm • €3 • ⓦ museum-kassel
.de • **Marmorbad** An der Karlsaue 20d • April–Oct Tues–Sun 10am–5pm • €4 with English audio-guide • ⓦ museum-kassel.de

The Karlsaue's Orangerie is now home to the **Astronomisch-Physikalisches Kabinett**, whose collection of clocks, globes and scientific instruments from the sixteenth to eighteenth centuries is fascinating. Pride of the collection is the *Augsburger Prunkuhr*, a staggeringly opulent clock built in Augsburg in 1683. A side pavilion houses the **Marmorbad**, which contains sinuous mythological sculptures in Carrara marble by Pierre Etienne Monnot (1657–1733).

Schöne Aussicht and around

On a low hill on the north side of the Karlsaue, **Schöne Aussicht** ("beautiful view") was once lined with Baroque mansions, of which only one survives. A handful of fine museums in this area – and lovely views over the Karlsaue – make it worth a visit.

Neue Galerie

Schöne Aussicht 1 • Tues, Wed & Fri–Sun 10am–5pm, Thurs 10am–8pm • €6 • ⓦ museum-kasssel.de

The **Neue Galerie** is Schöne Aussicht's principal attraction. Refurbished and reopened in 2011, it displays the city's impressive collection of art from 1750 to the present, including works by Tischbein, Lovis Corinth and the German Expressionists, installations by Joseph Beuys and a 1980 Warhol portait of Beuys himself. There are also models of various past documenta projects, including a wrapping by Christo.

Grimmwelt

On the Weinberg • ⓦ grimmwelt.de

A little to the west of Schöne Aussicht, a striking new home for the city's collections relating to the Brothers Grimm, **Grimmwelt**, will present the work of the world-famous lexicographers and collectors of fairy tales in an up-to-date, interactive way. Under construction as this book went to press, the museum is scheduled to open in mid-2015.

Museum für Sepulkralkultur

Weinbergstr. 25–27 • Tues–Sun 10am–5pm, Wed 10am–8pm • €5 • ⓦ sepulkralmuseum.de

The **Museum für Sepulkralkultur** is about as bright and cheery as any museum on the theme of death and burial could be, with an emphasis on the associated rituals, craft skills and folk art, including examples from non-European and non-Christian cultures. The lower level is devoted to memorials and burial grounds in the German-speaking world from the late Middle Ages onwards.

Hessisches Landesmuseum

Brüder-Grimm-Platz • Closed for refurbishment • ⓦ museum-kasssel.de

The eclectic collections of the **Hessisches Landesmuseum** range from pre- and early history to a surprisingly engrossing wallpaper museum and a more conventional collection of applied art, including displays of eighteenth-century Kassel porcelain. The Torwache annexe houses a collection of ceramics, jewellery, glass and furniture from 1840 to the present, including examples of Jugendstil, Art Deco and Bauhaus. At the time of writing the entire complex remained closed for refurbishment; a new building is planned for the wallpaper museum.

Wilhelmshöhe

Besucherzentrum Wilhelmshöhe Wilhelmshöher Allee 380, close to the terminus of tram #1 • Mid-March to mid-Nov daily 10am–5pm; mid-Nov to mid-March Tues–Sun 10am–4pm • **Besucherzentrum Herkules** Mid-March to mid-Nov daily 10am–5pm; mid-Nov to mid-March Tues–Sun 10am–5pm • Park free • ⓦ wilhelmshoehe.de

The exuberance of the palace and parks of **Wilhelmshöhe** is visible even from the city centre, for the flamboyant Baroque **Bergpark** climbs the hill in front of you along arrow-straight Wilhelmshöher Allee, which is aligned with the park. The steepness of the incline foreshortens the view, and it's only once inside it that you realize Wilhelmshöhe is as vast as it is spectacular. There are *Besucherzentren* (visitor centres) at the foot of the park by the tram terminus, and behind the Herkules-Oktagon at the top.

Herkules-Oktagon

Herkules-Oktagon viewing platform mid-March to mid-Nov Tues–Sun 10am–5pm; May to mid-Oct also open Mon • €3 • Bus #22 ascends to the Oktagon from Kassel-Druseltal at the terminus of tram #3; there's also plentiful car parking next to the Besucherzentrum (visitor centre) Herkules

Created on the whim of Landgrave Karl in the first decade of the eighteenth century by the Italian Francesco Guerniero, Wilhelmshöhe is dominated by the **Herkules-Oktagon**, an enormous fantasy castle topped by a pyramid on which stands an 8.25m-tall figure of **Hercules**, the work of the Augsburg coppersmith Jacob Anthoni. The choice of subject reflected Karl's not-so-modest view of his own qualities.

11

Wasserspiele

May to early Oct Wed & Sun 2.30pm; evening performance 1st Sat of month at 10pm June/July, 9.30pm Aug & 9pm Sept • Free

From the foot of the Oktagon, the stepped **Kaskaden** (cascades) descend for 400m; from May to early October, this is the scene of the best free show in Hesse, the **Wasserspiele**, as water is released at the top and slowly flows downhill. It takes around ten minutes to descend the Kaskaden, then disappears, reappearing over the **Steinhöfer** waterfall and under the picturesque **Teufelsbrücke** before finally re-emerging in front of Schloss Wilhelmshöhe to power a spectacular 52m-high **water jet**. The entire performance takes an hour, so that you can comfortably follow its progress downhill. In summer there's an illuminated evening performance on the first Saturday of the month.

Schloss Wilhelmshöhe

Schloss Tues & Thurs–Sun 10am–5pm, Wed 10am–8pm • €6 • Weissensteinflügel and Löwenburg March to mid-Nov Tues–Sun 10am–5pm; mid-Nov to Feb Fri–Sun 10am–4pm • Both €4 • ⓦ museum-kassel.de

The lower reaches of the park are dominated by **Schloss Wilhelmshöhe**, a massive Neoclassical pile built between 1786 and 1801 to plans by Simon du Roy for Landgrave Wilhelm IX. The central **Corps de Logis** houses the **Gemäldegalerie Alte Meister**, a heavyweight collection of old masters originally amassed by the Landgrave Wilhelm VIII of Hesse-Kassel and ranking with the best in Germany. Laid out over three floors, it is particularly strong in Flemish and Dutch works. The third floor of the museum is a treasure-trove of works by Rubens, Van Dyck, Jacob Jordaens and Rembrandt, with highlights including Rembrandt's tender *Jacob Blessing Ephraim* and *Manasseh* from 1656 and Rubens' *Flight into Egypt*, a delicate and modest-sized panel painting that lacks the theatrical swagger of his altarpieces.

The second floor displays Dutch painting of the sixteenth and seventeenth centuries, while German works on the first floor include a small Cranach portrait of a rather stout Martin Luther, Dürer's 1499 *Portrait of Elsbeth Tucher* and a number of works by Johann Heinrich Tischbein the Elder, including a portrait of Wilhelm VIII himself. The first floor also displays Italian, Spanish and French art, including canvasses by Titian and Tintoretto. The ground floor and basement are occupied by the **Antikensammlung** of Classical antiquities, as well as a series of eighteenth-century cork models of the monuments of ancient Rome.

Weissensteinflügel and Löwenburg

The only part of Schloss Wilhelmshöhe that preserves its original Neoclassical interiors is the **Weissensteinflügel** in the palace's south wing. At the end of the eighteenth century the Louis XVI and English styles were influential at the Kassel court, but the wing also displays the influence of the French Empire style dating from the time of Jérôme Bonaparte, youngest brother of the Emperor Napoleon, who ruled the short-lived Kingdom of Westphalia from Kassel between 1807 and 1813. During this period, Wilhelmshöhe was renamed Napoléonshöhe.

In a secluded setting southwest of Schloss Wilhelmshöhe is the **Löwenburg**, a picturesque mock-medieval castle containing the Hesse-Kassel armoury, a chapel and a number of rooms furnished in mock-antiquarian styles.

ARRIVAL AND GETTING AROUND   KASSEL

By train Fast, frequent ICE trains arrive at Kassel-Wilhelmshöhe station, which is midway between Schloss Wilhelmshöhe and the city centre. Destinations Frankfurt (2–3 per hour; 1hr 22min–2hr 2min); Fritzlar (1 daily; 35min); Fulda (2–3 per hour; 30–35min).

Public transport Public transport is provided by NVV (ⓦ nvv.de); a *Kurzstrecke* ticket for up to four stops costs €1.60, single tickets €2.70, and a *Tagesticket* (day-ticket) €6.20. Tram #1 runs along Wilhelmshöher Allee and links the city centre with the west of the city.

INFORMATION

Tourist office Wilhelmsstr. 23 (Mon–Sat 9am–6pm; ☎ 0561 70 77 07, ⓦ kassel-marketing.de), and in Bahnhof Kassel-Wilhelmshöhe (Mon–Sat 9am–6pm; ☎ 0561 340 54).

Discount card Either office can sell you a KasselCard, valid for two people for 24hr (€9) or 72hr (€12), and offering free public transport and reductions on museum entry.

ACCOMMODATION

★**Days Inn Kassel Hessenland** Obere Königsstr. 2 ☎ 0561 918 10, ⓦ daysinnkasselhessenland.de. Convenient for the city-centre museums and trams to Wilhelmshöhe, with 48 rooms, free wi-fi and lots of character: public areas are in a lovely 1950s style, rooms have retro 1950s furnishings and the hotel is a listed historic monument. **€69**

DJH Kassel Schenkendorfstr. 18 ☎ 0561 77 64 55, ⓦ djh-hessen.de. The city's youth hostel is close to the Vorderer Westen's bar and restaurant scene, with accommodation in doubles and four- or six-bed dorms, a cafeteria, disco and indoor games. Breakfast included. Dorms and doubles (per person) **€23.50**

Kurfürst Wilhelm I Wilhelmshöher Allee 257 ☎ 0561 318 70, ⓦ bestwestern.de. Tastefully refurbished nineteenth-century hotel next to Bahnhof Kassel-Wilhelmshöhe, handy for the Vorderer Westen, with a

bedframe wittily balanced atop its corner tower and comfortable, en-suite rooms with wi-fi and TV. **€76**

Kurparkhotel Wilhelmshöher Allee 336 ☎ 0561 318 90, ⓦ kurparkhotel-kassel.de. Modern, slightly anonymous hotel with bright, tastefully decorated rooms, a sauna, whirlpool and swimming pool, fitness room and a convenient location close to Wilhelmshöhe. **€137**

Schlosshotel Schlosspark 8 ☎ 0561 308 80, ⓦ schlosshotel-kassel.de. Four-star comfort in a modern hotel just across the road from the Wilhelmshöhe palace complex. Some of the rooms have balconies and all have flat-screen satellite TV and wireless internet. **€119**

Schweizer Hof Wilhelmshöher Allee 288 ☎ 0561 936 90, ⓦ hotel-schweizerhof-kassel.de. Smart, comfortable business-oriented hotel close to Wilhelmshöhe, with bright rooms furnished in a crisp contemporary style, wi-fi, laptop-sized safes and a gym and sauna. **€109**

EATING AND DRINKING

CAFÉS

Eberts Friedrich-Ebert-Str. 116 ☎ 0561 73 99 230, ⓦ eberts-kassel.de. Stylish all-day crêperie and café in the elegant Jugendstil surroundings of a former officers' mess. Breakfasts from €3.30, crêpes from €3.20, baked potatoes from €5.90 and main-course meat dishes for around €15. Mon–Sat 9am–midnight, Sun 10am–midnight.

Meet & Eat Obere Königstr. 7 ☎ 0561 92 01 96 88. Fast-food veggie and vegan café in the city centre, with falafel from €3.50, vegan doner kebabs from €4.50 and pizzas from €4.50, plus Lebanese salads, *börek* and veggie

burgers. Mon–Thurs & Sun 10am–10pm, Fri & Sat 10am–2am.

Schlosscafé Schlosspark 6 ☎ 0561 325 43, ⓦ schlosscafe-wilhelmshoehe.de. The pick of the Bergpark's refreshment stops, the *Schlosscafé* is a pretty spot for a cool drink on the sunny terrace after a visit to Schloss Wilhelmshöhe. Light meals – *Bockwurst* with salad, trout with horseradish – cost around €6.50. Tues–Sun noon–6pm.

RESTAURANTS

El Erni Parkstr. 42 ☎ 0561 71 00 18, ⓦ el-erni.de. Upmarket Spanish restaurant in the Vorderer Westen, with an elegant, all-white interior and a tree-shaded terrace fronting Parkstrasse. Tapas starters are mostly €7–10, fish and meat main courses from around €15. Daily 6pm–1am.

Fratelli Pizza Pasta Bar Friedrichsplatz 10 ☎0561 76 67 91 90. Modern Italian trattoria and wine bar opposite the Fridericianum, with foccacia sandwiches from €4, bruschetta from €4.50 and pizza or pasta from €7, plus salads and meat- or fish-based mains. Mon–Fri 11.30am–2.30pm & 5.30–11pm, Sat 11.30am–midnight, Sun 11.30am–2.30pm & 5.30–10pm.

Gambero Rosso Gräfe Str. 4 ☎0561 28 53 81, ⓦgamberorosso-kassel.de. Fresh pasta and wines direct from the Italian producers at this relaxed but stylish restaurant and wine bar in the Vorderer Westen. Seasonal specials start at €10. Mon–Sat noon–2.30pm & 6pm–late.

Orangerie Am Auerdamm 20b ☎0561 28 61 03 18, ⓦorangerie-kassel.de. Strategically located in the Orangerie with a broad terrace facing the leafy Karlsaue, this place serves breakfast until 1pm (from €5.50), as well as *Flammkuchen* (from €9.50), wraps, burgers and *Currywurst* plus a few more substantial mains. There's also a €22 Sun brunch until 3pm. April–Sept daily 10am–late; Oct–March Wed–Sat noon–late, Sun 11am–6pm.

BARS

Eigenart 116 Wilhelmshöher Allee 116 ☎0561 77 60 80 70, ⓦeigenart116.de. Bustling, stylish modern café/bar on a corner site in the Vorderer Westen, with generous ciabatta burgers from €6.90, pizza and pasta from €5.90, plus salads and meaty mains. Cocktails from €7; wines by the glass from €4.20. Mon–Sat 9am–late, Sun 10am–late.

Joe's Garage Friedrich Ebert Str. 60 ☎0561 186 86, ⓦjoes-garage.de. American-themed rock bar on the Vorderer Westen's main bar strip, with a variety of oldies nights and (Sept–March) occasional gigs by local bands. Mon–Thurs 11am–1am, Fri 11am–4am, Sat noon–4am, Sun noon–1am.

Suspekt Fünffensterstr. 4 ☎0561 104 522, ⓦcafe-suspekt.de. Smoky city-centre lesbian and gay café/bar, with a varied programme of events, including Seventies/Eighties/Nineties disco nights. Tues–Thurs 6pm–1am, Fri 6pm–2am, Sat 3pm–2am, Sun 3pm–1am.

NIGHTLIFE AND ENTERTAINMENT

Musikpark A7 Miramstrasse 74 ☎0561 95 38 03 40, ⓦmusikpark-a7.de. Kassel's biggest mainstream dance club is in the east of the city and comprises several different areas, including main dance club *Agostea*, the more intimate *La Vie* soul club & lounge and the Alpine-style *Mausefalle*. Thurs–Sat 10pm–late, plus Mon during holidays.

Staatstheater Kassel Friedrichsplatz 15 ☎0561 109 4222, ⓦstaatstheater-kassel.de. Modern city-centre auditorium that is the main venue for drama, ballet and classical music in Kassel, including performances by the Staatsorchester Kassel.

North Rhine-Westphalia

LANDSCHAFTSPARK DUISBURG-NORD

North Rhine-Westphalia

With its population of around eighteen million actually exceeding that of the neighbouring Netherlands, North Rhine-Westphalia (Nordrhein-Westfalen) is by far Germany's most populous Land, though it's by no means the biggest geographically. As the name suggests, it's an artificial construction, cobbled together by the occupying British after World War II from the Prussian provinces of the Rhineland and Westphalia. Perhaps that explains why, for all its size and economic clout, it lacks the sort of breast-beating regional patriotism found in Bavaria. Instead, loyalties tend to be more local: to the city – particularly in the Land's great metropolis, Cologne – or to the region, as in the Ruhrgebiet, which straddles the historic boundary between Rhineland and Westphalia.

Occupied at various times by the French and British and with Charlemagne's capital, **Aachen**, at its western tip, North Rhine-Westphalia is an outward-looking, European-minded place. Several of its cities have played a decisive role in European history: in the north, the handsome cathedral city of **Münster** was the scene for the signing of the Treaty of Westphalia which ended the Thirty Years' War, while in the south the university city of **Bonn** – birthplace of Beethoven – strutted the world stage more recently as capital of West Germany during the Cold War. Though it lacks the Alpine drama of Germany's south, North Rhine-Westphalia has its share of scenic beauty, along the mighty **Rhine**, in the charming **Siebengebirge** and in the wooded, peaceful **Sauerland**.

Urban attractions are nevertheless to the fore, particularly in thriving, multicultural **Cologne** and chichi **Düsseldorf**, its near-neighbour, rival and the Land's capital. The increasingly postindustrial cities of the Ruhr conurbation – such as **Duisburg**, **Essen** and **Dortmund** – also have their charms, not least in their inventive reworking of their rich industrial heritage. Further afield, the ham-and-pumpernickel wholesomeness of Westphalian towns like **Soest**, **Paderborn**, **Detmold** and **Lemgo** couldn't be less like the Ruhr, while along the **Lower Rhine** – around Kalkar and Xanten – the proximity of the Netherlands makes itself felt in place names, architecture and landscape.

Getting into and **around** the region is easy. Three major **airports** – at Cologne-Bonn, Düsseldorf and Dortmund – are well-connected internationally, while there's a dense web of **public transport** links, with the core of the region served by rail, U-Bahn and bus. This is also one of the easiest parts of Germany to explore by **bicycle**, with well-equipped Radstations at many train stations and well-signposted cycle paths along which to explore the countryside.

12

Highlights

❶ Cologne The great metropolis of western Germany is fascinating, free-spirited and enormous fun to visit. **See p.616**

❷ Schloss Augustusburg Piety takes a back seat to pleasure at this dazzling Rococo archbishop's palace. **See p.632**

❸ Haus der Geschichte, Bonn The remarkable story of the postwar German miracle, told in an engaging and imaginative way. **See p.636**

❹ Aachen cathedral Charlemagne's former court chapel is unique north of the Alps. **See p.643**

❺ Eating and drinking in the Altstadt, Düsseldorf Far more than merely "the longest

bar in the world", Düsseldorf's Altstadt has an almost Mediterranean élan on fine summer nights. **See p.658**

❻ Landschaftspark Duisburg-Nord Industrial heritage meets nature and science fiction at this remarkable, recycled steelworks. **See p.662**

❼ Folkwang collection, Essen The superstars of French and German nineteenth-century art, housed in elegant modernist premises designed by British architect David Chipperfield. **See p.667**

❽ Hermannsdenkmal, Detmold A winged, bearded warrior rises romantically above the wooded ridge of the Teutoburger Wald. **See p.682**

HIGHLIGHTS ARE MARKED ON THE MAP ON PP.614–615

NORTH RHINE–WESTPHALIA

N

NETHERLANDS

MÜNSTERLAN

Hengelo

Gronau

Burgsteinf

Rh

Coesfeld

Dülmen

Arnhem

Nijmegen

Emmerich

Kleve

Kalkar

River Rhine

Xanten

Recklinghausen

Kevelae

Gelsenkirchen

Oberhausen

Essen ⑦ Bochum

Duisburg ⑥

Mülheim

Venlo

Krefeld

Wuppertal

Düsseldorf

Mönchengladbach

Neuss ⑤

River Ruhr

Zons

Dormagen

Leverkusen

Maastricht

Cologne (Köln) ①

BERGISCHE LAND

Dreiländereck ④ Aachen

Düren

Brühl ②

Troisdorf

Bonn ③ Königswi

Euskirchen

Bad Honnef

Heimbach

Liège

BELGIUM

Monschau

Bad Münstereifel

EIFEL

Remagen

River R

0 ——— 25
kilometres

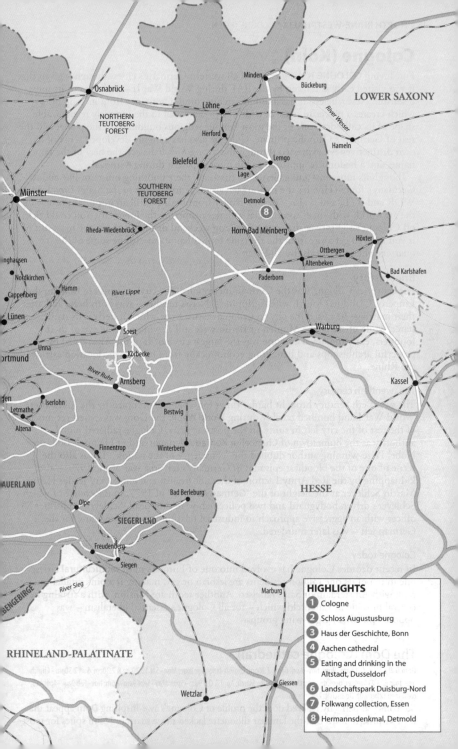

Minden

Bückeburg

LOWER SAXONY

Osnabrück

Löhne

River Wesser

NORTHERN TEUTOBERG FOREST

Herford

Hameln

Lemgo

Bielefeld

Lage

SOUTHERN TEUTOBERG FOREST

Münster

Detmold ⑧

Horn-Bad Meinberg

Höxter

Rheda-Wiedenbrück

Ottbergen

nghausen

Altenbeken

Bad Karlshafen

Nordkirchen

Paderborn

Cappenberg

Hamm

River Lippe

Lünen

Warburg

Soest

Korbecke

Kassel

Unna

rtmund

River Ruhr

Arnsberg

gen

Iserlohn

Letmathe

Bestwig

Altena

Finnentrop

Winterberg

HESSE

AUERLAND

Bad Berleburg

Olpe

SIEGERLAND

Freudenberg

Siegen

River Sieg

Marburg

BENGEBIRGE

RHINELAND-PALATINATE

Wetzlar

Giessen

HIGHLIGHTS

① Cologne

② Schloss Augustusburg

③ Haus der Geschichte, Bonn

④ Aachen cathedral

⑤ Eating and drinking in the Altstadt, Dusseldorf

⑥ Landschaftspark Duisburg-Nord

⑦ Folkwang collection, Essen

⑧ Hermannsdenkmal, Detmold

Cologne (Köln)

Fun-loving **COLOGNE** is the greatest of all western Germany's cities, though – given that it was visited early and often by the RAF during World War II – perhaps not its most beautiful. Nevertheless, it has a unique architectural inheritance from its long history which creates a powerful sense of continuity – above all in the instantly recognizable shape of its **cathedral**, one of the most famous religious buildings on the planet and the seat of Germany's Catholic primate. Cologne also has a highly developed sense of its own distinctiveness, expressed through the strong *Kölsch* dialect, the beer of the same name, and a hedonistic approach to life most apparent during **Karneval**.

Though its museums and galleries are first-rate, there's nothing museum-like about Germany's fourth city: it's the nation's television centre, home to the major broadcasters WDR and RTL, and is also – despite rivalry from Berlin – still an important centre for the art world, with small commercial galleries peppering the inner city. You could tick off Cologne's sights over the course of a long weekend or so, but to get the most out of it you need to get away from the riverside tourist haunts to explore some of the quarters where the locals live and play.

Brief history

For centuries Cologne was the German metropolis. The city's origins are Roman: the Emperor Claudius's fourth wife Agrippina – Nero's mother – was born here, and after their marriage he raised the city to Colonia status, from which it derives its name. Later, while upstarts like Munich or Berlin were still a twinkle in the eye of their founders, early **medieval Cologne** was the largest city north of the Alps, ruled by powerful archbishops and benefiting economically from its strategic location astride the Rhine.

The twentieth century

The twentieth century brought harder times for Cologne, occupied by the Allies after World War I and bombed terribly during **World War II**; the Dom was spared yet much of the rest of the city left in ruins. In the postwar years, Cologne radiated moral authority as the hometown of **Chancellor Konrad Adenauer** and of Heinrich Böll, the Nobel Prize-winning author dubbed the "conscience of the nation". It was also the scene of one of the bloodiest episodes in Germany's terrorist war of the 1970s – the kidnapping by the Red Army Faction of the industrialist and employers' leader Hanns Martin Schleyer at the height of the **"German Autumn"** of 1977, in the course of which Schleyer's driver, bodyguard and two policemen were shot dead. Schleyer – a former SS officer with an aggressive approach to industrial relations, and a hate figure for the German left – was later murdered.

Cologne today

In recent decades Cologne has evolved into one of Europe's most **multicultural** cities; one in ten of its one million residents are lesbian or gay, making it a pink citadel to rank with Amsterdam or San Francisco. Another tenth are Muslim, with a striking new central mosque in Ehrenfeld which – for all Cologne's essential liberalism – was opposed noisily by right-wing groups.

The Dom (Cologne cathedral)

Dom Daily: May–Oct 6am–9pm; Nov–April 6am–7.30pm; English-language tours Mon–Sat 10.30am & 2.30pm, Sun 2.30pm • Church free; tour €8 • ⓦ koelner-dom.de • **South tower** Daily: March, April & Oct 9am–5pm; May–Sept 9am–6pm; Nov–Feb 9am–4pm • €3, combined ticket with Domschatzkammer €6

So iconic, so perfectly realized does the profile of Cologne's awe-inspiring **Dom** appear that it's a surprise to learn that the familiar silhouette lacked those soaring, 157m spires for most

COLOGNE ORIENTATION

The **Dom** and the **Rhine** – both just metres from the Hauptbahnhof – are the obvious main points of orientation. Strictly speaking the entire **city centre** is Cologne's Altstadt, since the crescent of boulevards fringing the centre to the west, north and south marks the line of the old medieval fortifications, some of whose gates survive. But the area often referred to as the **Altstadt** – and which certainly has the most old-world atmosphere – is the tight network of lanes and squares around Gross St Martin and the Rathaus, south of the Dom. West of this area, the main shopping streets – **Hohe Strasse** and **Schildergasse** – run north–south and east–west respectively.

West of Neumarkt around **Rudolfplatz** is a fashionable district of designer shops and gay bars, while the **north** of the city centre has some of the most interesting museums and sights, but is – the **Friesenviertel**'s party scene aside – otherwise relatively quiet. So, too, is the **Severinsviertel** in the south. Cologne's neighbourhoods are known as Veedel or Viertel; two definitely worth exploring are the studenty **Zülpicher Viertel**, southwest of the centre – also known as the **Kwartier Lateng** – and the chic **Belgisches Viertel** just to its north. Further afield, **Ehrenfeld** is arty and multicultural, with some of the city's best clubs; while north of the centre, the Zoo and botanical garden offer an escape from the noise of the city. Across the river, **Deutz** has more greenery, plus classic views across the river to the Dom.

of its history. Construction of the Dom – whose design was inspired by the colossal French cathedrals of Beauvais and Amiens – was prompted by the transfer of the relics of the Three Magi from Milan in 1164. Work began in 1248, with the 50m-high choir consecrated by 1322, but stopped in 1560 and the church remained incomplete until the mid-nineteenth century, when neo-Gothic architect Ernst Friedrich Zwirner finished the job.

It's only when you get up close do you appreciate its sheer size, at which point the sooty towers resemble vast waterfalls of Gothic sculpture. You can climb the **south tower**, though be warned – there are 509 steps, and no lift. In the run-up to **Christmas**, a traditional market fills Roncalliplatz on the south side of the Dom, with others on Alter Markt, Heumarkt, Neumarkt and Rudolfplatz.

The interior

Once inside, the downside of the Dom being Germany's most famous church is apparent, as grumpy, red-robed officials struggle to maintain some sort of ecclesiastical decorum amid the seething mass of visitors. But look up and you'll forget the crowds, for the genius of the design lies in the way sheer height lends such delicacy and elegance to the structure of what is, by any measure, an enormous building. Five windows on the north side of the nave date from 1507 to 1509, though the Dom's oldest window, the Bible Window, dates from around 1265 and is in the Chapel of the Three Magi in the ambulatory. The cathedral's treasures include the very **Shrine of the Three Magi** that first inspired its construction; gorgeously gilded and bejewelled, the reliquary dates from around 1190 to 1225 and is behind the high altar.

On the north side of the ambulatory, the **Gero Crucifix** is the oldest remaining monumental crucifix in the western world; it dates from 970, and originally stood in an early predecessor to the Dom. The most recent addition to the Dom's artworks is the striking 19m-high abstract window by Cologne-based artist **Gerhard Richter**, installed in the south transept in 2007.

The Domschatzkammer

Domkloster 4 · Daily 10am–6pm · €5, combined ticket with south tower €6 · ⓦ domschatzkammer-koeln.de

The partly subterranean **Domschatzkammer** is accessed from the exterior of the cathedral on the north side, and has something of the air of a bank vault, which is hardly surprising given the priceless works of religious art it contains, or the fact that one of them – the jewelled, seventeenth-century **Sumptuous Monstrance** – was badly damaged by thieves in 1975. The treasury occupies a series of thirteenth-century vaults, and its

12

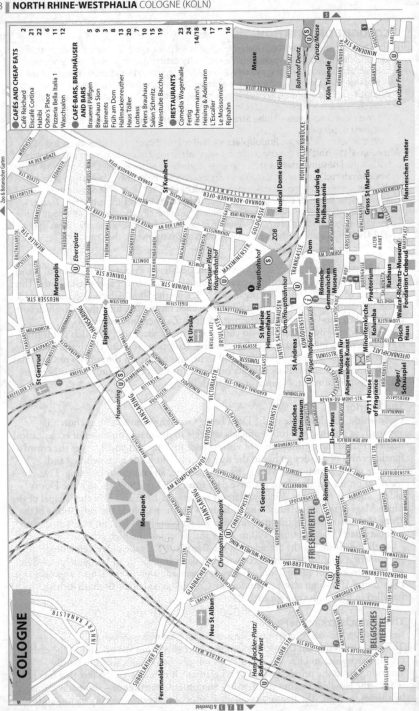

COLOGNE

● CAFÉS AND CHEAP EATS	
Café Reichard	2
Eiscafé Cortina	21
Habibi	22
Osho's Place	6
Pizzeria Bella Italia 1	11
Waschsalon	12

● CAFÉ-BARS, BRAUHÄUSER AND BARS	
Brauerei Päffgen	5
Brauhaus Sion	9
Elements	3
Früh am Dom	8
Hallmackenreuther	13
Haus Töller	20
Lorbass	7
Peters Brauhaus	10
Salon Schmitz	15
Weinstube Bacchus	19

● RESTAURANTS	
Comedia Wagenhalle	23
Fertig	24
Fischermann's	14/18
Heising & Adelmann	4
L'Escalier	17
Le Moissonnier	1
Riphahn	16

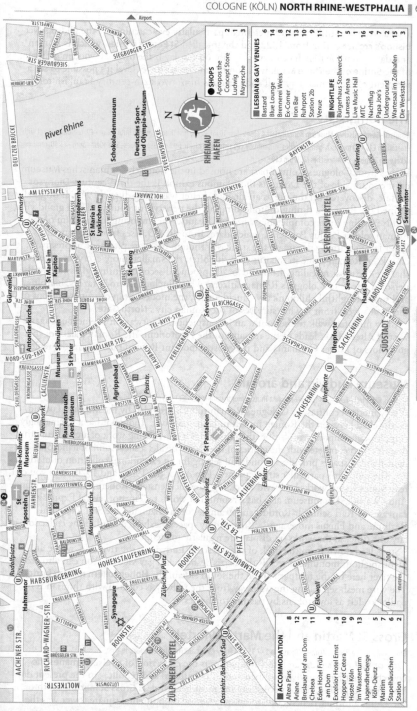

12

artefacts are beautifully lit and presented: particularly eye-catching are the gilded silver **bishop's crosier** dating from 1322 and the so-called **St Peter's crosier**, which is Roman and dates from the fourth century AD. Also on display is the original wooden structure of the **Shrine of the Three Magi**, while on the museum's lower level it's possible to see a fragment of the Roman city wall and the finds from two sixth-century Frankish tombs.

The Roman city

Römisch-Germanisches Museum Roncalliplatz 4 • Tues–Sun 10am–5pm, first Thurs in month until 10pm • €9, combined ticket with Praetorium €10 • ℗ roemisch-germanisches-museum.de • **Praetorium** Kleine Budengasse 2 • Tues–Sun 10am–5pm • €3.50, combined ticket with Römisch-Germanisches Museum €10

Riches from Cologne's Roman past are housed in the **Römisch-Germanisches Museum** on the south side of the Dom. Its most famous exhibit is the third-century **Dionysos mosaic**, discovered on the site as an air-raid shelter was being dug in 1941. It originally formed the floor of a dining room leading off the peristyle or courtyard of a grand villa, and is startling in its completeness, size and beauty. The imposing mausoleum of the Roman soldier Lucius Poblicius, which dates from 40 AD, rises from the museum's lower level to utterly dominate the staircase. Though there are plenty of impressive chunks of Roman stone in the museum, it's often the smaller, more everyday objects that are the most revealing, from the locally produced second-century glassware to the personal effects of Cologne's Roman citizens, which include mirrors, razors, hairpins and some delightful children's toys. Incidentally, the modest heap of stones in front of the Dom's west front is what survives of the Roman city's **North Gate**.

A few minutes' walk to the south, an inconspicuous doorway on Kleine Budengasse west of Alter Markt leads to the remains of the **Praetorium**, the Roman palace of the governors of Lower Germania and the most important Roman building in the region.

Museum Ludwig and around

Heinrich-Böll-Platz • Tues–Sun 10am–6pm, first Thurs in month until 10pm • €11 • ℗ museum-ludwig.de

A very modern contrast to Cologne's Roman ruins is provided by the **Museum Ludwig**, sandwiched between the Roman museum, Dom and river. Though it has a fascinatingly complex contemporary roofscape, the museum is a self-effacing work of architecture that doesn't try to compete with the glories of the Dom. Inside, a succession of handsome and light-flooded spaces provides a wonderful setting for an exceptional collection of modern art. The museum's particular strong point is Pop Art of the 1960s and 1970s, and you can feast your eyes on works by David Hockney, Roy Lichtenstein, Robert Rauschenberg and Andy Warhol. The museum also has a roomful of works by Picasso, several Expressionist canvases by Karl Schmidt-Rottluff and examples of the Bauhaus, De Stijl, Nouveau Réalisme and Fluxus movements. There is only space to exhibit a third of the collection at any one time, so the works on display are regularly rotated.

Steps lead down from the back of the Museum Ludwig to the riverside, where an inconspicuous **monument** recalls the Nazis' lesbian and gay victims. You can also cross the river here by the footpath along the south side of the **Hohenzollern railway bridge**. The wire mesh separating the walkway from the railway is covered with thousands of padlocks, left as love tokens by passing romantics.

Gross St Martin and the Martinsviertel

Gross St Martin Tues–Sat 8.30am–7.30pm, Sun 1–7.15pm • Free • ℗ romanische-kirchen-koeln.de

One of Cologne's great architectural glories is the collection of twelve **Romanesque churches** that have survived – albeit variously battered and rebuilt – to the present day. The most imposing, if not necessarily the most beautiful, is **Gross St Martin**, south of the Dom, a former Benedictine monastery whose monumental square tower was the dominant feature of the city's skyline until the Dom acquired its towers. The narrow lanes that huddle around it convey the atmosphere of medieval Cologne better than anywhere else in the city, though many of the **Martinsviertel**'s "medieval" houses only date from the mid-1930s, when the Nazis spruced up the hitherto unsanitary and poverty-ridden quarter. Genuinely old specimens include the much-photographed **Stapelhäuschen** in front of the church. Altogether more splendid are the Renaissance **Haus St Peter** on Heumarkt and the incredibly tall, double-gabled **Zur Brezel/Zur Dorn** on Alter Markt, which dates from 1580 to 1582.

The Rathaus

Rathausplatz 2 • Mon, Wed & Thurs 8am–4pm, Tues 8am–6pm, Fri 8am–noon • Free

The sprawling **Rathaus** occupies much of the space between Alter Markt and Rathausplatz. Seriously damaged during World War II, the complex now presents a dizzying array of styles, from Gothic to 1970s. Miraculously, the beautiful Renaissance **Rathauslaube**, or porch, built between 1569 and 1573 to the plans of Wilhelm Vernukken of Kalkar, was only lightly damaged during the war. Another surviving feature is the eight-sided, fifteenth-century Gothic **tower**. Highlights of the interior include the **Hansa Hall** dating from 1330 and the rich Renaissance decoration of the Senatssaal or Senate Hall, which escaped destruction by being removed for safekeeping during the war.

The Jewish quarter

In front of the Rathaus, the foundations of the medieval **synagogue** and **Jewish quarter** are currently the subject of further excavations, which will link with the Praetorium (see opposite) to form a new subterranean Archäologische Zone (archeological zone). Plans for the site, which include a proposed new Jewish museum in front of the Rathaus, have had a troubled history, with opposition focusing on the loss of a public square and on spiralling costs. A proposal for a local referendum on the subject was struck down by the city council in 2014, but construction of the museum has yet to begin.

The Wallraf-Richartz Museum

Obenmarspforten • Tues, Wed & Fri–Sun 10am–6pm, Thurs 10am–9pm, first Thurs in month until 10pm • €8, prices for temporary exhibitions vary • ⓦ wallraf.museum

The south side of Rathausplatz is dominated by the clean, modern lines of the **Wallraf-Richartz-Museum/Fondation Corboud**, beautifully laid out and curated in such a way that it offers a coherent lesson in art history. It has an important collection of medieval Cologne art, Flemish and Dutch masters, and French and German art of the nineteenth and early twentieth centuries. Highlight of the medieval collection is Stefan Lochner's *Virgin in the Rose Bower* (c.1440–42); among a considerable trove of Flemish and Dutch masters are works by Rubens, Van Dyck and a late Rembrandt self-portrait. German paintings from the nineteenth century include some typically symbolic works by Caspar David Friedrich and a masterpiece by Max Liebermann, *The Bleaching Ground*, from 1882. The Fondation Courboud collection of Impressionist and post-Impressionist works is the most complete in Germany, with works by Manet, Sisley, Cézanne and Van Gogh; a 1915 Monet *Water Lilies* is already well on the way to abstraction. The graphic collection includes drawings by Leonardo da Vinci, Albrecht Dürer and Auguste Rodin.

The southern Altstadt

Just behind the Wallraf-Richartz-Museum on Martinstrasse, the **Gürzenich**, a fifteenth-century banqueting hall, is another much-mauled but impressive survivor from

Cologne's medieval heyday, and is closely associated with the city's carnival festivities (see box, p.630). The neighbouring church of **St Alban** was left a ruin as a war memorial. A short walk to the south is another of the city's Romanesque churches, **St Maria im Kapitol** (Mon–Sat 10am–6pm, Sun 1–6pm; free), which is hemmed in by houses and so, despite its size, is as self-effacing as Gross St Martin is bombastic. The oldest parts of the church – which was built as a convent on the site of a Roman temple – date from the middle of the eleventh century. It has a trefoiled choir based closely on the plans of the Church of the Nativity in Bethlehem. The city's last surviving Romanesque merchant's house, the step-gabled **Overstolzenhaus**, is nearby at Rheingasse 8.

Museum Schnütgen and Rautenstrauch-Joest Museum

Cäcilienstr. 29–33 • Tues, Wed & Fri–Sun 10am–6pm, Thurs 10am–8pm, first Thurs in month until 10pm • Museum Schnütgen €6, Rautenstrauch-Joest Museum €7, combined ticket €10 • ⓦ museenkoeln.de

A few minutes' walk to the west of St Maria im Kapitol, the deconsecrated **Cäcilienkirche** provides a suitable setting for the **Museum Schnütgen**'s collection of medieval religious art. It shares a spacious foyer with the recently reopened **Rautenstrauch-Joest Museum**, Cologne's ethnographic museum. An imposing 1930s rice store from the island of Sulawesi guards the entrance to the collections, which are presented in innovative fashion and begin with musical instruments from Java before progressing to displays covering the Americas, Oceania, Africa and Asia.

The Rheinauhalbinsel and Rheinauhafen

The **Rheinauhalbinsel** jetty on the riverside is home to two museums, the child- and chocoholic-friendly **Schokoladenmuseum** (Tues–Fri 10am–6pm, Sat & Sun 11am–7pm, last entry 1hr before closing; €9; ⓦ schokoladenmuseum.de), and the more worthy but imaginatively presented **Deutsches Sport & Olympia Museum** (same hours; €6; ⓦ sportmuseum.de), whose highlights include displays relating to the 1936 Berlin and 1972 Munich Olympics, as well as winter sports, football and boxing. To the south of the museums, the quays and warehouses of the old **Rheinauhafen** have been transformed into an ultramodern, Docklands-style urban quarter with a traffic-free riverside promenade that's particularly popular with joggers.

Kolumba

Kolumbastr. 4 • Daily except Tues noon–5pm; closed first two weeks of Sept • €5 • ⓦ kolumba.de

Standing atop the war-shattered remains of the church of St Kolumba southwest of the Dom and incorporating the ruins into its design, **Kolumba** houses the art collection of the Diocese of Cologne. Though the theme of the collection is spiritual, this is no narrow display of conventional religious iconography, as the inclusion of kinetic sculptures by Rebecca Horn and of work by Joseph Beuys demonstrates. One of the museum's greatest treasures is Stefan Lochner's *Madonna with the Violet*; it's arguable, however, that the stunning building itself is at least as memorable as the collection, which it displays with lavish spaciousness, and there are superb views of the Dom from its upstairs windows. Across the street, the sweeping curve of the **Disch Haus** – a Weimar-era office building – has been beautifully restored and provides an excellent architectural foil to the museum.

The 4711 House of Fragrance

Glockengasse 4 • **Shop and museum** Mon–Fri 9.30am–6.30pm, Sat 9.30am–6pm • Free • **Fragrance workshops** Thurs 3pm (in German); other languages available on request • €35 • ⓦ galerie-glockengasse.de

Close by Kolumba is the **4711 House of Fragrance**, the premises of the famous manufacturer of Kölnisches Wasser – **Eau de Cologne** – which derives its brand name, 4711, from the number allocated to the house on Glockengasse by occupying French troops in 1796. The French connection is acknowledged by the carillon on the building's south facade, which plays the *Marseillaise* every hour on the hour. Inside, there's a small **museum** and a fountain of cologne, which you can dip into free of charge. They also offer **fragrance workshops**.

Museum für Angewandte Kunst

An der Rechtschule • Tues–Sun 11am–5pm, first Thurs in month until 10pm • €6, or €8 including temporary exhibitions • ⓦ museenkoeln.de

A short walk to the north of Glockengasse, the **Museum für Angewandte Kunst** presents the city's substantial collection of applied art, including the work of such big-name international designers as Charles Eames and Philippe Starck, alongside fine art by Mondrian, Kandinsky and others.

Kölnisches Stadtmuseum and around

Zeughausstr. 1–3 • Tues 10am–8pm, Wed–Sun 10am–5pm, first Thurs in month until 10pm • €5 with free English audio-guide, €7.50 including temporary exhibitions • ⓦ museenkoeln.de

A winged, gilded Ford car atop the medieval city armoury announces the **Kölnisches Stadtmuseum**, which takes an engrossing journey through Cologne's long history. Among its exhibits is a huge model of the city based on Mercator's 1571 plan, which shows that quite extensive areas within the walls were given over not to buildings, but to vineyards. There's also a model of one of the extraordinary log rafts that were once floated down the Rhine to satisfy the enormous demand for timber; these could be 300m long and had accommodation on board for the four to five hundred people needed to crew them. In the Middle Ages, seagoing ships could go no further upriver than Cologne, and the city's prosperity was greatly aided by the *Stapelrecht* – a law that stipulated merchants had to offer their goods for sale to the citizens of Cologne before they were allowed to transship them. It persisted until 1831. There's also a section on Jewish life in Cologne.

El-De Haus: the NS-Dokumentationszentrum

Appellhofplatz 23–25 • Tues–Fri 10am–6pm, Sat & Sun 11am–6pm • €4.50, English audio-guide €2 • ⓦ nsdok.de

Cologne's time under the Nazis is covered in depth at the **NS-Dokumentationszentrum** in the **El-De Haus** around the corner from the Kölnisches Stadtmuseum. Here, the crimes of the Nazi regime in Cologne are documented in the city's former Gestapo headquarters. The exhibition squarely demolishes the idea that the Nazis enjoyed no support in Cologne, and among the most chilling exhibits are the letters written by two elderly female residents of a retirement home, denouncing their young parish priest.

The northwestern Altstadt

West of the El-De Haus along Gereonstrasse is **St Gereon** (Mon–Fri 10am–6pm, Sat 10am–5.30pm, Sun 1–6pm; free; ⓦ stgereon.de), the most memorable of all Cologne's Romanesque churches thanks to the spectacular decagon at its heart, a monumental space which blends late Romanesque and early Gothic elements. It was reworked into its current form in the early thirteenth century, when the oval core of the church was already nine hundred years old. Some of its medieval frescoes have survived, making its interior less austere than some Cologne churches.

Nearby, the well-preserved **Römerturm** at the eastern end of Friesenstrasse was the northwest corner tower of the city's Roman fortifications. It dates from around 50 AD, and is decorated with mosaic-like stone patterns. The bars and restaurants of the attractive **Friesenviertel**, which stretches west along Friesenstrasse and south along Friesenwall, are the stamping ground of trendy types; the district also preserves some of the tall, narrow townhouses that were once characteristic of Cologne's inner city.

Rudolfplatz and around

At the western extremity of **the Ring** – the series of roads that mark the old city walls – one surviving medieval gate, **Hahnentor**, presides over bustling **Rudolfplatz**. By day the surrounding shopping streets are among the city's best: **Ehrenstrasse** is young and trendy, while the boutiques of **Pfeilstrasse** and **Mittelstrasse** are chic and expensive – don't miss the über-stylish **Apropos** concept store at Mittelstr. 12 (Mon–Sat 10am–7pm; ⓦ apropos-store.com), which is Cologne's air-kissing epicentre of designer fashion. At night, this area is the main hub of the city's nightlife, and also of its lesbian and gay scene.

At the eastern end of Mittelstrasse, a bronze of Germany's first postwar chancellor (and former Cologne mayor) Konrad Adenauer stands in front of the Romanesque church of **St Aposteln** (Mon & Wed–Sun 10am–1pm & 2–5pm; free); inside there's a small exhibit on the church's history, including its wartime damage and reconstruction. St Aposteln faces out over **Neumarkt**, the western limit of the central pedestrian zone and an important transport hub.

Käthe Kollwitz Museum Köln

Neumarkt 18–24 • Tues–Fri 10am–6pm, Sat & Sun 11am–6pm • €4 • ⓦ kollwitz.de

High above the Neumarkt Passage on the north side of Neumarkt is the small **Käthe Kollwitz Museum Köln**, which exhibits the largest existing collection of lithographs, drawings and watercolours by the antiwar artist, who was increasingly preoccupied by themes of death after her son was killed in Flanders in World War I. Her compassion for wider human suffering is evident throughout the museum.

The Belgisches Viertel and Zülpicher Viertel

West of the Ring, the beautiful Jugendstil apartment buildings of the **Belgisches Viertel** escaped wartime bombing and are now among the most sought-after in the city. Cologne's most fashionable district, it's a great place to linger over a *Milchkaffee* or glass of wine between extensive bouts of window-shopping in the area's numerous small boutiques, where you can buy everything from handmade shoes and jewellery to innovative men's and women's fashions from upcoming young designers. From Zülpicher Platz, Zülpicher Strasse heads southwest to define the **Zülpicher Viertel**, also known as the **Kwartier Lateng** or Latin Quarter, which in recent years has become a funky strip of student-friendly bars, restaurants and shops, thanks to its proximity to the university.

STUMBLING BLOCKS OF HISTORY

You first notice them almost by accident, as the sun catches the pavement and something glitters underfoot. Yet once you've spotted your first **Stolperstein** (ⓦ stolpersteine.de) – the name means, literally "stumbling block", you'll keep stumbling over more. The little brass plaques, memorials to individual victims of the Nazis, usually stand in front of the house from which that victim was taken, and are the work of **Gunter Demnig**, a Berlin-born but Cologne-based artist. Since 1996 he's laid 30,000 *Stolpersteine* in Germany and others in Poland, Austria, Hungary, the Czech Republic and the Netherlands among other places. They are particularly thick on the ground in the Zülpicher Viertel and Belgisches Viertel, close to the Roonstrasse synagogue; you'll sometimes stumble across a dozen or more in front of a single house. Incredibly moving, they're the antithesis of the big, official monuments to the Holocaust: they record the name, birth-date and fate – as far as it is known – of an individual. Chillingly, in many cases, the story is the same: deported and *verschollen* – missing, presumed dead. The placement of the stones outside the homes of the victims means the fate of entire families is often recorded. While many of the individuals remembered by the stones are Jewish, there are also *Stolpersteine* for political opponents of the regime, for the murdered Sinti and Roma, and for the Nazis' gay victims.

The Severinsviertel and Südstadt

On Chlodwigplatz at the southern tip of the Ring, the medieval **Severinstor** leads into the **Severinsviertel**, presided over by yet another Romanesque church, the **Severinskirche** (Mon–Fri 9am–6pm, Sat 9am–5.30pm, Sun 9.30am–noon & 3–5.30pm; free), and with something of the air of a separate town – if you've seen the Mercator plan in the Stadtmuseum, you'll understand why, for in the Middle Ages the Severinsviertel, though within the city walls, was separated from Cologne's centre by extensive vineyards. At Severinstr. 15, the tall, gabled **Haus Balchem**, dating from 1676, is one of the best-preserved historic merchant's houses in the city.

Across the Ring from the Severinsviertel the **Südstadt** is reminiscent of the Belgisches Viertel, if rather less trendy. It stretches northwest from the river towards the Zülpicher Viertel, and is an engaging mix of good restaurants, quirky boutiques along Merowinger Strasse, and Jugendstil facades in Teutoburger Strasse and Volksgartenstrasse.

Ehrenfeld

A stroll northwest from bustling Friesenplatz, on the liveliest section of the Ring, along Venloer Strasse and into **Ehrenfeld** is instructive for anyone wishing to get to grips with Cologne's multicultural character. A working-class neighbourhood that has acquired a bohemian overlay, it's one of the most cosmopolitan corners of the city, with everything from baklava bakeries to an Asian tea shop. Many of its residents are of Turkish origin, and it's here that Cologne's new central **mosque** has been built. Old industrial areas west of Venloer Strasse have been reworked as studio space for artists, and the area has many gay and lesbian residents. It wasn't always so tolerant: towards the end of World War II, the Nazis staged mass executions here of slave labourers and of Edelweisspiraten – members of an anti-authoritarian youth movement who refused to participate in the Hitler Youth. A mural next to the S-Bahn station on Schönsteinstrasse commemorates the victims.

The Zoo and Flora

Zoo Riehler Str. 173 • Daily: March–Oct 9am–6pm; Nov–Feb 9am–5pm • €17.50 • ⓦ koelnerzoo.de • **Flora** Amsterdamer Str. 34 • Daily 8am–dusk • Free • U-Bahn Zoo/Flora

North of the centre, Cologne's child- (and parent-) friendly **Zoo** and **Flora** – its sweetly old-fashioned botanical garden – are pleasant escapes from the bustle of the city on a fine day. The latter has tropical and arid hothouses, formal flowerbeds and a kitchen garden.

Deutz

A cable car, the **Kölner Seilbahn** (late March to early Nov daily 10am–6pm; €4.50 one-way, €6.50 return, ⓦ koelner-seilbahn.de), connects the Zoo with the **Rheingarten** park on the opposite side of the river in **Deutz** – the views en route are spectacular. The Rheingarten provides ample space for lazing in the sun, and also boasts an exclusive spa, the **Claudius Therme** (daily 9am–midnight; 2hr from €15). Deutz's **riverside** offers the classic view of Cologne's **skyline** across the Rhine – most dramatically from the observation platform atop the steel-and-glass **KölnTriangle** skyscraper, at Ottoplatz 1 on the eastern end of the Hohenzollernbrücke (May–Sept Mon–Fri 11am–10pm, Sat & Sun 10am–10pm; Oct–April Mon–Fri noon–6pm, Sat & Sun 10am–6pm; €3 ⓦ koelntrianglepanorama.de).

ARRIVAL AND DEPARTURE   **COLOGNE**

By plane Cologne-Bonn airport (ⓣ 02203 40 40 01, ⓦ koeln-bonn-airport.de) is southeast of the city, connected by S-Bahn trains every 20–30min, taking around 15min to the Hauptbahnhof.
By train The Hauptbahnhof is right in the centre of the city alongside the Dom.

12

Destinations Aachen (2–3 per hour; 33–57min); Amsterdam (every 2–3hr; 2hr 40min); Berlin (hourly; 4hr 23min); Bonn (up to 5 per hour; 17–29min); Brussels (9 daily; 1hr 48min); Dortmund (every 20–30min; 1hr 11min–1hr 26min); Duisburg (5 per hour; 34–47min); Düsseldorf (5 per hour; 21–30min); Düsseldorf airport (2–4 per hour; 30–38min); Essen (every 20min; 47min–1hr 5min); Frankfurt (every 30min–1hr 30min; 1hr 4min–2hr 20min); Frankfurt airport (1–2 per hour; 55min–1hr 15min); Koblenz (3 per hour; 53min–1hr 10min); Mainz (2 per hour; 1hr 44min–1hr 53 min); Munich (around 13 daily; 4hr 30min–7hr 24min); Münster (2–3 per hour; 1hr 46min–2hr 1min); Wuppertal (up to 4 per hour; 28–46min).

GETTING AROUND

By public transport Cologne is an enjoyable city to explore on foot, but sooner or later you're likely to make use of the public transport system (ⓦ kvb-koeln.de), which includes S-Bahn and U-Bahn metro networks – the latter emerging above ground at various points to become tramways, extending as far out as Bonn–Bad Godesberg (see p.638). A €1.90 *Kurzstrecke* ticket is valid for up to four stops; to travel further within the city you'll need a €2.80 *EinzelTicket*, or a €8.10 *TagesTicket*, which can be used from the moment it is validated until 3am the following day.

By bike Bike rental is available at Radstation, on the north side of the Hauptbahnhof at Breslauer Platz (Mon–Fri 5.30am–10.30pm, Sat 6.30am–8pm, Sun 8am–8pm; 3hr €5, 1 day €10, 2–4 days €8/day; ☎ 0221 139 71 90, ⓦ radstationkoeln.de), and at Colonia Aktiv, Gereonswall 2–4 (daily 10am–6pm; 3hr €9, 1 day €15, 2 days €25; ☎ 0221 34 66 95 57, ⓦ colonia-aktiv.de).

By taxi Taxi-Ruf Köln ☎ 0221 28 82, ⓦ taxiruf.de.

By car Car rental is available from: Avis, airport ☎ 02203 402 343, Hauptbahnhof ☎ 0221 913 00 63; Europcar, airport ☎ 02203 95 58 80, Hauptbahnhof ☎ 0221 139 27 48.

Sightseeing buses Cologne Coach Service (☎ 0221 979 25 70, ⓦ ccs-busreisen.de; €11) and Kölner City Tour (☎ 0221 270 45 66, ⓦ citytour.de; €13) offer sightseeing bus trips with English commentary.

Tourist train The Wolters Bimmelbahn offers chocolate-, zoo- or Christmas market-themed itineraries (☎ 0221 709 99 70, ⓦ bimmelbahnen.de; round trip €6).

INFORMATION AND TOURS

Tourist office Right opposite the Dom at Kardinal Höffner Platz 1 (Mon–Sat 9am–8pm, Sun 10am–5pm; ☎ 0211 221 34 64 30, ⓦ koelntourismus.de); it offers online accommodation booking through its website, though the tourist office staff can also help in person. You can get a Citisafari guide for smartphone for €12.90, or download a free app for Android or iPhone from the website. There's a souvenir shop in the basement.

Discount cards If you're anticipating museum-hopping, it's worth considering the Köln WelcomeCard, available from the tourist office (24hr/48hr: Cologne city €9/18; Cologne–Bonn region €24/48); it gives twenty percent off municipal museums, reduced entry to many others and unlimited use of the public transport system. You can also get a group card for up to five people (24hr/48hr: Cologne city €19/38; Cologne–Bonn region €49/98).

Boat trips Boats of the KD Köln-Düsseldorfer fleet (☎ 0221 208 83 18, wk-d.de) anchor in front of Gross St Martin and offer a variety of cruises all year round, including evening (€15.80) and dinner (€56) cruises and trips south past Bonn and the Siebengebirge (€21.20 return to Bonn, €32.60 to Bad Godesberg). Boats belonging to Kölntourist (☎ 0221 12 16 00, ⓦ koelntourist.net) follow similar itineraries (Bonn €18 return).

ACCOMMODATION

Cologne has scores of **hotels** in just about every category, though they can still get pretty busy if there's a major trade-fair in town, when prices also take an upward hike across the board. There are plenty of hotels right in the heart of the **Altstadt**, with a cluster of budget and mid-priced options north of the Hauptbahnhof and several swanky business-oriented offerings across the river in **Deutz**. The **Belgisches Viertel** has some stylish small hotels which make a sensible base if Cologne's nightlife or shopping are your priority.

HOTELS

Altera Pars Thieboldgasse 133–135 ☎ 0221 27 23 30, ⓦ alterapars-koeln.de. Comfortable, good-value hotel above a restaurant, just off Neumarkt and handy for the nightlife of Rudolfplatz and the Friesenviertel. Rooms have shower and WC, wireless internet and cable TV. €74

Ariane Hohe Pforte 19–21 ☎ 0221 759 88 02 10, ⓦ hotelariane.de. Pleasant, 3-star sister hotel to the Altera Pars, just south of the city's main shopping district. It's on the Rosenmontag parade route, with wi-fi in all areas. All rooms are en suite, with LCD TV. €90

Breslauer Hof am Dom Johannisstr. 56 ☎ 0221 27 64 80, ⓦ hotel-breslauer-hof.de. Bright, comfortable if slightly characterless rooms – all en suite – and a very central location just across from the Hauptbahnhof make this family-owned 3-star hotel good value when there's not a big conference or exhibition in town. €105

Chelsea Jülicher Str. 1 ☎0221 20 71 50, ⊛hotel-chelsea .de. "Art hotel" in the Belgisches Viertel, with an astonishingly eccentric roof-line, artworks by artists who actually have a connection to the place and a good café on the ground floor. The rooms are crisp, modern and minimalist in style, with bath or shower; some have balconies, and the most distinctive are built into the roof structure. Standard rooms **€98**, roof rooms **€118**

Eden Hotel Früh am Dom Sporergasse 1 ☎0221 27 29 20, ⊛hotel-eden.de. There's a funky, youthful feel to this modern boutique-style hotel next to the *Früh am Dom* (see p.628) and just across from the Dom itself. Facilities include wireless internet and a restaurant. **€125**

Excelsior Hotel Ernst Domplatz/Trankgasse 1–5 ☎0221 27 01, ⊛excelsiorhotelernst.com. Truly palatial city-centre hotel with a 140-year history. A member of the Leading Hotels of the World group, it's recently been refurbished with a conservative but up-to-date ambience, Asian and French restaurants and a piano bar. You can get cheaper deals through the hotel's website if you're flexible about when you stay. **€230**

★ **Hopper et cetera** Brüsseler Str. 26 ☎0221 92 44 00, ⊛hopper.de. Excellent, Belgisches Viertel boutique hotel in a converted monastery, with bright and stylish – if not particularly huge – rooms, a churchy mural in the breakfast room and a waxwork monk in the lobby. **€130**

Im Wasserturm Kaygasse 2 ☎0221 200 80, ⊛hotel -im-wasserturm.de. The most luxurious and architecturally audacious of Cologne's modern designer hotels really does occupy a converted nineteenth-century water tower, and numbers Brad Pitt and Madonna among past customers. **€164**

Maritim Heumarkt 20 ☎0221 202 70, ⊛maritim.de. Eye-catching modern architecture and a huge atrium distinguish this smart chain hotel on the south side of Heumarkt. It's also one of the city's most gay-friendly. **€106**

Stapelhäuschen Fischmarkt 1–3 ☎0221 272 77 77, ⊛kleines-stapelhäuschen.de. Charming Altstadt hotel/ restaurant rebuilt to resemble its seventeenth-century appearance, very near Gross St Martin. Rooms overlooking the river are the nicest. **€62.25**

HOSTELS

Hostel Köln Marsilstein 29 ☎0221 99 87 76 00, ⊛hostel.ag. Stylish combination of budget hotel and hostel with free wireless internet, 24hr reception and an excellent, central location. Breakfast is included and doubles come with bath and shower. Dorms **€37**, doubles **€89**

Jugendherberge Köln-Deutz Siegesstr. 5 ☎0221 81 47 11, ⊛koeln-deutz.jugendherberge.de. Large and functional modern HI hostel close to Deutz station, directly across the Rhine from the Altstadt. Dorms **€23.40**, doubles **€74.80**

Station Marzellenstr. 44–56 ☎0221 912 53 01, ⊛hostel-cologne.de. Large, privately run hostel just north of the station, with 24hr reception, no curfew, a kitchen and free internet. Dorms **€17**, doubles **€48**

12

EATING AND DRINKING

The **Altstadt** is the first port of call for most visitors looking for somewhere to eat or drink, and it's here that the traditional *Brauhäuser* are thickest on the ground, serving up hearty portions of eccentrically named Cologne specialities to help soak up the dainty glasses of local *Kölsch* beer (see box, p.628). Many of Cologne's most interesting and fashionable places to eat and drink are, however, on the western fringe of the centre, where **Hohenzollernring**'s raucous strip of bars, restaurants and cinemas provides the focus, but with maximum charm found in the streets of the **Belgisches Viertel** to the west. Studeny **Zülpicher Viertel** – the so-called Kwartier Lateng or Latin Quarter – is good for bars, but is above all the city's most fertile hunting-ground for cheap eats, while to the south there are some good options in the **Südstadt**.

CAFÉS AND CHEAP EATS

Café Reichard Unter Fettenhennen 11 ☎0221 257 85 42, ⊛café-reichard.de. This classy local institution is the pit stop for *Kaffee und Kuchen* in Cologne, serving breakfast from €6.90, delicious cakes and *Strudel* (€6.50) and hot food (from around €9) in elegant surroundings; there are fine Dom views from the terrace too. Daily 8.30am–8pm.

★ **Eiscafé Cortina** Hohenstaufenring 22 ☎0221 310 83 78. Classic Italian *gelateria* with huge windows, and a terrace fronting the Ring. The frozen yoghurt is particularly delicious; they also serve crêpes, waffles and pizza. Sundaes from €4.60. April–Sept Mon–Sat 9am–10/11pm, Sun 11am–11pm; Oct–March daily 10am–9pm.

Habibi Zülpicher Str. 28 ☎0221 271 71 41, ⊛habibi-koeln.de. Serving arguably the best falafel in Germany, this Lebanese restaurant in the student neighbourhood stays open for the late-night munchies. Takeaway falafel in bread €1.90; eat-in falafel platter with hummus & *tabbouleh* €6.70. Mon–Thurs & Sun 11am–1am, Fri & Sat 11am–3am.

Osho's Place Venloer Str. 5–7 ☎022 800 05 81, ⊛oshos-place.de. Bright, self-service veggie place, with Asian-influenced food, monthly *thali* evenings and a regular Sun brunch buffet. Daily lunch specials €8.40. Mon–Thurs & Sun 8am–10.30pm, Fri & Sat 8am–midnight.

Pizzeria Bella Italia 1 Friesenwall 52 ☎0221 277 46 22. It's nothing fancy, but this super-cheap Italian close to Rudolfplatz and the Ring is a dependable late-night refuelling stop at weekends, with pasta from €4, eat-in pizzas from €3.50 and takeaway mini pizzas for €1.50. April–Sept Mon–Thurs 11.30am–11pm, Fri & Sat 11.30am–1am, Sun 2–11pm; Oct–March Mon–Thurs 11.30am–10pm, Fri & Sat 11.30am–1am.

Waschsalon Ehrenstr. 77 ☏0221 13 33 78, ⊚cafe-waschsalon.de. Washing machines reworked as decor dominate this busy café, which offers a large range of breakfast options, plus *Flammkuchen* from €6.90 and salads and light savoury dishes from around €6. Mon–Fri 10am–1am, Fri & Sat 10am–3am.

RESTAURANTS

Comedia Wagenhalle Vondelstr. 4 ☏0221 35 55 89 10, ⊚comedia-wagenhalle.de. Chic, cosmopolitan bistro in an historic converted fire station, complete with firemen's poles. There's a lovely garden at the back; the restaurant and bar are attached to a theatre. Main courses around €10–20. Daily 5–11pm.

Fertig Bonner Str. 26 ☏0221 801 73 40. Hearty portions of French-accented bistro food, from *boudin noir* to confit of duck, dished up in unpretentious, pub-like surroundings south of the Severinstor. Main courses around €17.50–24. Daily 5–11pm.

Fischermann's Rathenauplatz 21 ☏0221 801 77 90, ⊚fischermanns.com. Asian, German and Mediterranean influences blend in the cooking of this trendy restaurant and cocktail bar, with dishes such as bavette pasta with speck, chives and chanterelles; main courses cost from €16, and there's a €38 set menu. There's also a sister restaurant in the chic Apropos concept store (see p.624). Mon–Thurs & Sun 6pm–2am, Fri & Sat 6pm–3am.

Heising & Adelmann Friesenstr. 58–60 ☏0221 130 94 24, ⊚heising-und-adelmann.de. Smart Friesenviertel restaurant and cocktail bar favoured by media types; the garden at the back is much in demand in fine weather. Main courses from €21; set menus €32.50 for two courses, €38.50 for three. Tues–Sat 6pm–10.30pm.

L'Escalier Brüsseler Str. 11 ☏0221 205 39 98, ⊚lescalier-restaurant.de. Highly respected French restaurant in the Belgisches Viertel, with affordable bistro food – including a bargain €24 business lunch – alongside its altogether more expensive gourmet creations. Tues–Sat noon–2pm & 6–10pm.

Le Moissonnier Krefelder Str. 25 ☏0221 72 94 79, ⊚lemoissonnier.de. Superlative French gourmet cooking – at a price – at this renowned two Michelin-starred restaurant in the north of the city. Main courses will set you back €40 and up, or there's a four-course weekday menu for €85. Tues–Thurs noon–3pm & 6.30pm–midnight, Fri & Sat noon–3pm & 7pm–midnight.

Riphahn Apostelnkloster 2 ☏0221 99 87 45 77, ⊚riphahn.com. Franco-German country cooking – with dishes such as lamb ragout with chickpeas or veal *Tafelspitz* in tomato vinaigrette – in a beautiful 1950s dining room pepped up with modern art. Main courses from around €18. Tues–Sat 10am–midnight, Sun 10am–6pm.

BRAUHÄUSER AND BARS

Brauerei Päffgen Friesenstr. 64 ☏0221 13 54 61, ⊚paeffgen-koelsch.de. Unlike the vast *Brauhäuser* near the Dom, this Friesenviertel favourite still brews on the premises, and it's considerably less touristy than some. Their *Kölsch* (€1.60) helps wash down Rhineland dishes such as *Himmel un Äd* or *Kölsche Kaviar*. Main courses from around €8. Mon–Thurs & Sun 10am–midnight, Fri & Sat 10am–12.30pm.

Brauhaus Sion Unter Taschenmacher 5–7 ☏0221 257 85 40. Cavernous *Brauhaus* belonging to the Sion brewery, rebuilt after wartime destruction in finest 1950s "traditional" style. It's more sedate than some, with sausages and local dishes such as *Dicke Bohnen* on the menu. Main courses around €9–13. Daily 10.30am–12.30am.

Elements Friesenstr. 16 ☏01512 127 76 85, ⊚elements-cologne.de. This smart cocktail bar in the thick of the Friesenviertel's nightlife quarter is a good bet for well-mixed drinks. The terrace is open from noon in fine weather for tapas or *Flammkuchen*. Tues–Thurs 8pm–1am, Fri & Sat 8pm–3am.

Früh am Dom Am Hof 12–18 ☏0221 261 32 15, ⊚frueh-am-dom.de. Located opposite the Dom, this

---

KÖLSCH – THE LOCAL ACCENT ON BEER

Kölsch is not only the name of the local Cologne dialect – one of the strongest regional accents in all Germany and positively mystifying to foreign visitors – but also of the city's deliciously refreshing, hoppy, top-fermented **beer**, traditionally drunk in tall, slim 0.2 litre glasses known as *Stangen*, though these days there's a certain amount of glass-size inflation going on to please German and foreign visitors accustomed to drinking their beer in larger measures. Brewery-owned or -affiliated *Brauhäuser* (or *Bierhäuser*) represent the traditional core of Cologne's eating and drinking scene, and there's a whole range of colourfully named **local dishes** to accompany the *Kölsch*, from *Kölsche Kaviar* (in reality blood sausage) to *Halver Hahn* (a cheese roll rather than the "half a chicken" the name suggests) and *Hämmche* (pig's trotter). The characteristically self-aggrandizing behaviour of the cheeky *Köbes* or **waiters** rounds off a highly distinctive, regional beer culture.

huge *Brauhaus* serves excellent food, including classic *Brauhaus* dishes like *Halver Hahn* and *Kölsche Kaviar*. Though it's frequently mobbed, the atmosphere in the labyrinthine interior is excellent and the cheeky waiters and general bustle are all part of the experience. Main courses from around €9. Daily 8am–midnight.

★ **Hallmackenreuther** Brüsseler Platz 9 ☎ 0221 51 79 70. Wonderful retro-Sixties decor and a peaceful location overlooking a leafy square make this trendy Belgisches Viertel bar a winner. There's Mediterranean-influenced food too, with light main courses around the €8–9.50 mark. Daily 11am–1am, Sat until 2am.

Haus Töller Weyerstr. 96 ☎ 0221 258 93 16, ⓦ haustoeller.de. Lovely, long-established *Brauhaus* close to Barbarossaplatz, nothing like as touristy as the Altstadt haunts but with plenty of atmosphere; there's draught *Päffgen Kölsch* to drink and Rhineland specialities such as traditional horsemeat *Sauerbraten* to eat (mains from around €20). Mon–Sat 5pm–late; closed July & August.

Lorbass Antwerpener Str. 34 ☎ 0221 16 86 33 41, ⓦ lorbass-bar.de. Refined, upmarket cocktail bar in the Belgisches Viertel where the red leather upholstery and liveried bartenders give an almost cinematic feel to the proceedings. Classic mixed drinks from €7.70; champagne cocktails €10. Wed–Fri 8pm–2am, Sat 8pm–3am.

Peters Brauhaus Mühlengasse 1 ☎ 0221 257 39 50, ⓦ peters-brauhaus.de. Big yet surprisingly cosy and intimate Altstadt *Brauhaus*, serving a large choice of Cologne delicacies to anchor down the own-brew *Kölsch*. Mains €12.40 up. Daily 11am–12.30am.

Salon Schmitz Aachener Str. 28–30 ☎ 0221 139 55 77, ⓦ salonschmitz.com. Elegantly decorated Belgisches Viertel bar that attracts a good-looking, trendy thirty-something crowd at all hours of the day. There's food (specials from €8.20) from the beautiful former butcher's shop next door, and a gorgeous ice cream parlour next to that. Daily 9am–3am.

Weinstube Bacchus Rathenauplatz 17 ☎ 0221 21 79 86, ⓦ weinstubebacchus.de. Charmingly unpretentious neighbourhood *Weinstube*, with a pretty terrace at the front, a good selection of German and international wines, and delicious *Erdbeerbowle* (strawberry punch) for €5.80. They also serve food, with main courses from €12.20. Mon–Sat 6pm–1am, Sun 6pm–late.

THE LESBIAN AND GAY SCENE

12

For all the recent headlines about the "death of the scene", Cologne's **lesbian and gay scene** remains one of the biggest in Europe, catering not just to the one in ten city residents who identify as lesbian or gay but also to regular weekend visitors from Düsseldorf, the Ruhr and further afield. Though clubnights take place at venues all over the city, there are two main focuses for the bar scene: the traditional bars attracting an older, mostly male clientele to the **Altstadt** area between Alter Markt and Heumarkt – also the focus for the summer's Christopher Street Day celebrations (see box below) – and the rather larger and more fashionable scene focused on **Rudolfplatz**. Pick up a free copy of the monthly *Rik* magazine from bars for comprehensive **listings** (in German) and good, clear maps to help you find it all. What follows is a selection of the most popular venues and clubnights.

CAFÉS, BARS AND CLUBS

Bastard Friesenwall 29 ☎ 0221 420 77 77, ⓦ bastard-bar.de. Café/bar in a *Hinterhof* close to Ehrenstrasse's shopping, and especially popular for its outside seating on two levels. Good-value food includes breakfasts from €4 and baked potatoes with salad from €3.50. Mon–Thurs & Sun 11am–1am, Fri & Sat 11am–3am.

Blue Lounge Mathiasstr. 4–6 ☎ 0221 271 71 17, ⓦ blue-lounge.com. Bar and dance club south of Neumarkt that is one of the city's liveliest mixed gay/lesbian venues, very popular with women. There are regular weekend *houseBEAT* and *queerBEAT* dance nights, plus various one-off events. Fri 9pm–5am, Sat 9pm–6am.

Brennerei Weiss Hahnenstr. 22 ☎ 0221 82 82 01 91, ⓦ brennereiweiss.de. Recently revamped restaurant which becomes more raucous and bar-like as the evening goes on, and is popular with both gay men and lesbians. *Flammkuchen* and light food from around €7; meaty main courses €8.60 up. Mon–Fri 5pm–late, Sat 1pm–late, Sun 11am–late.

Era Friesenwall 26 ☎ 0221 169 344 30, ⓦ cafeera.de. The smartest of the Rudolfplatz area's gay café-bars, and a good spot for a late breakfast. Coffee from €2.10; Aperol spritzers €5.40. Mon–Thurs 10am–1am, Fri & Sat 10am–2am, Sun noon–midnight.

Ex-Corner Schaafenstr. 57–59 ☎ 0221 233 60 60, ⓦ excorner.de. The absolute lynchpin of the gay scene's

---

CHRISTOPHER STREET DAY IN COLOGNE

Christopher Street Day (ⓦ colognepride.de) all but takes over the city in late June and early July, regularly attracting between 750,000 and a million people to see the colourful parade that snakes its way through the city. The parade has evolved into a summer equivalent of Rosenmontag (see box, p.630), with the fun by no means restricted to the lesbian and gay community.

so-called "Bermuda Triangle", this corner bar is one of a cluster just south of Rudolfplatz and is busy every night of the week. Cruisy, but jolly with it. Mon–Thurs & Sun 7pm–4am, Fri & Sat 7pm–6am.

Iron Bar Schaafenstr. 45 ☏0221 27 64 96 14, ⓦiron-bar.com. Excellent, spacious cocktail bar in the Rudolfplatz district with DJs and twice-monthly karaoke. It attracts a stylish, mainly male crowd. Tues–Thurs 6pm–late, Fri & Sat 8pm–late.

★**Ruhrpott** Balduinstr. 20 ☏0221 16 87 50 38, ⓦruhrpott-cologne.de. Smart, comfortable newcomer on the Rudolfplatz scene, attracting a mainly thirty-plus, bearish, gay male crowd. Mon noon–3pm, Tues–Thurs

noon–2am, Fri noon–4am, Sat 8pm–4am, Sun 8pm–2am.

Station 2b Pipinstr. 2, ⓦstation2b.com. Cologne's biggest men-only leather and fetish bar, with dancing on the ground floor, a cruising area in the basement and (depending on the event) a fairly strict dress code. Fri & Sat 10pm–late, Mon, Wed & Thurs various themed nights 7pm–1am.

Venue Hohe Str. 14 0221 630 695 55, ⓦvenue-cologne.de. Lesbian and gay club which hosts a variety of one-nighters, including the monthly *Poptastic*, which attracts a young crowd, and *HomOriental* Asian night. Fri & Sat 10pm–5am, Sun 6am–noon.

NIGHTLIFE AND ENTERTAINMENT

As befits a major city and media centre, Cologne is a superb place for **live music**, with everything from small clubs featuring up-and-coming bands to stadium-style venues for the monsters of the international rock circuit, as well as **jazz**, **opera** and **classical music**. The **club scene** is characterized by regularly changing themed nights, often in converted theatres or industrial premises, and, if your German is up to it, the city has a lively theatre scene. Cologne's German-language **listings magazine**, *Stadt Revue*, costs €3 from bookshops and newsstands.

CLUBS, CABARET AND LIVE MUSIC

Bürgerhaus Stollwerck Dreikönigenstr. 23 ☏0221 991 10 80, ⓦbuergerhausstollwerck.de. Multipurpose community arts centre in a vast former chocolate factory in the Severinsviertel, the venue for small-scale drama, comedy and cabaret.

E-Werk Schanzenstr. 36 ☏0221 967 90,

ⓦe-werk-cologne.com; tram #4 to Keupstrasse. Beautifully restored nineteenth-century power station northeast of the centre that's now a spacious live music venue for big-name acts.

Lanxess Arena Willy-Brandt-Platz, Deutz ☏0221 80 20, ⓦlanxess-arena.de; U-Bahn 1 or 9 to Deutz/Lanxess Arena. Purpose-built stadium-style venue – the

---

KARNEVAL IN COLOGNE

Cologne's biggest festival is without doubt **Karneval** (ⓦkarneval.de), which is celebrated with as much ritual and dedication to frivolity here as it is in Rio, filling the streets and bringing normal life to a standstill, never mind that the February weather in the Rhineland is nothing like as tempting as in Brazil. The so-called "fifth season" is officially launched each year at 11.11am on November 11, but Karneval doesn't really get under way properly until the New Year, with around six hundred Karneval-related events – including balls and *Sitzungen* or sessions, where *Bütten* (carnival speeches) are made – taking place between then and Ash Wednesday. The season reaches its climax with the **Tolle Tage** or "crazy days", beginning on the Thursday before Ash Wednesday with **Weiberfastnacht** or Women's Day. This is a bad day to wear a tie if you're a man, because it will get snipped off, the symbolism of which is somewhat obvious.

ROSENMONTAG

The **Rosenmontag** (Rose Monday) procession on the Monday following Weiberfastnacht is the undoubted highpoint of Karneval, with wonderfully silly costumes and floats, presided over by the *Prinz* (the master of ceremonies), the *Bauer* (a farmer) and the *Jungfrau* or maiden, who is represented by a man in drag (though this aspect was suppressed by the Nazis). Around a million people turn out to see the Rosenmontag **procession**, which takes around four hours to wind its way through the city centre, as sweets (*Kamelle*), bouquets (*Strüsjer*) and other goodies are thrown at the *Jecke* – the "fools" or spectators – from the passing floats, and all and sundry cry *Kölle Alaaf!* – the carnival greeting, which is a dialect derivation of "Köln über alles" or, freely translated, "up with/long live Cologne". In parallel with the official carnival events, there's a lively **alternative scene**, including a gay and lesbian element.

largest of its kind in Germany – for major rock concerts and other large-scale events including boxing tournaments and ice hockey matches.

Live Music Hall Lichtstr. 30, Ehrenfeld ☎0221 954 29 90, ⓦlivemusichall.de; U-Bahn Venloer Strasse. Don't let the name fool you – music here at weekends is as much about DJs spinning pop, rock and Eighties and Nineties oldies as it is about the gigs, which also take place on Wed. There's a *Biergarten* in the courtyard. Fri & Sat clubnights 9 or 10pm–late.

MTC Zülpicher Str. 10, Zülpicher Platz ☎0221 240 41 88, ⓦmtcclub.de. One of Cologne's more intimate venues, this studenty club in the Zülpicher Viertel features rock and metal bands live, plus DJ nights. Clubnights 10pm–late.

Nachtflug Hohenzollernring 89 ☎0177 400 09 01, ⓦnachtflug.com. Probably the best of several fairly mainstream clubs on the Ring between Zülpicher Platz and Christophstrasse, with DJs spinning mainly house, dance and R&B. Best for the monthly pan-sexual after-hours club, *Greenkomm* (entry €13), which runs from 6am on Sun morning – if you've still got the legs for it.

Papa Joe's Buttermarkt 37 ☎0221 257 79 31, ⓦpapajoes.de. This Altstadt jazz club claims to be Germany's oldest, with a sister bar on Alter Markt and a music policy that sticks mostly to old-time trad jazz and swing. Live jazz nightly. Daily 8.30pm–12.30am.

Underground Vogelsanger Str. 200 ☎0221 54 23 26, ⓦunderground-cologne.de; U-Bahn Venloer Strasse. Great for live gigs, especially rock and punk, the *Underground* also has a beer garden and a big indie/ alternative following. Wed–Sat 6.30pm–late; beer garden summer 6pm–late.

Wartesaal im Zollhafen Im Zollhafen 2 ☎0221 912 88 50, ⓦwartesaal.de. Slick new club, restaurant and terrace in Cologne's "Docklands", recently transferred from its old location next to the Hauptbahnhof and well-known for its long-established clubnights, including regular Depeche Mode, over-thirties and oldies nights. Clubnights Fri & Sat 10pm–late, plus occasional events on Thurs.

Die Werkstatt Grüner Weg 1b ☎0221 16 86 22 16, ⓦwerkstatt-koeln.de; U-Bahn #3 or #4 to Venloer Strasse/Gürtel. Hip club and live venue in Ehrenfeld, with DJs spinning indie, Britpop, hip-hop and electro. Clubnights 11pm–late.

CINEMA, THEATRE, OPERA AND CLASSICAL MUSIC

Hänneschen – Puppenspiele der Stadt Köln Eisenmarkt 2–4 ☎0221 258 12 01, ⓦhaenneschen.de. Cologne's famous puppet theatre has been established for 200 years and gives performances in the local *Kölsch* dialect, which even native German-speakers struggle to understand. Matinees generally 4.30pm, evenings 7.30pm.

Kölner Oper Offenbachplatz ☎0221 22 12 84 00, ⓦoperkoeln.com. One of the city's major postwar landmarks, Cologne's opera house is closed for much-needed restoration until at least 2015; performances in the meantime are being held at various venues including the Musical Dome Köln, rechristened Oper Köln am Dom (see below).

Metropolis Ebertplatz 19 ☎0221 972 62 97, ⓦmetropolis-koeln.de. Small cinema showing English-language films with the original soundtrack and German subtitles.

Musical Dome Köln Goldgasse 1 ☎0221 734 41 50, ⓦmehr.de. Purpose-built venue for big-name international musicals just north of the Hauptbahnhof; it is currently hosting Cologne's opera company until refurbishment of the opera house is complete.

Philharmonie Bischofsgartenstr. 1 ☎0211 28 02 80, ⓦen.koelner-philharmonie.de. The city's major classical concert hall is the home for two orchestras, the Gürzenich-Orchester and the WDR-Sinfonieorchester, as well as providing a venue for visiting big-name orchestras, jazz and pop concerts.

Schauspiel Köln Offenbachplatz ☎0221 22 12 84 00, ⓦschauspielkoeln.de. The city's most prestigious theatre company is housed in the same complex as the Kölner Oper and is performing at temporary venues – including an industrial zone in Mülheim – until 2015 at least, when its home base should be reopened.

12

DIRECTORY

Bookshops Mayersche at Neumarkt 2 (Mon–Sat 9am–8pm; ☎0221 20 30 70, ⓦmayersche.de) and Ludwig in the Hauptbahnhof at Trankgasse 11 (Mon–Sat 7am–10pm, Sun 8am–10pm; ☎0221 126 01 07) have English-language sections.

Left luggage At the Hauptbahnhof (€3 for 2hr, €6 for 24hr).

Medical services Emergencies ☎112; out-of-hours medical service ☎0116 117. There is a list of Cologne

hospitals, doctors and pharmacies on the city website ⓦstadt-koeln.de.

Pharmacies At the north exit from the Hauptbahnhof (Mon–Fri 6am–10pm, Sat 8am–10pm, Sun 10am–6pm); there's also a digital noticeboard here giving details of out-of-hours service.

Post office Breite Str. 6–26 (Mon–Fri 9am–7pm, Sat 9am–2pm).

Brühl

The industrial southern fringes of Cologne seem an unlikely setting for an outburst of fantasy, frivolity and surrealism, yet all are on display in copious quantities in the otherwise unassuming commuter-belt town of **BRÜHL**, home to one of Germany's most magnificent palaces and one of Europe's best theme-parks, as well as a museum devoted to the Dadaist artist, Max Ernst. Brühl is easily reached from the centre of Cologne, either by tram #18 or by train from Cologne's Hauptbahnhof, which takes less than fifteen minutes.

Schloss Augustusburg

Schloss Admission by guided tour only Feb–Nov Tues–Fri 9am–noon & 1.30–4pm, Sat & Sun 10am–5pm • €6 • ⓦ schlossbruehl.de • **Gardens** Open all year daily 7am–dusk • Free • **Jagdschloss Falkenlust** Same hours as Schloss • €3.50, English audio-guide €1 • ⓦ schlossbruehl.de

It was in 1725 that the elector and archbishop of Cologne, Clemens August, first commissioned a new palace on the ruins of a medieval moated palace, but the results – by Westphalian builder Johann Conrad Schlaun – were judged insufficiently fabulous for a member of the Wittelsbach dynasty, and so the Bavarian court architect François de Cuvilliés was commissioned to vamp things up. The result is **Schloss Augustusburg**, a Rococo Xanadu of extraordinary panache that is one of Germany's most magnificent palaces and a UNESCO World Heritage Site.

The Treppenhaus and reception rooms

The moment you see the breathtakingly lavish, ceremonial **Treppenhaus** (staircase) by Balthasar Neumann with its frothy rocailles and vivid stucco marble effects, you'll understand why this was Clemens August's favourite residence, for as you ascend the staircase the sheer exuberance of the design becomes apparent, even as you try to decide precisely how far over the top it all is. Napoleon, who visited in 1804, is said to have remarked that it was a pity the Schloss wasn't on wheels so he could take it with him. The dizzying reception rooms at the top of the staircase continue in a similar vein.

The gardens and Jagdschloss Falkenlust

The **gardens**, with their parterres and fountains, offer an outdoor equivalent to the indoor excess. An avenue leads across the park to the little lodge of **Jagdschloss Falkenlust** which, though smaller in scale than Schloss Augustusburg, is similar in spirit, and for which – unlike in the Schloss – you don't have to join a tour. Clemens August used it for entertaining and for trysts with his mistresses.

Max Ernst Museum

Comesstr. 42 • Tues–Sun 11am–6pm • €6 • ⓦ www.maxernstmuseum.lvr.de

Schloss Augustusburg aside, Brühl's other cultural claim to fame is the **Max Ernst Museum** near the station, which commemorates the work of the Brühl-born Dadaist and Surrealist artist, Max Ernst (1891–1976). In addition to early works and most of the artist's graphic output, the collection includes 36 so-called "D Paintings" which were birthday presents or love offerings to his wife, the artist Dorothea Tanning.

Phantasialand

Berggeiststr. 31–42 • April to early Nov daily 9am–6pm; late Nov to early Jan Wed–Sun 11am–8pm • Day-ticket €45 • ⓦ phantasialand .de • Shuttle bus from Brühl Bahnhof or the Stadtbahn (tram) stop "Brühl-Mitte" (€1.50 return)

The **Phantasialand** theme park is widely regarded as one of Europe's best. Its elaborately landscaped rides compare with Disney and include the African-themed, looping roller-coaster Black Mamba, and Talocan, a suspended top-spin ride with an Aztec theme. It's not all adrenaline-pumping thrills, however, and there are more sedate rides for younger children as well as a brace of log flumes and a beautiful old-fashioned carousel. In the evening there's also a glossy dinner show, *Fantissima*.

Bonn

The placid university town of **BONN** was "provisional" capital of West Germany for fifty years, from 1949 until the Bundestag and many government departments began relocating to Berlin in 1999. Bonn was dubbed "Federal Capital Village" for the sheer improbability of its choice as capital; likelier candidates included Frankfurt, which even built a parliament building to fulfil its anticipated role. But Bonn prevailed, and it was changed by the experience, so that by the time the federal government moved to Berlin it was no longer quite the "small town in Germany" of John Le Carré's Cold War spy story. The two houses of the German parliament may no longer reside here, but several ministries do, along with the United Nations and the headquarters of Deutsche Telekom, T Mobile and Deutsche Post.

Bonn's pleasant, traffic-free **Altstadt** benefits from its associations with **Ludwig van Beethoven**, who was born here, while the setting – at the beginning of a particularly scenic stretch of the Rhine – is a delight, and easily explored on foot. The modern city, by contrast, stretches far along the Rhine. Sandwiched between the city proper and its spa-town suburb of **Bad Godesberg** is the old government quarter, the **Bundesviertel**, and its strip of modern museums along the so-called **Museumsmeile**, planned before the Berlin Wall fell but which, in the event, proved to be a generous goodbye present to the city. Facing Bonn across the Rhine are the inviting, wooded hills of the **Siebengebirge** (see p.641) – a hugely popular destination for walkers and day-trippers alike, right on Bonn's doorstep.

12

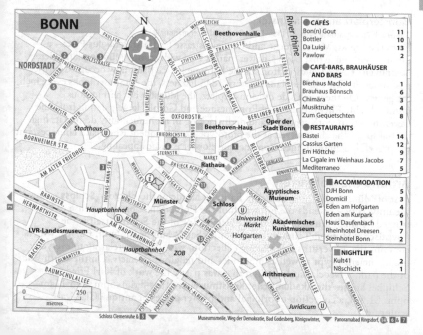

The Altstadt

Before 1989, the market stalls in front of the prettily Rococo eighteenth-century **Rathaus** were a potent symbol of the West German capital's lack of metropolitan swagger and, by implication, of the extent to which the Federal Republic had turned its back on the Nazi era's megalomania; visiting VIPs including Charles de Gaulle and John F. Kennedy appeared before Bonners on the Rathaus steps. Now stripped of symbolic importance, **Markt** remains the liveliest of the irregularly shaped squares that punctuate the Altstadt's meandering streets.

Beethoven-Haus

Bonngasse 20 • April–Oct daily 10am–6pm; Nov–March Mon–Sat 10am–5pm, Sun 11am–5pm • €6, audio-guide €2.50 • ⓦ beethoven-haus-bonn.de

To the north of Markt is the appealingly creaky **Beethoven-Haus** where Ludwig van Beethoven was born in an attic room in 1770. At the time, the city was the capital of the Electorate of Cologne, and Beethoven's father and grandfather had both been employed by the archbishop-electors as court musical director and court singer, respectively. Beethoven's father had promoted him as a Mozart-like child prodigy in Bonn, and by his early teens, Ludwig was already working as a court musician. In 1787 he travelled to Vienna to have lessons with Mozart, and in 1792 returned there to study under Haydn. The dissolution of the Electorate two years later – and hence the disappearance of his court position – turned what had been a study trip into permanent exile.

Pick up the English-language leaflet or an audio-guide to get the most from the museum's displays, which include family portraits, a Broadwood piano identical to the one presented to Beethoven by its London maker in 1817 and the ear trumpets the composer used as his hearing steadily deteriorated. In the so-called **Digitale Beethoven Haus** next door (same ticket & hours) you can use workstations to carry out Beethoven-related internet and intranet searches or visit a digital reconstruction of the composer's apartment in Vienna.

Münsterplatz and the Münster

Münster daily 7am–7pm; cloister Mon–Sat 10am–5.30pm• Free • ⓦ bonner-muenster.de

From the Markt, Markt Brücke and Remigiusstrasse lead past **Remigius-Platz** – a café-fringed square that hosts a flower market – to wide, sunny **Münsterplatz**. Here, **Beethoven's statue** stands in front of the Baroque palace that's now occupied by the post office; in Ernst Julius Hähnel's stern 1845 likeness, the composer looks every inch the genius. On the south side of Münsterplatz, the **Münster** is a harmonious, unmistakeably Rhenish fusion of Romanesque and Gothic, largely dating from the eleventh to thirteenth centuries and oddly lacking in monumentality despite its high central spire. The choir served as the prototype for subsequent Rhineland churches, but the peaceful, memorial-lined Romanesque **cloister** is more appealing.

Around the Hofgarten

East of Münsterplatz, the immense Baroque facade of the Electors' **Schloss** – now the university – extends the full width of the **Hofgarten**, a broad expanse of lawn fringed by small museums. In the Koblenzer Tor of the Schloss itself is the **Ägyptisches Museum** (Tues–Fri noon–5pm, Sat & Sun noon–6pm; €2.50), which contains the university's Egyptology collection, with displays relating to everyday life in ancient Egypt as well as mummies and religious artefacts. On the south side of the park, a Neoclassical pavilion that was partly the work of Karl Friedrich Schinkel houses the **Akademisches Kunstmuseum** (Tues–Fri 3–5pm, Sun 11am–6pm; €1.50), a collection of original and plaster copies of antique Classical sculptures.

The Arithmeum

Lennéstr. 2 • Tues–Sun 11am–6pm • €3 • ⓦ arithmeum.uni-bonn.de

At the southern corner of the Hofgarten is the **Arithmeum**, a beautifully presented exhibition that traces the history of arithmetic, from the clay tablets used in ancient Mesopotamia through various increasingly ingenious and beautiful mechanical calculating machines to the silicon chip. There's plenty of information in English, and the light-filled museum building is a delight.

Schloss Clemensruhe and Botanische Gärten Bonn

Botanische Gärten Bonn • Meckenheimer Allee 171 • April–Oct Mon–Wed, Fri & Sun 10am–6pm, Thurs 10am–8pm; Nov–March Mon–Fri 10am–4pm; glasshouses April–Oct Mon–Fri 10am–noon & 2–4pm, summer only also Sun 10am–5.30pm • €3 on Sun, otherwise free • ⓦ botgart.uni-bonn.de

From the western end of the Hofgarten, broad Poppelsdorfer Allee connects the Schloss with the Poppelsdorfer Schloss or **Schloss Clemensruhe**, the Electors' Rococo summer palace, completed in the eighteenth century by Balthasar Neumann and now part of the university. In summer it is the venue for concerts, while its gardens are now the **Botanische Gärten Bonn**, one of the oldest and largest plant collections in Germany. The **glasshouses** contain the world's largest water lilies.

The gracious **Südstadt** district southeast of the Schloss is full of grand houses that testify to Bonn's nineteenth-century status as one of Germany's wealthiest cities.

LVR-LandesMuseum

12

Colmantstr. 14–16 • Tues–Fri & Sun 11am–6pm, Sat 1–6pm • €8 • ⓦ www.landesmuseum-bonn.lvr.de

West of the Hauptbahnhof, the **LVR-LandesMuseum** takes a modern, thematic approach to its eclectic collections of regional interest. The most famous exhibit is the 42,000-year-old skull of a man discovered in a quarry at Neandertal near Düsseldorf in 1856; subsequently, Neanderthal – using the old German spelling of the place name – became the accepted term for the extinct species of pre-modern human to which he belonged. As well as the skull and other bones, you can see a reconstruction of his face. The museum also has extensive Roman displays and a collection of medieval religious art, including the expressive fourteenth-century Röttgen *Pietà*. There's also a fascinating collection of paintings and drawings exploring the allure of the "Romantic Rhine" in German and Anglo-Saxon art – works on display include J.M.W. Turner's *Hochkreuz and Godesberg* from 1817.

The Museumsmeile

From the Hofgarten, a boulevard named for three of Germany's political giants leads south through the **Bundesviertel** or former government district. It begins as Adenauer Allee, continues as Willy-Brandt-Allee and then becomes Friedrich-Ebert-Allee, named after the Weimar-era socialist who was Germany's first democratic president. The western side of this avenue constitutes the **Museumsmeile**, an impressive strip of museums that ensures Bonn's heavy-hitter status among Germany's cultural centres.

Museum Koenig

Adenauer Allee 160 • Tues & Thurs–Sun 10am–6pm, Wed 10am–9pm • €5 • ⓦ zfmk.de • U-Bahn Museum Koenig

The first museum on Museumsmeille is the **Museum Koenig**, a stately sandstone pile that was the venue for the first elected postwar national assembly on September 1, 1948. The museum's zoological exhibits have been given a child-friendly makeover, though the lack of English labelling limits its rainy-day appeal slightly – pick up the English-language leaflet at the entrance. Displays are grouped by habitat and include African savanna, rainforest and the Arctic; the Vivarium in the basement has live lizards, snakes and fish, as well as the Zwergmaus – a particularly tiny rodent.

Haus der Geschichte der Bundesrepublik Deutschland

Willy-Brandt-Allee 14 • Tues–Fri 9am–7pm, Sat & Sun 10am–6pm • Free • W hdg.de • U-Bahn Heussallee/Museumsmeile

A little way to the south of Museum Koenig, the **Haus der Geschichte der Bundesrepublik Deutschland** charts the history of the Federal Republic of Germany in a lively and entertaining way; as you leave the U-Bahn the first thing you see is the luxurious railway carriage used by chancellors Konrad Adenauer and Ludwig Erhard but originally built for Nazi bigwig, Hermann Göring. Rubble marks the start of the story in 1945, with grim footage of concentration camps and of destroyed German cities; it continues through the beginnings of democratic politics and of artistic rebirth to the 1950s Wirtschaftswunder – the "economic miracle" – the Cold War and division of Germany, and moves finally to the period post-1989.

The years of division are a strong focus, with an examination of the way both halves of Germany were bound into opposing ideological camps. Along with the political developments post-1989, recent German history is also examined in the light of globalization, the life of migrant groups and the increasing deployment of German forces overseas. It's not all dry politics by any means: along the way, fun exhibits like the 1950s-style ice cream parlour lighten the mood. Labelling is in English as well as German.

Kunstmuseum Bonn

Friedrich-Ebert-Allee 2 • Tues & Thurs–Sun 11am–6pm, Wed 11am–9pm • €7 • W kunstmuseum-bonn.de • U-Bahn Heussallee/Museumsmeile

The most architecturally refined of the area's museums is the **Kunstmuseum Bonn**, whose starkly beautiful modernist interior provides a fitting home for its collection of works by **August Macke** and the Rhine Expressionists. Macke, who was born in 1887 and killed in action in France in 1914, grew up in Bonn but was no mere "regional" artist, as his gorgeous, colour-filled canvases demonstrate: poignantly, the most confident are the 1914 *Tightrope Walker* and *Turkish Café*. The museum has a substantial collection of post-1945 German art, with works by heavyweights including Gerhard Richter, Georg Baselitz and Joseph Beuys, and there's a strong emphasis on photography, video installation and film.

Kunst- und Ausstellungshalle der Bundesrepublik Deutschland

Friedrich-Ebert-Allee 4 • Tues & Wed 10am–9pm, Thurs–Sun 10am–7pm • Prices vary according to exhibition • W bundeskunsthalle.de • U-Bahn Heussallee/Museumsmeile

The **Kunst- und Ausstellungshalle der Bundesrepublik Deutschland** next door to the Kunstmuseum provides a venue for large-scale touring art exhibitions and is big enough to host several simultaneously. Don't miss the striking roof garden, dominated by three ceramic-clad light spires and free to wander around if it's not being used as part of an exhibition.

Deutsches Museum Bonn

Ahrstr. 45 • Tues–Sun 10am–6pm • €5 • W deutsches-museum.de/en/bonn • U-Bahn Hochkreuz/Deutsches Museum

The **Deutsches Museum Bonn** is a resolutely contemporary museum of science and technology whose themed displays on research and technology in Germany since 1945 allow you to learn about medical and interdisciplinary research, the scientific achievements of the former GDR and the ethics of genetics – as well as find out how a car airbag works. There's a Transrapid hoverrail train in front of the main entrance.

Weg der Demokratie

Between the Museumsmeile and the Rhine, the **Weg der Demokratie** ("Path of Democracy") is a signposted walk through sites associated with Bonn's period as federal capital. It starts and finishes at the Haus der Geschichte (see above), and while the full itinerary is too exhaustive for all but the most obsessive fans of German democracy, a

stroll through the district underlines the former capital's low-key style, with leafy avenues and government buildings interspersed with suburban housing. The main landmarks are on Platz der Vereinten Nationen, a couple of blocks east of Willy-Brandt-Allee, where Günther Behnisch's glassy 1992 **Plenarsaal** replaced an earlier home of the Bundestag – the lower house of the German parliament – only to be rapidly superseded by the new Berlin Reichstag. The adjacent **Bundeshaus** is a Bauhaus-style 1930s teacher-training college that was adapted for parliamentary use to counter Frankfurt's rival claims; the **Bundesrat** – the upper house of the German parliament – sat in its north wing until 2000.

To the north, along Adenauer Allee, the 1860-built **Palais Schaumburg** was, from 1949, the official residence of the German chancellor; it was here in 1990 that representatives of East and West Germany signed the treaty on monetary, economic and social union. It remains the chancellor's official base in Bonn, though it is currently undergoing lengthy restoration. Behind it stands the modernist **bungalow** built for Chancellor Ludwig Erhard in 1963, which can be visited (Sun at 2 & 3pm; enquire at the Haus der Geschichte; passport required). Further north, the elegant white **Villa Hammerschmidt** is the president's official Bonn residence.

Bad Godesberg

For much of the twentieth century, diplomacy and **Bad Godesberg**, south of the centre, were synonymous, for its gracious villas found favour as embassies during Bonn's time as federal capital. The compact town centre is a slightly odd mix of spa-town prettiness and crass postwar development, fringed by leafy parks. Facing one of these on Kurfürstenallee is the graceful, late eighteenth-century **La Redoute**, a concert hall and ballroom where the young Beethoven played for Haydn.

Godesburg castle tower

Auf dem Godesberg 5 • April–Oct Wed–Sun 10am–6pm • €1, pay at restaurant • ⓦ godesburg-bonn.de

Looming above the town centre, the solitary surviving tower of the thirteenth-century **Godesburg** castle now accommodates an upmarket restaurant; if it's not being used for a private function, you can climb it for sweeping views over the town towards the river and Siebengebirge.

The Rhine and around

East of Bad Godesberg's U-Bahn station, stately Rheinallee leads to the banks of the **Rhine**, and some wonderful opportunities for walking, cycling and rollerblading with magnificent views of the Siebengebirge hills on the opposite bank. A **ferry** crosses from the Bastei at the end of Rheinallee to the **Königswinter** (see p.641) side of the river (Mon–Sat 6.05am–8.45pm, Sun 8.05am–8.45pm; one-way foot or car passenger €1.30, car and driver €2.70).

It was on the Bad Godesberg riverbank, at the **Rheinhotel Dreesen**, that Adolf Hitler and British prime minister Neville Chamberlain had their first meeting during the Sudetenland crisis in September 1938; Chamberlain stayed in the hilltop *Petersberg* hotel across the river, which can clearly be seen from the Dreesen. Following the river to the south brings you to the **Panoramabad Rüngsdorf** (May–Aug Mon–Fri 6.30am–8pm, Sat & Sun 11am–7.30pm; €4), a riverside open-air swimming pool and sunbathing meadow.

| ARRIVAL AND DEPARTURE | BONN |

By train Bonn's Hauptbahnhof is on the south side of the Altstadt.

Destinations Berlin (4 daily; 4hr 43min); Brühl (every 20min; 11–13min); Cologne (every 10–20min; 20–30min); Dortmund (hourly; 1hr 37min); Duisburg (2 per hour; 1hr–1hr 17min); Düsseldorf (2 per hour; 47min–1hr); Düsseldorf airport (hourly; 1hr 7min); Essen (every 2hr; 1hr 13min); Frankfurt (every 2hr; 2hr); Koblenz (every 20min; 32–45min); Mainz (every 20–40min; 1hr 23min–1hr 34min); Münster (1–2 hourly; 2hr 10min); Trier (2 daily; 2hr 12min).

GETTING AROUND

By public transport Public transport in and around Bonn is operated by Stadtwerke Bonn (wswb-busundbahn.de). A *Kurzstrecke* ticket (four stops or less) costs €1.90, a single CityTicket €2.80 and a *Tageskarte* €8.10. If you're going to Königswinter (see p.641) by public transport, note that it's in a different fare zone and you'll need a €3.80 CityPlus ticket. U-Bahn lines #16, #63 and #67 link the centre to the Museumsmeile and Bad Godesberg; if you're exploring the scenic Siebengebirge hills on the opposite bank of the Rhine, take line 66 towards Bad Honnef. A network of nine night-bus lines fans out from the Hauptbahnhof on the half hour after midnight until 4.30am.

By bike Radstation, Quantiusstrasse, behind the Hauptbahnhof (March to mid-Nov Mon–Fri 6am–10.30pm, Sat 7am–10.30pm, Sun 8am–10.30pm; mid-Nov to Feb Mon–Fri 6am–9pm, Sat 7am–8pm, Sun 8am–8pm; 0228 981 46 36, wradstationbonn.de; €10/day, plus deposit of €30–50; cheaper for multiple day rentals).

INFORMATION

Tourist office Windeckstr. 1 (Mon–Fri 10am–6pm, Sat 10am–4pm, Sun 10am–2pm; 0228 77 50 00, wbonn .de). There's a second tourist office opposite the Bahnhof in Bad Godesberg on Ria-Maternus-Platz 1 (Mon–Thurs 10am–6pm, Fri 10am–noon, Sat 10am–3pm; 0228 184 26 90, wbadgodesbergstadtmarketing.de).

Discount card If you're staying in Bonn it's worth buying the Bonn Regio WelcomeCard (valid 24hr: €9 city of Bonn, €12 greater Bonn, €24 VRS regional transport network), which gives free or reduced entry to museums and attractions in and around Bonn and unlimited use of public transport – how far the ticket will take you on public transport depends on the price band you choose.

ACCOMMODATION

DJH Bonn Haager Weg 42 0228 28 99 70, wbonn .jugendherberge.de; bus #600 (direction "Ippendorf") from the bus station to stop "Jugendherberge". Bonn's youth hostel is on the Venusberg hill south of the centre, on the edge of the Kottenforst nature reserve, with 28 wheelchair-adapted en-suite rooms. Dorm rooms are 4-bed and prices include breakfast and bed linen. Dorms €22.90, doubles €71.80

Domicil Thomas-Mann-Str. 24 0228 72 90 90, wdomicil-bonn.bestwestern.de. Stylish, modern hotel set around a garden courtyard in an attractive street of nineteenth-century houses a few minutes' walk from the Hauptbahnhof. €109

Eden am Hofgarten Am Hofgarten 6 0228 28 97 10, weden-bonn.de. Good-value, mid-range hotel in a peaceful setting on the southwest corner of the Hofgarten, with some proper singles as well as comfortable doubles, with shower, WC and TV. €85

Eden am Kurpark Am Kurpark 5a 0228 95 72 70, weden-godesberg.de. Very pleasant sister hotel of the Eden am Hofgarten, located opposite Bad Godesberg's Stadtpark; rooms have wi-fi, en-suite showers or bath and WC, phone and TV. There's also parking available. €85

Haus Daufenbach Brüdergasse 6 0228 63 79 44, whaus-daufenbach.de. Renovated and very central accommodation just off the Markt. All singles and doubles have WC, shower, phone and flat-screen TV. €96

Rheinhotel Dreesen Rheinstr. 45–49 0228 820 20, wrheinhoteldreesen.de. In an idyllic riverside location with wonderful views towards the Siebengebirge, this historic hotel is comfortable, upmarket and traditional. Rooms have bath and WC, internet, cable TV and free minibar; some doubles have balconies with views across the Rhine. There's also a splendid beer garden with river views. €125

Sternhotel Bonn Markt 8 0228 726 70, wsternhotel.de. Elegant hotel with a winning location in the very heart of the city and a choice of room styles, including suites and junior suites, each with wireless internet, satellite, safe and minibar. €145

EATING AND DRINKING

Central Bonn and Bad Godesberg both have their fair share of places to eat and drink, with some of the most interesting options in the **Nordstadt**, a formerly working-class district that is nowadays the city's bohemian quarter, peppered with small bars.

CAFÉS

Bon(n) Gout Remigiusplatz 2–4 0228 65 89 88, wbonngout.com. Stylish, modern Italian café/bar with a sunny terrace fronting the flower market. Serves good breakfasts from €3.60, light Italian dishes from €4.50 and main course salads from €13.90. Mon–Thurs 9am–midnight, Fri & Sat 9am–1am, Sun 10am–11pm.

Bottler Vivatsgasse 8 0228 90 90 29 99, wbottler-bonn.de. Classic French-style café in elegant Jugendstil premises, with home-made quiches and *croques* (€6.95 up), steak frites for €20.90 and a €12.90 Sun brunch. There's outdoor seating in the shadow of the thirteenth-century Sterntor. Mon–Sat 9am–10pm, Sun 10am–6pm.

12

Da Luigi Kaiserplatz 6 ☎0228 63 12 17. Italian-style ice cream parlour with a big outdoor terrace in a plum position at the beginning of the Poppelsdorfer Allee; ice cream €0.90 per scoop. There's another branch on Markt. Daily 10am–10/11pm.

Pawlow Heerstr. 64 ☎0228 65 36 03. Cult Nordstadt café/bar, by day a place to breakfast late (from €3.70) or linger over a *Milchkaffee*, by night livelier, when the music is eclectic and the action spills into the street outside. For those on a tight budget, there are small measures of wine from €1.70. Daily 10am–1am.

RESTAURANTS

Bastei Von-Sandt-Ufer 1, Bad Godesberg ☎0228 368 04 33, ⓦ bastei-bonn.de. Landmark restaurant and *Biergarten* on the Bad Godesberg riverside, with fabulous views of the Siebengebirge and seasonally changing Mediterranean-influenced menus: fish and meat main courses €19 and up. Restaurant daily noon–11pm; *Biergarten* Mon–Thurs 5–10pm, Fri & Sat 4–11pm, Sun noon–10pm.

Cassius Garten Maximilianstr. 28d ☎0228 65 24 29, ⓦ cassiusgarten.de. Bright, modern, sprawling vegan and veggie place opposite the Hauptbahnhof. Offers daily-changing hot vegetarian specials, buffet-style meals (pay by weight: 100g costs €1.70), and vegan ice cream from €1/scoop. Coffee from €2. Mon–Sat 8am–8pm.

Em Höttche Markt 4 ☎0228 69 00 09, ⓦem-hoettche.de. Gorgeously traditional *Gasthaus* right next to the Rathaus, with a history dating back to 1389 and a versatile menu of Rhineland specialities that includes both substantial main courses and lighter dishes. Main courses from around €11. Daily 10am–1am.

La Cigale im Weinhaus Jacobs Friedrichstr. 18 ☎0228 184 12 50, ⓦlacigale.de. This traditional *Weinhaus* in the Altstadt's pedestrian zone has been given a fine-dining makeover, with elegant decor and a weekly-changing menu with French and Italian influences. Lunch with wine €13.50, two courses €16.40, three €19.90; à la

carte from around €15. Mon–Thurs 11.30am–3pm & 6–10pm, Fri & Sat 11.30am–10.30pm, Sun 6–10.30pm.

Mediterraneo Heerstr. 98 ☎0228 90 91 89 05. Pleasantly informal Nordstadt restaurant, with risotto and pasta dishes for around €8.40–11 and plenty of fish and meat choices from upwards of €12. There's a pretty terrace in summer, and a sister tapas bar right across the street. Daily 11am–1am.

CAFÉ-BARS, BRAUHÄUSER AND BARS

Bierhaus Machold Heerstr. 52 ☎0228 963 78 77, ⓦ bierhaus-machold.com. Smart and historic Nordstadt *Bierhaus*, with own-brew draught *Dunkel* and *Naturtrüb* beers from €2.40, veggie dishes from €8.60 and meat or fish mains from €11.90. There's a small but pretty walled beer garden at the back. Mon–Sat 5.30pm–1am.

Brauhaus Bönnsch Sterntorbrücke 4 ☎0228 65 06 10, ⓦ boennsch.de. Packed Altstadt *Bierhaus* serving its own *Bönnsch* beer (from €1.70) along with typical Rhineland cuisine, simple *Flammkuchen* and burgers (€8–13). Mon–Thurs 11am–1pm, Fri & Sat 11am–3am, Sun noon–1am.

Chimära Wolfstr. 6 ☎0228 18 03 36 74, ⓦchimaera-bonn.de. Relaxed Nordstadt bar with plush upholstery, daily cocktail deals and an array of cultural events including literary readings, jazz and swing. Tues–Thurs & Sun 5pm–1am, Fri & Sat 5pm–3am.

Musiktruhe Maxstr. 40 ☎0228 69 39 31, ⓦ musiktruhe-bonn.de. Amiably grungy Nordstadt blues and rock bar, with occasional live bands, billiards, table football and darts, and a decent selection of bottled beers; Dom *Kölsch* €2.20, Paulaner €3.50. Mon–Sat 8pm–late.

Zum Gequetschten Sternstr. 78 ☎0228 63 81 04, ⓦzum-gequetschten.de. Traditional Rhineland *Brauhaus* in the Altstadt, with Gilden *Kölsch* and Jever on draught, serving Cologne and Rhineland specialities in a cheerfully traditional setting and, in summer, on an outside terrace. Main courses from around €10. Mon–Sat 10.30am–1am, Sun noon–10pm.

NIGHTLIFE AND ENTERTAINMENT

Beethoven features prominently on the city's **cultural** scene, with an annual Beethovenfest (ⓦbeethovenfest.de) in September. For what's-on listings (in German), there's a free monthly local magazine, *Schnüss*, available from the tourist office, where there's also a **box office** for tickets.

CLUBS

Kult 41 Hochstadenring 41, Nordstadt ☎0228 908 57 07, ⓦkult41.de. Arts and community venue in the Nordstadt hosting a varied programme of live bands, political talks, pub and social nights, and film.

N8schicht Bornheimer Str. 20–22 ☎0228 963 83 08, ⓦn8schicht.de. Amiable club close to the Stadthaus on the fringe of Nordstadt, with a music policy that ranges from pop, electro and dance music to chart hits and disco

classics. There's usually no dress code. Wed & Thurs 11pm–5am, Fri & Sat 10pm–5am.

THEATRE, OPERA AND CLASSICAL MUSIC

Beethovenhalle Wachsbleiche 16 ☎0228 722 20, ⓦbeethovenhalle.de. Riverside concert hall that is the city's main venue for classical concerts by the Klassische Philharmonie Bonn (ⓦklassische-philharmonie-bonn.de), Beethoven Orchester Bonn (ⓦbeethoven-orchester.de) and

Freie Philharmonie Bonn (ⓦphilharmonie-bonn.de). The Beethoven-Haus (see p.634) is used for chamber music concerts. **Oper der Stadt Bonn** Am Boeselagerhof 1 ☎0228 77 80 08, ⓦtheater-bonn.de. Modernist building by the river that is Bonn's main venue for opera, drama and dance; Theater Bonn also performs in the smaller Kammerspiele in Bad Godesberg.

The Siebengebirge

Facing Bonn and Bad Godesberg across the Rhine, the extinct volcanic domes of the **Siebengebirge** are perfect mountains in miniature. None rise higher than 500m, yet the hills are steep-sided and thickly wooded enough to create a plausible impression of alpine ruggedness. Much mythologized and immortalized in song, the Siebengebirge were rescued from destruction by quarrying in the nineteenth century and now comprise one of Germany's oldest nature reserves. There are in fact many more hills – 42 in all – than the name (which means seven mountains) would suggest, and several are topped by ruined fortresses, which merely adds to their mystique. The entire range is crisscrossed by hiking trails, including the 320km **Rheinsteig** long-distance path which passes through on its way from Bonn to Wiesbaden. Given their picturesque charm and close proximity to the Rhineland's big cities, the Siebengebirge are, not surprisingly, highly popular.

Königswinter

Strung out along the banks of the Rhine opposite Bad Godesberg, the small town of **Königswinter** has a neat waterfront lined with imposing hotels and a spanking modern **Sea Life** aquarium at Rheinallee 8 (mid-April to Dec daily 10am–6pm, last admission 1hr before closing; €14.95; ⓦvisitsealife.com). The main reason to visit the town, however, is to ascend the 320m **Drachenfels** (Dragon Rock), which rises above the riverfront resort of Königswinter and is the most popular of all the Siebengebirge's hills.

The Drachenfels

Drachenfelsbahn, Drachenfelsstr. 53 • Jan, Feb & 1st two weeks Nov Mon–Fri noon–5pm (on request), Sat & Sun 11am–6pm; March & Oct daily 10am–6pm; April daily 10am–7pm; May–Sept daily 9am–7pm; closed second half of Nov and all Dec • Trains every 30min March–Oct, otherwise hourly • €8 one-way, €10 return • ⓦ drachenfelsbahn-koenigswinter.de

Though it's not one of the Siebengebirge's higher hills, the reasons for the popularity of the **Drachenfels** are not hard to divine: it has a castle-topped prettiness, and rises high above the banks of the Rhine to give breathtaking views from its summit north over Bonn and Cologne – you'll see Cologne cathedral on a clear day – and south over the town of Bad Honnef. A cog railway, the **Drachenfelsbahn**, eases the ascent.

Schloss Drachenburg

April–Oct daily 11am–6pm; Nov–March Sat & Sun noon–5pm • €6 • ⓦschloss-drachenburg.de

To enjoy the Drachenfels to the full, take the train to the summit for the views from the castle ruins, then take the meandering footpath downhill, pausing halfway at **Schloss Drachenburg**, a fantastically spooky neo-Gothic mansion from whose terrace there are spectacular views downriver; you can visit the freshly restored period interiors and there's a museum of nature conservation in the Vorburg. There's also a bistro serving cakes, ice cream and full meals. If you don't fancy the descent on foot of the Drachenfels, there's a station on the cog railway close to Schloss Drachenburg.

Nibelungenhalle, Drachenhöhle and the Reptile Zoo

Mid-March to Nov daily 10am–6pm; Nov to mid-March Sat & Sun & Christmas holidays 11am–4pm • €5 • ⓦnibelungenhalle.de

A little further downhill from Schloss Drachenburg the **Nibelungenhalle** is no less extraordinary or gloomy. Built in Jugendstil style in 1913 to commemorate the

12

centenary of Wagner's birth, the little temple leads to a short tunnel – the **Drachenhöhle** – which is adorned by a 13m-high dragon representing the beast supposedly slain here by Siegfried in the tale of the same name which forms part of Wagner's opera cycle, *The Ring of the Nibelung*. The tunnel leads in turn to a **reptile zoo** (same ticket & hours), whose attractions include snakes and crocodiles.

ARRIVAL AND DEPARTURE   KONIGSWINTER

By U-Bahn Line #66 (direction Bad Honnef) from Bonn city centre.

By boat From Bonn's city centre the Bonner Personen Schifffahrt from Brassertufer quay (Am Alten Zoll; ☎0228 63 63 63, ⓦb-p-s.de; €7 one-way) can get you

there in 50min. Alternatively, from Bad Godesberg there's a car and passenger ferry that shuttles back and forth across the river (Mon–Sat 6.05am–8.45pm, Sun 8.05am–8.45pm; one-way foot or car passenger €1.30, car and driver €2.70).

Aachen

Few places can claim such proudly European credentials as **AACHEN** (known as Aix-la-Chapelle in French, Aken to the Dutch). Its hot thermal springs were known to the Celts and Romans, but it wasn't until **Charlemagne** took up residence in 768 AD that the city briefly took centre stage as the capital of his vast Frankish empire. At its height, this encompassed much of what would form – more than a millennium later – the original core of the European Union. But it didn't long

survive his death, and nor did Aachen's political importance, though for six centuries afterwards the city remained the place where German emperors were crowned. Charlemagne's chief legacy is the magnificent domed court chapel – now the city's **cathedral** and a UNESCO World Heritage Site – that is still the most splendid thing in the city.

During World War II, Aachen was the first German city in the west to fall to Allied invasion, after a six-week battle in the autumn of 1944 that laid waste to much of it. However, the cathedral escaped destruction and the heart of the city, at least, retains a pleasing sense of history. These days, Germany's most westerly city is a lively, medium-sized place, its municipal boundary forming the international frontier at **Dreiländereck** – the point where Belgium and the Netherlands meet – creating an easy-going and cosmopolitan feel, with the student population supporting a vibrant **nightlife** scene and the **spa** bringing in a steady stream of more genteel visitors. The centre is compact and walkable, with the main spa facilities and some museums a little way to the east.

The Altstadt

Aachen's ancient treasures – miraculous survivors of the 1944 destruction, in some cases heavily restored – cluster tightly at the heart of its **Altstadt**. The Dom is the obvious first port of call for visitors, but the city's focal point and central square is **Markt**, lined by café terraces that give fine views of the Rathaus, while the houses surrounding it are a mishmash of everything from Gothic to postwar modern.

The Dom

Dom Domhof 1 • Jan–March Mon–Fri 11am–6pm, Sat & Sun 12.30–6pm; April–Dec Mon–Fri 11am–7pm, Sat & Sun 12.30–7pm; English tour daily at 2pm • Free; tours €4 – buy tickets from Dominformation • **Dominformation** Opposite Schatzkammer in Johannes-Paul-II-Str. • Daily: Jan–March 10am–5pm; April–Dec 10am–6pm • ⓦ aachendom.de

Though its slightly eccentric exterior hints at the building's unique riches, the dark, Byzantine interior of Aachen's **Dom** nevertheless comes as a surprise. As you enter the cathedral through the massive, twelve-hundred-year-old bronze doors you're immediately presented with its great glory, the octagonal **palace chapel** built for Charlemagne and inspired by the churches of San Vitale in Ravenna and Little Hagia Sophia in Istanbul. It was the first domed church north of the Alps and though it was the work of Otto von Metz, Charlemagne himself contributed his own ideas to the design. If you can, take the **guided tour** as much of the interior is off limits for casual visitors and you'll only gain the most superficial impressions without it. In particular, it's only on the tour that you'll see the marble **Imperial Throne** in the upper gallery which was used for coronations for six centuries, from Otto I in 936 to Ferdinand I in 1531.

The vast twelfth-century gilded **Barbarossa chandelier**, which hangs low in the centre of the octagon, catches the eye, along with the nineteenth-century mosaics inside the dome high above; but the octagon's marble **pillars** are altogether more ancient, having been brought to Aachen from Rome and Ravenna with the permission of Pope Hadrian I. So prized are they that French troops hauled 28 of them off to Paris in 1815, where four can still be seen in the Louvre.

As the burial place of Charlemagne and a place of pilgrimage, the cathedral was embellished over the centuries with various chapels, and in the fourteenth century a soaring, light-filled Gothic **choir** – the so-called "Glass House of Aachen" – was added to ease the crush of visiting pilgrims. It houses the gilded thirteenth-century **shrine** that contains Charlemagne's remains. The choir's original **stained glass** was destroyed by hail in 1729; the present windows are post-1945, and replaced glass destroyed during World War II.

12

12

Schatzkammer

Johannes-Paul-II-Strasse • Jan–March Mon 10am–1pm, Tues–Sun 10am–5pm; April–Dec Mon 10am–1pm, Tues–Sun 10am–6pm • €5

The Dom's **Schatzkammer**, just around the corner from the Dom, has more than its share of treasures – indeed, it's regarded as the most important religious treasury north of the Alps. The gilded silver **bust of Charlemagne** looking every inch the emperor is perhaps the most recognizable of the hundred or so exhibits, though as it dates from 1349 – half a millennium after his death – it's scarcely a reliable guide to what he might have looked like.

Other treasures include the fabulous **Lothar cross** dating from around 1000 AD, and, richly adorned with gemstones, the extraordinary **Dreiturmreliquiar** – a triple-pinnacled fourteenth-century Gothic creation in gold – and a second-century Roman marble **sarcophagus** carved with scenes of the Rape of Persephone.

Rathaus

Markt • Krönungssaal daily 10am–6pm • €5, combined ticket with Couven Museum and Internationales Zeitungsmuseum €10

A short stroll north of the Dom and scarcely less imposing, Aachen's Gothic **Rathaus** looms over the Markt. Dating from the early fourteenth century, the building incorporates surviving sections of Charlemagne's palace, including 20m of the Granus tower on the east side, plus later accretions. The side facing the Markt is decorated with statues of fifty German emperors with another four on the east facade; 31 of them were crowned in Aachen. Above the main entrance, Charlemagne is to the right of Christ with a model of the Dom, with Pope Leo III – who consecrated it – to the left.

Inside, the splendid **Krönungssaal** on the first floor is where newly crowned emperors held their coronation banquets. Today it's where the Charlemagne Prize for services to European unification is awarded; interactive screens on the staircase give biographical details of the prize winners. The hall is decorated with mid-nineteenth-century **frescoes** on themes from Charlemagne's life by Aachen-born painter Alfred Rethel. Of the original eight frescoes, only five survived wartime damage. Copies of the imperial **crown jewels** are also on view; the originals are in Vienna.

Centre Charlemagne

Katschhof • Tues–Sun 10am–6pm • €5 • ⓦ route-charlemagne.eu

Aachen's new museum of local history, the **Centre Charlemagne**, occupies a site on the Katschhof, the former palace courtyard between the Dom and the Rathaus. Opened in 2014 to coincide with the 1200th anniversary of Charlemagne's death, it focuses on a few key periods in Aachen's history: the monumental Roman city that flourished until the end of the fourth century; Charlemagne's Aachen, when the city was the centre of the Frankish empire; the medieval period when Holy Roman emperors were crowned here; and the Baroque period, when Aachen experienced a Renaissance after a disastrous fire devastated the city in 1656. Also covered are the period of industrialization, and Aachen's chequered path from frontline city in two world wars to its present-day role as host city of the Charlemagne Prize.

Couven Museum

Hühnermarkt 17 • Tues–Sun 10am–6pm, 1st Sat in month 1–6pm • €5, combined ticket with Rathaus and Internationales Zeitungsmuseum €10, combined ticket with Ludwig Forum and Suermondt-Ludwig-Museum €10 • ⓦ couven-museum.de

A short walk from the Rathaus, the **Couven Museum** is a handsome old townhouse that is now a museum of bourgeois interiors from the Rococo to the Biedermeier. The Festsaal on the first floor is particularly lovely, with five tall windows giving views across to the Rathaus; so too is the elegant, early nineteeth-century Biedermeier furniture on the top floor. The reconstructed pharmacy on the ground floor alludes to the history of the house itself; there was a pharmacy on the premises as early as 1662.

Internationales Zeitungsmuseum

Pontstr. 13 • Tues–Sun 10am–6pm • €5, combined ticket with Rathaus and Couven Museum €10 • ⓦ izm.de

Just north of Markt in the fifteenth-century Haus Rupenstein on Pontstrasse is the **Internationales Zeitungsmuseum** (International Newspaper Museum). It was in this street in 1850 that Paul Julius Reuter founded his famous news agency, and the museum presents regularly changing exhibitions on the history, present and future of the print media on two floors. The museum's own collection on the upper floor includes items such as a rare surviving copy of Émile Zola's 1898 "J'accuse" letter to *L'Aurore* on the subject of the Dreyfus case, and a copy of the Nazi anti-Semitic newspaper *Der Stürmer*. There's also a section on the misuse and manipulation of text and pictures.

Beyond the museum, Pontstrasse is one of the liveliest streets in the Altstadt, stretching as far as the mighty **Ponttor**, a survivor of the medieval city's outer defences.

The Kurviertel and around

Northeast of the Altstadt along Monheimsallee, Aachen's elegant Wilhelmine **Kurviertel** (spa district) is dominated by the portico of the **Neues Kurhaus**, which houses the swanky **Casino Aachen** (table games daily 3pm–3am, until 4am Sat; slot machines daily 11am–2am; table games area admission €5, slot machines admission €1; ⓦ westspiel .de), for which you're expected to dress reasonably smartly. Behind the Kurhaus, the pretty **Stadtgarten** was the work of the great Prussian garden designer, Peter Joseph Lenné (1789–1866). On the far side of the park, the modern **Carolus Thermen** spa complex (daily 9am–11pm; from €11, with sauna from €22; ⓦ carolus-thermen.de) offers a full range of mineral water pools, steam baths and a Finnish-style sauna, with beauty treatments available and a choice of healthy restaurants.

Ludwig Forum für Internationale Kunst

Jülicher Str. 97–109 • Tues, Wed & Fri noon–6pm, Thurs noon–8pm, Sat & Sun 11am–6pm • €5, combined ticket with Suermondt-Ludwig-Museum and Couven Museum €10 • ⓦ ludwigforum.de • Buses #1, #21, #46 or #52 from Bushof

Located to the east of Corolus Thermen on grungy Jülicher Strasse, the **Ludwig Forum für Internationale Kunst** is a former 1920s umbrella factory whose glass-roofed building provides an ideal setting for regularly changing exhibitions of contemporary art, with masses of space for large-scale installations. The permanent collection is strong on American Pop Art, including Duane Hanson's life-size *Supermarket Lady* complete with shopping trolley and junk food, and Andy Warhol's *Saturday's Popeye* and *Campbell's Soup Can I*. There are also works by Ai Weiwei, Jean-Michel Basquiat and Keith Haring.

Suermondt-Ludwig-Museum

Wilhelmstr. 18 • Tues, Thurs & Fri noon–6pm, Wed noon–8pm, Sat & Sun 11am–6pm • €5, combined ticket with Couven Museum and Ludwig Forum €10 • ⓦ suermondt-ludwig-museum.de

South of the Kurviertel, the **Suermondt-Ludwig-Museum**'s eclectic art collection ranges from sublime medieval religious woodcarving to some seventeenth-century Dutch and Flemish masters and a selection of twentieth-century German art on the second floor that includes works by Max Slevogt, Max Beckmann, Lovis Corinth and Karl Schmidt-Rottluff. Highlights include Lucas Cranach the Elder's gory *Judith with the Head of Holofernes*, and there's some excellent modern stained-glass, too.

Dreiländereck

A popular short bike trip out of town is to the **Dreiländereck** – the meeting of the German, Dutch and Belgian borders, about 5km west of Aaachen. If you're coming by

12

car, the Dreiländereck is most easily reached via Vaals on the Dutch side, but the approach that cyclists take – along **Dreiländerweg** through rolling countryside – is pleasant by car too, though you'll need to park by the *Gasthäuser* some way back from the frontier and walk the rest of the way. The route veers right just before **Gut Fuchstal** and then winds up through woods to the frontier; you emerge just south of the meeting point itself, which is marked by a post – touchingly, it's very hard to work out which country you're in without reference to it. From 1816 to 1919 a fourth "country" abutted the other three. The tiny wedge-shaped territory of **Neutral Moresnet** was created after the Congress of Vienna to settle a territorial dispute between the Netherlands and Prussia. It was abolished by the Versailles Treaty after World War I and is now part of Belgium.

ARRIVAL AND GETTING AROUND | AACHEN

By train Aachen's Hauptbahnhof is on the south side of the city centre, from where it's a 5min walk north to Friedrich-Wilhelm-Platz.

Destinations Cologne (every 10–30min; 35–54min); Dortmund (every 22–38min; 2hr 38min); Duisburg (2 per hour; 1hr 45min); Düsseldorf (1–3 per hour; 1hr 21min–1hr 28min);Düsseldorf airport (1–2 per hour; 1hr 12min–1hr 36min); Essen (1–2 per hour; 1hr 36min–1hr 59min); Liège (1–2 per hour; 23–50min).

By public transport City buses (⟨w⟩avv.de) depart from the *Bushof* a few hundred metres northeast of the tourist office, at the corner of Kurhausstrasse and Peterstrasse. Though Aachen's historic centre is compact and walkable, a one-day *Tages-Ticket* (€7.40) may be useful if you're staying outside the centre; you can also get a one-day *Euregioticket* (€18) valid for the Aachen region and for cross-border travel far into Belgium and the Netherlands.

By bike Bike rental is available from the Radstation on the square in front of the Hauptbahnhof (Mon–Fri 5.30am–10.30pm, Sat & Sun 9.30am–1pm; €1/hr, €5/day; ☎0241 45 01 59 02).

INFORMATION

Tourist office Housed in the Elisenbrunnen, a Neoclassical spa colonnade by Karl Friedrich Schinkel on Friedrich-Wilhelm-Platz (Jan–March Mon–Fri 9am–6pm, Sat 9am–2pm; April–Dec Mon–Fri 9am–6pm, Sat & Sun 9am–4pm; ☎0241 180 29 60, ⟨w⟩aachen.de). You can book hotels in both Aachen and neighbouring Dutch towns through the tourist office website. The monthly *Klenkes* listings magazine (in German) is available from the office.

ACCOMMODATION

A&O Aachen Hauptbahnhof Hackländerstr. 5 ☎030 809 47 51 10, ⟨w⟩aohostels.com. Big new two-star hotel from the national hostel chain, close to the Hauptbahnhof and with family rooms available as well as doubles and singles. **€44.90**

Benelux Franzstr. 21–23 ☎0241 40 00 30, ⟨w⟩hotel-benelux.de. In a fairly quiet location midway between the Hauptbahnhof and Dom, this is a fairly smart if rather bland mid-range choice with some bright, spacious rooms. Facilities include a fitness room, parking and roof terrace. **€126**

Drei Könige Am Büchel 5 ☎0241 483 93, ⟨w⟩h3k-aachen.de. Modest-sized, boutique-style hotel in an unbeatable central location close to the Rathaus and Dom, with warm but tasteful colour schemes, wi-fi and satellite TV. **€120**

Euroregionales Jugendgästehaus Maria-Theresia-Allee 260 ☎0241 71 10 10, ⟨w⟩aachen.jugendherberge.de; bus #2 from stop "Miseror" a few hundred metres west of the Hauptbahnhof (turn left out of the station main entrance to reach it), to stop "Ronheide". Modern hostel south of the city centre, with accommodation in twin or family rooms and four- or multi-bed dorms; there are also some wheelchair-accessible en-suite rooms. Dorms **€26.40**, doubles **€69.80**

Hesse Friedlandstr. 20 ☎0241 47 05 40, ⟨w⟩hotelhesse.de. Renovated 3-star hotel facing a small park a few minutes' walk west of the Hauptbahnhof, with tastefully decorated, if slightly bland rooms, all with bath or shower and WC, internet and TV. It's one of the nicest options close to the station. Breakfast €10. **€69**

Ibis Budget Aachen City Schumacherstr. 12 ☎0241 99 77 52 20, ⟨w⟩ibisbudget.com. Impressive new outpost of the budget chain on a very central site close to the *Bushof* and tourist office, with good levels of comfort for the money and underground parking adjacent to the hotel. **€52**

Pullman Aachen Quellenhof Monheimsallee Allee 52 ☎0241 913 20, ⟨w⟩pullmanhotels.com. A classic historic grand hotel with a contemporary twist, Aachen's most prestigious address is right on the Kurpark between the casino and conference centre, and is the choice of visiting VIPs. **€163**

12

EATING AND DRINKING

Good places to eat and drink are scattered throughout Aachen's historic core: there's a concentration of atmospheric, traditional eating places in and around **Markt**, while **Pontstrasse** is where you'll find the liveliest of Aachen's bar scene. The local sugary treats are **Aachener Printen**, a type of gingerbread; sample it at *Leo van den Daele* (see below) or from *Nobis* at Münsterplatz 3, near the cathedral.

CAFÉS AND BARS

Café Kittel Pontstr. 39 ☎0241 365 60, ⓦcafekittel.de. Relaxed bohemian café-bar with inexpensive breakfasts (from €2.50) and simple hot food at student-friendly prices, with chilli for €4.50. There's a beer garden in summer. Mon–Thurs & Sun 10am–2am, Fri & Sat 10am–3am.

Domkeller Hof 1 ☎0241 342 65, ⓦdomkeller.de. Lovely old pub-type place close to the Rathaus, with Belgian beers, cocktails, a huge outside terrace and live music Mon from 8pm during student term-time. Mon–Thurs & Sun 10am–2am, Fri & Sat 10am–3am.

Egmont Pontstr. 1–3 ☎0241 40 77 46, ⓦegmont-aachen.de. Lovely, cluttered café close to the Internationales Zeitungsmuseum, with a slightly battered Art Deco look, a small terrace, a huge range of teas and soup-bowl-sized *Milchkaffees* (€3.30). Food ranges from cakes (€2.40) to baked potatoes and light savouries including *Zwiebelkuchen* (onion cake; €3.50). Mon–Sat 8am–late, Sun 9am–late.

Leo van den Daele Büchel 18 ☎0241 357 24, ⓦvan-den-daele.de. The dark, woody interior behind the glossy black-and-gilt shopfront is the classic place to stop for coffee and cakes in Aachen; breakfasts from €6.75. Mon–Sat 9am–6.30pm, Sun 10am–6pm.

Molkerei Pontstr. 141 ☎0241 489 82. One of a number of stylish café-bars that cluster around the Apollo cinema at the north end of Pontstrasse; it's busy much of the time and serves affordable food and cocktails to a fairly young crowd. Mon–Thurs & Sun 10am–1am, Fri & Sat 10am–late.

Ocean/Sowiso Pontstr. 164–166 ☎0241 401 93 30, ⓦsowiso-aachen.de. Trendy sports and cocktail bar in the thick of the Pontstrasse action whose student-friendly prices and leafy outdoor terrace make it a prime spot for alfresco lounging in fine weather. Daily 10am–late.

Vertical Kockerellstr. 13 ☎0241 900 67 81. Classy little wine-bar with high stools, a few tables outside in fine weather and thirty wines by the glass (from €2.70), many from prestigious wineries, plus a big rum and whisky selection and hot and cold food. Mon–Thurs 4pm–midnight, Fri & Sat 11am–1am.

RESTAURANTS

Am Knipp Bergdriesch 3 ☎0241 331 68, ⓦamknipp.de. Northern Altstadt stalwart with an enchantingly pretty interior and *Flammkuchen* (from €8.90) and hot German staples from around €16, though, despite claiming to be Aachen's oldest restaurant, it isn't quite what it seems – the building is a postwar reconstruction. Mon & Wed–Fri 5pm–1am, Sat & Sun 6pm–1am.

★**Postwagen** Krämerstr. 2 ☎0241 350 01, ⓦratskeller-aachen.de. Wonderfully atmospheric seventeenth-century restaurant attached to the Rathaus and run by the same team as the *Ratskeller*, serving good, hearty traditional dishes such as *Himmel en Erd* – blood sausage with mashed potato and apple – or *Sauerbraten* with raisins and *Printen* spices. Main courses from around €12. Daily 11am–10pm.

Ratskeller Markt 40 ☎0241 350 01, ⓦratskeller-aachen.de. Creative gourmet cooking in the elegant surroundings of the Rathaus's refurbished cellars, with the likes of Barbary duck breast with chickpea cassoulet; main courses à la carte €25, three courses €42.50, four €55. Daily noon–3pm & 6–10pm.

Zum Goldenen Einhorn Markt 33 ☎0241 326 93. Historic *Gasthaus* facing the Rathaus, with classy ambience and a mix of local and regional German specialities on its menu, from *Schnitzel* (around €11.50) to more sophisticated meat and fish mains from around €12.50. Daily noon–3pm & 6–10pm.

Zum Goldenen Schwan Markt 37 ☎0241 316 49, ⓦschwan-ac.de. Traditional *Gasthaus* that's just as atmospheric and historic as its neighbour the *Einhorn*, but more informal and generally cheaper, with German tapas from €8.50 and *Flammkuchen* from €9. Mon–Thurs, Sat & Sun noon–midnight, Fri noon–2am.

NIGHTLIFE AND ENTERTAINMENT

CLUBS AND LIVE MUSIC

Musikbunker Goffartstr. 26 ☎0241 53 21 80, ⓦmusikbunker-aachen.de. Live rock venue and club in the extraordinary setting of a vast World War II air-raid shelter. Weekend clubnights include Bass Wreckage drum & bass/dubstep night. Weekday gigs generally start at 8pm; clubnights Fri & Sat 11pm–late.

Starfish Liebigstr. 19 ☎0241 93 89 00, ⓦstarfish-aachen.de. Aachen's biggest dance club is northeast of the centre, just off Jülicher Strasse, with four dancefloors each with a different music style, from mainstream house to Eighties and Nineties hits, *Schlager*, disco, hip-hop and electro. Fri & Sat 10pm–6am.

12

THEATRE, OPERA AND CLASSICAL MUSIC
Eurogress Aachen Monheimsallee 48 ⊕ 0241 91 31 0, ⓦ eurogress-aachen.de. Modern conference centre in the Kurviertel that is also the venue for all manner of large-scale events, from rock and classical concerts to dance and live comedy.

Theater Aachen Theaterplatz ⊕ 0241 478 42 44, ⓦ theateraachen.de. The imposing Neoclassical Theater Aachen is the city's main venue for serious drama, opera and operetta; the Sinfonieorchester Aachen splits its concert performances between here and the Eurogress conference centre.

Wuppertal

Around 40km northeast of Cologne in the hilly Bergisches Land, **WUPPERTAL** is not so much a city as an amalgam of towns strung out along the narrow, wooded valley of the River Wupper; they united in 1929 and shortly afterwards adopted the name Wuppertal. Known internationally for its unique suspended-monorail system, the **Schwebebahn** (see box below), and for the **Tanztheater Pina Bausch** – one of the world's most renowned modern dance troupes – it's also the place where aspirin was invented, and was a major centre of the German textile industry. Despite some down-at-heel stretches Wuppertal is redeemed by its hilly, leafy site and by the survival of a large number of buildings from its nineteenth-century heyday, particularly in **Elberfeld**, which is the larger and more attractive of the two main centres, the other being **Barmen**, a little to the east.

Elberfeld

Wedged between the river and the high ground to the north, **ELBERFELD**'s compact knot of shopping streets contains a few dignified old civic buildings. As the larger of the city's two principal central districts, it's the nearest thing Wuppertal has to a conventional city centre.

Von der Heydt Museum

Turmhof 8 • Tues, Wed & Fri–Sun 11am–6pm, Thurs 11am–8pm; temporary exhibitions hours vary • €12, free 1st Thurs of month 5–8pm • ⓦ von-der-heydt-museum.de

Elberfeld's handsome former Rathaus from 1842 is now home to the **Von der Heydt Museum**, which displays a rotating selection from its impressive collection of big-name fine art, from sixteenth- and seventeenth-century Flemish and Dutch masters to the French and German Impressionists and a roll call of modern movements, including Expressionists, Fauvists, Cubists and Futurists. The graphic works include prints and drawings by Otto Dix, Karl Schmidt-Rottluff and Ernst Ludwig Kirchner, while postwar highlights include a couple of typically geometric works by Victor Vasarely, a Joseph Beuys self-portrait and works by Wuppertal-based British artist Tony Cragg; the bronzes in front of the museum are by him. The

---

WUPPERTAL'S SWINGING RAILWAY

The **Schwebebahn** system – suspended from massive girders above the course of the River Wupper – was an ingenious solution to the problem of providing a rapid-transit system in an extremely narrow valley where space was at a premium. The idea of Cologne engineer Eugen Langen, it was built in the 1890s. Kaiser Wilhelm II took the inaugural ride in 1900 and the system opened to the public a few months afterwards. It takes some getting used to, as the trains are noisy and sway from side to side in slightly disconcerting fashion, but the Schwebebahn has a good safety record, and on weekend afternoons you can take a "*Kaffeefahrt*" on one of the original 1900 trains, departing from Vohwinkel station (ⓦ kaiserwagen.de); book online or enquire at the tourist office. Tickets for ordinary journeys are as for other cities in the VRR regional transport network for the Rhine Ruhr.

museum also has an important collection of works by the Elberfeld-born nineteenth-century neo-Idealist Hans von Marées.

Luisenviertel

West of Elberfeld centre along Friedrich-Ebert-Strasse, the delightful **Luisenviertel** preserves many old weavers' houses, their simple slate-hung or clapboard facades giving them a somewhat North American look. The district's obvious focus is spacious **St Laurentiusplatz** with its Neoclassical, early nineteenth-century church, but pretty **Luisenstrasse** to the north is more enjoyable, with its antique, jewellery and clothes shops and relaxed cafés, bars and restaurants.

The Ölberg

From Luisenstrasse, ascend steep **Ortenbrucher Strasse** or the evocatively named **Tippen-Tappen-Tönchen** steps – so named for the noise the workers' wooden clogs made on them – to reach the Nordstadt or **Ölberg**, a well-preserved nineteenth-century residential district whose steep streets and elaborate facades provoke comparisons with San Francisco or Montmartre. It's popular with film-makers looking for intact period locations, and though by no means uniformly gentrified, it does have a bohemian flavour. In summer local artists hold Sunday **art fairs** on Otto-Böhne-Platz – check ⓦ nord-stadt.de for dates. The most grandiose of the district's old apartment houses are along its main artery, Marienstrasse.

Briller Viertel

Immediately to the west of the Olberg, the **Briller Viertel** was where the city's prosperous textile magnates built their opulent villas, and the streets have suitably important-sounding Prussian names to match the grand architectural details. **Roonstrasse**, the district's most photographed street, is a picturesque ensemble of gables, turrets, balconies and steps.

12

Barmen

Compared with Elberfeld's intact nineteenth-century streetscapes, the charms of **BARMEN** are modest – an Allied air raid in 1943 caused a firestorm that destroyed much of it – but there's enough to see there to justify a trip on the Schwebebahn.

Historisches Zentrum

Engelsstr. 10–18 • Tues–Sun 10am–6pm • €4 • ⓦ friedrich-engels-haus.de • Schwebebahn to "Adler Brücke"

Barmen's chief attraction is the **Historisches Zentrum**, which comprises a rather dry museum in the **Engels Haus**, commemorating the revolutionary Friedrich Engels, son of a wealthy local textile magnate, born nearby in 1820, and the altogether more engrossing **Museum für Frühindustrialisierung** (Museum of Early Industrialization), which tells the story of Wuppertal's early nineteenth-century rise as Germany's cotton metropolis. As the displays – which include a Spinning Jenny, a brace of Arkwright machines and a Crompton Spinning Mule – attest, the industry was initially dependent on British technology, but by the end of the century the city was producing its own looms. As in the UK, children formed most of the workforce; the city's great export success was blue-and-white gingham used to clothe Afro-American slaves. Nowadays the industry plays a subsidiary role in Wuppertal's economy, though it continues to produce specialist fibres for medical and other uses.

The Skulpturenpark Waldfrieden

Hirschstr. 12 • March–Oct Tues–Sun 10am–7pm; Nov–Feb Fri–Sun 10am–5pm • €10 • ⓦ skulpturenpark-waldfrieden.de • Bus #628 from Elberfeld or Barmen

High on a wooded slope between Elberfeld and Barmen is the **Skulpturenpark Waldfrieden**, an open-air exhibition of uncompromisingly abstract modernist sculptures in the park-like grounds of the **Villa Waldfrieden**, a postwar private house of strikingly original design. The brainchild of British artist Tony Cragg, the park displays 36 monumental works in bronze, stainless steel, stone and concrete – most but by no means all by Cragg himself – against a backdrop of deciduous trees and, in the spring, of cherry blossom, lilac and wisteria.

ARRIVAL AND INFORMATION

By train Elberfeld's Hauptbahnhof is on Döppersberg, just south of the traffic-free shopping zone.

Destinations Bonn (every 20min–1hr; 58min–1hr 21min); Cologne (every 5–24min; 28–48min); Düsseldorf (evey 15–25min; 20–31min).

Tourist office A short walk from the Hauptbahnhof in the City-Center, Schlossbleiche 40 (Mon–Fri 9am–6pm, Sat 10am–2pm; ☎ 0202 194 33, ⓦ wuppertal.de).

ACCOMMODATION

Art Fabrik & Hotel Bockmühle 16–24, Barmen ☎ 0202 283 70, ⓦ art-fabrik-hotel.de. Wuppertal's most interesting hotel is the arty and reasonably priced *Art Fabrik*, in a converted textile mill that once belonged to the Engels family and is now a protected historic monument. **€63**

Astor Schlossbleiche 4–6, Elberfeld ☎ 0202 45 05 11, ⓦ hotel-astor-wuppertal.de. A tasteful, central and comfortable 3-star *hotel garni* near the tourist office, offering 44 rooms with bath or shower, free wireless internet and satellite TV. Hotel guests also get free use of local public transport. **€63**

DJH Wuppertal Obere Lichtenplatzerstr. 70, Barmen ☎ 0202 55 23 72, ⓦ wuppertal.jugendherberge.de. Barmen's youth hostel is at the foot of a wooded nature reserve south of the town centre, with accommodation mainly in six-bed dorms, though there are some twin, three- and four-bed rooms. Dorms **€15.90**, doubles **€49.80**

Ibis Hofaue 4, Elberfeld ☎ 0202 870 40, ⓦ ibishotel .com. Very central outpost of the budget chain, close to the tourist office and city centre, with comfortable a/c rooms, free wi-fi and friendly staff. There's parking on-site too. Breakfast €10. **€55**

EATING AND DRINKING

By far the best choice of places for eating and drinking in Wuppertal is in the **Luisenviertel**, but there's a scattering of offbeat places in the quieter Ölberg and one or two worthwhile options in central Elberfeld.

Alaturka Luisenstr. 63a, Elberfeld ☎ 0202 30 84 13, ⓦ alaturka-restaurant.de. An excellent Turkish restaurant in the Luisenviertel, with a pretty courtyard and climbing roses. Set menus start at €21.90; main courses cost from €11.90, and include plenty of veggie choices. Tues–Sat 6pm–midnight, Sun 10am–3pm & 6–11pm.

★ **Café du Congo** Luisenstr. 118, Elberfeld ☎ 0202 31 62 13. Relaxed, arty Luisenviertel café-bar with an eclectic, chalked-up menu of well-executed main courses for €8–20, including the likes of chicken with grilled watermelon and teriyaki sauce, plus plenty of veggie choice. There's a pretty terrace across the street. Breakfast served until 3pm. Daily 11am–11pm.

Domhan Marienstr. 36, Elberfeld ☎ 0202 257 48 70, ⓦ domhan-wtal.de. Excellent Brit-style Ölberg pub with a friendly Scottish barman, occasional live music and a cosmopolitan selection of beer and whisky from Bitburger to Newcastle Brown. Daily 7pm–1am.

Engel Friedrich-Ebert-Str. 13, Elberfeld ☎ 0202 309 98 87. High-ceilinged café in a historic Luisenviertel house where Kaiser Wilhelm II was several times a guest. There's a weekend breakfast buffet for €7.90, baguettes from €3.90 and salads from €5.70. Mon–Thurs 8am–midnight, Fri & Sat 8am–2/3am, Sun 9am–midnight.

Mangi Mangi Rommelspütt 9a, Elberfeld ☎ 0202 612 75 351, ⓦ mangimangi.de. Excellent all-day café in Elberfeld's shopping district, serving a daily-changing menu of wholesome soups (€4.50), salads, veggie and meaty main courses (from €6.80). There's an imaginative breakfast menu, too. Mon–Fri 8am–6.30pm.

ENTERTAINMENT

When it comes to high culture, Wuppertal exceeds expectations, largely due to its association with avant-garde choreographer Pina Bausch (1940–2009), generally regarded as one of the greatest innovators in modern dance. Though frequent international tours spread the reputation of her dance company, **Tanztheater Wuppertal Pina Bausch** (ⓦ pina-bausch.de), worldwide, it retains its base in Wuppertal.

12

Historische Stadthalle Johannisberg 40 ☏0202 24 58 90, ⊛stadthalle.de. Wuppertal's magnificent concert hall was built in 1900 and still has its original, opulent interiors intact. It's the home base for the Sinfonieorchester Wuppertal. **Opernhaus** Kurt-Drees Str. 4, Barmen ☏0202 563

7600, ⊛wuppertaler-buehnen.de. Hosts opera and is the home venue for performances by Tanztheater Wuppertal Pina Bausch, which continues to perform Bausch's classic works in Wuppertal when it is not touring.

Düsseldorf

Chic **DÜSSELDORF** is not just North Rhine-Westphalia's capital but also its Knightsbridge or Upper East Side – a sophisticated, cosmopolitan city of swish hotels, contemporary art and designer labels, very different from the industrial Ruhr to the north. Though its surface glitter is underpinned by the business acumen of its banks and corporate headquarters, fashion houses and advertising agencies, it's the confident ease with which Düsseldorf enjoys its prosperity that strikes visitors most forcefully, from the Altstadt's bars and restaurants to the chichi boutiques on stately Königsallee. For all its glitz, Düsseldorf is an easy city to enjoy, but its pleasures don't necessarily come cheap. You'll probably notice the price differential if you arrive here after Cologne or the Ruhr.

Brief history

Düsseldorf's worldly flair is nothing new: when Napoleon passed through in 1806 he thought the city "a little Paris". First mentioned in the twelfth century, the village at the mouth of the River Düssel owed its subsequent rise to the Counts of Berg, whose Schloss dominated the Altstadt until it burned down in 1872. The city blossomed under Elector Johann Wilhelm of Pfalz-Neuburg (1658–1716), known as Jan Wellem, and by the time Napoleon arrived it had already spread in planned fashion beyond its historic core.

12

The Altstadt

All that remains of the castle of the Counts of Berg is a stumpy tower on riverside Burgplatz. Today the **Schlossturm** (Tues–Sun 11am–6pm; €3; ⊛freunde-schifffahrt museum.de) houses a **museum** on Rhine shipping and is topped by a café. Along with the distinctive spire of the nearby church of **St Lambertus** it forms the visual focus of the agreeably walkable **Altstadt**. The church's spire owes its twisted shape to the use of unseasoned timber when it was rebuilt after a lightning strike in 1815. Inside, the highlights are the rocket-like fifteenth-century Gothic tabernacle and the splendid Renaissance memorial to Duke Wilhelm V.

Andreaskirche

Andreasstr. 27 • Church Mon–Sat 7.30am–6.30pm, Sun 8.30am–7pm; mausoleum 1st Wed of month at 4pm • Free • ⊛dominikaner-duesseldorf.de

Swing east from Burgplatz and a short stroll brings you to the uplifting Baroque **Andreaskirche**, built for the Jesuits in the early seventeenth century and with a pretty

---

DÜSSELDORF ORIENTATION

The **Rheinuferpromenade** is the main pedestrian thoroughfare between the vibrant **Altstadt** in the north and the trendy **Medienhafen** to the south. Inland, swanky **Königsallee** (or Kö as it is known) runs south–north from the **Hofgarten** to Graf-Adolf-Strasse, with the peaceful **Carlstadt** to the west. Most of the city's sights are located between Kö and the river, though many of its hotels are to the east or south, and you may want to venture out of town to see **Schloss Benrath**.

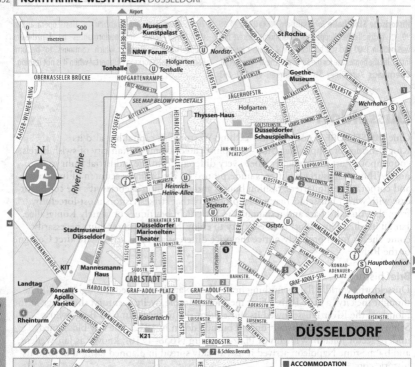

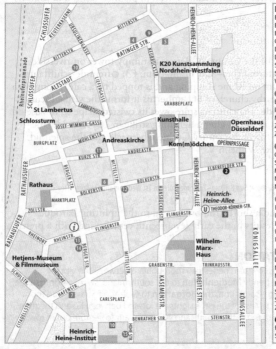

ACCOMMODATION

Backpackers Düsseldorf	7
Breidenbacher Hof	9
Burns Art Hotel	5
Carat Hotel	10
DJH Düsseldorf	4
Domo	6
Sir and Lady Astor	2/3
Steigenberger Parkhotel	8
Windsor	1

BRAUHÄUSER AND BARS

Brauerei Kürzer	11
Im Füchschen	9
M168	4
Zum Schlüssel	12
Zum Uerige	13

CAFÉS AND CHEAP EATS

Curry	6
Sattgrün	3
Münstermann's Kontor	15
Naniwa Noodles & Soups	1
Naniwa Sushi & More	2

RESTAURANTS

Berens am Kai	5
Fischhaus	14
Lido	7
Parlin	10
Robert's Bistro	8

NIGHTLIFE

Dä Spiegel	6
Nachtresidenz	2
Nähkörbchen	7
Rudas Studios	3
Schlösser Quartier Bohème	4
Stone im Ratinger Hof	5
Zakk	1

SHOPS

Kaufhof	2
Stilwerk	1

CREATIVE CAPITAL

North Rhine-Westphalia's capital punches far above its weight in matters cultural. It has latterly acquired some cutting-edge **architecture** by big names like Frank Gehry and Will Alsop to match its established reputation for **modern art**: Joseph Beuys, the enfant terrible of the postwar art scene, was a professor at the esteemed Kunstakademie, and the city's galleries are impressive. The Kunstakademie also nurtured the influential **Düsseldorf school of photography**, whose leading lights include Andreas Gursky, celebrated for his vast panoramic images. There's a strong **rock music** tradition here, the most famous local musical exports being synthesizer pioneers Kraftwerk and Eighties electropoppers DAF and Propaganda. Düsseldorf is Germany's **fashion** capital too, and it was in a local nightclub in the 1980s that supermodel Claudia Schiffer was discovered. Its greatest son was, however, neither rock star nor fashion plate, but the Romantic poet **Heinrich Heine**, who is commemorated by a museum.

icing-sugar stucco interior that's worth a visit. The church also houses a low-key **mausoleum** containing Jan Wellem's tomb.

Marktplatz and the southern Altstadt

Düsseldorf's favourite Elector, **Jan Wellem**, sits plump and pleased with himself astride his horse in front of the Renaissance **Rathaus** on Marktplatz, immediately to the south of Burgplatz. Legend has it that there wasn't enough metal to cast Gabriel di Grupello's splendid equestrian likeness – created towards the end of Jan Wellem's life – and that locals were forced to donate their best silver to complete it. To the east and south, the streets are animated day and night as tourists and locals descend on a vast array of bars, cafés and restaurants. **Carlsplatz** defines the Altstadt's southeastern tip with an excellent, lively **food market** (Mon–Fri 8am–6pm, Sat 8am–4pm).

Hetjens-Museum and Filmmuseum

Schulstr. 4 • **Hetjens-Museum** Tues & Thurs–Sun 11am–5pm, Wed 11am–9pm • €4 • ⓦ duesseldorf.de/hetjens • **Filmmuseum** Same hours • €5 • ⓦ duesseldorf.de/filmmuseum

Schulstrasse on the Altstadt's southern fringe is home to two museums. The **Hetjens-Museum** houses an impressively eclectic collection of ceramics from ancient times to the present day; star exhibits include a spectacular seventeenth-century blue faïence dome from Multan in Pakistan. Highlights of the **Filmmuseum** next door include the tin drum from Volker Schlöndorff's 1978 film of the same name, plus costumes from Peter Greenaway's *The Cook, the Thief, His Wife and Her Lover* and Werner Herzog's *Nosferatu*.

The Hofgarten and around

East of the Altstadt, an impressive string of museums and art galleries fringe the **Hofgarten**, a graceful, lake-studded park laid out in the eighteenth century and later extended by Napoleonic decree.

Kunsthalle

Grabbeplatz 4 • Tues–Sun 11am–6pm • €6 • ⓦ kunsthalle-duesseldorf.de

Just east of the Andreaskirche, on Grabbeplatz, the bunker-like **Kunsthalle** hosts big-name temporary exhibitions of modern art and is also home to the **Kunstverein**, which promotes the work of less established artists, and to the **Kom(m)ödchen**, a political cabaret (see p.660).

K20 Kunstsammlung Nordrhein-Westfalen

Grabbeplatz 5 • Tues–Fri 10am–6pm, Sat & Sun 11am–6pm, 1st Wed in month until 10pm • €8, combined ticket with K21 €17, free after 6pm 1st Wed in month • ⓦ kunstsammlung.de

Facing the Kunsthalle across Grabbeplatz is the sinuous, glossy black facade of the **K20 Kunstsammlung Nordrhein-Westfalen**, which houses an outstanding collection of

12

modern art including around a hundred works by Paul Klee as well as work by Joseph Beuys, a substantial Cubist collection including work by Braque, Léger and Picasso, and postwar American art from Pollock to Warhol. Temporary exhibitions are staged in the large Klee Halle on the ground floor, while the route through the permanent collection follows a meandering course. There's a free shuttle bus service between K20 and its sister gallery, K21 (see p.656).

Museum Kunstpalast

Ehrenhof 4–5 • Tues, Wed & Fri–Sun 11am–6pm, Thurs 11am–9pm • €5 • ⓦ smkp.de

A stroll through the western fringes of the Hofgarten past the imposing Kunstakademie and Expressionist 1926 Tonhalle (see p.660) brings you to the **Museum Kunstpalast**, worth a visit for its eclectic collection of modern and not-so-modern art. The **Gemäldegalerie** exhibits European painting from the fifteenth to the early twentieth century; the collection has its origins in the collection of the Elector Jan Wellem, and includes Rubens' *Assumption of the Virgin Mary* and *Venus and Adonis*, and works of the nineteenth-century Düsseldorf school, whose pleasing landscapes give light relief from the occasionally heavy-handed moral themes.

The **sculpture and applied art** collection includes fine examples of South German medieval woodcarving; the **graphic collection** ranges from Raphael to Joseph Beuys and Gerhard Richter; and the **modern collection** features classics by Franz Marc, Otto Dix and Ernst Ludwig Kirchner alongside more recent work. Not to be missed is the **Glasmuseum Hentrich**, with an encyclopedic glass collection that encompasses the Romans, Tiffany, Gallé, Lalique, and some superb contemporary Czech and German fine-art glass.

NRW Forum

Ehrenhof 2 • Tues–Thurs, Sat & Sun 11am–8pm, Fri 11am–10pm • €6 • ⓦ nrw-forum.de

Next door to the Museum Kunstpalast, the **NRW Forum** hosts excellent temporary exhibitions on subjects of contemporary cultural interest, from fashion to photography and advertising. With big international names – from Azzedine Alaïa to Kraftwerk – often in the spotlight, the shows have broad appeal.

Königsallee and around

A little of the Hofgarten's leafy charm continues south from the park along **Königsallee**, the lavish 82m-wide boulevard laid out along the course of the city's old fortifications at the beginning of the nineteenth century. The eastern side is probably Germany's prime spot for *flâneurs* or fashion victims, its 812m length an A-to-Z of international designer names from Armani to Ermenegildo Zegna, not forgetting Germany's own Jil Sander. A block east on Grünstrasse, the extrovert **Stilwerk** mall is filled with upmarket interiors stores.

Separated from all this by two avenues of trees and an ornamental moat, Königsallee's western side fringes the banking district and is more sober in style, though even here there is some glitz. The copper-roofed Jugendstil **Kaufhof** at the north end is the city's most imposing department store. It was designed for the Tietz chain in 1907–09 by Joseph Maria Olbrich, a leading light of the Viennese Secession and of Darmstadt's Mathildenhöhe Künstlerkolonie (see p.576).

The banking quarter

West of Königsallee, the broad, straight avenues of the banking quarter have an almost North American feel, an impression heightened by two Weimar-era skyscrapers – the 1924 **Wilhelm-Marx-Haus** on Heinrich-Heine-Allee and the 1922 **Haus der Stummkonzern** at Breite Str. 69, both of which blend Expressionist and brick Gothic elements to good effect.

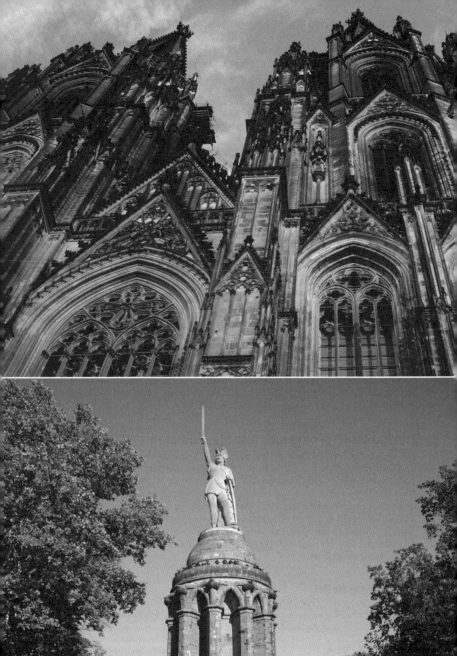

Carlstadt

Stretching towards the Rhine west of Kasernenstrasse is delightful **Carlstadt**, preserving among its antiquarian bookshops, art galleries and chic shops some of the handsome eighteenth- and nineteenth-century houses that have long made it a favoured residential district. One such house at Bilkerstr. 12–14 houses the **Heinrich-Heine-Institut** (Tues–Fri & Sun 11am–5pm, Sat 1–5pm; €4; ⍵ duesseldorf.de/heineinstitut) in the same street in which the poet (see box below) was born in 1797.

Stadtmuseum Düsseldorf

Berger Allee 2 • Tues–Sun 11am–6pm • €4 including temporary exhibitions • ⍵ duesseldorf.de/stadtmuseum

Carlstadt is fringed to the south by small lakes. On the north side of one of them, the **Stadtmuseum Düsseldorf** occupies the eighteenth-century Spee'sches Palais and its modern extension, presenting an engrossing overview of Düsseldorf's history, with labelling in English and German. Exhibits include a model of the long-vanished Schloss and a French passport dating from the Napoleonic occupation. You'll also see packaging from the Henkel company, whose Persil washing powder is Düsseldorf's most famous brand name.

K21 Kunstsammlung Nordrhein-Westfalen

Ständehausstr. 1 • Tues–Fri 10am–6pm, Sat & Sun 11am–6pm, 1st Wed in month until 10pm • €12, combined ticket with K20 €17, free after 6pm 1st Wed in month • ⍵ kunstsammlung.de

On the south side of a lake, the Kaiserteich – the former Rhineland parliament – now houses **K21 Kunstsammlung Nordrhein-Westfalen**. The conversion of the grandiose neo-Renaissance nineteenth-century parliament into a clean, white space with a vast atrium and over-arching glass roof is an audacious work of modern architecture. The city's main contemporary art gallery picks up where K20's collection of classical modernism leaves off, with a focus on German and international art since 1980. Installations, video art and photography are interspersed with works in oil or charcoal; among the artists featured are Nam June Paik, Andreas Gursky and the Liverpool-born, Wuppertal-based Tony Cragg.

The Rheinuferpromenade and Medienhafen

Düsseldorf regained its riverside in 1995 when the traffic-choked B1 highway was finally diverted into a tunnel. In its place, the **Rheinuferpromenade** makes for delightful strolling south from the Altstadt towards the **Medienhafen**, a revamped dockside district that's now one of the city's most visually striking. Admire the dignified stone facade of Peter Behrens' 1912 **Mannesmann-Haus** building before pausing for artistic and liquid refreshment at **KIT**, at Mannesmann Ufer 1b (Kunst im Tunnel: Tues-Sun & hols 11am-pm; 11am–6pm; €4; ⍵ kunst-im-tunnel.de), an inspired venue for contemporary art sandwiched between the two arms of the road tunnel, with a cool café/bar at ground level.

HEINRICH HEINE

The author of some of the loveliest verse ever written in the German language, **Heinrich Heine** was the son of prosperous, assimilated Jewish parents, and his Judaism was a theme not only during his lifetime – he converted to Christianity in 1825, declaring his act a "ticket of admission to European culture" – but also long after his death. Heine's books were among those burned by the Nazis in 1933 as they began to fulfil his prophecy that "There, where one burns books, one also burns people in the end." But not even they could ban his most popular work, the *Loreley*, which was tolerated – in poem form and in the musical setting by Friedrich Silcher – as a "folk song". Heine was deeply influenced by the spirit of the French Revolution, which he imbibed during the years of the French occupation of Düsseldorf. A radical and a trenchant critic of German feudalism, he spent much of his life in exile in Paris, and died there in 1856.

Rheinturm Düsseldorf

Stromstr. 20 • Mon–Thurs & Sun 10am–midnight, Fri & Sat 10am–1am • €5 • ⓦ guennewig.de

Beyond the Rheinkniebrücke the obligatory **Rheinturm Düsseldorf** (TV tower) looms above the North Rhine-Westphalia parliament, with an observation deck 168m above the river, a revolving restaurant and cocktail bar (see p.659) and illuminated portholes forming the world's largest decimal clock.

The Medienhafen

Over the past decade or so, the redundant harbour south of the parliament has been reinvented as the hip **Medienhafen**, with advertising agencies alongside slick nightclubs, restaurants and eye-catching buildings by celebrity architects. Particularly distinctive are the wobbly silver-and-white **Neuer Zollhof** towers by Frank Gehry; also notable is the **Stadttor**, which resembles a steel-and-glass Arc de Triomphe astride the entrance to the road tunnel. Though it's all undeniably developer-led, the Medienhafen is anything but sterile, and in the culinary stakes at least can give the Altstadt a run for its money.

Schloss Benrath

Benrather Schlossallee 100–106 • Mid-April to mid-Oct Tues–Fri 11am–5pm, Sat & Sun 11am–6pm; mid-Oct to mid-April Tues–Sun 11am–5pm; Corps de Logis occasionally closed for wedding ceremonies Wed & Thurs • Corps de Logis €9, Museum für Europäische Gartenkunst/Museum für Naturkunde €6 each, combined ticket for Corps de Logis and museums €12 • ⓦ schloss-benrath.de • Tram #701 from Jan-Wellem-Platz , U-Bahn #74 or S-Bahn #6 to Benrath

Southwest of the centre the pretty, pink ensemble of **Schloss Benrath** is arranged symmetrically around a large pond. Built between 1755 and 1770 for the Elector Carl Theodor by his French court architect Nicholas de Pigage in a style that is on the cusp between Rococo and Neoclassical, the complex has a doll's-house neatness that belies its size. The central **Corps de Logis** can only be visited on a guided tour. Once inside, it's apparent that the Schloss's modest external appearance disguises a sumptuous palace. The rooms display the same grace and lightness of touch as the exterior, though the circular domed hall aspires to monumental status. The prettily feminine garden-rooms are particularly delightful. The two service wings flanking the Corps de Logis both contain museums: the enjoyable **Museum für Europäische Gartenkunst** (Museum of European Garden Design) occupies the east wing while the rather less exciting **Museum für Naturkunde** (Museum of Natural History) is in the west wing. There's a classy café, and in summer the grounds are used for concerts.

ARRIVAL AND GETTING AROUND   DÜSSELDORF

By plane Düsseldorf's airport (ⓣ 0211 42 10, ⓦ dus.com) is north of the city, with a mainline ICE rail station linked by frequent trains to the Hauptbahnhof (5–12min).

By train The Hauptbahnhof is east of the centre.
Destinations Aachen (2 per hour; 1hr 25min); Bonn (3 per hour; 43min–37 min); Cologne (3–5 per hour; 23–31min); Dortmund (4 per hour; 50–58min); Duisburg (extremely frequent; 11–18min); Essen (extremely frequent; 26–33min);

Münster (every 30min–1hr; 1hr 15min–1hr 44min).
By public transport The bus, tram and U-Bahn system (ⓦ rheinbahn.com) fans out from the train station – useful if your hotel is any distance from the Altstadt. Travel up to three stops for €1.50 on a *Kurzstrecke* ticket, or throughout the city on a €2.50 Class A ticket. A €6.50 *TagesTicket* is valid from the moment you validate it until 3am the following morning.

INFORMATION

Tourist office Opposite the Hauptbahnhof at Immermannstr. 65b (Mon–Fri 9.30am–7pm, Sat 9.30am–5pm; ⓣ 0211 17 20 28 44, ⓦ duesseldorf-tourismus.de), or in the Altstadt at the corner of Marktstrasse and Rheinstrasse (daily 10am–6pm; ⓣ 0211 17 20 28 40).

Discount card The Düsseldorf WelcomeCard (24hr €9, 48hr €14, 72hr €19) offers free or reduced entry to museums and attractions plus unlimited use of public transport.

12

12

ACCOMMODATION

The tourist offices can help with finding accommodation, or you can book through their website. There's a glut of business-oriented **hotels** in Düsseldorf, mainly three stars or higher, with some truly luxurious options at the top of the market; genuine budget options are rather scarce, and prices rise across the board when there's a major **trade fair** or event on. The best hunting-ground for all prices is in the streets north and west of the Hauptbahnhof.

HOTELS

Breidenbacher Hof Königsallee 11 ☎ 0211 16 09 00, ⓦ capellahotels.com. The most über glitzy of all Düsseldorf's five-star hotels opened in 2008, though it harks back to the original *Breidenbacher Hof* of 1812. The style is traditional grand hotel with the luxury vamped up to the max. Breakfast not included. €324

Burns Art Hotel Bahnstr. 76 ☎ 0211 779 29 10, ⓦ hotel-burns.de. Crisp, clean lines and sober colours distinguish the rather masculine decor of this "art hotel" between Königsallee and the Hauptbahnhof. Weekend rates are lower, and they also have apartments to rent. €199

Carat Hotel Benrather Str. 7a ☎ 0211 130 50, ⓦ carat-hotel-duesseldorf.de. Solid 4-star comfort in a great location close to Carlstadt's shops and galleries and the Altstadt's nightlife. There's free wireless internet, and more expensive rooms have Nespresso coffee makers. €119

Domo Scheurenstr. 4 ☎ 0211 384 45 30, ⓦ nk-hotels .de. Fairly basic but good-value pension on the fifth and sixth floors of a tower between Königsallee and the Hauptbahnhof – don't be put off by the slightly seedy surroundings, as the hotel itself is perfectly OK, and also offers two- and three-bed apartments. Cheaper rooms lack WC. Breakfast included. Apartments (per person) €30, doubles €50

Sir and Lady Astor Kurfürstenstr. 18/22 ☎ 0211 93 60 90, ⓦ sir-astor.de. Stylish, intimate twin boutique hotels facing each other across a quiet street near the city centre. *Sir Astor*'s decorative theme is "Scotland meets Africa", while *Lady Astor* has a richer, more opulent feel. €80

Steigenberger Parkhotel Königsallee 1a ☎ 0211 138 10, ⓦ steigenberger.com. A dependable deluxe address with tasteful, conservative decor and a prime site between the Hofgarten, Altstadt and Königsallee shops. There's free internet and the hotel has a sauna and fitness complex, cigar bar and elegant restaurant. €208

Windsor Grafenberger Allee 36 ☎ 0211 914 680, ⓦ hotel.windsorhotel.de. Sister hotel to the *Sir and Lady Astor* east of the Hofgarten, with eighteen rooms handsomely decorated in traditional style behind an attractive Jugendstil stone facade. €85

HOSTELS

Backpackers Düsseldorf Fürstenwall 180 ☎ 0211 302 08 48, ⓦ backpackers-duesseldorf.de. Friendly, spacious hostel south of the centre, with accommodation in four, six-or ten-bed dorms, free internet access and no curfew. Reception 8am–10pm. Dorms €17

DJH Düsseldorf Düsseldorfer Str. 1, Oberkassel ☎ 0211 55 73 10, ⓦ duesseldorf.jugendherberge.de; U-Bahn to Luegeplatz, from where it's a 7min walk. Impressive modern hostel in the swanky suburb of Oberkassel west of the Rhine. Accommodation is in twin, four- or six-bed rooms, with some family rooms available. Dorms €23.40, doubles €74.80

EATING AND DRINKING

The **Altstadt** is the obvious first port of call for eating or drinking. Traditional *Brauhäuser* (microbreweries) dispense the distinctive, local top-fermented *Altbier*, while in summer elegant restaurant terraces give Berger Strasse a Mediterranean flair. Bolkerstrasse is the epicentre for raucous mainstream bars, while Ratinger Strasse to the north is more bohemian and charming. Elsewhere, **Immermannstrasse** is good for Japanese and other Asian restaurants, while the **Medienhafen** has some stylish and expensive options for both eating and drinking.

CHEAP EATS

Curry Hammerstr. 2 ☎ 0211 303 28 57, ⓦ curry-deutschland.de. Trendy *Currywurst* restaurant in the Medienhafen, with regular, spicy and Berlin-style variants of the streetfood classic, served with a variety of sauces including ketchup, chip sauce and aioli (€3–9). March–Nov Mon–Thurs & Sun 11.30am–11pm, Fri & Sat 11.30am–midnight; Nov–Feb daily 11.30am–10pm.

Münstermann's Kontor Hohe Str. 11 ☎ 0211 130 04 16, ⓦ muenstermann-delikatessen.de. Hugely popular Carlstadt lunch spot, expanded during 2014 to incorporate the delicatessen of which it was once part, with daily-changing specials, home-made cakes and plenty of lighter options. Mains from around €12. Tues–Fri 11am–10pm, Sat 11am–6pm.

Naniwa Noodles & Soups/Sushi & More Oststr. 55 ☎ 0211 16 17 99; Klosterstr. 68a ☎ 0211 83 02 222, ⓦ naniwa.de. Simple Japanese canteen selling cheap noodle dishes and soups from around €8; the sister restaurant across the street has more expensive sushi, sashimi and tempura. *Asahi* set menu with *gyoza*, miso soup, *kimchi* & beer €13. Noodles & Soup Mon & Wed–Sun 11.30am–10.30pm; Sushi & More Mon–Sat noon–10pm.

Sattgrün Graf-Adolf-Platz 6 ☎0211 876 33 90, ⓦsattgruen.de. Organic Asian-influenced vegetarian (and largely vegan) place close to Carlstadt and the banking district, with soups, pasta, couscous and rice-based dishes, plus a salad buffet. Small portion €6.90, large portion €9.50. There are branches in the Medienhafen and Flingern. Mon–Sat noon–5pm.

RESTAURANTS

Berens am Kai Kaistr. 16 ☎0211 300 67 50, ⓦberensamkai.de. The austere elegance of the Bauhaus-influenced decor ensures all attention is focused on the *haute cuisine* at this Michelin-starred Medienhafen restaurant. Set menus start at €85, rising to €149; for that you can expect dishes like filet veal with *beignet*, truffles and quinoa. There are five hundred bottles on the wine list. Mon–Fri noon–2pm & 7–10pm, Sat 7–10pm.

★**Fischhaus** Berger Str. 3–7 ☎0211 828 45 64, ⓦfischhaus-duesseldorf.de. Excellent, bustling Altstadt fish restaurant with sumptuous fresh seafood displays, brusquely efficient waiters and, in summer, a pleasant terrace at the front to watch the world go by. Main courses €14 up. Daily 11.30am–midnight.

Lido Am Handelshafen 15 ☎0211 15 76 87 30, ⓦlido1960.de. Memorably set on an ultramodern "island" in the Medienhafen, this stylish bistro offers modern European food with a French accent and plenty of seafood. Four courses €72; main courses à la carte around €36. Mon–Fri noon–2pm & 6–10pm, Sat 6–10pm.

Parlin Altestadt 12–14 ☎0211 87 74 45 95, ⓦparlin -weinbar.de. Urbane wine bar and restaurant in one of the Altstadt's more refined corners serving sophisticated modern bistro dishes beneath a spectacular stucco ceiling. Main courses around €20. Tues–Sat 6pm–midnight, Sun 5–11pm.

★**Robert's Bistro** Wupperstr. 2 ☎0211 30 48 21, ⓦrobertsbistro.de. Wonderfully unpretentious, long-established French bistro close to the Medienhafen, with

authentic choices such as confit of duck and *andouillette*; main courses €12.50–26.50. Tues–Fri 11.30am–midnight, Sat 10am–midnight.

BRAUHÄUSER AND BARS

Brauerei Kürzer Kurze Str. 18–20 ☎0211 32 26 96, ⓦbrauerei-kuerzer.de. The first new *Hausbrauerei* in the Altstadt for decades, serving its highly praised own-brew craft *Altbier* (€1.60) in stripped-back, contemporary surroundings without the usual *Brauhaus* kitsch. There's simple food too. Mon–Thurs 6pm–1am, Fri & Sat 6pm–5am, Sun 3pm–1am.

Im Füchschen Ratinger Str. 28 ☎0211 13 74 70, ⓦfuechschen.de. Civilized *Hausbrauerei* with excellent beer, a traditional atmosphere and an affordable menu of *Schnitzel*-and-*Sauerbraten*-type fare, with main courses around €9–15. It attracts a slightly younger crowd than some of its rivals. Mon–Thurs 9am–1am, Fri & Sat 9am–2am, Sun 9am–midnight.

M168 Rheinturm, Stromstr. 20 ☎0211 863 20 00, ⓦguennewig.de. The highest cocktail bar in Germany sits at the top of the Rheinturm TV tower, affording panoramic views over the Rhine and city. The innovative cocktails ensure it's not all just about the view. Mon–Thurs & Sun 10am–midnight, Fri & Sat 10am–1am.

Zum Schlüssel Bolkerstr. 43 ☎0211 828 95 50, ⓦzumschluessel.de. Vast and usually busy traditional *Hausbrauerei* on the Altstadt's liveliest street, serving hearty regional food alongside the *Altbier*; main courses from around €8. Mon–Thurs & Sun 10am–midnight, Fri & Sat 10am–1am.

Zum Uerige Berger Str. 1 ☎0211 86 69 90, ⓦuerige .de. Labyrinthine, wonderfully atmospheric Altstadt *Hausbrauerei* that spills outside in summer. It's not sophisticated, but the bitter *Altbier* is good and there's hearty food to mop it up (mains from around €11; light snacks from €2.40). Daily 10am–midnight.

NIGHTLIFE AND ENTERTAINMENT

Again the Medienhafen is a good spot for **nightlife** and **clubs**. Düsseldorf's **lesbian and gay scene** suffers from the city's proximity to Cologne, but there are a few convivial places in addition to the rather glum men-only offerings near the Hauptbahnhof. You can see the full panoply of performance in Düsseldorf, with everything from opera to cabaret and variety. The **theatre** tradition is strong: the great actor-director Gustav Gründgens, the subject of Klaus Mann's unflattering novel, *Mephisto*, was born here, while in the postwar years the Düsseldorfer Ensemble attracted such internationally renowned actors as Anton Walbrook and Elisabeth Bergner.

DÜSSELDORF FESTIVALS

In February, the city celebrates the climax of **carnival** with as much fervour as Cologne; in July the **Grösste Kirmes am Rhein** – an odd blend of folk festival and shooting fair – fills the river banks with old-fashioned funfair rides; and in September the **Düsseldorf Festival** brings dance, music and drama to various Altstadt venues, with a theatre tent on Burgplatz. Düsseldorf's **Christmas market** fills the Altstadt's squares from late November until 23 December.

12

CLUBS

Les Halles Schirmerstr. 54 ☎211 869 377 96, ⓦ les-halles.de. Stylish, vaguely "alternative" club and restaurant in a former freight depot, with inventive decor that mixes the opulent and the industrial, and a house and funk music policy. Fri & Sat 10pm–late, plus occasional Wed Nachtklinik nights for doctors, nurses and medical students 11.45pm–late.

Nachtresidenz Bahnstr. 13 ☎0211 136 57 55, ⓦ nachtresidenz.de. Huge city-centre club in a converted cinema, playing house, Latin, soul and disco beneath a 13m ceiling and with a "dress to impress" door policy. There's also a second, more intimate dancefloor, a smart lounge bar and a restaurant. Fri 11pm–late, Sat 10pm–late.

Nähkörbchen Hafenstr. 11 ☎0211 323 02 65, ⓦ karins-naehkoerbchen.de. The "little sewing basket" is an enjoyable, sing-along-style gay bar in the southern half of the Altstadt, with a soundtrack of cheesy German *Schlager* hits, karaoke and Eurovision. Wed & Fri 6pm–3am, Thurs 6pm–1am, Sat noon–4am, Sun 3pm–1am.

Rudas Studios Kaistr. 7 ☎0211 69 55 69 90, ⓦ rudas-studios.com. Upmarket club in a former film and recording studio in the Medienhafen, renowned for its excellent sound and for its Tues after-work parties. There's also occasional live music. Tues 8pm–late, Sat 10pm–late.

Schlösser Quartier Bohème Ratinger Str. 25 ☎0211 15 97 6150, ⓦ quartierboheme.com. Vast nightlife complex on the Altstadt's northern fringe, with something to suit most tastes – from a restaurant to a lounge and full-on disco – making it one of the city's hottest nightlife destinations, with queues at weekends. There's also occasional live music. Mon, Tues, Thurs & Sun 11am–1am, Wed 11am–3am, Fri & Sat 11am–5am.

Stone Im Ratinger Hof Ratinger Str. 10 ☎0211 210 78 28, ⓦ stone-club.de. Alternative club in what was once one of Germany's leading punk venues, with an eclectic music policy that embraces anything from indie to punk, garage to northern soul. There are also occasional live concerts. Clubnights Fri & Sat 10pm–late.

LIVE MUSIC

Dä Spiegel Bolkerstr. 22 ☎0211 323 74 90, ⓦ daespiegel.de. Long-established, noisy Altstadt bar with *Night Live* live-music venue on the first floor; rock and pop gigs kick off at 10pm. Mon–Fri 11.30am–5am, Sat 10.30am–5am, Sun 10.30am–5am (summer) or 11.30am–5am (winter).

Zakk Fichtenstr. 40 ☎0211 973 00 10, ⓦ zakk.de. Politically engaged cultural centre in a converted factory east of the Hauptbahnhof, with rock concerts, poetry, discos (including lesbian and gay events) and cabaret. Events on Sat night include *Schamlos* lesbian and gay night and *Zakk on the Rocks* rock disco. Gigs generally start at 8pm, clubnights at 11pm.

THEATRES, CONCERT VENUES AND CABARET

Düsseldorfer Marionettentheater Palais Wittgenstein, Bilkerstr. 7 ☎0211 32 84 32, ⓦ marionettentheater-duesseldorf.de. Puppet theatre presenting opera and children's classics like *Beauty and the Beast* as well as more serious pieces. Matinees 4pm, evening performances at 8pm.

Düsseldorfer Schauspielhaus Gustav-Gründgens-Platz 1 ☎0211 852 30, ⓦ duesseldorfer-schauspielhaus.de. Düsseldorf's main venue for serious drama, in an iconic, white modernist building just off the Hofgarten, with large and small auditoria and a youth theatre programme. Also presents modern dance.

Kom(m)ödchen Kay und Lore Lorentz Platz 44 ☎0211 32 94 43, ⓦ kommoedchen.de. Renowned political cabaret that attracts performers with a national reputation – worth catching, if your German is up to it.

Opernhaus Düsseldorf Heinrich-Heine-Allee 16a ☎0211 892 5211, ⓦ operamrhein.de. Both opera and ballet are presented at Düsseldorf's opera house, a notable building from the 1950s that is now a protected historic monument. It premieres several new productions each season.

Roncalli's Apollo Varieté Apollo-Platz 1 ☎0211 828 90 90, ⓦ apollo-variete.de. Old-style variety club, incongruously located beneath one of the main Rhine bridges, with everything from acrobats to clowns, jugglers and magicians.

Tonhalle Ehrenhof 1 ☎0211 899 61 23, ⓦ tonhalle.de. The city's principal concert hall – and the home base of the Düsseldorfer Symphoniker – in a landmark Weimar-era rotunda with excellent acoustics. There are regular matinees as well as evening concerts.

Duisburg

Straddling the Rhine at the point where the Ruhr empties into it, **DUISBURG** is the Ruhrgebiet's westernmost city and, with a population of half a million, its third largest. Surviving medieval defences point to a long history, but it was the Ruhr's nineteenth-century industrialization that transformed it into a major city, the largest inland port in Europe and a centre for steel, coal and engineering. From the

THE REINVENTION OF THE RUHR

A tough working-class cop with a complex personal history and a fondness for drink sounds like an unlikely rescuer for a depressed industrial region. Yet when Duisburg *Kriminalhauptkommissar* **Horst Schimanski** burst into German homes in the television series *Tatort* in 1981, initial outrage at his unorthodox methods quickly turned not just into adulation, but also to a resurgence of interest in the Ruhr's history and identity. Played by Götz George as a soft-centred macho with a combat jacket and huge moustache, Schimi's rise to cult status was greatly aided by the show's use of gritty Ruhr locations, and is credited with having rallied the region's morale, badly battered by the decline of its coal and steel industries from the 1960s onwards. Gradually the idea arose that the **Ruhrgebiet** – or **Ruhrpott** as it's affectionately known by its inhabitants – could be cool too.

Germany's largest urban area, the Ruhrgebiet consists of a string of interlinked towns and cities stretching east of the Rhine along the often surprisingly green valley of the Ruhr. It straddles both the historic boundary between Rhineland and Westphalia and the confessional divide – Dortmund was traditionally Protestant, Essen Catholic. The Ruhr's cities nevertheless have a shared history of sleepy provincialism abruptly transformed by coal and steel in the nineteenth century.

It is an important **footballing region**, with teams like Gelsenkirchen's Schalke and Borussia Dortmund numbered among the nation's most successful. In recent years the Ruhr has also burnished its **cultural** credentials. Rather than demolish and forget its redundant steelworks and mines, the Ruhr reinvented them as design centres, art galleries or museums, in the process creating some of the most strikingly original visitor attractions in Europe and providing a memorable setting for the region's stint as European Capital of Culture in 2010.

12

mid-1960s onwards the heavy industries declined, but Duisburg has faced its challenges with imagination, hiring British architect Norman Foster to oversee a remarkable physical transformation. Though it's no great beauty, the city's engrossing galleries, reworked industrial landscapes and funky, revitalized docks ensure it's worth at least a brief stopover.

The city centre and Altstadt

Duisburg's main thoroughfare is tree-lined **Königsstrasse**, rejuvenated in recent years by a trio of new malls but fairly lifeless outside business hours but for the blob of light around König-Heinrich-Platz; Niki de Saint-Phalle's jolly **Lifesaver fountain** adds a further splash of colour to the west. To the south, there's a brace of worthwhile **art museums**, while at the western end of the traffic-free zone is what remains of Duisburg's Altstadt. There's not much of any great age here save some sections of the **medieval town walls** and the stately **Salvatorkirche**, the city's main Protestant church, completed in 1415 and the final resting place of Flemish-born cartographer Gerhard Mercator (1512–94). The church forms an impressive architectural ensemble alongside the vast, early twentieth-century Rathaus next door.

Lehmbruck Museum

Friedrich-Wilhelm-Str. 40 • Wed, Fri & Sat noon–6pm, Thurs noon–9pm, Sun 11am–6pm • €8 • ⓦ lehmbruckmuseum.de

Set in a sculpture park on the southern fringe of the city centre, the **Lehmbruck Museum** houses a remarkable collection of modern sculpture in a pair of calm, pavilion-like structures. At the heart of the collection is the work of Duisburg-born **Wilhelm Lehmbruck** (1881–1919), regarded as one of the pioneers of twentieth-century sculpture and whose work, which focuses on the female form, is represented here by numerous busts, full-length figures and paintings. There are also works by a roll call of big international names, from Alexander Calder to Barbara Hepworth and Jean Tinguely, as well as a selection of German Expressionist paintings.

Museum DKM

Güntherstr. 13–15 • Sat, Sun & 1st Fri of month noon–6pm • €10 • ⓦ museum-dkm.de

A quiet side-street east of the Lehmbruck is home to the **Museum DKM**, which juxtaposes ancient art from Asia and the Middle East with contemporary Western and Asian art in a series of gallery spaces carved out of a 1960s commercial and residential block. There is work by Ai Weiwei, Ben Nicolson and Richard Serra among others, and the museum exhibits a substantial body of work by sculptor Ernst Hermanns.

The Innenhafen

Duisburg's Altstadt ends at the square brick **Schwanentor** bridge, which crosses the **Innenhafen**, the former dock that is now the focus of the city's regeneration. You can follow the dock northeast from the bridge to the **Kultur- und Stadthistorisches Museum Duisburg** (Tues–Sat 10am–5pm, Sun 10am–6pm; €4.50; ⓦstadtmuseum-duisburg.de), where the local history displays include a collection relating to the life and work of Mercator. Beyond it is the **Garten der Erinnerungen**, a strikingly tough postindustrial garden designed by Israeli artist Dani Karavan, with isolated chunks of dock architecture preserved like whitewashed specimens among the highly sculptural lawns and planters. Further east still, a row of preserved warehouses presides over the liveliest part of the Innenhafen, lined on both sides with big restaurants, cafés and bars.

MKM Museum Küppersmühle für Moderne Kunst

Philosophenweg 55 • Wed 2–6pm, Thurs–Sun 11am–6pm • €9 including temporary exhibitions, €6 for temporary exhibitions only • ⓦ museum-kueppersmuehle.de

A massive former grain warehouse at the eastern end of the Innenhafen houses the **MKM Museum Küppersmühle für Moderne Kunst**, Duisburg's museum of contemporary art, whose cool white spaces host touring exhibitions and are home to the Ströher collection of post-1945 German art, with works by major figures such as Georg Baselitz, Joseph Beuys, Anselm Kiefer, Sigmar Polke and Gerhard Richter.

The Museum der Deutschen Binnenschifffahrt

Museum Apostelstr. 84 • Tues–Sun 10am–5pm • €4.50 • **Museumsschiffe** Leinpfad • Easter–Sept Tues–Sun 10am–5pm • €3 • ⓦ binnenschifffahrtsmuseum.de • Tram #901 to Ruhrort Bahnhof or bus #907 to "Binnenschifffahrtsmuseum"

A Jugendstil former swimming pool in the dockside suburb of Ruhrort is home to Germany's largest museum of inland waterways, the **Museum der Deutschen Binnenschifffahrt**, which charts the history of inland navigation from the Stone Age to the present with the aid of models and full-sized boats. From Easter to September the visit is not complete without a stroll along the water's edge to the museum's floating collection of historic ships, the **Museumsschiffe**; these include the **Oscar Huber**, a splendid twin-funnelled paddle-steamer built in Duisburg in 1922.

The Landschaftspark Duisburg-Nord

Emscherstr. 71 • Open access to park; visitor centre Mon–Fri 9am–6pm, Sat & Sun 11am–6pm; guided tours Sat & Sun noon & 2pm, May–Sept also Wed 10am • Park free, tours €9 • ⓦ landschaftspark.de • Tram #903 from Duisburg Hauptbahnhof, then on foot along Emscherstrasse

In the north of the city is Duisburg's most original attraction, the **Landschaftspark Duisburg-Nord**, until 1985 a giant steelworks belonging to the Thyssen group. Since its decommissioning, nature has reclaimed large parts of the two-square-kilometre site, with rose gardens planted in former ore hoppers and trees growing up and through rusty blast furnaces, one of which can be climbed for a vertigo-inducing – though perfectly safe – closer look. The atmosphere is eerie, almost post-apocalyptic, yet it works, both as a park and as an awe-inspiring piece of industrial archeology. It's also a clubbing venue (see below) and **activity centre**, with alpine climbing gardens, a high ropes course, cycle trails (bike hire from €6) and Europe's largest artificial diving centre housed in a flooded gasometer. At weekends a stunning **light installation** turns it into pure science-fiction after dark.

ARRIVAL AND DEPARTURE   DUISBURG

By train Duisburg's Hauptbahnhof is at the eastern edge of the city centre, a short way from Königsstrasse.
Destinations Düsseldorf (up to 10 per hour at peak times;

11–18min); Essen (up to 9 per hour at peak times: 11–12min); Münster (1–2 per hour; 1hr 8min–1hr 26min); Xanten (hourly; 45min).

INFORMATION AND TOURS

Tourist office In the CityPalais mall, Königsstr. 39 (Mon–Sat 10am–7pm, Sun 10am–2pm; Nov–March closed Sun; ☏0203 28 54 40, ⓦduisburgnonstop.de). The office can help with accommodation.
Discount card The DuisburgCard, available from the tourist office, offers free travel on public transport and reduced-price admission to museums and other

attractions (24hr €9, 48hr €14, 72hr €19).
Boat trips Weisse Flotte, Calaisplatz 3 (☏0203 713 96 67, ⓦwf-duisburg.de), offers cruises from the Schwanentor bridge through Duisburg's vast inland harbour (March & Nov Sat & Sun noon & 2.15pm daily; April–Oct daily 10.30am, 12.45pm & 3pm; 2hr; €14).

ACCOMMODATION

Goldener Hahn Hohe Str. 26a ☏0203 34 87 88 88, ⓦkoesterduisburg.de. Family-run place close to the Hauptbahnhof with comfortable, renovated en-suite rooms above a restaurant, with shower, WC and cable TV. **€70**
Jugendherberge   Duisburg   Landschaftspark Lösorterstr. 133 ☏0203 41 79 00, ⓦduisburg-landschaftspark.jugendherberge.de. Duisburg has two youth hostels, but this is the one to opt for if you're visiting

the Landschaftspark, as it's next to the park, in a former Thyssen admin building. Dorms **€20.90**, doubles **€67.80**
Wyndham Duisburger Hof Opernplatz 2 ☏0203 300 70, ⓦwyndhamduisburg.com. Duisburg's most luxurious hotel since 1927, just off the central König-Heinrich-Platz and full of 4-star elegance. Facilities include wireless internet, sauna and fitness room and there are keen rates available via the website. **€109**

EATING AND DRINKING

The easiest bet for a place to eat and drink is the eastern end of the **Innenhafen**, with a row of slick and trendy places on both sides of the basin. In the city centre the **City Palais mall** has a good range of Italian and Asian options, and there's a scattering of interesting places in the **Dellviertel**, just south of the city centre.

Drei Giebel Haus Nonnengasse 8 ☏0203 268 59, ⓦdreigiebelhaus.com. Steaks and traditional German dishes in the historic surroundings of the city's only surviving medieval house, with the likes of pike-perch fillets in cream sauce or *Zwiebelrostbraten* of Angus beef. Main courses from around €11.50. Tues–Fri noon–2.30pm & 6–9pm, Sat 5.30–9.30pm, Sun noon–3pm & 5.30–8.30pm.
Faktorei Philosophenweg 21 ☏0203 346 83 79, ⓦfaktorei.de. Classy Innenhafen bar/restaurant with American & Argentinian steaks for €18.50–32.50 and fancy burgers, including the €14.80 saltmarsh lamb burger with rosemary. Tues–Sat 6pm–midnight.

Mezzomar Innenhafen 8–10 ☏0203 363 59 57. Modern Italian wine bar and restaurant on the north side of the Innenhafen, with a terrace facing the dock; it's part of a small Ruhr chain and a bit classier than its neighbours. Pizza from €6.90, pasta from €6.30, plus char-grilled meat and fish mains from around €11. Daily 9am–late.
Webster Brauhaus Dellplatz 14 ☏0203 230 78, ⓦwebster-brauhaus.de. Dellviertel *Hausbrauerei* with own-brew blond and brown beers, beer cocktails and a *Biergarten* in the shade of the church opposite. They serve food, too, from hearty *Brauhaus* staples to lighter fare including tapas; main courses from around €10. Mon–Sat noon–late, Sun 10.30am–late.

NIGHTLIFE AND ENTERTAINMENT

CLUBS AND LIVE MUSIC

Club:Machine In the Gebläsehalle, Landschaftspark Duisburg Nord, Emscherstr. 71 ⓦclubmachine.com. Electronic dance music in a spectacular industrial setting, with two dancefloors and various bars and lounges.

Club:Machine (€12) takes place up to four times a year; check the website or Facebook for upcoming dates.
Djäzz Börsenstrasse 11 ⓦdjaezz.de. Live music club with gigs most nights of the week and a far wider range of musical styles than its name suggests, with everything from jazz to rap

and electronic music. There are also DJ nights.

Goldengrün Realschulstr. 10 ☎0203 73 99 67 91, ⓦ goldengrün.de. Hip late-night Dellviertel DJ bar and live venue, popular with a young/studenty crowd, and with an eclectic music policy that ranges from Latin to Seventies disco, punk and countrybilly. Mon–Sat 8pm–5am, Sun 7pm–1am.

THEATRE AND CLASSICAL MUSIC

Mercatorhalle Duisburg im CityPalais Landfermannstr . 6 ⓦ mercatorhalle.de. The main venue for classical concerts by the Duisburger Philharmoniker (ⓦ duisburger-philharmoniker.de) is the Mercatorhalle in the CityPalais complex; undergoing renovation as this book went to press, it is scheduled to be reopened by the end of 2015.

Theater Duisburg Opernplatz ☎0203 300 91 00, ⓦ theater-duisburg.de. Duisburg's stately Neoclassical civic theatre hosts drama, opera and ballet and is (with Düsseldorf) the home base for the Deutsche Oper am Rhein.

Essen

First-time visitors expecting vistas of belching chimneys are likely to be surprised by **ESSEN**, for the Ruhr's "secret capital" is a modern, unashamedly commercial city with a modest forest of office towers and a vast central shopping zone. Though it contests with Dortmund the status of biggest city in the Ruhr, Essen is the one with the unmistakeable big-city feel, and it's this, as much as its central position in the region, that gives it an edge over its rival. It's an enjoyable place to spend a day or two, with plenty of high culture, a smattering of interesting sights including one UNESCO World Heritage Site, and a lively nightlife scene.

Basic orientation is straightforward: the **city centre** is immediately north of the Hauptbahnhof, with the main **cultural zone** to the south; further south still is some of the most enticing eating, drinking and sightseeing, while the gritty north preserves reminders of the city's industrial greatness.

The city centre

A sign on the roof of the **Handelshof** building opposite the Hauptbahnhof welcomes you to "Essen, the shopping city". Essen has long functioned as a business hub for the rest of the Ruhr, and much of its character still derives from a handful of imposing, early twentieth-century commercial buildings which, by their sheer solidity, testify to the confidence of the local business class in the years before the Depression. The 1929 **Deutschlandhaus** on Lindenallee is perhaps the pick of them, a slim, elegant Bauhaus proto-skyscraper with graceful rounded corners and a small internal shopping arcade. A cluster of Weimar-era monuments is also found along **Kettwigstrasse**, the city's main shopping street, which leads north from the Hauptbahnhof. Here, the much-loved 1928 **Lichtburg** cinema was forcibly "Aryanized" – expropriated from its Jewish owners – under the Nazis. Germany's largest cinema, it hides a beautiful 1950s auditorium behind its no-nonsense Bauhaus facade.

> **FROM COMEDY TO KRUPP**
>
> For many Germans, Essen's best-known son is **Heinz Rühmann** (1902–94), Germany's greatest screen comic, whose extraordinary film career spanned the Weimar Republic, Third Reich, Cold War and post-reunification eras and whose best-loved film – the school comedy *Die Feuerzangenbowle* – still enjoys *Rocky Horror*-style cult status more than seventy years after it was first shown. For the rest of the world, however, the city's name is synonymous with that of the **Krupp family**, the powerful steel-to-armaments dynasty whose rise mirrored the city's own ascent to industrial greatness during the nineteenth century, and whose commercial genius and questionable political judgement accurately reflect the experience of Germany in the first half of the twentieth century.

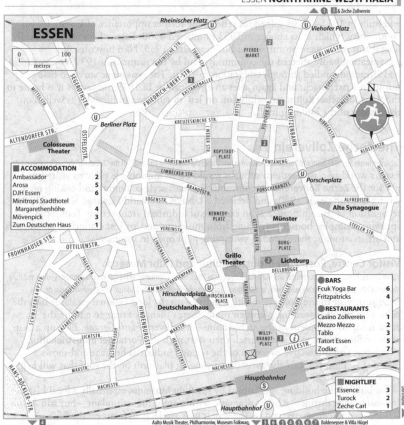

Münster

Burgplatz 2 • **Münster** Mon–Fri 6.30am–6.30pm, Sat & Sun 9am–7.30pm; no access for visitors during Mass • Free • ⓦ dom-essen.de •
Domschatz Tues–Sat 10am–5pm, Sun 11.30am–5pm • €5 • ⓦ domschatz-essen.de

Rather overshadowed by the surrounding commercial bombast, Essen's Dom –
commonly known as the **Münster** – was founded as a convent in 852 AD by Altfrid,
bishop of Hildesheim, and has a sturdy octagonal tower dating from around 1000 AD,
which survived both the fire that destroyed the rest of the church in 1275 and the
World War II bombing raids. The Münster's low, attenuated profile is partly an
accident of topography and partly the result of its curious physical attachment to a
second church, the tiny **Johanniskirche**, reached across the tenth-century atrium or
Paradies at the cathedral's west end. The Münster's treasury or **Domschatz** is well worth
a look: its treasures include the jewel-encrusted *Lilienkrone* – the crown reputedly used
to crown Otto III in Aachen in 983 AD – as well as a series of fabulous gilded crosses
dating from the tenth and eleventh centuries. The cathedral's most famous treasure,
however, is the **Goldene Madonna**, a graceful, gilded wood figure which dates from
around 980 AD and which has its own chapel in the main body of the cathedral.

Alte Synagoge

Edmund-Körner Platz 1 • Tues–Sun 10am–6pm • Free • ⓦ alte-synagoge.essen.de

A few hundred metres to the east of the Münster – marooned by speeding traffic
– stands the **Alte Synagoge**, one of Germany's largest. Designed by Edmund Körner

and built in 1911–13, its splendour reflects the former importance of Essen's Jewish community, which at its apogee in 1933 numbered 4500. Essen's Jews were politically liberal and many were prominent in business; after 1933, Nazi boycotts and Aryanization badly affected the community and by the summer of 1939 its population had already dwindled through emigration to 1650. The synagogue survived being burnt on Kristallnacht and again after an electrical fire in 1979; nowadays it is home to the **Haus Jüdischer Kultur**, an exhibition on Jewish culture and lifestyles as well as on the history of the building itself.

The Zeche Zollverein

Gelsenkirchener Str. 181 • Tram #107 (direction "Gelsenkirchen") from the city centre and alight at the "Zollverein" stop • ⓦ zollverein.de

Essen's working-class northern suburbs would be an improbable place to visit were it not for the **Zeche Zollverein**, an enormous Bauhaus-style coal mine and coking plant dating from the early 1930s and declared a UNESCO World Heritage Site in 2001 in recognition of its significance as an example of industrial architecture. Today, the sprawling complex houses everything from museums and art installations to restaurants and artists' studios; there's even a swimming pool open in summer.

Visitor Centre, Portal der Industriekultur and Ruhr Museum

Visitor Centre, Portal der Industriekultur and Ruhr Museum all daily 10am–6pm • Combined ticket for Portal der Industriekultur and Ruhr Museum €10 including temporary exhibitions, or €8 without; English audio-guide for Ruhr Museum €3 • ⓦ ruhrmuseum.de

Start your visit to the Zollverein with a journey up the long external escalator into the mine's former coal-washing plant; en route, there's plenty of time to admire the retro-futuristic grandeur of the architecture – it's all very *Flash Gordon*. Pick up a map at the **visitor centre** to orient yourself then start with the **Portal der Industriekultur**, which gives an interactive overview of the region's industrial heritage and shows a 360-degree film; you can also ascend to a viewing platform on the roof that will help you orient yourself.

The bulk of the building is occupied by the **Ruhr Museum**, essentially a local history museum made distinctive by its dramatic setting amid the redundant – but still *in situ* – hoppers and conveyors, and by the way it uses artefacts to focus on the life experiences of individual Ruhr dwellers. Its broad sweep encompasses war and industrial decline, the role of British and Polish migrants in the Ruhr's industrialization and the region's obsession with football. There's good labelling in English, and regular temporary exhibitions on Ruhr-related themes.

Red Dot Design Museum

Tues–Sun 11am–6pm, last entry 5pm • €6,€9 during temporary exhibitions • ⓦ red-dot-design-museum.de

The Zeche Zollverein's former boiler house was redesigned by Norman Foster to house the **Red Dot Design Museum**, the world's largest exhibition of contemporary design, with a changing selection of some 2000 products selected annually by international jury and encompassing anything from USB drives and power tools to electric bikes or furniture. Perhaps inevitably, it sometimes has the feel of a department store where you can't actually buy anything – though there is a gift shop at the entrance – and you'll probably find yourself questioning the merits of some choices. Nevertheless the displays are engrossing and make inventive, often witty use of the dramatic, vertigo-inducing space.

The Kokerei (coking plant) and The Palace of Projects

Palace of Projects Fri–Sun 11am–5pm • €4 • Ice rink Dec & early Jan Mon–Fri 3–8pm (10am–8pm during Christmas holidays), Sat 10am–10pm, Sun 10am–8pm; Fri Eisdisco 8pm–midnight • Day-ticket €6.50 • Pool July & Aug daily noon–6pm • Free

The Zollverein complex becomes less crowded the further you venture from the visitor centre, and by the time you reach the distant **coking plant** it's positively deserted. It's worth the trek, however, to see Ilya and Emilia Kabakov's eccentric art installation, **The**

Palace of Projects, which documents several of their projects, in the dark, echoing former salt store.

The **coking plant** itself is gargantuan, though without familiar architectural reference points it's difficult to grasp the sheer size of the place. Human scale is restored in December and January, when an **ice rink** opens in the shadow of the coke ovens. In summer there's an open-air **pool**.

South of the centre

South of the Hauptbahnhof, two of Essen's cultural jewels fringe the leafy Stadtgarten: the **Philharmonie** and the more eye-catching **Aalto-Musiktheater**, a characteristically white, elegant structure by the Finnish modernist Alvar Aalto, which opened in 1988. A short distance further south, the **Museum Folkwang** houses an exceptional collection of French and German art.

Museum Folkwang

Museumsplatz 1 • Tues–Thurs, Sat & Sun 10am–6pm, Fri 10am–10pm • €5, English audio-guide €4 • ⓦ museum-folkwang.de

The superb **Museum Folkwang** is reason enough for a visit to Essen. David Chipperfield's coolly understated modernist extension – which opened in 2010 – has created a series of spacious galleries grouped around serene internal gardens; the new building seamlessly incorporates the old, with separate areas devoted to nineteenth- and twentieth-century art, contemporary art, graphic art and temporary exhibitions.

The collection's undoubted highlight is the nineteenth- and twentieth-century section, kicking off with the Romantic period and works by Caspar David Friedrich and Karl Friedrich Schinkel before romping through a treasure-trove of French Impressionists and post-Impressionists: paintings include some wonderful late Van Goghs, Cézanne's *Le Carré de Bibémus* and Signac's pointilliste *Le Pont des Arts*. German Expressionist works include Schmidt-Rottluff's spiky *Leipziger Strasse with Electric Tram* from 1914 and the near-abstract *Forms at Play* by Franz Marc, painted the same year. The roll call of modernist greats continues with works by Braque, Léger, Picasso, Beckmann and Kandinsky; post-1945 highlights include work by Mark Rothko, Yves Klein and Gerhard Richter.

12

The Villa Hügel and around

Hügel 15 • Tues–Sun 10am–6pm • €5, villa leaflet in English €0.30, exhibiton leaflet in English €0.50 • ⓦ villahuegel.de • S-Bahn #6 to Essen-Hügel

The **Villa Hügel** is the Neoclassical mansion built between 1868 and 1873 to his own designs by industrialist **Alfred Krupp** (1850–87) in a lush, forested setting south of the city. It's reached by a meandering path through the park from the S-Bahn Essen-Hügel station, and is considerably bigger than photographs suggest; inside, the rooms are monumental in scale, if a little ponderous in style. Pick up a leaflet in English at the entrance, as you'll be lost without it.

Next to the main house, the former guesthouse now hosts an exhibition on the history of the Krupp dynasty, which attained greatness in the nineteenth century under the leadership of Alfred Krupp, only to acquire notoriety during the Third Reich under Gustav Krupp and his son Alfried Krupp von Bohlen und Halbach for their use of slave labour in the manufacture of armaments. An upstairs room deals with this dark chapter in the company's history, but the displays are in German only.

The Baldeneysee

Am Regattaturm, Freiherr vom Stein Str. 206a • Hourly cruises late April to early Oct daily 11.10am–7.10pm • €11 • ⓦ baldeneysee.com • S-Bahn #6 to Essen-Hügel

An obvious antidote to Essen's heavyweight attactions is a two-hour cruise on the **Baldeneysee**, an artificially widened stretch of the Ruhr just south of the Villa Hügel that makes for a popular summer excursion as well as a focus for rowing and sailing. The lake is fringed by low, wooded hills and is rather picturesque.

ARRIVAL AND GETTING AROUND

By train The Hauptbahnhof is at the southern edge of the city centre.

Destinations Cologne (up to 4 per hour; 51min–1hr 3min); Dortmund (up to 6 per hour; 21–23mins); Duisburg (up to 8 per hour; 10–18min); Düsseldorf (up to 8 per hour; 25–34mins); Münster (2–3 per hour; 50 min–1hr 6min).

By public transport To get to grips with this large city, you'll need to master the extensive public transport system, which includes bus, tram and U-Bahn (⊛evag.de)

as well as trains to the suburbs and neighbouring cities. Ticketing is integrated with other Ruhr communities through the VRR regional transport network: you can travel up to three stops for €1.50 on a *Kurzstrecke* ticket or through most of the city on a €2.50 Class A ticket. A €6.50 *TagesTicket* allows unlimited travel from the moment you validate it until 3am the following morning. *NachtExpress* night buses serve outlying districts after normal services have ceased, departing hourly from the Hauptbahnhof.

INFORMATION

Tourist office Opposite the north exit from the Hauptbahnhof at Am Hauptbahnhof 2 (Mon–Fri 9am–6pm, Sat 10am–4pm; ☎0201 887 23 33, ⊛essen-tourismus.de).

Discount card The Essen Card, available from the tourist office, offers free travel on public transport as well as reductions on museums and attractions (24hr €9, 48hr €14, 72hr €19).

ACCOMMODATION

Ambassador Viehofer Str. 22–23 ☎0201 24 77 30, ⊛ambassador-essen.de. Comfortable, slightly bland family-run hotel right in the central pedestrian zone, with private parking and some roomy singles. Handy for the city centre's nightlife scene. **€67**

Arosa Rüttenscheider Str. 149 ☎0201 722 60, ⊛hotel-arosa-essen.de. Classy modern 4-star hotel in a great location right on the Rü, but it's also close to the Messe, so watch out for price hikes during conferences and exhibitions. Various leisure-oriented package deals available. **€99**

DJH Essen Pastoratsberg 2 ☎0201 49 11 63, ⊛essen.jugendherberge.de; S-Bahn to Essen-Werden, then bus #190. Essen's youth hostel is in the pretty half-timbered suburb of Werden, south of the Baldeneysee. The bulk of the accommodation is in four- to six-bed dorms, but there are some doubles. Dorms **€20.90**, doubles **€67.80**

Minitrops Stadthotel Margarethenhöhe Steile Str. 46 ☎0201 438 60, ⊛mmhotels.de. Boutique-style hotel in a historic building in the garden suburb of Margaretenhöhe, southwest of the centre. Rooms are bright, modern and decorated with contemporary art, and come with minibars, a/c, en-suite shower and WC. Best rates are available at weekends. **€121**

Mövenpick Am Hauptbahnhof 2 ☎0201 170 80, ⊛moevenpick-essen.com. Slick, very central business-class hotel, with tasteful decor, spacious a/c rooms and remarkably good deals if you pick your dates. Breakfast not included. **€126**

Zum Deutschen Haus Kastanienallee 16 ☎0201 23 29 89, ⊛hotel-zum-deutschen-haus.com. A good budget option at the northern end of the city centre with a traditional German restaurant on the ground floor. Cheapest rooms share facilities, and there are some singles. **€55**

EATING, DRINKING AND ENTERTAINMENT

For laidback drinking and cosmopolitan eating, head south to Rüttenscheider Strasse (or **"Rü"** for short; U-Bahn #11 to Martinstrasse, or trams #101 or #107). There's a more raucous, younger edge to bars in the **city centre**, particularly around Viehofer Platz close to the university.

RESTAURANTS

Casino Zollverein Schacht XII Gelsenkirchener Str. 181 ☎0201 830 240, ⊛casino-zollverein.de. Stylish restaurant at the Zeche Zollverein beneath a spectacular, rough-hewn 6m-high concrete ceiling, with dishes such as rosemary polenta with smoked tofu, mushrooms and hazelnuts, plus a €29 Sun lunch buffet. Mains €15.50 up; steaks from €25. Tues–Sun 11.20am–midnight.

Mezzo Mezzo Kettwigerstr. 36 ☎0201 22 52 65, ⊛mezzomezzo.de. Casual but classy modern Italian in

the Lichtburg cinema, with mountainous *bruschette* from €4.10, enormous portions of pasta from €7.50 and excellent, if pricey, fish dishes, plus chalked-up daily specials. Mon–Sat 11am–midnight.

Tablo Huyssenallee 5, Essen-Südviertel ☎0201 811 95 85, ⊛tablo-restaurant.de. Critically acclaimed, stylish, modern Turkish restaurant close to the Philharmonie and Aalto-Musiktheater. Salads from €10, meat or poultry mains from around €16 and veggie dishes from €13.50. There's also fresh fish daily. Mon–Thurs 11am–11.30pm,

Fri & Sat 11am–midnight, Sun noon–11.30pm.
Tatort Essen Rüttenscheider Str. 182 ☎ 0201 32 03 99 80, ⓦ tatort-gastronomie.de. Bags of enthusiasm and a hand-written menu – featuring the likes of fennel and avocado salad with lightly cooked salmon and pomegranate, or turbot with lentils & Thai asparagus – set the tone at this Rüttenscheid gastro haunt. Mains from around €22. Mon 6–10.30pm, Tues–Sat noon–2.30pm & 6–10.30pm.

Zodiac Witteringstr. 41–43 ☎ 0201 77 12 12, ⓦ restaurant-zodiac.de. Charming veggie place in Rüttenscheid, a little off the beaten track but worth the trek for its reasonably priced Asian and European food. Main courses around €10–15. The pizza place next door at no. 43 is owned by the same people, with pizzas from €7. Zodiac Mon–Wed & Fri–Sun 6pm–midnight; pizzeria daily noon–midnight.

ON THE TRAIL OF THE RUHR'S INDUSTRIAL HERITAGE

The Ruhr has experienced the same structural difficulties faced by similar "rust belt" regions elsewhere, but it has risen to the challenge of reusing its redundant industrial sites in a very different way. Instead of bulldozing them, many have been preserved in acknowledgement of the historical significance and tourist potential of these so-called "cathedrals of industry". Today, a 400km road route and a well-signposted 700km cycle trail form the **Route der Industriekultur** (Industrial Heritage Trail; ⓦ route-industriekultur.de), linking former steelworks, coal mines and slagheaps to offer a fascinating insight into the technology of heavy industry, with a healthy injection of contemporary culture. Some of the most significant attractions are dealt with in the individual city sections in this chapter, but others are listed below.

You can **rent bikes** from one of the many cycle stations scattered across the region. There are two cycle hire networks: Nextbike's Metropolradruhr (ⓦ metropolradruhr.de; €1 for 30min) and RevierRad (ⓦ revierrad.de; €6 for 2hr). You have to register with Metropolradruhr and book in advance with RevierRad.

Aquarius Wassermuseum Burgstr. 70, Mülheim an der Ruhr ⓦ aquarius-wassermuseum.de; S-Bahn #S1 from Dortmund, Essen, Düsseldorf, Duisburg; #S3 from Oberhausen to Mülheim-Styrum, then a 10min walk. Built by August Thyssen in 1892–93 to provide a nearby ironworks with water, this splendid mock-medieval water tower houses a water-themed museum on fourteen levels. Entry €4. Tues–Sun 10am–6pm.

Deutsches Bergbau-Museum Am Bergbaumuseum 28, Bochum ⓦ www.bergbaumuseum.de. The world's largest museum devoted to the subject of mining, housed in a huge brick pile just north of Bochum city centre and dominated by a 63m-high winding tower that once graced Dortmund's Germania mine. You can climb it after you've toured the museum's displays, which include a substantial stretch of show mine. Entry €6.50. Tues–Fri 8.30am–5pm, Sat & Sun 10am–5pm.

Gasometer Arenastr. 11, Oberhausen ⓦ gasometer .de; bus or tram from Oberhausen Hauptbahnhof to Neue Mitte. This 117m-high gasometer next to the CentrO shopping mall was built in 1929 and now provides a spectacular exhibition space for large-scale works of art, as well as a viewing platform with panoramic views over the western Ruhr. Entry €9. Tues–Sun 10am–6pm.

Kokerei Hansa Emscherallee 11, Dortmund ⓦ industriedenkmal-stiftung.de; U-Bahn #47 from Dortmund Hauptbahnhof to Parsevalstrasse, then a 5min walk. This 1920s coking plant has been preserved

as a gigantic sculpture; a trail leads visitors into the imposing compressor house with its huge engines, and to the coal tower, from which there are panoramic views over Dortmund. Entry €8 with tour. April–Oct Tues–Sun 10am–6pm; Nov–March Tues–Sun 10am–4pm.

LVR-Industriemuseum Hansastr. 20, adjacent to Oberhausen Hauptbahnhof ⓦ industriemuseum .lvr.de. The former Altenberg zinc works now houses a permanent exhibition on heavy industry, with everything from giant ingot moulds, mill rollers and a steam locomotive to a 53-tonne steam hammer. Entry €4.50. Tues–Fri 10am–5pm, Sat & Sun 11am–6pm.

Schiffshebewerk Henrichenburg Am Hebewerk 2, Waltrop ⓦ lwl.org; bus #231 from Recklinghausen Hauptbahnhof, stop "Kanalstrasse". Opened in 1899 by Kaiser Wilhelm II, this impressive ship-lift at Waltrop north of Dortmund lifted barges 14m from the lower to the upper reaches of the Dortmund–Ems Canal. Attractions include a collection of preserved boats and barges. Entry €4. Tues–Sun 10am–6pm.

Zeche Zollern Grubenweg 5, Dortmund ⓦ lwl.org; train from Dortmund Hauptbahnhof to Bövinghausen. The most beautiful colliery in the Ruhrgebiet is an architecturally distinguished selection of Gothic revival and Jugendstil buildings. Restoration work on the main machine hall will be complete in 2015. Entry €6. Tues–Sun 10am–6pm.

12

12

BARS

Fcuk Yoga Bar Emma Str. 13 ☎0201 87 78 25 96, ⓦfcuk-yoga.de. Stylish, distinctive Rüttenscheid cocktail and cigar bar with chilled music and creative drinks such as Gin Basil Smash or Shanghai Strawberry Slam alongside more classic Bloody Marys and mojitos (cocktails from €7). Mon–Sat 6pm–2am.

NIGHTLIFE AND ENTERTAINMENT

CLUBS AND LIVE MUSIC

Essence Viehofer Str. 38–52 ☎0201 437 595 50, ⓦclub-essence.com. Classic big dance club in a converted cinema, hosting big-name guest DJs and live erotic dancing. There are two dancefloors plus a bistro and lounge. Fri 11pm–late, Sat 10pm–late.

Turock Viehofer Platz 3 ☎0201 490 37 80, ⓦturock.de. Grungy, trendy, student-friendly, city-centre rock club, disco and lounge, with regular live bands and, in summer, a big outdoor terrace. Clubnights Fri & Sat 10pm–6am.

Zeche Carl Wilhelm-Nieswandt-Allee 100 ☎0201 834 44 10, ⓦzechecarl.de. Cabaret, live music venue and arts centre housed in redundant mine buildings. The venue also hosts clubnights, including gothic, post-punk and new wave party *Nachttanz*. Clubnights generally Fri & Sat 10pm–late.

THEATRE AND CONCERT VENUES

Aalto Musiktheater Opernplatz 10 ☎0201 8122 200,

Fritzpatricks Girardet Str. 2 ☎0201 79 88 877, ⓦfritzpatricks.com. Boisterous Rüttenscheid Irish bar with the usual pubby trappings, sport on the big screen and regular karaoke nights. There's Guinness and Kilkenny on draught, a wide selection of Irish and Scottish whiskies and a steaks-to-burgers food menu. Mon–Thurs & Sun 11am–1am, Fri & Sat 11am–3am.

ⓦtheater-essen.de. This elegant Alvar Aalto-designed modernist theatre is the city's main venue for classical opera and ballet.

Colosseum Theater Altendorfer Str. 1 ☎0201 240 20, ⓦcolosseumtheater.de. Vast, converted former Krupp workshop preserving its industrial atmosphere but now staging musicals and other big-budget spectaculars, from comedy to rock concerts.

Grillo Theater Theaterplatz 11 ☎0201 812 22 00, ⓦtheater-essen.de. The stately old Grillo Theater is the city's most prestigious venue for classical drama, with a repertoire that ranges from Shakespeare to Thomas Mann, plus contemporary writing.

Philharmonie Huyssenallee 53 ☎0201 8122 200, ⓦphilharmonie-essen.de. The city's main concert hall, home venue for the Essener Philharmoniker as well as hosting classical and jazz performances by big-name visiting orchestras.

Dortmund

Perched at the Ruhr's eastern extremity, **DORTMUND** is a former free imperial city and Hanseatic League member that grew rich in the Middle Ages from its position on the Hellweg, a major trading route, before declining after the Thirty Years' War. In the nineteenth century it re-emerged from provincial obscurity thanks to coal, steel and beer: at one point only Milwaukee brewed more. All three industries declined in the late twentieth century and there's now just one major brewer, the Dortmunder Actien-Brauerei, plus a brace of smaller ones. Information and biotechnology are the economic motors of the "new" Dortmund, which seems to have mastered the transition from heavy industry relatively well; the old Union brewery with its giant illuminated "U" still looms over the city, but nowadays it houses art, not beer, and shares the skyline with a scattering of funky modern office towers. Nevertheless, the surviving medieval street pattern and a scattering of worthwhile sights ensure that Dortmund preserves a sense of its long history.

The city centre

Dortmund's compact, walkable **centre** is surrounded by a ring of streets following the course of the medieval walls, of which one vestige, the reconstructed **Adlerturm** on Ostwall, survives. It contains a children's **museum** of local history (Tues, Wed & Fri 10am–1pm, Thurs & Sun 10am–5pm, Sat noon–5pm; €2.50). The main east–west axis and principal shopping street follows the course of the medieval Hellweg and is known at its western end as Westenhellweg and in the east as **Ostenhellweg**. Here, a handful of prewar stone buildings provide the backdrop for two of Dortmund's four

surviving medieval churches, the looming, thirteenth-century **Reinoldikirche** (daily 10am–6pm; free) and the somewhat older **Marienkirche** (see below). The former is considered the city's principal church and is named after its patron saint, but the latter is the more interesting of the two.

Marienkirche

Kleppingstr. 3 · Tues, Wed, Fri 10am–noon & 2–4pm, Thurs 10am–noon & 2–6pm, Sat 10am–1pm · Free · ⓦ st-marien-dortmund.de

The twelfth-century Romanesque **Marienkirche** faces the Reinoldikirche across the street to the south. It's the oldest of the city's medieval churches and though it was heavily damaged during World War II its treasures were saved. Foremost of these is the radiant red, gold and blue Gothic altar triptych painted by local boy Conrad von Soest in 1420 and considered one of the masterpieces of German medieval art. It depicts scenes from the life of Christ and the Virgin Mary. What survives is incomplete: the panels were butchered in the eighteenth century to fit it into a new, Baroque high altar, which itself fell victim to a World War II air raid. Less battered by history is the *Berswordt Altar* in the north aisle, which dates from 1395 and depicts the Crucifixion. The sixteenth-century choir stalls portray human weaknesses – adultery, theft, excess, vanity and disobedience – in light-hearted fashion.

The Petrikirche and Propsteikirche

West along Westenhellweg, the fourteenth-century Gothic **Petrikirche** (Tues–Fri 11am–5pm, Sat 10am–4pm; free; ⓦ stptrido.de) lost its Baroque accretions to wartime bombs, leaving a plain, coherent setting for its chief treasure, an extraordinary sixteenth-century Flemish altar originally carved for the city's Franciscan monastery. The largest surviving Flemish altar of the period, it's also one of the largest works of Gothic church art anywhere. The nearby **Propsteikirche** (Mon 10am–7pm, Tues, Thurs & Fri 9am–7pm, Wed, Sat & Sun 9.30am–7pm; free) – which remained Catholic after the Reformation – is similarly austere following wartime destruction, but houses a winged altar dating from 1470 to 1480.

Museum für Kunst und Kulturgeschichte

Hansastr. 3 · Tues, Wed, Fri & Sun 10am–5pm, Thurs 10am–8pm, Sat noon–5pm · €5 · ⓦ museendortmund.de/mkk

Near the Hauptbahnhof on Hansastrasse, the eclectic and engrossing **Museum für Kunst und Kulturgeschichte** (Museum for Art and Cultural History) occupies the rotunda of an Art Deco former bank building. Friezes at the entrance depict the crises of the early 1920s, including the hyperinflation and the French occupation of the Ruhr, while inside there's a section on the city's history, a collection of religious art and paintings by Lovis Corinth, Max Slevogt and Caspar David Friedrich, among others. There's also a strong emphasis on applied arts, the result of the museum's origins as a pedagogic institution, charged with the task of improving the quality of Germany's manufactured goods, with everything from Meissen porcelain and Tiffany glass to groovy modernist furniture by Marcel Breuer and Verner Panton.

The Deutsches Fussballmuseum

Königswall · ⓦ fussballmuseum.de

Occupying a striking modern building on a prominent site opposite the Hauptbahnhof, the impressive new **Deutsches Fussballmuseum** opens in 2015 to celebrate all things associated with German football, not least four World Cup victories – the most recent in 2014 – and the worldwide renown of the Bundesliga, of which local favourites Borussia Dortmund are a prominent member. The aim is to engage with the cultural history of the game as much as with the individual historic exhibits, which will be displayed in five themed zones exploring different aspects of football, from the national team to trainers and tactics.

The Dortmunder U and Museum Ostwall

Leonie-Reygers-Terrasse 1 · Museum Ostwall Tues, Wed, Sat & Sun 11am–6pm, Thurs & Fri 11am–8pm · €5 or €8 with temporary exhibitions · ⓦ museumostwall.dortmund.de

Immediately to the west of the ring of medieval streets that defines the city centre, the **Dortmunder U** (ⓦ dortmunder-u.de) is a striking, early modernist tower built in 1926–27 for the Union brewery and long since regarded as the symbol of Dortmund. Redundant for many years, it now houses a number of arts and cultural organizations, the most important of which is the city's principal art museum, the confusingly named **Museum Ostwall**. The museum, relocated from its original site on Ostwall, presents its impressive collection of twentieth- and twenty-first-century art in reverse chronological order. Things kick off on the fourth floor, where the Fluxus movement of the 1960s forms the core of the display, which then regresses through Nouveau Réalisme back to Expressionism, with works by Ernst Ludwig Kirchner, Emil Nolde and Karl Schmidt-Rottluff. The fifth floor is devoted to the art of the last half-century, with works by Joseph Beuys among others; the sixth floor is used for temporary exhibitions.

North of the centre

North of the Hauptbahnhof and traditionally the wrong side of the tracks, Dortmund's **Nordstadt** is a sprawling mix of docks, industry and close-packed nineteenth-century housing that has lately acquired an arty, hip overlay. Though it's too big (and in places a bit too dodgy) for carefree strolling, it does repay selective exploration.

Mahn- und Gedenkstätte Steinwache

Steinstr. 50 · Tues–Sun 10am–5pm · Free · ⓦ ns-gedenkstaetten.de/nrw/dortmund

Close to the northern exit from the Hauptbahnhof, the **Mahn- und Gedenkstätte Steinwache** houses an exhibit on the Nazi terror in Dortmund in a former Gestapo prison. Dortmund's prosecutors were openly pro-Nazi even before Hitler came to power, siding with fascist thugs against the local police in a notorious 1932 case, in which the police, not their Nazi attackers, were put on trial. During the Third Reich, thirty thousand people were imprisoned in this building; in one of the cells you can see the names of some of the prison's many inmates scratched into the wall.

Brauerei-Museum

Steigerstr. 16 • Tues, Wed, Fri & Sun 10am–5pm, Thurs 10am–8pm, Sat noon–5pm • €2.50 • ⓦ museendortmund.de/brauereimuseum

The **Brauerei-Museum** is housed in the former machine hall of the Hansa-Brauerei and focuses on the commercialized, large-scale beer production for which Dortmund became famous in the nineteenth and twentieth centuries, in particular the glory years after 1950.

South of the centre

A ten-minute walk south of the centre along Hohe Strasse, the leafy **Kreuzviertel** (U-Bahn Saarlandstrasse) has the visual appeal much of the city centre lacks, particularly around Arnecke Strasse, Vincke Platz and Liebigstrasse. Here, lovely Jugendstil facades rise above relaxed neighbourhood cafés and bars, making this a good part of town to let the pace slip. Suitably refreshed, continue south to the **Westfalenpark** (daily 9am–11pm; €3), home to several attractions, from art exhibitions to the **Deutsches Rosarium** and its two thousand-plus varieties of rose. It's overshadowed by the city's 212m-high TV tower, the **Florianturm** (Mon–Sat 11am–10pm, Sun 9am–10pm; €2.50), which you can ascend for spectacular outdoor panoramas. West of the park, **Signal Iduna Park**, the 80,000-seat home of Borussia Dortmund, rises behind the **Westfalenhalle**, the city's largest live music and exhibition venue.

ARRIVAL AND GETTING AROUND   DORTMUND

By plane The airport (☎0231 92 13 01, ⓦdortmund-airport.de) is connected with the Hauptbahnhof by regular shuttle buses (hourly 5am–10.30pm; €6).

By train Dortmund's Hauptbahnhof is on the north side of the city centre.

Destinations Cologne (2–3 per hour; 1hr 10min–1hr 29min); Münster (2 per hour; 29–51min); Paderborn (every 2hr; 1hr 8min); Soest (every 30min; 37–47min).

By public transport If you're visiting museums outside the centre you may need to use public transport (ⓦ bus-und-bahn.de), which includes trams, buses and the U-Bahn, and is integrated with neighbouring cities in the VRR regional transport network for the Ruhr.

INFORMATION

Tourist office Opposite the Hauptbahnhof at Max-von-der-Grün-Platz 5–6 (Mon–Sat 10am–6pm; ☎0231 18 99 92 22, ⓦdortmund-tourismus.de). You can book accommodation and tickets for events through the tourist office website.

ACCOMMODATION

Ibis Dortmund City Märkische Str. 73 ☎0231 18 57 70, ⓦibishotel.com. Comfortable, if bland, modern budget hotel southeast of the centre and about a 15min walk from the best of the Kreuzviertel; rooms have WC and shower plus wireless internet and cable TV. It has three rooms equipped for people of limited mobility. **€79**

Jugendgästehaus Silberstr. 24–26 ☎0231 14 00 74, ⓦdjh-wl.de/jh/dortmund. Large, modern hostel right in the city centre, with plenty of doubles and four-bed rooms, as well as a small number of singles. Some rooms have internet; cheaper rooms share shower and WC. Open 24hr; check-in from 12.30pm. Breakfast included. Dorms **€27.30**, doubles **€66.60**

Pullman Dortmund Lindemannstr. 88 ☎0231 911 30, ⓦpullmanhotels.com. Upmarket modern hotel close to

Westfalenpark, the Signal Iduna stadium and the Kreuzviertel's bar and restaurant scene, with spacious, tastefully decorated rooms, internet access, a fitness centre, sauna and spa. Rates are cheaper at weekends. **€143**

The Grey Schmiedingstr. 11–13 ☎0231 419 103 00, ⓦthegrey-hotel.de. Stylish and affordable boutique hotel close to the Hauptbahnhof and Deutsches Fussballmuseum. The cool, understated grey decor reflects the hotel's name. **€89**

Union Arndtstr. 66 ☎0231 55 00 70, ⓦhotel.de. Pleasant, family-run hotel garni in a peaceful residential area a 10min walk east of the centre, with some good-value singles. Rooms have shower, WC, TV and phone. **€99**

EATING AND DRINKING

Eating and drinking in Dortmund divides between the **city centre**'s Italians and traditional brewery-owned places, and more relaxed offerings in the **Nordstadt** and **Kreuzviertel**, where boundaries between café, bar and restaurant tend to blur. Many of the city's best gourmet offerings, however, are in the outer **suburbs**.

12

RESTAURANTS

Jankas Lokal & Biergarten Braunschweiger Str. 22, Nordstadt ☎ 0231 840 46 06, ⓦ jankas-lokal.de. Trendy Nordstadt place with fresh produce from its own garden and an Italian- and French-influenced menu serving the likes of *vichyssoise*, *petits farcis* with lamb or veal in aspic with *sauce rémoulade*. Main courses €16–19; six-course tasting menu €45. Tues–Sat 6–11pm.

Kitchen Club Plauenerstr. 2 Kreuzviertel ☎ 0231 589 77 06. Bright, candy-coloured canteen-style neighbourhood restaurant with creative, good-value "Deutsche crossover" food, including salmon and scallop *shashlik* with mint yoghurt sauce plus plenty of veggie options. Mains from around €10. Daily 11am–11pm.

Pfefferkorn's No. 1 Markt 6 ☎ 0231 52 58 15, ⓦ no1 .pfefferkorn-restaurants.de. Darkly opulent, traditional restaurant that's a touch more refined than its neighbours, with an emphasis on steak. The menu's substantial selection of meat and fish options also includes *Matjes* herring for €11.90 and €12.40 *Schnitzels*. Daily 11am–midnight.

Schönes Leben Liebigstr. 23, Kreuzviertel ☎ 0231 33 04 52 27, ⓦ schoenes-leben-dortmund.de. Spacious, informal, all-day neighbourhood bistro/bar in the Kreuzviertel, with breakfasts from €5.50, pasta from €8.50 and more substantial meat and fish dishes from €15.90. Mon–Sat 9.30am–late, Sun 11am–late.

BARS

Brauereiausschank Zum Alten Markt Markt 3 ☎ 0231 57 22 17, ⓦ altermarkt-dortmund.de. Traditional trappings and old Westphalian specialities from around €9.50 are the order of the day at this brewery-owned city-centre beer hall, which also serves Dortmunder Thiers and Hövels beer. Mon–Thurs 10am–1am, Fri 10am–3am, Sat 9am–3am, Sun 11am–11pm.

Hövels Hausbrauerei Hoher Wall. 5–7 ☎ 0231 914 54 70, ⓦ hoevels-hausbrauerei.de. Big city-centre *Hausbrauerei* serving its own distinctive top-fermented *Original* beer that's neither *Pilsner* nor an *Alt*; from €2.80. There's also hearty German food from around €12. Mon–Thurs & Sun 11am–midnight, Fri & Sat 11am–1am.

SissiKingKong Landwehrstr. 17, Nordstadt ☎ 0231 728 25 78, ⓦ sissikingkong.de. Groovy ambience and music make this quirky café-bar a favourite among the Nordstadt arty crowd. There's also a short, Italian-influenced food menu, ranging from nibbles to main courses (around €10 up) and a club in the basement. Tues–Sun 6pm–late.

Subrosa Gneisenaustr. 56, Nordstadt ☎ 0231 82 08 07, ⓦ hafenschaenke.de. A battered, kitschy opulence, live bands and football on TV are the attractions of this arty, studenty Nordstadt bar. Mon–Sat 6pm–late, open earlier on Sat if there's Bundesliga; live gigs 7.30pm.

NIGHTLIFE AND ENTERTAINMENT

Domicil Hansastr. 7–11 ☎ 0231 862 90 30, ⓦ domicil-dortmund.de. A stylish blend of café-bar and serious jazz venue, with a bit of world music thrown in, all in a landmark Weimar-era building in the city centre.

Konzerthaus Dortmund Brückstr. 21 ☎ 0231 22 69 62 00, ⓦ konzerthaus-dortmund.de. Modern city-centre

concert hall that is the home of the Dortmunder Philharmoniker, and also provides a venue for visiting orchestras, choirs and pop acts.

Opernhaus Platz der Alten Synagoge ☎ 0231 50 27 222, ⓦ theaterdo.de. The major venue for opera and ballet in Dortmund; it also stages occasional concerts and musicals.

The Lower Rhine

North of Duisburg the Rhineland's heavy industry gives way to a peaceful, agricultural region dotted with small towns, the place names and flat terrain reflecting the proximity of the Dutch border. Under the Holy Roman Empire the **Duchy of Cleve** counted for something – famously supplying the English king Henry VIII with one of his wives – but these days the region is mainly of interest as an excursion from the Ruhr, with hourly trains from Duisburg making historic **Xanten** a magnet for day-trippers. Beyond it, placid **Kalkar** preserves a more low-key charm.

Xanten

With its reconstructed Roman monuments, teeming shops hawking clothes or assorted trinkets and a miniature tourist train doing endless circuits of the old town in the height of summer, it's easy to spot the tacky side of **XANTEN**, 45 minutes by train from Duisburg, which owes its name to a corruption of the Latin dedication "ad sanctos" ("to the saints"). Yet as the Roman connection suggests, it's one of the oldest towns in

Germany, the mythical birthplace of Siegfried – the hero of the *Nibelungenlied* (see box, p.527) – and still encircled by its **medieval defences**.

Dom St Viktor and the Stiftsmuseum

Dom March–Oct Mon–Sat 10am–6pm, Sun 12.30–5.45pm; Nov–Feb Mon–Sat 10am–5pm, Sun 12.30–5pm • Free • ⓦ stviktor-xanten
.de • **Stiftsmuseum** Kapitel 21 • Tues–Sat 10am–5pm, Sun 11am–6pm • €4 • ⓦ stiftsmuseum-xanten.de

Xanten's chief architectural glory is the imposing twin-towered **Dom St Viktor**, walled off from the rest of the Altstadt in the peaceful **Immunität**, or cathedral close, as if shunning the tourist hubbub outside. The Immunität's intriguing name reflects the fact that the area encircling the cathedral is independent of civil law. The cathedral has a splendid five-aisle Late Gothic nave and contains the grave of the eponymous St Viktor, a Roman-Christian legionnaire martyred in the fourth century. Like much of Xanten, the cathedral was grievously damaged in the final months of World War II; repairs were completed by 1966. Nestling in the lee of the Dom is the **Stiftsmuseum**, which houses the cathedral's treasures, including textiles dating back a thousand years, one of Europe's oldest monstrances and illuminated manuscripts.

SiegfriedMuseum

Kurfürstenstr. 9 • Daily 10am–5pm • €4 • ⓦ siegfriedmuseum-xanten.de

Xanten's connection to the mythical prince Siegfried and the *Nibelungenlied* – a masterpiece of medieval German literature (see box, p.527) – is explored at the **SiegfriedMuseum**, wedged between the tourist office and Dom, where you can not only find out more about who Siegfried was and how the *Lied* came to be written, but also how the *Nibelungenlied* has been used (and misused) in European politics.

LVR-Archäologischer Park and RömerMuseum

Siegfriedstr. 39 • Daily: March–Oct 9am–6pm; Nov 9am–5pm; Dec–Feb 10am–4pm • €9 • ⓦ www.apx.lvr.de

About a ten-minute walk from the cathedral, the reconstructed Roman defences of the **LVR-Archäologischer Park** give an undeniably powerful impression of the sheer size of the Roman settlement of Colonia Ulpia Traiana, which achieved urban status under Emperor Trajan around 100 AD. Once inside the park, you'll find the isolated re-creations of Roman architecture either intriguing or kitsch – there's even a Pompeiian-style restaurant where you can eat Roman dishes. The vast scale of the site is more readily apparent since the re-routing of the B57 highway, which hitherto sliced through it. The **RömerMuseum**, built on the site of the Grosse Thermen – the Roman town's public bath complex – is arguably the most rewarding part of the complex, the modern building's imposing dimensions corresponding to the size of the original. It houses the park's various archeological finds, including Roman weaponry and an ancient freight barge.

ARRIVAL AND INFORMATION   XANTEN

By train From Xanten's Bahnhof outside the medieval walls, Bahnhofstrasse leads directly to the tourist office in the Altstadt. Xanten is connected to Duisburg by regular trains (hourly; 45min).

Tourist office Kurfürstenstr. 9 (daily 10am–5pm; ☏ 02801 77 22 00, ⓦ xanten.de).

ACCOMMODATION AND EATING

Xanten's tourist hordes disappear at 6pm sharp and a delightful evening calm descends on the town, making an overnight stay a good way to experience the place at its peaceful best. There are some inviting and atmospheric accommodation options, and some good places to eat, too.

Gotisches Haus Markt 6 ☏ 02801 70 64 00, ⓦ gotisches-haus-xanten.de. This absolutely gorgeous step-gabled brick Gothic house offers a €12.90 three-course lunch menu Tues–Sat; otherwise there are crêpes, pasta and the likes of *Schweinebraten* with a *Kummel* glaze and Riesling *Sauerkraut*

for around €10. Tues–Sun 11.30am–10pm.
Hotel van Bebber Klever Str. 12 ☏ 02801 66 23, ⓦ hotelvanbebber.de. Lovely, historic hotel that's just far enough away from Markt to escape the worst of the tourist hubbub, with atmospheric public areas festooned with antlers

and 35 distinctive rooms furnished in country style or with antiques. **€109**

Hövelmann's Markt 31 ☏ 02801 40 81, ⊛ hotel-hoevelmann.de. Right on the main square, with views of the Dom and 24 tastefully decorated rooms with shower/WC, cable TV, free wireless internet and minibar. The smart and bright dining room offers dishes such as pink-toast duck with rhubarb and sweet potato ragout; main courses are around €18–25. Restaurant Mon–Sat noon–3pm & 6–11pm, Sun 11.30am–11pm. **€94**

Jugendherberge Xanten-Südsee Bankscher Weg 4 ☏ 02801 985 00, ⊛ xanten.jugendherberge.de. Xanten's youth hostel is some distance from the Altstadt alongside the Freizeit Zentrum Xanten water park, on the banks of the Xantener Südsee. Dorms **€23.90**

Klever Tor Klever Strasse; book through tourist information ☏ 02801 983 00, ⊛ xanten.de. There are three tastefully decorated self-catering apartments in this fourteenth-century gatehouse, which is part of the town's medieval defences. **€75**

Kalkar

Hourly buses take about twenty minutes to connect Xanten's Bahnhof with **KALKAR**. With a strollable Altstadt dotted with stepped gables and a central market square dominated by the fifteenth-century brick Gothic **Rathaus**, it's an attractive place, as sleepy as Xanten is lively and well worth a visit for the artistic and architectural riches left from its fifteenth- and sixteenth-century peak.

St Nicolai

April–Oct Mon–Sat 10–11.45am & 2–5.45pm, Sun 2–5.30pm; Nov–March Mon–Sat 2–3.45pm & Sun 2–5.30pm • Free • ⊛ stnicolai.de

The Late Gothic church of **St Nicolai** just off Markt contains a dazzling array of nine Gothic altars, including a splendid high altar commissioned in 1488 that took three craftsmen twelve years to complete. No less imposing is the wonderful *Sieben-Schmerzen-Altar* in the right aisle, carved by the Kleve craftsman Henrik Douverman, who came to Kalkar in 1515.

Städtisches Museum

Grabenstr. 66 • Summer Tues–Sun 10am–5pm; winter Tues 10am–1pm, Wed–Sun 10am–1pm & 2–5pm • Free

Behind Kalkar's Rathaus, the brick gabled house **In gen Stockvisch** dates from 1500 and is now the **Städtisches Museum**, with displays of local interest and a small collection of nineteenth- and twentieth-century art. It also hosts temporary exhibitions.

Schloss Moyland

Am Schloss 4, Bedburg-Hau • April–Sept Tues–Fri 11am–6pm, Sat & Sun 10am–6pm; Oct–March Tues–Sun 11am–5pm • €7 • ⊛ moyland.de • Bus #44 from Markt (10min)

West of town, the neo-Gothic **Schloss Moyland** houses the private art collection of the Van der Grinten brothers, close associates of Joseph Beuys, whose works form the core of the collection. The museum also mounts themed temporary exhibitions which highlight different aspects of the permanent collection.

ACCOMMODATION AND EATING   KALKAR

Brauhaus Kalkarer Mühle Mühlenstege 8 ☏ 02824 932 30, ⊛ kalkarermuehle.de. *Brauhaus* and restaurant in a preserved (and still functioning) eighteenth-century windmill on the fringe of the Altstadt, with a seasonally changing menu of game, meat and fish dishes from around €12, plus a few veggie options. Tues–Fri 11am–2pm & 5–11pm, Sat & Sun 10am–11pm.

Camping am Wisseler See Zum Wisseler See 15 ☏ 02824 963 10, ⊛ wisseler-see.de. Large 1000-pitch campsite on the shores of a bathing lake just to the north of the town. Open all year round, with pitches for tents and

space for caravans and campervans, plus chalets to rent. Pitch **€10**, plus **€6.50** per person

Hotel Siekmann Kesselstr. 32 ☏ 02824 924 50, ⊛ hotel-siekmann-kalkar.de. Small family-run hotel a short walk from Markt in the northern Altstadt, with eleven individually decorated guest rooms; there's also a restaurant and, in summer, a *Biergarten*. **€80**

Ratskeller Markt 20 ☏ 02824 24 60, ⊛ ratskeller-kalkar .com. Classy restaurant in the brick-vaulted cellar of Kalkar's town hall, serving meat and fish main courses for around €13.50; there's also a tiny terrace fronting Markt. Tues–Sun noon–2pm & 5.30–9pm.

Soest

Set in rich farming country fifty minutes by train east of Dortmund, idyllic **SOEST** was another medieval Hanseatic League member on the Hellweg, with trade links reaching as far as Russia. Cologne's archbishops founded a Pfalz or residence here around 960–965 AD, and were for centuries the town's overlords; Soest's fifteenth-century struggle to be rid of them triggered its decline and by 1500 its glory days were over, leaving an enchanting townscape of half-timbered houses and striking, sage-green sandstone churches whose charm even wartime bombs couldn't erase. Most of what's worth seeing is within the surviving **medieval defences**, a circuit of which makes a pleasant way to spend an hour or two.

Soest's particular culinary claim to fame is that it is supposedly the place where **pumpernickel** – the sticky, black rye bread so characteristic of Westphalia – was invented. The high point of Soest's calendar is the **Kirmes fair** which fills the Altstadt in early November; the Altstadt is also the setting for a **Christmas market** in December.

St Maria zur Wiese

Wiesenstrasse • April–Sept Mon–Sat 11am–6pm, Sun noon–6pm; Oct–March Mon–Sat 11am–4pm, Sun noon–4pm • Free • ⓦ wiesenkirche.de

Soest's distinctive green sandstone is seen to best effect in the sublime **St Maria zur Wiese**, a tall, graceful Late Gothic hall church, begun in 1313 and among the loveliest in Germany. Inside, you experience an almost overwhelming rush of colour from the green stone and vast stained-glass windows, one of which – the *Westfälische Abendmahl* – dates from around 1500 and shows Jesus and the disciples tucking into a Germanic Last Supper of beer, pork, pumpernickel and ham. For all its magnificence it has never been the town's main church, and its soaring (and fragile) twin spires rise above modest, villagey houses on the opposite side of the **Grosser Teich**, the town's millpond – still with an intact watermill – from the main body of the Altstadt.

12

Grünsandstein Museum

Walburgerstr. 56 • Mon–Sat 10am–5pm, Sun 2–5pm • Free • ⓦ gruensandsteinmuseum.de

Close encounters with Soest's mysterious green sandstone can be had at the **Grünsandstein Museum**, which has some beautiful specimens of Gothic carving to supplement its geological displays. The stone's colour varies from yellow-green to almost blue, depending on its mineral content; it was deposited on the shore of a warm sea ninety million years ago.

St Maria zur Höhe

Lentzestrasse • April–Sept Mon–Sat 10am–5.30pm, Sun noon–5.30pm; Oct–March Mon–Sat 10am–4pm, Sun noon–4pm • Free

South of St Maria zur Wiese near the Grosser Teich, Hohe Gasse leads to the late Romanesque **St Maria zur Höhe**, known as the Hohnekirche, which dates from around 1230 and is as squat as the younger church is lofty. It too has a beautiful interior, with rich frescoes showing Byzantine influence and the strange *Scheibenkreuz*, a cross on a carved wooden background that dates from 1200 and resembles the end of a beer barrel.

Osthofentor

Osthofentorstr. 2 • April–Sept Tues–Sat 2–4pm, Sun 11am–1pm & 3–5pm; Oct–March Wed 2–4pm & Sun 11am–1pm • €2, combined ticket for all Soest museums €3

Just to the east of St Maria zur Höhe along Osthofenstrasse, the sixteenth-century **Osthofentor** – sole survivor of the town's ten gates – houses a **museum** with displays on Soest's medieval history as well as the remnants of the municipal armoury.

THE SAUERLAND

Modest by Alpine standards, the swathe of unspoilt wooded hills known as the **Sauerland** nevertheless represents a precious taste of the great outdoors for the millions who live in North Rhine-Westphalia's major cities, as well as attracting holiday-makers from further afield. The region, which strays across the Land boundary into western Hesse, is above all popular for activities, from **hiking**, **mountain biking** or **Nordic walking** in the summer to **skiing** in the winter, while its artificial lakes – the target of the famous RAF "Dambuster" air raids during World War II – offer a focus for all kinds of water-based activities, from canoeing and fishing to swimming, sailing and windsurfing. If that's too energetic, you can take a sedate coffee-and-cake excursion aboard a comfortable cruise boat on the Möhnesee (ⓦ moehneseeschifffahrt.de).

Five natural parks together comprise almost three-quarters of the region's territory, crisscrossed by a number of themed hiking-trails such as the **Sauerland-Höhenflug** – a high-altitude route that takes in four 800m peaks – and the 240km **Waldroute**, which links the towns of Iserlohn, Arnsberg and Marsberg to provide a close-up view of the region's forests and fauna. For mountain-bikers, the 1700km **Bike Arena Sauerland** is the draw, supported by cyclist-friendly hotels and guesthouses. **Möhnesee** is the closest of the Sauerland lakes to Soest; from late April to early October a bike-carrying bus service – #R51 – takes around 25 minutes to connect Soest Bahnhof with the lakeside town of **Körbecke**. For more information (in German), visit the web portal ⓦ sauerland.com.

Burghofmuseum

Burghofstr. 22 • Tues–Sat 10am–noon & 3–5pm, Sun 11am–1pm • €2, combined ticket for all Soest museums €3

Soest's main local history museum, the **Burghofmuseum**, occupies a house in the southern Altstadt. Its displays include a section on everyday life in the Middle Ages and an air-raid shelter that gives a flavour of the town's experiences during World War II.

Markt and the central Altstadt

It's fun to get creatively lost in the Altstadt's picturesque lanes, some of which have colourful names, such as Elendgasse ("Misery Lane"). The central square, **Markt**, is dominated by a photogenic row of half-timbered houses, loveliest among them the **Haus zur Rose** with its beautiful, coloured fan decorations.

Soest's central architectural ensemble is on **Domplatz**, where the Baroque **Rathaus** stands between the green-tinged Romanesque **Petrikirche** (Tues–Fri 9.30am–5.30pm, Sat 9.30am–4.30pm, Sun 2–5.30pm; free) – with a couple of Crucifixion frescoes on the columns of the nave attributed to the Gothic painter Conrad von Soest (a Dortmund man, despite his name) – and the **St Patrokli Dom** (daily 10am–5.30pm; free), the town's thousand-year-old principal church. The Dom, an architectural show of strength by the Cologne archbishops, preserves beautiful Romanesque frescoes of St Patroclus, the town's patron saint, but otherwise shows obvious traces of postwar restoration.

Tucked behind the Dom on Thomästrasse, the tiny **Nikolaikapelle** (Tues–Thurs & Sun 11am–noon; free) has a lovely retable by von Soest. The chapel is usually locked, but the tourist office offers guided tours along with the Petrikirche and Dom.

ARRIVAL AND INFORMATION

By train Soest's Bahnhof is just north of the Altstadt; from here Brüderstrasse meanders south towards the Dom and Grosser Teich.

Tourist office In the watermill at Teichsmühlengasse 3 (Mon–Fri 9.30am–4.30pm, Sat 10am–3pm, Sun 11am–1pm; Nov–March closed Sun; ☏ 02921 66 35 00 50, ⓦ wms-soest.de). It provides information on the Sauerland (see box above) as well as on Soest itself.

ACCOMMODATION AND EATING

Brauhaus Zwiebel Ulricher Str. 4 ☏ 02921 44 24, ⓦ brauhaus-zwiebel.de. Atmospheric half-timbered *Brauhaus* with own-brew *Soester Hell*, *Dunkel* and *Weizen* beers, plus hearty portions of Westphalian specialities, fish and *Schnitzel*. Main courses from €9. Mon–Sat 11am–11pm, Sun 11am–10pm.

★**Café Fromme** Markt 1 ☎ 02921 21 07. Soest's prime spot for *Kaffee und Kuchen*, with a terrace on Markt and a lovely, timewarp 1950s interior. Breakfasts from €4.90, excellent cakes from €2.30 and ice creams from €3.20. Mon–Sat 9am–6.30pm, Sun 10.30am–6.30pm.

DJH Soest Kaiser-Friedrich-Platz 2 ☎ 02921 162 83, ⓦ djh-wl.de/de/jugenderbergen/soest. Soest's small youth hostel is immediately south of the Altstadt close to the Stadthalle, and easily reached on foot; there are a few family rooms alongside the four- to six-bed dorms. Check-in from 3pm. Breakfast included. **€22.60**

Im Wilden Mann Am Markt 11 ☎ 02921 150 71, ⓦ im-wilden-mann.com. Occupying a striking half-timbered house on the main square, with a bustling restaurant on the ground floor, this is the most central and best known of Soest's historic inns. **€88**

Pilgrim Haus Jakobistr. 75 ☎ 02921 18 28, ⓦ pilgrimhaus.de. Next to the town wall, this charming old place claims to be the oldest inn in Westphalia, dating from 1304. Rooms are furnished in a clean, modern style; some have beams. There are single, three- and four-bed rooms and a couple of apartments in addition to doubles. The restaurant is much the most imaginative of Soest's hotel dining rooms, offering the likes of pork stuffed with feta, leeks & walnuts for around €18, plus simpler Soest specialities from around €9.60. Restaurant daily noon–2pm & 5.30–10.30pm. Apartments **€130**, doubles **€98**

Paderborn

Religion and power meet at **PADERBORN**, where Charlemagne discussed his coronation as emperor with Pope Leo III in 799 AD. Its bishopric blossomed in the Middle Ages into a prince-bishopric and in 1929 into an archbishopric. The compact cathedral city remains a strongly religious place, with a theology faculty that traces its roots back to the Jesuit university founded by Prince-Bishop Dietrich von Fürstenberg in 1614. Its religious monuments, combined with its unique geographical location at the source of Germany's shortest river, make it an engrossing place for a short visit.

12

The Paderquellgebiet

Paderborn stands at the point where powerful springs bubble up from a limestone aquifer to form Germany's shortest river, the 4km-long Pader. An air raid on March 27, 1945, left Paderborn a smoking ruin, yet paradoxically the destruction had some positive consequences, enabling the city authorities to open up the hitherto densely built-up and rather malodorous area around the source to create the **Paderquellgebiet**, a delightful water garden right in the heart of the city.

The Ottonian Kaiserpfalz

Ikenberg 2 • Museum Tues–Sun 10am–6pm, 1st Wed of month until 8pm • €3.50, combined ticket with Diözesanmuseum €5 • ⓦ kaiserpfalz-paderborn.de

In 1963 demolition of war-damaged houses led to the sensational rediscovery of the **Carolingian Königspfalz**, the palace where Charlemagne held the first Frankish assembly on Saxon soil in 777 AD. Its foundations can now be seen between the cathedral and the **Ottonian Kaiserpfalz**, a rather successful 1970s resurrection of the Carolingian palace's eleventh-century successor, incorporating whatever of the actual palace survived. It houses the **Museum in der Kaiserpfalz** where you can see film footage of the 1960s excavations, a model of the city as it was in the eleventh century and – tucked inconspicuously beneath the museum – the gorgeous stone-vaulted Quellkeller, whose cool green waters are fed by three of the Pader's multiple sources.

Bartholomäuskapelle

Between the museum and cathedral stands the most substantial survivor of the palace complex, the eleventh-century **Bartholomäuskapelle**. It was the first hall church north of the Alps and reputedly the work of Greek builders. The interior is austere but elegant: there's almost no decoration except for the capitals on its six slender columns.

NUNS AND BEER

Paderborn's cathedral is dedicated to **St Liborius**, an early Christian bishop from Le Mans whose remains were transferred to the town in 836 AD. The obscure Gallo-Roman cleric is the focal point of the annual nine-day **Libori festival** in late July, when the golden shrine containing his reliquary is paraded through the streets and the city centre becomes a riotous mix of nuns and beer, attracting a million visitors.

The Dom

Domplatz • Mon–Sat 6.15am–6.30pm, Sun 6.45am–7pm; no visits during Mass • Free

The distinctive square tower and copper-clad spire of the cathedral, or **Dom**, dominate Paderborn's skyline. The construction of this monumental thirteenth-century hall church spanned the stylistic transition from Romanesque to Gothic: the great west tower is Romanesque, the nave – which has two sets of transepts – Gothic. The best way to enter the cathedral is down the steps from Markt on the south side through the **Paradies**, which in the Middle Ages served as a shelter for pilgrims en route to Santiago de Compostela.

The interior

Inside, it's the richness of the various tombs that catches the eye, particularly the splendid black-and-white Mannerist memorial to Prince-Bishop **Dietrich von Fürstenberg** by Heinrich Gröninger. The **cloisters** contain the celebrated sixteenth-century **Hasenfenster** or Hare Window, which, with great artistic cunning, depicts three leaping hares who share just three ears, though each hare somehow has a pair. At the cloister's northern exit is a moving **memorial** to the victims of the World War II air raids and in particular to the fourteen killed by a bomb which landed in the cloister on March 22, 1945. Mosaics by Paderborn artist Agnes Mann depict three young boys trapped in the burning city.

Diözesanmuseum

Markt 17 • Tues–Sun 10am–6pm • €3.50, combined ticket with Museum in der Kaiserpfalz €5 • ⓦ diozesanmuseum-paderborn.de

In front of the cathedral on the south side, the uncompromisingly modernist **Diözesanmuseum** presents its collection of religious art with considerable flair – Baroque angels from the destroyed 1736 *Libori Festaltar* soar above your head, while in the crypt-like cellar the treasures include the shrine of St Liborius itself.

The rest of the Altstadt

Beyond the museum, the city centre focuses on **Markt** – with its carefully restored gabled houses facing the cathedral – and **Rathausplatz**, dominated by the three flamboyant Weser Renaissance gables of the city's greatest secular building, the **Rathaus**. It dates from 1616 and was another of Prince-Bishop Dietrich's building projects. Just to the west, the gabled facade of the **Heising'sches Haus**, built for Burgomeister Heinrich Stallmeister around 1600, is almost as showy.

South of the Rathaus stand more fruits of Dietrich's building mania in the shape of the reconstructed **Gymnasium Theodorianum** and the formerly Jesuit **Marktkirche** next door, which has a sumptuous high altar, re-created after complete wartime destruction and finally completed in 2004. To the east, the beautiful cloisters of the eleventh-century **Busdorfkirche** are worth a look, while the city's finest half-timbered house, the **Adam und Eva Haus** on Hathumarstrasse, contains the local history museum (Tues–Sun 10am–6pm; €2.50), with graphic film footage of Paderborn after the air raids. As for the rest of Paderborn's centre, it's a mishmash of surviving and reconstructed historic buildings interspersed with postwar austerity housing and a few regrettable eye-sores, and is only intermittently picturesque.

12

Heinz Nixdorf MuseumsForum

Fürstenallee 7 • Tues–Fri 9am–6pm, Sat & Sun 10am–6pm • €7 • ⓦ hnf.de • Bus #11

From the city centre, a riverside path along the park-like banks of the Pader brings you after 3km to the **Heinz Nixdorf MuseumsForum**, which claims to be the world's largest computer museum and takes a broad perspective on its subject, the exhibits beginning with the development of writing in Mesopotamia around 3000 BC.

Schloss Neuhaus

Schlossstr. 10 • Free access • ⓦ schlosspark-paderborn.de • Bus #1, #8 or #11

Schloss Neuhaus, the former residence of the prince-bishops, lies 5km from the city centre along the Pader's riverside path, and is a popular walk from the city. The palace is set in a lavish, formal Baroque park with swirling parterres re-created in 1994 to their original design.

Schloss Wewelsburg

Burgwall 19, Büren-Wewelsburg • Tues–Fri 10am–5pm, Sat & Sun 10am–6pm • Erinnerungs- und Gedenkstätte free, Historisches Museum €3 • ⓦ wewelsburg.de • Bus #460 from Paderborn

Perched atop a wooded slope close to Paderborn's airport, the distinctive triangular **Schloss Wewelsburg** was built between 1603 and 1609 and served as a residence of the prince-bishops of Paderborn. The Renaissance castle is better known, however, as the focus of the creepy pseudo-religious cult built around the **SS** in the 1930s and 1940s by Heinrich Himmler, for which purpose it was extensively rebuilt after 1934 to include a shrine-like crypt and a ceremonial hall in the north tower. The former SS guardhouse is now the **Erinnerungs- und Gedenkstätte** with an exhibition tracing the development of the SS and examining its social structure, world view and crimes, concluding with a look at how postwar Germany dealt with its malign legacy. The castle also houses the **Historisches Museum des Hochstifts Paderborn,** laid out over three floors of the castle and charting the history of the Paderborn prince-bishopric.

12

ARRIVAL AND INFORMATION

PADERBORN

By plane Paderborn/Lippstadt airport (☎ 02955 770, ⓦ airport-pad.com) is southwest of the city, linked by bus (#S60, #460, #NE16; single €6.20) to the Hauptbahnhof.

By train Paderborn's Hauptbahnhof is west of the centre on Bahnhofstrasse. This continues as Westernstrasse, the city's main shopping street, to Marienplatz.

Tourist office Marienplatz 2a (April–Oct Mon–Fri 10am–6pm, Sat 10am–4pm; Nov–March Mon–Fri 10am–5pm, Sat 10am–2pm; ☎ 05251 88 29 80, ⓦ paderborn.de).

ACCOMMODATION

DJH Paderborn Meinwerkstr. 16 ☎ 05251 220 55, ⓦ djh-wl.de/jugendherbergen/paderborn. Paderborn's youth hostel is in a sprawling old building right on the fortifications at the northern entrance to the Altstadt, a short walk from the Paderquellgebiet and with accommodation in singles to eight-bed dorms. Breakfast included. Dorms €21.40

Galerie-Hotel Abdinghof Bachstr. 1 ☎ 05251 122 40, ⓦ galerie-hotel.de. The most romantic place to stay in Paderborn, in a sixteenth-century *Brauhaus* facing the

Paderquellgebiet. The pretty rooms have either bath or shower and WC plus flat-screen TV and free wi-fi. Cheaper deals at weekends. €95

Hotel Aspethera Am Busdorf 7 ☎ 05251 288 81 00, ⓦ hotel-aspethera.de. Smart, business-oriented option, next to the Busdorfkirche, hiding an eighteenth-century wine cellar beneath its modern exterior. Rooms are tastefully furnished in contemporary style. Cheaper deals at weekends. €108

EATING AND DRINKING

Kupferkessel Marienstr. 14 ☎ 05251 236 85, ⓦ kupferkessel-paderborn.de. The Michelin-listed *Kupferkessel* is the city's most elegant restaurant, with the

likes of Iberian pork cutlet with chanterelle *Spätzle* for around €25. Three courses €33.90, four courses €39.90. Mon–Sat noon–3pm & 6pm–midnight.

La Petite Galerie At the Galeri-Hotel Abdinghof, Bachstr. 1 ☎ 05251 122 40, ⓦ galerie-hotel.de. Quiches, chalked-up specials and a €55 three-course candlelit *Menu de l'Amour* with prosecco, all in arty surroundings, with a leafy terrace outside. High tea with dainty sandwiches, scones and cream costs €16.50. Daily 8am–10pm, snacks until 10.30pm.

Ostermann Café am Dom In the Diözesanmuseum, Markt 17 ☎ 05251 878 74 88, ⓦ www.cafe-ostermann.de. Paderborn's most sumptuous coffee-and-cake place, right next to the cathedral, with waffles from around €4.60 plus inexpensive soups, salads and quiches. Tues–Fri 9am–6.30pm, Sat 9am–6pm, Sun 10am–6pm.

Paderborner Brauhaus Kisau 2 ☎ 05251 28 25 54, ⓦ bono-gastronomie.de. The city's biggest beer garden, in a leafy waterside setting just to the northwest of the Paderquellgebiet, with Isenbeck beer plus *Spanferkel* and *Schnitzel* mains for around €10–16; steaks €21.50. Mon–Fri 5pm–late, Sat & Sun 11.30am–late.

Ratskeller Rathausplatz 1 ☎ 05251 20 11 33, ⓦ ratskeller-paderborn.de. Westphalian *Gutbürgerlich* cuisine in the atmospheric cellar of the city's Rathaus, with the likes of *Sauerbraten* in pumpernickel sauce or venison ragout with fresh mushroom dumplings for around €13–15, plus *Flammkuchen* and simpler fare from €7.80. Daily 11.30am–2.30pm & 6pm–midnight.

Detmold

High above **DETMOLD** on the forested ridge of the Teutoburger Wald, 35km north of Paderborn, stands a remarkable monument to one of the founding legends of the German nation-state, the *Hermannsdenkmal* – a solitary, wing-helmeted warrior raising his sword high over the canopy of trees. Detmold itself is a charming, attractive town, laid out around its Residenzschloss's watery moat.

The Hermannsdenkmal

March–Oct 9am–6pm; Nov–Feb 9.30am–4pm · €3 · ⓦ hermannsdenkmal.de · Tourist bus #792 from Detmold (weekends only)

The **Hermannsdenkmal** was the vision of one dogged obsessive, the sculptor Joseph Ernst von Bandel, a bust of whom stands outside the hut he occupied while struggling to complete the 53.46-metre-high monument, begun in 1838 and finally completed with financial support from the Prussian state in 1875. The copper-green warrior commemorates Arminius (or "Hermann"), chieftain of the Cherusci, who united local tribes in 9 AD to annihilate three Roman legions at the battle of Teutoburger Wald and thus struck an early blow for German unity. Though the impetus for Hermann's construction was blatantly nationalistic, these days he cuts a romantic figure, and there's no denying the beauty of the views from the platform at his feet.

LWL-Freilichtmuseum

Krummes Haus · April–Oct Tues–Sun 9am–6pm · €7 · ⓦ lwl-freilichtmuseum-detmold.de · Tourist bus #792 from Detmold (Easter–Oct weekends only)

A cycle path descends through the woods east of the *Hermannsdenkmal* to reach the **LWL-Freilichtmuseum** on the town's southern outskirts. Stretching over a ninety-hectare site it's Germany's largest open-air museum, assembling an evocative collection of rustic half-timbered buildings from across the region, along with the home of a Jewish family from the early years of the Third Reich and a 1960s petrol station. There are also temporary exhibitions on themes related to the life of the region.

Vogelpark Heiligenkirchen and Adlerwarte Berlebeck

Vogelpark Heiligenkirchen Ostertalstrasse · Mid-March to early Nov 9am–6pm · €7.70 · ⓦ vogelpark-heiligenkirchen.de · **Adlerwarte Berlebeck** Adlerweg · Mid-Feb to early Nov 9.30am–5.30pm · €6 · ⓦ adlerwarte-berlebeck.de · Access to both by bus #792 from Detmold (Easter–Oct weekends only)

To the south of the *Hermannsdenkmal*, the **Vogelpark Heiligenkirchen** is a family-friendly aviary and zoo with over three hundred species from around the world, including plenty of exotica; the daily feeding of the parrot chicks at noon and 4pm is a highlight for children. More avian attractions are found nearby at the **Adlerwarte Berlebeck**, where you can see eagles and other birds of prey in free flight.

Externsteine

Exernsteiner Str. 35 • Infozentrum Jan & Feb Sat & Sun 10am–4pm; March, Nov & Dec Tues & Thurs–Sun 10am–4pm; April–Oct 10am–6pm • Access to site €3, parking €2.50, Infozentrum free • Bus #792 from Detmold (Easter–Oct weekends only)

Detmold's final outlying attraction is the **Externsteine**, a series of strange sandstone pinnacles southeast of town with an intriguing religious significance: thought to have originally been a pagan site, the rocks were allegedly adopted by Christians in the Middle Ages as a substitute for the pilgrimage to Jerusalem. The modern **Infozentrum** helps explain the site.

Altstadt

Detmold is an undeniably pretty town, with hundreds of beautifully-preserved historic buildings in a variety of styles from slate-hung and half-timbered to Jugendstil. Lange Strasse, the classy **Altstadt**'s main street, is handsome enough, but for sheer cuteness it's hard to beat the row of half-timbered seventeenth-century artisans' cottages in quiet **Adolfstrasse**, east of Markt off Schuler Strasse.

Fürstliches Residenzschloss

Schlossplatz 1 • Hourly tours daily: April–Oct 10am–5pm; Nov–March 10am–4pm • €4 • ⓦ schloss-detmold.de

The centre of Detmold is dominated by the **Fürstliches Residenzschloss**, a fine example of the Weser Renaissance style. The seat of the princes of Lippe – an extinct principality of which Detmold was the capital – the Schloss is still in the hands of the family; its chief artistic glory is a set of Brussels tapestries depicting the battles of Alexander the Great.

Lippisches Landesmuseum

Ameide 4 • Tues–Fri 10am–6pm, Sat & Sun 11am–6pm • €5 • ⓦ lippisches-landesmuseum.de

Facing the Schloss across the watery Schlossteich, the **Lippisches Landesmuseum** is partly housed in the five-storey, sixteenth-century Kornhaus, where the wonderful timber structure provides an atmospheric setting for displays on local and peasant life, from room reconstructions and painted furniture to weaponry and regional costume – notable for the women's eccentric headgear. The top floor eschews the *völkisch* with a display of classic modern furniture tucked under the eaves.

ARRIVAL AND GETTING AROUND

DETMOLD

By train Detmold is 30km from Paderborn, to which it is linked by hourly trains (39min). The Bahnhof is northwest of the Altstadt: follow Bahnhofstrasse to Paulinenstrasse, turning right and continuing to its junction with Bruchstrasse, which leads into the Altstadt.

By bus At weekends from Easter to Oct the #792 tourist bus does the rounds of Detmold's outlying visitor attractions, with hourly departures (9.10am–5.10pm) from the Bahnhof. It also carries up to twenty bikes.

INFORMATION

Tourist office In the Rathaus on Markt (April–Oct Mon–Fri 9am–6pm, Sat 10am–2pm; Nov–March Mon–Fri 10am–5pm, Sat (Advent only) 10am–2pm; ⓣ 05231 97 73

278, ⓦ detmold.de). You can also obtain tourist information at the Lippisches Landesmuseum (see above), which is open on Sun.

ACCOMMODATION AND EATING

★**Detmolder Hof** Langestr. 19 ⓣ 05231 98 09 90, ⓦ detmolderhof.de. Absolutely beautiful family-run 4-star hotel in the centre of Detmold, with an

established, timeless air. The rooms are prettily decorated in a refined country style, with natural stone bathrooms. The classy restaurant serves the likes of

12

monkfish medallions with lemongrass and ginger sauce or fillet steak with shallot jus, with main courses around €20 up; there's also a three-course Westphalian menu for €32.50. Restaurant daily 11.30am–2.30pm and 6–10pm. **€139**

Gottis Bistro At the Lippischer Hof hotel, Willy-Brandt-Platz 1 ☎05231 93 60, ⓦ lippischerhof-detmold.de. Stylish hotel restaurant serving dishes such as pork fillet with spring leek risotto or *Matjes* fillet with bean salad; pasta from €11.50, meat or fish mains from around €17/18. Tues & Sat noon–2pm & 6–10pm, Wed–Fri 6–10pm, Sun noon–2pm.

★**Grabbe Café** Unter der Wehme 7 ☎05231 243 72. Very pleasant café in the former home of the Detmold-born dramatist and satirist, Christian Dietrich Grabbe

(1801–36). Breakfasts from €4.60, light meals including soups and salads (€3.30/€5.60), good cakes and outstanding home-made biscuits. Tues–Sat 8am–6pm, Sun 10am–6pm.

Hotel Brechmann Bahnhofstr. 9 ☎05231 256 55, ⓦ hotel-brechmann.de. Simple but tastefully furnished en-suite rooms in a nineteenth-century house close to the station and a short walk from the Altstadt; there's secure storage for bicycles. **€75**

Jugendherberge Detmold Schirmannstr. 49 ☎05231 247 39, ⓦ djh-wl.de/de/jugendherbergen/detmold. Detmold's youth hostel is on the town's outskirts close to the Freilichtmuseum, with an adjacent meadow for sports and barbecues and accommodation mainly in 4- to 7-bed dorms. Breakfast included. Dorms **€22.60**

Lemgo

LEMGO, 11km north of Detmold, draws day-trippers to see the architectural reminders of its Hanseatic League prime, its streets a photogenic blend of Weser Renaissance pomp and picturesque half-timbering. Not everything in the town's history is as charming as its appearance, however. Protestant after the Reformation, from 1583 to 1681 Lemgo was gripped by an anti-witchcraft frenzy that was cynically exploited by politicians. The last woman prosecuted for witchcraft, Maria Rampendahl, survived, but 254 men and women were not so fortunate.

The Rathaus and around

The **Rathaus** on Markt is no coherent set-piece but rather a delightful jumble of buildings dating from 1325 to 1612, with the star turn being the **Apothekenerker**, an exuberant Renaissance oriel window attached to the municipal pharmacy and decorated with images of eminent physicians from Hippocrates to Paracelsus. On the south side of the complex, the op-art zigzags on the **Zeughaus** (armoury) dazzle, while the terracotta-coloured **Ballhaus** (ballroom), which just predates the Thirty Years' War, completes the ensemble. Looming above the lot are the mismatched spires of the **Nikolaikirche**, resplendent in yellow ochre since its recent restoration.

From Markt, a stroll east along **Mittelstrasse** takes you past multicoloured half-timbering, the **Planetenhaus** with its astral decoration and the gorgeous **Haus Alt Lemgo** being particularly fine examples. South of Markt, Breite Strasse leads south past the Gothic **Wippermannsches Haus** from 1576, which may have lagged behind the architectural fashion of its day, but is another beauty. Off Breite Strasse on Stiftstrasse, the appealingly saggy Gothic Lutheran **Marienkirche** (Tues–Sun: summer 8am–6pm; winter 8am–4pm; free) is notable for a rare, seventeenth-century "swallow's nest" organ clinging to the church wall.

The Hexenbürgermeisterhaus

Breite Str. 17–19 • Tues–Sun 10am–5pm • €3, English audio-guide €1, combined ticket for all Lemgo museums €6 • ⓦ hexenbuergermeisterhaus.de

The last, bloodiest, wave of Lemgo's witchcraft trials was presided over by the notorious Hermann Cothmann (1629–83), the so-called Hexenbürgermeister or "witch mayor". His former home on Breite Strasse is a stunning example of Weser Renaissance architecture, built in 1571 and distinguished by a spectacular high gable and carvings that depict the virtues – including, ironically, charity. It houses the **Städtisches Museum Hexenbürgermeisterhaus**, where you can see instruments of torture, watch old films and learn more about some of the individuals caught up in the trials.

East of the Altstadt

East of Lemgo's Altstadt at Hamelner Str. 36, the **Junkerhaus** (April–Oct Tues–Sun 10am–5pm; Nov–March Fri–Sun 11am–3pm; €3, combined ticket for all Lemgo museums €6; ⓦjunkerhaus.de) is the eccentric work of nineteenth-century sculptor and artist Karl Junker; its elaborately carved interior is spooky enough to conjure up thoughts of those Lemgo witches. A little to the south at Schlossstr. 18, the moated late sixteenth-century **Schloss Brake** – a former residence of the Counts zur Lippe – houses the **Weserrenaissance Museum** (Tues–Sun 10am–6pm; €3; ⓦwrm.lemgo.de), which displays a fine collection of Renaissance paintings, furniture, silverware and other objects which helps put the town's architectural splendour in context.

ARRIVAL AND INFORMATION	LEMGO
By bus A frequent bus service (#790; every 30min; 29min) links Detmold with Lemgo's Bahnhof, which is at the southern entrance to the Altstadt. **Tourist office** Kramerstr. 1 (Mon–Fri 9am–5pm, Sat	9am–1pm; ☎05261 988 70, ⓦlemgo.net). To locate the office, follow Breite Strasse north from the car park just east of the station.

ACCOMMODATION AND EATING

Hansa Hotel Breite Str. 14–16 ☎05261 940 50, ⓦhansa-hotel.de. Simple but comfortable hotel right opposite the Hexenbürgermeisterhaus, with good-value en-suite rooms including seven singles. **€82**

Hotel Stadtpalais Papenstr. 24 ☎05261 25 89 00, ⓦhotel-stadtpalais.de. Lovely hotel in a Weser Renaissance building furnished with lots of antiques, including four-poster beds in some rooms; those in the extension are more contemporary. Rates are cheaper at weekends.The atmospheric *Brauhaus* is the place to tuck into Lemgo *Sauberbraten* with pumpernickel sauce or crisp-skinned pike-perch with horseradish & beer foam; main courses from around €13. Brauhaus Tues–Fri 5–10pm, Sat & Sun noon–2pm & 5–10pm. **€100**

Ristorante Vesuvio Papenstr. 32. ☎05261 3650, ⓦvesuvio-lemgo.de. Smart Italian restaurant in a spectacular gabled house in the Altstadt, with a big range of pasta from €6.80 and plenty of pizza choice from €7.80 up. Mon–Sat noon–2.30pm & 6–11.30pm, Sun noon–2.30pm & 5.30–11pm.

12

Münster

Bicycles rule in studenty **MÜNSTER**, which, with twice as many bikes as people, is Germany's most cycle-friendly city. Its history is intertwined with that of its bishopric, the name Münster deriving from the monastery founded at Charlemagne's behest in 793 AD, while in the twentieth century, Bishop Clemens August von Galen was one of the few prominent clerics to defy Nazi rule. In the Middle Ages Münster was a Hanseatic city; during the Reformation it experienced a brief, bloody tyranny under an extreme Anabaptist sect, but soon returned to the Catholic fold. In 1648, it was the venue for the signature of the Peace of Westphalia; later, during the Napoleonic wars, the city was briefly the capital of the French *département* of Lippe, before in 1816 becoming capital of Prussian Westphalia.

Built – or rather rebuilt – on a human scale, Münster is easy to explore on foot: defined by the continuous green **Promenadenring** along the line of the old defences, the **Altstadt** contains the main sights. Beyond it, you'll find fresh air and space to picnic around the **Aasee** lake southwest of the centre, and cool bars and restaurants on the **Stadthafen**'s waterside strip. Watch your step though, for those cyclists are not to be messed with.

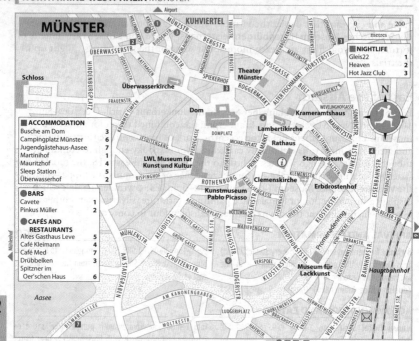

12

Prinzipalmarkt and the eastern Altstadt

With its steep stone gables and natty arcades, elegant, curving **Prinzipalmarkt** is as fine a street as any in Germany. It isn't quite what it seems, for wartime bombs devastated Münster and by 1945, ninety percent of the city's core was a ruin. Faced with the alternatives of starting afresh or trying to recapture some of the city's lost beauty, the authorities opted for the latter. Major monuments were rebuilt exactly as they had been, but others were reconstructed in a loose pastiche of historic forms. The mix works well.

The Rathaus

Prinzipalmarkt 10 • Friedenssaal Tues–Fri 10am–5pm, Sat & Sun 10am–4pm • €2

Flanked by the Renaissance **Stadtweinhaus** (1615) and Gothic **Haus Ostendorff**, Münster's fourteenth-century **Rathaus** was reduced to its lower storeys by wartime bombs, but rapidly rebuilt afterwards, and the delicate finials topping its high gable once again soar above Prinzipalmarkt. Step inside to see the **Friedenssaal**, the room in which on October 24, 1648, the Catholic half of the Peace of Westphalia was brokered – the Protestant faction was based in Osnabrück. Regarded as the first triumph of modern diplomacy, it ended the Thirty Years' War, recognized the sovereignty of the Netherlands and Switzerland and put Catholic and Protestant faiths on an equal legal footing. The room's magnificent sixteenth-century wood panelling and the 37 portraits of the key delegates are original, having escaped wartime destruction by being stored outside the city.

The Lambertikirche

To the north of the Rathaus the sooty openwork spire of the Late Gothic **Lambertikirche** is hung with a grisly garnish of three iron cages in which the bodies of Anabaptist leader Jan van Leiden and his lieutenants were exhibited in 1535 after their torture and execution under Prince-Bishop Franz von Waldeck. Leiden, who had proclaimed himself king of the "New Zion" in Münster, presided over a colourful, but bloody, period in which polygamy was a duty, money was declared obsolete and all property communal. The spire is nineteenth century, but the body of the church was built between 1375 and 1450 and is notable for the relief of the Tree of Jesse above the main portal. It was from the Lambertikirche's pulpit that on August 3, 1941, Bishop von Galen denounced the Nazis' euthanasia programme against the mentally ill. In the evening, a watchman blows a copper horn from the church tower (Mon & Wed–Sun 9pm–midnight, every 30min).

The Stadtmuseum and around

Salzstr. 28 • Tues–Fri 10am–6pm, Sat & Sun 11am–6pm • Free • ⓦ stadt-muenster.de/museum

The **Stadtmuseum** offers a well-displayed overview of the city's history, with grimmer exhibits leavened with more light-hearted displays, such as the original 1950s interior of the former Café Müller. Nearby lie the **Clemenskirche** and Baroque **Erbdrostenhof** – both the mid-eighteenth-century work of court architect Johann Conrad von Schlaun.

Museum für Lackkunst

Windthorststr. 26 • Tues noon–8pm, Wed–Sun noon–6pm • €3, free Tues • ⓦ museum-fuer-lackkunst.de

Occupying a Neoclassical villa just beyond the Promenadenring, the **Museum für Lackkunst** houses a unique collection of lacquerwork from two millennia, including examples from Europe, China, Japan and the Islamic world. It also hosts regular exhibitions of historic and contemporary lacquerwork.

St Paulus Dom

St Paulus Dom Mon–Sat 6.30am–7pm, Sun 6.30am–7.30pm • Free • ⓦ paulusdom.de • **Domkammer** Tues–Sun 11am–4pm • €3

Situated at the heart of the Altstadt, the immense **St Paulus Dom** is the largely thirteenth-century successor to a church built in the eighth century. Take a gentle circuit of the building before entering the west transept via the **Paradise** porch, which features late Romanesque sculptures of Christ and the Apostles.

Inside, the Dom impresses more through its unusual width than its modest height, and it is pleasingly austere save for some splendid memorials and a sixteenth-century **astronomical clock** in the ambulatory, constructed between 1540 and 1542 by the printer Theodor Tzwyvel, the Franciscan friar Johannes Aquensis and the wrought-iron craftsman Nikolaus Windemaker. Decorated with paintings by Ludger Tom Ring, the clock is divided into 24 hours, charts the position of the planets and is accurate until 2071. The Dom's artistic treasures can be seen on the north side of the cloisters in the **Domkammer**; they include an eleventh-century head reliquary of St Paul and a jewel-encrusted thirteenth-century cross reliquary.

LWL Museum für Kunst und Kultur

Domplatz 10 • Tues–Sun 10am–6pm • Permanent collection €2, temporary exhibitions €10, combined ticket €12 • ⓦ lwl-museum-kunst-kultur.de

Facing the cathedral across Domplatz, the eclectic **LWL Museum für Kunst und Kultur** houses a sprawling collection of fine and applied art from the medieval to the modern. An impressive new extension, opened in 2014, eases the space constraints that hitherto meant only a tiny fragment of the collection was on display at any one time. The museum's **Medieval** treasures include Conrad von Soest's *Saints Dorothea and Odilia*, created for the Walburgis convent in Soest, and splendid, late medieval carvings by Münster-born Heinrich Brabender, the great master of Westphalian sculpture at the turn of the sixteenth century.

The **Renaissance** is represented by paintings by Münster's own Tom Ring dynasty, but also by the *Wrangelschrank*, a spectacular inlaid cabinet made in Augsburg in 1566 and decorated with scenes from Roman wars. It was once the property of Swedish field marshal Carl Gustav Wrangel. The extensive **modern art** collection includes Impressionist paintings by Max Liebermann and Lovis Corinth, and Expressionist works from the Brücke and Blaue Reiter groups, with an emphasis on the work of Westphalian-born August Macke.

12

Kunstmuseum Pablo Picasso

Picassoplatz 1 • Tues–Sun 10am–6pm • €10 • ⓦ kunstmuseum-picasso-muenster.de

South of Domplatz the **Kunstmuseum Pablo Picasso** presents a regularly changing selection of graphic works by Picasso and his contemporaries in the Druffel'scher Hof, a rare surviving eighteeth-century patrician house now almost swallowed in the chic Münster Arkaden shopping mall.

The western Altstadt

Northwest of the cathedral, a lane leads across the diminutive River Aa to the **Überwasserkirche**, or Church over the Water, badly trashed by the Anabaptists in 1534. Its medieval sculptures were smashed and buried, but exhumed during excavations of the transept in 1898, and are now on view in the LWL Museum. The delightfully small-scale district beyond the church, known as the **Kuhviertel**, is one of Münster's liveliest quarters, with plenty of places to eat or drink. On the western fringe of the Altstadt, the stately Schloss is another of Johann Conrad von Schlaun's Baroque confections, built as the prince-bishops' residence between 1767 and 1787 and nowadays home to Münster's university.

Around the Aasee

South of the Schloss, spacious **Aasee** is Münster's chief recreation ground, with **boat trips** (mid-April to mid-Oct 10am–5pm; from €3.50; ⓦ aaseeschifffahrt.de) and an attractive shoreline for a picnic. On the north side of the lake, the **Freilichtmuseum Mühlenhof** (March–Oct daily 10am–6pm; Nov–Feb Mon–Fri & Sun 11am–4pm; €5) is a rustic assembly of buildings from rural Westphalia, including an eighteenth-century windmill.

12

ARRIVAL AND DEPARTURE

MÜNSTER

By plane Münster-Osnabrück airport (☎ 02571 94 33 60, ⓦ fmo.de) is at Hüttruper Heide north of the city; frequent buses (every 30min; 25–45min; €6.60) connect it to the Hauptbahnhof.

By train Münster's Hauptbahnhof is east of the Altstadt. To reach the tourist office, follow Windthorststrasse across the Promenadenring into Stubengasse, which in turn becomes Heinrich-Brüning-Strasse.

Destinations Berlin (1 daily; 3hr 37min); Dortmund (every 30min; 32–53min); Duisburg (2–3 per hour; 1hr–1hr 21min); Essen (up to 4 per hour; 55min–1hr 7min); Paderborn (every 30min; 1hr 28min).

INFORMATION

Tourist office Heinrich-Brüning-Str. 9 (Mon–Fri 10am–6pm, Sat 10am–1pm; ☎ 0251 492 27 10, ⓦ muenster.de).

Bike hire Radstation at the Hauptbahnhof (Mon–Fri 5.30am–11pm, Sat & Sun 7am–11pm; ☎ 0251 484 01 70, ⓦ radstation.de) rents out bikes for €8 per day.

ACCOMMODATION

HOTELS

Busche am Dom Bogenstr. 10 ☎ 0251 464 44, ⓦ hotel-busche.de. You'll scarcely get more central than this long-established, family-run place close to the Dom. Rooms are furnished in traditional Westphalian style and come with en-suite shower and WC plus TV and phone; some singles available. **€109**

Martinihof Hörstenstr. 25 ☎ 0251 41 86 20, ⓦ hotel-martinihof.de. Very central and reasonably priced *hotel garni*, with 31 singles, 21 doubles and some three-bed rooms, attractive if rather functional, and mostly with shower and WC. **€98**

Mauritzhof Eisenbahnstr. 17 ☎ 0251 417 20, ⓦ mauritzhof.de. Central and classy, this modern boutique-style hotel has 39 individually designed rooms, including seven suites, some with a balcony or terrace. Free wi-fi. **€102**

Überwasserhof Überwasserstr. 3 ☎ 0251 417 70, ⓦ ueberwasserhof.de. Attractive modern decor, good bathrooms and comfortable rooms, each with bath or shower, WC and cable TV. It's very handy for the Kuhviertel's bar scene too. **€122**

HOSTELS AND CAMPSITES

Campingplatz Münster Laerer Werseufer 7 ☎ 0251 31 19 82, ⓦ campingplatz-muenster.de. Well-equipped five-star site 5km east of the city centre, with internet access, shop and restaurant, cooking and laundry facilities.

Open all year. Pitch and two people, including power €28
Jugendgästehaus Aasee Bismarckallee 31 ☎ 0251 53 02 80, ⓦ djh-wl.de/de/jugendherbergen/muenster; bus #10 or #4, stop "Jugendgästehaus Aasee". Münster's HI hostel is southwest of the centre facing the Aasee lake, with singles and two- and four-bed rooms, including some adapted for wheelchair users. Reception 7am–11pm.

Breakfast included. Dorms €29.50, doubles €82.60
Sleep Station Wolbecker Str. 1 ☎ 0251 482 81 55, ⓦ sleep-station.de. Friendly, well-run backpacker hostel in a convenient position right next to the Hauptbahnhof, with accommodation in single, double or three-bedded rooms and four-, five-, six- or eight-bed dorms. Check-in 8am–12.30pm & 4–9.30pm. Dorms €16, doubles €46

EATING AND DRINKING

Münster punches above its weight when it comes to eating and drinking. There's a traditional or studenty vibe to the **Kuhviertel**'s offerings, slick modernity is the rule along the **Stadthafen**'s Kreativkai and there's a sprinkling of upmarket and atmospheric offerings in the **Altstadt**.

CAFÉS AND RESTAURANTS

Altes Gasthaus Leve Alter Steinweg 37 ☎ 0251 455 95, ⓦ gasthaus-leve.de. "Münster's oldest *Gaststätte*" is in fact a postwar reconstruction of the destroyed seventeenth-century original, but it's nevertheless an atmospheric place offering reasonably priced Westphalian specialities (around €8) and Pinkus Müller beer on draught. Daily noon–midnight.

Café Kleimann Prinzipalmarkt 48 ☎ 0251 430 64, ⓦ konditorkleimann.de. Classic *Kaffee und Kuchen* stop in a prime spot opposite the Lambertikirche, with luscious cakes from €3.40 and sweet and savoury pancakes from €4.90. There are a few tables facing Prinzipalmarkt and a few more on the narrow lane at the back. Mon, Tues, Thurs & Fri 10am–7pm, Wed & Sat 9am–7pm.

Café Med Hafenweg 26a, Stadthafen ☎ 0251 674 95 95. Good pizzas (from €6.50), generous portions of pasta (from €8) and an informal atmosphere attract a lively, young crowd to this vast dockside café-bar, though the service sometimes struggles to cope with the rush. Mon–Fri noon–2.30pm & 6pm–1am, Sat 6pm–1am, Sun noon–midnight.

Drübbelken Buddenstr. 14–15, Kuhviertel ☎ 0251 421 15, ⓦ druebbelken.de. The "olde worlde" atmosphere is laid on with a trowel at this darkly *Gemütlich* Kuhviertel place, in a half-timbered house with open fire and hearty Westphalian food – including *Schnitzel*, home-made *Bratwurst* and *Dicke Bohnen*. Mains from around €12. Mon–Fri 11.30am–2.30pm & 5.30pm–midnight, Sat & Sun 11.30am–midnight.

Spitzner im Oer'Schen Hof Königstr. 42 ☎ 0251 41 44 15 50, ⓦ spitzner.ms. One of Münster's top gourmet offerings, in the elegant surroundings of an eighteenth-century house, with creative dishes that combine Westphalian produce and Mediterranean influences. Main courses €25 up. Tues–Sat noon–2pm & 6.30–10pm.

BARS

Cavete Kreuzstr. 37–38, Kuhviertel ☎ 0251 414 35 16, ⓦ muenster-cavete.de. Münster's classic student pub, with a pretty exterior, grungy interior and salads, veggie dishes and pasta (all €7.90 up) to soak up the *Kölsch*, *Alt* or cocktails. Daily 6pm–late.

Pinkus Müller Kreuzstr. 4, Kuhviertel ☎ 0251 451 51, ⓦ pinkus.de. Vast *Gaststätte* owned by Münster's sole surviving brewery, with traditional trappings, a woody interior and Westphalian food (from €6.90) to accompany the beer; *Alt* €2.30. Mon–Sat noon–midnight.

12

NIGHTLIFE AND ENTERTAINMENT

CLUBS AND LIVE MUSIC

Gleis 22 Hafenstr. 34 ☎ 0251492 58 55, ⓦ gleis22.de. Studenty live-music venue and club close to the Hauptbahnhof, with DJ nights spanning everything from jazz, punk and indie to reggae and Balkan beats. Gigs 8.30pm, clubnights 10pm–late.

Heaven Hafenweg 31, Stadthafen ☎ 0251609 05 85, ⓦ heaven-lounge.de. Spacious and stylish dockside club in an industrial setting in Münster's docks, complete with a restaurant and, in summer, the *Coconut Beach* beach bar. The music policy spans house, electro, chart music, hip-hop and R&B. Restaurant Tues–Sat 6–11pm, club doors open 11pm.

Hot Jazz Club Hafenweg 26b, Stadthafen ☎ 0251 68 66 79 10, ⓦ hotjazzclub.de. Live music venue on the Stadthafen with a programme that embraces jazz, funk, soul, rock and reggae music, and with dancing on Fri and Sat from 10/11pm. There's also a dockside terrace and good-value food. Gigs generally at 8 or 9pm. May–Aug Mon–Sat 6pm–late, Sun 3pm–late; Sept–April Mon–Sat 7pm–late, Sun 3pm–late.

THEATRE

Theater Münster Neubrückenstr. 63 ☎ 0251 59 09 100, ⓦ theater.muenster.com. The city's main cultural hub, with large and small auditoria and a repertoire that extends to classical music, opera, serious drama, literary readings and dance.

Lower Saxony and Bremen

CAR TOWER, AUTOSTADT, WOLFSBURG

13

Lower Saxony and Bremen

If Lower Saxony is little known by foreign visitors, that's probably because it lacks the sort of definitive city- or landscape that helps to cement other German states in the mind. The second largest Land in Germany after Bavaria, it's a neutral ground, sharing more borders than any other state. Scenically, it's a region of rolling hills between low mountains and the plains at the Dutch border. Architecturally, too, it represents a middle ground that segues from the half-timbered country to a red-brick coast. It's tempting to put this lack of identity down to history. Niedersachsen, as Germans know it, only came into being in 1946 through the redrawing of the map by the British military.

Yet Lower Saxony has deeper roots. The name is a reflection of the Saxon tribe that populated the region long before Germany existed as a defined entity. This was the stamping ground of mighty Saxon duke Henry the Lion (Heinrich der Löwe), a European powerbroker of the twelfth century, and the state would probably have retained the name "Saxony" had his humbling not led to the slow migration of the Saxon powerbase up the Elbe to the state that now bears its name.

The watchword when touring, then, is diversity – both of attractions and in scenery that morphs from brooding highlands in the Harz (see p.217) via the undulating **Lüneburg Heath** to the salty air and mudflats of the North Sea coast. While the state benefits from a low population density, its eastern half is the most urban, partly due to state capital **Hannover**, the hub around which all life (and transport) revolves. But even this city of gardens and art is small fry in national terms, with just over half a million people. The second urban centre is **Braunschweig**, which preserves the monuments from its era as the powerbase of Henry the Lion.

Yet this most industrialized part of the state defies easy categorization. Within half an hour in either direction of Braunschweig lie destinations as distinct as **Wolfsburg**, definitively modern as the wellspring of Volkswagen, and the daydreaming former ducal town of **Wolfenbüttel**. The latter is as good an introduction as any to the small historic towns dotted throughout the state: UNESCO-listed **Hildesheim**; **Celle** with its pretty, half-timbered Altstadt; and the absurdly picturesque **Lüneburg**. **Hameln**, of Pied Piper fame, is another world again, with an Altstadt characterized by Weser Renaissance styles, and a hilly hinterland – the Weserbergland – which swoops south along the **Fairy-tale Road**. It's a popular cycling (and canoeing) touring route, taking in such picture-book half-timbered towns as **Hannoverisch Münden** which lies en route to **Göttingen**, the university town that stops the area south to Frankfurt from falling asleep in a surfeit of sunshine and small-town life.

Separated northwest on the flatlands where North Rhine-Westphalia bites a chunk out of the state is **Osnabrück**, the hub of western Lower Saxony state whose history of peace-broking may have contributed to its accreditation as the happiest city in Germany. The western half of the state above Osnabrück is the least interesting in

Highlights

❶ Hannover One of the finest Baroque gardens in Europe, good art galleries and a couple of drinking districts that let rip at weekends – the state capital proves culture comes in bars as well as museums. **See p.694**

❷ Follow the Fairy-tale Road Hameln of Pied Piper fame and Baron Münchhausen's Boden-werder are two stops on a route that swoops south beside the Weser River – a chance for slow travel by bike or canoe. **See p.711 & p.733**

❸ Autostadt, Wolfsburg The birthplace of the Volkswagen Beetle is less a factory than a motor-mad theme park that's a must for petrolheads. **See p.725**

❹ Celle Carved timbers by the tonne in a picture-book-pretty courtly town within easy reach of Hannover. **See p.727**

❺ Lüneburg Wonky red-brick buildings and beautiful squares in an idyllic small town that exudes provincial contentment. **See p.731**

❻ Bremen A relaxed small-scale city with a famously easy-going attitude, and a medieval village, fantastical Art Nouveau street, fabulous town square and boisterous bar district all within fifteen minutes' walk of each other – what's not to like about Bremen? **See p.738**

HIGHLIGHTS ARE MARKED ON THE MAP ON P.694

13

terms of scenery – much of the sparsely populated area incorporates East Frisia (Ostfriesland), which owes as much to Holland in landscape as it does in its dialect, Plattdeutsch. The reason to come north is **Bremen**, a splendid former maritime power which, with its North Sea port of **Bremerhaven**, represents a state in its own right – independent and fiercely proud of it.

Hannover

"Is Hannover the most boring city in Germany?" news weekly magazine *Der Spiegel* once asked. In a word, no, although **HANNOVER**, the capital of Lower Saxony, can appear every bit a faceless modern metropolis. When five of the world's ten largest trade fairs roll into town, up to 800,000 businesspeople wheel, deal, then disappear, the majority probably unaware that they had been in a state capital which, from 1814 to 1866, ruled a kingdom in its own right.

Eighty-eight air raids reduced Hannover from elegant aristocrat to war-torn widow and, with ninety percent of the centre reduced to rubble, the city patched up where possible but largely wiped clean the slate, leaving it without a coherent core. Nonetheless, it's a vigorous, ambitious city, a place with the bottle to reinvent itself through street art, from the *Nanas* at Hohen Ufer to its wacky bus- and tramstops. There are some vibrant art museums, too, and a bar and nightlife scene that is anything but boring. The city is at its best outside the centre: around the **Maschsee** lake for its **art galleries**, or in the celebrated **gardens** to the northwest. And it's at its most fun in

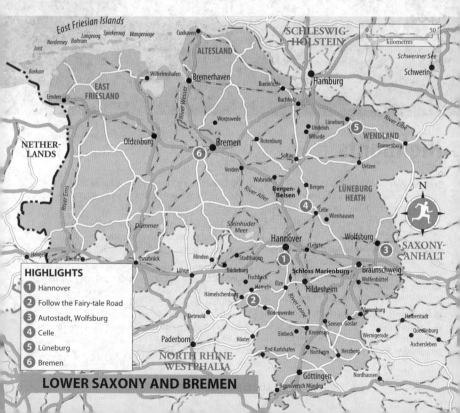

HIGHLIGHTS

1. Hannover
2. Follow the Fairy-tale Road
3. Autostadt, Wolfsburg
4. Celle
5. Lüneburg
6. Bremen

LOWER SAXONY AND BREMEN

13

HANNOVER AND THE BRITISH CONNECTION

It was 1700 and the English were in a bind: Queen Anne was old and her last child sickly. Parliament had scoffed previously at talk of a link between the Crown and the House of Hannover. But the legitimate claim of exiled Catholic James Edward Stuart, "the Old Pretender", had concentrated Protestant minds. In 1701 the **Act of Settlement** declared the crown to "the most excellent princess Sophia, electress and duchess-dowager of Hannover" on the grounds that Electress Sophia von der Pfalz was a granddaughter of King James I, adding a caveat that "the heirs of her body being Protestant". No matter that her son spoke no English, nor that his slow pedantic manner was spectacularly unsuited to the rough-and-tumble of the contemporary English court. Georg Ludwig, Duke of Brunswick-Lüneburg, elector of Hannover, became **George I** in 1714 to begin 120 years of joint rule by the House of Hannover.

Of the four Georgian kings of Great Britain, **George III** was the first to take any interest in his new territory. George I and II were content to appoint a "prime minister" to rule as their representative, accidentally taking the first step towards the modern British political system. By the time the Hanoverian dynasty got hands-on with the English-speaking George III, it was too late. A now-powerful parliament and fate – social unrest, the loss of the American colonies, not to mention the king's mental illness – got in the way. Those woes conspired to make him the most abused monarch in British history. Shelley wrote about "an old, mad, blind, despised and dying king", and liberal historians of the next century competed in their condemnation of him.

Yet it was not bad press that did for joint rule. Salic law forbade the accession of women to head the kingdom of Hannover, newly declared at the Congress of Vienna in 1814. So when William IV died in 1837, his brother Ernst August took up the crown in Hannover while his niece, **Victoria**, settled on to the throne in London.

outlying neighbourhoods: in the gentrifying restaurant and residential quarter **List**, the seedy **Steintor** bar strip, or in **Linden-Nord**, the multicultural hipsters' quarter.

Brief history

The seventeenth-century dukes of Calenburg revitalized the former Hanseatic League member, and Ernst August ushered in a **golden age** for his royal capital in the late 1600s. Court academic Gottfried Wilhelm Leibniz wowed Europe with his mathematical and philosophical theories and the arts blossomed, as did a Baroque garden seeded by the regent's wife, Sophia; Hannover's prize, it ranks among the finest in Europe. More significantly for British history, Sophia's parentage as granddaughter of James I of England saw her son, plain old Georg Ludwig, metamorphose into George I of Great Britain in 1714 to begin the **House of Hannover**'s 120-year stint on the British throne (see box above). Hannover became its own kingdom, with George III as its king, in 1814 when Napoleon's former territories were sorted out; the dream lasted until 1866, when the area was annexed by the Kingdom of Prussia, only to become part of the German Empire five years later, in 1871.

The Royal Gardens of Herrenhausen

Hannover only truly looks the part of historic royal capital in its **gardens**, a fifteen-minute walk northwest of Steintor. Of the quartet of gardens planned during the ducal tenure, **Welfengarten** abutting the city is the most forgettable, though popular with students who laze between lectures in the Welfenschloss at its east side, a preposterous piece of Gothic Revival with faux battlements.

Georgengarten

Georgengarten Open access • Free • ⓦ herrenhausen.de **Deutsches Museum für Karikatur & Zeichenkunst** Tues–Sun 11am–6pm • €4.50 • ⓦ karikatur-museum.de

More romantic than Welfengarten is the **Georgengarten** beyond, a public park whose neat lawns and mature trees are a model of the naturalistic English style that Romantics

13

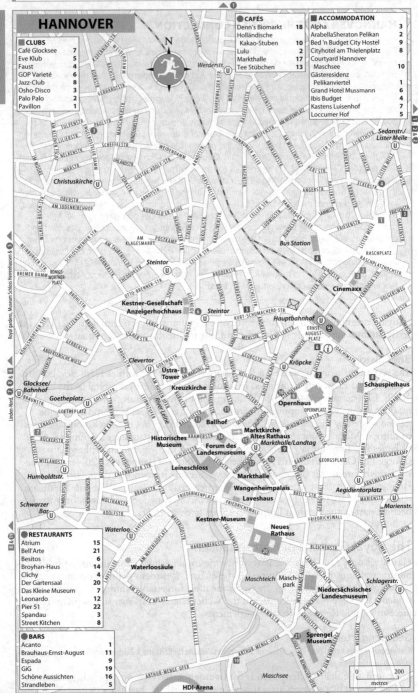

HANNOVER

■ CLUBS

Café Glocksee	7
Eve Klub	5
Faust	4
GOP Varieté	6
Jazz-Club	8
Osho-Disco	3
Palo Palo	2
Pavillon	1

■ CAFÉS

Denn's Biomarkt	18
Holländische Kakao-Stuben	10
Lulu	2
Markthalle	17
Tee Stübchen	13

■ ACCOMMODATION

Alpha	3
ArabellaSheraton Pelikan	2
Bed 'n Budget City Hostel	9
Cityhotel am Thielenplatz	8
Courtyard Hannover Maschsee	10
Gästeresidenz Pelikanviertel	1
Grand Hotel Mussmann	6
Ibis Budget	4
Kastens Luisenhof	7
Loccumer Hof	5

● RESTAURANTS

Atrium	15
Bell'Arte	21
Besitos	6
Broyhan-Haus	14
Clichy	4
Der Gartensaal	20
Das Kleine Museum	7
Leonardo	12
Pier 51	22
Spandau	3
Street Kitchen	8

● BARS

Acanto	1
Brauhaus-Ernst-August	11
Espada	9
GiG	19
Schöne Aussichten	16
Strandleben	5

conceived as a "walk-in painting". In the middle of the Georgengarten, the Baroque Georgenpalais houses the **Deutsches Museum für Karikatur & Zeichenkunst**, a museum dedicated to Wilhelm Busch, a Hannover-born nineteenth-century artist who dreamed of emulating Rubens but stumbled into fame as the father of the modern cartoon strip with *Max und Moritz*. Alongside his works are four centuries of satirical graphic arts, and every three months an exhibition of a luminary in the field; past masters have included Goya and Hogarth as well as modern political cartoonists.

The Grosser Garten and Museum Schloss Herrenhausen

Herrenhäuser Str. 4 • Daily: May–Aug 9am–8pm; Sept–April 9am–dusk; fountain displays April–Sept Mon–Fri 10am–noon & 3–5pm, Sat & Sun Mon–Fri 10am–noon & 2–5pm; museum daily 11am–6pm • €8 includes museum and Berggarten (€6 Oct–Feb) • ⓦ herrenhausen.de

Located beyond the Georgengarten, the modest Neoclassical **Schloss Herrenhausen** overlooks the Baroque **Grosser Garten**, the first garden in Hannover and still the best. Fired with inspiration after a visit to Versailles and aided by French master-gardener Martin Charbonnier, **Electress Sophia** – the consort of Ernst August, hailed by Leibniz as the greatest female mind of her age – transformed the kitchen garden of the royal summer palace into a horticultural masterpiece. "The Herrenhäuser garden is my life," she admitted, with good reason since the royals' open-air ballroom was thirty years in the making, finally complete in 1710. But what a stage: a precision-planted paean to the Age of Reason, surrounded by a moat that was plied by Venetian gondolas.

The garden

The orangerie and frescoed festival hall beside the palace survived wartime destruction. The heart of the garden beyond is the formal **Grosse Parterre**, with allegorical statues among the neat box hedge – the Cascade viewing platform adjacent to the palace provides an elevated view. In 2003 the garden's **grotto** received a shot of cultural adrenaline from New York artist Niki de Saint-Phalle, who inlaid Gaudí-esque ribbons of mosaic in rooms themed as Spirituality, Day and Life, and Night and the Cosmos, all bulging with her trademark cartoony sculptures.

As celebrated as the grotto is the **Grosse Fontäne**. Electress Sophia tasked the greatest engineering minds of her court with the problem of how to power a fountain to rival the Sun King's. The pump was cracked by English know-how; in 1720 a plume of water spurted 36m high and Europe marvelled. Today the pump has sufficient oomph to fling a jet of water 80m and the city continues to boast of having the highest fountain of any garden in Europe.

Museum Schloss Herrenhausen

Destroyed in World War II, the Schloss Herrenhausen was reconstructed in 2012 and now holds a conference centre and – in the two side wings – the **Museum Schloss Herrenhausen**. Partially underground, the new museum has a worthwhile exhibition on life in the Baroque era, with exhibits including the ornate sleighs that used to whizz the gentry around the gardens in winter, plus period art collections and an automatic pedometer designed by Leibniz in 1700.

Berggarten

Berggarten Daily: May–Aug 9am–8pm; Sept–April 9am–dusk • €3.50, combined ticket with Grosser Garten and Museum Schloss Herrenhausen €8 (€6 Oct–Feb) • ⓦ herrenhausen.de Sea Life Daily 10am–6pm • €16.50, less online • ⓦ visitsealife.com

The **Berggarten** on the other side of Herrenhäuser Allee is meagre stuff after the Grosser Garten. It was intended to house rare blooms in its greenhouses, some of which remain to house the largest permanent display of orchids in Europe. Laves's garden library, the Bibliothekspavillon, which is framed as you walk up Herrenhäuser Allee, flanks the other side of the entrance. He also designed a mausoleum of the Hannover kings which lies in front of a rhododendron thicket that blooms in late May. A popular attraction in the Berggarten is **Sea Life**, a kiddie-friendly aquarium and rainforest bubble.

13

Marktkirche and around

Hanns-Lilje-Platz 2 • Daily 9am–6pm • ⓦ marktkirche-hannover.de

The medieval **Marktkirche** – the southernmost example of north Germany's love affair with Gothic brick – is the heart of what's left of the Altstadt. The church's mighty tower powers up 98m as a launch pad for a spire – and ends instead in a pinprick. Why Hannover residents are so proud of this landmark is a mystery because their whimpering turret is a fudge, a miniature version of the architect's plans enforced by empty coffers and builders who, a contemporary chronicle relates, were "faint and taken of the sickness".

Severe wartime damage has swept the **interior** clean of later furniture to leave the austere monument erected in 1366. A Gothic Passion altar survives from the Reformation purges; behind, St George suffers his trials in medieval stained glass, and to the left, sprouting from a base like a gramophone trumpet, is an oversized fifteenth-century font featuring the Marktkirche's second saint, St James, with the staff and scallop shell of Santiago de Compostela pilgrims. Don't leave without taking a look at the 1959 **entrance doors**, on which sculptor Gerhard Marcks delivers a dramatic sermon on the "discordia and concordia" of modern German history, complete with a Nazi agitator, tanks, executions, corpses, rape, and a woman saving her child from a burning house only to see it succumb to hunger.

Altes Rathaus

On the south side of the Markt the rebuilt **Altes Rathaus** is a sideshow to the Marktkirche despite step gables that bristle with finials and layers of glazed and red brick, two styles favoured by the Baltic cities Hannover aped after it signed up to the Hanseatic League in 1386. Among the princes and heraldic arms depicted in a plaster frieze on the Schmiedestrasse flank, two burghers are locked in a game of *Luderziehen*, a medieval tug-of-war with ropes looped around their necks.

Around Holzmarkt

In the late 1800s, Jerome K. Jerome acclaimed Hannover for "handsome streets and tasteful gardens side by side with a sixteenth-century town where old timbered houses overhang the narrow lanes; where through low archways one catches glimpses of galleried courtyards". A faint echo of this is in **Kramerstrasse**, which runs between the Markt and Holzmarkt, and **Burgstrasse**, a suspiciously neat row of half-timbered fakes restored or rebuilt to replace the medieval streets obliterated by over eighty air raids in 1943.

Leibnizhaus

Holzmarkt 4 • Mon–Fri variable hours • Free

At the end of Kramerstrasse on Holzmarkt, **Leibnizhaus** is the rebuilt and relocated Renaissance mansion of philosopher **Gottfried Wilhelm Leibniz**. Leibniz asserted cheerfully that his job as ducal librarian to the Guelphic dukes in the late 1600s left spare hours for his leisure pursuits: inventing differential and integral calculus independently of Newton; honing theories of metaphysics; dreaming up a concept of cataloguing as an offshoot of a utopian universal library of thought; advancing theories of linguistics. His sharp mind also elevated his employer, Ernst August, to an elector after he unearthed tenuous links between the dukes and noble Italian stock of Este. The university-owned building is open erratically on weekdays; you can see Leibniz's letters to contemporaries such as Newton, plus essays and calculations showcased in the foyer.

Historisches Museum

Pferdestr. 6 • Tues 10am–7pm, Wed–Fri 10am–5pm, Sat & Sun 10am–6pm • €5, free Fri • ☎ 0511 16 84 23 52

On the corner of Holzmarkt, the **Historisches Museum** is an enjoyable wander through 750 years of town history: models and maps follow Hannover from a kernel trading

HANNOVER'S NANAS

Hohen Ufer promenade stretches along the River Leine, its name a nod to the "high banks" above the floodline that led to the founding of settlement "Honoevere" in the tenth century. On the opposite side of the river, three buxom belles pirouette like extras from a scene in *Yellow Submarine* as imagined by Picasso. For sober Hannover residents, the psychedelic **Nanas sculptures** created by New York artist **Niki de Saint-Phalle** in 1974 were not simply derogatory, they were expensive, too – with characteristic pragmatism, it was pointed out the *Nanas'* DM150,000 price tag could have paid for three rapid-response cars for doctors – and the people demanded Hannover's **Experiment Strassenkunst** (Street Art Experiment) conducted in the early 1970s be brought to a hasty conclusion. Inevitably, the bulging *Nanas* are now treasured as colourful icons of a largely faceless city. There's more of the artist's work in the Sprengel-Museum and the Grosser Garten (see p.701 & p.697).

outpost on the Leine onwards, including postwar footage of the devastation wrought by the Allies. On the ground floor, among the remnants of the former sixteenth-century armoury, a Rococo stagecoach straight from Walt Disney's *Cinderella* outshines the three other carriages that are on loan from the House of Hannover. The museum incorporates into its fabric the solid Beginenturm (1357) behind, a relic of the fortifications that girdled the medieval city.

The Ballhof and around

Britons will recognize the lion-and-unicorn crest on Duke Georg Ludwig's (King George I) former stables gateway, Tor des Marstalls, on the Historisches Museum's north side. Beyond the gateway and across Burgstrasse is the pretty **Ballhof** courtyard, named after a seventeenth-century sports hall (now the Lower Saxony State Theatre) in which Duke Georg Wilhelm swiped at shuttlecocks.

The Neues Rathaus and around

Friedrichswall, an arterial road that traces the former city walls, demarcates the former southern edge of the Altstadt. Stuttering chunks of the **medieval defences** remain like Morse code from the past: on the path between Georgswall and Osterstrasse, for example, or incorporated into the fabric of the Volkshochschule opposite the Neues Rathaus.

Neues Rathaus

Trammplatz 2 • Mon–Fri 8am–6pm, Sat & Sun 10am–6pm; dome lift March–Oct from 9.30am • Free, lift €3

The **Neues Rathaus** was built to replace the Altes Rathaus on the Markt, and what a town hall it is. Crowned by a dome of preposterous dimensions, its revivalist hulk so impressed Kaiser Wilhelm II that he officiated at the opening in 1913. Over six thousand piles prevent the fantastical behemoth sinking into marshy ground, and, although architect Hermann Eggert locked horns with city accountants over the interior (and lost), the Jugendstil entrance hall retains something of the exterior's grandiose scale, with a domed ceiling like a secular cathedral. Small wonder that it was here the birth of Lower Saxony was announced in 1946. Four models of the city trace Hannover's meteor-like path, from ascendant golden age with the arrival of the Guelph dukes in 1639 to the low of a postwar city reduced to rubble – this was one of the few buildings to survive with minimal damage. In addition, one of Europe's two inclined **lifts** curves around the cupola to the top of the dome, with spectacular views of the city and countryside beyond; come early or prepare to queue on sunny days.

13

> ## GOETHE AND CHARLOTTE KESTNER
>
> August Kestner (see below) was the most successful son of Charlotte Kestner, née Buff, who so captured the heart of a 23-year-old Goethe that she became immortalized in his *The Sorrows of Young Werther*, much to the chagrin of her future husband, who believed himself "grievously exposed and prostituted". Thomas Mann rendered a later, painfully polite meeting between Goethe and Charlotte as *Lotte in Weimar*.

Kestner-Museum

Trammplatz 3 • Tues & Thurs–Sun 11am–6pm, Wed 11am–8pm • €2.50–7, free on Fri • ⓦ kestner-museum.de

At the side of the Neues Rathaus is the **Kestner-Museum** and a six-millennia tour of decorative arts. The exhibits are founded on the collection of August Kestner, an art-loving chargé d'affaires of the Vatican, whose collection of Egyptian, Greek, Etruscan and Roman antiquities is updated with Art Nouveau and twentieth-century design classics.

The Maschsee

Directly behind the Neues Rathaus, the **Maschpark** and its **Maschteich** lake are a prelude to the 2.4km-long **Maschsee** lake, flanked to the east with a boulevard of trees and to the west by the Leine River. Hannover's nineteenth-century council had envied the Binnenalster lake in Hamburg and the town finally got its own artificial lake through a Nazi work-creation scheme: the regime's commemorative pillar remains at the north tip. Today the Maschsee is a focus for summer days, whether on a **cruise** from quays on all banks (Easter–Oct 10/11am–5/6pm; crossing €4, 1hr circuit of lake €7; ⓦ uestra-reisen.de), messing about in a sailing or rowing boat rented from a quay opposite the Sprengel-Museum (see opposite), dining in a couple of superb restaurants or spending lazy days on the Strandbad beach at the southeast corner. It takes around thirty minutes to walk along the foot-, cycle- and rollerblade path on the east bank; bus #267 plies a route down the same bank, or U-Bahn Altenbekener Damm lies a block across, midway down.

Niedersächsisches Landesmuseum

Willy-Brandt-Allee 5 • Tues & Thurs–Sun 10am–6pm, Thurs 10am–8pm • €4 • ⓦ nlmh.de

Founded in the mid-1800s, the **Niedersächsisches Landesmuseum** is the *grande dame* of Lower Saxony museums, with multiple personalities over its three levels. An aquarium and reptile house claim the ground floor alongside fairly musty ethnographical displays. Exhibits on the first floor track European civilization from prehistory to Roman and Saxon – the crowds inevitably gather around Roter Franz, a 300 BC pickled bog corpse named for his red hair – and there are the usual dinosaur skeletons and stuffed mammals in the natural history department.

Landesgalerie

The second-floor **Landesgalerie** steals the show. A Gothic Passion altar by Meister Bertram fizzes with characteristic vivacity, and there's a flowing *Mary and Child* by Tilman Riemenschneider, the genius of Late Gothic; nearby, Cranach studies his friend Martin Luther, alive and dead. Botticelli and Tiepolo star among the Italians, and the Dutch and Flemish masters are well represented: Bartolomeus Spranger teeters on the verge of Baroque with his saucy Bacchus tweaking the nipple of Venus; and look for Rubens' *Madonna and Child*, modelled, it's thought, on his first wife, Isabella Brant, and eldest son, Albert. Caspar David Friedrich provides a Phases-of-the-Day cycle, *Morning, Noon, Dusk* and *Evening*, and Monet glimpses Gare St-Lazare through thick swirls of steam. Collections of Max Slevogt, Lovis

Corinth, Worpswede's Paula Modersohn-Becker and Max Liebermann represent German Impressionism and early Expressionism.

Sprengel-Museum

Kurt-Schwitters-Platz • Tues 10am–8pm, Wed–Sun 10am–6pm • €7 • ⓦ sprengel-museum.de

Works in the nearby Landesmuseum are an overture to the twentieth-century art in the **Sprengel-Museum**, five minutes' walk south. Blockbuster exhibitions bolster a veritable Who's Who; expect all the big guns of the Blaue Reiter group (see box, p.347) – August Macke, Kandinsky and especially Klee, who gets a room to himself – plus savagely bitter canvases from Max Beckmann and displays of Munch and Oskar Kokoschka that are a tutorial in Expressionism. Their angst-wracked doom mongering is balanced by the empathetic humanism of sculptor Ernst Barlach and Surrealists such as Magritte and Ernst, or a few of Picasso's Cubist works. A selection from the world's largest collection of sculptures by **Niki de Saint-Phalle**, the American artist behind Hannover's *Nanas* (see box, p.699) and grotto in the Grosser Garten, are also on display; a new wing is under construction to house the full collection.

ARRIVAL AND DEPARTURE

HANNOVER

By plane Hannover international airport (ⓦ hannover-airport.de) is 9km northwest of the centre, linked by S-Bahn S5 to the Hauptbahnhof; a taxi will cost around €25.

By train The Hauptbahnhof (and bus station behind it) lies in the heart of the city, at the head of the pedestrianized high streets.

Destinations Braunschweig (every 45min; 30–45min); Bremen (every 40min; 1hr); Celle (every 15–30min; 20–45min); Goslar (hourly; 1hr–1hr 20min); Göttingen (every 20–40min; 35min–1hr); Hameln (every 30min; 45min); Hildesheim (every 30min; 25–35min); Lüneburg (hourly; 1hr); Osnabrück (every 2hr; 1hr 30min); Wolfsburg (every 15–30min; 30min–1hr).

GETTING AROUND

Public transport Tickets within Zone 1 – all you'll ever need – cost €2.35 for a two-hour single, €1.50 for a *Kurzstrecke* short-distance ticket valid for three stops on the U-Bahn (or five on a bus), €4.90 for a *TagesTicket* day-ticket, or €9.40 for a *TagesGruppenTicket* that covers up to five people.

Bike rental At the Fahrradstation (Mon–Fri 6am–10.30pm, Sat & Sun 8am–10.30pm) on the east side of the Hauptbahnhof.

City tour bus Departs from in front of the tourist office, stopping at six stops around the city (mid-April to Oct Mon–Fri 3 daily, Sat & Sun hourly; €13–15); the full tour takes 1h 20min.

Car rental All rental outfits except Avis unite operations in the *Reisezentrum* (travel centre) of the Hauptbahnhof. All also maintain a desk at the airport: Avis, Am Klagesmarkt ☎ 0511 12 17 40; Sixt ☎ 0180 525 25 25; Europcar ☎ 0511 363 29 93.

INFORMATION

Tourist office Directly opposite the Hauptbahnhof at Ernst-August-Platz 8 (Mon–Fri 9am–6pm, Sat & Sun 10am-3pm; Nov–March closed Sun; ☎ 0511 1234 5111, ⓦ hannover-tourism.de). As well as the usual information services, it can book accommodation for €2.50 per booking and sells the HannoverCard. Excellent touchscreen

Infopoints around town provide details on everything from hotels to nightlife, with links to maps.

Discount card The HannoverCard provides free travel on all public transport and discounts of around twenty percent on most sights and many opera and theatre tickets. A one-day card costs €9.50, a three-day card €17.50.

ACCOMMODATION

Unsurprisingly for a city known for trade fairs, hotels in Hannover are business-orientated. Be aware too that beds are hard to come by when the expense accounts roll into town. Worse, prices double, triple, then asphyxiate, and that's before they overcharge you for internet access – prices quoted below are for standard times, so book ahead or check with the tourist information office rather than trust it to chance.

HOTELS AND APARTMENTS

Alpha Friesenstr. 19 ☎ 0511 34 15 35, ⓦ hotelalpha .de. No minimalist understatement for the

Mediterranean-themed *Alpha*. Charming or chintzy depending on taste – marionettes may be a quirk too far – it undoubtedly offers a homely atmosphere and a quiet street behind the Hauptbahnhof. Breakfast extra. €84

Arabella Sheraton Pelikan Pelikanplatz 31 ☎0511 909 30, ⓦsheraton.de/hannover. North of the Hauptbahnhof by Listerplatz U-Bahn, the former factory that produced the famous Pelikan fountain pens is now the chief-executive's choice, a marriage of bold interior design and first-class comforts. Facilities include a gym with sauna. Breakfast extra. €164

Cityhotel am Thielenplatz Thielenplatz 2 ☎0511 32 76 91, ⓦsmartcityhotels.com. Funky retro-modernism at a budget price from a young hotel that's well located near the Hauptbahnhof – expect Verner Panton-style chairs and aluminium globe lights in renovated rooms; others are a little frumpy. €105

Courtyard Hannover Maschsee Arthur-Menge-Ufer 3 ☎0511 36 60 00, ⓦmarriott.de. An outpost of the international Marriott chain where, for an extra fee, rooms enjoy views down the Maschsee lake as well as a central location, the only hotel in Hannover to offer both. Otherwise standard classic-modern decor and efficient service. €171

Gästeresidenz Pelikanviertel Pelikanstr. 11 ☎0511 399 90, ⓦgaesteresidenz-pelikanviertel.de; tram #3, #7 or #9 to "Pelikanstrasse". Great-value apartments furnished in IKEA-esque fashion in an old brick warehouse; economy rooms are a squeeze, standards as worth the extra €20 for a couple. Facilities include a laundry and on-site bar. Long-stay rates available. The bad news is a location 4km north of the centre. €88

Grand Hotel Mussmann Ernst-August-Platz 7 ☎0511 365 60, ⓦgrandhotel.de. Opposite the station; large, modern rooms with oak parquet and clever space-saving bathroom design. Rooms have names instead of numbers, inspired by Hannover park photos. Ask for the special weekend deals. €149

Ibis Budget Runde Str. 7 ☎0511 235 55 70, ⓦibis.com. The functional en suites of the budget chain – moulded pod-like bathrooms and bunk beds for a child and two adults in tiny cabin rooms – make this an option best treated as a crash-pad. However, the location is central and it's one of the few bargains during a trade fair. €65

Kastens Luisenhof Luisenstr. 1–3 ☎0511 304 40, ⓦkastens-luisenhof.de. This five-star has been the *grande dame* of Hannover hotels for over 150 years; past names in the guestbook include opera singer Pavarotti and assorted visiting royals. Decor style is classic elegance in public areas, classic-modern in rooms. Service is immaculate. €199

Loccumer Hof Kurt-Schumacher-Str. 14–16 ☎0511 126 40, ⓦloccumerhof.com. Friendly, modern hotel right in the centre of the city which has rooms with idiosyncratic decor themed by elements and countries; if ever you wanted to wake to an alarm clock of the Dalai Lama singing, the "Tibet" room is your place. Others are in comfortable business style. €71

HOSTELS AND CAMPSITES

Bed 'n Budget City Hostel Osterstr. 37 ☎0511 360 61 07, ⓦbednbudget.de. Cheap dorm and private rooms, all fitted out with sturdy bunk beds, and many with TV, desk, fridge and private bathroom. Near the shopping streets and Markthalle, it's dead central too. Dorms €20, doubles €68

Blauer See Am Blauen See 119, Garbsen ☎05137 899 60, ⓦcamping-blauer-see.de; tram U4 to Garbsen to connect with bus #126 to "Waldschenke", then 1.5km walk to lake; by car exit junction 41 of the A2. The closest site to the centre is wrapped around a lake west of the city. A playground, fine beach and cable waterskiing will please parents and kids alike. Pitch €5.70, plus €8.90 per person

EATING AND DRINKING

Touristy Kramerstrasse and Knochenhauerstrasse offer choice in the centre, while style café-bars congregate around the Opernhaus. Better for eating are the locals' dining areas of **Lister Meile** and multicultural **Engelbosteler Damm**, north and northwest of the Hauptbahnhof respectively, and upmarket **Linden-Nord**, across the River Leine. For a picnic in the gardens, go to **delis** in the Markthalle (see below) or organic supermarket Denn's Biomarkt at Marktstr. 45 (closed Sun).

CAFÉS AND CHEAP EATS

Holländische Kakao-Stuben Ständehausstr. 2 ☎0511 30 41 00, ⓦhollaendische-kakao-stube.de. Be prepared to wait for a table on Saturdays because it can feel as if all Hannover has come to this historic, Dutch-styled café, all Delft tiles and blue-and-white china. Award-winning gâteaux and twelve varieties of cocoa make the wait worthwhile. Mon–Fri 9am–7.30pm, Sat till 6.30pm.

Markthalle Karmarschstr. 49 ⓦmarkthalle-in-hannover.de. A popular city-centre food hall that's an

excellent spot for a quick, quality bite or a good glass of wine at the end of the afternoon. Your options span the globe: from traditional sausages and *Currywurst* to Spanish tapas and South African *biltong* (beef jerky). Mon–Wed 7am–8pm, Thurs & Fri 7am–10pm, Sat 7am–4pm.

Lulu In der Steinriede 12 ☎0511 533 61 93, ⓦcafe-lulu.com. Come in summer and *Flammkuchen* (Alsatian-style pizza), *Schnitzels*, salads and tasty baguettes are served on a pretty cobbled square outside this café-bar a block east of the Lister Meile in the gentrified List neighbourhood. Mon–Sat 9am–1am, Sun from 10am.

13

★**Tee Stübchen** Am Ballhof 10 ☎0511 363 16 82, ⓦteestuebchen-hannover.de. Enchanting family-run throwback to nineteenth-century café society, all pea-green panelling and snug candlelit niches. There are over forty different teas to choose from, all served in large china cups, and delicious home-made apple cake. Also lovely for a glass of wine in the evening. Daily 10am–1am.

RESTAURANTS

Atrium Karmarschstr. 42 ☎0511 300 80 40, ⓦaltes-rathaus-hannover.de. The atrium is that of the Altes Rathaus – a bright courtyard protected by a glass roof – and the food is largely Mediterranean, typically upmarket bistro-style dishes. Together this makes for a sophisticated lunch destination for dishes such as spinach and ricotta ravioli or five-course menus for €15. Mon–Fri 9am–8pm, Sat till 4pm.

Bell'Arte Kurt-Schwitters-Platz 1 ☎0511 809 33 33, ⓦbellarte.de. The stylish restaurant of the Sprengel-Museum is beloved by an arty, older crowd for a contemporary Italian menu and a classic panorama over the Maschsee from its terrace; mains average €15. Tues–Sun 11am–midnight.

Besitos Goseriede 4 ☎0511 169 80 01, ⓦbesitos.de. Hipsters' courtyard place in the Steintor area that segues from a Spanish restaurant serving tapas and mid-priced grilled fish and meats (€15–19) to a cocktail bar. There's a touch of industrial chic to its main room and a courtyard space in summer. Daily 5pm–1am, Fri & Sat 5pm–2am.

Broyhan-Haus Kramerstr. 24 ☎0511 32 39 19, ⓦbroyhanhaus.de. Named for a Hannover brewer of the 1500s, this is the best option on Kramerstrasse, as traditional a tavern as you could want. Dishes are as time-proven as the decor: roast suckling pig with *Sauerkraut* is typical of a menu that changes once a century. Daily 11am–2am.

Clichy Wiessekreuzstr. 31 ☎0511 31 24 47, ⓦclichy.de. Behind an unpromising exterior near the start of the Lister Meile restaurant strip lies this small, elegant restaurant that comfortably marries tradition with first-rate contemporary cooking. Modern European cuisine leans towards France, all of it seasonal. Mon–Sat 6–11pm.

Der Gartensaal Trammplatz 2 ☎0511 16 84 88 88, ⓦgartensaal-hannover.de. At the rear of the Neues Rathaus, this bistro is as elegant a lunch spot as you can find in Hannover, with dining either in a spectacular hall or a terrace overlooking the Maschteich lake; parents rejoice – a playground is at its side. Summer cooking is light Asiatic or Mediterranean, changing to hearty German in cooler months. Daily 11am–10pm; mid-Sept to mid-May closes 6pm.

Das Kleine Museum Grotestr. 10 ☎0511 215 39 79. The crocodile screwed to the ceiling is just one of many odd objects brought home to this small French restaurant by its adventurer owner. The decent-sized, reasonably priced meals include a sheep cheese starter (€8) and chicken in honey-date sauce (€9). In summer, there's a nice terrace, in winter a cosy fireplace. A block south of the Leinaustrasse U-Bahn station in Linden-Nord. Mon–Thurs 5pm–1am, Fri & Sat 5pm–2am, Sun 5pm–midnight.

Leonardo Sophienstr. 6 ☎0511 32 10 33, ⓦweinstube-leonardo.de. A basement restaurant that is among the culinary highlights of Hannover thanks to the superb Italianate cooking of chef Carmelo Berardinelli, who conjures up dishes such as guinea fowl in grape sauce, *Wolfbarsch* in a pistachio crust or lamb from the Lüneburg Heath. Good value at average €19 for a main. Mon–Fri noon–3pm & 6pm–midnight, Sat 6pm–midnight.

★**Pier 51** Rudolf-von-Bennigsen-Ufer 51 ☎0511 807 18 00, ⓦpier51.de. A spectacular glass box on a pier that juts into the Maschsee midway down the east bank that's both a hip restaurant preparing expensive modern international cooking (meat and fish dishes €22) and a bar. There's a great terrace and also *Piergarten*, a beer garden with a snack stand for summer. Daily noon–midnight.

Spandau Engelbosteler Damm 30 ☎0511 12 35 70 95, ⓦspandauprojekt.de. The hippest spot of a multicultural restaurant strip 10min north of Steintor, this retro-styled place prepares Thai curries and Italian plates (around €9), plus organic buffet breakfasts at weekends, all at low prices. It morphs into a clubby lounge bar in the evening. Mon–Fri noon–1am, Sat & Sun 10am–1am.

Street Kitchen Limmerstr. 26 ☎0511 98 63 88 34, ⓦstreetkitchen-viet-cuisine.de. Fresh and great-value Vietnamese food in a stylish Linden-Nord restaurant; there's fried beef with red curry for €5.50, *pho ga* chicken noodle soup for €5.50. Reserve a table at weekends or be prepared to wait. Mon–Thurs & Sun noon–10pm, Fri & Sat noon–midnight.

NIGHTLIFE AND ENTERTAINMENT

Grungy bar-clubs can be found in the **Steintor** among the strip-clubs of parallel Reuterstrasse and Scholvinstrasse – it's fairly seedy but can be fun for boozy bar-hopping. The hippest scene is in **Linden-Nord**, a multicultural urban village west of the river with a bar on every corner – start at the junction of Limmerstrasse and Kotnerholzweg. For comprehensive what's-on listings pick up weekly **listings magazine** *Prinz*. Café-bistro *Café Konrad* at Knochenhauerstr. 34 and cocktail bar *Caldo* at Bergmannstr. 7 are good sources of information on the Hannover **gay scene**. The tourist office has a **ticket desk** for all entertainment events in the city.

BARS

Acanto Dragonerstr. 28 ☎0511 39 10 30, ⓦacantohannover.de. One of Hannover's most glamorous venues, this bar occupies the former royal stables, its high brick vaults drenched in washes of colour. "Celebrate with style" is the motto, helped by classic funk and soul, house and Latin plus clubnights at weekends. Glamorous adjacent restaurant *Basil* sets the mood for a sophisticated night out. Thurs & Fri 9pm–late, Sat 10pm–late.

Brauhaus-Ernst-August Schmiedestr. 13 ☎0511 36 59 50, ⓦbrauhaus.net. Part microbrewery whose speciality is unfiltered organic *Hanöversch Pils*, part restaurant serving hearty fare, part club for crowd-pleasing charts, disco and Schlager tunes – all in a sprawling institution that's popular among tourists and an older crowd. Mon–Thurs 8am–3am, Fri & Sat 8am–5am, Sun 9am–3am.

Espada Theaterstr. 14 ☎0511 32 23 38, ⓦespada-bar .de. A popular city-centre lounge bar serving everything from quality early breakfasts to late-night cocktails. Calm during the day, at weekend nights the atmosphere is buzzing, and bookings are recommended. Mon–Thurs 9am–midnight, Fri & Sat till 2am, Sun till 9pm.

★**GiG** Lindener Marktplatz 1 ☎0511 357 17 51, ⓦgig-linden.de; tram #9 to "Lindener Marktplatz". A former town-hall restaurant is now one of the most enjoyable bars in the Linden district, split over two levels and with eclectic thrift-shop-chic decor. It doubles as gig venue several times a week: alt-folk, jazz and rock. Mon–Fri 11.30am–2am, Sat & Sun 10am–3am.

Schöne Aussichten Röselerstr. 7 ☎0511 982 68 33. A lively city-centre beach bar on the top deck of a parking garage; there's sand to wiggle your toes in, great views over central Hannover, cocktails, food, and regular parties at the weekends. May–Sept daily 10am–midnight (closed if raining).

★**Strandleben** Weddingenufer ☎0511 123 570 95. "Beach life" just as the name says: deckchairs, parasols and sand between the toes on a bend of the Leine River south of the Georgengarten. Neutral ground for hipsters and counterculture alike; with a soundtrack of chilled funk, Brazilian and nu-jazz grooves, it makes a great warm-up for a night out in Linden-Nord a 10min walk away – follow signs for "Faust". May–Sept daily noon–midnight (closed if raining).

CLUBS

Café Glocksee Glockseestr. 35 ☎0511 161 47 12, ⓦcafe-glocksee.de. A mainstay of indie nights that also schedules a mixed programme of everything from electro to Fifties rock'n'roll via reggae, plus occasional gigs, usually of the rock or alt-folk variety. Occasional midweek 9pm–late, Fri & Sat 11pm–late.

Eve Klub Reuterstr. 3–4 ☎0152 094 584 67, ⓦeve-klub .de. Good-time grooves – Kool & The Gang, James Brown, Boney M and Prince – interspersed with the occasional Fat Boy Slim or Grandmaster Flash classic pack out the dancefloor in a small place with free entry. Bar daily 9pm–late; clubnights Fri & Sat 10pm–late.

Osho-Disco Raschplatz 71 ☎0511 642 27 85, ⓦosho-disco.de. Mainstream clubbing behind the Hauptbahnhof is the mainstay of "Baggi", as locals know this club. Expect club chart hits and disco house with the occasional party funk tune dropped for a young crowd. Decent bar areas too. Wed, Fri & Sat 10pm–late.

Palo Palo Raschplatz 8a ☎0511 33 10 73, ⓦpalopalo .de. Small fun club and bar behind the train station with a diet of soul, heavy funk and r'n'b, interspersed with the odd house or electro night. Occasionally has bands. Mon, Thurs, Fri & Sat 10pm–late.

LIVE MUSIC, CABARET AND THEATRE

Faust Zur Bettfedernfabrik 3 ☎0511 45 50 01, ⓦkulturzentrum-faust.de. Indie rock, ska-punk, reggae, metal, world music – you name it, this alternative cultural centre in a disused factory in Linden-Nord programmes the lot, alongside modern dance and art exhibitions plus clubnights in concert hall 60er-Jahre-Halle, plus a bar, *Mephisto*, and beer garden. Variable hours.

GOP Varieté Georgstr. 36 ☎0511 301 86 70, ⓦvariete .de. Aerobatic spectaculars and magic, song-and-dance numbers and comedy plus classic cabaret nights. The venue has a touch of 1930s dinner cabaret about its tables and chairs set on the main floor beneath a small stage. Tickets from €15. Tues–Sun, hours vary.

Jazz-Club Am Lindener Berge 38 ☎0511 45 44 55, ⓦjazz-club.de; tram #9 to Lindener Marktplatz, then 10min walk. Though fairly isolated midway between Linden Mitte and Linden Sud, this programmes a variety of acclaimed jazz names – past guests include Jan Garbarek and Lionel Hampton. Check the website or listings magazines as the schedule is erratic. Fri from 8.30pm–late, plus occasional midweek concerts.

Opernhaus Opernplatz 1 ☎0511 99 99 00, ⓦstaatstheater-hannover.de. The *grande dame* of Hannover high culture programmes major productions of opera from the likes of Wagner and Verdi plus ballet and

---

HANNOVER FESTIVALS

The highlight of the festival year is the largest **Schützenfest** (Marksmen's Festival; ⓦhannover .de/schuetzenfest) in Germany, held over ten days over the end of June and into July. Similar but more restrained is the **Maschsee** festival over nineteen days from the last Wednesday in July. The **Masala Festival**, North Germany's largest world-music festival (ⓦmasala-festival.de), is also in July.

13

classical concerts, then confounds the critics with crowd-pleasers like *The Rocky Horror Show*. Tues–Sun, hours vary.

Pavillon Lister Meile 4 ☎ 0511 235 55 50, ⓦ pavillon-hannover.de. A former shopping-centre behind the bus station, now a cultural centre with a varied programme of theatre and concerts: jazz, solo performances by past rock heroes and world music – it hosts the Masala world-music

festival in July (ⓦ masala-festival.de). Its buzzy café-bar *Café Mezzo* is a popular hangout too.

Schauspielhaus Prinzenstr. 9 ☎ 0511 99 99 00, ⓦ staatstheater-hannover.de. The leading stage for premieres and new productions in Hannover. The same company stages modern works in other venues throughout the city, notably at the two-stage Ballhof.

DIRECTORY

Cinema Multi-screen Cinemaxx (ⓦ cinemaxx.de) is behind the Hauptbahnhof on Raschplatz. Art house and repertory is screened in the Anzeiger Hochhaus (ⓦ hochhaus-lichtspiele .de) at Goseriede 9 – screenings are three or four times daily.
Hospital Marienstr. 37 ☎ 0511 28 90.

Markets A Saturday flea market (8am–4pm) sprawls along Hohen Ufer behind the Historisches Museum – tatty, cheerful fun that can even turn up the occasional bargain.
Police Raschplatz 1, behind Hauptbahnhof ☎ 0511 32 94 12.
Post Ernst-August-Platz 2, in front of Hauptbahnhof.

Hildesheim

For centuries **HILDESHEIM**, 30km southeast of Hannover, starred on the check-list of every cultured Grand Tour of Europe. It was medieval Germany writ large, its two Romanesque churches among the finest on the continent and its Altstadt a half-timbered fairy tale. So a night of firebombs on March 22, 1945, which ravaged the centre as the Allies targeted prestige cities to sap German morale during the war's

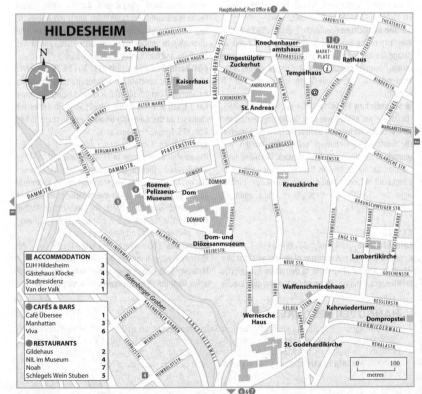

HILDESHEIM

■ ACCOMMODATION	
DJH Hildesheim	3
Gästehaus Klocke	4
Stadtresidenz	2
Van der Valk	1

● CAFÉS & BARS	
Café Übersee	1
Manhattan	3
Viva	6

● RESTAURANTS	
Gildehaus	2
NIL im Museum	4
Noah	7
Schlegels Wein Stuben	5

end-game, struck particularly hard. The town salvaged what it could and erected typically monstrous postwar rebuilds until, in 1984, the council took the unprecedented decision to re-create the former townscape. Uncharitably, then, the architectural highlights of Hildesheim are conscious antiquarianism at best, glorious fakes at worst. Yet UNESCO deemed the efforts worthy of its World Heritage list, an unexpected fillip to a beautification programme that seems likely to continue. Aside from the architecture, Hildesheim is a relaxed university town, pleasant, certainly, but also fairly provincial.

The Markt

Playing the game of superlatives, the great nineteenth-century academic, philosopher and all-round Prussian brainbox Wilhelm von Humboldt, who had seen a fair bit of Europe in his function as a diplomat, declared Hildesheim's **Markt** the most beautiful in the world. Hyperbole, perhaps, but the one-time mercantile showpiece of the city is once again pure camera-fodder since its rebuild in 1984, the only sign of which is its over-polished "medieval" buildings.

The Rathaus, Tempelhaus and around

The stone **Rathaus** at the Markt's rear was able to be patched up to return its Gothic form – an iron rod that measures an ell (a medieval length) of cloth remains embedded in blocks at the rear corner. The **Tempelhaus** patrician's house on the south side of the Markt has a turreted facade thought to derive from a Crusader's description of the Holy Land, while its name mistakenly refers to a Jewish temple that was thought to have stood here. The Renaissance oriel tacked on its front, removed during the war and therefore saved from damage, narrates the parable of the Prodigal Son. Continuing clockwise, conjoined Wedekindhaus, Lüntzelhaus and Rolandstift are all replicas, the former smothered in carvings, as is the Bäckeramtshaus (bakers' guildhouse) that opens the west side of the square.

Knochenhauer-Amtshaus

Markt 7 • Tues–Sun 10am–6pm • €3 • Ⓦ stadtmuseum-hildesheim.de

The source of all the "oohs" is the colossal **Knochenhauer-Amtshaus** (butchers' guildhouse) at the side of the Bäckeramtshaus. The current incarnation was completed in 1989 to the same plans and carpentry methods as the Gothic original, deemed through time-honoured tradition as "the most beautiful half-timbered building in the world". One reason is the playground of folkloric images – old and new – carved on gables that cascade from a peak 26m up. It's one of the few reconstructed buildings you can go inside as the home of a **Stadtmuseum** in the upper floors.

Andreasplatz

The firebombs that obliterated the Markt also did for **Andreasplatz** southwest, formerly considered its rival. In late 2007, a council motion was passed to reconstruct iconic medieval house, **Umgestülpter Zuckerhut** ("Sugarloaf House"); its inverted half-timbered stack – a medieval ploy to gain space on a small footprint – returned to a corner in 2010.

St-Andreas-Kirche

Andreasplatz 6 • Church tower May–Oct Mon, Tues, Thurs, Fri 11am–4pm, Sat 11am–6pm, Sun noon–4pm • €2.50

Andreasplatz is named for the **St-Andreas-Kirche**, rebuilt from its foundations with the four naves and ambulatory planned by the medieval builders but which proved beyond their technical know-how. The reason to visit is for the views from the tower, 75m up.

13 St Michaelis

Michaelisplatz 2 • Mon 8am–6pm, Tues 10am–6pm, Wed–Sat 8am–6pm, Sun noon–6pm • Free • Ⓦ michaelis-gemeinde.de

Of all Hildesheim's reconstructed ecclesiastical monuments, it is **St Michaelis** that receives most accolades. The UNESCO-listed church on a low hill west of Andreasplatz rises like a miniature city of towers and copper roofs, a vision of Jerusalem as conceived by its founder Bishop Bernward to venerate a fragment of the Holy Cross. The erudite bishop, a tenth-century aristocrat who tutored Emperor Otto III, lived just long enough to see his three-aisled basilica stand in 1022 as what turned out to be the pinnacle of Ottonian architecture, a bridging style that pioneers Romanesque. Bernward was canonized for his effort in 1192 – he lies in the crypt at the western end – and to commemorate the event a **rood screen** was carved to depict Bernward with a model of his church among angels and holy dignitaries. A superb work, it ranks among the masterpieces of German sculpture of the time. The church's other highlight is a ceiling of the **Tree of Jesse** inspired by manuscript illuminations. Yet what impresses as much is the architectural dignity of the basilica, achieved through its classically inspired adherence to quadrilateral measures. The nave is as wide as two transepts, and the church pioneers the so-called Lower Saxon style of alternating pillars and bulky columns, creating quadrangles to frame the transepts. The Baroque-styled **Magdalenengarten** to its west is a welcome bit of greenery in the city centre.

The Dom

Domhof • Daily 10am–6pm • Free, museum €6 • Ⓦ dom-hildesheim.de

UNESCO's salute to Hildesheim was the World Heritage accreditation of its **Dom**, seemingly caught in a temporal back-eddy within its romantic courtyard. Never mind the fudge of styles that obscures the early eleventh-century structure, its fame is twofold. Foremost in artistic merit are its **bronze doors**, displayed in a hall at the western end. Bishop Bernward commissioned the doors, each over 4.7m high and 1.2m wide, in 1015 for the St Michaelis church only for his successor, Bishop Godehard, to remove them as a processional portal for the new cathedral. Their sixteen-cell biblical cartoon-strip, cast from a sculpted sand mould, narrates the Old Testament from the creation of man to the fratricide of Cain, then the New Testament of Christ, with an almost Expressionist kinetic energy and wealth of background detail that is unparalleled in contemporary casting. Bernward also commissioned the **Christussäule** (Christ pillar) in the south transept soon after the doors' completion, and the same energy infuses the life story of Christ as it spirals up the 4m column. The well-travelled bishop clearly modelled his creation on Rome's victory pillar, the Trajan Column, although the top "Romanesque" capital is a clumsy attempt at beautification from the late 1800s. Also worth a look is Germany's oldest wheel-shaped **chandelier** (c.1055), forged by Godehard as a representation of the heavenly city of Jerusalem and hovering symbolically over the altar.

More artistic treasures, notably a couple of gold crucifixes, are displayed in rotating exhibitions in the **Dom Museum**. Look, too, for a gem-studded cross inlaid with gold filigree said to have been that of Saxon duke Henry the Lion.

Cloisters

The second source of the Dom's fame is the thousand-year-old **rose bush** in its **cloisters**. The story goes that Emperor Louis the Pious, son of Charlemagne, who raised Hildesheim to a bishopric in 815 AD, awoke from a nap while hunting one summer to find his Marian relics frozen fast to a rose bush. Detecting the hand of the divine, he vowed to found a diocese on the spot. Whether this is the same bush is a matter of some conjecture. Even if it is, what you see is growth that sprouted after the original was burned along with the cathedral in 1945 – a somewhat miraculous revival, perhaps, but a rose bush is still only a rose bush.

Roemer- und Pelizaeus-Museum

13

Am Steine 1–2 • Tues–Sun 10am–6pm • €10 • ⓦ rpmuseum.de

A former friary just southwest of the Dom serves as one wing of the **Roemer- und Pelizaeus-Museum**, a well-lit display of antiquities that would do credit to any European capital. Indeed, in 1912 the manager of Berlin's Egyptian Museum acclaimed its most famous exhibit, the life-size tomb statue of Hem-iunu, an Egyptian vizier c.2400 BC, as "the best figure I know of in Egypt", adding, "What a shame it will be relegated to the provinces." The pharaoh's man-boobs are an indication of his prestige. The museum's strength is a re-creation of a tomb and the largest collection of Egyptian jewellery in Germany. Smaller pieces, such as a four-thousand-year-old model granary in which labourers fill grain sacks, also intrigue, and there are displays from ancient Peru and imperial Chinese porcelain.

The southern Altstadt

While the bombs rained on the centre, the southern Altstadt was mostly spared, preserving a pocket of old Hildesheim. The charm begins at the bottom of Hinterer Brühl with early seventeenth-century **Wernersche Haus**, its beams carved with images of the virtues and vices, local heroes – bearded Charlemagne, Louis the Pious and St Bernward with his church. Opposite the house, **St Godehardikirche** is a well-preserved basilica erected in the fourteenth century in honour of the bishop who had been canonized earlier that century. He is depicted in the tympanum beside Christ. The interior is modelled on St Michaelis, its advance being the knotted capitals of its alternating Lower Saxon-style pillars.

East of the church the former Jewish ghetto – the **Lappenburg** district – is a photogenic nest of residential streets. Armourers' guildhouse **Waffenschmiedehaus** on Gelber Stern depicts its trade and what may be two Hebrew kings, while Kesslerstrasse beyond is a pretty jumble of half-timbering, ending in a square with a dramatic monument for the synagogue that stood here until *Kristallnacht* in 1938.

The Kehrwiederturm

The **Kehrwiederturm** that punctuates the skyline is a relic of the city's medieval fortifications, one celebrated in a legend about a noble virgin who used it as homing beacon to return through thick forest from her beloved knight. They say he was struck by lightning for the subterfuge romance. The yarn probably derives from a local tradition of annual donations to virtuous virgins, hence the maiden who proffers a laurel wreath on the city coat of arms.

Schloss Marienburg

Nordstemmen, 15km northwest of Hildesheim • Tours daily every 45min (audio-guides in English available) Easter–Oct 10am–5pm • €8 • ⓦ schloss-marienburg.de • Train to Nordstemmen (frequent trains), then 3km walk or connecting bus (Sat & Sun only)

Not in Hildesheim but an easy day-trip from it, **Schloss Marienburg** is as romantic a castle as you could wish for. It was intended both as a birthday gift from Hanoverian king Georg V to his wife Queen Marie in 1857, and a fantastical homage to the history of his Guelphic dynasty realized by one of Germany's finest neo-Gothic architects, Conrad Wilhelm Hase. Prussian annexation of his kingdom meant the ruler never got to enjoy his summerhouse – Marie lived there in semi-imprisonment for just under a year before she followed him into exile in Austria – but ancestral owner Prince Ernst August VI von Hannover occasionally resides here.

As an alternative to public transport, and to make a day of it, you could **cycle** from Hildesheim; it's 14km west on a good track – allow about an hour and a half each way. The tourist office in Hildesheim can provide advice and maps of the route. There's a restaurant at the Schloss.

The interior

The fantasy medieval aesthetic continues in an interior whose decor swings between neo-Gothic swagger – state halls such as the **Rittersaal** banqueting hall, furnished with silver chairs that Georg II commissioned from Augsburg goldsmiths in 1720, for example, or a spectacular **queen's library** which umbrella from a central pillar – and genuine romance in the children's bedroom **Salon der Prinzessinen** (Princesses' Salon), painted with scenes from *Sleeping Beauty*, apt for a palace that mouldered until 1945.

ARRIVAL AND INFORMATION HILDESHEIM

By train Hildesheim lies at a rail junction of the Hannover and Braunschweig lines. The Hauptbahnhof is around 500m due north of the centre.

Destinations Braunschweig (hourly; 25min); Göttingen (hourly; 30min); Hameln (hourly; 50min); Hannover (every 30min; 30min).

Tourist office In the Tempelhaus, Rathausstr. 20 (Tues–Fri 10.30am–6pm, Sat 9am–3pm, Sun 11am–3pm; Nov–March closed Sun; ☏ 05121 179 80, ⊕ hildesheim .de/tourismus). The tourist office's pamphlet guide, *Hildesheimer Rosenroute* (€1), covers most of the town's sights.

ACCOMMODATION

DJH Hildesheim Schirrmannweg 4 ☏ 05121 427 17, ⊕ djh-niedersachsen.de. Though in a bucolic location, the youth hostel is a fair hike from the centre and not served by direct transport. From the train station, take bus #1 to "Schuchstrasse", then change to a Bockfeld-bound bus #4 and alight at "Triftstrasse", from where it's a 15min walk uphill. Dorms **€22.50**, doubles **€53**

Gästehaus Klocke Humboldtstr. 11 ☏ 05121 17 92 13, ⊕ gaestehaus-klocke.de. Simple en-suite rooms with high ceilings and pine floors in a miniature Art Nouveau mansion of creaky staircases and stained glass – a true traditional guesthouse. It's located on a quiet residential street in the southern Altstadt, a short walk from St Godehard church. **€82**

Stadtresidenz Steingrube 4 ☏ 05121 697 98 92, ⊕ hotel-stadtresidenz.de. This suite-and-apartment four-star lies in a residential area 10min walk from the centre. Popular with older travellers for accommodation that is large, spotless and styled in a sort of upmarket homely decor, plus good breakfasts. Note that reception closes at 6pm unless by advance notice. **€106**

Van der Valk Markt 4 ☏ 05121 30 00, ⊕ hildesheim .vandervalk.de. Hildesheim's finest address marries design flair to old-world charm in a modern spa hotel spread over three reconstructed townhouses on the Markt. Exact service from the Van der Valk chain and fine breakfasts. Bear in mind that rooms overlooking the Markt get the bells and town market (from 5am on Wed and Fri) as well as the views. **€104**

EATING AND DRINKING

CAFÉS AND BARS

Café Übersee Almsstr. 33, corner of Wallstrasse ☏ 05121 29 97 22. Nicely laidback café and bar which sets wicker chairs and parasols outside on a terrace and in a modern interior. It comes recommended for cheap breakfasts and makes a pleasant spot for mellow drinking. Occasionally hosts weekend gigs. Daily 9am–midnight, Fri & Sat 9am–1am.

Manhattan Burgstr. 15 ☏ 05121 13 40 43. Over 300 cocktails and whiskies in what is considered among the best cocktail bars in Germany. Come early or order well in advance – you can wait an age for a drink to arrive when it's busy. Tues–Sun 9pm–late.

Viva Lucienvörder Str. 22 ⊕ cafeviva.de. Mellow, modern café in a quiet corner of the Altstadt near St Godehard church. A terrace over the canal and tables shaded by trees are pleasant spots to lose an hour over lunch – expect the likes of fresh soups or quiche, foccacia sandwiches and antipasti platters. Also nice for afternoon coffee or a quiet beer. Daily 8am–7pm.

RESTAURANTS

Gildehaus *Van der Valk Hotel Hildesheim*, Markt 4 ☏ 05121 30 00, ⊕ hildesheim.vandervalk.de. Sophisticated dining in the town's premier hotel, with an elegant dining room and a seasonal international menu plus a few upmarket local dishes like corn chicken with goat's cheese (€18.50); a union of modern and traditional styles. There's a nice terrace on the Markt as well, and you can start the night in the hotel's hip cocktail bar, *Havanna*. Daily noon–11pm.

NIL im Museum Roemer- und Pelizaeus-Museum, Am Steine 1 ☏ 05121 40 85 95, ⊕ nil-restaurant.de. The glass-walled restaurant and café of the museum is beloved by an older, arty set for its stylishly laidback vibe and modern Italianate cooking. Expect the likes of pork *saltimbocca* (€12.30) or home-made antipasti. Regular parties on weekend nights too. Mon 5pm–midnight, Tues–Sun 11.30am–midnight.

Noah Hohnsen 28 ☏ 05121 69 15 30, ⊕ noah-cafe.de. Glass-walled bistro and café with a terrace over the Hohnsensee lake that's popular with locals for sunny afternoons and weekend brunch buffets. Located 20min south of St Godehardikirche via Mühlengraben then across the footbridge, it's a nice destination for a walk. Mon–Sat 9am–11pm, Sun 10am–11pm.

Schlegels Wein Stuben Am Steine 4 ☎05121 331 33, ⓦschlegels-weinstuben.de. Tucked away behind the Roemer- und Pelizaeus-Museum, this historic house is the place to come for fine dining with charm to spare. It's installed in a 1500s house, with historic rooms as a backdrop for high-class, seasonal and regional cooking; there's a wine bar, too. Mon–Fri 5–11pm, Sat 6–11pm.

Hameln

Like Bremen with its town musicians, **HAMELN** (Hamelin) must say a daily prayer in praise of fairy tales. The rat-catcher-turned-child-snatcher not only gave the small town international fame but a ready-made promotional angle. A **Pied Piper** fountain gushes rodents and the tale (see box below) is re-enacted weekly in summer. Even the Marktkirche has a Pied Piper window. Whatever the yarn would have you believe, the town has more than its fair share of children, too, because the ploy works. Such is its popularity – the town receives over 3.5 million tourists per year – that Hameln isn't always the "pleasanter spot you never spied" as American Robert Browning describes in his poem of the tale. It is a good-humoured place, however, with few pretensions to greatness other than its historic Altstadt. It also serves as gateway to the lovely hill-and-river country of the **Weserbergland** south.

Along Osterstrasse

Whatever the fun of fairy tales, Hameln is also known for its Weser Renaissance style, a home-grown version of the Italianate known for elaborate facades. The best can be found along Osterstrasse, a street that opens with fine carving on the **Rattenfängerhaus** at no. 28, a former councillors' house built in 1602. Its "Ratcatcher House" moniker refers to the inscription on its side that relates the Pied Piper tale. The Rattenfängerhaus looks positively sober compared to the **Lesithaus** at no. 9, a confection of candy pinks, cream and sherbet yellows from whose sugary oriel Lucretia gazes distractedly, her modesty just about covered by a slip of cloth. It seems likely its architect designed the merchant's home to trump its older neighbour, the **Stiftsherrenhaus**, whose half-timbered facade is a riot of rosettes, twisted rope motifs, and biblical and astrological personalities, a very contemporary union of religion and superstition.

THE PIED PIPER LEGEND

Hameln, June 1284: A stranger in multicoloured clothes strikes a deal with the town council over payment to lift a plague of rats that has infested the town. He pipes the rodents to their deaths in the Weser, yet the council renege on payment. The stranger returns while the citizens are in church, and, dressed in a hunter's costume, exacts his revenge – 130 children follow his pipe from the town and are never seen again. Just two boys remain, one lame, the other deaf.

Germany's most **famous legend** was recognized in a stained-glass panel in the church as early as 1300. Academics agree the yarn is rooted in history – it is surely not coincidence that Hameln town records commence with the tragedy, which is reported as straight news a century later in a manuscript and given a date – June 26, 1284 – but hard facts remain elusive. The most plausible theory proposes nothing more fantastical than an exodus of citizens, Hameln "children" all, during colonization of eastern nations such as Pomerania and Prussia – the finger is often pointed at Count von Schaumberg who moved to Olmutz, now Olomouc in the Czech Republic. In the Grimm Brothers' account, compiled from eleven sources, the children founded a town in Transylvania. However, the presence of rats has led some scholars to propose a **mass migration** during the Black Death, a baton taken up by a theory that suggests the tale remembers an early plague in which the piper represents Death.

13

Museum Hameln

Osterstr. 8–9 • Tues–Sun 11am–6pm • €5 • ⓦ hameln.de/museum

Together, the Lesithaus and the Stiftsherrenhaus are home to **Museum Hameln**, with the usual town history displays perked up by a small section on the Pied Piper legend. Among its facsimiles is the earliest depiction of the narrative from the early fifteenth century with a jester-like piper standing above a tiny town as a crowd of kids march up a hill – one version of the story has the children disappear inside the cave and returned after a substantially inflated payment.

Markt and around

At the end of Osterstrasse is the **Markt**, town centre and venue for free **performances** (Sun at noon May to mid-Sept) of Hameln's legend by an eighty-strong local troupe. The **Marktkirche** is a postwar rebuild that is missable except for a stained-glass window of the Pied Piper tale, a replica of an original said to have been crafted within a lifetime of the event.

Pulverturm

Thielewall • March–Dec Mon–Sat 10am–1pm & 2–6pm, Sun 10am–5pm • €5, glass-blowing €18 • ⓦ glasblaeserei-hameln.de

Five minutes' walk north from the Markt is the **Pulverturm**, one of the last defence towers of the town's medieval fortifications; when beefed up into the strongest defences in the Kingdom of Hannover, they gained Hameln a reputation as a "Gibraltar of the North". The tower now houses a glass factory with **glass-blowing demonstrations** – visitors can try under supervision – and a shop.

ARRIVAL AND DEPARTURE

HAMELN

By train Hameln's Bahnhof is a 15min walk west of the Altstadt centre: follow Bahnhofstrasse to Diesterstrasse and turn left.

Destinations Hannover (every 30min; 45min); Hildesheim (hourly; 50min–1hr).

INFORMATION AND TOURS

Tourist office Deisterallee 1, on Altstadt ringroad, opposite the end of Osterstrasse (Mon–Fri 9am–6pm, Sat 9.30am–3pm (till 1pm Oct–April), Sun 9.30am–1pm; Nov–March closed Sun; ☏ 05151 95 78 23, ⓦ hameln.de).

River cruises Flotte Weser operates river cruises from a quay on the Weser Promenade south of the centre (mid-April to mid-Oct; ⓦ flotte-weser.de); some go south through the Weserbergland as far as Bad Karlshafen.

ACCOMMODATION

HOTELS

Altstadt-Wiege Neue Marktstr. 10 ☏ 05151 278 54, ⓦ hotel-altstadtwiege.de. The best option on a street with several, this friendly family-run *hotel garni* provides four rooms above its restaurant. Notwithstanding a four-poster in one room, the style is modern yet enjoyably quirky, with some custom-designed furnishings. Good breakfasts too. **€73**

Christenhof Alte Marktstr. 18 ☏ 05151 950 80, ⓦ christinenhof-hameln.de. What appears a traditional half-timbered house in a cobbled lane from outside is an efficient comfortable business hotel within. Decor in rooms is classic business style; facilities include a small counter-current pool in a historic brick cellar and a sauna. **€110**

Jugendstil Wettorstr. 15 ☏ 05151 955 80, ⓦ hotel-jugendstil.de. Period character in a high-ceilinged Art Nouveau house a block north of the Altstadt. Modernized and well-maintained rooms make this an appealing 4-star option – the owners claim former guests include Klimt and Toulouse-Lautrec. **€115**

★**Schlosshotel Münchhausen** Schwöbber 9, 7km southwest of Hameln, west of Gross Berkel ☏ 05154 706 00, ⓦ schlosshotel-muenchhausen.de. This Renaissance manor estate hotel makes a trip to Hameln worthwhile in itself. Colourful toile fabrics lift restrained decor in beautiful modern-country rooms in the Schloss; cheaper, less glamorous accommodation is in a restored tithe barn. The hotel also has a fine-dining restaurant, plus a German cellar number, and a spa and golf course. **€80**

Zur Krone Osterstr. 30 ☏ 05151 90 70, ⓦ hotelzurkrone .de. Beams bring character to the front rooms of this renovated seventeenth-century house that is superbly located on an arterial pedestrianized thoroughfare of the Altstadt. Those in the modern block behind are classic-modern in style. **€95**

HOSTELS AND CAMPSITES

DJH Hameln Fischbecker Str. 33 ☎05151 34 25, ⓦdjh-niedersachsen.de; bus #2 from the Bahnhof to "Wehler Weg". Two- to six-bed rooms in a hostel with a riverside location north of the centre – the Wesserradweg cycle path passes outside to link to the centre a 10min walk away along the river. Dorms **€21**, doubles **€49**

Fährhaus an der Weser Uferstr. 80 ☎05151 674 89, ⓦcampingplatz-faehrhaus-hameln.de. Though largely dedicated to caravans, this site has space for a few tents and the location on the west bank of the Weser appeals – there's a nice little beach-bar and pool for summer, too. It's located a 20min walk north from the centre. Pitch **€3.50**, plus **€4.50** per person

EATING AND DRINKING

Antiquitäten Cafe & Tee Kupferschmiedestr. 7 ☎05151 80 97 10. A charmingly old-fashioned cornershop café with a good selection of hot drinks – including local "rat dropping" tea – and cake. Mon–Thurs 10.30am–5.30pm, Fri & Sat 10.30am–2pm.

Böhmerwald Sudetenstr. 1 ☎05151 293 90, ⓦboehmerwald-restaurant.de. Hearty German and Czech fare served inside a former water-powered electricity plant along the Weser. There's trout for €7.60 and *Svickova*, veal marinated in wine (€13.50). Good river views from the summer terrace. Daily 11.30am–midnight.

Me Lounge Am Stockhof 2 ☎05151 407 92 80, ⓦmelounge-hameln.de. Smart, mainstream café-bar on the Weser with a large terrace over the river that is popular for summer dining and drinks. Mon–Thurs & Sun

9am–1am, Fri & Sat 9am–3am.

Rattenfängerhaus Osterstr. 28 ☎05151 38 88, ⓦrattenfaengerhaus.de. A famous *Gaststätte* that provides good *Bürgerlich* cooking (*Schnitzel* €14) in a traditional Hameln house – thankfully, the rat-themed cuisine is in name only (although there may be some truth in the name of fifty-percent-proof *Schnapps Rattenkiller*). Touristy, but that's half the point. Daily 10am–late.

Sumpfblume Am Stockhof 2 ☎05151 932 10, ⓦsumpfblume.de. A self-described "culture and communication station", which translates into a studenty riverside café near the Flotte Weser quay, serving snacks, burgers (around €6) and sandwiches. In the evening it becomes a bar, club and live music venue. Mon–Fri 4pm–late, Sat 2pm–late, Sun 10am–late.

Down the Weser River

The Weser River, the arterial waterway of the Weserbergland, forges south of Hameln into countryside pillowed by woods and rolling fields. It provides a great excuse for touring, swinging alongside the Weser on the B83 for much of the way to **Hannoverisch Münden**, swooping around broad meanders and hauling over wooded hills. Indeed, the journey is as much an attraction as the destinations en route.

GETTING AROUND   THE WESER RIVER

By bike The stretch of the Weser River between Hameln and Hannoverisch Münden forms part of one of Germany's most popular cycle routes, the Weserradweg (ⓦweser-radweg.info and ⓦweserradweg.de) – 150,000 cyclists a year can't all be wrong.

By canoe The Weser River is acclaimed canoeing country, but a swift current demands that you make the journey in reverse, heading north from, say, Bad Karlshafen; a local operator there (see p.715) provides canoe hire and transfers.

By ferry With careful juggling of timetables, you can make most of the journey south from Hameln by ferries of the Flotte Weser line (Easter–Oct; ⓦflotte-weser.de); they go to Bodenwerder (Wed, Fri and Sun), and from Höxter 30km south, linked by local buses, to Bad Karlshafen (Tues–Sun). Pick up timetables from the ferry quay in Hameln and all tourist offices in the area.

By bus Bus transport is fiddly: daytime-only bus #520 from Hameln goes via Bodenwerder to Holzminden to hook up with train services to destinations south.

Bodenwerder

Hameln has a piper; **BODENWERDER**, 20km south, has **Baron von Münchhausen**. The aged baron who told fantastical tales of feats such as riding cannonballs, travelling to the moon and pulling himself out of a swamp by his own hair (or bootstraps depending on who tells the story) is founded upon local baron Karl Friedrich Hieronymous von Münchhausen. The literary hero he became (see box, p.714) looms large in what is an otherwise unremarkable one-street village. Every third Sunday of the

13

> ## BARON VON MÜNCHHAUSEN
>
> While Hameln's Pied Piper is shrouded by folklore, the aged duke who spun fantastical tales of his daring is hard fact. Local baron **Karl Friedrich Hieronymous von Münchhausen** returned to his ancestral seat from Russian campaigns against the Ottomans in the mid-1700s to regale anyone who would listen with witty but exaggerated boasts of his exploits. With a pinch of traditional folk-tale and a generous helping of fantasy, these were cooked up in English in 1785 by Rudolf Erich Raspe as *Baron Münchhausen's Narrative of his Marvellous Travels and Campaigns in Russia*, then returned back to the original German and extended as *Wunderbare Reisen zu Wasser und zu Lande: Feldzüge und lustige Abenteuer des Freiherr von Münchhausen* (Marvellous Travels on Water and Land: Campaigns and Comical Adventures of the Baron of Münchhausen).
>
> It remains an enduringly popular text, a blend of historical shaggy-dog story and *Gulliver's Travels* fantasy. By way of example: our debonair hero is embroiled in conflicts around the globe – he single-handedly saves Gibraltar by hurling Spanish cannons into the sea and rides a cannonball to reconnoitre Turkish troops; journeys to a cheese island in a sea of milk; and is propelled with his ship to a harbour on the moon by a whirlwind – his second visit, apparently. Director Josef von Báky realized his exploits in *Munchausen* for Germany's fourth colour movie, shot in super-saturated colour in 1943, as did Terry Gilliam, whose special-effects spectacular, *The Adventures of Baron Munchausen*, was released to general critical indifference in 1988. Perhaps more damaging for the reputation of the genuine baron, who was not nearly as shameless as his literary namesake, is the illness named after him, **Munchausen syndrome**, a psychiatric disorder whose sufferers exaggerate or fake illness to win attention.

month, the **Grotto pavilion** where Von Münchhausen told his stories in his hunting room is opened to visitors – visits are coordinated through the **tourist office**.

Münchhausen Museum

Münchhausenplatz 1 • April–Oct daily 10am–5pm • €2.50

The odd cannonball in the **Münchhausen Museum** opposite the Rathaus struggles to live up to the narrative fantasy. More enjoyable are illustrations of the tall tales that are showcased near portraits of the real baron. Elsewhere bronzes of his exploits will entertain the kids. A fountain outside the museum has our hero astride the prize horse that was shot in half in battle – he didn't realize until water poured from its body as it drank (he sewed the horse up again). Another fountain on the pedestrianized main street depicts the baron riding his cannonball to spy out Turkish positions, while one block behind he hauls himself from a pond by his hair. The stories are staged in front of the Rathaus on the first Sunday of the month from May to October (from 2pm; free).

INFORMATION   **BODENWERDER**

Tourist office By the museum at Münchhausenplatz 1 (April–Oct Mon–Fri 9am–noon & 2–5pm, Sat 10am–12.30pm; Nov–Feb Mon–Fri 9am–noon; ☏ 05533 405 41, ⓦ muenchhausenland.de). A board outside the office lists accommodation options.

Bad Karlshafen

Snuggled into woodland on a meander 60km south of Bodenwerder, idyllic **BAD KARLSHAFEN** is a surprise after the half-timbered towns to the north. If its handsome white villas and broad streets seem to have been beamed across the border from France it is because the miniature Baroque town (actually, more oversized village) was planned by seventeenth-century Huguenot refugees from Languedoc and Dauphine who were guaranteed sanctuary and tax-free trading by Landgraf Karl von Hesse-Kassel. With the earl's death and the silting up of its canal at the confluence of the rivers Weser and Diemel, a town founded on wool and linen withered on the vine, and all that's left is the villas around a harbour in which lighters once tied up.

The **Deutsches Hugenotten-Museum** at Hafenplatz 9a (mid-March to Oct Tues–Fri 10am–5pm, Sat & Sun 11am–6pm; Nov & Dec Mon–Fri 9am–noon; €4) fills in the background with displays about the tyranny that followed Louis XIV's revocation of religious tolerance – there are some grisly copperplates of persecution – before tackling the town itself upstairs. There's also a model of the town that never materialized in the foyer of the **Rathaus**, located by the harbour, whose size hints at the planners' ambitions.

The tourist office provides maps of **walking trails**; arguably the best of the three planned routes is a river circuit to Helmarshausen 2km south via ruined Romanesque castle, **Krukenburg** (daily 10am–6pm; free).

INFORMATION AND ACTIVITIES
BAD KARLSHAFEN

Tourist office In the Rathaus, Hafenplatz 8 (Mon–Thurs 9am–noon & 2–4pm, Fri 9am–noon; ☎ 05672 99 99 22, ⓦ bad-karlshafen.de).

Canoe rental Local canoe operator Kanu Schumacher (☎ 05675 72 59 05, ⓦ kanu-schumacher.de), just up from the campsite on the far side of the bridge over the Weser, rents Canadian canoes by the hour – tributary River Diemel is a lovely spot to dip an oar – and provides transfers back from destinations all along the Weser. Overnight expeditions go to Hannoverisch Münden.

ACCOMMODATION

Campingplatz Bad Karlshafen Am Rechten Weserufer 2 ☎ 05672 710, ⓦ camper-karli-event.de. This large site spreads itself around a meander across the north bank of the river, to which it provides direct access. It also has a small pool and views to the town opposite, plus mod cons like wi-fi. Though popular with motorhomes, it reserves a large area of riverfront for tents. Pitch €4, plus €3.40 per person

Zum Schwan Conradistr. 3–4 ☎ 05672 10 44, ⓦ hotel-zum-schwan-badkarlshafen.com. This Baroque mansion – a former ducal residence that overlooks the inner harbour – is now a grand old-fashioned place, a mite frilly in its country-style decor perhaps, but recently modernized to add touches of contemporary design. Its period dining-room is splendid. €86

Hannoverisch Münden

As the marketing blurb mawkishly puts it, **HANNOVERISCH MÜNDEN** (better known as **Hann. Münden**), 40km south of Bad Karlshafen, is sited "where the Werra and Fulda kiss" to flow into the Weser River. Naturalist Alexander von Humboldt, who knew a thing or two about the world, having explored Russia and Latin America, declared it "one of the seven most beautifully sited towns in the world". Never mind the scenery, it's the **Altstadt** that wows: a picture-book-pretty jumble of over seven hundred half-timbered houses clustered beside those burbling rivers, and largely still girdled by its medieval fortifications. A tourist office booklet guides you around every carefully carved beam.

The Rathaus

Lotzestr. 2 • Debating hall May–Oct daily 8am–8pm; Nov–April Mon–Fri 8am–4pm, Sat 8am–2pm • Free

As ever, the place to begin explorations is the **Markt**, if only for a stone **Rathaus** whose chunky Weser Renaissance facade is an exercise in solidity among this streetscape of beams. At noon, 3pm and 5pm, a glockenspiel clunks out a ditty to accompany the tale of Dr Johann Andreas Eisenbart, a local hero who won national fame for a technique that cured cataracts with a needle. Jealous peers and his weakness for self-publicity have conspired to make his name a synonym for charlatan. During office hours you can look at the Rathaus's Renaissance debating hall when the council is not in session.

Welfenschloss

Schlossplatz • Jan–March & May–Dec Wed–Sun 11am–4pm; April Wed–Sun 1–4pm • €2.50

A building of particular note is the huge **Welfenschloss** beside the Werra River, a sober Weser Renaissance palace that houses the inevitable **town museum** covering river trade and local archeology – access to the frescoed ducal chambers is by tour through the

13

tourist office. A semicircular tower near the entrance is the most impressive of the town's **medieval defences**. Others are revealed on a walk around the Schloss's walls to reach the **Werrabrücke** over the river, from where you get a lovely view back into an Altstadt of swaying houses.

Tillyschanze

Late April to Oct Tues–Sun 11am–8pm; Nov–late April Fri–Sun 11am–6pm • €2.50

The best view of the town's rippling roofs is from a castellated viewing tower known as the **Tillyschanze**, sited on a hillside to the west, a twenty-minute walk from the Altstadt. There's a bar and restaurant at the site.

ARRIVAL AND INFORMATION	HANNOVERISCH MÜNDEN

By train Hannoverisch Münden lies on the Göttingen–Kassel rail line; the Bahnhof is east of the centre – head along Bahnhofstrasse.
Destinations Göttingen (hourly; 1hr); Kassel (hourly; 20min).

Tourist office In the Rathaus, Lotzestr. 2 (May–Sept Mon, Wed & Thurs 9.30am–5pm, Tues & Fri 9.30am–3pm, Sat 10am–3pm; Oct–April Mon–Thurs 9.30am–4pm, Fri 9.30am–1pm; ☎05541 733 13, ⓦ hann.muenden-tourismus.de).

ACCOMMODATION

★Aegdienhof Aegidiistr. 7–9 ☎05541 984 60, ⓦ fahrrad-hotel.de. In a renovated half-timbered house on one of the town's most photogenic squares, this place is a bargain for the arty touches it brings to a sort of rustic minimalism: stripped wood floors, beams, pine furnishings. The friendly young couple who own the place also offer apartments. €63

Alter Packhof Bremer Schlagd 10–14 ☎05541 988 90, ⓦ packhof.com. The first choice for an overnight stay is this former nineteenth-century warehouse that overlooks the Fulda River in a peaceful corner at the front of the

Altstadt. Renovated into a 4-star country hotel, it provides a comfortable stay that's upmarket without being too formal; "Comfort" class is worth the extra €10 for space. €129

Campingplatz Hann. Münden Tanzwerder 1 ☎05541 122 57, ⓦ busch-freizeit.de. On the river island that fronts the Altstadt, with views of the old townhouses opposite, the campsite couldn't be more central. Downsides are its popularity in summer and the proximity of tent pitches at the far tip to the road bridge across the river. Open April to mid-Oct. Pitch €4, plus €6.50 per person

EATING

Café Aegdius Aegidiplatz ☎05541 984 60, ⓦ aegidien-kirche.de. A new lease of life for the deconsecrated Aegidienkirche, this excellent café's design features – such as long teardrop lights and pew seating – sit easily in the medieval architecture; there's a pretty terrace, too. Food-wise, there are excellent breakfast buffets, plus light lunches and tasty nibbles. April–Oct daily 8am–6pm.

Die Reblaus Ziegelstr. 32 ☎05541 95 46 10, ⓦ die-reblaus.com. Lamb with courgette-feta rolls or home-made ravioli with cream cheese epitomize the Italianate

dishes (€15–20) of one of the town's finest restaurants. It maintains a large terrace on adjacent Kirchplatz in summer. April–Sept daily except Tues noon–2.30pm & 6–11pm; Oct–March Mon & Thurs–Sun noon–2.30pm & 6–11pm.

Ritter der Rotwurst Lange Str. 29 ☎05541 51 51, ⓦ schumann-feinkost.de. Although this has an attached restaurant, *Marktstube*, the first choice for this butcher's off the Markt is its *Imbiss-café*, where you can tuck into multi-award-winning sausages alongside tasty home-made soups. Daily except Thurs 11am–8.30pm.

Göttingen

GÖTTINGEN calls itself the "City of Science" (Stadt der Wissenschaft); it has nurtured forty Nobel Prize winners and institutions such as the German Aerospace Centre and the Max-Planck-Institutes. But don't let that put you off. For most visitors – and probably the majority of locals – the town is more about its café and bar culture than high culture. The root cause of both is the same: the **Georg-August Universität**. Founded in 1734 by Hannover elector Georg August, also known as King George II of Great Britain, the university grew into one of the intellectual think-tanks of Europe and boasted a roll-call of distinguished professors, among them Brothers Grimm, Jakob and Wilhelm. The university also brings a city-sized vibrancy to a medium-sized town. One in five of the 130,000-strong population is a student, nurturing a free-thinking liberalism that harks back to the Göttingen Seven, an academic grouping that dared to question the authority of Hannover king Ernst August in 1837. Students and easy-going attitudes also mean **nightlife** – perhaps the primary reason to visit, whatever the value of the Hanseatic heritage.

The Markt and around

Geographically, historically, socially, the focus of the small Altstadt is the **Markt**. At its centre is the **Ganseliesel** – "the most kissed girl in the world", as the tourist board never tires of quipping. By tradition, graduating doctoral students kiss the bronze lips or cheek of the demure goose-trader who is canopied in a wrought-iron thicket.

Altes Rathaus

Markt • Debating hall Mon–Fri 9.30am–6pm, Sat 10am–6pm, Sun 10am–2pm; Nov–March closed Sun

The Markt is dominated by its **Altes Rathaus**, a chunky Gothic building derived from a fifteenth-century renovation of a progenitor merchants' guildhall. The 1880s wall-paintings in the **debating hall** allude to that trading past with shields of Hanseatic League members, and add the sort of allegorical faux-medievalisms beloved by an empire busy rediscovering its past; four decades earlier, the same zeitgeist had inspired university professors Jakob and Wilhelm Grimm to compile traditional folk-tales.

Behind the Altes Rathaus rise the octagonal spires of the **St Johanniskirche**. The highest spire, at 62m, was probably the tallest student digs in Germany when it housed theology students – probably the noisiest, too, with the bells so close.

Barfüsserstrasse

Barfüsserstrasse, on the opposite side of the Altes Rathaus, retains a couple of houses from Göttingen's sixteenth-century heyday. Finest is the **Junkernschänke** on the corner of Jüdenstrasse (now a restaurant – see p.719); among its biblical panoply are portraits of the owner and his wife carved on the corner post.

St Jacobikirche

Jacobikirchhof 2 • Church daily 11am–3pm, tower until 6pm • Free, tower €2.50 • ⓦ jacobikirche.de

Pedestrian high-street Weender Strasse heads north of the Markt towards the **St Jacobikirche**. Once you've recovered from the shock of its interior – geometric stripes zigzag up its columns, a trick of the Middle Ages to create the illusion of distance – there's a fine high altar by a mystery master. Fully open, it presents the coronation of the Virgin as queen of heaven before an assembly of saints, among them church patron St James with his trademark scallop shell. When closed, you see either a sumptuous narrative of Christ, its scenes divided by pillars like rooms in a Gothic castle, or the life story of the patron, depending on which of the two sets of wings is shut. The newly renovated **tower** provides views over the Altstadt's roofscape in summer.

The former ramparts and Bismarckhäuschen

Bürgerstr. 27 • Tues 10am–1pm, Thurs & Sat 3–5pm, or by appointment • Free • ☎ 0551 48 58 44

A green belt girdles the town in place of the medieval ramparts that were begun in the mid-1300s. Indeed, the Altes Rathaus would have been larger had funds not been diverted to the defences. A stroll along the former ramparts takes just over an hour. En route you'll find the last tower of the rampart, the **Bismarckhäuschen**. Hearsay has it the 18-year-old **Otto von Bismarck** was banished to its squat garret for student

13

high-jinks in 1833 – a replica of his study is on display. Certainly Göttingen proved an unhappy year for the future Iron Chancellor. A Prussian aristocrat and snob, Bismarck looked down on his liberal colleagues, and seems to have whiled away most of his year there not studying law but duelling and boozing with an aristocratic fencing fraternity.

ARRIVAL AND GETTING AROUND   GÖTTINGEN

By train Göttingen is well-connected and serves as a connection between major cities. The Bahnhof is at the western edge of the centre.
Destinations Erfurt (6 daily; 1hr 40min); Frankfurt (every 30min; 1hr 50min); Hannover (every 30min; 40min); Kassel (approx hourly; 1hr); Weimar (6 daily; 1hr 55min).

By bike You can rent bikes at Velo-Voss in a bike-park (*Fahrrad-Parkhaus*) beside the Bahnhof (Mon–Sat 6am–10pm, Sun 8am–10pm). Note that the police routinely hand out fines for riders who ignore the no-cycling signs in the pedestrian centre.

INFORMATION

Tourist office In the Rathaus on the Markt (Mon–Fri 9.30am–6pm, Sat 10am–6pm, Sun 10am–2pm; Nov–March closed Sun; ☎0551 49 98 00, ⊛www.goettingen -tourismus.de).

Discount card The tourist office sells the GöCard ticket (1 day €5, 3 days €12), giving free public transport and discounts on museum entry and city tours.

ACCOMMODATION

Central Jüdenstr. 12 ☎0551 571 57, ⊛hotel-central .com. Central, indeed, with a location one block from the Markt and with modest design aspirations to boot: platform beds, art prints and exposed brickwork in public areas effectively disguise what is actually an older hotel – larger upper-level rooms with a bath are arguably overpriced. **€89**
Gebhards Goetheallee 22–23 ☎0551 496 80, ⊛gebhardshotel.de. The 4-star prestige address in Göttingen, a short walk from the Markt, features traditional elegance in public areas and up-to-date comfort in its rooms. Facilities include wi-fi throughout, a sauna/jacuzzi and an excellent restaurant. **€158**
Hostel37 Groner Landstr. 7 ☎0551 63 44 51 77, ⊛hostel37.de. This small and friendly hostel in a former doctor's clinic practically next to the Bahnhof is a good central budget option. Private rooms are small but

comfortable; dorm rooms have good bunk beds. The reception is manned between 3pm and 9pm. Linen is provided, and breakfast is €4 when available. Dorms **€18**, doubles **€46**
Kasseler Hof Rosdorfer Weg 26 ☎0551 72 08 12, ⊛kasselerhof.de. Located on a quiet residential street southwest of the centre beyond the Altstadt ring road, this family-run hotel provides modern en-suite rooms from the IKEA school of decor. Clean and good value for money, nonetheless. **€79**
Leine Groner Landstr. 55 ☎0551 505 10, ⊛leinehotel-goe.de. Comfortable for a short stay and popular with visiting academics, this place describes itself as a "boarding house", which translates into spacious if rather spartan split-level rooms with small kitchenettes in an Eighties block. It's a 15min walk behind the Bahnhof. **€93**

EATING AND DRINKING

A student town par excellence, Göttingen has a good spread of bars, from cosy traditional cocoons of wood to scruffy student common rooms. Similarly, student stand-bys such as cheap pizza and kebab places are gathered beside the university at the top of **Wilhelmsplatz**.

CAFÉS AND BARS

Cello Coffee Bar Weender Str. 87 ☎0551 999 55 77. "The world of espresso" is the motto of this local chain, which translates into twelve types of coffee – as well as fresh smoothies and tasty bagels. Cheap bagel and coffee deals are available for breakfast, best enjoyed in the pretty rear garden. Mon–Sat 9am–6.30pm, Sun noon–6.30pm.
Cron & Lanz Weender Str. 25 ☎0551 500 887 10, ⊛cronundlanz.de. The cognoscenti's choice for *Kaffee und Kuchen* in Göttingen is this splendidly old-fashioned café that's been going strong since the 1860s. Locals acclaim the

gâteaux and pralines of its *Konditorei* the best in town. Mon–Fri 8am–7pm, Sat 9am–7pm, Sun 1–6.30pm.
Gartenlaube Markt 7 ☎0551 473 73, ⊛cafe -gartenlaube.de. Overlooking the Rathaus, this is the kind of café-bar in which you could happily spend an afternoon, switching from coffee to beers and cocktails after dark. There's a terrace out front, and a nice shady garden at the rear for summer days. Mon–Fri 9am–2am, Sat 9am–3am, Sun 1pm–1am.
Monster Café Goethe-Allee 13 ☎0551 49 97 77 79. Exhibitions by local artists decorate a relaxed café-bar that's more alternative than other options in the centre.

Food-wise there's organic coffee, legendary breakfasts and "Monster Crepes"; for entertainment there's free wi-fi and board games. Mon–Fri 11am–8.30pm, Sat 10am–1am, Sun 10am–8pm.

Mr Jones Goethe-Allee 8 ☎ 0551 531 45 00, ⓦ mrjones -goe.de. Airy modern café-bar that overlooks the Leine canal. Prepares food throughout the day, then becomes a good option for refined drinking of large cocktails while DJs play a good-times funk and jazz soundtrack at weekends. Mon–Fri 11am–late, Sat & Sun 10am–late.

Sausalitos Hospitalstr. 35 ☎ 0551 508 48 27, ⓦ sausalitos.de. Housed in a large half-timbered former mill near the Bismarckhäuschen, this is a typically knockabout member of the Tex-Mex bar chain. It's especially popular among students for summertime drinking due to its "beach" beer garden. Daily 5pm–midnight, Fri & Sat 5pm–late.

RESTAURANTS

Bullerjahn Markt 9 ☎ 0551 307 01 00, ⓦ bullerjahn.info. The former town-hall restaurant has lofty whitewashed Gothic vaults with designer lampshades, while the terrace on the Markt is furnished with loungers and parasols. Pork with rocket and goat's-cheese crust (€15) is typical of a modern German menu – quality is good rather than gourmet. Mon–Thurs & Sun 9am–midnight, Fri & Sat 9am–1am.

Gaudí Rote Str. 16 ☎ 0551 531 30 01, ⓦ restaurant -gaudi.de. Airy, quietly stylish place located in a mews off Barfüsserstrasse. As the name suggests it serves tapas plates, but focuses more on a modern Mediterranean menu, not cheap at around €22 a main; pasta dishes are available for around €12 a plate, and the three-course lunch menus go for around €14–19. Decent wine list, too. Mon 6pm–midnight, Tues–Sat noon–3pm & 6pm–midnight.

Gauss Obere Karspüle 22, on Theaterstrasse above the Jacobikirche ☎ 0551 566 16. Easily the finest dining in town is in this cellar place, with short seasonal menus of contemporary German cuisine often fused with Asian flavours; mains cost roughly €28, with a €21 three-course "Nachtmenü" served between 9.30pm and 10.30pm. Service is excellent, whether in the stone-walled dining room or beneath trees on a summer terrace. Tues–Sat 6pm–midnight.

Junkernschänke Barfüsserstr. 5 ☎ 0551 384 83 80, ⓦ steakhouse-junkernschaenke.de. One of the oldest half-timbered houses in town, with biblical stories carved into the facade, hosts a large steak restaurant serving four types of beef steak at decent prices; count on €22 for a meal. Drinks are pricey however. Mon–Fri 9am–11pm, Sat till 1am.

Zum Szültenbürger Prinzenstr. 7 ☎ 0551 431 33. A great choice for solid eating at low prices is this historic *Gaststätte* whose single intimate dining-room is decorated with images of old Göttingen. Nothing fancy, just traditional home-cooking – typically *Schnitzels* and steaks with *Bratkartoffeln*, most plates costing under €10 – and beer on tap. Mon–Sat 11am–3pm & 5–11pm.

NIGHTLIFE AND ENTERTAINMENT

Göttingen has a vibrant club scene. Local **listings magazines** *Pony* or *37* are your best source of what's on; you can pick up copies in *Apex* (see below). As ever, weekends offer the greatest choice, but you should find something somewhere week-round. Wed night is **student night** – expect reduced or free entry to nightclubs and cheap drinks.

CLUBS

Alpenmax Weender Landstr. 3–7 ☎ 0551 370 61 30, ⓦ discofun.de/goettingen. The only club in town currently open on Mon and certainly the only one styled as an alpine ski-hut with mirrorballs. A mixed programme of clubnights caters to oldies (ie over-30-year-olds) as well as students, all with mainstream sounds and cheap to enter. Mon, Fri & Sat 10pm–late, Thurs 8pm–late.

JT Keller Am Wochenmarkt 6 ⓦ jt-keller.de. Friendly basement club attached to the Junges Theater whose music policy can swing from Eighties to electroclash to dubstep depending on who's in – check the website. Weekenders at the start of each month are always fun. Fri & Sat 11pm–late.

Savoy Berliner Str. 5 ⓦ club-savoy.de. A former bank building hosts mainstream clubbing in a warehouse-style main room with a penchant for glitterball glamour: generally house and soul veering into indie for students on Wed "Unight". There's a lounge bar in the basement. Wed, Fri & Sat 10pm–6am.

LIVE MUSIC AND CABARET

Apex Burgstr. 46 ☎ 0551 468 86, ⓦ apex-goe.de. Jazz, bossa nova, indie-folk plus comedy and cabaret in a cultural centre that usually programmes one event a week. At other times its relaxed café-bar gets the nod from a middle-aged arty set. Bar Mon–Sat 5pm–1am; events from 7pm.

Nörgelbuff Groner Str. 23 ☎ 0551 384 82 62, ⓦ noergelbuff.de. Four decades young, one of Göttingen's oldest nightclubs programmes a diverse range of clubnights plus interesting live-music nights usually once a week: there are regular slots from the house blues band plus a monthly funk-jazz jam and open-mic sessions. There's usually something on throughout the week in term-time but dates vary, so check the website. Midweek clubnights 9pm–late, Fri & Sat 10pm–late.

13

Braunschweig

After nearly a millennium of habit **BRAUNSCHWEIG** routinely tags itself "Die Löwenstadt". The lion refers to Saxon duke **Henry the Lion** (Heinrich der Löwe), a giant of twelfth-century Europe who commanded the last great independent duchy of fledgling Germany. His territory comprised a great swathe north to Kiel – he founded Lübeck and Lüneburg among other towns – and much of present-day Bavaria; Munich is another of his creations. His capital, however, was Braunschweig, and the high points of the state's second largest city after Hannover are intrinsically bound up with its founder, despite an illustrious history that again flared into brilliance in the mid-1700s as a ducal Residenzstadt.

Braunschweig is not the most instantly appealing destination in the state – as the epicentre of Lower Saxony's industry, it was badly damaged in 1944 – but as a major transport junction it is one you're sure to pass through and there are a couple of appealing day-trips to Wolfenbüttel (see p.724) and Wolfsburg (see p.725) within half an hour.

Burgplatz

If Braunschweig has a holy of holies it's **Burgplatz**, the heart of the Altstadt – or what's left of it – and the well-spring of its growth from which Henry the Lion ruled an empire. The Saxon lion king commissioned the leonine **Burglöwe statue** at its centre – said to be the first freestanding monument cast north of the Alps since the Roman occupation – as a symbol of his power and jurisdiction. The statue in the square is a

BRAUNSCHWEIG

RESTAURANTS
Das Alte Haus 8
Brodocz 4
Fried'rich 5
Mutter Habenicht 3
OX 7
Saz 1

BARS
Barnaby's Blues-Bar 6
Okercabana 9
Schadt's Brauerei
Gasthaus 2

NIGHTLIFE
42° Fieber 1
Brain Klub 2

ACCOMMODATION
Café am Park 5
Frühlings-Hotel 2
Penta 4
Stadthotel Magnitor 1
StadtPalais 3

replica; the original is housed in the Burg Dankwarderode (see below). Among the impressive buildings ringing Burgplatz are **Huneborstelsches Haus** and **Von Veltheimisches Haus**; carved with a playground of folkloric images, they are early 1900s rebuilds pieced together from older timbers.

Burg Dankwarderode

Burgplatz 4 • Tues & Thurs–Sun 10am–5pm, Wed 10am–8pm • €6 • ⓦ 3landesmuseen.de

A squat structure that boxes in the east side of Burgplatz, the **Burg Dankwarderode**'s out-of-the-wrapper Romanesque is an 1880s guess at Henry's first palace, based on excavations after a fire demolished the building. Its ground floor displays the medieval collection of the Herzog-Anton-Ulrich-Museum (see p.722), the star pieces among some eye-catching reliquaries being the *Burglöwe* statue that Heinrich had cast in 1166 and a cloak said to have belonged to his son, Otto IV. The Rittersaal is a fantastical piece of imperial pomp, a marvel of Romanesque arches and columns that re-creates the knights' halls of medieval fable.

The Dom

Burgplatz • Daily 10am–5pm • Free, crypt €1

In 1173 Heinrich returned from pilgrimage to the Holy Land and commissioned a mighty **Dom** as a repository for his souvenir relics and a burial place to honour his magnificence. His tomb lies at the heart of a basilica, the ruler cradling a model of his church on a slab (1235) that depicts him beside his English queen, Mathilde. Inspired by a German ruler who masterminded expansion east and never shy of a PR coup, Hitler ordered the tomb be opened in the 1930s, only to discover a small man with black hair, probably due to Henry's Italian lineage. Other members of the Welf dynasty lie in sarcophagi in the crypt. The absence of decoration elsewhere in the church only heightens the impact of smudgy thirteenth-century frescoes in the choir. Accidentally uncovered in 1845, their pictorial bible is imbued with all the smoke and mystery of the early Church. The colossal seven-arm candelabra inset with cloisonné enamel in front is another legacy of Henry – it was commissioned to sit over his tomb as a symbol of resurrection.

Braunschweigisches Landesmuseum

Burgplatz 1 • Tues–Sun 10am–5pm • €4 • ⓦ 3landesmuseen.de

Housed in a collonaded building opposite the Burg Dankwarderode, the German-only **Braunschweigisches Landesmuseum** tackles local and state history once you're beyond the dull displays on geographical origins – the years under Henry the Lion and as a duchy are more fun. An earlier replica *Burglöwe* stands in its foyer.

Altstadtmarkt

Altstadtmarkt, which started as a mercantile township of the fledgling settlement in the mid-1100s, served as a counterweight to the governmental authority on Burgplatz and flourished as a venue of trade fairs and parades as Braunschweig blossomed into a commercial medieval power.

The Rathaus

Altstadtmarkt • Mon–Fri 9am–5pm • Free

Pride and joy of the civic town was the L-shaped Gothic **Rathaus**, which wraps around Altstadtmarkt's far corner. A town museum within it fast-forwards through the centuries, taking in fashions, council silverware and early copperplates of the town. It takes second place to the Grosse Dornse council chamber on the first floor with its elegant balcony, where councillors gazed out at the citizens beneath, their authority confirmed by the surrounding statues of Welfen dukes – Heinrich and Mathilde are at the end opposite the church of St Martini.

13

Gewandhaus and St Martini Kirche

Only the **Gewandhaus**, the drapers' warehouse and trading hall which shuts in Altstadtmarkt's opposite side, can match the Rathaus in size. Its bulk reflects the prestige of the most distinguished guild in the city – a rich one, too, if the Renaissance facade added to the east end is any guide. The backdrop to the square is **St Martini Kirche**, the first church erected after the Dom, which served as a model before its rethink into Gothic. It hosts occasional art exhibitions.

The Magniviertel

Only the ducal **Residenzschloss** will detain you en route east of Burgplatz. Its huge Baroque facade, crowned by the largest quadriga in Germany – larger even than that on the Brandenburg Gate – reappeared in 2008 after a total postwar rebuild, only to front a shopping centre. The area's focus is the historic **Magniviertel**, a picturesque corner of half-timbered houses on cobbled lanes that escaped wartime destruction. Inevitably, it has gentrified, and become a popular bar and restaurant district. The area lies behind the Residenzschloss's right-hand corner beyond **Happy-Rizzi-Haus**, a candy-coloured complex by New York Pop Art artist James Rizzi – local opinion is divided over whether the cartoony complex is whimsically wacky or better suited to a Kindergarten.

Herzog-Anton-Ulrich-Museum

Museumstrasse • Closed for renovation until mid-2016 • ⓦ 3landesmuseen.de

Henry the Lion receives all the attention, but Braunschweig duke Anton Ulrich deserves much credit for masterminding a golden age of culture in the mid-1600s. His eclectic tastes are reflected by the diversity of the **Herzog-Anton-Ulrich-Museum**, a jackdaw's hoard presented as Germany's first public museum in 1754, four decades after the duke's death. He had impeccable taste. Among the fourth largest picture gallery of old masters in Germany are several Cranachs, including *Hercules and Omphale*, a warning about lust that sees the tempted hero ensnared like the partridges in the background. The duke also had an eye for Dutch works – Rubens and especially Rembrandt – and porcelain, including the world's largest private collection of Fürstenburg china, as well as fine Chinese lacquerwork. Elsewhere are European bronzes and furniture and antiquities. How much is on display depends on the progress of a protracted renovation programme; at the time of writing the museum was slated to reopen in 2016. Until then, two hundred choice objects are on show in Burg Dankwarderode (see p.721).

Bürgerpark

South of the Altstadt, the informal English-style **Bürgerpark** is a favourite escape from the city on sunny days, with a great summer "beach" bar (see opposite) by the Oker River. From May to September you can rent Canadian **canoes** at OkerTour (ⓣ 0531 270 27 24, ⓦ okertour.de; €10/hr) on a quay just east of John-F.-Kennedy-Platz.

ARRIVAL AND GETTING AROUND   BRAUNSCHWEIG

By train The Hauptbahnhof and the adjacent ZOB bus station lie a hefty 1.5km southeast of the centre: trams #1 or #2 or any bus bound for the "Rathaus" will whisk you into the fairly dispersed centre.

Destinations Göttingen (hourly; 55min); Hannover (every 40min; 30–45min); Hildesheim (every 30min; 25–30min); Wolfenbüttel (every 45min; 10min); Wolfsburg (every 30min; 15–30min).

Public transport Single tickets either cost €2.20 or are priced by time: a 1hr 30min *Einzelfahrschein* costs €2.40, a day-long *Tageskarte* is €6. Extend the zone to take in nearby Wolfenbüttel and Wolfsburg and day-ticket prices rise to €9 and €13.50 respectively.

INFORMATION

Tourist office Kleine Burg 14, near the Dom (Mon–Fri 10am–6.30pm, Sat 10am–4pm, Sun 10am–noon; Oct– April closed Sun; ☎0531 470 20 40, ⓦbraunschweig .de/touristinfo).

ACCOMMODATION

Café am Park Wolfenbütteler Str. 67 ☎0531 730 79, ⓦhotel-cafeampark.de. No frills, no chintz, just a bright and efficient cheapie a 10min walk south of the Altstadt ring road. Plain decor of white walls and pine furniture makes a virtue of its simplicity; the cheapest rooms share bathrooms. **€64**

Frühlings-Hotel Bankplatz 7 ☎0531 24 32 10, ⓦfruehlingshotel.de. Friendly, quietly stylish place in a nicely renovated late-1800s building with an excellent location in the central Altstadt – rooms at the top are fine. Some large suites have kitchenettes. **€159**

Penta Auguststr. 6–8 ☎0531 481 40, ⓦpentahotels .com. There's no escaping the boxy rooms, but the decor at this funky, central hotel has a playful touch and the atmosphere is relaxed throughout. **€104**

Stadthotel Magnitor Am Magnitor 1 ☎0531 471 30, ⓦstadthotel-magni.de. The most relaxing hotel in Braunschweig thanks to its location in the historic Magniviertel. With just 29 rooms, it styles itself as a modest designer number, with a restrained palette of cream, grey and pastel pink, the odd vintage find and statement headboards in some rooms. Also has a good restaurant. **€110**

StadtPalais Hinter Liebfrauen 1a ☎0531 24 10 24, ⓦpalais-braunschweig.bestwestern.de. The local 4-star outpost of the Best Western group has more character than is usual for the world's largest chain due to the fabric of its historic building. All you'd expect – modern, comfortable, seamless service, good breakfast buffet – plus a good location in the Altstadt. **€88**

EATING AND DRINKING

RESTAURANTS

Das Alte Haus Alte Knochenhauer Str. 11 ☎0531 480 35 03, ⓦaltehaus.de. Forget the name – there's nothing old about this modern side-street bistro. Its short, seasonal Mediterranean menu is the best in town, some locals say, with dishes like turbot with grapefruit and cream polenta. Mains average €25, three-course menus from €34. Tues–Sat 6pm–1am.

Brodocz Stephanstr. 2 ☎0531 422 36, ⓦrestaurant -brodocz.de. This long-standing local favourite in the pedestrianized centre serves exclusively fish and vegetarian dishes, including some Indian flavours; the vegetable-fish curry with rice is €19.50. All ingredients are organic, certified and gluten-free. It's at its best in summer when a pretty, half-timbered courtyard is open. Mon & Wed–Sat 11.30am–10.30pm, Tues 11.30am–3.30pm.

Fried'rich Am Magnitor 5 ☎0531 417 28. A cosy Magniviertel restaurant and wine bar that has a good reputation among older locals – fish dishes come recommended on a menu of light German cooking which also has snacks like camembert in beer batter. Nice rear garden for summer evenings. Tues–Sun 5pm–midnight.

Mutter Habenicht Papenstieg 3 ☎0531 459 56, ⓦmutter-habenicht.de. An old favourite for good-value eating in the Altstadt – it's been going strong since 1870. Most items on the traditional menu are priced under €15 and there's a choice of rooms, plus a small beer garden at the rear. Daily 11am–midnight.

OX Güldenstr. 7 ☎0531 24 39 00, ⓦox-steakhouse.de. The best steak in town in a smart speciality restaurant that has an American-style dedication to achieving the perfectly grilled cut of beef: eight different steak varieties are available, including a Porterhouse for two and a Kobe-style Wagyu filet (both €90). Carnivore heaven, with fish of the day for others. Daily noon–2.30pm & 6pm–1am.

Saz Am Neuen Petritore 7 ☎0531 135 14. A small, friendly restaurant serving large portions of fantastic Turkish food; the grilled meat and especially the lamb comes recommended – as do reservations, as it's frequently packed. Tues–Sun 5pm–midnight.

BARS

Barnaby's Blues-Bar Ölschlägern 20 ☎0531 356 95 60, ⓦbarnabys-bs.de. Boozy, smoky, intimate – this drinking den is everything a blues bar should be. An older crowd pack in on Fri for live bands, often fronted by musicians who perform with rock legends such as Eric Clapton, Bruce Springsteen or the Rolling Stones. Daily: May–Oct 3pm–late; Nov–April 5pm–late.

★**Okercabana** Bürgerpark ⓦokercabana.de. Not quite Brazil in Braunschweig, but *caipirinhas* are mixed nevertheless at this great city beach bar on the Oker River, a 10min walk behind the Volkswagen Halle (on Adenauer Strasse). Lounging central for families and hipsters alike by day, it segues into a laidback nightspot with DJs at weekends. Snacks available throughout the day. May to early Sept Mon–Fri 11am–midnight, Sat & Sun 10am–midnight.

Schadt's Brauerei Gasthaus Marstall 2 ☎0531 40 03 49, ⓦschadts-brauerei-gasthaus.de. Unpretentious traditional *Hausbrauerei* in a modern building just north of Burgplatz. It brews a *Pils*, *Weizen* and a seasonal beer, and doubles as a restaurant whose special is – what else? – pork roasted in beer (€12). Mon 5pm–midnight, Tues– Sat noon–midnight, Sun 5–10pm.

NIGHTLIFE AND ENTERTAINMENT

CLUBS

42° Fieber Kalenwall 3 ⓦ bs-nights.de. A medium-sized club with a friendly crowd and good music played at loud volume levels; you can expect chart hits, ladies' nights and Eighties theme parties. Fri & Sat 11pm–late.

Brain Klub Bruchtorwall 21 ⓦ brain-bs.de. An alternative, intimate and studenty place. Expect a leftfield mix of indie, electro, drum'n'bass and dubstep. Thurs–Sat 11pm–late.

THEATRE

Staatstheater Braunschweig Am Theater ☎ 0531 123 45 67, ⓦ staatstheater-braunschweig.de. The name is an umbrella for three stages – Grosses Haus, Kleines Haus and Haus Drei – which between them stage theatre and opera, both established works of the classical canon by the likes of Ibsen and Lessing, Strauss and Weber, plus new works. Occasional concerts, too.

Wolfenbüttel

Legendary libertine Giacomo Casanova spent "the most wonderful week of my entire life" there and Wilhelm Busch, father of the modern cartoon-strip, declared the place "marvellous". Yet still **WOLFENBÜTTEL** is not as well-known as it deserves to be. Having escaped war and mass tourism, this small town, with an ensemble of over six hundred half-timbered houses, has an almost fairy-tale quality, a blend of aristocracy and an erudite mindset that sees its museums publish websites in Latin. Partly responsible is the ducal House of Braunschweig which declared Wolfenbüttel a Residenzstadt in 1432. Under the Guelphic dukes' three-century tenure, high culture flowered and the royal town metamorphosed into the first planned town in Renaissance Germany. And when the dukes shifted back to Braunschweig in 1753 they sent Wolfenbüttel into a deep sleep from which it seems yet to awake – one reason to go.

The Schloss

Schlossplatz • Tues–Sat 10am–5pm • €7 • ⓦ schlosswolfenbuettel.de

When urban planners designed the town in the late 1400s, they created discrete districts for society's different strata. For the aristocracy, that neighbourhood was centred on the largest **Schloss** in Lower Saxony. Behind its facade, a model of elegant Baroque only slightly thrown off-kilter by a Renaissance tower, the private apartments of the last duke, the flamboyant Anton Ulrich (he of the Braunschweig museum), are a sumptuous parade of Baroque dercor – rich damask wall coverings, frothy stucco, rich marquetry panels inlaid with delicate ivory scenes – and decorative arts. The Zeiträume showcase later decorative art styles as part of historical displays of local history.

Lessinghaus and Herzog August Bibliothek

Lessingplatz • Tues–Sun 10am–5pm • €5 combined ticket for Lessinghaus and Bibliothek • ⓦ hab.de

Lessinghaus opposite the Schloss pays homage to its most celebrated resident, Gotthold Ephraim Lessing. The Enlightenment dramatist penned *Nathan the Wise* in his *maison de plaisance* when not working as ducal librarian of the **Herzog August Bibliothek** at the back of Schlossplatz. For a moment in history, Duke August the Younger pored over the largest library in Europe. "There is not a mountain range in which it is more pleasant to hunt," he said, and his 350,000-tome collection, bound in leather hides and shelved in a domed hall of marble pillars, is a bibliophile's dream.

Pride of place among such treasures as Descartes' *Tractatus de homine*, Cicero's *De officiis*, beautiful *livres de peintre* and Renaissance globes and maps in the basement goes to what was the world's most expensive book when it was bought at auction for the equivalent of €16.6 million in 1983, the *Welfen Evangeliar*, an illuminated gospel that Saxon duke Henry the Lion commissioned for the Braunschweig Dom in 1188. A facsimile is on display for all but one week of the year.

To the Stadtmarkt

13

Along Löwenstrasse off Schlossplatz, Wolfenbüttel relaxes as you enter the pretty, half-timbered Freiheit district, where court employees wedged themselves between royal and civic districts. Beyond Wolfenbüttel's narrowest house at Kleiner Zimmerhof 15 you can discover a remnant of a sixteenth-century canal system dug by Dutch engineers and known as "Little Venice" (Klein Venedig). Southeast of here the dukes' planned town, Heinrichstadt, is a formal grid centred on **Stadtmarkt**, with its bronze of August the Younger leading his horse. One-time home to courtiers and wealthy townsmen, it was modelled on piazzas of the Italian Renaissance, and the **Fachwerkhäuser** (half-timbered houses) along the north side are particularly elegant.

Hauptkirche

Kornmarkt • Tues–Sun 10am–noon & 2–4pm • €1 donation requested

East of Stadtmarkt, Reichsstrasse features a parade of houses from around 1600, as well as the **Hauptkirche**, which was completed in 1608 as one of the first to follow Luther's credo against visual distractions. Certainly the bright Mannerist interior where the dukes lie in state is a model of simplicity. But without such restraints for his facade, Schloss architect Paul Francke lets rip with Weser Renaissance frills and fine portals.

ARRIVAL AND INFORMATION

WOLFENBÜTTEL

By train and bus Wolfenbüttel falls within the public transport zone of Braunschweig, linked by buses and Regional Bahn trains; most visitors treat the town as a day-trip from there. The Hauptbahnhof lies a 5min walk south of the historic centre, Stadtmarkt.

Tourist office Stadtmarkt 7a (Mon–Fri 10am–6pm, Sat 10am–2pm; ☎ 05331 862 80, ⓦ wolfenbuettel-tourismus .de).

ACCOMMODATION AND EATING

Bayrischer Hof Corner of Brauergildenstrasse and Reichsstrasse ☎ 05331 50 78, ⓦ bayrischer-hof-wf.de. A small slice of Bavaria in sober North Germany, with a twee galleried dining hall, a beer garden and a menu that includes regional specialities like *Schweinshaxe* with *Sauerkraut* (€13). It also has a few cheap rooms for an overnight stay. Restaurant daily 11am–3pm & 5pm–midnight. **€77**

Wolfenbütler Brauhaus Stadtmarkt 3 ☎ 05331 88 27 34, ⓦ brauhaus-wolfenbuettel.de. Occupying a corner of the pretty main square, this microbrewery is the most appealing option for dining or drinking, especially when tables are set outside in summer. Four fresh beers are available to go with a menu of traditional dishes. Mon–Sat 11.30am–midnight, Sat & Sun 11.30am–9pm.

Wolfsburg

Around 121,000 people live in **WOLFSBURG**, along the main railway line to Berlin, but make no mistake, this is Volkswagen's town. Hitler's Ford-inspired dream of a Volkswagen (literally "people's car") was realized in 1937 as a sprawling greenfield factory began churning out the "Beetle", designed by Ferdinand Porsche. Aided by the economic pick-me-up of a postwar British military contract – an exception to enforced de-industrialization elsewhere – Volkswagen thrived, a fairy godmother of the German economy's rags-to-riches Cinderella story. As a result, Wolfsburg thrived, becoming Germany's richest city in 2013 with a GDP of €92,000 per person.

Autostadt

Daily 9am–6pm, till 10pm in Aug • €15, €7 after 4pm • Tours (book ahead): general tour €5–11; factory tour on production days €11, in English at noon; car tower tour €8; e-car test drive free; 4WD course €25–35 • ☎ 05361 400, ⓦ autostadt.de

Set beside the vast car plant behind the train station, Volkswagen's **Autostadt** car collection centre is a futuristic theme-park of museums and mobility-themed experiences, and a rev-head's paradise.

13

The five-storey **ZeitHaus Museum**, the most visited car museum in the world, celebrates milestones in gleaming automotive history (early cars that resemble horse carts, an Auto Union "Silver Arrow" racing car) and also its icons (an Art Nouveau Bugatti designed by Jean Bugatti himself, gorgeous Cadillacs and Chevys and the millionth Beetle). In futuristic **pavilions** behind, Volkswagen indulges in entertaining self-promotion for its brands, with a separate pavilion for each: Bugatti's bling; Lamborghini's power; reliable Skoda; dynamic Seat; futuristic Audi; and the quality and safety of Volkswagen. If you have toddlers in tow, there's a good motor-themed crèche in the **GroupForum** building, and, for older kids, a computerized driving course to complete in mini VW Beetles.

Autostadt's star attraction, the 1930s brick **factory complex** itself – which at 8.4 square kilometres is four times larger than Monaco – can be visited on production days on a factory tour. Another tour whisks you up in glass elevators to the top of one of the landmark cylindrical **glass towers** in which shiny cars await collection, and just outside the complex you can tackle the streets in a VW e-Golf or e-Up, or take on a challenging **4WD terrain course** in a VW Touareg or Tiguan.

AutoMuseum Volkswagen

Dieselstr. 35 • Tues–Sun 10am–5pm • €6 • ⓦ automuseum.volkswagen.de

Classic VWs are on show in the **AutoMuseum Volkswagen**, a twenty-minute walk east of the station. Exhibits include a *Herbie* Beetle that advertised the famous Disney films, the millionth VW campervan and world's first Scirocco, plus two interesting Golfs – one with two engines, the other with floats.

Phaeno

Willy-Brandt-Platz 1 • Tues–Fri 9am–5pm, Sat & Sun 10am–6pm • €12.50 • ⓦ phaeno.com

The **Phaeno** museum beside the station is unmissable thanks to its building by architect Zaha Hadid – a sort of futuristic take on Corbusier's modernism. Beneath its steel-girdered roof lies a playground of 250 interactive scientific experiments, zoned into themes such as wind and water, biology, technology or energy. Forty were designed by artists, making for exhibits that are often as aesthetic as they are educational – the *Feuertornado* (fire tornado) which creates a 7m flaming whirlwind is particularly impressive.

Kunstmuseum Wolfsburg

Hollerplatz 1 • Tues–Sun 11am–6pm • €8 • ⓦ kunstmuseum-wolfsburg.de

Wolfsburg's centre, south of Phaeno, would be spectacularly dull without the excellent **Kunstmuseum Wolfsburg**, which lies an uninspiring kilometre down the pedestrianized high street, Porschestrasse, from the station. Its focus is contemporary art: changing displays of a permanent collection that includes international names such as Warhol, Damien Hirst, Jeff Koons and Gilbert and George, plus modern German heavyweights like Neo Rauch, as well as big-name temporary exhibitions.

ARRIVAL AND INFORMATION

WOLFSBURG

By train The central Hauptbahnhof is on the lines from Hannover and Braunschweig east to Berlin, an easy stopover. The Autostadt can be reached across the bridge beside Phaeno; visitors en route to Berlin or elsewhere can use the Autostadt luggage lockers in the reception building.

Tourist office In the Hauptbahnhof (Mon–Sat 9am–6pm, Sun 10am–3pm; ☏ 05361 89 99 30, ⓦ wmg-wolfsburg.de).

Bike rental You can rent bikes at the Hauptbahnhof.

EATING AND DRINKING

Eating options abound **in Autostadt**, where there are several good café-restaurants – the *Currywurst* in the *Tachometer* restaurant is even manufactured in a dedicated VW butchery – plus fresh bread and cake at *Das Brot*, quality Italian food at *La Coccinella* and fine-dining at *Aqua* inside the hotel in the complex, and at *Chardonnay*.

Aalto Porschestr. 51 ☏ 05361 89 16 89, ⓦ aalto-wolfsburg.com. This modern bistro is part of the Alvar Aalto Kulturhaus, which lies opposite the Kunstmuseum and was designed by the Finnish architect. It's a good option for a coffee-break as much as for cheap Italian food: pizzas, pastas and salads, plus larger mains. Mon–Sat 10.30am–3pm & 6–11pm.

Awilon Hollerplatz 1 ☏ 05361 255 99. Within the glass-skinned Kunstmuseum, this cool bistro-restaurant rewards those who make the 1km journey south from the station. Expect the likes of shrimp and asparagus salad or scallops with a potato crust, all freshly cooked to order on a creative international menu. Tues–Sat 11am–11pm, Sun 10am–6pm.

Celle

CELLE is just half an hour from Hannover but the distance in atmosphere is centuries. While the bombs rained on the state capital, this small town emerged unscathed, a charming miniature of the seventeenth-century townscape lost in Hannover. As one of the finest half-timbered towns in Germany, Celle gets more than its share of tourists; indeed it's worth an overnight visit just to enjoy it free of day-trippers. However, it remains – just – more market town than museum piece. Either way, it owes its fame to the dukes of Braunschweig-Lüneburg. Banished from Lüneburg in 1378, the nobles crossed the Lüneburg Heide and made Celle an aristocratic Residenzstadt for nearly three centuries, encouraging the prosperity that built its streetscape. Celle is a testament that feudalism starts as a street plan: the ducal Schloss lies at the western edge of the Altstadt, whose parallel streets to the east run up towards it, a gesture of submission to the ducal yoke.

The Schloss

Schloss Tues–Sun 10am–5pm; tours April–Oct Tues–Fri & Sun 11am, 1pm & 3pm, Sat hourly 11am–3pm; Nov–March Tues–Sun 11am & 3pm, Sat & Sun also 1pm; notes in English available • €5, tours €7 • ⓦ residenzmuseum.de • **Schlosstheater** Tickets for performances are sold from a kiosk just behind the Rathaus at Markt 18 • ☏ 05141 905 08 75, ⓦ schlosstheater-celle.de

The moated pile the Braunschweig-Lüneburg dukes built for themselves sits aloof from the Altstadt proper, a beautifully proportioned Renaissance **Schloss** which stands on the same spot where Duke Otto the Severe erected a medieval tower residence in the 1200s to found a town. Exhibited as a museum of the Welf dynasty, state rooms and living quarters where the last duke, Georg Wilhelm, gave audience from his bed are a document of Baroque high-life, largely thanks to rich stucco confected by an Italian master, Giovanni Battista Tornielli. An upper floor features the rooms in which exiled queen, Caroline Mathilde of Denmark, youngest sister of Britain's King George III, lived out her final years as a semi-prisoner until 1775. Her crime was to fall for the court doctor after her husband, Danish King Christian VII, lost his wits. Her lover lost his head.

Schlosskapelle and court theatre

On tours you can also visit the lovely, intimate ducal **Schlosskapelle**, its Gothic architecture – a sole survivor of the original castle – all but lost behind a cacophony of Renaissance colour, not least in the paintings by Antwerp Mannerist Marten de Vos, whose allegorical *Temptation of the Holy Church* is to the left of the entrance. Tours also take in a miniature **court theatre** if no rehearsals are ongoing on the oldest Baroque stage in Germany, created in 1674 to stage commedia dell'arte and operetta.

Kunstmuseum Celle and Bomann-Museum

Schlossplatz **Kunstmuseum Celle** • Tues–Sun 10am–5pm • €5, free Fri • ⓦ kunst.celle.de • **Bomann-Museum** Tues–Sun 10am–5pm • €5 • ⓦ bomann-museum.de

The glass-skinned cube next to the Schloss is the **Kunstmuseum Celle**, whose night-time illumination of exhibits in the window – and colours that change its facade on the hour

13

– prompts its billing as the world's first 24-hour museum. Its largely post-1960s permanent art collection of works by modern giants such as Joseph Beuys reflects the tastes of Hannover connoisseur Robert Simon. Some space is also reserved for temporary exhibitions. Beside it, the **Bomann-Museum** documents rural and town lifestyles and includes a reconstructed farmstead and workshop.

The Altstadt

Celle's old town lies east as parallel streets that run up to the Schloss. All are worth a stroll for the row upon row of half-timbered buildings erected over two hundred years from the sixteenth century onwards to bequeath a streetscape that's among North Germany's most historic. Your introduction is likely to be **Stechbahn**, a broad artery and one-time ducal games ground that leads from the Schloss into the Altstadt. Duke Otto the Magnanimous is said to have come a cropper here during a joust in 1471 – a horseshoe outside the court chemist, Löwenapotheke, marks where he fell. At the end of Stechbahn, tourists pose for a holiday snap wearing the neck manacles that shamed miscreants in public in the 1700s, and quite overlook the venerable Gothic **Rathaus** beside it, remodelled in Weser Renaissance style in 1571.

Stadtkirche

Stechbahn • Mon–Sat 10am–6pm, Sun 11am–2pm; tower April–Oct Tues–Sat 10am–11.45am & 2–3.45pm • €1

Beside the Rathaus, the town's greatest monument, the **Stadtkirche**, received a makeover during renovation of the Schloss under the mastery of Tornielli, who here matches his craftsmanship with exquisite artistry: a stucco garden of flowers blooms on the barrel-vaulted roof, twelve apostles stride from pillars and in the choir he provides an intimation of paradise in the flowers that smother the original Gothic vaults. A pictorial Bible that wraps around the gallery and a Baroque organ played by Johann Sebastian Bach himself completes the picture. A 234-step tramp up the **tower** provides both views of Celle's roofscape and a platform for a town trumpeter (9.30am & 5.30pm).

Zöllnerstrasse and around

The finest **half-timbered** streets fan out east and south from the Rathaus. Upper storeys jut over the narrow streets to eke extra space and beams are carved with a carnival of allegorical figures and God-fearing maxims – "He who trusts in God has built well" is a favourite – in a typically late-medieval marriage of folklore and religious piety.

Zöllnerstrasse is a pictorial textbook of sixteenth-century beam decoration: its development traces from early step- or branch-and-tendril motifs, via zigzag ropework and rosettes to squiggles that ape clasps on furniture. Turn right from the end of Stechbahn instead, however, for **Hoppenhauer Haus** (1532) on the corner of Poststrasse and Rundestrasse, one of the ritziest pieces of carving in town, its scrollwork and rural scenes created as a statement of prestige by a ducal official. **Grosser Plan** further south is worth a look for a handsome – and usually quieter – wedge-shaped piazza. Some of the most enjoyable carving lies on less grand streets north of Zöllnerstrasse. Look at **Neue Strasse 11** for a bawdy monster that defecates coins in a sermon about the fate that awaits the avaricious in hell.

Synagogue

Im Kreise 24 • Tues–Thurs noon–5pm, Fri 10am–3pm, Sun noon–5pm • Free

The area southeast of the Altstadt was the town's Jewish ghetto, though you'd never know until you step inside the **synagogue**. The oldest in North Germany, it occupies a half-timbered house that survived *Kristallnacht* in 1938. Its original interior was destroyed during that Nazi purge and, poignantly, some articles for its replacement were donated by survivors of the nearby Bergen-Belsen concentration camp (see p.730), who worshipped here after liberation. A small museum within has an exhibition of local Jewish life.

Französischer Garten

From the Synagogue it's a five-minute walk to the **Französischer Garten** which borders the southern Altstadt. The name probably derives from the French gardeners employed by Duke Georg-Wilhelm; the mature parkland itself is in naturalistic English style.

ARRIVAL AND INFORMATION   CELLE

By train On the Hannover line, Celle's Hauptbahnhof lies a 15min walk west of the Altstadt via Bahnhofstrasse, which emerges at the rear of the Schloss.
Destinations Hannover (every 30min; 30–45min); Lüneburg (6 daily; 30–40min).

Tourist office Markt 14–16 (May–Sept Mon–Fri 9am–6pm, Sat 10am–4pm, Sun 11am–2pm; Oct–April Mon–Fri 9am–5pm, Sat 10am–1pm; ☎05141 12 12, ⓦ celle-tourismus.de).

ACCOMMODATION

HOTELS

Borchers Schuhstr. 52 ☎05141 91 19 20, ⓦ hotelborchers.com. What appears to be a half-timbered house from outside is actually a pleasant modern hotel at the heart of the the Altstadt. Some of the nineteen rooms open directly onto a garden; all are classic-modern in style. **€84**

Celler Hof Stechbahn 11 ☎05141 91 19 60, ⓦ cellerhof.de. A half-timbered house on one of Celle's finest streets hides relaxed business-style rooms with mod cons from the Wallbaum chain. Facilities include a Finnish sauna. You're paying mostly for a central location opposite the Stadtkirche – keep the window open and its trumpeter provides a reveille at 9.30am. **€97**

Fürstenhof Hannoversche Str. 55–56 ☎05141 20 10, ⓦ fuerstenhof-celle.com. Not just Celle's premier address but one of the finest in the area, housed in a Baroque palace just south of the Schloss. Modern-country decor is as elegant as its building, inspired by local themes – royalty, hunting, equestrian or heathland – and calm and five-star sophistication reign. **€130**

Götz Hannoversche Str. 28 ☎05141 278 80 72, ⓦ goetz-hotel-celle.de. The cheapest hotel in Celle has basic pine-furnished en-suite rooms – though nothing special, they are clean and perfectly acceptable for a bunk-down on a budget. Front rooms can be noisy due to the busy road outside. It's a 10min walk from the centre. **€50**

HOSTELS AND CAMPSITES

Campingpark Silbersee 4km north of the centre in Vorwerk suburb ☎05141 321 23, ⓦ campingpark-silbersee.de; bus #6, or off B191 by car. The nearest campsite lies among silver birch trees on the shore of a small lake. Facilities include laundry, a shop and a bar-restaurant, plus a playground and small beach to entertain the kids. Pitch **€3.60**, plus **€3.70** per person

DJH Celle Weghauserstr. 2 ☎05141 532 08, ⓦ djh-niedersachsen.de; bus #3 to "Jugendherberge" stop. Popular with school groups, who must feel at home in this former school. It's located on the western edge of the town a 20min walk from the centre. Four- to six-bed dorms share facilities. Dorms **€20**, doubles **€50**

EATING AND DRINKING

Endtenfang Hannoversche Str. 55–56 ☎05141 20 10, ⓦ fuerstenhof-celle.com. The Mediterranean-inspired creations served at the *Fürstenhof* hotel's restaurant have earned it a Michelin star 25 years running; dishes such as saddle of venison with walnuts and hibiscus jus are well worth a visit. The ambience is elegant yet informal and, praise be, there's decent portion sizing too. Four-course dinner menus start at €75; the three-course lunch on Fri or Sun is €65. Wed, Thurs & Sat 6.30pm–midnight, Fri & Sun also noon–2pm & 6.30pm–midnight.

Fachwerk Schuhstr. 25 ☎05141 278 82 55. Maximalist wallpaper, leather sofas, chandeliers, tapas plates and cocktails in a lounge bar in the Altstadt. While hardly

cutting-edge compared to city bars, this is as good an antidote to the heritage schtick as you'll find in the Altstadt. Wed–Fri 6pm–late, Sat & Sun 7pm–late.

Raths-Weinschenke Zöllnerstr. 29 ☎05141 226 05. Located in a pretty half-timbered courtyard, Celle's oldest and cosiest wine bar is a charmer, with half-barrel seats in its tiny interior. Foodwise, expect home-made platters of Italian salami and cheese and quiche. Tues–Fri 5–11pm, Sat noon–6pm.

Ratskeller Markt 14 ☎05141 290 99, ⓦ ratskeller-celle.de. A little pricey compared to most of its kin, but the town hall restaurant is renowned for high-quality regional cuisine – *Heidschnucken*, lamb grazed on the Lüneburg

13

Heath, is a speciality (€23). Dining beneath the Gothic arches of what is claimed as north Germany's oldest restaurant (1378) may be worth paying extra for too. Mon–Sat 10am–midnight, Sun 10am–3pm.
Schweine Schulze Neue Str. 36 ☎05141 229 44. A good option if the *Ratskeller* is too full or too formal, this

family-owned *Gästatte* has an excellent reputation for fine regional cooking, priced between €11 and €16. Dishes such as *Eisbein*, steaks and North Sea sole are served by a genial host in two snug historic dining-rooms. Mon–Fri 11am–3pm & 6pm–midnight, Sat 11am–4pm.

The Lüneburg Heath

Spread between Celle and Lüneburg lie the open landscapes of the **LÜNEBURG HEATH** (Lüneburger Heide). Sparsely populated and dotted with pretty Lower Saxon farming villages of red-brick and beams, the area has been mostly drained of its original moors to stand as a gently undulating, minimally farmed landscape. The heath is famed for the heather that lays a carpet of dusty purple from mid-August, auguring in a month of village fêtes to crown a Heather Queen: the week-long **Heather Blossom Festival** at Amelinghausen from the middle Saturday in August is the largest. Being mixed with broom, gorse and juniper, the heather also produces excellent honey and adds flavour to the shaggy Heidschnucke lambs, which are grazed here year-round. Some shepherds don traditional floppy hats and waistcoats for tourists.

Tourist offices in Celle (see p.729) and Lüneburg (see p.733) are your best sources of **information** on the heath; for pre-planning, area tourism website ⓦluneburger-heide .de is useful, though there's little in English.

Naturschutzpark Lüneburger Heide

The favoured grazing ground for local shepherds is the **Naturschutzpark Lüneburger Heide**, centred on the Wilseder Berg, a hill that at 169m is easily the highest point in the park. Alongside sheep, you can spy from its summit a couple of the huge megaliths that dot the area, known locally as **Hünengräber**, or giants' graves. The hill is accessed from the pretty village of Undeloh just off the A7 west of Lüneburg, but limited public transport makes visiting tricky without a bike or a car.

Vogelpark Walsrode

Walsrode • Daily: mid-March to Oct 10am–7pm; Nov–Feb 10am–4pm • €19, family ticket €59 • ⓦ vogelpark-walsrode.de

Apart from the walking tracks that crisscross the heath, the most popular attraction of the area is **Vogelpark Walsrode** near Walsrode village at the western fringe of the heath. What is claimed to be the world's largest bird park stages free-flight displays of raptors and condors to buttress other avian attractions – a raised tree walk, penguin enclosure and walk-through rainforest house where birds fly free, for example – and pleasant landscaped gardens.

Bergen-Belsen

Lohheide, near Belsen • Documentation centre daily: April–Sept 10am–6pm; Oct–March 10am–5pm; former camp area open 24hr; 3–4hr tours June to mid-Sept Thurs–Sun 2.30pm, Fri & Sat also 11.30am • Free • ⓦ bergen-belsen.stiftung-ng.de • Bus from Celle Bahnhof or Schlossplatz to the Bergen-Gedenkstätte stop (weekdays only); catch the first of the day to have enough time at the site before the return in mid-afternoon

The Lüneburg Heath's place in history is bound up with World War II. On a sunny spring morning on May 3, 1945, Field Marshal Montgomery accepted unconditional surrender of German forces in North Germany, the Netherlands and Denmark. It occurred barely a fortnight after the Allies had first reeled at Hitler's "Final Solution" in the **BERGEN-BELSEN** concentration camp 22km northwest of Celle. Established to hold prisoners of war in 1940 (around eighteen thousand Russian prisoners from the eastern front perished of hunger, cold and disease here in 1941–42) the camp became infamous as the SS detention camp in which fifty thousand Jews died, most of starvation and disease under its commanding officer, the "Beast of Belsen" Josef Kramer.

The excellent **documentation centre** at the Bergen-Belsen Memorial has an exhibition tracking the camp's history, including the postwar use of the soldiers' barracks as a "displaced persons' camp" for Jews emigrating to Israel. Even though a laudably restrained documentary of the liberation tackles the atrocities with thought-provoking interviews, the footage, which was screened in UK cinemas at the time, remains genuinely shocking. Much of the area has been reclaimed by silver birch and pine forest – the buildings were razed by the British to prevent a typhus epidemic – but that doesn't make a walk where the Allies discovered around twelve thousand unburied corpses on April 15, 1945, any less disturbing. Camp paths and the track of the outer fence cut like scars through the forest, and some barrack foundations remain visible. Similarly blunt statements of the dead within mass graves appal, even though the statistics are infamous. A haunting personal dimension is the memorial to teen diarist Anne Frank, who succumbed to typhus weeks before the liberation in March 1945. The documentation centre sells booklets to guide you around the camp, and free guided tours in English are offered in summer.

Lüneburg

Few small towns in North Germany are so improbably picturesque as **LÜNEBURG**. Almost anywhere you go in the Altstadt will be a small-town streetscape of film-set looks. Yet despite the richness of its architecture, the small town is founded on the prosaic. Local **salt mines** were already being worked by the monks of St Michaelis here in 956 AD, and when Lüneburg's citizens wrested independence from the Guelphic princes in 1371 and signed up to the mercantile Hanseatic League, exports of its "white gold" via Lübeck catapulted the town into the highest echelons of affluence. In its Renaissance golden era, Lüneburg was Europe's largest salt producer, only to shrink suddenly into obscurity as its Hanseatic market waned. Salt production ceased in 1980. The flip-side of stagnation, however, is preservation: without funds for building, Lüneburg has had to make do with an Altstadt full of Hanseatic step-gables and brickwork like twisted rope. Salt continues to shape the town today – subsidence of underground deposits causes the Altstadt to lean at decidedly woozy angles.

Lüneburg's Altstadt is ordered around two squares: **Am Markt**, the civic heartland above its historic port, the **Wasserviertel**; and elongated **Am Sande** at its southern end.

The Markt and around

The Roman moon goddess Luna that crowns the fountain on **Am Markt**, and the half-crescents on the exterior of the nearby Rathaus together suggest a romantic derivation of Lüneburg's name – but were actually a conceit dreamed up with the intellectual flowering of the Renaissance. "Lüneburg" is actually just a corruption of the Lombard *hiluni*, or refuge.

The Rathaus

Am Markt • Tours in German (English notes available) Tues–Sat 11am, 12.30pm, 2.30pm & 4pm, Sun 11am & 2pm • €5

No building expresses Lüneburg's former standing better than the **Rathaus**, begun in the thirteenth century and extended over five hundred years. The facade is Baroque at its most balanced, refined from the dull early variant but not yet smothered by Rococo froth, and here topped by a peal of Meissen china bells that chime the ditties of a Lüneburg composer, J.A.P. Schulz.

13

Within are rooms of, arguably, Germany's finest Renaissance town hall. City fathers saved the firework display of gilt and paint for the **Gerlichtslaube** (Court of Justice), with its inscription promising equal judgement for rich and poor and its stained glass of "nine good heroes", although it is run a close second by the beamed roof of the **Fürstensaal** (Prince's Hall). The real treasure is the **Grosse Ratstube** (Council's Great Chamber): it's not nearly as flash as preceding rooms, but its carving by Westphalian master Albert von Soest is first-rate Renaissance. One tympanum depicts the agonies of the damned in particularly vivid detail.

Heinrich-Heine-Haus

The gables carved as dolphins on **Heinrich-Heine-Haus** to the right of the Rathaus date from the same era. The house was home to the Romantic poet's parents – Heine is said to have penned his famous *Lorelei* here in the 1820s – but he was scathing about the cultural backwater that was contemporary Lüneburg, and pined in one letter for the "Makkaroni und Geistesspeise" (literally, "macaroni and spiritual food") of Berlin.

Around Auf dem Meere

Behind the Rathaus, via Waagestrasse, some of the most photogenic residential streets in Lüneburg lie off **Auf dem Meere**. **Untere Ohlingerstrasse** and **Obere Ohlingerstrasse** easily make up in Disneyesque charm what they lack in civic grandeur. Salt subsidence that has caused the streetscape to sway drunkenly also affected the area's **St Michaelskirche**; its pillars lean dangerously like a Gothic horror film-set.

St Nikolai

Head up Bardowicker Strasse at the Markt's northeast corner to reach the sailors' and artisans' church, **St Nikolai**. Although its 93m-high spire is a product of overzealous renovation in the late 1800s, the high Gothic nave fretted with star vaulting is genuine, best interpreted as a statement of pride by a merchant population at the high point of its prosperity. It's a sentiment repeated in the ambulatory on an altarpiece of the town from c.1444 – the earliest portrait of Lüneburg is recognizable by the crooked spire of St Johannis (see opposite) – and a nearby work that sees Abraham breaking bread outside medieval Lüneburg rather than the Promised Land.

The Wasserviertel

St Nikolai, the sailors' church, lies above the **Wasserviertel**. The clamour of Hanseatic trade in the port on the River Ilmenau has long been replaced by the buzz of dockside restaurants, although a 1330s cargo crane, a replica cargo-lighter moored in the river and a former herring warehouse topped with a lighter weathervane bear witness to its former life. A wander through streets above reveals fine merchants' houses; those on Rotenhahnstrasse are the oldest.

Am Sande

The second square in Lüneburg, elongated **Am Sande**, is ringed by step-gabled houses, many leaning dangerously due to salt subsidence. The square's most impressive building, the twin-gabled **Schwarzes Haus** (Black House), now the Chamber of Commerce and Industry, was built in 1548 as a brewery, during an era when malt rivalled salt in civic importance and Lüneburg boasted over eighty breweries.

Kronen-Brauerei

Heiligengeistr. 39–41 • Tues–Sun 1–4.30pm • Free • ⓦ krone-lueneburg.de

The old **Kronen-Brauerei**, on Heiligengeiststrasse off the west end of the square, retains a traditional brewery over several storeys at its rear; pick up leaflets in English to guide you through the process of traditional beer-making.

13

St Johannis

Am Sande is dominated by the brick church of **St Johannis**, or rather its 108m-high spire that is off-kilter by 2.20m; a dubious tale relates that a haycart thwarted a suicide jump by the distressed architect, who later slipped off his bar stool while celebrating his luck and died. Five naves create a spacious interior whose pillars frame a late medieval altar, its panels a sermon of Passion and Resurrection. More impressive is an organ that fills the rear wall. It inspired a young keyboardist named Johann Sebastian Bach to great things and remains one of the biggest and most sonorous in North Germany. Times of daily concerts are posted by the church door. Just by the church's corner, a neo-Gothic **water tower** (April–Oct daily 10am–6pm; €4) provides aerial views of Am Sande.

Deutsches Salzmusem and Salztherme

Deutsches Salzmuseum Sülfmeisterstr. 1 • May–Sept Mon–Fri 9am–5pm, Sat & Sun 10am–5pm; Oct–March daily 10am–5pm • €6 • Ⓦ salzmuseum.de • **Salztherme** Uelzener Str. 1–5 • Mon–Sat 10am–11pm, Sun 8am–9pm • 2hr from €7.90 • Ⓦ salue.info

From Am Sande, Heiligengeiststrasse leads eventually to Lambertiplatz, beyond which is the once all-important salt works. On a street just off here, in one half of a former warehouse (the rest is occupied by a supermarket), the **Deutsches Salzmusem** explains more than you're ever likely to want to know about salt production; enter through the train carriage. The salt infatuation continues further south in the saltwater baths of spa and pools centre **Salztherme**, ten minutes further south of Lambertiplatz via Sülztorstrasse.

ARRIVAL AND INFORMATION   LÜNEBURG

By train and bus Lüneburg's Hauptbahnhof and bus station lie east of its centre, with the Altstadt accessible from either end of Bahnhofstrasse in front.
Destinations Celle (6 daily; 35min); Hamburg (hourly; 30min); Hannover (hourly; 1hr); Lübeck (hourly; 1hr 10min).

Tourist office In the Rathaus on Am Markt (Jan–April & Nov Mon–Fri 9.30am–6pm, Sat 9.30am–2pm; May–Oct & Dec Mon–Fri 9.30am–6pm, Sat 9.30am–4pm, Sun 10am–4pm; ☏ 0800 220 50 05, Ⓦ lueneburg.info).

ACCOMMODATION

HOTELS

Altes Kaufhaus Kaufhausstr. 5 ☏ 04131 308 80, Ⓦ alteskaufhaus.de. Slick if a mite bland in its modern neutral decor, this hotel appeals for its Superior or Deluxe rooms – an extra €10 buys you picture-window views over the river to the Wasserviertel opposite. Throughout, you get brisk, smart service plus access to facilities such as a gym and spa. **€99**

Bremer Hof Lüner Str. 12–13 ☏ 04131 22 40, Ⓦ bremer -hof.de. Well-located hotel near the Wasserviertel with modern renovated rooms in a historic merchant's house. Rooms in a modern block behind are cheaper. **€93**

Einzigartig Lünertorstr. 3 ☏ 04131 400 60 00, Ⓦ hoteleinzigartig.de. Lüneburg's first design hotel shows off the fabric of its beautifully restored sixteenth-century house by the Wasserviertel. Nine minimalist rooms are cool without being frosty, a symphony of white, cream and dove-grey with pops of colour from designer pieces. **€142**

★**Haus auf dem Meere** Auf dem Meere 6 ☏ 04131 898 30 00, Ⓦ privat-zimmer-lueneburg.de. A half-timbered house has been renovated to create five snug studios for up two people in Lüneburg's most picturesque residential area. Cool grey and cream paintwork, wood floors and mixed-style furnishings create the feel of a stylish Scandinavian home. A real find and outstanding value. **€59**

Scheffler Bardowicker Str. 7 ☏ 04131 200 80, Ⓦ hotel -scheffler.de. Rooms are a little dull compared to the bags of character in the public areas of this inn near the Nikolaikirche, but this is a perfectly acceptable family-run hotel that well located just off the Markt. **€95**

HOSTELS AND CAMPSITES

DJH Lüneburg Soltauer Str. 133 ☏ 04131 418 64, Ⓦ djh-niedersachsen.de; bus #5011 or #5012 to "Scharnhornstrasse" drop you close by, but services are meagre in the evening. Typically large, modern youth hostel, popular with school groups; a third of the rooms are en suite. It's located south of the centre near the university. Dorms **€26**, doubles **€58**

Rote Schleuse Rote Schleuse 4 ☏ 04131 79 15 00, Ⓦ camproteschleuse.de. You can pitch a tent by the River Ilmenau and hire a canoe at this woodland campsite located 4km south of the centre; it's signposted off the main road south from the centre towards the B4, and also off the B4 near its junction with the B209. Pitch **€3.50**, plus **€7** per person

13

EATING AND DRINKING

★**Anna's Cafe** Am Stintmarkt 12 ☏ 04131 884 31 81, ⓦ annas-cafe.de. Relaxed café set just away from the waterfront of the Wasserviertel whose vintage chandeliers and elegant sofas are as charming as its waitresses. A delight for breakfasts, it also offers light bites such as *Flammkuchen* plus fresh modern gâteaux to go with good coffee. Daily 8am–9pm.

Mälzer Heiligengeiststr. 43 ☏ 04131 477 77, ⓦ maelzerbrauhaus.de. A house-brewed *Pils, Dunkels* and *Hefeweizen* that come in volumes up to a litre is one

reason to come to this popular, informal pub off Am Sande. Another is a cheap menu that swings from rumpsteak (€15.50) to *Currywurst*. Mon–Sat 9am–1am, Sun 11am–midnight.

Pons Salzstrasse Am Wasser 1 ☏ 04131 287 30 60, ⓦ pons-lueneburg.de. Once it was sailors; now students sup in the oldest pub in town, an appealingly scruffy place of crooked walls and eclectic furnishings by the Wasserviertel quay. It hosts occasional art exhibitions and prepares a short veggie menu. Daily 1pm–late; kitchen closes 11pm.

Osnabrück

Welcome to the happiest town in Germany. Last decade a nationwide poll found citizens of **OSNABRÜCK**, the largest city in western Lower Saxony, more content than those anywhere else in Germany, inspiring a marketing campaign in *Stern* magazine that declared "Ich komm zum Glück aus Osnabrück" ("I'm lucky to be from Osnabrück"). A friendly small-scale city of modest charm and with a university to prevent it stagnating, it has much to be happy about. The biggest festival of the year is **Maiwoche**, a ten-day extravaganza of music and entertainment, usually from the second Friday in May.

Brief history

In 1648 after more than four years of negotiations here and in Münster 60km south, Catholic and Protestant signatures dried on the Peace of Westphalia and the political and religious inferno of the Thirty Years' War was finally doused. Osnabrück has treasured its diplomacy of peace ever since. The city's two great sons, Justus Möser and Erich Maria Remarque, dreamed of ennobled, free workers and railed against war's insanity respectively, and today Osnabrück proudly declares herself "Die Friedenstadt" (**Peace City**), host of Nobel Peace Prize-winners Henry Kissinger and the Dalai Lama, home of the German Foundation for Peace Research and the national branch of child-relief agency Terre des Hommes. Perhaps it's no surprise that its finest museum-gallery pays homage to a Jewish artist murdered at Auschwitz.

The Dom

Domhof · **Dom** Daily 7am–7pm · Free · **Diözesanmuseum** Tues–Sun 10am–6pm · €5

In 780 AD, Charlemagne thrust his standard into the Hase's banks and vowed to bring Christianity to the Saxons on the far bank. Just as his pioneering mission grew into a town, so his church has swelled into the **Dom** that sits on its own square near Osnabrück's birthplace. Begun as a Romanesque basilica, it was built at a leisurely pace over five hundred years with each era stamping its mark, not all successfully. Renaissance builders enlarged the girth of the southwest tower rather than re-forge a prize bell, which was cast too large for it. Its smaller sister tower remains to lend the facade a lopsided appearance.

The **interior** speaks of strength and dignity in powerful Gothic columns and arches that parade to a luminous choir where the relics of French saints Crispin and Crispinian, who renounced Roman nobility for humble cobbling to spread the word, were venerated as Charlemagne's gift. The star pieces are the bronze font in the baptistry, cast in 1226, and Lower Saxony's largest *Triumphkreuz* (1240), a blaze of gilded evangelist symbols. There's also a fine, Gothic stone Madonna in the north transept, a picture of serenity as she tramples a serpent, and through iron gates that play tricks with perspective, a Late Gothic triptych (1517) is hidden in a chapel off the square ambulatory.

Diözesanmuseum

More masterpieces, including an ivory comb said to be Charlemagne's, are in the **Diözesanmuseum**. Among the Romanesque crucifixes studded with coloured jewels, Roman cameos and bishopric rings are devotional carvings by the Master of Osnabrück, the anonymous sculptor behind the city's most distinguished works of the Middle Ages.

The Markt

The spiritual heart of Osnabrück, the **Markt** is a triangle of cobbles lined with a colourful array of Hanseatic-style step-gabled facades. Apart from a quaint row of houses, the city's two main sights can be found here: the Gothic **Rathaus** and the soaring **Marienkirche**.

The Rathaus

Markt • Friedenssaal Mon–Fri 8am–7pm, Sat 9am–4pm, Sun 10am–4pm • Free

On the Markt's long side, kings and emperors glower from a stocky **Rathaus**, nineteenth-century newcomers despite their looks, erected to replace allegorical statues as Germany swaggered into a new empire; you have to admire the chutzpah of an empire that cast contemporary ruler Kaiser Wilhelm I as the right-hand man of Charlemagne at the centre. However, Osnabrück has reason to be proud of its Gothic hall. Envoys of the Protestant Swedish and German factions stare gloomily above the bench seats on which they hammered out the Peace of Westphalia (see box below) in the **Friedenssaal**. A replica of the famous deed is in the Schatzkammer alongside treasures like the fourteenth-century *Kaiserpokal* – the story goes that incoming councillors had to prove their worth by downing in one a draught from this gold goblet.

Marienkirche

An der Marienkirche 11 • Daily: April–Sept 10am–noon & 3–5pm; Oct–March 10.30am–noon & 2.30–4pm; tower Sun 11.30am–1pm • Free, tower €2

To the right of the Rathaus is the Stadtwaage guilds' weights and measures office and next to it Gothic church, the **Marienkirche**, whose haggard Christ splayed on a medieval *Triumphkreuz* commands attention, as does a Passion altar from Antwerp in the choir. Look, too, in the ambulatory for the tombstone slab of **Justus Möser** (1720–94). When not poring over the finances of the town's last prince-bishop, this articulate heavyweight of the German Enlightenment pioneered a vision of a state whose citizens were free of the dictates of sovereign rulers. Hailed as both a people's champion and an intellectual star, Möser is honoured with a memorial before the Dom. Before you ascend the tower for a view over the Markt, there's a Stations of the Cross cycle by Renaissance hero Albrecht Dürer, created five years before the Passion altar in 1510 and centuries ahead in artistry.

THE POOR SWORDSMITHS AND THE PEACE OF WESTPHALIA

Protestant factions met in Osnabrück's Rathaus for over four years to broker their half of the **Peace of Westphalia** (the Catholics were in Münster) and unpick the knotted conflicts of the **Thirty Years' War** that had brought German cities to their knees. Once signed by both, city fathers stood on the Rathaus steps on October 25, 1648, and proclaimed the carnage over, a declaration greeted at first with disbelief by the crowd, then by tears and a spontaneous outburst of hymns. As a contemporary pamphlet relates: "Osnabrück and all the world rejoices, the joyful people sing, Flags fly bravely … I am only sorry for the poor swordsmiths for they have nothing to do."

13

Erich Maria Remarque museum

Markt 6 • Tues–Fri 10am–1pm & 3–5pm, Sat & Sun 11am–5pm • Free

One of Osnabrück's favourite sons is Erich Maria Remarque, author of World War I classic, *All Quiet on the Western Front*. If your German's up to it, the text-heavy **Erich Maria Remarque museum** opposite the Marienkirche chronicles his life.

Around the Markt

Behind the Rathaus, the conjoined high-streets of **Krahnstrasse** and **Bierstrasse** house the best of the buildings that survived Allied bombs. At Bierstr. 24, the **Walhalla** hotel (see opposite) – formerly an inn that Erich Maria Remarque acclaimed for its "erstklassig Essen" (first-class eating) – hosts a troupe of saints and cherubs on its beams, beneath which the devil is caught squatting on a roasting chamber pot. At Krahnstr. 7, meanwhile, **Haus Willmann** has a relief of Adam and Eve.

More historic charm is in the nest of streets behind Bierstrasse known as the **Hegetorviertel**, which squirrels away Osnabrück's most interesting shopping and a modest bar district. All alleys thread to the eponymous **Hegetor** gate in the former city walls, a Neoclassical salute to soldiers who fought at Waterloo on its former outer side. Although Osnabrück's defence walls have disappeared, their embrace is felt when you emerge from the Hegetor onto a suddenly modern ring-road that replaces the old defences.

North of the Hegertorviertel, at the end of Bierstrasse at Hasemauer 1, the **Dominikanerkirche** (Tues–Fri 11am–6pm, Sat & Sun 10am–6pm; €3; ⓦosnabrueck .de/kunsthalle) now hosts modern art exhibitions in a Gothic church building.

Felix-Nussbaum-Haus and Kulturgeschichtliches Museum

Lotter Str. 2 • Tues–Fri 11am–6pm, Sat & Sun 10am–6pm • €5 • ⓦ osnabrueck.de/fnh

Directly opposite the Hegetor, the **Felix-Nussbaum-Haus** is a dialogue between architecture and art created by Daniel Libeskind. The architect behind Berlin's acclaimed Jewish Museum here creates a savagely oppressive building, its angular rooms slashed by windows, its long corridors sloping upwards to constrict the visitor in echo of the disorientation and oppression of Osnabrück-born Jewish painter Felix Nussbaum. His Surrealism-lite darkens into cadaver-like figures with the onset of Nazi persecution, when he was forced into hiding in Brussels and began to use pencil and charcoal for fear the smell of the turpentine to clean brushes might reveal his hideaway. More crushing is the despair of his final works: *Self-portrait with Jewish Identity Card* and *Triumph Of Death*, painted just before his death in Auschwitz in 1944.

Such is its impact, the Felix-Nussbaum-Haus almost entirely overshadows the rest of the **Kulturgeschichtliches Museum** (Museum of Cultural History) of which it is a part, a chronicle of local history in, among other things, weaponry, folk costume and sculpture. Its archeology wing features some Roman items unearthed from a garrison town near Detmold where Germanic tribes triumphed in battle and took a decisive step towards a fledgling country – a taster for the Varusschlacht Museum und Park Kalkriese to the north (p.738).

ARRIVAL AND INFORMATION   **OSNABRÜCK**

By plane Osnabrück shares an international airport with Münster, midway between the two cities about 40km southeast of Osnabrück. Minibus #X150 shuttles to the Hauptbahnhof (40min); expect to pay around €55 for a taxi to the centre.

By train The Hauptbahnhof is just outside the city walls to the southeast.

Destinations Bremen (hourly; 50min–1hr 10min);

Hannover (hourly; 1hr 5min–1hr 30min); Münster (every 30min; 25min).

Tourist office Just off the Markt at Bierstr. 22–23 (Mon–Fri 9.30am–6pm, Sat 10am–4pm; ☎0541 323 22 02, ⓦ osnabrueck.de).

Discount card The tourist office sells the *Kulturkarte* day-ticket (€8), for free public transport and entry into all museums.

13

ACCOMMODATION

Dom Kleine Domsfreiheit 5 ☎ 0541 35 83 50, ⓦ dom-hotel-osnabrueck.de. It's worth paying an extra €10 to secure larger suite-style rooms in this small business-styled hotel. If its inoffensive decor of pale-wood furniture and pastel walls are forgettable, the helpful managers and excellent location behind the Dom are less so. **€87**

Intour Maschstr. 10 ☎ 0541 96 38 60, ⓦ intourhotel .de. Modest but perfectly acceptable family-run three-star on a quiet side-street west of the Altstadt. While on the small side, all rooms are en suite and the fact that the Hegertor bars are a 10min walk away appeals. All in all, a simple, good-value choice. **€84**

Penthouse Backpackers Möserstr. 19 ☎ 0541 600 96 06, ⓦ penthousebp.com. North of the station on the top floor of an office block – hence the name – this is a friendly, small hostel, cheerfully shabby and with an outdoor terrace for barbecues. Eight- and ten-bed dorms, bright rooms (two en suite), laundry and free internet and breakfasts.

Note that check-in is 8–11am & 4–9pm only. Dorms **€16**, doubles **€40**

Steigenberger Hotel Remarque Natruper-Tor-Wall 1 ☎ 0541 609 60, ⓦ steigenberger.com/osnabrueck. Just outside the Altstadt on the city's inner ring-road, just north of Felix-Nussbuam-Haus, the premier address in Osnabrück maintains an air of relaxed elegance through a calm ochre-and-saffron colour scheme in its business-style rooms. Deluxe options provide a lot more space for relatively little money. **€126**

Walhalla Bierstr. 24 ☎ 0541 349 10, ⓦ hotel-walhalla.de. The connoisseur's choice, installed in a 400-year-old half-timbered inn at the heart of the town, has been modernized with an eye for modern interior design. Accommodation in the historic front half is equally historic in terms of space; rooms in the rear wing are larger and a mite more modern. Facilities include a small spa. **€119**

EATING AND DRINKING

The most central bar scene is in the west Altstadt streets by the Hegertor, the so-called **Hegertorviertel**. The *Mosquito* booklet (ⓦ mosquito-os.de), available from bars and the tourist office, is a good source of **listings**.

Café Läer Krahnstr. 4 ☎ 0541 222 44. *Die kunst zu geniessen* ("the art of enjoyment") is the punning mantra of this split-level café in a historic townhouse in the pedestrianized streets of the city centre. Cakes come highly rated by locals and there are usually a few organic home-made quiches and soups on offer for lunch. Mon–Fri 8am–6.30pm, Sat 7.30am–4pm.

Friche Blöcks Herderstr. 26 ☎ 0541 75 04 20 08, ⓦ fricke-bloecks.de. A gastropub in a residential area near the Felix-Nussbaum-Haus with a modern menu that swings from Mediterranean grilled lamb and couscous to a house-special pork cutlet marinated in tequila, lemon and sea salt. The stylish venue, with a small beer garden, is a pleasant spot for a refined drink among a young professional crowd. Mon–Sat 6pm–midnight.

Grüner Jager An der Katherinenkirche 1 ☎ 0541 273 60, ⓦ gruener-jaeger-os.de. A splendid old boozer at the southern end of the pedestrian streets, whose warren of traditional rooms – love that faux baronial hall – attracts a diverse crowd, from students at the nearby university to fifty-something drinkers via football fans for live

Bundesliga games. Food is so-so, but there are good cheap options on the same square. Mon–Thurs 11am–1am, Fri & Sat 11am–3am, Sun 2.30pm–2am.

La Vie Krahnstr. 1–2 ☎ 0541 33 11 50, ⓦ restaurant-lavie.de. Head chef Thomas Bühner creates a firework display of fragrance, aroma and texture in this three-Michelin-star restaurant – not simply one of the finest in North Germany, but a fixture among the most creative modern-European cuisine in Germany. Ingenious creations such as marinated cod tartar with lychee jelly and iced almond foam are balanced by traditional dishes like guinea fowl or langoustine with green tomato, iberico bacon and bulgur wheat. Reserve at least two weeks in advance. Menus from €140. Tues–Thurs 7–11pm, Sat & Sun noon–2pm & 7pm–midnight.

Rampendahl Hasestr. 35 ☎ 0541 245 35, ⓦ rampendahl .de. A brewery-restaurant just up from the Dom whose popularity at weekends shows how high is the regard locally for its delicious house beers – a good range of *Pils* and dark beers. The menu is typically unpretentious home-cooking, with lots of meaty plates and *Pfanne* dishes, and service is brisk. Mon–Sat 11am–midnight, Sun 11am–10pm.

Around Osnabrück

The environs of the city hold modest attractions for anyone who has made the effort to reach Osnabrück, sandwiched as it is between two layers of woodland and meadows designated as the UNESCO-listed **Geo Park TERRA.vita** (ⓦ naturpark-terravita.de). With a network of 2300km of walking trails and 1500km of tracks, this area is ideal for a **bike day-trip** – the tourist office can advise on rental and provide maps.

13

Varusschlacht Museum und Park Kalkriese

Venner Str. 69d, Bramsche-Kalkriese • April–Oct daily 10am–6pm; Nov–March Tues–Sun 10am–5pm • €7.50 • Ⓦ kalkriese-varusschlacht
.de • Bus #X275 from Osnabrück (Mon–Fri 4 daily, Sat 2 daily, Sun 1); by car take B218 towards Minden off A1

The premier attraction north of Osnabrück is **Varusschlacht Museum und Park Kalkriese**
at the Geo Park's northern edge, 20km north of Osnabrück. When a British major and
amateur archeologist unearthed a treasure-trove of Roman coins in 1987, he stumbled
upon the site where Germanic tribes triumphed over their Roman overlords in 9 AD – a
key skirmish in the so-called "Battle of the Teutoburg Forest" long thought to have taken
place southeast near Detmold. It was as much a very public defeat for ruler Publius
Quinctilius Varus, a "greedy, self-important, amateurish weakling", according to Roman
records, as it was a triumph for the fledgling German identity. Both the Second Reich
and Hitler mythologized the victorious Arminius as a symbol of national strength, quietly
skipping over that little was – nor still is – known about the Germanic commander.

The museum

A modern **museum** in a rusted-steel tower narrates the political tectonics of the conflict
and displays archeological finds, including a superb Roman cavalry mask. Its viewing
platform provides a view over the battlefield itself where the legions were ambushed
between woodland and marsh. As well as a replica section of Germanic rampart that
ripples away across the field, the site has three themed pavilions for different
perspectives on the area. A museum restaurant provides pseudo Roman and Germanic
dishes, although this is perfect picnic territory.

Tecklenburg

Twenty kilometres southwest of Osnabrück, at the far end of the Teutoburger Wald,
TECKLENBURG is small and uncomplicated, with an improbably picturesque Altstadt of
wonky half-timbered buildings and cobbled lanes. Its looks make it a popular weekend
trip, which in turn has introduced boutiques and cafés. Should you tire of loafing in
cafés on the idyllic Markt, you can peruse displays of folk culture in the
Puppenmuseum doll museum (2–5pm: April–Oct Tues, Thurs, Sat & Sun; Nov–
March Sat & Sun; €2.50; Ⓦ puppenmuseumtecklenburg.ev.ms) – follow the enamelled
cobbles from the Markt – or ascend to the ruins of a sixteenth-century **Schloss** above
the town. Partly rethought as Germany's largest open-air theatre, it hosts the
Tecklenburger Festspielsommer from May to September.

ARRIVAL AND INFORMATION

TECKLENBURG

By train Tecklenburg is linked by regular trains from
Osnabrück (40min; change at Lengerich).

Tourist office On the Markt (Mon–Fri 9am–5pm, Sat &
Sun 11am–4pm; Oct–April closed Sat & Sun; ☏ 05482 938
90, Ⓦ tecklenburg-touristik.de).

Bremen

Never mind that the donkey, dog, cat and cockerel celebrated in the folk tale (see box,
p.741) forgot all about their goal as soon as they had a roof over their heads, brochures
and innumerable souvenirs cheerfully proclaim **BREMEN** "die Stadt der
Stadtmusikanten" ("the Town of the Town Musicians"). A more eloquent insight into
what makes Bremen tick is that it is the smallest Land of the Federal Republic – a
declaration of Bremeners' independence that is a leitmotif of a 1200-year history.

Self-confidence and a university have made Bremen a liberal city free of conservative
hang-ups. Few southern-German cities would allow an architectural fantasy like
Böttcherstrasse to be dreamed up in their midst. As appealing, Bremen feels far smaller
than a place with a population of one million – only around half that number live

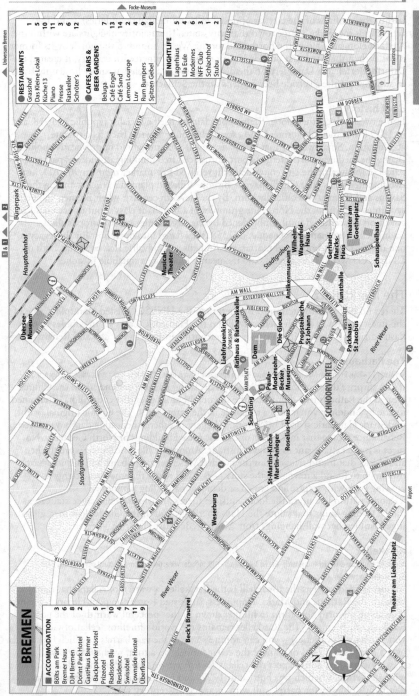

BREMEN

■ ACCOMMODATION

Bölts am Park	3
Bremer Haus	6
DJH Bremen	8
Dorint Park Hotel	2
GastHaus Bremer Backpacker Hostel	5
Prizeotel	1
Radisson Blu	10
Residence	4
Swissôtel	7
Townside Hostel	11
Überfluss	9

● RESTAURANTS

Grasshof	1
Das Kleine Lokal	5
Küche13	10
Piano	11
Presse	3
Ratskeller	6
Schröter's	12

● CAFES, BARS & BEER GARDENS

Beluga	7
Café Engel	13
Café Sand	14
Lemon Lounge	4
Luv	9
Rum Bumpers	2
Spitzen Gebel	8

■ NIGHTLIFE

Lagerhaus	5
Lila Eule	4
Modernes	6
NFF Club	3
Schlachthof	1
Stubu	2

13

within the confines of the city (as opposed to its municipal boundaries) – and the centre feels more like a large town than city-state. The majority of sights are within the **Altstadt** elongated along the north bank of the Weser, bound to the north by its former moat. When the city burst outside its defences in the nineteenth century, it created the **Ostertorviertel**, aka Das Viertel ("the district"), today a lively bar area whose only rivals in summer are the riverside beer gardens on the **Schlachte**.

Brief history

In the twentieth century alone, Bremen proclaimed itself a socialist republic in 1918, and in 1949 it was the only former Land except Hamburg to wrest back its city-state accreditation. Small wonder that Germans view it as a stronghold of provocative politics. Blame the medieval **port**. Bremen's port introduced free-thinking attitudes as part and parcel of the wealth the city enjoyed after it received free-market rights in 965 AD, just two hundred years after Charlemagne's Bishop Willehad planted a crucifix among the Saxons and Bremen was officially born. By the eleventh century, when Bremen was being acclaimed a Rome of the North, the grumbles of a merchant class about its ecclesiastical governors crescendoed until, emboldened by the city's admission to Europe's elite trading-club, the **Hanseatic League**, in 1358, they flared into open hostility. Its legacy is one-upmanship in bricks and mortar: the Rathaus and chivalric *Roland* statue, both on UNESCO's World Heritage list, and the nearby Dom, are a squabble in stone.

The Marktplatz

There's no better introduction to Bremen than the UNESCO-listed **Marktplatz**, one of the finest squares in North Germany. From the Hanseatic Cross set in cobbles to the flash patricians' houses, it is a paean to mercantile prowess in Rococo and Renaissance.

The Rathaus

Am Markt 21 • Tours in English Mon–Sat 11am, noon, 3pm & 4pm, Sun 11am & noon • €5; tickets from tourist office at Langenstr. 2

It's no surprise that a citizenry dedicated to declaring its independence from the Church created the **Rathaus** that dominates the square; the story goes that councillors determined its size by huddling voters into a rectangle in the early 1400s. The Gothic original, with trademark Hanseatic striped brickwork, is largely smothered beneath a flamboyant Weser Renaissance facade that makes this one of the prized buildings of North Germany. No piece is more extravagant than the balustrade. Among its allegorical images are the hen and chicks that found refuge from the flooded Weser on a sandbank and inspired Saxon fishermen to found a town – so the story goes – and reliefs that mock the clergy as a crowing cock with sceptre and crown or depict a man riding a bishop.

Rooms within live up to the looks outside: there's an ornate Renaissance staircase; model trading-ships that salute the Hansa heritage; and in the Güldenkammer, gilded Jugendstil leather wall-hangings from Worpswede artist Heinrich Voegler.

Ratskeller

Am Markt • Tours Jan & Feb Fri 4pm; March–Oct Fri 3pm & 4pm • €10, includes wine; tickets from the tourist office at Langenstr. 2 • Ⓦ ratskeller-bremen.de

Almost as renowned as the town hall is the **Ratskeller**, a warren of cellars that rambles beneath the Rathaus and Markt. Happiness, suggested Romantic poet Heinrich Heine, is escaping a North Sea storm to hunker down in the "peaceful warmth of the good Ratskeller of Bremen". The Ratskeller remains the world's foremost cellar of German wines (over 650 varieties) – you can admire some of the vast barrels in which it's stored over a meal (see p.748) or explore the cellar tunnels on a tour, washed down with a glass of wine. Just don't expect the cellar's *Rüdesheimer Apostelkeller*, the oldest drinkable wine in Germany, which was bottled in 1727, and be thankful it's not a glass from Germany's oldest wine barrel, still with its sixteenth-century wine.

Stadtmusikanten

Beside the Ratskeller's entrance, Bremen's very own fab four, the **Stadtmusikanten** (Town Musicians), pose in the pyramid that terrified a band of thieves and won them a home according to the folk tale popularized by the Brothers Grimm (see box below). Created by Bauhaus sculptor Gerhard Marcks in 1951, the bronze is Bremen's icon; they say it grants any wish made while holding the donkey's legs. Behind rise the spires of **Unser Lieben Frauen Kirche**, its stark three-nave interior a victim of Reformation purges.

Roland statue

The city's traditional hero is chivalric knight **Roland** (see box, p.208), Charlemagne's nephew and star of the medieval French epic *Chanson de Roland*. Since 1404, the symbolic stone guardian of civic rights has stood before the Rathaus and brandished a sword of justice at the Dom to champion the citizens' independence from the archbishops – the previous wooden statue was burned on behalf of the clergy in 1366. Local lore relates that so long as this 5.5m-high protector stands on his 10m plinth, the city's liberty is assured. Bar Napoleon, who occupied from 1810 to 1813 but respected the free-city status, and Hitler (who didn't), it's been proved right.

St Petri Dom

Sandstr. 10 **Dom** Mon–Fri 10am–5pm, Sat 10am–2pm, Sun 2–5pm • Free • **Dom Museum, tower and Bleikeller** Mon–Fri 10am–4.45pm, Sat 10am–1.30pm, Sun 2–4.45pm • Museum free, tower €1, Bleikeller €1.40 • Ⓦ stpetridom.de

The indirect cause of the Markt's showpiece architecture is the medieval **Dom** directly east. The archbishops erected its 98m towers in the thirteenth century as a sermon on the absolute authority of divine power – only for the independent burghers to reply with their *Roland*.

Within is an elegant sandstone organ gallery (1518) by Münster's Hinrik Brabender – a furiously bearded Charlemagne holds a contemporary model of the Dom with his bishop, Willehad, who converted the progenitor Saxon village on a sandbank in 787 AD. If the high choir above is open, you can ascend to see its painted ceiling and hunt out a church mouse carved on a south pillar, a joke by a stonemason. The Dom's eleventh-century forerunner survives in crypts at either end of the church; the east crypt retains a contemporary *Enthroned Christ* and Romanesque capitals that put pagan symbols of a wolf and snake cheek by jowl with a Christian flower of salvation. The star piece of Romanesque sculpture is the baptismal font (1220) in the west crypt.

Dom Museum and Bleikeller

The **Dom Museum** contains more sculpture alongside a panel by Cranach, archbishops' silk robes and ceremonial crosiers. You can also ascend one **tower** for an aerial view of the Markt. Beneath the southern cloister – a peaceful spot in the central city entered from outside the Dom – is the **Bleikeller** (Lead Cellar). A careless roofer, a Swedish general killed during the Thirty Years' War, a mystery countess and a student who lost a duel are among the eight mummies who gape from glass-topped coffins, desiccated by super-dry air on Bremen's highest sandbank, according to one theory. Whatever the truth, they've been a ghoulish attraction for at least three centuries.

BREMEN'S AWESOME FOURSOME

It was the **Grimm Brothers**, during their collation of Lower Saxony folk tales, who popularized the age-old story of the **Bremener Stadtmusikanten** (Town Musicians of Bremen). Once upon a time, so the story goes, a donkey, dog, cat and cockerel, fearful of the slaughterhouse and cooking pot in their elderly years, journeyed to Bremen to seek a future as musicians. At nightfall they sought shelter in a house only to discover it was occupied by thieves. Undeterred, our heroes form an animal pyramid, the cockerel at the top and donkey at its base, and unleash their first performance – a caterwaul of brays, barks, meows and crowing. The robbers flee from the banshee outside the door and the four settle down to live happily ever after.

13 ## Böttcherstrasse

Street tours (1hr) Sat 11.30am (in German), plus 1–3 times per month in English • €5; tickets/information at Sieben-Faulen-Laden shop at Böttcherstr. 9 • ☎ 0421 33 88 20 • Free English tour at ⓦ app.boettcherstr.de via the free "Sparer Dank" wi-fi network

Bremen boasted the first coffee shop in Germany (1673) and half the country's beans still enter through its port, Bremerhaven. So it seems fitting that it was a Bremen coffee baron, **Ludwig Roselius**, who funded the transformation of **Böttcherstrasse** southwest of the Markt into such an eccentric fantasy. Roselius made his fortune through decaffeinated coffee, *Kaffee Hag* – the story goes he stumbled upon the secret using beans that had been soused in sea water. In 1922, he commissioned a team of avant-garde artists, notably sculptor **Bernhard Hoetger**, to jazz up the then-derelict Gothic houses of Böttcherstrasse with cutting-edge Jugendstil, Art Deco and Expressionist styles. Soon after the opening of his 110m-long "Kunstschau" (Art Show) in 1931, the Third Reich condemned it as degenerate. Only Roselius's wily suggestion that it should stand as a warning against further cultural depravity saved it from demolition.

Reconstructed after the war, Böttcherstrasse still astounds for the invention of its impulsive brick work, the artistry of its sculpture and wrought iron and its weird globe lights – it's especially enigmatic when spotlit at dusk. Its overture is Hoetger's gilded relief **Lichtbringer** (Bringer of Light), which bathes the street's entrance in a golden glow. Midway along, where medieval craftsmen plied their trades in Handwerkerhof courtyard, Hoetger lets rip a kaleidoscope of Expressionist brickwork – circles, stripes and impassioned splurges – a bust of Roselius and a fountain which immortalizes Bremen's caterwauling musicians.

The Glockenspiel

Böttcherstrasse • Jan–April, except when frosty, noon, 3pm & 6pm; May–Dec hourly noon–6pm

A courtyard midway along Böttcherstrasse fills several times a day for a Meissen china **Glockenspiel**, which chimes while panels depicting craggy transatlantic pioneers – from Leif the Viking and Columbus to Count Ferdinand von Zeppelin – revolve in salute to the adventurous zeal of Bremen's Hanseatic merchants.

Atlantis-Haus

Böttcherstr. 2 • Staircase and Himmelsaal Mon 10am–noon & 2–4pm; ask at hotel reception • €3

Near the Glockenspiel, the **Atlantis-Haus** (now the *Radisson Blu* hotel – see p.746) has a spectacular, original Art Deco staircase that spirals up within blue glass bricks and bubbles in approximation of the lost city; it ends at the strikingly blue Himmelsaal hall with its curved blue-and-white glass ceiling.

Paula Modersohn-Becker Museum and Roselius-Haus

Böttcherstr. 6–10 • Both Tues–Sun 11am–6pm • €6 • ⓦ museen-boettcherstrasse.de

Designed by Bernhard Hoetger, the **Paula Modersohn-Becker Museum** was the first museum anywhere dedicated to a female artist. Her landscapes and portraits of the community at the Worpswede art colony (see p.750) are rendered in her distinctive rustic Expressionism, but no work is more haunting than a self-portrait painted on her sixth wedding anniversary in the self-containment of pregnancy, a year before she died, age 31, in 1907. Upstairs are sculptures and ceramics by Hoetger; he also cast the bronze sculptures for the foyer. Even if you don't visit the museum, there's free access to the first-floor terrace overlooking the Expressionist brick courtyard and street.

Roselius-Haus

The same ticket gets you into Roselius's revamped Gothic merchant's house, **Roselius-Haus**, part gallery, part representation of a Renaissance house where panels by Cranach and Westphalia's Late Gothic master Conrad von Soest fight a losing battle against rich wallpaper and fiddly furniture. A Pietà by the masterful Tilman Riemenschneider fares

13

better in an isolated alcove, a typically powerful work by Germany's greatest Late Gothic sculptor, which infuses Gothic piety with Renaissance humanism.

Along the Weser River

Böttcherstrasse emerges at the Gothic **St-Martini-Kirche** (see below) beneath which is a quay for **river cruises** (see p.746). It was the river port that propelled Bremen into the big time – hence the replica trading cog of Hanseatic merchants moored here in summer. The focus of the town's commercial activity was the **Schlachte** west of the quay. By the late 1700s, over three hundred dockers and porters toiled on a 400m-long harbour lined by inns. The river's silting forced the creation of sea-port Bremerhaven in the late 1800s, leaving the leafy harbourside promenade free as a strip of restaurants and bars (ⓦschlachte.de). When up to two thousand revellers descend on summer weekends, the vibe is more Mediterranean than North Sea.

St-Martini-Kirche
Martinikirchhof 3 • May–Oct 10.30am–12.30pm & 3–5pm • Free

The **St-Martini-Kirche** sits on the river, so its merchant congregation could nurture their souls without straying far from the ships that nourished their wallets – a typically practical mercantile approach to salvation. A window in the south aisle commemorates assistant preacher and Bremen son Joachim Neander. Wowed by a sermon he'd come to mock, the teenager renounced his larrikin past and became the best hymnal poet of the Calvinists – the church bells peal his *Lobe den Herren* (Praise the Lord). Alas his fame has been hijacked by his namesake, Neanderthal man, through a bizarre chain of events: the prototype human was unearthed in the Neandertal (spelled in the late 1800s Neanderthal), a valley near Düsseldorf so named because our hero briefly lived in a grotto here as a hermit.

Weserburg
Teerhof 20 • Tues, Wed & Fri–Sun 11am–6pm, Thurs 11am–8pm • €8 • ⓦ weserburg.de

Reached by a footbridge off the Schlachte, the **Weserburg** museum at the tip of river island Teerhofinsel houses modern art exhibits in former coffee warehouses. Its niche is as a collector's museum rather than a traditional art museum, with interesting interactions between private collections, generally from the 1960s, including Fluxus and Pop Art, to the cutting-edge present.

Beck's Brauerei
Am Deich 18/19 • 2hr tours in English Thurs, Fri & Sat 3pm • €10.50 • ☎ 0421 308 00 10, ⓦ becks.de/besucherzentrum

A five-minute walk upstream from the Weserburg on the south bank of the Weser River is **Brauerie Beck & Co**, which maintains a half-millennium tradition of brewing in Bremen. Though famous internationally, Beck's is a relative newcomer in Germany, having been founded by a local entrepreneur in 1873. Tours take in a museum, the storehouse and the brewhouse where Germany's premier export beer is produced, all washed down with three brews.

The Schnoorviertel

Southwest of the Dom, the former quarter of fishermen, sailors and craftsmen on the Weser's banks – the **Schnoorviertal** – is both the oldest residential district in Bremen and an urban village. Named after the narrow main street **Schnoor** (*snoor* is the Low German for "string"), it survived postwar modernists who proposed ripping the area down, and benefited from a preservation order that led to restoration of its cottages. Today the Schnoor is a photogenic quarter of upmarket boutiques, galleries and restaurants – touristy, certainly, but charming nonetheless. The area's gateway is the staircase down to **Lange Wieren**. Here barn-like **Propsteikirche St Johann** was built as a church by the

13

medieval Franciscan order; vows of poverty meant a spire was too great an extravagance. Beyond, Schnoor peels away as cute half-timbered cottages painted in chalky pastels.

Wüstestätte

Narrow **Wüstestätte** alley halfway down on the right is home to the quaint **Hochzeitshaus** (Marriage House) at no. 5. The tiny house originates from a medieval decree that couples from the surrounding area who married in Bremen had to spend a night in the city. More miniature still is the house at **Wüstestätte 3**: an outside ladder leads to a door on the upper storey rather than waste inside space on a staircase.

Further along towards the river quay, where pre-Reformation pilgrims bedded down before they embarked for Santiago de Compostela – hence the statuette of St James outside – the **St Jacobus Packhaus** at Wüstestätte 10 is Bremen's only remaining Altstadt warehouse. Inside, the **Bremer Geschichtenhaus** (Mon noon–6pm, Tues–Sun 11am–6pm; €6.90; ⊚ bremer-geschichtenhaus.de) spins through city history using costumed actors. All dialogue is in German, though.

Antikenmuseum

Marterburg 55–58 • Sat noon–5pm; closed July & Aug • €5 • ⊚ antikenmuseum.de

The only moment of high culture in the Schnoor is the **Antikenmuseum**, which lies uphill at the end of Schnoor. Its small but superb œuvre of finely decorated Grecian vases stands up to comparison with pieces in many major cities in the country.

East to the Ostertorviertel

Bordering the Schnoorviertel to the northeast, Ostertorstrasse ("East Tower Street") ends at Am Wall (literally "at the rampart"). If their names don't give it away, a map reveals the latter's semicircular route as a defensive wall that encircled the Altstadt until removed by Napoleon. Neoclassical guardhouses that replaced the eastern gate in the city defences now house museums, and the ramparts themselves are landscaped as the **Wallanlagen gardens** around the former zigzagging moat – an easy escape from the city in summer.

Architecturally, **Ostertorviertel** beyond testifies to boom-time Bremen of the late 1800s; residential side-streets such as Mathildenstrasse are chock-full of handsome fin-de-siècle villas erected by businessmen and bankers. Practically, "Das Viertel" today has reinvented itself again as the hippest quarter of Bremen, with a great nightlife that gets grungier the further you go along Ostertorsteinweg.

Kunsthalle

Am Wall 207 • Tues 10am–9pm, Wed–Sun 10am–5pm • €8 • ⊚ kunsthalle-bremen.de

Bremen hoards its art treasures in the **Kunsthalle** at the eastern end of Am Wall. Temporary exhibitions claim most space downstairs, including changing displays from a collection of over 220,000 prints, from Dürer to Degas via big guns like Tiepolo, Goya, Picasso and Beardsley. Upstairs, Cranach titillates under the pretence of mythology with one of German art's first erotic nudes, *Nymphquelle*. There's also a joint effort by Rubens and Jan Bruegel, *Noli Me Tangere*, a highlight among the Dutch and Italian works.

The Kunsthalle's pride is a gallery of **French and German Impressionism**. Delacroix prepares the ground with the largest collection outside France and lives up to Baudelaire's accolade to him as the last great artist of the Renaissance and the first of the modern. Thereafter are most of the big guns of French Impressionism – Renoir, Manet and two early Monets – followed by Cézanne and Van Gogh, whose *Poppy Field* throbs with natural vitality. Pick of their German counterparts are Lovis Corinth and Max Liebermann, Max Beckmann and insightful works by Paula Modersohn-Becker, who outshines everyone else among the otherwise whimsical Worpswede group.

13

Gerhard-Marcks-Haus and Wilhelm-Wagenfeld-Haus

Gerhard-Marcks-Haus Am Wall 208 • Tues, Wed & Fri–Sun 10am–6pm, Thurs 10am–9pm • €5 • ⓦ marcks.de • **Wilhelm-Wagenfeld-Haus** Am Wall 209 • Tues 3–9pm, Wed–Sun 10am–6pm • €3.50 • ⓦ wwh-bremen.de

Beside the Kunsthalle, **Gerhard-Marcks-Haus** showcases modern and avant-garde sculpture – temporary exhibits of big hitters such as Joseph Beuys, Georg Kolbe and France's Aristide Maillol sit alongside occasionally quirky works by the eponymous sculptor who crafted the Bremen musicians statue. **Wilhelm-Wagenfeld-Haus** opposite, documents design in all its guises – industrial, graphic, packaging and fashion.

Übersee-Museum

Bahnhofsplatz 13 • Tues–Fri 9am–6pm, Sat & Sun 10am–6pm • €6.50 • ⓦ uebersee-museum.de

The modern city is a jolt after the Altstadt. Closest of its widely scattered sights is the **Übersee-Museum** on Bahnhofsplatz. In the 1890s, Bremen merchants staged a grand exhibition of curios to show off their global reach. The ethnological museum it fathered groups around a pair of courtyards as a comprehensive tour of the continents. Exhibits are at their best when liberated from showcases: a Japanese garden and African village; a Polynesian paradise in huts, boats and palms; and a lovely early twentieth-century coffee merchant's shop. Newer exhibits tackle contemporary themes of globalization such as climate change, migration and human rights.

Bürgerpark and around

Behind the Hauptbahnhof lies over two square kilometres of landscaped lawns, cattle-grazed meadows and woodland. This is the **Bürgerpark** (ⓦ buergerpark.de), a lovely place to while away an afternoon in a rowing boat – **boat rental** is available from a kiosk on the southwestern Emmasee – or over a picnic. Other eating options are one-time summerhouse *Meierei* at the centre, and beer garden *Waldbühne* in the northeast. The park is also the starting point for the lovely 27km-long **Blockland-Runde** cycling route through rural meadowland; ask for the free map at the tourism office.

The parked UFO beyond the *Waldbühne* at the park's distant northeastern tip is child-friendly science centre **Universum Bremen**, Weiner Str. 1 (Mon–Fri 9am–6pm, Sat & Sun 10am–6pm; €16; ⓦ universum-bremen.de; tram #6 to "Naturwissenschaften 1" stop), whose hands-on exhibits tackle the big questions of humanity, the Earth and space.

Focke-Museum

Schwachhauser Heerstr. 240 • Tues 10am–9pm, Wed–Sun 10am–5pm • €6 • ⓦ focke-museum.de • Tram #4 or #5 to "Focke-Museum"

The **Focke-Museum** is largely overlooked, which is a shame for a complex whose well-presented exhibits span over a millennium of local history and culture. Bremen's obsession with the Weser River and trade is a leitmotif: exhibits chronicle the Hanseatic seafarers, and the elegant glassware and Fürstenberg porcelain prized by the merchant elite are displayed, appropriately, in an aristocrat's Baroque summerhouse. The original Rathaus statues of Charlemagne and the prince-electors are also here, balanced by displays of rural life in one of three historic half-timbered barns rebuilt in the parkland.

Airbus Defence & Space

Airbus-Allee 1, Bremen airport, 6km south of the city centre • Tours (2hr) in German Sat 2pm & 4pm; minimum age 10 • €16.50; reserve through the tourist office • ⓦ bremen-tourism.de/eads-astrium

The European Space Agency's largest single contribution to the International Space Station (ISS) – the Columbus module – was partly built in Bremen, at **Airbus Defence & Space** at the city airport. You can see a replica of the module (a science laboratory), and find out about life on the ISS on a once-weekly tour.

13

ARRIVAL AND DEPARTURE

By plane Bremen's international airport (Ⓦairport-bremen.de) is 6km south of the city centre; tram #6 links to the Hauptbahnhof in 15min; a taxi costs around €16.
By train The Hauptbahnhof and bus station behind it are a 10min walk north of the Altstadt.

BREMEN

Destinations Bremerhaven (every 40min; 35–50min); Hamburg (every 30min; 1hr); Hannover (every 30min–1hr; 1hr); Oldenburg (every 40min; 30min); Osnabrück (every 45min; 50min–1hr 15min).

GETTING AROUND

Public transport For attractions outside the centre you may need buses and trams (three-stop *Kurzstrecke* €1.30; singles €2.50–3 depending on zone; *Tageskarte* day-card €7.10–8.30); the tourist board's ErlebnisCARD (see below) may offer better value. Travel information and tickets are available at an information booth in front of the Hauptbahnhof (Mon–Fri 7am–7pm, Sat 8am–6pm, Sun 9am–5pm).

Bike rental There's a cycle centre and workshop beside the Hauptbahnhof at Bahnhofsplatz 14 (Mon–Fri 10am–6pm, Sat 10am–2pm).
Car rental All car rental operators maintain a desk at the airport and share an office at the Hauptbahnhof: Hertz ☎0421 55 53 50; Europcar ☎0421 17 35 10; Sixt ☎01805 25 25 25.

INFORMATION AND TOURS

Tourist office At the Hauptbahnhof (Mon–Fri 9am–7pm, Sat & Sun 9.30am–5pm; ☎0421 3080010, Ⓦbremen-tourism.de) and at Langenstr. 2 (Mon–Sat 10am–6.30pm, Sun 10am–4pm). Both have a good range of maps and brochures, rent out audio-guides (€7.50/day) and can organize English-language city walks.
Discount card Both offices sell the ErlebnisCARD (24hr €8.90, 48hr €11.50), giving free public transport and up to

fifty percent discount on admissions; each card also covers two children under 14. Group cards (24hr €18.50, 48hr €22.90) for up to five people are good value.
Boat trips Hal Över Schreiber (Ⓦhal-oever.de) and Weisse Flotte (Ⓦweisse-flotte.de) operate a variety of cruises on the Weser River: options include harbour tours, trips downriver to Bremerhaven (see p.749), and to North Sea stump Helgoland (May–Sept).

ACCOMMODATION

HOTELS AND PENSIONS

Bölts am Park Selvogtstr. 23 ☎0421 34 61 10, Ⓦhotel-boelts.de. A family pension on a leafy street behind the Hauptbahnhof, which maintains the aura of a former residential house of the 1930s. Decor is modern(ish), in pleasant inoffensive pastel shades, and most rooms are en suite; those with shared bathrooms are €10 cheaper. **€89**
Bremer Haus Löningstr. 16–20 ☎0421 329 40, Ⓦhotel-bremer-haus.de. An unassuming but pleasant small place in a quiet side-street location, that makes for a more personal stay than the usual chain hotel. Service is friendly, rooms are spotless and individually decorated, recently refreshed in a relaxed modern style. Buffet breakfasts are excellent. **€109**
Dorint Park Hotel Im Bürgerpark ☎0421 340 80, Ⓦdorint.com. The queen of Bremen's hotels is a palace of luxury whose elegant country-hotel atmosphere benefits from views across the landscaped Bürgerpark and an ornamental lake. All rooms come with a view, Superiors are worth the extra €30 for space and the suites are sensational. Price does not include breakfast. **€189**
Prizeotel Theodor-Heuss-Allee 12, ☎01805 69 77 49, Ⓦprizeotel.com. The "Designocracy" catchphrase translates as interior design for all in Bremen's first budget design hotel, located in a block behind the station. Design in this case means loud and funky, with Pop Art-inspired plastic furnishings in rooms, all with wi-fi. Prices vary by

dynamic pricing but represent great value. **€85**
Radisson Blu Böttcherstr. 2 ☎0421 369 60, Ⓦradissonblu.de/bremen. Art Deco notes such as the staircase and Himmelsaal (see p.742) seep in from Bremen's most famous street. Otherwise this is a 4-star business hotel with bright, modern rooms, and an impressive atrium with a good restaurant. **€159**
Residence Hohenlohestr. 42 ☎0421 34 87 10, Ⓦhotelresidence.de. Despite its link to the City Partner chain, this family-run 3-star hotel in a residential street retains a personal atmosphere through friendly staff and individual decor. Standard rooms are a mite business bland, while Superior class aspires to interior design, with statement walls and laminate wood floors. A good breakfast buffet, too. **€80**
Swissôtel Hillmannplatz 20 ☎0421 62 00 00, Ⓦswissotel.com/de/bremen. This glass-skinned outpost of the international chain appears every inch the slick business hotel, with cool minimalist decor in neutral shades. Yet it also serves as a fine holiday stay too, as evidenced by children's rooms with toys, and all in a good location close to the Altstadt. **€156**
Überfluss Langenstr. 72 ☎0421 32 28 60, Ⓦhotel-ueberfluss.de. Bremen's hip design hotel and far from cheap. You're paying for the coolest interior design in town – think glossy lacquered tables and big statement lamps in rooms that mix and match styles with flair – and facilities

13

like a spa and small pool. River views are worth the extra €15. €164

HOSTELS AND CAMPSITES

Camping am Stadtwaldsee Hochschulring 1 ☎ 0421 841 07 48, ⓦ camping-stadtwaldsee.de; Universität-bound tram #6 to station NW1, then bus #28 to "Station Campingplatz". The city's nearest campsite occupies a spacious lake-side site at the head of the Bürgerpark in the north of the city. Facilities include a bistro/bar and an on-site shop. If driving, take junction 19 off the A27. Pitch €4.50, plus €11 per person

DJH Bremen Kalkstr. 6 ☎ 0421 163 820, ⓦ jugendherberge.de. The official hostel, beside the Weser River in the western Altstadt, is a cool modern place, especially the glass-walled lounge with views over the river, but hugely popular with school groups. Dorms €30, doubles €70

GastHaus Bremer Backpacker Hostel Emil-Waldmann-Str. 5–6 ☎ 0421 223 80 57, ⓦ bremer-backpacker-hostel.de. Friendly hostel on a quiet side-street, a 5min walk from the Hauptbahnhof. It is bright and modern throughout, with not a bunk bed in sight in its six- and four-bed dorms. It also maintains a budget hotel with en-suite rooms around the corner (€79). Dorms €18, doubles €46

Townside Hostel Am Dobben 62 ☎ 0421 780 15, ⓦ townside.de. Lively hostel with impressive touches like free Fair Trade tea and coffee and water conservation measures. It's also superbly located for the Ostertorviertel bar scene – a good or bad thing depending on your preference. Dorms, including a women-only one, sleep four to nine, and there are all the usual facilities such as laundry and free wi-fi. Dorms €15, doubles €64

EATING AND DRINKING

Bremen's culinary scene divides roughly into four areas: the **Altstadt** and the **Schnoorviertel** are the choice for traditional restaurants; waterfront promenade **Schlachte** has modern chains; and **Ostertorviertel** has bistro-style restaurants. **Drinking** is focused in the latter two. Though dominated by chains, the Schlachte is great for bar-hopping in summer, while "das Viertel" along Ostertorsteinweg segues from restaurants to a grungy student vibe. Ten minutes north of its main drag **Auf den Höfen** is an intimate yard of restaurants and bars. As well as the listings below, there are good bars in *Lila Eule* and *Lagerhaus* (see p.748), while beer gardens on the Schlachte are hard to beat on sunny days.

CAFÉS, BARS AND BEER GARDENS

Beluga Auf den Höfen ☎ 0421 794 68 58, ⓦ beluga-bar .de. Lofty candlelit place that's popular with twenty-somethings for a boisterous night and a bop – whether that's because of a soundtrack of party house and Latin or because of cheap cocktails until 9pm is another matter. Also screens live matches of Werder Bremen football club. Daily 7pm–late.

Café Engel Ostertorsteinweg 31 ☎ 0421 696 423 90, ⓦ engelweincafe-bremen.de. Laidback bistro at the heart of Ostertorviertel. As the "Weincafé" tag suggests, it specializes in international wines and bistro fare for the Viertel's smarter residents. Mon–Fri 8am–1am, Sat & Sun 10am–1am.

★ Café Sand Strandweg 106 ☎ 0421 55 60 11, ⓦ cafe-sand.de. Beach culture in Bremen by a conservatory café-bar on a river beach – expect swimming and volleyball, beach towels and deckchairs on sunny weekends: the ideal city escape without having to leave. A passenger ferry shuttles from a quay on Osterdeich, near the junction with Sielwall for easy access to Das Viertel nightlife. Daily 10am–midnight.

Lemon Lounge Am Wall 164 ☎ 0421 514 88 55, ⓦ lemonlounge.de. Small, rather clubby bar that lies beyond an unprepossessing entrance door at the top of a spiral staircase. Its intimate space has a nicely louche atmosphere in which to get stuck into cocktails and there's a tiny dancefloor. Tues–Sat 6pm–late; July & Aug from 8pm.

Luv Schlachte 15–18 ☎ 0421 165 55 99, ⓦ restaurant-luv.de. The hippest of the many café-bars on the Schlachte manages to be all things to all people, both a beer garden and a contemporary bar, and a place to tuck into rack of Iberico pork as well as *Currywurst*. Nice breakfast spot, too. Mon–Sat 11am–1am, Sun 10am–1am.

Rum Bumpers Humboldtstr. 34 ☎ 0421 794 74 70. Boozey, dingy dive-bar with DJs, off the main strip, with a scruffy student atmosphere that seems pickled by countless lost weekends. The perfect place to start or end a night out. Try the liquorice *Schnapps*. Daily 6pm–1am, later at weekends.

Spitzen Gebel Hinter dem Schütting 1 ☎ 0421 330 68 98, ⓦ spitzen-gebel.de. Traditional drinking in the oldest *Bürgerhaus* in Bremen (1348), a cocoon of varnished old wood and brass that's barely large enough for its few tables. House speciality is a potent liqueur named "Sluk ut de Lamp", distilled to a secret recipe and hailed as a cure-all for everything from haemorrhoids to headaches. Mon–Thurs noon–midnight, Fri noon–2am, Sat 11am–2am.

RESTAURANTS

Grashoff Contrescarpe 80 ☎ 0421 147 49, ⓦ grashoff .de. Lovely Parisian-styled bistro with art on the walls, attached to an equally excellent deli. The laidback ambience and fine cooking that leans towards Mediterranean make this a choice lunch-spot for an arty middle-aged set. Expect to pay around €20 a main. Mon–Thurs 10am–8pm, Sat 10am–4pm.

13

Das Kleine Lokal Besselstr. 40 ☎ 0421 362 85 57, ⓦ das-kleine-lokal.de. Intimate restaurant whose ironic old-fashioned decor belies the experimental modern creations of Stephan Ladenberger. Only 36 diners at a time get to sample minimalist dishes that shift with the seasons – three-course menus start at €42. Tues–Sat 7–11pm.

★**Küche13** Beim Steinernen Kreuz 13 ☎ 0421 2082 4721, ⓦ kueche13.de. Run by a group of friends and infused with a love for food and hospitality, the menu of this modern Viertel restaurant changes weekly. Expect high-quality international dishes at high prices, *Zander* fillet in white wine sauce (€21.70) for example, or lamb in olive-basil crust with port wine sauce (€26.50). Tues–Sat 6pm–midnight.

Piano Fehrfeld 64 ☎ 0421 785 46, ⓦ cafepiano-bremen.de. An enduringly popular café-restaurant at the heart of the Ostertorviertel that's as popular with hipsters as young families. No wonder – it's cheap, friendly and unpretentious, with a simple menu of all-day breakfasts, steaks, pizza and pasta dishes, most priced under €10. Daily 9am–midnight.

Presse Langenstr. 31 ☎ 0421 336 28 22, ⓦ presse-bremen.de. An Italian-style grand café in the city centre, with high ceilings, newspapers, a bustling atmosphere and good coffee, snacks and bistro food. There's risotto for €12, and house speciality bouillabaisse fish soup for €14. Mon–Fri 10am–10pm, Sat 10am–11pm.

Ratskeller Am Markt ☎ 0421 334 79 27, ⓦ ratskeller-bremen.de. A tourist attraction in its own right, the veritable *Ratskeller* is a joy, with tables among the huge and historic carved wine barrels, and waiters in traditional garb. The surprise, then, is that the hearty local specials such as *Bremer Knipp*, a sort of Bremen haggis of pork and oat groats, come at good prices. Daily 11am–11pm.

★**Schröter's** Schnoor 13 ☎ 0421 32 66 77, ⓦ schroeters-schnoor.de. Founder Rainer Schröter has handed over to his son, Daniel, which seems only to have upped the ante of this local institution. Expect modern European dishes priced between €12 and €20 and prepared with flair – venison with chestnut couscous, beautifully presented turbot on radicchio – in this classy restaurant with a small rear garden. Daily noon–3pm & 6–11pm.

NIGHTLIFE AND ENTERTAINMENT

Glossy newsstand titles *Bremer* and *Prinz* provide more comprehensive **what's on listings** than the freesheets available in the tourist office. **Clubbing** in Bremen is good value – entry is usually around €6–8. A strip of clubs popular with teenagers lies on Rembertiring, east of the Hauptbahnhof; those in Ostertorviertel are more interesting. Most clubs only open on Friday and Saturday. For **classical music**, keep an eye on concerts staged in the city's churches, usually the Dom.

CLUBS

Lila Eule Bernhardstr. 10 ☎ 0421 794 06 64, ⓦ lilaeule .de. Grungy club that's been a mainstay of the alternative nightlife scene since its debut as a jazz den in the Sixties. Clubnights are raucous and fun – generally along the lines of alternative, disco-punk, electrorock, hip-hop, with the occasional soul/funk or Balkan beats party. They're also cheap – student night on Thurs is free and messy. Also hosts occasional gigs. Thurs–Sat 11pm–late.

Modernes Neustadtswall 28 ⓦ modernes.de. Bremen's best mainstream nightclub is housed in a former cinema in the Neustadt south of the Weser. Expect nights of indie or classic disco, funk and party house plus the occasional midweek gig, all ventilated by a sliding domed roof. Fri & Sat 11pm–late.

NFF Club Katharinenstr. 12–14 ⓦ nffclub.de. One of Bremen's best options for cocktail clubbing in the centre, where occasional visiting German names spin to the young crowd. Otherwise, resident DJs spin chunky house and electro in the Ibiza or Miami mode, with a mash-up of r'n'b and even ragga thrown in for good measure. Fri & Sat 11pm–late.

Stubu Rembertiring 21 ⓦ stubu.de. A multi-room palace to mainstream clubbing that is spread over five rooms at weekends, when it's usually busy with a young party crowd. The soundtrack ranges from hip-hop and r'n'b via chart sounds and electro. Daily 10pm–late.

LIVE MUSIC AND THEATRE

Die Glocke Domsheide 4–5 ☎ 0421 33 66 99, ⓦ glocke .de. Bremen's grand old concert hall is located behind the Dom in the centre and renowned for its fine acoustics. It hosts both the Bremener Philharmoniker and the acclaimed Deutsche Kammerphilharmonie, Bremen's chamber orchestra. Some jazz gigs are also scheduled.

Lagerhaus Schildstr. 12 ☎ 0421 701 00 00, ⓦ kulturzentrum-lagerhaus.de. An interesting programme of gigs – largely rock, indie and alt-folk – staged in a former squat venue that's been a bastion of the Viertel scene for over twenty years, largely due to its eclectic Warehouse Disco on Saturdays. Also has Latin nights, plus cultural events and a good bar popular with a clued-up young crowd.

Schlachthof Findorffstr. 51 ☎ 0421 37 77 50, ⓦ schlachthof-bremen.de. Rock music, cabaret and theatre as well as art and photography exhibitions and summer outdoor cinema in a cultural centre created from a former abattoir that is located north of the Hauptbahnhof. Its *Schlachthofkneipe* bar screens all Werder Bremen games (free). Bar daily 5pm–1/2am.

Theater am Goetheplatz Goetheplatz ☎ 0421 365 33 33, ⓦ bremertheater.com. The most prestigious stage in town hosts heavyweight opera, operettas and dance. The affiliated Neues Schauspielhaus

(Ostertorsteinweg 57a; same contact details) is the city's leading dramatic stage – expect modern classics and avant-garde. Nice touch: tickets are valid for buses and trams to and from the theatre.

Theater am Leibnizplatz Am Leibnizplatz ☏ 0421 50 03 33 (phone Mon–Fri 3–6pm only), ⦿ shakespeare-company.com. Home of the renowned Bremen Shakespeare Company, whose trademarks are bare stage or nonrepresentational theatre in productions that feature – and are created by – collaboration rather than a star director. It also stages occasional German classics.

Around Bremen

Within an hour's travel of Bremen are a couple of day-trips: **Bremerhaven**, fast reinventing itself from container port to tourist destination; and bucolic artists' colony **Worpswede**. Frequent transport links mean you're never stuck for a return, though you might be tempted to stay the night in Worpswede.

Bremerhaven

As its port silted, Bremen petitioned the King of Hanover to acquire the land between the Geeste and Weser rivermouths and so was founded **BREMERHAVEN** in 1827. The largest working port in Germany after Hamburg, it's no charmer – the centre was thrown up at rapid pace after 95 percent of the port was obliterated by air raids – and has long had a utilitarian air. This is, after all, the town that has the world's longest quay (4.9km) and is Germany's premier fishing port.

Yet "Fischstadt" is raising its game. Central harbours – the adjacent Neuer Hafen and Alter Hafen – have been renovated as a focus for two superb museums and billion-euro architecture projects such as the **Atlantic Hotel Sail City** (viewing platform €3), modelled on Dubai's signature *Burj Al-Arab* hotel.

Deutsches Auswandererhaus

Columbusstr. 65, Neuer Hafen • Daily March–Oct 10am–6pm; Nov–Feb 10am–5pm • €12.60 • ⦿ dah-bremerhaven.de

Reason enough for a visit to Bremerhaven is the **Deutsches Auswandererhaus** (German Emigration Centre), one-time European Museum of the Year, that documents the seven million New World émigrés who departed from the harbour between 1830 and 1974, the majority in the late 1800s, when Bremerhaven was the largest port of emigration in Europe. You receive a boarding card of a former émigré as you enter and pass through a series of stage-set dioramas to follow a transatlantic odyssey that took the first passenger steamers twelve weeks. In addition a cinema screens poignant documentaries on the immigrant experience and there's a free research centre with a database of German emigrants to the States. Imaginative, thought-provoking, occasionally moving and more relevant than ever in an era when debates about immigration are so divisive, this is highly recommended.

Historisches Museum

An der Geeste • Tues–Sun 10am–5pm • €5 • ⦿ historisches-museum-bremerhaven.de

You can find emigration-themed content and a German Emigrants Database in the town's **Historisches Museum** beside the bridge over the Geeste River. Incidentally, searches can be made on the German Emigrants Database website (⦿ dad-recherche .de), although full data records cost €15 per emigrant.

Klimahaus Bremerhaven 8° Ost

Am Längengrad 8 • April–Aug Mon–Fri 9am–7pm, Sat & Sun 10am–7pm; Sept–March daily 10am–6pm • €14.50 • ⦿ klimahaus-bremerhaven.de

Bremerhaven's climate-change theme museum, **Klimahaus Bremerhaven 8° Ost**, is a sci-fi-styled glass ellipse engineered for maximum energy efficiency, generating some of its own power through green technology. Less clear is the maze of themed areas within.

13

The idea is that exhibits track a circumnavigation via the eighth degree of longitude looking at climatic issues such as natural forces and weather or energy consumption. The re-creations of alpine, jungle, desert and Antarctic habitats (to name a few) entertain, and there are science experiments and infotainment games to occupy the kids, but adults may find many exhibits rather insubstantial.

Deutsches Schifffahrtsmuseum

Hans-Scharoun-Platz 1 • Daily 10am–6pm; Nov–March closed Mon • €6; historic vessels free with ticket or €1 per vessel/€3 for submarine • ⓦ dsm.museum

Prior to the opening of its new museums, Bremerhaven's pride and joy was the **Deutsches Schifffahrtsmuseum**, a maritime museum in Alter Hafen, the harbour that lies adjacent to Neuer Hafen. Its maritime displays in a modern complex are diverting, notably a section on the windjammers built in Bremerhaven until 1928 and what's left of a showpiece fourteenth-century Hanseatic cog that was wrecked offshore. Most of the eleven historic vessels in an adjacent harbour are open in summer, including a wartime submarine.

Zoo am Meer

H.-H.-Meier-Str. 7 • Daily: March & Oct 9am–6pm; April–Sept 9am–7pm; Nov–Feb 9am–4.30pm • €8.50

Opposite the Deutsches Auswandererhaus on the sea-side of the harbour wall, the **Zoo am Meer** has penguins, polar bears and Arctic foxes, among other animals, plus a large playground; its small size makes it especially child-friendly.

ARRIVAL AND DEPARTURE
BREMERHAVEN

By train Hauptbahnhof is in the southeast of the city, a 20min walk from the harbours to the northwest: take Friedrich–Ebert–Strasse, then pedestrianized Bürgermeister-Smidt-Strasse.

Destinations Bremen (hourly; 30–50min).
By boat Hal Över (ⓦ hal-oever.de) cruises from Bremen, though they're best made one-way, as a return will only give you two hours in Bremerhaven.

INFORMATION AND TOURS

Tourist office H.-H.-Meier-Str. 6, at the bridge between the Emigration and Climate museums (daily: April & Oct 9.30am–6pm; May–Sept 8am–6pm; Nov–March 9.30am–5pm; ☎0471 464 61 20, ⓦbremerhaven.de/tourismus).

Boat trips Cruises from Neuer Hafen run to the port and Columbus Quay (March–Nov daily; €10, ⓦ hafenrundfahrt-bremerhaven.de), from which millions of emigrants departed.

Worpswede

When Impressionist artists Fritz Mackerson and Otto Modersohn discovered it in the 1880s, **WORPSWEDE**, 26km north of Bremen, was just another village that eked out a living on the Teufelsmoor (Devil's Bog). Within ten years of the pair setting up their easels, inspired by its huge cloudscapes, it had morphed into an **artists' colony**, and today there are art ateliers plus smart crafts boutiques scattered throughout the village. Factor in bucolic walks, boat trips on peat barges beneath lung-busting skies and the journey from Bremen by vintage train, and you have the lazy day-trip par excellence.

Grosse Kunstschau

Lindenallee 5 • Mid-March to Oct daily 10am–6pm; Nov to mid-March Tues–Sun 10am–5pm • €7 • ⓦ worpswede-museen.de

For a sense of the early art colony in what was then just a peat-digging village, visit the **Grosse Kunstschau**, a Hoetger-designed gallery next to the main car park in the village centre. Of those early art pioneers – Fritz Mackerson, Otto Modersohn, Fritz Overbeck, architect and painter Heinrich Voegler, poet Rainer Maria Rilke, and Bernhard Hoetger of Böttcherstrasse fame (see p.742) – it is Paula Modersohn-Becker (Otto Modersohn's wife) who shines, although keep an eye open too for Voegler's Pre-Raphelite-inspired *Summer Evening*, which depicts the artist loafing on his patio.

Hoetger's eccentric **Kaffee Worpswede** (see below) nearby was derided by villagers immediately as "Café Verrückt" ("Café Crazy") – small wonder considering its fusion of traditional, Expressionist and tribal styles; don't miss the tent-like interior.

Worpsweder Kunsthalle

Bergstr. 17 • Mid-March to Oct daily 10am–6pm; Nov to mid-March Tues–Sun 10am–5pm • €4 • ⓦ worpswede-museen.de

The **Worpsweder Kunsthalle** next to the tourist office, 250m northwest of the Grosse Kunstschau, has an extensive collection of Worpswede art, from the early pioneers through to postwar artists. It also stages special exhibitions of contemporary arts and crafts.

Käseglocke

Feb–Dec Tues–Sun 11am–4/5pm • €2

As quirky as Hoetger's *Kaffee Worpswede* is the **Kaseglöcke** (Cheesebell) in the woods behind the Grosse Kunstschau. Created in 1926 for Edwin Koenemann, a failed artist who became the colony's first tour guide, the bulbous building is a fairy-tale cottage designed by Bruno Taut, with furnishings by Hoetger and Modersohn-Becker.

Barkenhoff

Ostendorfer Str. 10 • Daily 10am–6pm • €6 • ⓦ worpswede-museen.de

The creative hotbed of the colony's formative days was Voegler's home and studio, **Barkenhoff** – follow Lindenallee uphill from the Grosse Kunstschau, then take a path left off the right bend. Located beyond a front garden still recognizable as that from *Summer Evening*, the house features Voegler's works, which segue from Jugendstil to early Expressionism.

ARRIVAL AND GETTING AROUND	WORPSWEDE

By bus #670 runs to Worpswede from the Bremen bus station at frequent intervals (44min).

By train The historic Moor Express train runs from Bremen Hauptbahnhof (May–Sept 4 daily; €13 return; ⓣ 04792 93 58 20, ⓦ moorexpress.net); bicycles can be taken along.

Bike rental Available on the main road from Fahrradladen Eyl at Findorffstr. 28 (ⓣ 04792 23 23).

INFORMATION AND TOURS

Tourist office In the centre at Bergstr. 13 (May–Oct Mon–Thurs 11am–4pm, Fri & Sat 10am–6pm, Sun 10am–3pm; Nov–April Tues–Fri 11am–3pm, Sat 11am–3pm, Sun 11am–1pm; ⓣ 04792 93 58 20, ⓦ worpswede.de). There's an exhibition about the development of the village, and free brochures in English.

Boat trips Cruises aboard traditional peat barges known as Torfkahn (May–Oct; 1hr 30min; €9.50) sail from Neu Helgoland, 1.5km west of the centre. Booking is required; contact the tourist office for tickets and times.

ACCOMMODATION AND EATING

DJH Worpswede Hammeweg 2 ⓣ 04792 13 60, ⓦ jugendherberge.de. Traditionally-styled youth hostel among woodland west of the centre, within walking distance of the train and bus stations. Most of its four- and six-bed rooms or family, double and single rooms are en suite. Dorms €26, doubles €62

Haus im Schluh Im Schluh 35 ⓣ 04792 522, ⓦ haus-im-schluh.de. Pretty pension in a historic farmhouse once owned by Heinrich Voegler, whose art and furnishings decorate some rooms. All four guest rooms are defiantly old-fashioned: shared facilities, no mod cons like sinks – rooms have a china bowl and jug instead – no telephones and no TVs. Bliss. €75

Kaffee Worpswede Lindenallee 1 ⓣ 04792 10 28, ⓦ kaffee-worpswede.de. High prices are justified by the wonderfully wacky decor of Hoetger's café, as much as by a menu of quality modern-German cuisine (mains up to €30) – expect the likes of duck with fried mushrooms and gnocchi in cherry sauce. Pastas and *Schnitzels* are cheaper, at around €15. Wed–Sun 11.30am–10pm.

Village Bergstr. 22 ⓣ 04792 935 00, ⓦ village-worpswede.de. An appealing small hotel in the village centre with just nine individually decorated rooms, some with mezzanine bed areas. Relaxed modern design – old wood and rattan furnishings, fabrics in shades of olive and cream – lend the air of a peaceful country retreat. It also has a fairly priced bistro. Restaurant daily noon–2.30pm & 6.30–9.30pm. €136

Hamburg and Schleswig-Holstein

SYLT, NORTH FRISIAN ISLANDS

Hamburg and Schleswig-Holstein

14

Schleswig-Holstein is all about location. It is a Land made by the forces around it: west and east, the North and Baltic seas; north, Denmark. The former is realized as fine beaches and marram-grass dunes, candy-striped lighthouses, commercial ports on deep fjords, vast skyscapes and changeable weather. The latter reveals itself as a region that feels distinctly Nordic. Don't come looking for national stereotypes here. If anything, Schleswig-Holstein and neighbouring city-state Hamburg have a Scandinavian liberalism to make land-locked southerners appear prudish. The air of a separate country is compounded by a predominantly fish diet and a local dialect akin to Dutch, Plattdeutsch, that is almost as impenetrable to most Germans as it is to foreigners.

As ever, this distinct character was shaped by history. The peninsula was under Danish rule from the fifteenth century until the mid-1800s, when nationalist fervour inspired calls for independence among its German-speaking population. This posed the Schleswig-Holstein Question, which vexed some of the finest diplomatic minds in Europe. As British prime minister Lord Palmerston is said to have despaired: "The Schleswig-Holstein Question is so complicated only three men in Europe have ever understood it. The first was Prince Albert, and he is dead; the second is a German professor, and he is in an asylum; and the third was myself, and I have forgotten it."

Nowadays, Schleswig-Holstein is less political poser than bucolic backwater. Notwithstanding the Land capital **Kiel**, a brusque, working port, it is free of urban development, with its Baltic coast notched by fjords, its west coast wind-blown and wild, and everywhere canopied by colour-wash skyscapes that have long captivated artists such as Emil Nolde. Even **Lübeck** wears its history lightly. Sure, the one-time city-state has a tale as rich and complex as any plotline by local son Thomas Mann, yet at the core of its appeal is nothing more complicated than one of the most enigmatic old towns in Germany, with a heritage and sense of cultural worth handed down from its time as the head of the medieval Hanseatic League, the first pan-European superpower.

HOLSTENTOR, LÜBECK

Highlights

❶ **Hamburg** Both a rollicking port city and a boom-town media capital with thriving art and gourmet scenes, Germany's liberal second metropolis has a restless energy that makes up for its lack of historic looks. **See p.757**

❷ **Hamburg nightlife** From world-class opera to throbbing clubnights in portside dive-bars, from showstopper musicals to grungy gigs in a war bunker, sophisticated style-bars to dancing at dawn in the Sunday Fischmarkt. Revel in the contradictions. **See p.780**

❸ **Lübeck** The medieval queen of the Hanseatic League is as ravishing as ever – a small-town symphony that's as cultured as it is

charming. And all with a decent beach on its doorstep. **See p.783**

❹ **Schleswig** The former Viking stronghold of northern Europe has mellowed into an idyllic small town on a fjord with a blockbuster museum to boot. **See p.800**

❺ **Sylt** Never mind the weather, this North Sea watersports wonderland is also the most glamorous beach resort in the country, especially in Kampen village. **See p.808**

❻ **North Sea island-hopping** Regular ferries let you skip from Sylt to its sleepy sister-islands, bucolic Föhr and powder-sands paradise Amrum. **See p.814**

HIGHLIGHTS ARE MARKED ON THE MAP ON P.756

Once you've ticked off the cultural heavyweights of Hamburg and Lübeck, then Schleswig-Holstein is pure holiday country. With your own transport, you could lose a happy week on a circuit from Lübeck, bowling through small towns where coast meets country – places like cultured backwater **Eutin** among the lakeland of Holsteinische Schweiz, or erstwhile Viking stronghold **Schleswig**, relaxed, charming and home to a blockbuster museum that ticks all boxes. Powder beaches have transformed the **North Frisian islands** off the west coast into a treasured national playground, even though they are largely overlooked by foreigners in the stampede south. People-watching in **Sylt**, a sort of German Hamptons, or simply loafing around in *Strandkörbe* wicker seats in **Föhr** and **Amrum** are a defining part of the German coastal experience.

Even boomtime metropolis **Hamburg**, a state in its own right, finds space for beach bars from April to September, complementing a year-round nightlife that is as much a reason to visit as some of the finest galleries and museums in Germany. Without a car, it is your best transport hub, although rail links from Lübeck serve east-coast destinations as far as Kiel. Remember, too, that ferry services off the west coast permit island-hopping down the trio of North Frisian islands – the free-wheeling beach holiday in a nutshell.

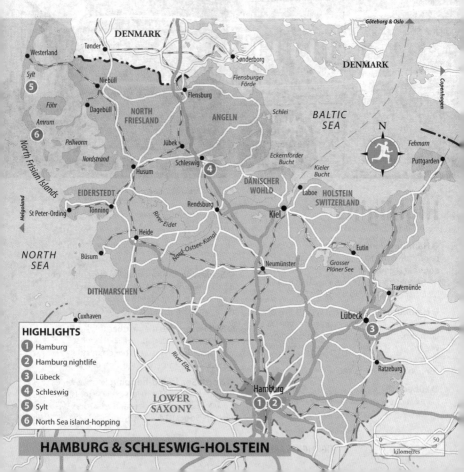

HIGHLIGHTS

1 Hamburg
2 Hamburg nightlife
3 Lübeck
4 Schleswig
5 Sylt
6 North Sea island-hopping

HAMBURG & SCHLESWIG-HOLSTEIN

Hamburg

HAMBURG suffers from image schizophrenia. To many of its tourists, Germany's second metropolis is simply sin city – a place of prostitutes and strip shows in the Reeperbahn red-light district – while in its homeland it is revered as a cosmopolitan, stylish city-state, rapaciously commercial and home to the highest head-count of millionaires in the country. Either way the cause is the same: through one of the greatest ports in Europe it has sucked in wealth – and probably vice – ever since a canny piece of diplomatic manoeuvring in 1189 led Emperor Friederich I to grant tax-free imports down the Elbe. Hamburg never looked back. The good times began to roll in the early Middle Ages after it fostered links with Hanseatic leader, Lübeck, and the city paused only to congratulate itself when declared a Free Imperial City by Emperor Maximilian I in 1510.

Today a restless boom-town, forever reinventing itself – its latest incarnation as a metropolis with an eco-conscience saw it named the Green Capital of Europe in 2011 – Hamburg still flaunts its "Freie und Hansestadt" (Free and Hanseatic Town) title. And that umbilical link to maritime trade continues in a sprawling container port that grounds the city, adding a no-nonsense robustness to the sophistication that has come with a postwar role as Germany's media capital. Though the port makes Hamburg fairly grimy in places, seedy even, it adds earthy flavours to the rich cosmopolitan stew. It brings dive bars to a city renowned for its arts and theatre; nurtures a strong counterculture movement alongside hip media types; and helps support a nightlife that is as raucous as it is refined. Even the drizzle that blankets the place for days at a time can't dampen its spirit.

The surprise, then, is that Hamburg is so manageable. Despite a population that nudges towards 1.8 million, just under a fifth of which has immigrant roots, Hamburg has the lowest population density of any European city. Only around a third of the land area is urban development; the rest is parks and water. Canals that once carried produce now provide breathing space among the offices as they thread from the mercantile heart on the Elbe's banks to the shimmering Alster lakes. The city's 2302 bridges are more than Venice, Amsterdam and London combined.

HAMBURG ORIENTATION

Most of the classic tourist sights are in the **city centre** clustered on the north bank of the Elbe. A fire in 1842, then Allied bombs a century later, wiped most historic architecture from the streetscape, yet pockets of history remain in places like the **Rathaus**, the heart of the city and fulcrum of its business and shopping districts, with luxury shopping to the north. The shopping high-street east leads towards the Hauptbahnhof and Hamburg's **Kunstmeile** ("Art Mile") of art and culture museums. A museum quarter is also emerging at the old port warehouse district, **Speicherstadt**, and adjoining **HafenCity**, although the two are worth a visit as much for their distinctive harbour architecture – old and new. The hub of current port activity is St-Pauli-Landungsbrücken, a fifteen-minute walk west.

However, Hamburg is at its best at its most local. For character look to residential districts: **St Georg** east of the Hauptbahnhof, which has gentrified from red-light district to a gay-friendly area centred on the restaurants and bars of Lange Reihe; or the exclusive quarters that fringe the **Aussenalster** lake – Rotherbaum and Harvestude on the west shore have smart, late 1800s villas, and are still Hamburg's des res among the well-heeled. West of the centre are **St Pauli**, the former port district of **Reeperbahn** fame, and to its north, the scruffy but rapidly gentrifying **Schanzenviertel**; together, these form the heartland of Hamburg nightlife, with the latter currently the epicentre of the Hamburg scene. Things become progressively quieter (and more expensive) as you shift downriver through the western riverside suburbs from **Altona** and **Övelgönne** to villagey **Blankenese**, where city tycoons occupy some of the most expensive real-estate in Germany.

14

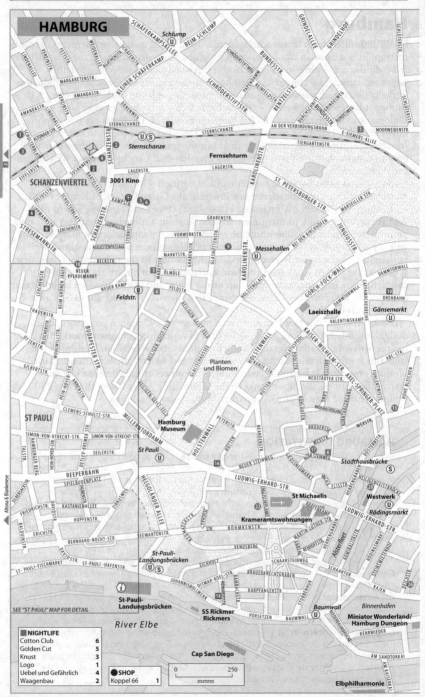

HAMBURG

NIGHTLIFE
Cotton Club	6
Golden Cut	5
Knust	3
Logo	1
Uebel und Gefährlich	4
Waagenbau	2

●SHOP
Koppel 66	1

0 — 250
metres

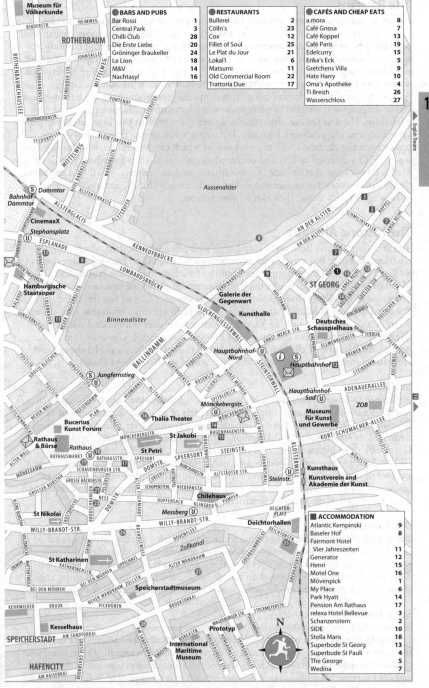

The Rathaus

Rathausmarkt • Guided tours usually every 30min Mon–Fri 10am–3pm, Sat 10am–5pm, Sun 10am–4pm; in English, 2 or 3 daily • €4

Forty-four years after the Great Fire of 1842 razed the Altstadt, city fathers began work on their morale-booster, a monument to inspire Hamburg's citizens and embody her revival. If the neo-Renaissance Rathaus oozes civic self-confidence today, it must have positively swaggered when completed in 1897. It isn't shy about boasting either: above a parade of German emperors are statues of the tradesmen who won the city's prosperity; protectress Hammonia casts an imperial gaze from above the balcony; and classical figures and wreaths of plenty adorn the bases of two flagpoles crowned with gold ships. Hard to believe, then, that only oak poles prevent this bombastic pile from subsiding into the sandbank beneath. The senate and city government still dictate policy from the Rathaus's 647 rooms, some of which can be seen on 45-minute guided tours. With a coffered ceiling and oversized murals of the city's founding, the Great Hall is a knockout. At the back of the Rathaus, on Adolphsplatz, you'll find the **Börse**, the current incarnation of Germany's first stock market (1558), and a revealing symbol of mercantile priorities at the heart of government.

The historic Altstadt

The area south of the Rathaus is Hamburg's wellspring: the location where Charlemagne rode out across a sandy hummock between the Elbe and Alster rivers in 808 and built the "Hammaburg" fort. South of Rathausmarkt, the **Trotsbrücke**, Hamburg's oldest bridge, marks the transition to the site of the first settlement on the other side of the Alster River, which explains its statue of Count Adolph III of Schauenburg, the nobleman who pulled off the 1189 tax concession that kick-started Hamburg's ascendancy. Like all good businessmen, he clinched the deal with a sweetener – a donation to the crusade of Emperor Frederick I. Opposite him is St Ansgar, the "Apostle of the North", who slotted in fourteen years as Hamburg's first archbishop from 831 between spreading the gospel to Vikings and Danes.

St Nikolai

Willy-Brandt-Str. 60 • Lift and documentation centre daily: May–Sept 10am–6pm; Oct–April 10am–5pm • €5 • ⓦ mahnmal-st-nikolai.de

The landmark of the Altstadt proper (or what's left of it) is the skeletal spire of **St Nikolai**. The Great Fire did for the original, then a century later Allied air command destroyed its replacement, and Hamburg left what remained as a peace symbol: Germany's third highest spire, a 144m-high neo-Gothic number that Sir George Gilbert Scott – the great English master of Victorian neo-Gothic – modelled on the steeples of the Dom in Cologne and Freiburg's Münster. A glass lift up the tower's blackened skeleton takes you to a viewing platform, and a documentation centre has sobering images of the wartime destruction.

Deichstrasse

Deichstrasse hints at Hamburg before fire and war, with a touristy row of gabled houses that were the homes and warehouses of seventeenth- and eighteenth-century merchants. Slip down a passage between them and you reach the Nikolaifleet; you don't have to stretch the imagination far to visualize the canal filled with ships, their crews heaving produce from the holds into warehouses via pulleys at the gables' peaks.

St Katharinen

Katharinenkirchhof 1 • Mon–Sat 10am–5pm, Sun 11am–5pm • Free • ⓦ katharinen-hamburg.de

Unmistakeable due to its twin-lantern Baroque spire, **St Katharinen church** was the focus of the medieval merchants' quarter; inside are a crucifix and a demure effigy of its saint, who clutches the spiked wheel on which she was tortured for daring to out-debate the pagan sages of Emperor Maxentius. Local folklore narrates that the replica of St Katharine's gold

OPERATION GOMORRAH, JULY 1943

The port that nourished Hamburg also made it a prime target for the Allies. In retaliation for earlier Luftwaffe raids, **British and US raids** wiped ten square kilometres of Hamburg off the map and obliterated eighty percent of the harbour during a week of relentless sorties at the end of July 1943. Over seven thousand tonnes of high explosives and incendiaries rained onto the city, **killing nearly 40,000 people**; by way of comparison, the famous Luftwaffe raid on Coventry killed 538.

As the flames sucked in oxygen, typhoon winds blasted western residential districts and the Germans had to create a new word to describe the apocalypse – **"Feuersturm"** (firestorm). Winds of nearly 1000°C set asphalt streets ablaze, trees were uprooted, cars flung into superheated air. "Every human resistance was quite useless," Hamburg's police chief reported later. "People jumped into the canals and waterways and remained swimming or standing up to their necks for hours… Children were torn away from their parents' hands by the force of the hurricane and whirled into the fire." Third Reich architect Albert Speer later revealed that Hitler and Hermann Göring had been shocked at the devastation. Even Air Chief Marshal **Arthur "Bomber" Harris** conceded that the attacks on the Reich's second city were "incomparably more terrible" than anything previously launched at Germany. Operation Gomorrah was well named.

crown, which wraps around the spire, was smelted from the booty of pirate Klaus Störtebeker, the bane of Hanseatic merchants until, according to legend, he was double-crossed and executed in Hamburg in 1401. It's said the folk hero's decapitated body rose and walked from the scaffold.

The Chilehaus
Pumpen

Hamburg is hardly short of unique architecture, yet the **Chilehaus** (1924) in the **Kontorhaus** (Counting House) business quarter still seems eccentric. Taking inspiration from the ships in the docks, Expressionist architect Fritz Höger married cost-saving brick with sleek Twenties style. And the ten-storey Chilehaus certainly has style, despite locals' quips about a flat iron. Look at it from where Burchardplatz meets Pumpen and Höger's ocean liner becomes apparant: the building's end forms a high bow, a Chilean condor acts as a figurehead and decks with railings jut out on either side. Its merchant owner, Henry Barens Sloman, earned his wealth through thirty years of saltpetre trade with Chile, hence the building's name.

St Jakobi
Steinstrasse • Mon–Sat 10am–5pm (from 11am Oct–March), Sun noon–5pm • Free • ⓦ www.jacobus.de

A giant among organs takes pride of place in the fifteenth-century church of **St Jakobi** on Steinstrasse. It is the largest surviving work of Arp Schnitger, a rising star of organ-building when he created it in 1693, and a talent now recognized as the best the Baroque era produced. Johann Sebastian Bach tickled the instrument's keys in 1720 while considering a position as resident organist. That it survives at all is a wonder. In World War I its case-pipes were melted for munitions and, after a 1944 air raid, all that remained of the church was its Gothic facade and a stump of tower. Other art treasures include the high altar of the Coopers' Guild, depicted at work in the stained glass above; the Fishers' Guild altar; and the fine altar of St Lukas. Look, too, for a sight of old Hamburg in a 1681 cityscape, the skyline pricked by Hamburg's spires as today.

St Petri
Mönckebergstrasse **Church** Mon–Fri 10am–6.30pm, Sat 10am–5pm, Sun 9am–8pm • Free **Tower** Mon–Sat 11am–5pm, Sun 11.30–5pm • €3 • ⓦ sankt-petri.de

Today's neo-Gothic **St Petri** stands on the foundations of a fourteenth-century church destroyed by fire in 1842 – the final insult after Napoleon's troops used the church as a stable and prison during their occupation of Hamburg from 1808 to 1814. Yet the church is home to Hamburg's oldest artwork, a bronze lion's-head door knocker cast in 1342. A calf-burning climb takes you to a peak in the church **tower** where you peer out through portholes for views of the Rathaus, the Alster lakes and the Elbe; anyone who suffers vertigo may want to think twice.

The Alster lakes and around

14

If the port characterizes the heart of the city centre, the **Binnenalster** and **Aussenalster** lakes define it. Created when the Alster rivulet was dammed in the thirteenth century, the lakes were ignored until the 1800s, when the city's wealthy burghers settled the area and strolled the lakes' banks. During a Sunday constitutional, families paraded their unmarried daughters ("Jungfern") beside the Binnenalster's banks on **Jungfernstieg**, still a pleasing promenade despite its current incarnation as a busy road.

Eligible offspring in tow or not, the 8km **Alsterwanderweg** path remains a popular walk around the adjacent Aussenalster lake – allow three hours for the circuit. The picture-postcard view across the Binnenalster to the city spires is from Lombardsbrücke. Alternatively, hop-on, hop-off tourist **ferries** (see box below) call at the nine quays around the lake every hour, and **cruises** tour into the canals of the wealthy northern suburbs; boards on the quay have details.

The lakeside enclaves around the Aussenalster are among the smartest in the city centre. **Rotherbaum** and **Harvestehude** remain as prestigious now as when they emerged in the late 1800s as the des res of business tycoons, their beautiful villas still home to the affluent and to foreign consulates. One favoured hangout is **Pöseldorf**, located just behind Fährdamm wharf in the northwest. Between lunch with Hamburg's media high-rollers and browsing boutiques and galleries, there is fine Jugendstil architecture in the side streets to discover – nowhere else in Hamburg boasts such a diverse mix of large white villas, courtyards and mews.

Museum für Völkerkunde

Rothenbaumchaussee 64 • Tues, Wed & Fri–Sun 10am–6pm, Thurs 10am–9pm • €7 • U-Bahn Hallerstrasse then 10min walk • ⓦ voelkerkundemuseum.com

The **Museum für Völkerkunde** is housed in a handsome building on Rothenbaumchaussee. An engaging collection of ethnology, it's strong on Africa and the Pacific, and offers an illuminating approach to its subjects, with interesting asides on cross-cultural exchange. In the Africa exhibition, for example, traditional culture and religion meet modern life in a display of football fetishes.

Museums of the Kunstmeile

Hamburg's art collections are displayed on a **Kunstmeile**, or "**Art Mile**", that arcs from behind the Hauptbahnhof to the Elbe. With work from classics to cutting-edge, pure art to decorative design and photography, there's something for everyone here, plus two

---

GETTING AROUND THE ALSTER LAKES

Tourist **ferry** provider ATG (ⓦ alstertouristik.de) offers a hop-on, hop-off day-ticket around the nine quays of the Alster lakes (April–Oct 10am–6pm; boats leave hourly; 1 stop €1.70, 5 stops €8.50, day-ticket €12), as well as cruises which take in both the lakes and the Fleet canals to the south (€12.50–15). You can also pick up a **pedalo**, **canoe** or **sailing dinghy** at rental outfits dotted around the Aussenalster: the most convenient is Segelschule Pieper (☎ 040 24 75 78, ⓦ segelschule-pieper.de), opposite the *Atlantic Kempinski* hotel. At the northern end of the lake, Bootshaus Osterndorf at *Café Isekai*, Isekai 13, Epplesdorf (☎ 040 47 34 61, ⓦ cafe-isekai .de), rents canoes for exploring the canals off the lake.

world-class collections in the Kunsthalle and Museum für Kunst und Gewerbe. The Kunstmeile label encompasses five venues – the Kunsthalle, the Museum für Kunst und Gewerbe, the Kunstverein, the Deichtorhallen and the **Bucerius Kunst Forum** (Tues, Wed & Fri–Sun 11am–7pm, Thurs 11am–9pm; €8; ⓦbuceriuskunstforum.de) at the right-hand shoulder of the Rathaus, which hosts temporary art exhibitions – although there are other private galleries en route. The year-long **Kunstmeile Pass** (€29) is available should you want to tick off all.

The Kunsthalle

Glockengiesserwall • Tues, Wed & Fri–Sun 10am–6pm, Thurs 10am–9pm • €10 • ⓦ hamburger-kunsthalle.de

Fresh from a modernization that restored its historic building, the world-class **Kunsthalle** (Art Hall) opens the Kunstmeile with a feast of paintings and sculpture, from medieval to modern, which takes at least half a day to digest properly. North Germany's premier artist pre-1400, Meister Bertram, gets star billing among the German medieval artists for his *Grabow Altarpiece*, once the high altar of St Petri (see p.761). This 36-panel work blazes with sumptuous colour and lively detail, especially the Creation of the Animals; a sheep has already got it in the neck as a portent of the Fall of Man. Look, too, for charismatic portraits by Cranach, and Rembrandt's early *Simeon in the Temple*, a highlight among a strong selection from the Dutch Golden Age.

Nineteenth-century Germans are well represented, with the big draw their Romantic-in-chief, Caspar David Friedrich, and his *Rambler above the Sea of Fog* and *Ice Sea*, both variations on his favourite themes of solitude and the power of nature. Beyond French Impressionists – Manet's scandalous courtesan *Nana*, enjoyable works by fellow Frenchmen Toulouse-Lautrec and Renoir – are Classical Modern works such as the warped eroticism of Munch's *Madonna*, more whore than holy, plus vigorous works by Expressionists of the Blaue Reiter (see box, p.347) and Die Brücke groups, as well as non-affiliates Beckmann and Klee and contemporaries like Picasso.

Galerie der Gegenwart

The post-1960s collection is in the **Galerie der Gegenwart** (Gallery of Contemporary Art; same hours & ticket), a white cube with a central, light-filled atrium, reached through a tunnel from the Kunsthalle. Modern giants rub shoulders with up-and-coming names: from established figures such as Andy Warhol, David Hockney, Joseph Beuys, Gerhard Richter and Richard Serra to the likes of Jeff Koons, Tracy Emin and key figures of German painting such as Georg Baselitz and Rebecca Horn.

The Museum für Kunst und Gewerbe

Steintorplatz • Tues & Fri–Sun 11am–6pm, Wed & Thurs 11am–9pm • €8 • ⓦ mkg-hamburg.de

In a scruffy area of St Georg south of the Hauptbahnhof, the vast **Museum für Kunst und Gewerbe** (Museum of Art and Crafts) is a treat. Over three floors is a treasure-trove of decorative arts, from antiquities to a who's who of modern interior design, alongside superb Renaissance and Baroque exhibits, fashions, poster art and graphics, plus objets d'art from the Islamic world and East Asia, all beautifully and innovatively displayed after a recent refurbishment.

ART ATTACK

Berliner artists who revel in their image as "poor but sexy" like to rib Hamburg as bourgeois and boring. It's a fair guess they haven't been to **Westwerk** (Admiralitätstr. 74; ⓦ westwerk.org). In the Fleetinsel region west of the Rathaus, this artists' collective has been defying convention since 1985. Today around thirty residents plus many more external artists produce and host exhibitions and occasional gigs here. Times and prices vary – check out the website to visit a venue that taps into Hamburg's counterculture spirit.

14

While the museum prides itself on the world's finest collection of early European **keyboards** on the ground floor – ask about the times of daily concerts when you buy your ticket – more enjoyable are the complete **period rooms**, including a Hamburg piano room in Louis XVI style, and a cabin-like nook that a lawyer who was nostalgic for his sea journey commissioned from St Petri and Rathausmarkt architect Alexis de Chateauneuf. More magnificent are the Jugendstil rooms assembled by the museum's first director at the 1900 World Exhibition in Paris. Justus Brinckmann conceived his acquisitions of furniture, wall hangings, textiles, lamps, decorative objects, even books, as a *Gesamtkunstwerk* (integrated artwork) and generously allowed the city council to pick up the bill for what was the largest purchase of contemporary works ever made by a German museum. Don't miss, too, the museum's latest room acquisition on the top floor, a fabulous Pop Art canteen created by Verner Panton for Hamburg's Spiegel Publishing House. All in all, highly recommended – allow half a day at least.

Private galleries along Klosterwall

Forming part of the Kunstmeile are exhibitions presented in a line of private galleries along Klosterwall: **Kunsthaus**, Klosterwall 15 (Tues–Sun 11am–6pm; prices vary; ⓦkunsthaushamburg.de), **Kunstverein**, Klosterwall 23 (Tues–Sun noon–6pm; €5; ⓦkunstverein.de), and **Akademie der Kunst**, also at Klosterwall 23 (Tues–Sun 11am–6pm; prices vary; ⓦakademie-der-kuenste.de).

Deichtorhallen

Deichtorstr. 1–2 • Tues–Sun 11am–6pm, first Thurs in month till 9pm • €9 • ⓦ deichtorhallen.de

The Kunstmeile concludes at the former fruit and veg market halls that now host the **Deichtorhallen**, Europe's largest contemporary arts space. Its six thousand square metres split between art in the Halle für Aktuelle Kunst and photography in the Haus der Photographie. Expect blockbuster solo exhibitions of internationally acclaimed painters and sculptors in the former, and photography retrospectives all the way back to the first pioneers in the latter.

St Michaelis church

Englische Planke 1 (Church) Daily: May–Oct 9am–7.30pm; Nov–April 10am–5.30pm • Viewing platform €4, crypt museum €4, combined ticket €7 • ⓦ st-michaelis.de (Nacht Michel "bar") Jan & Feb Fri & Sat 5.30–11pm; March & April, Nov & Dec Mon–Thurs & Sun 5.30–9.30pm, Fri & Sat 5.30–11pm; May–Oct daily 7.30–11pm • €10.50 • ⓦ nachtmichel.de

A city icon, **St Michaelis**, at the western edge of the city centre by Ludwig-Erhard-Strasse, is Hamburg's iconic church and no wonder: more than any other building, the "Michael" mirrors the city's irrepressible spirit. Burned down after a lightning strike in 1750, it was rebuilt in Baroque style only to be incinerated again in 1906 when a workman started a blaze with his blowtorch. In 1945, the Allies obliterated the roof and decor of church number three. Reconstructed again, it is now the finest Baroque church in North Germany.

The interior

With white-washed walls alleviated only by capitals picked out in gold, it's a typically plain Protestant affair; Martin Luther, whose statue stands outside, would have approved of its space and restraint. With his elevation of the spoken word, he would also have admired a pillar-free nave that provides a 2500-strong congregation with a clear view of a pulpit like a chariot. A "Multivision" show in the **crypt** traces the church through various stages of construction and destruction in images and mementoes. Here, too, you can pay homage at the grave of C.P.E. Bach, who succeeded Georg Philipp Telemann as its musical director; **organ concerts** are held at noon after Sunday mass.

Viewing platform

Perhaps the most rewarding attraction is the **viewing platform** 82m up, which provides one of the best views over Hamburg: the 360-degree panorama takes in Speicherstadt, the container port and shipping on the Elbe, the Alster lakes, and the five spires of the churches and Rathaus, which punctuate the skyline like exclamation marks. It is also open as the **Nacht Michel "bar"**, in reality just a night-time opening of the tower with a soft or alcohol-free drink included. While the view is magic, it's fair to say Luther would not approve.

The Krameramtswohnungen

The time-honoured sight behind the St Michaelis church is the **Krameramtswohnungen**, a street of seventeenth-century brick and half-timbered buildings almshouses where the shopkeepers' guild (the Krameramt) housed widows of its departed members. It's an atmospheric nook but a tourist trap.

Hamburg Museum

Holstenwall 24 • Tues–Sat 10am–5pm, Sun 10am–6pm • €9 • ⊛ hamburgmuseum.de

No surprise that the port looms large in the **Hamburg Museum**'s potted history of Hamburg and its citizens – there are models of the city's fleets, both Hanseatic merchant ships and transatlantic liners, and an opportunity to explore the bridge of a 1909 cargo steamer against a backdrop of the earliest colour footage of the port. Equally engaging are the re-created historic Hamburg interiors on the second floor, none more evocative of former mercantile pomp than the seventeenth-century quarters of a prosperous merchant from Deichstrasse. Elsewhere are exhibits of medieval religious sculpture salvaged from the churches, town fashions, an enormous model of Solomon's Temple – less a historical fact than an insight into the ideals of Baroque architecture – and, on the top floor, a 1950s model railway which whirrs into action at regular intervals. Most exhibits have annotations in English.

The Bismarck statue and city parks

Looming above the treetops opposite the Hamburg Museum is a 37m-high monument to **Otto von Bismarck** – the largest in Germany. The Iron Chancellor's strong-arm tactics wrestled back Schleswig and Holstein from Denmark in 1864, allowing Hamburg to resume its boast of being a "gateway to the world", which is why Bismarck gazes downriver towards the North Sea. The statue stands at one end of **Wallanlagen**, the first in a line of parks that replace the former city fortifications. The highlight is **Planten un Blomen**, in the centre north of the Musikhalle, a botanic garden and Europe's largest Japanese garden.

Speicherstadt and HafenCity

Not just the name, **Speicherstadt** (Warehouse Town), but also the cobbled streets and gables combine to make the district beyond Zollkanal (Tax Canal) a world apart from the city. The red-brick architecture – a deliberate nod to Hanseatic days – of the largest continuous warehousing in the world sprang up from 1885 to 1927, providing storage for a city that had recently signed up to the fledgling Customs Union (1888) of the Second Reich. An entire residential district was razed, and nearly 24,000 people displaced to make way for it. Trade has moved to deeper water, but a few importers still hoard goods tax-free in its warehouses – Europe's largest stock of Middle Eastern carpets is here, apparently – and so strict are preservation orders that goods are hoisted by block and tackle. A museum (see p.766) provides details of the area's past, but much of the

14

DESTINATION AMERICA

Such is the hubris of boom-town Hamburg that its role as the principal **emigration** point in Germany is largely overlooked. Yet the area opposite HafenCity was the last piece of Europe experienced by millions of Europeans and Russians. Nearly five million people embarked at Hamburg for a new life in the New World – almost 1.9 million people left during the peak period of mass migration between 1891 and 1914, when poverty and pogroms proved the final straw for many in southern and eastern Europe. A cholera epidemic that claimed ten thousand lives in three months prompted city authorities to demand that the emigration shipping lines relocate from the docks at St Pauli to Veddel island opposite Speicherstadt. Located beside the south exit of Veddel S-Bahn station, the last brick Emigrant Hall to house the masses is the centrepiece of the **BallinStadt museum**, Veddeler Bogen 2 (daily: April–Oct 10am–6pm; Nov–March 10am–4.30pm; €12; ⓦballinstadt.de), whose interactive exhibits seek to re-create the emigrant experience with dioramas that combine contemporary exhibits and personal narratives. Most emigrants were bound for the United States – a research area provides access to online records of émigrés from 1850 to 1934, plus a partner database with 34 million records.

---

pleasure is in simply nosing about, especially at dusk, when spotlit warehouses rising sheer from the waterways provide one of Hamburg's most evocative sights. You can also experience the area at water-level on **boat trips** from St-Pauli-Landungsbrücken (see box opposite) and Jungfernstieg (see box, p.762).

Speicherstadt museums

A growing number of warehouses have been recycled as attractions, many of them child-friendly – a godsend on rainy days. For a full quota of sights such as **Dialog im Dunkeln** (Tues & Wed 9am–5pm, Thurs 9am–8pm, Fri 9am–7pm, Sat & Sun 10am–7pm; €15–19; ⓦdialog-im-dunkeln.de), an experiential tour in which blind guides lead sighted visitors through darkened scenarios, pick up maps from the tourist information centre.

Speicherstadtmuseum

Am Sandtorkai 36 • April–Oct Mon–Fri 10am–5pm, Sat & Sun 10am–6pm; Nov–March Tues–Sun 10am–5pm • €3.60 • ⓦ speicherstadtmuseum.de

The two floors of the **Speicherstadtmuseum**, a former warehouse, are the best location to grapple with the area's past; there are photos and maps of the quarter's historical development plus hands-on exhibits of dockers' tools and imports to explain how coffee and tea was unloaded from lighters.

Miniatur Wunderland and Hamburg Dungeon

Kehrwieder 4 • **Miniatur Wunderland** Approx 8am–11pm but times vary by day and month; updated calendar on website • €12, advance purchase online recommended to guarantee a ticket • ⓦ miniatur-wunderland.com • **Hamburg Dungeon** Daily: July & Aug 10am–7pm, Sept–June 10am–6pm, April–Oct Sat till 7pm • €24 • ⓦ the-dungeons.de

A former warehouse at the front of Speicherstadt hosts two of the most popular kids' museums. Europe's largest model railway, **Miniatur Wunderland** – currently 1300 metres squared, with around nine hundred trains over its 13km of track – is slowly inching towards completion circa 2020. It's the minute detail that astonishes in the sections themed into pan-global areas, the largest of which is dedicated to Hamburg – many visitors lose up to four hours inside. The same building houses the **Hamburg Dungeon**, a franchise of the schlock-horror-fest with local themes.

International Maritime Museum

Kaiserspeicher B, Koreastr. 1 • Tues, Wed & Fri–Sun 10am–6pm, Thurs 10am–8pm • €12.50 • ⓦ internationales-maritimes-museum.de

The most relevant local attraction for Germany's principal seaport is the **International Maritime Museum** in Speicherstadt's southeast, with eight storeys of all things maritime. As impressive as the breadth of coverage – from navigation, sail and shipbuilding to oceanography via art and bone models crafted by prisoners of war, plus a pair of Nelson's cannon at the entrance, all presented in modern themed displays – is that many exhibits are the personal collection of Peter Tamm, former CEO of Europe's largest newspaper publisher, Hamburg-based Axel Springer Verlag.

Prototyp

Shanghaiallee 7 • Tues–Sun 10am–6pm • €9 • ⓦ prototyp-hamburg.de

For petrol-heads, **Prototyp**, a modern museum of pioneering motors, is a joy. Among the collection of vehicles from the Thirties to the present, many innovatively presented, are the world's oldest Porsche coupe, a Porsche 356, and Michael Schumacher's first Formula One racer. A cinema screens classic races through history and aspiring Schumachers will enjoy a race simulator in a Porsche 356.

HafenCity

Ever ambitious, Hamburg is shoring up its economic clout with a €5bn redevelopment of derelict docklands that has extended the centre by forty percent south and east of Speicherstadt. By its completion in 2025, the area is expected to provide sufficient office space for 40,000 people and 5500 apartments. Once Europe's largest construction site at 1.55 kilometres square, **HafenCity** has now taken shape as a showpiece district of steel-and-glass offices, residential quarters, modernist apartments cantilevered over former quays and urban parks – a must-see for any fan of modern architecture. **Kesselhaus**, at Am Sandtorkai 30 (Tues–Sun: May–Sept 10am–8pm; Oct–April 10am–6pm; free), acts as an information centre, with a scale model.

Elbphilharmonie

Am Kaiserkai • **Elbphilharmonie tours** Tours (in German) Sun 10am–4pm; tickets go on sale 2 months in advance on 1st of month • 90min • €8 • **Information centre** Magellan-Terrassen • Tues–Sun 10am–5pm • Free • ⓦ elbphilharmonie.de

The figurehead building over the Elbe, at the symbolic convergence of river, city and harbour, is the **Elbphilharmonie** concert hall at the tip of Am Kaiserkai. A bold design by Swiss architects Herzog & de Meuron of London's Tate Modern fame, it places a futuristic tower of glass on the shell of a brick industrial warehouse. It certainly looks visionary and should be worth a visit for the views from its public plaza 37m above the river when complete circa 2016. Best not to mention that the project has run €500m over budget and four years over deadline – yes, even in Germany. Guided **tours** of the project run on Sundays but often sell out months in advance.

HAMBURG HARBOUR TOURS

St-Pauli-Landungsbrücken (see p.768) is the embarkation point for **harbour tours** (Hafenrundfahrt) of Germany's largest harbour (the ninth biggest in the world), a must on any visit to Hamburg. In high season all manner of craft – from two-storey catamarans to replica Mississippi paddle-steamers – set off every half-hour to spend an hour or two nosing around the vast container and ship-repair port opposite or through the canals of Speicherstadt and HafenCity upriver. Prices average €18 for a two-hour tour. It's worth checking if an English commentary is available (many operators have an audio loop).

Particularly useful is the **Maritime Circle Line** from quay 10 (4 daily; €16; ⓦ maritime-circle-line.de), a hop-on, hop-off ferry that loops through the docks and the BallinStadt museum (see box, p.766), returning via Speicherstadt. Perhaps the biggest bargain are the municipal ferries operated by **HADAG** (ⓦ hadag.de), which are priced the same as other forms of public transport, so free with a HamburgCARD. Ferry #62 provides a great trip downriver before it terminates at the south-bank docks at Finkenweder, or you can disembark at Neumühlen/ Övelgönne, site of the best city beach, then walk back along the river. Ferry #73 goes deep among the container docks on the south bank.

The port

The massive stone blocks of **St-Pauli-Landungsbrücken** are an exercise in solidity for a city fond of brick. Four years after work on the quay began in 1906 the first ocean-going liner processed up the Elbe to moor alongside; the occasional cruise-ship still docks nearby, dwarfing everything else around. The centre of the action today is the wharves where ferries come and go to upriver districts or across the river; a balcony behind provides good views of the action.

14

SS Rickmer Rickmers

Überseebrücke • Daily 10am–6pm • €5 • ⓦ rickmer-rickmers.de

Looming above the wharves, the three-masted 1896 barque **SS Rickmer Rickmers** is an insight into the self-contained world of working ships a century ago. Four years' restoration work buffed her up from the mouldering hulk that lay in Lisbon until 1983; she was a reparation gift from the British to the Portuguese Navy, snatched during World War I off Chile to the disgust of her Hamburg owners.

From the varnished belay pins to the signalling flags neatly shelved in the navigator's quarters, the 92m windjammer is complete except for her 25 crew, and you sense their ghosts in the personal possessions in cabins or scratches scored by trouser buttons in the benches of the officers' mess.

Cap San Diego

Überseebrücke • Daily 10am–6pm • €7 • ⓦ capsandiego.com

Upstream from the *Rickmer Rees* and far less romantic, **Cap San Diego**, the "White Swan of the South Atlantic", ran all manner of cargo to South America. You can nose around from her deck to her engine room, and there are exhibitions on the history of the Hamburg South Shipping Line and emigration from Hamburg.

Hafenstrasse

The street behind the Landungsbrücken, **Hafenstrasse**, was the battle ground for fierce fighting between squatters and real-estate developers keen to exploit the "tenderloin of the port's border" during the 1980s. It's still in limbo as an artist's commune, a wellspring of counterculture where graffiti declaims "Kein mensch ist illegal" ("No one is illegal") and protest banners hang like battle colours among the rapid gentrification of St Pauli.

The Fischmarkt

Ten minutes' walk downriver from Hafenstrasse you pass the nineteenth-century fish auction halls that are the epicentre of the infamous Sunday **Fischmarkt** (see box below). This schizophrenic institution characterizes a mixed area undergoing rapid change: on

---

THE FISCHMARKT: A PARTY JUST FOR THE HALIBUT

Official records reveal the **Fischmarkt** as the city's oldest market, but that rather misses the point. Hamburg's Sunday market retains the same hours as when it began in 1703 – from 5am to 9.30am (from 7am Nov–March) – yet its focus shifted long ago. Just as it's doubtful that modern traders pack up to go to church as their predecessors did, so fish now takes second place to a mind-boggling sprawl of wares, from genuine bargains to tat, from fruit and veg to livestock. The story goes that in the early 1960s The Beatles received a police warning for chasing a live pig they bought here among the stalls.

Even that is civilized stuff compared to the action in the iron Fischauktionshalle. Where Altona's fishing fleet once sold its catch, late-night casualties from St Pauli cross paths with early birds, as everyone sinks a beer and bellows along to live rock bands while bemused tourists look on. Unless you're in a sympathetically booze-fuelled frame of mind, such raw exuberance at such an early hour can be hard to stomach. Fortunately, cafés on the first floor are a safe haven from where to watch the chaos.

the "Elbemeile" beyond, Stilwerk, a conglomerate of hip interior designers housed in a former malthouse, and stylish restaurants rub shoulders with fish wholesalers – Hamburg in a nutshell.

St Pauli

Here it is then, the Sündermeile (Sin Mile) counterweight to the Kunstmeile on the opposite side of the city. Hamburg's citizens are nonplussed that the **Reeperbahn** still attracts so much attention abroad. While the "Kiez" (the local term for the Reeperbahn area) is a far cry from the road where immigrant ropemakers weaved hemp warps for the docks (*Reep* is rope), and its seedy underbelly attracts more than the usual quota of dubious characters – a few don't seem far removed from those in Tom Waits's lowlife bar ballad, *Reeperbahn* – the area has come a long way from the rough dockers' quarter where sailors spent shore leave. Gone are the excessive prostitution and hard drugs that characterized the late 1970s, to be replaced by theatre venues and bars that trade on tourist-friendly titillation. Today drag queens act as tour guides and while an arts-squat commune on Bernhard-Nocht-Strasse/Hafenstrasse remains from the countercultural past, it now sits alongside a five-star hotel. A no-nonsense police force keeps crime figures among the city's lowest, too, despite the legion of stag parties.

Grosse Freiheit

The street-spanning neon along **Grosse Freiheit** recalls the area's rollicking Sixties prime, popularized during The Beatles' residence (see box, p.770). The street's name – Great

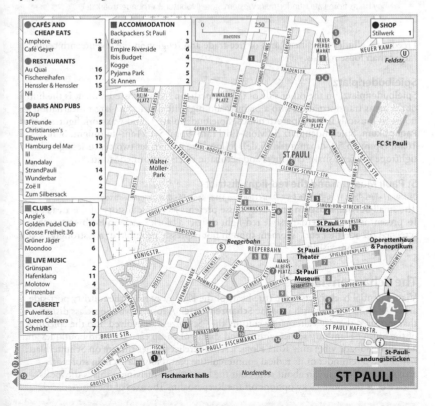

14

THE BEATLES IN HAMBURG

They arrived in Hamburg as amateurs in August 1960. They left two years and five visits later as a fledgling **Fab Four**. The Beatles have always acknowledged the debt they owe Hamburg. As John Lennon put it: "It was Hamburg that did it. We would never have developed so much if we'd stayed at home." Its red-light district area was also an eye-opener for the teenagers: "I was born in Liverpool, but I grew up in Hamburg," Lennon quipped.

Many of the shrines are still there to make St Pauli as holy as Liverpool for **Beatles pilgrims**. The boys' first address in the city was a squalid cell in a cinema, Bambi Kino (Paul-Roosen-Str. 33), that was convenient for gigs in the grimy *Indra* club (Grosse Freiheit 64). Here they earned thirty Marks a day each by entertaining sailors and strippers for up to six hours a day. The venue's manager, Bruno Koschminder, was unimpressed after their first lame performance and demanded they "Mach shau!" ("Put on a show!"). Lennon duly hung a toilet seat around his neck and George Harrison played in his Y-fronts. They transferred to nearby *Kaiserkeller* (Grosse Freiheit 64) and found haircuts from Hamburg's hip Existentialists, and a new drummer, Ringo Starr, then playing for Rory Storm and the Hurricanes.

This stint was truncated when Paul McCartney and former drummer Pete Best hung a lit condom outside their room, then spent a night in the Spielbudenplatz police station accused of arson before being deported. In truth, the tour was at a close anyway because 17-year-old George Harrison had been deported for being underage and the boys returned to Liverpool, billed as **"The Beatles: Direct From Hamburg"**. In 1961 the band returned to Germany for a 98-day run at the epicentre of all things beat, the *Top Ten Club* (Reeperbahn 136), and afterwards a seven-week stint at the *Star Club* (Grosse Freiheit 39), also host to Jimi Hendrix circa the release of *Hey Joe*. A short way along the Reeperbahn from a sculpture of the Fab Four at the entrance to the Grosse Freiheit (renamed Beatles-Platz), true Beatles devotees can follow in the boys' footsteps and buy their first cowboy boots from Paul Hundertmark Western Store (Nobistor 8; ⓦ hundertmark.de).

Freedom – alludes to a liberal area of free trade and religion in the seventeenth century, rather than loose morals.

Spielbudenplatz

Spielbudenplatz, on the other side of the Reeperbahn from Grosse Freiheit, is the hub of the area's transformation into a mainstream nightlife district. Its latest incarnation as home to musicals in the **Operettenhaus**, Spielbudenplatz 1, and waxwork figures in the **Panoptikum**, Spielbudenplatz 3 (Mon–Fri 11am–9pm, Sat 11am–midnight, Sun 10am–9pm; €5.50; ⓦpanoptikum.de), follows the pattern set two centuries ago when tightrope walkers, snake charmers and acrobatic riders performed stunts.

St Pauli Museum and the red-light district

Davidstr. 17 • Tues–Thurs 11am–9pm, Fri & Sat 11am–11pm, Sun 11am–6pm • €6 • ⓦ st-pauli-museum.com

The small **St Pauli Museum** on Davidstrasse presents a concise history of the area's past. Its present is the Amsterdam-style red-light district a block south on **Herbertstrasse**, screened off at either end. Women, though not expressly prohibited, are strongly discouraged from visiting.

The Schanzenviertel

Via residential backstreets – the true heart of the Kiez away from the touristy port-side area – St Pauli segues north into the **Schanzenviertel**. A former working-class district that nurtured the city's alternative culture, the "Schanze" has evolved into the epicentre of the hipster Hamburg scene, with a good spread of cheap eats, bars and boutiques and a scruffy laidback vibe; only Rota Flora, a semi-derelict former theatre on Schulterblatt, remains as a reminder of its radical counterculture past. Nowadays chain stores are arriving and locals moan about rents, but the bar-scene is thriving – this is the locals' choice over the more tacky options off the Reeperbahn. The axes of the district are

Schanzenstrasse and **Schulterblatt**, but there are also interesting boutiques in a former abattoir complex opposite Feldstrasse U-Bahn station and nearby **Marktstrasse**.

Altona

Altona is the Schanzenviertel wholeheartedly gentrified. It is the first in a series of ever more expensive districts west of the centre, an erstwhile working-class area of immigrant settlers that has been colonized by young families and style-conscious fifty-something hipsters – a sort of Hamburg-style Notting Hill, albeit less affluent. Much of the appeal is that Altona retains the feel of the separate town it was until the Nazis dragged it within Hamburg's jurisdiction in 1937. Before then, the free city of Altona was an upstart to its larger neighbour, even under Danish administration for two hundred years until 1864.

The Altonaer Museum

Museumstr. 23 • Tues–Sun 10am–5pm • €6 • Ⓦ altonaermuseum.de

South of the Bahnhof, a Baroque fountain on Platz der Republik hints at Altona's past glories as you head towards the **Altonaer Museum**. Models of fishing boats and ships' figureheads flag up the settlement's maritime roots, and there's an enjoyable showcase of eighteenth-century life in Schleswig-Holstein through rebuilt farmhouse rooms.

Övelgönne

The riverside district south of Altona is **Övelgönne**, one of the most prestigious addresses in Hamburg. Twenty or so restored craft nod at their moorings as an open-air harbour museum beside the city centre's best **beach**, where passing container ships provide waves and locals linger over lattes at the *Strandperle* café (see box, p.779).

Return towards the centre along the river and you're on the **Elbemeile**, a former fishing dock that is rapidly morphing into an epicentre of gourmet Hamburg. Part of this redevelopment is the cutting-edge **Dockland Office Building** on the Fischereihafen; from the top of its glass-and-steel wedge (steps up on the outside) – intended to suggest the superstructure of cruise liners – you get great views downriver.

Blankenese

Though **Blankenese** is the next *Elbvororte* (Elbe suburb) west of Övelgönne, it feels more coastal village than city suburb. The sea captains of old have long made way for captains of industry – probably the only people who can afford some of the most expensive real estate in Germany. For the tourist, there's little to tick off, which is a relief after the high culture of Hamburg, and Blankenese demands little more than time and a walk.

It'll take strong legs, though. The riverside area is known as the "Treppenviertel" (literally, "Steps quarter"), because Blankenese is a suburb of stairways – 58 in total – which spill off Blankenese Hauptstrasse then trickle like tributaries to the Elbe, threading through cottages, villas and modern designs shoehorned onto the hillside. A surprisingly fine **beach** fronts the river. Go west along Strandweg, past a few restaurants and cafés, and the sand becomes purer, the beaches more isolated, and you find the bizarre summer scene of beach balls and bikinis as the container ships chug past.

ARRIVAL AND DEPARTURE
HAMBURG

By plane Served by domestic and international carriers, Hamburg airport (⊕ 040 507 50, Ⓦ ham.airport.de) is around 8km north of the centre. The S-Bahn line S1 operates every 10min from the airport to the Hauptbahnhof (€2.85) between 4.30am and 12.15am. A taxi from the airport to the Hauptbahnhof will cost around €30.

By train The most useful of Hamburg's four train stations are the Hauptbahnhof, a 15min walk east of the Rathaus and a short way west of St Georg, and Bahnhof Altona in the west of the city. Depending on their direction of approach, some services also call at Bahnhof Dammtor north of the centre or Bahnhof Harburg in the south of the city.

Destinations Berlin (hourly; 1hr 40min); Bremen (every 30min; 55min–1hr 15min); Flensburg (10 daily; 2hr); Husum (every 45min; 2hr); Kiel (hourly; 1hr 15min); Lübeck (every 30min; 45min); Schleswig (10 daily; 1hr 35min); Westerland, Sylt (hourly; 3hr).

By bus The ZOB (bus station) is just southeast of the Hauptbahnhof on Adenauerallee.

By car Car parks are expensive in the centre – a large car park on Hafenstrasse, east of St-Pauli-Landungsbrücken, is a cheap alternative – although most hotels offer parking at reduced costs. If you leave a car in the suburbs check and recheck that your chosen spot is legitimate. Towing companies demand huge charges to release cars from a pound in Rothenburgsort.

GETTING AROUND

Walking around the city is pleasant enough away from the major thoroughfares but it requires stamina; as an idea of distances, from the Rathaus to St Michaelis church takes about 20min at a brisk pace. Public transport is run by HVV (ⓦ hvv .des) as a coordinated system of U- and S-Bahn trains and buses. All forms of public transport are priced by zone, although most of the time you're unlikely to go outside central zone A.

U- and S-Bahn Generally clean and efficient, trains are organized into colour-coded routes – underground (U) and express commuter (S) routes – and operate every 5min from approx 4am to 12.30am. In addition, three long-distance commuter lines (AKN) snake into outlying regions.

Night buses These operate between midnight and 5am; in theory conductors can pre-book a taxi for your stop.

Public transport tickets Current prices for all public transport are: €1.50 for a *Kurztrecke* (short hop); €2 for a single ticket; and €7 for a *Tageskarte* (day-ticket), or €5.90 if bought after 9am. A *Gruppenkarte* (group ticket) bought after 9am for up to five people of any age costs €10.80. Note, too, that three children under 15 can travel for free on an adult single ticket, and that the Hamburg CARD (see below) provides free travel.

By ferry An alternative way to reach the western suburbs – and do a bit of sightseeing in its own right – is by the Elbe river ferries from St-Pauli-Landungsbrücken. Boats to Altona or Övelgönne leave from Brücke 3 every 15min; prices are the same as those for trains and buses.

Non-municipal tourist services of the ATG Alster-Touristik line (ⓦ alstertouristik.de) circuit around the nine quays on the Aussenalster (see box, p.762).

By car International car rental agencies maintain bureaux in the Hauptbahnhof and at the airport.

By bike This is the fastest and most flexible means of travel over short distances within the centre thanks to a good network of cycle routes off the main roads, demarcated by red-paved lanes. Municipal StadtRAD bikes (ⓦ stadtrad.hamburg.de) are on the street throughout the city; hired using a credit card, they are free for the first 30min, then €0.08/minute up to €12/ day. Alternatively try Hamburg City Cycles in St Pauli at Karolinenstr. 17 (ⓣ 040 21 97 66 12, ⓦ hhcitycycles.de). You can take a bicycle on to any rapid-transit rail service (U-, S-, A-Bahn) for €3.50.

By taxi Taxis wait 24 hours a day at ranks on the Kirchenallee side of the Hauptbahnhof and outside St-Pauli-Landungsbrücken. To pre-book a taxi, try Taxi Hamburg (ⓣ 040 66 66 66).

INFORMATION

Tourist offices Hamburg Tourismus (ⓣ 040 30 05 13 00, ⓦ hamburg-tourism.de) operates four visitor information centres: at the Hauptbahnhof, Kirchenalle exit (Mon–Sat 9am–7pm, Sun 10am–6pm); at St-Pauli-Landungsbrücken (Mon–Wed & Sun 9am–6pm, Thurs–Sat 9am–7pm); and at terminals one and two of the airport (daily 6am–11pm). All can book just about anything in town, from hotels (€4 fee per person) to tickets for theatres and sightseeing tours. Their free maps are also a good source of information on the huge variety of bus and walking tours, the latter generally themed

along the lines of Hanseatic history, The Beatles, cuisine, the port and the Reeperbahn's bawdy past.

Discount cards All bureaux sell the Hamburg CARD, which provides free public transport and free entry or discounts on municipal museums, plus ten to thirty percent reductions on cruises, tours, theatre tickets and selected restaurants. Single tickets are currently: €9.50 for a one-day card, valid from 6pm the previous day; €22.90 for a three-day card; and €38.50 for a five-day card. Group tickets for up to five people of any age are a bargain at €15.50, €39.90 and €64.90 respectively.

HAMBURG STREET CRIME

Though far from dangerous compared with other European cities, Hamburg demands basic city sense, especially around the Hauptbahnhof: drunks mean the Kirchenallee exit, nearby Hansaplatz and Steintorplatz are not places to linger at night. The main safety issues around the Reeperbahn are pickpockets and foreign stag parties.

ACCOMMODATION

Accommodation in Hamburg is expensive – expect €150 average for a mid-range hotel and around €300 for top-end – but a new breed of excellent **budget design hotels** and hostels has recently emerged. Reservations are advisable for all. Where you stay depends as much on your plans as your budget. Hotels in the **city centre** provide sights on your doorstep, but leave you marooned from nightlife. Gay-friendly **St Georg** is another option (although beware bargain hotels around the Hauptbahnhof and Steintorplatz, the latter a minor red-light district). **St Pauli** and the **Schanzenviertel** are the best bets for hostels and nightlife. Private agency St Pauli Tourist Office, Beim Grünen Jäger 7–8 (☎ 040 98 23 44 83, ⓦ pauli-tourist.de), is a good source of budget **flatstays** in the area.

14

HOTELS AND PENSIONS
CITY CENTRE

Baseler Hof Esplanade 12 ☎ 040 35 90 60, ⓦ baselerhof.de; U-Bahn Stephansplatz or S-Bahn Dammtor; map pp.758–759. A comfortable 4-star hotel in the centre with hints of former grandeur, not least the lobby. Rooms are classic-modern business style (singles can be small), and the location is excellent for the price. **€135**

Fairmont Hotel Vier Jahreszeiten Neuer Jungfernstieg 9–14 ☎ 040 349 40, ⓦ fairmont.com /hamburg; U-Bahn Jungfernstieg; map pp.758–759. Less of a hotel than a Hamburg institution, this five-star founded in 1897 is a bastion of old-world traditional comforts and arguably the most luxurious address in the centre, with a brilliant range of restaurants, bars and cafés to boot. Breakfast extra. **€265**

Henri Bugenhagenstr. 21 ☎ 040 554 35 75 57, ⓦ henri-hotel.com; U-Bahn Mönckebergstrass Pauli; map pp.758–759. A super-central location and cool mid-century modern styling appeal in this Hamburg newcomer. Repro Fifties design pieces lend rooms far more character than most business hotels. Kitchenettes in larger studios. **€178**

Motel One Ludwig-Erhard Str. 26 ☎ 040 35 81 89 00, ⓦ motel-one.com; U-Bahn St Pauli; map pp.758–759. One of four Hamburg branches of this popular German chain – others are in Altona, by the airport and near the Alster lake – and typical of the budget design leanings: crisp, modern decor, with an attached lounge-café. **€86**

Park Hyatt Bugenhagenstr. 8 ☎ 040 33 32 12 34, ⓦ hamburg.park.hyatt.com; U-Bahn Mönckebergstrasse; map pp.758–759. The prestige address where Gwyneth Paltrow was seen in the sauna, Lenny Kravitz worked out in the gym, Christine Aguilera swam lengths and The Stones enjoyed the spa. Spacious rooms, effortlessly classy. **€225**

★**Pension Am Rathaus** Rathausstr. 14 ☎ 040 33 74 89, ⓦ pension-am-rathaus.de; U-Bahn Rathaus; map pp.758–759. A pension with twelve rooms, two-thirds of them singles and most with pine furnishings and wood floors that make a virtue of simplicity. Sure, the cheapest rooms share bathrooms – en-suites cost €70 – but it's astonishing value for the location; think "flashpacker" standards. Prices rise €5 at weekends. **€51**

SIDE Drehbahn 49 ☎ 040 30 99 90, ⓦ side-hamburg .de; U-Bahn Gänsemarkt; map pp.758–759. A five-star temple of interior design with space-age sofas above the courtyard foyer and crisp minimalist style in rooms of marble, glass and pale wood. **€153**

ST GEORG

Atlantic Kempinski An der Alster 72–79 ☎ 040 288 80, ⓦ kempinski.com; U-Bahn Hauptbahnhof-Nord; map pp.758–759. Long one of Hamburg's premier addresses, this five-star was created for transatlantic ocean-liner passengers and its foyer is a paean to Twenties glamour. Recently refurbished to offer smart Deluxe and Superior rooms only, plus superb suites – the Atlantic Suite starred in Bond movie *Tomorrow Never Dies*. Facilities are as luxurious as you'd expect. Cheaper online rates are available. **€247**

relexa Hotel Bellevue An der Alster 14 ☎ 040 31 11 30, ⓦ relexa-hotels.de; S-Bahn Lohmühlenstrasse; map pp.758–759. A reliable, comfortable mid-range option installed in a villa opposite the lake – the best rooms have water views. Breakfast extra. **€113**

★**The George** Barcastr. 3 ☎ 040 280 03 00, ⓦ thegeorge-hotel.de; U-Bahn Lohmühlenstrasse; map pp.758–759. Opened in 2009, this has established itself as one of the best addresses in St Georg. Style is hip and eclectic, an on-trend take on traditional British luxury, and service is superb. Also has a rooftop spa and the spectacular *Campari Lounge* roof bar overlooking the Alster. Some rooms also have lake views. Great value. **€140**

★**Wedina** Gurlittstr. 23 ☎ 040 280 89 00, ⓦ wedina .de; U-Bahn Hauptbahnhof-Nord; map pp.758–759. Five styles, from bo-homely to hip minimalism via plain modern business, in five buildings of a literary-themed hotel close to the restaurants and bars of Lange Reihe. Rooms are small but excellent – those in Green, Yellow, Blue or Pink houses have the most character, though Red House has a lovely garden. **€115**

ST PAULI AND THE SCHANZENVIERTEL

East Simon-von-Utrecht-Str. 31 ☎ 040 30 99 30, ⓦ east-hamburg.de; U-Bahn St Pauli; map p.769. An über-hip design number carved from a former iron foundry that offers real wow factor in public areas: the fluid organic forms make it feel like being inside a Dalí painting. The decor elsewhere is tasteful interior-design-style and there's a luxury spa. **€145**

Empire Riverside Bernhard-Nocht-Str. 97 ☎ 040 31 11 90, ⓦ empire-riverside.de; U-Bahn St Pauli

14

Landungsbrücken; map p.769. A copper-clad towerblock, this hotel is all about astonishing views of the port or city through floor-to-ceiling picture windows: go as high up its twenty storeys as you can get in compensation for the underwhelming minimalist decor. Cheaper online rates available. Breakfast extra. **€165**

Ibis Budget St Pauli Messe Simon-von-Utrecht-Str. 63–4 ☎040 31 76 56 20, ⓦaccorhotels.de; U-Bahn St Pauli; map p.769. Functional IKEA-esque rooms from the budget chain, either basic doubles or double-and-single bunk bed, but a good fallback at an excellent price. Adjacent sister hotel *Ibis* is a mite smarter. Dynamic pricing means rates vary by availability. **€62**

Kogge Bernhard-Nocht-Str. 59 ☎040 31 28 72, ⓦkogge-hamburg.de; U-Bahn St Pauli Landungsbrücken; map p.769. Grungy themed decor in a self-styled "rock 'n' roll hotel" above a bar – the streetside Show Room is one for exhibitionists. Actually, this is more hostel than hotel: rooms are tiny and can be noisy (they provide earplugs), so its appeal is the location in the Reeperbahn's heart. **€55**

Mövenpick Sternschanze 6 ☎040 334 41 10, ⓦmoevenpick.com; U-Bahn Sternscahnze; map pp.758–759. Created from a brick water tower, so with far more character than most chain franchises; there are bare brick walls in public areas and relaxed modern decor in the rooms, all with good bathrooms. The Tower Suite with 360-degree views is knockout if money is no object. Well located for the Messe trade-fair ground and nightlife in the Schanze, too. **€169**

My Place Lippmanstr. 5 ☎040 28 57 18 74, ⓦmyplace-hamburg.de; U- & S-Bahn Sternschanze or U-Bahn Feldstrasse; map pp.758–759. Evidence of the Schanze's gentrification, this place provides homely, modern, individually designed accommodation – well-maintained bright rooms or suites with a terrace – in a quiet street at the heart of the district. Great value. **€97**

Pyjama Park Reeperbahn 36 ☎040 31 48 38, ⓦpyjama-park.de; U-Bahn Reeperbahn; map p.769. Modern, friendly youth-hotel where graffiti art lends a sort of designer street-style. Has a mix of en-suite doubles plus private "Hostel" rooms that share a bathroom for groups of up to six. Doesn't get more central for the Reeperbahn. **€63**

St Annen Annenstr. 5 ☎040 317 71 30, ⓦhotel-st-annen.de; U-Bahn St Pauli; map p.769. Excellent, small hotel with a touch of designer flair about its classic-modern cherrywood furnishings. It benefits from a location on a quiet square that's close – but not too close – to the Reeperbahn nightlife. Nice garden, too. **€109**

Stella Maris Reimarusstr. 12 ☎040 319 20 23, ⓦhotel-stellamaris.de; U-Bahn St Pauli Landungsbrücken; map pp.758–759. From decor to room categories, nautical flair defines this small hotel in the port-side Portuguese quarter: cabin-sized "Seaman's rooms" with shared facilities are a steal for the price (€60) and even higher-grade standard "Officer" rooms are good value. **€97**

ALTONA AND THE WESTERN SUBURBS

Louis C. Jacob Elbchaussee 401–403 ☎040 82 25 50, ⓦhotel-jacob.de; S-Bahn Klein Flottbeck. An idyllic location on the Elbe, faultless service and classic elegance combine to make this a refined hideaway. Decor is inspired by Art Deco in spacious rooms, the best with river views. Its gourmet restaurant is sensational. **€198**

Strandhotel Strandweg 13 ☎040 86 13 44, ⓦstrandhotel-blankenese.de; S-Bahn Blankanese. Seaside and the city combine in a chic small hotel located beside the fine beach of Blankanese. The architecture of its Art Nouveau house is updated with on-trend design to create an address that exudes hip style without pretension. **€160**

HOSTELS

Most hostels are in the nightlife areas of St Pauli and the Schanzenviertel; others are in the St Georg area east of the Hauptbahnhof.

Backpackers St Pauli Bernstorffstr. 98, St Pauli ☎040 235 170 43, ⓦbackpackers-stpauli.de; U-Bahn Feldstrasse; map p.769. Small hostel run by St Pauli locals that's in a quiet residential street equidistant from the nightlife of St Pauli and the Schanze. Larger dorms are clean but rather cramped. Check-in is at the bar. Dorms are four- and eight-bed. Dorms **€17**; twins **€65**

Generator Steintorplatz 3, near the Hauptbahnhof, St Georg ☎040 226 35 84 60, ⓦgeneratorhostels.com; U-Bahn Hauptbahnhof; map pp.758–759. One of the new breed of hostel-hotels with modest design leanings, this place offers six- and eight-bed dorms, plus en-suite singles to quads. It's on the grungy Steintorplatz but has door-security. Dorms **€33.50**, doubles **€54**

Schanzenstern Bartelstr. 5, Schanzenviertel ☎040 439 84 41, ⓦschanzenstern.de; U-Bahn Sternschanze; map pp.758–759. It doesn't get more central for Schanze nightlife than this small hostel in a former factory. However, rooms – most private, all en-suite – are quiet, being six floors up. There's also a quiet courtyard space behind the hostel. Nice organic café, too. Dorms **€19**, doubles **€55**

★Superbude St Georg Spaldingstr. 152, St Georg ☎040 380 81 80, ⓦsuperbude.de; U-Bahn Berliner Tor; map pp.758–759. Industrial chic meets street style at this effortlessly cool, multi-award-winning hostel-hotel. Bright colours and upcycled furnishings such as beer-crate seats abound, plus there are nice extras like free fresh bread in a great kitchen area, and a Wii games

room. Rather isolated but bike hire is available. Dorms €16, doubles €60

★**Superbude St Pauli** Juliusstr. 1–7, Schanzenviertel ☎040 8079 15 820, ⍈superbude.de; U-Bahn Berliner Tor; map pp.758–759. The newest *Superbude*, with the same alternative, industrial-cool ambience as the *Superbude St Georg* yet even more popular with everyone from backpackers to young families and older groups due to the location – reservations are essential. Largely private rooms, styled like a budget design hotel. Dorms €16, doubles €72

EATING AND DRINKING

Hamburg has blossomed into a great gourmet centre, its role as a prosperous media metropolis nurturing discerning diners with a penchant for **eating** in style – traditional restaurants are thin on the ground compared to the rest of Germany – and an appetite for the next big thing. For the hippest new openings, source *Szene Essen & Trinken* (€8.50) at larger newsagents and some tourist information centres. There are two caveats. First, your options are more limited in the **city centre**, especially in the evenings. Streets such as touristy Deichstrasse and Colonnaden or squares such as Grossneumarkt provide choice in one location, as does the Portuguese Quarter, Ditmar-Koel-Strasse, near the port. The second caveat is that, notwithstanding student-budget dining in the Schanzenviertel, eating out in Hamburg is expensive. Cheaper brasserie and bar options are listed with cafés.

CAFÉS AND CHEAP EATS

CITY CENTRE

★**Café Paris** Rathausstr. 4 ☎040 32 52 77 77, ⍈cafeparis.net; U-Bahn Rathaus; map pp.758–759. *Très chic*, this French café-bistro in an Art Nouveau former butcher's accommodates a sophisticated crowd for brunch (recommended), pasta (€11) and *steak frites* (€21) or simply drinks. Worth visiting for its tiled interior alone. Mon–Fri 9am–11.30pm, Sat & Sun 9.30am–11.30pm.

Edelcurry Grosse Bleichen 68 ☎040 35 71 62 62, ⍈edelcurry.de; S-Bahn Stadthausbrücke; map pp.758–759. Trust Hamburg to up the ante of the humble *Currywurst*. Voted Germany's best in 2009, the spicy sausages served in this café come with various sauces: aioli, *sate*, honey-mustard, even good old ketchup. Mon–Sat 11am–10pm, Sun noon–8pm.

Ti Breizh Deichstr. 39 ☎040 37 51 78 15, ⍈tibreizh .de; U-Bahn Rödingsmarkt; map pp.758–759. Melt-in-the-mouth crêpes served by waiters in striped tops in a sweet Breton café and boutique. Secure a table beside the canal behind on a sunny day, order a bottle of cider and settle in for a fine afternoon. Daily noon–10.30pm.

Wasserschloss Dienerreihe 4 ☎040 55 90 82 640, ⍈wasserschloss.de; U-Bahn Messberg; map pp.758–759. In one of the most atmospheric corners of Speicherstadt, this is as famous for its tea obsession (burger with smoky Lapsang souchong-barbecue sauce, anyone?) as its historic building. Non-tea mains, cakes, and even coffee all feature on a mid-priced bistro menu. Daily 10am–10pm.

ST GEORG AND AROUND

★**a.mora** An der Alster, Atlantic-Steg ☎040 28 05 67 35, ⍈a-mora.com; U-Bahn Hauptbahnhof-Nord; map pp.758–759. On the quay before the *Atlantic Kempinski* hotel, this stylish café-bar unites unrivalled views over the Aussenalster with lounger-style eating: typically pasta, salads and toasties. Heaven for brunch or drinks on sunny weekends, though service can be a misnomer. Mon–Sat 9am–6pm.

Café Gnosa Lange Reihe 93 ☎040 24 34 04, ⍈gnosa .de; U-Bahn Lohmühlenstrasse; map pp.758–759. This quaint old-fashioned café of 1930s vintage, updated with chic modern furniture, offers light meals and home-made cakes. It's also a hub of the local gay community. Daily 10am–1am.

Café Koppel Lange Reihe 75 ☎040 24 92 35, ⍈cafe-koppel.de; U-Bahn Lohmühlenstrasse; map pp.758–759. Home-made vegetarian cooking prepared daily in the café of the Koppel 66 arts centre: expect pastas and couscous for around €7 and delicious cakes. The small garden is a lovely spot for a late breakfast. Daily 10am–11pm.

ST PAULI AND THE SCHANZENVIERTEL

★**Amphore** St Pauli-Hafenstr. 140, St Pauli ☎040 31 79 38 80, ⍈cafe-amphore.de; U-Bahn St-Pauli-Landungsbrücken; map p.769. A cool café-bar with views over the docks below plus nice touches like blankets for drinkers on the terrace. A little expensive but unbeatable for alfresco breakfasts or mellow drinking – beers, wines or delicious hot chocolate. Tues–Sun 10am–late.

Café Geyer Hein-Köllisch-Platz 4, St Pauli ☎040 239 36 12; S-Bahn Reeperbahn; map p.769. Proof that central St Pauli is not all boozing, this friendly café-bar on a pretty square has a nice line in relaxed urban cool. All food is prepared to order so settle in for a nice slow breakfast, weekend lunch or a quiet evening meal. Daily 10am–1am.

Erika's Eck Sternstr. 98, Schanzenviertel ☎040 43 35 45, ⍈erikas-eck.de; U-Bahn Sternschanze; map pp.758–759. A famous late-night *Schnitzel* stop, this traditional corner bar was intended for workers at the nearby abattoir but has become a Hamburg institution on a night out. Mon midnight–2pm the next day, Tues–Fri 5pm–2pm the next day, Sat & Sun 5pm–9am.

Gretchens Villa Marktstr. 142, Schanzenviertel ☎040 76 97 24 34, ⍈gretchens-villa.de; U-Bahn Messehallen; map pp.758–759. A pretty café on one of the most popular streets in the Schanze. It's beloved by late twenty- and thirty-something hipsters for its weekend brunches,

A TASTE OF HAMBURG

Cosmopolitan flavours rule in Hamburg, fusion food is a favourite. Nevertheless, many restaurants offer at least one time-proven traditional dish on the menu.

Aalsuppe The soup is largely vegetable despite the seeming reference to eel; "aal" means "all" in Low Saxon, apparently, though most chefs now add eel to avoid arguments.

Alsterwasser Fortunately not the water of the Alster lakes but shandy in a fifty-fifty ratio of beer and lemonade.

Bohnen, Birnen und Speck Literally, green beans, pears and bacon – a tasty, light dish that's ideal for summer.

Hamburger The world's favourite fast-food has its origins in the mists of time, but was introduced to the States in the late 1800s by emigrants from Hamburg, who knew it as a dockers' street-snack. Ironically another immigrant food, the doner kebab, is far more popular in the "home" town.

Labskaus A sailor's hash that minces corned beef, potatoes and beetroot and is topped with a fried egg and rollmop herring. The result: a bright pink stodge that locals swear cures hangovers. One theory also attributes the dish as the linguistic derivation of the Liverpudlian nickname "Scouser".

Rotes Grütze Rich dish made of red berries swimming in cream, popular in summer.

14

though is worth visiting as much for its excellent cakes. Tues–Fri 10am–7pm, Sat & Sun 11am–7pm.

Hate Harry Stresemann Str. 1, Schanzenviertel ☎ 040 41 35 59 24; U-Bahn Feldstrasse; map pp.758–759. Hate Harry? Not round here they don't. An outpost of the local Hatari group, this is a studenty bistro for informal eating: pizzas (€10) are recommended. Mon–Sat 6pm to late.

Oma's Apotheke Schanzenstr. 87, Schanzenviertel ☎ 040 43 66 20, ⓦ omas-apotheke.com; U-Bahn Sternschanze; map pp.758–759. Nothing fancy, just tasty, cheap (under €10) grub such as all-day breakfast, steaks, *Schnitzel* and jacket potatoes in a popular *Kneipe* that retains the vintage fittings of its original chemist's. Mon–Fri 9am–1am, Sat & Sun 9am–2am.

ALTONA

Hatari Eulenstr. 77, Altona ☎ 040 39 90 90 40; S-Bahn Altona. Daily specials chalked on the blackboard plus good-value gourmet burgers in a laidback gastropub, with eclectic vintage decor in its candlelit rear dining-room. The place to come for a pleasant, mellow night. Mon–Sat 6pm–late, Sun 7–11pm.

Das Knuth Grosse Rainstr. 21, Altona ☎ 040 46 00 87 08, ⓦ dasknuth.com; S-Bahn Altona. Buzzy airy café-bar at the heart of Altona, with magazines to browse, strange coffees to try (hazelnut latte, anyone?) and delicious cakes. Mon–Sat 9am–late, Sun 10am–8pm.

RESTAURANTS

CITY CENTRE

Cölln's Brodschrangen 1–5 ☎ 040 36 41 53, ⓦ cöllns-restaurant.de; U-Bahn Rathaus; map pp.758–759. Bismarck was a regular at this elegant gourmet restaurant of snug historic rooms. Expect expensive German *haute cuisine*: the oysters, fillet steak in port-wine sauce and sole with North Sea shrimps are local legends. Mon–Fri 11am–11pm, Sat 5.30–11pm.

Fillet of Soul Deichtorstr. 2 ☎ 040 70 70 58 00, ⓦ fillet-of-soul.de; U-Bahn Steinstrasse; map pp.758–759. Laidback cool in a canteen-styled hall at the Deichtorhallen, where an open kitchen prepares modern gastro dishes. Lunches are excellent value at under €10. Mon 11am–3pm, Tues–Sat 11am–10pm, Sun 11am–6pm.

Le Plat du Jour Dornbusch 4 ☎ 040 32 14 14, ⓦ leplatdujour.de; U-Bahn Rathaus; map pp.758–759. Top-notch classic French cuisine in a wood-panelled dining room with waiters in black-and-whites; service is exact but informal. Mains such as rabbit with Dijon mustard or scampi *à la provençale* average €20, plus good-value set menus. Daily noon–10.30pm.

Matsumi Colonnaden 96 ☎ 040 34 31 25, ⓦ matsumi .de; U-Bahn Stephansplatz; map pp.758–759. Japanese food and sushi that's rated by many connoisseurs as the best in Hamburg due to the freshness of its fish. Teriyaki costs around €10, sushi plates around €20 and sashimi €20–30. Tues–Sat noon–2.30pm & 6.30–11pm.

Old Commercial Room Englische Planke 10 ☎ 040 36 63 19, ⓦ oldcommercialroom.de; U-Bahn St Pauli/S-Bahn Stadthausbrücke; map pp.758–759. Touristy but enjoyable traditional dining in a historic restaurant with an interior as cosy as a cabin. The menu includes local classics like *Labskaus* alongside the usual fish. Mains €20–25. Daily noon–11.30pm.

★ **Trattoria Due** Grosseneumarkt 2 ☎ 040 35 71 51 40; U-Bahn Stadthausbrücke; map pp.758–759. On a square of neighbourhood restaurants, this cosy, historic Italian stands out for its atmosphere and fine kitchen. Expect black tagliatelli with *Zander* and calamari or tortellini with truffles (mains average €16). Lunch plates (around €8) are great value. Mon–Fri noon–11.30pm, Sat 4–11.30pm.

14

ST GEORG

★**Cox** Lange Reihe 68 ☎040 24 94 22, ⓦrestaurant-cox.de; U-Bahn Hauptbahnhof-Nord; map pp.758–759. The original home of *haute cuisine* in St Georg and as popular as ever. Modern decor nods to French brasserie style, and the menu is short, international and exquisite: expect the likes of roast lamb in lemon-thyme juice with artichokes for around €21. Mon–Fri noon–3pm & 7–11.30pm, Sat & Sun 6–11pm.

ST PAULI AND THE SCHANZENVIERTEL

Bullerei Lagerstr. 4, Schanzenviertel ☎040 33 44 21 10, ⓦbullerei.com; U-Bahn Sternschanze; map pp.758–759. A venture by TV chef Tim Mäzler, this cool industrial-chic place offers two options for two budgets: fine-dining menu in the main restaurant – steaks are excellent – or gourmet burgers and pastas at circa €10 a plate in a busy deli-café. Restaurant daily 6pm–midnight; deli daily 11am–midnight.

Lokal1 Kampstr. 25–7, Schanzenviertel ☎040 49 22 22 66, ⓦlokal1.com; U-Bahn Sternschanze; map pp.758–759. A superb local (obviously) whose understated style belies quality international dishes curated with love: iced red pepper soup with ginger, home-made pasta, bio Surf & Turf, delicious bread. Menus only: from €28 for two courses. Tues–Sat noon–2.30pm & 6–11pm.

Nil Neuer Pferdemarkt 5, Schanzenviertel ☎040 439 78 23, ⓦrestaurant-nil.de; U-Bahn Feldstrasse; map p.769. This galleried space (a former shop with a garden) has long been a first choice for good eating for an older Schanze clientele. Its modern international cuisine is priced at around €20 a main, great-value four-course menus €42. Daily except Tues 6–10.30pm.

THE ELBEMEILE

Au Quai Grosse Elbstr. 145 ☎040 38 03 77 30, ⓦau-quai.de; S-Bahn Königstrasse; map p.769. Hip riverfront dining, from the arch-pun of the name to the raw industrial concrete of its dining room and dishes like black cod with grilled watermelon (€25). The greatest selling point of all is the harbourside location – spectacular as dusk segues into dark. Mon–Fri noon–11pm, Sat 5pm–late (kitchen till 10.30pm).

Fischereihafen Grosse Elbstr. 143 ☎040 38 18 16, ⓦfischereihafenrestaurant.de; S-Bahn Königstrasse; map p.769. Among the fish wholesalers, Hamburg's original harbour fish restaurant remains the favourite for an older clientele out for a smart meal. Not cheap at €22–36 a main, though the harbour view is great if you can reserve a table. Daily 11.30am–10pm.

Henssler & Henssler Grosse Elbstr. 160 ☎040 38 69 90 00, ⓦhensslerhenssler.de; S-Bahn Königstrasse; map p.769. Steffen Henssler excels in modern Asian fish, while his son learned his trade in California. The result is creative fresh sashimi and sushi – straight and Californian fusion-style – plus grills served in a buzzy dining room. Mains €18–28. Mon–Sat noon–3pm & 6–11.30pm.

ALTONA

Eisenstein Friedensalle 9 ☎040 390 46 06, ⓦrestaurant-eisenstein.de; S-Bahn Altona. A Hamburg institution that is justly celebrated as much for its spectacular setting in a renovated brick industrial complex as for its pizzas (€11). Also has Italianate mains circa €22. A good option for a local night with a well-dressed crowd. Tues–Sat noon–2.30pm & 6.30–10.30pm.

FuH Fischers Allee 42 ☎040 390 05 66, ⓦrestaurant-fuh.de; S-Bahn Altona. From its charming staff to the whimsically mismatched decor, this place is eclectic and relaxed. Expect short creative menus pieced together from seasonal produce, usually with an updated local classic. Waits can be long when busy, mind. Tues–Sat 6–11pm.

★**Zur Traube** Karl-Theodor-Str. 4 ☎040 39 90 82 36, ⓦzur-traube-hamburg.de; S-Bahn Altona. Proper gutsy French dishes such as rack of lamb with a mustard crust at around €18 plus cheaper seafood pastas in what is said to be Hamburg's oldest wine bar (1919). Choose from a romantic downstairs dining room of candlelight and old wood or a modern first-floor space. Tues–Sat 6–11.30pm.

BARS AND PUBS

With everything from glossy hangouts to Szene drinking dens to dubious dive-bars above the port, Hamburg's drinking scene ticks all boxes. Like any major city, the turnover is rapid and bars can swing into, and out of, fashion within a few years. The bar scene focuses on the **Schanzenviertel**, its heart being midway up Schulterblatt and surrounding roads. The **Kiez** (central St Pauli) is another good choice, although the Reeperbahn area is derided by many locals as tourist fodder. The distinction between bar and nightclub blurs, with many of the former boasting a dancefloor and DJs at weekends. Similarly many cafés become laidback bars at night – good options for a relaxed night. Wherever you go, opening **hours** generally extend till at least midnight and can run until 5am or last wo/man standing at weekends in the nightlife districts.

CITY CENTRE AND ST GEORG

Chilli Club Am Sandtorkai 54, HafenCity ☎040 35 70 35 80, ⓦchilliclub.de; U-Bahn Baumwall; map pp.758–759. Actually a café-restaurant serving modern Asian food, but this place has the best waterfront terrace in HafenCity. DJs spin on Sat nights and in summer cushions are spread over the quay's steps for an alfresco chill-out room. Daily noon–1am.

Die Erste Liebe Michaelisbrücke 3 ☎040 36 90 18 08, ⓦersteliebebar.de; U-Bahn Rödingsmarkt; map pp.758–759. On a pretty square by the canal, this arty café-bar softens its minimalism with old pillars and wooden tables. A handy option for a central break; also serves pasta and sandwiches. Mon–Fri 9am–8pm, Sat 10am–6pm.

Gröninger Braukeller Willy-Brandt-Str. 47 ☎ 040 57 01 51 00, ⓦ groeninger-hamburg.de; U-Bahn Messberg; map pp.758–759. Old-fashioned cellar *Hausbrauerei* whose copper vats brew *Pils* and *Weizen* beers – top-ups keep coming until you put a beer mat over your glass. It also rustles up traditional pub-grub in large portions. Mon–Fri 11am–late, Sat 5pm–late, Sun 3–10pm.

Le Lion Rathausstr. 3 ☎ 040 334 75 37 80, ⓦ lelion.net; U-Bahn Rathaus; map pp.758–759. Boutique spirits, beautiful glasses – and a poorly marked entrance (press the bell in the lion's mouth): this high-class classic cocktail bar owned by one of Germany's leading mixologists, Jörg Meyer, has the lot. Cocktails €9–15. Mon–Sat 6pm–3am, Sun 6pm–1am.

M&V Lange Reihe, St Georg 22 ☎ 040 28 00 69 73, ⓦ mvbar.de; U- & S-Bahn Hauptbahnhof Nord; map pp.758–759. A traditional long bar that retains its cosy booth seating but is now a popular mixed-gay/lesbian spot for the city's scene; usually busy at weekends. Daily 5pm–2am.

Nachtasyl Alstertor 1 ☎ 040 32 81 42 07, ⓦ thalia-theater.de/nachtasyl; U-Bahn Mönckebergstrasse; map pp.758–759. A lofty lounge bar at the top of the Thalia Theater. Rarely crowded due to its city-centre location, but attracts everyone from businessmen to students and arty intellectuals. Also has funk-soul clubnights at weekends. Daily 7pm–late.

ST PAULI AND THE SCHANZENVIERTEL

20up Bernhard-Nocht-Str. 9, St Pauli ☎ 040 31 11 90, ⓦ empire-riverside.de; U-Bahn St-Pauli-Landungsbrücken; map p.769. The clue's in the name: twenty storeys up, the cocktail bar of the *Empire Riverside Hotel* provides astonishing port views. Pricey and busy at weekends, of course. Smart-casual dress code. Mon–Thurs & Sun 6pm–2am, Fri & Sat 6pm–3am.

3Freunde Corner of Wohlwillstr. and Clemens-Schultz-Str., St Pauli ☎ 040 53 26 26 39, ⓦ 3freunde-hamburg.de; U-Bahn Reeperbahn; map p.769. The authentic side of Kiez drinking, this corner bar has no glitz and no neon, just great cocktails at decent prices and a buzzy local vibe. Mon–Thurs & Sun 6pm–1am, Fri & Sat 6pm–3am.

Bar Rossi Max-Brauer-Allee 279, Schanzenviertel ☎ 040 43 32 21, ⓦ 13ter-stock.de; U-Bahn Sternschanze; map pp.758–759. A long-standing popular bar in the Schanze, decked out in scruffy retro style and soundtracked by house and techno from DJs as a warm-up for the club above. Arrive before 10pm if you want a seat at weekends. Mon–Thurs from 8pm, Fri & Sat from 7pm.

Christiansen's Pinnasberg 60, St Pauli ☎ 040 317 28 63, ⓦ christiansens.de; S-Bahn Reeperbahn; map

14

SUMMER BEACH-BARS

That locals have spent weekends on their river beaches since the late 1800s at least helps explain why no town in Germany does the city beach with such flair as Hamburg. The Elbe views help, of course, as does sand on the riverbanks. But even away from the river, bar owners import sand to create a little piece of coastal paradise, scattering deck chairs among the potted palms and adding a soundtrack of lazy funk and chilled house beats. The city's **beach clubs** – nine at the last count – operate daily in summer (roughly mid-April to Sept); the exception is *StrandPauli*, which opens year-round. Those on the river with views of the container port are quintessentially Hamburg.

Central Park Max-Brauer-Allee 277, Schanzenviertel, ⓦ centralpark-hamburg.net; U-Bahn Sternschanze; map pp.758–759. A surprising slice of beach lifestyle near the top of Schulterblatt provides sand between the toes and deck chairs in the urban heart of the Schanze. Mon–Thurs & Sun 10am–11pm, Fri & Sat 10am–midnight.

Hamburg del Mar Bei den St-Pauli-Landungsbrücken, St Pauli ⓦ hamburg-del-mar.de; U-Bahn St-Pauli-Landungsbrücken; map p.769. Spread over the top deck of a car park and not as successful as nearby *StrandPauli*, yet a good option nonetheless, with potted palms and rattan loungers, plus unobstructed views of the port opposite. Daily noon–midnight.

★ **StrandPauli** St-Pauli-Hafenstr. 89, St Pauli ⓦ strandpauli.de; U-Bahn St-Pauli-Landungsbrücken; map p.769. Utterly brilliant and very Hamburg take on Balearic, its palm-thatch bars, driftwood sun loungers and retro lamps part street-style, part castaway cool. The soundtrack is an eclectic blend of Latin, reggae and house, the views of the docks opposite unbeatable. Hamburg in a nutshell. Daily noon–midnight.

Strandperle Övelgönne 60, Altona ☎ 040 880 11 12, ⓦ strandperle-hamburg.de; S-Bahn Altona. For many locals the best Hamburg beach café: no fuss, just a shack on the sands where an older crowd and families nibble at *Flammküchen* and potato and sausage salads. Mid-March to Oct daily 10am–11pm; Nov to mid-March Sat & Sun 11am–dusk (all weather-dependent).

14

p.769. Hardly the most popular place in St Pauli, though that's half the appeal of this Manhattan-style dive bar of dark wood and red leather. Friendly barmen know their way around an astounding drinks list. Mon–Thurs 8pm–3am, Fri 8pm–4am, Sat 8pm–5am.

Elbwerk Bernhard-Nocht-Str. 68, St Pauli ☎040 657 914 20, ⊛elbwerk-hamburg.de; U-Bahn Reeperbahn; map p.769. Cheaper than the nearby *20up*, this smart civilized bar offers a similarly superb panorama over the port – a great choice if you can get a beanbag on the terrace. Mon–Fri from 5pm, Sat from 10am, Sun from 9am.

lil Neuer Pferdemarkt 4, Schanzenviertel ☎040 40 18 78 88; U-Bahn Feldstrasse; map p.769. A clubby bar that's less frantic than some of its neighbours, though it always feels like 2am inside. There's a chill-out lounge upstairs – another on the roof, too, in summer – and a small courtyard garden. Daily 8pm–late.

Mandalay Neuer Pferdemarkt 13, Schanzenviertel ☎040 43 21 49 22, ⊛mandalay-hamburg.de; U-Bahn Feldstrasse; map p.769. A chic option among the grungy bars of the Schanze that's popular with thirty- and forty-something couples. Good for a quieter drink… until it morphs into a small club at midnight. Wed–Sat from 8pm.

Wunderbar Talstr. 14–18, St Pauli ☎040 317 44 44,

⊛wunderbar-hamburg.de; U-Bahn Reeperbahn; map p.769. A classic if rather touristy mixed/gay bar that picks up a gear at weekends, when a young enthusiastic crowd squeeze in. Worth a visit if only for the camp boudoir interior. Daily from 10pm.

Zoë II Neuer Pferdemarkt 17, Schanzenviertel; U-Bahn Feldstrasse; map p.769. A.k.a. "Sofabar" because of its vintage sofas and tassled lamps – think Granny chic – in a distressed former shop. The antithesis to the relentless pace elsewhere, so good for a quiet night. Mon–Thurs 2pm–2am, Fri 2pm–4am, Sat noon–4am, Sun noon–1am.

Zum Silbersack Silbersackstr. 9, St Pauli; U-Bahn Reeperbahn; map p.769. A St Pauli tavern with a cult status in the 1980s, this is the last unreconstructed sailors' bar in the area – cheap, boozy and dingy. A period piece from 1949 in all but the prices. Mon–Sat from 3pm, Sun from 5pm.

ALTONA

Aurel Bahrenfelder Str. 157 ☎040 390 27 27; S-Bahn Altona. Lovely, candlelit corner-bar in the Altona–Ottensen area that pulls off the trick of being cool without pretension yet has drinks at decent prices – the *caipirinhas* are almost as legendary as the whale song in the toilets. Daily from 11am.

NIGHTLIFE AND ENTERTAINMENT

Hamburg rivals Berlin for nightlife. Freesheets in visitor information centres provide what's-on basics; they're especially useful for a rundown of which blockbuster musicals have settled in for a long run. But for a breakdown of the fun – clubnights, bands, art-house cinema and the gay scene – look to local **listings magazines** such as *Szene* (€3) or *Prinz* (€1.50), or check out their websites, ⊛szene-hamburg.de and ⊛hamburg.prinz.de. Visitor information centres at the Hauptbahnhof and St-Pauli-Landungsbrücken have **ticket** bureaux that can handle most mainstream venues, or try Ticketmaster-affiliate Kartenhaus at Schanzenstr. 5 (Mon–Fri 10am–7pm, Sat 10am–2pm; ☎040 43 59 46, ⊛kartenhaus.de).

CLUBS

Many live music venues also programme clubnights: *Grünspan* and *Hafenklang* (see opposite) host clubs at weekends. Be aware, too, that many clubs operate Thurs–Sat only, so double-check websites or local listings before you go. Either way, weekend clubbing in Hamburg doesn't get going until well after midnight.

Angie's Spielbudenplatz 27–28, St Pauli ☎040 317

88 11, ⊛angies-live-music-club.de; U-Bahn St Pauli; map p.769. A nightclub of the old school where a mainstream older crowd is powered along by good-times soul and funk plus classic rock and pop hits from an in-house band. Long-serving host Angie Stardust makes the occasional appearance. Thurs–Sat 10.30pm–late.

Golden Cut Holzdamm 6, St Georg ☎040 85 10 35 24,

GAY AND LESBIAN HAMBURG

It should come as no surprise that a liberal metropolis such as Hamburg has a thriving gay and lesbian scene. Its heart is the **St Georg** district, with a number of mainstream gay cafés and bars sited along main-drag Lange Reihe. *Café Gnosa* (see p.776) is a good source of information about what's on; there's usually a copy of local gay listings magazine *Hinnerk* (⊛hinnerk.de) knocking around. The best clubbing tends to be in one-nighters that shift between venues, many in St Pauli; again consult listings and local knowledge. Hamburg also has a separate but important leather scene – the annual Hamburg Leather Party (*Ledertreffen*), usually held on the last weekend in July by fetish club *Spike*, is a major event on the scene's European calendar.

@ goldencut.org; U-Bahn Hauptbahnhof-Nord; map pp.758–759. One of the few options in St Georg, this provides grown-up sophisticated clubbing for an older crowd – dress up to get past the doorman. House, soul and jazzy lounge tunes. Fri & Sat 11pm–late.

★**Golden Pudel Club** Am St Pauli Fischmarkt 27, St Pauli @ pudel.com; S-Bahn Reeperbahn; map p.769. A party crowd sardines into a glorified squat for everything from throbbing electro to dancehall – not the secret it was but still very alternative Hamburg, especially on Sat when the nearby Fischmarkt provides a perfect carry-on. Don't bother arriving before 1am. For weekday opening times see website. Fri & Sat 11pm–late.

Grosse Freiheit 36 Grosse Freiheit 36, St Pauli ☎ 040 317 77 80, @ grossefreiheit36.de; S-Bahn Reeperbahn; map p.769. Crowd-pleaser clubbing in several venues, including the *Kaiserkeller* made famous by The Beatles: expect nights of Eighties and Nineties, salsa, indie classics, and the occasional goth-industrial hammer-fest. Thurs–Sat 11pm–late.

Grüner Jäger Neuer Pferdemarkt 36, Schanzenviertel ☎ 040 31 81 46 17, @ gruener-jaeger-stpauli.de; U-Bahn Feldstrasse; map p.769. An attitude-free bar-club that provides a good-times mix of Motown, cheesy Eighties and Nineties rock and pop or indie depending on the night, all spun in a hunting-lodge-gone-disco. Cheap entry and frequent gigs, too. Mon–Thurs & Sun 8pm–late, Fri & Sat 11pm–late.

Moondoo Reeperbahn 136, St Pauli ☎ 040 31 97 55 30, @ moondoo.de; S-Bahn Reeperbahn; map p.769. An impressive DJ line-up, including international names, make this a credible (though more expensive) option on the Reeperbahn. Music is generally funky house, soul, nu disco, breaks. Thurs–Sat 11pm–late.

★**Uebel und Gefährlich** Feldstr. 66, Schanzenviertel @ uebelundgefaehrlich.com; U-Bahn Feldstrasse; map pp.758–759. Neither evil nor dangerous despite the name, but a flagship of Hamburg's alternative scene in the upper floor of a war bunker (love the friendly lift attendants), with a roster of clubnights – always worth checking out, though entry queues can be long. Midweek gigs as well. Fri & Sat 11pm–late.

Waagenbau Max-Brauer-Allee 204, Schanzenviertel ☎ 040 24 42 05 09, @ waagenbau.com; U-Bahn Sternschanze; map pp.758–759. A grungy favourite of the Schanzenviertel scene with breaks, super-heavy funk, dubstep, drum'n'bass and reggae. It's located beneath a railway – hold on to your drinks when a train passes. Fri & Sat 11pm–late, plus odd midweek nights 9pm–late.

LIVE MUSIC: ROCK, BLUES AND JAZZ

Uebel und Gefährlich (see above) hosts occasional international indie acts and *Grosse Freiheit 36* (see above) hosts gigs once or

twice a week: Damon Albarn, Elvis Costello, Little Dragon, Lily Allen and Rodrigo y Gabriela on our last visit.

Cotton Club Alter Steinweg 10 ☎ 040 34 38 78, @ cotton-club.de; U-Bahn Rödingsmarkt; map pp.758–769. Hamburg's original jazz club is a proper intimate jazz den, with barely room for a sextet on stage. Dixieland, New Orleans, blues and classic jazz are mainstays. Mon–Sat 8pm, Sun 11am–3pm.

Fabrik Barnerstr. 36, Altona ☎ 040 39 10 70, @ fabrik .de; S-Bahn Altona. A long-running venue carved from a former machine factory. Rock, blues, funk, world and jazz acts, with one or two major international names a month, attract an older clientele of knowledgeable musos. Generally 8pm–late.

Grünspan Grosse Freiheit 58, St Pauli ☎ 040 31 79 34 83, @ gruenspan.de; S-Bahn Reeperbahn; map p.769. Hamburg's oldest rock venue – today the self-proclaimed "Rockcenter No 1" – provides weekend clubnights and midweek concerts in a galleried hall. Past guests have included Babyshambles, Mogwai, Enter Shikari and Chimaira. Fri & Sat clubnights 11pm–late.

★**Hafenklang** Grosse Elbestr. 84, St Pauli ☎ 040 38 87 44, @ hafenklang.org; S-Bahn Reeperbahn; map p.769. Once the recording studio of Einstürzende Neubaten, this port-side venue has an underground vibe and an eclectic programme of concerts, often featuring touring international acts, that defies categorization. Also has kicking weekend clubnights, usually deep house/electro and drum'n'bass. Generally Mon–Thurs & Sun 8/9.30pm–late, Fri & Sat 11pm–late.

Logo Grindelallee 5 ☎ 040 41 33 88 09, @ logohamburg .de; U-Bahn Dammtor; map pp.758–759. A who's who of rock has played on the stage of this small venue, going strong since 1974. Today it has a soft spot for metal, but you're also likely to get rock, indie or folk. Around four gigs a week. Doors 8pm.

Knust Neuer Kamp 30, Schanzenviertel ☎ 040 87 97 62 30, @ knusthamburg.de; U-Bahn Feldstrasse; map pp.758–759. A former slaughterhouse in the Schanze now hosts a great mixed programme of alternative names in an intimate setting. Generally Mon–Thurs 7pm–late, Fri & Sat 8pm–late.

Molotow Holstenstr. 5, St Pauli ☎ 040 430 11 10, @ molotowclub.com; U-Bahn Reeperbahn; map p.769.

14

A NIGHT OUT IN HAMBURG: TOP 5

Le Lion
StrandPauli
Golden Pudel Club
Uebel und Gefährlich
Hamburgische Staatsoper

14

Shunted to new premises by a redevelopment of Spielbudenplatz, this place remains a bastion of the Kiez counterculture scene – hence the name, *Molotow*. Spunky rock and punk bands feature a couple of times a week and there are clubnights at weekends. Mon–Thurs & Sun 8pm–late, Fri & Sat 11pm–late.

Prinzenbar Kastanienallee 20 ☎040 31 78 83 45, ⓦprinzenbar.net; U-Bahn St Pauli; map p.769. Cherubs, mirrors, vast chandeliers: the neo-Baroque decor of this ballroom provides a fabulous setting for gigs – David Bowie played here – and a great alternative for the occasional tech-house clubnight. Gigs generally 7pm–late, clubnights Fri & Sat 11pm–late.

LIVE MUSIC: CLASSICAL AND OPERA

Hamburg has a well-deserved reputation for high culture that is maintained by one of the country's most prestigious orchestras – the Philharmonisches Staatsorchester (ⓦphilharmoniker-hamburg.de) – and the excellent opera house, the Staatsoper, currently under the baton of Australian Simone Young, a former critics' Conductor of the Year. The city's churches also host frequent classical music concerts, notably St Jakobi and St Michaelis.

★**Elbphilharmonie** Magellan-Terrassen ☎040 357 666 66, ⓦelbphilharmonie.de; U-Bahn Baumwall; map pp.758–759. Though still under construction, by 2016 this will be the showpiece cultural centre of Hamburg, an astonishing 2150-seat venue that promises fine acoustics to match its spectacular architecture and waterfront position in HafenCity.

Hamburgische Staatsoper Dammtorstr. 28 ☎040 35 68 68, ⓦhamburgische-staatsoper.de; U-Bahn Gänsemarkt/Stephansplatz; map pp.758–759. In the world's opera top-ten for most critics, its reputation bolstered under the stewardship of Simone Young. Also serves as a concert venue for the Hamburg Philharmonic until 2016 and has an acclaimed ballet company. Advance ticket sales from Grosse Theaterstr. 25 (Mon–Sat

10am–6.30pm).

Laeiszhalle Johannes-Brahms-Platz 1 ☎040 357 666 66, ⓦelbphilharmonie.de; U-Bahn Gänsemarkt; map pp.758–759. Beautiful neo-Baroque nineteenth-century concert hall with good acoustics and two spaces – the main hall and the intimate 1950s Kleines Saal for chamber music, jazz and chanson.

THEATRE, MUSICALS AND CABARET

Hamburg's weakness for show-stopper musicals in the New York and London mould provides an antidote to high culture. Tourist information can book tickets for whichever mega-budget production has settled in for a very long run – bear in mind that familiar international names will have been translated into German.

Deutsches Schauspielhaus Kirchenallee 39 ☎040 24 87 10, ⓦschauspielhaus.de; U-Bahn Hauptbahnhof-Nord; map pp.758–759. The largest stage in Germany is also one of the leading centres of the dramatic arts. Expect innovative productions of classics and modern plays. Shows from 7/8pm.

Pulverfass Reeperbahn 147 ☎040 24 78 78, ⓦpulverfasscabaret.de; S-Bahn Reeperbahn; map p.769. Sequins, ostrich feathers and heavy make-up in dinner-table variety shows performed by drag queens. However, very much a tourist rip-off – €20 a drink and bottles of wine for €50 – and expensive tickets at weekends. Shows daily 7.30pm plus May–Sept Fri & Sat 11.30pm.

Queen Calavera Gerhardstr. 6 ☎040 80 79 87 08, ⓦqueencalavera.com; S-Bahn Reeperbahn; map p.769. Tiny bordello-style burlesque club, where stripping – male and female – is performed without sleaze, all with a rockabilly or swing soundtrack. Thurs–Sat 9pm–3am.

Schmidt Spielbudenplatz 27–28 ☎040 31 77 88 99, ⓦtivoli.de; U-Bahn St Pauli; map p.769. Cabaret and variety, mostly comic, though with some dance acts. Dinner

---

SHOPPING IN HAMBURG

Hanseviertel The collective name for the seven arcades north of the Rathaus – accessed from Jungfernstieg, Poststrasse and Grosse Bleichen – which contain a wide range of retailers, cafés and restaurants. The area is a triangle of designer couture, which stretches north from the Rathaus to Gansemark.

Koppel 66 Koppel 66/Lange Reihe 75, St Georg (ⓦkoppel66.de). Jewellery, design, crafts and some art in a small collective accessed off two streets in St Georg.

Mönckebergstrasse The mainstay of high-street shopping in Hamburg is the "Mön", a broad pedestrianized street that spears between the Rathaus

and Hauptbahnhof with national and international chains.

Schanzenviertel The best bet for edgy fashions plus vintage boutiques. Marktstrasse in the so-called Karolinenviertel has some interesting outlets. The Saturday-morning flea market at its western end is all good fun, too.

Stilwerk Grosse Elbstrasse, St Pauli (opposite the Fischmarkt; ⓦstilwerk.de). A temple to style for addicts of interiors and couture, this former malt warehouse is now an effortlessly cool conglomerate of small designers, with seven floors of good taste.

cabaret venue *Schmidts Tivoli* (same contacts) stages *Heisse Ecke* (Hot Corner), a romanticized musical about Reeperbahn lowlife, while the building also hosts nightclub *Angie's* (see p.780). Mon-Sat 10am -7pm, Sun 2-7pm.

St-Pauli-Theater Spielbudenplatz 29 ☎ 040 41 71 06 66, ⓦ st-pauli-theater.de; U-Bahn St Pauli; map p.769. A charming small galleried theatre in the heart of St Pauli that hosts a varied programme of quality cabaret and comedy, plus the odd touring music-theatre show. See website for opening times.

Thalia Theater Alstertor 1 ☎ 040 32 81 44 44, ⓦ thalia-theater.de; U-Bahn Mönckebergstrasse; map pp.758–759. No pantomime or bedroom farces here, danke – this has emerged as one of Hamburg's most innovative theatres. Expect quality, aesthetically innovative contemporary drama.

The English Theatre Lerchenfeld 14 ☎ 040 227 70 89, ⓦ englishtheatre.de; U-Bahn Mundsburg. Classics from the likes of Shakespeare, George Bernard Shaw and Tennessee Williams plus modern works performed by a professional troupe in Germany's oldest English theatre. Sept–June Mon–Sat from 7pm.

CINEMA

"OmU" and "OoU" are the acronyms to find original-language films; the former has German subtitles. Evening newspaper *Hamburger Abendblatt* indicates original-language films with "OF" in its listings on Thursday and Saturday. Tickets average €8 and most cinemas offer midweek discounts.

3001 Kino Schanzenstr. 75–77 ☎ 040 43 76 79, ⓦ 3001-kino.de; U-Bahn Feldstrasse; map pp.758–759. In the heart of the Schanze district, this small art-house cinema screens quality international releases and shorts, old and new.

CinemaxX Dammtordamm 1 ☎ 01805 24 63 62 99, ⓦ cinemaxx.de; U-Bahn Gänsemarkt; map pp.758–759. The city's largest and most central multiplex cinema, located just west of Binnenalster, screens Hollywood blockbusters.

DIRECTORY

Consulates Canada, Ballindamm 35 ☎ 040 460 02 70; Ireland, Feldbrunnenstr. 43 ☎ 040 44 18 61 13; New Zealand, Domstr. 19 ☎ 040 442 55 50; South Africa, Palmaille 45 ☎ 040 38 01 60; UK, Neuer Jungfernstieg 20 ☎ 040 44 80 32 36.

Hospitals and medical Marien Krankenhaus, Alfredstr. 9; Universitätsklinikum, Martinstr. 52. Round-the-clock emergency doctors at ☎ 040 22 80 22. To locate the nearest 24-hour pharmacy call ☎ 0800 228 22 80 (free call, 24hr).

Internet All hostels and most hotels have internet access (always free in the former). Otherwise try Saturn department store, Mönckebergstr. 1 (Mon–Sat 10am–8pm); Aba Phone, Nobistor 16, St Pauli (daily 9am–10pm); 3x23 Internet-Café, Sternstr. 107–9, Sternschanze (Mon–Sat 10am–midnight, Sun 1pm–midnight).

Laundry Most hostels offer laundry. Otherwise there's St Pauli Waschsalon, Hein-Hoyer-Str. 12 (daily 6am–10pm), or Laundrette, Ottenser Hauptstr. 56 (Mon–Thurs & Sun 8am–midnight, Fri & Sat from 8am through the night); the latter is also a cool bar and café with internet.

Left luggage All train stations have lockers for up to 72hr.

Media Thalia's megastore at Spitalerstr. 8 maintains the largest foreign-language section in Hamburg; a second, smaller outlet is at Grosse Bleichen 19. English Books & British Foods in the Schanzenviertel (Stresemannstr. 169–167; ⓦ english-books-hamburg.de) is chock-a-block with secondhand tomes (and has a food outlet). Presse & Buche at the Hauptbahnhof and also Altona train station has a decent stock of international media.

Police At the Hauptbahnhof, Kirchenallee exit, and on Spielbudenplatz, St Pauli.

Post Dammtorstr. 14 (Mon–Fri 8.30am–6pm, Sat 9am–noon); Alter Wall 38 (Mon–Fri 9am–6.30pm, Sat 10am–1pm); Mönckebergstr. 7 (Mon–Fri 9am–7pm, Sat 10am–3pm); Susannenstr. 26 (Mon–Fri 9am–1pm & 2–6pm, Sat 9am–12.30pm).

Lübeck

Few towns on the North European coast preserve a sense of the glory of their medieval selves like **LÜBECK**. For over two centuries as flagship of the Hanseatic League (see box, p.785), it was one of the richest and most powerful cities in Europe, a Venice of the Baltic that lorded it at the head of a medieval trading-cartel with nearly two hundred

LÜBECK MUSEUM TICKETS

As well as the museum prices quoted here, all museums in Lübeck offer a deal on tickets whereby you pay full price for one, but can enter another museum for half-price within three days. All museums fall under the umbrella website ⓦ die-luebecker-museen.de.

14

LÜBECK

■ **ACCOMMODATION**
An die Marienkirche	6
Anno 1216	5
Atlantic	9
Campingplatz Schönböcken	1
CVJM SleepIN	10
DJH Altstadt	4
Jensen	8
Park Hotel Am Lindenplatz	7
Rucksackhotel Backpackers	2
Radisson SAS Senator	3
Zur Alten Stadtmauer	11

● **SHOPS**
Carl Tesdorpf	1
Niederegger	2

■ **NIGHTLIFE**
Hüx	2
TreibsAND	1

● **CAFÉS AND CHEAP EATS**
Café Affenbrot	6
Café Remise	13
Cole Street	4
Frøken Wildhagen	5
Niederegger	11

● **RESTAURANTS**
Haus der Schiffergesellschaft	2
Markgraf	3
Miera's	12
Ratskeller	9
Roberto Rossi im Schabbelhaus	8
Vai	14
Wullenwever	7

● **BARS AND INNS**
Im Alten Zolln	15
Kandinsky	10
StrandSalon	1

members, and which challenged policy of the Holy Roman Emperor himself. Mercantile wealth found its expression in architecture: from the oldest Rathaus in Germany – an expression of civic independence from the bishopric – to churches crowned by soaring spires or a streetscape of merchants' mansions. The highly decorative red-brick Gothic pioneered here served as a blueprint for the entire North European coastline, and it's a measure of the enduring splendour that Lübeck was the first town in North Europe to make it onto UNESCO's list in 1987. The league imploded in the late 1600s, puncturing Lübeck's status as a regional superpower, but by then its artistic legacy was as valuable as its architectural one.

The flipside of stagnation is preservation, and the delicately crumbling past is the town's main draw – Lübeck's appeal lies as much in side streets where houses lean at crazy angles as its architectural show-stoppers. It's no stuffy museum town, however. While it can be terrifyingly cultured, a vibrant university life balances the opera and classical music served in concert halls, and 20km north lies the chirpy resort of **Travemünde** for sand between your toes.

The Altstadt

The city moat preserves the **Altstadt** as a compact oval of streets. The twin axes around which all life revolved in Hanseatic Lübeck were league headquarters the Rathaus and the river port, and the pair remain a focus for most sights, while linking streets are characterized by the des res mansions of merchant patricians. The residential east Altstadt – today the student district – was that of artisans. While you can tick off the big sights, the joy of the Altstadt is that it is sufficiently compact to wander down whichever street looks interesting to explore. Indeed, stumbling upon the city's enchanting courtyard "villages" is part of the fun.

Holstentor

Museum Jan–March Tues–Sun 11am–5pm; April–Dec daily 10am–6pm • €6 • ⓦ museum-holstentor.de

There's no finer introduction to Hanseatic Lübeck than the iconic **Holstentor**. First impressions count, and the city pulls no punches with its fifteenth-century main gate. Its two fat towers, capped by cone-like turrets and joined by an arch with stepped gables, are so impressive a portrait of solidity that the Holstentor featured on the old 50DM note. Actually, it leans in all the wrong places like a collapsing sandcastle. Despite its wood piles, it gently sagged into the marshy ground beneath during construction in the 1470s and it was a close call whether it would be demolished entirely during a nineteenth-century revamp. Yet the facade remains one of Lübeck's

---

THE HANSEATIC LEAGUE

When the European Union was just a twinkle in history's eye, the **Hanseatic League** acted as a powerful pan-European bloc whose reach stretched from England to Russia, from Scandinavia to the German Alps. Such was its power, it issued ultimatums to sovereign states and launched its own fleet when diplomacy failed.

Saxon duke **Henry the Lion**'s guarantee of mercantile independence from the Church in 1159 established Lübeck as a base for North German trading guilds (**Hanse**; Hansa in English), and prompted mutual security deals at a time when there was no national government to safeguard trade. The momentum for a league proper began in 1241, when Lübeck, with easy access to Baltic trade routes, struck a deal with Hamburg on the North Sea to tie up exports of Lüneburg salt – a smart move in an era when states waged war over the "white gold". As their influence grew in a fragmented Europe, towns from Belgium to Poland signed up to benefit from the collective bargaining power, and league colonists established Hansa outposts in cities as far away as Aberdeen and Novgorod, trading league bills-of-exchange to the chagrin of commercial centres such as London. Throughout, Lübeck remained the headquarters for annual meetings and was the arbiter in Hansa law.

The league's primary directive to maintain trade routes inevitably led to its emergence as a political and military force. The merchant cartel **fixed prices** of essential commodities such as timber, fur, tar, flax and wheat. And after an international fleet of Hansa members united in 1368, Danish king Valdemar IV was forced to cede Scandinavian **trade rights** (and fifteen percent of his own profits) to the medieval superpower. The victory proved a high-water mark. Strong-arm tactics inevitably bred resentment, particularly among the great seafaring countries like England and Holland which had been deliberately excluded to favour the league's chosen markets. Both nations nurtured fleets to defeat the competition. New World trade routes leached away more influence and the chaotic Thirty Years' War in the 1600s was the final nail in the coffin for a league that was already crumbling from internal tension. Only nine members attended the last annual meeting in 1669, and when the league was formally wound up in 1862 only Lübeck, Hamburg and Bremen remained, which perhaps explains why each still declares itself a **Hansestadt**.

14

finest, with trademark rows of black and red bricks beneath the legend "SPQL" within, a vainglorious nod to the Romans' SPQR acronym, Senatus Populus Que Romanus ("the senate and people of Rome"). One tower holds a town museum – a model of the Altstadt c.1650 outshines every Hansa-era model ship and torture instrument beforehand.

The peaked facades beyond are former **warehouses for salt** from fellow Hanseatic Leaguer Lüneburg during the seventeenth and eighteenth centuries; salt was as valuable as an export as it was a preservative of food for merchants' sea journeys.

Theater Figuren Museum

Kolk 14 • **Museum** April–Oct daily 10am–6pm; Nov–March Tues–Sun 11am–5pm • €6 • **Marionettentheater** Performances generally Thurs–Sat 3pm, plus 7pm shows on Sat

From the wharf beyond the Holstentor, **Grosse Petersgrube**, a pleasing jumble of Gothic, Baroque and Rococo architecture, arcs up to the **Theater Figuren Museum** on side street Kolk, with displays of around a thousand puppets from Europe, Asia and Africa (plus a bizarre Michael Jackson marionette), as well as props from what it claims is the largest puppet collection in the world. Some feature in performances of its **Marionettentheater**.

Petrikirche

Grosse Petersgrube • **Gallery** Tues–Sun 11am–4pm • Free • **Lift** Daily: April–Sept 9am–9pm; Oct–March 10am–9pm • €3

The spire of the **Petrikirche**, a walloping five-nave Gothic church, towers over everything else in this corner of the Altstadt. Badly damaged by air raids in 1942 (see box below), it was patched up to serve as a gallery and concert venue – the space is as much an attraction as the art itself. A lift takes you to a platform 50m up with a great view of the flying buttresses of the Marienkirche, like sails among the waves of terracotta roofs.

The Rathaus

Entrance on Breite Strasse • Tours Mon–Fri at varying times, Sat & Sun 1pm • €4

If the Holstentor is a statement of prosperity tempered by the dictates of defence, the **Rathaus** is unfettered pride. It was begun to celebrate the town's new status as a Free City of the Holy Roman Empire in 1226, making it one of the oldest town halls in Germany and certainly one of the most impressive. The current building is a product of four centuries of home improvements. The first incarnation rises at the back of the Markt as three copper-clad turrets like candle-snuffers and a "show facade" that is punched by two holes so it survives winds off the Baltic Sea. On to its front is tacked a pure Renaissance lobby of Gotland sandstone, as white as icing after a recent scrub.

The **Langes Haus** on the side was built as a festive hall sometime in the fourteenth century. But the star piece is the **Neuen Gemacht** (New Chamber) above, added in

---

LÜBECK'S LUCKY ESCAPE

The night before Palm Sunday, 1942, war finally caught up with Lübeck as the Allies unleashed the first major **bombing campaign** on a German town. A U-boat training school and docks for Swedish iron ore provided a fig leaf of legitimacy, but in reality the raid was in retaliation for the Luftwaffe Blitz on British urban centres. The target was the Altstadt itself, its timbered buildings a trial run for a newly developed incendiary bomb. Nearly a fifth of the town, including showpieces like the Marienkirche, was destroyed in two days of raids, and Lübeck might have gone the way of Dresden had a German Jewish exile working as a liaison officer not tipped off his Swiss cousin about plans to raze the Altstadt entirely to sap public morale in 1944. That cousin was **Carl-Jacob Burkhart**, president of the Red Cross. Thanks to his efforts Lübeck was nominated as an official entry harbour for gifts to Allied POWs, and Bomber Command looked elsewhere for targets. Burkhart was later made an honorary citizen of Lübeck.

1440. With staccato turrets, wind-holes and heraldic crests of other Hansa members, it unites the best of the earlier Rathaus and throws in for good measure a stone staircase in Dutch Renaissance style on Breite Strasse.

The interior

The pick of the interior rooms is the swirling Rococo **Audienzsaal** where the Hanseatic League court passed sentence. Allegorical paintings portray the ten virtues of good government, and an oak door by local master-craftsman Tönnies Evers shows King Solomon pondering his judgement. The story goes that felons slunk out with heads hung low by the smaller door while the innocent left through the larger door with heads high.

Café Niederegger and Marzipan-Salon

Breite Str. 89 • Mon–Fri 9am–7pm, Sat 9am–6pm, Sun 10am–6pm • Free • Ⓦ niederegger.de

Lübeck is to **marzipan** what Dijon is to mustard, and opposite the Rathaus is the **Niederegger Café** – shop, café and, in a **Marzipan-Salon** above, a museum that combines modest history and a puff piece on a company that has made the sweet since 1806. A yarn relates that the sugary sweet was a happy accident confected by a local baker during a siege using his last four ingredients – sugar, almonds, eggs and rose water. Another tall tale that describes it as the bread of St Mark (*marcus panis*) explains the sugary loaves on sale inside. Facts – or at least guild records – show Lübeckers have imported almonds, the principal ingredient, since at least 1530, and today Lübecker marzipan is guarded with strict purity laws.

The Marienkirche

The **Marienkirche** behind the Rathaus is not only Lübeck's most impressive church, it's also the finest brick church in northern Germany. The merchant elite, their independence from the Church guaranteed by Saxon town-founder Henry the Lion, had a point to prove when they built it during the thirteenth and fourteenth centuries – it's no coincidence the church melds into the heart of civic power, nor that its two spires dwarf those of the bishop's Dom to the south. A minor collapse mid-build provided an excuse to switch from Romanesque into fashionable French Gothic; flying buttresses explode like ribs from the nave, seen at their best from the pedestrian street opposite, off Breite Strasse.

The interior

If its scale impresses from the outside – it's the third-biggest church in Germany – the interior inspires awe. Gothic **frescoes** of Christ and saints add colour to otherwise plain walls; the pastel images only resurfaced when the 1942 air raid that destroyed much of the church licked away the whitewash. Two **bells** that fell from the south tower during the raid remain shattered on the floor as a memorial to war dead. Also lost in the fire was the instrument of Lübeck's favourite organist, **Dietrich Buxtehude** (see box, p.788). The new Buxtehudeorgan, the world's largest mechanical organ, stars in concerts. There's superb visual art too. Behind the chancel in the **Marientiden-Kapelle**, a double-winged triptych altar from Antwerp depicts the life of St Mary in cobweb-fine carving.

LÜBECK'S MONIED MOUSE

In the Marienkirche ambulatory, a pair of sandstone Passion reliefs by Münster's **Hinrik Brabender** draw visitors mostly for a tiny mouse in the Last Supper scene. Apparently, like the ravens of London's Tower, Lübeck was secure so long as a rose bush bloomed beside the **Marientiden-Kapelle**. A mouse gnawed at its roots to create a nest, the plant wilted, and soon afterwards, in 1201, Danish king Waldemar II conquered the city for a quarter of a century. Smooth from wear, the tiny mouse is said to bring wealth to whoever touches it with their left hand.

> **BUXTEHUDE AND BACH**
>
> The improvisatory, fugal concerts of Marienkirche organist **Dietrich Buxtehude** were a sensation during his forty-year tenure from 1667. Such was their renown, in fact, that an ambitious young organist named **Johann Sebastian Bach**, from Arnstadt 320km south, took four weeks' leave to investigate in 1705. A variation on the story has it that Bach journeyed to take up Buxtehude's position but had a change of heart on learning his daughter's hand was part of the package.

14

Buddenbrookhaus

Mengstr. 4 • Daily: Jan–March 11am–5pm; April–Dec 10am–6pm • €6 • ⓦ buddenbrookhaus.de

Perhaps inevitably, plain old "Mengstrasse 4" no longer exists and in its place there is forever **Buddenbrookhaus**. **Thomas Mann** housed the declining merchant family of his Nobel Prize-winning debut, *Buddenbrooks*, in this, his grandparents' house – he was born and lived nearby at Breite Strasse 38. All that remains of the original is its late Baroque facade, but that hasn't stopped its postwar replacement from becoming a homage to Mann and his novelist brother Heinrich, with a museum about the family and their exile during the Nazi years, and above, the Landschaftsimmer (landscape room) and Speisesaal (dining room) of the novel furnished as Mann saw it in his mind's eye.

Such veneration is a far cry from the outrage expressed upon the book's publication in 1900. Many Lübeck citizens perceived themselves in his cast of decadent characters and Mann's description of Lübeck as a "mediocre trading centre on the Baltic Sea" probably won few friends.

Mengstrasse

Carl Tesdorpf: Mengstr. 64 • Mon–Fri 10am–7pm, Sat 10am–4pm • ⓦ tesdorpf.de

Downhill from Buddenbrookhaus, **Mengstrasse** holds some of Lübeck's grandest merchants' houses on a street that unites the two axes around which Lübeck revolved – Hansa government and harbour. One of the finest buildings houses restaurant **Roberto Rossi** at nos. 48–52 (see p.794), named after a master pastry chef who made his fortune by creating a "Hanseat" biscuit. He bequeathed the house to the city as a period piece, exactly the sort of self-aggrandizing Thomas Mann satirized. Further down, at no. 64 is the shop (Mon–Fri 10am–7pm, Sat 10am–4pm; ⓦ tesdorpf.de) where Germany's oldest wine importer, **Carl Tesdorpf**, has operated since 1678. Medieval salt-ships returned with casks of Bordeaux red, so they could be matured in local cellars as *Lübecker Rotspon* – Napoleon's officers acclaimed it far superior to the Bordeaux at home.

Haus der Schiffergesellschaft and around

No restaurant in Lübeck is more famous than the Renaissance-gabled **Haus der Schiffergesellschaft**, at Breite Str. 2. It was purchased by the Shippers' Guild in 1535, and their members' widows still benefit from the lease money earned through the restaurant inside (see p.794), a bosun's locker of maritime knick-knacks with rough tables, long wooden benches and the obligatory model ships, some over 2m long. If you can face the crowds, the self-styled "world's classiest pub" offers highly atmospheric dining.

This northeast corner of Lübeck is overlooked by most visitors yet is worth a visit for its tiny mews that bring romance to Lübeck's streetscape (see box opposite). **Hellgrüner Gang 28**, halfway along side-street Engelswich (off Engelsgrube), is among the prettiest of the ninety or so that remain; duck down its tunnel and you emerge into a hidden "village" of dead ends and courtyards.

The Jakobikirche

The north end of Breite Strasse is bookended by the **Jakobikirche**. Its original congregation of sailors and fishermen means its Gothic is far less flashy than that of the Marienkirche, although there are similar pastel frescoes, including a large St Christopher – the medieval belief was that anyone who saw it would survive the day, probably a ruse to guarantee attendance. Elsewhere a splintered lifeboat from the training barque *Pamir*, which sunk with all hands in 1957, is the centrepiece of a memorial to drowned mariners in the north chapel. The church's trump card is the **Brömbse Altar**, a subtle masterpiece by Hinrik Brabender, who carved himself into the Crucifixion scene – he wears a beret next to Mary Magdalene.

Heiligen-Geist-Hospital

Am Koberg • Tues–Sun 10am–5pm; closes 4pm in winter • Free

Opposite the Jakobikirche is the **Heiligen-Geist-Hospital**, Germany's oldest hospital (c.1260) and former pensioners' home. Its interior features superb frescoes: a fourteenth-century *Christ in the Mandorla* on the north wall with portraits of the hospice's patrons girdling the Son like an inner circle and an early fifteenth-century rood screen of the life of St Elizabeth. At the back is the Langes Haus men's ward where pensioners lived in tiny cabins until 1970, latterly without the daily prescription of three litres of home-brew their predecessors enjoyed until 1775.

Burgkloster: Europäisches Hansemuseum

Hinter der Burg 2–6 • ⓦ hansemuseum.eu

In a quiet corner of the Altstadt, the **Burgkloster** monastery was built to honour a battle oath that summoned Mary Magdalene to evict the Danes on July 22, 1227, if the *Chronicella Novella* of a Dominican historian can be believed. On our last visit it was in transition into a museum on the **Hanseatic League** – the values and ethics (or lack of them) of the medieval trading cartel as much as the league's origins and operation (see the box on p.785 for a primer). The previous museum's star exhibit, a Hanse merchant's hoard of gold and silver coins from over eighty international mints, is expected to remain.

Königstrasse

Spine-street **Königstrasse** runs almost the length of Lübeck. Adjacent to the Jacobikirche is a bronze of nineteenth-century poet **Emanuel Geibel**, who penned a ditty about the Mercury statue on the Puppenbrücke before the Holstentor. A rough translation reads: "On Lübeck's bridge is standing/ The god Mercury proud and fine/

COURTYARD CHARM

The **courtyards and mews** secreted behind the street fronts are one of Lübeck's most charming features. Though much of this housing was – and some still is – charitable, many developments were a ploy by landlords to develop the space between houses as the population exploded in the 1600s. By the end of the century, Lübeck's streetscape was riddled with 190 passageways like woodworm holes, into which were shoehorned tiny *Buden* (literally, booths) for artisans and labourers; the smallest in Lübeck, at **Hartengrube 36**, was 3.5m wide, 5m high and 4.5m deep. Charity seemed lacking even in some almshouses: during meetings in Haasenhof, widows enjoyed soft chairs while spinsters were only permitted wooden stools.

Today ninety or so courtyards remain. The most picturesque in the Altstadt are **Hellgrüner** (see p.788) **and Dunkelgrüner** Gang off Engelswich in the northwest, and Der Füchtingshof and Glandorpsgang off Glockengiesserstrasse in the east (see p.790). The tourist office organizes the occasional courtyard tour – useful, as entrance gateways can be locked – and some houses are available as idyllic holiday lets, again sourced via the tourist office. Ones for the photo album include:

- Von Höveln Gang (Wähmstr. 73–77)
- Lüngreens Gang (Fischergrube 38)
- Schwans Hof (Hartengrube 18)
- Von Dornes Hof (Schulmacher Str. 19, between Fleischhauerstrasse and Hüxstrasse)
- Haasenhof (Dr Julius-Leber-Str. 37–39)
- Grützmacherhof and Blohms Gang (20m north of An der Obertrave–Effengrube junction).

In every part, toned muscles form/ A statue Olympian/ In god-like contemplation/ To clothes he won't succumb/ So to all those people passing/ He bares his naked bum."

Museum Drägerhaus Behnhaus

Königstr. 9–11 • Tues–Sun: Jan–March 11am–5pm; April–Dec 10am–5pm • €6 • ⓦ museum-behnhaus-draegerhaus.de

Baroque merchants' houses **Drägerhaus and Behnhaus** are today merged as a museum of art and culture. Behind the pinched frontage, the Drägerhaus is an exercise in balanced refinement that speaks volumes about Lübeck high-life c.1800 – a fine backdrop for its displays of Classical furniture and objets d'art. The Behnhaus houses the town's gallery of Impressionist and Expressionist art. Notwithstanding moody seascapes by Caspar David Friedrich, standout sections include the brilliant works Edvard Munch produced during his time in Lübeck, work by Ernst-Ludwig Kirchner and Max Beckmann, and a room dedicated to local son, Friedrich Johann Overbeck, ringleader and most steadfast of the Nazarene artists who strived for high art through Italian Renaissance inspiration.

Willy-Brandt-Haus

Königstr. 21 • Tues–Sun: Jan–March 11am–5pm; April–Dec 11am–6pm • Free • ⓦ willy-brandt.de/haus-luebeck

"I always carried a piece of Lübeck inside me, wherever I had to go," said Willy Brandt, the German chancellor and twentieth-century statesman celebrated in **Willy-Brandt-Haus**. Though intended as a homage to a local son, the museum is more compelling as a document of the social tides that have swept through modern Germany, especially in sections that tackle the Ostpolitik which thawed icy relations with the GDR and won Brandt the Nobel Peace Prize – the certificate is displayed here.

Katharinenkirche

Corner of Königstrasse and Glockengiesserstrasse • April–Sept Tues–Sun 10am–5pm • €2

Built in the thirteenth century as a Franciscan monastery, museum-church **Katharinenkirche** is renowned for the chunky sculptures by Ernst Barlach on its facade. On the left, and titled, variously, *Woman in the Wind*, *The Beggar* and *The Singer*, their vivacious style reveals the influences of medieval carving and social empathy that shaped the Expressionist's works. Barlach would have cast all nine in a "Community of Saints" cycle had he not been condemned as "degenerate" by the Nazi regime in 1932, leaving Bauhaus sculptor Gerhard Marcks to finish the job after the war. Inside, half-hidden in the gloom on the west wall, Tintoretto's monumental *The Resurrection of Lazarus* is a souvenir picked up in Venice by a Lübeck merchant.

Glockengiesserstrasse

Away from the grand architecture around the harbour area and main thoroughfares – addresses coveted by the town's moneyed elite – Lübeck relaxes into cobbled backstreets. **Glockengiesserstrasse**, off Königstrasse, holds three of the town's most celebrated seventeenth-century **almshouse courtyards** (see box, p.789). Unmissable by its Baroque portal, **Füchtingshof**, at no. 23–27 (daily 9am–noon & 3–6pm; free), was a merchant's bequest to house mariners' widows; today 28 pensioners enjoy the mews of manicured flowerbeds and dusty pink walls. Further along, at Glockengiesserstr. 39, **Glandorps-Gang and -Hof** are the oldest of the town's charitable courtyards (1612).

Günter Grass-Haus

Glockengiesserstr. 21 • Jan–March Tues–Sun 11am–5pm; April–Dec daily 10am–5pm • €6 • ⓦ grass-haus.de

A small museum for fans of Günter Grass, a colossus of modern German literature who lives near Lübeck, the **Günter Grass-Haus** is light on traditional literary exhibits; its displays showcase instead the Nobel Prize-winner's etchings and bronze sculpture to tease out common themes.

Museumsquartier St Annen

St-Annen-Str. 15 • Jan–March Tues–Sun 11am–5pm; April–Dec Tues–Sun 10am–5pm • €6 • ⓦ mq-st-annen.de

This former convent in the south Altstadt is the pick of Lübeck's museums. The core of the **Museumsquartier St Annen** is the superb **St Annen Museum**, billed as "faith, society and art behind the facades of Lübeck". A room of predellas and altarpieces commissioned by Lübeck guilds is a delicate balance of overt wealth and espoused piety; the highlight is a Marienalter from the Heiligen-Geist-Hospital whose cobweb-fine carving seems modelled on the prints of contemporary artist Albrecht Dürer. More astonishing is a brilliant Passion altar by Flemish master, Hans Memling. That it was commissioned for a local merchant's private chapel says all you need to know about sixteenth-century affluence hereabouts. Well-displayed floors above showcase civic and merchant life and also re-create the spectacular entrance halls of merchants. And just when all this heritage seems cloying you emerge through a door into the very modern **Kunsthalle St Annen** gallery, whose concrete shell hangs modern art post-1945. All in all, highly recommended.

The Dom

Cross Mühlenstrasse to reach *Fegefeuer* (purgatory), heed a warning plaque of sinners simmering in *Hölle* (hell) and, good pilgrim, you are rewarded with *Paradies* (paradise) – the vestibule of the **Dom** in whose tympanum Christ sits as supreme judge. Saxon duke Henry the Lion laid the foundation stone of his only surviving monument in town in 1173, only for mercantile Lübeck to rebuff the newly arrived bishopric and found a civic centre around what became the Rathaus and Marienkirche. True, the Dom's Romanesque basilica with tacked-on Gothic choir can't match its rival for architectural flamboyance, but its bulk and twin towers impress. A whitewashed interior only boosts the impact of the fifteenth-century *Triumphkreuz* that fills an entire arch. It's the work of sculptor and painter Bernt Notke, a Michelangelo of the Baltic and a masterpiece of expressive figures that reveal more secrets the longer you study. Notke also designed the rood screen behind, another masterclass despite a seventeenth-century astronomical clock which throws it off kilter.

Travemünde

TRAVEMÜNDE at Lübeck's municipal boundary lives a double life as a major port and a small-fry **beach resort**. Bought for a song – Lübeckers paid 1060 Marks for the hamlet to safeguard their gateway to the sea – it became an opera. In the nineteenth century it was a German St Tropez as the nation went crazy for seawater bathing. High rollers, including that inveterate gambler Dostoevsky, tried their luck in a *belle époque* casino and Emperor Wilhelm II competed in the Travemünde Woch regatta. Thomas Mann took his holidays here, enthusing about "a paradise where I have undoubtedly spent the happiest days of my life", and Clara Wieck gushed to future husband Robert Schumann about sailing trips. While the casino and spa now house upmarket hotels, Travemünde contents itself as a modest holiday resort; it's less impressive than the Baltic resorts to the east, but its broad silver sands are pleasant to while away a sunny day in a wicker *Strandkörbe*, the hooded Rolls-Royce of beach seating.

SS Passat

Daily: Easter to mid-May & Oct 11am–4.30pm; mid-May to Sept 10am–5pm • €4 • ⓦ ss-passat.com • Passenger ferry by river mouth, and car/passenger ferry 400m upriver; €1.10 pedestrian, €3.40 car

From Travemünde's river channel, lined by fish restaurants, you can take a ferry across the river to the four-masted barque **SS Passat**, Germany's last windjammer and sister-ship to the ill-fated *Pamir* whose lifeboat is in Lübeck's Jakobikirche. Having rounded Cape Horn 39 times during her years circumnavigating the globe in the 1930s and 1940s, the 115m 1911-built barque is now on a permanent mooring on the Priwall peninsula, a wild conservation area with plenty of beach space.

ARRIVAL AND DEPARTURE

By plane Lübeck airport (☎ 0451 58 30 10, ⊛ flughafen-luebeck.net), 7km south of the centre, is served by international budget airline flights. Lübeck Flughafen train station is 300m from the terminal (hourly; €3), otherwise bus #6 stops nearby on Blankenseer Strasse (5am–11.50pm; €3); both provide access to the city centre. In addition, a shuttle bus to Hamburg coordinates with international flights of cooperating airlines such as Ryanair (1hr 15min; €11.50; ⊛ vhhpvg.de). Expect to pay around €20 for a taxi; ranks are outside the Hauptbahnhof and airport, or try Lübecker Funktaxen (☎ 0451 811 21) or Radi's Taxi (☎ 0451 442 44).

By train The Hauptbahnhof is a 5min walk west of the Holstentor and tourist office.

Destinations Eutin (every 30min; 25–30min); Hamburg (every 30min; 45min); Kiel (hourly; 1hr 10min); Ratzeburg (hourly; 20min).

By bus The bus station (ZOB) is just outside the train station.

By ferry Finnlines (⊛ finnlines.de) operates ferry services to Travemünde from several Finnish ports and to Lübeck from St Petersburg, while DFDS Tor Line (⊛ dfdstorline .com) sails to Lübeck from Riga, Latvia.

By car The largest car parks in Lübeck are by the Musik- und Kongresshalle on Willy-Brandt-Allee.

GETTING AROUND

By foot Although local transport is free with a HappyDay card (see below), it's easier to negotiate Lübeck's compact Altstadt on foot.

By train A rail branch line from the Hauptbahnhof runs to three stations in Travemünde: ferry terminal Bahnhof Skandinavienkai; Hafenbahnhof, in Travemünde town centre; and Strandbahnhof near the beach. Cruises operated by Könemann Schiffahrt (see below) are a more scenic option from April to early Oct.

By boat Könemann Schiffahrt sails to Travemünde (April Sat & Sun daily; May–early Oct 2 daily; €14 one-way, €20.50 return; ☎ 0451 280 16 35, ⊛ koenemannschiffahrt .de). Departures are from Drehbrücke, north of the other wharves at the end of Engelsgrube.

By bike Available from Bike & Tour, Geniner Str. 2 (⊛ fahrrad-laden.info), northeast of the centre.

INFORMATION AND TOURS

Tourist offices The excellent Welcome Center is halfway between the Hauptbahnhof and Holstentor at Holstentorplatz 1 (Jan–May, Oct & Nov Mon–Fri 9.30am–6pm, Sat 10am–3pm; June–Sept Mon–Fri 9.30am–7pm, Sat 10am–3pm, Sun 10am–2pm; ☎ 0451 889 97 00, ⊛ luebeck-tourism.de). It offers maps (€1), can book hotel accommodation and sells the HappyDay discount card (see below). It also stocks the German-language *Lübeck Rundum* book (€2.90) of shopping, restaurants, tours and A–Z local listings.

Discount card The HappyDay card provides free local transport and discounts or free entry to attractions; a 24/48/72-hour card costs €11/€13/€16.

Walking tours and guides Guided walking tours of the Altstadt in English (May–Aug Sat 11.30am; €10) depart from the Welcome Center. The Welcome Center also rents out audiovisual guides "led" by two locals (3hr €7.50; whole day €10); bring a passport or credit card as a deposit; the guide is also available as a free App – search for "iTour Lübeck".

Boat trips Cruises around the Altstadt moat are run by three companies from wharves by the Holstenbrücke. All operate daily departures (March to mid-Oct daily 10am–6pm; every 30min; around 1hr; €8) and since they operate identical routes on near-identical craft, you're best to hop aboard the next departure. Wakenitz Schifffahrt Quandt (☎ 0451 79 38 85, ⊛ wakenitz-schifffahrt-quandt .de) and Personenschiffahrt Reinhold Maiworm (☎ 0451 354 55) also operate 2hr trips down the Wakenitz River to Rothenhausen (March–Nov 2 daily; also July & Aug Sat & Sun every 2hr; €12 one-way, €16.50 return), where you can connect to a second ferry to Ratzeburg (see p.795); they depart from Moltebrücke, east of the Altstadt on the other side of the moat.

ACCOMMODATION

Rooms are at a premium during high season and early Dec for the Christmas markets. Private **holiday homes** squirrelled away in the Altstadt offer good-value apartments (€55–75) and charm in abundance, and can be booked through the tourist office or its website.

HOTELS
LÜBECK

★ **An die Marienkirche** Schüsselbuden 4 ☎ 0451 79 94 10, ⊛ hotel-an-der-marienkirche.de. Designer looks at low prices in a small, private hotel that has been modernized throughout. Rooms are simple and streamlined, with contemporary Scandinavian-style furnishings, and the location in the heart of the Altstadt is superb. **€89**

★ **Anno 1216** Alfstr. 38 ☎ 0451 400 82 10, ⊛ hotelanno1216.de. This elegant eleven-room hotel preserves plenty of original features from its past as a former merchant-aristocrat's residence and warehouse – beams in double rooms and Rococo plasterwork in magnificent suites (€258) – all with a superb location. Breakfast €7.50 extra. **€148**

Atlantic Schmeidestr. 9 ☎0451 38 47 90, ⓦatlantic-hotels.de/luebeck. Part business hotel, part modest design hotel for tourists, this 4-star outpost of the Atlantic chain has the usual streamlined decor in well-maintained modern rooms, and benefits from an excellent location. **€151**

Jensen An der Obertrave 4–5 ☎0451 70 24 90, ⓦhotel-jensen.de. Plain, classic-modern accommodation in a renovated harbourside merchant's house owned by the Ringhotel chain; the best front rooms enjoy views over the Stadt-Trave canal. **€109**

Park Hotel Am Lindenplatz Lindenpltaz 2 ☎0451 81 19 70, ⓦparkhotel-luebeck.de. One of several small hotels around the train station, this family-run place benefits from the high ceilings, stained glass and moulded cornice of its Art Nouveau villa. Standard classic-modern rooms, though spacious and comfortable, are a bit of a let-down afterwards. Komfort rooms (€115) are fresh and modern. **€89**

Radisson SAS Senator Willy-Brandt-Allee 6 ☎0451 14 20, ⓦsenatorhotel.de. The smartest outfit in the centre is this business-style hotel with wings, propped above the harbour and with all the facilities you'd expect from a five-star member of this chain. Facilities include a pool with views across to the old town waterfront, and breakfast is served on a canal-side terrace. Breakfast €13 extra. **€141**

Zur Alten Stadtmauer An der Mauer 57 ☎0451 737 02, ⓦhotelzuraltenstadtmauer.de. Child-friendly, colourful and relaxed, this small welcoming pension offers a relaxed stay in the southeast Altstadt. Rooms also come in three- and four-bed varieties; for decor, think pine furnishings and colourful walls. Singles share a bathroom. **€93**

TRAVEMÜNDE

Landhaus Bode Fehlingstr. 67 ☎04502 88 66 00, ⓦlandhausbode.de. A rather elegant stay, this, with Biedermeier-style accommodation in a small and hugely helpful hotel. It's well located opposite the train station, a short walk from the beach, and breakfasts are good. **€110**

HOSTELS AND CAMPSITES

LÜBECK

Campingplatz Schönböcken Steinrader Damm 12 ☎0451 89 30 90, ⓦcamping-luebeck.de; bus #7 stops outside. The nearest campsite is a surprisingly pleasant spot, with country views from its lower field, despite an unprepossessing suburban location 4km west of Lübeck. Pitch **€4**, plus **€5.50** per person

CVJM SleepIN Grosse Petersgrube 11 ☎0451 399 94 10, ⓦcvjm-luebeck.de. An exceptional Altstadt location makes this YMCA hostel in a renovated late-Gothic house worth considering; bright feature walls add zip to the eight-bed dorm rooms. The same house has three simple two-person apartments and a bar with jazz and folk gigs. Dorms **€22.50**, apartments **€65**

DJH Altstadt Mengstr. 33 ☎0451 702 03 99, ⓦdjh-nordmark.de. The smaller and most central of Lübeck's two youth hostels is mostly given over to two-bed rooms, so is an appealing option for couples on a budget. Dorms (four- or six-bed) are simple but comfy enough and the location in one of Lübeck's most prestigious streets is great. Dorms **€22.10**, doubles **€58**

Rucksackhotel Backpackers Kanalstr. 70 ☎0451 70 68 92, ⓦrucksackhotel-luebeck.de. A pleasant small independent hostel in the east Altstadt, full of homely student charm. It has two- to ten-bed dorms plus colourful, individually decorated twins. All share bathrooms. Disabled rooms available. Check-in after 5pm only. Dorms **€14**, twin **€38**

TRAVEMÜNDE

Travemünde Strandcamping Priwall Dünenweg 3 ☎04502 28 35, ⓦstrandcamping-priwall.de. A short way behind the SS *Passat* and disappointingly regimented for a campsite, with much of its area dedicated to caravans. Claim a tent site, however, and one of the best beaches in the area is a short walk away. Pitch **€9**, plus **€6** per person

EATING AND DRINKING

Lübeck's dining scene punches far above its weight, not just for cuisine but the number of restaurants in which the historic ambience is as much of an attraction as the food. Character doesn't always come cheap, so it pays to look to lunch menus for bargains. Budget eats lie in the pubs and student quarter in the east Altstadt.

CAFÉS AND CHEAP EATS

Café Affenbrot Kanalstr. 70 ☎0451 721 93, ⓦcafeaffenbrot.de. Part of the Werkhof warehouse complex, this bright buzzy vegetarian café with a cheerful colour scheme and a nice terrace is hugely popular for its good food at low prices; nothing costs over €10. Mon–Sat 9am–11pm, Sun 9am–10pm.

Café Remise Wahmstr. 43–45 ☎0451 777 73,

ⓦremise-luebeck.de. Chandeliers bring glamour to this courtyard café in a former factory. It's a popular choice with an older clientele for drinks as much as for breakfasts, snacks like home-made burgers (€8), pasta or thirty-day-aged Holstein steak. Mon–Sat 9am–midnight, Sun 9am–10pm.

★**Cole Street** Beckergrube 18 ☎0451 389 12 31, ⓦcolestreet.de. The antithesis of Lübeck's heritage schtick, this café-bar-cum-gallery has more than a touch of relaxed metropolitan cool to its vintage thrift-shop chic. Good breakfasts – weekend buffet breakfasts are busy – and coffee. Daily 12.30pm–late.

Frøken Wildhagen Beckergrube 90 ☎ 0451 48 91 71 63, ⓦ froeken-wildhagen.de. This Scandinavian-styled café provides a gentle start to the day, or makes an excellent coffee-stop. Expect good breakfasts, excellent coffee and home-made quiche and cakes. Tues–Sat 10am–6pm.

Niederegger Breite Str. 89 ☎ 0451 530 11 27, ⓦ niederegger.de. The more stylish and quieter outpost of the marzipan-maker is glass-walled into the Rathaus's Gothic arcades. However, we prefer the traditional oldies' favourite opposite, for *Kaffee und Kuchen* and, of course, marzipan. Mon–Fri 9am–7pm, Sat 9am–6pm, Sun 10am–6pm.

RESTAURANTS

★ **Haus der Schiffergesellschaft** Breite Str. 2 ☎ 0451 767 76, ⓦ schiffergesellschaft.com. Baltic fish – including a speciality *sole meunière* – and roast rack of lamb in rosemary sauce at the original oak-planked tables of the sixteenth-century sea-captains' guildhall; less a restaurant than a museum of Hanseatic history. Touristy but essential. Daily 10am–11pm.

Markgraf Fischergrube 18 ☎ 0451 706 03 43. Modern international cuisine such as organic veal on chantarelle mushrooms or red snapper on basil-mash potatoes with pesto in a sixteenth-century merchant's house; one room is traditional, the other reinvented into cool contemporary glamour. Tues–Sat 6pm–midnight.

Miera's Hüxstr. 57 ☎ 0451 772 12, ⓦ miera-luebeck .de. There's Italianate cooking in the restaurant above (from 6pm) but we prefer the buzzy garden bistro below which serves the likes of antipasti, beef stew or salmon with spring salad and lemongrass potatoes. Mon–Sat 10am–midnight.

Ratskeller Markt 13 ☎ 0451 720 44, ⓦ ratskeller-zu-luebeck.de. Beneath the town hall cellars and as historic as you'd hope, from the booth-style seating at the front to the smarter Hanse Saal with Hanseatic shields. Its menu is good honest German cooking: plenty of fresh fish plus sailor's mash *Labskaus* and speciality pork spare ribs with a caraway sauce. Daily 11.30am–11pm.

Roberto Rossi im Schabbelhaus Mengstr. 48–52 ☎ 0451 720 11, ⓦ schabbelhaus.de. A seventeenth-century merchant's house that rates high on the wow factor. Italian cuisine is not cheap – mains average €23, three-course menus from €46 – but dining here is about the setting as much as the cuisine. Mon–Sat noon–2.30pm & 6–11pm.

Vai Hüxstr. 42 ☎ 0451 400 80 83, ⓦ restaurant-vai.de. A flagship of modern dining in Lübeck but without the po-faced fuss of a gourmet restaurant. Expect interesting lobster with truffle mash as well as lamb or even *Schnitzel* (mains €19–28) served in the small, sleek dining room. A small rear garden opens in summer. Mon–Sat noon–10pm.

★ **Wullenwever** Beckergrube 71 ☎ 0451 70 43 33, ⓦ wullenwever.de. Dazzling Michelin-starred seasonal menus conjoured by Roy Petermann, accredited by the Jeunes Restauranteurs d'Europe. The dining room is as effortlessly elegant as you'd hope, plus there's a pretty garden for alfresco. Mains start at €30, three-course menus from €65. Pure class. Tues–Sat 7–11pm.

BARS AND INNS

Im Alten Zolln Mühlenstr. 93–95 ☎ 0451 740 45, ⓦ alter-zolln.de. A traditional German inn with panelled rooms for winter and a leafy terrace on which a middle-aged clientele people-watch (and ignore the traffic) in summer. It provides solid cooking and fresh beers. Mon–Thurs 11am–1am, Fri–Sun 11am–2am.

Kandinsky Fleischhauerstr. 89 ☎ 0451 702 05 62. A nicely knocked-about studenty bar that spills out into the cobbled street in summer. Both inside and out there's a laidback vibe, plus occasional jazz concerts. Mon–Wed & Sun 1pm–1am, Thurs–Sat 1pm–2am.

★ **StrandSalon** Media Docks, Willy-Brandt-Allee ☎ 0451 397 08 88, ⓦ strandsalon.de. A rather brilliant summer beach bar on the old docks, with all the requisites – sand between the toes, *Strandkörbe* seats, potted palms and several bars – plus a small swimming pool. It also hosts occasional gigs and clubnights at weekends. May–Sept daily noon–late.

NIGHTLIFE AND ENTERTAINMENT

Don't come to Lübeck for clubbing; notwithstanding bars, nightlife in the centre is negligible. Classical music fans are better served, with Marienkirche **organ concerts** having drawn luminaries such as J.S. Bach ever since Dietrich Buxtehude flexed his fingers (see box, p.788); check the church and tourist offices for what's on. **Listings** for all events are provided in free magazines in the Welcome Center; *Ultimo* also publishes listings online at ⓦ ultimo-luebeck.de.

CLUBS AND LIVE MUSIC

Hüx Hüxterdamm 14 ☎ 0451 766 33, ⓦ huex.de. While nothing to worry the superclubs, Lübeck's most central club pulls a regular crowd of twenties and thirties party-goers for a boozy unpretentious bop at weekends. Crowd-pleaser tunes of house classics, pop and indie and a glitterball to boot – all good fun. Fri & Sat 10pm–late.

TreibsAND Willy-Brandt-Allee 9 ☎ 0451 706 33 11, ⓦ treibsand.org. When Lübeck's heritage feels cloying, this grungy (sub)cultural centre is your place. Bookers programme a wide variety of acts at weekends but have a weakness for punk and über-noise metal. Fri & Sat 8.30pm–late.

THEATRE, OPERA AND CLASSICAL
Musik- und Kongresshalle Willy-Brandt-Allee 10 ☎0451 790 40, ⓦmuk.de. This modern canalside hall is the venue for the premier showstopper entertainments in Lübeck. The home of the Philharmonishes Orchester der Hansestadt Lübecker, it also stages touring musicals plus jazz and rock acts.
Musikhochschule Lübeck Grosse Petersgrube 17–29

☎0451 150 50, ⓦmh-luebeck.de. The premier music school in the state performs works of the classical repertoire, most works for chamber orchestra plus some opera. It's renowned for the Brahms Festival Lübeck, held over ten days in early May.
Theater Lübeck Beckergrube 16 ☎0451 708 80, ⓦtheaterluebeck.de. Lübeck's main venue for theatre, opera and dance is this Art Nouveau, three-stage venue. Expect anything from *Swan Lake* to *The Rocky Horror Picture Show* via regular classical music concerts.

14

Ratzeburg

With Travemünde ticked off, the finest day-trip from Lübeck is **RATZEBURG**, 23km south. Approach by boat in a summer heat-haze and it seems almost like a mirage: a cluster of red roofs and a green copper tower afloat in a lake. The trick is that the town is clustered on an island at the south end of the elongated Ratzeburger See. Indeed the geography inspired the town – the island's defensive possibilities caught the eye of Saxon duke Henry the Lion as he marched north to found Lübeck in the mid-1100s.

For all the cultural value of Ratzeburg's museums, the town's premier attraction is water, both in it – from a beach by the quay near the western bridge to the Altstadt – and especially on it. The **Ratzeburg See** is an acclaimed sailing centre; see the box on p.796 for details of rental companies.

The Dom
Domhof 35 • May–Sept Mon–Sat 10am–6pm; Sun noon–6pm; Oct–April Tues–Sun 10am–4pm, Sun noon–4pm • Free • ⓦ ratzeburgerdom.de

A bronze lion, copied from Henry the Lion's Braunschweig capital, stands outside his Romanesque **Dom**, located at the villagey north end of the small town; its massive tower bears the stamp of its Lübeck contemporary. The basilica's interior is bare to the point of asceticism but has a few noteworthy artworks: a thirteenth-century *Triumphkreuz*, a softly sculpted Gothic Passion altar in the chancel, and, to its left, the oldest choir stalls in North Germany (c.1200), including a chunky oak pew for the noble rears of Saxon dukes.

Kreismuseum and A. Paul-Weber-Museum
Kreismuseum Domhof 12 • Tues–Sun 10am–1pm & 2–5pm • €2, combined ticket with A. Paul-Weber-Museum €3 • ⓦ kmrz.de • A. Paul-Weber-Museum Domhof 5 • Same hours and prices • ⓦ weber-museum.de

The villagey knot of streets around the Dom affords a happy half-hour's idle. In Domhof, a former ducal summer mansion houses the **Kreismuseum**, a rather bizarre rummage through everything from local history to Fifties scooters via music boxes and militaria, all upstaged by the Rococo ballroom on the first floor. The adjacent **A. Paul-Weber-Museum** is a shrine to the twentieth-century illustrator, buried in Ratzeburg, whose first whimsical images slip into dark social commentaries and despair after he was detained by the Third Reich.

Ernst-Barlach-Museum
Barlachplatz 3 • April–Oct Tues–Sun 11am–5pm • €5 • ⓦ ernst-barlach.de

The **Ernst-Barlach-Museum**, beside the central Markt and the town church, honours the Expressionist artist behind the sculptures on Lübeck's Katherinenkirche who fell foul of

14

TRIPS ON THE RATZEBURG SEE

Sailing **dinghies** and **canoes** are available for rent from Ratzeburger Segelschule, Reeperbahn 4a (☎04541 31 18, ⓦratzeburger-segelschule.de); dinghies cost from €18/hour, canoes from €9/hour or €45/day. Schiffahrt Ratzeburger See, Schlosswiese 6 (☎04541 79 00, ⓦschiffahrt-ratzeburg.de), schedules **pleasure cruises** around the lake (€11) from April to October, departing from the quay west of the Altstadt.

FROM RATZEBURG BY BOAT

From May to October, Schiffhart Ratzeburger See (ⓦschiffahrt-ratzeburg.de) runs trips up **to Rothenhausen** (4 or 5 daily May–Oct; €8.50) at the northern tip of the Ratzeburg See, from where you can join a two-hour cruise back **to Lübeck** along the River Wakenitz with Wakenitz Schifffahrt Quandt (see p.792), a lovely trip through a channel choked with lilies. Boats to Rothenhausen depart from Schlosswiese (by the large car park beside the lake).

Hitler's purge on "degenerate art". A small museum in his boyhood home holds more of his empathic works.

ARRIVAL AND INFORMATION   RATZEBURG

By train Ratzeburg is on the Lübeck–Lüneburg line, its train station 2km west of the town centre; buses bound for the Rathaus stop outside on main road Bahnhofstrasse. Destinations Hamburg (every 30min; 40min); Kiel (every 30min; 1hr 10min).

Tourist office In the Rathaus at Unter den Linden 1 as you enter from the west (April & Oct Mon–Fri 9am–5pm; May–Sept Mon–Fri 9am–5pm, Sat & Sun 11am–4pm; Nov–March Mon–Fri 10am–4pm; ☎04541 800 08 86, ⓦratzeburg.de).

EATING AND DRINKING

Fischerstube Schlosswiese 2 ☎04541 823 37. A pretty spot by the ferry quay, with tables on the lawn beside the lake. Fish dishes are good in a no-frills way, and range from *Zander* from the lake to Baltic cod and sole in creamy mustard and dill sauces (mains €10–14). Mon–Thurs noon–3pm, Fri–Sun noon–4pm.

Köbke Reeperbahn 4a ☎04541 87 02 99. Breakfasts, light bistro plates such as chicken and rocket salad with chilli dressing and pasta in a modern café with a terrace beside the lake. Nice spot for a drink, too. It's beside the sailing school near the cathedral. Tues–Sun noon–8pm.

Eutin

As charming as its "Rosenstadt" (Town of Roses) moniker, **EUTIN** lies at the heart of the lumpy lakeland of Holstein Switzerland. It is a paean to small-town Germany: a gentle place to potter that also hints at its culture as a ducal town in the late 1700s, when it nurtured such rare talents as poet Johann Heinrich Voss, painter Johann Heinrich Wilhelm Tischbein and composer Carl Maria von Weber.

Schloss

Schlossplatz • Mid-April to Oct daily 10am–6pm • €5 • ⓦschloss-eutin.de

The princes who masterminded Eutin's transformation into a "Weimar of the North" were from the House of Schleswig-Holstein-Gottorf, and their moated **Schloss** is the town's star turn, looking better than it has in a century or so after restoration. Inside, the Baroque pile is furnished in the late Baroque, Regency and Classical styles that followed the rebuild from a late medieval progenitor; one highlight is the model ships gifted by a relative, Tsar Peter the Great.

The princes' naturalistic gardens behind are a pleasant spot to wander and host alfresco opera and musicals from July to mid-August – the **Eutiner Festspiele** (ⓦeutiner-festspiele.de) is one of Germany's most traditional classical music festivals.

14

TO KIEL BY CANOE

Aficionados hail Holstein Switzerland as **canoeing country**, and with stamina or time, you can paddle through an interconnected mosaic of lakes all the way to Kiel (see below) – the 50km trip has been done in a long day, but most people allow three or four. A booklet of the route, *Paddeln*, is available either from the tourist office or as a download from its website. Boote Keusen Sielbecker, Sielbecker Landstr. 17 (☎04521 42 01, ⓦboote-keusen.de), in the northerly suburb Eutin-Fissau, has Canadian canoes and can provide boat transport back from wherever you end up. A great trip.

Ostholstein-Museum

Schlossplatz 1 • April–Sept Tues–Fri 11am–1pm & 2–5pm, Sat & Sun 10am–5.30pm; Oct–Jan & March Wed–Fri 3–5pm, Sat & Sun 11am–1pm • €4 • ⓦoh-museum.de

The palace's former stables house the **Ostholstein-Museum**, whose modest displays on Eutin's time as regional cultural capital provide context to the castle. No surprise that the main exhibits feature the awesome threesome: portraits by Tischbein, Goethe's pal; the translations of Homer that Voss made in the spare hours from his day-job as headmaster of the town's best school; and scores by local son Weber, a pioneer of Romanticism famous for his operas.

ARRIVAL AND INFORMATION — EUTIN

By train The Bahnhof – with regular trains to Kiel (every 30min; 45–55min) and Lübeck (every 30min; 30min) – is a 5min walk west of the Altstadt via a path off Bahnhofstrasse.

Tourist office Markt 19 (Mid-May to mid-Sept Mon–Fri 9am–6pm, Sat & Sun 10am–2pm; mid-Sept to mid-May Mon–Fri 10am–1pm & 2–6pm, Sat 10am–1pm; ☎04521 709 70, ⓦholsteinischeschweiz.de/eutin).

ACCOMMODATION AND EATING

Brauhaus Eutin Markt 11 ☎04521 76 67 77, ⓦbrauhaus-eutin.de. A mainstay of everyday eating in Eutin, the town microbrewery produces three delicious beers under its St Michaelis brand, plus a range of good honest cooking, from local fish to pub classics such as Holstein *Sauerfleisch* or home-made spare ribs. Daily 11am–11pm, Jan from noon.

Das Kleine Hotel Albert-Mahlstedt-Str. 6 ☎04521 858 04 41, ⓦdaskleinehotel-eutin.de. The most pleasant stay in town is this small relaxed townhouse, with a homely

modern-country vibe: think vintage furnishings painted cream and grey, modern art, bright curtains and accent walls in rooms. **€100**

Schlossküche Schlossplatz ☎04521 70 95 50, ⓦschlosskueche-eutin.de. *Zander* with mussels cooked in vanilla and saffron or herb-crusted lamb are typical of the quality regional dishes served in the Schloss restaurant, its historic setting updated by smart Scandinavian style. Mains average €16. A nice spot for breakfast, too. Daily 11.30am–10pm.

Kiel

State capital **KIEL** feels a gritty urban sprawl in this region of coast and cows. Over ninety raids in 1945 alone unleashed such devastation on what was Germany's principal submarine base that the port at the end of a deep firth had to start from scratch when the smoke cleared. Its concrete blocks built at speed in the 1950s are not the place to look for history – when brochures flag up the first pedestrian street in Germany (Holstenstrasse in 1525), you know tourist authorities are struggling.

Though lacking the looks of Lübeck – the more obvious candidate for capital – Kiel was chosen because of the port that made its fortune. It became the imperial war-port in 1871, and when the Kiel canal (Nord-Ostsee-Kanal) opened to link the Baltic and North seas in 1895, Kiel controlled what was the biggest man-made waterway in the world. It remains the busiest, and shapes modern Kiel: workaday, unpretentious, resilient. Today, Kiel tags itself "Sailing City", a name it lives up to during international sailing regatta **Kieler Woche** in late June, a must for any sailing fan who wants to sail aboard a historic windjammer (book via tourist information, and reserve accommodation in advance). And while the town's few museums will pass a morning, Kiel is at its best around water, whether seen from the **Kiellinie footpath** or on **cruises** on the Kieler Förde (see box below).

Nikolaikirche

Arterial Holstenstrasse leads to former centre Alter Markt and the **Nikolaikirche**, a Gothic church that was modernized when rebuilt post-1945. A fourteenth-century font and the triumphal cross and altar from a century later survive, though it's a wonder anything was salvaged at all. Paradoxically the sword-wielding angel outside, *Der Geistkämpfer* (literally, "Fighter of the spirit"), by Expressionist Ernst Barlach, only made it through the war because it was condemned as "degenerate" by Third Reich arbiters of aesthetics; the regime forgot to smelt the bronze and it was later discovered buried near Lüneburg.

Kieler Schiffahrtsmuseum

Wall 65 • Mid-April to mid-Oct daily 10am–6pm; mid-Oct to mid-April Tues–Sun 10am–5pm • €3

Cut to the harbour from Alter Markt, and you reach the **Schiffahrtsmuseum** (Maritime Museum), located in a former fish hall akin to an upturned hull. There are enjoyable exhibits on the imperial navy past and in summer the ticket lets you on to historic tugs and steamers moored nearby.

Kunsthalle

Dürstenbrooker Weg 1 • Tues–Sun 10am–6pm, Wed till 8pm • €7 • ⓦ kunsthalle-kiel.de

Ten minutes north of the centre, beyond the Schlossgarten park, the **Kunsthalle** contains a surprisingly rich spread of paintings and sculpture from late German Romanticism through to Expressionism – Schleswig-Holstein resident Emil Nolde is well represented – and post-1960s art. Abundant natural light, organization by theme, a floor of antiquities including Attic vases and thoughtful temporary exhibitions add to the appeal.

Along the harbour promenade

The **Kiellinie footpath** threads off the busy dual-carriageway opposite the Kunsthalle as a broad promenade along the harbour; with its views of ships, sailing-school dinghies – every Kiel schoolchild receives free sailing lessons – and the docks opposite, this is Kiel at its best. There's a child-centred **aquarium** of Baltic and tropical fish at Dürstenbrooker Weg 20 (daily April–Sept 9am–6pm; Oct–March 9am–5pm; €3;

KIEL FERRIES AND CRUISES

Ferries of the SFK line (ⓦ sfk-kiel.de) ply the **Kieler Förde** harbour, shuttling between quays at Bahnhofsbrücke opposite the bus station and Laboe 18km east (€2.40 one-way, €8 day-pass) – useful disembarkation points are at Seegartenbrücke by the Schiffahrtsmuseum and Reventloubrücke at the northern end of the town centre. SFK also run **cruises** on the Kieler Förde (May–Oct Sat–Thurs 3 daily; 2hr; €13).

Arguably the best boat trip is that along the **Kiel canal**. Adler Schiffe sails on return day-trips to Rendsburg, 40km west of Kiel, aboard the *Adler Princess* (May–Oct 1 or 2 weekly; 4hr; from €37.40, including lunch; ⓦ adler-schiffe.de), and runs less frequent return-trips aboard the 1905-vintage paddle-steamer *Freya* soundtracked by a jazz band (April–Dec; 4hr; €53.40); go online for timetables.

ⓦaquarium-kiel.de), run by the university sea-science division. Most people, however, are content with the pool of **seals** beside the Kiellinie; feeding times are 10am and 2.30pm daily (except Fri). **Ferries** from the Reventloubrücke quay 300m or so beyond ply a return back to the centre (€3 one-way).

Schleswig-Holsteinisches Freilichtmuseum

Hamburger Landstr. 97, Molfsee • April–Oct daily 9am–6pm; Nov–March Sun 11am–4pm in good weather only • €7 • ☎ 0431 65 96 60, ⓦ freilichtmuseum-sh.de • Bus #500 or #504

Rather lost 6km southwest of the centre in Molfsee, the open-air **Schleswig-Holsteinisches Freilichtmuseum** contains around seventy traditional buildings plucked from the Land and gathered in miniature villages. It's as good a place as any for an overview of regional quirks; farmhouses retain original cottage furniture – notably the cabin-like beds in which whole families slept to ward off winter cold – and craftsmen demonstrate cottage industries such as pottery and basket-weaving in summer. Livestock adds to the bucolic charm.

The Kiel canal

The world's busiest man-made shipping channel, the **Kiel canal** (Nord-Ostsee-Kanal; ⓦkiel-canal.org) stretches for almost 200km from Holtenau, 2km north of Kiel, west to Brunsbüttel on the North Sea. Boat trips operate along the canal (see box opposite), but perhaps the easier way to sample the waterway is to visit the massive **locks** (*Schleusen*) at Holtenau – perhaps the most interesting part of the canal from an engineering perspective. Take bus #11 to the terminus at Wik. There's a viewing platform at the south side (daylight hours; €1), or you can take a free ferry to the north bank.

Laboe

Laboe at the mouth of the firth 18km from Kiel has few pretensions to be anything other than a minor beach resort and a yachting centre. Yet the fact that it can be accessed by SFK ferry from the city centre provides a decent day-trip: a chance to spread a towel on a suprisingly fine beach with a couple of nautical sights at hand.

Deutscher Marine-Ehrenmal and U995

Strandstr. 92 • Daily: April–Oct 9.30am–6pm; Nov–March 9.30am–4pm • Deutscher Marine-Herenmal €5.50, *U995* €4, combined ticket €8.50 • SFK ferry, or bus #100 or #120 from Kiel

The surprise behind the sands is the **Deutscher Marine-Ehrenmal**, which honours sailors (of all nationalities) who perished in both world wars. Architect Gustav August Munzer said his 72m-high brick tower, completed in the 1930s, was nonrepresentational, but it nevertheless resembles a vast ship's rudder-stock. Actually, the building is more impressive than the exhibits: beyond a sunken memorial hall are displays of navigation and a viewing platform. The site's technical museum is the **submarine** beached in front. The Hamburg-built **U995** is the world's last Type VIIC, the workhorse of the war that was immortalized in classic film *Das Boot*. It's just as claustrophobic within.

ARRIVAL AND DEPARTURE	KIEL

By train The Hauptbahnhof and bus station are adjacent at the southern end of the central shopping streets that stretch behind the harbour.

Destinations Eutin (hourly; 45min); Husum (hourly; 1hr 20min); Lübeck (hourly; 1hr 15min); Schleswig (hourly; 50min).

Tourist office A block north of the Hauptbahnhof at Andreas-Gayk-Str. 31 (Mon–Fri 9am–6pm, Sat 10am–2pm; ☎ 0431 67 91 00, ⓦ kiel-sailing-city.de); a bureau also operates at the train station (daily 8am–8pm). It provides maps and the information booklet *KursKiel*, and can book accommodation.

14

ACCOMMODATION

Atlantic Raiffeisenstr. 2 ☎0431 37 49 90, ⓦatlantic-hotels.de/kiel. A large 4-star business hotel with modest design leanings in modern rooms that have all the usual facilities. The real winner is the location on the harbour – lounge bar *Deck 8* has a great outdoor terrace. €179

Berliner Hof Ringstr. 6 ☎0431 663 40, ⓦberlinerhof-kiel.de. The best mid-range option in the centre is this old station hotel that has had a modest refurbishment: Komfort Plus rooms are bright and cheerful, with laminate floors and pops of colour from linen; Komfort rooms are older, with bland though acceptable business style. €105

Comfort Hotel Langer Segen. ☎0431 57 97 50, ⓦhotel-tomkyle.de. Good-value and well-maintained franchise of the Comfort chain on a sidestreet north of the centre. Its 37 rooms have been recently refurbished to offer rather plush business decor. €122

DJH Kiel Johannesstr. 1 ☎0431 73 14 88, ⓦjugendherberge.de. One of the largest youth hostels in the state benefits not just from efficient management and modern decor but an excellent location near the east bank of the harbour. Dorms €20.80, doubles €61.60

★**Romantik Kieler Kaufmann** Niemannsweg 102 ☎0431 881 10, ⓦkieler-kaufmann.de. Kiel's finest address north of the centre marries the old-world romance of its late 1800s garden villa to understated luxury in the rooms. Names in the guestbook include assorted European royals and politicians, including Chancellor Angela Merkel. Good restaurant, too. Breakfast extra. €147

EATING AND DRINKING

Der Bauch von Kiel Legienstr. 16 ☎0431 512 15, ⓦwww.derbauchvonkiel.de. A stylish brasserie that's a great choice, with the likes of duck in a herb sauce, pasta or home-made salmon and rocket quiche (mains €9–23) on a modern German menu. It's behind the Kleiner Kiel lake west of the centre. Mon–Fri 11.30am–late, Sat & Sun 6pm–late.

Louf Reventloualle 2 ☎0431 55 11 78, ⓦlouf.de/index.html. Whether as a restaurant or café-bar, this is one of the nicest spots in Kiel in summer, when deckchairs bring a beach vibe to a terrace with unobstructed harbour views. Menu-wise it's international and snacks. March–Sept daily 10am–midnight; Oct–Feb Mon–Sat 11.30am–11pm, Sun 10am–11pm.

Lüneburg-Haus Danische Str. 22 ☎0431 982 60 00, ⓦluneburghaus.com. A menu of affordable regional dishes such as Holstein *Sauerfleisch* (mains circa €13) offsets a more expensive continental menu (circa €24) while decor is stylish French bistro. A good choice in the pedestrian centre. Mon–Sat noon–3pm & 6–10pm.

Weinstein Holtenauer Str. 200 ☎0431 55 55 77, ⓦweinstein-kiel.com. The city's fine-dining address is a smart *Vinothek* 1km north of the centre – worth the effort for the few daily dishes of modern German cuisine beautifully presented. Mains average €21. Mon–Fri 11.30am–late, Sat & Sun 6pm–late.

Schleswig

SCHLESWIG should be one of the region's premier tourist destinations. That it is not is one more reason to make the journey. One of the most distinctive small towns in the state, it dozes on the banks of the broad Schlei fjord as a provincial backwater of around 25,000 people. Yet until the tenth century, Haithabu on the south bank of the Schlei was a hub of the Viking world. Founded in 800 AD, the "colony of the west" flourished at the crossroads of trade routes to North Atlantic and Baltic settlements, populated by a cosmopolitan cross-section of Europe and serving as a base for Christian missionaries to Scandinavia. Indeed, it is only due to its destruction in 1066 that Schleswig emerged opposite, roots that the town celebrates with rollicking **Wikingertage** (Viking Days; ⓦwikingertage.de) at the end of July/early August. With a bit of poetic licence there remains something of the Scandinavian about the **Altstadt**, a sleepy knot of cobbled lanes gathered on the fjord's northern shore, where red-brick fishermen's houses exude village charm. That Schleswig's holy trinity of must-see sights – **cathedral**, **palace** and the **Viking past** – is spread over a wide area only serves to underline that it is a town best savoured slowly. Make a day of it – perhaps two.

St-Petri-Dom

Norderdomstr. 4 · Mon–Sat 9am–5pm, Sun noon–5pm · Free

Only the **St-Petri-Dom**, its spire visible for miles, suggests Schleswig was ever anything other than the village on the Schlei it appears today. A modern-looking exterior – notably that eighteenth-century spire – belie a cathedral born as a twelfth-century basilica. Powerful Romanesque arches at the crossing spoke so eloquently of strength and permanence that they were moulded into the fabric of the later Gothic structure. They also retain medieval frescoes.

The artistic highlight, however, is the **Bordesholm high altar**. It took Hans Brüggemann seven years to create this audacious masterpiece from 1521, its cobweb-fine carving as detailed as the prints of Germany's Renaissance superhero Albrecht Dürer on which it seems based. Nearly four hundred individual figures fill its crowd scenes – a narrative of the Passion, Descent and Resurrection – each carved from the single oak block that produced its filigree canopy. The predella beneath is no less audacious. It's worth visiting in the morning when sunlight from a side window creates a play of light and shadow within the carvings. Brüggemann also carved the oversized St Christopher by the main portal, adjacent to a richly polychromed Magi (c.1300).

Holm

A sign of a fisherman announces **Holm**, one-time fishing village that stood on an islet until 1933; "holm" is an old Norse word for island. Although only a handful of fishermen continue to eke out a living from the Schlei and the "village" has merged into the Altstadt, the area retains a distinct atmosphere, notably at its core ringed by cute houses. Many have *Klöndören*, literally "natter doors", which divide horizontally to facilitate local gossip. In an area free of tourist tat, visitors are directed to the **Holm Museum** (daily 10am–6pm; free; ☏04621 93 68 20) by the fisherman sign, with photo exhibitions of village life. The waterfront beneath is as picturesque – all rickety pontoons and small boats whose swooping lines are not too far removed from the Viking craft of old.

Schloss Gottorf

April–Oct Mon–Fri 10am–5pm, Sat & Sun 10am–6pm; Nov–March Tues–Fri 10am–4pm, Sat & Sun 10am–5pm • €9 • ⓦ schloss-gottorf.de

When the bombs rained on Kiel in 1945, collections rich enough to warrant a trip in their own right went to Schleswig's ducal palace 2km west of the Altstadt. **Schloss Gottorf** is a magnificent setting for not just the finest museum in Schleswig-Holstein but one of the best all-rounders in northern Germany, not least because the palace is an impressive piece of sober North European Renaissance. The palace and outbuildings house large collections that tick most boxes – put aside at least half a day to see it quickly, or a full day should you break for lunch at the museum's restaurant.

Landemuseum für Kunst und Kulturgeschichte

The core of the **Landemuseum für Kunst und Kulturgeschichte** are the historic art, culture and archeology collections. They begin in the long hall of the palace's Gothic progenitor with medieval religious art: a retable by Hans Brüggemann of St-Petri-Dom fame and, in a following room, oils by Cranach the Elder – a celebrated *Fall of Man* and the darkly erotic *Lucretia*. Beyond Flemish art and Baroque furnishings upstairs is a reassembled Lübeck wine tavern from 1660 whose wooden panels are carved with images of Bacchus and boozy merriment such as a couple in bed surrounded by beaming cherubs. It also introduces a suite of restored palace rooms: the richly stuccoed Blauer Saal; the Schlosskapelle, a Renaissance gem lorded over by a ducal box hidden somewhere beneath frothy decoration; and the contemporary Hirschsaal festive hall named for its life-size stucco deer.

Elsewhere on the second floor are first-class Jugendstil decorative arts and folk art. Don't miss, too, imaginatively presented exhibits of the state museum of archeology on the third floor. Crowds gravitate towards the ghoulish bog corpses (*Moorleichen*) that are thought to be around two thousand years old, but whose expressions are far too lifelike for comfort – the jury is out over whether the deceased, one blindfolded, were sacrificed, executed or died peacefully.

Nydamhalle

Schloss Gottorf's most celebrated treasure is the **Nydam-Boat**, a thirty-man Viking longship c.350 AD housed in the **Nydamhalle** to the left of the palace. Why the slender 23m oak vessel ended up in its eponymous Danish bog is a subject of conjecture, although a plausible theory proposes it was intended as a sacrifice. Around two thousand contemporary artefacts are displayed with the ship, from weapons and clothing to Roman-Germanic gold jewellery.

Kutschensammlung, Kreuzstall and Galerie der Klassichen Moderne

The **Kutschensammlung** behind the Nydamhalle houses ducal coaches, while buildings on the other side of the palace fast-forward into the twentieth-century arts: regional artists plus crafts and design in the cross-shaped **Kreuzstall**, and a good spread of German Modernists in the **Galerie der Klassichen Moderne**. Highlights include the smudgy colour washes of Emil Nolde's landscapes, waggish lithographs by Beckmann, the work of Die Brücke artists (and a display of the African masks that inspired them), and characteristically empathetic works by Ernst Barlach (see box, p.851) and Käthe Kollwitz.

The Baroque Gardens and Gottorf Globe

April–Oct 10am–6pm • Gardens €2 or free with Schloss ticket, gardens & Globushaus €7

Behind Schloss Gottorf itself is the ducal **Baroque Garden** (Barockgarten), replanted as planned in the seventeenth century as the first terraced garden north of the Alps. The garden's geometric designs were intended as a paean to the Age of Reason and its scientific diversion was the **Gottorf Globe**. A keen academic, Duke Friedrich III commissioned a 3m globe to depict the world without and the heavens within. Court mathematician Adam Olearius completed his task in 1650; guests sat in candle-light as the stars span within, and Europe marvelled at this "astronomical wonder" – so much so that it was swiped by the Russians during the Great Northern War and presented to Tsar Peter the Great in 1713. With the original still in Russia, a near-replica stands in the small white building at the garden's south end, the Globushaus. Having surveyed the surface of the known world circa 1650, visitors cram inside to see the rotating night sky as understood by Renaissance scholars.

Wikinger Museum

Am Haddebyer Noor 5, Busdorf • Museum & replica dwellings April–Oct daily 9am–5pm; museum only Nov–March Tues–Sun 10am–4pm • €7 • ⓦ haithabu.de • Bus #4810 towards Kiel, alight at Haddeby; or take a ferry from Schleswig Stadthafen (Tues–Sun 5 daily; €3.50; ⓦ hein-haddeby.de)

Haithabu, the Viking settlement, lay directly opposite modern Schleswig on the south bank of the Schlei. Haphazard archeological excavations of the area gained momentum with the discovery of a Viking longship in 1980 – the impetus for the **Wikinger Museum** (Viking Museum). The ship – which is less complete than the one in Schloss Gottorf, but grafted onto a replica – occupies one of a series of buildings. Others house archeological finds that reveal the sophisticated domestic culture usually omitted in tales of rape and pillage. More fun are the **replica Viking dwellings** built within the original village earthwork beyond. The effect is a sort of miniature Viking open-air museum, where raised boardwalks lead around a settlement of workshops and homesteads gathered around a civic longhouse. In summer craftsmen don doublet and hose for demonstrations of trades practised in what was one of the largest crafts centres in northern Europe.

ARRIVAL AND INFORMATION

By train The train station is 3km southwest of the centre and 1km south of Schloss Gottorf – local buses #1 and #2 pass the latter en route to the centre.

Destinations Flensburg (every 45min; 30min); Hamburg (hourly; 1hr 40min); Husum (hourly; 30min).

By bus Inter-town buses drop you at the junction of Königstrasse and Plesenstrasse.

Destinations Kiel (every 2hr; 1hr 30min).

Tourist office At Plesenstrasse 7, near the west end of

SCHLESWIG

St-Petri-Dom (April, May & Oct Mon–Fri 10am–4pm, Sat 10am–2pm; June–Aug Mon–Fri 10am–6pm, Sat & Sun 10am–4pm; Sept Mon–Fri 10am–4pm, Sat & Sun 10am–2pm; Nov–March Mon–Fri 10am–4pm; ☎ 04621 85 00 56 57, ⓦ schleswig.de).

Bike rental Bike (and rollerblade) rental is available in the Altstadt at Knud-Laward-Str. 30 from Fahrradverleih Röhling (☎ 04621 99 30 30, ⓦ fahrradverleih-schleswig .de).

14

ACCOMMODATION

Bed & Breakfast am Dom Töpferstr. 9 ☎ 04621 48 59 91, ⓦ bb-schleswig.de. A two-hundred-year-old townhouse near the harbour with eight cottage-style en-suite rooms. Floral fabrics, antiques and wooden floorboards warm up a palette of cool Nordic greys and creams. **€90**

Campingplatz Haithabu Haddebyer Chaussee 15 ☎ 04621 324 50, ⓦ campingplatz-haithabu.de; bus #4810 or ferry from Stadthafen. The town campsite is on the south bank of the Schlei, at Haddeby, near the Viking Museum. Also offer a mobile home that sleeps four. Pitch **€9**, mobile home **€30**, both plus **€4** per person

DJH Schleswig Spielkoppel 1 ☎ 04621 238 93, ⓦ nordmark.jugendherberge.de. The town's youth hostel is in a modern block 1km northwest of Schloss Gottorf and

2km west of the Altstadt. Be warned: it's often overrun with school groups. Closed Dec–early Feb. Dorms **€40**

★ Hahn Lutherstr. 8 ☎ 04621 99 53 52, ⓦ hotelhahn .de. This small *hotel garni* north of the centre offers an elegant stay. Created from a nineteenth-century house, it is beautifully decorated – shades of French grey, taupe and cream, plus elegant design furnishing – and owners could not be more helpful. Superior rooms are worth the extra €20 for a splurge. **€109**

Schleiblick Hafengang 4 ☎ 04621 234 68, ⓦ hotel-schleiblick.de. A former fisherman's house by the harbour, this restaurant also provides water views from its top-floor rooms. Think personality over cutting-edge style in small but sweet pension-style rooms with a mixture of modern and vintage furnishings. **€80**

EATING AND DRINKING

Luzifer Königstr. 27 ☎ 04621 292 06, ⓦ luzifer-sylt.de. Serving no-nonsense pub-grub as a chain restaurant, this is also Schleswig's brewery, celebrated for its eponymous brew, "the divine beer of Vikings" apparently. Choose between the main hall and beer garden and order a large one because service can be slow when busy. Daily 9am–midnight.

Senator-Kroog Rathausmarkt 9–10 ☎ 04621 222 60, ⓦ senatorkroog.de. A *Gaststätte* near the Dom that's been going strong since 1884, with a warren of historic rooms

decorated in a Nordic palette of pale blue, grey and cream. Fish specials are bolstered by a decent selection of meat plates, all in hearty quantities. Tues–Sun 10am–midnight.

Zur Schleimöwe Süderholmstr. 8 ☎ 04621 243 09, ⓦ schleimoewe.de. Fish speciality *Gaststätte* in Holm – all the usuals plus seasonal local specials such as Schlei eel in dill sauce or a home-made *Rötes Grütze* berry dessert at good prices – in a traditional cottage setting. Daily 11.30am–2pm & 5–10pm.

Flensburg

Though just 30km north of Schleswig, the commercial port of **FLENSBURG** is centuries apart in atmosphere. Pressed hard against the border of former owner Denmark, the self-described "southernmost town of Scandinavia" is shaped by the deep-water port through which it has prospered, first as property of the Danish Crown – for centuries Flensburg outranked Copenhagen – then the German; it was claimed by Prussia in 1864, then threw in its lot officially in a plebiscite in 1920. Labels of cult local brew *Flensburger Pilsner*, with their royal Danish lions and merchant ship, sum up the history as succinctly as any icon. The trading past is also evident in the historic warehouse courtyards that burrow behind street-fronts. Notwithstanding these pockets, Flensburg has few airs or graces. Although starting to take tourism more seriously, it remains a typical small port: knockabout and straightforward. Everything of interest in Flensburg is in the **Altstadt** on the west bank of the Flensburger Förde harbour.

Museumsberg

Museumsberg 1 • April–Oct Tues, Wed & Fri–Sun 10am–5pm, Thurs 10am–8pm; Nov–March Thurs 10am–8pm only • €6, combined ticket with Schiffahrtsmuseum (see opposite) €8 • ⓦ museumsberg.flensburg.de

14

The town's repository of culture is spread over two houses above the tourist office and pedestrianized centre.

Heinrich-Sauermann-Haus

A local furniture tycoon, Heinrich Sauermann, scoured North Friesland to bring together the collection of farmhouse rooms reassembled in **Heinrich-Sauermann-Haus**. Despite their modest size and cabin-like bed alcoves, carved panels and Dutch-style Delft tiles reveal the former owners as wealthy families. Elsewhere there are displays of folk crafts and religious art, notably the Hütten altar (1517) whose predella depicts a yarn about the massacre of chaste English princess Ursula and companions for spurning the advances of a heathen king at Cologne.

Hans-Christian-Haus

In 1884 Sauermann hired an apprentice furniture-maker named Emil Nolde, and it's the mystical Expressionist painter he became who stars in a gallery of North Friesland painting in **Hans-Christian-Haus**, notably his sea sickness-induced recollection of a journey to the island of Anholt, *High Waves*. The gallery also includes landscapes and portraits by its eponymous leader of an artists' colony at nearby Eckendorfe, and Das Pariser Zimmer, a parlour presented to the 1900 World Exhibition in Paris as the pinnacle of German Revival style.

Merchants' courtyards

The town high street is pleasant enough, though pedestrian in both senses, worth a visit largely for the merchants' courtyards (**Kaufmannshöfe**) in side-alleys. The tourist board provides maps of the town's distinctive complexes, originally arranged around an elongated courtyard as harbourside warehousing or workshops. The oldest and most photogenic is **Kruse Hof**, a touristy but pretty medieval timewarp where craftshops are shoehorned beneath a beamed gallery. It's one of several along Rote Strasse, just uphill from the tourist office. Elsewhere, **Westindienspeicher** (West Indian Warehouse) at Grosse Str. 24 off the main pedestrian thoroughfare is more representative of the supply chain that shuffled imports uphill from the harbour to warehouses, then to the high street above. Courtyards at Holm 19, between Südermarkt and Grosse Strasse, and

---

RUMSTADT FLENSBURG

During the eighteenth century under Danish rule, Flensburg flourished as a **rum trader** founded on raw spirit imported from the Danish West Indies (now the US Virgin Islands). In a spirit-soused 1700s heyday that earned Flensburg the nickname "Rumstadt", up to two hundred distilleries refined a raw West Indies rum known as "Killdevil", then exported it to merchant sailors and whalers.

The last rum merchant to produce its own-brand rum is **Alt Johannsen**, off Nordermarkt on the pedestrian high street (Marienstr. 6; Mon–Fri 10am–6pm, Sat 10am–3pm; free; ⓦ johannsen-rum.de) – you can see the historic courtyard distillery and buy spirits in a shop. **Braasch**, one of the last specialist importers and blenders of Jamaican rums, has opened a small **museum** about the historic rum trade behind its own outlet at Rote Str. 26–27 (Mon–Fri 10am–6pm, Sat & Sun 10am–3pm; free; ⓦ braasch.sh).

half-timbered Norderstr. 22, known as **Künstlerhof** because of its artists' studios, are also attractive, and **Oluf-Samson-Gange** off Norderstrasse now seems far too lovely to have been a street of sailors and brothels.

Schiffahrtsmuseum

Schiffbrücke 39 • Tues–Sun: April–Oct 10am–5pm; Nov–March 10am–4pm • €6, combined ticket with Museumsberg (see opposite) €8 • Ⓦ schiffahrtsmuseum.flensburg.de

Rum receives a section alongside port history and trade in the **Schiffahrtsmuseum** (Maritime Museum) on the port. A small fleet of privately owned historic craft are moored opposite, and you can nose around whatever wooden craft is mid-build in a workshop nearby.

ARRIVAL AND INFORMATION

By train The Hauptbahnhof is a 15min walk south of the centre.
Destinations Hamburg (every 2hr; 2hr); Kiel (hourly; 1hr 15min); Schleswig (hourly; 30min).
By bus The bus station is at the south end of the harbour.
Destinations Husum (approx every 3hr; 1hr 10min).

FLENSBURG

Tourist office Rote Str. 15–17 (Mon–Fri 9am–6pm, Sat 10am–2pm; ☎ 0461 909 09 20, Ⓦ flensburg-tourismus .de). The office offers bike rental and also books private rooms (circa €50), one of the town's cheapest accommodation options.

ACCOMMODATION

Arcadia Norderhofenden 6–9 ☎ 0461 841 10, Ⓦ arcadia-hotel.de. The town's central business hotel is brisk and efficient, if rather lacking in character. No faulting the excellent location at the corner of the harbour, however. **€122**
Hostel Flensburg Zur Exe 23 ☎ 0461 90 90 833, Ⓦ hostel-flensburg.de; buses #1 or #5 to "Südermarkt", then #11 to "Mathildenstr". IKEA furniture rules in the en-suite rooms of this bright independent hostel 1km south of the centre; if driving from the centre, it's on the road towards Niebüll. Dorms **€20**, doubles **€60**
Ibis Budget Süderhofenden 14 ☎ 0461 48 08 920,

Ⓦ accorhotels.com. The usual functional accommodation of the budget hotel chain; tiny rooms but a decent no-frills option in the centre that's handily located beside the bus station. Dynamic pricing means rates vary – an electronic display in the window shows the day's price. **€65**
Strandhotel Glücksburg Kirstenstr. 6, Glücksburg ☎ 04631 614 10, Ⓦ strandhotel-gluecksburg.de. Thomas Mann took his holiday in 1919 at this stylish small spa-hotel behind a silver beach at the mouth of Flensburg's fjord. Today it offers individually decorated rooms finished in romantic Scandinavian style. Two-night minimum at weekends. **€229**

EATING AND DRINKING

Hansens Brauerei Schiffbrücke 16 ☎ 0461 222 10. Popular brewery tavern inn on the harbourfront that serves a delicious *Schwarz*, *Pils* and one seasonal brew. It also prepares passable but unexciting German cooking. Daily 11.30am–11.30pm, Fri & Sat 11.30am–2am, Sun 11.30am–midnight.
Porterhouse im Gnomenkeller Holm 3 ☎ 0461 221 16, Ⓦ gnomenkeller.de. As the name suggests, steak is the choice here, available in a variety of cuts, grill styles

and sauces. Add in the historic cellar setting and it is clear why this is one of the town's most popular choices. Mon–Thurs 11.30am–10pm, Fri & Sat 11.30am–11pm.
Die Weinstube im Krusehof Rote Str. 24 ☎ 0461 128 76. A historic bar at the end of Flensburg's oldest merchant's courtyard, this charming nook provides wines and a range of tasty *Flammkuchen* alongside old-world charm by the barrelful. Mon–Sat 10am–11pm.

Husum and around

Long tradition obliges that **HUSUM** is described as "the grey town by the sea", which seems unfair for a North Sea harbour whose facades are a rainbow of pastel yellow, green, blue and terracotta. Paradoxically its local hero is to blame. Nineteenth-century author and Husum resident Theodor Storm coined the tagline with *Die graue Stadt am Meer*, an affectionate poem that describes the spring and autumn pea-soupers that blow

14

off the North Sea to enshroud the town in grey fog. Yet the town's inner harbour is all about local colour. Houses painted in a palette of bright colours jostle for space behind fishing boats moored in the heart of the town as they have been since medieval days, when Husum was used by the Dutch as a short cut between the North and Baltic seas.

Schiffahrtsmuseum Nordfriesland

Zingel 15 • Daily 10am–5pm • €5 • ⓦ schiffahrtsmuseum-nf.de

While the harbour has maritime charm, the serious stuff is in the **Schiffahrtsmuseum Nordfriesland** at the back of the port. It serves as an introduction to the region's fishing and former whaling industries, its prize possession a sixteenth-century trading ship that was rescued from the harbour's mud in 1994.

Theodor-Storm-Haus

Wasserreihe 31 • April–Oct Tues–Fri 10am–5pm, Sat 11am–5pm, Sun & Mon 2–5pm; Nov–March Tues, Thurs & Sat 2–5pm • €3.50 • ⓦ storm-gesellschaft.de

Writer Theodor Storm's residence, **Theodor-Storm-Haus**, is on a side street off the harbour's rear left-hand corner. Exhibits on an author who is barely known outside of his homeland leave most foreigners nonplussed, but the house is mildly diverting as a document of upper-middle-class lifestyles in the late 1800s.

Schloss vor Husum

König-Friedrich V-Allee • March–Oct Tues–Sun 11am–5pm; Nov–Feb Sat & Sun 11am–5pm • €3.50 (gardens free) • ⓦ museumsverbund-nordfriesland.de

Schlossgang slips off Grosse Strasse a block behind the harbour to reach **Schloss vor Husum**, a Dutch Renaissance pile set in a park. Magnificent fireplaces hint at the former splendour of a now spartan interior; carved from wardrobe-sized pieces of alabaster, their reliefs are like miniature antique friezes, the mortal agonies of the damned depicted in vivid detail on that of the Rittersaal. Your ticket buys you into the **modern art exhibitions** (March–Oct) which occupy some of the rooms' interiors and the Dachgalerie in the attic.

ARRIVAL AND INFORMATION HUSUM

By train Husum Bahnhof is on the Hamburg rail line and located south of the centre, reached via Herzog-Adolf-Strasse.

Destinations Friedrichstadt (hourly; 10min); Hamburg (hourly; 1hr 40min–2hr); Niebüll (approx every 30min; 30min); Schleswig (hourly; 30min).

NORTH SEA HALLIGEN

For a hit of maritime air, take a cruise on the **Wattenmeer sea**, a World Heritage-listed maritime national park between the mainland and North Frisian islands. Most tours visit the **Halligen**: glorified sandbanks just 1–2m elevation above the high-water mark. Small wonder villages on the largest island, **Pellworm**, are ringed by defences like prehistoric earthworks.

FERRIES AND CRUISES

Ferry operator NPDG (☎04844 753, ⓦfaehre-pellworm.de; €11 return) operates five or six ferries a day to Pellworm from Nordstrand harbour 15km northwest of Husum. Departures are coordinated with the timetable of bus lines #1047 and #1091 from Husum (a combined bus-and-ferry ticket costs €21 return); tourist information in Husum has ferry timetables.

Alternatively, from mid-April to October, Adler Schiffe (☎01805 12 33 44, ⓦadler-schiffe.de; from €22) visits Pellworm and **Hallig Hooge**, the so-called King of the Halligen due to its huge size, on tourist cruises which also visit seal sandflats. Cruises usually run daily; book in advance via Husum tourist information.

Tourist office In the Altes Rathaus at Grossestr. 27 (Mon–Fri 9am–6pm, Nov–March till 5pm, Sat 10am–4pm; ☎ 04841 898 70, ⓦ husum-tourismus.de).

Wattenmeer national park office NationalparkHaus Hafen Husum, beside the harbour at Hafenstr. 3 (March–Oct Mon–Sat 10am–6pm, Sun 1–5pm; Nov–Feb Mon–Sat 10am–5pm, Sun 1–5pm; ☎ 04841 66 85 30, ⓦ nationalparkhaus-husum.de), has information on (and displays of ecology in) the Wattenmeer national park.

ACCOMMODATION AND EATING

Altes Gymnasium Süderstr. 2–10 ☎ 04841 83 30, ⓦ altes-gymnasium.de. The town's upmarket address is this five-star number near the Schloss in a nineteenth-century school. Decor in rooms is all traditional elegance and there are good spa facilities. **€179**

Dragseth's Gasthof Zingel 11 ☎ 04841 77 99 95, ⓦ dragseths-gasthof.de. Husum's oldest inn is a late sixteenth-century place at the harbour's back, with cabin-like rooms and a courtyard garden. The local delicacy on a well-priced menu is *Husumer Krabben* (Husum shrimp), sprinkled liberally on fish and blended into a creamy soup. Daily 11am–2pm & 5pm–late.

Husum Camping Dockkoog 17 ☎ 04841 619 11, ⓦ husum-camping.de. Rather spartan in style, yet its location – not far from a beach at the rivermouth – turns the town campsite into a holiday destination in high season. It's located 2km west of the harbour. Pitch **€6**, plus **€6** per person

Osterkrug Osterende 52–58 ☎ 04841 661 20, ⓦ osterkrug.de. Pleasant mid-range hotel and restaurant with modest designer leanings, all within easy walking distance of the town centre. Komfort-class rooms, refurbished in modest designer style, are worth the extra €5 over simpler Standards. **€130**

Friedrichstadt

The lazy day-trip par excellence from Husum is to the small town of **FRIEDRICHSTADT** at the confluence of the Treene and Eider rivers. Divided by a canal with a picture-postcard charm that Husum can only dream of, its grid of streets was created by Dutch religious refugees who were sheltered by Schleswig-Holstein-Gottorf duke Friedrich I in 1621. Given trade privileges, the merchants created the picturesque Dutch step-gabled houses on the Markt, most with the ornamental marks that identified owners before the town got round to numbers – a water lily, starry sky or windmill, for example. **Paludanushaus** off the Markt at Prinzenstr. 28 is the grandest residence in town; others are identified in a free leaflet stocked by the tourist office (see below). Walk left from the Markt along the canal and the **Alte Münze** (Old Mint: Tues–Sun: April, May & Oct noon–4pm; June–Sept 11am–5pm; €3) provides context as a municipal history museum. Across the canal, at the town's tip, you can hire **boats** to potter on the canals.

ARRIVAL AND INFORMATION   FRIEDRICHSTADT

By train Friedrichstadt is a stop south of Husum on a branch line, connected by hourly trains (10min).

Tourist office On the Markt (Mon, Tues, Thurs & Fri 10am–5pm, Wed & Sun 10am–2pm, Sat 11am–4pm; ☎ 04881 939 30, ⓦ friedrichstadt.de).

EATING

Holländische Stube Am Mittelburgwall 24–26 ☎ 04881 939 00, ⓦ hollaendischestube.de. The house special on a menu that includes North Sea fish is lamb grazed on the surrounding salt marshes; snacks like waffles and coffee are also available between 2pm and 5.30pm. Historic rooms and a terrace beside the canal add to the appeal. Mon–Sat 11am–10pm, Sun 5.30–9pm.

North Frisian islands

Scattered in the North Sea 6km off Schleswig-Holstein are the **North Frisian islands**. For centuries the islands' storm-battered villages eked out a living from farming and fishing, their thatched houses hunkered down behind sand dunes in defence against waves that occasionally washed away whole communities. Tourism replaced

14

agriculture as the premier source of income decades ago, yet even on Sylt the scenery is overwhelmingly bucolic-seaside. There are the same dune seas of marram grass and vast skies – blue and brooding by turns – that captivated artists in the early 1900s; there are the same thatched villages, even if many house boutiques and restaurants rather than fisherfolk; and there are the same colonies of sea birds and seals in the coastal **Nationalpark Schleswig-Holsteinisches Wattenmeer** (literally "shallow sea"), added to UNESCO's World Heritage list in 2009. This may be Germany's coastal playground, but it is more Martha's Vineyard than St Tropez – perhaps the reason why **Sylt**, the most popular and developed of the islands, stood in for Martha's Vineyard in Roman Polanski's 2010 film *The Ghost*. Sylt is centred on main resort **Westerland** and glossy village-resorts **Kampen** and **Keitum**. Sister islands **Föhr** and especially **Amrum** are rural retreats of homespun charm with little to do except stroll or cycle – not just good options to get around but sometimes your only ones.

Just bear in mind the **weather**. The islands are on the same latitude as Newcastle in northeast England or the southern tip of Alaska. Statistics tell their own story of changeable conditions as weather fronts barrel across the North Sea: although only fifteen days a year are free of prevailing westerly winds that can blow gale-force even in summer, the islands bask in 1750 hours of sunshine a year.

Sylt

New Yorkers weekend in the Hamptons. North Germans escape to **SYLT**. They've come en masse since the nation went crazy for seawater bathing in the mid-1800s, and today around 600,000 people a year swell a year-round population of 23,000, though thankfully only 50,000 at a time. In recent decades Sylt has carefully cultivated its reputation as a playground of the moneyed elite. Minor celebrities for decades have been caught in flagrante delicto here by the paparazzi, adding to the prestige of **Kampen** village.

Cross under grey North Sea skies to disembark in the main resort, **Westerland**, and you might wonder what all the fuss is about. The answer is a broad beach of pale quartz sand that fringes the entire west side of an elongated island tethered to the mainland by its railway. The sheltered east coast looks over mudflats of the Wattenmeer, while the north arm around the port of **List** is a sea of sand dunes. Flashy restaurants and boutiques aside, Sylt is an island of simple holiday pleasures: dozing in one of 11,000 *Strandkörbe*, the cute wicker beach-seats for two; dawdling through the lanes of postcard-pretty **Keitum**; nature walks among Germany's largest sand-dunes at List; sea cruises from **Hörnum** or any number of watersports; and, of course, people-watching at **Kampen**.

Westerland

After a century of promoting itself as the principal resort on Sylt, **WESTERLAND** has more or less destroyed itself. The progenitor late-1800s spa resort has been replaced by holiday-blocks and the sand dunes vanished long ago beneath paving slabs. What it has are all the facilities of a fully-fledged holiday mall – shops, restaurants, banks and supermarkets along pedestrianized main drag Friedrichstrasse, the latter two in short supply elsewhere on Sylt. As the hub of the public transport network it's also unavoidable. Its saving grace is a beach that's as fine as anywhere else on Sylt. Should you be stuck with kids to entertain on a rainy day, you could visit the **Sylter Welle** (daily 10am–10pm; €10; ⊕sylterwelle.de), an indoor fun-pool and sauna complex behind the beach at Sandstr. 32. Alternatively, fifteen minutes east of the centre on Gaadt is an **aquarium** (daily 10am–6pm; €13.50; ⊕syltaquarium.de) of tropical and North Sea fish with an underwater tunnel.

ACTIVITIES ON SYLT

No surprise on an island fringed by 35km of sand that the focus of all activity is the **beach**. The finest, whitest sands run the entire length of the west coast, access to which costs €3.50 and is payable as the *Kurtax* included in accommodation or as a *Tageskarte* if you enter as a day-tripper. Hooded **Strandkörbe** (beach seats), which come into their own in these breezy conditions, are available for rent by the day or hour on all beaches except those north of List on the Ellenbogen. Prevailing winds mean waves break on the west coast, while sheltered (though often muddy) strips of beach line the east – Königshafen lagoon northwest of List, or the peninsula south of Hörnum are safe for young children in rough conditions.

Walking aside, watersports are the main alternative to loafing on the beach. **Windsurfing** is excellent thanks to waves and smooth water on either side of the island – Sylt hosts the Windsurf World Cup in the last week of September. Other aquatic activities include **kitesurfing**, and, waves permitting, **surfing**. The principal surf break is at Westerland – a mid-tide A-frame known as Brandenburg is the most popular spot in Germany. Inland are **riding** centres, many of which provide beach rides; a leaflet from tourist information centres lists eight.

WATERSPORTS OPERATORS

Surfschule Camp One Dünenstr. 33, Wenningstedt ☏04651 433 75, ⓦsurfschule-wenningstedt.de. Has windsurfers, surfboards and kitesurfing gear. Lessons available. May–Oct.

Surfschule Sunset Beach Brandenburger Str. 15, Westerland ☏04651 271 72, ⓦsunsetbeach.de. Rents windsurfers, surf- and bodyboards, as well as stand-up paddleboards and sea kayaks. Lessons available. May–Oct.

Wenningstedt

Around 3km north of Westerland is the low-key and low-rise resort of **WENNINGSTEDT** – the crowds thin, the pace slows and no concrete slab is cemented anywhere near a fine beach. Beyond the village church on the far side of its central crossroads, the **Denhoog** (April & Oct Mon–Fri 10am–4pm; May–Sept Mon–Fri 10am–5pm, Sat & Sun 11am–5pm; €3.50, combined ticket to all Sylt museums €8.50) is an early Stone Age burial chamber constructed from granite dumped as glacial erratics; the top stone alone is estimated to weigh around twenty tonnes. Descend by stepladder and you reach the five-thousand-year-old main chamber.

Kampen

If Sylt has an image of chichi exclusivity, **KAMPEN** is to blame. For several decades it has filled pages in the gossip press as the holiday resort of money and celebrity. Expensive designer boutiques and galleries occupy the thatched Frisian houses. Slick bars and restaurants line Strönwai, aka Whiskeyallee; there are even a couple of nightclubs. Former holiday-makers Thomas Mann and Emil Nolde wouldn't recognize the old place. Window-shopping aside, the principal daytime activities are to walk up the **Uwe Düne** behind the village for a sweeping panorama from 57m up – Himalayan by local standards – or stroll beneath the ruddy sand **Rotes Kliff** (Red Cliff) that runs along the beach underneath. If that's too much effort laze beside the beautiful people at **Buhne 16** beach 1km north of central Kampen – not quite the status symbol it was two decades or so ago, but still fairly flash.

Keitum

There aren't many fishermen or farmers left in east-coast **KEITUM**, but ostentatious displays of wealth here have not yet reached the gung-ho levels of Kampen. The most photogenic village in Sylt, Keitum is a sleepy knot of lanes canopied by beech and chestnut trees. Once the island's leading settlement thanks to a sheltered location, it has a streetscape of traditional reed-thatched houses, most with the single high gable characteristic of Frisian architecture. A whaler built the eighteenth-century residence that houses the **Sylter Heimatmuseum**, Am Kliff 18–19 (April–Oct Mon–Fri 10am–5pm, Sat & Sun 11am–5pm; Nov–March Wed–Sat noon–4pm; €5, combined ticket to all Sylt museums €8.50), with modest exhibits of folk culture and island archeology, plus works by local artist Magnus Weidemann. Adjacent **Altfriesiches Haus** (same hours; €5) allows a nose around a reassembled early nineteenth-century house, a typical North Frisian example of Delft-style tiles and painted doors.

A fifteen-minute walk north of Altfriesiches Haus on the same lane is the church of **St Severin** (daily 9am–6pm; free), Sylt's ecclesiastical highlight, which has grown from a tiny Romanesque chapel of pink granite. It hosts chamber music concerts in summer: regularly on Wednesdays plus occasionally on weekends.

List

More small town than village, **LIST** at the tip of Sylt only stirs to life when passengers from Denmark disembark at its port. For a diversion, **Naturgewalten Sylt** by the harbour car park (daily: Jan–June & Sept–Dec 10am–6pm; July & Aug 10am–7pm; €12; ⓦmuez.de) styles itself as an "Experience Centre", which translates as multimedia child-friendly displays on natural forces that shape Sylt and its fauna. West of the town are Germany's largest sand dunes, the **Wanderdünen**, which roll east at around 4m per year. Walking paths embark through its mini-Sahara of bare sand ridges that rise up to 35m, fuzzed to a glorious purple by heather in late summer, or there are views of the exposed east flank on a poorly surfaced road to Weststrand; en route is one of Sylt's many **Strand Sauna** (daily Easter–Sept 11am–4pm; €15 day-ticket plus €2.50 parking) – the idea is to sweat up, then plunge into the North Sea. Good luck with that.

Ellenbogen

West of List, a side road at Sylt's most northerly point leads onto the **Ellenbogen** (cars €5), a privately owned "elbow" crooked around the north end of Sylt. Extending east, its dunes are empty except for lots of sheep and a handful of visitors to some of the quietest beaches on the island – the broadest, whitest strands are on the north and at the tip.

Hörnum

South of Westerland, you roll through the village of Rantum at the island's narrowest point before the straight run 11km south to **HÖRNUM** at the far tip. A broad, fine beach all the way along the western side of the route is accessible at intermittent points. At Hörnum you can walk 1km south to access an impressive sand-spit beach where Sylt finally peters out. Ever since herring fishermen embarked from here in the 1400s, the village has been centred on the island's largest port embedded behind the dunes and overlooked by a candy-striped lighthouse. Today it is the embarkation point for **cruises** (see box below.)

SYLT CRUISES AND WATTWANDERUNG

From mid-March to October, Adler-Schiffe (ⓦadler-schiffe.de) runs a huge variety of **cruises** from Hörnum. By far the most popular is to see **seal colonies** on mudbanks (daily at 2pm & Tues–Fri at 10.15am; 1hr 30min; €18) and to sister islands **Amrum** and **Föhr** (2 or 3 daily; from €27). Timetables are stocked in tourist offices on the island.

Perhaps the strangest day-trips from Sylt to the islands of Amrum and Föhr are the **guided walks** over the **mudflats** between the two islands run by Adler-Schiffe (late April to mid-Oct; €32). For two four-day periods each month, tidal heights allow Wattwanderung (literally "mud hiking") – you'll squelch barefoot between the two islands for around 2.5 hours on a day-trip that takes in both islands on a combination cruise and bus trip. Westerland tourist office stocks flyers with current trips – reservation is essential.

14

ARRIVAL AND DEPARTURE

SYLT

By plane Domestic airlines fly direct to Sylt airport, 2km east of Westerland.

By train Sylt terminal Westerland is on the Hamburg line. Because no roads run to the island, cars and motorbikes must be loaded onto Deutsche Bahn's SyltShuttle car train at Niebüll (roughly hourly 5am–9.40pm; €90 return or €77 midweek return (Tues–Thurs); ⊚ syltshuttle.de).

By ferry Adler Schiffe tourist ferries (☎ 01805 12 33 44, ⊚ adler-schiffe.de) link Hörnum to North Sea islands Amrum and Föhr (2–3 daily; from €27), which are themselves linked to the mainland by regular services. Though the latter mainland services are intended as return cruises, just going one-way works out cheaper than the cost of a train to Sylt and boat to the islands.

GETTING AROUND

By bus SVG buses travel to all destinations on the island approximately every 30min from a bus station outside the Westerland Hauptbahnhof; #1 and #5 go north to List via Wenningstadt and Kampen, #2 south to Hörnum, and #3 and #4 circle east to Keitum (singles €1.85–7.20, 3-day all-zone pass €23.50).

By bike On a 35km-long island where a 50m hill is mountainous, cycling is an excellent means of getting

about, and all buses have capacity for five bikes at the cost of a few euros. Bike rental is available at the Hauptbahnhof or in every village on the island; Fahrrad Leksus (☎ 04651 83 50 00) has outlets in Westerland at Lorens-de-Hahn-Str. 23, Bismarckstr. 9 and Norderstr. 42, plus two in Wenningstedt at Hauptstr. 8 and Westerstr. 20. Or try Sylt Bike (Keitumer Landstr. 12–14; ☎ 04651 446 31 03, ⊚ sylt-bike.de) beside Westerland train station.

INFORMATION

Website The website of the Sylt marketing board, ⊚ en .sylt.de, is useful for planning.

Westerland tourist office Beside Congress Centrum Sylt, Friedrichstr. 44 (Mon–Fri 9am–6pm, Sat 10am–5pm, Sun 11am–5pm; ☎ 0180 500 99 80, ⊚ westerland.de); second office in pavilion on Bahnhofsplatz (daily 9am–6pm; same contact details).

Wenningstedt tourist office Haus des Gastes, Dünenstr. 3 (Mon–Fri 9am–6pm, Sat 10am–noon, also Sun June–Aug 10am–noon; ☎ 04651 989 00, ⊚ wenningstedt.de).

Kampen tourist office At village centre on main road,

Hauptstr. 12 (Mon–Fri 9am–5pm, Sat 10am–1pm; ☎ 04651 469 80, ⊚ kampen.de).

Keitum tourist office Gurstieg 23 (Mon–Fri 9am–5pm, Sat 10am–1pm; ☎ 04651 33 70, ⊚ keitum.de).

List tourist office In the Kurverwaltung west of the port in the village centre (Landwehrdeich 1; Mon & Fri 9am–noon, Tues–Thurs 9am–noon & 1–5pm; ☎ 04651 952 00, ⊚ list .de); and in kiosk at harbour (May–Oct daily 10am–6pm).

Hörnum tourist office Kiosk at the port (Mon–Fri 9am–5pm, Sat 10am–1pm; ☎ 04651 962 60, ⊚ hoernum .de).

ACCOMMODATION

Accommodation is expensive in high season – a double in a modest hotel costs around €150 – and often booked long in advance, so local tourist offices are the best resources should you choose to wing it. They can also source **private accommodation** and holiday apartments (usually minimum three nights), which work out cheaper than a hotel for extended stays. Wherever you go, €3–4 is added to the day-rate as a **Kurtax**. In return you receive a ticket that permits free access to beaches and meagre discounts on some attractions.

HOTELS AND HOSTELS

WESTERLAND

DJH Westerland Fischerweg 36–40, 4km south ☎ 04651 83 57 825, ⊚ djh-nordmark.de. The best of the island's three youth hostels because of its fabulous location among the dunes south of Westerland – a 45min walk from the Hauptbahnhof or take a south-bound bus and walk across the dunes. Two- to four-bed en-suites available. Dorms **€23.50**, twins **€57**

★ **Long Island House Sylt** Eidumweg 13 ☎ 04651 995 95 50, ⊚ sylthotel.de. Crisp Nordic style in a bright, former residential house with a palette of fresh contemporary pastels, rooms individually furnished with a nod to the nautical and a small garden. Probably the most appealing mid-range address in Westerland. **€186**

Single-Pension Kirchner Trift 26 ☎ 04651 920 70, ⊚ singlepension.de. The cheapest private accommodation option in Westerland (if not Sylt) is this place on the main road south of the pedestrian centre, with glorified hostel-style single and double rooms, some singles with shared amenities, and a clientele of mixed ages. **€69**

WENNINGSTEDT

Pension Stick Berthin-Bleeg-Str. 2 ☎ 04651 424 33, ⊚ pension-stick.de. Good value in a modern pension. Decor in the ten rooms (four singles, six doubles) is homely, simple and modern. Add in the fact that the friendly young owner maintains a relaxed vibe and you have a fine base at an excellent price. **€80**

Wenningstedter Hof Hauptstr. 1 ☎04651 946 50, ⓦwenningstedter-hof.de. Rattan furniture and neutral colours characterize the good-value rooms of this comfortable family-run small hotel spread over three houses at the centre of the village. Hardly cutting-edge in island style stakes, but none the worse for it. **€120**

KAMPEN

Ahnenhof Kurhausstr. 8 ☎04651 426 45, ⓦahnenhof .de. A small hotel that has the same high standards and central location as other Kampen luxury addresses but without the asphyxiating prices. Smart country decor, a spa and a terrace with views of sand dunes and sea. **€195**

★ **Haus Rechel** Kroghooger Wai 3 ☎04651 984 90, ⓦhaus-rechel.de. Here's a shock: an affordable hotel among the exclusive establishments of Kampen. Actually, it's more homestay than hotel – a traditional thatched house of just seven en suites whose cottagey decor reflects the tastes of its charming elderly owner. Nice cottage garden to relax in too. **€100**

KEITUM

Benen-Diken-Hof Keitumer Süderstr. 3–5 ☎04651 938 30, ⓦbenen-diken-hof.de. Splendid, contemporary-country resort hotel of the Romantik group, its rooms and apartments scattered throughout several thatched houses. Facilities include a spectacular spa and golf course, both free for guests. Stylish rooms are classic-modern. **€206**

Keitumer Hafenhaus Kirchenweg 28 ☎04651 939 60, ⓦkeitumerhafenhaus.de. The former harbour office of a nineteenth-century sea captain now provides nine good-value holiday apartments for two that make up in cost-saving what they lack in modern style. And all with a garden down to the sea of the prettiest village on Sylt. A bargain. **€80**

CAMPSITES

Seven campsites behind the beach and low prices make camping an enjoyable option, weather permitting. All operate from Easter to October and are enormously popular – it's worth phoning if you're coming by bus in July and August. Bear in mind, too, that not all accept tents. Those below do.

Campingplatz Hörnum Rantumer Str. 31 ☎04651 835 84 31, ⓦhoernum.de. Arguably the most appealing site on Sylt due to a dedicated tent area embedded behind the dunes – a short walk leads you onto a mile of pure white-sand beach. There's also an on-site restaurant and a shop. Pitch **€6**, plus **€4** per person

Campingplatz Kampen Möwenweg 4 ☎04651 420 86, ⓦcampen-in-kampen.de. One of the better sites on the island because of its location among the dunes that rear up behind the site – a joy for the many young families who visit. Facilities include a large playground, a laundry and a shop selling basic foodstuffs. Pitch and one adult **€10**, plus **€3.05** per person

Campingplatz Rantum Hörnumer Str. 3 ☎04651 807 55, ⓦcamping-rantum.de. This place south of Westerland is a touch more expensive than other sites on the island because it's also better equipped: there's a restaurant, bakery and shop as well as a playground. Camping is in a tents-only meadow behind the dunes. Pitch **€7.50**, plus **€5** per person

EATING AND DRINKING

Though you can eat well on Sylt, **prices** are far steeper than the mainland. Expect to pay around €17 for a main course in most places, and around €25 in smarter restaurants; the prices in some could spoil a meal. Local chain **Gosch** rustles up tasty cheap fish in Westerland, Wenningstedt and List – look for its red lobster logo – and **beach cafés** are a great spot for lunch.

WESTERLAND

Alte Friesenstube Gaadt 4 ☎04651 12 28, ⓦaltefriesenstube.de. Charm by the cartful in the oldest house in Westerland, a 1680s cottage with an interior of Delft tiles and tables in a garden decorated with lanterns in summer. There's a first-class fish menu (written in Plattdeutsch), with mains averaging around €24. Service can be slow when busy. Tues–Sun 6–11pm.

Jorg Müller Süderstr. 8 ☎04651 277 88, ⓦhotel-joerg-mueller.de. The gourmet cooking of Jörg Müller, Germany's answer to Michel Roux, is reason enough to visit Sylt for some people. Expect classic flavours like sole with asparagus and mussels or organic kid goat with white beans and chanterelle mushrooms. Mains €38–58, four-course menus from €118. Reservations essential. Daily except Tues 6–10pm.

WENNINGSTEDT

Wonnemeyer Am Strand 1 ☎04651 452 99, ⓦwonnemeyer.de. Wenningstedt's own Café del Mar beach bar, with a raised terrace over the sands – a great choice for lunch or just to slurp a cold one. Find it by walking along the beach north of the village centre. Daily: Jan & Feb 11am–6pm; March to mid-June & Sept–Dec 11am–10pm; mid-June to Aug 11am–late.

KAMPEN

Buhne 16 Lister Str. 333, car park 500m north of Kampen ☎04651 44 68 27, ⓦbuhne16.de. Pastas, North Sea shrimp baguettes and *Currywurst* plus lunch specials such as seafood paella in a beach bar-café that epitomizes Sylt's brand of beach cool. Weekend DJs soundtrack barbecue evenings in summer. April–Oct daily noon–late.

Gogärtchen Stromwai 12, Kampen ☎04651 412 42,

14

ⓦgogaertchen.com. Don't be fooled by the traditional appearance. This is a Sylt institution that's a playground for the style-set. Come to sample plates like *Zander* with chorizo and saffron (€27) in the Frisian-style restaurant or to people-watch with a pizza (€16) in the bar. Daily from noon.

★**Kupferkanne** Stapelhooger Wai 7, Kampen ⓣ04651 410 10, ⓦkupferkanne-sylt.de. Breakfast, light lunches and fresh home-made cakes and mugs of coffee are on the menu. Yet you're also here to experience this famous café's enchanting Hobbity house and mazey terraces overlooking the sea. March–Oct daily 10am–6pm; Nov–Feb Mon–Thurs & Sun noon–5pm, Fri & Sat 10am–5pm.

KEITUM

Fisch-Fiete Wiedemannweg 3, Keitum ⓣ04651 321 50,

ⓦfisch-fiete.de. All manner of fish – from monkfish stew to green eel and sole – are served in a mid-priced restaurant with tables in the garden. An adjacent bistro-café offers cheap Frisian tapas plates and fish sandwiches. Mid-Feb to Dec daily except Tues: restaurant noon–2pm & 6–10pm; bistro noon–9pm.

RAMPEN

★**Sansibar** Hörnumer Str. 80, 3km south of Rampen, 10km south of Westerland ⓣ04651 96 46 46, ⓦsansibar.de. Beach-shack chic in a hip pavilion that's always busy in season and has tables among the dunes. It serves pastas, steak and fish for lunch (mains €14–24); dinners are more expensive. Classic Sylt – it even has its own bus stop – and hard to beat for a lazy lunch. Daily 10.30am–late.

Föhr and Amrum

Like Sylt, **Föhr** and **Amrum** are split between fine beach and the shallow Wattenmeer, a nutrient-rich sea of blues, browns and silvery light on the east coast. In other ways the southern islands couldn't be more different. Tranquil and cheaper, these small family-friendly islands are sleepy and rural. The hubbub disappears and in Föhr's largest village, **Wyk**, there's bedtime storytelling not DJs in the bandstand – a nod, perhaps, to former holidaymaker Hans Christian Andersen. By 10pm the whole place is asleep. Charming and uncomplicated, the islands have the innocent vibe of childhood holidays past, their main activities walking, cycling and building sandcastles on the beach.

Föhr

The largest island of the duo, **FÖHR**, lies in the shelter behind Sylt and Amrum as a sea of marshy flats that have christened it the "green island of the North Sea". Most of the 8650 population live in island "capital", **Wyk**, fronted by cafés along Sandwall esplanade. Sheltered from the prevailing weather on the southeast coast, it flourished briefly as a whaling base in the seventeenth and eighteenth centuries. Whaling looms large in the **Friesenmuseum**, Rebbelstïeg 34 (16 March to June, Sept & Oct Tues–Sun 10am–5pm; July & Aug daily 10am–5pm; Nov to 15 March Tues–Sun 2–5pm; €3.50 with accommodation *Kurkarte*, otherwise €4.50; ⓦfriesen-museum.de), fronted by a whalebone arch; inside there are paintings and harpoons plus very real butchery in a staged whaling documentary of the 1920s, as well as the usual items of local history and crafts, plus splendid folk costume decorated in silver jewellery.

A couple of **windmills** in Wyk, one at the museum, are the first indication of island landscapes that seem as Dutch as the local dialect, Fering (or Föhring). Indeed, Dutch know-how created the medieval dykes that cross-hatch an island that is only 5m above sea level at its highest point. One of the prettiest corners is **Nieblum**, 4km west of Wyk and dotted with the decorative thatched cottages of former whaling captains. Though it is now the most celebrated spot on the island, **Oevenum**, 3km north, runs it a close second in looks. Go south for sand – a good **beach** runs from Wyk along much of the south coast.

Amrum

Föhr seems almost lively compared to **AMRUM**. A one-road island of minimalist landscapes, 13km from marshy tip to sandy toe and never more than 1.5km wide, the most tranquil of the North Frisian group is effectively an oversized sandbank whose entire western half consists of the **Kniepsand**, Europe's widest beach, with ten square kilometres of white sand. Sheltered behind the dunes, a patchwork of woods and heath pillows the island's five **villages** composed of traditional Frisian cottages with a single high gable and tousled gardens. Most people rush it on a day-trip, but if you have time, Amrum is a lovely place to drop off the radar. Just outside Wittdün in the south of the island, the tallest **lighthouse** on the German North Sea rises candy-striped above the dunes (viewing platform Mon–Fri 8.30am–12.30pm; €1.50) while at the northern tip the island's largest village, **Norddorf**, feels almost busy. A 10km path behind the Kniepsand links the two.

Nebel

Should you tire of the beach (unlikely), **NEBEL** village midway up the east coast offers **Öömrang Hüs** (summer Mon–Fri 11am–1.30pm & 3–5pm, Sat 3–5pm; winter Mon–Fri 3–5pm; €3; w oeoemrang-hues.de), the prettily furnished house of an eighteenth-century captain – his ship is depicted in full sail on a tiled wall. He's probably buried in the village cemetery, its graves carved with ships under full sail. A model ship also hangs over the congregation in its St Clemenskirche.

ARRIVAL AND INFORMATION

By ferry from the mainland From mainland port Dagebüll, linked by train to Niebüll to the northwest, car ferries of WDR (w faehre.de) depart roughly every 1hr between Easter and Oct (reduced service in winter) to Wyk, the Föhr capital (€8.40 one-way per passnger), and every 2hr to Wittdün on Amrum (€12.20 one-way); it also sails between the two villages (€8.70). Return trips are around a third more expensive.

By ferry from Sylt Regular tourist cruises run by Adler-Schiffe (t 01805 12 33 44, w adler-schiffe.de) depart from

FÖHR AND AMRUM

Hörnum to both Amrum and Föhr (2–3 daily; from €27).

Föhr tourist office At Wyk ferry terminal (daily 10am–2pm; t 04681 300, w foehr.de) and in Post Trat, Nieblum (May–Oct Mon–Fri 9am–5pm, Sat 9am–noon, Sun 10am–noon; Nov–April Mon–Fri 9am–5pm; same contact details).

Amrum tourist office At Wittdün ferry terminal (May–June, Sept & Oct Mon–Fri 8.30am–5pm, Sat & Sun 9am–2pm; July & Aug Mon–Fri 8.30am–5.30pm, Sat & Sun 9.30am–5.30pm; t 04682 940 30, w amrum.de).

GETTING AROUND

By bus On Föhr, WDR (w faehre.de) operates a public bus service, while on Amrum a bus runs from Wittdün to Norddorf every 30min in summer (9am–6.30pm).

By bike Cycling is a joy on these flat islands; there are rental outlets by the ferry quays and in every village.

ACCOMMODATION AND EATING

As on Sylt, accommodation is subject to a €3 *Kurtax* added to the day-rate. In return you receive a *Kurkarte* that permits meagre discounts on some attractions.

FÖHR

★**Alt Wyk** Grosse Str. 4, Wyk t 04681 32 12, w alt-wyk .de. Superb modern cooking – such as lobster with shellfish tortellini and pak choi in lemongrass sauce – in a historic house just off the seafront. Outstanding for a holiday treat. Four courses €67, lunch menus €46. Feb & March Thurs & Fri from 5.30pm, Sat & Sun 12.30–2.30pm & from 5.30pm; April, May & mid-Oct to Christmas Wed from 5.30pm, Thurs–Sun noon–2.30pm & from 5.30pm; June to mid-Oct Mon & Wed from 5.30pm, Thurs–Sun noon–2.30pm & from 5.30pm.

Duus-Hotel Hafenstr. 40, Wyk t 04681 598 10, w duus-hotel.de. A reliable, well-maintained option in the old town of Wyk. Although fairly plain in this traditional place, the classic-modern accommodation is spotless and the location – moments from the harbour – is excellent; many rooms have harbour views. **€110**

Sternhagens Landshaus Buurnstrat 49, Oevenum t 04681 597 90, w sternhagenslandshaus.de. The rural

escape par excellence, this restaurant in a traditional Frisian house offers cosy cottage rooms, all en-suite and country-modern in style, in the eaves. **€145**

AMRUM

★**Campingplatz Amrum** Inselstr. 125, Wittdün t 04682 22 54, w amrum-camping.de. Pitch your tent on white powder sands with dunes for a windbreak in this simple campsite off the main road west of Wittdün village. Facilities include a shop, an *Imbiss* and a bar, plus a playground should the kids tire of sandcastles (unlikely). Closed Nov–March. Pitch **€5**, plus **€8** per person

Ual Öömrung Wiartshues Bräätlun 4, Norddorf t 04682 836, w uöw.de. There's Frisian charm everywhere you look in this small restaurant-hotel. Accommodation is simple and homely in the traditional thatched house, with pine furnishings and pretty bed-linen, or cool Scandi modern in a Suitenhaus. Rooms **€112**, suites **€174**

14

Mecklenburg-West Pomerania

CHALK CLIFFS, JASMUND, RÜGEN

Mecklenburg-West Pomerania

"When the end of the world comes, I shall go to Mecklenburg because there everything happens a hundred years later."
Otto von Bismarck

With only 1.8 million people in 23,170 square kilometres, no Land in Germany is as sparsely populated as Mecklenburg-West Pomerania (Mecklenburg-Vorpommeron). Bar the odd towerblock, the conjoined former duchies of Mecklenburg and western Pomerania, pressed into Poland, were barely developed under the GDR and, without any city worth the name, the state lay off the radar for most foreigners. Since reunification, however, its profile has grown alongside the fame of the quartzite beaches that fringe the longest coastline in Germany – 354km from the Trave River at Lübeck to Usedom on the border. That Berlin city-slickers now flee north for weekends on the coast is testament to an area that's on the up.

15

In fact, the coast is simply returning to form. During the late 1800s, Germany's first and second largest islands, **Rügen** and **Usedom**, were the preferred playgrounds of the German glitterati – the moneyed elite, assorted grand dukes and even the occasional Kaiser sojourned to dip an ankle at their smart sea-water bathing resorts. An injection of capital after decades of GDR neglect has brought a dash of former imperial pomp to both and also taken the resorts upmarket. Rügen is one of the most popular holiday destinations in the country, celebrated for its chalk cliffs above the Baltic Sea as much as its Bäderarchitektur (coast resort architecture of the *belle époque*).

Elsewhere, the Baltic coast is true Hanseatic League country (see box, p.785); the Backsteingotik architecture (decorative Gothic red-and-black brick) of the UNESCO-listed Altstadts in **Wismar** and **Stralsund** are wistful reminiscences of the former grandeur of this medieval mercantile power-bloc. There's some heritage, too, in **Rostock**, the state's largest city and its chief port, but you're more likely to visit for its bar scene, the superb beach at Warnemünde, or to use it as a launch pad for a superb Münster in **Bad Doberan** – a must-see for anyone with a passing interest in ecclesiastical architecture.

You don't have to travel far from the coast to enter a bucolic backwater whose ruler-straight roads are lined with avenues of trees and whose rape fields light the scenery gold in early summer. It's a place to drop off the radar, just as it was when favoured as a summer retreat from Berlin among Prussian aristos; many of their manors are open as grand hotels. The heart of the plateau is the **Mecklenburg Lake District** (Mecklenburgische Seenplatte) centred around Germany's second largest freshwater lake, Lake Müritz, and the **Müritz National Park**. Nicknamed the Land of a Thousand Lakes and home to the largest contiguous area of waterways in central Europe, its aquatic mosaic is beloved by canoeists and birdwatchers alike. Ducal seat turned state capital **Schwerin** at its western end is the only true town hereabouts, albeit pocket-sized and packing a cultural punch to match that of its fairy-tale castle; while **Güstrow**, another ducal seat, is dedicated to the memory of Germany's greatest Expressionist sculptor, Ernst Barlach.

Highlights

❶ Wismar An air of faded grandeur pervades the Altstadt of this splendid old Hanseatic port, with much of the atmosphere of Lübeck but none of its crowds. **See p.821**

❷ Bad Doberan Beautiful architecture and superb artworks make Bad Doberan's thirteenth-century Münster one of the finest medieval churches in the Baltic, while the steam train ride to the coast is one of the region's most fun days out. **See p.824**

❸ Rügen Charming small seaside resorts and Hitler's colossal holiday camp are side by side on Germany's biggest island, celebrated for its white cliffs, beautiful beech woods and mile upon mile of powder-fine sands. **See p.833**

❹ Schwerin Tour a fairy-tale palace that goes straight to the head. **See p.846**

❺ Canoeing in the Mecklenburg Lake District Play at being Huckleberry Finn for up to a week on canoe-and-camp adventures through a mosaic of interconnected lakes and channels. Slow travel at its finest. **See p.853**

HIGHLIGHTS ARE MARKED ON THE MAP ON P.820

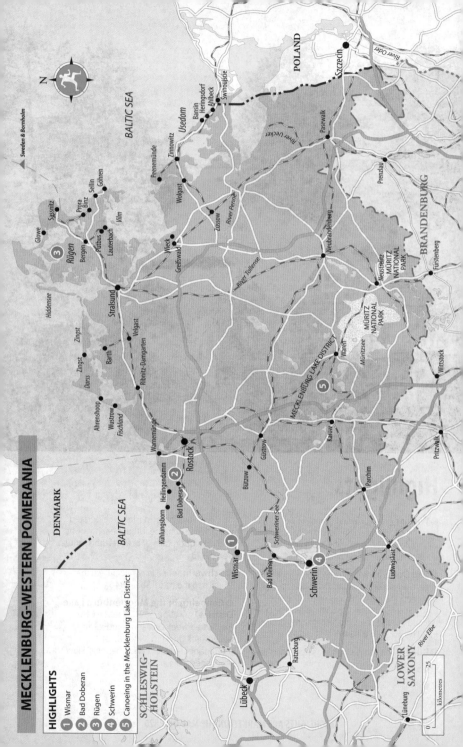

Wismar

Fate had it in for **WISMAR**. The first Hanseatic city east of Lübeck has similar looks to the league-leader on which it was modelled – the cobbled Altstadt is stuffed with gables and red-brick Gothic – and retains the harbour that made it a rich medieval port with considerable diplomatic clout. Unlike Lübeck, however, Wismar was conquered by the **Swedes** in 1648. On the ramparts of the empire, it suffered sieges, fire and pillage throughout the Swedes' 150-year occupation. By the early 1900s it was a backwater – perhaps one reason why film director F. W. Murnau used Wismar as a backdrop for his 1922 Gothic-horror classic, *Nosferatu*: shots include the prewar Markt and the vampire's ghostly ship drifting into the old harbour. Air raids in 1945 that obliterated two massive medieval churches and subsequent mothballing under the GDR were the final insult.

Since reunification, Wismar has taken tourism seriously and today it positively hums with quiet prosperity. It again declares itself a **Hansestadt** (Hanseatic town), and a major renovation programme has smartened up its Altstadt, something that elevated it onto UNESCO's World Heritage list in a joint application with Stralsund (see p.830). Yet Wismar remains refreshingly untouristy. Away from the set pieces, the historic streets have an air of glories past and are free of tour groups – just one more reason to go.

15

The Markt

The showpiece of Wismar's renovation is its cobbled **Markt**. Encircled by pastel-tinted facades, its scale as one of the largest town squares in north Germany testifies to the Hanseatic heyday. At its back is the Wasserkunst, a Dutch Renaissance pavilion for the town's water supply; water still trickles from the bronze merman and mermaid taps. Opposite is one of the finest Late-Gothic Hanseatic facades you'll see on the Baltic coast, the status boast of a burgher c.1380 despite the misleading "Alter Schwede" moniker. The conceit is maintained by replica "**Swedish heads**" (see box below).

Rathaus

Am Markt 1 • Museum daily 10am–6pm, closes 4pm on Sun Nov–March • Free

The only formal note among the Markt's pleasing jumble of facades is the Neoclassical **Rathaus**. Entered at the side, its original Gothic cellars feature a sixteenth-century mural of sailors slugging from wineskins (this was the council wine-cellar, after all), while historical exhibits provide a primer on the city's past: Hanseatic drinking tankards from an era when the port had two hundred breweries, as well as a splendid

---

SWEDISH HEADS AND OTHER YARNS

Nowadays Wismar is only too happy to point out evidence of its annexation by Swedish forces from 1648. Most prominent are the colourful "**Swedish heads**" scattered throughout the town. With their fabulous handlebar moustaches, rakish cravats and lion's-head caps worn over black curls, they present a dashing image in front of Alter Schwede on the Markt and the Baumhaus at the end of the harbour.

Whether they are actually Swedish is another matter. An original in Schabbelhaus is one of a pair that was mounted at the harbour entrance for a century until they were accidentally rammed by a Finnish ship in 1902. At the time they were known as the "Old Swedes". But because documents mention "The Swede" harbour boundary from the 1670s, their origins remain a mystery. Historians date them to approximately 1700, the time of the Swedish occupation of Wismar, and suggest they are a Baroque depiction of Hercules. The most plausible theory suggests they were mounted on a Swedish merchant ship, possibly glaring from the stern or mounted before the captain's quarters. However, another suggestion moots that their name derives from their "**Schwedenköpf**" (literally Sweden head) haircut, short for its time and a powder-free style as a sign of enlightenment.

polychromed tomb-slab of a Swedish major general, Helmuth Wrangel. Before you leave the Markt area, restaurant *Zum Weinberg* behind the Rathaus at no. 3 is worth a look for its well-preserved hallway of a Renaissance wine-merchant.

St-Marien-Kirche

St Marienkirchhof • Daily: April–June, Sept & Oct 10am–6pm; July & Aug 10am–8pm; Nov–March 11am–4pm • Free

The area west of the Markt was once known as the Gothic quarter. Then came the twelfth and final air-raid of 1945. Only the square tower of **St-Marien-Kirche** remains, a massive 80m edifice mounted with a clock donated by Wrangel – he of the Rathaus tomb-slab. Notwithstanding tours that ascend the landmark tower several times a day, it is put to use as an exposition on contemporary church-building, with a stereoscopic film on, and demonstrations of, medieval construction.

Fürstenhof

Heading away from the Markt beyond the St-Marien-Kirche, you pass the **Fürstenhof** on Vor dem Fürstenhof, erstwhile seat of the Mecklenburg dukes whose take on Italian Renaissance appears distinctly frothy in a region of brick. Terracotta plaques on the public face present images of the Trojan Wars, then, privately within the courtyard, relax into folkloric scenes of feasting and pig-wrestling supposed to represent the tale of the Prodigal Son.

St-Georgen-Kirche

St Georgen-Kirchhof • Daily: April–June 10am–6pm; July & Aug 10am–8pm; Nov–March 11am–4pm • Free

Powering above the Fürstenhof is the **St-Georgen-Kirche** whose scale is a testament to the wealth of the Hanseatic craftsmen and merchants who funded it. Seriously damaged in the war – it was still a weedy shell in 1990 after reunification – the largest church in Wismar was completed again in 2010 after a €35 million rebuild. Notwithstanding a few merchants' tomb-slabs carved with ships in full sail, the soaring interior is raw brick and all the more atmospheric for it. It serves as an exhibition space and concert hall.

Heiligen-Geist-Kirche

Lübsche Str. Strasse • April–June Mon–Sat 10am–6pm, Sun noon–6pm; July & Aug daily 10am–8pm; Nov–March Mon–Sat 11am–4pm, Sun noon–4pm • €1 donation requested

Opposite St-Georgen-Kirche, Grosse Hohe Strasse leads north to east–west spine-street Lübische Strasse and the **Heiligen-Geist-Kirche**. The medieval hospital church was modelled on that of Hanseatic League leader, Lübeck, its unsupported Renaissance roof painted a century or so later with Old Testament scenes. Look, too, for a painting by the altar in which Wismar's seventeenth-century skyline is just visible through the rigging of a merchant galleon.

Welt-Erbe-Haus

Lübsche Str. 24 • Daily: April–Sept 9am–5pm; Oct–March 10am–4pm • Free

Although **Welt-Erbe-Haus** (World Heritage House) flags up Wismar's addition to the UNESCO list, it is better understood as an interactive look at town history through the architectural fabric of a 700-year-old house. So, interactive audiovisual displays narrate the town's development alongside information on the renovation of the Welt-Erbe-Haus itself. The highlight is a 1820s salon with hand-painted wallpaper that depicts Telemachus's journey to Calypso.

The north Altstadt

The sleepy historic streets of the north Altstadt are backwater Wismar at its best. Propped by flying buttresses at its centre, **St-Nikolai-Kirche** is the only one of Wismar's medieval churches that stood intact in 1945. At 37m high, its giddy nave seems out of all proportion to surrounding houses – explained by the town's Hanseatic past and the fact that this was the church of seafarers, who formed the bulk of the town's medieval population when St Nikolai was built in the late 1300s. A Baroque makeover stripped much of the original Gothic; remnants include medieval murals of a Tree of Jesse and St Christopher, a high altar in a side chapel, and a fourteenth-century font.

Schabbellhaus

Corner of Schweinsbrücke and Fischergrube • Check with tourist office for new hours and price

By the Schweinsbrücke (Pigs' Bridge) topped by playful porkers over the Grube canal, **Schabbelhaus** – an above-average museum of town history – is scheduled to reopen in autumn 2016 after protracted renovation. Its most infamous exhibits are the mummified "dead hands"; a staple of medieval prosecutors, these were hacked off a murder victim and presented in court – literally an accusing finger from the grave. There are also fine copperplates of the Altstadt, guild treasures and one of the original Swedish heads (see box, 000). Previously, notes in English were provided in all rooms.

15

Alter Hafen

Follow the Grube canal downstream from the St-Nikolai-Kirche and you reach the medieval **Alter Hafen** (old harbour) fronted by the Wassertor, last of five medieval gateways in the town defences through which Nosferatu crept with his coffin. When not at sea, a replica medieval trading-cog is open for inspection (no set hours; free) – during summer it embarks on three-hour **sailing trips** a couple of times a week (€25; ☎03841 30 43 10, ⓦ poeler-kogge.de).

ARRIVAL AND DEPARTURE   WISMAR

By train The Bahnhof is near the harbour at the northeast edge of the Altstadt.

Destinations Rostock (hourly; 1hr 10min); Schwerin (hourly; 30–40min).

INFORMATION AND TOURS

Tourist office A helpful office is at Lübsche Str. 23 (daily: April–Oct 9am–6pm; Nov–March 10am–4pm; ☎03841 194 33, ⓦ wismar.de). They have a good stock of English-language themed leaflets, including a tour around Swedish monuments.

Bike rental Available at the train station (platform 2C) from municipal operator Wismar Rad (March–Oct).

Boat trips Boats of Reederei Clermont tour the harbour (May–Oct daily every 30min; 1hr; €11.50; ☎03841 22 46 46, ⓦ reederei-clermont.de), and sail three times a day (April–Oct) to Poel island (€18 return), a pretty, bucolic backwater 10km north of Wismar on the opposite side of the Wismar Bight.

ACCOMMODATION

Chez Fasan Bademutterstr. 20 ☎03841 21 34 25, ⓦ pension-chez-fasan.de. The cheapest beds in central Wismar are in this good-value pension spread across three houses in the central Altstadt, a block behind the Rathaus. Though plain, rooms are nonetheless perfectly adequate. Breakfast extra. **€47**

DJH Wismar Juri-Gagarin-Ring 30a ☎03841 326 80, ⓦ jugendherbergen-mv.de; bus #C or #D to bus stop "Philipp-Müller-Strasse/Krankenhaus". Installed in a hall-like building and passable for a cheap bed, if rather isolated a 20min walk west of the centre. En-suite doubles, two disabled-access rooms, plus dorms with shared facilities. Dorms **€21.40**, doubles **€61.80**

Fründts Schweinsbrücke 1–3 ☎03841 225 69 82, ⓦ hotel-stadtwismar.de. This mid-range place represents excellent value for money. Sure, accommodation is plain, but it's spacious and comfortable, and Komfort class verges on luxurious – a bargain for the €8 extra. **€68**

Reingard Weberstr. 18 ☎03841 28 49 72, ⓦ hotel-reingard.de. A pleasant pension in a side street, complete with wood floors and a pleasing bygone style in individually decorated rooms. Probably not worth the extra expense over other hotels, but this is one of the few options with homely character. **€89**

Stadt Hamburg Am Markt 24 ☎03841 23 90, ⓦ wismar.steigenberger.de. Part of the Steigenberger chain, this business hotel is the plushest address in town, with brisk service, 4-star standards and a fine location on the Markt; good views from the rooftop spa, too. The downside is the bland chain decor. Breakfast extra. **€109**

EATING AND DRINKING

As ever on the German coast, boats moored at Alter Hafen rustle up cheap smoked-fish sandwiches.

Alter Schwede Am Markt 19 ☎03841 28 35 52, ⓦ walter-schwede-wismar.de. Tuck into Baltic fish specialities such as roast eel and herring with cranberry cream or Mecklenburg *Rippenbraten* (roast pork stuffed with apple and plums) in the oldest *Bürgerhaus* in Wismar – it's touristy but it also gets the locals' vote for quality regional cooking. Daily 11.30am–late.

★**Avocados** Hinter dem Chor 1 ☎03841 30 33 33, ⓦ avocados-wismar.de. Rather brilliant little organic bistro opposite Schabbelhaus that prepares fresh, creative vegetarian dishes. A daily menu is chalked on the board, but expect dishes like bulgar wheat with fried mushrooms or *Spätzle* with cheese, plus curries, pastas and risottos – all at bargain prices. Times vary, generally Mon–Fri 11am–4/5pm, Sat 10am–4pm.

Café Glücklich Schweinsbrücke 7 ☎03841 796 93 77. In an area of interesting crafts and arts shops, this pretty café is a great pit stop for coffee and decadent home-made cakes such as white chocolate with raspberries. Mon & Sun 9am–6pm, Tues–Sat 9am–8pm.

To'n Zägenkrog Ziegenmarkt 10 ☎03841 28 27 16, ⓦ ziegenkrug-wismar.de. Once named one of the best fish restaurants in the state, this is certainly among the most charming in its bygone nautical decor, especially the cabin-like Kajüte room. The daily catch from Wismar and Poel island is prepared simply in creamy sauces. Daily 11am–10pm.

Volkskammer Ziegenmarkt 1 ☎03841 25 28 55. One of the most unusual drinking spots in town, this is a shoebox of a bar, where every surface is covered with memorabilia of GDR days. Shame the same can't be said of the beer prices. Mon–Fri from 7pm, Sat from 8pm.

Bad Doberan and the beach resorts

"Münster, Molli, Moor und Meer" the tourist board trills happily to tick off the attractions of **Bad Doberan**: its minster, the Molli (train), a moorland health centre and the Baltic beach resorts of **Heiligendamm** and **Kühlungsborn** 15km northwest. None is really worth a journey on its own, but together they comprise a happy day-trip that's easily accessible from Rostock.

Bad Doberan

The pull of history is ever present in **BAD DOBERAN**. Leafy and light-hearted, it blossomed into a summer spa resort in the early 1800s under the guidance of the Mecklenburg dukes. Pale Neoclassical edifices from the resort's formative years line August-Bebel-Strasse; now council offices and a hotel, the buildings are worth a look for their foyers. Spa-goers strolled in the park opposite, **Kamp**, and took the waters in its two Chinese-style pavilions that add an unexpected rakish air. The smaller Roter Pavillon holds a gallery, the Weisser Pavillon a café. By 1886, spa-goers were all aboard the Molli steam engine to add sea bathing to their water cures. The **Mecklenburgische Bäderbahn Molli** (see opposite), to give the splendid narrow-gauge train its full name, chuffs hourly through high-street Mollistrasse – one for the photo album – on its way to Heiligendamm and Kühlungsborn.

The Münster

Klosterstr. 2 • **Münster** March, April & Oct Mon–Sat 10am–5pm, Sun 11am–5pm; May–Sept Mon–Sat 9am–6pm, Sun 11am–6pm; Nov–Feb Mon–Sat 10am–4pm, Sun 11am–4pm • €3 • **Café** Daily 1–5pm • ⓦ doberanermuenster.de

Alongside a day-trip to the beach aboard the Molli train, the **Münster** is undoubtedly the premier reason to visit Bad Doberan – the fourteenth-century Cistercian church is arguably the crowning achievement of ecclesiastical Gothic architecture in the Baltic. Completed in a fusion of Hanseatic and French high-Gothic styles, the abbey church is poised where architectural form is stretched to its limits yet unencumbered by the embellishments to follow. Nowhere is this clearer than at the crossing, whose two tiers of arches are arguably the church's most graceful feature. Having come through the Reformation without a scratch, the **furnishings** are as impressive; a leaflet provided on entry pinpoints 22 artworks, including what is claimed as the oldest existing wing altar (1300), crowned by flamboyant Gothic spires, and an audacious tabernacle. Also within the grounds are a curious octagonal ossuary known as the *Beinhaus* (bone house) and a complex of agricultural buildings, one of which contains a café.

Heiligendamm

The Molli's second stop is **HEILIGENDAMM**, founded in 1793 when local duke Friedrich Franz I decided to tap into the popular (and lucrative) cure of sea-water bathing. The result was Germany's first **bathing resort**; the legend "Happiness awaits those who are cured after bathing" is carved above the main bathhouse. The "white town on the sea", most of which dates from 1814–16, remains as spotless as when created – and as exclusive, too, after the bathing complex was renovated to create one of the Baltic's grandest stays, the *Grand Hotel Heilgendamm* (⍟grandhotel-heiligendamm.de). The spa, restaurants, and several bars (including one on the beach) are all open to guests.

Kühlungsborn

The Molli's terminus, **KÜHLUNGSBORN WEST**, is a relaxed resort backed by woodland. The largest beach resort in Mecklenburg, it bills itself as the "Seebad mit flair", the latter provided by Jugendstil villas along Ostseeallee, a backdrop to the longest **promenade** in Germany – 4.8km of it, extending either side of a pedestrianized core at the pier, along a beach with tidy rows of *Strandkörbe* wicker seats.

ARRIVAL AND GETTING AROUND

By train Trains run hourly from Rostock and Wismar, timed to coincide with departures aboard the Molli.

Molli steam engine The Molli runs throughout the year, linking Bad Doberan to the beach resorts of Heiligendamm and Kühlungsborn (late April–Oct 11 daily; Nov–March 5 daily; Heiligendamm €9 return, Kühlungsborn €13 return; ⍟molli-bahn.de).

INFORMATION

Bad Doberan tourist office Severinstr. 6 (mid-May to mid-Sept Mon–Fri 9am–6pm, Sat 10am–3pm; mid-Sept to mid-May Mon–Wed & Fri 9am–4pm, Thurs 9am–6pm; ☎038203 62 154, ⍟bad-doberan-heiligendamm.de). The office stocks timetables for the Molli train.

Kühlungsborn tourist office Ostseeallee 19 (May–Sept Mon–Fri 9am–6pm, Sat & Sun 10am–4pm; Oct–April Mon–Fri 9am–4pm, Sat & Sun 10am–1pm; ☎038293 84 90, ⍟kuehlungsborn.de). The office is also your best source of accommodation in summer.

ACCOMMODATION AND EATING

Prinzenpalais Alexandrinenplatz 8, Bad Doberan ☎038203 731 60, ⍟prinzen-palais.de. Views of the Molli train as it chuffs to its terminus are available from the front rooms of this smart hotel in a historic spa building. All rooms are quietly luxurious, with modern decor. **€104**

Zum Weissen Schwan Am Markt 9, Bad Doberan ☎038203 778 20, ⍟zumweissenschwan.de. Fine dining without the fuss, this place gets rave reviews locally. Dishes are modern German – Baltic fish cooked in white wine or lemon oil, or lamb in a red wine sauce (average €20) – and beautifully presented. May–Sept Tues–Sun noon–2pm & 6–11pm; Oct–April Tues–Sun 6–10/11pm.

Rostock

Too small to be truly dynamic, too large to be quaint, **ROSTOCK** is the principal city in Mecklenburg-Western Pomerania. The most important port on the German Baltic has been everything from a powerful Hanseatic trader to a major ship-building port at the head of the deep-water Warnow River. Its townscape bears the scars of Allied bombers and GDR planners alike. Even the reunification welcomed elsewhere proved a bitter pill when it ended the subsidies that had sustained the ship-building industry, prompting mass unemployment.

Although pockets of historical charm remain in the **Altstadt**, an oval cat's-cradle of streets above the harbour, and renovation has buffed up the centre, the core is unlikely to detain you for more than half a day. The Kröpeliner Tor-Vorstadt (aka the **KVT**) district, where a 12,000-strong student population helps fuel the liveliest nightlife on the German Baltic, is one reason to hang around. Otherwise there's nearby **Warnemünde**, a chirpy sister resort with one of the finest beaches in Germany. Warnemünde also hosts the town's best **festivals**: regatta week Warnemünder Woche (ⓦwarnemuender-woche.de), straddling the first and second weeks of July, and classic sail extravaganza Hanse Sail (ⓦhansesail.com) in early August.

15 The Altstadt and Neuer Markt

The egg-shaped Altstadt remains visible on maps even if bombs and urban development removed much of the medieval town-wall itself. Air raids pulverized the old town's heart, **Neuer Markt**, which is too spacious by half thanks to the GDR weakness for a grand civic space. Nevertheless, planners restored its historic architecture: on the east side stands the **Rathaus**, a Baroque porch smothered over a turreted Gothic facade which is just visible behind the pink sugar-icing. Opposite the Rathaus is a rebuilt row of townhouses: the prettiest picture in Rostock.

The Marienkirche

Neuer Markt • May–Sept Mon–Sat 10am–6pm, Sun 11.15am–5pm; Oct–April Mon–Sat 10am–5pm, Sun 11.15am–12.15pm • Free

The defining monument of the Altstadt is the impressive bulk of the **Marienkirche**. It would have been bigger still had the basilica not collapsed mid-build in 1398, forcing a return to the blueprints to create a cross-shaped footprint of equal-length transepts and nave. Aside from a gloriously over-the-top Baroque organ shoehorned theatrically above a ducal gallery, the church's prizes are a bronze font (1290) propped on representations of the four elements, and a superb **astronomical clock** behind the altar. Built in 1472, the upper face shows a 24-hour clock, monthly star signs and seasonal chores, while the lower face is a blur of planetary movements. Visit at noon and Jesus and the Apostles circle around into Heaven, while Judas has the door slammed in his face.

Universitätsplatz and around

Pedestrianized high-street Kröpeliner Strasse, the former market thoroughfare, forges west off Neuer Markt to open at Universitätsplatz and the **Brunnen der Lebensfreunde** (Fountain of Happiness), an uncharacteristic piece of GDR jollity. The wedge-shaped square is named for north Germany's oldest university (1419) whose current incarnation is a handsome neo-Renaissance pile at the rear. Kröpeliner Strasse concludes at the **Kröpeliner Tor** (daily 10am–6pm; €2), oldest of the city's former 22 gateways; its lower sections date from 1280.

Kulturhistorisches Museum

Klosterhof 7 • Tues–Sun 10am–6pm • Free • ⓦ kulturhistorisches-museum-rostock.de

In a quiet courtyard behind Universitätsplatz, former Cistercian monastery Kloster-zum-Heiligen-Kreuz houses the town museum, the **Kulturhistorisches Museum**. Beyond modest exhibits from its medieval origins on the ground floor you're rewarded with an altar that depicts the Three Magi arriving in Rostock by ship in 1425; its image of defences and the skyline pierced by the Petrikirche spire is the first portrait of the medieval town. Above are displays of glass and Flemish china, guildhouse goblets and artwork, including works by Expressionist, Ernst Barlach (see box, p.851).

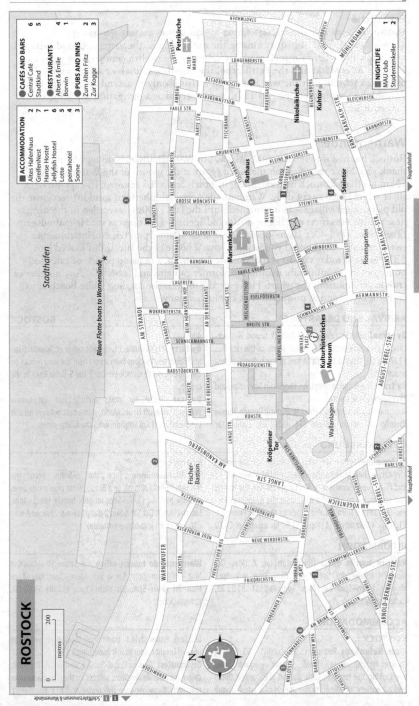

ROSTOCK

0 — metres — 200

Stadthafen

Blaue Flotte boats to Warnemünde

Schiffahrtsmuseum & Warnemünde

Hauptbahnhof

Hauptbahnhof

15

ACCOMMODATION	
Altes Hafenhaus	2
GreifenNest	7
Hanse Hostel	1
Jellyfish Hostel	6
Lotte	5
pentahotel	4
Sonne	3

CAFÉS AND BARS	
Central Café	6
Stadtkind	5
RESTAURANTS	
Albert & Emile	4
Borwin	1
PUBS AND INNS	
Zum Alten Fritz	2
Zur Kogge	3

NIGHTLIFE	
MAU club	1
Studentenkeller	2

Petrikirche

Nikolaikirche

Kuhtor

Rathaus

Steintor

Marienkirche

Kulturhistorisches Museum

Wallanlagen

Köpeliner Tor

Fischer-Bastion

Petrikirche

Alter Markt • May–Sept Mon–Sat 10am–6pm, Sun 1–6pm; Oct–April Mon–Sat 10am–4pm, Sun 1–4pm • tower €3

There's a gentle pull of history among the quiet lanes of the eastern Altstadt, draped over a low hill where Rostock made its debut in the twelfth century. The area's kernel is **Alter Markt** and the **Petrikirche**, the one-time church of sailors and fishermen rebuilt after the war and worth a visit if only to ascend an elevator to a 44m-high viewing platform. Its 117m tower served as a navigation mark for sailors for centuries.

Warnemünde

Rostock has had it tough since the *Wende*, but **WARNEMÜNDE** is doing very nicely, thank you. Since reunification the beach resort at the mouth of the Warnow River 13km north of Rostock has flourished, its hotels and villas restored, its expansive silver-white beach swept daily. Warnemünde's original fishermen wouldn't recognize the old place. Their village – as it remained until the late 1800s – is recalled in the streets near the tourist office; one house at Alexandrinenstr. 31 is open as the **Heimatmuseum** (Tues–Sun: April–Oct 10am–6pm; Nov–March 10am–5pm; €3; ⓦheimatmuseum -warnemuende.de), should you wonder what a home of the late 1800s looked like.

The heart of today's resort is harbourside **Am Strom**, a nonstop parade of cafés and boutiques in the miniature mansions of former captains and fisherfolk. Any number of **cruises** embark from the wharf. However, the focus is the dazzling white **beach** at its end – as broad and as powder-fine as any in Germany.

ARRIVAL AND DEPARTURE   ROSTOCK

By plane Domestic airlines fly to Rostock airport, Rostock-Laage (ⓦrostock-airport.de), 28km south of the city. Bus #127 (€5.50) links to the city. A taxi to the centre will cost around €50.

By train The Hauptbahnhof, on the Berlin line, is around 1km south of the centre.

Destinations Bad Doberan (hourly; 20min); Bergen, Rügen (hourly; 1hr 40min); Berlin (14 daily; 2hr 20min–2hr 40min).

By ferry Ferries connect to a wide range of Scandinavian and Baltic destinations from a port near the river mouth on the east bank (ⓦrostock-port.de); the S-Bahn links to the centre.

By car Useful car parks include one on Grosse Wasserstrasse, off Neuer Markt, and a vast outdoor area at the harbour off Am Strande, with cheap day-rates.

GETTING AROUND

By tram The centre is walkable, but trams (ⓦrsag-online .de) can be handy. From the Hauptbahnhof, trams #2, #5 and #6 run up to Steinstrasse and Lange Strasse, the former two continuing to Schröder Platz near the Kröpeliner Tor-Vorstadt (KTV). Tram #4 also heads to the KTV. Prices are €1.50 for a *Kurzstrecke* (4 stops), €1.90 for a single or €4.70

for a day-pass.

To Warnemünde Take the S-Bahn from the Hauptbahnhof (20min), or a Blaue Flotte river cruise from Rostock harbour (June–Sept roughly hourly 10am–4pm; March–May & Oct Sat & Sun 2 daily 11am & 2pm; one-way €10, return €14; ⓦblaue-flotte.de)

INFORMATION

Rostock tourist office Universitätsplatz 6 (May–Oct Mon–Fri 10am–6pm, Sat & Sun 10am–3pm; Nov–April Mon–Fri 10am–5pm, Sat 10am–3pm; ☎0381 381 22 22, ⓦrostock.de).

Warnemünde tourist office Am Strom 59 (May–Oct Mon–Fri 10am–6pm, Sat & Sun 10am–3pm; Nov–April Mon–Fri 10am–5pm, Sat 10am–3pm; ☎0381 54 80 00, ⓦrostock.de).

ACCOMMODATION

ROSTOCK

Altes Hafenhaus Strandstr. 93 ☎0381 493 01 10, ⓦaltes-hafenhaus.de. Small, rather elegant hotel overlooking the harbour, with stained glass, wood floors and art gallery all adding to the appeal of a late Baroque building. Room style is traditional, though enlivened by pops of bright colour in soft furnishings. €99

GreifenNest August-Bebel-Str. 49 ☎0381 877 56 18, ⓦgreifennest.de. A relaxed address for the post-backpacker market midway between the centre and KTV bar district.

Pleasant simple doubles and excellent family rooms, some en suite. Also provides a spacious modern lounge and kitchen, and small backyard with hammocks. €60

Hanse Hostel Doberaner Str. 96 ☎0381 25 29 99 80, ⓦhanse-hostel.de. Friendly family-owned hostel run by young staff, all an acceptable stagger (or a short ride on tram #4) from Rostock's bar scene. Bright and spotless, it has two- to eight-bed dorms as well as cheap singles and doubles, free internet access and a small yard with barbecue. Dorms €14, doubles €56

Jellyfish Hostel Beginenberg 25-26 ☎0381 444 38 58, ⓦjellyfish-hostel.com. Modern hostel in a nineteenth-century townhouse where spacious rooms and design details lift the four- to eight-bed dorms and doubles (some en suite). Also has a good kitchen and lounge. A great budget option in the centre. Dorms €17, doubles €56

Lotte Wismarsche Str. 1a ☎0381 377 92 92, ⓦstadtpension-rostock.de. This is a comfortable pension close to Rostock's bar scene. The watchword is eclectic: think rough walls, stripped pine floors and the occasional antique. Not to all tastes but if thrift-shop style is your thing, you'll be charmed. €65

pentahotel Schwaansche Str. 6 ☎0381 497 00, ⓦpentahotels.com. Superbly located just off – and accessible from – the pedestrianized high street, this glass-skinned-style hotel follows the penta chain's trademark

eclectic decor and relaxed ambience, plus has nice touches like on-demand films. Dynamic pricing produces wide price ranges. €129

Sonne Neuer Markt 2 ☎0381 497 30, ⓦrostock .steigenberger.de. The executive's choice is this member of the Steigenberger chain – with all the comfortable mod cons you'd expect of a four-star, and with a great location on Neuer Markt. Breakfast costs €25 extra. €139

WARNEMÜNDE

Am Leuchtturm Am Leuchtturm 16 ☎0381 543 70, ⓦhotel-am-leuchtturm.de. Located by the lighthouse of the name, this is a small hotel on the beachfront with sea views from most of its 35 rooms. Bright and breezy decor in blue and yellow, and spacious dimensions. €179

DJH Warnemünde Parkstr. 47 ☎0381 54 81 70, ⓦjugendherbergen-mv.de. Five-star standards and a broad sweep of silver sands just across the road makes this hostel in a former weather station one of the most popular in the state. Most rooms and dorms are en suite. Dorms €31.80, doubles €73.40

Strandhotel Hübner Seestr. 1 ☎0381 543 40, ⓦhotel-huebner.de. There are more luxurious hotels in Warnemünde, but none have the beach location of this modern resort hotel. Add in sea views (worth paying extra for) and superb spa and pool facilities for a fine stay. €185

EATING AND DRINKING

While **Rostock**'s central Altstadt is largely bereft of good eating opportunities, there are options in streets above the harbour. In **Warnemünde**, Am Strom is chock-full of fish restaurants whose menus could be photocopies, while Mühlenstrasse has cheaper café-restaurants away from the happy hordes. The Rostock drinking scene is focused in the Kröpeliner Tor-Vorstadt (**KVT**) west of Schröder Platz around Leonhardstrasse.

ROSTOCK

CAFÉS AND BARS

Central Café Leonhardstr. 22 ☎0381 490 46 48. Laidback modern brasserie in the heart of the Kröpeliner Tor-Vorstadt scene that is a great spot for breakfast, a light meal or a mellow drink. Long a hub of the KVT scene. Mon–Thurs 2–10.30pm, Fri 2–11pm, Sat 11am–11pm, Sun 11am–10.30pm.

Stadtkind Leonhardstr 5 ☎0381 252 67 50. Don't worry about the name, which translates as "City Boy". With its black-and-white tower-block imagery, beige leather banquettes and a large corner-terrace, this lounge-bar attracts a clientele of relaxed hipsters for a quiet drink. Daily 7pm–late.

RESTAURANTS

★**Albert & Emile** Altschmeiderstr. 8 ☎0381 493 43 73, ⓦalbert-emile.de. Perhaps the most romantic meal in Rostock, where old wood and candlelight suggest a classic French bistro (its owners hail from Bordeaux) but

the seasonal dishes (mains circa €18) are actually international, interesting – zucchini blossom stuffed with young vegetables and crayfish is typical – and always home-made. Great wine list, too. Tues–Fri noon–2pm & 6.30–11pm, Sat 6.30–11pm.

★**Borwin** Am Strande 2 ☎0381 490 75 25, ⓦborwin -hafenrestaurant.de. While not cheap (mains around €20), this harbourside restaurant with a great terrace is a popular choice, as much for its casual ambience – the terrace is almost smart beach-shack – as its five-star fish menu. The day's catch is chalked up on a board outside. Daily noon–midnight.

PUBS AND INNS

Zum Alten Fritz Warnowufer 65 ☎0381 20 87 80, ⓦalter-fritz.de. Tasty home-made German pub food like *Schweinshaxe* or Mecklenburger *Rippernbraten* (rolled pork with dried fruits) and fine fresh beers are served by this microbrewery, which has a large terrace by the harbour in summer. Daily 11am–midnight.

15

Zur Kogge Wokrenter Str. 27 ☎ 0381 493 44 93, ⓦ zur-kogge.de. Touristy but fun historic harbour-*Gaststätte*, whose splendid galleried interior has stained glass and immaculately varnished booths like cabins. A menu of predominantly fish dishes is not as expensive as you'd expect. Jan–March Mon–Fri 4–11pm, Sat noon–midnight; April–Dec daily 11.30am–midnight.

NIGHTLIFE

MAU club Warnowufer 56 ☎ 0381 202 35 76, ⓦ mauclub.de. Harbourside club that programmes a mixed bag of gigs and clubs at weekends. Expect gigs from folk to punk via indie, and clubnights that can be anything from indie to doom-metal; best check before you enter. Fri & Sat: gigs 7/8pm–late, clubnights 10pm–late.

WARNEMÜNDE

Schusters Seepromenade 1 ⓦ schusters-strandbar.de. The chill-out spot of choice in Warnemünde is this beach-bar at the end of Am Strom, near the old lighthouse. Its sunloungers, potted palms and cocktails are as close as it gets to St Tropez hereabouts, with prices to match. Daily 11am–late.

Studentenkeller Universitätsplatz 5 ☎ 0381 45 59 28, ⓦ studentenkeller.de. One of Rostock's long-standing venues, this cellar bar schedules student-friendly nights of party tunes and oldies, and has free entry on Tues, otherwise on the first hour after opening. Times vary, usually Tues, Wed & Fri–Sat 8pm–late.

15

Darss-Zingst peninsula

Artists have long acclaimed the vast land-, sea- and skyscapes of the conjoined **Darss** and **Zingst** islets that arc east of Rostock. In the late 1800s, they founded an artists' colony in Ahrenshoop, which must have been a surprise for the fishing village. Today the peninsula is a backwater of gentrified holiday villages treasured by north Germans as a nature getaway. With kilometres of wild beach and birdlife in the **Western Pomeranian Boddenlandschaft national park** (ⓦ www.nationalpark-vorpommersche-boddenlandschaft.de) and chic boutiques in thatched houses, the peninsula is a fine way to lose a day between Rostock and Stralsund.

Ahrenshoop is the focus for shopping and culture alike, a chic village-resort which maintains its artistic credentials in a slew of galleries. The new **Kunstmuseum Ahrenshoop** in the village centre (daily: March–Oct 11am–6pm; Nov–Feb 10am–5pm; €8; ⓦ kunstmuseum-ahrenshoop.de) is the best, focusing on the early decades of the colony when artists sought refuge from the Nazi regime in this remote corner. There are at least ten other galleries in the village that hang works by today's artists: **Kunstkaten** (generally daily 10am–1pm & 2–5/6pm; ⓦ kunstkaten.de), occupying a traditional house on Strandweg, has been going strong for over a century.

The rest of the peninsula is almost wilfully low-key by comparison: a place for simple pleasures like strolling and cycling. A popular option is the eastern tip beyond Zingst, where Europe's largest **crane roost** – up to 50,000 birds – occupies the coastal marshes to the south (the Bodden of the national park's name) in spring and autumn. Bike hire is available at a hut by the car park.

INFORMATION   DARSS-ZINGST PENINSULA

Ahrenshoop Kirchnersgang 2 (April to mid-June & mid-Sept to Oct Mon–Fri 9am–5pm, Sat 10am–3pm; mid-June to mid-Sept Mon–Fri 9am–6pm, Sat & Sun 10am–3pm; Nov–March Mon–Fri 9am–4pm, Sat 10am–3pm; ☎ 038220 66 66 10, ⓦ ostseebad-ahrenshoop.de).

Stralsund

STRALSUND's fate is to be en route to one of Germany's favourite holiday destinations. Many people slow to marvel at its silhouette of mighty church towers, then whiz on to Rügen – and nor do the town's shipbuilding suburbs suggest you do otherwise. However, within lies a cobbled kernel Altstadt which is as evocative of a Hanseatic past as more acclaimed members of the medieval league. During its fourteenth-century golden age, Stralsund ranked second only to Lübeck. Indeed, it was chosen as a venue in which to broker the 1370 "Peace of Stralsund" deal between the league and Denmark that represented the league's high-water mark. The legacy is a UNESCO-listed streetscape where gabled Gothic showpieces are interspersed with Baroque monuments from its two centuries as property of the Swedish Crown. Ringed by water, without the crowds of nearby Rügen, the most westerly town of western Pomerania ticks over at sleepy pace, with only a commercial port to ensure it's no museum piece.

Alter Markt

The heart of the old town, **Alter Markt** does little to dispel the illusion of Stralsund as a pocket of history. The ensemble of church and Rathaus clearly took its cue from that of Lübeck, its focus being the **Rathaus**. It's a pinnacle of Hanseatic Gothic brick, whose stage-flat show-facade bristles with peaks and turrets and is punched by rosettes to let the Baltic winds through. Swedish occupiers refashioned its two buildings into a Baroque galleried courtyard, carving its columns with fruit and adding the impressive portal at the side. **Wulfhamhaus** at Alter Markt 5 is Stralsund's finest Gothic townhouse, its facade a deliberate mirror to the Rathaus opposite.

15

St Nikolaikirche

Alter Markt • April, May, Sept & Oct Mon–Sat 9am–6pm, Sun 1–4pm; June–Aug Mon–Sat 9am–7pm, Sun 1–4pm; Nov–March Mon–Sat 10am–4pm, Sun 1–4pm • €2

The Rathaus was conceived in tandem with the adjacent **St Nikolaikirche**, also built in the fourteenth century. All furniture is eclipsed by a frothy Baroque high altar by Berlin's Andreas Schlüter, with a triangular Eye of God spitting lightning above a boiling cloud of putti. Around the ambulatory at the back of the choir is one of Europe's earliest astronomical clocks (1394), its bearded craftsmen pictured at a side-window, and the only surviving medieval guild altar, the *Pew of the Novgorod Traders*, with an image of Russian hunters harvesting squirrel pelts for a Hanseatic merchant, on the right.

The harbour

Off Alter Markt, gabled merchants' houses peel back along Fährstrasse – which linked the two hubs of medieval life in Stralsund, port and government – to the once-shabby **harbour**, now reviving through tourism. Before the arrival of the Ozeaneum aquarium, the area's highlight was windjammer **Gorch Fock I** (daily: April–Sept 10am–6pm; Oct–March 11am–4pm; €4.50; Ⓦgorchfock1.de), which lies opposite on a semi-permanent mooring; for an extra €11 (April–Sept) you can ascend the ratlines to a yard arm 12m above the deck.

Ozeaneum

Daily 9.30am–6pm, until 8pm June to mid-Sept • €16 • Ⓦ ozeaneum.de

The showpiece of the harbour is the striking **Ozeaneum** aquarium, one of the main draws of Stralsund. Providing wow factor among the child-friendly exhibits are full-size models of whales and a 2.6-million-litre tank of North Sea life; other aquaria include Baltic and Atlantic seas, including an underwater tunnel. It's at its best when crowds ease in late afternoon.

Meeresmuseum and Kulturhistorisches Museum

Mönchstr. 25 **Meeresmuseum** Daily 10am–5pm, closed Mon Oct–May • €9 • Ⓦ meeresmuseum.de • **Kulturhistorisches Museum** Daily 10am–5pm, closed Mon Nov–Jan • €6

Before the Ozeaneum, Stralsund's pride and joy was its **Meeresmuseum** (Oceanographic Museum) in a former Dominican priory south of the Alter Markt (via Ravensberger Strasse). Small in scale, it remains one of Stralsund's most enduringly popular attractions for children, largely because of its 45 tanks of tropical sea life, including turtles.

Sharing the building (though with a different entrance) is town history collection the **Kulturhistorisches Museum**. Exhibits of medieval art and regional finds are small beer beside the architecture – the former refectory, canopied by vaults and muralled at its centre with what appears to be a beaming potato, is beautiful. Upstairs rooms fast-forward through four centuries of interior decor. Your ticket also buys you into **Museumshaus** at Mönchstr. 38 (same hours), a restored merchant's house (1320) which retains its original hoist.

St Marienkirche

Neuer Markt **Church** Mon–Sat 9am–6pm, Sun noon–6pm • Free • **Tower** Mon–Sat 10am–5pm, Sun noon–5pm • €4

One way to understand the **St Marienkirche** at the south end of the Altstadt is as a merchants' riposte to the government Nikolaikirche – traders funded it and no building better expresses mercantile confidence during the late 1300s. If the Baroque caps and sheer bulk impresses outside, the volume awes within, rising 33 vertiginous metres to constellations of star vaulting as you enter. You can also wind up the 366 steps of a tight spiral staircase to a 90m-high viewing platform in the tower.

ARRIVAL AND INFORMATION   STRALSUND

By train The Hauptbahnhof is west of the Altstadt. Walk over causeway Tribseer Damm and you reach Neuer Markt, the southern axis of the town linked by Mönchstrasse to its centre, the Alter Markt. Large churches on both squares are handy homing-beacons.
Destinations Binz, Rügen (14 daily; 50min); Greifswald (every 30min; 20min); Neubrandenburg (hourly; 1hr

30min); Züssow (every 30min; 40min).
Tourist office Alter Markt 9 (May–Oct Mon–Fri 10am–6pm, Sat & Sun 10am–2pm; Nov–April Mon–Fri 10am–5pm, Sat 10am–2pm; general ☎ 03831 246 90, accommodation ☎ 03831 24 69 69, ⓦ stralsundtourismus.de).

ACCOMMODATION

Altstadt Pension Peiss Tribseer Str. 15 ☎ 03831 30 35 80, ⓦ altstadt-pension-peiss.de. Small, friendly place near Neuer Markt that's one of the most appealing options away from the harbour area, with good, modern rooms of wood floors and colourful fabrics, plus a small rear garden. **€115**
Hafenresidenz Seestr. 10–13 ☎ 03831 281 12, ⓦ hotel-hafenresidenz.de. Views in this stylish modern four-star on the harbour are either of the Altstadt or across the bay – the terrace is a lovely spot for breakfast in summer. The building, a former pump house, lends a touch of industrial chic. Facilities include a spa and gym. **€121**
Hostel Stralsund Reiferbahn 11 ☎ 03831 28 47 40, ⓦ hostel-stralsund.com. Bright, independent hostel a 10min walk east of the harbour. Coloured accent walls add character to the crisp Scandi style in the two- to six-bed rooms; there are no bunks except in the largest dorm, and

doubles are probably the biggest bargain in town. Also has laundry, internet, a barbecue area and bike rental. Dorms **€16**, doubles **€46**
★**Scheelehof** Fährestr. 23-5 ☎ 03831 28 33 00, ⓦ hotel-stralsund-scheelehof.de. Just off Alter Markt, this boutique 4-star spa hotel, carved from several interconnected medieval merchant houses, is a joy. Dashes of artistic flair bring character to modern rooms that are either neutral or nod to former Hanseatic days, while the wetroom-style bathrooms are excellent. Upper storeys offer the best views. **€114**
Sund-Camp Altefähr Am Kurpark 1, Altefähr ☎ 038306 754 83, ⓦ sund-camp.de. The nearest campsite is on Rügen island on the other side of the harbour. Ferries of Weisse Flotte shuttle from the harbour (daily late April to Oct; ⓦ weisse-flotte.de) or there's a year-round local bus service. Pitch **€5.50**, plus **€5.50** per person

EATING AND DRINKING

The harbour has emerged as an eating district, with several **fish restaurants** providing tables on the old wharves. For a snack, the inner harbour has the usual boats serving fresh smoked fish and sandwiches. No one comes to Stralsund for **nightlife**, yet the port area provides pleasant drinking in summer.

Monopol Mühlenstr. 55 ☎03831 203 45 54, ⓦkaffee-monopol.de. The best coffee in town, say locals, comes from this little *Roasterie* off Alter Markt: think mid-century modern style and cool jazz. Mon–Fri 10am–6pm, Sat 10am–1pm.

Das Torschliesserhaus Am Kütertor, off Mühlenstr. ☎03831 29 30 32, ⓦtorschliesserhaus-stralsund.de. In an old house adjacent to the town's medieval walls, this popular place has rustic decor over two levels and a *Gutbürgerlich* menu that, while solid rather than spectacular, comes at low to moderate prices. Daily noon–3pm & 6–11pm.

Wulflamstuben Alter Markt 5 ☎03831 29 15 33, ⓦwulflamstuben.de. The mid-priced German menu here covers all bases, and quality is consistently good. But where this place – in one of the town's finest patrician houses

– really scores is its location opposite the Rathaus, perfect for alfresco dining in summer. Daily 11am–11pm.

Zum Goldenen Anker An der Fährbrücke 8 ☎03831 28 05 45. The closest Stralsund comes to a pub is this harbour bar beside the *Gorch Foch I* barque that's just the right side of shabby. It's cosy in winter, and in summer its terrace gets the sunset. Daily from 4pm.

Zum Scheel At the *Scheelehof* hotel, Fährstr. 23–5 ☎03831 28 33 112, ⓦhotel-stralsund-scheelehof.de. Spectacular dining in a modernized Renaissance merchant's hall, all red-brick and beams. It's a stylish backdrop for modern-German cooking: expect the likes of cod in citron-butter or braised beef cheek with smoky apple on a short menu (mains circa €20, three-course menus €51); lunch menus offer great value. The hotel's *Scheel's Labor* cellar bar is ideal for an aperitif or nightcap. Daily noon–11pm.

Rügen

Ever since the Romantics eulogized an island where coast and country collide, **RÜGEN** has held a special place in German hearts. The great, good and fairly unsavoury of the last two centuries – Caspar David Friedrich, whose paintings did more than any poster to promote its landscapes, Brahms and Bismarck, a couple of Kaisers and assorted grand dukes, Thomas Mann, Hitler and GDR leader Erich Honecker – not to mention millions of families, have taken their holidays on an island renowned for chalk cliffs, 56km of silver sands and beautiful deciduous woodland. Notwithstanding a newfound sheen as coastal resorts reassert themselves as the fashionable bathing centres they were in the early 1900s, Rügen is timeless and uncomplicated, with an innocent, Famous Five quality. Largely protected as a biosphere reserve, its rural southeast is a gorgeous preindustrial landscape where a steam engine chuffs around small beach resorts and inland villages knot around lanes shaded by ancient trees.

Those on a flying visit usually only tick off premier resort **Binz**, a classic Baltic holiday destination renowned for its handsome Bäderarchitektur, and the Jasmund peninsula's **Königstuhl**, a chalk cliff immortalized by Friedrich. Do so and you may be forgiven for wondering what the fuss is about – together, they are the busiest destinations on Rügen, and can be overcrowded. With an area of 926 square kilometres, Germany's largest island has less-populated corners to discover. Places like **Putbus**, not so much a planned town as a Neoclassical folly writ large; smaller resorts near the rural **Mönchgut peninsula**; or the **Jasmund National Park**'s chalk cliffs cloaked in spacious forest. There are curios such as **Prora**, Hitler's former holiday camp, or the former fishing village of **Vitt** in the windswept northwest. And then there are places like **Hiddensee**, a car-free sliver of land just off the west coast that may be the most idyllic spot in the area.

ACTIVITIES ON RÜGEN

Should you tire of promenading or loafing in a *Strandkorb*, any number of activities operators will be happy to help you pass the days. Tourist offices have maps of **hiking trails** around all resorts; recommended easy day-hikes include the rural Mönchgut peninsula south of Göhren, its tip protected as a biosphere reserve, and the cliffside route through the Jasmund National Park from Sassnitz to the Königsstuhl. Reederei Ostsee (ⓦreederei-ostsee-tour.de) schedules **tourist cruises** from Binz and Sassnitz past the Stübenkammer to Kap Arkona several times daily (April–Oct; 4hr; €20). And numerous small providers offer **sailing**, **kite- and windsurfing** and **riding**. The tourist office in Binz is the best all-island reference, with racks of flyers.

15

15

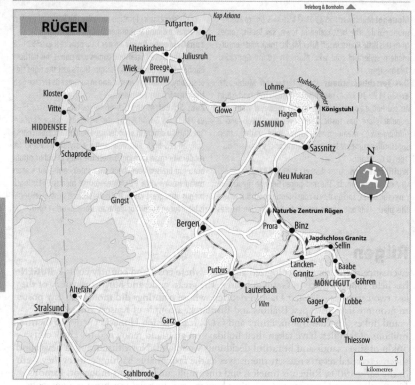

Binz

BINZ, or Ostseebad Binz to give the most celebrated former bathing resort its full title, is Rügen's holiday capital. If tourist mini-trains, cafés, boutiques and all the adjuncts of a jolly holiday resort are not to your taste, this is not your place in peak season. High-rise it is not, however. Friendly and approachable, Binz is instead characterized by the **Bäderarchitektur** of its time as a fashionable sea-water bathing resort in the early 1900s. Central shady streets are lined with the former villas of German high society, adorned with carved verandas and wrought iron, all splashed with a uniform coat of white paint. The result is pure holiday architecture – light-hearted rather than ostentatious. Now as then, the heart of the seafront promenade is the palatial **Kurhaus** (now a five-star hotel – see p.839), where nineteenth-century bathers sipped spa waters. At its shoulder, at the end of main drag Hauptstrasse, is the requisite pier, and in front of it all is 5km of fine white sands, all scattered with wicker *Strandkörbe* seats.

Jagdschloss Granitz

2km south of Binz • May–Sept daily 9am–6pm; Oct & April daily 10am–4pm; Nov–March Tues–Sun 10am–4pm • €6 • ⓦ jagdschloss-granitz .de • Naturbe-Prora-Express tourist land-train from Binz pier (every 45min high season, every 2hr low season; €8 return; ⓦ jagdschlossexpress .de); *Rasender Roland* steam train (approx hourly; ⓦ ruegensche-baederbahn.de); shuttle land-train from *Rasender Roland* terminus €3

In the 1830s, four decades before any sea-water bather wetted an ankle, island aristocrat Prince Wilhelm Malte I rebuilt his hunting cabin on Tempelberg hill south of the village to create **Jagdschloss Granitz**. The centrepiece of the dusty-pink neo-Gothic castle is a 38m tower designed a decade later by Prussian architect Karl Friedrich Schinkel, whose viewing platform permits good views. The story goes that Malte only requested the tower to settle a dispute over island property rights – the Swedes finally agreed to his terms that he could keep whatever he could see from his lodge.

Located around 2km south of Binz, the lodge is most easily accessed on the Jagdschloss-Express tourist-train that runs from Binz pier via the resort centre to the entrance. Alternatively, the steam train *Rasender Roland* stops at a terminus downhill from the castle, or there's also a car park; it takes around fifteen minutes to walk the 2km up to the castle from either unless you take the shuttle land-train.

Prora and around

Sea-bathers were not the only ones impressed by the good beach that extends from Binz to **PRORA** 3km west. In 1936 Hitler chose the site for a holiday camp (see box below) and while some blocks are finally being renovated, much of Prora's fascination is simply as a raw, unsanitized curio. The beach on the other side is as fine as ever and spared the 20,000 holiday-makers the Nazis intended – the antidote to the crowded sands in Binz.

15

Dokumentations Zentrum Prora

Objektstr. Gebäude 1 • Daily: March–May, Sept & Oct 10am–6pm; June–Aug 9.30am–7pm; Nov–Feb 11am–4pm • €6 • ⓦ proradok.de • Naturbe-Prora-Express tourist land-train from Binz pier (at least hourly Easter–Oct; €7 return; ⓦ jagdschlossexpress.de)

The most rigorous overview of Prora's past is **Dokumentations Zentrum Prora**, which exhibits German-only display boards on the resort's conception and construction, plus an illuminating thirty-minute subtitled documentary that confronts the issues over current use. Notes in English are available.

KulturKunststatt Prora

Daily: summer 9am–7pm; winter 10am–4pm • €6.90 • ⓦ kulturkunststatt.de • Naturbe-Prora-Express tourist land-train from Binz pier (at least hourly Easter–Oct; €7 return; ⓦ jagdschlossexpress.de)

Around the corner from the Dokumentations Zentrum is **KulturKunststatt Prora**, a banner title for six oddball private collections spread over six storeys, including the **NS-KdF Museum** with an 18m model of the completed holiday complex, and **NVA Museum Prora**, which looks at Prora's use by the National People's Army from 1952.

Naturbe Zentrum Rügen

2km west of Prora • Daily: May–Sept 9.30am–9.30pm; April & Oct 9.30am–5.30pm; Nov–March 9.30am–4.30pm • €9.50 • ⓦ nezr.de • Naturbe-Prora-Express tourist land-train from Binz pier (at least hourly Easter–Oct; €7 return; ⓦ jagdschlossexpress.de)

Bizarrely, the decades that this corner of Rügen spent off-limits as a GDR military zone helped preserve its rich biodiversity: a mix of pasture, woodland, wetland and coastal habitats. At the **Naturbe Zentrum Rügen**, 2km west of Prora, a rather dry, family-orientated

---

HITLER'S HOLIDAY CAMP

The apogee of the Nazis' "KdF" or *Kraft durch Freude* ("Strength through Joy") movement was their **seaside resort** at Prora on the east coast of Rügen. Known as **Kolos** ("Colossus"), it was built to provide R&R for the German people – up to 20,000 at a time – before the nation's forthcoming military expansion east. However, construction stalled upon the outbreak of hostilities in 1939 – ironically, the only families to stay here were those bombed out of Hamburg by the RAF in 1945 – then, under the GDR, it was off-limits as a **military base**. The camp is classic dictatorial architecture – megalomaniac in size, brutal in style – its six-storey reinforced-concrete blocks arcing away behind the coast for over three miles. It takes over twenty minutes just to cycle along the length of the entire complex. Having slowly fallen into ruin for decades as the debate raged over its future, several of the blocks are now being renovated as holiday apartments, and one building at the north end has been rehabilitated as Europe's largest **youth hostel** (see p.840).

exhibition highlights the local flora through interactive displays. However, the centre is really just a prelude for its 1.2km **forest canopy walk**: a raised boardwalk winds up through mixed forest to a 40m viewing tower with views over Rügen.

Göhren and the Mönchgut peninsula

If Binz has the crowds, **GÖHREN**, at Rügen's east tip, has the beaches. The modest little resort spills downhill on either side of a headland to two fine strands: **Nordstrand**, home to the town's pier, is the most developed and sweeps along the shore framed by cliff headlands, while on the east side is quiet **Südstrand**. The resort is almost somnambulant compared with Binz, its only sights two modest adjacent museums on the high street that flag up the village's roots as a fishing and farming settlement: the **Heimatmuseum**, in an 1850s farmer-fisherman's house at Sandstr. 1 (daily: May & June Tues–Sun 10am–5pm; July–Oct Mon–Sat 10am–5pm; Nov & Dec erratic opening; free; ⓦmoenchguter-museen-ruegen .de), traces Göhren's metamorphosis from prehistory via Slavic settlement to Rügen's third largest resort; while nearby **Museumshof** (open erratically) is a low-eaved farmstead complex housing rickety carriages and agricultural implements.

South of Göhren, the remote **Mönchgut peninsula** pokes a finger of lovely countryside into the Baltic. Another effortless expanse of sand lies south of Südstrand, while on the other side are sheltered bays on the Hagensche Wiek. Pretty village **Gross Zicker**, meanwhile, stands at the head of a protected upland of wildflower heath and meadow, **Zikersches Höft**, crisscrossed by walking trails.

Putbus and Lauterbach

PUTBUS is a surprise among the villages and wheat fields of south Rügen. Prince Wilhelm Malte I was ahead of his time when in 1818 he gave Rügen its first bathing resort. His plan was not merely villas behind the beach, but a small Neoclassical spa-town. With its classical layout and solid white boxes, the self-proclaimed "White Town of Rügen" fancies itself a cut above other island villages, boasting of its cultural weight and "Italianische charme".

Its core is the **Circus**, where smart townhouses encircle a self-congratulatory obelisk to mark the town's completion in 1836. West along main road Alleestrasse, Rügen's only **theatre** is a splendid statement of princely delusions, with a portico fit for a city and an interior of wrought-iron balconies (free tours, times posted by side entrance). The Markt at its shoulder is a similarly noble space. For himself, the prince commissioned Berlin's finest architect, Johann Gottfried Steinmeyer, to design a Neoclassical Schloss. The GDR regime saw instead a symbol of feudal repression and dynamited the lot in the 1960s – the story goes a local mayor wanted to impress visiting top brass. Nevertheless, a handsome **orangerie** and, most impressively, the mature **Schlosspark** itself remain. The former doubles as the tourist office (see p.839) and a gallery. The latter's naturalistic gardens are a lovely spot for an amble.

A road that arrows ruler-straight from the Schlosspark is channelled past the tiny port of **LAUTERBACH** by an avenue of trees towards an impressive span of Doric columns that front the bathhouse of Malte's original spa resort, today a smart spa-hotel (see p.840).

Jasmund

If any one area is responsible for Rügen's transition from bucolic backwater to holiday haven it is **JASMUND**. A thumb of woodland and fields poked into the Baltic, much of it protected as the UNESCO-listed **Jasmund National Park** (ⓦwww.nationalpark -jasmund.de), the peninsula north of Binz is famous for its wooded chalk cliffs. These are the **Stubenkammer** popularized in works by Romantic painter Caspar David Friedrich, a stretch of cliffs that extends for several kilometres.

15

The Königsstuhl

Nationalpark-Zentrum Königsstuhl Daily: Easter–Oct 9am–7pm; Nov–Easter 10am–5pm • €7.50 • ⓦ koenigsstuhl.com • **Shuttle bus** Daily: Easter–Oct roughly every 30min 9.20am–7.20pm; Nov–Easter 10.20am–5.20pm • €1.65 one-way, €3.20 return

The most celebrated section of the Stubenkammer is the mighty **Königsstuhl** cleft that juts from the cliffs – the name "king's stool" derives from a folk tale that whoever scaled its 117m face could claim Rügen's throne. Partly thanks to Friedrich, the Königsstuhl is a landmark lodged in the national consciousness, though whether an artist who eulogized raw nature would have set up his easel today is a moot point because the Königsstuhl is one of Rügen's premier natural attractions.

Access is from a car park by the main road at **Hagen**; the car park for the *Gasthaus* opposite is cheaper for day-long stays should you intend to walk in the area. From Hagen's car park you can either walk 3km through beech woods – look out for the earthwork Herthaburg, the remains of a ninth-century Slavic fort – or take a shuttle bus to reach the **Nationalpark-Zentrum Königsstuhl**, with child-friendly multimedia displays and a panoramic cinema which screens a wraparound film on fauna and flora. Far better is the real thing outside – the fabled cliff and a mesmerizing seascape that shimmers startling shades of jade on sunny days. Visit as early as you can to avoid the worst crowds; the sight was still accessible out of hours at the time of writing. You can also avoid it altogether and walk twenty minutes south to **Victoria-Sicht** through beautiful ancient beech woods. The name comes courtesy of Kaiser Wilhelm I who visited in 1865 with his daughter, later Britain's Queen Victoria.

The Königsstuhl is also accessible by direct buses from nearby Sassnitz (see below), which is also the starting point for the lovely **Hochuferweg trail** (see box below) that wends its way for 9km along the clifftops to the Königsstuhl.

Sassnitz

SASSNITZ is usually overlooked in the rush to the Königsstuhl. Yet Rügen's principal port – part commercial and fishing harbour, part maritime-themed tourist attraction – was one of the first seaside resorts on the island. This is only apparent in the town's kernel, a lovely tangle of lanes north of the harbour; if driving, continue ahead as the through-road bends sharp left towards the Jasmund National Park. In recent years it has acquired a number of interesting galleries and jewellery ateliers – another reason to stop.

Kap Arkona

The wind-blown Wittow peninsula is as far north as Rügen gets. It's a remote spot of undulating fields, with a long beach along the isthmus to Jasmund and chalk cliffs at **Kap Arkona** (ⓦ kap-arkona.de) at the island's northern tip. The surprise is that mass tourism has arrived here too, for there are some modest attractions accessed from

---

THE HOCHUFERWEG TRAIL TO KÖNIGSSTUHL

The most celebrated walk on Rügen is the 9km **Hochuferweg** trail from Sassnitz (see above) to the Königshstuhl. Named among the top ten walks in Germany, it's a fairly easy clifftop walk that offers time to appreciate this landscape's beautiful ancient beech forest and palate of jade sea, green leaves and white chalk.

The easiest start is from a car park on main road Stubenkammerstrasse at the northwest end of Sassnitz. A path forges through beech forest for 2km, then cuts towards the coast and the Wissower Klinken cliffs – the Ernst-Moritz-Arndt-Sicht viewpoint 1km north offers good views. Another couple of hours further north along the cliffs, at Victoria-Sicht, you glimpse the **Königsstuhl**, then soon afterwards stroll from an empty track into the crowds at the spur itself.

The trail presses on to Lohme, or buses #14, #20 and #23 return to the Sassnitz car park from the Königsstuhl car park at Hagen. The tourist office at Sassnitz (see p.839) sells hiking maps.

15

HIDDENSEE ISLAND

"Dat söte Länneken" sighs the marketing material of **Hiddensee island** (ⓦ seebad-hiddensee .de) off the west coast of Rügen. "The sweet little land", 16km long, only 300m wide at its narrowest point, the second sunniest spot in Germany after Usedom (1805 hours average a year) and entirely car-free, remains the popular outing it was since day-tripping artists visited in the early 1900s. Most people potter in the vicinity of the island's three villages – **Kloster**, **Vitte** and **Neuendorf** – which together account for the year-round 1100 population. **Kloster** is the pick of the bunch for looks and a fine beach.

However, what appeals most are the windswept landscapes that give the Hiddensee a sense of space and clear horizons. None are difficult to access by bikes, which can be rented in every village for around €10 a day, or horse-and-cart trips offered in summer. The premier destinations are the meadows in the north known as the **Dornbusch**, their wide skyline punctured only by a lighthouse at the highest point. A single road meanders south of island "capital" Vitte through swathes of protected flowering heath to **Neuendorf**, from where a track continues towards a second lighthouse. Wild heath beyond slowly peters out into the Gellen, a sandbank popular with birdwatchers.

Access is by **ferries** of Reederei Hiddensee (☎0180 321 21 50, ⓦ reederei-hiddensee.de). These operate from Schaprode to all villages several times a day (€15.30–17.70 return) and also from Stralsund three times a day (€18.90–19.70 return).

gateway village, **Putgarden**. Here you'll find a vast visitors' car park for the cape, an information office, bike hire (€6/day) and a mini-train (one-way €2, €3.50 return) that pootles 2km north on the only road to the sights at the cape's tip.

The Schinkelturm and Neuer Lechturm

Kap Arkona **Schinkelturm** Daily 10am–6pm • €2 • **Neuer Lechturm** Daily 11am–5pm • €3

One benefit of Rügen's coming under Prussian rule in 1815 after two centuries of serfdom under the Swedish Crown was a navigation light to warn of shallows off the cape. Built in 1827, the **Schinkelturm** is a stubby red-brick rectangle named for its architect, Berlin's Karl Friedrich Schinkel, with missable displays on optics and German lighthouses, and views from the top of its iron staircase. The panorama is a little better from the **Neuer Lechturm** nearby which, at 35m, is over 15m higher than its forerunner.

The Burgwall

Kap Arkona • Daily 10am–4.45pm • €1

Near the lighthouses is what's left of the **Burgwall**, a fort of the Slavic tribes who occupied the island from 500 AD. Danish chroniclers in the twelfth century wrote about discovering sculptures of a four-headed deity after their conquest of the stronghold. Only earthworks providing views east remain of what is thought to have been a religious site.

Vitt

Reached after a kilometre on the path beyond the Burgwall, **VITT** harks back to the traditional villages all but lost elsewhere on Rügen. Gathered in a cleft above a shingle beach, the picture-postcard fishing hamlet traces its origins to a settlement trading with the Slavs – many of its thatched houses perpetuate an ancient rune-like numbering system. There's a pretty *Gaststätte* here, too, for lunch. By the hamlet's entrance, an octagonal chapel has an altarpiece of Christ plucking St Peter from the seas, copied from Dresden's Phillip Otto Runge, and a naive mural of villagers gazing into a stormy sea. The road from here triangulates back to Putgarden, either a 1km walk or a jaunt by horse and cart.

ARRIVAL AND DEPARTURE   RÜGEN

By train The mainland rail-line terminates in Sassnitz, though there are direct services to Binz (see p.834) from major rail points.

Destinations Berlin (1 daily; 3hr 50min); Hamburg (2 daily; 3hr 40min); Rostock (2 daily; 2hr); Stralsund (approx 12 daily; 50min).

By ferry International ferries from Sweden and Denmark sail to Sassnitz, the island's principal port.
By car Rügen is linked to Stralsund by the Rügenbrücke suspension bridge. If arriving from the east you could take the Autofähre Glewitz car ferry from Stahlbrode near Greifswald to the south tip of Rügen.

GETTING AROUND

By train All resorts on the south and east are served by standard rail services, plus the charmingly named *Rasender Roland* steam train ("Racing Roland"; ⑳ ruegensche -baederbahn.de). It runs from Lauterbach to Göhren 5 times a day (6 from Putbus), plus shuttles approximately hourly along coastal resorts from Binz to Göhren. Prices range by distance from €1.80 to €9; bikes can be carried for €3.

By tourist train The Naturbe-Prora-Express tourist landtrain (⑳ jagdschlossexpress.de) shuttles from Binz to Prora and Naturbe Zentrum Rügen at least hourly between Easter and October. The maximum return fare from Binz is €3.50.

By bus Island-capital Bergen is the hub of a local bus service operated by RPNV (⑳ rpnv.de). There's access to most areas (including the Königstuhl car park; every 45min), and services run roughly every 20min between destinations such as Bergen and Binz. Single fares range from €1.55 to €8.30, and bikes cost an additional €1.90; a Rügen day-card is €12.10.

By ferry Expensive but enjoyable tourist cruises are operated by a number of lines, including Reederei Ostsee-Tour (⑳ reederei-ostsee-tour.de), Adler Schiffe (⑳ adler-schiffe.de) and Weisse Flotte (⑳ weisse-flotte .de). Most ply routes from Göhren to Sassnitz via Sellin and Binz between May and October, with up to 11 departures a day between, say, Binz and Sassnitz. Panoramic cruises also go to the Stubenkammer's chalk cliffs from Sassnitz. Timetables are in tourist offices and are posted on piers where ferries dock, or consult ⑳ ruegen-schifffahrt.de.

By bike Largely flat, with dedicated cycle lanes off main roads, Rügen is a joy to cycle, the only caveat being rough cobbles in some inland villages. Cycling maps *Radeln auf Rügen* are available in tourist offices, and bikes can be rented at the Bahnhof of each resort. Most RPNV buses transport bikes, as does the *Rasender Roland* steam train.

INFORMATION

Binz tourist office In the Haus des Gastes, Heinrich-Heine-Str. 7 (April–Oct Mon–Fri 9am–6pm, Sat & Sun 10am–6pm; Nov–March Mon–Fri 9am–4pm, Sat & Sun 11am–4pm; ☎ 038393 14 81 48, ⑳ ostseebad-binz.de).

Göhren tourist office On the high street at Poststr. 9 (April–Sept Mon–Fri 9am–7pm, Sat & Sun 10am–6pm; Oct–April Mon–Thurs 9am–noon & 1–4.30pm, Fri 9am–3pm; ☎ 038308 667 90, ⑳ goehren-ruegen.de). A second information point operates from the pier at Nordstrand (mid-May to Sept daily 9am–noon).

Putbus tourist office In the orangerie on the main throughfare, Alleestr. 35 (May–Oct daily 9am–5pm; Nov–April Tues–Sat 10am–5pm; ☎ 038301 431, ⑳ putbus.de).

Sassnitz tourist office The most convenient office is beside the Stadthafen harbour at Strandpromenade 12 (daily 10am–6pm; ☎ 038392 64 90, ⑳ insassnitz.de). The other at Bahnhofstr. 19a (Mon–Fri 9am–6pm, Sat 10am–6pm, Sun 2–6pm; ☎ 038392 669 45) is handy for the Bahnhof above the port.

ACCOMMODATION

All resort **hotels** add a daily €1.50–2 *Kurtaxe* to the tariff. **Campers** are well served – a free brochure from tourist offices lists fourteen sites across the island. The tourist offices listed above are a godsend for sourcing accommodation if you wing it in high season. They're also a good source of **private rooms** or holiday homes and apartments; for a group, the latter work out cheaper than a hotel over a week.

BINZ

Ceres Strandpromenade 24 ☎ 038393 666 70, ⑳ ceres-hotel.de. A glamorous design and spa hotel styled in metropolitan minimalism – masculine shades of black, grey and cream – and with high-tech toys such as flat-screen TVs, wireless internet and sound systems in rooms. A smart restaurant serves cosmopolitan cuisine. €238

DJH Binz Sandpromenade 35 ☎ 038393 325 97, ⑳ jugendherbergen-mv.de. Excellent, modern youth hostel with four- to eight-bed rooms that's a bargain considering the location behind the beach, and absurdly popular as a result, so reservations are essential. Smaller dorms are available as twin rooms (€4.80/person extra) if space permits. Dorms €28.60

Imperial Strandpromenade 20 ☎ 038393 13 80, ⑳ krain-loew-hotellerie.de. The beachfront location and good-sized accommodation are the appeal of this small 3-star hotel in an early 1900s villa. Its 27 rooms are fairly plain but clean and comfortable. €120

Kurhaus Binz Strandpromenade 27 ☎ 038393 66 50, ⑳ tc-hotels.de. This five-star flagship resort hotel of the Travel Charme chain occupies the former palatial spa of Binz's heyday. Public areas aspire to bygone glamour while rooms are elegant and modern. Facilities include several pools and spa areas plus restaurants. €240

15

Nymphe Strandpromenade 48 ☎ 038393 122 00 00, ⓦ hotel-nymphe.de. The presence of a large iMac in every room tells you all you need to know about this small design hotel on the seafront: crisply styled modern rooms with throws of aqua or lemon to lift the neutral decor, plus a small spa. Good value. **€134**

Pension Haus Colmsee Strandpromenade 8 ☎ 038393 214 25, ⓦ hauscolmsee.de. Here's a shock: a budget stay in a historic seafront villa. Family-owned, this place provides simple but cheerful rooms with painted pine furnishings plus sea views for an extra €10. Reservations essential; minimum 3 nights in high season. **€82**

PRORA

DJH Jugendherberge Prora Mukraner Str. Gebäude 15 ☎ 038393 668 80, ⓦ jugendherbergen-mv.de. Its massive renovation completed in 2011, one block of the Nazis' Baltic family resort is open as Europe's largest youth hostel – 400 beds in 96 crisp modern rooms, all with a sea view. Dorms **€31.80**, doubles **€73.40**

GÖHREN

Inselhotel Rügen Wilhelmstr. 6 ☎ 038308 55 50, ⓦ inselhotel-ruegen.de. Faultless mid-range resort hotel that is comfortable yet rather bland. Still, the decor is inoffensive, and the price good for a location 150m from the beach. The two-bed apartments are great value considering they're almost twice the size of doubles. Apartments **€112**, doubles **€110**

Regenbogen Am Kleinbahnhof ☎ 038308 901 20, ⓦ regenbogen-camp.de. Rügen's largest campsite, but invariably busy nonetheless due to facilities like a spa and kids' playground. Well located among woods behind Nordstrand, and near the *Rasender Roland* train station. Closed Nov to mid-Dec. Pitch (two people) **€29**, pitch (single people) **€15**

Strandhaus 1 Nordstrand 1 ☎ 038308 250 97, ⓦ strandhaus1.de. A simple hostel-style pension above a restaurant that provides modern(ish) rooms, some with sea views, directly behind the beach; there's one family room. The bar can be noisy at weekends, so best to join in the fun. **€83**

EATING AND DRINKING

BINZ

Fritz Schillerstr. 6 ☎ 038393 66 33 33, ⓦ fritz-braugasthaus.de. A great option for a casual meal, this outlet of a regional chain prepares mid-priced meals like *Schnitzel* and cheap home-made burgers as well as beers from its microbrewery. The real USP is the large terrace. Daily 11am–11pm.

nixe Strandpromenade 10 ☎ 038393 66 62 00, ⓦ nixe .de. This hotel restaurant, styled in metro-cool, provides

PUTBUS AND LAUTERBACH

Badehaus Goor Fürst-Malte-Allee 1 Lauterbach ☎ 038301 882 60, ⓦ hotel-badehaus-goor.de. Smart spa hotel in the Neoclassical Badehaus of Prince Wilhelm Malte's original resort. The plush modern rooms rather struggle to match the building's promise but the vibe is calm, and the spa facilities excellent. **€136**

★ **Im Jainach** Am Yachthafen 1, Lauterbach ☎ 038301 80 90, ⓦ im-jaich.de. Clean-lined Scandinavian design and breakfast terraces beside the water in immaculate well-equipped holiday houses in Lauterbach marina, either floating or raised on piles. Small in size, but this is the great escape par excellence. **€149**

Wreecher Hof Kastanienallee, Wreechen ☎ 038301 850, ⓦ wreecher-hof.de. A lovely getaway, this is a small hotel pillowed in the countryside south of Putbus. It spreads throughout a complex of thatched houses, with pretty country-style decor and a small spa and pool centre. **€119**

SASSNITZ AND LOHME (KÖNIGSSTUHL)

Krüger Naturcamping Jasmunder Str. 5 ☎ 038302 92 44, ⓦ ruegen-naturcamping.de. Nature rules in this mellow campsite beside woodland 500m west of the Königsstuhl car park, by the turn-off to Lohme – its owner runs a shuttle bus or you can walk the 3km direct to the Königsstühl. Basic facilities, but there's a simple bar with snacks on-site. Closed Nov–Easter. Pitch **€3**, plus **€7** per person

★ **Panorama-Hotel Lohme** An der Steilküste 8, Lohme ☎ 038302 91 10, ⓦ lohme.com. Comfortable (though bland) classic-modern rooms, a first-class restaurant and uninterrupted views of the sun sizzling into the Baltic from its veranda – all in all one of the most appealing hotels in this corner of Rügen, and unmatched for escapism. **€89**

Waterkant Walterstr. 3, Sassnitz ☎ 038392 509 41, ⓦ hotel-waterkant.de. A good-value seaside hotel in a garden villa whose classic-modern rooms may be fairly plain but are well-maintained, spacious and modern(ish); a room with a sea-view balcony will set you back €85. The lawns provide a broad panorama over the port. **€70**

some of the finest dining on the island, according to *Michelin* critics: expect the likes of *Zander* with aubergine cream plus Asiatic-inspired flavours created from regional seasonal produce (mains €20–35; menus from €56). May–Aug daily 6pm–midnight; Sept–April Tues–Sun 6–11pm.

★ **Strandhalle** Strandpromenade 5 ☎ 038393 315 64, ⓦ strandhalle-binz.de. This vintage hall is a Rügen legend, both for its wonderfully eccentric decor and for the cooking of Toni Münsterteicher – from the likes of *Zander*

with wasabi foam that has wowed Michelin gourmets, to house classics like Baltic cod with a potato-rosemary crust. Daily: April–Oct noon–11pm; Nov–March 6–11pm.

GÖHREN
Fischklause Sandstr. 14 ☎ 038308 256 21, ⓦ haus-karlsruhe.de. This cosy fish restaurant, tucked off the main high street, has an excellent reputation locally. Though waits can be long, they're worth it for delicious mains such

as cod in mustard sauce or Baltic wild salmon. Tues–Sun 5–late; closed Wed Oct–April.

SASSNITZ
Gastmahl des Meeres Strandpromenade 2 ☎ 038392 51 70, ⓦ gastmahl-des-meeres-ruegen.de. Rich cherrywood and bright brass lend a smart nautical air to this traditional fish restaurant by the harbour and tourist office. Daily noon–11pm.

Greifswald and around

A compact Altstadt is one sign that **GREIFSWALD** was always a bit player in the Hanseatic League; another is the lack of grand edifices compared to those of fellow leaguers. Instead it is north Germany's second oldest university, **Ernst-Moritz-Arndt-Universität**, that is the focus of a neat town you can tick off in a lazy day. Thanks to its large student population, Greifswald has a youthful energy out of all proportion to its size, and a few bars to boot. The pretty Altstadt was immortalized in the paintings of local son Caspar David Friedrich.

The Markt and around

Thanks to a now-forgotten Third Reich commander who surrendered to the Red Army without a shot in 1945, Greifswald's pretty **Markt** retains its pastel-tinted gables and Hanseatic patricians' houses; the most impressive is at no. 11, a turreted Christmas tree patterned by a brick lattice of lancet arches. All buildings are secondary to an oxblood-red Baroque Rathaus that fills the centre.

Marienkirche
Brüggstr. 35 • Mon–Fri 10am–6pm, Sat 10am–3pm, Sun 1–3pm • Free

Poking above the Markt's northeast corner, the **Marienkirche** on Brüggstrasse is unmissable because of a stubby tower that earns it the nickname "Fat Mary". Though the oldest of the town's three churches was built to celebrate the signing up to Lübeck's Hanseatic charter in 1250, no original artwork remains, nor did later furnishings survive Napoleon's troops one cold winter in the early 1800s. A Renaissance pulpit inlaid with images of Reformation heroes is a rare piece in an otherwise bare church.

Dom St Nikolai
Nikolaikirchplatz • May–Oct Mon–Sat 10am–6pm, Sun 3–6pm; Nov–April Mon–Sat 10am–3.30pm, Sun 11.30am–2.30pm • Free, tower €3

The city's ecclesiastical highlight is the **Dom St Nikolai**, a great heap of Gothic brickwork whose turreted tower buds into a series of Baroque bulbs rising behind the Markt. Friedrich loved it, setting up his easel in Greifswald wherever he could contrive to include its romantic silhouette. The whitewashed interior of "Long Nicholas" is a disappointment after such a promising overture, worth a visit only to ascend 264 steps to a viewing platform in the tower.

Pommersches Museum
Rakower Str. 9 • Tues–Sun 10am–6pm; Nov–April closes 5pm • €5 • ⓦ pommersches-landesmuseum.de

There's much to enjoy in this modern museum off the Markt, not least that most of its exhibits are in a creatively restored medieval monastery. Beautifully lit archeology and town exhibits unfold in the cellars – for once a compelling journey through history that culminates in a Renaissance tapestry commissioned by a local grandee to celebrate the arrival of Luther's new creed in Pomerania. As impressive is an art gallery whose star is, inevitably, **Caspar David Friedrich**. A representative cross-section of his works are on display, showcasing his favourite theme of natural splendour while also demonstrating his draughtsmanship in a coloured sketch of the Markt c.1818.

Wieck

While the old harbour northeast of the Markt brings a maritime tang into central Greifswald, **WIECK**, 4km to the east, is your place for the smack of salt air; in summer the two are linked by passenger cruises (3 daily), or buses #5, #6 and #7 go from outside the train station. Now lined by cafés and restaurants, the former fishing village has a resort feel around its pretty harbour spanned by a Dutch-style lifting wooden bridge. Opposite the bridge, Studentenstieg leads to what's left of a Cistercian monastery (Kloster) in **Eldena**. For a dyed-in-the-wool Romantic like Friedrich, the Gothic ruin was a wistful embodiment of melancholy, a leitmotif of decay. Even without his rose-tinted glasses it's a pretty spot for a picnic.

ARRIVAL AND INFORMATION   GREIFSWALD AND AROUND

By train On the Stralsund and Berlin lines, Greifswald Hauptbahnhof lies immediately west of the Altstadt. To reach the Markt turn left along Bahnhofstrasse then right at the elbow on to Lange Strasse, which becomes the high street.
Destinations Berlin (9 daily; 2hr 45min); Stralsund

(hourly; 20–25min).
Tourist office On the Markt in the Rathaus (March & April Mon–Fri 9am–6pm; May, June & Sept Mon–Fri 9am–6pm, Sat 10am–2pm; July & Aug Mon–Fri 9am–6pm, Sat & Sun 10am–2pm; Nov–Feb Mon–Fri 9am–5pm; ☎ 03834 52 13 80, ⓦ greifswald.de).

ACCOMMODATION

GREIFSWALD

Hôtel Galerie Mühlenstr. 10 ☎ 03834 773 78 30, ⓦ hotelgalerie.de. The best stay in the centre is this glass-skinned design hotel managed by a gallery owner – rooms are named after former exhibitors. Decor is of the streamlined minimalist variety, and most of the modern art on the walls is for sale. Excellent location just off the Markt, too. **€108**
Kronprinz Lange Str. 22 ☎ 03834 79 00, ⓦ hotelkronprinz.de. The traditional address favoured by an older clientele and visiting executives, rather dated in decor (and staff can be stuffy too) although it's comfortable

enough in the 4-star rooms and the location by the Altstadt's pedestrian high street is good. **€120**

WIECK

majuwi Yachtweg 3, Wieck ☎ 03834 83 02 950, ⓦ majuwi.de. Modern youth hostel on Wieck harbour – the name refers to its former title, the Maritimes Jugenddorf Wieck. It's a mite institutional, with modest Ikea-style dorms and doubles, all en-suite. Inevitably popular with school groups. Dorms and doubles (per person) **€26**

EATING & DRINKING

GREIFSWALD

Café Pariser Kamaunenstr. 20 ☎ 03834 32 02, ⓦ pariser-greifswald.de. Ramshackle place that's more scruffy scout-hut than student dive-bar – one to love or loathe, depending on your taste. Mon & Tues 3–9pm, Wed–Sat 8pm–late.
Fritz Markt 13 ☎ 03834 578 30, ⓦ fritz-braugasthaus .de. The Greifswald outpost of this regional brewery chain is probably the most popular address in town, with good-value traditional dishes. No faulting the setting either, in a Gothic merchant house on the Markt – idyllic on the terrace in summer. Daily 11am–midnight, Fri & Sat till 1am.
Mitt'n Drin Domstr. 53 ☎ 03834 89 95 14. Cocktails and club sounds in a modern bar near the Dom, a hangout for students and a mid-twenties and thirties crowd – a popular warm-up at weekends. Term-time daily 9am–late, otherwise 11am–late.

WIECK

Büttner's Am Hafen 1a, Wieck ☎ 03834 887 07 37, ⓦ buettners-restaurant.de. Dishes such as fried *Zander* fillet with wild garlic cream-cheese ravioli (€24) are typical of the regional and seasonal menus in this elegant restaurant at Wieck harbour: informal, but with immaculate service. Tues–Thurs from 5pm, Fri–Sun from noon.
★ **Fischer-hütte** An der Mühle 8, Wieck ☎ 03834 83 96 54, ⓦ fischer-huette.de. Ingredients come straight off the boat and into the pan at this rustic fish restaurant with tables by the harbour and a maritime-rustic interior. Blackboard specials are always worth investigating, alongside a regular menu that includes the likes of *Zander* with horseradish cream sauce. A popular weekend lunch spot. Daily 11.30am–11pm.

15

Usedom

Second to Rügen in terms of size, **USEDOM** is overshadowed by its larger sister as a Baltic resort, too. This low-lying undulating island, around 50km long and only split from the mainland for much of its length by the narrow Pennestrom channel, lacks the scenic variety of its much-mythologized neighbour. Yet during the early 1900s Usedom was a summer playground for a wealthy elite in resorts that now brand themselves the **Kaiserbäder** (literally "Emperor's Baths"). Since reunification **Bansin**, **Heringsdorf** and **Ahlbeck** have renovated their handsome Second Empire villas and Art Nouveau hotels to recapture some of that imperial pomp and shake off an image as workers' playgrounds acquired in GDR decades; regime top-brass claimed private villas on the spurious legal grounds they were for the benefit of trades unions. Each resort has its own market, from families to pensioners to spa-goers. What keeps them all coming is 42km of fine sand, spread up to 70m deep along the north coast and drenched in more sunshine than anywhere else in Germany, an average 1906 hours a year.

Historisch-Technisches Museum Peenemünde

Peenemünde • Daily: April–Sept 10am–6pm; Oct–March 10am–4pm • €8 • Ⓦ peenemuende.de • UBB train (Ⓦ ubb-online.com); change at Zinnowitz

Imperial glitz aside, Usedom's place in history is as the world's first rocket test-site. Between 1936 and 1945, technicians developed liquid-fuelled jet engines at **PEENEMÜNDE** at Usedom's northwest tip – the result was the V-1 rockets which blasted London (see box below). Subsequently occupied by the Red Army, then operational as a GDR base until 1990, the huge red-brick power station today contains the **Historisch-Technisches Museum Peenemünde** – for many, reason enough to visit Usedom. Even if the museum's claims that Peenemünde was the birthplace of space travel are somewhat disingenuous – the rocket was always a military goal – its interactive exhibits and video are a surprisingly engrossing insight into the technological breakthrough and its consequences. Half of the vast power station has also been restored to document the site's development from fishing village to temple of industry.

The Kaiserbäder

Europe's longest promenade runs for 8km between the three Usedom resorts, known as the **Kaiserbäder**. The westernmost of them, **BANSIN**, is as low-key as it is low-rise. Historic architecture is restricted to the odd Jugendstil villa; its pier is nothing more flashy than a glorified gangway; and a mellow vibe makes it popular with young families.

Heringsdorf

Far more commercial than Bansin is **HERINGSDORF**, 2km east. That "Herring village" should boast the longest pier in continental Europe – 508m in length, albeit a replica of the original that burned down in 1958 – says something of the resort where

---

ROCKET-PROPELLED AIR RAID

At 3pm on October 3, 1942, the prototype A4 rocket soared to an altitude of 85km and the Space Age had arrived. Originally intended for a jet plane, the **rocket technology** developed at Peenemünde (see above) was hijacked by the Nazis to develop the V-1 and V-2 *Vergeltungswaffen* (vengeance weapons) – "flying bombs" that rained on London in 1944, shortly after the Allied air-raids destroyed the original site and forced production to shift to the Harz region.

emperors Friedrich III and Wilhelm II sojourned. A fishing village in the 1820s, it flourished as Germany went crazy for sea-water bathing in the 1880s, and retains many of the splendid villas and hotels that made it the St Tropez of the Baltic. GDR urban planners blighted the centre with breeze-block architecture around Platz des Friedens, but elsewhere is pure Baltic Bäderarchitektur; Delbrückstrasse has some of the finest villas.

Ahlbeck

More than any other, it is final Kaiserbad **AHLBECK** that is quietly transforming itself into a swish spa destination. It is the oldest of the trio, welcoming a moneyed clientele from the 1850s three decades before its rivals. Pride and joy of the town is a photogenic pier that was built in 1888 and has been embraced as an icon for the island.

ARRIVAL AND GETTING AROUND   USEDOM

By train All national train services go to Züssow on the Stralsund and Greifswald line to connect with the local Usedomer Bäderbahn (UBB; ⓦ ubb-online.com) which shuttles along all resorts several times a day; change at Zinnowitz to go northwest to Peenemünde.
By bus Local buses ply routes along coastal resorts at regular intervals.

By ferry Adler-Schiffe cruisers run between the three Kaiserbäder resorts (May to early Oct; from €9.50 day-card; ⓦ adler-schiffe.de).
By bike With generally flat terrain, cycling is a good option, though you will be forced on to roads at times. Bikes can be rented in all resorts, generally from the Bahnhof, and can be transported on UBB trains for a minimal charge.

15

INFORMATION

Tourist offices The Haus des Gastes by the pier, Bansin (ⓣ 038378 470 50); Forum Usedom at Kulmstr. 33, Heringsdorf (ⓣ 038378 24 51); and Dünenstr. 45, Ahlbeck (ⓣ 038378 49 93 50). Hours for all are roughly Jan–March, Nov & Dec Mon–Fri 9am–4pm, Sat & Sun 10am–noon; April, May & Oct Mon–Fri 9am–5pm, Sat & Sun

10am–3pm; June–Sept Mon–Fri 9am–6pm, Sat & Sun 10am–3pm. The website for the Kaiserbäder resorts is ⓦ drei-kaiserbaeder.de. All three offices can book private rooms (circa €50) and apartments in historic villas – a good first port-of-call without a reservation in high season, when accommodation is in short supply.

ACCOMMODATION

DJH Heringsdorf Puschkinstr. 7–9, Heringsdorf ⓣ 038378 223 25, ⓦ jugendherbergen-mv.de. Usedom's only hostel is this outpost of the national youth hostel, split between two Art Nouveau houses behind the beach. All doubles and dorms (up to five-bed) are en suite and there's also disabled access to a couple of rooms. Dorms **€31.80**, doubles **€73.40**
Fortuna Kulmstr. 8, Heringsdorf ⓣ 038378 470 70, ⓦ hotel-fortuna.kaiserbaeder.m-vp.de. This hotel in a late nineteenth-century villa offers great value; though simple, rooms are immaculately maintained, and mod cons include free wi-fi and a sauna – and all 2min walk from the beach. **€80**

Residenz Bleichröder Delbrückstr. 14, Heringsdorf ⓣ 038378 36 20, ⓦ residenz-bleichroeder.com. The place to live out fin-de-siècle fantasies is this neo-Baroque mansion built for a financial adviser to Bismarck. Fabulously over-the-top furnishings are a paean to imperial pomp; the best rooms have four-posters and roll-tops. Also has holiday apartments in adjacent modern blocks. **€105**
Seehotel Ahlbecker Hof Dünenstr. 47, Ahlbeck ⓣ 038378 6 20, ⓦ seetel.de. Luxurious spa hotel of the Romantik chain where the sumptuous period decor matches the grand seafront building; the best rooms have a seafront balcony. Prices almost halve in off-season. **€217**

EATING

★**Kulm Eck** Kulmstr. 14, Heringsdorf ⓣ 038378 225 60, ⓦ kulm-eck.de. What appears a simple, historically styled bistro-restaurant is actually one of the premier culinary addresses on the island, serving creative fresh cuisine. Adventures à la carte prove expensive, while three-course €39 menus offer good value. April–Oct Tues–Sun 6pm–midnight.

Lutter & Wegner Kulmstr. 3, Heringsdorf ⓣ 038378 221 25, ⓦ l-w-berlin.de. An outpost of the upmarket Berlin bistro, located in the heart of the resort near the tourist office. Famous for its *Wiener Schnitzel* (€19.50) and *Tafelspitz*, all served with brisk efficiency; it has a good wine menu, too. Daily 11am–midnight.

Usedomer Brauhaus Platz des Friedens, Heringsdorf ☎ 038378 614 21. Smarter than your average microbrewery, this is a respite from more stylish places in the resort, with solid pub dishes like *Schweinshaxe* and *Leberkäse* (mains €7–12), plus five beers to try. Daily noon–midnight.

Schwerin

Encircled by lakes and with a fairy-tale Schloss that goes straight to the head, **SCHWERIN** punches far above its weight. Although the names of Puschkinstrasse and Karl-Marx-Strasse give away the past, its time as a GDR backwater was a hiccup in its history. Crowned as the capital of Mecklenburg-Western Pomerania in 1990, Schwerin has settled back into its time-honoured role as the state's cultural dynamo. After Saxony's Henry the Lion swatted aside an early Slavic settlement on its islet in 1160, the dukes of Mecklenburg took up residence in the fourteenth century, then moved in and out of their royal seat for nearly five centuries. Chosen as the duchy residence over Ludwigslust (see p.849) in 1837, Schwerin blossomed into a cultural heavyweight with a vigorous arts scene and showpiece architecture, not least that impressive **Schloss**. The legacy of that period lingers, and today Schwerin, the smallest state capital in Germany, fairly hums with quiet prosperity – a pocket-sized city with the airs and architecture of a historic capital yet none of its urban grit.

The Altstadt

Heart of the Altstadt, **Am Markt**, is as good a place as any to start a tour, boxed in on opposite sides by the **Rathaus**, with the mock battlements beloved of the 1800s, and the Neoclassical **Neues Gebäude**, home to a café and art exhibitions. Both reveal more eloquently than words the town's aspirations as it flourished under Mecklenburg-Schwerin Grand Duke Paul Friedrich Franz II in the mid-1800s.

Dom
Am Dom 4 • Mon–Sat 10am–5pm, Sun noon–5pm • Free • ⓦ dom-schwerin.de

North of the square stands the Gothic **Dom**, a royal lion by its gateway honouring Saxon duke Henry the Lion, the twelfth-century power-broker who founded an earlier cathedral here. The centrepiece of high lancet arches in its whitewashed interior is a fifteenth-century *Triumphkreuz* taken from Wismar when its Marienkirche was bombed; its gold and green buds are intended as an allegory of the crucifix as a tree of life, although there's not much triumphal about its weary Christ. The tombs of Mecklenburg dukes lie in the choir aisle, the finest carved by an Antwerp master for Duke Christopher in the northern chapel.

Schelfstadt
Northeast of the Dom, on the right bank of the Pfaffenteich lake, is **Schelfstadt**, a quiet quarter of half-timbered streets planned as a separate craftsmen's village in 1705, then swallowed into Schwerin's urban sprawl. Today it's an atmospheric villagey spot to loaf about, browsing crafts and design shops on Münzstrasse, or nosing into the Baroque parish church Schelfkirche or temporary art exhibitions in **Schleswig-Holstein-Haus**, Puschkinstr. 12 (daily 10am–6pm; €3).

Galerie Alte & Neue Meister
Alter Garten 3 • Mid-April to mid-Oct Tues, Wed & Fri–Sun 10am–6pm, Thurs noon–8pm; mid-Oct to mid-April Tues, Wed & Fri–Sun 10am–5pm, Thurs 1–8pm • €8 • ⓦ museum-schwerin.de

A rebuild of Schwerin's Schloss freed up space in the former gardens for the ducal art gallery. Full marks to the Mecklenburg dukes: their collection in the **Galerie Alte & Neue Meister** would do any city proud. Beyond Cranach's lovely *Venus and Amor as*

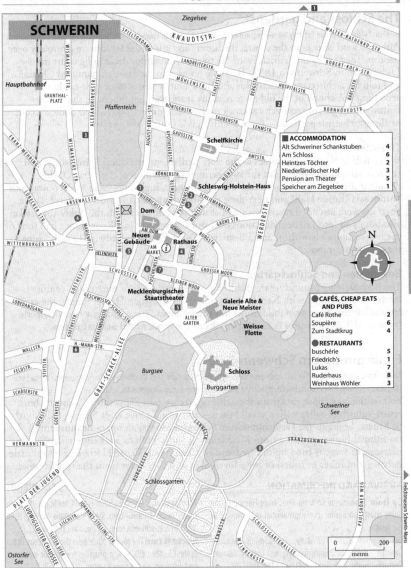

SCHWERIN

Ziegelsee

Hauptbahnhof

Pfaffenteich

Schelfkirche

Schleswig-Holstein-Haus

Dom

Neues Gebäude

Rathaus

Mecklenburgisches Staatstheater

Galerie Alte & Neue Meister

Weisse Flotte

Burgsee

Schloss

Burggarten

Schweriner See

Schlossgarten

Ostorfer See

Freilichtmuseum Schwerin-Mueß

N

15

■ ACCOMMODATION

Alt Schweriner Schankstuben	4
Am Schloss	6
Heintzes Töchter	2
Niederländischer Hof	5
Pension am Theater	5
Speicher am Ziegelsee	1

● CAFÉS, CHEAP EATS AND PUBS

Café Rothe	2
Soupière	6
Zum Stadtkrug	4

● RESTAURANTS

buschérie	5
Friedrich's	1
Lukas	7
Ruderhaus	8
Weinhaus Wöhler	3

0   200
metres

Honey Thieves is a wealth of sixteenth- and seventeenth-century Dutch and Flemish painting that includes names like Rubens, Rembrandt and Hals, and the world's finest collection of Jean-Baptiste Oudry, a French court painter whose series of exotic animals was originally commissioned for the royal gardens at Versailles. Gainsborough represents British portraiture with a full-length Mecklenburg royal, Queen Charlotte, and Caspar David Friedrich kicks off the nineteenth century, while in the twentieth-century section there are Ernst Barlach sculptures and a superb collection of Duchamp's ready-made artistic jokes.

The Schloss and gardens

Lennéstr. 1 • Mid-April to mid-Oct daily 10am–6pm; mid-Oct to mid-April Tues–Sun 10am–5pm • €6, gardens free • ⓦ schloss-schwerin.de

After the solid edifices in the centre, the turrets and gilt of the **Schloss** are gloriously over the top. They are Paul Friedrich Franz II's treat to himself for decamping court from Ludwigslust to Schwerin in 1837. The duke pointed to the Loire's Chambord Château and told his architects to remodel his ancestors' Dutch Renaissance-style castle accordingly. A chunk of the old place remains at the rear, but otherwise this is pure fantasy: a polyglot of architectural exotica – fairy-tale turrets, onion-bulb domes, a couple of almost Moorish pavilions – topped with a gilded turret like a crown.

The interior

While half of the palace doubles as the state parliament, the ducal living, social and ceremonial quarters all exhibit the swaggering excess typical of their era. Of the decadent display of gilt, stucco and carving on show, highlights include the outrageous **Thronsaal** (Throne Hall) and next-door the **Ahnengalerie** (Ancestors' Gallery) whose portraits were intended to awe visitors before their audience with the duke. Your ticket also buys you into smaller collections of historic weaponry in a Renaissance hall (one of the few sections left within) and a display of Duke Christian Ludwig II's early china, then a status symbol.

Burggarten and Schlossgarten

The **Burggarten** surrounding the Schloss is a splendid piece of nineteenth-century landscape gardening, with Neoclassical statuary by Christian Daniel Rauch, the artist trusted for the grandest public works in Prussia, a handsome wrought-iron orangerie (now a café) and a grotto. A causeway links to the modernized **Schlossgarten**.

Freilichtmuseum Schwerin-Muess

Alte Crivitzer Landstr. 13 • Tues–Sun: late April–Sept 10am–6pm; Oct 10am–5pm • €4 • ⓦ schwerin.de/freilichtmuseum • Weisse Flotte (ⓣ 0385 55 77 70, ⓦ weisseflotteschwerin.de) boats to Muess depart from a quay adjacent to the Schloss

Follow the lake shore east from the Schlossgarten – past Zippendorf, a south-shore resort-suburb of villas with a small beach – and you'll arrive after 5km at the suburb of Muess, home to the **Freilichtmuseum Schwerin-Muess**, an open-air museum of traditional houses plucked from Mecklenburg and rebuilt as a lakeside village – the blacksmith forge is fired up on Wednesday. Cruisers of Weisse Flotte line also shuttle here on a number of tours, or for a lovely day out, hire bikes from the tourist office.

ARRIVAL AND INFORMATION   SCHWERIN

By train Schwerin is on train lines from Hamburg, the Baltic coast and Berlin; its Hauptbahnhof is northwest of the centre.

Destinations Berlin (12 daily; 2hr 25min); Hamburg (hourly; 50min–1hr 20min); Ludwigslust (hourly; 30min); Rostock (hourly; 1hr); Stralsund (every 2hr; 2hr).

Tourist office The tourist office is at 14 Am Markt, the main square (Mon–Fri 9am–6pm, Sat & Sun 10am–4pm; ⓣ 0385 592 52 12, ⓦ schwerin.com). It hires bikes (€20/day).

Discount card The tourist office sells the Schwerin-Ticket (24hr €5, 48hr €7), which provides free public transport and discounts on the town's sights.

ACCOMMODATION

Alt Schweriner Schankstuben Am Schlachtermarkt 9–13 ⓣ 0385 592 53 13, ⓦ schankstuben.de. This half-timbered restaurant doubles as a small hotel with rooms that open on to one of the prettiest squares in the centre. Expect plain, pastel-tinted, modern accommodation and views to the Dom for an extra €10. **€94**

Am Schloss Heinrich-Mann-Str. 3 ⓣ 0385 59 32 30, ⓦ hotel-am-schloss.m-vp.de. A comfortable mid-range

stay in the centre. Classic-modern business rooms in the main block are of the blonde wood and stainless steel fittings variety, while those in an adjoining annexe are smaller but with more character; some have old beams. **€86**

Heintzes Töchter Wederstr. 49 ⓣ 0385 479 29 68, ⓦ hostel-schwerin.de. Good-value doubles, triples and four- and nine-bed dorms in Schwerin's only independent hostel, a homely place 5min walk from the Schloss.

Check-in is 4–8pm, but it's worth calling the owner who's often off-site. Dorms €15, doubles €48

Niederländischer Hof Alexandrinenstr. 12–13 ☎0385 59 11 00, ⊚niederlaendischer-hof.de. Schwerin's finest hotel, overlooking the Pfaffenteich lake and effortlessly relaxed in its old-world elegance. Public areas allude to a late-1800s country hotel, and rooms are smart, the best at the front overlooking the water. Its restaurant is likewise highly rated. €139

Pension am Theater Theaterstr. 1–2 ☎0385 59 36 80, ⊚schwerin-pension.de. This small pension is a favourite with touring actors in the theatre opposite. For everyone else, it provides cheerful, modern(ish) accommodation in a superb location. Simple but excellent value. €76

Speicher am Ziegelsee Speicherstr. 11 ☎0385 500 30, ⊚speicher-hotel.com. Relaxed designer style, a spa and lake views in a former grain warehouse on the Ziegelsee 1km north of the Schloss. There are fluffy bathrobes and spacious rooms with modern Italianate decor, plus a sauna and gym. €110

EATING AND DRINKING

buschérie Buschstr. 9. ☎0385 39 45 60 92, ⊚buscherie.de. Ignore the yuppie-wine-bar decor, this small restaurant provides the finest classic-modern cooking in town. Expect the likes of scallop salad, fish of the day or liver in port and rosemary sauce (mains €16–26). Daily 11am–11pm.

Café Rothe Puschkinstr. 14 ☎0385 557 13 05. With its *belle époque* style and classic house-made confectionery and *gâteaux*, this is as traditional a location as you could wish for mid-afternoon *Kaffee und Kuchen*; hot chocolate hits the spot on cold days. Mon–Sat 7am–6pm, Sun 1–6pm.

Friedrich's Friedrichstr. 2 ☎0385 55 54 73, ⊚restaurant-friedrichs.com. One of the better options for relaxed dining. To suit its nineteenth-century villa, the decor style is vintage brasserie but the cooking is well-prepared and modern. A front terrace facing the lake adds to the appeal in summer. Daily 9am–11pm.

Lukas Grosser Moor 5 ☎0385 56 59 35, ⊚restaurant-lukas.de. A modern restaurant that specializes in mid-priced fish and seafood – trout, mixed fish platters of *Rotbarsch*, *Zander* and salmon, or monkfish spaghetti. Also offers steaks and potato dishes. Daily 11am–10pm.

Ruderhaus Franzosenweg 21 ☎0385 20 24 12 59, ⊚ruderhaus.info. Heaven in summer because of its lakeside terrace – come for the legendary Sunday brunch and dishes like steak with whisky aïoli or *Maränen* (freshwater fish) with pak choi (mains €12–18), or simply for ice creams and coffee. Tues–Fri from 4pm (from 2pm July & Aug), Sat from noon, Sun from 10.30am; closed Feb.

Soupière Puschkinstr. 59 ☎0385 484 80 44. Tasty home-made soups and stews such as Mecklenberg potato and bacon, spicy goulash, summer tomato or delicious Thai fish soup are served up with bread at low prices. Eat in a modern café or take away – great for a quick bite. Mon–Sat 11am–4pm.

Zum Stadtkrug Wismarsche Str. 126 ☎0385 593 66 93, ⊚altstadtbrauhaus.de. The local brewhouse, installed in a 1930s hall, has eleven varieties of beer served in volumes up to a litre, plus solid pub-grub at low prices, some of its dishes cooked with a malt crust. Daily 11.30am–11pm.

Weinhaus Wöhler Puschkinstr. 26 ☎0385 55 58 30, ⊚weinhaus-woehler.de. A historic inn whose stained glass and wooden partitions date back to the mid-1800s – hugely atmospheric if not too cheap (mains on the largely traditional menu cost around €18). There's also tapas and cocktails in a modern atrium café (Tues–Sat 5pm–1am), a snug wine-bar and a leafy summer garden. Daily 11am–midnight.

Schloss Ludwigslust

Mid-April to mid-Oct daily 10am–6pm; mid-Oct to mid-April Tues–Sun 10am–5pm • €3.50, gardens free • ⊚schloss-ludwigslust.de • Ludwigslust Bahnhof is on the Schwerin line; from the station, Bahnhofstrasse segues into Friedrich-Naumann-Allee which leads to the Schloss

Until Grand Duke Paul Friedrich Franz II shifted court to Schwerin 35km north, **LUDWIGSLUST** was the heart of the Mecklenburg-Schleswig court, realized as a spacious planned town laid at the feet of the **Schloss Ludwigslust**. His predecessor, Grand Duke Friedrich I, commissioned the first court palace in the hunting grounds of his father Christian Ludwig, and was dogged by money problems almost as soon as the building began in 1772 – as the joke went, Ludwig's Lust (pleasure) was Friedrich's Arbeit (work). Behind the majestic, late Baroque facade is the same humble brick used for the courtiers' houses on approach road Schlossstrasse. Architect Johann Joachim Busch was even more creative within. In place of stucco and carved wood, he used papier-mâché, euphemistically named Ludwigsluster Carton. The pinnacle of his achievement is the **Goldene Saal**, a Louis XVI-style galleried ballroom fit for a Cinderella ball whose gilded Rococo mouldings are all glorious fakes. Even the reliefs of putti above the door turn out to be *trompe l'oeil*. A carved grandfather clock and *Venus de'Medici* in later rooms also prove to be papier-mâché. Many of the oils, however, are genuine works by French court painter Jean-Baptiste Oudry.

The palace gardens

The garden that extends behind the Schloss was landscaped in naturalistic style by the ubiquitous Peter Joseph Lenné. Maps from the Schloss pinpoint various oddities to discover: a grotto, a tea pavilion and church, fountains, statuary, two mausoleums, a bizarre monument to Friedrich's favourite horse (Pferdedenkmal), and the Schweizerhaus, a Swiss-style summerhouse for Duchess Louise that is now a daytime café.

The Stadtkirche

Ahead of the Schloss you cross a broad grass oval ringed by palace-workers' cottages to reach the **Stadtkirche**. Its severe classical facade is another of Busch's, and inside he is equally theatrical: a floor-to-ceiling altar painting of the *Annunciation* rises behind gold papier-mâché candlesticks and at the rear is a ducal gallery like an opera box. "Friedrich the Pious" himself lies in a plain sarcophagus in the centre – they say it took 24 horses two days to drag its granite slab from a nearby village to be carved.

Güstrow

Once a capital of the Mecklenburg duchy, **GÜSTROW** lives in its dotage as a pretty, provincial small town on the fringes of Mecklenburg's lake country. For centuries its hero was Albrecht von Wallenstein, a duke who distinguished himself as supreme commander of the Habsburg armies during the Thirty Years' War. Today, however, Güstrow declares itself Der Barlachstadt ("The Barlach Town") in honour of Expressionist sculptor **Ernst Barlach** (see box opposite), who spent half of his life here and whose humanist works chime more comfortably with our age. In his wake have come a few galleries that add to the appeal of Güstrow's cobbled lanes.

The Altstadt

The centrepiece of the **Altstadt** is the Markt, filled back-to-back by an oversized Baroque Rathaus and the **Pfarrkirche St Marien**. The sixteenth-century furnishings in the parish church testify to Güstrow's early wealth as a ducal capital, not least the Gothic high altar by Brussels' Jan Borman. Above hangs the triumphal cross, thanks to Ernst Barlach – the artist, inspired by the energy of medieval sculpture, urged the town council to restore the fifteenth-century work from a storeroom where it had been consigned for being too crude. He also contributed the child-like *Angel of Hope* terracotta plaque on the right-hand pillar beneath.

Dom

Philipp-Brandin-Str. 5 • April to mid-May & mid-Oct to mid-Nov Tues–Sat 10am–noon & 2–4pm, Sun 2–4pm; mid-May to mid-Oct Mon–Sat 10am–5pm, Sun 2–4pm; mid-Nov to March Tues–Sat 11am–noon & 2–3pm, Sun 2–3pm • Free

The best introduction to Ernst Barlach is the **Dom** southeast of the Markt in one of the most picturesque corners of the Altstadt. Hidden in the half-light of the north aisle, his

ERNST BARLACH

Ernst Barlach (1870–1938) is the finest artist no one knows outside Germany. Empathetic and with a keen sense of pathos, the Expressionist sculptor and graphic artist was the son of a country physician in a village near Hamburg. He studied sculpture in Dresden and Paris, then travelled. It was a trip across the **Russian steppes** in 1906 that made him. His sketchbooks filled with exaggerated facial expressions – tortured, helpless, radiant, primitive – based on the peasants he met. In them he saw an intense Christian humility that chimed with his passion for German medieval art. These sketches served as the basis of his vigorous, simplified works whose archaic power and inner spirituality has sometimes seen Barlach pigeonholed as "modern Gothic".

The horrors of **World War I** only intensified his humanism – Barlach, by now a reader of Dostoyevsky and Tolstoy, quickly lost his early enthusiasm for war as a means to shake up the ruling elite – and by 1930 he was a leading figure of German art, commissioned for a large war memorial in **Magdeburg Cathedral**. Such socialist leanings did not square with the militaristic hubris of the **Nazis**, however. His bronze of *Christ and St Thomas* was labelled "Two Monkeys in Nightshirts" in their Munich exhibition "Entartete Kunst" (Degenerate Art) in 1937, and many of his works were smelted. He died in Rostock a year later and was buried beside his father in Ratzeburg (see p.795). Like fellow Expressionist and "degenerate" Käthe Kollwitz, Barlach's place in the German canon was restored after the war: direct and accessible, his works have an empathy and humanism that strikes a chord today.

Flying Angel levitates, eyes closed, towards the Divine. How the Third Reich regime could condemn this serene angel as "degenerate art" is a mystery, yet the original, the most famous work of Germany's premier Expressionist, was smelted down, though not before a cast had been taken in secret – this copy was recast after the war. He also created the apostle plaque and *Crucifixion* in the same aisle, both less appealing than kinetic sculptures of the Apostles by A Lübeck master in the nave; Barlach cited them as an influence. Other eye-catchers in the Gothic three-nave basilica are in the choir: swaggering Renaissance funerary monuments of Mecklenburg dukes – Duke Ulrich and his wives from Denmark and Mecklenburg kneel in front of a ducal family tree – and a Gothic high altar by Hamburg's Hinrik Bornemann.

Güstrow Schloss

Franz-Parr-Platz 1 • Mid-April to mid-Oct daily 10am–6pm; mid-Oct to mid-April Tues–Sun 10am–6pm • €5 • ⓦ schloss-guestrow.de

The ducal **Güstrow Schloss** is a splendid pile that synthesizes Italian, French and German styles as an expression of founder Duke Ulrich's sophistication. Although Napoleon and the Nazis, who used one of Germany's finest Renaissance palaces as a prison, have taken their toll, renovation has restored the fine stucco in the south wing, especially in the first-floor Festsaal whose hunting scenes seem to spring into action as you look. Most of the palace houses a mixed bag of sculpture, painting and objets d'art, the most valuable pieces sited on the ground floor by Tintoretto and Maerten de Vos. The latter's *Menagerie* is testament to the fad for exoticism that gripped imaginations during the Age of Exploration, hence his image of a unicorn (dismissed as dubious even at the time) set in the recently discovered West Indies.

Getrudenkapelle, Atelierhaus and Ausstellungsforum-Graphikkabinett

All April–June, Sept & Oct Tues–Sun 10am–5pm; July & Aug daily 10am–5pm; Nov–March Tues–Sun 11am–4pm • Getrudenkapelle €4, Atelierhaus & Ausstellungsforum-Graphikkabinett €6, combined ticket €9 • ernst-barlach-stiftung.de • Atelierhaus can be reached by bus #252 or via the Barlachweg footpath which branches right off main road Plauer Strasse

The world's most extensive collection of works by Barlach is shared between three gallery spaces outside the centre. The most convenient is the **Getrudenkapelle** on Getrudenplatz just northeast of the Altstadt; Barlach's works are displayed in the grounds of a deconsecrated Gothic chapel – an ideal foil for his medieval-influenced sculpture. Sited 4km east of the centre above the Inselsee lake, Barlach's studio

15

Atelierhaus, with a modern glass gallery attached, reveals the artist's profound humanism in works such as *Singing Man*, while the adjacent **Ausstellungsforum-Graphikkabinett** hangs Barlach's graphics.

ARRIVAL AND INFORMATION   GÜSTROW

By train On the Schwerin and Rostock lines, Güstrow Bahnhof is 10min north of the centre of the Altstadt.
Destinations Schwerin (hourly; 30min); Stralsund (hourly; 1hr); Waren (every 2hr; 55min); Wismar (hourly; 1hr 10min).

Tourist office Beside the Schloss on Franz-Parr-Platz (May–Sept Mon–Fri 9am–7pm, Sat 10am–5pm, Sun 11am–5pm; Oct–April Mon–Fri 9am–6pm, Sat 9.30am–1pm; ☎03843 68 10 23, ⦿guestrow.de).

ACCOMMODATION AND EATING

Burg Schlitz Hohen Demzin ☎03996 127 00, ⦿burg-schlitz.de. Luxury reigns in the most spectacular of several manor hotels in the vicinity of Güstrow – unbeatable for Cinderella romance. Turn south at Teterow, 20km east of Güstrow. **€198**

Gästehaus Am Schlosspark Neuwieder Weg ☎03843 24 59 90, ⦿gaestehaus-guestrow.de. The best deal in the city centre provides simple, spotless modern rooms in three categories, all en suite and some with kitchenettes, in a converted hospital just south of the Schloss. Breakfast not included. **€50**

Kurhaus am Inselsee Heidberg 1 ☎03843 58 00,

⦿kurhaus-guestrow.de. A few kilometres from the centre en route to Atelierhaus, this hotel benefits from its tranquil location beside the Inselsee lake. Within are smart traditional rooms, all brass and cherrywood furniture, and exact service, plus a spa. **€110**

Verdura Krönchenhagen 12 ☎03843 46 67 60, ⦿bistro-verdura.de. On a street with several eating options, this modern organic bistro-café prepares a short daily menu, often vegetarian: expect home-made pasta with spring vegetables, home-made meatballs or fish on Fri (mains €6–9). Mon–Fri 11am–3pm.

Müritz National Park

The natural heart of Mecklenburg Vorpommeron are the two swathes of forest, heath and moorland that make up the **MÜRITZ NATIONAL PARK** (Nationalpark Mürtiz) around the Baroque backwater of **Neustrelitz**. By far the largest area is that to the west of the town, which represents nearly three-quarters of the park's total 322 square kilometres and is characterized by its large pine forests and open moorland, although there are also ancient beech woods in the Serrahn area east of Neustrelitz. The focus west is water, namely the **Müritzsee**, which at 115 kilometres squared is the second largest lake in Germany after Lake Constance. Most of its reed-choked east shore falls within the park boundary, as do over a hundred smaller lakes lying further east – one reason why this is known as the "Land of a Thousand Lakes". Not surprisingly, the park is a haven for water birds: ospreys and white-tailed sea eagles breed in the area, and storks and cranes stalk among water lilies in the shallows. Sky-blue moor frogs are usually heard rather than seen, while red deer roam the remote woodland areas.

Waren and around

The draw of Lake Müritz has turned **WAREN** on its north shore into a modest resort. It is the natural base from which to explore the area, whether on the abundant lake cruises that depart from its quay, or by car or bike. Its only tourist attraction, the **Müritzeum** nature discovery centre (daily: April–Oct 10am–7pm; Nov–March 10am–6pm; €7.50; ⦿mueritzeum.de), with Germany's largest freshwater aquarium and displays on local ecology, is as good an introduction to the lake as any. Otherwise explore the real thing: pick up maps at the tourist office then tour a necklace of lakes and villages on a road that tracks the east shore.

Your best chance of spotting the ospreys and sea eagles that breed here is to seek current information from a park centre at **FEDEROW**, 7km south of Waren (April–Oct daily

CANOEING THE MECKLENBURG LAKE DISTRICT

For many visitors, the appeal of inland Mecklenburg is the **Mecklenburgische Seenplatte** (Mecklenburg Lake District) where you can play at being Huckleberry Finn on **canoe-and-camp expeditions** through a mosaic of lakes between Neustrelitz and Lake Müritz. The longest route begins at the Zierker See directly west of Neustrelitz then traces a large U to end at Schillersdorf west, paddling around 15km a day between camps; you need around a week to cover the lot. However, the area abounds in short circuits of two or three days. Regional tourism brochure *Das blaue Paradies* (Ⓦdas-blaue-paradies.de) has some suggestions, otherwise maps of routes are provided by the many **rental outlets** in the park; as well as those detailed below, lists are on the national park website or can be sourced at tourist offices. As an idea of prices, for a Canadian two-man canoe expect to pay €30/€70/€130 for one/three/six days. Good sources for planning include the Mecklenburg Lake District website Ⓦmecklenburgische-seenplatte.de, and regional web portal Müritz Online, Ⓦmueritz.de.

CANOE AND CAMPING OPERATORS

All of the following offer guided tours on request. Note that outfits only operate from April to October and that camping is in designated sites only.

Haveltourist ☎03981 247 90, Ⓦhaveltourist.de. Offers combination rental-and-camp deals in its nine campsites throughout the area from a base at *Havelberge Camping and Holiday Resort*, 5km southwest of Neustrelitz near Gross Quassow.

Kanu Mühle ☎039832 203 50, Ⓦkanu-muehle.de. Two train stops from Neustrelitz in Wesenburg.

Kanustation Mirow ☎039833 220 98, Ⓦkanustation.de. Four train stops from Neustrelitz.

15

9am–6pm; ☎03991 66 88 49), then continue to an observation station a few kilometres beyond at **SPECK**. Ospreys visit between March and October only, sea eagles are present year-round. Arguably the most spectacular avian show occurs in the second half of October, when thousands of cranes fatten up before their long migration south to Spain and Africa – marshland around the Rederangsee lake south of Federow is a favourite roost.

Beyond Speck, the road descends to a forest track (no stopping in cars) to **GRANZIN**, an isolated village whose farmers coin an easy euro by hiring **canoes** (May–Sept) on a lake.

ARRIVAL AND INFORMATION

MÜRITZ NATIONAL PARK

By train Neustrelitz is on train lines from Neubrandenburg and Rostock among others; Waren has direct train services from Rostock.

By bus Müritz-Linie (€9 bus day-ticket; Ⓦnational parkticket.de) loops southwest from Waren to Boek on the east bank of the Müritz lake. If you come by car, be aware that driving is prohibited within most of the park area; the route to Granzin is open.

Tourist offices There's an office in Waren at Neuer Markt 21 (May–Sept daily 9am–8pm; Oct–April Mon–Fri 9am–6pm, Sat 10am–3pm; ☎03991 74 77 90, Ⓦwaren-tourismus.de), which also sells park maps and can book accommodation in the area, much of it in holiday homes; and another in Neustrelitz at Strelitzer Str. 1 (May–Sept Mon–Fri 9am–6pm, Sat & Sun 9.30am–1pm; Oct–April Mon–Thurs 9am–noon & 1–4pm, Fri 9am–noon; ☎03981 25 31 19, Ⓦneustrelitz.de).

ACCOMMODATION

Kleines Meer Alter Markt 7, Waren ☎03991 64 80, Ⓦkleinesmeer.de. Classy small hotel near the waterfront whose designer style is of the warm, relaxed variety; think ash furniture, brushed steel and calm neutral colours. It also has a good restaurant serving modern European dishes. <u>€115</u>

BRANDENBURG GATE

Contexts

History

For most of its history Germany has been a geographical rather than a political term, used to describe a collection of minor states with broadly common interests and culture. Their roots can be traced back almost three millennia and for much of the last two thousand years Germanic peoples have held sway over large areas of Western Europe north of the Alps. However, it wasn't until the late nineteenth century that a drive to unify most German-speaking lands began to define Germany's modern-day political history. Since its inception as a defined country in 1871 Germany has often been at the forefront of international politics, competing with France, Britain, Italy, Russia, Japan and the US on the world stage, most notoriously during the conflicting ambitions that brought two world wars. Their legacy, along with that of the Holocaust, defined Germany for much of the second half of the twentieth century – battle-scarred and divided in two at the frontline of the Cold War. It is only relatively recently, following reunification, and the move of the political capital back to Berlin in 1999, that the country feels like it is finishing the process of rebuilding, not only physically with legendary Germanic industriousness, but also in terms of national pride. With most of this process complete, Germany is once again at the forefront of international politics, at the heart of the European Union and ever more engaged worldwide.

Beginnings

Archeologists estimate the area that covers modern-day Germany has been inhabited for about 60,000 years, and there is evidence of hunter-gatherer activity dating from about 8000 BC, with more substantial remains of Stone Age farming settlements evident from 4000 BC onwards. It was around 750 BC that tribes speaking **Germanic languages** came from Scandinavia. Over the next thousand years or so their influence increased across all the territories of Europe, which were largely in **Roman** hands; by the late fifth century AD they had effectively taken over as the continent's most powerful force – replacing the western Roman Empire with a number of **Germanic successor states**. Of these, the **Franks** proved the most successful and by the ninth century they commanded most of modern Germany, as well as France and northern Italy.

Circa 750 BC	**9 AD**	**4th Century**
Germanic tribes from Scandinavia and Celtic tribes from the south migrate to present-day Germany	Battle of Teutoburg Forest that sees three legions massacred by tribal leader Arminius and ends Roman expansion ambitions	Great migrations across Europe cause culture clash

The early Germans

The first Germans came from what is now Sweden and Denmark – possibly driven by climate change, by expanding populations and a desire to conquer less-well-organized peoples in the south. Circa two thousand years ago, these Germanic people came to dominate all territories north of the Danube, an area so large they formed distinct **tribes**. Other peoples coexisted in the region, particularly Celtic tribes in southern Germany, who seem in time to have gradually integrated into German culture, rather than being conquered or displaced.

These early Germans lived in wooden houses, practised mixed settled farming and ate a gruel of seeds and weeds, but were not without sophistication. They had a class system, in which chiefs and powerful warriors dominated each tribe, worshipped war gods such as Odin (Wodan), to whom they sacrificed defeated enemies, and were buried with jewellery and fine weapons. The various tribes were allied to one another through particular religious cults, their annual festivals doubling as opportunities to trade and peaceably settle disputes.

Roman coexistence

Around the time of the birth of Christ, the **Romans'** expansion north brought them into contact with Germanic tribes. In around 12 BC Roman forces crossed the Danube and Rhine in a fierce campaign that saw the massacre of three Roman legions by the Germanic leader Arminius in 9 AD. Unsurprisingly, the Romans decided these barbarians were too much trouble, so consolidated their power by dotting frontier garrisons along both rivers – one later grew to become the city of Koblenz.

While border raids were a part of life, an alliance system with some German tribes created a porous frontier that allowed free trade and travel. Cultural cross-fertilization was inevitable: Roman money began to be used; free Germans served in Roman armies; and Roman farming and pottery techniques plus general goods appeared in German society. A degree of literacy also spread north and by around 350 AD a written form of Gothic had developed, which Christian missionary Wulfila used to translate the Bible.

This progress produced more powerful Germanic tribes, which grew into two strong military confederations: the **Alemanni** on the Rhine and the **Goths** on the Danube.

The great migrations

From the late fourth century, Europe's uneasy stability was thrown into disarray by the arrival of nomadic, mounted, non-Germanic Huns from the east. A powerful destabilizing force, they encouraged – along with climatic changes, growing populations and adventurousness – the easternmost Germanic peoples, the Visigoths and Ostrogoths, to head west into central Europe and the Roman Empire.

And so began the hundred years of the **great migrations** during which time displaced tribes sought new lands in a process that involved giant battles and pillaging as much as travel. The journey of the **Visigoths** – a tribe of about 80,000 – was among the most spectacular. Driven west from Ukraine they initially settled in the Danube region until local hostility sent them packing. They fought and pillaged through Greece and Italy – sacking Rome in 410 – then moved west to colonize the French coast around today's Toulouse and a good part of the Iberian peninsula. Other Germanic tribes on the move included the Suebi and Vandals, who established themselves in Spain and later in North

410	754	768–814
The Visigoths sack Rome in their rampage south	Death of Germanic missionary St Boniface	Charlemagne conquers much of Germany as king of the Frankish empire; its capital is Aachen

Africa. The Ostrogoths moved from the Black Sea to today's Hungary, then Italy, while the **Burgundians** moved from northern Germany through the southwest of the country and finally to southeastern France – as celebrated in the *Nibelungenlied* (see box, p.527).

Successor states

The overstretched Roman Empire was forced to compromise to resolve most territorial questions in Europe, and it consented to Germanic successor states such as the Visigothic and Burgundian kingdoms. Meanwhile, the Franks, Frisians, Saxons, Thuringians, Alemanni and Bavarians emerged, all the product of smaller tribes clubbing together to defend themselves against the Huns. As the western Roman Empire crumbled they integrated the Roman provincial population into their own, fusing a Germanic military with Roman administrative skills that would establish taxes and legal powers for these German rulers.

The Franks

Among these new Germanic tribes, the **Franks** proved themselves the strongest. From their fifth-century tribal lands in today's Belgium, they began to expand south and east, particularly under King Clovis (482–511) of the **Merovingian** dynasty. In 751 the **Carolingian** dynasty took over and continued to expand under their greatest leader, **Charlemagne** (768–814), who made Aachen – now Germany's westernmost city – his capital. At the time of his death the Frankish empire took up most of modern-day France, Germany and northern Italy.

The success of the Franks' expansion and consolidation lay in allowing conquered regions to be governed semi-autonomously by dukes of mixed Frankish and indigenous background, who all swore ultimate allegiance to the Frankish king. The conversion of the Franks to **Christianity** and their subsequent missionary zeal also helped immensely, providing the support of Christians in conquered regions and an administrative means of control which could be spread throughout the empire.

One of the most influential missionaries was **St Boniface** (c.675–754), who converted much of Germany and helped integrate it into the Roman-Frankish church by the time of his martyrdom in northern Frisia. Thereafter the only areas of Germany that needed a concerted effort were the lands of the pagan Saxons, who stood in the way of eastward expansion. The process of bringing them to heel was particularly brutal. As soon as Charlemagne's army moved on from their victories, the Saxons would revolt, slaughter Frankish officials and priests, and raid as far west as they could. Charlemagne in turn would punish the offending tribes; on one occasion in 782 he executed 4500 Saxons at Verden.

The Holy Roman Empire

Frankish empire-building effectively ceased after Charlemagne and the territories he had controlled were divided into three kingdoms ruled by his grandsons. One, the **East Frankish Empire**, covered the greater part of modern Germany and would become known as the **Holy Roman Empire**. Initially governed by **Louis the German** (804–876), it assumed a German identity, helped by Louis's cultivation of German language and literature, which included the translation of the Gospels.

804–76	**962**	**1152–90**
A distinct German language and literature emerge under Frankish king Louis the German	The Pope crowns Otto the Great king of Germany and emperor of the Holy Roman Empire as the Saxon ruler cements Germany as a kingdom	As Frederick I – Frederick "Redbeard" – focuses on Italy, central authority collapses slowly into princely states

This emergent German culture helped bind the Holy Roman Empire, but the main forces holding it together were the cooperation of territorial rulers and the Church. Over the empire's thousand-year history both forces progressively weakened, producing an ever more complex situation in which territories increasingly fought among themselves. The underlying problem was the piecemeal power structure, in which a mosaic of different interests could politik, feud and scheme. The tug of war initially went in three directions – between the **territorial rulers**, the **elected king** (or emperor if crowned by the pope) and the **Church** – but soon spread throughout wider society in struggles between various subgroups including the **petty aristocracy**, **knights** and **prelates**. One particularly divisive factor was the Germanic custom of splitting estates between sons, rather than passing them to the eldest, which created ever smaller territories. Meanwhile economic development created ever larger, more powerful and independent **cities**.

Inevitably, central authority weakened – not helped by an erosion in Crown lands and revenues as dynasties gave away imperial possessions as bribes to secure the re-election of their descendants. The financial and law-enforcing power of the king – the foundation of royal authority elsewhere – was in any case negligible, leading to growing lawlessness and petty wars across the empire. In the sixteenth century this dynamic took a new and even more divisive turn as the **Protestant Reformation** split the Church. Great, lengthy, brutal and costly wars ensued, retarding the economic and social development of German states and effectively ending the Holy Roman Empire as a political power while European neighbours – particularly Britain, France, Spain and the Netherlands – began to develop global empires.

The Saxons (911–1024)

By 911 the Carolingian dynasty had effectively died out and all power devolved to local leaders: Saxon, Frankish and Bavarian dukes, among others, met at Forchheim in Franconia to elect a new king. In 919 they chose **Henry the Fowler**, the first of a line of Saxon kings, who reasserted Germany as a single empire and cemented the kingdom with vast military prowess. The Saxons were particularly effective under **Otto the Great** (reigned 936–973) when they subdued the Magyar (Hungarian) invasions and continued **eastward expansion**. Between 955 and 972 he founded and richly endowed an archbishopric at Magdeburg as a missionary base, and led savage military campaigns against the polytheistic Slavic Wends, who – like the Saxons two hundred years earlier – tenaciously resisted Christian conversion with brutal consequences. Otto's reign also included the conquest of Rome, forcing the pope to crown him emperor in 962, and beginning a tradition of giving the East Frankish Kingdom the imperial title. Otto enjoyed a good relationship with the Church, which he energetically built up in order to disrupt the secular lords' jurisdictions. By loading bishoprics and abbeys with endowments and privileges he gradually turned bishops and abbots into princes directly answerable to the king. Though this helped with governance, it built a powerful new force which in the coming centuries would be part of the empire's undoing.

The Salians (1024–1125)

After the Saxons, the **Salian** dynasty from Rhenish Franconia controlled the empire for the next hundred years, but had a much worse time of it. They struggled against the

1348–49	1356	1438
A quarter of the population is wiped out by an epidemic of plague	The Golden Bull, Germany's first constitutional document, fixes the imperial electoral process following an earlier declaration that ended the pope's role as king-maker	With the election of Albrecht II, the Austrian-based Habsburg dynasty emerges as a major European force

increasing authority of territorial princes and deep financial problems, which were largely the result of Saxon gifts to the Church. At the same time the **Gregorian reform movement** emerged. It argued for the separation of State and Church as spiritual power should not be purchasable, so fundamentally contradicted the empire's constitutional basis; as both sides fought through polemical writings, nobles were driven to take sides. When **Henry IV** (1056–1106) came to the throne aged 5, a free-for-all ensued throughout the empire. When he came of age, Henry's attempts to recover Crown lands began a period of costly civil war which lasted almost twenty years and embroiled the pope who, at one stage, excommunicated Henry.

One lasting feature of German society to come out of all this chaos was the creation of a class of **knights**: soldiers from ecclesiastical estates who served the king as a small private army.

The Hohenstaufens (1125–1268)

Henry V, the last Salian, died childless in 1125, leaving an empire that could no longer dominate European politics, so got almost no material benefit from the **Crusades**. The empire entered more than two decades of competition between the Swabian **Hohenstaufens** and the Saxon **Welfs** until the two dynasties were united by marriage and the birth of **Frederick I** (Frederick Barbarossa, "Redbeard"; reigned 1152–90) who was careful to maintain good relations with all the big dynasties – one effect of which was the elevation of **Austria** into a duchy as a way of evening the power balance.

But Frederick spent most of his reign preoccupied with conquering Italy, leaving Germany without an effective central authority and encouraging another period of chaos, during which time ducal authority was eroded by bishops and princes. These upstarts then built a rash of castles, toll stations, mints and mines, and took judicial command. None wanted the election of a strong king, who would threaten their growing independence, so a trend was set of selecting weaker or preoccupied regents. In the short term, it ushered in the **Great Interregnum** (1250–73), a period of chaos in which there was effectively no central power, until the papacy intervened and established an electoral process whereby the Holy Roman Emperor was chosen by seven leading princes.

Hohenstaufen rule also saw ceaseless conquering and colonizing to the east. The Slavic Wends were finally overwhelmed and Germans from every level of society migrated east.

The early Habsburgs and the Luxembourgs (1273–1437)

In the thirteenth century the **Habsburgs**, a fledgling dynasty that came to dominate much of the western world and outlive the Holy Roman Empire itself, made a brief appearance. Though initially weak as emperor, Rudolf I (1273) made sufficiently canny dynastic acquisitions like Austria, Holland and Zeeland to worry the electoral princes. They plumped instead for the House of **Luxembourg**, not a unanimous decision, so one that produced yet more inter-prince wars. These disputes were only resolved with the Declaration of Rhens (1338) which established election by a majority vote, and the **Golden Bull** of 1356, a basic constitutional document that fixed the electoral body at seven: the archbishops of Mainz, Cologne and Trier, the count palatine of the Rhine, the king of Bohemia, the margrave of Brandenburg, and the duke of Saxony – who all received far greater judicial and financial powers.

1471	1472	1517
Albrecht Dürer, arguably the greatest artist of the North European Renaissance, is born in Nuremberg	The court painter Lucas Cranach the Elder is born in Franconia	Martin Luther nails his 95 Theses to a church door in Wittenberg to launch the Reformation

From 1347, the Luxembourgs inherited Bohemia, providing them with vast wealth with which to shore up their imperial position, but also distracting them from the needs of the empire. As a consequence, **city leagues** appeared across Germany and beyond – including the Hanseatic League (see box, p.785), the Swabian League, and the Rhenish League. Cities clubbed together to defend their interests and establish trading agreements, forming powerful and often wealthy secular powerbases across Europe. Their interests often clashed with those of the princes over things such as the loss of rural labour – which became particularly acute when the **Black Death** (1348–49) killed around a quarter of Germany's population. The consequent loss of revenue was one reason for the raising of princely tolls on civic trade to the point where tensions turned into war in 1388. While the conflict produced a stalemate, it led to the disbandment of most city leagues by imperial intervention.

The Habsburgs (1438–1648)

A marriage between the Luxembourgs and Habsburgs united the dynasties and brought another **Habsburg** to the imperial throne in 1438. Albert II ushered in an almost unbroken line to the end of the Holy Roman Empire. Initially the dynasty shored up its power with ambitious marriage alliances, expanding out from Austria to include the Netherlands, much of Italy, Spain (with all its New World colonies), Bohemia and Hungary – perhaps the most troublesome possession of all, given the repeated attacks by the Ottoman Empire. Since Germany was not the main source of their power, the Habsburgs' interests lay elsewhere: **Frederick III** (1440–93) was more preoccupied by astrology; and **Maximilian I** (1493–1519) was a naive idealist – he once seriously approached the Ottomans with the idea that Turks and Christians might settle their differences in a medieval tournament. The most powerful Habsburg of all, **Charles V** (1519–58), was blunt on his priorities: "I speak Spanish to God, Italian to women, French to men, and German to my horse." The feeling was largely mutual, and the prince-electors enjoyed a powerful protector who had little time to intervene.

Nevertheless, under the Habsburgs there was some much-needed reform of the imperial government. The central administration expanded and appointed permanent professional councillors, trained in centralizing Roman law, many at the newly founded **universities**, which included Heidelberg (1386), Rostock (1419) and Tübingen (1477). Meanwhile the **estates** met at the Diet of Worms in 1495, where they outlawed private feuds, created a supreme imperial chamber court and imposed a new imperial tax. Even though territorial rulers and city magistrates held much of the real power on the ground, the centralized, bureaucratic expansion, increasingly extravagant courts, larger armies, incessant war, and a grasping, corrupt Church all served to increase the financial burden at every level of society.

The Reformation

Economic resentment was inevitable and the outburst of one monk in Wittenberg struck a chord across society. **Martin Luther**'s (see box, p.202) objections to the profligacy of the Church were outlined in his **95 Theses** (1517) which challenged papal authority as the sole interpreter of the Bible, the only source of religious truth for Luther. When he was called to explain himself before Charles V at the Diet of Worms

1555	**1618–48**	**1685**
Following decades of unrest, the Peace of Augsburg allows rulers to decide the religion of their principalities	The Thirty Years' War rips Germany apart in a pseudo-religious conflict and the subsequent peace deal confirms independent states	Johann Sebastian Bach is born in Eisenach

in 1521, he became a German hero. Nor was he alone in rejecting authority. Any ruler who adopted the new creed could expect to profit hugely in power and wealth by taking ownership of the Church within their states. The general public – newly informed of revolutionary ideas by the recent invention of the printing press (see box, p.530) – fused Luther's vehemence with a general hope for social improvement. This prompted the large-scale **rebellions of 1525** that saw knights, peasants, farmers and the urban poor mount armed insurrections to improve their lot. However, Luther was no social radical. He argued that a hierarchical society was God's will and the rebellions quickly fizzled out.

The religious revolution of Luther and his supporting regents and cities continued unchecked, however, as Habsburg attention was fixed on wars against France and the Turks, who captured much of Hungary and Vienna in 1529 under Süleyman the Magnificent. By the mid-1520s a number of German cities and states had severed ties with Rome and formally turned Lutheran. The reforms agreed in the **Diet of Speyer** (1526) resulted in a state church in every Lutheran territory whose members were dubbed **Protestants** because of their protest against imperial attempts to revoke the Speyer ruling. The **Diet of Augsburg** in 1530 saw the presentation of the **Augsburg Confession** authored by Philipp Melanchthon, a definitive statement of Lutheran beliefs that, as far as Catholic theologians were concerned, represented too deep a rift for reconciliation. With its foundations laid, Lutheranism further integrated the church into state politics and everyday life.

Division, war and collapse

One immediate effect of the Diet of Augsburg was the formation of the **Schmalkaldic League** (1531), a military grouping of Protestant rulers, preparing the way for a century of almost constant strife. The Lutherans sought to ensure their survival and extend their sphere of influence, as did the Catholics, who included the Habsburgs and of course the papacy, bent on recovering power and confiscated properties. To strengthen their cause the Catholic Church organized the **Council of Trent** (1545–63), which spearheaded a Catholic **Counter-Reformation** from Spain and Rome and produced authoritative dogmas that formally pronounced the papacy to be the only legitimate arbiter of Biblical interpretation. Founded in 1534 and bent on recovering lost ground, the militant **Jesuit** order was extremely active in Germany.

A series of religiously inspired wars and peace treaties began in 1545, when the first clash between Protestant and imperial forces resulted in the 1555 **Peace of Augsburg**. This determined that whoever governed a territory decided its legitimate faith – Lutheranism or Catholicism – for everyone in the jurisdiction. Good news for Lutheranism, bad for Calvinists who followed a more radical form of Protestantism from Switzerland and whose subsequent alienation prompted them to push hard to gain recognition as they made major territorial gains in the 1560s and 1570s.

Tensions continued to escalate and by the early seventeenth century Germany was divided into competing military alliances: the **Protestant Union** (1608) and the **Catholic League** (1609). Both looked to foreign powers for support, vastly increasing the scale of the ensuing **Thirty Years' War** (1618–48). In the course of the war, Spain fought for the Catholics, while France, England, the Netherlands, Bohemia, Denmark and Sweden weighed in for the Protestants, albeit often to stymie the Habsburgs rather

1756	**1770**	**1774**
Frederick the Great triumphs in the Seven Years' War to confirm Brandenburg-Prussia as a new European superpower	Ludwig van Beethoven is born in Bonn	Johann Wolfgang von Goethe pens the book that would catapult him into history, *The Sorrows of Young Werther*

than out of any religious conviction. However, the European powers could ill-afford their mercenary armies, so they made promises of loot and allowed unprecedented brutality: in 1631 two-thirds of the 20,000-strong population of Magdeburg was massacred by imperial troops. The war also saw the Swedes rampage around Germany, taking most towns in southwest Germany, including Heidelberg. For German society, the war was catastrophic: around three million of Germany's twenty million population died in the war or in the epidemics that followed the general economic collapse.

It took the **Peace of Westphalia** (1648) to finally end the bloodshed. This brought territorial gains to Sweden and France, confirmed that rulers determined the religion of their lands (although they had to keep it as it was in 1624), and permitted some religious tolerance, including of Calvinism. It also guaranteed almost unlimited sovereignty to German princes, thereby dividing the Holy Roman Empire into hundreds of autonomous political entities and ending it as a political unit.

The age of absolutism (1648–1871)

By removing much of the power of the Holy Roman Emperor and the papacy, the Peace of Westphalia established territorial sovereignty for German rulers. These numbered around three hundred principalities, over fifty imperial cities, and almost two thousand counts and knights, with the smallest unit – the Swabian Abbey of Baindt, with a few hundred acres, 29 nuns and a princess-abbess – having many of the same rights as the largest. Germany's history became that of the thousands of these smaller histories as petty rulers legislated, taxed, allied with each other and foreign powers, and fought at will. As princely courts strengthened, many copied the absolutist rule and lavish indulgences of the intensely fashionable (and powerful) French **King Louis XIV** (reigned 1661–1715). German rulers like Saxony's Augustus the Strong, to name just one, flattered themselves with Baroque palaces and adopted elaborate French court ceremonies, food and conversation. They courted an international nobility and welcomed foreign cultural innovations like opera. When added to the cost of large armies and proliferating bureaucracies, these ruinously expensive courts were an enormous burden on the people. Louis XIV expanded his influence across the border by other means, marching east to establish the Rhine as France's new border in the late seventeenth century. Whole German towns were laid to ruins in the process. Inevitably, development – economic, social and political – slowed. While other European powers enlarged colonies and developed democracies, Germany was barely even a concept.

The exception to all this overindulgence and provincialism was **Prussia**. Through austerity and militarism it grew increasingly powerful, eventually replacing Austria as the dominant German power. And it was out of its industrialization and a European-wide **social revolution**, that war and diplomacy finally created a country called Germany.

The rise of Prussia

The meteoric rise of **Brandenburg-Prussia** from the ruins of the Thirty Years' War was, to say the least, unpredictable. The ruling house of Hohenzollern had little in resources and was sovereign over a patchwork of sparsely populated territories widely scattered from their capital in Berlin between modern-day Poland and the Rhineland.

1785	1791	1806
Friedrich Schiller pens *An die Freude*, better known as the *Ode to Joy* of Beethoven's 9th Symphony	Friedrich II aggrandizes his capital with Berlin's Brandenburg Gate, built as a symbol of peace	The Prussians are overthrown by the French and Napoleon reorganizes German territory

The Prussian route for success was to build a flourishing mercantile economy by offering skilled European refugees protection. Those who came included Jews, South German Catholics, 20,000 French Huguenots and resettling Dutch colonists. Prussia became one of Europe's most tolerant states, even though it was all to support autocratic rule and a disciplined permanent army. **Frederick William I** (1713–40) perfected the Prussian scheme – strong government, productivity and militarism – by enforcing spartan conditions. Laws limited luxuries (even theatre was eventually banned) and most court servants were fired. This tight fiscal ship furnished the "soldier-king" with an army of 80,000 men, the continent's fourth largest after France, Russia and Austria. While the army marched and drilled, a draconian work-ethic was drubbed into the populace; Frederick took to walking Berlin and personally beating anyone he caught loafing.

His son **Frederick II** (1712–86) added a degree of sophistication, encouraging learning and culture by sponsoring leading figures of the German Enlightenment, including playwright Gotthold Ephraim Lessing and philosopher Moses Mendelssohn, abolishing torture and reducing taxes on the poor. Yet Frederick not only maintained the Prussian military tradition, he began to deploy its might. Most gains were at Austria's expense. Its 100,000 troops were spread too thinly – over much of the modern-day Czech Republic, Hungary and Poland and (after 1714) the southern Netherlands and the duchy of Milan – and it was weak from long wars against France and the Ottoman Empire. The Austrians were also troubled by a succession crisis as Charles VI sought to persuade the world to accept his daughter, **Maria Theresa**. Sensing vulnerability, Frederick II annexed Silesia in the **War of the Austrian Succession** (1740–48), which saw the outnumbered Prussian armies prove themselves a superior force. Austria, Saxony, France and Russia were startled, and responded by starting the **Seven Years' War** in 1756. Prussia won that, too, confirming it as a new Central European power and earning Frederick the epithet "the Great".

Napoleonic occupation

The Revolutionary and Napoleonic wars that followed the French Revolution of 1789, during which **Napoleon** advanced across the continent, confirmed both the immense military power of France and the decrepit nature of the Austrian Habsburg forces. By 1806, Austria had lost so much ground that Francis II laid down the imperial crown and pronounced the end of the Holy Roman Empire after a thousand years – though in practical terms it had long since finished. Prussia found itself alone and was quickly routed by the French in two simultaneous battles at Jena and Auerstädt (October 14, 1806). Berlin was occupied two weeks later.

Once in control, Napoleon began to reorganize German lands: Prussia lost almost half its territory and population, and France occupied the left bank of the Rhine and compensated displaced rulers with possessions elsewhere. This, and Napoleon's goal to establish a chain of satellite states east of the Rhine, precipitated a frantic redrawing of political boundaries. Dozens of small political entities – free cities, imperial knights, ecclesiastical territories – fell into the hands of neighbours, particularly Napoleon's satellites, including Bavaria and Württemberg which he made into kingdoms, and Baden and Hesse-Darmstadt which became grand duchies. Napoleon also introduced state reform, streamlining ministries, allowing nobles to trade and making guild

1812	1813	1848–49
Academics Jakob and Wilhelm Grimm collect and publish a collection of folk tales	After decades of liberal reform, the aristocracy resume power via the Congress of Vienna but also reinstate Prussia as a player	The European year of revolutions is marked in Germany by a first, ultimately unsuccessful attempt to create a democratic national assembly

membership more accessible. He also forced almost all states – except Austria and Prussia – into a confederation. All of this unwittingly prepared the way for Germany to centralize, strengthen and nation-build.

Restoration, reform, revolution and reaction

The collapse of Napoleon's empire – a triple-whammy of defeat by Russia, Prussia and Austria at the **Battle of Leipzig** in 1813, the restoration of the French monarchy and his final defeat at Waterloo in 1815 – led to a new European order being drawn up at the 1814 **Congress of Vienna**. The attending parties maintained many of his streamlined borders and governments, but since democracy and national self-determination were anathema, it was mostly an exercise in re-establishing the old order.

However, the French Revolution had awakened in Germany the first stirrings of **liberalism**. So, although the next fifty years were peaceful and stable, open **rebellion** also increased. Students rose up as revolutionary *Burschenschaften* (fraternities), political parties emerged and society became increasingly urban as Germany **industrialized**. In 1848 economic depression, urban unemployment and major crop failure coincided, causing famine across northern Europe. One consequence was mass emigration to the New World; another was open rebellion among the working classes. The authorities' response was to restrict the rights of assembly, enlarge police authority and intensify censorship, thereby stifling intellectual and cultural life. However, more progressive governments recognized a need for **constitutional reform** to win the support of educated citizens. Constitutions were duly instigated in Bavaria and Baden (1818), Württemberg (1819) and Hesse-Darmstadt (1820). Prominent liberals were appointed to many state ministries, precipitating a slow programme of liberal reform in many parts of Germany.

Bismarck and German unity

The Congress of Vienna was also hugely significant in restoring Prussia as a power-broker. The agreements gave it land along the Rhine, making it pivotal in the defence of Germany's western boundary, and giving it the great iron and coal deposits of the Ruhr. Consequently, its industrial might grew at a furious pace, in part because of the development of an ever-expanding free-trade area called the **Zollverein**, or customs union, which, from 1834, produced a degree of German economic unity and gave Prussia a powerful new weapon in its struggle against Austria.

But Prussia's most powerful weapon to achieve German unity was **Otto von Bismarck**. The elevation of this conservative statesman to Prussian chancellor in 1862 immediately upset liberals, but Bismarck proved visionary, with a talent for political statecraft. In 1866, using the excuse of division of the duchies of Schleswig and Holstein as spoils of a brief Danish war, Bismarck embarked on the **Seven Weeks' War** with Austria. Armed with a brilliant strategist, Helmuth von Moltke, and a deadly breech-loading needle gun, Prussia won quickly, tipping the balance of power within Germany in its favour.

Bismarck then harnessed a growing sense of nationalism to strengthen Prussia's militarism. Opposition to Napoleonic rule in Germany had kindled the first German nationalist sentiments, and illustrated their potency. They had helped nurture the **Romantic movement**, which celebrated German spirit and tradition unlike the cold rationality of the French Enlightenment. From this grew notions of what it meant to

1871	1870s–80s	1876
Prussian Chancellor Otto von Bismarck engineers German unity following a spat with Austria, and an elected parliament (Reichstag) is born	Following worldwide economic depression, around four million Germans emigrate to the New World	Audiences endure fifteen hours and four operas in the first performance of Richard Wagner's *Ring of the Nibelung* at Bayreuth

be German and the idea that all Germans should be unified in a single state. So having defeated Austria, Bismarck used the burgeoning national identity to cajole and bully his neighbours into joining a **North German Confederation**, in which Prussia had about four-fifths of the territory, population and political control. A national currency and uniform commercial and financial practices and laws were quickly introduced. By addressing the frustrations of middle-class Germans, Bismarck defused their demands for greater political freedom while strengthening the position of the state and Prussia.

German unity lay just around the corner. France was already nervous about its newly united and strong neighbour, and when Bismarck altered a telegram sent by the foreign office of Prussian king Wilhelm I to the French government, it declared war. As Bismarck had hoped, the German nation rallied behind Prussia. Germany's southern states – particularly Bavaria, Württemberg, Baden and Southern Hesse – quickly joined the Franco-Prussian War, forcing Paris to capitulate in 1871. The peace gave Germany Alsace-Lorraine. More importantly, Bismarck used the patriotic fervour to negotiate with southern states and achieve political consolidation. So while Prussian guns bombarded Paris, a greater victory took place: **Wilhelm I** was proclaimed **emperor** of a united nation, beginning a powerful new empire under the Hohenzollerns.

The German Empire (1871–1918)

Once established, the German Empire quickly became Europe's leading power; its rapid economic expansion made the German economy second only to the United States by 1914. This new-found might prompted Germany to enter the **colonial** race. It was far too late to pick up anything of economic value, but by entering the fray it increased foreign mistrust, leading inexorably towards the catastrophe of World War I. Germany's defeat forced the abdication of the emperor and left it crippled.

Industry and society

Prussia, in commanding three-fifths of Germany's land and population and providing its emperor, dominated the united Germany. With typical efficiency, it created national institutions and freed up trade, prompting an unprecedented boom, then an equally sudden bust due to worldwide **depression in 1873**. Two million Germans left for the Americas in the 1870s, a trend that continued into the 1880s even as industry began to recover, in part thanks to cartels in heavy industry and protective import tariffs. By the 1890s the economy had turned around, emigration dropped off and Germany began to exceed Britain in steel production – from having only half its capacity in the 1870s.

Urbanization followed industrialization. By 1910 more than half of Germany's population of 41 million lived in cities; the population of Berlin alone doubled to two million between 1890 and 1900, leading to the construction of thousands of tenement buildings in working-class districts. The working class grew rapidly and union membership reached 3.7 million in 1912. Yet workers still lacked full political rights and sanitary living conditions, fermenting support for the revolutionary Social Democratic Party (**SPD**), the chief dissenters within the Reichstag.

They proved the chancellor's undoing. When the party posted enormous gains in the 1890 elections, Bismarck was seen as too old-fashioned and was forced to resign by the Kaiser, a humiliation for the former Iron Chancellor.

1885	1886	1890
Karl Benz creates his Patent Motorwagen, widely recognized as the first proper automobile	Bavaria's Ludwig II dies, leaving his fabulously theatrical retreat Schloss Neuschwanstein still incomplete	The new Kaiser Wilhelm II dismisses Chancellor Otto von Bismarck to usher in an erratic foreign policy that leads to war

Foreign policy

Bismarck had left an impressive legacy in foreign affairs. He had forged a series of **alliances** to protect the fledgling German Empire in the shifting power games of Europe. Central to this was to ensure the diplomatic isolation of France – with its grudge against Germany – and to maintain the stability between Austria-Hungary and Russia, who were increasingly on the verge of conflict over the Balkans after the disintegration of the Ottoman Empire.

Bismarck's successors abandoned this policy, however. The alliance with Russia was dropped, allowing France to end its isolation and ally with them. The plan was to make Germany a global power and it meddled everywhere, including in China and Turkey. Germany's navy went from negligible to one that rivalled Britain's in just over a decade, and the country acquired Togo, Cameroon and parts of modern-day Namibia, Tanzania, New Guinea and a few Pacific islands – all minor prizes that didn't justify the naval cost. Moreover the British felt threatened, leading them to negotiate alliances with Japan in 1902, then France in 1904 and Russia in 1907 to form a Triple Entente that left Germany surrounded.

Austria was Germany's only major ally – an alliance that immediately caused trouble upon the assassination of the Austrian heir to the Balkan throne, **Archduke Francis Ferdinand**, by a Bosnian Serb in June 1914. The Serbs and their Russian allies mobilized against the Austrians and their German allies, and the continent tipped into chaos.

World War I

When war broke out, no one imagined new military technologies would unleash such carnage as to result in some 37 million casualties, including sixteen million dead. Some two and a half million Germans would lose their lives. Instead German civilians greeted the outbreak of hostilities in 1914 with enthusiasm – only confirmed pacifists or communists resisted the intoxication of patriotism. The political parties agreed to a truce, and even the Social Democrats voted in favour of war credits.

Germany's calculation that France could be knocked out before Russia fully mobilized soon proved hopelessly optimistic, and Germany found itself facing a war on two fronts – the very thing it dreaded. As casualties mounted on the stalemated western front, rationing began to hit poorer civilians and disillusionment set in. From the summer of 1915 popular protests began as ordinary people turned against the war as being for the benefit of the rich at the expense of the poor.

Surrounded and blockaded, with Italy (1915) and Romania (1916) joining against them, Germany and Austria faced an almost impossible situation. The German government, like those of its enemies, found it safer to demand ever-greater efforts rather than admit the pointlessness of earlier sacrifices. Its generals, Ludendorff and Hindenburg, sought mobilization of the whole country, until more than eleven million men were in uniform. After a severe winter in 1916–17, Germany was unable to feed itself. Malnutrition – even starvation – was not uncommon and fuel shortages left the population vulnerable to an **influenza epidemic** that swept Europe. Around half a million Germans died in the epidemic that killed at least fifty million worldwide.

After a promising last great offensive in spring 1918, almost a million American troops arrived in France and German **defeat** was inevitable by autumn. Knowing the

1895	1901	1914–18
Wilhelm Röntgen detects X-rays in Würzburg	Marie Magdalena von Losch is born in Berlin – she becomes famous thirty years later as movie femme fatale Marlene Dietrich	World War I pits Germany, Austria and Turkey against their neighbours, with disastrous consequences. Kaiser Wilhelm abdicates

Allies would refuse to negotiate with the old absolutist system, Germany's supreme general, Ludendorff, declared a democratic, constitutional monarchy whose chancellor would be responsible to the Reichstag not the Kaiser. A government was formed under Prince Max von Baden. It agreed to extensive reforms, but it was too little too late for the bitter sailors and soldiers on the home front, where the contrast between privilege and poverty was stark. At the start of November, the Kiel Garrison led a naval mutiny and revolutionary workers' and soldiers' soviets mushroomed across Germany. Realizing the game was up, **Kaiser Wilhelm II abdicated**.

The Weimar Republic (1919–33)

Though humiliated, defeat allowed Germany to regroup, emerging from chaos to a new democracy with the **Weimar Republic**. Despite having the most modern and democratic constitution of its day, the burden of 1920s economic instability proved too much, and the global depression of the early 1930s finally broke the fledgling republic. A new wave of political strife fostered extremism and helped sweep the Nazis to power.

Abdication and the Weimar constitution

Following the abdication of the Kaiser, power passed to the SPD leader **Friedrich Ebert**. However, the revolutionary soldiers, sailors and workers who controlled the streets, inspired by the 1917 Bolshevik success in Russia, favoured a Soviet-style government and refused to obey Ebert's orders. A deal was struck with the army, which promised to protect the republic if Ebert would forestall a full-blooded socialist revolution – which

THE ARTS IN THE 1920S

"A world has been destroyed; we must seek a radical solution," proclaimed young architect Walter Gropius on his return from the front in 1918. In a remarkable response to the political and economic chaos of Germany during the 1920s, the arts flourished in a dazzling display of creativity. Gropius went on to found the famous **Bauhaus** school, initially in Weimar, then Dessau (see p.197), pioneering the modernist aesthetic which had begun to assert itself in the late nineteenth century.

In visual art the **Dada** shockwave rippled through the decade and George Grosz satirized the times in savage caricatures, while **Expressionism** concentrated on emotional responses to reality rather than reality itself. In **music** composers like Arnold Schoenberg rejected centuries-old traditions of tonality, while in **theatre** Bertolt Brecht's bitterly satiric *Dreigroschen Oper* ("Threepenny Opera") compared modern capitalism to the gangster underworld. Germany also became a global centre for the newest of the arts: **film**. Between the wars Germany produced legendary films such as Fritz Lang's *Metropolis* and Robert Wiene's *The Cabinet of Doctor Caligari*, which championed distorted sets and unusual camera angles to probe disturbing truths.

Meanwhile in popular culture, all-singing, all-dancing musicals, featuring platoons of women in various states of undress took off and the Berlin **cabaret scene** had its heyday – as celebrated by Berlin residents such as Christopher Isherwood, whose tales of the time were turned into the musical *Cabaret*. But not everyone welcomed the bawdiness or the modernist attack on tradition and the Nazis mercilessly put an abrupt end to all this "cultural bolshevism" in the 1930s.

1918	1919	1919
Kurt Eisner declares Bavaria an independent socialist republic, but is assassinated within months	The Weimar Republic introduces the most progressive liberal and democratic reforms in the world	Walter Gropius founds the Staatliches Bauhaus institute of design, art and architecture in Weimar

was threatening in the form of a **Spartacist uprising** in Berlin in early 1919. This uprising was put down by the **Freikorps** – armed bands of right-wing officers and NCOs from the old imperial army – and the Spartacist leaders, Karl Liebknecht and Rosa Luxemburg, were duly murdered, establishing a dangerous precedent for political violence. Elections in early 1919 confirmed the SPD as leaders of the country – with 38 percent of the vote – and made Ebert president.

Weimar, the country town that had been the wellspring of the German Enlightenment, was chosen as the venue to draft a national constitution; Berlin was tainted by monarchic and military associations. The **constitution** drawn up was hailed as the most liberal, democratic and progressive in the world. While it incorporated a complex system of checks and balances to prevent power becoming too concentrated in parts of government or regions, it crucially lacked any clauses for outlawing parties hostile to the system. This opened the way for savage attacks on the republic by extremists at both ends of the political spectrum. In 1920, Freikorps units loyal to the right-wing politician Wolfgang Kapp marched on Berlin, unopposed by the army, and briefly took power in the **Kapp putsch**; by the end of 1922 there had been nearly four hundred political assassinations, the vast majority of them traceable to the right.

Amidst such turmoil, and with public opinion divided between a plethora of parties, all Weimar-era governments became unwieldy coalitions that often pursued contradictory policies and had an average life of only about eight months, producing a weak framework that later readily allowed the extremists in the far-right Nazi party to take control.

The Treaty of Versailles

Much of the history of Germany in the 1920s was determined by the Allies and the harsh terms imposed by the **Treaty of Versailles**: Alsace-Lorraine was handed back to France, who would temporarily get the coal-rich Saarland region to aid reconstruction. In the east, Germany lost a large chunk of Prussia to Poland, giving the latter access to the Baltic, but cutting off East Prussia from the rest of Germany. The overseas empire was dismantled. But what aggrieved Germans most was the treaty's war-guilt clause which held Germany responsible "for causing all the loss and damage" suffered by the Allies in the war. This was seen as a cynical victors' justice, yet provided the justification for a gigantic bill of **reparation payments** – a total of 132 billion gold marks.

Economic collapse

With the economy badly battered by the war and postwar political chaos, Germany struggled to meet reparation payments and in 1922 France and Belgium occupied the Ruhr in response to alleged defaults. The German government's response was to call a national strike in January 1923, which proved to be the final straw, sending the mark plummeting in the worst **inflation** ever known: a loaf of bread that cost 10,000 marks in the morning would cost 3,000,000 marks by nightfall; restaurant prices rose as customers ate. By November 15, 1923, it took 4.2 trillion German marks to buy an American dollar.

The mark was finally stabilized under a supremely able foreign minister, **Gustav Stresemann**, who believed relief from reparation payments was more likely to come from cooperation than resistance. The Allies, too, moderated their stance, and, realizing

1920	1922	1923
First international Dada Fair in Berlin, a landmark in the avant-garde cultural life of Weimar-era Berlin	Nosferatu stalks the silver screen for the first time in F.W. Murnau's Expressionist horror classic	Punitive reparation demands create rampant inflation: 4.2 trillion marks buys just one American dollar

Germany needed to be economically stable in order to pay, devised the **1924 Dawes Plan** under which loans poured into Germany, particularly from the US. The economic surge that followed lasted until the **Wall Street Crash** of October 1929. With this, American credit ended, wiping out Germany's economic stability, and the poverty of the immediate postwar period returned with a vengeance.

Political extremism and the rise of the Nazis

Everyone suffered in the economic troubles of the Weimar period. Hyperinflation wiped out middle-class savings, and six million people were unemployed by 1932. Increasingly, people sought radical solutions in political extremism, and support for two parties that bitterly opposed one another but shared a desire to end democracy grew: the **communists** and the **National Socialist German Workers' Party** (NSDAP), or Nazis. While red flags and swastika banners hung from neighbouring tenements, gangs from the left and right fought in the streets in ever-greater numbers, with the brown-shirted Nazi **SA** (*Sturmabteilung*) stormtroopers fighting endless pitched battles against the communist **Rote Frontkämpferbund** (Red Fighters' Front). The threat of a return to the anarchy of the postwar years increased Nazi support among the middle classes and captains of industry (who provided heavy financial support) because they feared for their lives and property under communist rule. Fear of the reds also meant little or nothing was done to curb SA violence against the left. The growth of Nazi popularity was also attributable to Hitler's record as a war veteran, his identification of Jews as scapegoats, his promise to restore national pride, and even his own charisma. Meanwhile, the communists found it difficult to extend support beyond the German working classes.

By September 1930, the communists and Nazis together gained nearly one of every three votes cast and in the July 1932 **parliamentary elections** the Nazis took 37 percent of the vote – their largest total in any free election – making them the largest party in the Reichstag; the communists took fifteen percent. Nazi thugs began attacking Jewish shops and businesses and intimidating liberals into muted criticism or silence. But what eventually brought the Nazis to power in 1933 was infighting among conservatives, who persuaded the virtually senile president and former field marshal Paul von Hindenburg to make Hitler chancellor. This move was based on a gamble that the Nazis would crush the left but fail to form an effective government, so that within a few months Hitler could be nudged aside. Hitler became chancellor on January 4, 1933, and Berlin thronged with Nazi supporters bearing torches. For the vast majority of Berliners it was a nightmare come true: three-quarters of the city had voted against the Nazis at the last elections.

The pretext for an all-out **Nazi takeover** was provided by the **Reichstag fire** on February 28, 1933, which was likely started by them, rather than the simple-minded Dutch communist Marius van der Lubbe on whom blame fell. An emergency decree the following day effectively legalized a permanent state of emergency, which the Nazis quickly used to start crushing the communists and manipulate the 1933 **elections** in which the Nazis won 43.9 percent of the vote. Though short of a majority, this was attained by arresting the communist deputies and some SPD leaders to pass an **Enabling Act** that gave the Nazis dictatorial powers. Hitler was only just short of the two-thirds majority he needed to legally abolish the Weimar Republic. The SPD

1923–25	**1925**	**1926**
French and Belgian troops occupy the Ruhr in response to German defaults on reparations payments	German foreign minister Gustav Stresemann negotiates the Locarno treaties with the western powers to renounce military aggression between France, Belgium and Germany	Germany joins the League of Nations

salvaged some self-respect by refusing to accede to this, but the Catholic centrists meekly supported the bill in return for minor concessions. It was passed by 441 votes to 84, hammering the final nails into the coffin of German parliamentary democracy. With Hindenburg's death in the summer of 1934, Hitler merged the offices of president and chancellor, declaring himself **Führer** of the German Reich and introducing an absolute dictatorship.

Nazi Germany (1933–45)

After gaining power in 1933, Hitler established a regime so brutal it has attracted an overwhelming, almost ghoulish, level of interest ever since. The Nazification of German society was rapid, and as the country remilitarized, Nazi Germany soon embarked on a ruinous crusade to conquer Europe and exterminate Jews, Roma (Gypsies), homosexuals and others. Hitler's aggressive foreign policy led to World War II (1939–45), the loss of which was even more devastating and humiliating for Germany than the first.

Government and society

Once in absolute power Hitler consolidated his control, removing opposition and tightening the Nazi grip on all areas of society. All other political parties were banned, unions disbanded, and leaders of both arrested and sent to **concentration camps**. On May 11, 1934, the Nazis shocked the world by burning thousands of books that conflicted with Nazi ideology, and the exodus of known anti-Nazis and those with reasons to fear them began in earnest: Bertolt Brecht, Kurt Weill, Lotte Lenya and Wassily Kandinsky joined the likes of Albert Einstein and George Grosz in exile.

The machinery of state was quickly and brutally Nazified as the party put its own men into vital posts in local governments throughout Germany. A series of political executions took place, including those on June 30, 1934, which included a purge of their own ranks and which became known as the "**Night of the Long Knives**".

Given the suppression, fear, exodus and the tightening grip of Nazi control on all areas of life, the atmosphere in Germany changed irrevocably. The unemployed were drafted into labour battalions to work on the land or build Autobahns; the press and radio were orchestrated by Joseph Goebbels; children joined Nazi youth organizations; and Gestapo spies were placed in every area of German society. Even non-Nazis couldn't escape the plethora of organizations that developed across every area of life, from riding clubs and dog breeders to the "Reich Church" and "German League of Maidens". Everywhere the Nazis tried to implement order and dynamism, a process that reached its zenith during the **1936 Olympics**, which raised Germany's international standing and temporarily glossed over the realities of Nazi brutality.

World War II

Throughout the 1930s the Nazis made **preparations for war**, expanding the army and gearing the economy for war readiness, to dovetail with Hitler's foreign policy of obtaining Lebensraum ("living space") from neighbouring countries by intimidation. From 1936 onwards Hitler even spent much time with his favourite architect, Albert Speer, drawing up extensive plans for a remodelled and grandiose Berlin, to be called "Germania", once it became the capital of the world.

1927	**1928**	**1929**
Günter Grass, the father of modern German literature, is born in Lübeck	Premiere of Bertolt Brecht's and Kurt Weill's *Threepenny Opera* in Berlin	The revolutionary German ocean liner *Bremen* sets a new world speed record for a crossing of the Atlantic

The road to war was swift. To little international protest the German army occupied the **Rhineland** (demilitarized under the Treaty of Versailles) in 1936, annexed **Austria** in 1938 and a few months later dismembered **Czechoslovakia** with Britain's and France's consent. Encouraged by this appeasement, Hitler made demands on Poland in 1939, hoping for a similar response, particularly since he had signed a nonaggression pact with his ultimate enemy, the Soviet Union, to ensure Germany could avoid a war on two fronts. But two days after the German invasion of **Poland** – dubbed the Blitzkrieg ("lightning war") – on September 1, Britain and France declared war in defence of their treaty obligations.

The outbreak of **World War II** was greeted with little enthusiasm in Germany, though the fall of France on July 18, 1940, caused jubilation. Up to that point Germany had suffered little from the war, and the impact of wartime austerity was softened by Nazi welfare organizations and a blanket of propaganda. In any case, with Gestapo informers believed to lurk everywhere, open dissent seemed impossible.

Having quickly gained direct or indirect control of large swathes of Europe, Hitler began a new phase in the war by breaking his pact and invading the **Soviet Union** on June 22, 1941, then declaring war on the USA after his Japanese allies attacked the American base at Pearl Harbor. The German army rapidly advanced into the Soviet Union, but the six-month Battle of Stalingrad in the hard Russian winter of 1942–43 turned the war and sent the German army into retreat.

In the spring of 1943 German cities began to suffer their first heavy **air raids**, and by the end of the year, bombardments became a feature of everyday life in many German cities. Apart from chipping away at Nazi power, the destruction also intensified **underground resistance**. Despite the Gestapo stranglehold, some groups managed minor successes and several failed attempts on Hitler's life were made, particularly in the 1944 **July Bomb Plot**. The **Normandy Landings** in June 1944 marked the major turning-point on the western front, with Germany in retreat and fighting on two fronts.

On May 8, 1945, the German armed forces surrendered to the **Red Army** in Berlin and the world began to count the cost of its second world war. Some 67 million lives had been lost, among them seven million Germans – or around one in ten of the population. Almost every city had been reduced to rubble and in many Soviet-occupied zones this was just the beginning, as the Soviets unleashed an orgy of rape and looting.

The Holocaust

It was only with the conquest of Germany that the full scale of Nazi atrocities became apparent. Hitler's main aim, along with expanding German borders, had long been to "cleanse" the world of those who did not conform to his social and racial ideals. Their persecution began with the start of Nazi rule and soon extended beyond political intellectual opponents to embrace a wide range of groups – including active church members, freemasons, homosexuals, Roma, the disabled and most notoriously, the Jews – who in 1933 numbered around half a million in Germany. In 1934 the SA began to enforce a **boycott of Jewish** businesses, medical and legal practices – and these turned into bare-faced attacks on Jewish shops and institutions by SA men in civilian clothes on November 9, 1938, in a night of savagery known as **Kristallnacht.** Thereafter the Nazis enacted anti-Semitic laws confiscating property and making life

1930	1933	1933
The UFA film *The Blue Angel* makes an international star of Marlene Dietrich	National Socialist leader Adolf Hitler is elected German chancellor and quickly establishes a dictatorship	The Reichstag is set ablaze, a Dutch radical is framed and Hitler seizes dictatorial power as Führer

difficult and dangerous for German Jews. Those who could, emigrated to countries beyond German control and escaped the Nazi "Final Solution" decided at the **Wannsee conference** in 1942 – to systematically exterminate all Jews in German-controlled territories in **concentration camps**. Those within Germany – including Sachsenhausen (see p.119), Dachau (see p.359) and Bergen-Belsen (see p.730) – were mainly prison and forced-labour camps, which had often been established early on in the Nazi regime, while those designed specifically for mass extermination were for the most part in the occupied territories. Of the eleven million estimated to have been murdered in the Holocaust, **six million** were Jewish, around 160,000 of them German Jews. Around 15,000 Jews survived in hiding in Germany, assisted by Germans who risked their lives to help them evade being rounded up onto trains bound for concentration camps.

Occupation and the Cold War (1945–89)

Having been brought down by the Allies, Germany was split between the USA, UK, France and Russia into four zones of occupation. Tensions between the western Allies and Russia led, in 1949, to the founding of capitalist and democratic West Germany and Soviet-dominated communist East Germany. That division remained in place as part of the Iron Curtain which divided Europe as the world fought a Cold War.

Occupation

The **Potsdam conference** from July 17 to August 3, 1945, was held to decide Germany's borders. The main losses to prewar Germany were to the east where all territory east of the rivers Oder and Neisse – old Prussian lands – became part of Poland or the USSR. These made up around a quarter of Germany's lands and turned a fifth of its population into refugees, as the German populations here and in the Czech Republic became subject to revenge attacks and were forced to flee west into Germany.

This compounded a German postwar situation that was already bleak. Agriculture and industry had virtually collapsed, threatening acute shortages of food and fuel just as winter approached and a weakened civilian population fell prey to typhus, TB and other hunger-related diseases. The Allies did what they could, but even by the spring of 1947 rations remained at malnutrition levels. Crime soared. In Berlin alone, two thousand people were arrested every month, many of them from juvenile gangs that roamed the ruins murdering, robbing and raping. In the countryside bandits ambushed supply convoys heading for the city. The winter of 1946–47 was one of the coldest since records began. People froze to death aboard trains and Berlin hospitals alone treated 55,000 people for frostbite.

Thereafter things gradually improved with the help of **Marshall Plan** aid, while the process of demilitarization and de-Nazification agreed at Potsdam continued as **trials in Nuremburg** (1945–49) brought dozens of Nazi war criminals to justice. But one issue that divided opinion at Potsdam was the reinstatement of democracy. The Soviet Union had already taken steps towards establishing a communist administration under **Walter Ulbricht** and the SED (Sozialistische Einheitspartei Deutschlands) in their zone of occupation before the war was over.

1934	1935	1936
All political opposition is silenced in the Night of the Long Knives	First prototype of the Volkswagen Beetle, designed by Ferdinand Porsche	The Nazis score an international PR coup as Berlin hosts the Olympic Games

The birth of the two Germanys

In 1948 tension mounted as the Allies introduced economic reform in the western half of Berlin, which now formed an island within Soviet-occupied Germany. The Russians cut off electricity supplies to the city and severed road and rail links during the **Berlin blockade** as they attempted to force the western Allies out of Berlin. In the end the greatest weapon proved to be American and British support. On June 26, 1948, they began the **Berlin airlift**, flying supplies into the city to keep it alive against the odds for almost a year until the Russians relented.

Within six months, the political division of Germany was formalized by the creation of two rival states. First, the British, French and American zones of occupation were amalgamated to form the **Federal Republic of Germany** (May 1949), based on a federal system that gave significant powers to its eleven constituent states. The Soviets followed suit by establishing the **German Democratic Republic** on October 7. As Berlin lay deep within GDR territory, its eastern sector naturally became the GDR capital. But the Federal Republic chose Bonn, and West Berlin remained under overall Allied control.

The 1950s

Throughout the 1950s **West Germany**, under Chancellor Konrad Adenauer, recovered from the ravages of war astonishingly quickly to become Europe's largest economy. Meanwhile the **GDR** languished, partly as the result of the Soviets' ruthless asset-stripping – removing factories, rolling stock and generators to replace losses in the war-ravaged USSR. The death of Stalin in 1953 raised hopes that pressures could be eased, but instead the government unwittingly fuelled smouldering resentment by announcing a ten percent rise in work norms, causing workers to band together in the **1953 uprising**, which was brutally suppressed. So as the economic disparity between East and West Germany worsened throughout the 1950s, West Berlin became an increasingly attractive destination for East Berliners, who were able to cross the city's zonal borders more or less freely. This steady population-drain undermined prospects for development in the GDR, as 2.5 million workers – often young and often highly skilled – quit the GDR during the 1950s for the higher living standards and greater political freedom of the West.

The 1960s

By 1961, the East German regime was desperate, and rumours that the Berlin border might be sealed began to circulate. Shortly after midnight on August 13, 1961, it was, with the city divided by the **Berlin Wall**, which went up overnight, and then further strengthened to form the notorious barrier or "death strip" between the two countries (see box, p.83). Despite outrage throughout West Germany and formal diplomatic protests from the Allies, everyone knew that a firmer line risked war.

As life grew more comfortable in **West Germany**, society began to fragment along generational lines. The immediate catalyst was the wave of student unrest in 1967–68, when initial grievances against conservative universities grew into a wider disaffection with West Germany's materialism. The APO, or extra-parliamentary opposition, emerged as a strong and vocal force criticizing what many people saw as a failed attempt to build a true democracy on the ruins of Nazi Germany. Another powerful strand was anti-Americanism, fuelled by US foreign policy in Southeast Asia, Latin

1937

1939–45

The German airship *Hindenburg* explodes over Lakeheath, New Jersey, ending the era of long-haul travel by airship

Hitler invades Poland and the world tips into the chaos that becomes World War II. Eleven million are estimated to have been murdered in the Holocaust, while air raids on Hamburg create a fire storm, killing more than 40,000

America and the Middle East. Both viewpoints tended to bewilder and enrage older Germans and although the mass-protest movement fizzled out towards the end of the 1960s, a new and deadlier opposition – the **Baader-Meinhof** group – would emerge in the 1970s, unleashing a wave of terrorism few could sympathize with.

The 1970s and 1980s

Germany's place in the international scene changed considerably around the turn of the 1970s. Both superpowers hoped to thaw relations, while West German elections brought to power **Willy Brandt**, a chancellor committed to rapprochement with the GDR. In 1972, the Federal Republic and the GDR signed a **Basic Treaty**, which bound both states to respect each other's frontiers and sovereignty. In return for diplomatic recognition, the GDR allowed West Germans access to friends and family across the border, which had effectively been denied to them (barring limited visits in the mid-1960s). However, the freedom to move from East to West was restricted to disabled people and senior citizens.

So, throughout the 1970s and early 1980s relations between West and East Germany remained cordial, despite a resumption of frostiness in US–Soviet relations, which heightened concern about **nuclear weapons**. Antinuclear activists protested during the Berlin visit of US President Ronald Reagan in June 1981, as part of a new radical movement throughout West Germany. Concern about the arms race and the environment was widespread; feminism and gay rights commanded increasing support. Left-wing and Green groups formed an **Alternative Liste** to fight elections which formed the nucleus of **Die Grünen**, the Green Party, which remains a significant presence in German politics.

East Germany remained relatively quiet. The new East German leader, **Erich Honecker**, who was regarded as a "liberal", succeeded Walter Ulbricht in 1971. Under him, living standards improved and there was some relaxation of the regime's tight controls on society. But the changes were mostly trivial: escapes continued to be attempted and the vast **Stasi** (see p.92) was as strong as ever in its surveillance and persecutions.

Die Wende

The year 1989 ranks as both one of the most significant years in German history and one of the most unforseeable. Yet in under twelve months **Die Wende** ("the turn") transformed Germany. With little warning East Germany suddenly collapsed in the wake of the general easing of communism in the Eastern Bloc of the late 1980s. The Berlin Wall came down on November 9, 1989, symbolizing an end to the Cold War, making a lifetime's dream come true for most Germans – above all, those living in the East. Events then followed logically and briskly: the union of the two Germanys; the reassertion of Berlin as capital; and the start of a process to put those responsible for the GDR's crimes on trial.

The first holes in the Iron Curtain

When, in 1985, **Mikhail Gorbachev** became the new Soviet leader and began his reformist campaigns, glasnost and perestroika, their initial impact on East Germany was slight. The SED regarded them with deep suspicion, so while Poland and Hungary

1949	**1954**	**1969**
Germany officially divides into the Allied-affiliated Federal Republic of Germany and Soviet-controlled German Democratic Republic	The Berlin Wall is erected almost overnight, then strengthened by a "death strip"	Formation of pioneering electronic group Kraftwerk in Düsseldorf

embarked on the road to democracy, Erich Honecker declared that the Berlin Wall would stand for another fifty or a hundred years if necessary. The authorities also banned pro-glasnost Soviet magazine *Sputnik*.

Nevertheless, as the decade wore on some signs of protest began to emerge: the **Protestant Church** provided a haven for environmental and peace organizations, whose members unfurled banners demanding greater freedom at an official ceremony in Berlin in January 1988. They were immediately arrested, imprisoned, then expelled from the GDR. It fell to other Eastern European countries to make the *Wende* possible: in 1988 Hungary took down the barbed-wire fence along its Austrian border, creating a hole in the Iron Curtain, across which many East Germans fled. A similar pattern emerged in Czechoslovakia.

The October revolution

The East German government's disarrayed response to reform elsewhere galvanized into action thousands of people who had previously simply tried to make the best of things. Fledgling opposition groups like the **Neues Forum** emerged, and unrest began in Leipzig and Dresden and soon spread to Berlin.

Then, at the beginning of October, at the pompous official celebration of the GDR's **fortieth anniversary**, Gorbachev stressed the need for new ideas and stunningly announced that the USSR would not interfere in the affairs of fellow socialist states. Protests and scuffles along the cavalcade route escalated into a huge demonstration as the day wore on, which the police and Stasi brutally suppressed. Thousands of arrests were made, and prisoners were subjected to the usual degrading treatment and beatings. The following week, nationwide demonstrations came close to bloodshed in **Leipzig**, where 70,000 people marched through the city, forcing the sudden replacement of Erich Honecker with Egon Krenz as party secretary, who immediately announced that the regime was ready for dialogue. The exodus via other Eastern Bloc countries and the pressure on the streets kept rising, culminating on November 4, when East Berlin saw over one million citizens demonstrate, forcing authorities to make hasty concessions, including dropping the requirement for GDR citizens to get visas to visit Czechoslovakia – in effect, permitting emigration: within two days fifteen thousand had reached Bavaria – bringing the number of East Germans who had fled the country in 1989 to 200,000.

The Wall opens

The **opening of the Berlin Wall** was announced almost casually, on the evening of Thursday, November 9, when Berlin party boss Günter Schabowski told a press conference that East German citizens were free to leave the GDR with valid exit visas, which would henceforth be issued without delay. Hardly daring to believe the puzzling announcement, Berliners on both sides of the Wall started heading for border crossings.

Huge crowds converged on the Brandenburg Gate, where the Volkspolizei gave up checking documents and simply let thousands of East Germans walk into West Berlin. An impromptu street party broke out, with West Berliners popping champagne corks and Germans from both sides of the Wall embracing. On the first weekend of the opening of the Wall 2.7 million exit visas were issued to East Germans, who formed

1972	1972	1977
Palestinian terrorists slaughter Israeli athletes at the Munich Olympic Games	FDR Chancellor Willy Brandt's Ostpolitik thaws frosty relations with the East	Red Army Faction terrorism reaches a crescendo in the "German autumn"

mile-long queues at checkpoints. West Germans – and TV-viewers around the world – gawped at streams of Trabant cars pouring into West Berlin, where shops enjoyed a bonanza as East Germans spent their DM100 "welcome money", given to each of them by the Federal Republic. By the following weekend, **ten million visas** had been issued since November 9 – an incredible statistic, considering the whole population of the GDR was only sixteen million.

The road to reunification

In the weeks that followed, the formidable Stasi security service was dismantled and free elections in the East agreed on, for which the SED hastily repackaged itself as a new, supposedly voter-friendly PDS – Partei des Demokratischen Sozialismus (Democratic Socialist Party) – partly by firing the old guard. The next initiative came from the West when **Chancellor Kohl** visited Dresden on December 19, addressing a huge, enthusiastic crowd as "dear countrymen" and declaring a **united Germany** his ultimate goal. As East Germans discovered that West Germany's standard of living eclipsed anything in the GDR, and found out exactly how corrupt their government had been, they concurred – with the result that the GDR's first free elections on March 18, 1990, returned a victory for a right-wing alliance dominated by the Christian Democratic Union and Kohl.

The **economic union** was hammered out almost immediately and the GDR began rapidly to fade away. With confirmation that a united Germany would respect its post-World War II boundaries, the wartime allies agreed to reunification. After an all-night Volkskammer session on August 23 it was announced that the GDR would become part of the Federal Republic on **October 3, 1990**.

The 1990s

December 2, 1990, saw Germany's first nationwide elections since 1933. Nationally the CDU, in coalition with the FDP (Free Democrats), triumphed easily. One surprise was that the PDS secured 25 percent of the vote in eastern Berlin on an anti-unemployment and anti-social-inequality ticket.

In 1991 vastly unpopular tax increases in western Germany had to be introduced to pay for the spiralling cost of unification. As the year wore on, and unemployment continued to rise, Kohl's honeymoon with the East ended. He became reluctant to show himself there, and when he finally did, in April, he was greeted by catcalls and egg-hurlers.

Ill feeling between easterners and westerners (nicknamed **Ossis and Wessis**) also became apparent and increased throughout the decade. West Germans resented the tax increases and caricatured easterners as naive and lazy. East Germans resented patronizing western attitudes and economic inequalities that made them second-class citizens, so mocked westerners for their arrogance and materialism. Feelings got worse as it became apparent that the ever-increasing cost of reunification had pushed the German economy into recession. As the instability of the transitional period began to ebb, the pursuit of those responsible for the GDR's repressive crimes began in earnest, particularly as Stasi files were opened to the public. **Trials** throughout the 1990s brought Politbüro members, border guards, even sports coaches who'd doped players without their knowledge, before the courts.

1982	1985	1989
Death of film-maker Rainer Werner Fassbinder aged 37 in Munich	Boris Becker becomes the first un-seeded player and the first German to win the men's singles of the Wimbledon tennis championships	Mass exodus of citizens via Eastern Bloc countries leads to the fall of the Berlin Wall

On June 20, 1991, a Bundestag decision to relocate the national government to Berlin ushered in a new era: a tremendous task, and one undertaken in the late 1990s with the usual German thoroughness.

Germany today

At the start of the twenty-first century, Germany finally appeared to be healing the wounds of the turmoil and division of the twentieth. With its cities rebuilt and democracy established throughout the country, centred on its new capital in Berlin, the economy resurgent, and memorials completed to the victims of the Nazi atrocities, Germany could project a friendly, youthful and dynamic image to the world as it hosted the football **World Cup finals in 2006**. The event, which put the nation back at ease with its own patriotism, seems to have coincided with a new phase of its history, in which it explores its place in international politics, completes the restructuring of its welfare state and comes to terms with economic and social inequalities – both between its eastern and western halves and across society, with the specific challenge of addressing the issues faced by the large number of immigrants, particularly Turks, who have settled in Germany since the 1950s.

Politics

Current German politics continues to be dominated by two parties: the moderately left-wing **SPD** and a centre-right alliance led by the **CDU**. From 1998 to 2005 the government was led by SPD chancellor Gerhard Schröder, the world's first ruling coalition that included an environmental party, the Green Party, in a government that included the popular Green maverick Joschka Fischer. Naturally the government was environmentally aware and reform-minded, making an agreement to switch off all Germany's nuclear reactors by 2022. But elsewhere, reforms of the welfare state were hampered by a lacklustre economy, which led to the call for an early election in 2005. The result was a political stalemate that could only be broken by a centre-right SPD–CDU "grand coalition" under the CDU's highly gifted leader **Angela Merkel**, an East German fluent in Russian and with a doctorate in quantum physics. This government has increasingly pursued a more ambitious foreign policy – building on the trend of the previous government which deployed German troops for the first time since World War II in peace-keeping missions in Kosovo and Afghanistan. At the same time, Germany's rejection of the Iraq War worsened its relationship with the US and effectively put its campaign for a seat on the UN Security Council on hold.

At home Merkel's progress was constantly hampered by bickering within the grand coalition and by party politics. Germany's deep exposure to the global **financial crisis** in 2007–08 lowered voter expectations and helped strengthen the coalition, which was initially united in its fiscal rescue packages. While Merkel secured another four years in office in 2009, internal rifts over the bankrolling of foreign debt to shore up the now-stricken euro currency became public and her party was hammered in local elections. In 2010, the loss of North-Rhine Westphalia saw the coalition lose its majority in the upper house, and the following year the CDU lost the state of Baden-Wüttermberg for the first time in six decades. The CDU and its Bavarian partner the CSU staged a comeback to win 42 percent of the vote in the 2013 federal

1990	2001	2002	2003
Chancellor Helmut Kohl leads a reunited Germany as Berlin is named capital the next year	German troops are deployed in Afghanistan in their largest non-European deployment since 1940	Germany discards the Deutschmark for the Euro	Wolfgang Becker scores a hit with his film *Good Bye Lenin!* and unwittingly unleashes a tidal wave of GDR nostalgia

OSTALGIE

Nostalgia for the East, or rather *Nostalgie* for the *Osten*, has produced **Ostalgie**, a hybrid word for a phenomenon that's been gathering momentum throughout the old East Germany. Though the sentiment might originate with those who remember the collapsed country, a nostalgia for the iconography of communist East Germany also has a kitsch appeal for younger Germans and visitors, spawning a mini-industry in Berlin.

The meaning of *Ostalgie* is a little nebulous, as it has slowly redefined itself since the *Wende*. What started as a nostalgia for the securities of a communist state among sixteen million East Germans thrust into capitalism became an expression of discontent and identity. It was a protest at the quick eradication of a unique East German culture and its absorption into the West – a process that implied that all things Western were superior, and tended to mock everything from the East as backward and naive.

So *Ostalgie* became a way to affirm that some aspects of the GDR were worth celebrating; that – despite the many shortcomings of the state – it had also produced rewarding moments in people's lives. Champions of the GDR also point out that it was progressive in areas where the West still needs to improve: scarcity lent more value to consumer goods and created a society that was less wasteful, decadent and environmentally unfriendly.

These days *Ostalgie* stretches far beyond political debates, and the film **Good Bye Lenin!** in 2003, with its nostalgic and comedic celebration of 1970s GDR kitsch and innocence, was as important a catalyst as any. In its wake, the celebration of cult GDR icons – particularly the **Ampelmann** of East German pedestrian crossings and the fibreglass **Trabant** – became popular. There's also been a revival of some GDR products, including foods, household products and cosmetics made by companies that had gone out of business when Western goods flooded the market.

elections, their best electoral result since the heyday of Helmut Kohl. But their coalition partner – the FDP – crashed out of the Bundestag as it failed to secure the necessary five-percent threshold to win seats, forcing Merkel's faction to enter into a grand coalition with the opposition SPD.

After almost a decade as chancellor the position of Angela Merkel – familiarly known as *Mutti* ("Mummy") – seems unassailable. Dominant at home, she is also increasingly regarded as the senior political figure on the European scene, as Germany has used its economic muscle and diplomatic nous to carve for itself a leading role in the European Union's responses to both the Euro crisis and the unrest in Ukraine.

Economy

Germany's economy is the fifth largest in the world. The country is the economic hub of the European Union (and home to the **European Central Bank**), so its performance has far-reaching consequences throughout the continent. Niche sectors such as innovative high-tech design have flourished in the past decade even if performance in industry has been disappointing, despite many ageing patriarchs making way for younger and more dynamic management and a restructuring of the labour market. This is particularly true in the east. Here, the problem remains the death of manufacturing and the absence of anything to replace it, as well as a welfare mentality. Industry still complains of high taxes and complicated red tapes but despite this Germany continues to vie with China and the United States for the title of world's

2005	2006	2009
GDR-raised Angela Merkel becomes the first female Chancellor of Germany	The FIFA World Cup at last allows hosts Germany to reclaim the national flag for a new generation	Romanian-born German writer Herta Müller wins Nobel Prize for Literature

largest exporter. As other western economies slid into debt and recession post-2007, Germany's underlying strength – and industrial prowess – kept it relatively insulated from the economic storm, with unemployment reaching a post-reunification low in 2011. Continued Eurozone weakness and the economic outfall from the Ukraine crisis nevertheless seemed to be pushing Germany towards recession in 2014.

Society

The German-hosted 2006 football World Cup marked the moment when a new generation of patriots proudly waved the German national flag for the first time in over half a century. Nevertheless, the country faces similar social problems to other European nations, especially in eastern Germany as a continuing hangover from reunification. **Depopulation** is a threat as skilled labour simply moves west for work. This is particularly true for women, who are generally better qualified: in some eastern German towns around half the young women have left. Those who remain appear to be forming a new underclass: low-skilled, often jobless and whose poverty is a fertile ground for political extremism. The ultra-right-wing National Partie Deutschland (National Party of Germany; NPD) has seats in two east-German state legislatures – and another far-right party has deputies in Brandenburg – and racist attacks have accompanied this.

Following the temporary immigration and subsequent settling of "guest workers" in the 1960s, Germany has a **Turkish population** circa four million-strong, including many second-generation German-born citizens caught between two cultures. Often living in the poorest neighbourhoods with the worst schools, much of their frustration and anger at society is voiced through petty crime and gangs. However, there are signs that the Turkish population is now established – kebabs now rival sausages as a favourite German fast-food, and there are large mosques in cities like Cologne, Berlin and Hamburg. In western Germany initial fears about Islamic extremism following 2001 receded, only to resurface again later with the rise of Islamic State in Syria and Iraq, the emergence of home-grown jihadists and of a new variant of anti-Semitism, this time linked to the Israeli-Palestinian conflict.

Angela Merkel insists economic and social integration of immigrants is "decisive" for Germany's wellbeing despite a speech in 2010 whose soundbite – that attempts to build a cohesive "multikulti" (multicultural) society had "utterly failed" – obliterated more nuanced messages about the need for skilled immigrant labour. It is probably no coincidence that the speech was made before local elections. A more successful face of multicultural Germany is **Cem Özdemir**, the Turkish-German co-chairman of Germany's Green Party since November 2008. As a charismatic late-40s family-man with an ethnic-minority background, he seems the kind of candidate who might represent the face of the ever-more-powerful modern Germany – environmentally minded, as sensitive to hyphenated identities as it is to remembering its past, and playing the central role in Europe's future.

2010	2013	2014
The Reichstag approves contribution to a €22.4bn bail-out for debt-ridden Greece, resulting in heavy electoral losses for the government	An international poll names Germany as the world's most admired country	The Eurosceptic Alternative für Deutschland party wins 7 seats in the European Parliamentary elections. Germany win the 2014 FIFA World Cup.

Books

What follows is a short selection of some of the best books about Germany; those indicated by the ★ symbol are particularly recommended. Most are readily available, but those currently out of print are signified with (o/p).

GENERAL

★ **John Ardagh** *Germany and the Germans.* Astute and illuminating characterization of almost every aspect of Germany – its history, politics and national psyche.

TRAVEL WRITING

Patrick Leigh Fermor *A Time of Gifts.* Evocative account of a 1933 walk from Rotterdam to Constantinople by one of the greatest British travel writers, as he passes through a Nazifying Germany.

Heinrich Heine *Germany: A Winter's Tale.* Heine writes about his journey from exile in Paris to his Hamburg home, with insightful snatches about early nineteenth-century Germany along the way.

Jerome K. Jerome *Three Men on the Bummel.* Semi-fictional account of three disorganized English gents travelling around Germany at the turn of the twentieth century.

★ **Mark Twain** *A Tramp Abroad.* Wickedly witty and well-observed commentary on the author's late nineteenth-century travels through Germany.

ART AND ARCHITECTURE

Peter Adam *The Art of the Third Reich.* Engrossing and well-written account of the official state art of Nazi Germany – with over three hundred illustrations.

Wolf-Dieter Dube *The Expressionists.* A good general introduction to Germany's most distinctive contribution to twentieth-century art.

Frank Whitford *Bauhaus.* Comprehensive and well-illustrated guide to the architectural movement that flourished in Dessau.

FILM

Sabine Hake *German National Cinema.* Painstakingly researched and rewarding historical account of film.

Klaus Kreimeier *The UFA Story.* Readable account of the rise and fall of Germany's greatest film company, which at its zenith in the early 1930s was second in international importance only to Hollywood.

HISTORY

GENERAL HISTORY

Andreas Nachama, Julius H. Schoeps and Golo Mann *The History of Germany since 1789.* Regarded as the best standard work of German history, written by Thomas Mann's historian son.

Hermann Simon (eds) *Jews in Berlin* (o/p). Packed with source material of every kind, this well-illustrated book charts the troubled history of Berlin's Jews between 1244 and 2000.

HOLY ROMAN EMPIRE

Geoffrey Barraclough *The Origins of Modern Germany.* Solid and insightful analysis of medieval German history – well written, too.

Heiko A. Oberman *Luther: Man Between God and the Devil.* Psychologically intriguing biography of Martin Luther.

THE GERMAN EMPIRE

David Blackbourn *The Long Nineteenth Century: A History of Germany, 1780–1918.* Good coverage of the period in which Germany emerged as a nation-state.

Roger Chickering *Imperial Germany and the Great War, 1914–1918.* Readable introduction to World War I Germany.

A.J.P. Taylor *Bismarck: The Man and the Statesman* (o/p). Engrossingly well-written biography of probably Germany's shrewdest-ever politician.

Hans-Ulrich Wehler *The German Empire, 1871–1918.* General history of the period, which explores the links between the empire and Nazi Germany.

WEIMAR GERMANY

Alex De Jonge *The Weimar Chronicle: Prelude to Hitler* (o/p). While not the most comprehensive account of the Weimar Republic, this is far and away the liveliest, spiced with eyewitness memoirs and engaging detail.

Peter Gay *Weimar Culture: The Outsider as Insider.* An engaging look at the intellectual and cultural brilliance of 1920s Germany.

NAZI GERMANY

★**Anon.** *A Woman in Berlin.* A female journalist's remarkable war diary, chronicling the fate of Berlin's vanquished in the closing days of the war, when looting and gang rape were part of daily life.

Antony Beevor *Berlin: the Downfall 1945.* A fine synthesis of many sources to provide a riveting account of how the city's defences crumbled and its civilians suffered, with few harrowing details spared.

★**Christabel Bielenberg** *The Past is Myself* (o/p). Few memoirs of the war years in Germany have quite the gripping pace or novel-like readability of this celebrated account of life in Berlin and the Black Forest by the British-born wife of a lawyer associated with the July 20 plotters around Count von Stauffenberg.

George Clare *Berlin Days 1946–1947* (o/p). British-army translator who recounts time spent in Berlin at what the Germans called the *Nullpunkt* – the zero point – when the city, its economy, buildings and society, began to rebuild almost from scratch. Packed with characters and observation.

A.C. Grayling *Among the Dead Cities.* Controversial but readable weighing up of the case for and against the Allied bombing raids against German cities, by a distinguished British philosopher.

Thomas Harding *Hanns and Rudolf.* Written by the great nephew of Hanns Alexander (the Hanns of the title), this book traces the very different lives of the German-Jewish Hanns and the Nazi Rudolf Höss, commandant of Auschwitz, whom Hanns hunted down after the war and brought to trial.

Raul Hilberg *The Destruction of the European Jews.* Learned and comprehensive study of the Nazi extermination of Jews.

Ian Kershaw *Hitler.* The definitive biography of the dictator.

W.G. Sebald *On the Natural History of Destruction.* An exploration of literary Germany's postwar taboo on the effects of Allied bombing on German cities, written by the late German-born but England-based author who remains among Germany's most lionized modern authors.

★**William Shirer** *The Rise and Fall of the Third Reich.* A classic, written by an American journalist stationed in Berlin during the Nazi period. Despite its length and occasionally outdated perceptions, the book is full of insights and easy to dip into, thanks to an exhaustive index.

Peter Wyden *Stella* (o/p). Gripping story of a young Jewish woman who avoided deportation and death by hunting down Jews in wartime Berlin for the SS. The author, who knew Stella, traces her life story and tries to untangle the morality.

POSTWAR HISTORY

★**Anna Funder** *Stasiland: True Stories from Behind the Berlin Wall.* Engrossing account of the experiences of East Germans who found themselves entangled with the GDR's State Security Service (Stasi).

★**Timothy Garton Ash** *The File: A Personal History.* Garton Ash lived and worked as a journalist in East Berlin in 1980, making him the subject of surveillance and a Stasi file. He tracks down the file and interviews informers using an informal style to marvellously evoke the era. *We the People* (US title: *The Magic Lantern*) is his first-hand account of the fall of the Wall.

Peter J. Katzenstein (ed) *Tamed Power: Germany in Europe.* A look at how Germany uses the European Union to express its political and economic power.

Charles S. Maier *Dissolution: The Crisis of Communism and the End of East Germany.* Excellent investigation of the collapse of the GDR.

David E. Murphy et al *Battleground Berlin: CIA vs KGB in the Cold War.* A detailed account by participants of the tense skirmishing between the spies of the two superpowers.

FICTION

Anon. *The Nibelungenlied.* Germany's epic poem (see box, p.527) of violence and vengeance; a heroic legend comparable in scope to the *Iliad.*

Alfred Döblin *Berlin-Alexanderplatz.* Unrelenting stream-of-consciousness epic about the city's proletariat.

★**Hans Fallada** *Alone in Berlin* and *Little Man, What Now?* Two novels from one of the forgotten greats of twentieth-century German literature, the first the story of a grieving couple's lone protest against the Nazis in wartime Berlin, the latter a moving tale of love and hardship at the time of the Great Depression – a huge international hit at the time.

★**Theodor Fontane** *Effie Briest.* This story of a woman's adultery in the second half of the nineteenth century offers a vivid picture of Prussian mores, with the sort of terrible and absurd climax that's virtually unique to Fontane and to German literature.

Johann Wolfgang von Goethe *The Sorrows of Young Werther.* Small novella on suicide that's probably the easiest introduction to the work of Germany's most celebrated literary genius.

Günter Grass *Dog Years; The Tin Drum; The Flounder.* The most celebrated contemporary German author, who specializes in fables that explore the German psyche in the aftermath of Nazi Germany and World War II. However, rather than being uncomfortable and dark, most of Grass's work is very readable thanks in part to many witty touches. His 2008 autobiography *Peeling the Onion* revealed for the first time a level of personal guilt, as the author had served in the Waffen SS, the elite Nazi army.

Jacob and Wilhelm Grimm *Complete Grimm Tales.* Collection of folk and fairy-tales by the most famous purveyors of the art form. One of the best places to understand Germany's Gothic sense of itself.

Hans Jakob Christoffel von Grimmelshausen *Adventures of a Simpleton.* Probably the finest seventeenth-century novel: an epic tale that follows its hero through various adventures in the era of the grisly Thirty Years' War.

★ **Christopher Isherwood** *Goodbye to Berlin.* Set in the decadent atmosphere of the Weimar Republic as the Nazis steadily gain power, this collection of stories brilliantly evokes the period and brings to life some classic Berlin characters. It formed the basis of the films *I Am a Camera* and *Cabaret.*

★ **Wladimir Kaminer** *Russian Disco: Tales of Everyday Lunacy on the Streets of Berlin.* Collection of stories that are snapshots of Berlin through the eyes of a Russian immigrant from Moscow – unusual, entertaining and well written. Kaminer has since become a local celebrity, DJing "Russendisko" nights at *Kaffee Burger* (see p.103).

Klaus Mann *Mephisto.* Klaus Mann's relocation of the Faust legend to Nazi Germany was a lightly-disguised attack on the career of the actor and theatre director Gustav Gründgens, later made into a film starring Klaus Maria Brandauer.

Thomas Mann *The Magic Mountain.* Mann's most celebrated book, a well-observed critique of the preoccupations of pre-World War I society. *Buddenbrooks*, about the decline of a bourgeois family from his native Lübeck, tackles similar themes.

Ulrich Plenzdorf *The New Sufferings of Young W.* Satirical reworking of Goethe's *The Sorrows of Young Werther*, set in 1970s East Berlin. When first published it pushed against the borders of literary acceptability under the old regime with its portrayal of alienated, disaffected youth.

★ **Erich Maria Remarque** *All Quiet on the Western Front.* Classic World War I novel: horrific, but written with a grim sense of humour.

Bernhard Schlink *The Reader.* A tale of sex, love and shame in postwar Germany as a young man tries to comprehend the Holocaust and his feelings for those involved; winner of the Fisk Fiction Prize – and made into a film starring Kate Winslet. Schlink has also written a string of successful detective novels featuring a septuagenarian private eye, Selb.

Film

Before World War II, Germany's film industry was second only to Hollywood's; post-1945, the industry subsided into nostalgia and Heimat-obsessed kitsch. The new wave of the 1970s changed that as directors like Wim Wenders and Rainer Werner Fassbinder put German film back on the international art-house circuit. Since 2000, a younger generation of film-makers has had great success re-examining Germany's recent history. Films indicated by the ★ symbol are particularly recommended. All are available on DVD – some (without subtitles) from Amazon's German website (ⓦamazon.de).

PRE-1933

The Blue Angel Josef von Sternberg's screen adaptation of Heinrich Mann's novel *Professor Unrat*, filmed in English and German versions, made an international star of Marlene Dietrich.

Das Cabinet des Dr Caligari Highly stylized silent horror classic, with distorted sets in Expressionist style. Made just after World War I, it was one of the first horror films to find international success, and was highly influential.

★ **Die Drei von der Tankstelle** and **Der Kongress Tanzt (The Congress Dances)** London-born Lilian Harvey was 1930s Germany's screen sweetheart, and these evergreen musicals show her at her peak: the former is a tale of love and rivalry during the Depression, the latter an escapist fantasy set in Vienna during the Congress of 1815. Filmed in German, French and English versions, it was a worldwide hit; the polyglot Harvey starred in all three.

M Fritz Lang's classic 1931 crime thriller stars Peter Lorre as a serial killer and paved the way for Lang's later success in Hollywood as a maker of film noir.

Metropolis Fritz Lang's pioneering big-budget sci-fi epic was one of the silent era's most ambitious movies, and though it almost bankrupted the UFA studio at the time its appeal has proved enduring.

Nosferatu F.W. Murnau's 1922 terrifying Expressionist version is the earliest film depiction of the Dracula story.

Viktor und Viktoria Reinhold Schünzel's tale of a woman who becomes a star by pretending to be a man pretending to be a woman was remade in 1982 with Julie Andrews. The original is a sparkling piece of late Weimar film-making, released just after the Nazi rise to power.

THIRD REICH

★ **Allotria** and **Bel Ami** Viennese actor/director Willi Forst made elegant comedies that kept their distance from the regime; these are two of the most enjoyable. The latter – an adaptation of Guy de Maupassant's novel – echoes the rise of Dr Goebbels, with its tale of a journalist who builds a political career while bedding a succession of beautiful women.

Die Feuerzangenbowle The most beloved of all German comedies is an escapist, back-to-school affair that takes the uncontroversial line that schooldays are the best days of your life. It stars Heinz Rühmann.

Münchhausen As the war turned against Germany, UFA cranked up its efforts to maintain morale with big-budget colour epics like this tale of the aristocratic fantasist Baron Münchhausen, with a script by banned author Erich Kästner.

Triumph of the Will and **Olympia – Fest der Völker** and **Fest der Schönheit** Leni Riefenstahl's innovative and influential documentaries – the former an adulatory record of the 1934 Nuremberg rally, the latter two about the 1936 Berlin Olympics – demonstrate her mastery of technique, but underline her role as the Third Reich's cinematic propagandist of choice.

Zu Neuen Ufern and **La Habanera** Hugely popular star vehicles for Zarah Leander, the Swedish actress and singer who was Nazi Germany's substitute for Dietrich. Beautifully directed by Detlev Sierck, who left immediately afterwards to forge a Hollywood career (as Douglas Sirk) making big-budget melodramas such as *All that Heaven Allows* and *Magnificent Obsession*.

POSTWAR

Die Brücke In the dying days of World War II, a group of teenage boys are given the senseless task of defending a bridge against the American invaders. Perhaps the most powerful anti-war film made in Germany.

★ **Der Hauptmann von Köpenick** The film version of Carl Zuckmayer's play – based on a true story – about a small-time crook who hoodwinks the authorities by donning military uniform.

Das Mädchen Rosemarie The true story of the murder of a high-class prostitute in Wirtschaftswunder-era Frankfurt – a rare slice of social realism from an era that often preferred its films escapist.

NEW WAVE

Das Boot Claustrophobic tale of death, comradeship and derring-do, set aboard a U-boat in World War II.

The Enigma of Kaspar Hauser Also titled *Every Man for Himself and God Against All*, Werner Herzog's beautifully shot take on the Kaspar Hauser legend features an unforgettable performance from Bruno S. as a mirror to the failings of a society who'd try to figure him out.

Fear Eats the Soul Fassbinder's homage to Douglas Sirk is a remake of *All that Heaven Allows*, transposed to the Federal Republic to tell a story of forbidden love between a middle-aged German woman and a young immigrant.

★**The Lost Honour of Katharina Blum** Volker

POST-REUNIFICATION

★**Aimée and Jaguar** The unlikely but true love story between a Nazi mother and a young Jewish woman in wartime Berlin is a real three-hankie weepie.

Downfall Based on the diaries of Hitler's secretary, this claustrophobic tale of the last days of the Nazi regime is set in Hitler's bunker, and features a powerful performance by Bruno Ganz as the ranting, broken dictator.

The Edukators A 21st-century addendum to Germany's turbulent countercultural past, this compelling – and very contemporary – take on the moral complexities of capitalism follows a trio of young activists way out of their depth in an ad hoc kidnapping of a local fatcat.

Good Bye Lenin! Funny and moving tale of a devoted

Die Mörder Sind Unter Uns *The Murderers are Among Us* was the first postwar German film, made at Babelsberg in the Soviet zone of occupation that was later to become the DDR, and starring a young Hildegard Knef.

Schlöndorff and Margarethe von Trotta's adaptation of Heinrich Böll's novel is a powerful indictment of the destructive power of the tabloid press, still relevant today.

★**Mephisto** István Szabó's Hungarian/German co-production brings Klaus Mann's Nazi-era reworking of *Faust* stunningly to life, with a spellbinding central performance by Klaus Maria Brandauer as Hendrik Höfgens, the actor who sacrifices his principles for his career.

★**Wings of Desire** Wim Wenders' tale of an angel who falls in love and opts to become mortal is one of the truly great Berlin movies, set in the still-divided city not long before reunification and filmed in both colour and black-and-white.

communist who suffers a stroke in East Germany and awakens in post-reunification Berlin, and of the lengths her family go to in order to spare her the shock of discovering the truth.

★**The Lives of Others** A cinematic counterblast to *Good Bye Lenin!*'s cuddly nostalgia, Florian Henckel von Donnersmarck's tale of Stasi surveillance and its impact on an intellectual couple was equally successful internationally.

Run, Lola, Run Tom Tykwer's critically-acclaimed crime caper about Lola's twenty-minute dash to save her boyfriend's life moves at a breathless pace, with the central dilemma replayed over and over.

Popular music

Germany's prowess in classical music is famous. Its contribution to popular music is less recognized outside Germany, yet has often been surprisingly influential. Choices indicated by the ★ symbol are particularly recommended.

KRAUTROCK

Can *Tago Mago*. Ambitious double album from early Seventies Krautrock pioneers that fused jazz, electronic and rock elements to innovative, surprisingly funky effect.

★ Kraftwerk *Autobahn*. An all-time classic and a hymn to the open road from the Düsseldorf-based pioneers of electronic music.

Popol Vuh *The Werner Herzog Soundtracks*. Though not the definitive box-set it might have been, this anthology of music from some of Werner Herzog's best films is as compelling an introduction as any to the otherwordly compositions of Krautrock mystic Florian Fricke.

Tangerine Dream *Phaedra*. The electronic soundscapes of Tangerine Dream's first Virgin album helped the band break through to international success.

EURODISCO AND DANCE

Donna Summer *Love to Love You Baby*. Summer's made-in-Munich epic is a languid symphony of disco erotica, stretched across an entire album side.

★ Giorgio Moroder *From Here to Eternity*. Not content with masterminding Donna Summer's rise to stardom, the Munich-based Moroder released his own album of electronic floor-fillers to worldwide commercial and critical success.

Sash! *It's My Life*. Hit-stuffed album by one of the masters of the Nineties electronic dance scene; includes *Ecuador!* and *Encore une Fois*.

Silver Convention *The Very Best of Silver Convention*. All the hits from the Munich-based female trio who were the first Eurodisco outfit to have a Billboard #1 with *Fly, Robin Fly*.

Sven Väth *Accident In Paradise*. Ambient/techno classic from the Frankfurt-based king of German techno.

NEUE DEUTSCHE WELLE AND THE EIGHTIES

Die Ärzte *Debil*. 1984 debut album by the Berlin-based punk band whose melodic sound and humorous (and often controversial) lyrics have brought them massive success in the German-speaking world, though they're relatively unknown outside it.

DAF *Alles ist Gut*. Hard-edged post-punk electro from the Düsseldorf-based aesthetes who were among the more influential (and lusted after) German acts of the time.

Einstürzende Neubauten *Ende Neu*. This 1996 album is one of the most listenable by the Berlin-based band who blend punk with industrial and electronic sounds, often using self-made instruments and found objects. The lovely single *Stella Maris* is a long way from the band's "difficult" reputation.

Klaus Nomi *The Collection*. Talented but tragic avant-garde counter-tenor who was one of the most distinctive artists of the early Eighties before succumbing to AIDS.

Nena *The Collection*. A one-hit wonder outside Germany, at home Nena was a star of power pop; *99 Red Balloons* is here, but there's much else besides, including the immensely catchy *Nur geträumt*.

Nina Hagen *The Very Best Of*. All the hits from the fairy godmother of German punk, including her take on Zarah Leander's wartime anthem *Ich Weiss, es Wird Einmal Ein Wunder Geschehen*.

★ Propaganda *A Secret Wish*. Gorgeous Eighties electropop from the Düsseldorf-hatched label mates of Frankie Goes to Hollywood.

Scorpions *Crazy World*. The Hannover-based rockers scored a worldwide hit with the haunting single *Wind of Change* from this 1990 album, capturing the mood of the moment as the Cold War came to an end.

Die Toten Hosen *All die ganzen Jahre*. All the hits from the Düsseldorf band who are the most internationally successful German punks.

CONTEMPORARY

Die Fantastischen Vier *4:99*. The second album by the Stuttgart-based pioneers of German rap, containing their breakthrough single *Die Da*.

★ Peter Fox *Stadtaffe*. Cracking album from the coolest of German rappers, including the incredibly catchy hit *Haus am See*.

Rammstein *Sehnsucht*. Second album by the Berlin heavy rock outfit who have scored massive success in Germany and internationally thanks to their driving, contemporary sound, which blends epic guitar riffs with elements of techno.

Rosenstolz *Kassengift*. One of the most accessible albums by Berlin-based duo – currently on sabbatical – whose gay fanbase and catchy electro melodies invite comparisons with the Pet Shop Boys.

Silbermond *Nichts Passiert.* Hailing from Bautzen in eastern Germany, Silbermond have hit big with a catchy light rock/pop sound; this 2009 album includes the single *Krieger des Lichts*, which has become a staple of radio playlists throughout the German-speaking world.

Söhne Mannheims *Wettsingen in Schwetzingen.* Recorded as part of MTV's Unplugged series, this live album by the Mannheim-based R&B band spawned a monster version of their hit *Das hat die Welt noch*

nicht gesehen. Singer Xavier Naidoo is also a successful solo artist.

Tokio Hotel *Scream.* The first English-language album by the young Leipzig band who combine considerable teenybop appeal with quite a hard, rocky sound.

Wir Sind Helden *Von Hier An Blind.* Radio-friendly, guitar-driven indie-pop, from the group who were the darlings of the German music scene until they split in 2012. Includes the single *Nur Ein Wort.*

German

English speakers approaching German for the first time have one real initial advantage, which is that German – as a close linguistic relative of English – shares with it a lot of basic vocabulary. It doesn't take long to work out that the Milch for your breakfast Kaffee comes from a Kuh that spends its life eating Gras in a Feld, or that Brot is nicer when spread with Butter. Two things conspire to give German a fearsome reputation among non-native speakers, however. The first is the grammar: it is complex – many Germans never really master it properly – but for the purposes of a short stay you shouldn't need to wade too deeply into its intricacies. The second is the compound noun – the German habit of creating enormously long-winded words to define something quite specific.

These aren't as difficult as they first appear, since they're composed from building blocks of basic vocabulary, so that, if you break them down into their component parts, you can often puzzle out the meaning without recourse to a dictionary (all nouns are written with a capital letter, by the way). German uses the same alphabet as English, with the exception of the letter ß ("scharfes S"), pronounced like "ss". The vowels o, a and u can be modified by using the Umlaut to ö, ä and ü, changing the pronunciation. Like any major language, German has considerable regional variation. Of the dialects you may encounter, the hardest to understand are Bavarian, Kölsch (the dialect of Cologne) and Plattdeutsch, which is spoken along the North Sea coast. The most correct German is considered to be the version spoken in and around Hannover.

PRONUNCIATION AND GRAMMAR

Unlike English, German is written more or less phonetically, so that once you understand how the vowels and consonants are pronounced there's rarely any ambiguity. Exceptions include foreign words that have been incorporated into German – including, in recent years, a great many from English. German pronunciation is clipped and clear, which makes it an ideal language for singers and rappers. Equivalent sounds below are in British English.

VOWELS AND UMLAUTS

a long "a" as in farther; short "a" as in hat
e long "e" as in lay; short "e" as in ten
i long "i" as in meek; short "i" as in pin
o long "o" as in open; short "o" as in hop
u long "u" as in loot; short "u" as in foot
ä is a combination of a and e, sometimes pronounced

like e in set (eg Hände) and sometimes like ai in laid (eg Gerät)
ö roughly like a long or short version of the vowel in sir
ü no exact equivalent; roughly a long or short version of the vowel sound in few

VOWEL COMBINATIONS

ai as in pie
au as in mouse
ie as in tree

ei as in pie
eu as in boil

CONSONANTS AND CONSONANT COMBINATIONS

ch is pronounced like Scottish "loch"

g is always a hard "g" sound, as in "go", except in the word ending –ig (eg Leipzig) when it is like a very soft German –ch

j is pronounced like an English y

s is pronounced similar to, English z; at the end of a word like s in glass before a consonant like "sh" (eg Straße)

sch is like English "sh"

th is pronounced like English t

v is roughly f

w is pronounced like English v, except at the end of the word, as in the Berlin place-names Kladow and Gatow, which rhyme with pillow

z is pronounced ts

GENDER AND ADJECTIVE ENDINGS

German nouns can be one of three genders: masculine, feminine or neuter (der, die or das). Sometimes the gender is obvious – it's der Mann (the man) and die Frau (the woman) – but sometimes it seems baffling: a girl is das Mädchen, because Mädchen – "little maiden" – is a diminutive, and diminutives are neutral. There are some hard and fast rules to help you know which is which: nouns ending in -er (der Sportler) are masculine; -ung, -heit, -keit or -schaft are feminine (die Zeitung, die Freiheit, die Fröhlichkeit, die Mannschaft). Definite (der/the) and indefinite (ein/a) articles and adjective endings can change according to the precise grammatical role in the sentence of the noun, which is where things start to get complex. If in doubt, stick to der or das for single items: once there is more than one of anything, it becomes die anyway.

POLITENESS

You can address children, animals and, nowadays, young people (but only in relaxed social situations, and really only if you're the same age) with the familiar "du" to mean "you". For anyone else – and particularly for older people or officials – stick to the polite "Sie"; if they want to be on familiar terms with you, they'll invite you to do so – "Duzen wir?" Incidentally, unmarried German women often prefer to be addressed as "Frau", the word "Fräulein" to describe a young, single woman being considered nowadays old-fashioned and rather sexist.

WORDS AND PHRASES

GREETINGS AND BASIC PHRASES

Good morning	Guten Morgen	There	Da
Good evening	Guten Abend	Open	Geöffnet/offen/auf
Good day	Guten Tag; Grüß Gott (southern Germany only)	Closed	Geschlossen/zu
		Over there	Drüben
		This one	Dieses
Hello (informal)	Servus (southern Germany only); Hallo	That one	Jenes
		Large	Gross
Goodbye (formal)	Auf Wiedersehen	Small	Klein
Goodbye (informal)	Tschüss (but also, Servus)	More	Mehr
Goodbye	Auf Wiederhören (telephone only)	Less	Weniger
		A bit	Ein bisschen
How are you? (polite)	Wie geht es Ihnen?	A little	Ein wenig
How are you? (informal)	Wie geht es dir?	A lot	Viel
Yes	Ja	Cheap	Billig
No	Nein	Expensive	Teuer
Please/ You're welcome	Bitte/Bitte schön	Good	Gut
Thank you/Thank you very much	Danke/Danke schön	Where is …?	Wo ist …?
Do you speak English?	Sprechen Sie Englisch?	How much does that cost?	Wieviel kostet das?
I don't speak German	Ich spreche kein Deutsch	What time is it?	Wieviel Uhr ist es?; Wie spat ist es?
Please speak more slowly	Könnten Sie bitte langsamer sprechen?	The bill, please	Die Rechnung, bitte! (or Zahlen, bitte!)
I understand	Ich verstehe	Separately or together?	Getrennt oder zusammen?
I don't understand	Ich verstehe nicht	Receipt	Quittung
Where?	Wo?	Where is the toilet?	Wo ist die Toilette, bitte?
When?	Wann?	Women's toilets	Damen/Frauen
How much?	Wieviel?	Men's toilets	Herren/Männer
Here	Hier		

Shower	Dusche	Week	Woche
Bath	Bad	Month	Monat
Is there a room	Haben Sie noch ein	Year	Jahr
available?	Zimmer frei?	Weekend	Wochenende
I'd like a room for two	Ich hätte gern ein	In the morning	Am Vormittag/Vormittags
	Zimmer für zwei	Tomorrow morning	Morgen früh
I'd like a single/	Ich hätte gern ein	In the afternoon	Am Nachmittag
double room	Einzelzimmer/Doppel		/Nachmittags
	zimmer	In the evening	Am Abend
When does the next	Wann fährt der nächste	Seven thirty	Halb acht (ie half before
train to Berlin leave?	Zug nach Berlin?		eight)
		Quarter past seven	Viertel nach sieben

NUMBERS

		Quarter to eight	Viertel vor acht
1	eins	Now	jetzt
2	zwei	Later	später
3	drei	Earlier	früher
4	vier	At what time?	Um wieviel Uhr?
5	fünf	Monday	Montag
6	sechs	Tuesday	Dienstag
7	sieben	Wednesday	Mittwoch
8	acht	Thursday	Donnerstag
9	neun	Friday	Freitag
10	zehn	Saturday	Samstag/Sonnabend
11	elf		(northern Germany)
12	zwölf	Sunday	Sonntag
13	dreizehn	January	Januar
14	vierzehn	February	Februar
15	fünfzehn	March	März
16	sechzehn	April	April
17	siebzehn	May	Mai
18	achtzehn	June	Juni
19	neunzehn	July	Juli
20	zwanzig	August	August
21	ein und zwanzig	September	September
22	zwei und zwanzig	October	Oktober
30	dreissig	November	November
40	vierzig	December	Dezember
50	fünfzig	Spring	Frühling
60	sechzig	Summer	Sommer
70	siebzig	Autumn	Herbst
80	achtzig	Winter	Winter
90	neunzig	Holidays	Ferien
100	hundert	Bank holiday	Feiertag
1000	tausend		

TRANSPORT AND SIGNS

Abflug	Departure (airport)
Abreise/Abfahrt	Departure (more generally)
Ampel	Traffic light
Ankunft	Arrivals
Ausfahrt	Motorway exit
Ausgang freihalten	Keep clear/no parking in
	front of exit
Ausgang	Exit
Autobahn	Motorway

DAYS, MONTHS, TIME AND SEASONS

Today	Heute
Yesterday	Gestern
Tomorrow	Morgen
The day before	Vorgestern
yesterday	
The day after tomorrow	Übermorgen
Day	Tag
Night	Nacht

Baustelle	Roadworks (on Autobahn etc)
Einbahnstraße	One-way street
Eingang	Entrance
Fähre	Ferry
Führerschein	Driver's licence
Fußgängerzone	Pedestrian-only zone
Grenze	Border
Kein Eingang	No entrance
Lärmschutz	Noise abatement (in connection with speed limit)
Nicht rauchen/ Rauchen verboten	No smoking
Notausgang	Emergency exit
Pass	Mountain pass

Plakette	Colour-coded sticker for cars, which you'll need if travelling into some major city centres
Raststätte	Fuel stop on the Autobahn, usually with a café or restaurant
Reisepass	Passport (but also Pass)
Stau	Traffic jam
StaugefährStaugefahr!	Possibility of traffic jams
Tankstelle	Petrol station
Umleitung	Diversion
Unfall	Accident
Verboten	Prohibited
Vorsicht!	Attention!/Take care!

A FOOD AND DRINK GLOSSARY

BASIC TERMS

Breakfast	Frühstück
Lunch	Mittagessen
Coffee and cakes	Kaffee und Kuchen – a mid-afternoon German ritual, equivalent to English afternoon tea
Supper, dinner	Abendessen
Knife	Messer
Fork	Gabel
Spoon	Löffel
Plate	Teller
Cup	Tasse
Mug	Becher
Bowl	Schüssel
Glass	Glas
Menu	Speisekarte
Wine list	Weinkarte
Set menu	Menü
Course	Gang
Starter	Vorspeise
Main course	Hauptgericht
Dessert	Nachspeise
The bill	Die Rechnung
Tip	Trinkgeld
Vegetarian	vegetarisch
I'm a vegetarian	Ich bin Vegetarier

COOKING TERMS

blau	boiled
eingelegt	pickled
frisch	fresh
gebacken	baked
gebraten	fried, roasted
gedämpft	steamed
gefüllt	stuffed
gegrillt	grilled

gekocht	boiled (also more generally means "cooked")
geräuchert	smoked
geschmort	braised, slow-cooked
gutbürgerlich	traditional German
hausgemacht	home-made
heiss	hot
lauwarm	lukewarm
kalt	cold
roh	raw
am Spiess	skewered
Topf, Eintopf	stew, casserole
überbacken	with a hot topping (especially cheese)
zart	tender (eg of meat)

BASICS

Belegtes Brot	sandwich
Bio	organic
Brot	bread
Brötchen	bread roll (or Semmel)
Butter	butter
Ei	egg
Essig	vinegar
Fisch	fish
Fleisch	meat
Gemüse	vegetables
Honig	honey
Joghurt	yoghurt
Kaffee	coffee
Käse	cheese
Marmelade	jam
Milch	milk
Obst	fruit
Öl	oil
Pfeffer	pepper
Sahne	cream

Salz	salt
Scharf	spicy
Senf	mustard
Soße	sauce
Süßstoff	artificial sweetener/ aspartame
Tee	tea
Zucker	sugar

SOUPS AND STARTERS

Blattsalat	green salad/salad leaves
Bohnensuppe	bean soup
Bunter Salat	mixed-salad
Erbsensuppe	pea soup
Flädlesuppe, Pfannkuchensuppe /Frittatensuppe	clear soup with pancake strips
Fleischsuppe	meat soup
Gulaschsuppe	spicy thick meat soup with paprika
Gurkensalat	cucumber salad
Hühnersuppe	chicken soup
Kartoffelsalat	potato salad
Leberknödelsuppe	clear soup with liver dumplings
Linsensuppe	lentil soup
Sülze	brawn
Suppe	soup
Wurstsalat	sausage salad

MEAT AND POULTRY

Backhendl	roast chicken (south Germany)
Bockwurst	chunky boiled sausage
Bratwurst	grilled sausage
Cordon Bleu	a Schnitzel stuffed with ham and cheese
Currywurst	sausage served with tomato ketchup and curry powder
Eisbein	boiled pigs' hock
Ente	duck
Frikadelle, Bulette	German burger
Gans	goose
Geschnetzeltes	shredded meat
Gyros/Dönerkebap	kebab
Hackfleisch	minced meat
Herz	heart
Hirn	brains
Hirsch, Reh	venison
Huhn, Hähnchen	chicken
Jägerschnitzel	cutlet in wine and mushroom sauce
Kassler Rippen	smoked and pickled pork chops

Kohlroulade	cabbage leaves stuffed with mincemeat
Kotelett	cutlet, chop
Lamm	lamb
Leber	liver
Leberkäse	baked meatloaf
Lunge	lungs
Nieren	kidneys
Rindfleisch	beef
Sauerbraten	braised pickled beef (or horse, in which case the menu description will specify "vom Pferd")
Schaschlik	diced meat with piquant sauce
Schinken	ham
Schweinebraten	roast pork
Schweinefleisch	pork
Schweinshaxe	roast pig's hock (knuckle) (south Germany)
Speck	bacon
Truthahn	turkey (also "Puter")
Weißwurst	Veal sausage seasoned with lemon zest and parsley
Wiener Schnitzel	thin cutlet in breadcumbs: either veal ("vom Kalb") or pork ("vom Schwein")
Wienerwurst	boiled pork sausage
Wild	wild game
Wildschwein	wild boar
Wurst	sausage
Zigeunerschnitzel	cutlet in paprika sauce
Zunge	tongue

FISH

Aal	eel
Forelle	trout
Garnelen	prawns
Hecht	pike
Hering, Matjes	herring
Hummer	lobster
Kabeljau	cod
Karpfen	carp
Krabben	shrimps
Lachs	salmon
Muscheln	mussels
Rotbarsch	rosefish
Saibling	char
Scholle	plaice
Schwertfisch	swordfish
Seezunge	sole
Thunfisch	tuna
Tintenfisch	squid
Zander	pike-perch

PASTA, DUMPLINGS AND NOODLES

Kasnocken	cheesy gnocchi (south Germany)
Kloß, Knödel	potato dumpling
Maultaschen	a form of ravioli
Reis	rice
Semmelknödel	bread dumpling
Spätzle	German pasta

VEGETABLES

Blumenkohl	cauliflower
Bohnen	beans
Bratkartoffeln	fried potatoes
Champignons	button mushrooms
Dicke Bohnen	broad beans
Erbsen	peas
Grüne Bohnen	green beans
Gurke	cucumber or gherkin
Karotten, Möhren	carrots
Kartoffelbrei	mashed potatoes
Kartoffelpüree	creamed potatoes
Kartoffelsalat	potato salad
Knoblauch	garlic
Kopfsalat	lettuce
Lauch (or Porree)	leeks
Maiskolben	corn on the cob
Paprika	green or red peppers
Pfifferling (or Eierschwamm)	chanterelle mushroom
Pellkartoffeln	jacket potatoes
Pilze	mushrooms
Pommes frites (or just Pommes)	chips/French fries
Salzkartoffeln (Petersilienkartoffeln)	boiled potatoes (with parsley)
Reibekuchen (Kartoffelpuffer)	fried potato cake
Rosenkohl	Brussels sprouts
Rote Rübe	beetroot
Rotkohl	red cabbage
Rübensalat	turnip salad
Sauerkraut	pickled cabbage
Spargel	asparagus
Tomaten	tomatoe`s
Weißkohl	white cabbage
Wok-Gemüse	stir-fried vegetables
Zwiebeln	onions

Fruit

Ananas	pineapple
Apfel	apple
Aprikose	apricot
Banane	banana
Birne	pear
Brombeeren	blackberries
Datteln	dates
Erdbeeren	strawberries
Feigen	figs
Himbeeren	raspberries
Johannisbeeren	redcurrants
Kirschen	cherries
Kompott	stewed fruit
Melone	melon
Obstsalat	fruit salad
Orange	orange
Pampelmuse (or Grapefruit)	grapefruit
Pfirsch	peach
Pflaumen	plums
Rosinen	raisins
Schwarze Johannisbeeren	blackcurrants
Trauben	grapes
Zitrone	lemon

CHEESES

Emmentaler	Emmental cheese
Käseplatte	cheese board
Quark	low-fat soft cheese
Schafskäse	sheep's cheese
Weichkäse	cream cheese
Ziegenkäse	goat's cheese

DESSERTS AND BAKED GOODS

Apfelstrudel (mit Sahne)	apple strudel (with fresh cream)
Berliner	jam doughnut
Dampfnudeln	large yeast dumplings served hot with vanilla sauce
Eis	ice cream
Gebäck	pastries
Kaiserschmarrn	shredded pancake served with powdered sugar, jam and raisins
Käsekuchen	cheesecake
Keks	biscuit
Krapfen	filled doughnut
Kuchen	cake
Lebkuchen (also Printen)	spiced gingerbread
Nüsse	nuts
Nusskuchen	nut cake
Obstkuchen	fruitcake
Pfannkuchen	pancake
Schlagsahne	whipped cream
Schokolade	chocolate
Schwarzwälder Kirschtorte	Black Forest gateau
Torte	gateau, tart

Glossary

Altstadt Old town (often synonymous with town centre)

Aufzug Lift, elevator

Bahnhof Train station (Hauptbahnhof is a main or large railway station)

Barock Florid architectural style of the seventeenth and eighteenth centuries, of Italian origin

Berg Hill, mountain

Biedermeier Elegant early nineteenth-century style of architecture, dress and furnishing, contemporary with English Regency and US Federal

Brauerei, Brauhaus Brewery

Brücke Bridge

Burg Castle

CSD/Christopher Street Day Gay pride festival

DDR Deutsche Demokratische Republik, the former East Germany

Denkmal (or Mahnmal) Monument

Dom Cathedral

Einkaufszentrum Shopping mall

Elector Prince or bishop who, during the time of the Holy Roman Empire, had a vote in deciding who the new emperor should be

Fachwerk Medieval half-timbered building style

Fasching Carnival

Festung Fortress

Flughafen Airport

Frühstückspension A small bed-and-breakfast hotel

Garten Park or garden (but **Anlage** or **Park** are also used)

Gasthaus, Gaststätte (also **Wirtshaus**) An inn, restaurant or bar

Gemütlich Cosy, welcoming

Gondelbahn Gondola: a cable car with small cars – usually for no more than four, seated, passengers

Gotik Medieval style of architecture characterized by arched windows and soaring pinnacles; neo-Gothic is the nineteenth-century revival of the style

Gründerzeit A period of economic and industrial development in mid-nineteenth-century Germany

Hanse, Hanseatic League Medieval trading alliance that linked cities along the Baltic and North seas with inland cities in northern and western Germany, Poland and the Baltic republics

Hausbrauerei Microbrewery

Hof (also **Innenhof**) Courtyard

Höhle Cave

Hotel garni A hotel that serves breakfast, but otherwise has no restaurant

Jugendstil German equivalent of the Art Nouveau style, also sometimes known as Secession

Kirche Church

Kirmes Folk festival (west Germany/Rhineland)

Kneipe Bar

Krankenhaus Hospital

Kunst Art

Kurhaus Assembly rooms: the social, rather than medical, heart of a spa town, often with a concert hall or casino; the spa facilities are known as **Thermen**

Land/Länder The German equivalent of states or provinces; **Länder** is the plural

Luftmalerei Literally "air painting": a southern-German form of trompe l'oeil fresco applied to the exterior of buildings

Markt/Marktplatz Market, marketplace – the principal square of a medieval town will often be known simply as **Markt**

Marstall Stable block

Neoklassik A form of architecture drawing inspiration from ancient Greece and Rome

Neue Sachlichkeit "New Objectivity" – rationalist, modern style of architecture and design dating from the 1920s and early 1930s and strongly associated with the Bauhaus design school

Neustadt "New town" – often used simply in relation to Altstadt, and thus often not particularly new

Palais Palace

Polizei Police

Rathaus Town or city hall

Ratskeller A restaurant or beer hall beneath a city hall

Rokoko Rococo, elegant but florid development of the Baroque style, characterized by shell-like decorative forms know as rocaille

Residenzstadt Town that was the seat of an ecclesiastical or lay prince or other ruler

Rolltreppe Escalator

Sammlung Collection (eg of art)

Schatzkammer Treasury

Schlepplift Pommel lift (on ski slope)

Schloss Noble residence – it can be a palace or a castle

Seebrücke Pier

Seilbahn Cable car

Sesselbahn Chairlift

Strand Beach

Tiergarten (Zoo) Zoo

Viertel Quarter or city district

Weinstube Wine bar

Weser Renaissance A style of Renaissance architecture specific to northwestern Germany

Wilhelminisch Relating to the era of the Kaisers

Zeughaus Arsenal

Small print and index

Rough Guide credits

Editor: Claire Saunders
Layout: Ankur Guhar, Pradeep Thapliyal
Cartography: Swati Handoo
Picture editor: Michelle Bhatia
Proofreader: Diane Margolis
Managing editors: Natasha Foges, Alice Park
Assistant editor: Sharon Sonam

Production: Janis Griffith
Cover design: Nicole Newman, Emily Taylor, Ankur Guha
Editorial assistant: Rebecca Hallett
Senior pre-press designer: Dan May
Programme manager: Gareth Lowe
Publisher: Joanna Kirby
Publishing director: Georgina Dee

Publishing information

This third edition published April 2015 by
Rough Guides Ltd,
80 Strand, London WC2R 0RL
11, Community Centre, Panchsheel Park,
New Delhi 110017, India
Distributed by Penguin Random House
Penguin Books Ltd,
80 Strand, London WC2R 0RL
Penguin Group (USA)
345 Hudson Street, NY 10014, USA
Penguin Group (Australia)
250 Camberwell Road, Camberwell,
Victoria 3124, Australia
Penguin Group (NZ)
67 Apollo Drive, Mairangi Bay, Auckland 1310,
New Zealand
Penguin Group (South Africa)
Block D, Rosebank Office Park, 181 Jan Smuts Avenue,
Parktown North, Gauteng, South Africa 2193
Rough Guides is represented in Canada by Tourmaline
Editions Inc. 662 King Street West, Suite 304, Toronto,
Ontario M5V 1M7
Printed in Singapore

MIX
Paper from
responsible sources
FSC™ C018179

Help us update

We've gone to a lot of effort to ensure that the third edition of **The Rough Guide to Germany** is accurate and up-to-date. However, things change – places get "discovered", opening hours are notoriously fickle, restaurants and rooms raise prices or lower standards. If you feel we've got it wrong or left something out, we'd like to know, and if you can remember the address, the price, the hours, the phone number, so much the better.

Please send your comments with the subject line "**Rough Guide Germany Update**" to ✉mail @uk.roughguides.com. We'll credit all contributions and send a copy of the next edition (or any other Rough Guide if you prefer) for the very best emails.

Find more travel information, connect with fellow travellers and plan your trip on Ⓦroughguides.com.

ABOUT THE AUTHORS

Jeroen van Marle grew up in England, studied in the Netherlands, learnt Romanian and moved to Eastern Europe, where he bribed a Russian consul with cognac, hitch-hiked between St Petersburg and Bulgaria, and founded the ⊕InYourPocket.com city guide in Bucharest. He's currently based in Berlin, where he works on guidebooks and travel articles. Follow Jeroen on Twitter at @jeroenvanmarle.

James Stewart (⊕jamesstewart.biz) is a freelance journalist for international media and the author of over ten guidebooks. He has written about Germany for newspapers, magazines and guidebooks for over a decade, and continues to discover new backwaters with every visit. He has yet to find a German beer he doesn't like.

Neville Walker has been fascinated by Germany since first visiting on an exchange trip in his teens. A freelance travel journalist, he has contributed to Rough Guides to Austria, France, London and Provence & the Côte d'Azur, and is the author of *Rough Guides Directions Gran Canaria*. He lives in London and Austria.

Christian Williams grew up in a divided Germany and has maintained strong links with the country ever since. As a freelance writer he has written or worked on various other Rough Guides, including Berlin, Austria, Tenerife, Canada, Colorado and the USA.

Acknowledgements

Jeroen van Marle Many thanks to Claire Saunders and Alice Park at Rough Guides. Special thanks: in Saxony to Christoph Münch and Martin Nagel in Dresden; Susann Palm in Leipzig; Almut Neumeister in Chemnitz. In Thuringia: Kerstin Neumann and Franz Sander in Erfurt; Anja Dietrich in Weimar. In Lower Saxony: Lisa Ulsamer in Hannover; Lino Santacruz, Alexandra Lucka and Philipp Dörfler of the Volkswagen Autostadt in Wolfsburg. And to Soulafa for the Sächsische Schweiz hikes, and everything else.

Neville Walker Thanks to Geoff Hinchley and Adrian Khanna, and to Claire Saunders and Alice Park at Rough Guides.

Christian Williams wishes to thank Neil and Gülnur in Berlin for their bottomless hospitality – as usual; Grace Scott for her energetic help in Freiburg; and fellow authors for all their support – particularly Jeroen for his Berlin tips. A big thanks also goes to all those involved in the book at Rough Guides and to Claire Saunders for her meticulous and well-considered editorial input.

Readers' updates

Thanks to all the readers who have taken the time to write in with comments and suggestions (and apologies if we've inadvertently omitted or misspelt anyone's name):

Daniel Bamford, Nick Cotterell, Menno Fenger, D.J. Koopmans, Jean O'Neill, Hollie Panther, Paul Senior, Tim Shepherd, Steve Simpson, Ryan Taylor, Michael J. Thompson, Lieske van der Torre, Isobel Williams.

p.16 Alamy Images: Bildarchiv Monheim GmbH (cl); Ray Roberts (cr); Cephas Picture Library (b)
p.17 Corbis: Dietrich Rose (t); Marcus Fuehrer (c); Lukas Barth (b)
p.18 SuperStock: Carola Koserowsky (t). Alamy Images: DIZ Munchen GmbH (cr). Corbis: Steven Vidler (cl); Jose Fuste Raga (b)
p.19 Corbis: Steven Vidler (tl); Xu Xiaolin (c). Robert Harding Picture Library: Peter Schickert (b)
p.20 Robert Harding Picture Library: M& G Therin-Weise (t). SuperStock: Siepmann (c). Alamy Images: Agencja Fotograficzna Caro (b)
p.21 SuperStock: Movementway (tl). Corbis: Bob Krist (tr); Fridmar Damm (br). Robert Harding Picture Library: Richard Maschmeyer (bl)
p.22 Alamy Images: imagebroker (tr). Corbis: Matthias Hiekel (tl); Bob Krist (bl). Getty Images: Eurasia (br)
p.23 Alamy Images: Iain Masterton (t). SuperStock (c). Alamy Images: Gunter Kirsch (b)
p.24 Corbis (tl)
p.128 Corbis: Paul Hardy (c)
p.131 Corbis: RenÈ Mattes (t)
p.159 Corbis: Jose Fuste Raga
p.184 Corbis: Carmen Redondo
p.187 Corbis: Yves Forestier (t)
p.203 Getty Images: JENS SCHLUETER (t). SuperStock: Siegfried Kuttig (b)
p.228 SuperStock (c)
p.231 SuperStock (t)
p.255 SuperStock: Stengert Nico (t); Sabine Lubenow (b)
p.276 Corbis: Adam Woolfitt (c)
p.279 Corbis: Enrico Nawrath (t)
p.307 SuperStock: Widmann (t); Alamy Images: David Bagnall (b)
pp.330–331 Corbis: Franz-Marc Frei
p.333 Corbis: Steven Vidler
p.353 Corbis: Hugh Rooney (t). Getty Images: Stringer (b)
pp.378–379 Robert Harding Picture Library: Dr. Wilfried Bahnmuller / Image Broker

p.381 Alamy Images: Scott Kemper (t)
p.407 AWL Images: Alan Copson (t). SuperStock: Pritzch (b)
p.424 Corbis: Mario Cipriani (c)
p.427 Daimler AG: (t)
p.447 SuperStock: Markus Keller (t); STELLA (b)
pp.480–481 Alamy Images: Kuttig - Travel - 2
p.483 Schwarzwälder Freilichtmuseum Vogtsbauernhof/ Karl Schlessmann: Karl Schlessmann
p.516 Corbis: Frank Lukasseck (c); Frank Lukasseck (br)
p.519 SuperStock: JTB Photo (t)
p.556 SuperStock: Christian WauerF1 ON (c)
p.559 Alamy Images: David Sanger photography (t)
p.583 Alamy Images: LOOK Die Bildagentur der Fotografen GmbH (t). SuperStock: Martin Moxter (b)
p.610 Corbis: Claudius (c)
p.613 Alamy Images: MiRafoto.com (t)
p.636 Corbis: Ralph Richter (br)
p.655 Robert Harding Picture Library: peter schickert / Image Broker (b)
pp.690–691 Robert Harding Picture Library: H. & D. Zielske /LOOK
p.693 Corbis: Mario Cipriani (t)
p.705 SuperStock (tl). Getty Images (b)
pp.752–753 SuperStock: Sabine Lubenow (c)
p.809 Alamy Images: Kuttig - Travel (t). Corbis: Frank Lukasseck (b)
pp.816–817 Corbis: Karl-Heinz Haenel
p.819 Corbis: Karlheinz Oster (t)
p.841 Getty Images: Ulf Boettcher (t). SuperStock: Sabine Lubenow (b)

Front cover and spine: *Lüftmalerei* in Mittenwald, Bavaria © Corbis: Alan Copson
Back cover: Bavarian Alps © Corbis: Frank Lukasseck (t). Frankfurt am Main skyline © AWL Images: MATTES RenÈ / Hemis (bl). Grosser Garten, Herrenhausen, Hannover © Alamy Images: Ernst Wrba (br)

Index

Maps are marked in grey

Map symbols

The symbols below are used on maps throughout the book

✈	Airport	◆	Place of interest	▬▬▬	Motorway road	▨	Building
✉	Post office	🏛	Monument	▬▬▬	Main road	⬭	Stadium
ⓘ	Information office	♟	Castle	▬▬▬	Minor road	▢	Park
@	Internet	⌒	Arc	▬▬▬	Pedestrianized road	⊞	Cemetery (Christian)
⊞	Hospital	⊙	Statue	▪▪▪▪	Funicular railway	⊟	Cemetery (Jewish)
⊠	Entrance	⌃⌃	Mountain range	✡	Synagogue		
Ⓤ	U-Bahn	▲	Mountain peak	⚑	Church (regional)		
Ⓢ	S-Bahn /subway	)(	Bridge	✚	Church		

Listings key

■	Accommodation
●	Café/cheap eats/restaurant/ bar/beer garden
■	Nightlife/gay and lesbian nightlife
●	Shop